Canadian Professional Pilot Studies

Phil Croucher

"Never allow your ego, self-confidence, love of flying, pressure from a customer, boss or co-pilot, or economic need to interfere with your good judgement during any stage of a flight. There is no amount of pride, no thrill, pleasure, schedule or job that is worth your licence or your life and the lives of your passengers. Complacency kills, and so does being a cowboy." John Bulmer

About the Author

Phil Croucher holds JAA, UK, UAE and Canadian professional licences for aeroplanes and helicopters and over 8500 hours on 37 types, with a considerable operational background, and training experience from the computer industry, in which he is equally well qualified. He has at various times been a Chief Pilot, Ops Manager, Training Captain and Type Rating Examiner for several companies, including a CRM Ground Instructor. He currently writes the safety column for *Heli-Ops* magazine. His flight experience includes VIP/Corporate, airline/scheduled, police, EMS/ambulance, high/low level photo, longlining, mountain flying, seeding, powerline & gas pipeline survey, and offshore.

Phil has also been successfully publishing his own computer books for over twenty years, and, on discovering the poor quality of ground study material available to pilots in Canada when converting his UK licences, decided to transfer his skills and form his own training and consultancy company to produce them for the worldwide market. The results can be seen at **www.electrocution.com.**

Andrew Sweet

TOC

Contents

If this page is a photocopy, it is not authorised!

© *Phil Croucher, 2007*

If this page is a photocopy, it is not authorised!

INTRODUCTION

0

Just as important as the exams is the interview panel, and this is the book for those who want to deal with both - its purpose is to help you become a professional, for which the exams are but a step on the way - doing the bare minimum to pass them makes you ill-prepared to be a pilot, which is not fair to future passengers and painfully obvious to employers, who certainly expect you to have more than basic knowledge. In fact, on flight tests, examiners treat you as a company pilot, so you will want to give the best impression.

This is the fifth edition of a book that has been very well received - much has been added after suggestions from many readers. As before, a lot of the contents are based on common questions asked during recurrent training, and known exam questions. In fact, there's a lot you *don't* get taught in flying school, including going for a job, and a lot you *should* be taught, were it not for time constraints.

The contents include the usual subjects, that is, radio, weather, law, flight planning, etc., up to the ATPL, as well as INRAT and IATRA, since the subject matter is essentially similar and the difference is only about 10% between them all, so there's real value here, especially as many professional tips and tricks are included to make your transition to a professional as easy as possible. IATRA is for CPL holders who want to add a first 2-crew aircraft to their licence. They are essentially mini-ATPL exams for complex aircraft.

To save space, information readily available in the exam and that is already in common publications has been left out, to make way for more useful stuff (there's a perfectly good explanation of weather charts and symbols in the TC AIM that needs no help from me or anyone else). Thus, in addition to this book, you will need the AIM/AIM and the *Canada Flight Supplement* (CFS), which has details of all the aerodromes available, plus a lot of other stuff besides (you will need it for your flight test anyway, and you will be expected to know your way round it *very* well). Both will be available from the local pilot shop or lying around the flying school.

Many instructors have helped with the book, especially Jeff Mitchell, and readers, such as Brian Marsh, who did some preafrooding (joke) with many contributions, and my thanks to them are extended here.

A basic knowledge of maths and physics is assumed, particularly in these areas:

- Trigonometry, especially Pythagoras
- Algebra, particularly transposition of formulae
- Ratios/Percentages
- Properties of Circles
- Indices

DIFFERENCES

There are some things to note for people coming to Canada from the JAA world (Europe). First of all, the place is big, and there are vast areas where you don't need to (or cannot!) speak to anyone on the radio at all, although it is always a good practice to do so when you can (you listen out mostly on 126.7 or 123.2 MHz). Many airfields don't have a tower, but use a common, or even mandatory, frequency for blind transmissions. In some areas, a controller will cover several aerodromes (from miles away) and, although you will be using the radio, your messages might well be relayed by telephone, so don't be surprised if they take a little time to reply.

Also, because of the remoteness, you also have to tell people where you're going, ranging from filing a full-blown flight plan, to leaving a message with a "responsible person" who undertakes to tell the authorities should you disappear.

The transition level is very high, at 18,000 feet. Flight duty times are longer, and they are part of the exams.

Lastly, QFE is not used because many aerodromes are at high elevations and the readings would be off the altimeter scale, so get used to knowing the elevation!

STUDYING

It has been found that, within two days, if it isn't reviewed, people remember less than 70% of any subject matter they have studied. By the end of the month, the figure falls to 40%. On the other hand, if it's looked over again within 2 days, then 7, you should be above the 70% level until the 28th day. Another review then should make it remain long-term. In fact, short and frequent bursts of study are more effective than one long one - the brain appears to like short "rests" to assimilate knowledge. Constant reviewing is the key, especially for a short time at the end of each day.

(Source: *Ohio State University*).

The real work is done after the lectures, on your own, which is something that university students know all about. However, here are a few tips:

* Allow yourself plenty of time - don't do everything at the last minute. This means that you need a good routine

* If you study during the day, review it in the evening

* Get plenty of rest

Then you need to practice, practice and practice the exams. There are no questions in this book (known ones have been worked into the text), but you can download some for free from our web site at **www.electrocution.com**, and there are more at **www.aerotraining.com**. Sample performance charts are in the Transport Canada study guides, at **www.tc.gc.ca**.

It has come to our notice that Transport Canada examiners use this book as a reference to generate questions for the CPL fixed wing exams.

EXAMS & TECHNIQUE

Unlike in Europe, you can turn up at any Transport Canada office and ask to take them.

Apart from a couple of remote offices with slow internet connections, the exams are computer-delivered, with necessary charts and diagrams on paper. The questions are presented one at a time, and can be bookmarked for later return, and you can jump around as much as you wish (the software keeps track of time and what you have answered). The exams are scored immediately and the results printed on site.

You have to get an overall pass mark and a minimum in each section. The Commercial Exam takes 3.5 hours and needs a pass mark of 60% on 100 multi-choice questions. The ATP takes the same time, but needs 70% out of 80. INRAT (needed for the ATP) gives you 50 questions in 3 hours, needing 70% to pass. IATRA and HATRA have 50 questions, to be done inside 2 hours.

* **Rule No 1**: *Know your subject!*

* **Rule No 2**: *Don't take the exams before you're ready - they will still be there tomorrow!*

Although you might use sample questions, don't just learn the answers, but read around them (the whole point of this book), and use variations on them to keep your mind flexible. If you rely on feedback from other people, you need some luck to get the same questions they got - if you know how to do things from the bottom up, or why things happen, you don't need luck (or a good memory!)

In the exam room, use scrap paper to write down any formulae you actually remember. Go through the questions once, and answer those you absolutely and positively know the answer to (in Flight Planning, do the chart questions first - there's a list on the front of the exam paper). Do the rest more carefully, looking for where the marks are, remembering that it's entirely possible to get the answer to one question in the text of another, or even some nearly identical, and you will pick them up in the overview. There's plenty of time, certainly enough to read each question twice. For example, correct numbers may be given in the choices available, but with the wrong units, so read the questions carefully! Some questions are worded negatively, such as "What will *not* cause hypoxia?" Also be careful of double-thinking - that is, you might not be offered the ideal answer, but have to choose from a poor selection (flaws in some answers may allow you to use a process of elimination to find the right answer).

With a question you are not sure of, cover the answers with some scrap paper, read the question (carefully!) and answer it to the best of your ability. Then uncover the answers and see which one fits the best. If there's more than one, go for the most correct. Where no answers are correct, isolate the least wrong one. If you don't know the answer at all, you are not penalized for a wrong answer so you might as well take your best guess.

Although there's a time limit, it's actually quite generous, and nobody cares how quickly you pass, just as long as you do, so don't rush, either.

HUMAN FACTORS

Aircraft are getting more reliable so, in theory at least, accidents should happen less often. Unfortunately, this is not necessarily the case, so we need to look somewhere else for the causes.

Believe it or not, accidents are very carefully planned - it's just that the results are very different from those expected, based on the idea that the folks who had them were doing things that made complete sense to them at the time (*Dekker*, 2006). The reason for studying this subject is to help you *generate countermeasures against anything that may affect your decision-making capabilities,* and to *seek a safe interface between human and system components* (because you become part of the machine), with *due allowance for human performance*, which is defined by the International Civil Aviation Organisation, or ICAO, (which more or less governs aviation worldwide) as *Human capabilities and limitations which have an impact on the safety and efficiency of aeronautical operations.* The essential problem is that our bodies are not constructed to live under the conditions imposed by aviation. In the air, physical and psychological stresses occur on top of the normal stuff of everyday life that should be taken note of in order to do our jobs properly. Minor illnesses, stress, fatigue, alcohol and caffeine can all affect your performance as a pilot, and there are even regulations* to cover their use, all discussed later in this section.

To this end, you must be medically fit and be certified as such by a physician at regular intervals (your professional licence is not valid without a Class 1 medical certificate, which is valid for 12 months if you are under 40 and 6 months if you are over, except when multi-crew, when it goes back up to 12 months).

You may not act as flight crew if you know or suspect that your physical or mental condition renders you unfit to do so. In other words, you may not exercise licence privileges once you are aware of a decrease in your medical fitness that makes you unable to exercise them safely. *Medicals are only valid if you meet the initial issuing requirements.* A Board of Inquiry or insurance company may interpret the words "medically fit" a little differently than you think if you fly with a cold or under the influence of alcohol or drugs.

In any case, you should talk to a medical examiner as soon as possible in the case of:

- admission to a hospital or clinic for over 12 hours
- surgery or other invasive procedures
- regular use of medication
- regular use of correcting lenses

In addition, you should inform the authorities in writing of significant personal injuries involving your capacity to act as a member of a flight crew, or illness that lasts for more than 21 days (after the 21st day), or pregnancy. In these cases, your medical is suspended, but it can be reinstated after an examination, or if you are exempt from one. It can be given back directly after pregnancy.

*You also have a common law duty of care to people in and around your aircraft.

ACCIDENTS

A *reportable accident* occurs when:

- anyone is killed or injured from contact with the aircraft (or any bits falling off), including jet blast or rotor downwash
- the aircraft sustains damage or structural failure
- The aircraft is missing or inaccessible

between the time any person boards it *with the intention of flight*, and all persons have disembarked. This does not include injuries from natural causes, which are self-inflicted or inflicted by other people, or any to stowaways hiding in places not normally accessible to passengers and crew. *Significant* or *Substantial Damage* in this context essentially means anything that may involve an insurance claim, but officially is damage or failure affecting structure or performance, normally needing major repairs.

Under ICAO, a *fatal injury* involves death within 30 days. A *serious injury* involves:

- more than 48 hours in hospital within 7 days
- more than *simple fractures* of *fingers*, *toes* and *nose*
- lacerations causing nerve or muscle damage or severe haemorrhage
- injury to any internal organ
- 2nd or 3rd degree burns or any over 5% of the body
- exposure to infectious substances or radiation

An **incident** is any happening other than an accident which hazards or, if not corrected, would hazard any aircraft, its occupants or anyone else, *not* resulting in substantial damage to the aircraft or third parties, crew or passengers. In other words, a dangerous event, but without any serious consequences.

An accident is the end product of a chain of events, so, in theory, if you can recognise the sequence it should be possible to nip any problems in the bud. A common saying is that "the well oiled nut behind the wheel is the most dangerous part of any car". Not necessarily true for aviation, perhaps, but, in looking for causes other than the hardware when it comes to accidents, it's hard not to focus on the pilot (or other people - e.g. the human factor) as the weak link in the chain - around 75% (between 70-80%) of accidents can be attributed to this, although it's also true to say that the *situations* some aircraft (and people) are put into make them liable to misfortune, particularly with helicopters - if you continually land on slippery logs, something untoward is bound to happen sometime!

The current teaching is that the human factor is the weak link at the root of most accidents (remove the bad apple and the problem goes away), but it isn't the whole story. Circumstances can also be involved, and even experienced pilots can get caught out. Take, for example, one who is tasked to do two flights in an afternoon, the first one with a light load of two people and the second with four. It would seem logical to fill the helicopter up with enough fuel to cover both flights, since the loads allow it and the schedule is tight between the flights, so you can save some time by not refuelling. But what happens if the first passengers are late, or don't even turn up at all? You are then faced with doing the second trip with more fuel than you would normally plan for to allow for safety margins, even though you might be within the machine's weight limits. Of course, you could defuel, but that can be a major inconvenience when you are the only one there and the

passengers are waiting in the usual car-park-as-a-passenger-lounge! Thus, it is not necessarily a person's character, but their circumstances that can be at the root of an accident, as has been proven by many psychological studies involving prison guards.

The "safety record" of an airline can also be nothing but a numbers game. Take a flight from Los Angeles to New York with two hundred passengers on board - the distance is 3000 miles, so they have flown 600,000 passenger-seat miles. With 150 on the flight back, you get 1,050,000, for being in the air for only 9 hours! If they have 20 aircraft doing that five days a week, and injure one passenger, they can say it happened only once in 105,000,000 passenger-seat-miles, which is still only 900 hours! Having said that, when flying, you are still safer by over 9:1 against driving or 300:1 over riding a bicycle on the road! Currently, the accident rate is *around 1 per million aircraft movements.*

However, it is impossible to design out all the system errors that could arise, so no system is safe all on its own - it still depends on people for its operation, and safety is not the only goal they have to achieve (Transport Canada's statement that a safety management system is a "businesslike approach to safety" does not mean that company profits, etc. should be taken into account, but that safety procedures should be integrated into the company's normal business practice). Granted, some people in any system may have an "attitude" problem, as discussed later, but it is definitely not the only factor!

And if you are thinking that safety might be expensive, review the consequences of an accident:

- Fatalities and/or injuries
- Customer relations & company reputation suffer
- You need alternative equipment.......
- ....while still making payments on the one you just crashed
- Any schedule gets screwed up
- The insurance is increased
- You end up with unwanted attention from the media and the authorities

Even if you don't get that far, it still costs $15,000 for an airliner to return to the gate, or $500,000 to shut down an engine in flight in terms of lost revenue and other indirect costs, such as hotels for passengers. It even costs $100 or so just to start the engine of a Bell 206, so it shouldn't be done lightly! Such losses are uninsured and cost the airline industry as a whole over $36 billion in 2001.

**It takes about 178 seconds for a
non-IR rated pilot to lose control.

THE HUMAN FACTOR

The emphasis on the human element in relation to accidents was recognized in '79 and '80, where over 500 incidents relating to shipping were analysed, and 55% were found to be related to human factors. Did you think that was *1979 & 80*? It was actually in *1879* and 80! In fact, as well as the iceberg, the *Titanic* had to dodge the *Deutschland*, which was floating around the shipping lanes, having run out of coal (it also nearly collided with the *New York* on its way out of Southampton). Since then, through the *1980s* and 90s, aviation accidents in the USA were analysed in depth, and it was found that *crew interaction* was a major factor in them since, nearly 75% of the time, it was the first time they had flown together, and nearly half were on the first leg, in situations where there was pressure from the schedule (over 50%) and late on in the duty cycle, so fatigue was significant (doesn't everything happen late on Friday afternoon?)

The Captain was also flying 80% of the time. The problem is, that it's not much different now - 70% of aircraft accidents in the USA in 2000 were pilot-related, based on mistakes that could easily be avoided with a little forethought, and it was more or less the same figure way back in 1940. Now, the figure worldwide is around 80%.

The majority of accidents studied by the Flight Safety Foundation occurred while a plane was taxying, or during the takeoff and initial climb, or during the approach and landing at the other end:

"Half of all worldwide commercial jet accidents between 1959 and 1994 with known causes occurred during final approach and landing, a phase representing only 4% of total flight time. Of the 439 final-approach-and-landing accidents with known causes, 383 (78.1%) included flight crews as a primary causal factor. This percentage was far in excess of any other primary causal factor."

Thus, the accident rate is highest during takeoff and landing, but as a percentage of flight time, it is highest in the cruise, usually because the machine hits something in the way - one of the highest causes of accidents is *Controlled Flight Into Terrain*, or CFIT, where a serviceable aircraft under the positive control of the crew interacts with something solid. However, for the exam, *the phase of flight most prone to accidents is intermediate and final approach.*

In other words, 60% of accidents occur during the 4% of time spent nearer the ground.

For helicopters, most fatal accidents happen in IMC**, or at least they did between 1991-2000 in the USA, according to the Flight Safety Foundation. A study of 147 accidents found that 58% occurred in IMC, and human error was the primary cause in 68%.

Otherwise, contributory factors may include:

- Pilots disregarding the rules
- Omitting important actions at critical stages
- Lack of situational awareness
- Press-on-itis

Others could be poor planning and/or flying and decision making practices, or inadequate evaluation of the weather. Up to 8% of accidents are also due to maintenance errors.

If air traffic continues to grow at the present rate, we will be losing 1 airliner per week by 2010, and even more GA aircraft - the Australian authorities are looking at 1 helicopter per week, which is why Human Factors training is now an ICAO requirement, with the syllabus drawn from many sources, including Psychology, Engineering, Physiology, Medicine, Sociology, Biology and others.

One problem is that the sort of mistakes that cause accidents do not arise directly from situations where HF is relevant, but from within individual pilots - if you want to be technical, they arise from *intrapersonal* (inside oneself) rather than *interpersonal* (between two people) causes. Modern life is stressful enough - we are all hostages to other peoples' expectations and attitudes, and it often seems that, within an hour of waking up, we have an attitude all of our own, by the time the toast has been dropped (face down) and everyone's had their bite out of you. You should not let what happens outside it into the cockpit - one function that checklists perform is to help keep your mind on the job and exclude outside influences.

It has also (finally) been realized that traditional methods of flight instruction have been missing something - the assumption has always been that, just because you have a licence, you know what you are doing, or that good, technically qualified pilots (or doctors, for example) make good decisions as a matter of course (I know many stupid doctors!) Naturally, everybody on the shop floor has always known that this is not necessarily so, and a lot of experienced pilots make mistakes, so experience is not the answer, either. In fact, experience can be a harsh teacher, assuming you heed its lessons anyway, so ways have had to be found to use training instead, hence the ICAO requirements for Human Performance training, which is meant to *increase the safety and efficiency of flight operations* and *maintain the well-being of the people involved.* This means that manipulating the flying controls is less than half of the training required to be a competent pilot.

Currently, aeronautical decision making is seen as a function that comes under standard psychological theory and practice (*Brecke*, 1982; *Stokes and Kite*, 1994). In fact, research into the human factors related to aircraft accidents and incidents has highlighted decision making as a crucial element (*Jensen*, 1982; *O'Hare, Wiggins, Batt, and Morrison*, 1994). The irony is that people who are aware that such training is a Good Thing do not need the courses - the sort that should most benefit are like the Enstrom owner who mentioned to his shocked engineer that he didn't like the look of two bolts in the tail rotor assembly, so he turned them round and shortened one of them, since it was longer than the other. After patiently explaining during wall-to-wall counselling that the reason why one bolt was longer was for balance purposes, and that they were inserted one way round for a reason, the engineer suggested the owner-pilot went elsewhere.

As with most other things, aviation is more of a mental process than a physical one. For example, it takes much longer to become a captain than it does to become a pilot, and CRM/PDM/Human Factors* training aims to shorten the gap by substituting training for experience. Almost the first thing you have to take on board is that not everyone does things the same way as you do, as a result of which, compromises have to be made in order to get the job done. Another is that, when operating by yourself as single pilot, feedback is missing, which is useful, when multi-crew, for making decisions. The only real replacement for this is reviewing your flights and discussing them with colleagues, which is more difficult for helicopter pilots, because of the lack of meeting places (but licensed premises are good).

Single Pilot Operations

Single pilot operations demand much higher standards, because they typically take place in unstabilised machines with the least accurate instruments in the worst weather. To achieve the higher standards of competency and discipline that single pilot operations demand, you must:

- Maintain a positive attitude

- Maintain medical fitness

- Be less willing to accept unserviceabilities

- Spend more time on planning & preparation, so you have a yardstick by which your flight can be compared when you do an after flight review - be prepared for eventualities before they happen!

- Maintain situational awareness

- Maintain a stricter observance of legal requirements - resist commercial pressure

- Be more willing to ask for help, especially with clearance readbacks

- Make more use of checklists and SOPs. If you have to design them as well, make them easier to read

- Workload Management, especially at critical moments. Make sure you have the right equipment in the first place, you know its capabilities, and that you use it properly:

  - Manage time - use relatively slack periods in the cruise to prepare for busy ones during the arrival. Prioritise!

  - Manage the cockpit - get the maps in the right order! Make sure they are folded properly! Ensure you have a map holder, writing instrument, stopwatch, etc. Don't throw the departure plates away too soon, in case you have to return to the field after takeoff

  - Use the autopilot in busy airspace, in a monitoring role rather than a controlling one. Do not use it until established in flight and certainly not below 400 feet

  - Make more effective use of the GPS. Instead of just putting in waypoints, and therefore pushing more buttons in flight, put them all into a route so that the screen changes automatically as you pass waypoints

  - Tune and use normal navaids as well as GPS

  - Before you operate a switch or press a button, make sure it is the right one

  - Cross check the readings for logic!

  - Be critical of your performance so you can improve the next flight

EVOLUTION

Since the problem of crew co-operation needed to be addressed, management principles from other industries, such as Quality Assurance and Risk Management, were distilled into what is mostly called *Crew Resource Management*, prompted, in Canada, at least, by three accidents, one of which was at Dryden, which was also instrumental in new Canadian icing laws being passed.

On the day concerned, the weather was forecast for generally unsettled and deteriorating conditions, with a lowering cloud ceiling and freezing precipitation. The Fokker F-28 landed late in the day, and behind schedule, which so far sounds like a typical day in aviation. Because the APU wasn't working, they had to keep one engine running, as there was no external start facility at Dryden. After refuelling, and when the passengers had been loaded, another 10 turned up, which meant that fuel had to be taken off. Since the engine had to be kept running for another 35 minutes, once all that was over, they needed more fuel, so there was another short delay to take more on. The Company required both engines to be shut down to stop ice being ingested into running engines, so no de-icing was available, since one had to be kept running in place of the APU. The flight crew had also recently converted from Convairs, which are very forgiving when it comes to taking ice, so perhaps they thought they could use that experience on the super-critical wing of the F-28.

By now it was snowing heavily, and the F-28 had to wait at the holding point while a Cessna in distress landed. The takeoff roll was eventually begun 70 minutes behind schedule. After a slower than normal acceleration, the aircraft rotated and took off briefly, to settle back down on the runway. After a second rotation, it managed to get off the ground, passing the end of runway at only 15 ft. The whole exercise ended in a fireball of orange flames.

Dryden Crash - Photographer Unknown

For up to 2 months beforehand, and especially within the previous five days, the aircraft had been subject to multiple unserviceabilities, including smoke in the cabin and oily smells. It could have been grounded, but there was pressure to keep to the schedule and getting another would have involved a delay. Maintenance deferred the repair of the fire detection system and a red placard, reading *APU unserviceable*, was placed on the APU panel. Although he bears the final responsibility, the Captain sure

didn't get much help from elsewhere (it didn't help that there was no ATC either - clearances at Dryden are given from Winnipeg, which is a four-hour drive away, aside from the fact that the airport authority was trying to cut down on the fire fighting equipment, so there was chaos at the incident itself - *author*).

As it happens, most weather-based accidents in small aircraft involve inadvertent entry into cloud by people with only the basic instrument training required for the commercial licence. Next in line is icing. With regard to jet transports and executive jets, it's CFIT (*Controlled Flight Into Terrain*), and the figures are 50% and 72%, respectively. GPWS marked a substantial decrease in hull loss rates in the 80s, after a TWA 727 hit a mountain near Washington DC in 1974, killing 92 people (only two months earlier another plane nearly hit the same mountain). From 33 such accidents in 1964, the figure fell to just 8 in 1984, although this is still too high.

Around 40% of fatal accidents were in aircraft without it.

CRM was actually developed from the insights gained after installing Flight Data Recorders and Cockpit Voice Recorders, when crews were not considered to be assertive enough, and Captains not receptive enough. CRM back then could probably best be summed up in the phrase "I'm the Captain - you're not!", which leads to situations where, although it's part of the First Officer's job to monitor and challenge the Captain, where necessary, a failure to do so could be down to the Captain's management methods, because that's where the rest of the crew take their lead from.

Prompted by a NASA workshop in 1979, United Airlines started to include the training, and not just for pilots. The goal was *synergism*, meaning that the total performance of a crew should be greater than the sum of its parts, or each crew member (like Simon & Garfunkel, or Lennon & McCartney, who are talented enough by themselves, but so much better as a group). For example, when you combine two radio frequencies, you get two more above and below. If you combine two singers, there is a third voice in there somewhere. It's all a matter of vibration, and it's the same with people, or flight crews. There is an extra buzz when a team is working well together.

As an example, until the mid 1960s, the French night mail crews routinely made landings at night in dense fog using standard instrumentation. Their regularity of service was 98%. A British journalist (*Flight International*) wrote in 1964 that one night they got down to 70 feet and saw only one light. At 100 feet they had seen nothing, but when no lights were seen, crew sympathy was such that no word

"The least experienced press on, while the more experienced turn back to join the most experienced who never left the ground in the first place."

was necessary to agree on a change of plan and go down further. The crew knew what the Captain had in mind.

To achieve such synergy, members of any team must feel that they and their opinions are valued, and understand their roles. Since, in most companies, the teams change from day to day (or flight to flight), the whole organisation must therefore foster teamwork, *from the top down*, and attempt to reduce the effects of jagged edges between people (in other words, the relatively simple concept of learning to live with others and allowing for their differences, which involves sharing power on the flight deck, at the very least, as *multi-crew* means what it says - the real point is that *everyone* should know what's going on). The behaviour of people in a company is very much a reflection of the management, in our case the commander, so there is an obligation to foster a positive working environment, which, essentially, means not being surly or miserable - the cockpit culture should allow anyone on board to speak up if they feel they have to.

Referring back to the Dryden accident, the significant amounts of snow on the wings were noticed by a flight attendant and two airline captains who were travelling as passengers, but who did not communicate the problem to the pilots. The flight attendant later said that she was concerned by the snow, but because she had been put off by company pilots in similar situations in the past, she decided not to go to the cockpit. Although the immediate cause of the Dryden accident was the accumulation of snow and ice on the wings during a delay in obtaining takeoff clearance, it was determined that the event was triggered by 17 inadequate corporate processes.

A reading of the accident report on the Air Florida flight that hit a bridge and ended up in the Potomac would also be instructive - the FO was clearly sure that something was wrong (icing) but didn't like to say so.

Like it or not, you are part of a team, even if you are the only one in the cockpit, and *you* have to fit into an established system, especially when IFR.

The CRM concept evolved from the original *Cockpit* Resource Management, through *Crew* Resource Management, where Decision Making became more important, into a third generation, which involved cabin crews, etc., and introduced aviation-specific training, as a lot of what served previously was very much psychology-based, but it is very difficult to escape psychology in just about every walk of life these days, and now aviation is no exception - all airlines use selection tests, as do many corporate employers. In fact, 90% of aviation casualties in World War I were down to human factors, and in World

War II they started testing to weed out people who had questionable decision-making skills, so it's not really new.

CRM then became integrated into all flight training, and an element is now met on nearly all check rides, with a complete syllabus cycle taking place over three years. In the US, the fourth generation can take the form of an *Advanced Qualification Program* (AQP) tailored specifically to individual company needs. Now we are in the fifth generation, which attempts to become universal and cover national culture, and concentrate more on *Threat & Error Management,* which is further discussed below. A further development could be to change the name (yet again) to *Company* Resource Management, where other departments get involved in the same training. The benefit of this for Air Aurigny (in the Channel Islands) has been improved communication between departments and a sharpening up of the whole operation once people saw what everybody else had to cope with - turnaround times became shorter, which made a direct contribution to the bottom line. However, as mentioned above, the general principles of CRM have been around for some time - Field-Marshal Montgomery wrote that the best way to gain a cohesive fighting force was efficient *management* of its components, and he certainly succeeded in getting the Army, Navy and Air Force to work together. However, as far as definitions go, you could call it *Cockpit* Resource Management when you're single pilot, and *Crew* Resource Management when you're not.

Previously, you might have been introduced to the concept of *Airmanship*, which involved many things, such as looking out for fellow pilots, doing a professional job, always doing pre-flight inspections, etc. In other words, actions relating to being the "gentleman aviator", or exhibiting professional behaviour as an airman, which involves discipline, skill, knowledge (of yourself and the aircraft), risk management, etc.

These days, especially when multi-crew, there are new concepts to consider, such as *delegation, communication, monitoring* and *prioritisation*, although they will have varying degrees of importance in a single-pilot environment. In fact, the term "pilot error" is probably only accurate about a third of the time; all it really does is indicate where a breakdown occurred. There may have been just too much input for one person to cope with, which is not necessarily error, because no identifiable mistakes were made. Perhaps we need a new phrase that occupies the same position that "not proven" does in the Scottish Legal System (somewhere between Guilty and Not Guilty).

Note: Airmanship is still a valid concept, and should be treated with as much respect as the regulations!

Anyhow, the aim of this sort of training is to increase flight safety by showing you how to make the best use of any resources available to you, which include your own body (physical and psychological factors), information, equipment and other people (including passengers and ATC), whether in flight or on the ground, even engine handling or using the humble map - copilots are trained for emergencies, for example, so they can be used instead of automatically taking over yourself when something happens - like a human autopilot, in fact. Using a GPS for navigation, and ignoring the other navigation aids or the map, is bad CRM.

You should be able to make better decisions after being introduced to the concepts, principles and practices of CRM, or Decision Making, with the intention of reducing the accident rate even further. That is to say, we know all about the hardware, now it's time to take a look at ourselves. Aircraft have limitations - so do you! An *accident-prone person*, officially, is s*omebody to whom things happen at a higher rate than could be statistically expected by chance alone.* Taking calculated risks is completely different from taking chances. Know your capabilities, and your limits. Things that can help, particularly with single-pilot operations, are:

• *Knowledge* - know the flight manual, and its limitations

• *Preparation* - do as much as you can before the flight - Is that runway *really* large enough to stop in if one engine fails? Has all the servicing been done? Is the paperwork correct? Visualise the route from the map - and fold it as best you can for the route. Got enough batteries for the GPS? Do you know the Minimum Safe Altitude if you get caught in cloud? And who to call?

It has been noticed that pilots who receive decision-making training outperform others in flight tests and make 10-15% fewer bad decisions, and the results improve with the comprehensiveness of the training. Remember that your training cannot cater for everything. Instead, as with licences everywhere, you are given enough training to be able to make decisions for yourself, hence the importance of decision making training.

CRM/PDM courses are supposed to be discussion-based, which means that you are expected to participate, with the intention that your experiences will be spread around to other crews. This is because it's quite possible never to see people from one year to the next in a lot of organizations, particularly large ones, and helicopter pilots in particular have no flying clubs, so experience is not being passed on. In fact, if you operate in the bush, you might see some of your colleagues during training at the start of the season, and not see them till the end, if at all. Even when single-pilot, you still have to talk to management and engineers, and to people even more important - the customers!

In short, CRM/PDM is the effective utilisation of all available resources (e.g. crew members, aircraft systems and supporting facilities) to achieve safe and efficient operation - the idea is to enhance your communication and management skills to achieve it. In other words, the emphasis is placed on the non-technical aspects of flight crew performance (the so-called *softer skills*) which are not part of the flying course but which are also needed to do your job properly - those associated with teamwork, and smoothing the interfaces between members of a team.

Captaincy

As we said before, you could loosely call this stuff airmanship, with an element of common sense, but the new term is *Captaincy*, as flying is a lot more complex now than when the original term was more appropriate.

The elusive quality of Captaincy is probably best illustrated with an example, using the subject of the Critical Point. If you refer to *Flight Planning*, you will find that it is a position where it takes as much time to go to your destination as it does to return to where you came from, so you can deal with emergencies in the quickest time. In a typical pilot's exam, you will be given the departure and destination points, the wind velocity and other relevant information and be asked to calculate the CP along with the PNR (*Point of No Return*), which is OK as far as it goes, but tells you nothing about your qualities as a Captain, however much it may demonstrate your technical abilities as a pilot.

Now take the same question, but introduce the scenario of a flight across the Atlantic, during which you are tapped on the shoulder by a hostess who tells you that a passenger has got appendicitis. First of all, you have to know that you need the CP, which is given to you already in the previous question. Then you find out that you are only 5 minutes away - technically, you should turn back, but is that really such a good decision? (Actually, it might not be, since it will take a few minutes to turn around anyway). Commercially, turning back would be disastrous, and here you find the difference between being a pilot and a Captain, or the men and the boys, and why CRM training is becoming so important.

A Captain is supposed to exhibit qualities of loyalty to those above and below, courage, initiative and integrity, which are all part of the right personality - people have to *trust* you. This, unfortunately, means being patient and cheerful in the most trying of circumstances, and even changing your own personality to provide harmony within the crew, since it's the objective of the whole crew (as a team) to get the passengers to their destination safely. As single crew, of course, there is only you in your cockpit, but you still have to talk to others. In this context, the word "crew" includes anybody else who can help you deliver the end product, which is:

. . Safe Arrival!

Safety Management Systems

A safe arrival is only as good as the system behind it - this would include the pilot who doesn't abuse the machine, the engineers who take pride in their work, the support staff in the operations office who don't overload the pilot with work they should be doing, and a management culture that allows people to approach their jobs in a manner that fosters safety and professionalism over short term customer satisfaction, and who are proactive (trying to stop the next accident) rather than reactive (wiping up the mess after the last one). To do this, various layers of paperwork have been developed over the years, culminating in a Safety Management System. Although companies are obliged to have certain systems in place, such as operations manuals or Quality Systems (see *Aircraft Operations*), they don't go far enough. The ops manual, for one thing, is a one-way document, and readers are simply expected to comply with its requirements.

A Quality System goes a step further by having someone monitor the system and produce a slight amount of feedback to management (and occasionally from staff), but this has limitations before it starts, because the system on which it is based was originally for manufacturing processes, with the intention of producing low return rates, which don't lend themselves well to a service industry such as aviation. It is a generic management system standard which doesn't have much to do with the end product, except for ensuring its production under sound management procedures, "leading to efficiency and consistency, and, ultimately, cost reductions".

However, in order to allocate resources to improve safety, management needs timely information. For this, you need a system that starts at the bottom, allows information to flow both ways, and is non-punitive.

So Is It Working?

A study that examined 558 airline mishaps between 1983-2002 was conducted by the Johns Hopkins Bloomberg School of Public Health in the United States. It revealed that there are 40% less incidents involving pilot error, attributable to better training and technology that aids pilot decision making.

"I used to be indecisive, but now I'm not so sure!"

DECISIONS, DECISIONS
••

The best way out of trouble is not to get into it, which is easier said than done with an intimidating passenger or management. You, the pilot, are the decision-maker - in fact, under the Chicago Convention, your word is law when in flight, but the other side of the coin is that you are responsible for what goes on.

Aviation is noticeable for its almost constant decision-making. As you fly along, particularly in a helicopter, you're probably updating your next engine-off landing point every five seconds or so. Or maybe you're keeping an eye on your fuel and continually calculating your endurance. It all adds to the many tasks you're meant to keep up to date with, because the situation is always changing. In fact, a decision *not* to make a decision (or await developments) is also a decision, always being aware that we don't want indecision. To drive a car 1 mile, you must process 12,000 pieces of information - that's 200 per second at 60 mph! It has to be worse with flying, and possibly over our limits - our capability of processing information is actually quite marginal, being able to deal with only one thing at a time, and it is vulnerable to fatigue and stress - the most demands are at the beginning and end of a flight, but the latter is when you are most tired (your heart rate is most just after landing).

Decision making in emergencies requires distribution of tasks (i.e. delegation) and crew coordination, but a good decision depends on proper analysis of a situation........

Information Processing

The way we interpret information on which we base decisions can be quite complex. With optical and aural stimuli, *the processing is done in the brain*, which uses past experience to interpret what it senses - it therefore has expectations, and can pre-judge a situation. In fact, as accident reports routinely show, in high stress conditions, the brain may even blank out information not directly concerned with the task in hand. Certainly, the processing

"Most people are woefully inadequate processors of information, who stumble along ill-chosen paths to reach bad conclusions"

of information before it is brought to our conscious attention is done in such a way as to protect our self-esteem and confidence. In other words, when people act contrary to their self-identity, anything that doesn't pass through that filter is either rejected or made to fit.

Information processing usually means the interpretation of signals from the sensory organs by the brain, which can be selective. It is the process of receiving information through the senses, analysing it and making it meaningful. This is represented by the diagram below.

In the process, physical stimuli, such as sound and sight, are perceived, given attention and received into sensory memory for final interpretation by the brain, where it can be worked on by *Short Term* (STM) or *Long Term* Memory (LTM). Some processes can bypass all that completely, such as motor programs, which operate subconsciously.

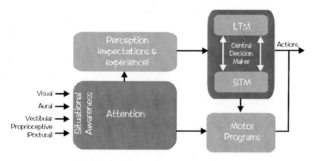

Although there may be lots of input, there is only one channel out of the Central Decision maker, which must be shared when things are busy. Anything not currently being attended to is held in short term memory.

The system works also in reverse, in that feedback on the results of any actions can be used to improve knowledge and future judgement.

Perception at this point means converting that information into something meaningful, or realising that it's relevant to what you're doing. What comes out depends on past experience of those events, your expectations, and whether you're able to cope with the information at that time (or are even paying attention to the situation). Good examples are radio transmissions from ATC, which you can understand, even if you can't hear them properly, because you expect certain items to be included, and you know from experience that they're bad anyway. The danger is that you may hear what you want to hear and not what is actually sent! (see *Communication*, later).

Rscheearch sohws taht it deosn't mttaer in waht oredr the ltteers in a wrod aeappr, the olny iprmoatnt tihng is taht the frist and lsat ltteer be in the rhgit pclae. The rset can be

a taotl mses and you can sitll raed it wouthit a porbelm. Tihs is bcuseae the huanm mnid does not raed ervey lteter by istlef, but the wrod as a wlohe.

Physical stimuli, such as sound and sight, are received and interpreted by the brain. *Perception* at this point means converting that information into something meaningful, or realizing that it's relevant to what you're doing. What comes out depends on past experience of those events, your expectations, and whether you're able to cope with the information at that time (or are even paying attention to the situation). Good examples are radio transmissions from ATC, which you can understand, even if you can't hear them properly, because you expect certain items to be included, and you know from experience that they're bad anyway. The danger, of course, is that you may hear what you want to hear and not what is actually sent! (see *Communication*, later). As mentioned above, the human body is not a good multi-tasker, and to keep the various balls in the air over a typical flight, we must learn to *prioritise* and switch rapidly between tasks, which depends on how much attention the primary task is demanding. This can be reduced by using standard procedures, as with R/T and SOPs - the less thought secondary tasks require, the less attention they take up, especially when an external event happens to upset those well-made plans and flood the system.

Memory

Memory is a feature in human information processing. We need it to learn new things - without it, we could not capture information, or draw on past experience to apply it in new situations (i.e. remembering). Thus, there are three processes involved in using memory, *input (or encoding), storage* and *retrieval*, any one of which can fail and make you think you're losing your memory, though this can depend on whether the items are placed in *short term* or *long term* memory. However, to encode something in the first place, it must be given *attention*, which ultimately depends on whether it can be *perceived* against all the other stuff going on. This means that much of what we are exposed to never even enters the memory, and thus is not available for recall. As a result, what are often called memory problems are really lapses in attention.

In 1951, Dr. Wilder Penfield began a series of scientific experiments in which he proved that, by touching the temporal cortex with a weak electrical probe, the brain could be caused to play back some past experiences, and the feelings associated with them, despite the patients not normally being able to recall them. He came to the following widely accepted conclusions:

- The brain acts like a tape recorder, and whilst we may forget some experiences, they are recorded somewhere

- The brain also records the feelings associated with the experiences, and they stay locked together

- A person can exist in two states simultaneously (patients replaying hidden events and feelings could talk about them objectively at the same time)

- Hidden experiences when replayed are vivid, and affect how we feel at the time of replaying

- There is a connection between mind and body, or a link between the biological and the psychological

Anyhow, most psychologists (by no means all!) agree there are 3 types of memory:

INSTINCT

What Jung called "race memory", gives an immediate (gut reaction) response to a stimulus, like being hard-wired. Some psychologists call this *sensory memory*, as it provides a raw reaction to sensory input (like a knee jerk). That is, it can retain information long enough to allow you to decide whether a stimulus is important or not, or whether it is for the eyes or ears. The perception of a streak of light as opposed to a series of dots when a lighted cigarette is moved across a darkened room would indicate its existence, which allows us to pay attention to one thing whilst being aware of and able to process events in wider surroundings (the *Cocktail Party Effect* is a good example). *Iconic Store* is where visual images are kept for about half a second. *Echoic memory* (for the ears) might last for between 250 milliseconds up to a few seconds. The *Haptic Store* retains physical senses of touch and internal muscle tensions. The reason for the slight delay is so that you can string connected events together and remember a series of words as a structured sentence.

Information that is not lost from sensory memory is passed on to..........

SHORT TERM MEMORY (STM)

Otherwise known as *working*, or *active*, memory by later theorists, this is for data that is used and forgotten almost instantly, or is used for current information (actually, nothing is ever forgotten, as any psychologist will tell you, but the point is that Short Term Memory is for "on the spot" work, such as fuel calculations or ATC clearances, and figures greatly with situational awareness, which can follow short term memory's limitations). STM can only handle somewhere between 5-9 items at a time (that is, 7

± 2), unless some tricks are used, such as grouping or association (*chunking*), meaning that what can be held in short term memory depends on the rules used for its organisation, which are in long-term memory. Mnemonics are also good (such as HASELL), since STM appears to like words, albeit taking things rather literally - words will be recalled exactly, and in the order they were processed, unlike in long term memory, which may recall their *meaning* instead. Data in short term memory typically lasts about 10-20 seconds, and is affected by *distraction*, and is probably what Einstein was referring to when he thought that as soon as one fact was absorbed, one was discarded (there are only 27 lines to the Xanadu poem, because Coleridge was disturbed by the milkman).

Note: Don't expect to remember short term information - *always write clearances down*, although you should be able to keep it in your head long enough for you to do so!

Because the capacity of short-term memory is so limited, items must clamour for attention, which may be based on *emotion*, *personal interest*, or the *unusual*. As mentioned, you can extend working memory's capabilities, either by *rehearsal* (mental repetition), or *chunking* (associating items with each other), or breaking up the information into sequences, as you might with a telephone number. The sequence of letters ZNEBSEDECREM becomes a lot easier to remember once you realise it is MERCEDES BENZ backwards, and suddenly your short term memory has 5 or so spaces for more information.

Just to prove that short term memory really is limited in its holding capacity, read out the following 15 words to a few people, taking one or two seconds per word, and get them to write down as many of them afterwards as they can remember. Most people will get 7 of them, and some (around 55%) will include *sleep*, even though it wasn't there in the first place, proof that we sometimes hear what we want to hear, and that eyewitness testimony can be suspect, which is why the test was developed in the first place (by Washington University in St Louis). The words are: *bed, rest, awake, tired, dream, snooze, wake, blanket, doze, slumber, snore, nap, peace, yawn, drowsy*. However, expertise can increase short term memory capacity, as does timing - NASA researchers found that football players learning tricky new manoeuvres did so better at 3 in the afternoon rather than 9 in the morning. The early session was as bad for learning as if the players had had only three hours' sleep the night before.

Note: Some say that it is not necessarily working memory's capacity that is lacking, but its *processing ability*.

Short term memory impairment occurs at 12 000 feet, but it can be affected as low as 8 000 feet.

Ultra short term memory lasts for about 2 seconds, and acts like a buffer, in that it stores information until we are ready to deal with it in its proper time slice, although it may actually be handled by control processes such as rehearsal, or repetition.

Unfortunately, you cannot do any chunking or association without ....

LONG TERM MEMORY (LTM)

This is where all our basic knowledge (e.g. memories of childhood, training, etc.) is kept - you might liken it to the unconscious, with more capacity and ability to retain information than short-term memory - its storage capacity is regarded as unlimited, and possibly consists of several interlaced systems, such as *semantic memory, generic memory, episodic memory* (from specific events), plus *procedural memory.* LTM works better when dealing with information that has special relevance or meaning, whereas short-term memory is more meaning-free. Where training is concerned, many processes can be carried out automatically in LTM, with little thinking. Repetition (or *rehearsing*) is used to get information into it, combined with organising it, placing it into some sort of context or associating it with an emotion (when studying, concentrate on the *meaning* rather than the subject matter). The time of day also has an effect - schoolchildren were better at immediate recall of a story read to them at 9 AM, but could recall more details if they were read to at 3 PM. Storage of information in LTM would thus appear to be better in the latter half of the day.

Knowledge stored in long-term memory should be pre-activated (with *planning* and *anticipation*) so it can be available when required and have the access time reduced.

The reason why long term memory is needed for association purposes is because it contains the rules that give the items meaning. For example, chess players can have extraordinary short term memory for positioning of pieces, *if the rules in long-term memory, are obeyed.* Upon random positioning, short term recall reverts to normality. People with brain damage (after accidents, etc.) can often remember only one type of information, which supports the idea that the above types of memory are quite distinct, and that data can go directly into long term memory.

It is interesting to note that the nervous system has a rhythm of arousal that peaks around 20:00, and long-term memory improves as arousal is heightened, reaching a peak late in the day. Short term memory, however, reaches

its zenith around 10:00-11:00 - it's about 15% more efficient in the morning and 15% less in the evening.

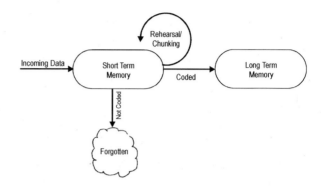

Perception

This is the process of giving meaning to what is sensed, or *interpreting, organizing* and *elaborating* on the input. After *visual* or *oral* perception comes *cognitive* perception, or understanding, leading to *expectations* or *mind set. Set* is a tendency to respond in a certain way, in line with expectations based on past experience - *perceptual set* relates this to the perception process. Variations on this theme could come from:

- The **stimulus** itself. For example, the moon at the horizon appears larger than when overhead, even though the image on the retina will be the same, because many of the visual cues for greater distance occur when it is viewed near land

- The **situation,** or the context in which an image is viewed. The figures 1 and 3 could be seen as the letter B if they were included together in a list of letters (like on number plates)

- The **state of the perceiver** with regard to motivation or emotion, or memories and expectations. If you are hungry, pictures of food can appear to be brighter, and the colour of a drink can affects the taste of the contents

Perception therefore happens in the brain, after a *stimulus* has been detected by the sense organs. The process by which sensory information gets to the brain (that is, transforming input into electrochemical energy) is called *transduction.* The brain distinguishes between them by paying attention to the part of it that is activated. The *Gestalt Theory* relates to perception and organisation.

However, the world is full of information that can be picked up by our senses - what makes us pay attention to some in particular? The answer is that there is a minimum level of stimulation that must occur before anything is noticed, so we are bound by the limitations of our sense organs. These are sample values for most humans under ideal conditions:

- *Sight* - A candle flame seen from 17 miles away

- *Touch* - a bee's wing falling on your cheek from 1 cm away

- *Taste* - 1 teaspoon of sugar in 2 gallons of distilled water

- *Smell* - 1 drop of perfume in a three-roomed house (1:500,000)

- *Hearing* - The ticking of a watch in a room 20 feet away

A shark, on the other hand, can sense one drop of blood in thousands of gallons of water!

Sensory stimulation is the first stage in the information process. The *absolute threshold* is the minimum level of stimulation (for a sensor) at which a stimulus is noticed, for 50% of the time. The increase in stimulation required for us to notice a change between two stimuli (for 50% of the time) is the *difference threshold* or the *Just Noticeable Difference* (JND), which involves *Weber's Law*, which states that, as the strength of an original stimulus increases, the magnitude of the change must also increase for a JND to be perceived. The JND threshold is therefore variable, in that it depends on the background against which changes are detected, and the strength of the original stimulus. Thus, changes between two thresholds may not be noticed and may build up in flight to extreme attitudes, hence the need to watch those instruments. If a sensory threshold *increases*, sensitivity *decreases*. Raising the perceptual threshold of a sensory organ means *lesser sensitivity*.

Proprioceptors ("seat-of-the-pants sense") do not orient you to your surroundings, but inform you of the relative motion and relative position of your body parts. *They can give false inputs to body orientation when visual reference is lost.* Subcutaneous (i.e. under the skin) pressure receptors are stimulated by pressure on the corresponding body parts when sitting, standing or lying down.

A stereotypical and involuntary reaction of the organism on stimulation of receptors is called a *reflex*.

Attention

All the stimulation in the world is no good if you ignore it! Attention is a limited resource that can be affected by *distraction*, *selectivity* or *motivation*, which is where habit takes over. You can omit essential actions after interruptions in your work, because you are not paying attention. You can

also include actions that are associated with the interruption in the original sequence of actions. A *premature exit* (relevant for engineers) is the termination of a job before everything is complete.

As mentioned above, the human body is not a good multi-tasker, and to keep the various balls in the air over a typical flight, we must learn to *prioritise* and switch rapidly between tasks, which depends on how much attention the primary task is demanding. This can be reduced by using standard procedures, as with R/T and SOPs - the less thought secondary tasks require, the less attention they take up, especially when an external event happens to upset those well-made plans and flood the system.

DIVIDED ATTENTION

This is the alternative management of several matters of interest at (almost) the same time, as when monitoring the progress of a motor program on a relatively subconscious level whilst making a radio call (time sharing). In this case, some tasks may suffer at the expense of others, especially if they are similar in nature.

SELECTIVE ATTENTION

With this, you give greater attention to one or more sources of input out of several. Such a selective mechanism is required because the resources of the Central Decision Maker (why can't they just call it the brain?) and short-term memory are limited. It is the process during which information is sampled to see if it is relevant, which makes you able to detect information meant for you, such as your callsign, even if you are not specifically monitoring the source.

THE COCKTAIL PARTY EFFECT

This describes the ability to focus your listening attention on a single talker amongst a mixture of background noise, ignoring other conversations (*Arons*, 1992; "The cocktail"). According to *Clifford* (2005), the effect can occur when we are either paying attention to one of the sounds around us, and when it is invoked by a stimulus which grabs our attention suddenly. For example, if someone the other side of a party room calls out your name, you notice that sound and respond to it immediately, whilst still paying some attention to the original group (the inability to select a signal from the ambient context is a symptom of hearing loss). Or, during a conversation in the cockpit, you respond to your callsign. As it happens, much of the early work about this can be traced to problems faced by air traffic controllers in the early 1950's, when they received many messages simultaneously over loudspeakers - it was very difficult to distinguish single voices from the many.

Colin Cherry, at MIT in 1953, conducted perception experiments in which subjects were asked to listen to two different messages from speakers at the same time, and try to separate them. It was revealed that our ability to separate sounds from the background is based on the *characteristics* of the sounds, like the gender of the speaker, or the direction from which the sound is coming, pitch, or the speaking speed, although spatial differences in the location of the sources greatly assists this ability. "Our minds can be conceived as a radio receiving many channels at once"; each channel perceives a kind of sound, but we can pay attention to only one channel at a time because of our limited capacity, so there is an audio filter in our brain which selects the channel to which we should pay attention from many kinds of sounds perceived. This is *Broadbend's Filter Theory*.

FOCUSSED ATTENTION

Where you focus on a single source and avoid distraction, with the danger of missing something important.

SUSTAINED ATTENTION

This is the ability to stay alert over long periods of time, often on one task.

VIGILANCE

The amount of attention given to a task is directly influenced by the amount of vigilance, which is defined as the degree of activation of the Central Nervous System.

Adaptation

This effect is common with instrument flying. Adaptation occurs when the response to a stimulus decreases after being exposed to it continually. The sense of smell is quickest to adapt, but IFR pilots know this happens with the sense of balance as well (the *leans*).

What Is A Decision?

A decision is supposed to be the end result of a chain of events involving judgment, after which you choose between alternatives. The process involves not only our eyes and ears which gather data, but our attention, which should not be preoccupied all the time. The human body is not a multi-tasker, and to keep track of what's going on it's necessary to split your attention for a short period between everything, typically a split second at a time, having prioritised all the tasks that need to be completed.

Risk assessment, discussed at the end of this section, is part of the process, as is timing, as a good decision that is made too late is useless, although this does not mean that you should become impulsive.

Although decision making is a *systematic and analytical process* involving several steps, things often seem to happen all at once, so it's important not to get fixated on one thing at the expense of another, which is typically what happens when flying under stress. Gather all the information you can in the time available or, better still, get in the habit of updating information you're likely to need in an emergency as the flight progresses, especially when single-pilot, because then you will have much of the information you need in place. For example, when faced with an anticipated period of time pressure, such as starting an instrument approach, the strategy should be to prepare for it by getting the weather in advance, considering alternatives, etc. This helps to activate the relevant information in long-term memory, as part of the preparation and prioritisation process.

There are three elements to the evaluation process. *Diagnosis* comes first (which is more of a skill than is thought), followed by the *generating of possible solutions* and the *assessment of any risks*, further described below. When evaluating a situation, you should stay as cool as possible and not let emotions cloud your decision - that is, do not let false hopes affect your thinking, as they might if your engine fails over trees - you first have to get over the idea that you will hit something! Once you have all the information, of course, there is no point in delaying the making of the decision, which must be followed by action! When other crewmembers are involved, time should always be taken to explain the reasons for a decision, even if it is after landing.

A poor decision is often attributed to faulty reasoning. For example, from the fact that cats and dogs both have four legs, you might conclude that a cat is a dog. Alternatively, if a pilot comes from a broken home, and you know that people who come from broken homes are social misfits, you might also conclude that the pilot concerned is a social misfit. In this case, your faulty conclusion arises from a *false premise*, because not all people from broken homes are social misfits. In addition to misinterpreting a premise, you might rely on cherished beliefs rather than logical analysis, where you know that a certain part of an engine is prone to give problems, but, when troubleshooting, you automatically assume that the part is causing the problem, and don't look anywhere else for the cause (*stereotyping*).

There are two types of reasoning, *deductive* and *inductive*. In the former, you progress from the general to the specific, and *vice versa* with the latter.

Some steps involved with making a decision are to:

- **G**ather all relevant information - using your senses (which may be wrong)

- **R**eview it

- **A**nalyze alternatives, keeping situational awareness (the big picture)

- **D**ecide and Do - make your choice and act on it, although other factors may affect the quality of your decision and your ability to implement it

- **E**valuate the outcome - and be prepared to start all over again

Note: CRM's function, in the guise of better crew interaction, is actually to facilitate the decision making process, but the popular conception is the opposite, i.e. that CRM is part of DM. You will notice that the problem solving comes first and the decision making comes late in the process, at the *Decide & Do* stage.

The point about decision-making, as distinct from problem solving, is that the possible solutions are already known - you are faced with various alternatives, from which you have to make a choice. Problem solving involves reconciling a present position with a goal, with no obvious way of getting there - it is an attempt to achieve the goal through a series of logical stages, which might include defining the problem, generating possible solutions and evaluating them, which leads to the decision-making process - the last two options above. Problem solving has two types of thinking associated with it: *Convergent* thinking brings information together, and *divergent* thinking generates different answers to one problem. The former requires more initial effort, whereas the latter requires more work towards the end (see *Judgement*, later in this section).

The above decision making steps are not rigid, but may be merged or even repeated in a situation. For example, when adverse weather is ahead, you might get the updated weather, then vary the route or land to wait it out. Then you might get airborne and find you have to do it all over again, but this time land for refuelling, before getting airborne once more. The whole thing can be a continuously evolving process, which can be made quicker if some experience has already been gained, hence the value of training, which can allow you to make short cuts.

However, in normal life, what usually happens with a decision is that the thinking comes afterwards. If you go shopping for a house, for example, you might look at the outside and decide you like it there and then, until you discover that there is a factory around the corner that works all night, or the shops are too far away to walk to, or the neighbours are nasty. Or you take the line of least resistance and follow the actions that seem to work as far as you can - only when you have bought some time, or see that your actions are not leading anywhere, do you think about changing things - this is often what happens in an aviation emergency. You are more decisive when you can make sense of the selections available, which includes cutting down the list to manageable proportions, as the more choice you have, the more you tend to take the easiest path, and too much choice is known to affect decision making. Because decisions often must be made quickly, we may concentrate on a few relevant facts, perhaps relying on intuition or rules of thumb as short cuts, based on previous experience. Two circumstances where past experience can hinder decision making include *mental set* (or *rigidity*), where an older solution is used, even when more efficient ones exist (which could be called *reproductive* thinking, rather than *productive* thinking), and *functional fixedness*, where we fail to see other solutions than the normal ones (in other words, think out of the box).

Training can reduce the need for making decisions - after all, the reaction to engine failure is pretty much cut and dried. However, there are many decisions that can be made before that point to reduce the after effects, such as choosing a good position in case something happens.

Influences on making choices can include *randomness* (flip a coin), *routine* (helps with small decisions), *rules* (start No 1 engine on odd days) and *outside influences*, say from spouses or friends. The trouble is that our brains were designed for a more simple life, with decision making taken completely out of the loop (if you came across a dinosaur, you ran - simple!) With the vast amount of choices available to us these days (just try ordering a sandwich in Subway) we have to think as well - either rationalise our decisions or risk making bad ones. The result is that we choose not to choose, or rationalise a decision afterwards, based on our prejudices and expectations. Another problem is that many decisions are beyond our awareness.

Neurophysiologists Benjamin Libet and Bertram Feinstein at Mount Zion Hospital in San Francisco recently measured the time for a touch stimulus on a patient's skin to reach the brain as an electrical signal. Patients also had to press a button once they became aware of being touched. The brain registered the stimulus in 0.0001 of a second, and the button was pressed inside 0.1 second. The interesting bit is that the conscious awareness of either event was not registered for nearly half a second, indicating that the decision to respond arose unconsciously. It has also been found that the brain generates signals for moving muscles 1½ seconds *before* you decide to do so.

Analysing decision-making steps in detail is inappropriate in the midst of an emergency. Sometimes we have to make rapid-fire decisions under high pressure and with little information, but you may be surprised to hear that you might not actually need that much information, especially with proper training, rules and rehearsal.

For example, many instructors are able to size up a student in less than a minute when it comes to deciding whether they will get their pilot's licence or not. Girls know in the first few moments of a date whether it will go anywhere (women's intuition), and policemen have their hunches. Sportsmen, too, try to be in something they call The Zone, otherwise known as the present moment, because that's where things are happening. It's where they can operate with little conscious thought, and where they ignore what could be or might have been. Sports psychologists like Debbie Crews help athletes to balance their brains to better control the backhand, the penalty kick or the golf swing. It's only when they stop listening to the analytical left brain and allow themselves to go with the flow of the instinctive right brain that they find their best performance.

It should also be noted that the kind of decisions that can have far-reaching effects are actually quite small. Say you have just landed in twilight, and it is reported that your port and starboard navigation lights are not working. These, of course, are required equipment when flying at night. Do you shut down and wait for an engineer to fix them, or stay overnight and try again in the morning?

Or do you take off in what is still officially daylight and pretend to yourself that they stopped working while you were in flight, relying on ATC radar to tell you about other traffic, and *vice versa*, and put the landing light on, figuring that if it were on under normal circumstances, people wouldn't see the navigation lights anyway?

Anyhow, the normal process is to recognise a change, assess alternative actions, make a decision and monitor the results. This can be enhanced with *awareness of undesirable attitudes*, learning to *find relevant information*, and *motivation* to act in a timely fashion.

In fact, just to introduce yet another essential acronym, decision making can be based on the DECIDE* model, which consists of these steps:

- **D**etect
- **E**stimate
- **C**hoose
- **I**dentify
- **D**o
- **E**valuate*

*The importance of the *Evaluate* step is to be able to step back and not necessarily press on - the problem is called *plan continuation bias*, which is a tendency to continue with what you are doing when changing circumstances require a new plan. It is otherwise called *press-on-itis*, (or *get-home-itis*) which is a phenomenon that is very common in bad weather. Whatever it's called, it has the effect of increasing the workload right when it should be eased, which diminishes your ability to think ahead.

Other influences include:

- *Belief Perseverance* - the tendency to cling to a belief, even if the evidence suggests otherwise

- *Entrapment* - when you've gone too far to withdraw from a situation, say, due to the costs involved

- *Overconfidence* - overestimating the accuracy of current knowledge

- *Expectancy* - or *Perceptual Set*, which can affect the perception of the world and what you do with the information. That is, your brain constructs its model of the world according to what it should be, and not what it is

- *Framing* - or the way information is presented (a 50% success rate is the same as a 50% failure rate)

Each decision you make eliminates the choice of another so, once you make a poor one, a chain of them usually follows. In fact, a decision-making chain can often be traced back up to and over fifty years, depending on whether the original cause was a design flaw (the F-15 and F-16, for example, are functionally identical to fly, except that the speed bands go the opposite way in each aircraft).

Another factor is the data itself; if it's incomplete, or altered through some emotional process, you can't base a proper decision on it. So:

- Don't make a decision unless you have to (which does not mean waiting until the last minute, but using the time you need *within the time available*)

- Keep it under review once you've made it

- No decision can be a decision (but watch for indecision)

Most important, though, is to be prepared to *change* a decision! (the Captain in the Dryden Accident should not have tried to take off a second time). Of course, by definition, the nature of most incidents means there's no time for proper evaluation, and you have to use instinct, experience or training. In this respect, there are two decision-making processes that affect us, both of which really speak for themselves - *ample-time* and *time-critical*.

Ample-Time Decision Making

You start with the awareness of a situation, which means having some idea of the big picture (similar to the continual updating mentioned above). The situation is developing slowly and you have time to start thinking up alternative courses of action. A good example is flying towards a warm front - once you start seeing the tell-tale clouds, you know that one is close, so you have to start thinking of returning to base or risk having to wait it out if you get caught. You might change your route to go towards it initially, so in the latter parts of the journey you are flying towards the clearer weather.

SITUATIONAL AWARENESS

As mentioned, this is "the ability to accurately perceive what is happening in- and outside the aircraft, plus the ability to understand the meaning of different elements in the environment and the projection of their status in the near future." To do this successfully, you have to know how things *should* be to recognise what's wrong!

Situational awareness refers to your knowledge of all relevant information, past or present, conscious or unconscious, which includes your cultural background. The information that contributes to situational awareness comes in through the senses, and is transformed by the brain into a mental model of the situation, through the process of *perception*. Unfortunately, perception can be modified by past experiences and current expectations, so someone else's interpretation of a situation can be quite different from yours, if only because they have had different life experiences. Situational awareness is therefore highest when perception approaches what passes for reality.

Note: This difference in viewpoints is one reason why communication is so important, because it is essential that all the crew are on the same page.

The main constituent is *vigilance*, or monitoring a situation without lapses in attention, which both uses up energy and processing power. In short, what the layman would call being alert. *Hypervigilance* occurs with a high workload, and the overwhelming of people with information, where it is difficult to latch on to what to prioritise first. *Hypovigilance* is a lack of attention to detail, as you might get when underwhelmed with detail, or bored.

For a good example of situational awareness, imagine yourself overtaking two trucks, one behind the other, in your car. The one behind is going faster than the one in front, and you know that there is a lot of momentum involved in driving a truck, so you figure it isn't going to slow down, but is more likely to want to overtake instead. You therefore expect the rear truck to want to occupy the lane you are in, so you either slow down, speed up or move over to the next lane to give it room (advanced drivers call this *reading the road*). In aviation terms, it can be likened to keeping a mental picture of what aircraft are around you, and what they are doing, by listening to ATC transmissions. SA involves knowledge of the past, present and future, and requires anticipation, so you need *vigilance* and *continual alertness*, with regard to what *may* happen on top of what *is* happening, which is difficult at the end of a long day. Being a pilot, most of the information you will base a decision on comes from your instruments and navigation equipment, but this can be affected by your physical state, discussed below.

The various levels of situational awareness are as follows:

- **Monitoring** - where you are just keeping abreast with events, and are only reacting to information presented by flight instruments. It is easy to fall behind the aircraft, especially when reading the newspaper on the flight deck. It is also important to understand the differences between *active* and *passive* monitoring.

  - **Passive monitoring** is indirectly attending to stimuli by conditioned, involuntary, reflexive responses, i.e., driving your car while thinking about other things. Under these conditions you will only be pulled back to the primary task when something alarming and/or distracting intervenes, such as lights, horns, certain types of signs, emergency situations, etc. From a physiological perspective, passive monitoring involves the subcortex portion of the brain which is associated with reflex activities and automatic responses

- **Active monitoring**, on the other hand, is consciously and selectively attending to a primary task, such as flying while listening to ATC, while checking your instruments and looking for trouble, as it were, also known as being *proactive*. It involves the cerebral cortex and requires commitment, energy, and effort, which can best be achieved through a mindset that recognises the importance and technique of active monitoring. The improvement in awareness, however, will be significant

- **Evaluate** - A slightly more proactive regime

- **Anticipate** - Being ahead of the game, and the highest level of situational awareness

Time-Critical Decision Making

Where decisions have to be made quickly, based on past experience or training, there is often no time to be creative or think up new solutions. In other words, time dictates your decision, and this is where checklists and SOPs can help, because they will be based on other peoples' experience (training should make your actions as near to reflex as possible, to make way for creative thought).

STANDARD OPERATING PROCEDURES

Drills, as per the Ops Manual, and checklists do the same thing on a different scale. Their purpose is to provide a framework on which to base good decision-making, as well as making sure you don't forget anything. SOPs are there to provide standardisation in situations where groups are formed and dissolve with great regularity, such as flight crews, as supported by checklists and briefings.

Standard Operating Procedures (SOPs) in a multi-crew environment are essential for consistent and predictable responses to routine and emergency situations. They also provide for enhanced morale (meaning less friction) between crew members that is often caused by doing things differently. For pilots who are in training, or new to the Company, they will help to ensure faster integration.

In fact, there are many reasons for SOPs (and checklists), including:

- A logical order of events

- Improvement in communication

- Better error management

- Better workload management and prioritisation

- Better situational awareness

- Improvements in cross-checking

- Limits or acceptance tolerances are set

- Conflict resolution (see under *Communication*)

The development of procedures makes pilots more effective and reliable in their activities - a process called, predictably, *procedural consistency*.

Although a checklist doesn't contain policy, it does at least stimulate activity, since the first response of most people in an emergency is to suffer acute brainfade. Either that, or you shoot from the hip, which is equally wrong. Checklists and drills are in the Company's Ops Manual and are intended to be followed to the letter (although they are not always based on the Flight Manual drills, which are there to comply with the requirements of the C of A). Whilst they have their uses, though, they cannot cater for every situation, and you may have to think once in a while. In such circumstances, it pays to have prehandled many emergencies (i.e. updating landing sites as above), but, otherwise, actions take place in two modes, the *conscious* and the *automatic*. The former can be slow and error-prone, but has more potential for being correct. The latter is largely unconscious and therefore automatic, but it only relies on a vast database of information (or experience), and is not creative of itself - a problem that may affect inexperienced pilots.

MAKING PLANS

Where time is critical, such as whether to stop or go at V_1 or TDP, it pays to have a plan ready in case something goes wrong, which is where your training, plus a preflight briefing comes in (run it through your head by yourself if there's nobody else there). This helps you to visualise the process - golfers see the ball going into the hole before they hit it, and Bell teach you to visualise an engine-off landing before you do one. However, there's no point in having a plan if you don't *execute* it! Many accidents happened because the original plan wasn't followed.

Group Decision Making

Many decisions are made collectively, particularly in families. In theory, therefore, a more cautious element should be built in to the process, with a greater chance of all information being recognised and considered, for more consistency. As it happens, group decisions are *more extreme* than those of the individual, meaning that an inclination to be cautious or risky will be increased.

This is the *group polarisation effect*.

A unanimous group will exert strong pressure to conform - if even one person dissents, the conformity is much less marked. Thus, a minority can influence a group if it maintains a consistent position without appearing to be rigid, arrogant or dogmatic. Although single-pilot, you are still part of a group - a *peer group* of other pilots, and the effects are just the same. Many accidents have occurred because people have worried more about how they look to their colleagues than taking the right actions.

People will try to live up to group norms (e.g. teenagers), which can be set quite quickly, even in a group that hasn't met much before (initial behaviour can leave a lasting impression). *Differences of opinion should be regarded as helpful.*

NORMS

A norm is an unwritten rule that is followed by the majority of a group, as opposed to a habit, which is peculiar to one person. Norms are therefore a code of behaviour (or a culture) which can be very powerful, as humans tend to like being in groups, and rejection is a danger if you don't conform to them. For example, it may be the norm in your company that people who make mistakes are ridiculed.

Norman

A *positive norm* (see left) is one where expected behaviour is condoned and contributes to the betterment of the group. For example, washing down a helicopter after a flight, even if it isn't your job. A *neutral norm* is one that is neither positive or negative, which does not detract nor enhance an accepted standard, so there is no great impact. A *negative norm* is a short cut or accepted practice that detracts from safety and which is accepted or tolerated by the majority of a group, which is why Chernobyl exploded - the engineers left out most of the safety procedures when they were trying an experiment. Drinking and driving used to be a good example, and in the days of the *Titanic* it was normal practice to steam straight ahead at high speed, even though the rules said they shouldn't (many ships also didn't batten down their hatches until they were well under way).

Responses

Following a decision, based on a stimulus, there is a response. However, one resulting from excessive pressure is more likely to be based on insufficient data and be wrong than a more considered one, assuming time permits. If you make a rushed decision, you are more likely to overlook analysis of the current situation and apply a decision prepared earlier, although you shouldn't change a plan unnecessarily; a previously made one based on sound thinking is more likely to work than one cooked up on the spur of the moment, provided, of course that the situation is the same or similar. A correct, rather than rapid, reaction is appropriate.

Response times will vary according to the complexity of the problem, or the element of expectation and hence preparedness (we are trained to expect engine failures, for example, but not locked controls, so the reaction time to the former will be less). Pushing a button as a response to a light illuminating will take about 1/5 th of a second, but add another light and button and this will increase to a second or so. An unexpected stimulus increases reaction time to nearly 5 seconds. There is a time delay between perceiving information and responding to it, which is typically 3.4 seconds. The reason we don't take this long to answer people in normal conversation is because we anticipate what they are going to say, which could lead to misinterpretation if you don't have body language to help, as you might get with using radio.

Dr. Daniel Stern studied a movie of Muhammad Ali at 24 years of age fighting in Frankfurt. He found that just over half of Ali's left jabs were faster than 9/50 of a second. His opponent, Mildenberger, threw left jabs faster than that for about a third of the time he was in the ring. They were too rapid to be traditional stimuli and responsi (joke). Obviously, Ali did not signal his punches, yet nearly all of his blows were blocked or avoided. In fact, he only won by a technical knockout. The answer is that Mildenberger's brain was decoding Ali's predicted behaviour patterns and anticipating them.

Similarly, in life, our actions can overlap in time and appear to be simultaneous, when, actually, they are not.

LEARNING & PERFORMANCE

In simple terms, learning can be defined as a *long-term change in behaviour based on practice and experience*, whether its other peoples' (reading, studying) or your own. You are *skilled* when you:

- Train or practice regularly

- Know how to manage yourself

- Know how to keep resources in reserve for the unexpected

According to Tony Kerr, skills come at four levels:

- **Level 1**, which is good enough to be safe

- **Level 2** includes effectiveness, such as being able to fly in your local environment by yourself

- **Level 3** is efficiency

- **Level 4** is precision and continuous improvement

Left to themselves, most pilots will only ever reach Level 2 without additional training.

The effect of experience and habit (see under *Judgement*) on performance can be positive or negative. Your performance is better when you are relaxed, independent of the time of day.

The word *behaviour* refers to how people act, or react, in particular circumstances. Behaviour in the form of action is one end result of information processing.

Rasmussen isolated three levels of behaviour with respect to the performance of tasks in his *SRK model*, in which errors can occur at all three:

Automatic

SKILL-BASED

This is based on practice and prior learning, to become part of the "muscle memory", or *motor programs*, of your body (as when learning the piano), meaning that reactions are largely unconscious and automatic, or routine. As such, it does not require continuous conscious monitoring, but it can lead to **environmental capture**, that is, doing something because it's always done and not because it's the right thing to do. You could also end up with the right skill in the wrong situation (**action slip**), meaning pulling the flap lever instead of that for the gear. In addition, you might not catch new stimuli when operating largely in automatic mode, and one other disadvantage is that it is difficult to explain (and thus pass on) to other people. Modification of skill-based learning

requires it to be relearnt at a deep level, so experienced pilots are more affected. In order not to make mistakes, you need to know that you are prone to errors at this level when you are preoccupied, tired, or otherwise distracted, so you need to be consciously aware of your actions. A good example is using the switches on the main panel of the AS 350 - you should read them first, because each one is different!

Wiegman & Shappell have shown that over 80% of general aviation accidents can be attributed to skill-based errors, meaning that the pilots were not flying properly, and that currency was an issue. Automation does not help!

If you approach an airfield under VFR, at a prescribed altitude, exactly following the approach procedure, and you encounter no unexpected or new problems, you would appear to show skill-based behaviour. In a co-ordinated turn, most of your activity is skill-based, as is the choice of the moment you select the gear down.

ASSOCIATED ERRORS

- Errors of Routine

- Environmental Capture

- Action Slip

Conscious

RULE-BASED

This relies on previously considered courses of action, and follows procedures, like checklists and SOPs, so it is a slower process, and more sequential. The rules are kept in *long term memory* (see below), requiring the *decision channel* and working memory for execution - an inexperienced pilot may have a problem with this if the rules are imprecise and assume a minimum level of knowledge for them to be used properly.

What usually happens when an accident occurs is that the brain goes smartly into neutral whilst everything around you goes pear-shaped. Checklists can help to bridge the gap of inactivity by giving you something more or less correct to do whilst psyching yourself up and evaluating information ready for a decision. The US Navy, for example, trains pilots to stop in emergencies, and reset the clock on the instrument panel, which forces them to relax, or at least, not to panic. Rule-based behaviour is generally robust, which is why procedures and rules are important in maintenance. However, you can use the wrong procedure as a result of misdiagnosis. Of course, you could always forget the procedure.

Once the application of a rule resolves the problem, you revert to automatic mode.

ASSOCIATED ERRORS

- Errors of Technical Knowledge
- Commission
- Departure from SOPs
- Interruptions
- Violations

Unsuitable rules, or situations when the rules do not apply, determine the transition from rule-based to knowledge-based activity......

KNOWLEDGE-BASED

This can rely on previous experience, but involves mostly knowledge, since it arises from the need to cope with new or unexpected situations, and knowledge is all you have to fall back on, so your primary weapons are *thinking* and *reasoning* (it's probably the only aspect that machines cannot cope with, and why we still need humans in the cockpit). When problem-solving, the transition from rule-based to knowledge-based activities is governed by the *unsuitability of known rules for the problem posed*. This is the sort of stuff you apply if you need to think things through, or maybe work on the *why* so the *how* becomes apparent, because there are no rules that you can apply to the situation. Inexperienced pilots are more likely to make knowledge-based mistakes when they are forced into knowledge-based behaviour in situations that have not been encountered before. They refer to information more than experts do when carrying out the same task. Thus, errors at this level arise from making diagnoses without full knowledge of a system, such as mistaking the sound of an engine blowing up for a tyre burst.

ASSOCIATED ERRORS

- Confirmation Bias, which is the tendency to search for information to confirm a theory, while overlooking contradictory information. It can be likened to making the ground fit the map, rather than accepting the fact that we are lost. You could also look upon it as a tendency to *ignore information that confirms a decision is a poor one*.

Factors That Affect Learning

Motor programs are stored routines that enable patterns of behaviour to be executed without continuous conscious control. According to *Anderson*, the acquisition of such expertise has three stages, namely: *Cognitive, Associative* and *Autonomous* or, in other words, you start with a theoretical knowledge of what needs to be done, move through practice, to where the knowledge is completely in memory (although I have never felt that learning the complete alphabet was necessary before learning to read). In aviation terms, in the first (or *cognitive*) phase, an instructor might talk about skills you will acquire, including the task, typical errors and target performance. Next comes the *associative phase*, where techniques are demonstrated and learned, and errors are gradually reduced. The *Autonomous* or *Automatic* stage is where you have it down pat.

The *quality* of learning is promoted by *feedback*. Otherwise, these factors may help in getting an instructor's message (for example) across:

- Personality
- The Environment
- Motivation
- Review (Recency)
- Fatigue
- Technique & Instructional Ability
- Age - Learning may not be so easy after about 60

ERRORS & VIOLATIONS
. . . .

Murphy's Law comes in several parts:

- If something can go wrong, it will, at the worst possible moment
- Nothing is as easy as it looks, and it always takes longer (and costs more) than expected
- If equipment is designed so that it can be operated wrongly, sooner or later, it will be

An error, officially, arises when a planned sequence of activities fails to achieve the intended outcome, where random external intervention is not involved. *Latent* errors, such as an unnoticed waypoint error in a GPS database, have consequences that lie dormant, and are difficult to recognise (or foresee) because of the time lag between their generation and occurrence, while *Active* errors, which are committed *at the human/system interface*, have consequences that are felt almost immediately, which is how they can be detected. In fact, human error can be present at four levels:

- *unsafe acts* (errors & violations)

- *predispositions* to unsafe acts

- unsafe or inadequate *supervision*

- *organisational influences*

> Latent errors are hard to prevent, but at least should be made visible by a Safety Management System

One working definition of human error is *"where planned sequences of mental or physical activity fail to achieve intended outcomes, not attributable to chance."* Another is *"the mismatch between the intention and the result of an action."*

Some errors can be *random*, or unpredictable, and will happen whatever you do, and others will be inherent in the system, called *design errors*. They occur because the system has not been thought out properly, so they should ultimately be predictable if someone eventually gets their thinking cap on. Thus, it is important to realise that errors don't just arise from the human parts of the system, but can result from the system as a whole (*Dekker*, 2006).

Errors can also be classified into those that can be quickly identified and corrected, with minimal consequences, and those that are more serious, such as a wrong entry into a GPS which can affect a whole flight.

Systematic errors are consistent, *random* errors have no specific pattern, and a sporadic error is a one-off that is very far removed from the rest of any related events.

Internal Influences
Origins of *representative errors* include:

- *Sensing Errors*. Errors must be detected for them to be reacted to - a good example is airspeed, which is often inferred from the surroundings, as when flying in mountains

- *Perceptual Errors* arise when interpretation is faulty, as influenced by context, data and expectancy

- *Action Slips*. When the wrong sequence of actions occurs (raising the gear instead of flaps)

- *Decision-Making*. Undue weight may be given to one factor, leading to a wrong conclusion

- *False Hypothesis*, like the Air Transat Airbus that ran out of fuel over the Atlantic, where computer indications of low fuel were ignored

- *Distraction*. This can lead to false assumptions - the whole crew of the 1011 that crashed into the

Everglades assumed the aircraft was under control while they dealt with a landing light problem. The solution is to prioritise actions and learn not to be influenced by interruptions

- *Motivation and Arousal*. Unmotivated or under-aroused people may commit more errors

External Influences
Human factors concerns the interaction between people and machines, procedures, and the environment:

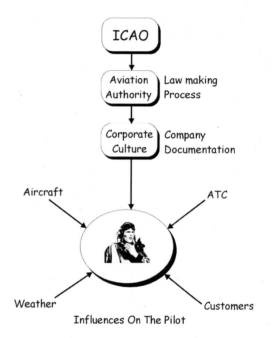

Influences On The Pilot

All of it is exemplified by.........

THE SHEL MODEL
This concept was originally presented by a psychologist called Edwards. Proper application of it can help prevent errors

. The letters of the word *SHEL* stand for *Software, Hardware, Environment* and *Liveware*, which represent influences on the typical pilot. *Hardware*, naturally enough, is the mechanical environment, *Environment* covers such things as hypoxia, temperature, etc., whilst *Software* covers checklists, etc. *Liveware* copes with interactions between the pilot and other people, including the pilot himself.

LIVEWARE-HARDWARE

The 3-needle altimeter was a classic example of poor design that led to accidents. EFIS/ECAS displays are also not entirely satisfactory because, although they present relevant information, they fail to show patterns and trends, and it is harder to read digits than it is to
read analogue dials, where you get used to a picture of needle positions, and any misplaced are easily noticed. When you have to read numbers, it takes a second or two to interpret the information. *Analogue presentation is most suitable for qualitative or comparative information.*

LIVEWARE-SOFTWARE

Liveware-software problems can occur when documentation is poorly written and presented, such as a pilot having problems with a checklist. Checklists ensure that the aircraft is in the proper configuration for a particular stage of flight, and that you haven't forgotten anything. To use them properly, *you need to be aware of what they are trying to achieve.* Refer also to *Multi Crew.*

LIVEWARE-ENVIRONMENT

Noise, vibration, temperature and heat all need to be carefully controlled, as do work patterns and shifts that fail to take account of sleep disturbance and jet lag. A poor working environment will affect motivation, and it is worth remembering that good working environments start from the top of the company downwards.

LIVEWARE-LIVEWARE

Poor relationships or communication between crewmembers have led to disasters. See *Parent-Adult-Child,* under *Communication.*

AUTOMATION

The brain's limitations, in terms of speed of computation and the ability to multi-task (i.e. none!) began to be recognised as early as 1959, when the Boeing 707 was first rolled out. This was when it was realised that pilots could soon begin to exceed their design capabilities, which meant the assistance of various black boxes was required.

However, a lot of work can be done for you by computers, which are just electronic machines - the man-machine system is meant to *relieve pilot workload and increase time for supervision.* To avoid wrong decisions, *a system should at least be able to report malfunctions.*

But how much control should be given to black boxes? If they have too much, the cockpit becomes boring and errors can go unnoticed amongst the monotony. Although

automation can conserve resources and attention, it can result in routine errors, or *slips,* such as when programming waypoints into the system. Machines can wait for infrequent information without getting bored, and can perform long-term control and set values, again, without getting bored, but people can exercise judgement, make better decisions and detect unusual conditions, whilst getting bored very easily.

On the one hand, automation is a good thing, because it can take much of the routine work away from you, and flight management systems can operate an aircraft very fuel-efficiently. For example, the FADEC on the Bell 407 helicopter (fuel control thingy) incorporates a lot of monitoring functions. On the other hand, it can induce a feeling of *automation complacency* (too much reliance on the machine) and lead you not to check things as often as you should (*reduced vigilance*), or push the envelope, as when using a GPS in bad weather - with much of the navigation task taken away from you, it is very tempting to fly in worse weather than you can really cope with (flying in bad weather is like sex - the further you get into it, the harder it is to stop). As your visual clues decrease, your mental processes focus more on trying to see where you're going and less on flying until you eventually lose control, at a point where trying to fly on instruments is no help out of trouble because you are not mentally prepared for it.

You can avoid *automation complacency* by regarding systems as *one more crewmember that needs to be cross-checked.*

A high degree of automation may alter traditional tasks so much that your attention and competence is reduced once you are out of the loop. Thus, communication and coordination call for a greater effort from the crew. The trouble is that we rely on machines so much, and their rapidity of change adds to our stress, as described by Alvin Toffler in his book, *Future Shock.*

However, one major benefit is the integration of many sources of information and its presentation in a clear and concise manner (sometimes!), as with the glass cockpit, and providing a major contribution towards situational awareness, as long as you keep a mental plot going, as the information presented can be highly filtered. Put more in exam language, *the use of modern technology in glass cockpits facilitates feedback from the machine via more concise data for communication on the flight deck.* So there.

ERGONOMICS

Under this heading comes cockpit design and automated systems, being associated with the human/workplace interface. Here's an illustration of how bad design can be the start of an *event chain*:

> *A relatively inexperienced RAF Phantom (F4) pilot had a complete electrics failure, as if being over the North Sea at night in winter wasn't stressful enough. For whatever reason, he needed to operate the Ram Air Turbine, but he deployed the flaps instead, as the levers were close together.*
>
> *Of course, doing that at 420 knots made the flaps fall off the back, and the hydraulic fluid followed. Mucking around with the generators got the lights back on, and he headed for RAF Coningsby, with no brakes. Unfortunately, on landing, the hook bounced over the top of the arrester wire, so he used full afterburner to go around in a strong crosswind, but headed towards the grass instead. The pilot and navigator both ejected, leaving the machine to accelerate through 200 knots, across the airfield at ground level.*
>
> *Meanwhile, the Station Commander was giving a dinner party for the local mayor in the Mess, and the guests had just come out on the steps (near the runway), in time to watch the Phantom come past on the afterburner, with two ejections. The mayor's wife was just thanking him for the firework display as it went through a ditch, lost its undercarriage and fell to bits in a field.*
>
> *The Fire Section had by this time sent three (brand new) appliances after it without any hope of catching up, but they tried anyway. The first one wrote itself off in a ditch because it was going too fast, the driver of the second suddenly put the brakes on because he realized there had been an ejection and that he might run over a pilot on the runway, at which point the number three appliance smashed into the back of him.*

We are in a similar situation - how many times have you jumped into the cockpit of a different machine, to find the switches you need in a totally different place? This doesn't help you if you rely on previous experience to find what you need (in emergencies you tend to fall back to previous training), so the trick is to know what you need at all times, and take the time to find out where it is (*read the switches*, like you have to in the AS 350).

Another example of design being a factor in an accident is what happened to a V22 (US Marine tilt rotor), which had the power controls changed to resemble those of the Harrier, because the Colonel in charge used to fly them. When another pilot with a helicopter background used the machine, and had a reverse-control problem, he used the control in the opposite sense, got more power when he was expecting less, and crashed.

Threat & Error Management

Flights can be affected by threats and errors, or *hazards that can reduce the normal safety margins*. Managing threats and errors during a flight is part of the function of TEM which includes airmanship but also includes training, checklists, briefings, and CRM to allow you to monitor things properly (CRM applies more general concepts).

Threats are events or hazards that are outside the control of the pilot, for which good situational awareness is a good antidote. Such threats might include the weather (density altitude), other traffic, obstacles, etc. Errors can be intentional or unintentional, but they still need management in order not to affect the safety of the flight. Mistakes in the flight paperwork are good examples, but pilots have been known to shut down the wrong engine!

Countermeasures include planning, anticipation, briefings, cross-checking, proactive monitoring, assertiveness, prioritisation of tasks to reduce the workload, etc.

Error Management could be regarded as a counter-measure against bad decisions. New pilots naturally make mistakes - experienced pilots tend to have monitoring errors, and are more likely to think they are flying an older type. There are three lines of defence against errors:

- Avoiding them in the first place (that is, not getting into a position that requires your superior skills to get out of). This requires a great deal of situational awareness and, by implication, active monitoring of the situation

- If they happen, detecting and trapping errors before they are significant

- Sorting out the mess afterwards

Error management accepts that mistakes happen, and adopts a non-punitive approach to minimise the effects (which does not mean that you should break the rules on purpose!) Evidence of this can be seen in the establishment of anonymous reporting procedures, such as CHIRP in the UK and the *Aviation Safety Action Program* (ASAP) in the US.

The *Zero Defect Program* tries to eradicate errors by encouraging very high levels of motivation with rigid training and checking, although it ignores the influence of external errors. The *Error Cause Removal Program* tries to anticipate them. There have also been attempts to remove the human from the system altogether (although someone still has to program the computer!) However, whoever is in charge has finally combined reducing the causes of errors, with reducing their *consequences*. That is, as mentioned before, they have finally realized that sh*t happens, or that it is impossible to eliminate mistakes, and have tried to make clearing up the mess easier. For more details, read Professor James Reason's book, *Human Error*, in which he points out that the sequence of human events in an accident can be likened to several slices of Swiss cheese (the stuff with holes in), with the holes as opportunities for accidents. The slices actually represent layers between management decision making and the incident concerned, but this should not be taken to mean that all accidents stem from management! On the day that the holes line up, something will happen, so if you can recognise the sequence, you should, in theory, be able to pull some of the holes out of line, and prevent an accident. One Australian fire fighting pilot went to transmit, pushed the wrong button and dropped his water bucket instead. He landed, picked it up and went home for a couple of days, figuring that he must be tired and he was better off out of it.

Unfortunately, the chain can sometimes not be broken in time. This is from an anonymous accident report:

"After twelve accident- and incident-free years flying single engine helicopters across western Canada and the U.S., I was feeling quite confident about my abilities as a pilot. I enjoyed my work, I was receiving regular compliments from customers for getting their work done safely and efficiently, and my company recognized my hard work with promotions, endorsements, cash bonuses, and pay-raises. Life was treating me well.

I hadn't had a visit from the proverbial "Murphy" yet.

The fire season had just started when I returned from a relaxing three-month holiday with my family. My first two days back to work were on a remote forest fire with a Bell 206 - a routine task in familiar territory. I had hauled firefighters and their equipment many times before, and dumped countless buckets of water on fires. I flew the allowed maximum of 8 hours on each of the first two days. At the end of each day, I flew my helicopter to the nearest company base, where I filled out my logbooks, had supper, and had a good sleep in an air-conditioned motel room. The summer was looking busy and profitable.

On the third day, I went back to the same fire after having had a good breakfast and feeling well rested. It was an unusually hot day with some wind, so I was hoping for some of my favourite work on a fire-water bucketing. However, after I set 20 firefighters out to work, the fire boss had me sling in camp gear, as he expected this to be a campaign fire. I was a bit sceptical of this, as I was worried that I might be expected to stay in the rough camp. The truck driver had dumped all the camp gear at the staging area, and I had nobody to help load up the nets and roll barrels. That meant that every time I arrived at the staging

point, I had to get out of the helicopter, load the nets and attach my longline. It was hot, dry, and smoky, and I was getting hungry and irritated. But I wasn't going to let the fire boss know that my frustration level was getting high, as I enjoyed the job and didn't want any complaints about me. I certainly wasn't going to allow another pilot - or worse, a competitor - take this dream job away from me. By the time I had all the camp gear flown in from the nearest road staging point and picked up the crews, my flight log showed I had flown 7.6 hrs - just enough time remained for me to return to base. I was hungry, thirsty, hot, tired and dirty, and looked forward to a shower, dinner and an air-conditioned motel room.

I informed the fire boss of my pending "time-exed" status. He said that the camp cook had seen some bears in the area, and asked me to stay at the camp for a few more hours, even though I was nearing the end of my 12-hour duty day. So, in the spirit of cooperation, I put on a brave face and helped the fire crew set up the tents. While they were eating, I carried boxes of groceries, rolled barrels of fuel, cleaned up my helicopter, and fixed a loose wire on my longline. I didn't worry about getting something to eat, because, after all, I was going back to town for a hot meal and a shower at the motel.

After my 12-hour duty day had expired, the fire boss asked me to stay the night, as he was concerned about bears in the area. I made one more round trip to the staging area with him for some more fire fighting equipment and to look for the bears. Twenty-four revenue hours in three days would be a good pay cheque. When we got back to camp, the camp cook told me that there was nothing left for supper. As it was now getting dark and I had flown my maximum hours as well as exceeded my duty day, I had no choice but to grin and bear it. There was no hot supper, shower, or air-conditioned motel room for me that night, but I wasn't going to complain. However, no supper was just the start of the bad news, as I was then told that there was not sufficient room for me in any of the sleeping tents, but I could sleep in the supply tent. Being a resourceful pilot, I pulled out the emergency sleeping bag from the helicopter, and looked in the supply tent. Nothing but gravel and some broken boxes of dry macaroni. I didn't want to be called a whiner, so I made the best of it.

I spent a cold, uncomfortable night lying on gravel with no mattress or pillow, listening to rodents eat the spilled macaroni. I was up at 3 a.m., wishing I had never taken this particular job. I was hungry, dirty, sweaty, and in desperate need of a shower and a change of clothes. Everybody else was sleeping, and I didn't want to make any noise in the kitchen tent looking for something to eat and drink, so I cleaned my helicopter some more, carried out a real thorough pre-flight inspection, and stood up some fuel barrels in anticipation of another busy day.

At about 6 a.m., the cook was up, and I asked if I could get something to eat or at least to drink. "Get out of here! You (expletive deleted) pilots think you are so important! I'll call you when breakfast is ready and not a minute sooner!" Good morning to you, too.

At 7 a.m. just as the regular firefighters were sitting down for breakfast, the local fire centre called on my handheld VHF-FM radio to inquire if I was available for initial attack on another fire. I checked with the fire boss, who decided to accompany me. The helicopter was full of fuel, but my stomach wasn't. Still, getting out of that grumpy cook's way was most appealing.

We worked on the second fire for about 4 hours before another helicopter showed up to relieve me, and the fire boss and I returned to our camp low on fuel. By this time, there were 20 firefighters ready to go to work. I re-fuelled and set out the crew and their equipment in about 2 hours of flying time. The crews understood that I needed to refuel the helicopter, but I still had not had supper, breakfast, a shower, or anything to drink. Just as I was about to shut the helicopter down for some badly needed nourishment, the fire boss came running over and informed me that I had to go to the staging area to pick up a radio operator and some more supplies. OK, one more trip, and then I could get something to eat and drink.

I began to give the new radio operator my standard safety briefing, but she informed me that she didn't need one. One of those types. Back at camp, a pressing need to deliver some lunches to the fire line meant another delay in getting some food and drink. My level of frustration was getting a higher every minute. By this time, fire activity was picking up, and I was confident I could keep going. The radio operator was cluttering up our already congested radio frequency with many requests to "say again." The impatience in the voices of the firefighters echoed my frustration with her incompetence and poor attitude.

Back at camp, I politely asked for a break so I could get something to eat and drink. The fire boss wasn't happy about my request, as he only had one helicopter to work with, but he accepted. In the middle of my two-minute cool-down, a very excited firefighter with an irritating high-pitched voice screamed on the radio, "Help me! I'm getting burned to death!" I quickly did another hot re-fuelling, and the fire boss jumped back in. A quick reconnaissance of her area showed she was in no immediate danger, but the fire boss advised me to keep an eye on her. Then the usual requests were coming in to us by radio, "Tell Dave to turn up the pump. Bring me a strangler." "I need some water buckets over here." "Bring me some more hose." By this time, my mouth was very dry and my stomach was feeling like it was going to collapse. The possibility of fatigue and frustration

getting in the way of sound judgment never crossed my mind, as I just wanted to please the customer.

As we were circling the fire, the fire boss told me he needed me to work late that night, as he was going to require me to sling in some more groceries and camp supplies after I picked up the crews. I thought, "Marvellous. Here I go again, another day without being able to sit down for a real dinner. By the time I finish, there won't be enough daylight left to fly back to town for a good night's sleep, so it'll be another night in that tent. And how am I going to fudge my logbooks to avoid showing that I exceeded my flight and duty time limitations?"

The next task was to move a firefighter and some hose from the top of a hill to another location. As we approached the grassy knoll, I could see the firefighter carrying the hose across a steep slope with some burned-out stumps. Not an ideal location, but picking him up there would save him walking 200 ft up the hill, and get me closer to food and drink.

At this point, it seemed like my peripheral vision was getting rapidly narrower. The area was tight, and there were a lot of stumps, but nothing I recognized as being overly hazardous. I was not able to advise the firefighter of my plans because of the steady radio chatter, but as I approached, I saw him crouch down. My thoughts were, "Perfect, this guy is a pro. He can see that I am going to pick him up here, and he's making it easy for me. This will go really smoothly. I'll do a quick toe-in landing with him at my left rear door, and he can jump right in. What a way to impress the fire boss!"

I was hot, hungry, thirsty, and sweaty, my shirt and helmet were sticking to me like glue, and I hadn't slept for about 34 hours. Not a very glamorous situation. I informed the radio operator that we were picking up Bravo 10 at pad 7. After what seemed like an eternity on a very busy radio, I got the reply, "Roger, copy you picking up Bravo 7 at pad 10." More frustration.

Just as I was about to settle the front of the skids between some stumps, I remembered that I still needed to correct the radio operator's misunderstanding. Then the high-pitched voice came over the radio again, "Hurry up! Help me! I'm getting burned to death!" The radio chatter really picked up now, as all 20 firefighters offered their advice at the same time. The fire boss, who was sitting on my left side, said, "Let's hurry and check up on her!" Fatigue, hunger, thirst, and high mental workload combined to turn me into an unthinking robot. Compulsive instinct was replacing sound decision making.

As I closely monitored the position of my main rotor near a tree, and the front right skid inches from a stump, I heard the fire boss gasp on the live intercom. I looked up to see what the problem was, and the firefighter who had seemed to be making my toe-in landing so easy had just stood up and was moving up *the hill with the roll of hose, just as he had been told to do, right under the main rotor!*

And how I was now out of options. My brain failed to function, and it seemed like I was viewing the world in black and white. I was completely out of energy. All I could do was pull on the collective and hope I could lift the helicopter up before the unsuspecting firefighter walked into the rotor. This is the time that Murphy decided to pay his visit. My right skid hooked the stump, and even though I had been well trained to avoid pulling collective in this situation, the combination of an impending decapitation and sheer fatigue meant that this long chain of events resulted in a classic dynamic rollover. One fine helicopter destroyed, but thankfully no injuries.

Looking back on the situation now, I had had every opportunity to shut the flight operations down until I had something to drink and eat, or I could even have requested a relief pilot because I was very tired. It's funny how customers tolerate delays to refuel the helicopter, as they see running out of fuel as a serious hazard, but the pilot is regarded as a machine who doesn't need to sleep, eat, or drink.

This account of the events leading up to a preventable accident is not an attempt to blame the firefighters. The cause of this accident was my decision to perform a tight toe-in landing among some stumps, rather than wait one or two minutes to pick the firefighter up at a much better location. This was a day when normal decision-making processes were affected by hunger, dehydration, accumulated stress and fatigue- factors that I have personally found to be in abundance on many job sites, but especially fires. The regulators at Transport Canada have tried to enforce rest time with complex flight and duty time regulations, but this was a situation where the pilot was severely fatigued, but well within the regulations.

Now when I read accident reports in the Vortex, I imagine there were usually a lot of human factors that resulted in the accident besides just the last few seconds before the terrible sound of the rotor blades hitting the ground; customer pressures, company pressures, or worst of all, self-imposed pressures. One thing I have learned from my experience on that terrible day is that I never want to be hanging in an upside down helicopter again.

Recognize that fatigue is hazardous, admit when you are tired, and break the chain of events!"

Recognizing an *Error Chain* will not necessarily mean that an accident will actually occur, but detecting the holes in the cheese slices lining up should be cause for concern and spark off an investigation. However, bear in mind that the events in an error chain may not happen one after the other, and may not even depend on each other. There could be months between incidents. There seem to be somewhere between 4-7 links in the average error chain, which, looked at another way, means you have up to seven opportunities to stop an accident.

The non-punitive approach to errors (hopefully used in Safety Management Systems) is there to encourage people to report them, so that others don't repeat them. There's no point, for example, in introducing penalties into a reporting system (so that if you report yourself, you get punished!), because no errors will be reported. All it will do is make the Safety Officer look good!

SITUATIONAL AWARENESS

Situational awareness, or being aware of what's going on, is your biggest weapon against errors. Pilots who read newspapers on the flight deck are behind the aircraft, as are those who devote too much attention to detail.

Physical Influences

These are the influences that your body is subjected to.

THE ENVIRONMENT

Conditions under which an aircraft is operated, including:

- Lighting

- *Noise* (can affect motivation - see below)

- *Temperature*. You may be remote, in a busy area, or just bl**dy cold. You can feel cooler because moisture is evaporating from your skin at an advanced rate in dry air - humidity needs to be 60% at 18°C for comfort. For temperature, the human body operates comfortably between 18-24°C, but it needs to maintain a core temperature of 37°C, with very little deviation allowed. A 3-4° difference can lead to death

- *Weather*. Doing inspections out in the cold

TIME

Pressure to keep to deadlines.

AIR QUALITY

Not only can haze or mist reduce visibility, it can also be irritating, or smelly, or deadly. CO (carbon monoxide) is a colourless, odourless gas which has a half-life of about 6 hours at sea level pressures, so a quarter of the original amount is present after 12 hours. It typically gets into the cockpit from faulty exhausts, but also comes about where something is burning without an adequate air supply, or where combustion is incomplete. One characteristic symptom of CO poisoning is cherry red lips. Use 100% oxygen to recover.

NOISE, VIBRATION & TURBULENCE

Prolonged amounts of any of these is fatiguing and annoying - noise is particularly prevalent in helicopters, especially with the doors off. Vibration at the right frequency (8-12 Hz) causes back pain, as anyone who has flown a Bell 206 will tell you. The others include:

- 1-4 Hz - Affects breathing (1/10-2 Hz affects the vestibular apparatus)

- 4-10 Hz - Chest and abdominal pain

- 8-12 Hz - Backache

- 10-20 Hz - Headaches, eye strain, throat pain, speech disturbance & muscular tension

- 30-40 Hz - Interference with vision

Otherwise, resonance of body parts can result from vibrations between 1-100 Hz.

WHOLE-BODY VIBRATION

WBV can be experienced in two ways; through an instantaneous shock with a high peak level (enough to jar you out of your seat, as with turbulence) or through repeated exposure to low levels of vibration from regular motion, as with a helicopter with one rotor blade out of alignment. Its relevance here is its contribution to fatigue (low-frequency vibrations of moderate intensity can induce sleep), but the most common effect of WBV is lower back pain and inflammation that can lead to degeneration of discs or trapped nerves. However, of particular importance to longliners, is the increase in its effects from twisted sitting postures, which increases stress and load on the neck, shoulder and lower back (the main purpose of lumbar support is to produce an even pressure on the discs by allowing the lower spine to curve naturally). For example, vibrations between 2.5 and 5 Hz generate strong resonance in the vertebrae of the neck and lumbar region. Helicopter vibration has a peak power at frequencies around 5 Hz. Vibration from engines can cause micro fractures in vertebrae, disc protrusion, nerve damage and acute lower back pain. Otherwise, short-term exposure has only small effects, such as slight hyperventilation and increased heart rate, plus increased muscle tension from voluntary and involuntary contraction (tenseness dampens the vibration).

Acute effects (short-term exposures) include headache, chest and abdominal pain, nausea and loss of balance. *Chronic effects* (long-term exposures) include degenerative spinal

changes, lumbar scoliosis, disc disease, degenerative disorders of the spine and herniated discs.

FLICKER

This occurs when light is interrupted by rotor blades (see *Flicker Vertigo*, below). It can cause anything from mild discomfort to fatigue, and even convulsions or unconsciousness. Flicker certainly modifies certain neuro-physiological processes; 3-30 a second appears to be a critical range, while 6-8 will diminish your depth perception (the Germans set their searchlights to flicker, during World War II, to get up the nose of bomber pilots). Hangovers make you particularly susceptible.

Violations

Whilst errors tend to be unintentional, violations are more deliberate acts, usually committed in the interests of speed or convenience. Technically, they are *deliberate deviations from rules, procedures or regulations*, although unintentional violations occur when the person concerned is unaware of a rule or procedure. *Routine violations* eventually become the normal working practice. *Situational violations* arise out of particular circumstances, including time pressure, workload, inadequate tools or facilities, or anything that prevents the normal procedure being followed. *Optimizing violations* concern breaking the rules for the hell of it (couldn't they think of a better name?) *Exceptional violations*, according to James Reason, are inevitable, when the normal rules no longer apply.

Whether violations occur is down to the attitudes, beliefs, norms and company culture. Aside from ignoring safety rules on any task, they put the rest of the system in jeopardy because it is written on the assumption that the rules will be followed.

THE BODY

The human body is wonderful, but only up to a point. It has limitations that affect your ability to fly efficiently, as your senses don't always tell you the truth, which is why you need extensive training to fly on instruments - you have to unlearn so much. The classic example is the "leans", where you think you're performing a particular manoeuvre, but your instruments tell you otherwise. However, although the sensors in the eyes and ears are actually quite sensitive, the brain isn't, and does not always notice their signals. Sometimes it even fills in bits by itself, according to various rules, which include your expectations and past experience. Thus, at each stage in the perception process, there is the possibility of error, because we are not necessarily sensing reality. For example, the reason why there is a *white balance* setting on a digital camera is because the brain interprets what is white in its own way and compensates all by itself - indoor bulbs actually glow quite red, and an overcast sky might have some blue in it, despite what you think you see. If the camera doesn't compensate, your pictures will be tinted the wrong way. The diagram on the right shows how limited the range of visible light is against the spectrum of electromagnetic waves available. If the full spectrum were 2 yards long, visible light would occupy 1/32 of an inch.

But why do you need to learn about the body? Well, parts of it are used to get the information you need to make decisions with, and, of course, if it isn't working properly, you can't process the information or implement any action based on it. In the single-pilot case, it needs to be efficient because there is nobody else to take over if you get incapacitated. Also, presumably, you want to pass your next medical!

G Tolerance

If you pull back on the controls, your body (after Newton) wants to carry on in a straight line, but is forced upward by the seat, which feels the same as if you were being pushed into it. This extra pressure is called G, and it affects the whole body, including the blood, so the heart must change its action to keep the system running.

The body can only cope with certain amounts of G-force, which arises from the effects of *acceleration*, that increase your weight artificially. When there is no acceleration, you are subject to 1G. We are often subject to acceleration forces beyond our design limits, hence some illusions when the mind misinterprets the proper clues. *Linear acceleration* (Gx) is what you get in crashes, and causes illusions in the pitch axis - under forward linear acceleration, you might think you are climbing. *Radial acceleration* (Gz) occurs while turning, and *angular or transverse acceleration* (Gy) happens when the rate of rotation changes, and which affects your sense of balance.

Short-term acceleration lasts for less than 1 second. Negative G acts upwards and can *increase the blood flow to the head*, leading to *red out*, facial pain and slowing down of the

Cosmic Rays	
Gamma Rays	
X Rays	
UV	Light Waves
Visible Light	
IR	
Radar	
FM	Radio Waves
TV	
AM	

heart. In addition, your lower eyelids close at -3G. Positive G is more normal, but will *drain* the blood, with the obvious consequences, including loss of vision, called *grey out*, at +3.5 G. This could end up as *black out* and unconsciousness at +6 G.

Both are affected by hyperventilation, hypoxia, heat, hypoglycaemia, smoking and alcohol, discussed later. The *valsalva manoeuvre* can be used to help cope with high G (close your mouth, pinch your nose tight and blow out, which increases the pressure in the mouth and throat. At the same time, try to swallow or move your lower jaw), or you could use a pressure suit. During substantial +G forces, the order of symptoms is: *grey-out, tunnel vision, black-out* and *unconsciousness*.

Impact-wise, the body can tolerate 25G vertically and 45G horizontally - if you don't wear shoulder straps, tolerance to forward deceleration reduces to below 25G, and you will jack-knife over your lapstrap with your head hitting whatever is in front of it at 12 times the speed of it coming the other way. *Long duration acceleration* lasts for more than one second.

Your ability to withstand G forces is reduced by:

- obesity
- low blood sugar and
- hypoxia

amongst other things, because they affect the action of the heart. Increase long term + G tolerance by tightening your abdominal muscles, ducking your head (bending forward) and performing a kind of pressure breathing. A tilt-back seat is also useful, because it provides a supine body position that keeps the heart and brain at the same horizontal level that makes the heart work less.

Dem Bones

The skeleton does not keep the body upright - it works the other way round. Muscle tone dictates how you carry yourself, and the bones inside provide support.

Body Mass Index (BMI)

This is supposed to relate your weight to your height, and is calculated by dividing your weight in kg by your height, in metres^2. If it is over 25, you are overweight, and over 30, you are obese, which could lead to heart disease and reduce your ability to cope with hypoxia, decompression sickness and G tolerance.

The acceptable range is 20-25 for men and 19-24 for women.

The Central Nervous System

Whatever your body gets up to, the processes involved must be coordinated and integrated. This is done by the central nervous system, with a little help from the endocrine system. Although making an approach to land might seem to be automatic, the control responses that occur as a result of input from your eyes and ears, and experience, plus the feedback required from your limbs so that you don't over control, are all transmitted over complex nerve cells (*neurons*) for processing inside the CNS, which consists of the brain and spinal cord, though, for exam purposes, it also includes the visual and aural systems (eyes and ears), proprioceptive system (the so-called "seat-of-the-pants" sense, which works off postural clues) and other senses.

A Neuron or Nerve Cell

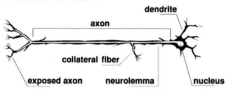

Cells communicate with a combination of electrical and chemical signals. Chemical ones either diffuse between cells (*neurotransmitters*) or are disseminated in the blood (*hormones*) to act on more distant parts of the body. Neurons don't touch each other directly - if a message needs to be transmitted, a neurotransmitter (of which there are over 50 types) carries it across the small gap between them, having been triggered by an electrical signal. Modern drugs pretend to be neurotransmitters by providing a "key" to the receptor's "lock". The connection between neurons is a *synapse*.

PERIPHERAL NERVOUS SYSTEM

This connects the Central Nervous System with the sense organs, muscles and glands, and therefore with the outside world. The PNS is divided into:

- the **somatic** nervous system, which contains the peripheral pathways for communicating with the environment and control of skeletal muscles, and

- the **autonomic** nervous system, which regulates vital functions over which you have no conscious control, like heartbeat and breathing (unless you're a high grade Tibetan monk, of course), or anything that is not to do with skeletal muscle. The ANS in turn consists of the:

  - **sympathetic**

  - **parasympathetic**

nervous systems. The former prepares you for fight-or-flight (see *Stress*, below) and tends to act on *several organs at once*, while the latter calms you down again, *acting on one organ at a time*. Being under the influence of fight-or-flight is like being in a powerful car in permanent high gear, which you can't do all the time - you need rest & relaxation to allow time for the parasympathetic system to kick in, such as meditation, or a snooze in the back of the helicopter. Being in such a high state of readiness all the time produces steroids, and can lead to depression. It is actually a pain in an emergency in a complex aircraft, where you have to force yourself to sit still and think your way through the problem (of course, many emergencies demand immediate action, but you get the picture).

The Brain

The brain is a switchboard, which is constantly in touch with the 639 muscles inside the body. It can also store vast amounts of information - the Hungarian physicist and mathematician John van Neumann calculated that the brain stored around 2.8×10^{20} bits of information over the course of the average lifetime! Although the brain is only 2% of the body mass, it takes up to 20% of the volume of each heartbeat - its blood supply needs to be continuous, as it cannot store oxygen. Many of the brain's departments merge into each other, and work closely together, but it still has three distinct areas, namely the *central core*, the *limbic system* and the *cerebral hemispheres*.

The brain itself doesn't register pain (but the scalp and skull should be deadened with a local anaesthetic if you want to go poking around!) When their temporal lobes were stimulated (behind the temples), epileptic patients were able to recall past episodes in vivid detail. However, when rats had various parts of their brains removed, they were still able to remember their way round a maze, which would suggest that, although memories are stored in the brain, they are distributed around the whole organ, rather than being allocated specific locations (people who have head injuries don't seem to forget halves of novels, or who their families are). Maybe each part of the brain contains enough information to reconstruct a memory, in the same way that a fragment of a hologram contains the complete image that the whole hologram contains. Paul Pietsch flipped the brains of salamanders around (upside down, etc.) and found that they behaved perfectly normally whichever way round they were.

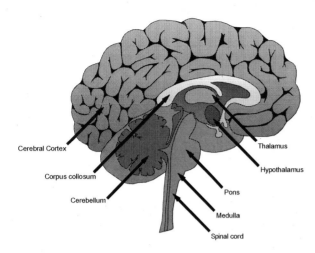

Cerebral Cortex

Corpus collosum

Cerebellum

Thalamus

Hypothalamus

Pons

Medulla

Spinal cord

Generally, the brain has a three-layer hierarchical structure, with the lower levels, at the base of the skull, taking care of mundane stuff like breathing and walking. Emotional management centres like the amygdala take care of hunches and instinct, whereas answering questions like "where shall I park this helicopter?", are left to the neurones up in the cerebral cortex, just above your eyebrows. Decision making is handled in the rear of the brain. In an emergency, the amygdala takes the brain's resources and dedicates them to the task in hand - it arouses all the circuits so you can make a decision as fast as possible. In summary, the "lower" level deals with the basic survival stuff, while the "higher" ones allow more complex processes, but they all work together.

- The **Central Core** includes most of the brain stem, starting at the *medulla* where the spinal cord widens as it enters the skull. The medulla controls breathing and some reflexes that keep you upright. Also, the nerves coming from the spinal cord cross over here, so the right side of the brain is connected to the left side of the body, and *vice versa*. Slightly above the medulla is the *cerebellum*, which concerns itself with (smooth) coordination of movement. The *thalamus* consists of two egg-shaped groups of nuclei. One acts as a relay station for messages, and the other regulates sleep and wakefulness. Just below that is the *hypothalamus*, which regulates endocrine activity (through the pituitary gland) and maintains normal body functions, in terms of temperature, heart rate and blood pressure, which are disturbed when under stress. For example, the body's core temperature should be between 35-38°C (normal is 37°C). It is maintained through mechanisms such as *vasorestriction* (narrowing of blood vessels), *sweating*,

shivering, or *goose pimples*, when hot or cold. Due to its role in responding to stress, the hypothalamus is also known as the *stress centre*.

- The **Limbic System** wraps itself round the Central Core and is closely connected to the hypothalamus. Part of it, the *hippocampus*, would appear to have something to do with short-term memory, in that, when it is missing, people can remember things that happened long ago, but not recently. Researchers have also discovered pleasure centres here. The Limbic System is often called the *interbrain*, as it has structures that communicate with both the higher and lower brain centres.

- The **Cerebral Cortex** is the final layer that allows the development and storage of analytical skills, verbal and written communication, emotion, memory and analytical thought.

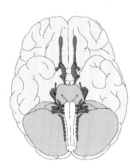

Cerebral Hemispheres consist of the "grey matter" you see when looking at a picture of the brain. Each half is basically symmetrical, but the left and right hemispheres are interconnected (through the corpus callosum), with women having more connections between them than men, which accounts for their ability to think of several things at once, often contradictory. Each hemisphere has four *lobes*. The hemispheres work in different ways, leading to two types of thinking:

- *Left Brain*, or logical - governs language, skilled in mathematics

- *Right Brain* - conceptual. The artist type

Note that, although the two hemispheres work differently, they still work very much together.

Unlike muscles, which only react to stimulation, the brain has several constant electrical rhythms. The dominant one consists of alpha waves, and an increase in brain activity creates beta waves which are faster, but of less voltage. These are associated with the focussing of attention and problem-solving, so they make stress arousal more possible. There are also theta waves and delta waves, the latter being slow and usually only detectable during sleep.

The Endocrine System

This system consists of glands, such as the pituitary or adrenal glands, which secrete hormones into the bloodstream. Like neurotransmitters, hormones are only recognized by certain types of cell, although they act over longer distances. The endocrine system has some relationship to the stress response, since it is controlled by the hypothalamus - as various areas of the hypothalamus are stimulated, the pituitary and some parts of the parasympatheic nervous system spring into action.

The adrenal glands also increase the heart and stimulate other physical responses. There is one sitting over each kidney. The pituitary initially secretes the hormone ACTH (adrenocorticotrophic hormone) into the bloodstream from where it ends up at the adrenal cortex, which itself wakes up to secrete *cortisol* and *aldosterone*, which more or less constitute the stress response.

Vision

LIGHT

Referring back to the electromagnetic spectrum, you will recall that, as radio waves get higher in frequency, they approach the lower reaches of visible light, which is what is detected by your eyes. This indicates that radio and light waves are of the same nature, so the eye can be viewed as a specialised kind of radio receiver, or at least a frequency analyser, so the work of converting light into an electrical impulse that can be sent to the brain suddenly does not seem quite so hard. Sub-ranges within the range of visible light are detected as colour, with the lowest frequency being red and the highest violet, in this order: R O Y G B I V. Their combination creates white light, and black is the absence of any radiation, so black and white do not exist as "colours" at all.

The nature of the atom is discussed more fully in Section 3, but, essentially, when an electron is knocked away from its inner orbit round the atom's nucleus, one from a further orbit replaces it. In doing so, it has to adapt to a slower speed, giving up high frequency radiation in the process, and the more energy that is given up, the higher that frequency is. As well, the closer to the nucleus this happens, the more energy is surrendered.

All electromagnetic energy is produced by the movement of electrons into holes in the inner orbits of different atoms by a kick of energy coming from outside. In the case of light, this energy mostly comes from the Sun. For example, shifting the orbit of an electron in a sodium atom will create a yellowish light, while steely blue comes from a mercury atom. You see objects in daylight because they are able to detect radiations from the movement of their electrons. The use of heat, as obtained with fire, or applying electricity to a filament in a light bulb, has the same effect. However, no such artificial means can enable you to see the visible spectrum in its correct proportions. Red will only appear as red when the light shining on it contains the frequencies that can agitate the electrons in atoms that are able to give off red light. A London bus, therefore, reflects only the red frequencies and fails to reflect the rest. If the light striking the bus contained no red, you would not be able to see it.

Vision is your primary (and most dependable) source of information - 70% of the information you process enters the visual channel. It gets harder with age to distinguish moving objects; between the ages of 40 and 65, this ability diminishes by up to 50%. However, this is only one limitation, and we need to examine the eye in detail to see how you overcome them all.

THE EYE

Vision is your primary (and most dependable) source of information - 70% of the information you process enters the visual channel. It gets harder with age to distinguish moving objects; between the ages of 40 and 65, this ability diminishes by up to 50%. However, this is only one limitation, and we need to examine the eye in detail to see how you overcome them all.

The eye is nearly round, and its rotation in its socket (and focussing) is controlled by external muscles. It has three coatings, or layers of membrane; the *sclerotic*, which is transparent at the front; the *choroid*, which lines the sclerotic and contains tiny blood vessels, and the *retina*, which is the light sensitive bit that detects electromagnetic waves of the frequency of light, and converts them to electrical signals that are interpreted by the brain, and which is sensitive to hypoxia.

The transparent part of the sclerotic is the *cornea*, behind which is the *lens*, whose purpose is to bend light rays inwards, so they focus on the retina. The lens, iris and cornea control the amount of light entering the eye through the *pupil*, which is the black bit inside the colored iris. It appears black because any light that does not get absorbed by the retina is usually absorbed by a layer behind it called the *retinal pigment epithelium*, as if you didn't know already. If it wasn't, your vision would be blurred by randomly scattered light. Redeye occurs when not all the light can be absorbed and some is reflected back.

```
                                    SCLERA
AQUEOUS
HUMOR                                        RETINA

CORNEA                                       VITREOUS
                                             HUMOR
PUPIL
                                             FOVEA
LENS

IRIS
                                             OPTIC
SUSPENSION                                   NERVE
LIGAMENT
         CILLIARY              OPTIC DISC
         MUSCLE                (BLIND SPOT)
```

70% of light is refracted by the cornea, and 30% by the lens. The more your iris is open, the less *depth of field* you have, so in darkness it is hard to see beyond or before the point of focus, and you may require glasses to help (the depth of field in photography is an area either side of the focus point in which everything is sharp. The wider the aperture, or iris, the shorter this distance is, and *vice versa*).

The retina is composed of ten very thin layers, with nerve endings that act as light sensors (actually, *neurons*) which are called *rods* and *cones*, in the ninth. Their names arise from the way they are shaped. Each is more efficient than the other in different kinds of light. Cones are sensitive to day or high-intensity light and rods are used at night or in low-intensity light. As the periphery of the retina consists mainly of rods, peripheral vision is less precise because they only see shades of grey and vague shapes (you see colors because the vibrations they give out are strong enough to wake the cones up, and the brain mixes the colors received by them. The most common color blindness is red/green). The rods contain *visual purple*, also known as *rhodopsin*, which builds up over a period of 30-45 minutes as light decreases until the approximate level of moonlight, which is when the rods take over from the cones. As rods are sensitive to shorter wavelengths of light, in very low light, blue objects are more likely to be seen than red (neither will be in color), which is why cockpit lighting is sometimes red because it affects the rods used for night vision less than white light.

Light waves from objects in the *right* visual field fall on the *left* half of each retina, for transmission to the *left* cerebral hemisphere, and *vice versa*. This is so that each side of the brain has input from both eyes at once.

The *optic nerve* carries signals from the eye to the brain. The point where it joins the retina is mostly populated with cones, which work best in daylight and become less effective at night, or where oxygen levels are reduced (which is significant for smokers, whose blood has less oxygen carrying capacity), so you get a blind spot in the direct field of vision, which is why you see things more clearly at night if you look slightly to the side of what you need to see. You don't normally notice the blind spot because the brain superimposes the images from each eye.

Once light falls on the retina, the visual pigment is bleached, which creates the electrical current. However, once bleached, the pigment must be reactivated by a further chemical reaction, which is called *nystagmus*, caused by the eye jerking to a new position, there to remain steady. The movement period is edited out by the brain, and the multiple images are merged, so continuous vision is actually an illusion, as an *after image* is produced when light falls on the retina - that is, the image of what you are looking at remains there for a short period, as light has a momentum (try it by closing your eyes and looking at the picture that remains). As the eye does not need to be seeing constantly (and can therefore be regarded as a detector of *movement*), it can spend the spare time in repair and replacement of tissue. 30-40 images per second are taken in the average person, and an image takes about 1/50th of a second to register. It has also been discovered that, when we blink, the visual cortex in the brain (the bit that interprets what the eye sees) closes down for that period. As it happens, if 90% of a rat's visual cortex is removed, it can still perform quite complex tasks that require visual skills. Similarly, a cat can have up to 98% of its optic nerves severed without much effect.

All this means you *see with the brain*, giving a difference between *seeing* and *perceiving*. It also means that vision problems can arise from the brain's processing ability and not the eyes themselves. This is because the eye's optical quality is actually very poor (you would get better results from a pinhole camera), hence the need for the brain, which can actually modify what you see, based on experience, and so is reliant on expectations. If the brain fills in the gaps wrongly, you get visual illusions. **Less than 50% of what you see is actually based on information entering your eyes!** The remainder is pieced together out of your expectations of what you should be seeing. For example, your mind can get so accustomed to seeing a given set of words that your unconscious can edit out what is really there and make you see what you expect to see, as experienced by writers who can miss a prominent typographical error for ages (if you see any in this book, please let me know!) Pilots used to seeing a certain instrument picture can miss any changes in the same way.

An aircraft heading towards you can disappear from sight. A high speed aircraft approaching head-on will grow the most in size very rapidly in the last moments, so it's possible for it to be hidden by a bug on the windscreen for a high proportion of its approach time (you might only see it in the last few seconds). Lack of relative movement makes an object harder to detect.

You should be able to see another aircraft directly at 7 miles, or 2.5 miles if it was 45° off - at 60° it's down to half a mile! The reason why you must scan is because the eye needs to latch on to something, which is difficult with a clear blue sky, or on a hazy day. With an empty field of vision, your eyes will actually focus at relatively short distances, anywhere from between 56 cm ahead (*Aviation Week*) to 3-10 metres ahead, and miss objects further away (*empty field myopia*). In other words, you effectively become short-sighted (myopic). The ratio of looking in- and outside should be 5:15 seconds.

Close your left eye and stare at the dot in the middle of the grid above with your right eye. As you move the page back and forth along your line of vision (about 10-15 inches away), the right one will vanish because it is falling inside your blind spot. Now close your right eye and stare at the dot on the right. The one on the left will vanish as well, but all the lines on the grid will remain intact. This is because your brain is filling in with what it thinks should be there.

Thus, there are gaping holes in what we think we see - if we are only seeing about half of what is out there, what are we missing? How many readings on our instruments do we not see at all?

The eye/brain combination is therefore not trustworthy, as it can tinker with its world view before you become conscious of it. In fact, visual information entering the brain is modified by the temporal lobes before being passed on to the visual cortices (*Pribram*).

The eye can, however, react quickly to changes in light, although it is slow to adapt from light to dark because *visual purple* needs to be created, a process requiring Vitamin A, of which the retina contains enormous amounts - having too little could result in night blindness. The changeover from light to dark takes about 20-30 minutes and should always be allowed for when night flying (some say 30-45 minutes - actually, the cones take 7 minutes, and the retina can take up to 45).

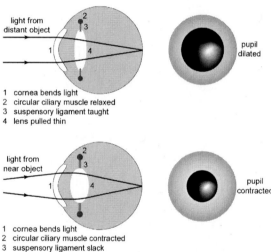

1 cornea bends light
2 circular ciliary muscle relaxed
3 suspensory ligament taught
4 lens pulled thin

1 cornea bends light
2 circular ciliary muscle contracted
3 suspensory ligament slack
4 lens more circular

The only part of the eye that sees perfectly clearly is in the centre of the retina, an area not much larger than a pinhead, called the *fovea centralis*, where the first eight layers of the retina are missing, so the rods and cones are directly exposed to light (that is, the light doesn't have to battle through the first layers) for clearer vision at that point. It is the area of best day vision, and no night vision at all. The area of sharp vision is therefore very small, at 4 feet, the size of a small coin. 5° away from the foveal axis, it reduces by a quarter, and one-twentieth at 20° away.

© *Phil Croucher, 2007*

Outside of that area, vision is quite blurred - if you look at the top part of this page, for example, you will not be able to see the rest clearly without shifting your vision. The illusion of seeing large areas clearly (that is, more than two words at a time) comes from the rapidity of shifting - attempting to do this otherwise means seeing without focussing, and results in eyestrain. Sometimes your eye and brain can get out of the habit of looking at one point together. Vibrations can also cause blurred vision, from *tuned resonance oscillation of the eyeballs.*

Best night vision

Best day vision

You must therefore look directly at an object to see it best. At night, though, look slightly to one side, as the rods that are sensitive to lower levels of light are outside the fovea, at the peripheral of the retina (scan slowly as well). The eye's ability to read alphanumeric information is limited to the foveal area of the retina.

There are three types of vision, and night vision involves the latter two:

- *Photopic*, which occurs by day or in high-intensity lighting, using mostly cones, as the rods bleach out and become less effective. Objects can be detected with peripheral vision, but central vision is mostly used anyway, because that's where the cones are

- *Mesopic*, for dawn, dusk and full moonlight, using both rods and cones. color perception reduces as the cones start to work less well, and off-centre scanning gets the best results

- *Scotopic*, for low light, and where vision becomes approximately 20/200 (see below). As the cones don't work at all, you get a night blind spot, so you have to look to one side to see an object properly

FIELD OF VIEW

The field of view of each eye is about 120° left to right, and about 150° up and down. There is an overlap of 60° in the centre where binocular vision is possible, and which has a blind spot about 5° wide where the optic nerve leaves the eyeball and there are no rods nor cones (see below). The brain normally fills in the blanks.

The picture below shows the field of view of a pair of eyes looking straight ahead. The white bit in the middle represents the fovea of each eye, and the light grey area is what is seen by the eye on that side. Stereoscopic vision is possible within the white area. The dark grey area is the cutoff by the brows, cheeks and nose.

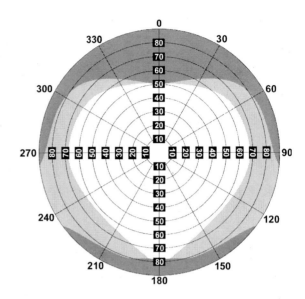

VISUAL ACUITY

Normal vision is described as 20/20, meaning that you can see at 20 feet what a normal person can see at 20 feet. If the ratio, as a fraction, is greater than 1/1, visual acuity is better than normal, so 6/4 means you can see at 6 m what a normal person can only distinguish at 4 m. On the other hand, 6/9 is poor: Normal people can detect at 9 m what you cannot see above 6 m.

Clarity of vision is affected by:

- light available

- size and contours of objects

- distance of an object from the viewer

- contrast

- relative motion

- the clarity of the atmosphere

Visual acuity at high altitudes can be affected by anaemia, smoking, carbon monoxide poisoning and hypoxia.

DEPTH PERCEPTION

This, useful when slinging, is the process of forming 3D images from 2D information, in our case, 2 sets, from our eyes - and it's all done in the brain, as mentioned before.

Binocular clues rely on both eyes working together in four main ways:

- *Retinal Disparity* -also known as *stereopsis*, this is the main cue to depth perception, and it depends on the difference in images received by each eye - look at this page with each eye separately - each one will have a different aspect. The brain fuses the two images to get a 3D result and analyses the differences between them to deduce distance. This disparity gets greater when objects are close. If you hold one index finger close to your eyes, and the other one further away but behind, the closer one will seem to shift its position more when you look at them with one eye closed at a time. This is because the angle between the eyes is greater

- *Accommodation* is a muscular clue to distance, from the change in curvature of the lens, which gets thicker as you focus on nearby objects and flattens with distant ones (with the *ciliary muscle*)

- *Convergence* is another muscular clue where the eyes point more and more inward as an object gets closer (like on eye tests). That is, each eye sees an object from a different angle. By noticing this angle of convergence, the brain produces depth information over 6-20 feet. You judge speed by the rate of change of the angle of convergence

However, the effects of convergence and accommodation are relatively negligible.

Monocular clues, used for longer distances (over 200 m), are most subject to illusion, and include:

- *relative size* (larger objects appear to be closer)

- *overlap* (an object covered by another looks to be further away)

- *relative height* (lower objects look closer)

- *texture gradient* (smooth surfaces look further away)

- *linear perspective* (more convergence means more distance)

- *shadowing*

- *relative brightness* (nearer objects are brighter)

- *aerial haze*

- *aerial perspective* (difference in focus and colour)

- *motion parallax* (nearer objects appear to move more)

For example, the dark shape on the left is actually a half-moon shape, and it is level with the other one, even though it looks like it is further away.

Optical illusions may occur when any of the above cues are missing. With reference to brightness, it has been shown that a pendulum swinging in a straight line in front of a person with one eye covered is actually seen as swinging in an ellipse.

After *Gold* (1976), differential size is the dominant cue at far distances, movement parallax at intermediate ones, and stereopsis up to 17 m (more if you fixate on the object).

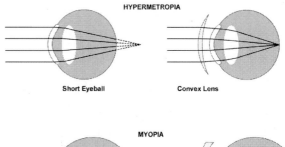

HYPERMETROPIA

Short Eyeball   Convex Lens

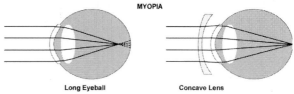

MYOPIA

Long Eyeball   Concave Lens

DEFECTIVE VISION

The major causes of defective vision are:

- *Hypermetropia* - where the eyeball is too short, and images focus behind the retina (farsightedness). Requires a convex lens

- *Myopia* - where the eyeball is too long, and images focus in front of the retina (short sight). Needs a concave lens

- *Presbyopia* - the lens hardens, leading to *hypermetropia* and difficulty in focussing, with lack of accommodation (comes with old age)

- *Cataracts* - the lens becomes opaque

- *Glaucoma* - increase in pressure of liquid in the eyeball interferes with accommodation

- *Astigmatism* - unequal curvature of the cornea or lens

If the point of focus happens in front of the retina, short sightedness, or myopia, results. You get long sightedness with the point of focus behind the retina. Both conditions cause blurred vision, which is correctable by glasses, that vary the refraction of the light waves until they focus in the proper place.

OPTICAL ILLUSIONS

Illusions exist when what you sense does not match reality. They occur because our senses are limited, especially when it comes to the demands of flight - the missing bits tend to get filled in by the brain, sometimes wrongly. Looking directly at an object under water is difficult, because light rays bend due to refraction as they pass the surface and the object appears to be displaced:

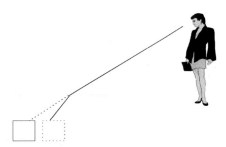

This has obvious parallels with looking at a runway through a wet windshield.

In the image below (the Ponzo illusion), the two horizontal lines are the same length, but your perspective cues are off.

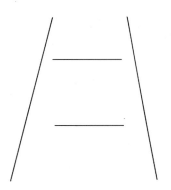

On the radar screen, the two aircraft tracks look to be safely separate, but they are not.

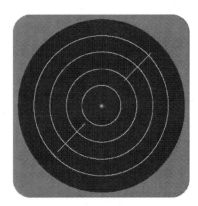

One classic illusion for pilots is *whiteout*, which is defined by the American Meteorological Society as:

"An atmospheric optical phenomenon of the polar regions in which the observer appears to be engulfed in a uniformly white glow".

That is, you can only see dark nearby objects - no shadows, horizon or clouds, and you lose depth perception. It occurs over unbroken snow cover beneath a uniformly overcast sky, when the light from both is about the same. Blowing snow doesn't help, and it's particularly a problem if the ground is rising. *Flat light* is a similar phenomenon, but comes from different causes, where light is diffused through water droplets suspended in the air, particularly when clouds are low. *Objects seen through fog or haze will seem to be further away.*

A good fixed wing example of an optical illusion is a wider runway tending to make you think the ground is nearer than it actually is:

A narrow runway delays your reactions, possibly leading to a late flare and early touchdown. In the diagram above, all three landing strips are the same distance and angle away from the aircraft, but the one on the left is wider and shorter (looks nearer, and low on the glideslope, so you might carry out a higher approach) and the one on the right is longer and thinner (looks further away and high on the glideslope, so you might go lower and land short while you try to keep the same sight picture). Thus, a pilot used to a runway 27 m wide, who lands on one 42 m wide, will think he is nearer than usual and tend to fly a lower and flatter approach with a tendency to undershoot, with a high roundout.

The illusions you might get with sloping ground include:

Problem	Illusion	Risk
Downslope	Too low	High approach
Upslope	Too high	Low approach
Rain	Closer	Low approach
Narrow	Too high	Low approach
Wide	Too low	High approach & flare
Bright lts	Too low	High approach

An approach to a downsloping runway should be started higher, with a steeper angle, because the perceived glide path angle is smaller than that of the actual glide path. However, the slope away from the aircraft presents a smaller image to your eyes, and you see less of the runway, so you try to see more by flying too high to correct the apparent undershooting. An approach to an upsloping runway should be started lower, at a shallower angle - good reasons why you should use VASIS when provided.

Helicopters A and C both see an approach path of 5 degrees. Boeing researchers found that a big black hole effect at night could cause a curved approach, so the trick is to avoid long approach paths.

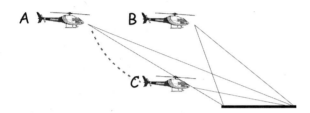

If an object is brighter than its surroundings (a well-lit runway), you will think you are closer to it, so on an approach, you might start early and be lower than you should. In haze, objects appear to be further away because of their lack of brightness.

Even going to the cinema is an optical illusion; still frames are shown so quickly it looks as if movement is taking place - the switching is done in the brain, in alliance with the eye's *persistence of vision*, which is the ability to retain an impression of the shape, colour and brightness of an image for a fraction of a second after light from the image stops being received. *Vectional illusions* are caused by movement, as when sitting in a railway carriage and wondering whether it's the train next to you or the one you're in that is moving (this is called the *illusion of relative movement* in the exam, but is actually *Motion Parallax*) - helicopter pilots can experience something similar when hovering close to moving water. The *waterfall effect* happens while hovering or in slow flight at low altitudes. The downwash causes the air to pick up water and displace it upward at the edge of the blades and downward directly under them, so you might see drops of water going down in your field of vision to give you a climbing sensation. A corrective manoeuvre to descend will put the helicopter in the water. Illusions met during taxying can come from *relative movement* and *height of the cockpit above the ground*.

When mountain flying, it's often difficult to fly straight and level because the sloping ground around affects your judgment. Similarly, you can't judge your height when landing on a peak:

One of the optical illusions you might come across at night is the apparent motion of a stationary object (*autokinesis*) which isn't helped by rain on the windscreen. Apart from reducing visibility, it's a particular threat when fixing your position by a single light source. When little or no light is on the surface and a prominent one comes into view, it may seem that the light is above the horizon, which could lead you to pitch into a steep attitude in keeping with the resulting false horizon. The light source may also appear to change color. Autokinesis gives the illusion that an object is moving, when it is actually your eye, typically encountered when staring at a single light in the dark. It could make you think that a star is an aircraft.

Sometimes the effect is not much more than an uncomfortable climbing sensation even when you're straight and level, but an obscured windscreen could make objects appear lower than they really are. This will be more apparent with high intensity runway lighting, which may also give you the same effect that actors have on stage, where they can't see the audience through the bright lighting. The lack of normal contrast will also upset your altitude perception, making you feel further away and higher than you are. As a result, on a final approach you could find yourself too low and fast. Approaching a rig, particularly, the lighting will appear as a straight line above 1 nm away, an ellipse as you get closer, then a circle close to. As you have no depth perception, the closing speed is very hard to judge until very close, and pilots will either come to the hover just short or go steaming past and have to pitch nose-up to stop themselves overshooting. *Distortion* occurs when viewing objects through a windshield covered with rain, where water is thicker near the bottom (nearer to the windshield), causing a *prismatic effect* - like looking through a base-down prism, which tends to make objects look higher or closer. Raindrops on a windscreen can double the apparent size of lights outside and make you think you are closer.

The solution is to use every piece of sensory information you can, including landing lights and instruments (if you keep two lights in view, and the lower one goes out of sight, your view of it has been obstructed, so go up until you see them both again). Problems will arise if several of the above factors affect you at once, especially if the landing point is sloping - this is where more frequent cross-referencing of altimeters is important.

Illusions of interpretation (*cognitive illusions*) are associated with the task of mental construction and environment. One of the major protective measures against illusions is *comprehensive briefing and debriefing.*

NIGHT MYOPIA AND NIGHT PRESBYOPIA

Night myopia (nearsightedness), also known as *twilight myopia*, causes some people who are slightly myopic in daylight to become more so after dark.

Presbyopia is a condition in which the crystalline lens of your eye loses its flexibility, which makes it difficult to focus on close objects. Also known as *red light presbyopia*, night presbyopia occurs in presbyopic individuals who are subjected to red light, which is found in some cockpits during night operations. Red light has the longest wavelength, so when you try to read instruments or charts in red light, the demand for accommodation is more than if you were using white light, making it difficult to read small print. In effect, your depth of field is reduced.

Vitamin A deficiency can cause night blindness because it is needed for the regeneration of visual purple. Night vision can be reduced above 8,000 ft.

SPACE MYOPIA

Also known as *Empty Field Myopia*, this describes myopia experienced when there is nothing to look at outside the cockpit, as mentioned previously.

Ears (Vestibular System)

The ears allow you to hear and assist you to maintain balance. They are important because an auditory stimulus is the one most often attended to. How many times do you answer the phone when you're busy, even though you've ignored everything else for hours?

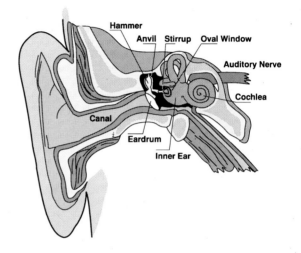

The eardrum is the boundary between the outer ear and the inner ear. Sound waves make the eardrum vibrate, and the vibrations are transmitted by a chain of linked bones in the middle ear known as the *hammer, anvil* and *stirrup* (collectively, the *ossicles*) to the *cochlea* in the inner ear (via the *oval window*), which is full of fluid. As you climb and outside air pressure reduces, the eardrum will bulge outwards, and *vice versa*. Such pressures can affect the balance mechanism. The difference in pressures is equalised by air leaking out through the *Eustachian Tubes,* which are canals that connect the throat with the middle ear; and their purpose is to equalise air pressure. When you swallow, the tubes open, allowing air to enter, which is why swallowing helps to clear the ears when changing altitude. Blocked Eustachian tubes can be responsible for split eardrums, due to the inability to equalise pressure. Since the eardrum takes around 6 weeks to heal, the best solution is not to go flying with a cold, but commercial pressures don't always allow that. If you have to, make sure you use a decongestant with no side effects.

The cochlea is the coiled bit in the right hand side of the diagram above - it is a tube which narrows progressively. There are thousands of fibres of different lengths inside it which vibrate in sympathy at different frequencies.

The fibres are linked to the brain and, as with sight, it is now, when the signal reaches the brain, that we "hear". Ear defenders reduce noise levels by up to 40 dbA and ear plugs by only about 20 - of course, wearing either doesn't help with communication!

As some of the fibres get damaged (through too severe vibration), the ability to hear the frequency they cover goes (they do not regenerate). You can recover from some deafness, such as that caused by illness, but not that caused by damage to the fibres in the fluid. See *Deafness*.

The *semicircular canals* are what we use to keep balanced *on the ground*, because they monitor angular accelerations. However, orientation in the air depends largely on vision, discussed under *Disorientation*, below. The canals are arranged at right angles to each other and use the fluid in the *inner ear*, which acts against sensory hairs with chalky deposits on the end to send electrical signals to the brain so you can tell which way is up. The semicircular canals sense angular acceleration, while the *otolith organs* on the top of the cochlea in the inner ear pick up changes in linear movement. The otolith organs consist of the *utricle*, for horizontal movement, and the *saccule*, for vertical.

The inertia of otoliths (which are small particles made up of a gelatinous matrix and calcium carbonate in the viscous fluid of the saccule and utricle) causes them to stimulate hair cells when the head moves. The hair cells send signals down sensory nerve fibres which are interpreted by the brain as motion. The problem is that, because our bodies are designed to operate on the ground, the vestibular system is more suited to stop-go motion and cannot register sustained motion very well.

Additional sources of positional information include *somatosensory receptors* inside the skin, joints and muscles. As they respond to pressure and stretching signals, they can be an important source of information about your equilibrium. They are called the "seat of the pants" sense because it was thought that you could tell which way was up by the seat of your pants sensing the most pressure. *The seat of the pants sense is completely unreliable as an attitude indicator when your body is moving in the aerial environment.*

The audible range of the human ear is 20 Hz to 20 KHz, with the most sensitive range between 750-3000 Hz. However, one exam question allocates a range of 16 Hz to 20 KHz (in such questions, the word *approximately* is used).

DEAFNESS

Hearing actually depends on the proper working of the *eighth cranial nerve*, which carries signals from the inner ear to the brain. Obviously, if this gets damaged, deafness results. The nerve doesn't have to be severed, though; deterioration will occur if you don't get enough Vitamin

B-Complex (deafness is a symptom of beriberi or pellagra, for example, which comes from Vitamin B deficiency).

There are two types of hearing loss:

- *Sensori-neural*, where the ability to process sound is lost. In aviation, high-tone deafness from sustained exposure to jet engines is very common. *Presbycusis* is hearing loss with age, where the high tones go first. *Noise Induced Hearing Loss*, or NIHL, occurs through prolonged exposure to loud noise, usually 90 db and above.

- *Conductive Hearing Loss* is caused by interference with the transmission of sound waves from the outer to the inner ear. In other words, it is damage to the physical hearing mechanism, which can include hardened ear wax!

DISORIENTATION

This refers to a loss of your bearings in relation to position or movement, and it is more likely to happen when you are subject to colds, in IMC, and frequently changing between inside and outside visual references. The "leans" is the classic case, which occur because your semicircular canals get used to a particular sustained motion in a very short time. If you start a turn and keep it going, your canals will think this is normal, because they lag, or are slow to respond. When you straighten up, they will try to tell you you're turning, where you're actually flying straight and level, to create a *vestibular illusion*. Your natural inclination is to obey your senses, but your instruments are there as a cross-reference. In fact, the whole point of instrument training is to overcome your dependence on your senses. Particularly dangerous is recovering from a spin of 2-3 turns, where, without visual reference, you think you are actually turning the opposite way and enter another spin when you try to correct it. Eventually an extreme nose-up condition results, which turns into an extreme nose-down attitude and a tight graveyard spiral before entering Terrain Impact Mode. To combat the leans, close your eyes and shake your head vigorously from side to side for a couple of seconds, which will topple the semi-circular canals (the official exam answer is *to rely on your instruments*).

When flying, you are always subject to illusions, especially when carrying out extreme manoeuvres and/or at night. The input from your senses is interpreted (rightly or wrongly) by both your conscious and subconscious minds. The former handles the visual aspects, and the latter all the rest, through the peripheral nervous system, part of which, if you remember, runs your body automatically.

When the subconscious becomes confused about your position in space (it assumes you are on the ground), the only link between you and reality is the visual system linked to the conscious mind, which is a lot slower and less capable in its processing ability. This is why you must rely on your instruments when you get disorientated.

During linear acceleration, you can get the impression of pitching up or climbing (*somatogravic illusion*), making you want to push the nose down. This is because the fluid in the inner ear flows backwards. The eyes help to overcome this, but at night, with no visual clues, say on takeoff, this can be mistaken for a steep climb in which you put the nose down and could hit the ground. The effect is more pronounced at night going into a black hole from a well-lit area, unfortunately confirmed by the artificial horizon, which suffers from the same effect. You get a pitch-down illusion from deceleration. The danger here is that lowering the gear or flaps causes the machine to slow down, which makes you think you are pitching down and want to bring the nose up, which could cause a stall at the wrong moment on approach.

In fact the brain gets its information from:

- The eyes

- The inner ear (otoliths)

- Positioning of the skeleton and muscles (proprioceptive clues)

The *coriolis illusion* with relation to vertigo is easily demonstrated with a revolving chair - sit in one, and get someone to spin it while you have your chin on your breast. When you raise your head sharply, you will find yourself on the floor inside two seconds. This has obvious parallels with flying, so make all your head movements as gently as possible, especially when making turns in IMC, or picking up a pen from the cockpit floor, as one exam question puts it (mention of fluid, above, implies that if you are dehydrated, you may also get spatial disorientation - if you feel thirsty, you are probably already 5% there).

You can get problems from colds, etc. as well, particularly a spinning sensation caused by a sudden difference in pressure between the inner portions of each ear. *Aerotitis*, or *Barotrauma of the middle ear* is a mismatch of pressure on either side of the eardrum which is more likely to occur *when flying with a respiratory infection during a descent* (exam question). It usually *comes with a reduction in hearing ability and the feeling of increasing pressure* (another one).

One countermeasure against aerotitis is to close your mouth, pinch the nose tight and blow out, to increase pressure in the mouth and throat. At the same time, try to swallow or move lower jaw (*Valsalva manoeuvre*).

Airsickness is a sensory conflict within the vestibular system accompanied by nausea, vomiting and fear.

A steady light flickering at around 4-20 Hz can produce unpleasant and dangerous reactions, including nausea, vertigo, convulsions or unconsciousness, which are possibly worse when you are fatigued, frustrated, or in a state of mild hypoxia. Military helicopter pilots are tested for *Flicker Vertigo* during selection, as the Sun flashing through the rotor blades can be a real problem (flicker reflected from spinning rotor blades can cause spatial disorientation and/or nausea when looked at for a longer period of time). When being affected by flicker, you should turn off the strobe lights.

The Respiratory System

This consists of the lungs, oronasal passage, pharynx, larynx, trachea, bronchi, bronchioles and alveoli.

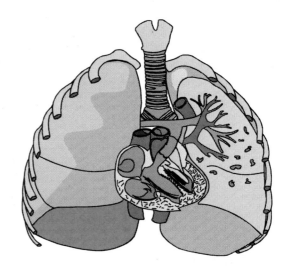

The two lungs are separated by the heart, airways and the major blood vessels in the centre of the chest, all of which are enclosed by the chest wall, which is a combination of ribs, cartilage and muscle. Each lung is covered by a thin, moist tissue called the *pleura*, which also lines the chest wall. The lungs and chest wall are elastic, but as you breathe in and out, the lungs recoil inward while your chest wall expands outward. These two opposing forces create a negative pressure in the pleural space between the rib cage and lung. If air enters that space, from in- or outside the lungs, the pressure can cause all or part of the affected lung to collapse.

The whole system performs various functions, including:

- acting as a blood filter or reservoir

- acting as an air filter, warmer and humidifier

- contributing to heat loss through ventilation

Internal Respiration exists when the chest cavity is expanded or contracted by its muscles so that air rushes into the lungs to fill the empty space (or rushes out), due to the pressure gradients that are created between the mouth or nose and the alveoli, from where oxygen is diffused (actually, pushed, under pressure) into the *haemoglobin* in the blood. At altitude, the space available is the same, but there is less air to fill it, and proportionately less oxygen, hence the need for supplementary supplies (there will also be less pressure to force the oxygen into the blood, even with a 100% supply). The oxygen thus absorbed is carried to the tissues of the body, especially the brain, which is the most sensitive organ to its lack. The blood is then pumped around the body by the heart. Waste products in the form of carbon dioxide go the other way, via plasma to the lungs, or *from the blood to the alveoli* - it is the carbon dioxide (and acidity) level in the blood that regulates respiration, which is monitored by several chemical receptors in the brain that are very sensitive to CO_2.

Breathing is controlled by the autonomic nervous system, but it can change according to your activity. Breathe with your stomach and chest - not only does this fill the lungs better, but it also stimulates blood flow in the liver. The normal rate of breathing is around 18 times a minute, exchanging 0.35-0.65 litres of air. (i.e. ½ ltr on average). The *tidal volume* (also known as V_T) is the volume of an individual breath (in and out) during quiet breathing. It averages about 500 ml, or cm^3, for some exams (whatever the units are, the maximum for a man is 2500, and 1500 for a woman). The total capacity of the lungs of a normal healthy person is around 6 litres, of which around 2½ remains after breathing out.

The spreading of gas particles to fill a container is called *diffusion*. *Graham's law* states that, under the same conditions, the rate of diffusion of a gas is inversely proportional to the square root of its density. Thus, hydrogen will diffuse 4 times faster than oxygen does under the same conditions of temperature and pressure.

The diffusion of oxygen into the blood depends on *partial pressure* (that is, its pressure in proportion to its presence in the mix - it follows *Henry's Law* and, presumably, *Dalton's*) so, as this falls, oxygen assimilation is impaired. Although the air gets thinner, the ratio of gases remains the same, so there is still 21% oxygen at 35 000. However, even if you increase the proportion of oxygen to 100% as you climb,

there is an altitude (around 33 700 feet) where the pressure is so low that the partial pressure is actually less than that at sea level, so just having oxygen is not enough, because, as altitude increases, the partial pressure of water vapour and carbon dioxide in the lungs also remains the same, reducing the partial pressure of oxygen in the lungs still further (the partial pressure of CO_2 in the alveoli is *lower* than it is in the blood). Also, at altitude, other gases dissolved in the blood, such as nitrogen, may bubble out and cause the bends or similar effects.

From 0-10 000 ft you can survive on normal air; above this, an increasing amount of oxygen is required, up to 33 700 feet, at which point you require pure oxygen to survive (breathing 100% oxygen at that height is the same as breathing air at sea level. At 40 000' it is the equivalent of breathing air at 10 000 feet). Above 40 000 the oxygen needs pressure, meaning that you must exhale by force (also, exposure to 0_3 becomes significant).

Having said all that, your learning ability can be compromised as low as 6 000 feet (*Source*: RAF).

Breathing	First Signs	Death
Air'	10,000 ft	22,000 ft
100% Oxygen'	38,000 ft	43,000 ft
Pressure Oxygen	45,000 ft	50,000 ft

OXYGEN

Pure oxygen is a colourless, tasteless, odourless and *non-combustible* gas that takes up about 21% of the air we breathe (it is actually quite corrosive - it belongs to the same chemical family as chlorine and fluorine, so too much is toxic). Although it doesn't burn itself, it does support combustion, which is why we need it, because the body turns food into heat, in the process producing water and waste as by-products. As we can't store oxygen, we survive from breath to breath.

How much you use depends on your physical activity and/or mental stress - for example, you need 4 times more for walking than sitting quietly. The proportion of oxygen to air (21%) actually remains constant up to about 9 km, but its *partial pressure decreases* because the barometric pressure does. However, water vapour and CO_2 have a constant partial pressure, so you can see that, at some point, they will restrict the partial pressure of oxygen.

At about 15 240 m (49 707 feet), the combined pressure of water vapour and CO_2 in the lungs is more or less equal to barometric pressure and gas exchange is not possible. At 19 202 m (62 630 feet), when the water vapour pressure of body fluids equals the barometric pressure, bubbles form in just about every part of the body that contains a liquid (ebullism). In short, the liquids in your body start to boil!

No extra oxygen is required below 5 000 feet, as 95% of what you would find on the ground can be expected there. However, at over 8 000 feet, you may find measurable changes in blood pressure and respiration, although healthy people should perform OK.

Lack of oxygen leads to.......

HYPOXIA

This is a condition where the oxygen concentration in the blood is below normal, or where oxygen cannot be used by the body, but anaemia can produce the same effect, as can alcohol. There are several types of hypoxia:

- *Hypoxic Hypoxia* arises from insufficient partial pressure, and is what people normally mean when they refer to the subject in general. It is otherwise known as *hypoventilation*, and has four stages:

  - *Indifferent*, with slight effects on dark adaptation, as low as 5000 feet

  - *Compensatory*, where the body tries to increase the oxygen intake through faster breathing & heart rate, etc.

  - *Disturbance*, where the body cannot keep up, and you get headaches, blue skin, etc.

  - *Critical*, where you are close to incapacitation

- *Anaemic Hypoxia* is a reduction in the blood's carrying capacity

- *Stagnant (Ischaemic) Hypoxia* comes from poor blood circulation

- *Histotoxic Hypoxia* exists where the body cannot utilise oxygen, possibly due to toxics, like cyanide

Night vision (which is most sensitive to lack of oxygen) is significantly reduced (by more than 25%) at 15 000 feet with *compensatory hypoxia*.

So, there may really be too little oxygen, or you don't have enough blood (haemoglobin) to carry what oxygen you need around the body - you may have donated some, or have an ulcer. You might also be a smoker, with your haemoglobin blocked by carbon monoxide (*anaemic hypoxia*). A blockage of 5-8%, typical for a heavy smoker, gives an equivalent altitude of 5-7000 feet before you get airborne! Short-term memory impairment starts at 12 000 feet. In short, and for the exams, hypoxia is a *reduced partial pressure* in the lungs. To help compensate for it, *descend below 10,000 feet*, breathe *100% oxygen* and *reduce your activity.*

The effects of hypoxia are similar to those of alcohol, but classic signs are:

- *Personality changes.* You get jolly, aggressive and less inhibited

- *Judgement changes.* Your abilities are impaired; you think you are capable of anything and have much less self-criticism

- *Muscle movement.* Becomes sluggish, not in tune with your mind

- *Short-term memory loss,* leading to reliance on training, or long-term memory

- *Sensory loss.* Blindness occurs (colour first), then touch, orientation and hearing

- *Loss of consciousness.* You get confused first, then semi-conscious, then unconscious

- *Blueness*

In summary, you can expect *fast & heavy breathing, impairment of vision, muscles* and *judgement.*

The above are *subjective* signs, in that they need to be recognised by the person actually suffering from hypoxia, who is in the wrong state to recognise anything. External observers may notice some of them, but especially lips and fingertips turning blue and possible hyperventilation (see below) as the victim tries to get more oxygen. However, the normal reaction to lack of oxygen, such as panting, does not appear, because there is no excess CO_2. As with carbon monoxide poisoning, the onset of hypoxia is insidious and can be recognised only by being very aware of the symptoms, which are aggravated by:

- *Altitude.* Less oxygen available, less pressure to keep it there

- *Time.* The more exposure, the greater the effect

- *Exercise.* Increases energy usage and hence oxygen requirement

- *Cold.* Increases energy usage and hence oxygen requirement

- *Illness.* Increases energy usage and hence oxygen requirement

- *Fatigue.* Symptoms arise earlier

- *Drugs* or *alcohol.* Reduced tolerance

- *Smoking.* Haemoglobin has an affinity for CO (carbon monoxide) 210-250 times that of oxygen

OXYGEN REQUIREMENTS

The oxygen to be carried, and the people to whom masks should be made available, varies with *altitude, rate of descent* and *Minimum Safe Altitude*. The latter two are dependent on each other, in that it's no good having a good rate of descent if the MSA stops you. It may well be that, although you're flying at a level that requires fewer masks, the MSA may demand that you equip everybody.

Preflight stuff includes ensuring that oxygen masks are accessible for the crew, and passengers are aware of where their masks are. Check the security of the circular dilution valve filter (a foam disc) on all of them, together with the pressure. Beards will naturally reduce their efficiency. Briefings should include the importance of not smoking and monitoring the flow indicator. All *No Smoking* signs should be on when using it. If you know you will need oxygen at night, it's best to start using it from takeoff.

There are three types of oxygen supply, *continuous flow, diluter demand* and *pressure demand* (refer to the *Air Law* chapter for legal requirements). For a diluter demand system, the *regulator* controls the amount of pure oxygen mixed with air. You start to become physically affected from lack of oxygen above 6,000 ft. In a *steady flow system*, oxygen is fed to a mask with a face piece and a plastic bag that can expand. The bag is a *rebreather*, because it allows air to be reused to a certain extent. Flow must be adjusted for different altitudes. If it is not enough, the flow indicator will show a red line. *Demand* oxygen systems only provide it when the person inhales.

In a climb, in a non-pressurised aircraft with no supplemental oxygen, you will pass the critical threshold at around 22,000 feet. Using 100% oxygen without pressure, expect hypoxia at approximately 38,000-40,000 feet - this is the same as breathing ambient air at 10 000 feet.

PRESSURE CHANGES (BAROTRAUMA)

Aside from oxygen, the body contains gases of varying descriptions in many places; some occur naturally, and some are created by the body's normal working processes. The problem is that these gases expand and contract as the aircraft climbs and descends. Some need a way out, and some need a way back as well.

- Gas in the ears normally vents via the Eustachian tubes. If these are blocked (say with a cold), the pressure on either side of the eardrum is not balanced, which could lead (at the very least) to considerable pain, and (at worst) a ruptured eardrum. It is called *aerotitis.*

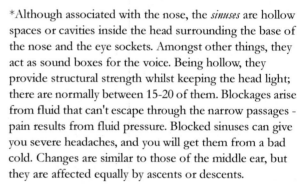

- Sinus* cavities are also vulnerable to imbalances of pressure, and are affected in the same way as eardrums are. *Aaerosinusitis* is caused by differences in pressure between the sinus cavity and the ambient air.

- Gas in the gut can be vented from both ends

- Teeth may have small pockets of air in them, if filled, together with the gums. Although dentists nowadays are aware of people flying, and pack fillings a lot better, the public don't fly every day, as you do, so be sure. High altitude balloonists actually take their fillings out

*Although associated with the nose, the *sinuses* are hollow spaces or cavities inside the head surrounding the base of the nose and the eye sockets. Amongst other things, they act as sound boxes for the voice. Being hollow, they provide structural strength whilst keeping the head light; there are normally between 15-20 of them. Blockages arise from fluid that can't escape through the narrow passages - pain results from fluid pressure. Blocked sinuses can give you severe headaches, and you will get them from a bad cold. Changes are similar to those of the middle ear, but they are affected equally by ascents or descents.

MOTION SICKNESS

Vertigo is the result of *Coriolis Effect*. It is caused by a mismatch between the information sent to the brain by the eyes and ears. Accelerating from straight and level flight may give the impression of pitching up (climbing), because the sensors in the inner ear perceive the body weight as going rearwards and downwards. As the most dependable source of sensory information is your eyes, believe your instruments. *Pilot's Vertigo* is dizziness and a tumbling sensation that arises when making head movements in a tight turn, or a sensation of rotation coming from multiple irritation of several semicircular canals. Aside from being *a sensory conflict within the vestibular system accompanied by nausea, vomiting and fear*, airsickness can also be caused by vibration, when the body (i.e. the skull), is vibrated at frequencies less than 0.5Hz, which is common in turbulence. Keeping the head still and closing the eyes helps.

Medications and alcohol can have similar effects. It's well known that lying down when drunk causes the ceiling to revolve, and this can lead to stationary objects appearing to move when standing upright. This is because the brain detects the movement of fluid in the inner ear and tries to rationalise things through the eyes. In other words, eye movements are used to compensate for head movement - the difference between the specific gravities of alcohol and inner fluid is enough to cause the sensors to move and be wrongly interpreted as a head movement. Since your head is not really moving, it looks as if the rest of the world is. This effect can be reproduced days after drinking only a couple of pints of beer, long after the alcohol is undetectable in the blood.

DECOMPRESSION SICKNESS

This results from the formation of nitrogen bubbles in bodily tissues and fluids after a cabin pressure loss at high altitude. In other words, where pressures are low, nitrogen in the blood comes out of solution (typically above 18,000', but more so at 25,000'), just like when you open a fizzy drink. Bubbles can form, and are especially painful in the joints, as you find with the *bends*. Other symptoms include the *creeps* (skin), *chokes* (lungs) and the *staggers* (brain). All this derives from *Henry's Law*. Unfortunately, the bubbles do not redissolve on descent, so if you are affected you may need to go into a decompression chamber. At the very least, you should *descend as low as you can and land as soon as possible*.

Diving before flight should be avoided, as extra nitrogen is absorbed while breathing pressurised gas, which will dissolve out as you surface again. When you go flying too soon, this is accentuated, and the symptoms can appear as low as 8,000 feet. A diver 30 feet under water is under twice the normal sea level pressure. Don't fly for 24 hours if you've been SCUBA diving, or 48 hours if the dive was very long, say over 4 hours.

Factors that *decrease* resistance to DCS include *SCUBA diving*, *obesity* and *old age*. If you get pains in the joints *within a few hours of landing*, see a doctor as soon as possible.

TIME OF USEFUL CONSCIOUSNESS

When you climb, oxygen levels fall, but the CO_2 levels in your blood do not, so the brain does not know it has to compensate. Otherwise known as *Effective Performance Time*, the *times of useful consciousness* (i.e. from *the interruption of the oxygen supply to when you are exposed to hypoxia*) are quite short:

Height (feet)	Seated	Moderate Activity
18 000	40 mins	30 mins
20 000'	10 mins	5 mins
25 000'	5 mins	3 mins

Height (feet)	Seated	Moderate Activity
30 000'	90 secs	45 secs
35 000'	45 secs	30 secs
40 000	25 secs	18 secs
43 000'	12-15 secs	12 secs

Note: Questions will not give you an exact height figure, but one in between, meaning you will have to interpolate. The figures depend on cabin pressure altitude, vary individually, and are affected by physical activity, strength and time of decompression

*You need to be taking steps within 5-6 seconds.

You won't pass out inside the times given above, but you will be pretty much useless in the cockpit unless you get your oxygen mask on and select 100% oxygen, preferably in a rapid and controlled descent to below at least 10,000 ft cabin altitude. If you don't, you will be in a state of *negative aspiration*, because the partial pressure of oxygen at that height will be much lower than that in your blood, and the pressure gradient will force it into your lungs, there to be sucked out even further due to Venturi effects (air will be pulled out by airflow over the hole). The figures above will therefore be *reduced* (by about half) in a *rapid decompression*, so check the exam question for the magic words. Typically, they will move down a slot. *Sufficient oxygen saturation of the blood ends at 88%.*

If you cannot get lower, be alert for decompression sickness, as it may occur even with a good supply of oxygen. Very rarely, lung damage can be caused by rapid depressurisation, which can be avoided by breathing out.

Another definition states that TUC is the amount of time an individual can perform flying duties efficiently with inadequate oxygen supply, or the time from the interruption of the oxygen supply or exposure to an oxygen-poor environment, to the time when useful function is lost (it is *not* the time to total unconsciousness). The exam says that TUC is: *The time during which you can act with physical and mental efficiency and alertness from when you are exposed to hypoxia, or when you lose the available oxygen supply.*

HYPERVENTILATION

This is simply overbreathing, or exhaling more than you are inhaling, where too much oxygen causes carbon dioxide to be washed out of the bloodstream, where the plasma gets too alkaline, and the arteries reduce in size, meaning that less blood gets to the brain.

Unconsciousness slows breathing down so the CO_2 balance is restored, but falling asleep is not practical! The usual cause is worry, fright or sudden shock, but hypoxia can be a factor - in fact, the symptoms are similar to hypoxia and include:

- Dizziness
- Pins and needles, tingling
- Blurred sight
- Hot/Cold feelings
- Anxiety
- Impaired performance
- Loss of consciousness

The last one is actually one of the best cures, since the body's automatic systems take over to restore normality. Whenever you are unsure of whether you are suffering from hyperventilation or hypoxia, treat for hypoxia, since this will almost always be the root cause - reach for the oxygen mask. You can treat hyperventilation by *talking aloud through the procedure to calm the emotions and reduce the rate of breathing*.

The Cardiovascular System

This is made up of the heart, arteries, arterioles, capillaries, veins and blood. It is a transport system that links the external environment to the tissues and distributes essential substances, such as hormones, oxygen and nutrients around the body. It also removes carbon dioxide and other waste products from the tissues and delivers them to the lungs, kidneys and liver.

The system is capable of anticipating physiological and metabolic demands by increasing heart action before it is actually required.

THE HEART

This item is pear-shaped, and found lying slightly to the left inside the thoracic cavity. It is surrounded by a protective membrane which contains a fluid filled cavity called the *pericardium*, which prevents friction between the heart and the surrounding tissues.

The heart consists of 2 pumps, side by side, each having an *atrium* (at the top) and a *ventricle* (underneath), and separated by the *septum*. The right atrium receives blood from the veins and passes it to the right ventricle, which pumps it under low pressure via the *pulmonary artery* to the lungs. At the same time, the left atrium receives blood from the lungs and the left ventricle pumps it under high

pressure to the arteries, via the *dorsal aorta*, so it has the thickest muscle walls (*myocardium*) to deal with it. Thus, the pumps do their work in phase, but deliver blood in series, throughout the body in one direction only, according to William Harvey, court physician to Charles I (blood vessels have internal non-return arrangements in the shape of valves that stop the blood going back the other way. Muscular activity and breathing push the blood along.). There is normally no direct transfer of blood between the pumps.

Cardiac muscle can contract rhythmically without nervous input, in a *myogenic rhythm*. The "pacemaker" is in the right atrium.

Arteries carry oxygenated blood *from* the heart to the body (the *pulmonary artery* goes straight to the lungs) whilst veins return blood *to* the heart (again, the pulmonary vein has a direct connection from the lungs) at a lower pressure.

Note that, although blood from the heart is oxygenated, and that to the heart is de-oxygenated, the pulmonaries are reversed. In other words, pulmonary circulation carries deoxygenated blood from the right side of the heart to the lungs, and oxygenated blood back to the left side of the heart. A second circulation, known as *systemic circulation*, carries oxygenated blood from the left side of the heart to the head and body. The right side receives deoxygenated blood from the body. In this way, oxygenated and deoxygenated blood is kept separate - the blood alternates between the two circulations.

Arteries eventually turn into *arterioles* which eventually break up into minute vessels called *capillaries* that allow the diffusion of small molecular substances like oxygen, vitamins, minerals, water and amino acids to nourish cells.

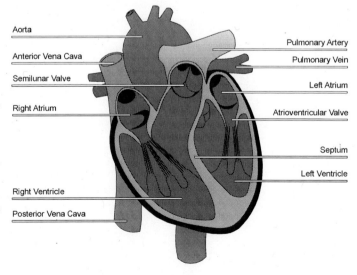

Carbon dioxide and water pass the other way in a process called *capillary exchange*.

The rate of contraction, or *pulse rate*, is around 72 (70-80) beats a minute when at rest. The pulse rate is influenced by *adrenalin*, *physical exercise* and the *treatment of glucose in the blood*. As the ventricle pumps about 70 ml of blood per beat, *cardiac output* is about 5 litres a minute (actually 4.9-5.3). Cardiac output is the volume of blood pumped per minute by each ventricle, and represents the total blood flow through the pulmonary and systemic circuits. It comes from the *stroke volume* and *heart rate* (increments in heart rate contribute more than stroke volume).

BLOOD

This is a liquid made up of:

- 55% colourless plasma, for transporting CO_2, nutrients and hormones, and

- 45% blood cells, which come in three varieties. *Red cells* transport oxygen via *haemoglobin*, and *white cells* (*leukocytes*) fight infection. *Platelets* are for clotting blood. All are produced in *bone marrow*, which capacity diminishes as we grow older

CO_2 in solution forms a weak carbonic acid which also helps to maintain the blood's acid balance. The amount of haemoglobin in the blood depends on the amount of oxygen in the lungs. Reductions in the amount of haemoglobin available reduces the blood's ability to transport oxygen (to cause anaemia). This could arise from either less red blood cells or the concentration of haemoglobin in them. Haemoglobin has an affinity for CO (carbon monoxide) of 210-250 times that of oxygen.

ANAEMIA

Anaemia means that you do not have enough functional haemoglobin, there being too few red blood cells, and a limited capacity to transport oxygen (more iron often cures it). *Anaemic Hypoxia* is the lack of oxygen resulting from anaemia.

BLOOD PRESSURE

This is the amount of force that the blood exerts on the vessel walls. It is sensed by bundles of nerves in cavities called *sinuses*. There are two sets in the main arteries to the brain, and another on the aorta, the *carotid* and *aortic sinus pressoreceptors*, respectively, but you knew that already. The brain varies secretions of two hormones in response to their signals, to regulate blood pressure by narrowing the arteries. As with electricity, the rate of blood flow through a vessel depends on the pressure gradient from one end to the other, plus the resistance encountered (which works the same way, too, in terms of series *vs* parallel!) The

amount of resistance to blood flow depends on the *vessel dimensions* and *blood viscosity*.

The *systolic blood pressure* is the peak pressure as blood is pumped from the left ventricle into the aorta. The *diastolic pressure* is the lowest, produced when resting between beats - it is an indication of the resistance of the small arteries and capillaries to blood flow, or the load against which the heart has to work. The World Health Organisation says that "normal" blood pressure lies between 100-139 mmHg (systolic) and 60-89 mmHg (diastolic) - something like 120/80 (120 over 80 for the exam). However, "standard" values are 100 and 60 mg, or 100/60, with the limits regarded as 160 and 100 mmHg, or 160/100. The higher the figures are, the harder the heart is working, and the greater is the risk of stroke and coronary heart disease.

As you get older, the systolic pressure should be roughly 100 plus your age in years. The arterial pressure in the *upper arm* is equivalent to the pressure in the heart, which is why it is used to check your pressure in medicals. The heart does not rest in the same way as do other muscles - instead, it takes a mini-rest for a microsecond or two in between beats. Heart muscles get their own blood from the *pulmonary arteries*.

Blood pressure has important links to diabetes (below).

HYPERTENSION & HYPOTENSION

This is known as a silent killer, as blood pressure is persistently elevated with no external symptoms - blood vessel walls, heart and other organs may be severely damaged without you knowing. It is the culmination of many factors, including your weight, diet, bad habits and family history. There is no cure, but prevention is possible.

Hypotension, on the other hand, is any blood pressure that is below the normal expected for given environment. It is a relative term because blood pressure normally varies greatly anyway with *activity, age, medications* and *underlying medical conditions*. Neurological conditions that can lead to low blood pressure include: changing your position from lying down to the more vertical (*postural hypotension*), stroke, shock, lightheadedness after urinating or defecating, Parkinson's disease, neuropathy and simply fright. Non-neurologic conditions that can cause it include: bleeding, infections, dehydration, heart disease, adrenal insufficiency, pregnancy, prolonged bed rest, poisoning, toxic shock syndrome and blood transfusion reactions.

DEEP VEIN THROMBOSIS (DVT)

This is a blood clot (thrombus) that develops *inside* a deep vein, usually in the lower leg, but also the arm, where it can cause pain. Blood clots that form in superficial veins that lie under the skin are called *superficial thrombophlebitis* and are much less serious.

In most cases, the clots are small and do not cause any symptoms, as the body can gradually break down the clot. However, larger clots may partially or totally block the blood flow in the vein and cause symptoms such as:

- swelling of the calf, which is usually different from the mild ankle swelling that many people get during long haul flights

- pain in the calf, or calf pain that is noticeable, or worse when standing or walking

Although they are not always a sign of DVT, if you experience clots, you should seek medical advice. There is evidence that long haul flights (i.e. lasting four hours or more) may increase the risk of DVT as a result of prolonged immobility, which can happen during any form of long distance travel, whether by car, bus, train or air. Potential complications include:

- *Pulmonary embolism*, when a piece of the blood clot breaks off and travels in the bloodstream to become lodged in the lungs and block blood flow, hours or even days afterwards. It may cause chest pain and shortness of breath

- *Post thrombotic syndrome* happens if a DVT damages the valves in the vein, so that instead of flowing upwards, the blood pools in the lower leg. This can result in pain, swelling and ulcers on the leg

Anticoagulant medicines are the most common treatment, which alter certain chemicals in the blood to stop clots forming so easily. Otherwise, you should:

- exercise your legs at least every 2-3 hours - starting with the muscles of your lower legs (which act as a pump for the blood in the veins) while sitting - pull your toes towards your knees then relax, or press the balls of your feet down while raising your heel.

- wear loose-fitting clothing

- keep hydrated with water rather than alcohol and caffeinated drinks

- wear graduated compression stockings

HEART DISEASE

Heart disease can be grouped into 3 categories:

- *Hypertensive* - from high blood pressure, working the heart harder so it gets enlarged (anxiety, etc.)

- *Coronary*, or *Arteriosclerotic* - hardening of the (coronary) arteries through excessive calcium, or cholesterol, which again makes the heart work harder (bad diet). The essential problem is that the coronary blood supply is blocked or restricted, and oxygen does not get to the affected cells, which die. Then you do, if enough are affected. This is known in the trade as a *myocardial infarction*. *Arteriosclerosis* exists where a build-up of fatty material in the linings of the coronary arteries makes them narrower. The fatty linings get harder as calcium deposits are added. The main result is *angina*, a symptom of which is a severe chest pain which radiates out to the left arm and up to the neck and jaws. The pain will go when you relax. Where the fatty lining disturbs the smooth blood flow, a clot may form to block the veins. The resulting *heart attack* would lead to *circulatory shock*, or a failure of the blood supply.

- *Valvular* or *rheumatic* - where valves are unable to open or close properly, allowing back pressure to build up (old age)

To reduce the risks of heart disease, double your resting pulse for at least 20 minutes 3 times a week. However, a recent US study has suggested that, although this will lengthen your life by around two years, that two years will be spent on the extra exercise! Otherwise, stop smoking, reduce stress and watch the diet........

The Digestive System

Digestion is the chemical process of breaking down the food you eat into substances that can be absorbed through the walls of the intestines, and transported to the rest of the body via the bloodstream, moving in a controlled fashion from the mouth to the other end. The stomach contains hydrochloric acid for this purpose, and the stomach lining is able to heal (from scratches, etc.) within 24 hours. The method by which energy is made available to the organism is called *Metabolism*.

The process starts in the mouth, where food is chewed and mixed with saliva that starts to break down starches. After being churned in the stomach, the food is moved through the intestines by a rhythmic muscular movement called *peristalsis*, which is controlled by numerous automatic reflexes. The centres that control hunger and appetite are in the hypothalamus and are closely related to pleasure and unpleasure. Since hunger and satiety are emotional states, the operation of the digestive system can be affected by other emotions, especially those that arise from stress - certainly, where anger, resentment and aggression are involved, the stomach will increase its production of hydrochloric acid.

Stress arousal will also affect peristaltic rhythm. You get diarrhoea if the food is moved so fast through the intestines that water cannot be absorbed, and constipation if the food moves so slowly that too much is absorbed.

DIET

The body's main fuel is glucose, which can either be converted from different types of food, or eaten directly. Levels of glucose are regulated by the *pancreas,* which secretes *insulin* to reduce blood sugar levels by getting it into cells or converting it into fat if there's no room.

The body's three sources of nourishment include:

- *Carbohydrates*, which are converted into glucose to provide energy and which consist of:

  - Simple sugars

  - Complex sugars

  - Starch

- *Fats* (and oils), which produce twice as much energy as carbohydrates for the same weight, but which are harder to digest

- *Proteins*, which are constructed from amino acids, not all of those required being carried in the body. Animal protein has to be broken down into peptides and amino acids before being reconstructed into what the body needs

Trace elements should be obtained through a balanced diet, which is *not* a pint in either hand! Breakfast should bring in about 25% of the daily calorie intake.

Note: It should be pointed out that sugar is one of the most harmful substances we can put into our bodies on a daily basis, and there is almost no processed food that does not contain it - even baked beans. Certainly, there is hardly a cereal product without it (did you ever wonder why cereals are fortified with vitamins? It's because they are all taken out first! The problem is that manufactured ones are never as good as the real thing). Sugar that is not needed to maintain adequate glucose levels and replenish stored glycogen in the liver and muscles is converted to fat, by insulin, which also tends to block the conversion of

fat back to glucose, so a high insulin level makes it difficult to remove the fat it created in the first place. The problem is that, on the average Western diet, our insulin levels are almost permanently high, which is something that our bodies are simply not built to cope with - the pancreas needs a rest! Thus, we should try to eat so that large spikes of insulin are not generated, which can be difficult in a normal pilot's lifestyle. That is, insulin should be injected into the bloodstream under more controlled conditions - processed foods are converted into glucose *very quickly*, which is the real problem. The type of carbohydrate you eat will determine how this happens (the Atkins diet works because it doesn't trigger insulin). As well, sugar has no vitamins, so it is unable to process itself in the body, and has to borrow what it needs from other sources, which will create a deficit of Vitamin B.

After reading most of the diet books around, the following conclusions can be drawn:

- It is not necessarily the fat you eat, but the fat created from sugar that is bad for your health

- Don't eat anything processed - which is usually anything "white", or at least with white flour in

- Eat fruit by itself - although fruit contains sugars, they also contain enzymes and other beneficial substances, and don't stimulate so much insulin (around a third, in fact). However, once you combine fruit with other food, you get the full non-benefit. Also, fruit is digested mostly in the small intestine, and eating it after a large meal causes this to be delayed, with fermentation that causes indigestion

- If you drink alcohol (in moderation!), dry (low sugar) red wine is best

- Exercise, but not so much that you need to eat a lot to produce the glucose you need

- Don't eat a heavy meal just before going to bed - calorie consumption is different in the evening

- Drink lots of fluid (not with sugar or caffeine in! Caffeine can pull calcium out of your bones)

- Eat lots of fibre and water-based food, such as fruit, greens, tomatoes, etc. in their raw state - try for around 70% of your total diet

And if you thought sugar was bad - think about monosodium glutamate, or MSG, as found in most foods under the name *hydrolized vegetable protein*. MSG is injected into rats to make them morbidly obese so they can be experimented on. It triples the amount of insulin created by the pancreas, so if you need proof that insulin can be bad for you, this is it. You will find MSG in most foods because it is addictive, and makes you want to eat the same stuff again, which is presumably why, after eating a Chinese meal, you want another one 2 hours afterwards (Chinese meals are notorious for containing MSG).

HYPOGLYCAEMIA

The most common problems (in the normal pilot's lifestyle, anyway) are low blood sugar (*functional hypoglycaemia*), or eating too much (*reactive hypoglycaemia*), caused by missed meals and the like. Although you may think it's better to have the wrong food than no food, be careful when it comes to eating choccy bars in lieu of lunch, which will cause your blood sugar levels to rise so rapidly that too much insulin is released to compensate, which drives your blood sugar levels to a *lower* state than they were before - known in the trade as *rebound hypoglycaemia*. Here, the sugar is pushed into all cells of the body and not specifically reserved for the Central Nervous System. Apart from eating "real food", you will minimise the risks of this if you eat small snacks frequently instead of heavy meals after long periods with nothing. Complex (slow release) carbohydrates are best, like pasta, etc.

Hypoglycaemia is bad enough in the short term, but long-term can be regarded as a *disease*. Although not life threatening, it is a forerunner of many worse things and should be looked at. The important thing to watch appears to be the suddenness of any fall in blood sugar, and a big one can often trigger a heart attack. A high protein diet will tend to even things out, as protein helps the absorption of fat, which is inhibited if too much insulin is about. Warning signs include shakiness, sweatiness, irritability or anxiety, difficulty in speaking, headache, weakness, numbness or tingling around the lips, inability to think straight (or lack of concentration), palpitations and hunger. At its worst, hypoglycaemia could result in coma, but you could also get seizure and fainting. Eat more if you exercise more.

HYPERGLYCAEMIA

This is the opposite of the above (and precedes it), an *excess* of blood sugar. Symptoms include tiredness, increased appetite and thirst, frequent urination, dry skin, flu-like aches, headaches, blurred vision and nausea. This condition causes dehydration, so have fluids around to help you. Also, decrease stress.

WATER & DEHYDRATION

You need water to:

- regulate body temperature
- circulate nutrients & oxygen and remove waste products from cells (there is 4 times more lymph than blood)
- prevent kidney stones, constipation and some urinary and colon cancers

The accepted figure is 8-10 glasses per day, which is around one for every two waking hours, plus more if you are exercising, as water is lost through respiration and sweating as well as urination. On an average day, you lose about 1 litre of water through various means, but this can increase to 5 when it is hot. The Israeli army calculates it to be nearer 20.

The comfort range of the human body is 21-27°C with an associated relative humidity of 50%. *Too hot* is defined as over 32°C, where blood vessels dilate to get rid of the heat and the heart cannot keep up, so you begin to feel tired. Below about 10°C, your body can lose heat quicker than it can be produced.

Note: Hunger and thirst share the same signals to the brain, so try drinking water first!

DIABETES

Glucose in the blood provides energy, but sometimes the body cannot either produce the insulin in the first place that is required to get it into the cells (*Type 1* diabetes), or make use of it in the best way (*Type 2*). The former tends to appear in people under 40, and the latter in people over 40, although they can occur in either. Both can be treated by diet and/or insulin injections. Exercise is good, too, as it uses up blood sugar that would otherwise need insulin to get rid of it.

Since insulin is needed to get glucose into your cells, it follows that, if this is not done, blood sugar levels can be dangerously high. In the short term, you may be tired, thirsty, urinate frequently (and get dehydrated), have blurred vision, headaches and tingling fingers and toes. More long-term, blood vessels can get damaged from high blood pressure and cholesterol levels. So important is this, that, if you were on a desert island with a bottle of blood pressure pills and a bottle of diabetes pills, you'd better take the blood pressure pills first! High blood pressure will tend to push proteins through the kidney walls, to be detected in urine.

ALCOHOL

There is only one rule - **flying and alcohol don't mix!**

Whilst nobody should object to you taking a drink or two the evening before a flight, you should remember that it can take over 3 days for alcohol to clear the system (it remains in the inner ear for longest). Within 8 hours of a planned departure, you should not drink alcohol at all. The maximum blood level is officially 0.2 mg per ml, a quarter of the driving limit in UK, but it's not only the alcohol that causes problems - the after-effects do as well, like the hangover, fatigue, dehydration, loss of blood sugar and toxins caused by metabolisation, etc. Many alcoholic drinks also have an odd range of chemicals in them. The body even produces its own alcohol - around 0.04 mg per 100 ml.

Although it appears otherwise, alcohol is not a stimulant, but an *anaesthetic*, which puts to sleep those parts of the brain that deal with inhibitions - the problem is that these areas also cover judgement, comprehension and attention to detail. In fact, the effects of alcohol are the same as hypoxia, dealt with elsewhere, in that it prevents brain cells from using available oxygen. One significant effect of hypoxia in this context is the resulting inability to tell that something is wrong.

It takes the liver about 1 hour to eliminate 1 unit of alcohol from the blood. Officially, alcohol leaves the body at 15 milligrams per 100 ml of blood per hour. A blood alcohol level of 60 mgm/100 ml will therefore take 4 hours to return to normal. 1 unit is, or used to be, considered the same as 1 measure of spirit, a glass of wine or half a pint of beer. The number of units per week beyond which physical damage is likely is 21 for men and 14 for women.

Although passengers get cabin service, persons under the affluence of incohol or drugs, of unsound mind or having the potential to cause trouble should not be allowed on board - certainly, no person should be drunk on any aircraft (people aren't generally aware that one drink at 6000 feet is the same as two at sea level). This is not being a spoilsport - drunks don't react properly in emergencies and could actually be dangerous to other people, which is why I always get an aisle seat - I don't have to get round people in the way. Therefore, it's not just for their own good, but that of others as well. If you need to get rid of obstreperous passengers, you can always quote the regulations at them (or even use sarcasm), but don't forget to fill in an Occurrence Report.

Crew members must not:

- Consume alcohol less than 8 hours before the specified reporting time for flight duty or the start of standby
- Start a flight duty period with a blood alcohol level over a certain level
- Consume alcohol during the flight duty period or while on standby

Note: Most regulations are worded so that you can have a drink 8 hours before reporting time, but you must also not have alcohol in your system.

Australian researchers compared the effects of alcohol and fatigue on performance. They found that being awake for 17 hours in a row is as bad as a blood alcohol concentration of 0.05%. The limit for driving in Canada, for example, is 0.08%.

The first step for curing alcoholism is the admission that you are an alcoholic, and the willingness to accept treatment.

MEDICATIONS

Although the symptoms of colds and sore throats, etc. are bad enough on the ground, they may actually become dangerous in flight by either distracting or harming you by getting more serious with height (such as bursting your eardrums, or worse). If you're under treatment for anything, including surgery, not only should you not fly, but you should also check that there will be no adverse effects on your physical or mental ability, as many preparations combine chemicals, and the mixture could make quite a cocktail. No drugs or alcohol should be taken within a few hours of each other, as even fairly widely accepted stuff such as aspirin can have unpredictable effects, especially in relation to hypoxia (it's as well to keep away from the office, too - nobody else will want what you've got). Particular ones to avoid are antibiotics (penicillin, tetracyclines), tranquilisers, antidepressants, sedatives, stimulants (caffeine, amphetamines), anti-histamines and anything for relieving high blood pressure, and, of course, anything not actually prescribed. Naturally, you've got to be certifiable if you fly having used marijuana, or worse.

Too much aspirin can cause gastric bleeding.

ANAESTHETICS

All procedures requiring local or regional anaesthetics disqualify you for flying for at least 12 hours.

The worst type of inapacitation, on finals or anywhere, is gradual, or insidious

BLOOD DONATIONS

Pilots generally are discouraged from giving blood (or plasma) when actively flying, because a donation may lead to a reduced tolerance of altitude. Some dental anaesthetics can cause problems for up to 24 hours or more, as can anything to do with immunisation. If you do give blood, try to leave a gap of 24 hours, including bone marrow donations. Although your arm will fill back up in a very short time, and for most donors there are no noticeable after-effects, there is still a slight risk of faintness or loss of consciousness. After a general anaesthetic, see the doctor.

Having donated blood, you should *rest supine for about 15-20 minutes, drink plenty of fluid and not fly for 24 hours.*

FOOD POISONING

Food poisoning can also be a problem, and not just for passengers - the standard precaution (like in *Airplane!*) is to select different items from the rest of the crew, even in the hotel, or at least eat at different times.

SMOKING

There are over 200 harmful chemicals in cigarette smoke, which are more concentrated in *sidestream smoke,* or that which has not been filtered through the main body of the cigarette, so passive smokers face the worst risks (cigarettes release ten times more air pollution than a diesel engine - it is a Group A carcinogen). Here are some of the chemicals involved and some common places they may also be found:

- Carbon monoxide (car exhausts)

- Arsenic (rat poison)

- Ammonia (window cleaner)

- Acetone (nail polish remover)

- Hydrogen cyanide (gas chambers)

- Naphthalene (mothballs)

- Sulphur compounds (matches)

- Formaldehyde (embalming fluid)

- Butane (lighter fluid)

Otherwise, the addictive substance in tobacco is *nicotine,* and the substance that stops the alveoli doing their work is *tar.* There is also carbon monoxide (CO), which has a better affinity with haemoglobin than oxygen does. Nicotine reduces the diameter of the arteries, which stimulates the release of adrenalin, to increase heart rate and blood pressure.

MISCELLANEOUS

Don't forget to inform the authorities (in writing) of illnesses, personal injuries or presumed pregnancies that incapacitate you for more than 21 days. Pilots in accidents should be medically examined before flying again.

Incapacitation

There is always a danger that whoever is in the other front seat may become incapacitated; in the obvious case, they collapse and fall across the controls. Less noticeable is the sort that comes with boredom or lack of mental stimulation on longer trips, where you may physically be in the cockpit but mentally miles away. Even disorientation during instrument flight is included. There's not much you can do against the first type aside from levelling the aircraft and returning to a safe flight path, then ensuring that the unfit pilot cannot interfere. Call for a passenger to help if need be and tell ATC what's going on. Land as soon as you can *under the circumstances,* which is not as daft as it sounds - it might be prudent to divert to a place with better aids or weather, which is further away, despite what the Company says about landing where they've got a base. *Do not* be rushed into an approach before you are ready, especially at an unfamiliar airfield. Your greatest responsibility is to the passengers.

Incapacitation can be *gradual* or *sudden, subtle* or *overt, partial* or *complete* and may not be preceded by any warning. It is mostly caused by acute gastro-intestinal disorders. According to the "Two Communications Rule", you are deemed to be incapacitated if you do not respond appropriately to a second verbal communication associated with a significant deviation from a standard operating procedure or flight profile. You should not be reluctant to take control if you have to.

PARTIAL OR GRADUAL

Symptoms that might affect your handling ability, to the extent that you have to hand over control, could include severe pain (especially sudden severe headache or chest pain), dizziness, blurring or partial loss of vision, disorientation, vomiting or diarrhoea (airline food again!)

TWO PILOT

You must immediately inform the other pilot and hand over control, then inform the destination, base or whoever else and divert, bearing in mind the nature and severity of the symptoms and the availability of medical facilities. Naturally, as with any emergency, the company would prefer you to carry on (minimum inconvenience to the passengers) or return to base (minimum inconvenience to them), but appendicitis waits for no man! You should not take control again, and your harness must be locked to stop you falling over the controls if you get worse.

SINGLE PILOT

You should react before any illness becomes severe enough to affect your handling, so an immediate radio call is essential. The first consideration must be for the safety of the passengers, so medical assistance for you must be a lesser priority, though the former may well depend on the latter.

SUDDEN OR COMPLETE

This may be subtle or overt, and give no warning; Murphy's Law dictates that fatal collapses occur during approach and landing, close to the ground. Detection of subtle incapacitation may be indirect, that is, only as a result of some expected action not being taken, so when you die maintaining your body position, the other pilot may not even notice until the expected order of events becomes interrupted.

TWO PILOT

Crew members should closely monitor the flight path, especially during takeoff, initial climb, final approach and landing, and immediately question any deviations. The fit pilot should assume control, assuming the controls are not interfered with, which is why you should always wear full harness, which should be locked in place and the seat slid back if there is any trouble, as a matter of priority (use passengers or other crew if required). First aid should be delayed until the immediate problems are sorted out, then the aircraft should be landed as soon as practicable.

Disease

You often fly to places with very low standards of hygiene and/or disease-carrying insects. Although not good for you in the long run, on such occasions, processed and packaged food can be a real lifesaver, as can bottled water. As with many things in life, prevention is better than cure - for malaria, certainly, a good tactic is to avoid being bitten (by the female Anopheles mosquito) in the first place, by wearing appropriate clothing, even though it is hot. Yellow fever is also insect-borne, but can be vaccinated against. Hepatitis A is transmitted by contaminated food or water, as is cholera. Tetanus is spread through bacteria in the form of spores via a puncture in the skin.

It is a misconception that illness starts when the symptoms first appear. There are often more subtle signs that are mostly ignored for some time. Changes in emotions are a good example, as are attitudes and

personality traits - some personality types are more prone to illness than others.

There are various types of disease:

ORGANIC DISEASE

Infectious diseases (e.g. colds & flu) are communicable, meaning that they can be transmitted from one host to another, and are regarded as acute, and short term. The microorganisms concerned (viruses, bacteria, fungi, parasites, etc.) cause their damage by releasing poisons or toxins and reproducing in enough numbers to interfere with the normal operation of the body.

Non-infectious diseases are typically caused by processes within the body, such as degeneration or heredity factors, but may include bad nutrition or a noxious environment. They are regarded as chronic.

PSYCHOSOMATIC DISEASE

These diseases stem from mind-body interaction, although a *coping reaction*, which is often confused with a psychosomatic illness, is a closing down of a bodily system as a reaction to stress - typical cases are deafness and blindness, but physical disabilities count, too. Some lifestyles promote psychosomatic illness, and knowledge is the best prevention.

The **psychogenic** variety refers to a physical disease caused by emotional stress. That is, there is organ damage, but without invasion or degeneration. These might include backaches, or migraines, or bronchial asthma, which often appears just before stressful periods in peoples' lives.

The **somatogenic** disorder works differently, in that an emotion such as anger or fear may bring down the immune system enough to allow a microorganism that may already be present to gain an influence, for which stress would be a catalyst.

PSYCHOLOGICAL FACTORS

Or, in other words, that which influences, or tends to influence, the mind or emotions. We are concerned with them, because they can influence the way we interpret information on which we base decisions. The thing is, with both optical and aural stimuli (discussed above), the *processing is done in the brain*, which uses past experience to interpret what it senses - it therefore has expectations that will exert an influence.

Modern technology, in the shape of automation, allows us to achieve more in less time and has led to lifestyles of constant change, which is something that humans don't like in general, anyway. Coping with change can be a major cause of stress, which pulls down your immune system and may act as a catalyst for an already-present organism to take a hold.

Stress

Flying is stressful, there's no doubt about that, but should stress be a problem? It's arguable that a little is good for you; it stops you slowing down and keeps you on your toes; this is the sort associated with success. The *Yerkes-Dodson Model* suggests that people can become complacent when they do not have enough stress in their lives, and their performance increases when they become subject to a little but, when something unusual or unexpected happens and their responsibilities start to pile up, the stress can become too much and they start to lose control - the harder they run around, the less they get done, and a vicious circle begins. We don't have time to rush! The model uses a graph of performance against arousal with an inverted U-shape which shows that, as arousal increases, performance increases to an optimum point, after which it falls off:

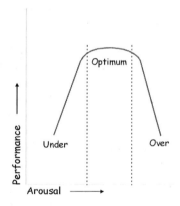

One definition of complacency is: "Self-satisfaction accompanied by a loss of awareness of danger." Once an activity becomes routine, you relax and reduce your mental effort, so the dangers are highest with the most skilled people. *Automatic behaviour* is most likely to result in complacency. High performers *remain vigilant, cross-check* their performance and *correct errors* before they are significant.

The optimum arousal state is 115-145 heartbeats per minute. After 145, motor skills start to break down. After 175, the forebrain (which has something to do with decision making) is superseded by the mid-brain.

behaviour becomes more aggressive and blood is withdrawn into the body (from the brain and immune system) to restrict your bleeding if something happens. What happened to Rodney King in Los Angeles occurred *after* a high speed chase. This is why you rehearse emergencies, because, when under stress, you may well revert to former training - watch out for those levers in the wrong place on the new machine (e.g. *reversion*)! An overstressed pilot may show mental blocks, confusion, channelized attention, resignation, frustration, rage, deterioration in motor coordination, and fast speaking in a high-pitched voice.

Excessive stress (or *dis*tress) can lead to fatigue, anxiety and inability to cope, and is associated with frustration or failure. Long term stress can affect your immune system, and, over the course of a career, can lead to failing medicals earlier than you should (you can measure stress by looking for cortisol in the urine. It is produced by the adrenal gland, which can get enlarged under prolonged stress). In fact, there is a large body of evidence to indicate that stress is behind many modern illnesses, certainly headaches, asthma, hypertension and heart disease.

In short, stress disturbs the body's *homeostasis*, which is the body's thermostat when it comes to its comfort and efficiency. The word comes from the Greek *homeos* and *stasis*, meaning *similar* and *condition*, respectively, and describes a state of the body where a stable equilibrium of internal functions exists. Homeostasis preserves the body's internal sameness, particularly with heat, by resisting and smoothing out changes. Since it allows the body's internal environment to be independent of the external one, it gives the organism a great amount of flexibility, especially with time, so we can interact more freely with the outside world without being tied down.

Stress enables you to adapt to encountered situations - it is the body's response to a *stressor*, which is an internal or external stimulus that is interpreted as a threat to the body's equilibrium, and prepares it for action in various ways, such as concentrating blood in the core of the body, releasing chemicals that make blood clot quicker, tensing muscles, etc. The reason why stress is a problem for the human body is evolutionary - the autonomic nervous system, if you remember, works as a whole unit, which may have been OK when coming across a mammoth, but not for the more everyday stuff we have to cope with today that is present in a more or less relentless stream. That is, a physical response to an emotional or physiological threat is inappropriate, because the effects take too long to dissipate with no physical action.

Fight or flight responses are bodily changes that prepare it for action - adrenalin starts to pump and many other changes take place as well, including a rise of sugar and fats in the blood (including cholesterol, from the liver), endorphins (from the hypothalamus), faster respiration, thicker blood (more oxygen), tense muscles and stopping of digestion, so more blood can be diverted to where it is needed. All this happens very quickly, but it cannot be maintained for long - if it is, the body can be adversely affected. Muscles can only contract or relax, and it takes a specific procedure to make them relax properly - this does not necessarily include going to the cinema! The problem is that just thinking about a defensive action can cause you to adopt a posture without consciously realizing it. This is how hidden fears or anger can create muscle tension, especially in the cardiovascular or digestive systems. Stress disorders are caused by chronic, long term overactivity.

With heightened awareness of a threat, you can get extreme visual clarity and tunnel vision - the mind shuts down all the stuff it doesn't need to deal with, including the bowels (yuk!) In fact, most people have one cerebral hemisphere dominant when under stress, as can be detected from their reactions. For example, a right-brain dominant person faced with a situation is more likely to want to run away from it. A left-brain dominant person, on the other hand, could get lost in the details - humour, a right brain activity, would be a good antidote in this case. Using only one hemisphere means that, on encountering a problem, you become less capable of solving it.

Stress and preoccupation have their effects; a PA31 pilot was doing a cargo flight with three scheduled stops, but he did not refuel or even shut down at any of them, so both engines stopped after the last delivery. He was anxious to get home as his wife was in hospital. This illustrates how stress can cause a *narrowing of the focus*, or a fixation on one problem to the exclusion of others. It also illustrates some of the sources of stress, which can include:

- Personality
- Family
- Occupation
- Situation

and their combinations, which are discussed fully below. In a complex task, high levels of arousal *narrow the span of attention* and *make you fixate on smaller areas of attention*. When under stress, because you cannot concentrate, your judgement becomes impaired, and you make rash decisions, just so the problem can go away. Mainly, though, you lose perspective.

GENERAL ADAPTATION SYNDROME

The biological reaction to stress, which the organism is mobilised by, is, after Selye, the *General Adaptation Syndrome*, where *adaptation* means *the tendency of the body to fight to restore homeostasis against forces that upset the body's natural balance.*

The GAS consists of three phases:

- *Alarm Phase* - where the stressor causes a fall in resistance. Stress hormones (adrenalin) will cause a massive release of glucose into the blood, an acceleration of pulse and blood pressure, and an increase in the rate and depth of breathing, but no specific organ system is affected

- *Resistance Phase.* The stress response is channelled into the specific organ system or process most capable of dealing with or suppressing it. It is characterised by activation of the autonomic nervous system and the appearance of psychosomatic disorders over time. The parasympathetic nervous system uses cortisol to convert fat into sugar to prolong the mobilisation of energy in the body

- *Exhaustion Stage.* The organs or process dealing with the stressor break down and we return to the generalised format of the alarm stage. This needs time to get rid of waste products created by the above processes

As an example, the body can adapt to high blood pressure without constantly going into the alarm stage, but kidney and heart damage will eventually cause a problem as the resistance is forced into a stronger system.

WHAT IS EXCESSIVE STRESS?

Anything that has a sufficiently strong influence to take your mind off the job in hand, or to make you concentrate less well on it. Not only are you not doing your job properly, but subconsciously feel guilty about it, too, which is enough to set up a little stress all of its own. We all like to feel we are doing the best we can possibly do, and it disturbs our self-image to feel that we're not. Consequently we get angry at ourselves for being in such a position, which increases the stress, which further takes us away from the job, etc.

Common situations causing stress include grief, divorce, financial worries, working conditions, management pressure, pride, anger, get-home-it is, motivation (or lack of), doubts (about abilities, etc.), timetable, passengers' expectations, etc. In fact, there are many life events in a long list, with each item weighted with *Life Change Units* (LCUs) according to its stress-producing capacity. They range from death of a spouse (100 LCUs) to minor violations of the law (11 LCUs). A visit from the in-laws rates 29! The current list is called the *Life Change Events Scale*, which can be grouped for convenience as follows:

- *physical* (environment, temperature)
- *physiological* (fatigue, illness)
- *emotional/psychological* (divorce, death, etc.)

There are many types of difficult people, but the most common you will encounter is the bully, from both ends of the spectrum (it has been known for Captains to get violent). Bullies are insecure, and jealous. Anyhow, under stress, because you cannot concentrate, your judgement becomes impaired, and you make rash decisions, just so the problem can go away. Mainly, though, you lose perspective.

All the above leads to anxiety, which is really based on fear, if you think about it (fear of people not liking you, of losing your job, etc.), but the common denominator is *change*, regardless of whether it is desirable or not. As anxiety itself can cause stress, you get a circulating problem. People have their own ways of dealing with stress, so what works for one does not necessarily work for someone else. This is possibly because of the evaluation of the stress that that particular person has, i.e. whether they feel they can cope and their perception of the problem. It is *perception* of demands and abilities, rather than actual problems that affect the individual. If you *feel* you are capable, or in control, your stress level will be relatively low. The more helpless you feel, the more stress.

Symptoms of stress include:

- Anxiety and apprehension, depression, gloom, mood swings
- Detachment from the situation
- Failure to perceive time
- Fixation of attention
- Personality changes
- Voice pitch changes
- Desire for isolation
- Reduced cognitive ability
- Poor emotional self-control
- Unsafe cavalier attitude
- Anger

STRESS MANAGEMENT

Referring back to the list of life events as stressors above, they all have one common denominator - change! You will cope with stress better if you learn to cope with change first, then modify *your* position relative to the stressor.

In fact, you can be affected by stress in these areas:

- **Adaptation**. Life is full of change, but this is a particular problem with customers, and the lack of planning on their part. Many pilots visualise a task up to a week before they get going, but it commonly changes at the last minute! Bad weather can also be included under this heading

- **Frustration** (too many people in the way, or thwarting of your goals). Pilots, in particular, have to reconcile the demands of two influential groups of people, namely customers and management

- **Overload**, so much to do, with so little time, particularly during a complex approach to an airfield. A level of demand that exceeds your capacity to cope (delegation helps)

- **Deprivation** (boredom or loneliness). Long flights watching the autopilot

- **Biological/Personality** (anxiety, etc.)

- **Nutritional** (lack of proper diet). A stress prone diet includes sugar, caffeine and salt, and leads to vitamin depletion, especially B and C, because stress uses up the body's supplies that are needed to process sugar into energy. Salt regulates the body's water balance - too much leads to fluid retention, which leads to high blood pressure. Caffeine stimulates the body in the same way that stress does

- **Noise and vibration** - refer to *Whole Body Vibration*, above

- **Smoking**

Since most of the above occur simultaneously, it can be seen that stress has a wide scope, with no simple solution - it is actually a *lifestyle* problem, which means that one of the most effective means of stress management is to switch to one that eliminates or avoids such stressors. You could change your daily routine, eat more healthy food, change your job or partner, or even your personality (however, you can never really get rid of them all).

The first thing is to recognise the situation, then eliminate the factors causing your stress (you could also use drugs that act on the autonomic nervous system, but these almost always have side effects and can be addictive, so you also have to deal with withdrawal). I like black humour myself, and some people favour eating, meditation or biofeedback machines that help them reduce their heart rate, etc., but most either adjust to the situation, or change it, or their thinking about it, or walk away. Since the primary fight or flight response is physical, which takes hours to undo, one of the quickest methods would be to get enough physical exercise to use up the chemicals that have been placed in your bloodstream, although exercise can also be a stressor if you include an element of competition.

However, the willingness to recognise stress and to do something about it must be there; for example, if you don't admit there's a problem at home, there's not much you can do! It is not weakness to admit you have a problem - rather, it shows lack of judgement otherwise. As previously mentioned, it's your *attitude* towards stress that counts, not the situation itself, as other people may be able to cope with it very well. If you have the usual fight-or-flight symptoms over a relatively minor incident, you are stressed! This energy has nowhere to go and you end up in overdrive, with a very easily ignited short fuse to push you over the edge (see *Anger*).

- *Action Coping* means taking positive action to cope with the source, including removing yourself from the situation, addressing the problem or altering the situation enough to reduce the demands

- *Cognitive Coping* involves reducing the *Perceived Demand*, maybe by rationalisation or consulting with a friend or colleague. Denial of the problem comes under this heading, but is not recommended

- *Symptom-Directed Coping* involves treating the symptoms rather than the cause of stress, say by drinking (exercise is better)

Fatigue

The human system is not well suited to being continuously alert for events that are unlikely to happen, especially after staying awake for long periods so that, if the event does happen, you are less able to deal with it. Indeed, there is some evidence to suggest that several shorter periods of 3-4 hours during the 24 hours of a day are better for you than one 8 hour period of sleep.

Prolonged exposure to fatigue can bring down your immune system and make you quite ill. Like the frog in a saucepan of warm water that is getting hotter, you don't

usually notice until you collapse in a heap at the end of the flying season. Helicopter pilots are especially prone to fatigue, due to the high workload and intense decision making, and vibration (see *Whole-body Vibration*). The Canadian government compares four hours' worth to eight hours' hard labour and double that when longlining (not including the normal A-B stuff, of course, and naturally, fixed wing pilots on short sector work have similar strains, without the vibration).

Fatigue is typically caused by delayed sleep, sleep loss, desynchronisation of normal circadian rhythms and concentrated periods of physical or mental stress or exertion. Working long hours, during normal sleep hours or on rotating shifts, all produce fatigue to some extent. As mentioned elsewhere, Australian researchers compared the effects of alcohol and fatigue on performance. They found that being awake for 17 hours in a row is as bad as a blood alcohol concentration of 0.05%, which is close to the legal limit for driving.

Symptoms of fatigue may include:

- diminished perception (vision, hearing) and a general lack of awareness

- diminished motor skills and slow reactions

- problems with short-term memory

- channelled concentration - fixation on single possibly unimportant issues

- being easily distracted by unimportant matters

- poor judgement and decision- making, leading to increased mistakes

- abnormal moods, erratic changes, depressed, periodic elation and energy

- diminished standards

Most people need about 8 hours' sleep, and you can do with less for a few days, creating a *sleep deficit*, but it's not only the amount of sleep you get, but *when* you get it that counts, so fatigue is just as likely to result from badly planned sequences of work and rest, or being too long away from base without a day off. A surprising amount (over 300) of bodily functions depend on the cycle of day and night - we have an internal (*circadian*) rhythm, which is modified by such things, which, oddly enough, is 25 hours, although there are actually several body clocks that might run for slightly more or less than that. You naturally feel best when they're all in concert, but the slippery slope starts when they get out of line. For example, one reason why people feel under par on Monday mornings is because they have let their body clocks run free over the weekend, instead of using the usual timegivers (*zeitgebers*), like alarm clocks and observing the cycle of night and day. Thus, when your alarm clock says it is 7 o'clock on Monday morning, your body thinks it is around 4 o'clock and still wants to carry on sleeping.

The best known desynchronisation is jet lag (*circadian disrhythmia*), but it also happens when you work nights and sleep during the day. Bright light can fool your body into thinking it's day when it's not. One day for each time zone crossed is required before sleep and waking cycles get in tune with the new location, and total internal synchronisation takes longer (kidneys may need up to 25 days). Even the type of time zone change can matter - 6 hours westward requires (for most people) about four days to adjust - try 7 for going the other way! This Eastward flying compresses the body's rhythm and does more damage than the expanded days going west; North-South travel appears to do no harm.

Symptoms of jet lag are tiredness, faulty judgement, decreased motivation and recent memory loss. They're aggravated by alcohol, smoking, high-altitude flight, overeating and depression, as found in a normal pilot's lifestyle. In view of all this, you have a maximum working day laid down by law, intended to ensure you are rested enough to fly properly (see *Flight Time & Duty Limitations*).

The two types of fatigue are *acute* and *chronic*, the former being short-term, or more intense, and the latter arising from more long-term effects, like many episodes of acute fatigue, typically found after a long spell of fire suppression. Acute fatigue usually affects the body, and just needs a good nights' sleep to sort things out, whereas the chronic variety can have a mental element, where you might not want to see an aircraft ever again. It typically happens after you've had no rest, food or recreation for some time, as mentioned in the example under *Error Management*, above. Symptoms are insomnia, loss of appetite, and even irrational behaviour. To control its effects, try rest, exercise and proper nutrition.

Foods low in carbohydrate or high in protein help fight fatigue, especially "healthy" ones, like fruit or yoghurt, or cereals, such as granola. Coffee, of course, contains caffeine, which keeps you awake (as does tea), but too much can lead to headaches and upset stomachs. People who drink unleaded coffee (decaffeinated) still report unpleasant side effects, as the process that removes caffeine is allegedly just as harmful, but in different ways. Caffeine has a half-life of about 3 hours, and although it might not stop you getting to sleep, it will affect its quality.

Trivia: ICAO Annex 1 excludes coffee and tobacco from the definition of psychoactive substance, but Coca Cola, Pepsi, Tea, and other substances containing caffeine, are not excluded.

SLEEP

Nobody really knows what sleep is for, but the current working hypothesis is that it is necessary to *restore and replenish the body and brain*. However, if that were the only reason, you would sleep less after a slack day and more after a busy day, but the amount does not seem to vary, although people do need different amounts - Margaret Thatcher only slept 5 hours a night as Prime Minister. As far as resting the body goes, you can do that in front of the TV, so it seems to be a mental thing.

Sleep is actually a state of altered consciousness, in which, although paralysed, you don't lose awareness of the external world, as any mother will tell you (it's actually where your brain focusses internally - consciousness seems to depend on certain regions of the brain stem for its function). It is part of a daily cycle which is 25 hours long - that is, the sleeping and waking rhythm is about an hour longer than the normal day of 24 hours, which itself is a mean figure anyway (*Moore-Ede, Sulzman & Fuller*, 1982). This is why flying West is easier on the system than flying East - the body's rhythm is extended the right way. Various factors, such as cycles of night or day, keep the natural 25-hour tendency in check. Normally, this *circadian rhythm* works with body temperature, so the body is coolest when it is hardest to stay awake, around 05:00. Thus, sleep is harder to achieve as body temperature rises.

1 hour of quality sleep equals 2 hours of activity, and you can accumulate up to 8 hours on a credit basis - that is, each sleeping hour gains 2 credit points and each hour awake loses one, to give you a *sleep debt*, which is the cumulative effect of not getting enough sleep. Although you can accumulate 30-40 hours of sleep debt, your performance will still suffer while under its influence.

Thus, 8 hours' sleep overnight means you will be ready for sleep again 16 hours after waking. If your work pattern is disrupted, you can increase your "credit rating" with a short nap in the back of the helicopter. Alcohol interferes with sleep because of its diuretic action - repeated use disturbs sleep on a long term basis, to give you insomnia. It's worth noting that a shave is about equal to 20 minutes' sleep, in terms of refreshing you, and washing your face or brushing your teeth are also good, as is moving around for 5-10 minutes. A person suffering sleep loss is unlikely to be aware of personal performance degradation, which may

*Paradoxical sleep is so called because the EEG readings are very similar to those of someone who is awake

be present for up to 20 minutes after a nap. The effects of sleep deprivation increase with workload and altitude.

Clinical Insomnia is being unable to sleep under normal conditions. *Situational insomnia* arises out of the circumstances, like sleeping in a strange bed or time zone (*circadian desynchronisation*). Although insomniacs may think they don't sleep at all, they actually spend their time in stages 1 and 2. *Sleep Apnea* stops people breathing for short periods up to a minute, and *Narcolepsy* makes them drop off at any time of the day.

Wilse Webb, a behaviourist, tried to persuade rats to stay awake when they would normally be asleep, but they would go back to their normal sleep routine once he stopped "reminding" them, which would suggest that the natural amount of sleep is regulated internally (he tried it with humans, too). The fact that how long you sleep depends on when you sleep also suggests that there are two components of the sleep system, and the former function is not an internal rhythm, but takes account of habits and routines - when these are taken away, people tend to sleep in shorter bursts. So, sleep can be resisted for a short time, but various parts of the brain will ensure that, sooner or later, sleep occurs. A Boeing 707 overshot LA International at 32,000 feet over the Pacific ocean after the whole crew had fallen asleep (one was only roused by ATC setting off alarms in the cockpit).

When we are asleep, the higher regions of the brain lose the ability to communicate - parts of the cerebral cortex which mediate perception, thought and action disconnect (*Science*, Sep 30 2005). It has been found that electronic signals do not pass beyond certain stimulated cells during sleep, so the brain "breaks down into little islands that cannot talk to one another." Conscious thought may therefore depend on the ability of the brain to integrate information, and REM sleep (see below), at least, may be a way of allowing the brain to defragment isolated pieces of information collected and processed during the day. Thus, the main role of deep sleep could be to allow for physical recovery and reconstitution of neural energy reserves.

TYPES OF SLEEP

The sleep process is characterised by five stages that take place over a typical cycle of about 90 minutes.

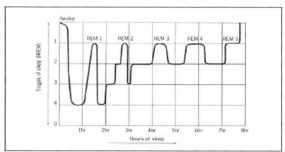

Figure 1   Typical Cycle of Stage 1-4 (NREM) sleep and REM Sleep in the Course of a Night

Source: UK CAA

Stage 1 sleep is the light sleep you get into just after dozing off. It only lasts a few minutes before you go into Stage 2, which takes up between 40-60% of total sleeping time. Stage 3 takes up 3-12%, while Stage 4 occupies 15-35% (you get to Stage 3 when delta waves are over 20% of the total wave count, and Stage 4 when they get to 50%). In all this process, you get deeper and deeper into it and it is progressively more difficult to be roused to wakefulness. It takes about 15-30 minutes to get into Stage 4, and you stay there for about 30-40 minutes before going back up through to Stage 1, the whole process lasting about 90 minutes. After this, you enter the first stage of REM sleep, so the sequence is 1 - 2 - 3 - 4 - 3 - 2- REM - 2 - 3 - 4 - 3 - 2 - REM and so on.

In *Rapid Eye Movement* (or *paradoxical**) sleep, the body and brain become active, heart and metabolism increase and the eyes shift, hence the name. The first REM period is between 5-10 minutes long, but the length of each period increases through the night (you could get up to four REM sessions per night, on average). Long term lack of REM sleep is not good for general health.

All this is an *ultradian* rhythm, which comes from the Latin *ultra dies*, or "outside a day". It would appear that REM sleep (*Rapid Eye Movement*) refreshes the mind, and *Slow Wave* (NREM) sleep refreshes the body, and you are more refreshed if you wake up during the former (Stages 3 and 4 are known as *slow wave* sleep, after the patterns on an EEG, and you are more groggy if you wake up then). With REM sleep, the brain is awake in a virtually paralysed body, so you are nearly awake anyway, and it is more difficult to get back to sleep for the next hour (but it is easier to wake up then). Sleep deprivation experiments suggest that if you are deprived of stage 1-4 or REM sleep, you will show

© Phil Croucher, 2007

rebound effects, meaning that, in subsequent sleep, you will make up the deficit in that particular type, particularly dreaming. The nature of fatigue may determine the stages required. For example, you might need extra slow-wave sleep after physical activity. People who have been without sleep for relatively long periods only seem to have needed relatively short periods of sleep to catch up with no ill effects. Alcohol degrades paradoxical (REM) sleep.

There appear to be three neurotransmitters involved with the sleep-dream clock, which are the same as those in the hypothalamus that convert light signals into time signals and regulate the pineal gland. For interest, they are *norepinephrine*, *serotonin* and *acetylcholine*.

In the same way that you are nearly awake during REM sleep, there are times during the day when you are nearly asleep, or it is at least easier to go to sleep. Up till 1500, the cycle is around every 90-120 minutes, but it gets wider after that (siesta time!)

COMMUNICATION

The first cockpit tool that tends to suffer from stress is communication. Any relationship needs it to be successful. In fact, there is hardly any job in which it can be ignored. Lack of it can affect your physical health - in the 13th century, for example, Emperor Frederick experimented by cutting some babies off from all communication, instructing their nurses to stay silent. The babies all died. A study was once done on graduates of Stanford University, to find out what makes a great engineer. The responses indicated that technical expertise formed only 20% of the ingredients for success - *the rest was due to people skills.*

Thus, your ability to communicate will account for over 80% of your success in any walk of life. However, your current methods of communication have more than likely been based on responses learned through childhood, and can almost certainly be improved. What happens is that you build a facade, either for emotional protection or because you have to behave in certain ways in order to get what you need (food, comfort, etc.), which does not necessarily have anything to do with the person that you

really are. From that stems the playing of games and manipulation, hurting and punishment until you grow into a full-blown control freak. To be sure, personality plays some part, but most behaviour patterns are learnt. Luckily, communication skills can be learnt, too.

Communication in aviation is important because customers, for instance, should know exactly what your helicopter can and cannot do or, more particularly, what you will and will not do (this is especially important with heliskiing!) For some reason, a fork lift driver who says that only 50 packages can be carried is believed, but helicopter pilots are automatically assumed to be lying - most customers think that all you need to do is put in extra gas to lift the load.

Communication is defined as the ability to put your ideas into someone's head and be sure of success, or to exchange information without it being changed. Or both. Unfortunately, even under ideal conditions, only about 30% is retained, due to inattention, misinterpretation, expectations and emotions. Your team needs to know what you want done, especially in an emergency, and requires feedback as to progress and satisfaction of your expectations. This could be through the spoken word or body language (in fact, 7% of all communication is accomplished verbally, 38% by unconscious signals, such as tone of voice, and the remainder (55%) by non-verbal means, i.e. body language). Officially, around 80% of all communication is achieved by factors other than words, otherwise known as *metacommunication*, which consists of those tools, other than the words, which complement them in order to communicate.

The ancient Greeks thought of communication between two people in three parts:

- *Ethos* - character (and credibility) of an individual. Its essence is in the degree of trust in the words the listener believes

- *Pathos* - emotional content

- *Logos* - the logical content, and the least influential part of the whole process - it will only be listened to when the other two are clear. You can be as correct as you wish, but if character and emotion are missing, your message will not get across

Implicit communication means that various interpretations may be placed on the information, whilst *explicit communication* has no ambiguity. Verbal communication may be either *social* or *functional*. The former helps to build teamwork, and the latter is essential to flying, or operating, an aircraft. For a spoken or written message to be understood, the sender has to make sure that the receiver is using the same channel of communication, and language, and can make out the message's meaning. The *channel of communication* is the medium used to convey the message. For the spoken word, this might be face-to-face, the radio or intercom.

So, communication is the exchange of thoughts, messages or information by various means, including speech. The elements of the process are the *sender*, the *message*, the *receiver* and *feedback*. The perceptions and background of people at either end may influence things - as in the Life Of Brian, a person at the back of a congregation might hear: "Blessed are the cheesemakers" instead of "Blessed are the peacemakers".

Effective Communication

This demands certain skills, in no particular order:

* *Seeking information* - good decisions are based on good information, so we need it to do our jobs effectively - particularly with reference to finding out what the customer actually wants

* *Problem solving*, especially in collaboration with other people

* *Listening* - active listening means not making assumptions about what the other person is saying, or what they really mean, so it *promotes a constructive solution of interpersonal conflicts*. You need to be patient, question and be supportive. Even low-time pilots have opinions! We can listen at up to 1200 words per minute, so our inability to listen is not physical, but mental. It takes practice to listen properly (especially, don't interrupt!)

* *Stating your position* - or *assertiveness skills*, which does *not* mean being aggressive! In other words, making sure the other person knows your viewpoint (ask yourself - would *you* listen to yourself?)

* *Resolving differences* - conflict resolution. Almost always, the best way to do this is ensure that the results are best for everyone concerned

* *Communication skill selection*, or how to perform the communication you need

* *Providing feedback*

Body Language

The fact that somebody isn't talking does not mean they are not communicating (some female silences can be quite eloquent!) It is said that 7% of communication is accomplished verbally, 38% by unconscious signals, such as tone of voice, and the remainder (55%) by non-verbal means, such body language. In fact, before language was invented it was the only way to get your point across. It's certainly the most believed means of communication, since it will most likely reflect the true feelings of the person concerned.

Non-verbal communication can accompany verbal communication, such as a smile during a face-to-face chat. It may be acknowledgement or feedback (a nod of the head). It can also be used when the verbal type is impossible, such as a thumbs-up when it's noisy. Body language can be very subtle, but powerful. For example, the word *No* with a smile will be interpreted quite differently from one accompanied by a smack in the mouth.

More typically, you can use the body language of the guys on the ground to let you know if your load has reached the ground - if they are looking up, it hasn't yet! (see below).

Non-verbal communication may also include written information or notes, between pilots or the flight-deck and cabin crew, but technology makes this even more important - it is the main way that systems speak to you - newer displays present data graphically. Unfortunately, the side-by side seating arrangements in the cockpit tend to lessen the effects of body language, so the choice of words (and their packaging) assumes a greater importance.

Note: Elements of body language should not be taken in isolation - folded arms may not mean hostility, but that the other person is merely cold. Always interpret body language based on three or four indications.

POSTURE

This is also an important part of an unspoken message. The way you sit or stand can show others a lot about how you are feeling. However, posture needs to be read with other clues, such as.....

GESTURES

These can be used in threatening or submissive ways (teachers point fingers a lot). Head movements, facial expressions and eye movements can be included here (or lack of eye movement if someone is ignoring you).

PROXIMITY & DISTANCE

Our personal comfort zones vary in size according to the person we are talking to - for example, you might stand further away from your boss than from a colleague, which can be used as a way of finding out seniority. The same effect can happen by your positioning - somebody in charge is more likely to place themselves at the head of a table. Those who want to influence that person will try to sit as close as possible, and those at the bottom of the pecking order will be furthest away.

"Those that think they are important will sit where they think they ought to sit. Those that are important will sit where they like."

QUESTIONS

Asking questions gives the impression that you are listening. Actually, the person who asks questions controls any conversation, because, once asked, the other person's mind flies to the answer, and you are in charge for as long as it takes to finish it. Open-ended questions require an extended answer, such as how long is a piece of string? They are best for getting a conversation going. Closed questions require a specific answer, such as *Yes*, or *No*, and can be used to bring a conversation to a conclusion.

AURAL CLUES

These include the words themselves, how quickly they are spoken, and the sound or pitch of the voice, not forgetting the "ums" and "ahs" that people use when they are nervous. A good ploy is to stop listening to words and start listening to the tone. For example, you could emphasise each word in turn of the following sentence and have a different meaning every time:

I never said your dog was ugly
I *never* said your dog was ugly
I never *said* your dog was ugly
I never said *your* dog was ugly
I never said your *dog* was ugly
I never said your dog *was* ugly
I never said your dog was *ugly*

Thus, it's not what you say that may cause a problem, but how you say it! In an emergency, you must use the proper language, so ATC can react properly, otherwise you won't get help but an increase in paperwork after you land!

SOUNDS

You don't need words to convey a message - a deep sigh can say much, as can grunts and groans. In addition, the pitch and pace of a voice can be very expressive.

LISTENING

It is estimated that we spend 45% of our time in listening. ¾ of it is heard imprecisely, and ¾ of the remainder is forgotten within three weeks. It has also often been said that hearing is done with your ears, whereas listening is done with the mind. *Active Listening* means doing it in such a way that whoever is speaking thinks you are hearing and understanding them, and you appreciate the feelings behind the words.

"Power" communicators have high levels of empathy. The key steps to proper listening include:

- *Listen* (with all the signals)
- Pause
- *Question* for clarification (How do you mean, exactly?)
- Paraphrase

Psychologists have a phrase, *Unconditional Positive Regard*, meaning that they always react in a positive and supportive non-judgmental way - they don't become angry or upset, but continue to smile and nod, which is obviously why people go to them in the first place.

Active Listening means doing it in such a way that whoever is speaking thinks that you are hearing and understanding them, and that you appreciate the feelings behind the words (yeah, right).

SUMMARY

To get on with other people, work with them, and influence them, you need to have a *rapport* with them. Thus, you should watch for facial expressions, posture and gestures (e.g. arms folded in defence, or looking at their watch while you are speaking) in order to get a grip of how receptive someone is to you. To influence someone, you might smile, make non-committal grunting noises, speak in a warm and friendly tone and make your posture indicate interest in what they are saying.

Barriers To Communication

Individual styles, body language and speech patterns all have their part to play in communication, and you need to be sensitive to and aware of their nuances. You also need to be aware of anything that might stop communication taking place.

Barriers to communication include:

- a reluctance to ask questions
- the influence of authority
- difficulty in listening

not forgetting making assumptions, and anger, described below. You, therefore, have to put people at their ease and make them think they can talk to you or ask questions. In fact, there can be *lack* of communication and *poor* communication. The former might be a young first officer who is very computer-literate, but doesn't tell you what he's doing. The latter, someone that tells you there is a problem, but not what it is. However, an important component is speech - the words you say often have completely the opposite effect to what is intended, because they simply mean different things to different people. In addition, when people speak, the words become coded into some sort of indirect expression. This is because we grow up learning to be politically correct in order to get what we need from other people, thus hiding your real self behind some sort of language barrier and continual demands not to show emotion. For example, when a child asks questions at bedtime, the meaning behind the words is a request to stay a little longer. All too often, we take words at face value and confuse the real meanings for their presentation, if only because the real meat of any conversation tends to come at the end. Listeners have problems, too, because people have filters through which words have to struggle to be understood.

It is difficult for humans to say exactly what is in their minds or hearts, and to listen without being distracted or distorting what is heard.

Responses that spoil communication include:

- *Judging*, which includes:
  - Criticizing, or constant fault-finding

- Name calling, or labelling - putting people into a box
- Diagnosing
- Praise, when used to manipulate

- *Solution-giving*. If you are the kind that takes over, the message you are really sending is: "You are incompetent. Let me do it. I know what I'm doing" which undermines self-esteem. Variations on this theme might include:
  - Ordering/Coercing
  - Threatening
  - Moralizing. Mothers, especially, are good at this
  - Interrogation (excessive questioning)
  - Advising - another self-esteem reducer

- Avoidance
  - Diverting. Bringing the conversation round to your own concerns, or focussing attention on yourself
  - Logic, which keeps others at an emotional distance
  - Reassurance, when it makes people feel stupid

If one party to the process is under stress, the more positive responses above will play their part in reducing communication.

ANGER

Anger held in becomes resentment - the trick is not to express it destructively. When you are angry your body pumps out adrenalin, and cortisol, which depresses your immune system, so being angry can have long-term health effects. Although "losing it" in a grand display can make you feel better, it is only temporary and a huge exhaustive low follows as the hormones leave your system. You'll probably also have to sort out the mess with the other people! Aggressive people are more susceptible to heart attacks, clogged arteries and higher cholesterol. However, anger is also an effective means of blocking communication. This is because there are four types of angry person, each with their own language:

- those who are generally non-malicious, whose anger is quick to boil and just as quick to dissipate
- those who are slow to anger, but keep a list of everything you did or said wrong since 1929

- those who just like being angry
- those who relish the after effects rather than the argument

If you learn more about your own makeup, you will be in a better position to avoid setting other people off. It will help you step back and *resolve* a conflict, if you can't avoid it in the first place. If you remember, the body is not built to be in fight or flight mode as much as it is these days. You will therefore not be surprised to hear that it takes very little effort to trigger off an angry reaction after even the most trivial event. Such emotional triggers can easily make people explode, but, at the very least, will affect the way you assess situations and react to them, or, more importantly, make decisions. Emotions carry so much force and influence that they rule your actions before you calm down enough to think rationally.

As for health, one study at the Ochsner Clinic in New Orleans reports high levels of hostility in many heart attack victims, who also had higher levels of weight, cholesterol, anxiety and depression. Stress brought on by rage can also affect memory, creativity and sleep. Bacterial infections can increase during angry episodes, and you lay yourself wide open to upper respiratory problems, like flu.

People overcome anger in many ways:

- Eating
- Displacement (taking it out on the dog)
- Talking (a lot)
- Exercise (kill the tennis ball)
- Writing
- Yelling and screaming
- Swearing
- Sulking

Laughter or humour is a good defuser of anger, as is reminding yourself that it won't matter in a week anyway. Another good way to defuse it is to acknowledge the other person's reasons for being angry, because it is, at bottom, a frustrated demand for attention. In fact, to be effective, a display of anger must satisfy *all* of the following:

- It must be directed at the target, with no retaliation
- It must restore a sense of control or justice
- It must result in changes of behaviour or outlook
- It must use the same language (see above)

Otherwise, it will be completely non-productive. For the best results from any conflict, everyone needs to feel they are a winner (because the loser is still wound up). In our case, our customers need to feel they have come off best, and it's up to us to make them think they are, even if they're not.

Note: Anger also makes you blind to reason!

Behavioural Styles

People trying to get their way may try to put you off-balance in many ways (this happens in interviews as well). Mothers, especially, use guilt, but, in the aviation world, you are most likely to come across bullying customers or management.

Bullies choose people who will go to great lengths to avoid conflict, typically a low-time pilot in a first job who doesn't want to lose it. The problem is that, somehow, these people seem to sense your vulnerability, probably because they are insecure and/or jealous themselves. Unfortunately, your behaviour can make it worse, and it is the only thing you have any control over.

If you behave negatively, the other person has control of the situation, which is why they do it! Your negative reaction is their expected response, so if you do something different, by asking them why they are angry, for example, it puts *them* off balance! You can then try to direct the situation the way you want it.

A long-term remedy to this is to increase your self-esteem. Again, this can be sensed by other people, and will go a long way towards nipping awkward situations in the bud. Lt Clifton James was used as a double for Monty during WWII, and he wrote that it wasn't until he became Monty inside (i.e. with no visible change on the outside) that the whole thing began to work.

Use the following steps in any altercation:

- STOP! Remain calm and don't react with gut feelings. Get all the facts!
- Defuse the situation
- Ask questions that give the impression you really care - acknowledge their anger or concerns, and fix the problem if you can

Here are some suggested behavioural styles:

- *Assertive*. These people have respect for themselves and others and are not afraid of sticking up (politely) for themselves. Being assertive is not the same thing as being aggressive

- *Aggressive.* These people have no respect for other people, and have no problem expressing their anger, although they will blame others for it

- *Passive.* These people have no respect for themselves and excessive respect for others. They very rarely stand up for themselves

- *Passively Resistant.* These are passive people who actually try to stick up for themselves, but they use manipulative games to do it, because they still have to learn deal with people up front (watch their body language)

- *Indirectly Aggressive.* These people use underhanded methods to get their way, such as by doing jobs improperly so they won't get asked to do them again, or by using backhanded sarcastic comments, the silent treatment or gossiping, etc.

- *Passive Aggressive.* These people feel one way, but act in another - they might look happy when they are seething inside. They deny anger because it makes them feel powerless.

STUCK IN THE MIDDLE

People trying to get their way may try to put you off-balance in many ways (this happens in interviews as well). Mothers, especially, use guilt, but, in the aviation world, you are most likely to come across bullying customers or management.

Bullies choose people who will go to great lengths to avoid conflict, typically a low-time pilot in a first job who doesn't want to lose it. The problem is that, somehow, these people seem to sense your vulnerability, probably because they are insecure and/or jealous themselves. Unfortunately, your behaviour can make it worse, and it is the only thing you have any control over.

If you behave negatively, the other person has control of the situation, which is why they do it! Your negative reaction is their expected response, so if you do something different, by asking them why they are angry, for example, it puts *them* off balance! You can then try to direct the situation the way you want it.

A long-term remedy to this is to increase your self-esteem. Again, this can be sensed by other people, and will go a long way towards nipping awkward situations in the bud. Lt Clifton James was used as a double for Monty during WWII, and he wrote that it wasn't until he became Monty inside (i.e. with no visible change on the outside) that the whole thing began to work.

Use the following steps in any altercation:

- STOP! Remain calm and don't react with gut feelings. Get all the facts!

- Defuse the situation

- Ask questions that give the impression you really care - acknowledge their anger or concerns, and fix the problem if you can

Laughter or humour is a good defuser of anger, as is reminding yourself that it won't matter in a week or so anyway.

PARENT-ADULT-CHILD

However, more common patterns are based on Eric Berne's *Transactional Analysis*, in which he postulates that people in any interaction take on one of three roles, *Parent*, *Adult* or *Child*, according to the circumstances. TA starts with the premise that people have multi-faceted personalities, which often conflict with each other.

Eric Berne stated that, when two people meet, there will be an interaction, in that one of them will speak to the other through a *Transaction Stimulus* (the reaction from the other person is the *Transaction Response*). The person sending the Stimulus is the *Agent*, and the person responding is the *Respondent*. In other words, there is a *contractual* approach, with rights and responsibilities on each side, and *expectations*.

Berne also said that people are made up of the three alter ego states mentioned above (which, naturally, do not have the same usage as found in normal language):

PARENT
This is the conditioning that comes from authority figures, like our real parents, teachers, older people, next door neighbours, relatives, etc. Phrases like "you will never amount to anything!" remain in our consciousness to affect us for the rest of our lives. They can be removed, but not easily - later psychologists have suggested that the *exact phrase* must be used, hence the difficulty, as you can't remember what it was anyway! Absorbing mannerisms in this way is called *introjecting*. As mentioned before, we often have to behave in certain ways in order to survive, which have nothing to do with our real personalities.

ADULT
This refers to our ability to think for ourselves. The adult starts to form when we are around ten months old, and is how we keep our Parent and Child under control. The Adult deals with the *here and now* and sees things how they *are*, not how they should be, or in terms of what we

project onto others. In other words, there is no unhealthy baggage from the past.

CHILD

This is the emotional body within each of us that usually is a series of replays from childhood. When anger or despair overcomes reason, the Child is in control. It is no easier to change than the Parent.

Our feelings at the time of an interaction determine which of the three states we will use, and to communicate successfully with someone, you must be able to detect which state they are in, as successful communications must be complementary. For example, if the stimulus is Parent to Child, the response should be Child to Parent (the ideal is Adult-Adult, if you want a rational conversation!)

If a crossed transaction occurs, there is an ineffective communication, and either or both parties will be upset. For the relationship to continue smoothly the agent or the respondent must rescue the situation with a complementary transaction.

Later, the original three Parent-Adult-Child components were sub-divided to form a new seven-element model, principally during the 1980's by Wagner, Joines and Mountain. This established *Controlling* and *Nurturing* aspects of the Parent mode, each with positive and negative aspects, and the *Adapted* and *Free* aspects of the Child mode, again each with positive an negative aspects.

Men Vs Women

It's not politically correct to acknowledge that men and women think, speak and decide differently, but it's true nonetheless.

THINKING

It has been mentioned elsewhere that women have more connections between the left and right halves of their brains. Since men do not, they tend to compartmentalise, that is to say, they are more able to leave home affairs behind when they go to work, and *vice versa*. In other words, once in a compartment of their lives, they can better remain there to the exclusion of anything else.

Women, on the other hand, see things more holistically, or globally - they connect things up more. They can see underlying detail and relationships more clearly, but may not be able to visualise objectives or goals properly.

Thus, if an issue is not resolved in the cockpit, a male pilot may go home, leaving things on hold while he opens the "home" compartment, and could even have forgotten

about it next time he gets back in the cockpit. A female pilot, however, might continue thinking about the issue until some closure is achieved.

SPEAKING

Women have a style that is more historical, presented in a narrative-type fashion. Thus, there is more detail in what they say, and they may ask questions in general conversation that men would actually find intrusive or demeaning, or even threatening. The end of the story comes at the end. For women, the purpose behind a conversation is to build rapport and provide help, while for men, it's to report facts, and the end might come at the beginning of a conversation, and without much detail, hence the frustration when a man asks a question of a woman, expecting the answer straight away, but actually getting it over the next five minutes. On the other side of the coin, a long email that gets a 4-word reply can be just as frustrating for a woman.

If you are a woman, and you see a man's eyes glaze over while you are speaking, it's not because he doesn't care about what you are saying - he is tuning out the irrelevant bits until you get to the bottom line. Speaking louder and slower will not change things, and adding more detail will only get an interruption! Try giving the bottom line first, then asking if more detail is required.

Don't use hints, either. The question "Would you like a coffee?" from a female to a male really means "I would like a coffee." Similarly, saying something like "Would you amend this publication, if you've got time?" leaves many options open, and will likely mean it doesn't get done at all. Being more direct would get more results - men are not mind readers, although they should, of course, learn to listen more attentively, and between the lines!

Radio Procedures

Professional languages use a limited vocabulary, to which the context provides meaning, reducing the risk of ambiguities. In Aviation, using non-standard phraseology can be fatal. The phrase:

> *"Advise ready for taxi, use caution, company pushing out of XYZ"*

is not a clearance to pushback, even though it might sound like one. Similarly, an instruction to conduct runup checks on the other side of a runway you would have to cross to get there is not a clearance to do so. The words *"request Federal Aid"* in one message were interpreted to mean that a hijack was in process, rather than the intended request for FAA clearance expressed in a joking fashion. The figures 210 by themselves could mean a Flight Level, a heading, or a speed to be maintained.

Communication in aviation could serve several purposes:

- Allocation of responsibilities

- Establishing common goals - you don't want people doing their own thing without you knowing

- Making sure that everyone has the same idea of what the problem is

- Collecting feedback

- Direction of attention

Here is an example of poor communication, with some CRM and fatigue factors thrown in. In 1977, in very poor visibility, a KLM 747 smashed into a Pan Am 747 which was backtracking the runway at Tenerife, and 583 people died *on the ground*.

The two 747s were originally parked on the holding area for runway 12, which was full from other aircraft which had diverted there after a terrorist bombing at Las Palmas airport, which was where both aircraft were originally going to. The Pan Am 747 finally got clearance to move, but the parallel taxiway was overcrowded, and the KLM 747 was blocking the holding area exit, so they had to wait for it to move. And if that wasn't bad enough, the weather was beginning to deteriorate (the airport was 2,000 ft high in a hollow between mountains) and the runway centreline lights weren't working.

By 16:30 the Pan Am crew had been on duty for 10¾ hours, but were only going to do a short 25 minute hop to Las Palmas. The KLM crew, on the other hand, had been on duty for 8¾ hours, but were going to Amsterdam (via Las Palmas), and were under pressure not to exceed their duty time (if they got stuck there, they would also need hotel rooms for 250 passengers and the next day's schedules would be missed). In addition, the Captain, whilst an experienced trainer, had been used to simulators, and had no recent route experience.

At 16:51 the KLM requested start-up, and the Pan Am received its start clearance shortly afterwards. Because of the northwesterly wind, both aircraft had to enter the runway from the holding area and taxi to the far end, over 2 miles, for takeoff the opposite way on runway 30.

The KLM was cleared to taxi at 16:56 but was told to hold short of the runway 12 threshold and to contact *approach* on 119.7 MHz, which they did, and received clearance to taxi back down the runway and exit at the third turn-off, then continue on the parallel taxiway to the threshold of

30. The first officer thought they said *first exit*, but the controller amended that almost immediately after the read-back. The KLM was directed to backtrack the runway all the way, then turn around at the end in the direction of takeoff. The FO acknowledged, but the Captain was beginning to miss radio calls, and it was difficult to keep track of their position anyway. One minute later, the KLM Captain radioed the approach controller (who could see nothing), and asked if they were to leave the runway at Charlie 1 taxiway. Once more they were told to continue straight down the runway.

The Pan Am received taxi instructions on the *ground* frequency of 118.7 MHz, being directed to hold at the threshold of 12, then follow the KLM. They were supposed to backtrack and leave by the third exit, but the ground controller's heavy Spanish accent did not help their understanding, and it was easier just to obey than try to decode every instruction (they actually wanted to stay where they were).

At 17:02, the KLM heard the Pan Am call approach and request confirmation of the backtrack instruction. "Affirmative," was the answer, "taxi into the runway and leave the runway third, third to your left, third."

By now the Pan Am crew had been on duty for over 11¼ hours, and the KLM crew over 9¼ hours, of which nearly 4 had been waiting on the ground. The visibility had dropped to as low as 100 m and it was difficult to spot the exits. In other parts of the airfield, it was down to zero. Captain van Zanten (KLM), when approaching Charlie 4, again asked his FO if this was their turn off, but the FO repeated the instruction to backtrack all the way to the end. The KLM crew had switched on the wipers and could see lights, confirmed by the FO: "Here comes the end of the runway."

"A couple of lights to go", replied the Captain. Approach then asked them to state their position.

17:02:56: PAN AM

- *I think we just passed Charlie 4 now*

17:03:01: ATC

- *OK. At the end of the runway make a 180 and report ready for ATC clearance.*

Meanwhile the Pan Am crew were asking for confirmation that they were to leave the runway at the third exit.

17:03:36: ATC

- *Third one sir, one, two, three, third, third one*

17:03:39: PAN AM

- *Very good, thank you*

The Pan Am was asked to report clear of the runway and the reply was its call sign. They could not see the markers, so were unsure of how many turnoffs had gone past. Meanwhile, the visibility had lifted enough for takeoff, and the KLM captain was anxious to get away quickly in the gap. By now the Pan Am was approaching Charlie 3 and nobody could see anything.

At 17:05:28, the KLM captain stopped at the end of the runway and immediately opened up the throttles. What happened next took around a minute:

- KLM F/O: *Wait a minute we don't have an ATC clearance*
- Captain: *No, I know that, go ahead ask. Throttles closed*

17:05:44 KLM RT (asking for takeoff and ATC clearance at the same time)

- *Uh, the KLM ... four eight zero five is now ready for take-off ... uh and we're waiting for our ATC clearance*

The Pan Am arrived at Charlie 3 just as the KLM's ATC clearance was being read back. They had missed their designated taxi route and were continuing down the runway, and were still about 1500 m from the threshold, out of sight of the KLM. The KLM crew's desire to depart helped them overlook the fact that the Pan Am had not called clear of the runway, as instructed.

17:05:53 ATC RT

- *KLM eight seven zero five uh you are cleared to the Papa Beacon climb to and maintain flight level nine zero right turn after take-off proceed with heading zero four zero until intercepting the three two five radial from Las Palmas VOR*

Before the ATC transmission is complete the KLM Captain says *Yes* and opens up the throttles, holding the aircraft on the brakes until the RPMs stabilise.

17:06:09 KLM RT

- *Ah roger, sir, we're cleared to the Papa Beacon flight level nine zero, right turn out zero four zero until intercepting the three two five and we're now (at take-off)*

As the F/O was still reading back the clearance the captain released the brakes and said *Lets go, check thrust.* This caught the F/O off balance and, during the last moments of his read-back, became noticeably more hurried and less clear. The rapid statement was ambiguous

enough to cause concern and the controller and Pan Am FO replied at the same time:

17:06:18 ATC RT

- *OK*

17:06:19 PAN AM RT

- *No .. eh*

As the Pan Am called to make their position clear, the two spoke over the top of each other:

17:06:20 ATC RT

- *Stand by for take-off, I will call you*

17:06:20 PAN AM RT

- *And we're still taxiing down the runway, the clipper one seven three six*

17:06:19 - 23 - the combined PAN AM and ATC communications caused a shrill noise in KLM cockpit - the last two messages were not heard by the KLM crew

17:06:25 ATC RT

- *Roger Papa Alpha one seven three six report when runway clear*

For reasons best known to himself, the controller used the call sign *Papa Alpha* instead of *Clipper.*

17:06:29 PAN AM RT

- *OK, we'll report when we're clear*

17:06:30 ATC RT

- *Thank you*

All that was lost to the KLM pilots busy with the takeoff, but the flight engineer tentatively inquired of the situation:

17:06:32 - KLM cockpit

- *Is hij er niet af dan? (Is he not clear then?)*

17:06:34 - KLM cockpit (Captain)

- *Wat zeg je? (What do you say?)*

17:06:34 - KLM cockpit (F/E)

- *Is hij er niet af, die Pan American? (Is he not clear that Pan American?)*

1706:35 - KLM cockpit (Captain)

- *Jawel. (Oh yes. emphatic)*

The copilot also answered in the affirmative and the flight engineer did not press things. The KLM continued taking off into the path of the Pan Am, on whose flight deck the crew were alarmed enough to comment although they were not aware that the KLM had started to take off:

PAN AM Captain:

- *Let's get the hell out of here*

PAN AM FO:

- *Yeah, he's anxious, isn't he?*

PAN AM F/E:

- *Yeah, after he held us up for an hour and a half, now he's in a rush*

The flight engineer had no sooner finished speaking when the Pan Am captain saw the KLM's landing lights, coming straight at them through the cloud bank.

PAN AM Captain:

- *There he is . . . look at him . . . that . . . that son-of-a-bitch is coming*

PAN AM FO:

- *Get off! Get off! Get off!*

Captain Grubbs (Pan Am) threw the aircraft to the left and opened up the throttles. The KLM FO, meanwhile, was calling V_1. Four seconds later, they spotted the Pan Am trying to scramble clear:

17:06:44 - KLM started rotation

The tail struck the ground and....

17:06:47 - KLM cockpit (Scream)

17:06:50 - Collision

In fact, the KLM 747 got airborne, about 1300 m down the runway, but almost immediately slammed into the side of the Pan Am, with its nosewheel over the top and its number one engine, on the extreme left, just grazing the side. The fuselage skidded over the top, but its main landing gear smashed into the Clipper's number three engine. Some passengers managed to escape by the openings that appeared in the Clipper's fuselage, whilst others jumped down on to the grass at the side of the runway. The flight crew, plus two employees in the jump seats, escaped through what was left of 1st class.

The KLM's main landing gear sheared off, and it sank back on to the runway about 150 m further on, where it skidded for another 300 m and slid to the right, rotating clockwise through 90°. Both fires lasted until the afternoon of the following day.

One problem was that the KLM captain heard the words *cleared* and *takeoff* in the same reply from ATC, although *cleared* only applied to the departure. As a result of this incident, in Europe, at least, the word *takeoff* is only used when you are actually cleared to do so - till then, the word *departure* is used.

CRM ISSUES

During the whole process, the KLM captain was very concerned about breaking the new Dutch flight time & duty regulations. These were quite rigid, and allowed the Captain no judgement or flexibility. Indeed, they carried severe penalties, including imprisonment and loss of licence. This is why the refuelling was done at Tenerife, so that there would be no delay when they eventually got to Las Palmas. This, of course, delayed the Pan Am for over an hour, because the KLM aircraft was blocking their exit. Both crews now had pressure they didn't need.

The major reasons for the accident (which was down to the KLM captain, who took off without clearance) were:

- Increased stress as the KLM captain's problems escalated (and focussing of attention - *author*)

- Deteriorating weather

- Two transmissions occurring simultaneously so that the KLM captain did not hear the Pan Am crew say that they were still on the runway

- Language problems

- Communication confusion between the Tower and the Pan Am about intersections

- Unusual traffic congestion that led to the short cut of taxying down the runway

Stuff like that should just never happen.

Cultural Factors

What's normal for one person isn't for others - in many countries, red is an extremely unlucky colour. Even within our own trade, there are fixed wing and rotary pilots, military versus civilian, jet against piston, etc., each with their own ways of thinking.

Organisational Factors

That is, the people we work for, or with. An organisation is a structure within which people work together in an organised and coordinated way to achieve certain goals, and the culture of the organisation can have a significant bearing on how people perform within it. Their goals may conflict, for example, resources may be insufficient, as may planning or supervision. We all know about pressures, commercial or otherwise.

Good Judgement is based on experience.

Experience is based on bad judgement!

JUDGEMENT

In short, judgement is process of choosing between alternatives for the safest outcome. Factors that influence the exercise of good judgement include:

- *Lack of vigilance* - vigilance (that is, keeping an eye on what's going on) is the basis of situational awareness. You need to keep a constant watch on all that is going on around you, however tempting it may be to switch off for a while on a long navex. Monitor the fuel gauges, check for traffic and engine-off landing sites, all the time

- *Distraction* - anything that stops you noticing a problem, for example, slowly backing into trees while releasing a cargo net. Keep pulling back from the situation to reaffirm your awareness of the big picture

- *Peer Pressure* - we all like to be liked, whether by people in or outside your own company. Do they want you to fly overweight? Or fly in darkness, even though they are late back? Being too keen to please is part of a self-esteem problem. *Do not take on other peoples' problems!*

- *Insufficient Knowledge* - although you can look the regulations up in a book, this is not always the most convenient solution, so you need a working knowledge of what they contain, including checklists and limitations from the flight manual, etc. We don't all have an aircraft library, or have the time to refer to it even if there was one

- *Unawareness of Consequences* - this is an aspect of insufficient knowledge, above. What are the consequences of what you propose to do? Have you thought things out thoroughly?

- *Forgetfulness of Consequences* - similar to the above

- *Ignoring the Consequences* - again, similar to the above, but more of a deliberate act, since you are aware of the consequences of your proposed actions, but choose to ignore them

- *Overconfidence* - this breeds carelessness, and a reluctance to pay attention to detail or be vigilant. Also, it inclines you to be hasty, and not consider all the options available to you. This is where a little self-knowledge and humility is a great help

Fascination

This is where pilots fail to respond adequately to a clearly defined stimulus despite all the necessary cues being present and the proper response available. A study in the 1950s (*Clark, Nicholson, and Graybiel*, 1953) classified experiences in 2 categories:

- **Type A**. This is fundamentally perceptual, where you concentrate on one aspect of the total situation to such a degree that you reject other factors in your perceptual field. Pilots become so intent on following a power line, for example, that they don't see the tower lines in the way

- **Type B**. Here, you may perceive the significant aspects of the total situation, but still be unwilling or unable to make the proper response

Habits

These are part of our lives; many are comforting and part of a reassuring routine that keeps us mentally the right way up. Others, however, are ones we could well do without, but the trouble is that they can be very difficult to break, because the person trying to break them is the very person trapped by them. We learn habits as children, simply in order to survive. Despite our true nature, we quickly find out that if we want food, or attention, we have to behave in certain ways, depending on the nature of our parents; in some families getting noticed demands entirely different behaviour than in others, mostly opposite to what we really are, which is one source of stress, the question of your true personality. In certain circumstances, habits can be dangerous - if you can't do anything about them, we need at least to be aware of them.

Habit can make you go for a familiar routine rather than trying for the best results - for example, *reversion* can occur after a pattern of behaviour has been established, mainly because you get so used to doing it - you may accidentally carry out a procedure you have used for years, even after recurrent training, which is quite possible under stress, but it can happen under normal circumstances - a Beaver pilot reverted to the piston-engined variety after a long spell on the turbo version, and ran the tanks dry before changing over, a normal practice in the bush, which caused quite a stir among the passengers in the airline he was flying for.

Training is all very well, but don't let it limit your thinking. Also, don't confuse *stereotyping* with *probability*. You can always accept a probability that certain actions will solve a similar problem to one you've had before, but stereotyping implies that the same actions work every time.

If you give an engineer a fuel load without planning for it, based on the fact that you always use that load, that is a *decision bias* based on habit (*frequency bias*).

Attitudes

Flying requires considerable use of the brain, with observation and/or reaction to events, both inside and outside the aircraft. Psychology and aviation have been used to each other for some time; you may be familiar with selection tests and interviews. Part of why accidents happen is that some people are accidents waiting to happen! This depends on personality, amongst other things, and we will look at this shortly. However, personality is not the only factor to be aware of on the flight deck. Status, Role and Ability are also important. Having two Captains on board, with neither sure of who's in charge can be a real problem! Either they will be scoring points off each other, or be too gentlemanly, allowing an accident to happen while each says "After you, Nigel". How do you sort out the mess if you have someone in the left seat who is a First Officer pretending to be a Captain, and someone in the other seat who is a Captain pretending to be a First Officer?

Your *personality* is based on heredity, childhood, upbringing and experience. It could be defined as the unique organisation of characteristics which determine the typical or standard behaviour of an individual. The word *attitude* refers to how you respond to another person, situation or organisation, and is the way we look at life, or the sum total of the meaning and values we give to various events. *Attitude* plus *behaviour* results in your *personality*. Your attitudes are the product of *personal disposition* and *past experience*. *behaviour* is the outward result of attitude and personality combined, and is adaptable. These attitudes have been identified as undesirable for the accident-prone person to possess:

- **Impulsivity**. Doing things without forethought - not stopping to think about what you're doing and ignoring the consequences. For example, a pilot and passengers who are anxious to get to their destination for a business presentation when thunderstorms are reported to be in a line across the route exhibit this attitude when they want to hurry and get going, before things get worse. Apply your training! *Slow down and think first!*

- **Anti-authority**. These people don't like being told what to do. They may either not respect the source of the authority, or are just plain ornery (with a deep source of bottled-up anger). Very often

there's nothing wrong with this - if more people had questioned authority, we wouldn't have had half the wars, or we wouldn't get passengers pressurizing pilots to do what they shouldn't. However, regulations have a purpose. They allow us to act with little information, since everything is supposed to be predictable, although that doesn't mean that rules should blindly be obeyed - sometimes breaking the rules saves lives. The DC10 that had an engine fall off during takeoff could have kept flying if the nose had been lowered a little for speed, instead of being set at the "standard" angle of 6°, as per the simulator, which, in this case, stalled the aeroplane. An official example of anti-authority is a pilot who neglects to renew medicals or ratings, or maintain records and logbooks, but my own opinion is that there's an element of laziness in there as well. The real anti-authority person is one who ignores the Chief Pilot's instructions and feels constrained by rules & regulations. This attitude is demonstrated when the passengers arrive almost an hour late for a flight that requires a reservation and the pilot considers that those rules do not apply. The antidote is to *follow the rules* (mostly!)

- **Invulnerability**. People like this think that nothing untoward can happen to them, so they take more risks, or push the envelope - humility is the antidote, or the realisation that it *could* happen to you. One instructor I know cures people who insist on flying VFR helicopters in IMC conditions by taking them up into cloud (in a twin) and showing them how incapable they are of instrument flying, even though they can do the occasional turn with the foggles on. The point is taken! *Repetitive tasks must be done as if they were new every time, no matter how tedious they may be* - you can guarantee that the one time you don't check for water in fuel, it will be there! You display this trait if, during an operational check of the cabin pressurization system, you discover that the rate control is inoperative and disregard it and depart on the trip because you think you can handle the cabin pressure yourself

- **Macho** people are afraid of looking small and are always subject to peer pressure, which means they care a lot about what other people think of them, leading to the idea that they have a very low opinion of themselves. Thus, they take unnecessary chances for different reasons than so-called Invulnerable people, above. These are typically the high-powered intimidating company executives who have houses in the middle of nowhere with no navaids within miles of the place. Such people may subconsciously put themselves in situations where they push the weather to test their own nerve. This is demonstrated if, while on an IFR flight, you emerge from a cloud to be within 300 feet of a helicopter and fly a little closer, just to show him. The antidote is *don't take chances*, or think you can fix things on the fly. You must stick up for yourself, with management and passengers

- **Resignation**. The thought that Allah (or luck) will provide is OK, but the Lord only helps those who help themselves - you've got to do your bit! If you want help to win the lottery, buy the ticket first! The antidote is to realise you *can* make a difference, or to have more confidence in your abilities. *Complacency* (mentioned in some reference books) would come under this heading

As you can see when you compare the opposites, each side of each coin above is as bad as the other - we should be somewhere in the middle, with a possible slight bias towards anti-authority and paranoia (you don't want management or customers putting you in invidious positions, and neither do you want them trying to kill you).

The first step in neutralising a hazardous attitude is to recognise hazardous thoughts. Label the thoughts as such and correct them by stating the corresponding antidotes.

Pilots must also learn to avoid some classic behavioural traps:

- *Peer Pressure*, which prevents evaluating a situation objectively

- *Mind Set*. Allowing expectations to override reality

- *Get-There-Itis*. This is actually a fixation, which clouds the vision and impairs judgment, combined with a disregard for alternative action

- *Duck-Under Syndrome*. Sneaking a peek by descending below minima, related to descending below MORA

- *Scud Running*. Trying to maintain visual contact while trying not to hit the ground - or going VFR when you really should be IFR

- *Getting Behind the Aircraft*. Allowing events to control your actions rather than the other way round, leading to.........

- Loss of Situational Awareness

- Getting Low On Fuel

- Poor Planning

- *Pushing the Envelope*. Exceeding design limitations in the belief that high performance will cover overestimated flying skills, or relying on manufacturer's fudge factors to go overweight

WHAT TYPE OF PERSON IS A PILOT?

Having decided what product we are selling (safe arrival), we can now talk about the best kind of person to produce it. We certainly have more intelligence than the average car driver. Or do we? Passing exams doesn't mean you're capable of doing a decent job or handling a crisis. There are stupid solicitors, professors, you name it. I have flown with 17,000-hour pilots who I wouldn't trust with a pram, and 1,000-hour types with whom I would trust anything.

I think it's fair to say that the public typically think of pilots (when they think of them at all) as outgoing types, often in the bar and having a lark, an image from all those World War II movies, and if you were cold, hungry, tired, frightened and inexperienced, you would probably behave that way, too, but life today is quite different.

A pilot should be a synthesis of the following headings:

- *Meticulous* - being prepared to do the same thing, the same way, every time, and not get bored, as that's the way you miss things

- *Forward Thinking* - in the same way that an advanced driver is ready to deal with a corner before going into it, the advanced pilot knows the load underneath will carry on if the helicopter slows down, and positions the controls properly

- *Responsible* - the "responsible position" that you hold as a commander is one where you act with minimum direction but are personally responsible for the outcome of your activities. In other words, you are responsible for the machine without being directed by any other person in it

- *Trustworthy* - people must be able to *trust* you - all of aviation runs on it. You trust the previous pilot not to have overstressed the machine, or to really have done 4.3 hours and not 6. Signatures count for a lot, and, by extension, your word

- *Motivated*. Motivation is a drive to behave in a particular fashion. It is an internal force which can affect the quality of performance, although excessive motivation together with high levels of stress will limit your attention-management capabilities. In short, you can get fixated

WHAT IS COMMON BETWEEN COMPETENT PEOPLE?

- *Intelligence*

- *Personality.* This can be defined as "The sum total of the physical, mental, emotional and social characteristics of an individual". Generally, to be accident prone, you are either under- or overconfident. With the former, situations will tend not to be handled properly, and with the latter, situations not appreciated properly. You might also be aggressive, independent, a risk taker, anxious, impersonal, competitive, and invulnerable, with a low stress tolerance, which, when you think about it, are all based on attention-seeking and fear. However, where personality really counts is during interactions with other people; behaviour breeds behaviour. Crews are frightened to deal with the Captain, and Captains won't deal with crews

- *Leadership vs teamwork.* Leadership has been defined as facilitating the movement of a team toward the accomplishment of a task, in this case, the crew and the safe arrival of their passengers. This is a better definition than "Getting somebody to do what you want them to do" which implies a certain amount of manipulation, something more in the realm of management as a scientific process. A Leader, as opposed to a Manager, is a more positive force, inspirational, nurturing and many other words you could probably think of yourself

- *Personal qualities* to passengers and colleagues

FLIGHT DECK MANAGEMENT
••

What sort of personality do you have? Do you leave everything to the last minute? Are you a placid type, or nervous and anxious? Do you have a low self-image or are you on the arrogant side? Do you succumb to pressure? Are you strong enough to stand up to the Chairman of the Board who insists he must get there NOW? It's better to ask for help and look stupid, than not to ask and risk looking worse. Unfortunately, the ability to laugh at yourself and not feel uncomfortable when you've cocked things up only comes with a certain degree of maturity. As you get older, you accept that mistakes are made; there's

no shame in that, even the most experienced pilot couldn't fly at one time - the trick lies in not making the same mistake twice, or at least ensuring that the ones you make aren't the fatal ones.

Groups

Groups behave differently from individuals. That is to say, a person may carry out different actions in concert with others than would be done solo - there is strong pressure *just to conform* when in a group, regardless of what the group gets up to, with a resulting high possibility of riskier decisions. Synergy arises from a group with a high degree of co-operation, where people in the group are motivated to support each other. Thus, groups are more likely than individuals to make decisions concerning risk, known as *risky shift*. In other words, if you put known risk takers together, the chances of them taking risks are amplified out of all proportion. *Conformity* concerns the likelihood of an individual to go along with a group decision, even if it is wrong, and it has been proved that the situations people are in, rather than their native personalities, make them behave as they do (vicious prison guards, etc.). The idea of being integrated into the team, to be recognised as a leader, or to avoid conflicts, may lead to a disposition to agree with decisions made by others. A request is more likely to be complied with if a greater one has previously been denied or a lesser one accepted (*compliance*).

Crew decision making is most efficient if all crew members adapt their management styles to meet the demands of the situation. *Cohesion* within a group is a major advantage in times of difficulty - but with too much, groupthink can have negative results.

When people work together to achieve common goals, the way they react together and the resulting harmony (or lack thereof) can have a significant effect on the outcome of their activities. In this respect, people can be *person-oriented* (focussed on keeping the team happy) or *goal-oriented* (focussed on getting the job done), after *Blake & Manton's Grid Theory*. A person too severely person-oriented is likely to run a laissez-faire cockpit (see overleaf), and one too goal-oriented may trample roughshod over peoples' feelings in trying to get the job done (1/9). On the other hand, a person who scored as 9/1 would be more interested in the task or goal with little interest in people, and would be authoritarian, expecting obedience at all times. A 1/1 person is not interested in the task or the people involved.

A 5/5 person would "go along to get along" but would not get the best out of any situation. At the top, a 9/9

If this page is a photocopy, it is not authorised!

person is a team manager who gets the task done by making the best use of individual members of the team.

The ideal professional pilot is person and goal oriented. However, helicopter pilots are generally goal oriented, which adds motivation and pressures (largely self-induced) to "get the job done" to impress customers and peers. Thus, helicopter pilots have an increased tendency to take risks, with a lower tendency to conform and a higher tendency to achieve (Flight Safety Foundation).

LEADERS & FOLLOWERS

Leadership has been defined as *any behaviour that moves a group closer to attaining its goals* or, in the words of Henry Kissinger, *the art of taking people where they would not have gone themselves.* It can arise out of personality (as with a born leader), a situation, or the dynamics of a group itself (interaction).

A leader's ideas and actions influence the thoughts and behaviour of others. Through example and persuasion, and understanding the goals and desires of the group, the leader becomes a means of change and influence. The quality of leaders depends on the success of their relationship with the team. A Leader, as opposed to a Manager, or Administrator, is a positive force, being inspirational and nurturing. Leaders see the big picture, people, empowerment, and opportunity, and expect outperformance. They display emotional resolve, control their actions, think before they act, and accept responsibility for their actions before placing blame on others. Administrators see detail, risk, budget and *control*, and require merely compliance and no mistakes.

Unfortunately, many seem to forget that most people know what their job is, and want to do it well, and that it's management's (in this case, the Captain's) function to create the proper environment for them to do it in, then get out of the way and let people work things through, although people should not work unsupervised. If you keep checking on them (and therefore distracting them) they will eventually tell you anything just to get you off their backs and you will end up working with false information, and look even worse to your boss. A major part of this is setting a good example - if the Captain turns up neatly dressed and organized, it shows his attitude towards the work in hand, or demonstrates expectations.

An effective leader should perform certain functions, including *regulating information flow, directing activities, motivation* and *decision making. Synergy* allows the group to appear greater than the sum of its parts, or crew members,

in our case. It's a new name for an old concept - for example, Montgomery wrote this years ago:

> *"The real strength of an army is, and must be, far greater than the sum total of its parts; that extra strength is provided by morale, fighting spirit, mutual confidence between the leaders and the led and especially with the high command, the quality of comradeship, and many other intangible spiritual qualities."*

You will get the best out of your staff if their goals align with those of your Company, and that happens when you give them the ability to make decisions, or assume responsibilities. Any problems are 99% down to bad leadership. Remember that you're not as concerned with what people get up to when you're there, but what they do when you're not there! It's all about giving people respect, which is reflected in your body language and tone of voice. Experienced doctors make mistakes, but only a very low proportion of them are actually sued. These are usually the ones that didn't treat their patients properly. People tend not to sue people they like! The real measure of people lies in how they treat their subordinates - management's function is to serve! In short, if you want your staff to look after you, you have to look after them.

There is a difference between *leadership*, which is acquired, and *authority*, which is assigned - although, optimally, they should be combined - the authority of the Captain, or Chief Pilot, should be adequately balanced by assertiveness from the crew. *A follower's skills should be exorcized in a supporting role that does not undermine the leader.* If special skills are held, sometimes the follower becomes the leader!

Monty also wrote this:

> *"The acid test of an officer who aspires to high command is his ability to be able to grasp quickly the essentials of a military problem, to decide rapidly what he will do, and then to see that his subordinate commanders get on with the job. Above all, he has got to rid himself of all irrelevant detail: he must concentrate on the essentials, and on those details and only those details which are necessary to the proper carrying out of his plan - trusting his staff to effect all the necessary co-ordination."*

Out of the military context, it is equally applicable to flight crew. Just remember - leadership has nothing to do with management!

Blake & Moulton classified leadership styles as follows:

- *Country Club* - everyone's friend

- *Team Leader* - someone who allows subordinates a certain amount of responsibility but is prepared to take over as and when necessary, and is not afraid to make uncomfortable decisions

- *Impoverished* - someone who is indecisive and who doesn't like making waves

- *Authoritarian*

AUTHORITY GRADIENTS

There is some risk involved when, for example, a very senior captain is paired with a very junior first officer. Aside from the potential lack of communication, what happens when the captain relies on experience that the f/o doesn't have to take short cuts? How is the f/o expected to monitor the process?

A *laissez-faire* cockpit exists when a passive approach by the captain allows decisions, choices and actions to be made by other crew members, with a major risk of an *inversion of authority*. A *self-centred* cockpit is one where crew members tend to do their own thing without telling the others what is going on. An *autocratic* cockpit is described by the captain's excessive authority, considerably reducing communication and consequently the synergy and cohesion of the crew. A captain running an autocratic cockpit is normally overloaded.

However, an effective flight deck (*synergetic cockpit*) exists when decisions are taken by the captain with the help and participation of the other crew members. In this case, a *democratic* and *cooperative* leadership style is characterised by the leader, when conflicts arise, trying to clarify the causes and reasons of the conflict with all persons involved. The team spirit of a crew depends on pilots respecting each other and striving for the same goals.

The advantages of coordination are redundancy, synergy and clarification of responsibility. Coordinated cooperation allows for synergy between the captain and copilot, synchronised actions and the distribution of responsibilities. *Coaction* is a mode of cooperation which recommends working in parallel to achieve one objective.

Multi-Crew

This term means that more than one person is flying the aircraft, and implies that they should be doing so as a team, which is defined as two or more people working together to perform a task as one. It is *not* the same as two superstars in the same cockpit working with each other!

Early multi-crew aircraft would need as many as five people on the flight deck, but modern ones can get by with two, both of whom can sometimes take on the tasks of the people who are not there now. For example, inertial navigation systems and GPS have reduced the need for a navigator, and FADECs and other automation have eliminated the flight engineer.

However, there are still so many tasks in a typical flight deck environment that they cannot all be done by one person effectively, hence the need for *delegation*, which implies that someone must set the tasks to be performed and monitor them. That person is the Captain.

A Captain has full control and authority in the operation of the aircraft, without limitation, over other crewmembers and their duties during flight time, whether or not valid certificates are held for the functions of those crewmembers. With that position comes responsibilities, not least of which is allowing other persons in the team a chance to develop (i.e. let the P2 get on with the emergency), and the need for humility, as when recognising that someone else may actually be better than you at doing what's required, and accepting that they may do it in a different way. Also, as mentioned, there is the need to be a leader, and motivate, rather than drive, people - in other words, set tasks and objectives, but not necessarily the way they are done.

Crews take their lead from the Captain. Positive influences that First Officers have reported include:

- Good attitude towards the job and the company

- Neat, professional uniform

- Good briefing skills

- Encouraging crews to speak up and/or express their opinions

Negative ones are:

- Quiet demeanour

- Negative attitude to job and Company

- Failure to state expectations

- Negative reaction to input

- Inability to admit mistakes

In return, the crew should provide positive support (if you're a First Officer, regardless of what your company says, it's your *job* to monitor the Captain and mention it if you think there's anything wrong, which is not to say you should be on the Captain's back - he is still the Boss and you could become a flight safety hazard).

With proper multi-crew operations, everyone should take the responsibility for the work of the team as a whole. Thus, any problems become *crew problems*.

The multi-crew concept is meant to provide a higher level of safety by:

- reducing the workload by sharing tasks (a governor runaway on the Bell 212 requires the co-ordinated efforts of two people handling the throttles to be done properly)

- allowing better quality decisions, because actions should be discussed

- allowing better error management by increasing situational awareness

In order to do this properly, certain things need to be established, namely are you a group of individuals working together or a fully functioning team? There is a subtle difference! These stages can turn one into the other:

- *Inclusion*, where individuals feel they are part of a team, and are motivated to do their best

- *Control* - who is exerting it, and how?

- *Trust*, which must be achieved as quickly as possible. Crew members need good reason to justify their trust in the leader and each other

All the above can be promoted with good crew briefings, during which you can show that you are comfortable in authority and can promote communication, and are prepared for the day's activities, establishing roles without making the boundaries too rigid. The first briefing during the assembly time before a trip is when the group decides in very short order how difficult each other will be to work with, particularly the Captain!

For example, if the Captain decides to ignore certain procedures, or even cut them out altogether (doing it "his" way), the rest of the crew will be wondering what else will be ignored. A quick, curt briefing is likely to set up barriers, as is one that is at odds with subsequent actions.

The usual briefings include:

- **Crew Briefing**, before the flight, which is an opportunity for its members to knit together when they first meet. One trick I use when meeting lots of new students for the first time (I used to do seminars for computer technicians) is to catch them having their first coffee, give one of them a soft ball and get them to throw it amongst themselves for a short time. It's a great ice-breaker, and pretty soon they are all chatting amongst themselves. It makes them less afraid of talking in the classroom and asking questions - that is, it makes them more likely to get involved, because

the last thing you want is a lot of puddings sitting there. It applies to flight crews as well

- **Departure**, during which routes are discussed

- **Pre-takeoff**, covering actions in emergencies

- **Approach**, routes and emergencies - for example, what to do if the glideslope goes out - do you carry on as a localiser only approach, or go around?

The latter three generally involve only the pilots.

CHECKLISTS

These will have been written for normal and abnormal situations. The latter are specific events, with their own checklists, which means that sometimes you have to be creative and try to combine them if you have multiple emergencies! An abnormal situation should positively identified before any action is taken, *after the aircraft is under control*. The crew member identifying it should call it out, then the PF should call for the appropriate checklist (not just "the checklist"!) Items should be called by the PM (Pilot Monitoring, or PNF, in some companies), and the PF should respond if and when it is understood.

Each person involved should have their own area of responsibility - items that are irreversible or complex should be agreed upon by both pilots.

Using a checklist before starting is a contribution to safety because the concentration required reduces distraction from personal stress.

Below is an example of the sort of checklist that comes out of a typical Chief Pilot's office. At first sight, it would appear to do the job quite well, but closer inspection reveals that it could do with a little tweaking here and there. For example, it is not obvious what are headings and what are not.

<u>**FIRE**</u>

Immediate Actions:

ON GROUND:	
Respective EMER OFF sw[1]	Open switch guard, press and release
Fuel Prime Pumps	Both OFF
Engines	OFF
Rotor Brake	ON
Battery	OFF
Passengers	Evacuate

IN FLIGHT:	
OEI flight condition	Establish
Respective EMER OFF sw[1]	Open switch guard, press and release
Affected engine	Identify, then OFF
Passengers	Alert
Check for signs of fire	
Warning light off	LAND AS SOON AS POSSIBLE
Warning light on	LAND IMMEDIATELY

Considerations

1. Respective engine will be automatically cut off. ACTIVE will illuminate on the EMER OFF sw panel and F VALVE CL will illuminate on the CAD.

"I have never taken disagreement as
an indication that I am wrong"

Enoch Powell

Here is the same checklist, tweaked:

FIRE

Immediate Actions

On Ground
1.	Switch guard	Open, press and release
2.	Fuel Prime Pumps	Both OFF
3.	Engines	OFF
4.	Rotor Brake	ON
5.	Battery	OFF
6.	Passengers	Evacuate

In Flight
1.	OEI flight condition	Establish
2.	Switch guard	Open, press and release
3.	Affected engine	Identify, then OFF
4.	Passengers	Alert
5.	Fire	Check for signs
6.	LAND AS SOON AS POSSIBLE	

Considerations
1. Respective engine will be automatically cut off. ACTIVE will illuminate on the EMER OFF sw panel and F VALVE CL will illuminate on the CAD.

It didn't take much effort to improve things, with a little spacing and layout.

Assertiveness

The feeling of being in control, with resultant self-esteem, has health implications - a study of civil servants found that the death rate of those in lower status jobs was three times higher. Everybody has a personal space around them, one which includes thoughts and attitudes, and culture. In other words, maintaining an appropriate emotional distance is just as important as maintaining a physical one. You do this by not putting people down, or asking too many questions, offering unwanted advice, swamping them with affection, etc. In short, allowing somebody, including yourself, to be their own person. To see what I mean about personal space, sit down next to someone on a park bench. There will be a point beyond which you do not feel comfortable going past. Only when another person sits on the bench do you feel able to bunch up closer (there is also a respectful distance behind cars, hence people getting wound up when you get too close behind them).

Thus, there are many opportunities for others to invade your space, and you often have to defend it. This is known as being *assertive*, which should not be confused with being *aggressive* - assertion is a way of defending your space non-destructively - whether you do this aggressively is up to you! It is a positive and productive expression of yourself. People who allow others to invade their space, on the other hand, are *submissive*. Submission brings less responsibility and conflict, of course, and usually brings more approval, but many people use it as a form of

control. Nevertheless, very often, the most appropriate role for a Captain is the submissive one, in order to get the job done.

Of course, asserting yourself with a customer or management can lead to a loss of job! Or getting seven bells kicked out of you! This is a real event:

"Had the opportunity to work with some real bone headed customers once - anyway, it was blowing a gale just after we had moved into a new campsite, raining also. The camp boss says its time to sling the gear off the beach up to the campsite, around 1/4 of a mile. My suggestion of waiting for the wind to die down falls on deaf ears and the comment to me was: "If you don't want to sling it up here you can go down and start carrying it up here". This after bending over backwards for these jerks for the last 30 days, so I told him if things go bad the load will be punched. His reply: "Whatever."

Well I tell them the loads will have to be light as the pick up point is upwind of the drop off site, and short of hovering backwards for a 1/4 mile, turning downwind will be some fun. Well, two loads go as reasonable as one can imagine with the wind, rain and pilot with a bad attitude - now for the last load - and its just a beauty - plywood on the bottom and assorted junk on top. Unknown to me at the time was my own personal toolboxes (2).

Well, getting it up was a bear, with maybe 10 torque to spare. I try to hover sideways with it...no luck...drags me to the ground....going all the way backwards was a good way to run into something near the camp, so let's try flying this crap and doing a mile wide turn. She gets going okay and into translation okay - up to 30 mph - okay - start do do the wide turn okay now going downwind like a bat out of hell, trying to push enough cyclic to keep her flying. No way! The airspeed hits 0 and we start to sink - the torque is at 100%, so as calm as one can be at this moment in time, I know that this load is not long for the world. Try turning into wind, no way will she turn - heading for the ground - left hand ready for the emergency release in case the electric one fails, going to wait for the last minute before punching it off - about 10 feet from the ground - bombs away, gain control of old Betsy again, calmly park her near the camp, shut down, blades are still turning when the camp boss and his cohorts come over and now are saying that I did that on purpose and want to kick the crap out of me.

Well, seeing as they outnumbered me 6-1, I calmly announced that if they should like to join into fisticuffs, get in line! As I drew a line in the dirt, I said I would gladly oblige them - one at a time. After no one took up my offer and I tried explaining what I had told them before this dog and pony show got started, they shuffled off and I went over to see what had become of the bomb load. To my displeasure I found what was left of my toolboxes....flattened to about six inches high....

If you assert yourself wrongly, you will generate a defensive response from the other person, and a request to reorganise two short words into a well-known phrase or saying. In other words, if you push, you will get pushed back, because the other person will not want to admit that they have affected your life, or are wrong. One pilot took off in a helicopter in bad weather, ignoring his wife who asked him not to take their son (he didn't wish to appear as if he was listening to what she said). The helicopter crashed into the side of a hill and killed them both. An expensive way to prove your point.

This is where a sympathetic approach from you will help - certainly allowing enough time for the other person to reply, and to listen - then make your point again. It may take more than ten attempts to get your message across.

A bullying customer invades your space by attacking your self-belief and current values - how do you clear them out? Conflict is an *emotional* thing, and you have to defuse the emotion first to make any progress. This is because, if you remember, the fight-or-flight response puts people under pressure and they are not in a mood to listen until that is over. First of all, treat the other person with respect. You won't need to say much - they will see your attitude towards them by your body language, eye contact, etc. Listen to the *meaning* of what they have to say. They won't appreciate a parrot-fashion repetition of their words, but if you paraphrase them, they may think you are listening!

Conflict management involves the participation of all involved parties in finding an acceptable collective solution.

Many accidents would not have happened if the Captain had been challenged properly, which makes the primary cause of the accident actually the secondary one. Is the failure to do so the FO's fault, or the Captain's?

So how should a First Officer challenge a captain? Does he drop a hint, or simply make a plain statement of fact?

"*Carelessness and overconfidence are often more dangerous than deliberately accepted risks*"

Wilbur Wright

A skilled pilot who takes risks is a bigger problem than an average one who is prudent and cautious

RISK MANAGEMENT

When the links in an error chain start to come together, the risk starts building. Uncertainty about a situation can often indicate risk.

One definition of risk is the chance that a situation, or the consequences of one, will be hazardous enough to cause harm, injury or loss. Another is that a *risk arises every time a person is in the presence of a hazard*. Health & Safety legislation defines a hazard as something that could be dangerous to persons or property, and risk in terms of the chance that that hazard could actually cause damage. The goal of whoever operates the *Safety Management System* in your company is to:

- Identify any hazards that might be encountered (e.g. wet helidecks)
- Identify the risks associated with them (spinning helicopters)
- The level of risk for each scenario
- Apply rules or design SOPs that will minimise the risks

It's worth pointing out that hazards need not be technical - there are business risks, too, such as when a company is growing quickly and can be exposed to cashflow problems, where safety might get a lower priority against simply surviving. There may be a high staff turnover, or you may have a disproportionate amount of inexperienced pilots that need proper supervision. A proactive safety manager looks for such problems before they start.

To have absolutely no risk, of course, we shouldn't take off at all, but that's not what we're here for, so we have to have some method of evaluating risk against a yardstick to get the job done, or balance profitability with safety. *Risk management* is the key, best used in an ample-time decision-making situation, where time is not critical. For example, in a helicopter, it can be more dangerous to avoid the height/velocity curve (say when coming out of a confined area) than to be in it for a few seconds. Part of the pilot's job is to decide which of the risks presents the least hazard - that is, is there a greater risk of colliding with something when coming out of the clearing than having an engine failure? Is it better to take off downwind into a clear area, or into wind with a lot of obstructions? In other words, Risk Management means measuring the degree of harm against that of exposure - the more you have to lose, the less risks you want to take.

Risk Management, therefore, is a decision-making tool that can be applied to either eliminate risk, or reduce it to an acceptable level, preferably before takeoff (things that stop you eliminating risk entirely would either be impracticality, or money). With it, you have to first identify a hazard, analyse any associated risks, make a decision and implement it (with a *risk strategy*) and monitor the results, with a view to changing things if need be. However, this depends on the *perception* of a risk, and the difference between yours, the management's and the customer's can be quite startling. Outside influences include weather, traffic and obstacles. Internal ones can be maintenance, fatigue, or the culture of the company.

Analysing Risk

There are many aspects to analyzing risk:

- Where is it?

- How likely is it to happen? A *High Probability* means it is likely to happen. *Medium* means it has a fair chance of happening, *Low* means it is possible, but not probable, and *Very Low* means it will almost certainly not happen (but never say never!)

- How significant is it? That is, what are the consequences? *High* indicates irreparable harm. *Medium* means a significant impact, and *Low* means just inconvenience

- What are the priorities? An HH risk, meaning that not only is something likely to happen, but, when it does, will cause irreparable harm to people or property, needs attention first

The assessment of risk in a particular situation will be based on subjective perception and evaluation of situational factors. What this means in English is that the difference between perceived and actual risk depends on the amount of control you think you have, and familiarity. For example, it is a lot more risky to ride a bike through a busy city than it is to live near a nuclear power station, yet people still ride bikes along boulevards and don't want to live near reactors. The former situation allows you more control (you can always get off and walk) and is more familiar. Your perception of control is influenced by your fear of the unknown.

Risk is equal to *probability* multiplied by the *consequences* of what you propose to do, and your *exposure*. You essentially have four choices - either not do the job, mitigate the effects of the risk, transfer it (buy insurance) or eat it (absorb the effects yourself). *High risk* means a high probability of death, damage or injury, requiring

appropriate procedures - possibly with none available at all and you have to think on your feet, which is where your training comes in. *Low risk* is a normal situation, where normal precautions are enough.

You could always try and prehandle situations - that is, make as many decisions as possible ahead of time, as part of your flight planning - most important, though is to leave yourself a way out. For example, always be aware, when dropping water, that you may have to get out of a hot hole with the load on - don't assume that the bucket will work and you will be light enough to escape! Is the weather closing in behind you? Have you gone into a confined area and boxed yourself in? Mountain pilots *always* have a way out - even after they've landed.

You might find it strange not to accept a risk of engine failure and a possible wire strike after you've just been hovering Out of Ground Effect in hostile terrain for the last 15 minutes, but this is the fine line in the world of helicopters. In the words of one senior pilot: "We do what we have to do, when we have to do it, in the calculated risk sense, but we never take a single risk we don't have to…"

Risk Checklist

These are only suggested headings - there could be many more........

- What equipment will you be using?

- Is it the correct equipment for the job?

- Is it in good condition?

- Is the load dangerous or awkward?

- What will it fly like?

- How much does it weigh?

- What condition is it in?

- Is the pilot qualified and current?

- Does the pilot have his mind on the job?

- Is the pilot rested?

- Is the destination sequence clear?

- Is it in a confined area? Are there obstacles?

- Are people on the ground trained & briefed?

- Performance requirements?

- What's the weather like? Marginal?

- Weight & Balance calculated?

- Is there any pressure from the customer, management, or the schedule?

PRINCIPLES OF FLIGHT

It's almost impossible to explain new terms as they arise without spoiling the flow of the text, although they are all explained in it somewhere. Here are some to start with, in a semi-logical order:

DEFINITIONS

The basis of this subject is the *conservation of mass*, of which the *continuity equation* is an expression. The *Law of Conservation of Mass* (from Lavoisier) states that mass can be neither created nor destroyed (but it may change its form into something that is not desired, such as heat with an engine) or that, in a chemical reaction, the total mass of the reacting substances is equal to the total mass of the products formed. In a steady flow process, meaning where flow rates don't change over time, this means that inflow should equal outflow, or what goes in must come out, whatever might happen in the middle. *Le Chatelier's principle* is a consequence of this - when a balanced system is subjected to a change in conditions, it adjusts itself to try and oppose the change. If you want to use the smallest possible force on an object, or want to obtain the largest possible velocity, the *Impulse-Momentum Equation* states that an impulse given to a particle causes a change in momentum of that particle. Obvious, really.

- **Vector** (Quantity) - A quantity that has *magnitude* and *direction* (a *scalar quantity* has magnitude only). Two vectors can be combined to produce a *resultant* (see right). A good example of a vector is a.....

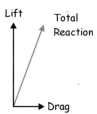

- **Vector Diagram** - a picture of a vector with an arrow showing the direction the force is acting in. Such a diagram could be used to depict the forces round an aerofoil, or in navigation, to show the effects of wind on a track or heading

- **Velocity** - rate of change of position in a given direction

- **Inertia** - This is a resistive force that gives a body the tendency to remain at rest, or at least carry on with what it's doing - in other words, not to change its present state, or to maintain a constant velocity, and be hard to stop or get moving. This should not be confused with *Momentum* (next), since even bodies at rest have inertia (Galileo argued that the only difference between constant velocity and zero velocity is magnitude, so he shifted the focus of attention from an object's position to how that position was changing). To change an object's current state, a force must be applied, proportional to the mass of the body concerned, in that the heavier something is, the more force you need to shift it. When mass changes, inertia changes, too

- **Momentum** - the quantity of motion in a body, or a tendency to keep right on going, similar to *kinetic energy*, except that kinetic energy is defined by work, and momentum is defined by impulse (kinetic energy is that arising from motion). The *Law of Conservation of Momentum* states that, when no net external forces are acting on a system of objects, the total vector momentum of the system remains constant. Being a vector quantity, momentum concerns the velocity of a body as well as its mass, so the relevant formula is *momentum = mass x velocity*, which denotes how much is moving and how fast. If mass or velocity increase, the momentum increases and you need a bigger force to change the body's state of motion. For example, a heavy helicopter hovertaxying at a high rate of knots requires larger handfuls of power to stop than if it were going at walking pace. Of course, you could also use a relatively small force for a longer time. The small letter p is used to signify momentum, and the conventional units used are kg and m/s (see also *Newton's Second Law*, overleaf)

Note: If you integrate the rate of change of momentum with differential calculus, the formula *mass x velocity* (mv) becomes $\frac{1}{2}mv^2$, which will become significant in the following pages.........

When two forces are applied to a point, their resultant is the diagonal of a parallelogram based on that point

- **Acceleration** - the rate of change of motion in speed and/or direction (velocity), or the change in velocity divided by the time interval. If you change one or the other, or both, the object is accelerating, as with a turning helicopter. Note that, although the word *acceleration* refers to any change in velocity, the word *deceleration* is also used to indicate a decrease. The acceleration of a falling body is 32 feet per second, per second, but the SI unit is metres per second, squared (m/s^2)

- **Equilibrium** - a state of balance between forces, or zero acceleration, as with a helicopter in a steady vertical climb or straight & level flight

- **Rotors** - the lift producing surfaces of a helicopter, the equivalent of wings on an aeroplane

- **Force** - that which can cause a change in motion of a body: Four forces act on an aircraft in flight, called *Lift*, *Weight*, *Thrust* and *Drag*, discussed later but, for now, lift makes a flying machine go up, weight makes it go down, thrust makes it go forward, and drag tries to stop it. The unit of force is the Newton, after Sir Isaac, mentioned shortly. Under Newton's first law of motion, a moving body will travel along a straight path with constant speed (that is, with constant velocity) unless it is acted on by an external force. When circular motion is involved, the constant force acting on a body that pushes it toward the centre is *centripetal force*, which acts inwards along a radius of a curve.

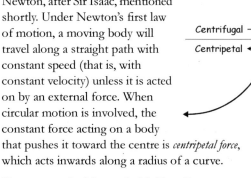

Centrifugal →
Centripetal ←

However, under Newton's third law (for every reaction there is an equal and opposite reaction), you need to balance centripetal force with something going the other way. *Centrifugal force* is a fictitious force that acts *outwards* from an axis of rotation, or along a radius of a curve. It increases with *mass*, the *square of rotational speed*, and the *distance from the axis*. Being fictitious, centrifugal force does not act on the body in motion - the only one involved is centripetal force. It is the *removal* of centripetal force that allows a blade to fly from the hub when it is released

- **Stall** - where an aerofoil (a wing or a rotor blade) starts to be less efficient at producing lift, when it is inclined sharply upwards and its speed is too low so, instead of cutting its way smoothly through the

air, as it would normally do at a higher airspeed and a lower angle, it leaves a turbulent partial vacuum behind

- **Mass** - the quantity of matter in a body, with *matter* being any physical property having volume. Mass can be a measure of how difficult an object is to start or stop, or otherwise influence. The word *weight* is often used instead, but that is just force arising from gravity, or the attractive force of a large object, such as the Earth. Newton defined mass in terms of inertia, in that the mass of a body is a numerical measure of the inertia that a body possesses - the greater a body's mass, the greater the force needed to move or stop it. A *slug* is a unit of mass that accelerates at 1 ft/sec when acted on by a force of 1 pound. Mass is equal to weight divided by the acceleration due to gravity.

- **Energy** - the ability of a given unit of mass to do work, measured in Joules. The amount of energy in a body comes from the work it can do. An aircraft can have three types of energy - *potential energy*, which comes from height, *kinetic energy*, which comes from movement, and *chemical energy*, which comes from the engines. For example, a hovering helicopter has no kinetic energy, miniscule potential energy and lots of chemical energy. One in straight and level flight has heaps of all three. A reduction in chemical energy will cause a descent. Energy is measured in terms of weight multiplied by distance (such as ft-lbs)

- **Work** - Work is movement *against resistance*, which may loosely be called the mechanical form of energy, since it is also measured in terms of weight against distance. Work is done when a force moves a body in the direction that the force is acting. If an object doesn't move despite a force being applied, no work is done, although "work" in the casual sense has obviously been done. The unit of work is the *Joule*, or 1 Newton metre. A hovering helicopter is not doing any work!

- **Viscosity**. This is an expression of the internal friction of a fluid, which is associated with the resistance of layers adjacent to each other.

- **Power** - this is the rate of doing work, and is measured in Watts, so it is the number of Joules consumed divided by the time taken

- **Mach Number** - The ratio between TAS and the local speed of sound, discussed in *AGK*

- **Angle Of Attack** - The angle at which the chord line of the aerofoil meets the relative airflow coming the other way

A *geometry limited* aircraft is one which cannot use the full rotation angle on takeoff because the tail might scrape the runway - mostly found with stretched versions.

Newton's Laws Of Motion

Newton formulated three laws of motion that govern all material bodies and which are also relevant to flight:

- *A body will continue in its state of rest, or uniform motion in a straight line, unless acted on by an external force.* Put another way, *an object at rest (or in motion) will remain at rest (or in motion at that velocity) until acted upon by an external force.* It's otherwise known as *Inertia*, mentioned above. In other words, you must apply a force to make an object move or change its direction. The effect of a constant force will be to change the object's *velocity* rather than its *position* by a constant amount. Since air has mass, it can be considered as an object

- *The rate of change of motion (of a body) is directly proportional to the force acting on it, and inversely proportional to the body's mass.* A body whose motion is changed by an outside force will accelerate in the same direction as that force at a rate in direct proportion with it. That is, the *acceleration* of a stream of air when it is deflected by an aerofoil is proportional to the aerofoil's momentum - if its speed doubles, so does the air's acceleration in the direction it is forced to go. On the other hand, if the *mass* of air doubles, its acceleration halves. Thus, motion is started, stopped or changed by causing the forces that act on an aircraft in flight to become unbalanced. Acceleration (or rate of change) therefore depends on how large the unbalanced force is and how much mass the body has. As a result of this law, the strength of a *force* depends on *mass* multiplied by *acceleration*

- *If one body exerts a force on another body, the second body will exert an equal and opposite force on the first body,* popularised as: *For every action, there is an equal and opposite reaction.* This law is made use of by propellers and jet engines to drive aeroplanes forward, and means that forces exist in pairs

AIRFLOW

Air is a liquid medium, meaning that it behaves rather like water, as is shown by submerged aircraft, which will "fly" to the bottom of the sea, miles away from where they splash down, a principle to remember during mountain flying. As mentioned in *Meteorology*, the atmosphere can be regarded as an "ocean" of air, which can therefore flow and change its shape but, unlike water, it is compressible, although, for aerodynamic purposes, at slow speeds (below the speed of sound), it is considered to be incompressible. As it has mass, air can exert force, and do work, and transfer energy. As a quantity, it is normally measured in cubic feet.

The speed at which an object moves through the air is called the *airspeed*, and it doesn't matter whether the air flows over it, or the object itself moves - the effects are the same, so even if you tie a rotor blade down, a strong wind acting on it will still make it want to fly up. The path an object takes through the air is called the *flight path*, and the air going the other way is the *relative airflow* or *relative wind* - they always oppose each other.

The Boundary Layer

Up to a certain critical airspeed, air flowing over or around a body will hug its shape and be quite well-behaved, flowing in a *laminar* fashion (that is, smoothly layered), after which it breaks up to form vortices that may interfere with any lifting action. the reason it hugs the body is that it speeds up to follow the body's shape, which makes its pressure less than the atmospheric pressure, which will keep it against the body's surface. This is discussed more fully later.

If you've ever been through a car wash, and your car is still wet, you may have noticed droplets of water remaining quite still on the bodywork, no matter how fast you drive. This happens on aerofoils as well - large specks of dust will remain on a wing even through a Transatlantic flight.

The layer in which this happens is called the *boundary layer*, which, in practice, doesn't exist much farther back than the thickest part of an aerofoil. Friction makes air in the lower areas of the boundary layer slow down progressively, until, at the surface, its relative speed could be zero, hence the specks of dust mentioned above being unaffected.

Looked at another way, an object moving through air pulls a few air molecules along with it, at around the same speed as the object. Molecules slightly further away will also be pulled along, but at a slightly lower speed, and so on. The layer of air that extends from the surface of the object to where nothing is dragged along at all is the *laminar boundary layer*, which is typically about half an inch thick up to the *transition point*, where it becomes the *turbulent boundary layer*, and around three inches thick. This creates a wedge of air that resists the aerofoil's movement in the shape of *drag*, which is dealt with in a few pages' time. The transition point moves *forward* with speed (and angle of attack), which is something to do with the Reynolds number, and more of the blade becomes affected by the turbulent area, which increases the amount of skin friction. The point where the turbulent airflow leaves the surface to create wake turbulence (see *Operational Procedures*) is known as the *separation point*.

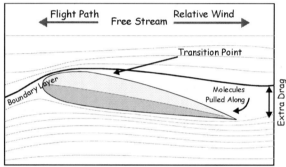

SUMMARY

The Reynolds number expresses the ratio of pressure forces against viscosity forces in the flow of a fluid - it is dimensionless, meaning that it has no limits. Fluid flow is turbulent when the RN is greater than 2000. Flow is laminar below that

The forces around aerofoils include a pressure force against the surfaces and friction along them, so the airflow will be slowed down to greater or lesser degrees, according to their smoothness. The layer of air immediately in contact with the surface is slowed down the most and subsequent ones less until it reaches the *free stream flow rate*. This boundary layer is divided into *laminar* (streamlined) flow and *turbulent* flow - the latter has more kinetic energy and the strongest change in velocity close to the surface. The point where it goes from laminar to turbulent is the *transition point*, where the layer thickens to create extra drag, that will try to stop the aerofoil moving through the air.

THE AEROFOIL

This is the official name for a wing, or any other device that creates a lift reaction out of the air. The aerofoil's purpose is to deflect a stream of air by making the air go faster over its top surface, which, for various reasons discussed shortly, has the effect of bending the airflow in a downwards direction.

In order to get airborne in the first place, the lift created must always be more than the weight of the aircraft - in the cruise, of course, when everything should be in balance, lift and weight will be equal. The shape of an aerofoil viewed from above is known as its *planform*, and it could be *rectangular*, *tapered* (from root to tip), *elliptical*, *delta* or *swept back*. Large, wide aerofoils, for example, are good for large transport aircraft, and short, stubby ones will be found on fast sports aircraft.

The *aspect ratio* of a wing is the relationship between its length and width, or *span* and *chord* (actually the square of the span divided by the wing area). You could have two aerofoils of equal surface area but different aspect ratios, depending on what they were designed for. The higher the ratio (the longer the wing relative to its width), the more lift you get, with *less* induced drag at the *tips*, but the wings are not so stiff and are best used at low speeds. Glider wings have high aspect ratios.

The *chord line* is the *straight* line joining the leading and trailing edges of an aerofoil. The curvature over the top is commonly called the *camber*, although technically the term refers to the distance between the chord line and the *mean camber line*, which is drawn midway between the upper and lower surfaces, so it will still be curved anyway, unless the aerofoil is symmetrical. *The camber line of a biconvex symmetrical section is common with the chord line.*

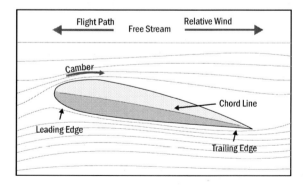

Thickness is a measure of the greatest distance between the chord and mean camber line, and the Thickness/Chord ratio of an aerofoil section is expressed in *percentage of chord*.

Increasing the camber on the upper surface will make the air speed up more over it. The camber is there to minimise drag, or smooth things out a bit, as there would otherwise be severe vortices above if the aerofoil were a flat plate.

The complete force produced by an aerofoil is the *total reaction*, which can be split into two vectors, called *lift*, which acts at right angles to the airflow, and *drag*, which acts parallel to it.

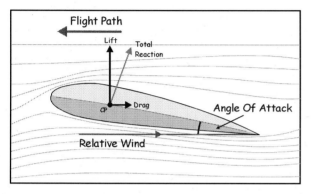

In the diagram below, the thrust and lift vectors are longer than those for their opposites, weight and drag, so you will fly forwards and upwards (the lift vector also has to combat a slight tail down force which helps with stability). You will also notice that the lift/weight and thrust/drag vectors are offset from each other. This is to create *couples* around the lateral axis (i.e. across the aircraft) to produce pitching moments when lift and thrust are taken away (as with an engine failure), placing the machine in the correct attitude. They will be balanced in normal flight by forces produced by the tailplane, so there will be an extra down force from the rear when in flight. If an aircraft has a low thrust line (that is, below the drag line), an increase in thrust results in a nose pitch up moment, which will reduce the stalling speed to a lower figure. This is because the pitch up moment assists the tailplane with the force generated by a forward C of G (it is similar to moving the C of G to the rear). The tailplane workload is reduced, so stalling speed is decreased.

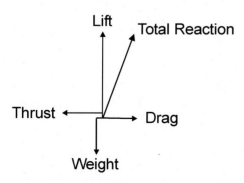

Angle Of Attack

The *angle of attack* is the angle at which the aerofoil meets the air, or, more technically, at which the chord line (the straight one that joins the leading edge with the trailing edge) meets the relative airflow - do not confuse it with the *angle of incidence*, where the chord line meets the longitudinal axis, which is a *mechanical angle* as opposed to an aerodynamic angle, and is discussed further in AGK.

You can either fly at a high speed with a small angle of attack, or a slow speed with a high one, up to the accepted maximum of around 15° but, as the angle of attack increases, there is more frontage to the airflow, increasing drag markedly, and lift decreases again.

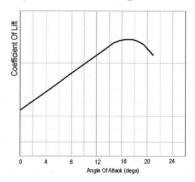

By changing the angle of attack (through the position of the aerofoil), you can control lift, airspeed and drag.

Stalling

The stall is a condition where an aerofoil cannot support an aircraft in the air (although, to be technical, lift is still being produced, but it is not enough). It always happens at the same angle of attack. The *stalling angle* is that *above which* the aerofoil stalls, or above the point at which lift is at its maximum. Although lift is still being produced after that angle, the aerofoil has a hard time producing it, and it is not enough to support the aircraft.

As mentioned before, the accepted maximum angle of attack is about 15°. After that, the air flowing round the aerofoil breaks up badly, making it unable to create enough lift, as well as creating large amounts of drag. The reason the stall happens in the first place is because the air under heavier pressure underneath the wing finds it easier to creep *forwards* over the upper surface from the trailing edge as the angle against the relative airflow increases.

In other words, boundary layer separation is produced from the *adverse pressure gradient*, when the low energy air flows in the *reverse* direction to the free stream, from where it forces itself under the normal airflow and makes it separate from the upper surface. At the trailing edge the air curls round and tries to force itself under the lower pressure air that is rushing towards it. This is made easier as the aerofoil assumes a more vertical position approaching the stall (if you were to attach some wool to the trailing edge, you would see it point *forwards*, well before the stall).

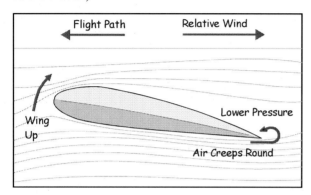

The probability of this happening increases with angle of attack and Mach number, so if the Mach number is high, the relevant angle of attack will be lower.

As the aerofoil comes into the stall, it starts to pitch down as the airflow starts to react about the midpoint of the lower surface instead of at 25% of chord.

ANGLE OF ATTACK (ALPHA) SENSORS

Although the stalling TAS may vary (from weight, load factor and power), a wing will always stall at the same angle of attack (*Alpha*). Because speeds are often an imprecise measure of attitude, the Alpha angle is used instead on military and jet transport aircraft (and by the Wright Brothers). It is also used by flight control computers and the aircraft data recorder.

VANE SENSORS

These are vanes that line up with relative airflow, clear of wash from wings or engine pods, usually one on each side of the nose. Their position relative to zero alpha is measured by a transponder and sent to the flight systems.

PRESSURE SENSORS

These are aerofoil sections with pressure measuring holes symmetrically above and below the leading edge. The chord line is at zero alpha, so the difference in recorded pressure between the upper and lower sets is the angle of arrival of the airflow. A pressure transducer changes this to electronic data and calculates alpha (you could also use the pressure differential to move a paddle in a box, with paddle position converted to alpha electronically).

Centre Of Pressure

The *Centre of Pressure* (CP) is a theoretical point on the chord line through which the resultant of all forces (i.e. the total reaction) is said to act. It moves forward steadily as the angle of attack increases, until just before the stalling angle, when it moves rapidly backwards. The range can be as much as 25% of the chord length. However, while being easier and cheaper to make, symmetrical aerofoils generally produce less lift than asymmetric ones, as well as having less than desirable stall characteristics. The reason the CP is at about 25% of chord is that more lift is generated near the leading edge than at the trailing edge.

The Centre of Gravity is an imaginary point around which the aircraft is balanced, and the aft limit of the safe range is normally just forward of the C of P anyway. The forward limit is determined by how much stability and how high a stalling speed you want. If the C of G is too far forward, the couple between it and the C of P will be long enough to produce a large nose down pitch from the lift/weight vectors. There will then be a longer distance between the C of G and the elevator, which will tend to make the machine longitudinally overstable (see *Stability*, below), meaning that you will need more control input to pull the column back on landing, and you may run out of range. For optimum fuel efficiency, though, it should be somewhere near the aft limit, because less tail-down force is required, and a lower angle of attack, and less drag. For more about the C of G, see *Flight Planning*.

A wing always stalls at the same angle of attack, but stall speed varies in proportion to aircraft weight (thus, if you pull out of a dive, you artificially make the machine heavier, so stall speed increases). With a jet, the stall angle of attack is essentially the same with power on or off, as prop wash can delay separation because it re-energises the boundary flow, at least at the wing roots.

Light aircraft base their stall speed on V_{SO} and V_{S1}. Heavier ones use a reference stall speed, V_{SR}, which is defined by the manufacturer, and which may not be less than a 1G stall speed. It must also be at least 2 kts or 2%, whichever is greater, above the speed that any device that pushes the nose down operates (e.g. a stick pusher). In either case, the stall warning is supposed to come on 6 kts before the stall.

To start off with, a wing is placed at an angle on the airframe called the *angle of incidence*, which is purely a figure out of the designer's head, although there are advantages in having it as small as possible, in that you can improve visibility and reduce drag in the cruise because the nose will not be so high (in practice, it is set at the best *lift/drag ratio*, or the point when you get the most lift for the least drag). This angle may vary throughout the length of the wing, being maximum at the root and minimum at the end, in a process called *washout* (or *washin* if you go the other way. The difference is that the former decreases lift and the latter increases it). The angle of incidence changes this way because the outer edges of the wing (or propeller, which acts on the same principle) will be moving faster than the rest in some manoeuvres (a turn, for example), creating more lift and stress. In addition, washout allows the outer parts of the wing to still be creating lift at slower speeds when the inner edges are stalled, as they might be when landing. You can get a similar effect by changing the *shape* of the wing from root to tip. In short, with washout, the angle of incidence at the wing tips is less than at the root, resulting in a gradual torsional twist. The tips now reach their stall angle of attack later, when the inboard sections of the wing do. Too much washout may zero or negative lift at small alpha angles, as when in the cruise.

Note: Other ways of stopping wing tips stalling too early include having the outboard sections of leading edge devices extend automatically within certain alpha values, to re-energise the flow over the top surface of the wing immediately aft of them, which delays the breakup of the streamline flow until more inboard areas have stalled (it also improves outboard aileron effectiveness near the stall). *Wing fences* inhibit the spanwise flow of air out toward the tips by effectively splitting the wing into two sections, isolating their effects from each other. They produce a trailing vortex that rotates in the opposite direction to the usual wing tip trailing vortex, which scours away the local boundary layer (see below). The *Saw Tooth* (or *Dog Tooth*) does the same by producing a sudden change in chord length as a notch at the leading edge (that is, the end of the wing suddenly juts forward), as used on military jets such as the F4 Phantom. *Vortilons* are small fences under the leading edge that shed vortices like a wing fence does. Engine pylons can do this. *Vortex Generators* are small vertical plates that rise above the wing surface to re-energise the boundary layer and inhibit the outward flow of the boundary layer. *Shark teeth* are found on near the root, on inner leading edges within the stagnation region at normal pitch attitudes. They stick out into the upper airflow, causing turbulence, and stall the inner wing section before the tips.

Bernoulli's Theorem

Put simply, to produce lift, the airflow will hit the underside of an aerofoil, to be forced downwards, forcing the aerofoil up, which is similar to carrying a large piece of plywood in a strong wind. That the air flows downwards can easily be proven by flying low over some ground fog or a field full of wavy crops, where you will see a disturbance that can only have come from downflowing air. However, this is a bit of a brute force solution, so the aerofoil will also be shaped to help things along, taking advantage of the *venturi effect*, which is credited to *Daniel Bernoulli*, and which is a principle made use of in carburettors and air-driven instruments. Bernoulli found that the pressure of a fluid decreases where its speed increases or, in other words, *in the streamline flow of an ideal fluid, the quantity of energy remains constant,* and a change in speed results in an opposite change in pressure, so a reduction in one means a balancing increase in the other, and *vice versa.* Bernoulli's theorem is a statement of the conservation of energy, and fluid flow increases in direct inverse proportion to the reduction in area that it has to flow through (notice how water will flow faster if you squeeze the end of a hose). Thus, the total amount of energy remains constant, although its form may change.

If you take a tube with a smaller diameter at its centre than at either end, and blow air through it, the pressure in the centre becomes less because the speed increases and the pressure decreases. In this case, the air forced around the obstructions in the middle has to increase speed because it is taking a longer path to keep up with the rest, and the pressure at that point decreases. On an oil rig, or any similar system involving lots of piping, the decreased pressure can be used to operate a switch or a valve.

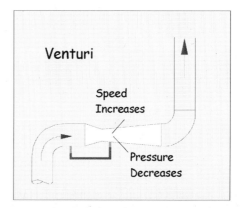

If you take the top half of the above-mentioned tube away, the phenomenon still works on the remaining (lower) half, which looks like the top surface of an aerofoil (a layer of undisturbed air is supposed to replace the missing part of the tube). You can see this yourself by taking a large piece of paper and folding it back over the top of your hand, keeping hold of it with your fingers. If you blow across the top, the paper will rise. Similarly, a high wind will lift the roof from a house rather than blow it off. Used sideways, this is how yachts use the wind to get along. The aerofoil will therefore have a natural tendency to go up or, looked at another way, to pull air down, to the low pressure area on the top and help the brute force effect.

Note, however, that this applies to *subsonic air*, which is assumed to be incompressible, so such pressure changes can take place without apparent changes in density. Also, this is a closed system, and assumed to be frictionless. If it were not, the same molecules of air have no incentive to meet up at the other end - those taking the longer route may be up to 30% of the distance away from their original fellows, depending on the angle of attack, and therein lies a problem, in that there is then no reason for the pressure to reduce, but we shall be returning to this shortly. For exam purposes, since *the speed of the flowing air (on top of the aerofoil) is increased, its pressure is reduced.*

This system also pulls fuel into a carburettor, and it's also the reason why a door closes by itself if left slightly ajar - there is less pressure in the gap between it and the door frame as the air moves through it. As the Titanic was proceeding at high speed, it may also have invoked the venturi effect to pull the iceberg towards it.

Just to reinforce the point - as air flows round an obstruction and does not pile up against it (like sand would), the same mass must flow away as flows towards it. As the obstruction makes the distance longer, the flow must accelerate to keep up, exchanging *potential energy* for the *kinetic energy* of movement. The reduction in potential energy shows up as a reduction in pressure.

Note the *stagnation point* at the *point of impact* just under the leading edge, where air molecules are given the choice of going over or under an aerofoil, so between the top and bottom edges, there is only a difference of one molecule. In terms of laminar flow, the molecule that is sent under just goes with the flow and is held against the wing by air pressure. The one that goes over the top, however, tends to get pulled away by the lower pressure, and has a harder time keeping next to the surface. This is not helped by the dents, scratches, rivets and generally rough surface of the average working aerofoil, which help give it a bumpier ride. The creation of circulation in the first place is sometimes called the *Magnus Effect*, which is a mechanically induced circulation familiar to golfers, where lift can be generated by a spinning ball.

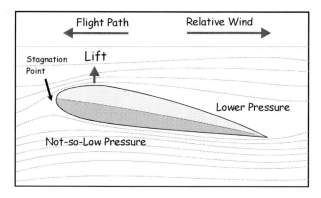

The pressure at the stagnation point is *static + dynamic pressure*, the components of *total pressure*. In fact, Bernoulli's equation can be written like this, where *pt* = total pressure, *ps* = static pressure and *q* = dynamic pressure:

$$pt = ps + q$$

Of course, all this can be proved mathematically. In physics, the formula for kinetic energy (that arising from movement, and measured in Joules) is:

$$\tfrac{1}{2}\text{Mass} \times V^2$$

Where *V* stands for *Velocity*. That is, the faster an object of a given weight moves, the more kinetic energy it has (remember the formula's derivation from calculus). In aerodynamics, we know that air has mass, because it consists of molecules that can exert pressure (against your hand in a wind, for example), so we can replace *Mass* in the formula above with *air density*, which uses the Greek symbol *rho*:

$$\tfrac{1}{2}\rho V^2$$

The more dense the air is, the more molecules that are available to push against an object. Combine that with speed, and you get *dynamic pressure*, which is represented by the above formula. Given that the total pressure is constant, if you increase the speed, the dynamic pressure will automatically increase, provided density remains constant. Therefore, static pressure will decrease (total pressure - dynamic pressure = static pressure). The abbreviation for the above formula is the symbol **q**.

Around two thirds of the total lift is said to come from the reduced pressure effect across the top of an aerofoil, not forgetting the less-reduced (therefore higher) pressure underneath. That is, the pressure above a wing is a *lot* lower than ambient pressure, and that below is *only slightly* lower, although they are signified by - and +, respectively. For exam purposes, half the lift from a wing is typically produced in the first ¼ of the chord length.

FURTHER DISCUSSION

The above is the dumbed-down official explanation of how an aerofoil produces lift, and the one expected by the examiners, but it doesn't explain how a plane will fly inverted, or how super-thin wings generate so much lift, or how it is that the rotor blade that invariably goes up the quickest out of your reach when you want to tie them down is the one with the wind blowing *backwards* over it! In short, there is something missing. If you feel you might be confused by the next few paragraphs, come back to it after you've passed your exams ☺.

The reason why air flows faster over the top of a wing, especially since the molecules don't meet up with the ones they started with, is that it speeds up *because* the pressure is lower, and not the other way around - Bernoulli's process may start things off, but something else must take over.

For example, the length of the path taken by air flowing over the top of the wing of a Cessna 172 is only about 1.5% greater than it is under the wing, so only about 2% of the needed lift would be developed at 65 mph (indeed, 2% is the figure calculated by aircraft modellers as to the *complete contribution* to lift from Bernoulli).

On those figures, it would appear that the minimum speed for the wing to develop enough lift to keep the 172 in the air is over 400 mph, or, looked at another way, the path length over the wing would have to increase by 50% if you kept the same speed. The wing would then be as thick as it is wide!

What's more likely to be happening is that the air bending around the top of the wing (because it is speeding up) is pulling the air above it into the vacuum, sucking air from the front of the wing and shooting it down and back toward the trailing edge. It is therefore the top surface of the wing that is the critical part, and the force we call "lift" is really the opposite of the downward trend of the air.

So how does the wing divert the air downwards?

There are three possible explanations for this. One is that, as the air hits the leading edge of the aerofoil, it is forced upwards and compressed. This *upwash* is therefore at a higher pressure, so there is a differential between the leading and trailing edges, which will assist with the acceleration of air from front to back (notice that the new angle created by the upwash will tend to produce a lower true angle of attack).

Secondly, in 1910, Henri Coanda built an aircraft which used an air compressor powered by a reciprocating engine. He injected fuel into the compressed air and obtained an afterburner which provided thrust. Metal plates were installed to deflect the exhaust flames away from the plywood fuselage, but they drew the flames toward themselves instead. Theodor Von Karmen, one of the foremost aerodynamics theorists of the time, at the University of Gottingen, realised that this was a new discovery and named it the *Coanda effect*. Coanda later found that a sheet of fluid discharged through a slit onto an extended and rounded lip will attach itself to the curved surface and follow its contour, and that a shoulder made of a series of short flat surfaces, at specified angles to each other and with a certain length, can bend a jet stream around a 180° arc. This is in keeping with Newton's laws, which also dictate that an attractional force exists between all masses, which gets stronger as the masses are increased, and weaker as the distance between them increases, although the bodies concerned do not automatically move towards each other, as they may be prevented from doing so by other forces that are greater. In addition, the deflected airstream *sucks up air from the surroundings* - as the jet flowed around the shoulder, it pulled in up to 20 times the amount of air in the original jet.

Thus, a stream of air (or other fluid) coming from a nozzle tends to follow a nearby curved or flat surface, if it is gentle, which is why teapots tend to dump their contents anywhere but in the cup if you pour slowly.

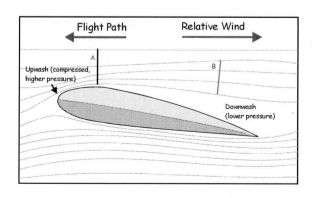

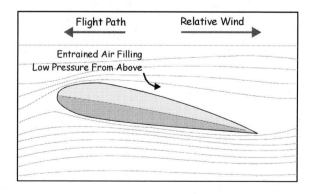

© Phil Croucher, 2007

The fluid follows the curved surface on top because of *viscosity*, or *resistance to flow* (remember the boundary layer, above). The viscosity of air is small but it is there, and enough for air molecules to want to stick to the surface of a wing, as is proved by the water in the car wash, or the dust sticking across the Atlantic.

Thirdly, an aerofoil produces wingtip vortices that curl inwards from the edge as the higher pressure from underneath the wing interacts with the lower pressure air from above, to produce a downward flow on the inside that is stronger at the wingtips than at the root (NASA).

FORCES IN FLIGHT

The four forces acting on an aerofoil are *Lift* & *Weight* (mentioned above), and *Thrust* & *Drag*. The parts of each pair oppose each other, and must be balanced for straight and level flight. In an aeroplane, they would resolve into something like this diagram:

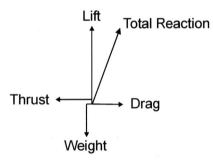

Where the points of action do not correspond, a couple is created that will affect the aircraft attitude. The aeroplane will rotate about the C of G.

Lift

Lift is "generated" when a mass of air is accelerated downwards. You could therefore argue that it is not a force, but a *reaction*. With reference to an aerofoil, Lift is said to act through the *Centre of Pressure* at 90° to its drag and the relative wind. You can increase lift in four ways, in this order:

- Increase speed for more reaction over the top surface

- Increase the angle of attack (up to the stalling point)

- Increase the lift producing areas

- Fly in denser air (that is, fly lower, or in a colder air mass)

As mentioned, the Centre of Pressure is a theoretical point where the aerodynamic forces are supposed to act (it's the equivalent of the C of G for the whole aircraft), and its position varies with the angle of attack. It's usually around 25% of the way from the leading edge, but it moves *forward* as the angle of attack is increased. With an unsymmetrical aerofoil, upper surface lift can act through a different point than lower surface lift, which causes the CP to move or, rather, produces a couple, since there will be a Centre of Pressure for the upper and lower surfaces. In a symmetrical aerofoil, the two vectors tend to be opposite each other. Forward movement of the CP is regarded as unstable, while rearward movement is stable.

Note: The CP's most forward point is just before the stalling angle, and airflow is at its maximum velocity at the CP in level flight. The *aerodynamic centre* is the point on the chord line about which no change in pitching moment is felt when the angle of attack changes, or where all the reactions in streamlined flow, including lift, drag and pitching or twisting forces are concentrated - it is fixed as long as the airflow is streamlined, as opposed to the CP, which is an older term and more theoretical. The aerodynamic centre and the Centre of Pressure must remain as close to the feathering axis (see *AGK*) as possible to stop the blade being forced to bounce around and affect the controls.

LIFT FORMULA

You will not be surprised to hear there is a formula for calculating lift, which is:

$$L = C_L (\tfrac{1}{2}\rho V^2) S$$

where:

- L=Lift

- C_L = the *coefficient of lift*, or the product of aerofoil design (shape) and angle of attack, or relative pressure distribution. In other words, its ability to deflect air, so this can vary between aerofoils. The coefficient will be at its maximum at, or just before, the stall, which you can see from the formula - if it (C_L) increases on one side, the other side (L) will increase also, until lift can no longer be produced. Similarly, reducing speed (V) will decrease lift (L). Thus, to keep the same lift, you have to change the angle of attack (C_L) if you change the speed, and *vice versa*. A symmetrical aerofoil, when in line with the RAF, will provide no lift, or, rather, *when the angle of attack is zero, the C_L will be zero.* Unsymmetrical aerofoils, on the other hand, might produce lift at a zero angle of attack or even at negative pitch

- The ½ is either there to represent the average of a body's velocity between the start and end of its travels, or is part of the results of integration

- ρ (rho) = air density

- V = TAS. True Airspeed depends on Indicated Airspeed (IAS) and air density, which decreases with altitude, so you need a higher TAS to get the same lift as you go up. The aircraft encounters less resistance, or drag, in front of and around it. In a descent, the increasing *rho* makes the air more dense, so you get more drag, more friction, and the machine decelerates. Thus, TAS could be viewed as a function of the resistance found when flying in the air. If the angle of attack does not change, other things being equal, lift varies with the square of the IAS, that is, if airspeed doubles, lift is multiplied by 4 (if you double IAS in level flight, C_L will be 0.25)

- S = the surface area. Aeroplanes use flaps and slots, etc. to increase the wing area

Weight

The opposite of lift, and a force acting through the Centre of Gravity. In a climb, this will acquire a rearward component which is below, parallel to and in the same direction as drag, and must be added to it. Notice that, because of the geometry, in a straight, steady climb, lift is less than weight, which must be compensated for with power (the load factor also becomes less than 1, something like 0.98). In fact, in a vertical climb, lift is zero, because you are replacing it with engine thrust.

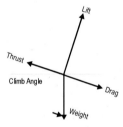

Thrust

The force that makes the aircraft move through the air, and the opposite of....

Drag

You could use a specially designed thin wing called a *laminar flow aerofoil* with a later transition point. It has a more pointed leading edge and is nearly symmetrical, being thickest about halfway across (50% chord, if you want to be technical). One disadvantage is that the transition point moves more rapidly forward when it stalls.

Anyhow, back to drag, which is a force that tends to slow an aircraft down, acting in the opposite direction to thrust, parallel to the relative airflow. As it retards motion and increases fuel consumption, it also affects range, endurance and maximum speed. In order of priority, drag can be split up into various components:

- **Induced Drag**. Sometimes called *Vortex Drag* or *Lift Dependent Drag* (LDD), this comes from the air's reaction to the aerofoil, or is induced from the creation of lift, when air at different pressures mixes at the trailing edge, so it comes from lift-producing surfaces (wings) and varies with angle of attack, so the slower the aerofoil is moving, the more induced drag you will get, because you have to shift more air in a shorter distance (however, *if no lift is induced, there is no induced drag*. Similarly, *the more lift there is, the more induced drag there is*). It may come from tip vortices, for example, and is inversely proportional to the square of the velocity, that is to say, halving air velocity increases induced drag four times. Tip vortices make up a considerable portion of induced drag, which is reduced by increasing airspeed, using long, narrow wings (with high *aspect ratios*), or by reducing the lift coefficient, which itself can be done with washout or design. In addition to distributing lift more evenly, *washout* reduces the angle of attack at the tips, which reduces induced drag (it can also be reduced by *taper, camber* or *aspect ratio*). In the picture below, you will notice a slight difference in angle between the upwash and downwash (*A* and *B*), which is the amount of induced drag.

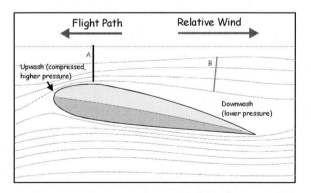

Induced Drag increases as an aircraft pulls out of ground effect on takeoff, as the ground will interfere with vortex formation, and can be affected by the aspect ratio of the wing.

Winglets are small vertical aerofoils on the wingtip that cut down induced drag by reducing the area of the wing tip affected by vortices - side forces make  the wing span larger at the expense of a small increase in form drag (winglets are actually a compromise between gaining extra lift and making sure the wings don't hit the hangar doors). The fences at the tip reduce the spill of high pressure air beneath the wing to the lower pressure above. They also create two smaller vortices (at the base and the tip), instead of one big one, for less drag and wake turbulence. They are most effective at low speed and high alpha, where induced drag is highest, and during the cruise when heavy with fuel and angle of attack is greater. They improve the range of long-range aircraft (like the 747-400) more than short-range commuter jets, but the 777 doesn't need them.

In fact, any method of stopping vortices from being generated by air spilling over wing tips improves efficiency - these may include wing tip tanks, wing tip plates, or droop tips (a tip tank raises and drops the wingtip at the same time). In other words, to reduce induced drag, the *effective* span must be greater than the *actual* span. In summary, induced drag varies with Taper, Sweepback, Altitude, Aspect Ratio, Angle of Attack, and Speed. It arises from making air accelerate to cause a differential pressure above and below the wing as well as wing tip spillage, so it all starts with Camber.

- **Parasite Drag** comes from anything moving through the air that is not actually creating lift, like the fuselage or undercarriage. Unlike induced drag, it *increases* with speed (the square of the velocity - see *Profile Drag*, below) and consists of:

  - **Interference Drag**, or the result of the interaction between components and the fuselage. In other words, if you added the various types of drag together, the result would be less than the total - interference drag is the difference

  - **Profile Drag** (or *zero lift drag*) consists partly of **Form Drag**, which results from the shape

of any body moving through the air, due to eddies formed when the streamline flow is disturbed - a flat piece of wood held perpendicular to the airflow is a good example. It is the backward force created by the difference between the stagnation point at the leading edge of the aerofoil and the lower pressure at the trailing edge. Form drag is minimised by *streamlining*. **Skin Friction** (or *surface friction drag*) is also a factor. Profile Drag is also called *Pressure Drag*, and in some books is often used to mean *parasite drag*

Aileron Drag, from downgoing ailerons, causes a yaw in the opposite direction to the bank. *Wave drag* comes from shock waves in high speed flight, from energy drag and boundary layer separation (the energy for a temperature rise across a shockwave is a drag on the aircraft).

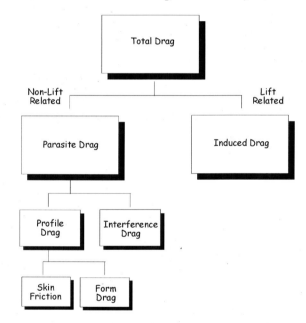

The best shape for a streamlined body is not sharp at the front, but rounded at the front and sharp at the rear so that the airflow behind does not separate.

DRAG FORMULA

Guess what? There's a formula for drag, too, which is similar to that for lift:

$$D = C_D (\tfrac{1}{2}\rho V^2) S$$

Drag will also increase with speed, although it is virtually unchanged with altitude (that is, it does decrease, given the same angle of attack, but you need more lift at height, so more angle of attack, and more drag).

Note: The V^2 factor takes it out of all proportion once you get out of the low speed regime - an aircraft at 150 kts encounters 100 times the drag found at 15 kts. This "square law" means that small increases in speed need larger amounts of thrust.

C_D, being the drag coefficient, represents the potential of a body to interfere with smooth airflow over it. Like with lift, shape is the most important factor, not size, and the angle of attack must also be considered. Otherwise, the remainder of the formula works as it does for lift.

LIFT/DRAG RATIO

Induced and Parasite drag are products of angle of attack, and they both vary with it. The airspeed where drag is at a minimum can be seen from a graph which compares total drag to parasite and induced drag.

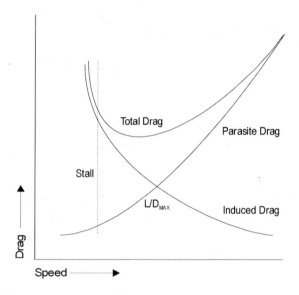

You can see that, as speed increases, parasite drag increases, but as speed reduces, *induced drag increases* (thus, both ways increase total drag). Since the lift is remaining the same, the lowest point on the total drag curve, near where they cross, is the best lift/drag ratio, or L/D_{MAX}. The amount of lift you get against the cost of the drag is used to determine the efficiency of an aerofoil for particular angles of attack, so you can calculate such items as max cruising or gliding ranges. Since C_D and C_L are involved, we are really talking about the shape and angle attack of the aerofoil, respectively. The shape will stay constant, so the L/D ratio changes as a function of the angle of attack.

The speed range below L/D_{MAX} in a jet is the *speed unstable regime*. That above it is the *speed stable regime*. Jets,

unfortunately, make their approaches in the former, because they have a higher V_{MD} (minimum drag speed), but this is eased by using flap, which reduces V_{MD} by moving total drag to the left (more parasite drag - flap increases parasite drag more than it does induced drag). The two regimes actually refer to speed and the power required to maintain it. In the speed stable regime, power is added to increase speed, as normal. In the speed unstable regime, however, power has to be added to maintain a *slower* speed, and there is less of a tendency to return to trim speed anyway, so control movements must be more precise (if airspeed increases, there is an excess of power and speed will increase even more - if it decreases, there is not enough power and the aircraft will tend to a further decrease). However, parasite drag is a function of speed, and induced drag arises from the angle of attack. If you increase weight, induced drag increases because you need a higher angle of attack to maintain the same speed (there will be little change with parasite drag). This moves the total drag curve to the right, increasing V_{MD}. So, if induced drag increases, V_{MD} happens at a higher speed, and if parasite drag increases, it occurs at a lower speed.

Tip: At V_{MD}, profile drag equals induced drag. You can use this to work out fuel flow if you remember that induced drag is proportional to the square of the weight. For example, if aircraft weight reduces by a factor of (say) .9, you would square that and reduce induced drag by the answer (profile drag does not change with mass), which is .81. Thus total drag becomes 99.19, which is a factor you can apply to fuel flow.

Then again, if you get a question like this:

> Two identical aircraft are flying at the same speed and altitude and have the same SFC. If aircraft 1 has a mass of 130000 Kg and a gross fuel flow of 4300 Kg/ hour, what is the gross fuel flow of aircraft 2 if the mass is 115000 Kg?

You could probably solve it with a simultaneous equation, or do something with proportion on your flight computer. The answer is 3804 Kg.

The drag curve is plotted against *Equivalent Airspeed* (EAS), which is IAS with pressure sensing errors and compressibility thrown in, which at V_{MD} is insignificant anyway, so the curve will not change with altitude or temperature. Increasing EAS increases the mass of air affected by the wing and the time during which it is affected by the wing, which reduces wingtip vortex strength and induced drag. Ice reduces lift and increases parasite drag. *Ground effect* (which you get within about one wingspan of the ground) results in more lift because it reduces induced drag (by reducing wingtip vortices), and explains why you need a higher angle of attack as you fly out of it on takeoff.

Power required is equal to Drag x TAS, but V_{MD} produces the lowest drag, not the lowest *power required* (V_{MP}), which is lower. Best glide endurance thus occurs at V_{MP} (for the minimum sink rate, but best glide range gives minimum glide angle).

POWER REQUIRED

If you climb at a constant IAS, you must increase TAS to maintain it, therefore power required increases as you climb. This comes from the formula:

```
Power Required = Drag x TAS
```

It derives from the fact that *Power* (the rate of doing *Work*) is equal to *Force* x *Distance* (i.e. Work) divided by *Time*.

See also *Fuel Management* in the *Performance* chapter.

SUMMARY

Parasite Drag only varies with speed and is directly proportional to V^2. So if a question asks you how much parasite (or profile) drag increases if speed is increased by 10%, you will know how to figure it out (10% is the same as multiplying by 1.1, which squared is 1.21, so drag increases by 21%).

Induced Drag varies with Lift, Speed and Aspect Ratio, is inversely proportional to Aspect Ratio and V^2 (so multiply by $1/V^2$), and directly proportional to $Lift^2/C_L^2/Weight^2$.

STABILITY

The stability characteristics of an aircraft describe its ability to return to its flight path after a disturbance without input from the controls. The *static stability* is the *initial* tendency (and essentially concerns one oscillation), while the *dynamic stability* concerns the *overall*, or long-term, tendency, after a series of oscillations - having one type of stability does not necessarily lead to the other, although you cannot have dynamic stability without static stability. Its significance lies not just with you nudging controls by accident, but in turbulence, which has the most to do with knocking your machine off its flight path. Stability and controllability are opposite sides of the same coin - the more of one you have, the less of the other you get.

If *positive stability* is a tendency to return to the flight path, *negative stability* tends to move it further away in increasing movements.

You could then say the aircraft is unstable. This could be a problem when the increasing oscillations lead you to stall or dive. A badly placed C of G can make a previously stable aircraft unstable. *Neutral stability* occurs where the oscillations are constant around the original flight path, or the aircraft stays in whatever new attitude it ends up in. Most aeroplanes have positive static stability in pitch and yaw, and are near-neutral in roll.

Stability in the pitching, rolling and yawing planes translates to *longitudinal*, *lateral* and *directional*.

Longitudinal Stability

This will be affected when a vertical gust hits you and causes a pitching moment affecting stability around the *lateral* axis. The Centre of Gravity (the imaginary point around which the aircraft is balanced) is designed to be ahead of the centre of pressure, to make the plane nose heavy so that, without engine power, the machine adopts the correct gliding attitude. In the cruise, the tailplane's negative lift balances this tendency, so it's the primary source of stability in pitch, with the C of G as a close second - as it (the C of G) moves aft, the aircraft becomes the less stable in roll and pitch. Stability in pitch is therefore a function of the tailplane - if the nose pitches up, it should produce enough lift to put the nose down again, and *vice versa*.

A forward C of G shift increases stability.

Lateral Stability

This makes you *roll* when hit by a gust from the side. You get it if the wings are not level across their span.

The *dihedral* is the angle between the wings and the horizontal, looked at from the front, where the wingtips are higher than the roots. It is supposed to enhance stability in the roll plane (lateral) - if the flight path is disturbed, and you sideslip, the lower wing produces more lift to restore level flight because of the increased angle of attack. If you had your hands on the controls all the time, of course, like the Wright Brothers, you wouldn't need it.

In fact, the term dihedral is commonly used instead of *lateral dihedral*. Longitudinal dihedral refers to the relationship between the angles of incidence of the wing and tailplane (or *canard*), which contribute to longitudinal stability.

Anhedral is the opposite, where the tips of the wings are lower in the horizontal than the roots (see left). Anhedral *reduces* lateral stability. In the Falcon, where it is used on the tailplane, it improves low speed flying qualities by reducing the effect of wing downwash.

In a high wing aircraft, the keel effect of the fuselage acts like a pendulum to pull it back to normal. *Sweepback* also helps, and is discussed under *High Speed Flight*, but it increases lateral stability, making the aircraft behave as if it had a greater degree of dihedral.

Directional Stability

This comes from fins, and makes you *yaw* when hit by a gust from the side. A sweptback wing also affects this, when one wing presents a longer leading edge to the airflow if the aircraft is yawed, producing more drag on the opposite side of the yaw and slowing it down, yawing it back. The fin acts like a weathercock to keep the aircraft straight - if it yaws, the surface is struck more from the side to force the nose back.

One reason for the roll from using the rudder by itself is the dihedral effect, otherwise known as the *secondary effect of rudder*, if you remember your instructor's lessons, or *rolling moment due to sideslip*. The wing on the outside of the turn goes faster, produces more lift and goes up, to start the roll. Sweepback increases lateral stability, making the aircraft behave as if it had a greater degree of dihedral.

Dutch Roll

A combined effect of disturbing the yaw and roll axes, with more roll than yaw (if it were the other way round, it would be called *snaking*). It occurs when lateral stability is stronger than directional stability.

Essentially, the machine rolls in one direction and yaws in another - but the roll happens before the yaw when a sideslip happens. In a sideslip, the effective span of the wings is changed and the forward one creates more lift for a short time, because it presents more of a span to the airflow than the other. This makes it rise, hence the roll. However, the increased lift also creates more drag to pull the wing back, starting an oscillation. A dorsal or ventral fin will reduce Dutch Roll by increasing directional stability and lateral *dynamic* stability while decreasing lateral *static* stability.

Spiral Stability

If you release the controls in a turn, the machine will either wind into the turn or come out of it by itself, indicating negative or positive spiral stability, respectively.

MANOEUVRES

Note: As this book is also meant to be of some help to instructors, these discussions mostly concern small aircraft, as used on the average flight test.

Taxi

Before you get to take off, you have to get from where you are to the runway, and return when you land. The "roads" that get you there are called *taxiways*, and they are usually identified with letters, such as *Taxiway Alpha*, or *Taxiway Bravo*, etc. You will be told the sequence to use when you first get clearance from ATC to start moving. The clearance may involve crossing a runway or two to get to the one you want - you should still check to see that nobody is using them! Clearance to *enter* your runway is entirely separate - *taxi* clearance is only to get you there.

To get started, you may need what seems like a lot of power, but this will reduce to a very small amount once the wheels start rolling. The first thing you do then is test the brakes with a small dab on the toe pedals, and bring the machine to a stop.

Once under way, the machine will want to head into wind - it is only held straight by friction from the tyres, but you can help by positioning the controls. Moving the control column into the wind direction deflects the ailerons so that they help control direction. A high wing aircraft with the wind coming from one of the rear quarters (SW, SE, etc.) should also have its elevators down (i.e. control column forward), but this is also true to a lesser extent for other aircraft. On a rough surface, pull the control column back, to protect the prop.

It is usual to initiate a turn to the left and right, if there is no opportunity to do so anyway, to check the instruments. The artificial horizon should always be level, and the compass and DGI increasing and decreasing according to the turn. The needle and ball (or turn coordinator) should also indicate the correct direction.

Try not to use the brakes to turn - you should be able to use the rudder pedals by themselves. Wearing out the brakes costs money, and you don't want to do this unnecessarily. Use them smoothly at all times. It is considered to be bad practice to use high power to taxi, and use the brakes to slow you down. A brisk walking pace is recommended. If you do use a brake to turn, the inside wheel should not be stationary, or the tyres will wear.

Takeoff

You should normally do this into wind as much as possible, although circumstances sometimes dictate otherwise - check your Flight Manual for the maximum crosswind limits your machine can take, but most can handle 90° of crosswind at 20% of the stalling speed.

Line up on the runway, and check that the compass and DGI show the right numbers. You should not experience any yaw to the left in a nosewheel aircraft unless the nose is lifted, as it would be for a soft field takeoff (it will reduce slightly once the tail comes off the ground in a taildragger). Keep full power on until at least 500 feet off the ground, at best rate of climb speed, unless you have obstacles, in which case use best angle speed.

In a crosswind, position the ailerons as if you were turning into wind, which will stop the wind wing rising. You can reduce this as speed is gained. Once airborne, you must stay airborne (because of the sideways movement if you settle again), and you must come off cleanly in the first place. Then make a coordinated turn into wind, until you have the right heading for the drift.

Where space is limited, you have to accelerate as quickly as possible and configure for a takeoff at slow speed, which means using some degree of flap (check the Flight Manual). To get maximum acceleration, you need maximum power without movement, which means both feet on the brakes. Assuming the power is what the Flight Manual says you should expect, release the brakes gently and raise the nose when you reach the correct liftoff speed.

Another way (used by bush and mountain pilots) is to keep the flaps up during the backtrack, and increase power to get as much speed as possible in the turn. Once you have speed on the takeoff roll, select full flaps and away you go (full flaps create drag, so you want them up as soon as possible - you can do this very slowly while still in ground effect, keeping the nose down).

Soft and rough surfaces need more distance, and the idea is to do as much as possible on solid ground so you can get off without stopping, otherwise you might get stuck. You need the nose high, or at least the weight off the nosewheel, so your liftoff speed will be slower than

normal, close to the stall. Fly level with wheels just off the ground until you have the speed for climbing.

When trying to get over obstacles, be prepared for a change in the wind that may stop you getting over them.

The Circuit

This is not just a way of making sure that everyone follows the same one-way route around an airfield, but also a good exercise in precision flying. The existence of the circuit is the reason why airfields have to be avoided by a minimum distance. In Canada, there are different ways of joining the circuit, depending on whether you need a radio or not for a *Mandatory Frequency* (MF) or *Aerodrome Traffic Frequency* (ATF). Control zones, with control towers, are obviously MF areas, but some lesser ones have only an aerodrome advisory from a Flight Service Station or a remote FSS, and they too are MF areas. In an MF area, everyone must have a radio and be communicating on the MF. Other aerodromes have nothing, or perhaps a UNICOM which has no authority or responsibility. They are not MF areas even though they have some assigned Aerodrome Traffic Frequency for use if you have a radio.

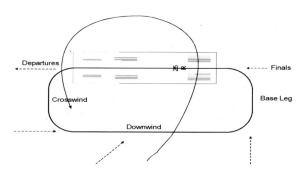

The takeoff phase lasts until 500 feet, where you make a 90° turn crosswind to level off at circuit height (usually 1000 feet, but check, in case they surprise you). Another 90° turn takes you downwind, and you report being on the downwind leg when more or less abeam the tower. You also do your pre-landing checks, but leaving the landing gear for the base leg, which is another 90° turn at the end of downwind.

While in the circuit, keep a good lookout and be very aware of your position relative to other aircraft, adjusting your spacing as necessary. Use the downwind leg to plan your final approach, according to conditions.

Join the circuit either straight into the downwind, or from the upwind (dead) side into mid-downwind (merging level into the downwind leg from the inactive side, having made a descending left-hand turn from at least 500 feet above

DO NOT TRY TO TURN BACK TO THE FIELD IF THE
ENGINE FAILS ON TAKEOFF - LAND STRAIGHT AHEAD.

READ THAT AGAIN.

AND AGAIN.

PRINCIPLES OF FLIGHT
Manoeuvres

circuit height). When crossing the aerodrome to check for landing information (to see the windsock, etc.), you must do so well above circuit height (at least 500' above). With an aerodrome advisory service available inside an MF area, join at 45° into the downwind, on base leg, or directly into final on a slow day.

You leave the circuit straight ahead (terrain permitting). In an MF area you must announce that you are departing the circuit (CAR 602.100). Don't make any turns until clear, after reaching circuit altitude.

Straight and Level

This is the basis of all other flight attitudes - many pilots regard doing it well as a matter of professional pride, which makes sense, as it is where they spend most of their flying life.

Correct small amounts of yaw (less than 10°) with rudder only - larger amounts need aileron as well to prevent rolling. In a similar vein, small changes in altitude are less than 100 feet, for which you can just use the elevator. Larger amounts need power as well.

After initiating a manoeuvre, it will continue unless you centralise the controls, so, having started a turn, for example, return the controls to where they started when you get to the position you want.

Turns

A "proper" turn is one in which the aircraft is in balance, and there are no acceleration forces, unless you are climbing and descending deliberately. That is, there is a constant rate of change of direction, maintaining height, and the forces acting on the machine are in equilibrium. You turn by making the aircraft bank in the required direction with ailerons.

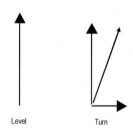

Level   Turn

Having done that, some of the lift force is applied to the turn, so the lift vector is reduced. As you make a turn in the diagram on the right, the original lift vector (on the left) has to be split as a side element is added to pull you into the turn (on the right). The side element is *centripetal force*, which acts towards the centre of the turn. The total lift is the resultant of them both (the diagonal line), but you can see that the vertical lift vector has reduced and needs some of compensation to maintain the lift, or the aircraft will descend.

You must therefore apply some backwards control column movement to force the tail down and the nose up, at the cost of a little speed (if you want to keep the same speed, you must apply power). Thus, you can increase lift by either increasing speed or the angle of attack. There will also be a yawing moment applied the opposite way to the turn, because the upgoing wing has more aileron in the airflow, and is producing more drag to slew the nose round (*adverse aileron yaw*). This will need a little rudder movement to keep the ship straight, although this can be allowed for in modern designs by adjusting the movement of the ailerons, or the shape, like the Frise aileron, which produces a counter drag from a lip that appears underneath the wing when it is moved upwards. You will also need a slight force to stop the machine turning, as the outside wing is moving faster and producing more lift.

The greater the rate of turn, the more the lift must be increased to maintain height, and the more the weight artificially increases to keep the forces balanced, which is one good reason for not being overweight, because you never know when you will need the power. At 3G, for example, the weight is the equivalent of *three times* what it would be in straight and level flight.

A turn will continue unless the controls are centralised. The nose drops because the lift vector moves away from its opposition to gravity (weight). You can either increase speed or the angle of attack, but the latter is preferable, although power is required for steep turns (see below). To judge the right angle of attack, you must get used to the position of part of the aircraft against the horizon (usually the nose or instrument panel), which will be different in a left or right turn. In practice, as long as you keep that position, you will stay level during the turn, only checking the altimeter occasionally to make sure, because you should keep the lookout going. Remember that a bigger angle of attack means more drag, that requires a bigger angle, and so on.

Centrifugal force will tend to alter the longitudinal axis of the aircraft against the arc of the curve. Look at the turn coordinator. A slip or skid will alter the wing's lift-producing characteristics and force you into unwanted adjustments.

You need to start rolling out slightly before the point at which you wish to end up, otherwise you will overshoot - you will be turning (at an increasingly lesser rate) all the time you are rolling out. To roll out of a turn on a selected heading, lead by half the angle of bank, that is, for a 30° bank, roll out 15° before the desired heading. Use small angles of bank for small heading changes. Usually half the number of degrees of heading change is enough. The approximate angle of bank to produce a rate one turn may be calculated with 10% KIAS + 7. Add 5 instead of 7 for statute miles per hour. Use ailerons and rudder, and relax the back pressure, otherwise the new lift vector from the turn will still be active and you will climb.

Climbing turns should be no more than 15°. The load factor increases with bank angle, as does the stalling speed. Also, lift is lost with bank, reducing the climb capability. The right turn will be less severe, due to torque and slipstream effects.

You can use greater angles of bank when descending (up to 30°) because the load factor is less than it would be in the climb. However, the nose will drop more as you roll in, and the nose attitude will be different as it will be lower at the start. Avoid a steep turn and a dive, or you will end up in a spiral dive.

Lessons involving steep turns are more about how to recover from them than performing them, since they can easily turn into spiral dives, although they should be done as well as possible, since they are good for co-ordination. However, there are many other reasons for steep turns, such as avoiding traffic (where you don't go all the way round) or getting out of a valley with bad weather in it, where you just want to go back the way you came as quickly as possible. A combination can also be used to slip through the only gap in a layer of cloud, remaining VMC, so you will be descending as well.

Steep turns are officially over 30° of bank, but they are much harder to do between 45-60°. A "normal" one, as an exercise, is 360°, rolling out on a specific heading (or landmark), maintaining altitude.

Get into a good cruise, as an extra speed margin is useful for helping the machine cope with the extra loads imposed on it. Do a HASELL check (see below). Roll into a turn and add power as you go through about 30° (climb RPM or higher), but sometimes you get a better turn by leading with throttle. This helps with the extra load and drag.

Use elevator back pressure to maintain the nose attitude against the horizon. Control the turn with aileron and rudder. Check the VSI and altimeter to see if you are keeping altitude (±100'), but this is very much a secondary check compared to the nose position. Do not use back pressure alone to stop the nose pitching down, as this will just tighten the turn - use the ailerons and rudder as well, to reduce the bank angle a bit.

When rolling out, anticipate your desired heading by about 20°. The ideal way is to use the ailerons, relax the back

pressure and reduce power at the same time, but in the early stages, power can be left till last. Be prepared to adjust the aircraft for up to 30 seconds afterwards, so it can settle down.

If TAS is increased in a turn, but bank angle is kept the same, the radius will increase. If TAS is kept the same, but bank angle is increased, the radius decreases. Thus, if you increase speed and want the same radius, you must increase the angle of bank. An increase in weight reduces the radius (if power is not applied), because a higher angle of attack is required for the extra lift, which reduces the speed. Wind affects the *apparent* radius.

Spiral Dives

These can be entered into from turns or spins. The turns can be inadvertent, as when trying to fly on instruments without experience, or flying low and slow without proper training. If the nose drops in a steep turn, so you are descending in a turn with high power, you will be very near the start of a spiral dive.

Although you shouldn't have your head too much in the office, it's actually your instruments that will give you the best clue as to what is happening. Your speed will be increasing, and altitude falling, both at increasing rates. Engine and propeller noise will increase as well.

In this situation, pulling back on the control column is the wrong thing to do, since it will just pull you tighter into the turn. Instead, quickly and firmly (no harsh movements!) pull the power back. Then use aileron and rudder to straighten up. Since you immediately get more lift, the nose will go up, so be prepared to relax the elevator back pressure as well (gently and carefully).

Climbing

When climbing, putting the nose up causes the speed to decrease, so you get less lift, despite the higher angle of attack, even though the thrust vector is inclined upwards, and contributes a small amount. Thus, you need more power to keep going up. However, full power wastes fuel and overheats the engine - save it for emergencies, and taking off.

There are various types of climb, including *best rate*, *best angle*, *normal* and *enroute*. The first gives you the most height in a given time, and the second gives you the most height in a given distance, useful for clearing obstacles (the angle will increase in a headwind). Both, however, will make the engine run hot if used for too long, so a normal climb should be resumed as soon as possible, not only for better cooling, but because it also gives you better forward visibility to help with your lookout. An enroute climb uses a little extra power to climb at just under normal cruise speed, so you don't reduce your groundspeed too much.

The procedure to enter a climb is to change add *Power*, change *Attitude*, and *Trim*, in that order (APT to level off). In general, keep the panel or cowling slightly above the horizon, and level before the selected altitude, at 10% of the climb rate, so going up at 500 fpm means you must start to level 50 feet beforehand.

Air density (affected by height, temperature and moisture) will have an effect on your climb performance and instrument indications - this is discussed later on.

CLIMB GRADIENT

To maintain a steady speed in a climb, the retarding forces (the rearward part of weight, and drag) must be balanced by an equal amount of thrust:

```
T = D + W sin Gamma
```

Gamma is the *Climb Angle*. Because, for small angles, sin is about equal to tan, you can get an approximate formula for climb gradient:

$$\text{Climb Gradient} = \frac{T - D}{\text{Weight}}$$

The greatest gradient comes with the biggest difference between thrust and drag and the least weight. Multiply the number obtained with the above formulae by 100 to get a percentage gradient. Multiplying it by TAS to get rate of climb:

$$\frac{\text{Power avail} - \text{Power reqd}}{\text{TAS}}$$

is the same thing, but, 1 kt = 101.3 ft/min (approx 1/0.987). For small angles of climb the ROC is approximately the % gradient x the TAS, so you could use:

$$\text{FPM} = \frac{(\text{TAS x \%})}{0.987}$$

However, propeller-driven aircraft have a different power available curve (see above), in that power available decreases with height, and power required stays the same as for a jet. The *service ceiling* for a prop-driven aircraft is where the rate of climb falls to 100 fpm, and for a jet, 500 fpm. With increasing altitude, excess power and rate of climb decrease. At the absolute ceiling, power available equals power required, excess power and rate of climb are zero and the two curves are parallel.

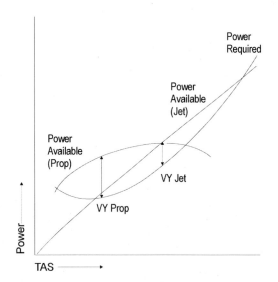

When climbing at a fixed IAS, angle of attack remains constant. When the Mach number remains constant, however, IAS reduces and angle of attack increases.

When coming out of the climb to level off into the cruise, reduce power only when you have the height and speed that you want. For example, in a jet, cruise power is set only after you have reached a speed of about .01 faster than the desired cruise speed, so you would accelerate to, say, .86 Mach before you reduced power to settle at .85 for the cruise. If you let the speed fall below the target, you use more power (and fuel) to get back up there.

Descent

There are two types of descent, *power on* and *power off*. In the latter situation, the recommended glide speed in the Flight Manual will give you the maximum range (don't raise the nose to stretch the glide!). A power on descent is used for more precise control, as when aiming for a runway. To initiate descent, the procedure is to use Power, Attitude and Trim. When you reduce power, the nose pitches down, but you should not let the speed increase. There will be some yaw to the right, caused by the diminishing slipstream. To keep straight, note the attitude and any items in the windscreen with constant bearing (your landing spot). During the descent, open the throttle occasionally, both to keep the engine warm and to clear any ice forming in the carburettor. Lowering the flaps or landing gear will steepen the angle of descent.

You use power to level, as just pulling the nose up will eventually lead to further descent (watch for left yaw - the nose will pitch up, due to the trim position). As with the climb, anticipate the level by 10% of the rate of descent.

FORCES IN A DESCENT

When either lift or thrust are removed, weight or drag parts of the couples will create a nose-down pitching moment. The horizontal component of weight described above turns the other way, and effectively becomes thrust. Although the lift vector is reduced, it is still close to its normal size. It follows that, if power is used in the descent, the less the forward component of weight needs to be to equal drag, and the smaller the gliding angle is. If the speed is kept the same, the rate of descent is lower.

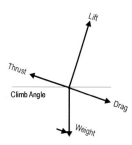

If drag is increased for any reason, you have to increase the forward component of weight to compensate, which means increasing the gliding angle, or making the glide steeper. If weight is increased, there is no change to the gliding angle, and hence range, but speed and rate of descent increase.

Approach & Landing

A good landing depends on a well set-up approach, during which a lot happens, so you must be constantly aware of what's going on. The landing spot should be kept in the same relative position on the windscreen for a constant angle of approach. The idea is to land with rear wheels first on a nosewheel aircraft, and all wheels together on a taildragger.

Keep your hand on the throttle, because when you need power, you need it *now.*

Somewhere between 15-30 feet, you should start the flare, or roundout, by pulling the control column back, having closed the throttle first. Keep pulling back until the aircraft settles onto the ground (when you should actually start to flare is difficult to describe, but my own preference is when I seem to be going too fast). When very close to the ground, further backward movement of the control column slows you down rather than keeps your height, and you would keep it back once a tailwheel aircraft is on the ground. You can relax the pressure with a nosewheel machine, for some weight on the nosewheel to assist with steering.

Crosswind landings are more difficult than takeoffs, because the controls are less responsive (there is no airflow over them from the powered prop). There are two methods of counteracting drift until the final moments, and different machines have their own preference. One is to keep a wing down into the wind direction while keeping

in line with the runway using the rudder (the *sideslip*, below). The other, which is my own choice, is to crab in, with the nose offset into wind and the wings level - the machine is straightened with rudder just before the touchdown, with a touch of into-wind aileron (the 777's undercarriage can take what looks like a 60° crab angle and be kicked straight *after* touchdown - I've seen the video). Although the sideslip avoids wear and tear on the aircraft, it does mean cross-controlling and more drag, and when you can't see the runway until the last minute (say with low ceilings), you can't correct for crosswind properly. Passengers will find the crab method more comfortable anyway (if you try the slip in a 737, you will hit the runway with an engine nacelle). Whatever method you use, though, get the weight on the wheels, start braking and get the flaps up as soon as possible.

For a short field approach, leave the power on until the landing flare is completed - in other words, "drive" it on to the ground, then get the flaps up straight away. Before going in, however, bear in mind that the takeoff run will always be longer - can you get out again?

Be prepared for quick deceleration on soft or rough ground, and watch for the nosewheel - keep the weight off as long as possible. You might want to do a low approach first for inspection purposes, and to chase the sheep off.

Slipping

To get down more quickly without increasing airspeed, you can use the slipping manoeuvre, which exists when you bank, as if to turn, but you actually keep straight with rudder (the *forward slip*). The *sideslip* can be used when landing in a crosswind, to keep straight down the approach.

Stalling

As the aerofoil comes into the stall, it starts to pitch down as the airflow starts to react about the midpoint of the lower surface instead of at 25% of chord.

Because of the above, the quoted stalling speed in the flight manual is the "clean" speed, which occurs in a straight and level glide at maximum weight with no gear and flaps down. As an exercise, it's the point at which the nose drops down when the elevator is pulled all the way back to the stops. Since you stall the aircraft onto the ground every time you land, practice gained here can only serve to improve subsequent arrivals on the runway.

To do the exercise in straight and level flight, do the HASELL check, place the carb air into hot, and reduce power to zero. Keep the nose level with the horizon, and be prepared for the controls to become mushy and ineffective. Do *not* use rudder, except very sparingly to keep straight, or you might end up in a spin, and you don't learn to get out of those until the next lesson. Allowing it to yaw is just as bad as using too much rudder, so don't use aileron, either, because yaw is a secondary effect of roll. In addition, aileron drag will only make it worse.

Keep pulling the elevator back, in attempt to maintain height. About 5-10 kts before the proper stall, you might hear the stall warning going (if you've got one), or feel a little buffeting in the controls. This is the aircraft protesting that it can't stay up, and that it is reaching the critical angle of attack - turbulent air is hitting the elevator and other controls.

At the stall, the nose will pitch down, usually just after the elevator reaches its full limit of travel backwards. The dropping could be relatively mild, or quite severe, depending on the design of the aircraft (sometimes you don't even notice it!).

The point to realise is that, in dropping the nose, the angle of attack improves enough to get lift again, and the aircraft starts flying, even if you keep the control column back, but we want to recover, so relax the back pressure, and note how much height is lost during the exercise, once you recover the cruise attitude. It will be around 350 feet, quite critical near the ground, so applying power just after relaxing the back pressure will reduce this to a minimum, sometimes down to below 100 feet.

Spinning

When spinning, the aircraft is out of control in all three axes of flight. It results from uneven stalling, so a spin is basically a stall that is not straight. That is, you are turning and descending with one wing (the downgoing one) in a permanent stall, hence the spin. The effect is a continuous roll, which causes yaw. Left to itself, the aircraft will not recover, as long as the one wing remains stalled.

You can't use aileron to get out of a spin, because aileron drag makes the condition worse, but rudder is available, so you shove in a bootful in the opposite direction to the turn, until the yaw stops. Then relax the back pressure on the elevator to pitch the nose down and reduce the angle of attack on the stalled wing (this may be done at the same time, depending on the machine). Do not use ailerons, and pull out of the dive once you have some airspeed. Then apply power as necessary. However, the aircraft must stall first, so if you avoid stalling you won't get into a spin. To start a spin deliberately, shove in some rudder at the point of the stall.

Before performing any manoeuvres, however, you should do:

The HASELL Checks

Remember these, as they are useful throughout your flying:

- *Height* - are you high enough to do the exercise and recover if something should happen, without hitting the ground?

- *Airframe* - clean - flaps are in, undercarriage is up, etc.

- *Security* - hatches and harness all secure (i.e. doors closed and seat belts done up), no loose articles in the cabin that could fly about, etc.

- *Engine* - fuel is on, and enough for what you want to do, with temperatures and pressures OK, carb heat green, etc. (carb heat should be on before reducing power below a certain RPM, as it won't have enough power to defrost if any already exists).

- *Location* - no good wondering where you are when the engine stops, better find out now! Also, make sure you are not over anywhere you are not supposed to be, like congested areas, water, etc., and you are in a position to make a forced landing should you have to.

- *Lookout* - make sure there is no traffic above, below or around. Do a turn to make sure, but not a steep turn at this stage, because you will learn how to do them later!

Low and Slow

This manoeuvre, which is defined as operating somewhere between stall and endurance speeds, can kill the unwary. It's commonly used on pipeline inspections, or police patrols, and is especially dangerous with steep turns. When banking hard over, your lifting aileron is fully deflected, so you can turn. Unfortunately, it's also producing maximum drag, which will tend to cause an adverse yaw in the opposite direction, that is, the aircraft wants to go right, but is being forced left, or whatever. In contrast, the aileron on the other wing has very little profile above it, so is producing very little drag. It isn't just the ailerons - the wing rolling motion doesn't help, but the point is that, if you don't use rudder to counteract this, the wing causing the yaw slows down and produces less lift, which stops it rising as told to by the aileron. The other wing moves faster, and gets more lift. The end result is that you roll the wrong way, or at least the Wright Brothers did.

Modern design methods have reduced the risks in the normal flight envelope, but when in extreme situations, such as in a steep turn, near the stall (and don't forget that a stall can happen at any speed with the wrong angle of attack) it may well catch you by surprise if you use the ailerons too abruptly, especially when the lifting wing stalls and puts you in a spin, which is just what you don't want at 200 feet (remember the aileron's purpose is to temporarily increase the angle of attack).

Tip: Use ailerons *last* out of a steep turn. Put the control column forward and use opposite rudder first, remembering that the controls are much less effective at slower speeds.

This can also be a problem when taking off from a short strip, with both wings at a high angle of attack. Sharp movement one way or the other will increase the angle on the lifting wing and stall it the wrong way. Again, modern design has improved matters, but try it a *long* way off the ground and see what I mean.

LOAD FACTOR

The total lift divided by the total weight, the ratio being 1:1 in level unaccelerated flight. In other words, the weight carried by a wing (or rotor disc) expressed in terms of G, which can be expressed as *apparent weight*, because it can vary with the stage of flight.

When you turn, the aircraft tries to continue in a straight line, and a force is needed to point it towards the centre of the turn - this would be Centripetal Force, which must be generated by extra lift from the wings. In effect, the (upwards) lift vector is reduced by the same amount, which needs to be compensated for. In a 60° banked turn, therefore, the amount of lift you need is doubled, so the load factor becomes 2. This can also be increased temporarily by sharp manoeuvres or gusts and turbulence (a gust with a speed of 66 feet per second will change the angle of attack at 200 kts by as much as 11°, which will either lift you very quickly or cause a stall).

Here is a chart expressing angles of bank against load factors:

Angle	Factor
0°	1
15°	1.04
30°	1.15
45°	1.41
60°	2
75°	4

In a level turn, load factor depends only on the angle of bank (for any given angle, the load factor remains constant). The rate and radius of turn, however, depend on airspeed as well. The rate of turn decreases if angle of bank is decreased or the airspeed increased. The radius of turn decreases if angle of bank increases or airspeed decreases and vice versa.

Use this formula to calculate the stalling speed for an angle of bank:

$$V_{SO} \text{ in turn} = V_{SO} \times V_{LF}$$

PROPELLERS

These are just aerofoils with a twist in them (*washout*) to spread the lift evenly over the whole length, as the tips run faster than the centre and need less angle of attack (the word *pitch* is sometimes used loosely to describe this). In fact, as far as the exams are concerned, the blade is twisted to *keep the local angle of attack constant along the blade*. The basic propeller is averaged to cope with many flight conditions, so is not perfect for them all, particularly the takeoff. The real problem is that you have to make the engine run faster for more performance from the prop, and engines work best within a certain speed range. Not only that, once the airflow becomes more than the propeller can cope with, thrust decreases.

Officially, a propeller's function is to convert crankshaft rotary movement into thrust, by moving a large column of air backwards, to propel the aircraft forward. As a propeller is an aerofoil, the thrust it creates is equivalent to the lift produced by a wing - it's just used differently. A *tractor* (at the nose) will propel fast, turbulent air over the lifting surfaces, whereas a *pusher* (somewhere behind the fuselage) provides better high speed performance because it doesn't produce so much drag. On the other hand, the tractor bites into clean air, while a pusher spins in air that is already disturbed.

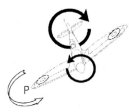

A rotating propeller creates various forces which may be allowed for in the design stages, including *gyroscopic precession* (see *Instruments*), where lifting the tail tends to make the nose yaw to the left. Torque results from the airframe going the opposite way to the direction of rotation (see left). The effect is to produce a roll, which is countered by washout on the upgoing wing.

The blade going down pulls more at high angles of attack, resulting in *asymmetric thrust* (also known as the *P factor*). Where the propellers rotate the same way on a light twin (such as the PA 23), the failure of one engine may cause more problems than the other would - in the case of the Aztec, the downgoing blades are on the right side, since the propellers rotate clockwise from the rear, so there is more of a turning moment if the left engine fails, as the longer thrust line from the downgoing blade of the right propeller is further away from the longitudinal axis.

The left engine in this case is called the *critical engine*, because its loss creates the most adverse conditions. Later aircraft (such as the Navajo Chieftain) have contra-rotating propellers (that is, the right engine rotates to the left). Watch for the designation of parts for particular engines with L or R so they go in the right place (the critical engine for a jet is the upwind one). The other thing to note is that the slipstream going back over the flight controls will also be asymmetric, and parts of some controls will be more responsive. The Trident I and the Boeing 727 (1963) were an attempt to remove asymmetric handling problems and make takeoffs in low visibility more of a possibility. They had three engines at the rear with the horizontal stabiliser high on the tail fin. However, engine failure increases the possibility of damage to the others because of their close proximity, and the fuel pipes run through the fuselage from the wings to the engines. There was also the potential to deep stall, which is discussed later in this chapter (see *Sweepback*).

The critical engines on jets are the outboard ones. Since the longest arm creates the biggest yawing moment, if one fails, a large one is generated. A crosswind on takeoff makes things worse, where the wheels act as a pivot while

the tail acts as a vane to weathercock the nose into wind. With a crosswind from the right, No 4 engine (on the far right) would be the critical one, and *vice versa*.

In a propeller-driven twin, somewhere between 60-80% of the lift from a wing comes from the prop wash over it (hence the difference between power-on and power-off stall speeds). If one engines stops at a slow speed, the affected wing will stall (power-off stall speed is *higher*), so you not only get asymmetric thrust, but asymmetric lift as well, resulting in a yaw *and roll* towards the dead engine. You must bank into the good engine to regain the lift that was lost.

For unsupercharged engines, V_{MC} (minimum control speed) decreases with altitude, so you can maintain directional control at lower airspeeds than at sea level. Nevertheless, do not practice stalls with one engine out, or you might lose it. This is because, with full power on the working engine, the machine will tend to roll as well as yaw into the inoperative one as airspeed drops below V_{MC}, and gets worse as speed is reduced. Aileron drag will increase the yaw, leading to a violent roll if a stall occurs. Banking at least 5° into the good engine ensures controllability above V_{MC} and minimum drag for best climb performance, because the lift will be inclined in the same direction to provide a small turning force that allows less rudder, reducing drag and giving you some leeway for later problems should they arise. Stall characteristics will not be degraded, either. The ball should not be in the centre - in fact, it should be displaced slightly towards the lower wing.

Increasing thrust on the operating engine will increase yaw, as will displacing it further from the centreline. Drag from a windmilling propeller will have the same effect, but bear in mind that the propeller is also turning the dead engine against all those cylinders - one very good reason for feathering it. Reduced lift arising from the reduced slipstream adds to the yawing tendency. Because the wing with the good engine goes faster it develops more lift and could lead to a sideslip and a spiral dive if the situation is not corrected immediately with rudder, the dead prop feathered and full power applied to the live engine.

Approaches and landings with an engine out should be essentially the same as for normal ones, and while on the subject of light multis, takeoff should be at least V_{MC} +5, followed by an acceleration to best rate of climb speed (V_Y) which should be maintained with takeoff power until a safe height. Note that V_{MC} is the minimum airspeed at which you can control the machine when the critical engine isn't working and the other one is producing full power. Thus, there is no guarantee that you can maintain altitude, let alone climb - you can only expect to maintain heading. V_{MC} is marked with a red line on the ASI, and V_{YSE} (best ROC with one engine out) with a blue one. *Propeller efficiency* is the ratio of thrust divided by brake horsepower, or the difference between what power is available from the engine to what is actually used.

Thrust is greatest before brake release and reduces with speed (because angle of attack decreases), so you get maximum thrust when stationary on the ground and minimum (with maximum drag) with maximum forward speed. Thrust also bends blades forward, while *torque* bends them against the direction of rotation.

Slipstream results from rotating air going round and round the fuselage until it eventually hits the tail fin, forcing it one way or the other (thus causing yaw), depending on which way round the propeller is going (see left). It is most prominent at low airspeeds with high power settings, and can be reduced by offsetting the fin, as most of an aeroplane's life is spent in the cruise. Outside of that, simply use rudder.

The *propeller torque reaction* will force a wheel into the ground on takeoff and cause the aircraft to steer wrongly - for example, with a clockwise rotating propeller (seen from behind), the airframe will want to go the other way and put pressure on the port wheel. This will cause a yaw to the left. Actually, it is in the same direction as the slipstream effect, above. With a tailwheel aircraft, you will get gyroscopic precession as the tail is lifted - the force applied to the top of the prop disk is felt 90° away in the direction of rotation, to cause a yaw. The downgoing blade also travels further, being at an angle, and will produce more lift for the same effect.

Remember that, although torque and slipstream produce roll and yaw, they ultimately produce yaw and roll as secondary effects.

Geometric pitch is how far a propeller should move forwards in one rotation - the *effective pitch* is how far it actually moves. The difference between the two is *propeller slip*, and is a measure of the efficiency or otherwise of the process. The *pitch angle* is that between the blade's chord line and its plane of rotation. The *helix angle* is between the resultant airflow and the plane of rotation. The surfaces of a propeller are the *thrust face* on the rear, and *pressure face* on the front.

Solidity describes the amount of propeller you can see against air, from the front. The more blades there are, or the higher the chord, the more "solid" it is. Thus, if you put in a larger engine, you would have to increase solidity to compensate, or absorb power from the engine. You could fit another prop (counter-rotating), or make the present blades bigger, but the most efficient way is to increase the number of blades.

Constant Speed Propeller

Otherwise known as a *Variable Pitch Propeller*, this performs pretty much the same function as the gearbox does in a car, in that it "maintains engine RPM over varying conditions of road", or flight, in this case (a fixed pitch prop's RPM varies, and must be controlled in extreme circumstances, say, in a dive). The gearbox (or constant speed prop) is there because engines work best within a certain range of RPM - going too fast or too slow is not good for them. In other words, a constant speed propeller can have its pitch adjusted for varying conditions. Most are hydraulically operated with a centrifugal governor operating a control valve that lets oil in to make the pitch coarser or releases it for fine pitch (best for takeoff). Coarse pitch is used for the cruise because the blades move a longer distance per rotation due to the higher angle of attack.

The *centrifugal twisting moment* is a component of centrifugal force that tends turn the blades into fine pitch. The *aerodynamic twisting moment* is the opposite, tending to coarse pitch (the blade's CP is in front of the pitch change axis). They both act in the same direction in a dive.

If the engine fails, and feathering is not available, select fully coarse.

COUNTERWEIGHTS

These can be used to force the blades into increasing their angle of attack. The angle is reduced by oil pressure, so when it is lost, the blade angle will increase, although there may be an automatic feathering system. Thus, with counterweights, loss of oil pressure feathers the blades. Otherwise, they go into full fine pitch. Now you have more choice - you can operate at high RPM and low manifold pressure, and *vice versa*. Using lower RPM in the cruise (with higher manifold pressure) helps fuel consumption, since the engine is going round fewer times per minute, and the losses from friction are less than at high RPM. However, using too much MP against low RPM will damage the engine and risk detonation.

OIL CONTROL

Turboprops use oil-controlled systems - the power levers control the torque and the prop levers control pitch and RPM, very similar to a piston. Higher oil pressure creates flatter pitch and higher RPM, so if an engine fails, and you lose oil pressure, the blades will feather, which is where you want them to be anyway. Springs or compressed nitrogen may assist the feathering.

The *primary governor* uses a valve controlled by the prop levers that uses flyweights to control oil going to the hub. If RPM decreases, the flyweights slow down and are drawn inwards, since they are normally held out by centrifugal force against springs. This allows more oil in to reduce the pitch. The *overspeed governor* increases blade angle automatically if the primary governor fails, to control RPM. It is usually a relief valve. The fuel-topping governor also prevents overspeed, but only within a small margin of lever settings. It adjusts fuel flow instead.

The *Beta range* (or *ground range*) is the range of the power lever aft of the centre of its quadrant (the prop lever remains forward as set for landing), used to put the props nearer flat pitch for ground manoeuvres. This is because a lot of thrust is generated even at idle, unlike piston-engined planes, which produce very little. The *beta valve* bypasses the primary governor to send more oil to the hub, and allows the power lever to control only prop pitch in beta range, as opposed to its normal torque. *Low pitch stops* or hydromechanical locking devices stop the propeller entering Beta range or even reverse pitch in the cruise. In reverse range, the power lever controls pitch and torque. The *Alpha range* (in the forward part) has the opposite function.

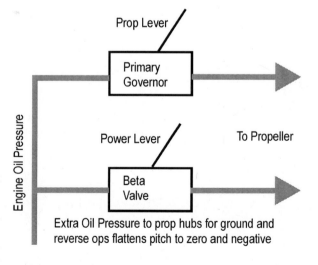

Extra Oil Pressure to prop hubs for ground and reverse ops flattens pitch to zero and negative

With one lever, power output and propeller RPM are controlled at the same time. There is a lever for residual control, called the *condition lever*, which sets the propeller for normal flight, that is, handing over control to the power lever, and for starting and feathering.

HIGH SPEED FLIGHT

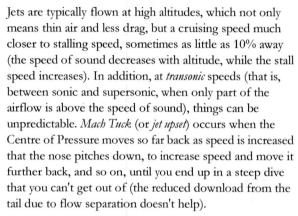

Jets are typically flown at high altitudes, which not only means thin air and less drag, but a cruising speed much closer to stalling speed, sometimes as little as 10% away (the speed of sound decreases with altitude, while the stall speed increases). In addition, at *transonic* speeds (that is, between sonic and supersonic, when only part of the airflow is above the speed of sound), things can be unpredictable. *Mach Tuck* (or *jet upset*) occurs when the Centre of Pressure moves so far back as speed is increased that the nose pitches down, to increase speed and move it further back, and so on, until you end up in a steep dive that you can't get out of (the reduced download from the tail due to flow separation doesn't help).

The *Pitch Trim Compensator* (or *Mach Trimmer*) continually deflects the horizontal stabiliser slightly more than is needed to maintain longitudinal stability and allow M_{MO} to increase, to take advantage of favourable drag figures. It also helps with confusing control problems as speed gets really high, when the nose-down tendency means not pushing the control column forward, but pulling it back. It provides enough of an input in the other direction to still give a progressive increase in push force as Mach number is increased.

Using rudder at high subsonic mach numbers can result in opposite yaw, because the faster wing gets a substantial increase in drag to produce the effect. The Yaw Damper monitors directional control requirements and inputs very small amounts of rudder at the earliest opportunity (there is an indicator in the cockpit that tells you what it is doing, but it only shows damper input).

The general idea is to get the fastest possible speed for the least possible drag, ending up with the least possible fuel burn. Various methods have been devised to help with this, described below.

Subsonic flight means up to about 0.75 Mach, or the critical Mach Number (M_{CRIT} - see below), the maximum airspeed at which no airflow reaches the speed of sound. Here, the air has time to divide before the aerofoil comes along. Transonic flight is somewhere between M_{CRIT} - 1.3M, where there is a mix. Supersonic is between 1.3-5M.

When waves cannot move ahead of the source, they bunch up and form a *Mach wave*, ahead of which the air has no time to divide to accommodate the aerofoil or moving body. The "normal" Mach wave is not a shock wave, but a line dividing areas where the source can be "heard" and areas where it cannot. It is at right angles to the direction of movement. Supersonic flight lies between 1.2-5 Mach, and above that, you go Hypersonic. When supersonic, an *oblique* Mach wave is formed, which acts as yet another boundary over which a wave cannot pass. Since it is three-dimensional, a *Mach cone* is formed.

The problem is that, although an aircraft may be flying just below the speed of sound, the air above the wings could be above it, because lift generation depends on the acceleration of air. One problem with Concorde was that the air going into the engine intake had to be slowed down a *lot*, otherwise the engines wouldn't work properly - it was eventually done with computer-controlled intakes. In addition, large waves produce a temperature increase which makes the local speed of sound go up - the initial speed of propagation of the pressure wave is at that speed.

As a reminder, the flow over the aerofoil initially moves into a region of lower pressure, courtesy of Bernoulli,

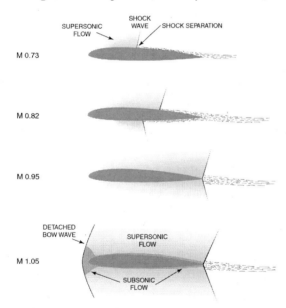

SUPERSONIC FLOW
SHOCK WAVE
SHOCK SEPARATION

M 0.73

M 0.82

M 0.95

DETACHED BOW WAVE
SUPERSONIC FLOW

M 1.05

SUBSONIC FLOW

which is how things should be, but as it nears the trailing edge it encounters a higher pressure from the adverse pressure gradient and has to work harder, so it decelerates. If the adverse gradient becomes too great, flow separation occurs and the aerofoil stalls. When it finally reaches the speed of sound, a shock wave will form where the flow decelerates, as behind it, the pressure waves are moving

forward from the adverse pressure gradient. It therefore forms where the two airflows meet.

A shock wave is a sudden discontinuity is air temperature and pressure, in which there is a considerable increase in density, pressure and temperature that causes the boundary layer to separate into a shockstall. The shock wave acts as if you had just deployed the spoilers - there is a marked increase in drag because the size of the disturbed wake has increased. In fact, the energy required for this comes from forward speed, so it is the equivalent of a drag penalty. The lower surface shock wave forms later because the lower camber is less, but this means that it is more forward than the upper one. This causes the Centre of Pressure to move aft, to move further aft when the shockwaves reduce the lift at the root. The resulting pitching moment only increases the aerofoil's speed and makes things worse.

Normally, pressure disturbances move ahead of an aerofoil and give the air particles in the way plenty of warning. Although being compressed, they are still moving, but as the aerofoil itself gets near the same speed, they can no longer do so because of the shock wave. Eventually, once above the speed of sound, a bow wave is formed in front, which is detached because of the high pressure at the stagnation point.

All changes in velocity and pressure will take place *sharply & suddenly*, which is another good reason for being smooth on the controls.

The shock wave sitting on the trailing edge may also affect the flying controls - in an aeroplane, the ailerons can freeze, as originally found by Spitfire pilots who put their machines into a high speed dive.

The *Critical Mach Number* (M_{CRIT}) is the highest speed you can get without supersonic flow (about M0.72) or, to put it another way, the speed at which any part of the airflow over the upper wing becomes supersonic in level flight and where shock waves form (that is, it first reaches, but does not exceed it). M_{CRIT} actually marks the lower end of the band of Mach numbers where a local one may be supersonic, thus marking the boundary between subsonic and transonic speeds. It follows that, the less the air is accelerated over the wing, the higher M_{CRIT} can be, which is done either with a lower camber or a higher sweep.

The 747's centre of lift shifts *forward* as it gets near to Mach 1, so it will rear up and bleed off speed instead of going into a dive. The solution with the Lockheed TriStar is to use an elevator that is combined with the horizontal stabiliser, and not hinged - the whole stabiliser moves as a unit to produce a force strong enough to pull the machine out of a high speed dive. The DC-10 uses the traditional hinged method, but relies on its general flying qualities to get it out of trouble.

If a *shock stall*, as it's called, occurs on both wing roots at the same time, there is a loss of lift and downwash on the tail, which thus becomes less effective, with separation of the boundary layer at about M 0.82. At this point (M_{MO}), there is a pressure and temperature increase behind the shock wave, causing a sudden increase in drag (called *Drag Rise* or *Drag Diversion*). In swept wing aircraft, the centre of pressure moves aft as well, contributing to the tail lifting tendency, or the Mach Tuck, mentioned above (if the wing tips stalled first, the C of P would move inward and

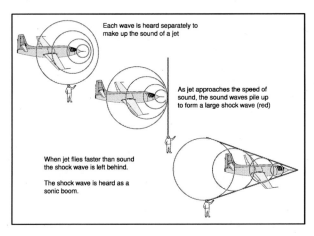

forward, ending with a pitch-up motion). Fuel consumption increases as well. *Shock waves cause wave drag.*

Mach Buffet (or *control buzz*) arises out of turbulent air from the wings hitting the tail surface, caused by the shock waves on top of the wing. The *low speed buffet*, which can be violent, means you are near the conventional stall - it occurs at *higher* speeds with altitude. The *high speed buffet*, on the other hand (which may involve a complete loss of elevator control), occurs at *lower* speeds with altitude, so at some stage the buffets will merge, at the *aerodynamic ceiling*. The margin between them (called *coffin corner*) is reduced by G forces caused by turning and turbulence, and you will want to choose a level that gives you enough breathing space, typically within 5 kts of stalling or reaching M_{CRIT}. Reducing weight or altitude will help with this. Watch out for a chart in the Flight Manual that shows the upper and lower boundaries against gross weight, altitude and bank. Select the chart based on forecast turbulence or expected manoeuvre load, and enter with a PA and Mach number. Extend along the pressure altitude line until the gross weight curve is reached then, using the PA/M intersection

as the reference, measure off the decrease in KIAS to the low speed side and the increase in KIAS to the high speed side of the chart. The speed range between high- and low-speed buffet increases in descent at constant IAS.

The *Limiting Mach Number* is the highest speed at which the aircraft becomes noticeably uncontrollable.

M_{MO} is the *Maximum Mach Operations Speed*. It is displayed on the ASI by a self-adjusting red-and-white needle called a *barber pole*, showing the local speed of sound - as air cools with height, it will fall. On the PFD, it is at the top of the airspeed tape (the small green circle is the stalling speed).

Speed Control

In the early stages of a climb, your flight path and speed are governed by performance regulations, so the amount of fuel you use cannot be altered. With an engine out, jets, or heavy aircraft, at least, climb initially at V_2 until at least 400 feet above the aerodrome, which is flap retraction height. In this situation, with a problem, you would normally land back at the departure aerodrome or its alternate, after dumping fuel to get the landing weight down. Otherwise, with all engines operating, you would normally progress through V_2, V_3 and V_4 to flap retraction height, then reduce pitch for acceleration and climb. As flaps and slats are retracted, you would typically aim for V_{ZF} + 10 kts (Zero Flap speed) until 3,000 feet, then go for enroute climb speed.

Around M0.7 - M0.8, there is a point where you change from a fixed IAS to a fixed Mach number, whereupon TAS and IAS start to reduce (this altitude may be selected by the company, and will be in the ops manual). For a fixed Mach number at a fixed level, IAS stays the same when moving into colder air, but TAS will decrease by around 1 kt per °C, and vice versa. A fixed Mach number is a percentage value of the speed of sound, so TAS will follow the same rules - that is, it will increase and decrease in line with temperature, other things being equal. However, long range cruise uses a variable Mach number according to aircraft weight, so light weights mean a lower Mach No, and vice versa. If temperature and FL remain unchanged, Mach No (and TAS) will decrease as fuel burns off.

At high subsonic speeds, the shock wave starts to change the shape of the power curve, at M_{CDR}. There is no effect on the climb as long as this is above V_Y, but, with altitude, M_{CDR} decreases with EAS until it coincides with V_Y. It is possible to continue the climb (assuming power is available) until EAS falls below V_X towards some sort of minimum control speed (and hold it until M_{MO}), but this is your absolute ceiling, or *coffin corner*, where stall speed and M_{CRIT} merge, and you cannot vary your speed or altitude.

V_Y is usually accepted as being equal to or greater than V_X.

The *service ceiling*, which is lower than the absolute ceiling, is where the climb rate (for a jet) falls to 500 fpm, although you may also be limited by the *pressurisation ceiling*, which is a structural limit on the fuselage. The service ceiling for a prop-driven aircraft is where the rate of climb falls to 100 fpm. Turboprops can maintain power better with height than pistons but, otherwise, there is little between them.

MAXIMUM RANGE SPEED

This gives you the most lift for the least drag, for the most economy, and the most distance for altitude lost. Flying either side of that speed will decrease the range when gliding. The Lift/Drag Ratio comes from dividing lift by drag. The angle of attack for the best ratio varies with the design of the wing, but is around a third to a quarter of the size of the stalling angle. It never changes, but, without an angle of attack indicator, you need an indirect method of guesstimating it, such as speed, which may have to be increased slightly with weight, reducing your range, as you will be using more power, and hence fuel, to attain it.

The biggest factor concerning your range will be the wind, which will reduce your groundspeed when on the nose, causing you to use more fuel. However, a slight increase in airspeed, say 5-10%, will get you there sooner with only a slight effect on fuel consumption.

MAXIMUM ENDURANCE SPEED

This gives you the most time in the air for least amount of fuel, which is useful when waiting for the weather to clear, or when asked to hold clear of a control zone, but, in practice, it gives you little or no controllability, so there will be a recommended endurance speed in the flight manual, which is a few knots above. The endurance is longer the lower you can fly (allowing for safety, of course), and turbulence and flaps will affect the speed considerably. There is more drag with endurance speed than there is with range speed, which is higher.

LONG RANGE CRUISE

LRC is higher than maximum range speed, and is used as the standard speed for cruise. Boeing and Airbus say that it is 4% faster than best range speed for 99% of the range. There are advantages (mainly commercial) to using it, the main one being money, because, as well as fuel, you save time by flying the route faster. Although this gives a slightly higher fuel burn, the cost of the airframe time is way higher. LRC is also a better speed in a headwind.

Supercritical Wing

The purpose here is to delay the formation of the shockwave for higher subsonic speeds by having a very thin wing. The top surface is relatively flat (so shock wave formation is delayed and M_{CRIT} increased), there is a blunt leading edge and a negative rear lower surface, to recover some of the lost lift from the upper surface (it also stabilises the flow and reduces drag from separation at the trailing edge.

However, there are practical limits to how thin a wing can be - for one thing, you have to get the fuel and landing gear in, and there are structural problems, too, so........

Sweepback (Positive Sweep)

A swept wing is angled forward or aft from a right angle to the fuselage (usually aft, as with Concorde). Wing sweep affects stability with a dihedral effect that tends to roll the aircraft out of a sideslip. Now it is more to do with high speed flight, above about 70% of the speed of sound, since engine power alone will not take you much above the Critical Mach Number.

A 30° sweep will increase M_{CRIT} up to about M 0.75. The idea is to make the wing appear thinner than it really is - coming at the air from an angle instead of head-on reduces the brute force effect, and allows some speed without the air going supersonic - in other words, you get an effective lower camber by making the air travel for longer, and the wing behaves just like a thin one.

In point of fact, once you sweep the wing, the chord line is no longer parallel to the direction of flight, and the velocity across it is less. The air velocity now has two components, one parallel to the wingspan, which is ignored because it has no chordwise velocity, and the other whose size depends on the sweep angle. For example, a 37° sweep produces a chordwise flow that is 80% of the free stream speed. 45° produces 71%, so the wing thinks it is flying at a slower speed.

However, although they suffer from less drag and are less susceptible to turbulence, sweptback wings produce less lift, which means flying faster to compensate, a problem when taking off and landing, hence the use of *high lift devices*, such as *slats* and *slotted flaps* (their purpose is to increase lift at low airspeeds and delay stall until a higher angle of attack - Concorde has longer legs and a droop nose instead). Although you could increase the speed as far as the wing is concerned, other parts of the aircraft might slow you down.

There is also a tendency towards Dutch Roll (see below), which means the machine rolls in one direction as it yaws in another, which arises out of sideslipping with yaw. When this happens, the effective span of the wings is changed and the forward one creates more lift for a short time, because it presents more of a span to the airflow than the other one. This makes it rise, hence the roll. However, the increased lift also creates more drag to pull the wing back, starting an oscillation. Subsonic machines should not use rudder to correct this. A *Yaw Damper* (often essential equipment in terms of a *Minimum Equipment List*) uses gyros to sense and correct changes in yaw. Pilot indications are the damper's inputs only, not total rudder movement (exam).

Something else that comes with sweptback wings is the *Deep Stall*, where the nose pitches *up*, and the loss of lift causes a descent, so you are going down, or rather, wallowing down, either slightly backwards or level (straight wing aircraft pitch nose down and go out of a stall automatically). This increases the angle of attack, taking the wings deeper into the stall, hence the name. With sweptback wings, the airflow tends to migrate out towards the wing tips, producing a thick low-energy boundary layer over them which separates very easily as the angle of attack increases. Thus, the stall occurs first at the tips, because the air approaching the leading edge deflects upwards (*upwash*), increasing the effective angle of attack (the tips are thin as well). The stalled air moves forwards and inwards as alpha is increased toward the stall speed, which also reduces aileron effectiveness.

As the tips are further aft than the roots, this means a loss of lift in the rear, moving the C of P forward, leading to the nose-up tendency. How easy it is to recover depends on the tailplane. A T-tail is in turbulent air from stalled wings, so it will be of less use (if at all) in getting the nose down than a conventional low-wing one.

Thus, on T-tailed, rear-engined aircraft, the nose pitches up at the stall, which not only makes things worse, but drops the engines into the turbulent flow from the wings as the stall develops, which makes them surge. In June 1966, a Trident I fell prone to all this and deep-stalled during testing, eventually flopping onto the ground. As a result, aircraft prone to deep stall now have a stick pusher as well as a shaker, some with automatic full throttle select, to stop entry into the stall (Learjets 31, 31A and 55C have *Delta Fins* which improve directional stability, enough so

you don't need yaw dampers). Deep stalling is an example of negative pitch stability.

Other problems with sweptback wings include the fact that airflow nearer the tips will curve in to approach the wing more at right angles,  reducing the sweep angle and making the tips flex more from the increased loading. The higher Mach number also has compressibility effects, risking a stall from shock.

The greatest acceleration takes place at the root, because that's where the thickness/chord ratio is greatest. As it beats against the fuselage, it is compressed, producing weak compression waves which may coalesce further out and create their own rear shock wave and greater than expected transonic drag.

FLYING BIG AEROPLANES

Heavy jet operations demand different piloting skills which were established with the advent of the B-47 bomber.

There is hardly any margin between power on and power off stall speeds.

Planes driven by jet engines are very slick, in that there is no automatic drag effect from reducing power as you would get when a propeller is involved, so there is a tendency to overspeed when you couple that with powerful engines. This means that constant attention is required (speed brakes help!) As mentioned elsewhere, it's like driving a powerful car in permanent high gear, so autopilots are routinely used to keep such aircraft under control and within performance and structural limits. Flying by the numbers is very important, as is strict adherence to procedures established by testing. Altitude changes too small to be detected on instruments can cause rapid changes in speed and altitude, particularly important at altitude where the stalling speed increases markedly.

The long wheel base can be a problem with taxying, and you can often lose sight of the taxiway.

Fuel

Fuel consumption is also high - long delays on takeoff can reduce your range by hundreds of miles. However, climbing is more rapid and consistent than it is with piston engines, which run out of puff quite soon and which have to have their power reduced anyway to avoid overheating.

Drag varies with EAS, which is what keeps the wing in the air. TAS increases relative to EAS with altitude, so the higher you are, the less drag there is and you cover more miles for the for the fuel required to overcome the drag.

Engines

Most engine run best at 90%, and being very high up is where maximum power will be at that figure.

To increase power, you have to remember to give the engine time to spool up, with a little delay between applying power and seeing the result, which again means you need more anticipation. In addition, if you reduce power, then increase it again, the engine will spin down to a low RPM then wind all the way up again. This is why, on approach, that relatively high thrust is maintained against all those lift-and-therefore-drag-producing devices, so the power is there when you need it.

The Airframe

Jets have high speed, low drag wings which demand special handling. Large aircraft also have high inertia, because they have more momentum, which is the product of force multiplied by velocity. Any force applied to change that momentum will have a lesser effect than it would against a piston engined machine, and the machine will carry on doing something wrong while you make a correction, so you cannot now afford to wait until a situation has developed before doing something about it. A good jet pilot corrects a problem almost before it happens! Such anticipation is why you need to know the numbers (power settings against flap settings), plus the associated trim changes.

Control forces are a lot higher, so the control surfaces will have balance arrangements. However, even this is not always enough, and brute force in the shape of hydraulics is needed. For any failure, there will be a reduction in controllability which must be thoroughly understood.

You need to know your weight fairly accurately, because it affects the operational characteristics. For example, an extra 10 000 lbs could mean around 4 knots less speed and some embarrassment when the takeoff speed figures have been wrongly computed (you really need to be accurate within 5 000 lbs for takeoff, which means a possible error margin of 2 knots).

Using fuel from a swept back wing produces a large forward change in C of G as fuel is consumed so big jets need a wider C of G range with which to work and a correspondingly wider range of travel for the elevator. The elevator, of course, is subject to stalling, so the variable

incidence tailplane was developed to keep the elevator within the proper aerodynamic range.

Note: Variable incidence tailplanes are extremely powerful!

Stall speed increases as the C of G moves forward, typically by about 5 knots. At a forward C of G, the tail has to produce a downward force, which increases the weight that the wings have to support.

A propeller provides airflow over the wing, which is very useful for fixing bad approaches in the final moments! Jet engines are positioned underneath the wing and do not provide this luxury. Thus, you can only get extra lift for a jet by increasing the speed of the whole aircraft, which can only be done with a *rapid* injection of power from the engines. As we know, they can be slow to respond.

Thus, there is less of a margin between power off and power on stall speeds.

"The pilot who masters the simple engineering principles of his aircraft, who understands the why behind the reaction - immediately elevates himself to a new level of competence and safety"

AIRFRAMES, ENGINES & SYSTEMS

3

The airframe is the complete structure of an aircraft, without engines and instruments. It will be as light and as strong as possible, because many forces are encountered in flight, like *compression*, *tension*, *torsion*, *shearing* and *bending*, so materials such as wood, aluminium, titanium, fabric and carbon fibre are used to cope with them (aluminium is too soft by itself, so it will be mixed with copper, manganese or magnesium for strength). Instead of being solid, where bulk is needed, a *honeycomb construction* will help to keep things light. This is a framework made of short hexagonal tubes covered over both open ends by metal sheeting. The airframe will be held together with aluminium alloy *rivets*, which are light, small and strong *in shear*. They are installed in the first place with special equipment. The condition of covering paint is a good indication of that of the rivet underneath - black stuff is powder from *fretting* against the aircraft skin. Loose rivets can indicate vibration.

Tension
Compression
Shear
Torsion

You can also get corrosion where dissimilar metals are used together. Corrosion happens where a metal breaks down into various compounds, either by chemical or electrolytic action, or movement, such as fretting, stress or erosion. Where a steel bolt is used to hold an aluminium panel together, you will get *galvanic* corrosion when moisture or some other electrically conductive substance acts as an electrolyte to form a "battery", where the aluminium, which is an anode, deteriorates when it receives metal ions from the steel bolt, or the cathode (there's more about this kind of stuff in *Electricity & Magnetism*). In this case, you would see a white, powdery surface. This effect gets worse with temperature and humidity, so the worst thing you can do with a wet aircraft in this respect is put it into a warm hangar (the same goes for your car, which is made up of panels dissimilar enough to cause a reaction when they get wet. Salts from the road conduct electricity better and only make things worse). This is a lesser reason why good bonding between aircraft surfaces is so important. Engineers can prevent such corrosion with zinc-based paints, or by using a suitable jointing compound, or electrically isolating panels. For example, if your battery is held against an aluminium firewall with a steel bracket, and the battery leaks, corrosion will start as soon as the battery's electroclyte meets the two metals, so a barrier between them will be cheap preventive medicine.

Also, copper and cadmium are relatively close in terms of electrical potential, so steel terminals should be cadmium plated if you want to use them with copper cabling. On the other hand, aluminium and magnesium will corrode easily because they are far apart electrically.

The Fuselage

The *fuselage* is where the pilot, passengers and cargo are placed, and to which any wings, tailplanes, and engines are attached:

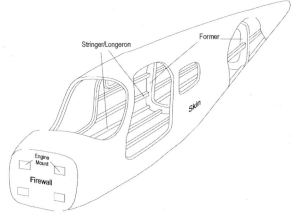

Older aircraft will be made of a *truss construction*, or *frame and skin*, where aluminium or steel tubing is joined in a series of triangular shapes, then covered with metal or fabric, in which case the metal acts merely as a cover, making no contribution towards the strength of the assembly. Instead, each part is made strong enough to take a certain load (mostly tension or compression) by itself. Unfortunately, this makes them relatively heavy - another disadvantage is that crossbracing takes up a lot of space.

If this page is a photocopy, it is not authorised!

© Phil Croucher, 2007

Canadian Professional Pilot Studies   3-1

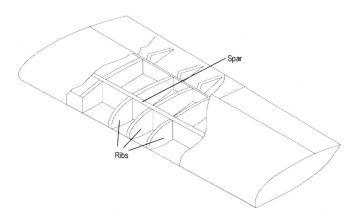

More modern machines use *monocoque*, which is a development of *stressed skin*, where the outside covering is rigid and takes the stresses of flight, and supporting devices inside, like *formers* held together by *stringers*, or *longerons*, help keep it in shape (see above).

Formers (or *frames*) are assembled one after the other, changing in size as required. They will absorb torsion and bending loads. Longerons (or stringers, which are shorter and tend to run just between formers) run fore and aft, keeping the formers together, spreading the load between them and stiffening the structure in general. *Bulkheads* are similar to formers, but tend to be found at either end of a fuselage, or a compartment, or when more strength is required. A *firewall* can be a bulkhead, being a fireproof partition that separates an engine compartment from the cabin. It is normally made of stainless steel, and on an aeroplane the engine is bolted to it.

An egg is a good example of a monocoque structure, which is handy, as *cocque* is French for *eggshell*. Monocoque therefore means *single shell*. Aside from saving weight, the big advantage of monocoque is that it leaves more space inside the aircraft. Older flying boats, made of wood, were among the earliest examples, but large-diameter aircraft cannot use this method because the skin would be too thick. Semi-monocoque is a compromise which uses longerons to take some of the strain.

In a wing, *ribs* are the equivalent of formers, and they are held in place with *spars*, which perform a similar function to longerons. Modern wings will also contain fuel tanks, which may or may not contribute to the strength of the wing. Tailplanes and elevators are made in a similar way.

FATIGUE & STRESS

Maintaining the structural integrity of an aircraft is important for flight safety, aside from reducing maintenance and minimising costs. The statistical probability of losing an aircraft through structural failure should not exceed 0.001.

Design Philosophy

This will determine the life of an airframe. For example, you could establish the *safe life* as 25% of the time taken to destructive failure. The length of the safe life may depend on such items as:

- the *number of landings* (stress on the gear)

- *hours flown* (components wear out)

- *calendar time*. Some turbine engines have 3000 hrs TBO, but also a date limitation of 10 years

- *cycles*, which are usually more relevant with pressurised aircraft

Components are either *structural* or *non-structural*. Structural items are load-bearing, meaning that they directly absorb the loads of flight. Otherwise, in any machine, doors, panels, etc. are non-structural. Structural failure can occur through the forces that arise from normal flight manoeuvres, plus turbulence and landing, etc., but threats to structural integrity also include overstressing, and operational hazards, such as bird strikes and corrosion.

FAIL SAFE

Fail Safe means that no one part of a system takes the complete load, which will have multiple paths to be absorbed - components are able to accept the loads placed on nearby components if they fail. For example, part of a fuselage may be made of two items instead of one, so cracks can be tolerated for a short while, say up to the next service inspection.

DAMAGE TOLERANCE

Damage tolerance accepts that production flaws might exist, and they are detected and fixed before they become critical. It does not have the redundancy of Fail Safe. Instead, it spreads loads over a wider area and makes the strain more bearable, so that, in theory, cracks do not start in the first place.

Strains & Stresses

Force is the product of mass multiplied by acceleration, and the mass of an aircraft in flight may be regarded as more or less constant (except for fuel usage, which will be relatively small), so the forces encountered in flight may be expressed in terms of acceleration, with the largest changes taking place in the vertical axis, which can be measured with accelerometers.

The general term for the force of attraction between molecules (of the same kind) is *cohesion*. It is a short-range force, and if you break something, gas molecules attaching to the surfaces of each broken part stop them rejoining. The force between molecules of different kinds is *adhesion*.

The *tensile strength* of a material depends on its cohesion. It is the maximum amount of tensile stress a material can be subjected to before it fails, the definition of failure varying according to the material and design philosophy. The *Yield Strength* is stress that a material can withstand without permanent deformation. Where this is not clear (ductile metals other than steel typically do not have a well defined yield point) it is usually when permanent deformation of 0.2% of the original dimension will result. *Ultimate strength* is the maximum stress a material can stand.

If a metal rod can be drawn through a small hole and turned into a wire, it is *ductile* (one gram of platinum can stretch to nearly 600 km!) Metals that can be hammered or rolled into sheets, on the other hand, are *malleable*. In both processes, the metal's cohesion is strong enough to allow it to hold together while its shape is changed.

When opposing forces are applied to an object, its size and shape can alter. An object's ability to return to its original size or shape when external forces are removed is known as *elasticity*. For example, a rubber band will normally return to its original shape after being stretched, but if it is overstretched will be unable to. This can happen to metals used in aircraft as well. When a substance is on the verge of becoming permanently changed, it has reached its *elastic limit*.

Two terms describe the elastic properties of a substance:

- **Stress** is the tendency to recover the original shape. The applied force will change the distance between molecules by pushing or pulling them together or apart. The molecular forces restore the original spacing when the force is removed

- **Strain** is the relative amount of deformation produced in a body under stress, in terms of *elongation*, *shear* or *volume* (a structure is officially strained when it cannot withstand a force applied to it). The deformation measured against the original shape produces a *strain ratio* which indicates how much of a strain there is

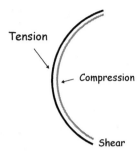

Flexure (bending) and torsion (twisting) are combinations of elongation and compression strains. A straight beam bent into a curve undergoes compression on one side and elongation on the other. The layer of material in the centre is unaffected, except at the ends, where they will tend to shear.

However, the rubber band's ability to resume its shape also depends on a relatively short time of stretching, so, even if the amount of stretching is within limits, if it's done for a long time, deformation could still take place. This elongation is also called *creep*, which can be affected by the material used, the load applied, the duration of stress and the temperature, since warmth can make material more pliable. A sudden increase in strain is called *shock loading*.

Metal Fatigue

Applying a load to a metal produces a stress, measured from the load itself divided by the cross-sectional area. *Ultimate stress* is where the metal will fracture, after the application of a single load, but repeated loads *well below* the level of ultimate stress will eventually have a similar effect, called *metal fatigue*. This is because aircraft have to be as light as possible, for obvious reasons, and the metal has to work harder. It will be subject to *alternating loads* and *load reversals*.

The points where fasteners are used to join parts together will be even more exposed. The local stress at any round hole in a sheet of metal under tension is 3 times the average. Fatigue cracks have three stages - *initiation*, *growth* and *final fracture*. Once started, corrosion helps a crack grow faster. A small hole is usually drilled at the end of a crack to stop it spreading (called *stop drilling*).

With metal, cracks almost always start on the surface of a structure that has anything out of the ordinary, such as sharp corners, fastener holes or just discontinuity of shape. With composite materials, fatigue is not a consideration at stress cycles around 80% of ultimate stress, because the individual elements tend to fail rather than the structure itself. In this case, cracks will not appear, but the structure will weaken gradually, as opposed to suddenly, as with metal.

AEROPLANES

Aeroplanes are either low wing (below), or high wing, (further below), which may have *struts* to keep the wings up, as well as internal bracing. Both types are also called *cantilever*, or *semi-cantilever*, (if a cantilever wing contains fuel, the highest bending moments are at the root).

Aeroplanes are single- or multi-engined, with fixed or retractable undercarriages, if they are landplanes, skis if they land on snow, and floats if they operate on water*:

A *monoplane* has one pair of wings, while a *biplane* has two (the Red Baron's triplane had three. I forget what Snoopy had). The shape of a wing as viewed from above is its *planform*, and could be *rectangular*, *tapered* (from root to tip), *elliptical*, *delta* or *swept back*. Large, wide ones, for example, are good for large transport aircraft, and short, stubby ones will be found on fast sports aircraft (a *rectangular planform* gives the highest local lift coefficient at the root).

The *aspect ratio* of a wing is the relationship between its length and width, or span and chord. You could have two wings of equal surface area but different aspect ratios, depending on what they were designed for. The higher the ratio (the longer the wing relative to its width), the more lift you get, with less induced drag and downwash (as with gliders), but the wings are not so stiff and are best used at low speeds. Big wings mean you are subject to drag forces automatically (try carrying a large plank of wood around in a high wind).

An aeroplane's rated strength is a measure of the load the wings can carry without being damaged. Light aircraft can take total loads in three categories:

- *Normal*, 3.8 x the gross weight
- *Utility*, 4.4 x gross weight
- *Acrobatic*, 6 x gross weight

Naturally, there is a safety factor involved, but the above should not be exceeded. Normal or utility categories do not allow manoeuvres with high positive and negative load factors. Bank angles would normally be inside 60°.

FLIGHT CONTROLS

When airflow over them is high, the controls, when moved, have a positive feel. They are less responsive at slow speeds, which is a point to remember when low and slow (also, because of the nose high attitude, the control surfaces may not have any airflow over them at all, which is why some aircraft have the tail at the top of the fin). In fact, the effectiveness of any control depends on its distance from the Centre of Gravity, the size of the control surface, its speed through the air and the degree of movement. Control surfaces can be activated by cables and pulleys, rods, tubes, hydraulics or electrical signals. Because of the high loads, jets often need hydraulic assistance to move control surfaces (see *Hydraulics*, below).

Fly By Wire systems detect movement of the controls, and transducers send signals over electrical cables to the system concerned, which will be a self-contained unit in the relevant location. There is some controversy as to whether the programmers actually talk to pilots, but the systems seem to work very well. If nothing else, they save weight, and maintenance, and can create more space in various locations, particularly the cockpit. Sometimes, sidesticks replace conventional control columns, as on the A-320 Airbus. *Q-Feel* uses static and pitot inputs to prevent overstressing of powered controls. Redundancy is achieved by having multiple pathways for signals, or multiple computers for the same task, and the computers are continually self-checking.

Anyhow, the controls will move the aircraft in one of three axes - pitching (nose up or down), rolling (wings up or down) or yawing (nose left or right). They do not move in isolation, however - an adjustment in one causes a secondary effect in another and must be allowed for, as we shall see in the discussions below. For example, an uncontrolled yaw eventually results in a roll, because one wing will be moving faster and will generate more lift on that side.

Primary Flight Controls

These move an aircraft in pitch, yaw and roll. The elevator, rudder and ailerons are attached by hinges to the tailplane (or horizontal stabiliser), fin and wing trailing edges, respectively.

A *Canard* is a horizontal stabiliser mounted on the front of the aircraft - it has the advantage of a longer moment arm, so the stabilising surfaces can be smaller:

The elevator controls *pitching* (where the nose goes up and down) by increasing the angle of attack above or below the tailplane, according to whether it is raised up or forced down by movement of the control column in the cockpit (if the column is pushed forward, the elevator is forced down into the airflow underneath the stabiliser, the angle of attack is increased, the tail rises because more lift is created and the nose goes down, and the opposite if pulled back). Sometimes, there is no elevator, but the whole stabiliser is moved, in which case it is a *stabilator*.

A *variable incidence* tailplane (as opposed to a fixed incidence one, with an elevator and trim tab) allows for more powerful trim.

The rudder does much the same thing, but sideways, to make the nose *yaw*, or move left and right. It is controlled by the foot pedals - whichever one goes forward moves the rudder to that side, where more lift is created and the fin is forced sideways in the appropriate direction, to produce a flat turn with a skid (you don't use the rudder to turn, but to fine tune one initiated by the ailerons, or stop it going the wrong way - see *Low and Slow*).

The ailerons make the aircraft roll around the nose. If you move the control column to the left, the right aileron goes down, increasing the angle of attack on that side, and the left one goes up, decreasing it, causing a roll in the same direction. To counteract Aileron Drag, which comes from the downgoing aileron, you might see *frise* or *differential* ailerons used. With the former, the downgoing aileron is streamlined. The latter moves the down aileron through a smaller angle. In fact, the frise aileron's hinge is offset, so a portion of the leading edge of the downgoing aileron sticks out into the airflow, to create a little drag to reduce adverse yaw. It also produces a slot (i.e. a gap between it and the rear of the wing) to smooth out the airflow over it.

Large aircraft may have multiple ailerons, with one set disabled at certain speeds - the 767's (outboard) second set

on each wing is locked at 240 kts, since only smaller ailerons are needed at high speeds (or aileron deflection can cause a wing to twist around its torsional axis, enough to reduce the angle of attack and make them ineffective). Beyond *aileron reversal speed*, you get a negative value and the roll will be the opposite of what you expect.

Aileron snatch results from the Centre of Pressure moving rapidly from airflow oscillating over the aileron at high angles of attack. It is prevented by placing a rubber seal between the aileron and the wing. Roll spoilers (see below) can either assist or replace ailerons.

Secondary Flight Controls

These include *flaps*, *spoilers*, *slats* and *tabs*.

TRIM

Depending on the net result of power and control positions, it may take more physical force to keep the aircraft in a particular attitude. That is to say, for any combination of power and control position, they will move freely with a certain range, but take a lot of force to go outside of it - an increase of speed from the trimmed position at low speed has more effect on stick force than it does at high speed. These extra forces can be *trimmed out* with a wheel or similar device in the cockpit which operates a very small control surface in the elevator (for example), so you have a control surface within a control surface. Such a trim tab is hinged at the rear of the starboard elevator and is usually controlled by two handwheels through a chain, cable, rod and gear system in the *opposite* direction to the elevator (when the autopilot is engaged, pitch adjustments are made by a *servo motor* connected to the tab). The wheel moves the surface up or down in the airflow, which moves the elevator the opposite way and does the work you would otherwise have to do to keep it there. If the trim wheel is moved forward, it forces the trim surface upwards, which creates more lift between it and the elevator, which therefore is forced down, creating more lift underneath the tail which lifts and forces the nose down. The thing to remember is that the control column, when moved forward, moves the elevator *down*, whereas the trim wheel moves its attached surface *up*. If the elevator gets jammed, the controls reverse. As they are independently controlled, *trim tabs remain fixed* for all positions of the controls they serve.

Power affects trim tabs, as more airflow varies the sensitivity of the controls. Reducing power makes the nose pitch down because the trim tab has become less effective and cannot hold the nose in position.

High-lift devices *increase lift* and *reduce the stall speed*, so takeoff and landing speeds are reduced.

Trim surfaces may also be found on rudders, depending on the complexity of the machine, which helps when you have to fly with one engine out.

You may occasionally see a *fixed trim tab*, which is there to provide a fixed amount of trim to make the machine fly true (it may be one wing low, for example, from the factory). It must only be altered by an engineer.

A *servo tab* is on the inside of the port elevator, and works in a similar way, except that only the tab is moved by controls, and the force of the airflow over it makes the primary surface move. Its function is therefore to assist in moving large control surfaces, rather than holding them in one position. Servo tabs move in the *opposite* direction to the surfaces they are attached to, through a mechanism on the port elevator torque tube. Normally, when control forces are light, the tab is part of the elevator, but when they exceed 25 lbs, a spring compresses to deflect the tab and produce an aerodynamic force to aid movement of the elevator. If the surface to which they relate jams, you get *control reversal*. A *control tab* does a similar job, but is manually controlled - it is only there for when the hydraulics fail and you need help with control movements.

An *anti-balance* or *anti-servo* tab moves *automatically in the same sense as the main control*, and is there to increase the force required to move it, so the further it is deflected, the greater the force (the angle of attack increases at a greater rate on the tab). This both aids the control's return to neutral and (more importantly) stops it moving to full deflection from aerodynamic forces, thus resisting over-controlling and resultant overstressing of the aircraft, especially when controls have low aerodynamic loading. It also makes hydraulically boosted controls more effective. It is outboard of the spring tab on the port elevator.

A *servomechanism*, by the way, is a closed loop control system in which a small power input controls a much larger power output in a strictly proportionate manner.

Interesting Aside: One of the Dambusters' Lancasters had to get home using only trim controls, after an aileron cable snapped, with flat turns from the rudders (Shannon said afterwards that it was a better landing than usual).

BALANCE
At high speeds, control surfaces may flutter because of buffeting, especially if the wings are flexible with a high aspect ratio. To prevent this, a streamlined balancing weight (usually lead) is fitted forward of the control surface's hinge. It may be inside the control surface itself, or fitted externally (*Mass Balance*). Sometimes, part of the control surface is placed forward of the hinge line, so that

airflow hitting it will help the pilot move the controls (known as *aerodynamic balance*).

FLAPS
These are hinged devices on the trailing edges of wings, inboard of the ailerons, that temporarily increase the lift producing areas for certain modes of flight, like landing, and sometimes takeoff (not in the PA 31, or aircraft without enough power to overcome the extra drag that reduces acceleration), where you might be going very much slower than normal and need a boost - in fact, *flaps produce the same lift at lower speed by increasing the upper camber and the negative pressure underneath* because the chord line moves further down at the rear and changes the angle of attack against the relative airflow (pushing the nose down restores the original angle).

Thus, the reason for using flaps (or any other low speed lift-producing device) is to change the shape of the type of wing required for high speed flight into one suitable for low speed flight, otherwise you would need several miles of runway to get airborne. Or land, in which case you would need sturdier (and heavier) undercarriages.

Flaps increase the lift *available*, but not the lift *delivered*, which means that induced drag hardly changes, although parasite drag does, so V_{MD} is reduced to help with the speed unstable regime for a jet. For a prop-driven aeroplane, the minimum drag speed gets below approach speed anyway, providing speed stability. However, there is a point beyond which the extra surface structure in the airflow produces more drag than lift, which is made use of when deliberately trying to bring the speed down, as with a short field landing, or increase the angle of approach without much sacrifice in speed. Sometimes, the ailerons are made to move in sympathy with flaps.

Various flap designs create different effects (all try to reduce drag), but the *Fowler flap* is generally considered to be the most efficient - they do not just drop down from the wing, but slide out from the back.

Slotted	16°	65%	energises flap boundary layer / nose-down pitching moment	
Fowler	15°	90%	increases wing area / strong nose-down pitching moment	
Triple Slotted Fowler	22°	110%	energises flap boundary layer / increases wing area / powerful nose-down pitching moment / complex mechanism	

LEADING & TRAILING EDGE COMBINED			
Slat & Slotted Flap	25°	75%	energises boundary layer / pitching moments offset
Slat & Triple Slotted Fowler	28°+	130%+	best combination for high lift / energises boundary layer / pitching moments offset

FLAP TYPE	TYPICAL STALL ANGLE	TYPICAL INCREASE IN $C_{L_{max}}$	REMARKS
	15°		effects of all flaps depend on shape of basic aerofoil in the first place
Plain	12°	50%	nose-down pitching moment
Split	14°	60%	more drag than plain flap / nose-down pitching moment / now uncommon

DEVICE	TYPICAL STALL ANGLE	TYPICAL INCREASE IN $C_{L_{max}}$	REMARKS
Slat	22°	60%	energises boundary layer / nose-up pitching moment
Krueger Flap	25°	50%	fitted on lower wing leading edge inboard and hinge forwards / loss of lift whilst deploying / nose-up pitching moment
Slotted Wing	20°	40%	energises boundary layer / now uncommon

The *Krueger flap* (as used on a 747) extends *forward* from the inboard leading edge of swept wing aircraft. It has a folding nose to vary the effective camber. An alternative is the *drooped leading edge flap*.

There is a *maximum flap extension speed*, as they are not designed for high speed flight. Lowering flaps generally forces the nose down, as they make the centre of pressure move backwards, but sometimes they affect the airflow over the tailplane enough to go nose-up. Once lowered, flaps should not normally be raised until actually on the ground. On missed approach, they should be raised after power is applied, in easy stages. The aircraft becomes less stable when flaps are extended, because the lateral CP moves inboard, so it becomes more manoeuvrable in roll. Longitudinal stability is decreased.

Should flaps operate *asymmetrically* (that is, one side works, but the other doesn't), the aircraft will roll to the retracted side, though less so with leading edge flaps. If it happens, immediately select flaps up and apply appropriate aileron and rudder, but this is a good reason for only selecting flap in small quantities in the first place!

OTHER WING DEVICES

Slats are small aerofoils that open forward of the main one to smooth out the airflow, or guide it over the top of the wing at an optimum angle, rather like those small triangular sails do at the front of square-rigged ships. When the angle of attack is high, they do this automatically (low pressure just behind the leading edge sucks them out. They are pushed back in by air pressure when the angle is low). They are usually found near the wing tips on the leading edge to help with lateral control. *Slots* are openings a little bit back of the leading edge of a wing that allow high pressure air underneath the wing to pass through them at high angles of attack to the low pressure area, to re-energise it and extend the laminar flow by reducing eddies. This reduces loss of lift and drag, and increases the stalling angle of attack. Slots may go across the length of the wing, or just where the ailerons are.

A *Wing Fence* is a small vertical fin a couple of inches high running the length of the chord on the upper surface of a wing that stops air moving towards the tips at high angles of attack (swept wing) or controls the airflow around the flaps (straight). Either way, handling is improved at slow speeds and help is given with the stall. *Vortex generators* reduce the drag from supersonic flow over the wing - they create a strong vortex to introduce high velocity, high energy air near the surface to reduce or delay separation. In other words, they mix boundary airflow with high energy airflow just above the surface.

Speed brakes on high performance aircraft allow you to keep the engines running enough not to shock them when power is reduced (see *Engine Handling*, later), and to produce decent descent rates, as modern aircraft are very slick. They create drag without altering the shape of the wing, essentially producing the same effect as introducing a barn door into the airflow, though not as big, of course (they are flat panels on the upper wing). If they go up on one wing, the wing will drop, since it is producing less lift than the other. Thus, the aircraft rolls in the direction of the *upgoing* spoilers. The downgoing wing puts the aileron up to counteract adverse aileron yaw, so: "Roll spoilers up, aileron up - DOWNGOING WING". Their operation can be *symmetrical* or *asymmetrical*.

As an extension of this, *spoilers* are there to spoil the airflow on the upper or lower surface of a wing, taking away the lift. They may work with the ailerons and assist with their control (in which case they are being used as a flying control) or may be linked with the brakes to increase the weight on the wheels, helping with the braking action and making sure the machine doesn't bounce back up in the air again (ground spoilers are effectively speed brakes that kill lift once on the ground). Selecting reverse thrust automatically deploys them on an abandoned takeoff.

On some aircraft, like the MU-2, spoilers are used instead of ailerons, as they are less complicated and more effective anyway (you need new crosswind landing skills). Ailerons and spoilers usually have separate control columns.

Note: Spoilers should be used *only* after the aircraft has touched down on the runway! Just before touchdown, you need all the lift you can get!

Fly By Wire

A modern airliner is a collection of computers with a fuselage round them, which should give you pause for thought if you've ever had to look after a network, as I have. For example, there are around 150 assorted computers and controllers on an A 320 Airbus (including one to flush the toilet), the main one being the *Flight Management System*, which provides navigational data and controls the autopilot, the autoland system, etc. The 777 has a similar setup.

The idea is that the flying surfaces are controlled by signals sent along wires rather than traditional cables and

pulleys, which has the obvious benefits of saving weight (and fuel and maintenance, thus costs) and automating the cockpit, but introduces problems with software quality and control and adds another item to the checklist, namely the software version. The 777, for example, had only one team of programmers using identical programs, whilst the Airbus consortium used several teams writing staggered ones, on the basis that a bug is less likely to appear over several sets of redundant code (flight control software runs over 132,000 lines).

ENGINES

An engine is a device for converting the stored energy of fuel into useful work. In an internal combustion engine, the fuel is burnt in a confined space called the *combustion chamber*. The increase in temperature produces an increase in pressure which is used to operate the engine.

In doing this, a quantity of air is sucked in and mixed with fuel, compressed, set on fire and slung out of the back (*suck, push, bang, blow* for short or, more technically, *induction, compression, power* and *exhaust*. The difference is that the power comes from the ignition stage in the piston, and the exhaust stage in the turbine, which is always ignited, whereas the piston only does so when the spark plugs operate. The turbine is also a whole lot lighter, and spins a lot faster. This process is not very efficient - if it was, exhausts would be cold (any engine will waste as much energy in heat as the power produced - the approximate thermal efficiency of a 4-stroke engine is 30%). The mechanical energy may drive electrical, hydraulic and pneumatic systems as well, which is why engines are also called *powerplants*.

Sometimes, however, engine output is actually too great for the transmission, so the manufacturer will *derate* it to make sure it doesn't damage anything. Often, derating provides a power reserve in emergency (as with the Bell 407), but its purpose is actually to better match the engine and transmission at altitude, or to provide a wider range of altitudes at which they can work together.

Aside from the engine itself, there are a few subsystems:

- Cooling
- Lubrication
- Ignition
- Fuel supply and carburation, which mixes the fuel with the air

Reciprocating Engines

A typical piston engine consists of a series of identical cylinders which can be arranged in many ways, according to what the engine is going to be used for. A radial engine has its cylinders arranged in a circle, with the pistons inside them attached to the crankshaft in the centre. In this case, the cylinders stay still, and the crankshaft moves, but earlier engines kept the crankshaft still while the cylinders moved. As you can imagine, maintenance was interesting!

Most modern light aircraft, including helicopters, now have their cylinders opposite each other (*horizontally* or *vertically opposed*), to cancel some opposing forces out:

but many still have them in line or in a V formation. Some engines are even upside down, like in the Chipmunk.

An aero engine has two spark plugs per cylinder, which are powered by independent *magnetos*. When doing power checks before takeoff, they are checked against each other for power and whether they actually are independent - there should be a discernible drop in RPM (around 100) when one magneto is switched off. If the RPM figure stays the same, they are interconnected somehow (when running up, set the magnetos to *Both* between testing each one singly to allow the engine to stabilise at the proper RPM and to burn off any oil and fuel that may have accumulated on the plugs that have been switched off. Any rough running at this point usually indicates fouled plugs which are typically cleared by leaning the mixture for a while).

Another difference is that car engines are a lot smoother (some diesel engines won't upset a coin standing on edge). However, car engines are not used in aircraft because they are not built to run continuously at 60-75% power, or more when taking off. A car engine typically uses 15% of its maximum power even on the motorway, and very rarely

tops more than 80%. In addition, car engines produce their maximum power at high RPM, whereas an aircraft engine would do this at around 2500-3000 RPM.

As the cylinders in an engine are the same, we will look at one shortly to see how they work. Note, however, that, although aircraft engines work in a similar way to car engines, they are designed to run slower (to reduce internal stresses) and are made of sturdier construction, so the chances of mechanical failure are minimised. Ignition and cooling systems are also different, but they are dealt with elsewhere in this section.

The *cylinder* in which the piston slides up and down is just that, being a large hole drilled in the engine casing and lined with steel for increased wear resistance, but it is closed at the top end by the valves (one for the *inlet* and one for the *exhaust*), to provide an airtight seal. Inside are also two spark plugs, and a *piston*, which slides up and down to provide an action like a pump, since it pulls air and fuel in, and pushes the burnt exhaust gases out. Its function is to be a *sliding gastight plug*.

As the piston is meant to be gastight, and no fit is perfect, there will be two or three rings round it (the *scraper* ring at the bottom is for cleaning) to mate against the cylinder wall and stop movement of anything from one side of the sealed portion to the other because, on the one hand, the engine will not produce full power if the burnt gases leak out and, on the other, oil will get through to the head from the lubrication system, mix with the fuel and air and cause a lot of bluish grey smoke (if you are getting mysterious oil leaks from your car, and everything appears to be done up underneath, check your piston rings, as they may be allowing pressurised gases through to the sump to force the oil out). The piston will be very slightly tapered towards the top, so that its sides will be parallel with the cylinder walls when it gets hot. In this respect, the piston's crown and skirt do not have the benefit of the cooling that the cylinder wall gets from whatever system is in use. Thus, heat can only escape from the piston to the cylinder wall through the intervening film of oil, or the air inside the crankcase.

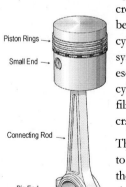

Piston Rings →
Small End →
Connecting Rod →
Big End →

The piston is attached by its big end to the *crankpin* on the *crankshaft*, via the *connecting rod* (or conrod, for short), which goes to the *small end* at the top (if either end goes, the engine will suddenly start clattering loudly). The piston is attached to the small end with a *gudgeon pin*.

The crankshaft is not straight, but is offset for each piston connected to it one after the other, so the up and down (reciprocating) movement of the piston is translated into rotary motion. The crankshaft has *main journals* at each end which are placed into *main bearings*, where they rotate.

The *throw* is actually of the diameter of the crank pin circle, which is equal to the stroke of the piston, but the word is often used as an alternative to the *crank radius*, or the distance the crank pin is offset from the main journals (the word *throw* is also used to mean a crank pin plus its associated webs and main journals).

At the front of the crankshaft will be a *flywheel*, which is a large heavy disc designed to keep the crankshaft turning through those cycles where energy is not produced (only one stroke out of four produces any energy).

In simple terms, pressure is introduced on the upper surface of the piston by burning a mixture of fuel and air in the confined space at the top of the cylinder. The pressure is released when the piston sops moving at the bottom of the cylinder by opening an exhaust valve to let the pressurised gases out.

Before the fuel is burnt, however, it must be vapourised and mixed with air, which is the job of the carburettor, discussed later.

The crankshaft will rotate clockwise (from the front) as the piston is pushed downwards to the lowest point of its travel, where the centres of the gudgeon pin, crank pin and crankshaft will all be in a straight line (the crank pin will be directly under the centre of the crankshaft). As any pressure from the piston will have no turning effect on the crankshaft, this position is called a *dead centre*, in this case the Bottom Dead Centre, or BDC). The Top Dead Centre (TDC) exists at the other extreme of the piston's travel. The TDC is an important factor in the timing of the spark that ignites the fuel/air mixture, mentioned later.

Movement of the piston from one dead centre to another is known as the *stroke*, and there are two strokes of the piston to every revolution of the crankshaft.

The diameter of the cylinder is the *bore*, and a *square engine* is one where the stroke equals the bore. A *short stroke* engine (i.e. most aircraft engines) *permits lighter construction* (exam) and reduces vibration. The difference between BDC, where the piston is at its maximum travel downwards, and TDC, where it is up as far as it can get, is the *compression ratio*, which is an expression of the number of times the volume above the piston *before* compression is greater than that *after* compression. It is equal to the total volume above the piston at BDC divided by the *clearance volume* at TDC (the space above the piston at TDC is called the clearance volume). The *total volume* above the piston at BDC consists of the clearance volume and the *swept volume*.

The formula for multi-cylinder engine displacement is:

```
piston area x stroke x no cylinders
```

The space between the crown (top) of the piston and the cylinder head, into which the fuel/air mixture is pulled and later compressed, is called the *combustion chamber*, which naturally gets larger and smaller as the piston goes up and down. Piston crowns generally have a concave surface, but may be convex if it is intended to reduce the size of the combustion chamber to produce more power.

At higher compression ratios, temperature increases at a slower rate than pressure, so at pressure ratios of say, 16:1, the small temperature gain is lost in the inefficiencies introduced by the rise in pressure. 16:1 is good for diesel engines - petrol engines must have a typical ratio of 8:1 (with 100 octane fuel) because the heat from compression would cause pre-ignition, described below.

Picture: Inside of typical 4-stroke engine

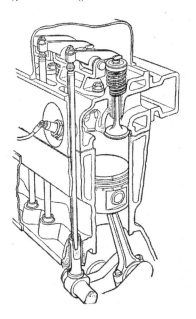

DETONATION & PRE-IGNITION

In being compressed, the mixture gets warmer, making it more disposed to ignite when the spark plug fires. Unfortunately, some mixtures get so warm that they can ignite without the spark (as with diesels), which will not only increase the operating temperature unnecessarily, but cause harm to the engine from shock waves, because the piston gets the effects of the power stroke when it doesn't expect it (pound for pound, fuel is more explosive than dynamite). Typically, the "hammer blow" will hit the piston on its way up the compression stroke, i.e. early, rather than when it is going down on the power stroke.

Having said that, ignition normally happens just before Top Dead Centre, to allow the flame to build up. In other words, burning of the fuel/air mixture starts in the latter part of the compression stroke and carries through to the early part of the power stroke. The flame front is accelerated by having two spark plugs in the cylinder - heat is released more rapidly and the pressure rise is quicker.

Detonation is a condition of *unstable combustion*, where the mixture burns too quickly and explodes, rather than expanding smoothly. It takes place *after* ignition has occurred, at high pressure and temperature in the unburned part of the mixture ahead of the flame front, where many isolated areas of ignition may exist at the same time. Aside from using unsuitable fuel or having an inadequately cooled engine, detonation can also arise from excessive carbon deposits in the cylinder, which can increase the compression ratio slightly.

Typical symptoms of detonation are vibration and loss of power. Although this is similar to pre-ignition, mentioned below, the two are intertwined and detonation can occur at any time.

It's otherwise known as *pinking*, because it sounds like that. You will hear it in your car if you make it work too hard (try going uphill in high gear). Detonation can cause the temperatures inside the cylinder head to rise to the melting point of the components inside it, with the piston usually going first. The hot gases will leak past the piston rings, pressurise the crankcase and blow the oil out. Net result: seized engine and holes in the pistons. Open the wallet!

Pre-ignition occurs when the mixture burns *before* it is supposed to be ignited by the spark plug, and which may cause, or be caused by, detonation (especially hotspots). Put another way, the spark plug may fire too late, and gases may leave the combustion chamber while they are still burning, leading to localised hotspots and detonation.

Thus, it is a product of overheating, especially where the mixture has been leaned too much (meaning that the engine is not being cooled adequately), and there are lead oxybromide deposits lying around inside the combustion chamber which are likely to be glowing bright red (more from misuse of the throttle than the mixture control, as when increasing power without adjusting the mixture). This is the reason why engines sometimes won't stop.

OCTANE RATINGS

Because of these problems, piston engines use fuel with an *anti-knock additive*, which used to be lead, to ensure that fuel ignites smoothly, and doesn't explode, and to stop it igniting before it's meant to. In the days before carburettors, fuel was much more volatile, and could be ignited ten feet away. Lead, of course, is no longer politically correct so, in cars, at least, the timing of engines is adjusted to produce the same effect with unleaded fuel.

The aviation industry still uses it, though. The "LL" in 100LL stands for *low lead*, but there is still about four times more than is needed. As well as the lead (as TEL - *Tetra-Ethyl Lead*), a scavenging agent (*Ethylene DiBromide*, or EDB) is added to ensure that the lead is vapourised as far as possible, ready to be expelled from the cylinder with other gases, otherwise the lead deposits would stick to the insides. This is not 100% successful, but the results are best at high temperatures and worst at low ones - the unwanted extras result in fouling of spark plugs, heavy deposits in the combustion chamber, erosion of valve seats and stems, sticking valves and piston rings and general accumulation of sludge and restriction of flow through fine oil passages, so it makes you wonder which is worse (in fact, petrol is not the only fuel you can use - Japanese Zeros used to outfly American aeroplanes because they used ethyl alcohol). The *octane rating* reflects the ability of fuel to *expand evenly*.

Higher octane fuels allow higher compression ratios than are possible with "normal" fuels without detonation. If fuel of a lower octane rating than is recommended in the Flight Manual is used, you should never use full throttle.

If detonation occurs, *reduce manifold pressure* and *enrich the mixture*.

Trivia: TEL is actually a liquid gas, which forms lead oxides *when it is compressed*. It was developed by a subsidiary company (Ethyl, Inc) of General Motors and I G Farben sometime before WWII, although the basic idea was thought of around 1921. In June, 1940, just before the Battle of Britain, you could only get TEL through the Anglo-American Oil Company, or Esso - the fuel concerned was called BAM 100. When British fuel was changed from 87 octane to 100 after working around the US *Neutrality Act* which banned its sale, German pilots got a real surprise, because British aircraft could suddenly climb a whole lot quicker (German planes could use 80-ish octane fuel anyway).

More Trivia: The unstable elements of petroleum have more hydrogen than carbon in their molecules. Octane (named after eight carbon atoms) results from reordering the atoms of a hydrocarbon.

When stored for long periods, the octane rating will decrease slightly if there is a lot of evaporation. Also remember that it isn't the fuel that burns, but the vapour given off from it - a lot of fuel is actually wasted, even in modern engines, because the fuel droplets going in are not fully vapourised.

COOLING

The gases burning in the engine can produce temperatures as high as 1500-2000°C. This will be absorbed by the various engine parts according to the temperature itself, the surface area exposed and the duration of the exposure. If left unchecked, this heat could cause those parts to distort and malfunction, or even cause pre-ignition or detonation. The function of the cooling system is therefore to remove heat from the engine at a high enough rate to keep its temperatures within safe working limits (note that overcooling can produce as many problems as undercooling - you need heat to vapourise the fuel, for example, and you don't want water vapour condensing on the insides). Liquid contaminants, such as water, have to be boiled off, at over 100°C.

AIR COOLING

Heat radiates directly into the air from the warm parts. Fins on a cylinder head, for instance, increase the surface area through which this can happen. The best engines for this tend to be those that allow the same amount of airflow over each cylinder, such as radials, but others, such as in-lines or those with a V formation may need fans and shrouds to assist the process, or their cylinders would have to be very far apart to let air through.

LIQUID COOLING

You need around 2000 times more air to remove a given amount of heat from an engine than you would if you used water or a suitable liquid.

There is a jacket around the warm parts, and the space between them is filled with a liquid such as water, with ethylene glycol added to solve certain limitations. This is pumped through a radiator which sticks out into the airflow to cool it down before it recirculates. Because all this has to be heated, the engine takes a little longer to warm up, and there is also the extra weight of the liquid and fixings to consider, not to mention leaks, extra maintenance and the possibility of freezing in cold weather, which is why water is not generally used, but a liquid that does not freeze in low temperatures or boil at high ones (frozen water expands and will crack the engine block). The boiling problem can also be solved by operating the system under pressure, for which you also need a *thermostat*, which is a bypass valve that regulates the movement of fluid in and out of the radiator.

Plain water is not used because it freezes on cold nights and expands, which can crack the engine. It also has a corrosive effect. Instead, it is mixed with glycol to increase its boiling point and lower its freezing point.

Tip: An *Exhaust Gas Temperature* gauge (EGT) is a fast-reading instrument that lets you know what the flame in the combustion chamber is up to. It responds almost instantly to changes in power and the fuel/air mixture. The *Cylinder Head Temperature* gauge (CHT), on the other hand, measures the core temperature near one of the combustion chambers, so it reacts more slowly and may not represent the whole picture, especially when there is only one carburettor supplying several cylinders and one may be hotter than the others. The *oil temperature gauge* (which reacts very slowly to changes) is the best measure of how heat is balanced around the engine, which means that having the correct amount of oil in it is essential, if only for cooling purposes. However, having too much oil can be just as much a problem as having too little, as it can creep up the pushrod tubes and pick up heat directly from the cylinders.

EFFICIENCY

Power developed inside the cylinders is known as *indicated horse power*. *Mechanical efficiency* is how good the engine is at converting that at the cylinders to power at the shaft, or brake (shaft) horse power.

THE CARBURETTOR

This is a device that mixes fuel and air in the correct proportions, vapourises it and delivers it to the cylinders via the *inlet manifold* (that is, an inlet that serves manifold, or many, cylinders). It uses the Venturi principle (see *Principles of Flight*), which states that, as the speed of air increases over a restriction, the pressure reduces.

The fuel (main) nozzle, which is connected directly to the fuel system through a series of pumps and jets, is inside the low pressure area, so the fuel in the line is sucked out and vapourised as it is forced to expand (this also cools the area, so be careful with carburettor icing, which can form well in advance of any other type). In fact, if you could make one small enough, there's no reason why you couldn't use an air conditioning unit to achieve the same effect. It would certainly work better than a carburettor.

There is a fuel strainer upstream of the needle valve (not shown). The diffuser ensures that the fuel flow is kept directly proportional to the volume of air flowing through the choke, preventing the main jet from supplying excessive fuel as engine speed is increased.

Just before the carburettor ends and the inlet manifold begins is a *butterfly valve*, which is best compared to a coin in a tube - when the throttle is closed, the butterfly valve is closed, and *vice versa*. One problem is that fuel splashes against it and condenses, which doesn't help with vapourisation or atomization much.

Even when the butterfly is fully open, though, there is still resistance to the flow of fuel from its sideways presentation. New car engines have eliminated it altogether by making the throttle increase the inlet valve opening time to get the same effect.

Anyhow, when the butterfly is closed, the engine still needs to be fed with fuel, so there is an *idle jet* that bypasses it to keep the engine ticking over. It also helps the venturi, since the airflow at idle is quite small (the jet is actually a hole next to the butterfly, and it's sometimes called the *slow running jet*). Also, when you need power in a hurry, there is a small lag due to inertia between the time you open the throttle and the time the engine starts to speed up, because the air supply responds more quickly than the fuel does, which gives you a *weak cut* (a momentarily weak mixture), so a small squirt of fuel is delivered separately to compensate, from an *accelerator pump*. When starting an engine from cold, therefore, resist the temptation to pump the throttle, because all you will do is flood it with large drops of fuel. A better tactic, if you need the throttle open, is to do so v e r y s l o w l y, so the pump doesn't kick in.

To start a flooded engine that has a carburettor, place the mixture control in cutoff, with the ignition switch off, and the throttle open until the fuel has been cleared.

Because aircraft go up, and air gets less plentiful at height, there is a danger of the fuel/air mixture getting out of balance as you climb - the engine will not work at all if the ratio of fuel to air is not correct. A mixture that has too much fuel against air is *rich*, while one the other way round

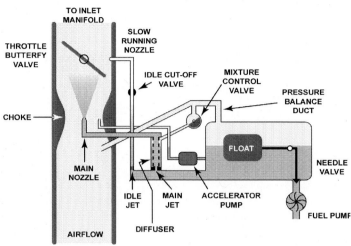

is *weak*. The *mixture control* is provided to adjust for this as you increase altitude - for example, you would have it set fully rich for takeoff and landing. The "normal" mixture is about 15:1 of air to fuel by *weight*, but this is not critical over a wide range. However, a ratio of 18:1 would be considered weak. The *mixture ratio* is that between the *masses* of *fuel* and *air* entering the *cylinder* (air to fuel).

The mixture control's main purpose is to adjust fuel flow to get the correct fuel/air ratio - it corrects for variations resulting from reduced air density at altitude. Leaning makes the engine run hotter and give you more power for less fuel; a 112 hp aircraft cruising at 4000 feet and 85 knots might burn 5 gallons an hour when rich, but only 4.5 when leaned, giving a range of 116 miles as opposed to 100 - a saving, or an increase, of 16%. The mixture control's secondary function is to cut fuel from the engine on the ground when you want to stop it (you don't just switch the magnetos off). The *Idle Cut Off* (ICO) in the carburettor is joined to the mixture lever with a *Bowden cable*. When the lever is operated at the end of a flight, the engine is starved of fuel, and stops.

Note: Most normally aspirated engines can be leaned at any altitude when the power is set *below* about 75% (cruise power for Lycomings is normally between 55-75%). Thus, leaning off at more than cruise power (i.e. in the climb) should *not* be carried out, as many engines rely on a rich mixture for cooling. It may save fuel, but petrol has a high latent heat content, and the excess fuel reduces the temperature when it evaporates.

MANIFOLD PRESSURE

The manifold pressure indicates the power output of a piston engine, being the density of the fuel/air mixture in the inlet manifold, or, in other words, its thermal energy. In an unsupercharged engine, it will drop with height for a given throttle setting, because there is less atmospheric pressure to push the useful charge into the cylinder, and you must keep opening the throttle to compensate (the gauge will indicate lower than atmospheric pressure when the engine is running, because it is showing the engine's *suction*, and the MAP sensor is in the induction system. When idling, the figure is about 12 inches). Eventually, you will get no more power, at the *limiting altitude*, which is kinda fun when you still have to get into a landing site at altitude when the only controls that have any effect are the cyclic and pedals.

The *service ceiling* is the altitude at which you can achieve 100 fpm rate of climb. The *absolute ceiling* is when you can only (just) maintain level flight.

You can extend the service ceiling by *supercharging* or *turbocharging*, discussed below. High MAP and low RPM makes an engine work too hard, and means severe wear and damage, so be careful to observe the limits.

Humidity has an effect, too, although it is less with turbines. The more water there is in the air, the less air gets into the engine, therefore the mixture is richer and burns slower. The point is that performance graphs do not show this, so factor them by around 10% if the air is wet, say after a shower. You will get the most engine power when it's cold and dry, in high pressure conditions.

Note: Boost pressure is generally considered to be any manifold pressure above 30 ins Hg.

FUEL PRIMING

A *fuel primer* is a small hand pump designed to put neat fuel directly into either the induction manifold (near the combustion chamber) or the inlet valve port before you start in the cold to promote the presence of fuel vapour that will ignite to start the engine (very rarely do you need to prime a warm engine). They are not there with fuel injection systems.

Tip: Since the fuel primer injects fuel straight into the cylinder, you can use it to put fuel into your engine if it quits because of carb icing.

Aside from the fire hazard, excessive priming should be avoided because it washes lubricant off the cylinder walls.

CARBURETTOR ICING

This is actually one aspect of *induction system icing*. The other two are *fuel icing*, arising from water suspended in fuel, and *impact ice*, which builds up on the airframe around the various intakes that serve the engine.

Even on a warm day, if it's humid, carburettor icing is a danger, especially with small throttle openings where there's less area for the ice to block off in the first place (as when descending, etc.) Also, the temperature drop (between the OAT and that in the venturi) can be anywhere between 20-30°C, so icing (in an R22, anyway) can happen even when the OAT is as high as 21°C (70°F), or more. Tests have produced icing at descent power at temperatures above 30°C, with a relative humidity below 30%, in clear air. Because it is more volatile, and likely to contain more water, you can expect more fuel and carb icing with MOGAS than AVGAS.

Carb icing usually arises from the action of the venturi in the throat, just before the butterfly valve, which regulates the amount of fuel into the engine. You will remember the venturi's purpose is to accelerate airflow by restricting the size of the passageway, which has the effect of reducing the pressure and pulling the fuel in. Unfortunately, this process also reduces the temperature, as does the fuel vapourisation, hence the problem (the lower temperature means greater relative humidity, and closeness to the dewpoint, and the vapourisation takes its latent heat from the surroundings, making the situation worse). In fact, the vapourisation (and cooling) can carry on most of the way to the cylinders, causing the problem to persist, especially with the butterfly semi-closed, which produces another restriction and more of the same. Any water vapour under those conditions will turn directly to ice. Note also that warm air produces *more ice* because it holds more moisture.

With smaller engines, use full settings for every application - that is, carb heat either on or off, with no in-betweens - the greatest risk is at reduced power. Out of Ground Effect (OGE) hover performance charts for helicopters usually assume the carb air is cold (the R22 requires carb heat below 18" MP). In fact, when heat is applied, an engine will typically lose around 9% of its rated power.

Rough running may increase as melted ice goes through the engine. Also, be careful you don't get an overboost or too much RPM when you reselect cold. Of course, aeroplanes have some advantage if the engine stops from carb icing, as the propeller keeps the engine turning,

BELOW 18" M.P. IGNORE
GAUGE & APPLY FULL
CARB. HEAT

giving you a chance to do something about it. In a helicopter, due to the freewheel that allows autorotation, the practice of only selecting hot air when you actually get carb ice may not be such a good idea - usually, a gauge is used with a yellow arc on it, showing the danger range. Use carb heat as necessary to keep out if it.

The other peculiarity with regard to helicopters is that power tends to be used as required on takeoff, whereas aeroplanes use full throttle. This makes helicopters more vulnerable to carb icing, as the butterfly opening is smaller, and easier to cover with ice, which is particularly apparent on the first takeoff of the day, when the engine and induction system are still cold. If it is filtered, your carb heat may be used to preheat the induction system during the engine warm-up.

Carb heat reduces air *density*, so the mixture gets *richer*.

FUEL INJECTION

Most of the above problems with the carburettor are avoided with fuel injection, where fuel is metered directly in an atomised state to the cylinders according to power requirements, automatically taking air density into account. Ice is not formed because there is no venturi to cause temperature drops (there's no carburettor in the first place, as it is replaced with an engine driven pump).

The fuel is also atomised more thoroughly as it is forced through a small nozzle at high pressure. The whole process is more precise than a carburettor, which uses a more scattergun approach when it comes to delivering fuel to the cylinders - some would get excess fuel in the process of ensuring that each one gets a minimum amount. As a result of fuel injection, engine response is quicker and smoother, fuel efficiency is improved (you need less fuel for the same power output), and exhaust emissions are cleaner.

The fuel injector consists of a nozzle and a valve. The mechanics of the system exist much further back, and the process of delivering the fuel is known as **fuel metering**.

More fuel than is required is forced into a **governed fuel chamber**, which is separated by a diaphragm from the **metered fuel chamber**. Thus, the pressure in the governed chamber is always constant (any excess goes through a relief valve).

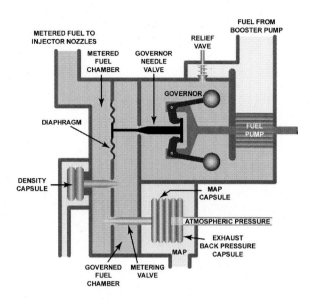

METERED FUEL TO INJECTOR NOZZLES — METERED FUEL CHAMBER — GOVERNOR NEEDLE VALVE — RELIEF VAVE — FUEL FROM BOOSTER PUMP — GOVERNOR — DIAPHRAGM — FUEL PUMP — DENSITY CAPSULE — MAP CAPSULE — ATMOSPHERIC PRESSURE — EXHAUST BACK PRESSURE CAPSULE — MAP — GOVERNED FUEL CHAMBER — METERING VALVE

As the governor rotates, its bobweights open a **needle valve** to allow the fuel to proceed into the **metered fuel chamber** where the difference in pressure between the governed and metered chambers acting on the diaphragm is used to try and close the needle valve and balance its movements. The pressure across the diaphragm is proportional to the square of the RPM, so the fuel flow through the jets ends up varying with engine speed. The fuel flow through the **main jet** is governed by *boost pressure* and *exhaust back pressure*. Increasing the boost (with the throttle) compresses a series of evacuated **MAP capsules**, which makes the main metering needle withdraw from the main jet to increase the fuel flow through it because the hole gets bigger (the needle is tapered to automatically control the mixture strength).

Normally, as atmospheric pressure falls with altitude, the exhaust gases find it easier to escape, as the pressure differential between the inside and the outside of the engine is larger. This improves volumetric efficiency because more of the fuel/air mixture can be pulled in. In a carburettor, the extra depression automatically pulls more fuel into the throat to keep the mixture correct but, in an injected system, some compensation is needed, otherwise the mixture would be weak (the improved volumetric efficiency makes more air in the manifold available to be drawn into the cylinders). This is provided by **back pressure capsules**, which are connected internally to atmospheric pressure, and externally to the MAP capsules. As altitude increases, the back pressure capsules are compressed by the greater difference between MAP and atmospheric pressure, opening the main needle valve.

To compensate for the reduction in density of the inlet charge when the temperature increases, a thermometer bulb in the inlet manifold controls the position of a second capsule-controlled needle valve. The capsule chamber is connected to the thermometer bulb by a liquid-filled capillary tube. When the manifold air temperature increases, the liquid expands, compresses the capsule and closes the needle valve, reducing the fuel flow to match the air density.

A common problem with fuel injected engines is blocked jets, from dirt in fuel. A lesser one, but still significant, is difficulty in starting, particularly on a hot day, when the feed pipes lie across the top of the engine and consequently get warm, with the fuel inside them evaporating nicely and creating a vapour lock, so you need a short burst of fuel pressure to prime the lines.

Tip: If the primary airway is blocked (ice, or a bird), alternate air in the cabin will change the source.

An electric fuel injection system will be backed up by a mechanical one. One benefit of this is being able to use it without the engine running, which is useful for priming.

SUPERCHARGERS

The power from a piston engine depends on the *weight* of the fuel/air mixture in the cylinder. This will naturally reduce with height because there is less atmospheric pressure to force it in. If you can force air into a cylinder under a pressure that is higher than atmospheric you can get a greater mass of air into the cylinder.

 A supercharger is a centrifugal air pump (that is, it has a *radial compressor*) run directly from the engine crankshaft (at a much faster speed!) through step-up gearing, situated between the carburettor and the inlet manifold. The supercharger's function is to *extend the service ceiling of the aircraft*, by compressing the fuel/air mixture to *maintain sea level power at altitude*, or to increase normal power lower down. It works by giving the air a high velocity which is gradually reduced as it passes through diffuser vanes, which provides the higher pressure. However, this forced induction only really works in a particular temperature range, and a supercharger can use up a lot of engine power. The essential point to remember is that the extra air is sucked through the carburettor, and *then* blown into the cylinder. The result is that the air is already half-compressed before it enters the combustion chamber, thus helping the adiabatic heating process and allowing a smaller compression ratio to be used.

Supercharging is therefore a two-stage compression process. Although some work is wasted and the efficiency of the cycle is reduced, the overall result is an improvement in power of around 40% for the same fuel consumption.

Automatic boost control uses an evacuated capsule to vary the engine RPM, which controls the speed of the supercharger and the manifold pressure, which ultimately controls the weight of charge entering the cylinder. The capsule is exposed to inlet pressure while being linked to the throttle via an oil operated servo piston. When the capsule is compressed, the throttle is partly closed, and *vice versa*. The oil comes from the engine lubrication system.

When the engine starts, the induction manifold pressure falls to a low value which is sensed by the capsule, which expands, to make oil flow below the servo piston, which is forced to the top of its stroke. If the throttle is opened any more, the capsules compress and the oil supply is eventually cut off, then directed above the piston, to make it go down and close the throttle. In this way, the boost cannot rise above the *Rated Boost,* which can be exceeded with an override system for takeoffs and emergencies.

When things are in equilibrium, any tendency for pressure to fall in the inlet is counteracted by a progressive opening of the throttle because more oil is introduced underneath the servo piston until you reach the altitude where the throttle is fully open. This *rated altitude* is that, above which, the induction manifold pressure *falls,* just like it does with a normally aspirated engine. The *full throttle height* is the altitude up to which a given boost setting can be maintained at a given engine RPM, so the lower the boost pressure you select, the higher it can be maintained by the automatic system. The rated altitude is also full throttle height at rated boost and normal RPM for that boost.

With superchargers, engine speed should be kept as low as possible to minimise losses from friction and adiabatic heating, which will cause the charge's density to reduce, followed by the engine power. You get maximum efficiency with the throttle fully open and the engine RPM as low as it can be without causing detonation.

Two-speed superchargers, which use variable gearing, are an attempt to overcome the problems of operating the engine at high speeds at high altitudes.

Note: Superchargers (and turbochargers) need special attention, particularly when they are older, as under- or overboosting (when applying full power or descending rapidly) can cause significant damage.

TURBOCHARGERS

A turbocharger also increases pressure in the inlet manifold, but its compressor is powered by exhaust gases which are deflected from their normal course outwards by a valve called a *wastegate,* which is sensitive to altitude. When the wastegate is closed, the engine is being turbocharged, that is, the exhaust gases are turning a turbine wheel which drives an *impeller* at the intake *before* the carburettor, so the air is being blown *into* it, as opposed to being sucked out by a supercharger. In this way, the engine doesn't lose power by driving it through geared shafts. Since the exhaust is involved, *preflight checks should include security of the pipes,* so that carbon monoxide doesn't get into the cabin. Automatic waste gate control is done with engine oil pressure acting against a spring, which opens the gate at low altitude. Oil closes it at high altitude, although, at low engine power it will be closed anyway, to conserve pressure (turbochargers are lubricated with engine oil). The *critical altitude* is the pressure altitude at which it is fully closed. Above it, power will fall in line with the manifold pressure. The waste gate actuator controller is *downstream* of the actuator.

If the waste gate seizes with the throttle fully open during a descent, there is a danger that the Manifold Air Pressure may exceed the maximum value.

Turbochargers provide a constant air *pressure* to the engine (not air density), but the air temperature is increased from the compression so, at higher temperatures, the density provided to the engine is less anyway. *Turbocharger intercoolers* (between the compressor and throttle) are there to prevent detonation at high altitude. They use ambient air to cool the intake air.

Controls should be moved smoothly and not too rapidly, and in the correct sequence. Turbocharger *boostrapping* (or *hunting*) is an overreaction to rapid throttle movement, leading to large pressure fluctuations and overboosting. A pressure relief valve in the induction manifold cures it. The turbocharger controller can also be damped.

One advantage of a turbocharger is that it makes power available less dependent on altitude. One disadvantage is that they are easy to overboost.

Tip: To preserve turbocharger life, let the engine run for a little while before shutting it down (check the flight manual for minimum times - usually 2 minutes), to stabilise the temperature and reduce the chances of distortion or oil coking on hotspots.

IGNITION

Near the end of the compression stroke, you need a spark with enough energy to ignite the fuel/air mixture in the cylinder provided at just the right moment. The spark must actually occur before TDC to suit modern engines that work under a various loads over a wide speed range, because you need to allow for the burning fuel to build up to its maximum pressure. In early engines, this timing adjustment (advancing or retarding) used to be done by the pilot, but now it is done automatically.

The whole mechanism that provides the spark at the critical moment consists of spark plugs, leads, magnetos, switches, etc., in duplicate (one magneto will serve one plug per cylinder, and the second the others). The duplication is actually for efficiency, as the magneto doesn't work that well at low RPM, but a side benefit is, obviously, safety. The magneto, which is actually a small generator that uses a permanent magnet, is a device with a transformer and all the circuitry to boost the low voltage primary current (24-28 volts) to one large enough to jump across a small gap at the plug electrodes. A car has similar items, but not in one unit. The other difference is that a magneto works as long as the engine is turning it - there is no need for external influence. This is done with the help of *magnetic induction*, or the relative movement of a magnetic field around a conductor, and *vice versa*, in which a current is induced, as described in *Electricity & Magnetism*, later in this section.

Note: The ignition switches in the cockpit ground the magnetos to Earth through the *primary circuit,* because they cannot be switched off (they work as long as they spin), so they must be treated as live. Ground connections can fail!

The components of a typical magneto consist of a permanent magnet, primary and secondary windings over a core, some way of making the magnetic field move (rotation of the magnet or the core), contact breaker points, a capacitor and a distributor.

ROTATING ARMATURE

In a *rotating armature* magneto, a rotor (armature) rotates in the gap between two ends of something resembling a horseshoe magnet. The armature is actually an engine-driven shaft, which is surrounded by two sets of coils, a *primary* then a *secondary* winding. As it spins, the flux along the armature reverses continually as the two poles of the armature rotate inside the magnetic field. The primary coil oscillates in sympathy with the flux reversals, and a current is induced in the secondary coil wrapped around it, because the primary field is expanding and collapsing - the essential point is *movement*. The ratio between the coils is significant, which is how such a high voltage is generated. The primary has thicker wire, but the secondary wire is hair-thin (all covered under *Electricity & Magnetism*, below).

ROTATING MAGNET

For engines with a lot of cylinders (over 6), a rotating magnet magneto is more efficient because it can produce more flux reversals per rotation. In this case, the primary and secondary windings are around the horseshoe magnet (which is now the armature) and the rotating part is a four-lobe magnet. This both increases the flux reversals and reduces the chances of the windings becoming undone through centrifugal loading at high speeds (in this case, you get four flux reversals and sparks per revolution, so it runs at ¼ of the engine speed).

CONTACT BREAKER

Inside the primary circuit of both types of magneto is a set of contact points that act as a switch whose function is to make the flux reversals more abrupt, since they are not good enough to produce a clean signal by themselves. The speed at which the lines of force intersect the windings is one of the determining factors in the voltage produced - the faster you can move the field, the more voltage you can produce so, in order to induce a large voltage, the magnetic field must be collapsed quickly, since it is easier to collapse it than to create it. Left to itself, the magnetic field would expand slowly, so there is comparatively little voltage induced by it into the secondary winding.

The magnetic field is collapsed almost instantaneously by opening the points, with the consequent generation of very high voltage in the secondary winding. However, when the points open, the collapsing magnetic field induces a current in the primary, in the opposite direction, large enough to jump a small air gap, such as the one between the just-opening points. The tiny spark is enough to erode metal away from them, but the condenser can absorb it, and store the excess current until the circuit is made again, where it is released harmlessly. Without the condenser, the current would bounce back and forth in the primary winding, stopping the magnetic field from collapsing properly.

The separation of the points has to take place in strict timing with the maximum primary current, to ensure that all this is done at maximum intensity. The points are opened by a *rocker arm*, which is moved by a cam as many times per revolution as there are lobes on the cam. The rocker arm is returned to its normal position with a spring.

DISTRIBUTION

The high voltage generated is fed (from the secondary coil) to the plugs by a *distributor*, which is essentially a rotor spinning inside a cap at the end of the magneto holding heavy screened cables going to the plugs.

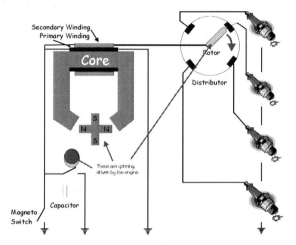

The rotor contacts each cable in turn, but they are not matched to the plugs in order, as one cylinder would receive the spark at the wrong time.

Instead, the cables are arranged out of order, on a four-cylinder engine as 1342 or 1243).

Note: If the internal half-speed wheel that drives the distributor fails, you can expect extreme rough running because the sparks will be delivered to the plugs in the wrong order. The solution is to turn off the offending magneto, which will allow you to land without turning the engine off - include it in your engine failure checks.

THE 4-STROKE (OTTO) CYCLE

With this method, one complete stroke of the piston carries out each of the operations involved, namely *induction, compression, power* and *exhaust*.

It all starts with the piston at *Top Dead Centre* (TDC), ready to start moving down while sucking in a fuel/air mixture from the carburettor, through the inlet valve, which has just opened (left, below). On top of the suction created by the piston's downward movement, atmospheric pressure helps to force the fuel and air in (when it is less, a supercharger or turbocharger helps).

The valve closes as the piston reaches Bottom Dead Centre (BDC), so the chamber is filled to maximum. With both valves closed, the piston starts moving up again (right, above), compressing and therefore heating the mix, as well as increasing its density, which helps the flame ignite quicker because the particles are closer together (the heating helps to increase the pressure).

For a very short period the volume remains relatively constant while the spark plug fires and causes the pressure and temperature to increase rapidly as the fuel ignites.

The spark plug actually fires just before TDC, with a spark from a high-voltage electric current provided by the magneto, which is rotating in sympathy with the engine. It is timed this way to give the fuel time to catch fire, and produce the optimum expansion at 10° *after* TDC, which is when it is actually required. Under power (i.e. at high speeds) the spark can occur as much as 30° beforehand (when idling, it is more like 10°).

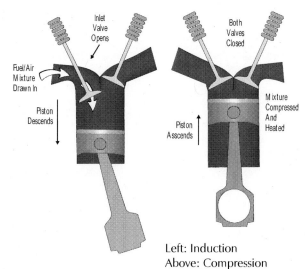

Left: Induction
Above: Compression

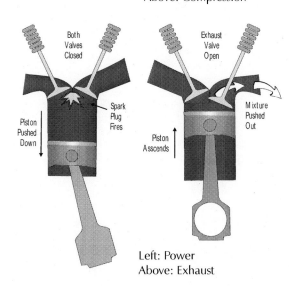

Left: Power
Above: Exhaust

The ignited gases expand adiabatically, and the temperature drops because the volume increases as the piston is forced downwards, in a smooth movement, making the crankshaft rotate, plus whatever is attached to it (left, above). Then the crankshaft's rotation, assisted by the flywheel, forces the piston up again with the exhaust valve open to let the burnt gases escape (right, above).

Note that, although there were four cycles, the crankshaft only went round twice.

DIESEL ENGINES

Diesel engines do not require spark plugs or carburation - instead, fuel is injected at high pressure just as the temperature increases at the end of the compression stroke, so volatility is not a good quality for the fuel, as it needs to be as incompressible as possible. The original idea was to operate the engine at constant pressure, but this is difficult to maintain, so part of the fuel is burnt at constant volume, as with the Otto cycle, and the remainder is burnt at constant pressure.

TIMING

The cylinder head (which is bolted to the top of the engine casing) contains valves which must open and close at precise times to allow the fuel/air mixture in and exhaust gases out (*fuel* or *inlet* valves, and *exhaust valves*). Valves are hollow, or partly filled with sodium pellets to encourage heat transfer, especially the exhaust valve. They will have two springs to help return them to their original position - the second is there to reduce valve bounce.

As it turns, the crankshaft will turn a smaller version of itself, called a *camshaft*, which rotates at *half the crankshaft speed*, and is linked directly to the valve rocker at the top of the cylinder by a long metal rod, the bottom end of which is enclosed in a *tappet* (to save wear). The top end of the rod hits the valve rocker directly, pushing the valve open. As the engine gets hotter, these rods expand, so there is a little clearance to allow for this, called the *valve rocker clearance* (valve rockers are *not* tappets). If the valve rocker clearance is too large, the valve will not open so much, which will reduce *volumetric efficiency*. If the gap is too small, there will be loss of compression because the valves won't close properly. Hydraulic tappets take up the slack automatically so you don't have to keep adjusting the valve rocker clearance.

The volumetric efficiency is the measure of mass charge to the theoretical mass charge at ISA if the engine were stationary. That is, the degree to which the cylinder is filled with new mixture at full throttle, as compared to an equivalent amount of atmosphere. It is rarely more than 80%, due to various leakages and losses, hence the need for supercharging (the volume of gas in the cylinder always weighs less than when it left the carburettor. The difference determines volumetric efficiency).

Some engines have an *overhead camshaft*, so called because it sits on top of the engine and opens the valves directly, that is, without a complicated linkage that can be a real limitation as to how fast the engine can go. It is extremely important to check the cam chain or belt regularly, because it also stops valves falling into the cylinders and welding themselves to the pistons.

Below: Overhead Camshaft Engine

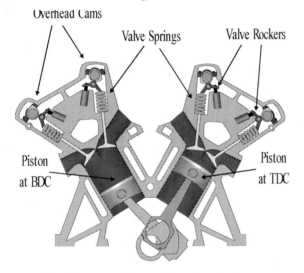

Normally, when an engine gets hot, the cylinders get longer and might get longer than the push rods (unless they are made of a material that expands very quickly), which means that the valve clearance will increase. With the overhead camshaft, any valve expansion keeps pace with the cylinder and makes the valve clearance decrease.

In theory, the fuel/air mixture should enter the cylinder during the piston's travel from TDC to BDC (top to bottom), with the exhaust gases leaving it between BDC to TDC, but things are not quite as simple as that! In practice, a small part of the piston's up and down movement is immaterial relative to the work done - this is called *ineffective crank angle*. In other words, it is a short period where the valves may as well be open as not.

As an engine is complicated, with a lot happening in a short time, some anticipation here and there doesn't go amiss. Opening valves early is called *valve lead*, and being

late is called *valve lag*. When they are both open at the same time, you get *valve overlap*, where the exhaust gases on their way out reduce the pressure in the manifold, which helps to pull in the incoming fuel/air mix (this is more effective at altitude, where the atmospheric pressure is lower). Valve overlap also promotes easier valve timing.

Opening the inlet valve early means that it will be fully open as the induction stroke starts, which overcomes the fuel/air mix's inertia, so there is no time lag between the piston moving down and the mix actually moving, to allow it to keep up with the piston. Its momentum when the piston finally stops at BDC means that as much of the mix as possible is crammed in and the valve closes *after* BDC to make sure.

At the end of the power stroke, as its force weakens, you may as well open the exhaust valve early so that the remaining internal pressure can force the gases out early. It closes late to take advantage of the gas's momentum.

Advancing the timing means moving the spark further *before* other events in the cycle. An *impulse coupling* in the magneto provides a high energy *retarded* spark during startup, as the engine is rotating very slowly at that point (magnetos do not work well at low RPM), and the spark needs to occur *later* than usual so the piston is beyond TDC as the gases start to burn and exert their pressure (this also reduces the chances of a kick-back). In the coupling, flyweights react against two stop-pins in the magneto housing as the engine (and magneto shaft) is turned over. The locked flyweights hold the magneto still whilst a spring is wound up until a certain amount of rotation has occurred, when projections on the housing release the flyweights. The spring then unwinds and spins the magneto to produce the spark. Once the engine fires, centrifugal force holds the flyweights away from the stop pins.

Ignition is automatically advanced as RPM increases, and retarded when starting up (the spark is intensified as well).

Note: A *hydraulic lock* (hydraulicing) occurs when there is some liquid in the cylinder when you start up that is equal to, or greater than the swept volume, and which stops the piston moving during the compression stroke, when both valves are closed. Damage (usually a broken connecting rod) occurs once the preceding cylinders have fired since the piston is forced against the liquid, which is incompressible. In a radial engine, the fluid is likely to be oil, in the bottom cylinder. In a horizontally opposed engine, however, the liquid is more likely to be accumulated fuel, in one of the forward cylinders. Be careful when operating the fuel boost pump during a failed start, and do not over-prime on sloping ground.

Turbines

As mentioned previously, the same principles apply to jet engines as reciprocating ones, only they're applied in a different way. They also use cheaper fuel, because compression is not a factor in producing the power, although avgas can sometimes be mixed with jet fuel (see the Flight Manual), at the expense of reduced maintenance periods, because it doesn't lubricate the fuel pumps so well (also, there is a lot of crud left on the turbine blades from the anti-knock additives, and, being a thin fuel, avgas will "bubble out" quicker at lower altitudes). Since compression can be ignored, and most of the airflow is used for cooling anyway, a high relative humidity has little effect on the output of a jet, which is a hot, thin and fast stream of air, although you would be wise not to try to lift too much after a heavy shower has passed through. Also, jet engines run on a continuous cycle, whereas a piston engine relies on a precisely timed sequence of individual events, with all the bits flying back and forth violently. In contrast, jet engines just spin round, although their "simplicity" relative to infernal combustion engines depends hugely on their quality of design and manufacture.

Propellers are only efficient up to certain speeds, below which jets use too much fuel relative to the work done - the airstream provided by a propeller is of a large diameter and moves around the same speed as the aircraft it relates to. The output from a jet engine, on the other hand, is hot and thin, and very much faster, which is why it's fuel-inefficient (it's also noisy, and like driving a car in permanent high gear. The noise comes from hot air meeting the cold air outside the aircraft too quickly). At higher speeds, say above 350 kts, jets are best only because propellers don't work at all, due to the prop tips approaching supersonic speeds (the Spitfire nearly managed Mach 1, but the lift reduced after a certain point). Officially, piston engines are best below about 217 kts (250 mph), turboprops between 217-390 kts (250-450 mph) and jets above that (although turbofans are like large propellers). Jet engines also do not work best when inlet air exceeds Mach 1, so high-speed jets use variable *ramps*, or *cones*, in the inlet to create a shock wave that slows the air down.

Turboprops (or turboshafts) are a good solution, where the output of the turbine drives a propeller shaft, but your top speed is still limited, hence the *fanjet*, or *turbofan*, which is simply a low speed propeller (with lots of blades) enclosed in a duct, so you don't waste power in the shape of

air that spills centrifugally out of the sides. This not only gives better thrust (actually, more than double), but also provides cooling, and less noise, because the temperature differential between the gases and the air is not so great. They are called *bypass engines* because the bulk of the air bypasses the core of the engine - the *bypass ratio* is the difference between the amount of air accelerated only by the fan against that passing through the engine. The end result is a large, relatively slow-moving column of cold air enclosing a thin, hot and fast exhaust. Total thrust is from the fan and the engine, but the greater part comes from the fan, with help from the duct. The back end of the engine runs a lot hotter, though, even white-hot in the early days. Low bypass (or turbojet) engines are noisiest from behind, and high bypass is noisiest from the front. The fan blades, as a point of interest, are built to bend and recover if they get struck by anything up to a 4 lb goose (in fact, an RB 211-535 engine on a 757 once sucked in and spat out four Canada geese without even a burp). The amount of air used for cooling is another reason why humidity has less effect on the performance or otherwise of jet engines.

Power is varied by changing the amount of fuel supplied to the engine. Put simply, turbine engines create continuously expanding gases, the energy from which is used for propulsion. Thrust is equal to the change in momentum of the air entering and leaving them. That is to say, thrust is measured by the acceleration of the air through a jet engine. As momentum is the product of *mass x velocity*, any increase in either will increase thrust in proportion, so, other things being equal, an increase in airspeed leads to more air being compressed at the intake and a greater mass of air entering the engine. However, because the air is slowed down before being accelerated again, the resulting *intake momentum drag* reduces the potential thrust. Low bypass engines suffer from this initially, but thrust will increase slightly but steadily above

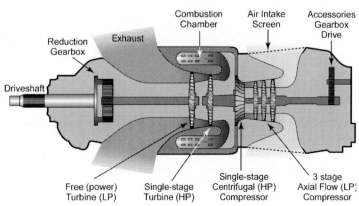

Reduction Gearbox · Exhaust · Combustion Chamber · Air Intake Screen · Accessories Gearbox Drive · Driveshaft · Free (power) Turbine (LP) · Single-stage Turbine (HP) · Single-stage Centrifugal (HP) Compressor · 3 stage Axial Flow (LP) Compressor

M0.5 as mass flow increases. High bypass engines, on the other hand, have reduced thrust as Mach number increases. Jet thrust decreases generally with altitude, and temperature has its effect in TGT (*Total Gas Temperature*) limitations. If this stops you applying more power, a lower OAT allows a little more RPM, and throughput of air, and thrust. Of course, if it's very cold outside, you will hit compressor RPM limits before the TGT. Either way, thrust has a finite limit. At high temperatures, thrust varies with temperature, but below about ISA +15°C thrust is independent of it and remains constant (the engine is known as *flat rated*). The 737 uses N_1 (compressor RPM) as an indication of power, but others use EPR, explained in the *Compressor* section, below. Note that *power* is a measure of *thrust* x *speed*, so it is not the same as thrust.

Speaking of 737s, if you increase N_1 of a CFM56-3 engine from 80-90%, you will add about 5000 lbs of thrust. From 30-40%, you will add only about 1000 lbs of thrust, so the Thrust/N_1 curve of a jet engine is logarithmic. Engine thrust is approximately proportional to engine speed$^{3.5}$, against speed^2 for a prop aircraft.

Equivalent Shaft Horsepower (EHSP) is a measure of power for a turboprop. Some get up to 15-25% of their thrust from the exhaust, and EHSP adds this to shaft horsepower to get a total figure. ESHP will decrease as density altitude gets higher. You usually get a turboprop's minimum specific fuel consumption somewhere between 25,000-35,000 feet (the tropopause). As thrust depends on angle of attack with a propeller, it decreases as speed is increased because the angle of attack is reduced from the airflow. However, the equation of *thrust* x *speed* is still valid.

The five basic parts of a jet engine are the *inlet*, the *compressor*, *combustor*, *turbine* and *nozzle* (the bit joining the compressor to the combustor is called the *diffuser*). They could be combined or doubled back on themselves in some engines, to save space. The PT6 (see picture overleaf) has a "backwards" design, with the compressor at the rear so that the power section is nearest the propeller gearbox. It is a free turbine, so maintenance is easier, as the two parts of the engine are separate. In a PT6-driven turboprop, the power turbine governor reduces fuel flow to stop the power turbine overspeeding.

Note: With the PT6, be careful during flight at high angles of attack, like when practising stalls or trying a short-field landing, because the air enters at the back. If wind shear is encountered and the stall warning sounds, increase torque *carefully* until above around 400 pounds (it varies between engines). Otherwise, you could get asymmetrical acceleration.

Another name for a jet engine is a *gas producer*. In a turbojet, this would be where the story stops, because the thrust is used to propel the machine forward directly. In a turboprop, the stream of hot gases is intercepted by a turbine, and used to drive a propeller gearbox. Unfortunately, about 2/3 of the energy produced is used simply to keep the engine running. Most of the rest is used by a power turbine for propulsion, leaving enough energy to ensure the gas falls out of the engine by itself, so you don't need extra components to drain more energy.

The speed at the tips of all rotating aerofoils in the engine is carefully governed to keep the airflow from creating shock waves.

In simple terms, the jet engine operates continuously, by drawing air in through the intake and into the compressor, in which there is a ring of rotating blades called *rotors* followed by a ring of stationary ones called *stators*, whose purpose is to slow the air down to compress and heat it. Since this increase is small, there may be one or two more rotor/stator sets (called *spools*) to go through before the air reaches the combustion section (spools can be driven by their own turbine and connecting shaft). Each spool will be numbered from N_1, through N_2, and so on.

Some N_1 air can be made to bypass the whole engine - in this case, the N_1 compressor may be so big that it is called a *fan*, which is more like a large propeller with lots of small blades. Anyhow, what air there is left in the engine core now enters the combustion chamber, where it is mixed with fuel and burnt. The expanding gases are guided through convergent guide vanes which direct it onto the turbine blades at the optimum angle. The turbine blades rotate and drive any compressors to which they are attached while the remaining air leaves the engine as a fast, hot stream.

THE INLET

Strictly speaking part of the airframe, this is where air enters the system. Its function is to convert ram-air pressure (from forward movement) into static pressure, ready for the compressor. In fact, the air enters the nozzle at less than the flight speed and is further slowed before the compressor (below) causes a substantial rise in pressure and temperature.

The air travelling through the inlet may well include other odds and ends, like sand (in the desert) dust, leaves, etc.

Fine screens can combat this, but they restrict airflow and can have an effect on performance. A *particle separator* uses centrifugal force from inlet air to create small swirls that pick up small particles and drop them into a sediment trap (like a vacuum cleaner). They work with snow as well.

THE COMPRESSOR

This is a rotating mass of impellers or blades, designed to take vast quantities of air, compress it (and therefore heat it) for direction to the combustor (see below), so it's an air pump, sometimes with the weight of air delivered determined by the engine RPM. That is, for any specified RPM, the air volume will be a definite amount. The temperature rise across the compressor could easily be 555°C and the compression ratio nearly 10:1 for a centrifugal compressor, and 25:1 for an axial (which means more thrust for the same frontal area).

Note: The air being so hot has some significance if the fire detection system in your machine is set to trigger off at a similar temperature, as a compressor leak could give you a false fire indication.

The **axial compressor** has a ring of rotating blades called *rotors* followed by a ring of stationary ones called *stators*, or *stator vanes*, whose purpose is to slow the air down to compress and heat it by bending and shaping it into the right position for the next compressor wheel. Pressure is gradually increased as the air is forced into smaller spaces created by further blades downstream (temperature and pressure *increase*, while velocity *decreases*).

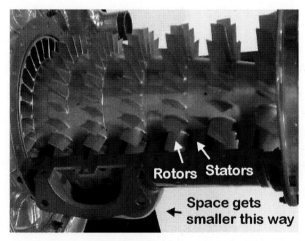

Rotors Stators

Space gets smaller this way

Each rotating wheel with its set of stators is a *stage*, so several together (on a shaft) constitute a *multistage compressor*, used because the heat increase is relatively small and needs boosting.

A dual compressor, on the other hand, would have stages in tandem, but on different shafts at different speeds, to produce higher compression ratios. The first in line would be the low pressure compressor (N_1), driven by the low

pressure turbine, which would also be the slowest, via the low pressure shaft, which rotates inside the high pressure shaft, which performs the same function for the high pressure compressor (N_2) and turbine. The N_2 shaft runs the opposite way to N_1, so the torques counteract and cancel each other out, relieving stress on the engine mounts. In some engines, N_2 is the intermediate shaft and N_3 the high power. Being the smallest, N_3 is the one started first.

The whole combination of shafts and compressor is known as a *spool*.

The *compression ratio* is the difference between the pressure of the air as it comes out of the compressor and the pressure at the engine inlet - it should always be higher than the back pressure from the turbine, or the airflow could go the wrong way - that for a centrifugal compressor is 4:1. The *Engine Pressure Ratio* (EPR), on the other hand, is the difference between air pressure coming out of the turbine compared to that at the compressor inlet, or an indication of thrust obtained by sensing pressure at various stages in the engine (depends on the aircraft). It is the normal measure of power output for turbojets or turbofans, except for the 737, which uses N_1 (turboprops use *torque*, with balanced oil piston or phase shift sensing systems in the gear reduction, measuring the force applied to a propeller over a distance of rotation). The EPR gauge shows you the ratio of the tailpipe (jetpipe) pressure to the compressor inlet pressure, and it will overread if the P1 probe is blocked. Maximum EPR for any stage of flight is calculated by computer, and it is easy to go over the indicated value. If performance allows, a reduced EPR may be used to save engine wear.

Inlet Guide Vanes direct air onto the first rotor of the compressor. They are closed at idle and fully open at about 70% engine RPM.

As its name implies, the **centrifugal compressor** uses impellers to fling air *outwards* into channels leading to the combustion chamber. It has a *high compression ratio by stage* and a *large diameter*, so it will tend to make an engine shorter, but wider.

Some engines have a small valve that opens when the engine starts, to correct the airflow so that the compressor blades do not stall (a *compressor bleed*) - for maximum efficiency, and because engines have to react quickly, you need to operate as close to the stall as possible. At low RPM, the engine is naturally is not able to pump as much air, so you need to "unload" it during start and low power operations. A bleed air system makes it see less restrictions by staying open until a certain pressure ratio is obtained. Other engines may use a bleed to prevent stalling when the throttle is opened too quickly.

A *compressor stall* reduces efficiency, meaning less power. Simply put, it is a stalling of the compressor blades when their angle of attack gets too much, which could happen if you pull power too quickly. A *cold stall* only affects a few blades, whereas a *hot stall* involves them all, and may mean severe damage from the hot gases coming out of the combustor when the airflow becomes reversed inside the engine (as the air is being compressed, it will try to spring back the way it came, as might happen if the intake gets blocked). In a *transient stall*, you will just hear the odd bang (and a bigger one when a blade flies through the side), but in a more steady stall, there will be a roaring sound and severe vibration with a sound like a machine gun, but mostly, you should just hear a coughing sound from the engine. About the only things you can do are to reduce the fuel flow and angle of attack on the compressor blades, or increase speed. In fact, the compressor is an ideal place from which to tap small amounts of air (compressor bleed air) for other purposes, such as cooling, pressurising of oil systems or operating anti-ice systems. However, when doing this, the exhaust temperature will tend to rise slightly. For anti-ice systems, the bleed is taken from the back end of the compressor (that is, compressor discharge air) that has already been heated from compression. It will typically flow through the compressor shell and hollow struts, and the inlet guide vanes.

The *diffuser* connects the compressor with the combustion section (next). The cross-sectional area of the engine increases here, which slows the air down and attains the highest pressure in any part of the engine, to make sure that the hot gases that are created in the combustion section don't go backwards (it converts kinetic pressure to static pressure). The diffuser in a centrifugal compressor makes pressure rise at constant velocity.

COMPRESSOR SURGE

For maximum efficiency, and because engines have to react quickly, you need to operate the compressor blades as close to the stall as possible. However, the stalling involved is not quite the same as that on an aerofoil, as compressor blades cannot change their position relative to the airflow they meet. They are affected by an *effective* angle of attack, which depends on the velocity of the airflow and the speed at which the blades are moving.

Some engines have a small valve (a *compressor bleed*) that opens when the engine starts, to correct the airflow so

that they do not stall - at low RPM, the engine is naturally not able to pump as much air, so you need to "unload" it during the start and low power operations so that the air does not hit the blades at the wrong angle. A bleed air system makes it see less restrictions by staying open until a certain pressure ratio is obtained. The same effect can be obtained with *Variable Inlet Guide Vanes* or *Variable Stators*, but these are more likely on aeroplane engines.

A compressor stall reduces engine efficiency, meaning less power. A *cold stall* only affects a few blades, whereas a *hot stall* involves them all, and may mean severe damage from the hot gases coming out of the combustor when the airflow becomes reversed inside the engine (as the air is being compressed, it will try to spring back the way it came, as might happen if the intake gets blocked). In a *transient stall*, you will just hear the odd bang (and a bigger one when a blade flies through the side), but in a more steady stall, there will be a roaring sound and severe vibration with a sound like a machine gun, but mostly, you should just hear a coughing sound from the engine. In the extreme, compressor surge is accompanied by loud banging noises and severe engine vibration.

About the only things you can do are to reduce the fuel flow and angle of attack on the compressor blades, or increase speed. Common causes of surging (which ultimately lead to less air relative to fuel) are:

- Rapid increase in fuel flow when RPM increases
- Low engine RPM
- Air going into the engine from the wrong direction, say in a crosswind, or restricted (say from icing)
- Contaminated or damaged compressor blades

Symptoms of surging include:

- Loss of thrust
- Odd noises & vibrations
- RPM fluctuations
- Increased TOT
- Burning gases out of various orifices

The compressor is an ideal place from which to tap small amounts of compressor bleed air for other purposes, such as anti-ice, cooling or sealing, where back pressure is used to stop other gases going the wrong way. However, when doing this, the exhaust temperature will tend to rise slightly. For anti-ice systems, the bleed is taken from the back end of the compressor (that is, compressor discharge air) that has already been heated from compression. It will typically flow through the compressor shell and hollow struts, and the inlet guide vanes.

THE COMBUSTOR

Generally, the air is divided into two streams here, one for burning, and the other for cooling. What air is left in the engine core after compression enters the combustion chamber, where it is mixed with fuel and burnt. There are two types of airflow in the combustion section, in the *Primary* and *Dilution* zones, but many manufacturers call them *Primary*, *Secondary* and *Tertiary* for more accuracy.

Once the flame is lit by the spark igniter during engine start, it stays that way till the engine is shut down (you could say that the engine is on fire all the time, and it's only when it becomes uncontained that it becomes an emergency). The engine is spun initially by air from a high pressure bottle or APU (or even a V8 for the SR-71, or a starter/generator) and the sparks ignited when the airflow is high enough to keep the temperatures down at the back end. As the combustion chamber has a fixed size, the hot air must increase speed to escape.

An *auto relight* system is designed to restart the engine should it flame out, providing a continuous spark from the igniter all the time it is switched on.

THE TURBINE

This is where hot air flows through, and the highest temperatures in the engine are at the start of the turbine inlet (the gases have just left the combustion section). The reason why the Turbine *Outlet* Temperature is measured is because it is simply too hot for a thermocouple to survive anywhere else (although, in the Bell 206, the temperature is actually measured *between* the turbines). Instead, a more severe limit is imposed on the TOT to protect the turbine(s) at the other end. The heat is kept within limits with cooling air extracted from the compressor, which is driven by the turbine through a connection.

A red triangle, or dot, or diamond on an engine instrument face or glass indicates the maximum limits for high transients, as found when starting

In a *free turbine* engine, used in turboprops, the exhaust goes through two turbine stages; a compressor turbine,

and a power turbine. That is, there is no direct connection between the exhaust from the engine and the gearbox it drives. There is always a reduction gear system to reduce high RPM from the power turbine.

In a *direct drive* system, the propeller is driven directly by the compressor shaft through a reduction gear. You can tell the difference between the two when the propellers are stopped - those driven by a free turbine will be in the feathered position, whereas those driven directly will be in fine pitch. *Start locks* fix the blades at 0° to reduce drag, and therefore strain, when the engine is started. They are metal pins that are held open with centrifugal force.

The turbine uses energy to drive the compressor, so temperature and pressure drop in this section.

One of the most important instruments in your cockpit is the Turbine, or Exhaust Temperature gauge, which shows the heat coming out of the back end. It is particularly important during starting because, if the battery is too weak to spin the engine properly, there will be less airflow through it, and not as much cooling available, leading to a hot start and an expensive repair as the back end melts. During flight, on hot days, this temperature may well be the limiting factor in the amount of payload you can take.

Turbine blades wash in. They are hollow, so they can be cooled with HP air (on the forward face of the blades, it forms a labyrinth to stop hot gases reaching the turbine wheel - on the rear, the exhaust cone acts as a screen). The most common method of fitting them to the wheel is with the *fir tree*.

Turbine *blade creep* is a change in blade length, which can be done deliberately with bleed air that changes the temperature of the casing to reduce the clearance for more power (*Turbine Active Clearance Control*). If you overtemp the engine, however, the change will be permanent - because the engine is not spinning so fast when you start, you are allowed more temperature as there is less risk of this happening.

Pressure, density and temperature decrease through a turbine, while velocity remains constant.

THE NOZZLE

Because the nozzle restricts the air flow, it makes the gases flow faster to provide better thrust. *Nozzle Guide Vanes* convert pressure energy to kinetic energy, impart the highest speed possible to the gas and direct it at the correct angle to the turbine, and guide the surplus air trapped in turbines overboard.

REVERSE THRUST

A *thrust reverser* will reverse the flow of exhaust gases outside the engine to help the brakes when stopping, up to slightly less than 50% of the engine's rated power, because it is not possible to deflect gases efficiently through 180 degrees. Because aircraft must stop in a specified distance with one engine out, meaning that reverse thrust will not be available anyway, flight planning calculations do not take thrust reversal into account - in fact, the reduction in distance with it working is actually not that large. Their main use is to relieve the strain on the brakes, as performance calculations are based on maximum braking (which is not used routinely), aside from allowing the brake to run cooler in normal use, and help with contaminated runways (as well as backing away from the gate, although this can put ground staff at risk). The process is most effective at high speeds, and pulls all sorts of crap into the engines at low speeds, so it should be engaged early (you could also get surging from the re-ingestion of hot air). Only a few (older) aircraft will allow reverse thrust to be deployed in flight, and you would typically use 75% of N_1 as a throttle setting (only use 100% in emergency). Normally, *squat switches* in the main undercarriage sense weight on the wheels, and allow an isolation valve controlling bleed air from the compressor to open once the throttles are at idle (the controls will be piggy-backed onto the normal thrust levers, so they are to hand when required). A reverse thrust door warning light on the instrument panel comes on when the reverse doors are unlocked.

Typically, on jet aircraft without bypass, *clamshells* forming part of the tailpipe block the escape of exhaust gases to direct them forward. *Buckets* can also be introduced directly into the exhaust stream to force it back over the top and bottom (these are hydraulically operated). Both types have to stand a lot of heat. *Cascade* types are used with high bypass engines, because there is usually little ground clearance. In this case, the equivalent of clamshells operate *inside* the engine to redirect cool bypass air out of the sides. *Petal Door reversers* do much the same.

Turboprop power levers are lifted back past an idle gate on the quadrant. This puts the propellers into negative pitch after initially increasing drag by flattening it. Engine power will increase as negative pitch is applied.

Reversers should not be used until the nosewheel touches down, since their use shifts the weight on to it.

ENGINE POSITION

On a modern jet, the engines are slung in pods underneath the wings, which not only provides a cleaner wing shape, but also helps to pull the wing down in flight, so the wing itself can be made of lighter construction. However, trying to roll near the ground can damage them! Engines at the rear minimise asymmetric problems, but wings need to be made stronger, and are therefore heavier. Engines are also closer together (a failure of one could damage the others) and the fuel pipes have to run through the fuselage.

Fuel

Jet and piston fuels mix differently with contaminants (particularly water), which is due to variations in their specific gravities and temperature. The specific gravity of water, for example, is so close to Avtur that it can take up to 4 hours for it to settle out, whereas the same process may take as little as half an hour with Avgas. As a result, there is always water suspended in jet fuel, which must be kept within strict limits, hence two filtration stages, for solids and water. The latter doesn't burn, of course, and can freeze, but it's the fungi that gather round the interface between it and the fuel that is the real problem - it turns into a dark-coloured slime which clings to tank walls and supporting structures, which not only alters the fuel chemically, but will block filters as well. Not much water is required for this - trace elements are enough, although, in reduced temperatures, dissolved water will escape as free water, and look like fog. Water in jet fuel is the reason for icing inhibitors, which will combine with the water and lower its freezing point, so that ice crystals do not form and block the lines. However, fuel heaters are more popular these days.

Each day before flying, and when the fuel is settled, carry out a water check in aircraft and containers. Collect samples in a transparent container and check for sediment, free water or cloudiness - if there is only one liquid, ensure it is not all water. Aviation fuel is "clean" if a one-quart sample is clear of sediment when viewed through a clean, dry, clear glass container, and looks clear and bright. Aircraft parked overnight should ideally have their tanks completely filled to stop condensation, but this is impractical if you expect a full load the next morning and don't have room for full fuel as well, in which case be prepared to do extensive sampling from the tanks (although the amount of water found under these circumstances in a small aircraft is unlikely to be more than a tablespoon).

The reason why long-term storage is not good for fuel (up to two years for drums is the accepted maximum) is partly because of daily temperature changes. When it is warm, the fuel expands and some of the vapour-air mixture is driven out. When it gets colder, the fuel contracts and fresh air is sucked in, to mix with more vapour. As the cycle repeats itself, the fuel inside gradually loses its effectiveness. Humidity will mean that water vapour will get in, too, and condense into liquid. The presence of oxygen will also cause a soluble gum to form, and insoluble black particularates, which become more apparent when fuel evaporates. TEL will oxidise into an insoluble white mass. Containers should be filled to 95%, and sealed tightly, in a place where the temperature is mostly below 80°F, out of direct sunlight - the 5% airspace allows room for expansion.

Fuel's volatility increases with altitude and temperature, so it will evaporate away quicker. This can cause *vapour locking*, where a bubble may form in the pipes and stop the fuel flowing. Increasing the pressure in the pipes helps with this, which is why boost pumps are installed.

AVGAS

Aviation gasoline is made of lighter hydrocarbons and has a specific gravity of around 0.72. It is coloured this way:

Colour	Fuel
Red	80/87
Blue	100LL
Green	100/130

JET FUEL

This is less volatile than AVGAS, but will still catch fire, given the chance - technically, it has a higher flash point, but a lower freezing point, and it gets more viscous as it cools, so gets harder to pump. At the freezing point, the hydrocarbons turn into waxy crystals. The specific gravity of jet fuel is between 0.75 to 0.84, but most flight manuals peg it down to 0.79.

Jet A, standard for commercial and general aviation (in the USA, at least), is narrow-cut kerosene, usually with no additives. Jet A1 has a lower freezing point and possibly (but rarely) something for dissipating static, and inhibiting fungus. It is used for long haul flights where the temperature gets very low. Jet B is a naphtha-type fuel made by blending straight-run kerosene with lower-boiling distillate, so it's wide-cut, lighter (i.e. less dense) and has a very low flash point (it's actually 2/3 kerosene and 1/3 naphtha, but in emergency you can swap the naphtha for avgas to get pretty much the same thing). It contains static dissipators, and is mainly used by military aircraft - the FCU may need to be adjusted if you want to use it.,

although it is being phased out, at least by Esso. Its only significant demand these days is in really cold places.

Try not to mix Jet A and Jet B - the mixture can ignite through static in the right proportions, as Air Canada found when they lost a DC-8 on the ramp in the 70s. The static can come simply from movement of fuel through the lines (it has to cross many materials). Jet A weighs about 5% more per litre than Jet B, but it gives you a longer range, as turbines work on the weight of the fuel they burn, not the quantity (hence the use of kg/hr for fuel flow, for example). So, if you load the same amount of fuel, your machine will weigh more with Jet A, but if you fill the tanks, you will use fewer litres and less money (this is one reason, aside from lubrication qualities, for not using AVGAS - its specific gravity is lower. However, AVTUR has more water in suspension and residual wax that must be heated to stop it blocking pipes).

JP4 is like Jet B but also has a corrosion inhibitor and anti-icing additives. It was the main military fuel but is being superseded by JP8, at least in the USA, for the Air Force. JP5 has a higher flashpoint than JP4, and was designed for US navy ships. It is similar to Jet A.

Fuel Control

Fuel heating devices are fitted upstream of the main fuel filters (on the engine) to prevent ice forming from water in the fuel.

In a twin jet, fuel booster pumps are inside a *feeder box* (or collector tank) which always has a small amount of fuel inside to keep the pumps submerged - aside from lubricating the pumps (which is why using avgas is such a problem), it stops *cavitation*, which is, essentially, bubbles in a fluid. In a pump, increased velocity reduces the pressure at the inlet, often below vapour pressure, so it "boils", allowing air to mix with it. Since this can block the pump and reduce performance, it has the equivalent of a heart attack. The pumps themselves operate on a low-ish pressure, to help the fuel get from the strange places it is kept in to the engine-driven fuel pump, especially when the lines pass through unpressurised areas.

FCU

The *Fuel Control Unit* does more or less the same job as a carburettor on a piston engine, except it uses springs and bobweights to meter fuel according to demand.

FADEC

The initials stand for *Full Authority Digital Electronic Control*. It's just a computer that controls the fuel system, based on information from various sensors, such as exhaust temperature, engine RPM, control movement, etc. (typical inputs are TGT, EPR/N_1, autothrottle/thrust management and EICAS/ECAM). The end result is a more precise control of propeller speeds under varying flight conditions, particularly with reference to overspeeding. Other benefits include automatic starting, better care of the engine (so more time between overhauls) and reduction of pilot workload through automation. Being a computer, it is software-based, and one preflight check is to ensure that the right software is loaded. Also, as it's a computer, it can monitor many parameters, hence more caution lights.

It will typically consist of two main items, the *Engine Control Unit* (ECU), on the airframe, with a processor inside, such as a 486 (powerful, huh? There is also the *Hydro Mechanical Unit* (HMU) on the engine, which functions rather like the old-style FCU when the FADEC is disabled. There will also be sensors and relays for the transmission of information around the system. Many signals will be repeated to the relevant instruments.

A FADEC has the following functions:

- Flow regulation
- Automatic starting sequence
- Transmission of engine data to the pilot's instruments
- Thrust management and protection of limits
- Monitoring thrust reversers
- Prevent overtemperature or overspeed

Engine Handling

One of the biggest things to unlearn when transitioning from piston to turbine is to keep your finger on the starter button once things start happening (with a piston, you tend to take your finger off straight away when the engine starts) - now you take your finger off when the engine becomes self-sustaining. Before then, it relies heavily on the battery or APU to keep it turning. It follows that, if the battery is weak to start with, the engine won't spin as fast, the airflow is reduced, the whole process becomes hotter and you could melt the back end with a hot start. You should always check the voltage available from the battery *before* starting a turbine engine. A *hung start* exists when the engine fails to accelerate to normal idle RPM. It just sits

there, weakening the battery and leading to a hot start. You get a *wet start* when the engine doesn't light off at all.

Pulling full power just because it's there is not always a good idea. Limitations may be there for other reasons - for example, the transmission might not be able to take that much. Excessive use of power will therefore ruin your gearbox well before the engine (and will show up as metal particles in the oil). Many turbine failures are the result of pulling too many cycles from minimum to maximum N_G, so if you don't need 100% torque, it's best not to use it.

Maximum Continuous Power is the setting that may be used indefinitely, but any between that and maximum power (usually shown as a yellow arc on the instruments - see left) will only be available for a set time limit.

While I'm not suggesting for a moment that you should, piston engines will accept their limits being slightly exceeded from time to time with no great harm being done. Having said that, the speed at which the average Lycoming engine disintegrates is about 3450 RPM, which doesn't leave you an awful lot of room when it runs normally at 3300! Turbines, however, are less forgiving than pistons and give fewer warnings of trouble because of the closer tolerances to which they are made. This is why regular power checks (once a week) should be carried out on them to keep an eye on their health. The other difference is that damage to a piston engine caused by mishandling tends to affect you, straight away, whereas that in a turbine tends to affect others down the line.

Apart from sympathetic handling, the greatest factor in preserving engine life is temperature and its rate of change. Over- and under-leaning are detrimental to engine life, and sudden cooling is as bad as overheating - chopping the throttle at height causes the cylinder head to shrink and crack with the obvious results - the thermal shock and extra lead is worth about $100 in terms of lost engine life. In other words, don't let the plane drive the engine, but rather cut power to the point where it's doing a little work. This is because the reduced power lowers the pressure that keeps piston rings against the wall of the cylinder, so oil leaks past and glazes on the hot surfaces, degrading any sealing obtained by compression. The only way to get rid of the glaze is by *honing*, which means a top-end overhaul. For the same reasons, a new (or rebuilt) engine should be run in hard, at least at 65% power, but preferably 70-75%, according to Textron Lycoming, so the rings are forced to seat in properly. This means not flying above 8000 feet density altitude for non-turbocharged engines. Richer mixtures are important as well. Also, open the engine compartment after shutting down on a hot day, as many external components will have suddenly lost their cooling. With some turbine engines, you have to keep a track of the number of times you fluctuate between a range of power settings because of the heat stress.

When levelling in the cruise, the combination of increased IAS and throttling back cools the engine rapidly, so close the cowl flaps beforehand. Don't use them as airbrakes, either, but to warm the engine after starting and to cool it after landing (allow temperatures to stabilise before shutdown, especially with turbochargers).

In the cruise, better fuel consumption may be obtained at slower speeds and lower power settings, at the cost of extended running time, so you might not really save that much. For example, leaning to 10° lean of peak Exhaust Gas Temperature (EGT), without exceeding the maximum, loses about 5 knots. Typically, CHT probes are fitted to one cylinder of the engine, which is not necessarily the one that reaches peak temperature first, even though it may end up as the hottest, so a margin of 25° rich of peak may still not be enough to stop another cylinder from getting too close to peak for comfort, or even lean.

One consideration with using low power when it's very cold is that the engine may not warm up properly and water that forms from combustion may not evaporate, so oil won't lubricate properly.

The reason the temperature cools either side of the peak reading is that on the one hand (rich), there is too much fuel and, on the other (lean), there is too much air (having said that, the hottest CHT is between 25-50° *rich* of peak EGT, because that's where the peak cylinder pressure occurs, with a high rate of heat transfer to the cylinder head, so you need to lean past it). However, although being lean of peak works, there is much more potential for causing damage to the engine if it is mismanaged - it needs more monitoring to be used effectively, as the temperature at the exhaust will still be high, which is not good for the valves, and particularly acute with high performance turbocharged engines - Australian authorities found that leaning causes lead oxybromide deposits to cling to various parts inside the combustion chamber, which could become hotspots and cause detonation (the lead appears as a result of chemical changes in avgas as it burns). At richer settings, the lead either doesn't form or is swept out of the cylinder (this may be true for lower performance engines, too).

Don't forget to enrich the mixtures before increasing power when at peak EGT or when increasing to more than 75% power. Move the engine controls slowly and smoothly, particularly with a turbocharged engine. Harsh movements that (on older engines) will result in a cough and splutter and having no power can be embarrassing.

Although many flight manuals state that as soon an engine is running without stuttering it's safe to use it to its fullest extent, try warming up for a few minutes before applying any load, at least until you get a positive indication on the oil temperature (and pressure) gauges. This ensures a film of oil over all parts, and no excessive wear. In addition, when the oil is cold, its pressure will be higher, and too much throttle will only endure that the pressure valves will let unfiltered oil into the system (high oil pressure spikes are also bad for the oil cooler).

Even better, warm the engine before you start it, because the insides contract at different rates - in really cold weather the cylinders may have the grip of death on the pistons and cause some strain when you turn the starter (manufacturers tend to suggest preheating around -10°C, but many pilots do it around 0°C. Don't forget the oil cooler, as warm oil from the engine meeting cold oil inside might also cause a burst). Equally important is not letting an engine idle when it's cold, as it must be fast enough to create a splash of oil inside (about 1,000 RPM is fine).

After flight, many engines have a rundown period which must be strictly observed if you want to keep it for any length of time. As engines get smaller relative to power output, they have to work harder. Also, in turbines, there are no heavy areas to act as heat sinks, like the fins on a piston engine, which results in localised hotspots which may deform, but are safe if cooled properly, with the help of circulating oil inside the engine (75% of the air taken into a turbine is for cooling). If you shut down too quickly, the oil no longer circulates, which means that it may carbonise on the still-hot surfaces, and build up enough to prevent the relevant parts from turning. This coking up could seize the engine in 50 hours or less.

The reason for reduced thrust on takeoff, by the way (not recommended for pitons), is to increase engine life, not reduce noise, as you end up nearer the ground in the process and keep the noise level the same anyway.

If the starter light remains on after you release the starter button on a piston engine, you should shut it down, as it indicates that the starter is still engaged with the engine and is being driven by it (starter systems don't have fuses).

Lubrication

Friction can be quite handy, but not inside an engine! Without some way of making the various surfaces rub smoothly against each other, they would get hot, and suffer from scoring damage. Oil actually does many things, including *cooling, cushioning, flushing, lubrication* and *sealing*, and there are two methods of its application:

- *Film Lubrication*, where a thin film of oil between two surfaces stops them touching. This film has three distinct layers, the outside two of which cling to each surface, and the middle one moves between them, providing some sort of cushioning. The thinner the oil is, the easier the movement is

- *Boundary Lubrication* is a state of near breakdown where the film above is reduced to next to nothing.

There are also two types of system, *wet* or *dry sump*.

WET SUMP

This is very simple, because the engine oil is kept in a sump which is under (and part of) the engine, where the crankshaft and other moving parts rotate, splashing it all around (*splash and mist*). It is generally thought that a pump is not used in wet sump system, but they can be, as with the Piper Cherokee. Wet sump systems are not used on modern aero engines, as the bearings will be starved of oil when the aircraft is inverted.

DRY SUMP

A dry sump system keeps the oil in a tank *outside* the engine, and the oil is force fed around under pressure to where it is needed - the sump in this case is used merely as a collector for stray oil dripping off the components inside. The *scavenge pump* (which pulls oil *from* the engine) has a greater capacity than the pressure pump to keep the sump dry, or to stop oil accumulating in the engine, especially after an unusual attitude, where oil might not necessarily be in the collection area until the machine is righted again, and the pump must cope with the surge (also, overnight, the crankcase drains into the sump and there will be oil remaining when the machine is started if the pumps were the same size). In addition, because air gets mixed with oil as it does its work, it becomes frothy, gaining a greater volume, which the scavenge pump has to handle (in a piston engine, the oil is sprayed around inside the crankcase. In a jet, the bearings are in small chambers, in which the oil is kept inside by pressurised air trying to get in through the chamber seals. Gears meshing together don't help).

In practice, the scavenge pump is 25-30% larger than the pressure pump, which is fed from the tank. The scavenge filter is between the engine and the scavenge pump, so any particles are removed. The oil cooler is between the scavenge pump and the reservoir, in the return line to the tank after the scavenge pump.

Pumps themselves are usually mesh gear types, where one gear is driven, which drives the other, to force oil round the outside of the gears within their housing: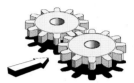

The next stop is the oil filter or oil screen, both of which have bypass valves to allow (unfiltered) oil through to the engine should the filter or screen become blocked. Mostly, this would happen because of lack of engine preheating or too much throttle on starting, but, occasionally, bits from the engine might cause it.

After passing through the filter, oil pressure is regulated by the *oil pressure relief valve*, which compensates for oil pump speed and viscosity variations with engine speed changes through the tension on its spring - in fact, engine oil pressure is adjusted by changing the spring pressure. One symptom of problems with the relief valve is *lower than normal oil pressure*, with *steady oil temperature.*

Oil is cooled by pumping it through an oil cooler, which works just like a radiator. An oil filter is used to trap any impurities, and the pressure relief valve is there to make sure it doesn't get too high (if the pressure increases, due to a blockage, maybe, the valve opens and dumps the oil back to the tank).

Chip detectors are small magnets that attract slivers of metal suspended in the oil. Sometimes, they are connected to a warning panel in the cockpit in which a light glows if the sliver makes a circuit across the detector. It's always a good idea to be prepared to land straight away if you see a chip light come on, and some flight manuals say do so immediately, although this is less of a trend for legal reasons (some pilots have landed immediately in some really stupid places). If the light is for a transmission system, keep it loaded, as unloading a disintegrating transmission has been known to make the situation worse (if you can land next to a pub, the engineers like it better!)

Engine oil reservoirs are sometimes at the front of the engine because the hot oil can heat the air intake.

An engine that is not used enough develops corrosion very quickly on the inside, and rust flakes, which are very abrasive, will circulate when the engine is started, which is why you have to change the oil even when you don't fly a lot. Another reason is an increased water content, which will have an acidic effect once it mixes with the by-products of combustion. The most wear takes place in the first seconds of a cold start, after the oil has been allowed to settle. Priming will wash whatever oil is left off the cylinder walls, so don't do too much, and maintain minimum RPM to let the oil circulate. The pressure will be high just after starting, but will reduce to normal once the engine warms up. Excessive oil pressure is acceptable *for a few seconds* on a cold day. In fact, after starting a cold engine, particularly in winter, you can allow the oil pressure not to rise for 30 seconds, because it may be too thick to get through the passages until it gets warm. Otherwise, you should shut the engine down immediately.

Oils come in various thicknesses, or *viscosities*, which measure resistance to flow. The lower the viscosity number, the thinner it is, so you would use 120 oil in Summer, 100 in Fall or Spring, 80 in Winter and 65 in the Arctic. To keep the oil thin, in the cold, one trick is to pour a few litres of petrol into the oil system just after closing down at night, so it is very thin in the morning and you can start the engine. By the time the oil has warmed up, the petrol has evaporated and you can carry on (but check your flight manual to see if this *Oil Dilution* is acceptable for your machine).

Mineral oil has no additives and is used in new engines. Detergent oil has chemicals added to help with cleaning, etc., including keeping particles suspended. *Do not mix the two.* Synthetic oils have one drawback, in that they hold contaminants longer. Another is that their temperature range is quite critical - watch those instruments!

When flying, oil temperature and pressure gauges work with each other (they are measured after the pump and before the engine). If the pressure is low, you can either expect the temperature to rise because it is working harder, or reduce because there is less going over the temperature detector. Check your flight manual, but it also depends on whether oil is leaking, or the detectors are near each other.

ELECTRICITY & MAGNETISM

Nobody really knows what electricity is, but everyone knows what it does - its effects have been known for a very long time. The term comes from the Greek word for amber, which is *elektron*.

Atomic Theory

The word *atom* derives from the Greek *a tomos* which means "not cut", or that you can't reduce (or cut) the atom into anything smaller. A collection of atoms is a *molecule*, which is the smallest part of an object that retains its identity. By the time Einstein came along, it had been discovered that atoms are both a lot smaller and a lot bigger than originally thought. If you enlarged an apple until it became the size of the Earth, for example, the atoms inside would be the size of cherries (and the atmosphere would have the thickness of clingfilm). Gold leaf has the thickness of about 5 atoms - if this book were printed on gold leaf, and you multiplied it by four, the total thickness would be that of a single sheet of paper.

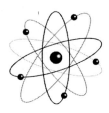 The diagram on the left is a loose depiction of the inside of an atom. The large ball in the middle is the *nucleus* and the smaller ones spinning rapidly round it are a cloud of *electrons*, which are negatively charged particles and around 2,000 times smaller in size. The nucleus consists of positive- and neutrally charged particles, called *protons* and *neutrons*. The neutrons are electrically neutral (they consist of a proton and an electron which cancel each other out) and keep the protons together, since particles of a like charge are repelled. As an example of how large atoms can be, if the nucleus were the size of the apple above, the first electron would be found anywhere between *1-10 miles away*, and be hardly visible at that.

In an atom, there should be an equal number of electrons to protons, to make it electrically neutral, which is why an extra electron (or a hole caused by one leaving), is balanced immediately. An atom with one extra is *negatively* charged, because electrons are labelled as negative, and with one missing is *positively* charged, or "carrying a positive charge", which is a bit of a misnomer as all it has done is lost an electron. This is called *ionisation*, because an unbalanced atom is called an *ion*, which we will come across later in the *ionosphere* that surrounds the Earth. Some components, like transistors, depend on the movement of electrons or holes (missing electrons) one way or the other.

None of the particles inside an atom are physical in nature, but are actually electromagnetic charges, or tiny whirlwinds of electromagnetic force. The negative electrons are held in place by the positive protons with *electrostatic attraction,* as particles with opposite charges attract each other. If the electron stays within the atom, the lines of force representing the attraction are self-contained, but once it leaves, lines of force are evident between them, to create a kind of electrical "tension" which is made use of in radio transmissions. Electrons spin round the nucleus at around 600 miles/second so, bearing in mind the relative distances above, you can see that they work quite hard! In fact, they move so quickly round a nucleus that they give the *illusion* of a more solid construction, in the same way as a lighted cigarette end moved round and round gives the illusion of being a solid circle because our senses don't work fast enough to detect the difference.

So, an atom:

- is not solid

- is mostly full of nothing

Electrons spinning round an atom occupy *energy levels,* or *shells,* rather like the orbits of the planets around the Sun. The first shell can hold up to 2 electrons, and the second up to 8, but it's always the *outer shell* that is important. Unbalanced electrons in the last shell of any atom are those that determine its *valency,* and are therefore called *valence electrons* (valency is the property of atoms to combine with or displace others). Valence electrons can be dislodged easily by applying stress in the form of heat or a magnetic field, which is how electrical current is produced.

Electrickery

Put very simply, if you line up a series of atoms (as in an electrical cable) and add an electron to the first one, it will repel those already there and push one electron out, which joins the next atom, and so on down the line until an electron falls off the last atom in the cable, giving you a very slow electric current as you make the electrons move along a *conductor,* which is described later. However, one electron has such a small charge that, in order for anything to be detectable, you need a basic charge to work with, such as the *coulomb,* which consists of 6.28×10^{18} electrons. The abbreviation for a coulomb is *C*.

When the electron is drawn in to the cable, at first there is a difference in potential (pressure) between that end and the other end, creating a *potential difference* between them. In other words, the new electrons have potential energy

due to their position, and the flow of electricity is like that of wind moving from high to low pressure, once it is set in motion. That's where the resemblance ends though, because it is the *lack* of electrons at the positive end that creates the difference in pressure to start the movement. A positive charge has less electrons (or pressure), so it will attract free electrons from the other end of the cable, from where they will be repelled, but only if there is a *complete circuit* where the electrons so absorbed can be passed along to the negative side. Transferring a bunch of electrons to a place and leaving them there sets up a stress (field) which is only relieved when the electrons are allowed to flow back. The stress is the p.d. measured in volts. However, the work we have to do to create such a "pressure" is also measured in volts, otherwise known as *electromotive force,* which could be viewed as the difference in the number of electrons at each end of the conductor.

Note: Electromotive force (emf) is a cause and potential difference (p.d.) is an effect, although they tend to be used synonymously since they are both expressed in volts. Electrons respond to emf *immediately,* so when the force is taken away, they stop right away.

You can maintain p.d. (or voltage) with a generator or a battery, which can be regarded as a voltage pump, or a voltage store, respectively.

There are three types of electricity:

- That which stays right where it is, or **static electricity,** although it does move when it jumps across small gaps, which static electricity is prone to do. There is an electric force between any two bodies that are close together without contact. Since this force does not move, it is called static, meaning electricity that is going nowhere in particular. However, it does have its uses - electrostatic principles are used in spray guns. *Static discharge wicks* are used on aircraft to dissipate it, because the airframe is used as an Earth return for electrical components, and develops its own static potential. On the ground, a conducting bead in the tyres will do the same job (skids do it automatically). Static (and sparks) are the reason for bonding an aircraft and a refuelling vehicle together, and aircraft surfaces to each other (corrosion is an indication that it isn't working)

- That which goes in one direction, usually at one speed, called **Direct Current**. Sources of DC include friction, heat, pressure, magnetism, photoelectricity and chemical action, as in batteries

- That which flip-flops back and forth to form a wave pattern, or **Alternating Current**

The essential point is *movement*, since nothing much happens when everything is still, but it is the last one, AC, with which we will be concerned when it comes to radio.

INSULATORS & CONDUCTORS

Some atoms don't have much of a hold on their outer, or free electrons, and allow them to move easily, especially when subjected to heat or an electrical field - the materials made up of such atoms are called **conductors**. Copper is the best, but gold is commonly used because it doesn't tarnish in a hurry and cause bad connections. A gas can also conduct electricity, as with fluorescent lighting.

The Earth is also considered to be a conductor, but only because it has an unlimited supply of electrons that it can supply or accept, which allows current to flow in the metallic parts of a circuit. By using Earth as a return path for electrons, you can transmit electricity with only one cable (although Nikola Tesla did it with none at all!)

Atoms that keep a tight hold of their electrons and allow no movement at all are found in **insulators**, which are used to keep conductors from touching each other, otherwise electricity would flow where you don't want it - if electricity takes such a *short circuit* it generates massive heat, with the obvious consequences. Good examples of insulators are glass, or plastic coating round a cable.

SEMICONDUCTORS

Diodes or transistors, which are typical semiconductors, and usually made of silicon, lie in between conductors and insulators, in that they can be either, depending on how they are used. Normally, silicon atoms will link up together to share their valence electrons, creating a bond so strong that they will not be dislodged. The resulting *crystal* is therefore a good insulator. However, the bond between these atoms can break down under heat or the flow of electricity, which can cause the electrons to loosen and create the ability to conduct.

Increasing conductance can also be done by *doping*, or adding an impurity with one more or one less electron in its outer shell than is contained in the silicon, which degrades the stability of the crystal. If there is an extra electron in the dopant, it is an *N-type* semiconductor (*N*=negative). If one is missing, it is a *P-type* (positive). Boron makes holes in P type material, and phosphorous makes extra electrons in N-type material. The most common type of transistor* has an N-P-N junction.

*Transistors form the basis of the on-off switches used in logic circuits. Since a small amount of current going into a transistor can control a larger amount going out, they can also be used for amplification.

This principle is also the basis of the diode, which only allows current to flow in one direction, to give you the electrical equivalent of a non-return valve, something that is useful in voltage regulators and rectifiers, and for protecting circuits.

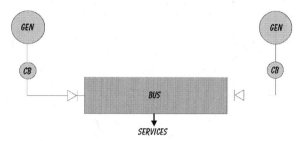

For example, in the diagram above, each line from the generator to the electrical bus (see *Busbars*) is protected by its own circuit breaker (CB), or fuse. However, there is also a diode, acting as a non-return valve, which is there to protect the generator from the *other* side - anything happening in the bus will not be passed through the diode to the generator.

CIRCUITS

Any combination of a conductor and a source of emf which allows electrons to travel round in a continuous stream is called an *electrical circuit*.

Electricity needs a complete circuit with which to operate - if it is broken, the circuit becomes *open* (as opposed to *closed*), and no electricity will flow. Mostly, the fuselage is used as an Earth return for electrical components on an aircraft, which means that you only need one length of cable to the component, which can otherwise be directly connected to the airframe. This saves weight and space, because you don't need a separate cable to complete the circuit, which is called a *dipole*.

Further weight savings can be made by using busbars, described later.

SERIES

A series circuit exists when the elements in it are connected end to end, creating *one path* for the current to flow in. Thus, an identical current will flow through every part of the circuit (meaning that every component must also be capable of handling the maximum current).

However, some emf is used up as the electrons flow through the components, creating a *voltage drop*, after Kirchhoff's second law, mentioned later, which states that all the voltage drops in a closed circuit are equal to the total voltage applied to the circuit.

PARALLEL

A parallel circuit has more than one path in which current can flow - you could think of its components as being connected side by side - that is, *across* the voltage source (a common term for this is a *shunt* connection). In this case, the voltage across the components will be the same, while the *current* will change with the value of resistance.

In a parallel circuit, the loss of one component does not result in the circuit failing.

COMPLEX

Simply a circuit where the components are connected in combinations of series-parallel.

Batteries

Certain chemicals, when they are combined with some metals, can cause electrons to flow as direct current, until all the electrons disappear from the metal, causing it to eventually get eaten away - since the atoms comprising the metal lose electrons, they cease to be the same atoms and therefore cease to exist in their former state - if you could put the electrons back, you would regain your metal plate, and recharge the battery.

Actually, a battery is a *collection of cells*, which typically have a charge of about 2.1 volts each (lead-acid), or 1.2 (Ni-Cad), hence the need to combine them in order to do anything useful. A NiCad needs 19-23 cells to be the equivalent of a 12v lead-acid battery, which has 6 cells for a charged voltage of 13v and a generator voltage of 14v. Knowing how to do this is handy when you are out in the field with a discharged battery and you are trying to connect two car batteries together to start your aircraft. A *primary cell* is one which is used and disposed of when finished with, and a *secondary cell* can be recharged.

BATTERY CAPACITY

An aircraft battery's purpose in life is to maintain a power supply under transient conditions, help with short term heavy loads and supply total power for a short time in emergencies, on top of being used to start the engine. However, it needs the right conditions in which to do this - when it's very cold, at least use a battery warmer, or even remove the battery and keep it warm. At -30°C, your battery has less than half its power to start an engine that needs 350% more effort to get going! This is because, when it is cold, a battery's internal resistance increases.

The battery itself will be rated in terms of Ampere-Hours (amps multiplied by hours), meaning that it's supposed to provide a certain amount of current (expressed in *Amperes* - see later) for a certain number of hours when fully charged, though it is never wise to rely on any battery for more than about 20 minutes (officially, they should last for at least 30).

Note: This is particularly relevant if your aircraft has an EFIS display, or a FADEC! It won't do the warning lights much good, either.

To get an idea of your aircraft's capabilities, add up the number of devices that use power (check the circuit breakers) and divide them into the amp/hour rating. So, if your devices collectively use 45 amps (see below), and your battery supplies 45 amp-hours, you should be able to get an hours' use out of it. When faced with such an emergency, it is usual to use the navaids, for example, to get a position fix, then turn them off until you start feeling a little lost, then turn them on again until you are once more certain of your position. The same with radios. This will get a little extra time out of your battery.

Without wishing to pre-empt the *Amps* section below, the definition of electrical current is the amount of charge flowing down a wire per second, expressed as:

$$\text{Current} = \frac{\text{Charge}}{\text{Time}}$$

Therefore current is a time-derived value, meaning that its value takes time into account, so a current of 45 Amps = 45 seconds' worth of electrical charge. A battery delivering 45 Amps for 2.5 hours could then deliver 90 Amps for 1.25 hours (double the current, but only for half the time) or 22.5 Amps for 5 hours (half the current, but for twice as long). Or any combination in between. The battery's rating is therefore 112.5 Ampere-hours.

A flat battery has maximum internal resistance, which will generate lots of heat when an alternator or generator attempts to charge it (on a bench, only a very small current is used). It is therefore not a good idea to continue flight if your battery gets discharged! In any case, it should be replaced before the next flight. One problem is, for it to work, an alternator needs current from a battery, and your machine's electrics won't work if it isn't there.

The polarities of a battery are positive and negative, marked plus (+) or minus (-), or coloured red and black, respectively, and electrons flow from the negative (-)

electrode, through circuit the battery is connected to, back to the positive (+), because the negative end has the most electrons (the terms are indeed misleading, and the words *positively charged* even more so, but they were coined a long time ago and it's a hard thing to change). If you join batteries in *series*, that is, one after the other, with the positive of one connected to the negative of the next (left, below), you will get a voltage which is the *sum* of them both, but with the *current capacity* of one.

If you join them in *parallel*, with the positive and negative connected to each other (right, below) you would get the *voltage* of one battery, but the *current capacity* of *all* of them, so you can use them for longer.

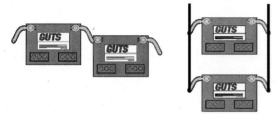

Since a typical aircraft runs on a 24-volt system, you would therefore connect two (12v) car batteries in series (better yet, two sets in parallel). Be aware, though, that terminals are different sizes to stop them being confused, so you need an adapter to connect them up in the middle (jumper cables may open up and spark when a load is applied).

Ensure that batteries have a load on them before completing a circuit.

CHARGING

A battery cell is made up of *electrodes* surrounded by *electrolyte*. Different materials are better or worse at this job, so you might get more or less voltage out of one type of battery or another, but the most common is zinc-carbon for daily use in flashlights, etc. The two types used in aircraft are *lead acid*, as found in cars, and *NiCad*, as found in portable computers. People who use both will already understand the difference but, in simple terms, the lead acid's output tends to fall off steadily with discharge, whereas a NiCad can pump out a constant power until it can do no more, as well as recovering more quickly, so it's good for starting turbines.

The **lead-acid** battery is made of Lead Peroxide (+) and Lead (-) plates, with an electrolyte made of sulphuric acid (37%) and water (63%). The plates will turn into lead sulphate as electrons are lost, hence the term *sulphated*, which describes a fully discharged battery. The electrolyte also loses its dissolved sulphuric acid and becomes primarily water. You can counteract any spilled electrolyte with sodium bicarbonate.

When uncharged, the positive electrode of a **NiCad** cell is nickelous hydroxide, and the negative is cadmium hydroxide. In the charged condition, the positive electrode is nickelic hydroxide, and the negative metallic is cadmium, meaning that the chemical reaction is in the plates. The electrolyte is *potassium hydroxide*, which is only there to provide a path for the current flow - it plays no part in the chemical reaction. If you spill any electrolyte from a NiCad, you can neutralise it with *dilute boric acid*.

During the latter part of a charge cycle, and during overcharge, nickel-cadmium batteries generate oxygen at the positive (nickel) electrode and hydrogen at the negative (cadmium) one (at full charge), which must normally be vented. To allow the system to be overchargeable while sealed, the battery is built with excess negative capacity so that the positive electrode reaches its full charge first. Since the negative electrode will not have reached full charge, it will not give off any hydrogen.

However, NiCads have short memories, in that if you keep charging them up when they have only discharged a little way, they will begin to think they have a lesser power rating, so to stop them causing hot starts they need regular *deep cycling* to keep them awake. Thus, although it's good practice to start a helicopter, for example, from a battery cart, to preserve the ship's battery for better reliability in remote places, occasionally a battery start is good for the system as it will help to eliminate the memory effect. The actual term is *voltage depression*, where there is a slight dip in the voltage near the end of a discharge. The dip goes below the normal output voltage, which makes you think the cell has actually discharged - a common occurrence with home movie cameras! As the battery is charged, the voltage depression point moves toward the beginning of the discharge period.

Another problem with NiCads is that they can spontaneously combust when too much current is drawn and then replaced, a process called *Thermal Runaway*. This is why some helicopters have a *Battery Temp* caution light on the warning panel which means you must land *immediately*, before the battery catches fire and takes other stuff with it, if it doesn't actually burn its way through the airframe and fall out. Yet another problem is that a NiCad cell will lose about 1% of its charge per day.

Note: Lithium Ion batteries, as found in most modern laptops and Portable Electronic Devices, can overheat and burst into flame. In 2004, they were banned in the US as cargo on passenger planes, but, due to the combination of the manufacturing process, where even a nano-sized particle of dust can cause a problem, and the falling quality control due to the economic climate, the incidents have been increasing, so be wary about putting such devices in a remote baggage compartment, as found on the Bell 212.

Because the electrolyte remains unchanged, there is no way to tell the real state of a Ni-Cad's charge by checking its relative density. Checking the voltage is no good, either, because a NiCad can produce a constant voltage for some time, even when discharged. On the other hand, a *hydrometer* can be used to check the specific gravity and hence the state of charge of a lead-acid battery, but not when it is installed in the machine, in case the acidic electrolyte gets spilled (hot electrolyte is 1.25 fully charged, and 1.3 when cold). In this case, the open and closed circuit voltages are compared (e.g. on-load and off-load). The CCV will fall significantly as charge diminishes. Otherwise, you can use a *voltmeter* while a load is applied.

During engine operation, the battery is recharged with a *generator* or an *alternator*, based on DC or AC, respectively, which will put out more voltage than the battery (typically 28v in a 24v system, or 42v in a 36v system) to make sure that the battery doesn't drive the generator. The *voltage regulator* is there to stop the battery being overcharged or the system being overloaded. There may be a warning light in the cockpit to indicate that this is happening, and that you are getting battery power only.

An alternator will charge at low RPM (a generator doesn't much), but some helicopters, notably the Bell 206, use a *starter/generator* to save space, despite this advantage (the same unit is used to spin the engine on startup, and switched over when it's running to become a generator). If an alternator were used, you would need yet another item attached to the engine. Alternators and generators are discussed later.

CIRCUIT PROTECTION

When power is used in a material that resists its flow, heat is created. If the material becomes too hot, it may either change its composition, expand, contract, or burn. Electrical equipment is rated according to the amount of power it can handle, and is protected in several ways.

Note: The *Battery Master Switch* controls the power to all circuits, and there will be others to control smaller groups of equipment, such as the *Avionics Master Switch*, for the radios and navaids. The Battery switch may well be in two parts, one for the battery itself, and the other for the alternator circuit. Circuits will be otherwise protected by *fuses* or *circuit breakers*, which are designed to interrupt the flow of current where specific conditions that generate a lot of heat exist. One difference between the two is that a

fuse will blow *before* the full fault current is reached, and the circuit breaker will trip afterwards, in which case both it and the item protected must be able to take the full fault current for a short time.

Circuit protection devices should only be reset once, if at all, since there will have been a reason for them blowing in the first place, especially if your aircraft has aromatic polyamide cable!

FUSES

A *fuse* is a deliberately weak part of a circuit that is designed to fail if a problem occurs, thus protecting the rest of the circuit and saving the trouble of replacing wiring in odd places - all you do is change the fuse. Technically, a fuse is a *thermal device wired in series with the load protected*, meaning that it *melts* because it *overheats* from *excess current* (cables get warm as current flows). Fuses are rated in amps, and are placed as close to a power distribution point as possible to minimise runs of unprotected cable.

Generally, the lowest rated fuse is selected consistent with reliable operation, but for emergency equipment (meaning anything that will affect the safe operation of the aircraft), the highest rating is used consistent with cable protection.

You must carry a certain amount of spare fuses.

Note: When starting, the starter switch will activate a *solenoid* (see *Magnetism*) which is just a bigger switch that can handle more current, to let enough current through to turn the engine, so the starter switch in the cockpit really only operates another switch in the engine compartment. Since the current is large (60 amps), there is *no fuse protection*, which is why there is a *starter light*.

CIRCUIT BREAKERS

A circuit breaker is relatively slow acting, and can be used in AC and DC circuits. It is a button that pops out when a fuse would otherwise break (see right), so it is a *resettable mechanical trip device*, activated  by the heating of a bimetallic strip element, where one metal expanding more than another pops it open. A *trip-free* circuit breaker will trip even if it is held in, and therefore does not remake a circuit. A magnetic one is a *quick tripping response protection system*. A *flush fit* circuit breaker cannot be manually tripped or pulled.

Circuit breakers are not designed to protect equipment as such - rather, they are there to protect the cabling and connectors which are not easy to replace and may be quite old and/or inaccessible if a fire starts.

Note: Try not to use a circuit breaker as a switch. In some aircraft, this cannot be avoided, but it is still not good practice. In addition, if one pops out, and you can live without the service, *do not reset it*, as you do not know the reason why it popped in the first place - this especially applies with the fuel system! Only reset it if you really need the item concerned to get you home. There are a lot of instruments in the average aircraft that do not need electricity with which to function.

REVERSE CURRENT RELAYS

As the name suggests, these are designed to operate whenever current flows in the reverse direction, to protect components from backfeeds caused by internal faults.

Amongst other places, they are found in DC generating circuits and consist of two coils wound on a core, plus a spring-controlled armature and contact assembly. When the generator voltage builds up to a value that exceeds the battery's, the shunt winding of the relay produces enough magnetism to attract the core and close the contacts.

However, when the generator voltage falls below the battery voltage, the battery starts to discharge through the generator (i.e. the current reverses), so the current in the series-field winding, and thus the voltage across the series-field winding, also reverses, to cause the magnetic field to reverse. As a result, the relay armature is pulled up by its spring tension and the contacts open, to disconnect the generator from the battery.

Amps

The flow of electrons in a conductor (i.e. the *current*) is expressed in terms of *amperes*, or *amps*, which is defined as the movement of 1 coulomb per second. In other words, the more electrons that move along a wire in a given time, the higher the current is, so if you increase the voltage, current will increase by default, other things being equal. Put more technically, *current will increase with voltage if the resistance, or opposition to flow, remains constant*. It follows that to control the current, you can vary either the voltage or the resistance.

Amps are measured in series (to measure the current through the load) with an *ammeter*, or *loadmeter*, both useful devices for checking if your battery is being charged, but presenting the information in different ways. An ammeter's needle (right, below) should always be showing in the + side of the gauge (not too much!), to show a positive charge going into the battery. This type of ammeter shows you how much is going both ways. With the battery on and the engine off, the needle will show a negative reading in the minus range or, in other words, a

discharge. If a discharge is shown with the engine running, the generator is not up to the job and the difference has to be made up by the battery. Switch things off until you get a positive reading. The other type (left, below) is also called a *loadmeter*. Since its display starts at zero, it will only show you what the alternator (or generator) is putting out. With the battery on and the engine off, it will read zero.

The *peak startup draw* (when the load is first applied) is always heavier than that used by a device when it is running. Typically, when you switch on the generator after starting an engine, the loadmeter will read high at first, then decrease as the battery becomes topped up. Only after reaching a certain figure on its way down should you switch the electrical services on.

Volts

If you move an electron to an electrically neutral body, you will have to do progressively more work to add others, because of the repellent force of those already there. When 1 joule of energy is needed to move 1 coulomb of electricity (1 amp), the Potential Difference is 1 volt.

Once a body is charged this way, it is "pressurised" (for want of a better word), and the potential energy is called the *potential difference* (p.d.) when it refers to a difference in energy, or pressure, between two points. You can get a continuous flow of electrons if a potential difference is maintained across the two ends of a conductor that is isolated from Earth. When internal resistance is ignored, the p.d. between 2 points is the same as the emf. Thus, you can look on volts as similar to water pressure. Either way, it is measured with a *voltmeter*, which you use to check the state of your battery before starting a turbine engine.

Resistance

Even a good conductor slows electrons down, because a new electron joining an atom meets a certain amount of repellent force. The longer and thinner the conductor is, the more this opposition will be (called *resistance* and expressed in *ohms*). 1 ohm allows 1 amp to flow when 1 volt is applied. Thus, resistance is calculated in terms of the emf required to push a certain current through the conductor, numerically equal to the number of volts needed to drive 1 amp of current (volts per ampere). A resistor slows down electrons in the *entire (series) circuit*, not just where the resistor is, where you would expect them to build up like a dam, then accelerate afterwards!

The symbol for resistance is Ω (omega), but in diagrams the zigzag symbol given overleaf is used.

Note: The symbol for resistance can mean a specific component or the amount of resistance present. In circuit diagrams, the straight connecting lines are assumed to have no resistance.

In formulae, resistance is signified by the letter *R*. Current flowing through a resistance causes heat from the friction of electrons moving against each other. The more work you make electricity do, the hotter things get, which is how electric fires work. If you make it work harder, you get light as well, hence light bulbs. Electrically, resistance in metals reduces down to a certain temperature, after which it rises again. For insulators, and semiconductors on the other hand, resistance *increases* as temperature is reduced (you get a *positive temperature coefficient* when resistance increases with temperature).

This quality is made use of to measure temperature with a *thermistor*, which is a thermally-sensitive resistor. Extra heat energy causes increased random movement of electrons, so resistance to current flow is increased, linearly with most metals.

Thus, resistance is *directly proportional* to *temperature* and *conductor length*, and *inversely proportional* to *cross-sectional area*, so the warmer, longer and thinner a cable is, the more resistance it has. Putting resistances in series makes the cable longer, and placing them in parallel increases the cross-sectional area.

Resistors are used in electrical circuits to generate heat, limit current, or vary voltage. They are therefore associated with the *dissipation* of energy, and power will be used up when they are in a circuit. Power used against resistance cannot be recovered - storing electricity so it can be used again is done with capacitors (in DC circuits), discussed below.

Capacitance

Resistors control current and voltage in a direct fashion, but there are other ways they can be varied, with capacitors and inductors, the latter being discussed later.

Normally, potential energy is associated with a physical property called *elasticity* or *stiffness*, which can be represented by a stretched spring. Electronically, potential energy is stored in a capacitor, which consists of two

plates separated by a *dielectric*, which can be air or some sort of insulator in a traditional circuit, but also fuel in a capacitive fuel gauging system.

The unit of capacitance is the *Farad* (F), named after Faraday. It represents 1 amp for 1 second with a change of 1 volt stored as 1 joule of energy. As it happens, this is too large to be used in circuits (the capacitor concerned wouldn't even fit into a room), so *microfarads* (μf), representing millionths, are used instead.

The things to remember are that capacitors will appear to pass AC, but block DC (as long as there is a steady charge on the plates), and they store energy. The reason AC current appears to pass is because the capacitor is being supplied with a varying voltage which can induce a charge in the other plate.

Once a capacitor becomes fully charged, its two plates carry equal and opposite charges. It acts as an open circuit to direct current because, as it reaches the maximum charge and therefore matches the supply voltage, the current becomes zero. Thus, if you don't want any (direct) current to flow, you simply charge the capacitor. If the source of current is taken away, the voltage stays where it is, but will leak away in the reverse direction over time so, until this happens, capacitors behave like miniature batteries, since a capacitor preserves a difference of potential between its plates for a short time. This is how you can change the batteries in your PDA without backup power (capacitors are also used in computer memory cells to store information, and as suppressors on electric motors, or in magnetos).

A voltage across the capacitor will build up an electric field between the plates; although current doesn't flow, the field will still exist because the electrons are trying to move, and there will be a "strain" on the dielectric between the plates (hence the word "tension", as in *High Tension*). This all stops when the capacitor voltage is equal to the supply voltage, where one plate will have a negative charge, and the other a positive charge.

As a capacitor charges, there is less voltage available to drive the current, so the rate of charging slows down. Thus, theoretically, the capacitor is never fully charged, but for all practical purposes it does so in a very short time.

INDUCED CHARGES

You will recall that a negatively charged item has an *excess* of electrons, and a positively charged one has a *deficit*. If you take a positively charged body (that is, one with more holes than electrons in its atoms) and bring it close to a neutrally charged one, there will be a migration of negative

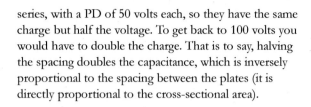

electrons towards the new body (the blue is the negative quality). This is called an *electronic tide*.

If you move the positively charged sphere back and forth, the tide will do likewise. These are called *induced charges*, brought about by a process of *induction*. Since electrons are moving, one way or another, you now have a drift of electrons called an electric current. Note that the electrons do not all rush completely to one side - the centre of the neutral body will remain neutral, that is, the negative charge will gradually increase from the centre to the end. Since the electrons have all moved over, there are holes in the atoms on the other side of the neutral body, and there is a similar gradient from the centre to the positive end.

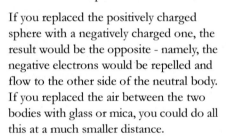

If you replaced the positively charged sphere with a negatively charged one, the result would be the opposite - namely, the negative electrons would be repelled and flow to the other side of the neutral body. If you replaced the air between the two bodies with glass or mica, you could do all this at a much smaller distance.

CAPACITY

The capacity of a capacitor depends on:

- the **dielectric** used. Mica, for example, has 6 times the capacity of dry air and glass three times. The reason that solids are more effective than air is that, when the charge starts or stops, a momentary flow of electrons begins or ends, even if the material involved is an insulator. This wouldn't happen if there was nothing there at all. This increase is called *permittivity* (see below)

- **distance** between the plates

- the **parallel surface area**

Thus, capacitance is more when the plates are nearer to each other, or larger. With many parallel plates, it is the area of one plate multiplied by the number of layers of dielectric, or the area of one plate multiplied by the number of plates, minus 1.

If you had 100 volts between two plates and introduced a third one between them, you would get two capacitors in

series, with a PD of 50 volts each, so they have the same charge but half the voltage. To get back to 100 volts you would have to double the charge. That is to say, halving the spacing doubles the capacitance, which is inversely proportional to the spacing between the plates (it is directly proportional to the cross-sectional area).

PERMITTIVITY

Permittivity is the quality of a material that allows it to store an electrical charge - for example, a material with high permittivity can store more of a charge than one with lower permittivity. It is a physical quantity that describes how an electric field affects and is affected by a dielectric, or *a constant of proportionality that relates the electric field in a material to the electric displacement in that material.*

Thus, permittivity relates to a material's ability to transmit (or "permit") an electric field - as mentioned above, solids are better at being a dielectric than air, and the increased permittivity allows the same charge to be stored with a smaller electric field (and a smaller voltage), leading to increased capacitance. This is how capacitive fuel measurement takes place, using the difference between fuel and air as a dielectric.

Ohm's Law

This describes the fixed relationship between voltage, current and resistance, and is therefore very useful for finding the unknown factor of current, voltage or resistance in a circuit if you have forgotten the relevant measuring instrument! It does not apply to all conductors, but is valid for practically all metals if the temperature remains constant. Essentially, it says that *the current passing through a conductor in constant temperature conditions is proportional to the potential difference across the conductor.*

The symbols for its elements in the formula are *I* for current (amps), *R* for resistance (ohms), *V* for voltage, and they come together in this formula:

$$E \text{ (or } V, \text{ or } PD) = I \times R$$

or (rearranged slightly):

$$I = \frac{V}{R}$$

If one element is constant, the others will vary - for example, if resistance remains constant, current flow will increase as emf is increased. On the other hand, given a constant emf, current flow decreases as resistance increases. Current flow is therefore *directly proportional* to emf and *inversely proportional* to resistance.

If this page is a photocopy, it is not authorised!

Ohm's Law states that the voltage drop across a resistance is equal to the current flowing through it, multiplied by its value, so, if you have a 24 volt battery (as in most aircraft), and a load has 12 ohms of resistance, there are 2 amps of current:

```
24 = I(2) x 12
```

Small currents may be measured in *milliamperes* or *microamperes*, which mean a thousandth or a millionth of an amp, respectively.

Note: Standard units should be used; milliamps, millivolts, etc., should all be changed to amps, volts and ohms.

This formula can be useful in many ways - if you had a break in a cable run, your ammeter would indicate a different current than if the cable were unbroken. Since you know the voltage, you can divide it by the current to get the resistance. As the cable will have a known resistance per foot you can calculate how far down the fuselage you need to start looking.

Alternatively, given that the resistance of an aluminium cable is about 60% greater than a copper conductor of the same length and cross section, if you were to replace a copper cable with an aluminium one, you could use the formula to calculate how much larger the replacement would have to be.

Tip: When solving Ohm's Law problems, it is always helpful to draw a diagram of the circuit, with all the known facts, then look for elements for which you know two values. Use Ohm's Law to find the third, and combine that answer with another unknown, etc. Series circuits with two or more resistances can usually be simplified into an equivalent one that is easier to work with.

Power (Watts)

The *rate* at which the work of moving electrons about is done is called *electrical power*, represented by the letter P, which is measured in *Watts*, after James Watt (the Watt is the SI derived unit of power, equal to one joule of energy per second). However, energy consumed in overcoming resistance is converted into heat or light, which *rate of energy conversion* (into another form of energy) is really what engineers mean when they use the word *power*.

Power consumed (wattage) is determined by whatever voltage is measured multiplied by the current (in amps):

```
P = V x I
```

In general, for maximum power transmission, V and I must naturally be as large as possible. However, the current is limited by the size of the wire and the voltage by the insulation. It is easier and cheaper to make a line with good insulation, so you can transmit a higher voltage, than to make one capable of carrying high current, as power loss is proportional to the square of the current, and the amount of current should be as low as possible.

Busbars

The lighter an aircraft is, the better, so it's impractical (if only for weight saving) to run a wire from the battery (and back) to every component it supplies (in a *dipole circuit*). A better solution is to run a single (big) wire to a distribution point and then (via fuses or circuit breakers) to any electrical appliances, to serve all of them from the end of that line, and use the fuselage as an Earth return, which is what a busbar system is all about.

Physically, an electrical busbar (*bus* for short) is a metal bar with provisions to make electrical contact with a number of devices that use electricity. Electrically, it's a conduit between components, like the memory bus in a computer. There's nothing to stop you having main buses supplying secondary ones, but the whole system must ensure that problems on or near it do not endanger any components connected to it, so services connected to a supply busbar are normally in parallel, to enable isolation and keep voltages equal (isolating individual loads *decreases* current consumption).

Busbars can be split, so that isolation is possible, to protect delicate equipment from large variations in electrical power, such as found when starting. In many aircraft, something like the Avionics Master Switch would serve as the link between two busbars, but you could also use a relay, which would open automatically when the starter switch is activated.

Note: The Avionics Master Switch would also be a circuit breaker (discussed below), and ia also useful for reducing wear on the switches of the radios and navaids.

For isolation purposes, components are graded in order of importance, namely *vital*, *essential* and *non-essential*.

- **Vital** services, like emergency lights, or engine temperature gauges (in the AS 355), will be wired directly to the battery bus, so they will work when the battery relay is switched off (there may be a *secondary battery switch* for just these items to stop the battery running down when the ship is unattended). The term *hot bus* or *direct bus* means that the bus is live even when the generators are not working (that is, it is directly connected to the battery), so you must switch devices attached to it off when you close down (as with the left fuel boost pumps in the Bell 407 or 206L). The hot bus not only allows items to be powered if alternators or generators fail, but also allows the engine(s) to be started when they are not working anyway

- **Essential** services, like those needed for flight, will still be powered if a generator or alternator fails

- **Non-essential** services are things like galleys which can be isolated in an emergency for load-shedding purposes

Most multi-engined aircraft have left and right main buses, and a battery master bus for a few essential items, but there the similarity ends. There are so many variations that it's difficult to keep track, and getting acquainted with a new type of aircraft can be quite difficult, especially when the Flight Manual is less than perfect. It helps in these cases to understand the philosophy behind buses, which are notoriously complicated.

Below is a typical example, without circuit protection devices, earth returns and battery, for simplicity.

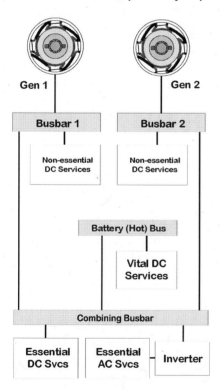

Each generator has its own busbar with non-essential services connected to it, or those that don't matter if one fails. Both are ultimately connected in parallel to a central

(combining) busbar which carries the essential services, so they will always have at least one source of power. The battery is also connected to the combining busbar, so it can be charged, yet still supply the essential components if both generators fail.

Essential things to know about buses are what they power, how to reroute power to them and how to isolate them, a bit like fuel tanks. All aircraft must have standby electrical power systems, in case the normal one goes down. For small ones, this is usually the main battery, which is oversized for this reason. The problem is, it's time-limited, as mentioned above. Usually, each power source will run its own set of buses, but there will be ways of rerouting it to others if the source fails. Duplicated items will usually be powered singly from different buses.

Magnetism

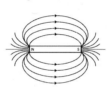

A magnet is a ferrous substance, typically a soft iron bar, that has lines of magnetic force running through and around it in the shape of a *magnetic field* (the Earth is a magnet as well). The lines are called the *magnetic flux*, expressed by the Greek letter φ (phi). The *flux density* is the number of lines within a magnetic field, and the flux is stronger where the lines are closer together. The symbol for Flux Density is *B*. Flux is measured in *webers*, or *Wb*.

A region called the *bloch wall* stops the lines mixing in the middle (no, they don't mix, and neither do they cross. In fact, lines of magnetic flux always form closed loops and behave like stretched elastic bands, in that they are always trying to shorten themselves. This property is made use of in electric motors, as we will see shortly).

Iron, nickel and cobalt are the only elements to be strongly attracted by a magnet.

All magnets have a North and a South pole, and two North poles will repel each other - North and South poles attract each other. If you therefore had a bar magnet, its South Pole (traditionally red) would point towards the Earth's (magnetic) North pole. This is what a compass is all about, discussed more fully under *Instruments*. The thing to remember, though, is that the South Pole is marked as North, because that's the end that points North.

ELECTROMAGNETISM

When electrons flow through a conductor, particularly a coil, a magnetic field forms around it, in the form of concentric circles that rotate clockwise. The greater the current flow, the greater the strength of the magnetic field. Conversely, if a conductor, particularly soft iron, is moved within a magnetic field, current can be made to flow in the conductor. This is called *electromagnetic induction* (from Faraday), as current is induced from the movement of an electronic tide. Thus, a changing magnetic field around a conductor produces an electric current in the conductor, with the size of the voltage being proportional to the rate of change of the magnetic field. *Lenz's law* extends this by stating that the changing magnetic field surrounding a conductor gives rise to an electric current whose own magnetic field opposes it.

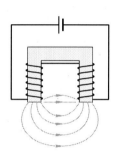

On the left is a picture of an electromagnet, which is created when current flows in coils wrapped around a soft iron core which acts as a *former* (as used in magnetos). When wire is wrapped round an iron bar, the bar becomes a magnet for as long as a current flows (the iron bar doesn't actually have to be there, but the field from the coil without it is much weaker). Nearby pieces of iron will also be affected, such as the diaphragm in a headset, whose in and out movements can cause your eardrum to vibrate in sympathy. You can also use this principle to operate switches.

The interesting thing to note at this point is that, when the current is stopped, the collapsing magnetic flux induces an electric current in the coil, so we get something for free. The amount of emf so induced is proportional to the rate or speed at which the conductor is cut by the flux. This is the basis of how generators and transformers work.

Magnetic reluctance is similar to resistance in an electrical circuit, except that it doesn't consume power. Hard iron in this respect will not pass flux easily, so it has a high reluctance and is therefore not easily magnetised. *Magnetic permeability* is the opposite, characterised by soft iron, which is easily magnetised.

THE SOLENOID

The word *Solenoid* actually refers to a long coil of insulated wire, but as they are often wrapped around a moveable metal core, thus creating an electromagnet, its common usage means a *solenoid switch*, or *solenoid valve*, such as those used to operate starter motors, or operate valves that switch fluid around a hydraulic system. When electricity is passed through the coil, a magnetic field is created, and the core will be drawn in, so a solenoid could be defined

as a device that turns energy into linear motion, typically used as a remote switch. Such a system could be used to operate a starter, for example, because a starter draws so much current that a normal switch, as found in the average cockpit, would burn out, so the cockpit starter switch operates a solenoid, which can handle the current, and which operates the machinery concerned. As well, you don't need to lay large cables everywhere - you only need them thick enough to operate the solenoid. In this way, a small switch can start a large reaction in a remote location.

The core is pulled back against a spring, so when the power is switched off and the magnetic field collapses, the core is returned to its original position. The Agusta 109 uses solenoid switches in the cockpit, that are held on by the solenoid as long as current flows. When it stops, the switch reverts to the off position.

The strength of a solenoid can be increased by adding more turns or current, or using a soft iron core.

THE RELAY

This does a similar job to a solenoid, but it is used for low-current switching or interruption of electrical current, typically used in conjunction with a voltage regulator. It doesn't have a moveable core, but the force produced by an electromagnet moves switching contacts back and forth, either automatically or manually.

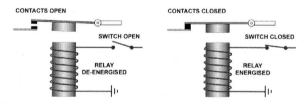

When a relay opens or closes, there is arcing between the moveable and stationary silver alloy contacts, which causes pitting on their surfaces, and extra resistance between them, which means extra heat, extra arcing, and so on, plus a lower voltage under load that will need extra amperage to complete the same task. If the component controlled by the relay is also faulty, there may be more of a current draw than the relay is rated for.

A normally open relay has its contacts open when it is de-energised. A normally closed one is the opposite. If a turbine engine starter relay fails in the open position, the starter/generator will not turn the engine. If it fails closed, the starter/generator will turn as soon as the battery is switched on.

Direct Current

As previously mentioned, this is electricity (current and voltage) that goes in one direction only. It can be produced in many ways, but aviators are concerned with electromagnetism and chemical action (see *Batteries*).

THE GENERATOR

Generators use magnetism to create DC. Faraday found that the magnetic field had to be *changing* to induce a current in a nearby circuit. A simple generator exists when a coil of wire (i.e. a conductor) is spun between the poles of a magnet to induce a current in the loop.

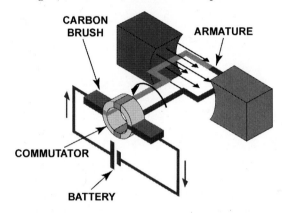

The magnet can be permanent*, or an electromagnet formed from battery current or the generator's own, of which more in a moment. The current so generated is actually AC, and can be converted to DC with a *rectifier* or by mechanical means at source, in which case the ends of the rotating coil are attached to a *commutator*.

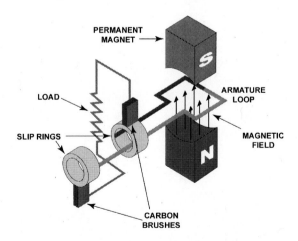

Note: The blue and red blocks in the diagram above are magnetic poles.

The commutator is really the slip rings used in an alternator, shown above, split into two halves which are placed opposite and insulated from each other, each being attached to one end of the rotating loop through *brushes*, so called because the original designs used copper brushes as contacts, but which have now been replaced by spring-loaded carbon blocks which simply wear out and are replaced from time to time. Thus, a commutator is a *mechanical means of periodically reversing current*, or an automatically reversing switch, which is ideal for converting the AC from the loop into DC, otherwise the current would reverse every time the coil moves through the plane perpendicular to the magnetic field. So, as the loop rotates, the current reverses continually - the commutator changes the connection as it does so.

As the rotor spins, the brushes contact each segment in turn, just as the current flow stops and is about to go in the other direction (actually twice per cycle). In this way, the polarity of the brushes remains constant, as does that of the commutator, and DC voltage is produced. The two parts of the commutator are insulated from each other, but they are short-circuited by the brushes as they pass through the zero voltage points.

However, the supply in the simple generator pulsates (called *commutator ripple*), which can be minimised with more loops and connections, or more poles through which the coil(s) can rotate. More complex generators have more than one commutator to ensure a smooth output and a constant supply.

Problem 1 is that the generator is driven by an engine, which will run at different speeds, so the next step is to keep the coil rotating, but inside a soft iron *electro*magnet which can have a variable current passed through it to vary the strength of the magnetic field in sympathy with the engine. The coils of wire in the electromagnet are known as the *field winding*, and the current inside it is the *field current*. The field current can be controlled by a variable resistance, which in turn can be controlled with engine speed. Clever, huh?

When the field current is taken from the generator itself, it is *self-excited*. When it is provided through the Master Switch, generator voltage will drop to zero when the switch is turned off.

In summary, the output of a generator depends on the *number of turns in the armature*, the *strength of the field current*, the *rotation speed of the armature*, and the *supplied load*.

*Any small generator using a permanent magnet is commonly called a magneto.

The types available are:

- **Permanent magnet**

- **Separately excited**

- **Self-excited**:

  - **Series wound** - the armature, field coils and external circuit are all joined up, so you need *fewer* turns in the field windings (the field current is large). As the load increases, so does field strength, to generate more voltage up to the saturation point. Series generators are not suitable for parallel running, as they are not self-regulating

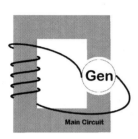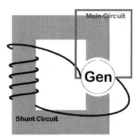

  - **Shunt** (parallel) **wound** (right above), across the field circuit, with a *large* number of turns in the field windings, so less current is needed (the word *shunt* means that some of the current will be shunted past some components). Only a small part of the armature current flows through the field coils - the rest flows through the load. As the shunt field and the armature are part of a closed circuit that is independent of the load, the generator is excited even when there is no load across the armature

  - **Compound wound** - one field coil in series (for the load) and one parallel with the armature (for the field). Compound generators were designed to overcome the drop in voltage that occurs in a shunt generator when the load is increased

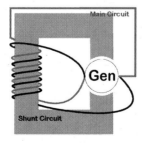

Most generators used in aircraft are *self-excited shunt wound*, with which there is always *residual magnetism* in the core, which is enough to get the whole process started (once it is rotating, the self-excitation takes over), but if it is lost or reversed, say through excessive heat or shockloading, it can be restored by briefly passing a current through it, a process known as *flashing the field*. Smaller aircraft can get their DC by using rectified output from a frequency wild AC generator, in which silicon diodes are used as a bridge rectifier, but these have no residual magnetism, so they need DC from the ship's battery to self-excite.

A *brushless generator* is two generators on the same shaft in the same casing. One is an exciter, and the other the main generator. It can self-excite with permanent magnets, or a permanent magnet generator.

OVERVOLTAGE

Overvoltage could arise if there is a fault in the field excitation circuit of a generator. A resistor, whose resistance decreases as current increases, is used to help disconnect the generator from the busbar with the aid of a sensing coil and armature assembly. The coil is connected in series with the resistor, in the generator shunt field circuit. Under normal conditions, the resistance in the sensing coil circuit is high enough to keep the contacts closed, but if an open circuit occurs in the sensing line, the current will increase and "trip" the resistor, increase the magnetic field in the coil and operate relays that disconnect the generator from the busbar.

LOAD SHARING

Multiple generators are operated in parallel because, if the associated engine fails, there should be, in theory, no interruption in the primary power supply. Since each one should take an equal share of the load, their output voltages must be as near equal as possible. This is done with an *equalising current* varied by *voltage regulators,* which are variable resistances connected *in series* with the field coil so they can vary the *field excitation*.

Voltage regulators maintain voltage within the normal operating ranges, but if an overvoltage occurs, relays will trip to take the protected machinery offline.

The carbon pile is a stack of carbon discs which vary their resistance according to the amount of compression on them. The larger the compression, the lower the resistance and *vice versa*. The stack is biased towards full compression (least resistance) by spring tension. An electromagnet is placed under the stack (i.e. voltage control coil) which influences the tension of the spring against the discs, and is in parallel with the generator output, so the current flow will be proportional to the generator voltage. As the current varies in the coil, it will increase or decrease the strength of the magnetic field, to vary the compression effect of the spring. This affects the current flow and the strength of the field coil until the required output voltage of the generator is achieved.

Carbon Pile Voltage Regulator

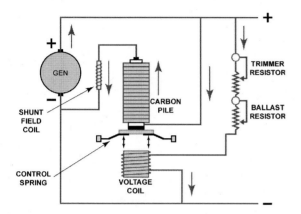

With the vibrating contact version, voltage is controlled by rapidly switching a fixed resistance in and out with an electromagnet (voltage coil) opening a pair of normally spring loaded closed contacts:

When generator output voltage is low, the current flow through the voltage coil is not enough to open the contact points, through which current flowing through the field winding will take the path of least resistance, thereby increasing field strength and generator output. The contacts will open at a predetermined current flow through the voltage coil (electromagnetic effect). Field current now flows through the fixed resistance causing its value to fall, to produce an output voltage of the required level. This process is repeated rapidly, the contacts opening and closing between 50 and 200 times a second, effectively maintaining a steady voltage.

Vibrating Coil Voltage Regulator

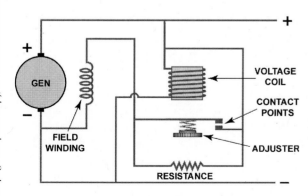

Summary: Generators are paralleled through their field circuits, and each one has a voltage regulator. Regulators compensate for varying RPM and load by adjusting variable resistance in the field winding which controls the flux density. They are *in parallel* with the *armature* and in *series* with the *shunt field coil*. A warning light indicates that the generator is undervolting.

DC MOTORS

These are essentially the reverse of DC generators. The field winding is carried around the inside of the casing, around pole pieces on the way. The armature, which is magnetised and revolves inside, has a commutator on the front, to which brushes are pressed to take off any current produced. A simple motor with a single armature coil would be impractical, because it will have neutral current positions and a pulsating torque, so a large number of coils is used instead, and the commutator is split into a corresponding number of pieces.

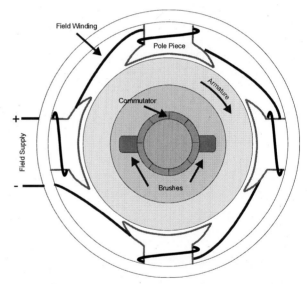

The commutator plays a very important part in the operation of a DC motor because it causes the current going through the loop to reverse at the instant unlike poles are facing each other, which causes a reversal in the polarity of the field, so that repulsion exists instead of attraction and the loop carries on rotating.

Since every current has an associated magnetic field, the one produced in the field winding as it is energised is repelled by the field already on the armature and the motor starts to spin. As mentioned previously, lines of magnetic flux behave like elastic bands, in that, when they are displaced, the tendency is to push back and create a force which starts the movement.

The job performed by a motor can depend on its *speed* or *torque* characteristics. The turning force (or torque) that a DC motor produces arises from the interaction of the magnetic field around the armature coils with the main field, so torque will vary with the strength of the main field and the armature current. Controlling the field current controls the motor speed, but when they are first started, DC motors have no back emf, so a resistor is connected in series with the armature to limit the current to a safe value in the early stages. The resistance is gradually reduced as speed builds up.

Series wound motors have a high starting torque as all the current is used, and the magnetic flux will be strong. They must have a load applied, because the back emf is not enough to stop it accelerating to destruction. Shunt wound motors, being wired in parallel, have a low starting torque, and will eventually settle at a normal operating speed. They are used when a fairly constant speed under varying conditions is required. A compound wound motor can have a high starting torque, and will not overspeed. If the field windings are connected so that the flux acts in opposition, the machine is known as a *short shunt*, and will behave like a series motor. If the flux is strengthened, it is a long shunt machine, with the constant speed characteristics of a shunt motor.

A *split field* motor can rotate forwards and backwards, which is useful when you want to operate something in two directions. The (series wound) field windings go in opposite directions and are controlled by a double throw switch to reverse the polarity as required.

To keep weight down, DC motors often have to work harder, so they require cooling periods after intensive operation. On the Bell 206, for example, you are only allowed 3 attempts at starting, with a 30-second gap between them. Then you have to wait 30 minutes before trying again.

STARTER/GENERATORS

These units combine two functions, those of a generator and a DC motor, which saves both weight and space. The DC motor function is used to start the engine, then the unit is switched over to be a generator at a predetermined speed, after a short wait (1 minute in a Bell 206), to allow the system to stabilise and the battery to recover before it receives a charge. A *changeover relay* is used for the process.

Because generators don't work well at low speeds, they are usually used in turbine engines, as they run at high RPM.

Alternating Current

There is a point beyond which the size and weight of DC components become a disadvantage, as well as the power loss you get when transmitting electricity over longer cable runs. With DC, you would have to have a very high starting voltage over a long run to get only a relatively small voltage at the other end. AC voltage can be stepped up and down with *transformers*, which is how power can be transmitted over long distances (transformers don't work with DC). When the voltage is increased in this way, the current is decreased, *but so is the resistance* (see *Ohm's Law*, above), so the power moves more easily. When it arrives at the other end, the situation can be reversed. Even if you retain the higher voltage and lower current, the same amount of power is available.

Alternating Current is electricity that reverses its polarity (and direction) several thousand times a second and continuously changes magnitude. That is, while the "positive" wire is negative, the "negative" wire is positive, and so on, alternating between the two (because of the potential for confusion, in AC circuits the positive wire is called *live*, and the negative wire is called *neutral*).

In an aircraft, AC is typically used to power flight instruments, and fuel quantity systems. The essential point is *movement*, and many devices, such as light bulbs, only care that electrons move, and not which way they move, in order to work.

If you can imagine changing the connections to a battery very quickly from one terminal to the other, you would get the same effect as AC, but the results would be jerky, and the waves square, because there would be a 90° rise when on, and a 90° drop when off. In contrast, transitions from an alternator are smooth and look like *sine waves*, as shown overleaf (AC current is assumed to be in the form of a sine wave unless otherwise stated). As there is only one frequency, it would sound like a continuous tone if you could hear it. The rate at which it varies is called the *frequency* which, in a typical North American home, is 60 cycles/second, or 60 Hertz (1 Hertz is equal to one cycle per second). In Europe, it is 50 cycles per second. When it comes to radio, try millions of cycles (the higher alternating frequencies for radio and radar are produced with *oscillators*, which consist of quartz crystals that vibrate at a high rate when placed under physical stress, in this case electrical).

A *cycle* is a complete transition from zero through a peak, down to a trough and back up to zero, so the more cycles you can fit into a particular time scale (the higher the frequency), the shorter the length of the wave is.

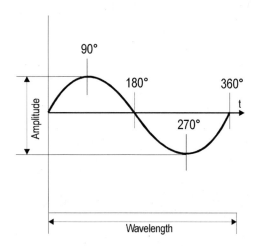

The difference between the peak (or crest) and the trough of a wave is the *amplitude* (or, loosely, volume). When the *frequencies* of two waves coincide, they are *in phase*. When they don't, they are *out of phase* by whatever angle is created when the second wave start its cycle (see next column).

Picture: Phase Difference

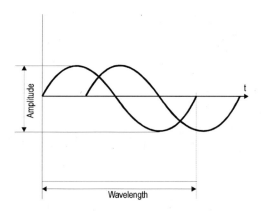

Phase difference is the basis of finding your direction with the VOR. In any case, current usually lags behind voltage in an AC circuit (see *Reactance*, below).

The simpler form of AC, as found in the home, is good enough for light bulbs, etc., because the human eye is not quick enough to catch the flickering effect, and the bulb will stay warm anyway while the power drops and rises again, but electric motors, as used for gyroscopic instruments, need a more constant source of power. Aside from that, a single phase generator is uneconomical because a lot of winding space would be wasted.

Three-phase AC is essentially three AC lines running in parallel, with their peaks a third of a cycle behind each other to reduce the changeover effect. In such *polyphase*

systems, loads can draw power at a uniform rate, so the machine runs steadily under a uniform torque because the power peaks and zero values do not coincide.

Although you can use any number of phases, most of the advantages are available with three, which is why three-phase is in general use (it was designed by the US military over 50 years ago). With it, three coils are at 120° (electrical degrees) to each other, so the voltages differ in phase by the same amount. Electrical degrees are used because there is more than one coil per phase, and you get more than one electrical cycle for each geometrical cycle.

When the voltage is at peak value at one phase, that of the others is at half peak value in the opposite direction, so the sum of all three voltages is zero. Using 400 Hz (as opposed to 50 or 60) means that smaller and lighter components can be used, albeit with some induction loss, but weight savings are more important with aircraft. You need 4 sets of wiring for a 3-phase system (3 live plus a neutral), but they are smaller, so you still save weight.

Phases may be wired in *mesh* (*delta*) or *star* arrangements. With a mesh, the three coils are in series, to form a closed circuit in the form of a triangle, so you don't actually need a neutral connection. The star has one end of each coil joined to a common point in the middle (the neutral), with which you get two voltages - a line voltage between any two phases, and a phase voltage between line and neutral. With both systems, however, only three wires are needed.

Advantages of polyphase systems include:

- The power rating increases with the number of phases. Each additional one increases total AC power as a function of the square root of the number of phases, so 115 volts multiplied by the square root of three will give you over 199 volts from a 3-phase system, hence the 115/200 designation

- Heating loss and the line voltage drop are less than that with a single phase

- Loads can draw power at a uniform rate

- AC Generators can work in parallel

- Each phase can be connected separately to different loads

- Fewer copper coils are needed to generate the necessary current, which allows for a smaller and lighter alternator

Constant Frequency AC systems run at 400 Hz (the most used frequency in aircraft). 6-pole systems run at 8000 RPM, and 8 pole at 6000 RPM.

Note: With AC, at higher frequencies (e.g. VHF level), the current flows on the *outside* of the cable, because that's where the electrons congregate, increasing the resistance (many times) because the effective cross-sectional area is reduced. This reduces the strength of a signal, and is called the *skin effect*. It can be counteracted with stranded wire.

REACTANCE

Reactance is part of the total opposition to the flow of AC, or the AC behaviour of capacitors and inductors. It is similar to resistance in a DC circuit and is also expressed in ohms, just to confuse matters, but the energy is always returned to the circuit and not dissipated as heat, as it would be with resistance. *Inductive reactance* is the opposition inside an inductive circuit, and *capacitive reactance* exists in a capacitive circuit.

RESONANCE

The frequency of an AC voltage applied to a series circuit determines its reactance or, put another way, the quicker the changes in current, the more opposition is experienced. If the inductive reactance is larger than the capacitive (usual for higher frequencies), the circuit is inductive and the voltage leads the current. If the capacitive is the larger reactance (for lower frequencies), the circuit is capacitive, and the voltage lags behind the current. Somewhere in the middle, the reactances will be equal and that of the circuit will be zero, meaning that impedance will be minimum, and equal to the "normal" circuit resistance (R), so the voltage across the circuit and the current in it will be in phase. This condition is *series resonance* which occurs at the circuit's *resonant frequency.*

A resonant, or *tuned*, circuit is one where the inductive and capacitive reactances (that is, concerning voltage and current) are equal, and cancel each other out because they have opposite polarity. The principle is made use of in radio to tune in to a frequency, where the tuning knob is connected to a *variable capacitor.* This means that an alternating current is required - an inductor in a DC circuit would have no effect, aside from the normal resistance in the wire wrapped round the coil.

Since such a circuit presents a low opposition to a voltage at the resonant frequency, the current is large, so the circuit can differentiate between voltages at different frequencies. In other words, it is *selective.*

CAPACITIVE REACTANCE

A capacitor in an AC circuit builds up a charge as supply voltage rises, which opposes and reduces current flow, so that, when the maximum supply voltage is applied, current will be zero. As the supply voltage falls, the capacitor starts to discharge, hitting a maximum discharge rate when the supply voltage is zero. This means that current is maximum when voltage is zero and *vice versa*, or current leads voltage by 90°. In the picture below, as the voltage rises rapidly at A, the current starts to flow into the capacitor (grey line), and decreases down to zero when the voltage is maximum at B. From B to C, the capacitor is discharging in the opposite direction reaching its maximum at C, when voltage is zero, and so on.

This *capacitive reactance* is the opposite of inductance, mentioned below. It is measured in ohms, as it opposes current flow, and is inversely proportional to AC frequency, meaning that when frequency is high reactance is low, and when frequency is low reactance is high. Capacitors therefore act as low resistances to high frequencies and high resistances to low frequencies.

INDUCTANCE

This is an electrical property that resists changes in *current*. A main (varying) current going through a coil will produce a magnetic field around the coil as a whole, resembling that of a bar magnet. It will also produce a self-induced magnetic field around the wire of which the coil is made, which will cut the next loop in line as it grows and spreads, and induce a current in opposition to the main current, stopping it from rising too quickly.

When the circuit is broken, and the current (and magnetic fields) start to collapse, the "local" electrons will go the same way as the main current, strengthening it so that it collapses slowly. Inductance is the degree of this self-induction, and it can happen between complete circuits that are near to each other (see *Transformers*).

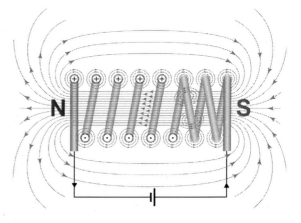

Note that there is no induction if the current is steady, so if DC is used, there will only be an effect as the switch is closed and opened, hence the use of contact points in magnetos.

In summary, as every circuit carrying a current has an associated magnetic field, it follows that, as that magnetic field varies with the current, it will induce yet another current into the system as it interacts with the loops next to it. Currents flowing in opposite directions tend to cancel each other out, and when the wire is wound into a coil, each added turn makes the current flow again in the same direction.

An inductor's action in an electrical circuit is therefore rather like a flywheel, in that, when voltage is applied to one, it takes time for the current to reach a steady value, and for it to die down when the current is switched off, so it can smooth out variations. This ability to "store" energy in a circuit is due to inertia.

The unit of inductance is the *Henry*, and its symbol is L.

IMPEDANCE

Impedance is the complete opposition to AC flow, consisting of normal resistance combined with reactance (capacitive* and/or inductive). Its symbol is Z, and its value is always greater than resistance, except at resonance, when $Z = R$. *Impedance is the vector sum of resistance against reactance.*

In a circuit with resistance only, current varies in the same manner and at the same time as the alternating emf does, so they are in phase. Inductive reactance has the opposite effect to capacitive reactance, because one lags voltage by 90° and the other leads by 90°, respectively, so they can be 180° apart and cancel each other out (subtracting one from the other gives the total reactance). You are therefore left with plain resistance current.

Impedance matching (as used in avionics) means that a device works best when a circuit to which an input or an output is connected has the same impedance as the input or output. A low impedance circuit should not be connected to a high impedance one without allowing for power losses, hence the use of transformers (the connection between a 75 ohm coaxial TV cable and a flat TV twin lead, which has an impedance of 300 ohms has a transformer in it. The turns ratio is 2:1).

THE ALTERNATOR

To create AC, you can vibrate a conductor near a magnetic field, and *vice versa*, or rotate it, as is done in an alternator (on modern aircraft, however, the term *AC generator* is often used instead). You can also use an *inverter*, which is described under *Power Conversion*, below. Alternators work in the same general fashion as generators, but use *slip rings* instead of commutators so that the periodic current reversals are not modified. Each end of the loop is connected to a separate ring.

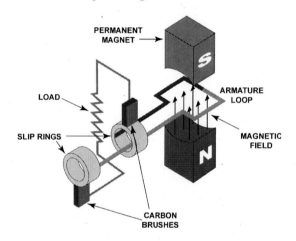

There are two types of alternator, one with a revolving armature and one with a revolving field. The former resembles the DC generator insofar as the armature rotates inside a stationary magnetic field. The latter, on the other hand, has a stationary armature winding so that the output can be connected directly to the load, as opposed to going through slip rings (insulation is easier). Instead, the slip rings are used to convey the field current to the coil, which is where the rotating field comes from.

The field windings are in the case and the magnets used to induce current in them are on the rotor, since this improves performance (a stationary armature is called a *stator*, and the rotating field magnets are *rotors*). Circuit current is taken from the stator at the high generated voltage without using slip rings or brushes, but they are used to get the much lower exciter voltage to the rotor.

The output is regulated by varying the current to the field windings. A *voltage regulator* senses the alternator output and adjusts the field current when voltage rises above a set value (typically 28.5 v). The current is cut off around 2000 times a second.

A single phase alternator has the armature conductors as one winding, across which an output voltage is generated. Multiphase (or polyphase) alternators have two or more electrically separate single phase windings symmetrically spaced around the stator. This would be 120° apart for a three phase alternator. However, instead of there being six cables, as you would expect, three of them (one from each phase) are connected into a star or delta arrangement. Where they connect is called the *neutral* and the voltage from this point to any of the line leads will be the *phase voltage*. The total voltage across any two line leads is the vector sum of the individual phase voltages, and the line voltage will be 1.73 times the phase voltage.

Alternators need battery power to function (they cannot self-excite), which is why flying with a dud battery can be problematical*. Alternators (or AC generators) are also lighter than generators and do not suffer from arcing at the commutators, since they don't have them, and radio interference is therefore lessened.

*Alternators come with on-off switches, voltage regulators, over-voltage protection, field switches and voltmeters. The on-off switches can isolate the alternators from the electrical system and should be turned off if the alternator fails. If an alternator is switched on and does not produce power, try turning the field switch on to excite the alternator.

INVERTERS

Inverters are used to produce AC from DC supplies. *Rotary* ones use a DC motor to drive an AC generator. *Static* inverters do the same thing electronically, and are much more common. They use an oscillator circuit to produce *single phase* AC. A *power conditioner* may also be used to regulate varying AC power coming from the varying speed of the engine. Some Gulfstreams use them, and the equipment on some modern aircraft is designed to use varying AC power.

POWER CONVERSION

TRANSFORMERS

Transformers are a special application of inductance, used in magnetos (or the coil in a car) to boost voltage from 24-28v to whatever is needed to jump across the gap of a spark plug. They consist of electrically separate coils on a common iron core in the same magnetic field which are *magnetically coupled* when an induced EMF is created in one (the *secondary*) by a change of current in the other (the *primary*). That is, an alternating current in the primary coil sets up an alternating magnetic flux in the iron core, which induces an alternating emf in the secondary coil, but in the opposite direction. In this way, we can create an electrical current without moving conductors and magnetic fields around each other, as you would with a generator or alternator. A reverse current is also induced in the primary.

This is *mutual inductance*, which is greatest when one coil is wound round the other, and least when they are at right angles. The voltage induced depends on the relative number of turns between the windings - if they are the same, the two voltages will be the same, and they will vary in exact proportion to the extra on either side.

A transformer converts AC at one frequency and voltage to AC with the same frequency and the same or a different voltage. In fact, they can be used for three purposes:

- Isolating parts of circuits from others, with a *one-to-one* transformer

- Raising or lowering voltages. A *step-up* transformer has more windings in the secondary coil and will increase voltage. A *step-down* is the opposite

- Matching impedances

Voltage transformers have their primary windings in parallel with the supply voltage, and *current transformers* have them in series.

Here is a simplified picture of the ignition circuit for one spark plug, with a step-up transformer in the middle.

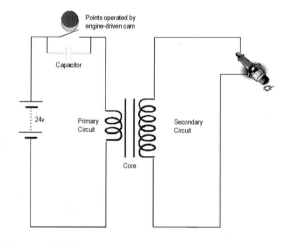

DC FROM AC (RECTIFIERS)

AC is used when it comes to generating large amounts of power, but most radio and computer equipment uses DC, and 12v at that. That part of the problem is easy - a transformer can be used to step the voltage down (or up) as required. Then a *rectifier* is used to covert the AC into DC by extracting the peaks from the AC waveform.

The diode can be a *half-wave* rectifier, in which current will flow only on alternative half-cycles (left, below):

Four diodes are used (*anti-phase*) for full wave, since the resulting voltage pulsates. A capacitor smooths the final result, inside a *filter circuit*. There might be a *bleeder resistor* across the capacitor's terminals to ensure it discharges when the power is switched off.

AC FROM DC
See *Inverters*, above.

POWER

For DC, where voltage and current are always in phase, power consumed is derived simply from the product of voltage and current - the unit of power is the watt, or the product of 1 volt and 1 ampere. However, with AC, it is derived from the product of current and *only that part of the voltage that is in phase with it*. Thus, the phase relationship between voltage and current is what actually determines an alternator's power output.

If the phase angle is zero, meaning that there is only resistance in the circuit, the voltage and current values reach their maxima together, and the power measured is in straight Watts. If they are 90° out of phase, so that either of them is zero when the other is maximum, the real power would be nothing. Any angle between 0° and 90° modifies the apparent power by a *power factor*. This means that the effective power you get from an alternator is always less than it could be, or never greater than unity (except in a pure resistive circuit when everything is in phase). You need to take account of the difference between effective power and apparent power, and the result is expressed as a ratio:

```
Power factor = KW (Effective Power)
               KVA (Apparent Power)
```

Thus, the traditional **volts x amps** formula becomes:

```
watts = volts x amps x power factor
```

If the current lags the voltage, the power factor is said to be lagging, and *vice versa*.

The Power Factor is the ratio between the power in Watts of a circuit and the volt-ampere, being the cosine of the phase angle between current and voltages. It determines what percentage of the supplied power is used up in Watts, and what percentage is returned to the source as wattless power*.

*The difference between apparent and true (effective) power is sometimes called "wattless power", since it produces no heat or light but still requires current flow. This arises from any component of current flow that is

90° out of phase with voltage (the part of current that is in phase is called the power component).

Effective (or *True*) *power* is also known as *Real power*, and is power resulting purely from the current flow due to resistance in the AC circuit. It is expressed in Kilowatts (kW). Apparent power, or *Reactive load* is the *Wattless load* which is the vector sum of the inductive and capacitive currents and voltage in the system expressed in KVAR (Kilo-Volt-Amperes-Reactance). In other words, it is the work done to overcome reactance, which is wasted. The more that voltage and current are out of phase, the more this will be.

Typical output would be between 30-90 kVA for the largest aircraft, so, if a 90 kVA AC generator has a power factor of 0.75, what is the useful output? 67.5 KW.

As an example, a 1.84 kW load supplied with a power factor of 0.4 would require a 20A cable, while the same load supplied at unity would only need an 8A cable.

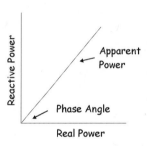

If you plotted Reactive Power against Real Power, and the phase angle is known, you could use Pythagoras to find the quantities of the remaining vectors (in a phasor diagram). Of course, you could also use the cosine of the phase angle.

Most loads are inductive in nature, so it would seem logical to add a capacitor in parallel to the load to improve the power factor

Since the voltage and current are constantly changing, it is difficult to measure the power output of AC, so you need some arbitrary measure which, in this case, comes from the mean value of many instantaneous measurements.

The power used in an AC circuit is the average of all the instantaneous values of power (or heating) in a complete cycle. That is, the instantaneous values of voltage and current are multiplied together to find the instantaneous values of power, which are then plotted over a given time to create a power curve. In a circuit which is in phase, the curve will be entirely above the zero axis, because two positives or two negatives make a plus. However, when the circuit is not in phase, the result is a negative. Inductors and capacitors store energy during one part of the voltage cycle and feed it back later (inductors store energy as a magnetic field and capacitors as an electric field).

Because the AC waveform is not square, its peak voltage must be 1.414 times that of DC to have the same energy (1.414 is the square root of two). The equivalent, or *effective*, AC voltage to match a DC one is the *root mean square* (VRMS). In the diagram below, the shaded area inside the curve over the square DC wave has the same energy as the shaded parts outside the curve.

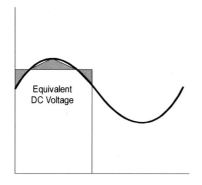

Equivalent DC Voltage

LOAD SHARING

This does not apply to *frequency wild* systems. Alternators are frequency wild if their RPM is not controlled, so such items would only be used on systems which are not affected by frequency, such as heating or non-fluorescent lighting, on simple aircraft where the primary supply is DC (that is, those that are driven directly by the engine). As frequency wild alternators cannot be paralleled, their phase relationship is unimportant. Having said that, you could rectify the frequency wild output, then push it through an inverter.

Constant frequency generators, on the other hand, are designed for these conditions. Where multiple AC generators are used on the same task, in parallel, their speeds must be kept fairly constant. If two, or more, become out of balance, in that one starts to supply a higher voltage than the other, a current will flow between them, and the one with lower voltage will be driven, causing a stress on the drive shaft, which may break, since it has a deliberately *weak link*, the mechanical equivalent of a fuse. Since the engines cannot be relied upon to maintain a constant speed, there needs to be some sort of interim arrangement using a *variable ratio drive mechanism*.

The *Constant Speed Drive Unit* controls an AC generator's rotational speed, and ultimately frequency and voltage. It may be cooled with ram air or its own internal oil supply. The CSDU is connected to the engine by a clutch (the *CSD disconnect*) which can be operated at any RPM, but preferably at idle, to reduce loads. Internally, it uses fixed and variable displacement hydraulic units, and a

differential gear. Real loadsharing control is effected by adjusting the torque at the output drive shaft.

Reactive load imbalances are corrected by controlling the exciter field currents delivered by the voltage regulators.

AC MOTORS

DC motors can suffer from problems with the action from commutation, and using an AC motor can be a lot less troublesome - many can operate without slip rings. They are particularly suited for constant speed operation, since their speed is determined by the *frequency* of the AC supplied, which generates a rotating magnetic field, although their speeds can be variable within certain limits.

There are three main types of AC motor - the *synchronous*, the *induction*, and the *series*, or *commutator* motor, which is most commonly found in domestic appliances. A synchronous AC motor, for example, can be found in a Bell 206 for transmitting engine RPM information to the gauge in the cockpit. Synchronous and induction motors work on the basis that AC supplied to the stator produces a rotating magnetic field that turns the rotor in sympathy. The rotation happens because the magnetic fields arising from the 3-phase supply are out of phase and therefore produce a shifting effect in the resultant field.

SYNCHRONOUS

A synchronous motor is an electric motor with its speed strictly proportional to (i.e. synchronised with) the frequency of the operating current, which is usually three-phase AC. If you took the rotor away, and replaced it with a compass, the compass would rotate in the same direction and speed as the rotating magnetic field set up by the stator winding. The rotor is supplied with DC current that creates an electromagnet with North and South Poles.

Without complex electronics, these are essentially constant-speed motors. Synchronous motors cannot start without being driven, or having their rotor connected as a self-starting circuit. That is, since the field is already rotating at the eventual speed (it rushes past the rotor poles so quickly that the rotor does not have a chance to get started, so the rotor is repelled first in one direction and then the other), the motor must be accelerated before it can synchronise, so it needs a separate starting mechanism. This is done mostly with a small induction motor, or equivalent windings incorporated inside, around a *squirrel cage*, which is called that because it looks like those things that hamsters run around in. The bars are copper or aluminium, shorted together by rings at each end (apparently you can get better starting and quieter running if the bars are slightly skewed).

A low voltage is induced in the windings by the rotating three-phase stator field and a relatively large current flows in the squirrel cage to create a magnetic field that interacts with the rotating field of the stator. The rotor begins to turn, and the motor starts. Once the squirrel-cage windings bring the rotor to near synchronous speed, a DC field to the rotor is energized, which makes it act like a bar magnet to lock the rotor in step with the rotating field. Full torque is developed, and the load is driven.

Once operating at synchronous speed, the magnetic field is rotating at the same speed as the rotor, so no current will be induced into the squirrel cage windings and they will have no further effect on the motor. The DC is applied in the first place by a mechanical switch that operates on centrifugal force.

Synchronous motors are used to keep a constant speed between no load and full load.

Single Phase AC Motors

These produce a pulsating magnetic field, as opposed to the rotating one from a 3-phase motor.

Since all AC motors require a rotating field to start, single phase motors have two windings that are electrically separated by about 90 degrees, called the *start* and *run* windings, whose fields create a rotation effect - a capacitor in series with the start winding does this nicely, but you could also make the start winding with a high resistance and the run winding with a high inductance. Once rotation is established (at about 80% of full load speed), the start winding is disconnected by a centrifugal switch.

Because both windings carry currents that are out of phase with each other, this is also known as a split-phase motor.

Induction

The squirrel cage is only used in a synchronous motor to get the thing started - otherwise the rotors in synchronous and induction motors are quite different, although their stator construction is near-identical (the rotor in an induction motor is self-contained and does not have power supplied to it at all).

The induction motor gets its name from the AC currents that are induced in the rotor circuit by the stator's rotating magnetic field that make it want to turn. The most common winding is the squirrel cage, but another type has coils in the rotor slots, to produce a *wound rotor*.

The induction motor is also known as an asynchronous motor.

SYSTEMS

There are various ways of operating the rest of the aircraft, described below. The motive power for these systems mostly comes from the engine (with independent backup), and you will find them working singly, or in combination, frequently with one type of system controlling another (electric switches controlling hydraulic rams, for example). It is important to know which way any system goes when it fails - that is, does it fail open or fail closed?

A basic system of whatever type (which needs to be a closed loop) will consist of a *reservoir* to contain whatever flows around it and provide the secondary function of ensuring that the delivery is constant and consistent, with no highs or lows, or shocks (this could also be done with the equivalent of an *accumulator*). There will also be a *pump* to return the stuff to the reservoir, but a high pressure pump can also pressurise the system to stop nasties getting in. To keep everything clean there will be a filter somewhere and, finally, some sort of motor could be powered by the system to do work. There are two variables in any system - the amount of stuff in the system and its pressure. You can use a small amount at high pressure or a larger amount at a lower one.

Note: While electrical systems are covered under the above, they are discussed in Chapter 7, *Electricity & Radio*.

Oxygen

Oxygen systems are for emergencies concerning depressurisation or smoke and toxic gases. In a *steady* or *continuous flow* system, oxygen is fed to a mask with a face piece and a plastic bag that can expand. The bag is a *rebreather*, because it allows air to be reused to a certain extent, as the rate you breathe is related to the pH value in your blood, which, if you are hyperventilating, is extremely low (low CO_2). Breathing into the bag brings the CO_2 to normal levels.

Flow must be adjusted for different altitudes. If it is not enough, the flow indicator will show a red line. *Demand* oxygen systems only provide oxygen when the person inhales (flight crew only) - the *demand valve* operates when you breathe in. Chemical oxygen generators use sodium chlorate and iron filings.

Oxygen masks should drop down at 14,000 feet. Main systems work at 1800 PSI. The oxygen supply in a smoke hood should last for 15 mins.

Fuel Supply

The simplest system is gravity feed, which needs the fuel cells to be above the engine to work properly. Modern design requirements, however, mean that fuel cells are in all manner of strange places, and come in many different shapes and sizes (together with a C of G system all of their own). Typically, they are in the wing, and are not actually a tank - instead, the wing is sealed so it can contain fuel, with the ribs and spars inside also acting as baffles (known as a *wet wing* system).

Because of this, various methods are used to get the fuel from there to the engine, all involving fuel pumps and filters. Each engine will have its own pump, but there will also be a *boost pump*, at the tank, to pressurise the fuel slightly and prevent vapour locks, as some lines may pass through unpressurised parts of the aircraft. Boost pumps are lubricated by the fuel they work on, so don't run them dry or you will burn them out.

Fuel tanks are vented to atmosphere, to prevent a vacuum forming inside the tanks as the fuel level is reduced. The vents might be in the fuel cap, or be an overflow pipe in the tank. If the gauge reads more than it should, there's too much venting - you've likely left the fuel cap off!

Turbine aircraft at high altitudes use fuel heaters (actually heat exchangers based on bleed air or engine oil) to melt the ice crystals that form in the fuel up there.

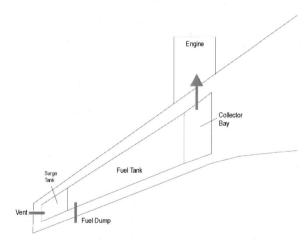

Fuel systems are typically designed as left and right halves so that contamination on one side does not spread to the other, although you are still able to transfer (crossfeed) to opposite engines in an emergency, or for trim purposes.

Jet engines typically burn up to five times more fuel at takeoff power than in the cruise at high altitude. To cope with peak demands, a *collector bay* (or a *header tank*, same

thing) collects the input from several wing tanks to ensure an uninterrupted fuel supply as the aircraft moves around in flight - in other words, it acts like a relay tank. *Surge tanks* near wingtips also control fuel movement. *Clack valves* live in the baffles in fuel tanks - they operate like a cat flap to allow fuel to drain to centre tanks. *Flapper valves* are spring-loaded doors that prevent reverse movement of fuel back to the main tanks from the collector bay.

Pressure refuelling is used because it does not require fuel caps to be open when it's raining, and the aircraft's fuel pumps can remain idle when auxiliary tanks are filled. An automatic shut off valve can also be used to prevent overfilling, but the equipment does add an extra 100 lbs or so the weight of a typical small jet.

Hydraulics

Moving the controls directly on large jets is physically impossible, so hydraulic units called *Power Control Units* (PCUs) are employed to do it instead. Movement of the controls operates control valves that allow a metered amount of hydraulic fluid through to move the controls a specific distance. Since this supplies no feedback for you to tell whether you are moving the controls too much, artificial feel units are built in to do this in proportion to the control movement.

Liquids have minimal compressibility, meaning that, when pressure is applied, it will be pretty much taken up throughout the whole system. In fact, *Pascal's Principle* states that static pressure exerted by a fluid is the same on all surfaces touched by it, so additional pressure is transmitted equally, assuming that the fluid concerned is confined and doesn't compress. This makes it a useful way of transferring movement round corners and into strange places, as the forces produced by a hydraulic system can be very powerful, hence their use to reduce the forces that would otherwise be required to move the flying controls. If you input 20 lbs of force into a piston with an area of 1 square inch, the output on a 10 square inch piston will be 200 lbs, so the total pressure inside the system remains equal. However, the smaller piston must move for 10 inches to make the larger one move for 1 inch.

In addition, cables stretch and linkages wear. If you add friction to the mix, much of your control input, if you use traditional methods, will not even get to the surface concerned. Hydraulics can therefore provide an alternative, lighter weight, solution to the problem of moving large or difficult to move control surfaces. As well, in larger aircraft, you don't need large electric motors and drive chains that will draw large amounts of power.

Part of an *accumulator's* job is to store pressure that can be used for a short time if the main system fails - that is, you can still operate the controls for a few seconds, at least enough to bring the speed back to where the forces are controllable. You can also think of an accumulator as a shock absorber, since a valve opening in a highly pressurised system makes quite an impact on the lines.

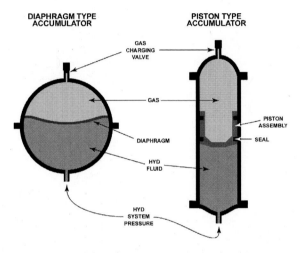

An accumulator is a cylinder in which a piston separates hydraulic fluid pressure from air which is also under pressure, being charged up on the ground. If the air pressure is to high, there will be less fluid in the system, and more on/off cycles as the pump kicks in and out. If it is too low, you can expect rapid fluctuations in pressure as surges are not absorbed - the piston will also hit against the stops and cause *hammering*, which should be investigated immediately. A *cutout valve* will sit between the pump and the accumulator. When the pump is pressurising the system, it will be closed and when the accumulator is doing the work, it will open, so fluid can be dumped back to the reservoir. When a jack gets as far as it can go, a *pressure relief valve* may be present to allow fluid to bypass the jack and unload the pump. The *cracking pressure* is that at which the PRV opens.

HYDRAULIC FLUID

Speaking of shocks to the system, hydraulic fluids are specially made to withstand high pressures and temperatures without vapourising, so make sure you use the proper stuff. The ideal hydraulic fluid should be incompressible, have a low viscosity, have good lubrication properties, be non-flammable and non-toxic, have a low freezing point and a high boiling point, with no foaming. It should also be compatible with the seals and materials used, that is, it should not cause corrosion. Being coloured

helps as well, so that leaks show up better. Did I mention stability? I thought not.

The three main types are *vegetable*, *mineral* or *synthetic*, and they are coloured straw, red or green/purple, respectively. Synthetic fluid becomes acidic if overheated (although it has a wide temperature range), and will attack electrical insulation. It will also be harmful to the skin and eyes. Mineral-based fluid can be flammable, so if it leaks out, it can catch fire, especially if the leak is in the form of a spray (*hydraulic fuses* prevent fluid loss from leaks downstream). In addition, it is hostile to rubber, so synthetic seals must be used.

JACKS

The basic system will have a *jack*, with a control attached to direct the fluid into whichever end of the jack is desired to move, a *pump* and a *reservoir*. Single-acting jacks move in one direction only, and are pulled back to their original position non-hydraulically, such as with a spring. Double-acting jacks can move either way according to which way hydraulic fluid is injected - the *spool valve* diverts system pressure to whichever side of an actuator it is needed. The power from the actuator depends on the pressure in the system and the size of the piston.

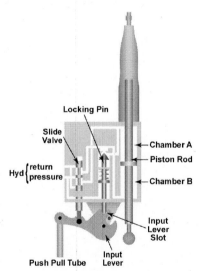

In a *fully powered* system, the controls will only activate the spool valve, and the fluid pressure will move the actuator concerned. When the servo moves, a feedback linkage closes the spool valve to trap hydraulic fluid inside the working cylinder. With an *irreversible* flight control system, the trapped fluid causes a hydraulic lock that freezes the controls so that the control surface cannot move them.

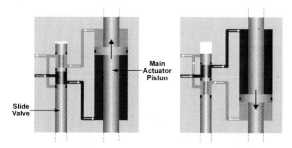

For a *boosted* system (i.e. similar to power steering), the input and output will be connected to the control linkage, as shown above, so the pilot's efforts will be assisted by a set percentage, such as 4:1, which will apply 4 units of servo power for every one from the cockpit.

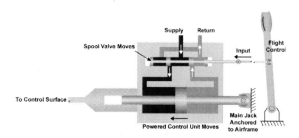

Thus, if hydraulic power is lost, you can still move the controls (boosted controls also provide some feedback).

If a jack is *compensated*, the area either side of the actuator piston is identical. An uncompensated jack is used in situations where the force required to do the job is more one way than the other, for example, with undercarriages, which are harder to pull up than to let down.

PUMPS

The engine drives the pump, which moves the fluid out of the reservoir and applies pressure to it - the fluid is slightly pressurised as it enters the pumps to prevent *vapour lock* (exam question). A de-aerator removes air bubbles from the system. The reservoir is also pressurised to prevent *pump cavitation*. A system without an accumulator will typically use a *constant displacement pump*, which moves a given amount of fluid per revolution. When higher pressure is required, a *spur gear displacement pump* will be used. If the pump starts and stops as the required pressure is reached and falls, it is a *variable displacement* type. It does not need a cutout valve, but does need a bypass to relieve the pressure if the pump fails.

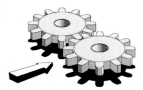

NON-RETURN VALVES

As the name implies, these allow fluid to move in one direction only.

THE SHUTTLE VALVE

Sometimes, fluid must come from more than one source to meet the demands of a complex system. At other times, an emergency system provides pressure if the normal system fails (the emergency system will usually actuate only essential components). The shuttle valve isolates the normal system from an alternate or emergency one. A typical *shuttle valve* contains three ports— normal system inlet, alternate or emergency system inlet, and an outlet. Inside, there is a sliding part predictably called the shuttle, whose purpose is to seal off an inlet port, which itself will contain a *shuttle seat*. When a shuttle valve is in its normal position, fluid can flow freely from the normal system inlet port, through the valve, and out through the outlet port to the actuating unit. The shuttle is seated against the alternate system inlet port and held there by normal system pressure and the *shuttle valve spring*, where it remains until the alternate system is activated. Fluid under pressure is then directed from the alternate system to the shuttle valve, forcing the shuttle to seal off the normal inlet port. Fluid from the alternate system then has a free flow to the outlet port.

The shuttle may be one of four types: *sliding plunger, spring-loaded piston, spring-loaded ball,* or *spring-loaded poppet.*

UNDERCARRIAGES

Landing gear is there to take the shock of landing, so it isn't transferred to the airframe. Of course, it also helps you get around on the ground. The retractable variety produces less drag in flight, at the expense of complication - they are mostly hydraulically operated. As with transmissions, the system will have its own oil system, in this case hydraulic fluid, and a backup system should it decide not to work. This can be operated manually, or by an air bottle. Otherwise, landing gear is made up of *struts,* that are attached to the fuselage, and which have the wheels attached to them (in tailwheel aircraft, struts are fitted slightly ahead of the C of G - otherwise, they will be slightly behind). For shock absorption, an *oleo strut* contains a piston and a cylinder, moving together inside hydraulic fluid. There are holes in the piston to allow fluid through and damp down the shocks. There may be nitrogen or dry air instead of fluid. Another function of a strut is to force the tyre on to the ground.

With wheels, there will be brakes, used for stopping, and sometimes steering (not recommended in a multi-engined aeroplane - use differential engine power instead).

BRAKES

Brakes work by applying friction to the wheels to slow them down and stop them rotating, converting kinetic energy into thermal energy in the process (in other words, the brakes get hot). They are operated by toe brakes that are at the top of each rudder pedal, operating the brakes on the wheels on their respective sides. This allows differential braking if it is required to help the rudder.

When disk brakes are used, the operating process is similar to that of the rotor brake. The energy rating of the brakes must match or exceed the kinetic energy generated at maximum landing weight and speed. On large aeroplanes, a *brake temperature monitor* will indicate whether the brakes are overheating or not. If they are, they will suffer from *brake fade*, and not work so well. Brake fade happens when the disks glaze from heat, and drum brakes suffer most from it. In fact, one of the jobs of the PM (*Pilot Monitoring*, or what used to be the *Pilot Non Flying*) is to note the time that maximum brake pressure is applied during an aborted takeoff and have the brake cooling chart handy, which will state when the brakes can be used again (sometimes you can't even taxi off the runway for a while). Wheels will also have thermal relief plugs that will melt and deflate the tyre, to stop it bursting. Even a light aircraft at 500 kg and touching down at 60 kts can produce enough energy to boil 2 cans of beer in standard ISA conditions!

There will be a *master cylinder* for each brake pedal, a reservoir, the brakes themselves and connecting pipes. The toe pedal activates the master cylinder directly, and a piston inside forces fluid along the lines to activate the brakes. Small aircraft use single disk brakes, and large ones use multi disks. The former can be checked visually for wear, and the latter use *wear indicator pins*. Carbon disk packs not only act as a heat sink, but they are much lighter, so they save weight. Brake units must be changed after a rejected takeoff at high weight and speed.

Antiskid systems monitor deceleration and release the brakes at intervals to prevent the wheels from locking. A control unit compares the rotation of each wheel with what it should be on a dry runway. If it is less than 85%, valves are opened to release the brakes. Each wheel has a speed measurement device.

ABS

Anti-skid protects tyres from the effects of skidding, to give you maximum braking, especially on slippery runways where hydroplaning may be a problem. An anti-skid computer compares the wheels' rate of slowdown against perfect conditions. If they are slowing down too quickly, ABS relieves enough hydraulic pressure to stay within model limits. Do not release brake pedal pressure during the landing roll - you should hold constant pedal pressure and let ABS do the work.

AUTOBRAKES

Once armed, the brakes will come on automatically once the wheels spin-up after touchdown. The setting dictates the degree of deceleration desired (1 is light), with 1 or 2 being normal. The rate of deceleration is detected by the INS, and braking effort is adjusted by the autobrake computer. If you apply significant pressure to the brake pedals during the landing roll with Autobrakes operating, it will assume you wish to take over manually.

Transmissions

This is how you get the power from the engines to the propellers. Because some engines work at higher speeds than other components, there is also be an element of reduction. Transmission systems will also have their own, self-contained oil supply. Torque in a turboprop is measured at the *reduction gearbox*.

Pneumatics

We have seen elsewhere that flight instruments are operated by air, as are deicing boots. Compressed air is used for many purposes on older aircraft, such as operating the landing gear, doors, flaps, etc., all things that are generally now done with hydraulics, but air is still useful in other ways. Although it is more compressible than hydraulic fluid, a good reason for using it instead is that you already fly through it, so you don't need to carry it in storage tanks, or need return pipes and systems, as it can be exhausted to the atmosphere. This saves weight.

Auxiliary Power Unit

The APU is a turbine engine that delivers power or compressed air, and is not intended for direct propulsion. In other words, it's a spare engine that runs the air and electrical systems when the aircraft is on the ground, or in emergency when in flight, through a gearbox or something. It saves you relying on ground power units. Sometimes, you can use the APU to power air conditioning, etc., so the main engines can give a little extra if you are heavy. It will be found in an unpressurised area, typically in the tail section, behind a firewall. Starting will be done from the ship's batteries, or one specifically for the APU. It is ready for loading 1 minute after the blue (AVAIL) light comes on. It can be shut down 2 minutes after working without load.

Being a turbine, an APU qualifies as one of the most powerful vacuum cleaners around, so loose articles, etc. should not be around. Also, they are noisy, so ear defenders should be worn.

ENGINE STARTING

Modern turbines are spun over until they are self-sustaining, with compressed air (or a starter/generator), commonly bled from the APU, to start the No 1, or Master, engine, which is then used to start any others through a crossfeed system of pipes and valves. Any electric motor used for this purpose would be too heavy! Early jets would use the exhaust from another machine to spin an engine over for starting.

Compressed Air

This can be created by a compressor powered by an engine, or come from storage bottles on the aircraft.

A compressor consists of a piston inside a cylinder, much like one in a reciprocating engine. There are even cooling fins, as air heats up when it is subject to pressure (compressors will also be positioned to get the maximum benefit from air cooling).

When the piston descends, air is sucked in through an inlet valve at the top of the cylinder. There is a *delivery valve* about halfway down the chamber, through which air from the previous upstroke is forced as the piston descends - it will have got there through a *transfer valve* in the top of the piston, which allows air through when it gets compressed as the piston goes up. Continuous delivery happens because the space underneath the piston is small, and the excess goes out directly through the delivery valve. Valves are spring-loaded.

A *high pressure relief valve* is fitted near the compressor to keep it warm, so it doesn't freeze up. Its purpose is to protect the system by allowing excess air to escape if a component fails and blocks things up. Although it is adjustable, it is *not* the way to control the pressure! That's done with the *pressure regulating valve*.

Also near the compressor is an *anti-freezer* full of methanol, which stops ice forming from the moisture in the air being compressed. An alternative solution is a *dehydrator* with silica crystals in, that absorb any moisture.

An air bottle acts as a temporary supply of pressure when the system is overloaded or switched off - it gets charged up during normal operations, although the system is filled before flight through a *ground charging valve*. The pipes going into the bottle actually extend inside by about 4 inches (forming *stack pipes*), so that oil or water that escapes the relevant traps doesn't get out.

Cabin Pressurisation

Contrary to popular belief, a pressurised cabin is not an airtight container - rather, it makes use of *outflow valves*, or *variable discharge valves*, that allow pressurised air to escape in an orderly fashion, depending on whether the First Officer remembers to set the controls or not. Think of it as a large paper bag with a hole in the end - the inside pressure is maintained as long as you keep blowing a constant mass flow of air into it (in our case, however, engine bleed air is used). The reason the cabin is not airtight is that plugging all the holes caused by routing cables, etc. through the cabin would be very inconvenient and expensive. On most modern airliners, cabin pressure is maintained by *regulating the leaving airflow*.

Note: Not all of the airframe is pressurised - some baggage compartments are often outside the "pressure vessel", which usually includes the cabin and cockpit.

Note: A bullethole is likely to be accepted as just one more leak. A much larger hole, however, appearing rapidly, will cause a rupture in the cabin wall.

The desired cabin altitude is usually set before takeoff, and it will "climb" automatically to it afterwards at an assigned rate, more slowly than atmospheric pressure (exam question). Typically, there will be two gauges in the cockpit, one to show the cabin's rate of climb (looks like a VSI), and the other with two needles, one to show the cabin altitude and a smaller one to show the ratio of the cabin pressure to the outside.

A system's efficiency is measured by its *max diff*, or *maximum differential* for short, which is the maximum ratio of cabin pressure to outside air pressure that the system can maintain. On the dial mentioned above it will be marked with a line. The maximum operating altitude comes from the maximum positive cabin differential pressure at the maximum cabin altitude (exam question). The pressurisation cycle concerns the rise and fall of differential pressure. The VSI will show a descent as cabin pressure is increased.

Just in case a modern system fails, you will need to know how to revert to doing it manually, so a few calculations are in order. To find out the cabin rate of climb, find the change in altitude, then the time taken to get to the one you want. Then divide the change by the climb time. So, if you start at 2,000 feet airfield elevation and want a cabin altitude of 8,000 feet, you divide the resulting 6,000-foot difference by the time taken to get to the real altitude of, say, FL 250.

Remember: The cabin can descend (or ascend) at a different rate than the airframe!

When descending, remember that cabin altitude must decrease proportionally with the real altitude so that both reach sea level (or airfield elevation) at the same time, so apply whatever you calculate as the time for descent to the cabin altitude as well (this is important, because a pressurised airframe can be stressed during a landing, although some aircraft are always slightly pressurised. Not only that, it can be hard to open the doors). Modern systems need to know the destination elevation at TOD so it can be worked out automatically.

Positive pressure relief valves dump excess pressure overboard when max diff is exceeded (they work at 1 PSI). *Negative pressure relief valves* stop the outside air pressure getting above that of the cabin (½ PSI) - they keep cabin pressure to a minimum level for when the cabin can't catch up, as with a fast descent. They may sometimes be called *pressurisation safety valves*, or *inward relief valves*, respectively. *Dump valves* allow you to manually dump the pressure in an emergency, which could be from a system failure or smoke in the cabin. *Squat switches* on the landing gear make sure the cabin is depressurised before takeoff and after landing (it activates the dump valve). A *ditching valve* closes all valves to stop water getting in. The *ditching control* closes the outflow valve.

The maximum cabin pressure altitude is 8,000', or 15,000' in case of failure. Normal rates of change are 500 feet per minute in the climb, and 300 in descent. A depressurisation warning system must be fitted over 25,000 feet.

Ground tests include pumping up the pressure until the max diff is reached and checking that the discharge valves operate. When the discharge valves are isolated, increase pressure slowly to check the safety valves.

All this inflating and deflating of cabins places a stress on the airframe, of course, as a result of which the life of an airframe can be limited by cycles, to save embarrassing incidents when the rivets fail.

Air Conditioning

An environmental control system should provide a favourable atmosphere for instruments and equipment, aside from allowing the crew to work in comfort. Conditioned air is controlled in respect of *temperature* and *pressure*, particularly below ambient temperature, and cabin air should be changed continuously at 1.5 kg/min to prevent the buildup of CO_2, water, dust, fumes and smells.

The normal flow rate in a large cabin should normally be 1 lb per seat per minute, but at least 0.5 lbs if any part of the (duplicated) system fails. In emergency, this can drop to 0.4. Any duplication is there to ensure that the minimum rate is maintained.

Cabin temperature should be kept within a range of between 18-24°C, with relative humidity around 30%. The ideal should be 18° and 60%.

Of course, in helicopters, the above requirements are modified somewhat, as very few helicopters have air conditioning anyway, due to the weight penalty. In the Bell 206 it is a small belt-driven widget attached to rear of the accessory drive.

There are several parts to the average air conditioning system, including the *air supply, flow control, cooling* and *heating systems, temperature control* and *distribution*.

They all work in the same way, by initially compressing a liquid, and taking some of the heat created by that process away by running cool air past it. When that air is expanded again, it absorbs heat from the environment and makes it cooler, with the amount of cooling being proportional to the change in volume.

Note: *Heat always flows from the hot to the cold substance.*

AIR SUPPLY & VENTILATION

At the basic level, air is drawn into the cabin and mixed with a supply of warm air for the right temperature. How air is sucked in depends on the system being used:

RAM AIR SYSTEMS

Ram air can cool a cabin directly, being allowed in through valves which regulate airflow typically coming in through the nose. If ram air is not available, for example, when on the ground, a blower could circulate the air instead.

Ram air is used on small, unpressurised machines not needing much throughput, with any heating either coming from the engine exhaust (by using a muff) or a unit that is self-contained - fuel burnt in it provides the heat, which is mixed with ram air through simple control valves (otherwise known as *punkah louvres*, after the punkah wallah in India, who waves a fan about).

The air itself is scooped in through an inlet in the nose or on the fuselage. Ram air ventilation may be provided throughout the cockpit and cabin through a series of ducts in windows and doors.

RAM AIR AND COMPRESSORS (OR BLOWERS)

These are used in conjunction with ram air, or instead of it when on the ground. They can be driven by the engine, to pump ram air from the wing leading edge or engine fairing into a system similar to the Bleed Air system, below. However, there will also be filters and silencers.

ENGINE BLEED AIR

Here, a a supply from the high pressure (i.e. hot) end of the compressor of an engine (or the APU, on a large pressurised aircraft) is tapped. Being hot (200-400°C), it needs to be cooled, so the air passes through a shutoff valve (used for isolation purposes), then to a pressure-reducing valve to calm things down before proceeding to the cold air unit.

Another benefit of using compressor air is that it is relatively uncontaminated, from either dirt or fumes, although filters are used anyway.

HEATING

Heating can come from a compressor bleed (most common in heavy helicopters), be electrical, or come from a separate source, such as the Janitrol heater. The simplest system uses a muff round the exhaust that makes air flowing through it warmer, on its way to the cabin. As a result, there is a danger of carbon monoxide poisoning if the exhaust is faulty.

Slightly more complicated is what can best be described as a flame in a tube, under some control, of course, around which air is forced (the *Janitrol*). These need a rundown period which should be observed, otherwise carbon will form on the igniter and stop it from firing up again.

As mentioned above, a compressor heats air up through pressure, and a butterfly valve can restrict airflow for the same result (*choke valve*). However, because of the availability of cold air, it is easier to cool down hot air than the other way round. A turbine powered machine can use bleed air from an engine, which can be mixed with outside air to regulate the temperature.

SYSTEMS

Systems can be based on air or vapour cycles:

AIR CYCLE

This system is used with engine bleed air. Although light and inexpensive, air cycle systems do not provide enough mass flow for machines with high cooling needs, so low pressure air is used. It is called and *air cycle* system because it uses ambient air for cooling, which at altitude is cold anyway and, since you're already flying through the stuff, you don't have to use up fuel by carrying lots of refrigerant.

There are three main types of cold air unit used with air cycle systems:

- **Bootstrap**. The bootstrap (or turbo-compressor) uses a **P**rimary heat exchanger (for pre-cooling against the ambient air temperature), the **C**ompressor section of the cooling turbine (to boost pressure and temperature to provide a significant pressure drop across the turbine, and for improved efficiency, because it is easier to work on air that has been pre-cooled), a **S**econdary heat exchanger (which also uses outside air as a coolant to remove the unwanted temperature rise across the compressor) and the expansion **T**urbine (PCST), which extracts work from the air by driving the compressor, and the resulting expansion cools the air further (if you reduce the pressure, temperature reduces as well). *The maximum temperature drop is in the second exchanger.* After the air has been cooled, any water vapour in it will naturally condense out, to form fog or high humidity, so the air leaving the expansion turbine is passed through a water separator, which uses

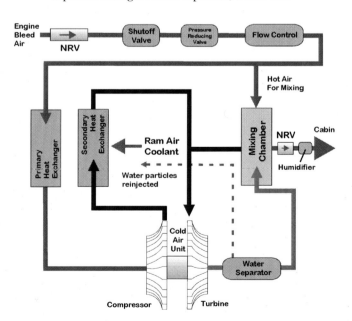

centrifugal force to throw the water particles into a coalescer bag that absorbs the moisture, which can be injected into the outside air entering the secondary heat exchanger to improve its performance. The air can now be combined in a mixing chamber with some uncooled engine bleed air to warm the air to any desired temperature

- **Brake Turbine**. Here, the initial tapping pressure is higher and the charge air goes directly to the turbine through a single heat exchanger. The compressor (which is driven by the turbine) takes in outside air (at low [pressure), but expels it through a restriction, so a back pressure is created on the compressor which brakes the turbine (hence the name) to provide energy conversion that removes heat from the charge air. As there is only one heat exchanger, the system is lighter, and the mass flow/weight ratio is better, but it cannot be used on the ground unless the output from the compressor is fed into the ducting downstream of the heat exchanger

- **Turbofan**. This is a further refinement of the Brake Turbine. A turbine drives a fan (not a compressor) so it can be used on the ground

VAPOUR CYCLE

A vapour cycle system, which uses its own refrigerant, can supplement an air cycle system, as it can be used without the engines running (being essentially a refrigerator, it also has its own compressor). It is self-contained, and mainly used on small aircraft. Vapour cycle systems use least power, and can place cool air accurately, but they can also reduce humidity, which is why they might be chosen over other systems.

With them, a gas refrigerant (usually Freon) is made to alternate between a liquid and a gas as it is pumped round, collecting heat at one end of the system, which is removed when the vapour is converted to liquid under pressure at the other end (when the gas is pressurised, it condenses into a liquid, which is why another name for the heat exchanger is a *condenser*). It therefore works by "moving" heat from one place to another, being compressed, cooled, expanded and heated, in that order.

The power required to do this depends on the difference in temperatures and the amount of air to be treated, and the temperature change depends on the rate of compression or expansion.

The liquid used in the system (the *refrigerant*) will have special properties, such as a low boiling point and the

ability to change state readily from liquid to vapour, and *vice versa*. You control the temperature around the system by varying the pressure of the refrigerant at any point.

Freon normally boils at 4°C. Although water is actually the lightest refrigerant, with the highest latent heat value, its boiling point is too high for best use.

You need a large quantity of latent heat to make a liquid change its state to a gas. If you can manage to accompany this change of state with expansion, you can suck a lot of heat from the atmosphere. This expansion takes place inside an *evaporator*. As air flows over it, heat will be extracted from the air.

In a more complex system, a *compressor*, which is driven by the engine, can compress the refrigerant vapour to increase its pressure and temperature, and therefore its boiling point. The compressor keeps a difference going between the low and high pressure sides of the system by increasing the pressure of the refrigerant going into the condenser, and reducing the pressure in the evaporator, to aid expansion.

The vapour is transferred to a *condenser*, which is a heat exchanger (like a radiator in a car) that uses external airflow to cool the refrigerant enough to turn it into a liquid (i.e. condensing it), so that it gives up its latent heat into the ram air. Water is removed now to stop the system corroding.

This liquid moves through an expansion valve to reduce its pressure and boiling point before it goes into an *evaporator*, where the process happens again. The *expansion valve* is a metering device that responds to temperature to increase or decrease the flow of refrigerant.

In other words, the evaporator is another heat exchanger that sucks heat from the air going into the cabin as it passes over the expanding (and therefore cooling) refrigerant. It is actually a long, thin tube, coiled as appropriate to save space. The air now gets so cool that you need water traps downstream to stop the system freezing from the moisture.

The water extractor and humidifier are downstream of the cold air unit.

In an *open circuit* vapour cycle system, evaporated refrigerant is lost to atmosphere, and wasted. In a *closed circuit* system, as found in those square units in motels, it is recycled by evaporation and condensation.

Deicing

Strictly speaking, de-icing systems are turned on after a bit of ice has built up, whereas *anti-icing* systems try to stop it forming in the first place. Examples of the former include the inflatable rubber boots on wing leading edges (already discussed under *Icing*). Anti-icing systems include those round engine intakes, which are fed with a bleed from the compressor, and pitot heating. Also, electrical power is used to heat the wing leading edges of smaller jets, together with sundry items such as windscreens, OAT probes, propellers, etc.

Larger jets use hot N_2 bleed air, or *thermal* anti-icing, where a second inner skin is used to provide a small gap between it and the leading edge, through which heated air is ducted to warm everything up. The hot air itself can come from compressor bleeds, or heating ram air through a heat exchanger in an engine exhaust, as found on many turbo-props. Air can also be blown past a cylinder in which a fuel/air mixture is burned. The air is cycled round the surfaces to reduce the maximum demand at any moment. Whatever is used, as with other uses of bleed air, they still take engine power, so are used in flight only.

Engine intake icing can occur well above 0°C, as air entering the engine accelerates and cools in the intake. The Bell 206, for example, requires engine anti-icing to be on when in visible moisture below 5°C. Fuel tanks are not heated, as the freezing point of Jet A1 is around -50°C, but fuel on its way to the engines is heated with a fuel/oil heat exchanger, which also cools engine and hydraulic oil.

Fluid de-icing is more common on small, propeller-driven aircraft, but can be found on older turbo-propellers. The *weeping wing* allows deicing fluid to creep out of tiny holes in the leading edge of the surface affected but, if the aircraft is too small, the supplies you need to carry can easily make you overweight.

EFFECT OF ICING ON TOD POINT

With jets, if you expect icing during the descent, you should start earlier, because you will need to run the engines faster to supply the bleed air, so the descent profile will be flatter.

Fire Detection

Fire is a chemical reaction involving rapid oxidation or burning of a fuel. It has three elements - fuel, oxygen and the heat. Take one away and it stops, although it's fair to say that cold does more to put out a fire than anything else. With dangerous goods, you can get fire from the reaction of flammable materials with an oxidising agent - you don't necessarily need a source of ignition. Although the atmosphere's oxygen content is 21%, fire only needs 18% to burn.

- A **Class A** fire is an ordinary one, that is, of normal combustible material on which water is usually effective (e.g. solids, like wood and paper, but not metal - see Class D). Symbol: *Triangle*

- A **Class B** fire is in a flammable liquid, such as oil or grease, or anything that melts to create a flammable liquid or vapour. Symbol: *Square*

- A **Class C** fire is electrical, or *anything near an electrical supply*, for which you need a non-conducting extinguisher (e.g. don't use foam or water). Thus, in any building, you should always consider C. Symbol: *Circle*

- A **Class D** fire covers other materials, like metals, that *may* burn, such as magnesium, titanium, potassium or sodium, as used in fireworks or aircraft. Use Dry Powder, which will absorb the heat from the material. Halon should not be used on burning metals because, at the high temperatures involved, it could form phosgene, which is a poison gas.

For B and C, you could use either CO_2 or Dry Powder (which ruins the avionics), but the fumes may be toxic, so you will need plenty of ventilation afterwards. The extinguisher colour codes are black and blue, respectively (foam is cream). You can use Halon (BCF) on anything, especially in the cockpit, if you're allowed to use it.

Note: In a cargo hold, you should turn off the ventilation (i.e. air conditioning) first!

Trivia: The numbers relating to Halon refer to the number of atoms in the basic molecule - for example, Halon 1211 has 1 Carbon atom, 2 Flourine, 1 Chlorine and 1 Bromine, hence its official name of bromochlorodifluoromethane (BCF).

To help you identify the source, smoke associated with electrical fires is usually grey or tan and very irritating to the nose or eyes (it doesn't smell too good, either). Anything else (say from the heater) tends to be white, but you may get some black from upholstery. If you think you have an electrical fire, it's no good just using the extinguisher, because you may be treating the symptom and not the cause, although there is a school of thought that advocates not using an extinguisher at all if you can possibly help it, due to the fumes and stuff you have to breathe in until you land, particularly with Halon/BCF which has been banned from everywhere else except aviation for this very reason (unfortunately, it's darn good at putting out fires!) Whatever you do, transmit a Mayday before it's too late - you can always downgrade it afterwards. Bear in mind also that your first strike with your extinguisher is the best, because the contents and pressure decrease from then on.

A couple of points not related to the exams, but still useful knowledge:

- Fire doubles in size every two minutes

- Never tackle a blaze that is bigger than you

- Fire extinguishers are only meant for small fires, and even then they should be used to help give you an escape route

- Always have an escape route behind you

- Only hold the handle on a CO_2 extinguisher, or you will get frostbite

SYSTEMS

A *Resistive* fire detection system consists of two independent loops of wire placed around the area to be protected, which both have to be activated to guard against false alarms - an AND logic gate (see *Computers, Etc*) helps with the decision-making process. A central electrode surrounded by crystal filler sits inside a capillary tube, and the two ends are brought together at a junction linked to a Wheatstone Bridge (no current flows because it is an endless loop). The capillary tube is earthed to the aircraft. As temperature increases, the resistance of the filler material drops, allowing the electricity to run to Earth via the capillary tube. The resulting flow unbalances the bridge and sends a signal to the warning panel. Sometimes, however, these can short out, particularly on misty or humid days, or if the capillary tube gets crushed, and create false alarms (escaping compressor bleed air from a turbine engine can do this, too). Another system uses the resistance drop to allow the current to increase enough to energise the warning system.

The wires in a *capacitance* system look identical to those in a resistive system, but the central electrode is connected to an amplifier unit which charges the central electrode for a set time then discharges it into the measuring unit, where its capacitance is compared with a reference value. In a fire, the capacitance will increase with temperature. The measuring unit senses this and sends a signal to the warning panel. If the fire wire earths out, the loss of capacitance will prevent a fire warning from being given (this is a *no-fault* system).

A fire detector that operates on the *rate of temperature rise* is a *thermocouple system*. If two lengths of wire made of two different metals are joined end to end (i.e. paralleled), and one end is heated, an electrical current will flow from the hot end to the cold end, and back again. In fact, current will increase with heat to a point, then decrease, then rise again, so there is a slight similarity with alternating current. In an aircraft, the potentially hot area could be the engine compartment, and the cooler area the cockpit. When a fire starts, current increases in the hot end, with the rise compared to a reference. Bimetal strip detectors are arranged in *series*, and they *open* during a fire.

Gas can be used as well. In the *Systron Donner* system, a responder unit contains two pressure switches and a core of titanium hydride. The rest of the unit is filled with helium which keeps one of the pressure switches closed, known as the *averaging gas*. A drop in gas pressure causes the switch to open, which is how you know if the unit has failed. When a fire starts, the titanium hydride will give off hydrogen gas, which will raise the internal pressure to close an alarm switch.

Fire detection systems are on the essential bus, meaning that they get priority for electrical current. Each engine will typically have its own warning light, but they will share an audio alarm, such as a bell. When a fire handle is pulled, various valves and gates are closed in preparation for operating the fire bottles (below).

When a fire is detected, put an oxygen or smoke mask on, if you have one, then bring on essential electrics one at a time until the smoke appears again. For a piston engine, turn off the fuel selector, or move the mixture to ICO, so the engine can run dry and stop. Then switch off the ignition.

On a jet, close the engine thrust lever, move the start lever to cutoff and pull the appropriate fire warning switch (after confirming you've got the right one!). This should cut off the fuel, but if the warning still carries on, rotate the fire warning switch in one direction and hold it there for a second to activate the extinguisher. Wait 30 seconds. If the warning is still on, rotate it the other way for the other extinguisher. If that doesn't work, bear in mind that structural failure of the wing will be imminent after about two minutes if the fire is uncontrolled, which is a sobering enough thought to make you commence emergency descent IMMEDIATELY, no matter how good it looks (having said all that, you could consider delaying actuation until you've no reason to suspect a false alarm; that is, unless you can actually see signs of a fire).

For a turboprop, the procedure is similar, except you will need to feather the prop.

In the cabin, in the air or on the ground, the priority is to get out, as soon as possible, because if the flames don't get you, the fumes will. The only difference between the two is how quickly this can be done, and what you can do about it.

The engine fire warning system on a multi-engined aircraft has an individual *warning light* and *bell* (with EICAS or ECAM, there might be a warning message on the screen, such as **FIRE ENG 1**). The fire handle warning light is there to help make sure you've got the right engine - it goes out when the detected fire is out.

Heat sensors can be found in many engine compartments, with smoke detectors in cabins, toilets, or anywhere convenient. Infra red systems may detect the light from flames or glowing metal (also used by railways to detect hot wheels).

Jet engine systems are divided into three zones:

- *Zone 1* surrounds the hydraulic pumps, ancillary gearbox, engine lubrication oil reservoir, fuel control unit, etc. Zone 1 is the most likely place for a fire to start and is the only one with fire detection and remotely operated fire extinguishers. To reduce the chance of fire spreading, the zone is kept at a lower pressure than other bays by a ventilation system

- *Zone 2* is where compressor blades could touch the engine case and create a metal fire, indicated via the engine vibration monitoring system. This zone is hotter than Zone 1

- *Zone 3* is the hottest Zone, as it surrounds the engine and jet pipe behind the combustion chamber. A bulkhead separates it from Zone 1

If a combustible fluid or gas has to pass through a hot zone, it must go through a double-skinned pipe).

CARGO COMPARTMENTS

If there is a fire in the compartment in the lower half of the fuselage, turn off the ventilation. Similarly, in an air-conditioned hold, turn off the air conditioning. You

should not use oxygen masks when the cabin is affected by smoke, because it allows the smoke to mix with the oxygen. Compartments must have provisions for safeguarding against fires according to these classifications:

CLASS A
A fire is easily discernible to crew at their stations, and all parts of must be easily accessible in flight (e.g. a passenger compartment, or cockpit). There must be a hand fire extinguisher for each compartment.

CLASS B
Typically an avionics bay or similar, enough access must be provided in flight to enable crew to effectively reach the whole compartment and its contents with a hand extinguisher, and the compartment must be able to contain hazardous amounts of smoke, flames, or extinguishing agent. There must be a separate smoke or fire detector system to give warning at the pilot or flight engineer station, a hand fire extinguisher, and it must be lined with fire-resistant material.

CLASS C
These compartments do not conform with the other categories. There must be a separate smoke or fire detector system to give warning at the pilot or flight engineer station, with a built-in extinguishing system controlled from them, because they are remote. It must be able to contain hazardous quantities of smoke, flames, or extinguishing agents. Ventilation and draft must allow extinguishing agents to control any fire. It must be lined with fire-resistant material, except that additional service lining of flame-resistant material may be used.

CLASS D
A fire in one of these is completely confined without endangering the safety of the aeroplane or occupants. Class D compartments must:

- contain hazardous quantities of smoke, flames, or noxious gases

- control ventilation and draughts so fires do not go beyond safe limits

- be completely lined with fire-resistant material

Consideration must be given to the effects of heat on critical parts nearby.

CLASS E

On cargo aeroplanes, cabin areas may be classed as E, which must:

- be completely lined with fire-resistant material.

- have separate smoke or fire detection systems to give warning at pilot or flight engineer stations.

- have a means to shut off ventilating airflow to or within, and the controls for it must be accessible to the flight crew in the crew compartment.

- be able to contain hazardous quantities of smoke, flames, or gases.

Crew emergency exits must be accessible under all conditions.

Smoke Detection

Smoke detectors in the home are very useful for telling you when the toast is done. In aircraft, however, the detection of smoke is one of the ways in which fire is detected, and is particularly important. Detectors are required in unmanned compartments and toilets, but are typically found in baggage compartments that are remote from the cabin.

Tip: Speaking of remote baggage compartments, be aware that talcum powder, if it escapes from a passenger's baggage, can set off a smoke alarm, as can dust.

Smoke detectors work in two ways:

- *Ion detection systems* use a bit of radioactive material that bombards oxygen particles in the surrounding air with alpha particles. Ions are thus created which allow a small current to pass through the air across the chamber (somewhat like a fluorescent light tube). Smoke will block the passage of current because they absorb the alpha particles. This blockage is detected and used to trigger an alarm

- *Optical detection systems* use a current of air drawn through a labyrinth with a lamp at one end and a photoelectric cell at the other. The labyrinth ensures that the one cannot be seen by the other directly. Smoke and fumes, however, allow light to refract and reflect and be seen by the photoelectric cell, to create an electrical current which can be used to trigger an alarm. The system is tested with a relay switch that lights a bulb next to the photoelectric cell

Fire Extinguishing

The fuel and ignition must be shut off first - it's done automatically when the discharge handle is pulled. In a jet, the contents of at least two CO_2 fire bottles can be directed to any engine. For example, use bottle 1, pull the handle and turn it to the left. Turn it to the right to discharge bottle 2. The EICAS/ECAM will display an **ENG BOTTLE 1** (or 2) **LOW** message.

APU

The APU will cut off its own fuel supply, shut the ventilation doors and shut down (actually, the extinguishing agent is discharged automatically, but will be withheld until the fuel is off and doors are closed, so that any air that might promote the fire is isolated). There is an aural warning horn in the front wheel well to warn ground personnel that the APU extinguisher has been discharged.

ON THE GROUND

Engine fire drills may vary considerably between different types, and these will have to be memorised, but there are some general points that can be made. One is, before evacuating the aircraft, make sure the parking brake is off, so it can be moved somewhere safer if things get out of hand, always being aware that it could run off by itself, as well! If the fire has been caused by spilt fuel, has spread to the ground under the wing and the other engine has been started, taxi clear of the area (or more specifically, the fuel on the ground) before evacuation, keeping the fire on the downwind side. If the other engine has not been started, evacuate first, carrying out what drills you can.

Always approach hot landing gear from the front or rear (the safest extinguisher for wheel fires is dry powder).

If you can, use the radio to summon help, and take the extinguisher. Remember that human beings *en masse* need very different handling than when encountered singly. In the air, initial actions are similar everywhere - after performing vital actions from memory (identifying the source, etc.), refer to the checklist to see if you haven't forgotten anything.

For an engine jet pipe fire on the ground, do a *Dry Motor Cycle* (run the engine without the igniter working).

Fuel Jettison

This system allows you to dump fuel when you are heavier than landing weight, and have to land in a hurry.

A fuel jettison system is needed on every aircraft, unless it is can do what amounts to a 15-minute circuit between takeoff and landing again. The system must be able to bring you down to landing weight within 15 minutes, and it should be done either over the sea or above 10,000 feet agl, but it is an emergency procedure, so these should not be too rigidly observed - exceptionally, you can do it over 7,000 feet agl in Winter and 4,000 in Summer. ATC should always be informed.

It is not a good idea to do it near thunderstorms, however, or in turbulence. The *No Smoking* light should be on and passengers briefed and radio silence observed as much as possible, especially with HF.

Autopilots, etc

In large aeroplanes, the autopilot is used for almost every manoeuvre except for taxiing and takeoff, and landings if you don't have autoland. This is because the tolerances for navigation and aircraft separation are very tight, whether you're in a departure or arrival procedure or simply flying long distance in RVSM airspace. Probably the only time you will fly the machine completely in manual is on your initial interview!

An automatic pilot ensures piloting and guidance in horizontal and vertical planes, stabilising and monitoring movement around the C of G. Those in large aeroplanes control attitudes in pitch, roll and yaw and are known as *3-axis* (a *2-axis* controls pitch and roll, and a single-axis roll only), and will even handle an engine failure.

Autopilots have two basic modes, called *Lateral Mode* (HDA) and *Vertical Mode* (VS). A full *Autopilot and Flight Director System* (APFDS), or *Automatic Flight Control System* (AFCS), may consist of the autopilot, auto throttle, yaw damper and Flight Director, described below.

You should be able to maintain an altitude or heading, intercept and follow a radial or localiser and keep to a descent pattern (that is, control vertical speed). However, when following a radial, the results can often be unsettling to passengers, as the system chases the needle too much. A better solution is to use the heading bug and chase the needles yourself so you don't spill the coffee (near the VOR cone of confusion, the roll channel temporarily switches to heading mode). When being engaged, and without selecting a particular mode, an autopilot enables stabilisation with attitude hold, or maintaining vertical speed and possibly automatic trim. In a selected axis capture mode, it gives a bank attitude input proportional to the deviation between the selected heading and the current heading, but not exceeding a given value (in other words, governed to a rate of bank).

Autopilots use gyroscopes to detect changes in the flight path (they may go unserviceable frequently, because many aircraft are moved before the gyros have a chance to stop). Any attitude change is sensed by a rate gyroscope which precesses and produces an output signal proportional to the rate of change. A controller computes a corrective signal and sends it to servo which moves the appropriate flight control and feeds back its position to the controller so actual and required movement can be compared. As the original attitude is gradually restored, the gyroscope output and error signal are gradually removed and the controller the pitch command. This is a *closed loop* system which needs feedback to work (in this case an *inner loop*, so a three-axis autopilot would have at least 3 inner loops). Control inputs from external sources form *outer loops*, which are there for control, while an inner loop's function is to stabilise.

Autopilot outputs ultimately act on control servos, whose control inputs will be electronic, but the power required to do the job can be hydraulic (main controls) or electric (secondary systems, like trim). *Torque limiters* stop servos from operating flying control surfaces too rapidly or through too great a range. If torque becomes excessive, a spring-loaded coupling and friction clutch will limit it.

An autopilot cannot be engaged when there is a fault in the power supply, the controlled-turn knob is not set to centre-off, there is a synchronization fault in the pitch channel, or a fault in the attitude reference unit.

The *yaw damper*, which suppresses Dutch roll, controls the rudder, with the angular rate about the vertical axis as the input signal. The signal for a given rate of oscillation is varied inversely with airspeed. The yaw damper indicator supplies the pilot with information about yaw damper action on the rudder.

Control Wheel Steering, as fitted to Boeings, allows inputs from the control column to be made with autopilot engaged, and the new attitude will be held automatically - if you engage the CWS of a conventional autopilot and carry out a manoeuvre in roll, when the control wheel is released, the autopilot maintains the attitude obtained at that moment. It can be used in pitch or roll, or both.

Touch Control Steering needs the autopilot to be disengaged with a switch whilst attitude is set. It is maintained on re-engagement.

Interlocks stop the autopilot taking over if the system isn't ready, and cause it to disengage on failures. A slaved power control circuit can synchronise itself, so when it fails, it stops the automatic pilot from engaging. Synchronization of the autopilot control channel system enables the prevention of jerks during engagement, and functions in the heading, navigation and approach modes.

LOOPS

The *inner loop* of a system concerns itself with events internal to the aircraft, such as movement of controls, and their disturbances in pitch, roll and yaw, etc., so it is only concerned with stability.

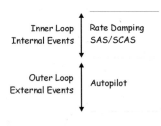

| Inner Loop Internal Events | Rate Damping SAS/SCAS |
| Outer Loop External Events | Autopilot |

The *external loop* deals with stuff affecting the machine from the outside world, including airspeed, altitude and track, so is there for *control*.

CONTROL LAWS

These are rules that the autopilot computer has to follow, determining how it interprets a performance demand against a control response, but they also determine the fundamental response of the aircraft and set safety limits for automatic flight (that is, the control law will protect the aircraft from overstress or overspeed). Put more simply, control laws allow a fly-by-wire system to position the flight controls for the most efficient response. They are electrical algorithms that figure out the proper electrical signals to be sent to the electrohydraulic actuators.

For example, the control law of a transport aeroplane autopilot control channel may be defined as *the relationship between the computer input deviation data and the output control deflection signals* (don't blame me, I didn't write it).

DIRECT CONTROL LAW

This is the basic mechanical connection between input and output - a nose-up pitch demand applied and held will initiate a nose up pitch rate. As natural stability comes in to oppose the increase in angle of attack, the pitch rate will slow to zero and the aircraft will hold a new attitude. That is, the machine will obey your direct control inputs.

PITCH RATE DEMAND/ATTITUDE HOLD LAW

In this system, a nose-up pitch input applied and held will react as above, but the computer will continuously increase elevator deflection to maintain a constant pitch rate. With zero pitch input there will be zero change, so zero pitch input is an attitude hold condition. This means that, in a positive alpha vertical gust, attitude will not change, but the extra lift will balloon the aircraft above the intended flightpath. The disadvantage is that flightpath is

not maintained under zero input and continual autopilot control inputs are needed.

G DEMAND/FLIGHTPATH HOLD LAW

This depends on level flight being a constant 1G flightpath. Increased G makes the aircraft go up, and reduced G makes it go down. In response to a nose-up pitch input, the computer initiates a demand for more G and calculates the necessary elevator angle. Thus, a pitch input calls for a flightpath change and zero pitch input is a flightpath hold demand. This is inherently good for maintaining a defined flightpath, but there is an inherent lag in response from gusts, which leads to sharp and rapid computed corrections, particularly at low speed.

AUTOMATIC TRIM

The function of automatic trim is to:

- Reduce to zero the hinge moment of the entire (elevator) control surface to relieve the load on the servo-actuator

- Maintain the stability & manoeuvrability trade-off in the flight envelope

- Transfer a stabilised aeroplane to the pilot during disengagement (that is, ensure it is properly trimmed when the autopilot is disengaged)

- For pitch, cancel the hinge moment of the elevator

AUTOTHROTTLE

The autothrottle's job is to maintain constant engine power or aeroplane speed - it can catch and maintain N_1, EPR and IAS or Mach number.

AUTOLAND

The autopilot intercepts of a localiser beam at a constant heading. Vertical speed is maintained according to radalt height between 50' and the ground.

Note: Autoland is intended for conditions of low visibility, meaning fog, with little wind. It is *not* designed for crosswinds over 15 kts, hand flying, or turbulence!

Semi-automatic mode with respect to landings means that the autopilot maintains the ILS and the autothrottle maintains a constant speed until DH, to disengage automatically at around 100'. *Automatic Mode* maintains the ILS until the flare, the autothrottle decreases thrust at around 30 ft, and the flare and ground roll are performed automatically. An automatic landing system that keeps operating (that is, still allows the approach, flare and landing to be completed automatically) after a failure below alert height is *Fail Operational*, although it will then operate as *Fail-Passive*, meaning that the landing must be continued manually if something else fails (a fail-passive system produces no significant out-of-trim condition or deviation of flight path or attitude after a failure, but the landing is manual). If there is a secondary independent guidance system to help with the manual landing, you have a *fail-operational hybrid* system. There must be 3 autopilots for fail operational, and 2 for a fail passive. With only one autopilot for climbing, cruising and approach, the system is also fail-passive.

During a Cat II automatic approach, height information is supplied by a radio altimeter. From about 50 ft, vertical speed is maintained according to radio altimeter height.

On an autopilot coupled approach, Go Around mode is engaged by pushing a button on the throttles. When an automatic landing is interrupted by a go-around, the autothrottle reacts immediately upon pilot action on the TO/GA (Take-off/Go-around) switch to recover the maximum thrust, the autopilot monitors the climb and the rotation of the aeroplane, ad the pilot retracts the landing gear and reduces the flap to reduce the drag.

STICK SHAKER/PUSHER

This is a device fitted to the yoke as an aid to prevent stalling - when the angle of attack, or alpha, approaches a critical value, the stick is made to shake as a warning to the pilot. If this is ignored, the stick pusher applies down elevator. They became essential equipment with the introduction of swept wings and T-tails.

USING AN AUTOPILOT

Typically, before takeoff, you would engage the Pitch, Roll and Yaw channels, plus the Flight Director so you can see what inputs are required (the full autopilot is not normally switched on for takeoff or landing, unless you have a suitable operational one, as used with SAR. At this stage you will actually be using the SCAS).

Engagement of an autopilot is not possible when:

- The electrical supply is faulty
- The turn control knob is not set to centre off
- There is a synchronisation fault
- There is a fault in the attitude reference unit

If you ever want to fly the machine yourself, you must use the *Disengage* button on the cyclic to release the system's grip of death on the controls.

The power switch for the autopilot may well be disguised as the Flight Director, with three selections:

- **OFF**, which speaks for itself
- **FDIR**. The Flight Director's job is to reduce your workload by indicating the manoeuvres required to execute, achieve or maintain a flight condition. It does this by presenting data as control commands to show you the *optimal way to achieve your flight path*. In other words, the flight director gives you directions about *how to position of the controls* rather than the attitude of the aircraft. This means you get no information about the flight path, for which you need a separate navigation display. When the FD bars centralise, you have only made the proper control inputs, not reached the optimum flight path! The flight director can be used without the autopilot, although the autopilot can use the FD to tell you what it's doing (on a helicopter, the autopilot follows the FD)

    Remember: The FD doesn't tell the aircraft what to do - rather, *command bars* show you what control inputs are required:

    All you need to do is align them as they move.

    Note: In this mode, you are doing the flying, not the autopilot!

- **AUTO**. The autopilot will fly the machine according to your selections below

Here is a list of some of the buttons available and their functions. Note that some will not be present on simpler autopilots, or they may be labelled differently!

- **WLV**. The Wing Leveller simply holds the wings level while you figure out what to do next. It's a handy button to punch in an overload situation and will hold the wings at the current level of bank, or level them for you if you engage it with less than a certain figure, typically 7°
- **HDG**. Heading Hold follows the heading bug on the HSI or DG. To turn, simply move the heading bug to the desired direction and the machine will follow. **Tip:** Ensure the heading bug is in place before engaging the HDG button, or the machine will seek the heading!
- **LOC**. The Localizer will fly an ILS localiser, which is more sensitive than a VOR radial, such as is used with the NAV button. Pushing this button just arms the system - *your current HDG mode will remain in force until the localiser needle starts to move into the centre*. At that point, the LOC will go from

ARMED to ACTIVE, and start flying for you, disengaging any previous modes

- **G/S**. Flies the glideslope portion of the ILS, in the same way as LOC handles the Localiser

- **ALT**. Holds the current or pre-selected altitude. If you hit this button, the system will maintain the altitude you are currently sitting at, if the figures in the altitude selection dial. However, you should dial in the assigned altitude in the altitude window well before you get there and use V/S or FLCH to get there

- **V/S**. Holds a constant vertical speed. To climb or descend, push VS (*Vertical Speed*) and select the rate of climb or descent with a knob on the VSI. This will disable ALT, if selected. Once at the required altitude, reselect the ALT button to maintain

- **SPD**. Holds a pre-selected airspeed

- **FLCH**. Flight Level Change is commonly used to change altitude by allowing you to add or take away power while holding an airspeed. This is like SPD, but, if you have auto-throttle, FLCH will automatically add or take away power

- **PTCH**. Use Pitch-Sync to hold the nose at a constant pitch attitude, in the same way you would use the Wing-Leveller

- **VNAV**. Vertical Navigation will fly automatically loaded altitudes from the FMS so you can follow route altitudes

- **BC**. The Back Course is a second *localiser* that works in the opposite sense to the proper ILS. You use it to fly along the extended centreline once you have missed the runway and have to carry out a Missed Approach. However, some airfields save money by making you to use the Back Course as a proper ILS, although you won't have a glideslope. When coming back in the other way, everything is back to front. Pushing this button reverses all the commands to make it look right. It does nor work with an HSI

- **NAV** (or **VOR**). This keeps you coupled to a selected radial on the HSI, which must naturally be slaved to whatever navaid you are using. The problem is that it can chase the heading too much, and will overshoot and come back rather than make small adjustments to creep up on the selected heading. It is often more practical and comfortable for passengers to use HDG mode and

move the heading bug yourself if time permits. In addition, you have better roll rates and maximum bank angles in HDG mode

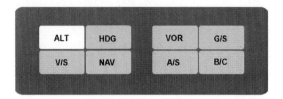

In the picture above, the light behind the ALT button is illuminated, indicating that the height-keeping function has been selected. Together with the HDG button, this is the most used function. So much so, that these are usually the automatic selections when the thing is switched on in the first place, to maintain pitch and roll.

VS, FLCH and HDG all do stuff the moment they are engaged. Others, like ALT, G/S and LOC, on the other hand, sit there on standby (armed) until they intercept the altitude, glideslope or localiser required. That is, *they will not do anything until then*.

EXAMPLE

You set the machine up straight and level at 3,000 feet and push the ALT and HDG buttons. Now you can take your hands off and read the instructions, as the autopilot will maintain that level and whatever heading you set with the heading bug until you tell it otherwise. Now you want to climb to 6,000 feet, so you need to dial this figure into the altitude window. (you would also set your cleared altitude before you take off.

How you want to get to there determines what button you push next. You could hit the vertical speed (V/S) button, then select a rate of climb on the VSI until you get to the selected altitude. This mode should be disengaged automatically on reaching it.

FLCH or SPD, on the other hand, will pitch the nose up and maintain the currently indicated speed, leaving you to add power as needed. Again, this mode should disengage automatically when you get to the selected altitude.

AIRCRAFT HUSBANDRY

You can tell how well pilots treat their machines by the maintenance costs. Even something as small as caging gyros before you turn them on can make a difference to the company's bottom line long-term.

Don't forget taxying procedures, such as not using the brakes too much, or using aircraft momentum when turning corners to save using the engine. Engine runups (like on power checks) should be done into wind for better engine cooling and least strain on the prop, and away from loose items on the ground, both to protect people behind and the prop itself, as the airflow around the tips will tend to pull bits of gravel etc towards it, and cause damage.

Controls

Control locks are devices attached to flying controls (external) or control columns (internal), to stop them moving on the ground and protect them from gust and high wind damage. Together with covers, they should be used when convenient (especially when winds are high, in which case consider picketing as well), and all doors, hatches and windows should be closed when the aircraft is left unattended.

Control stops are devices that restrict a control's range of operation.

Anti-collision Lights

These should be switched on immediately before starting engines, but it is suggested (like the military) that this be done immediately the aircraft is occupied, always having due regard for the capabilities of your battery (speaking of which, always leave the anti-col light switches on when leaving the aircraft, because that lets you know you've left the Master switch on).

Tyres

Aircraft tyres have a lot to cope with, including high speeds, heat, abrasion and high braking loads. Most are bias-ply, with multiple layers of nylon ply at alternating angles to the tread centreline (in radial tyres, the ply runs at 90°, which helps with cornering). When tyres touch the runway, and have to spin rapidly in a short time, they can

creep round the wheel rim. Aside from stressing the tyre, it can also force the valve assembly to one side, so it is usual to monitor *creep* by checking the alignment marks on the tyre that are placed on it when the tyre is fitted. If the movement reaches half the width of the paint marks, it's time to consult an engineer. A red spot is used to match up the tyre with the rim when balancing, and a grey/green one is an *awl hole* that allows trapped gas between plies to escape. A speed rating is present if a tyre is rated above 160 mph.

Cold tyres are rejected if they are over 10% below pressure. Between 5-10%, they can be reinflated and checked the next day, then rejected if they are still more than 5% below.

Tip: You might get a spot check of tyre pressures on a check ride. You may have checked them the night before, but it gets colder overnight!

The tyre inflation pressure in the flight manual is for when the aircraft is not supported by aircraft weight. About 4% should be added to compensate, and there is a tolerance of 5-10% either way.

Hot tyres are rejected if they are more than 10% below the loaded pressure of other tyres on the same leg. A tyre 5% below can be reinflated, but must be rejected if it reaches the same value. Under-inflated tyres wear most on their shoulders. You can go down to the depth of the pattern (on patterned tyres), or the marker tie bar or 2 mm above the bottom of the wear indicator on ribbed tyres.

A *tubeless tyre* has no air tube and is easier to balance. Other advantages over tubed tyres are a lower risk of bursting and better adjustment to wheels. They are vented to release air trapped in the casing during manufacture or by normal permeation through the inner liner. The vent positions are marked by green or grey dots on the lower side wall. Up to 5% pressure loss over 24 hours is OK, and pressures should be checked daily (ideally before every flight). Air can escape either through the valve or the carcass (not tubeless). Tyres should be inflated with dry nitrogen, because there is a reduced pressure change with altitude.

Oil Cans

These come sealed so you need a special implement to open them. Actually, you can use a screwdriver, but whatever you use, don't bang it down on the lid, but *gently* prise it open. This stops you getting slivers of metal in the oil which may disagree with your engine. Also, shake the can, especially if it has been sitting, so any anti-icing additive that has settled gets spread through the mixture.

FLOATPLANES

Although in flight the differences between a floatplane as opposed to a landplane are quite subtle (less stable directionally, not so much aileron required in a sideslip), it is on the surface of the Earth that the differences become most marked. So marked, in fact, that you also need training in seamanship as well as airmanship (you now have to watch for currents - a 10 kt current against a 15 kt wind will produce the same wave height as a 25 kt wind).

The obvious difference is the floats, which are attached to the fuselage with struts. Floats typically use a riveted aluminium construction, with internal compartments (rather like the Titanic!) which will have a fitting through which you can pump out any stray water. The step compartment will contain the most water simply because it has the most seams and rivets where it can get in (it is also the strongest part of the assembly).

It follows that you need special equipment, such as:

- a **powerful engine** to cope with the extra weight and drag of the floats. One that allows you to take off from grass with three-quarter power in a "normal" aeroplane should be OK. The extra weight also means that the useful load is decreased, as are the rate of climb and the cruising speed. Also get a **propeller** with a larger diameter and finer pitch

- **floats**, of proper size! If they are too long you will not be able to rotate properly. Short ones catch every bump from the waves - less than two wave lengths over the length of the float is considered as being too rough for takeoff

Each float has a retractable water rudder at the rear, with connections to the rudder pedals for slow taxying. There is a cable in the cockpit that raises and lowers the rudders as required - you use a hook on the side of the fuselage to keep it in place when they are raised. Water rudders are naturally not very effective at slow taxi speeds.

- **bilge pump**, for emptying floats, especially before the first flight of the day. Water in floats will affect the aircraft's centre of gravity and all-up weight, and handling characteristics. Learn the number of strokes needed to empty a compartment so you can gauge the amount of water you are shifting. Too much should be investigated

- **life jackets**

- **paddle**

- **anchor**

- **mooring lines**

- **fuel filter** and **water detection equipment**

- **bush pilot gear** as appropriate - sunnies (non-polarised), sensible shoes (smooth soles with no studs), waders (for when you have to beach the machine), etc

- **spare person** (optional) to undo mooring lines, etc., unless you do this from the cockpit

Definitions

- *Under Way.* Where the aircraft is not fastened (moored) to any fixed object, whether or not a qualified person is at the controls, and regardless of direction

- *Sailing.* Under way and being manoeuvred by wind or water currents only

- *Stationary.* The aircraft is being held in one position with engine thrust

- *Taxying.* Being manoeuvred under way in a forward direction with engine thrust

- *Lines.* Lengths of rope of whatever description used to moor the aircraft

- Bridle. A Y-shaped set of lines used to moor an aircraft to a buoy or when using an anchor. The two legs of the Y are secured to each float

Preflight

Your preflight should include security of the struts and floats, plus a check for obstructions, wind, etc. *before* you start taxying, because you will have no brakes! You need to make sure you won't drift into anything if the engine doesn't start, or you have to start it without any restraints, and that there is a clear path for the takeoff (small boats are very likely to get in the way!)

In a fast flowing river, get your helper to put you at a 30 or 45° angle to the current flow.

With no control inputs, the aircraft will always point into the wind, and the stronger the wind is, the more difficult it will be to control.

Look for bands of flat water near the shore whose thickness will tell you the wind strength (the line between them and the shore tells you the direction). Whitecaps mean wind speeds over 9-12 knots.

Engine Start

Any propeller swinging must be done from behind.

Taxi

Keep the aircraft as slow as possible when taxying downwind, as more speed means more spray. If you are taxying against the current, turn for takeoff after the intended takeoff point. If going with the current, begin your turn beforehand.

The wind will also increase any rolling tendency so be careful when crosswind as well.

You will use various combinations of the following during takeoff and landing.

IDLE (NORMAL) TAXI

In this mode you have forward momentum and the water rudders are your primary method of steering. Speed is up to around 8 kts.

The engine is running very near to idle speed and there is hardly any spray coming off the floats because you are not moving fast enough (the controls are also held fully back to keep the prop away from bow waves and spray). However, in strong winds, the water rudders are less effective and you need......

SAILING MODE

Here, you use the wind (against the normal rudder) to move the aircraft about, so the water rudders will be up, and their cables hooked to the side of the fuselage. You can also use some aileron drag to help with directional control, plus paddles, and get more sail area by lowering flaps or opening doors. In strong winds, the air rudder has more effect, and you may need more room to turn and possibly more prop wash to overcome wind effect.

Tip: If you need to keep the engine running for whatever reason (it may not be a good starter), you can reduce engine speed further by turning off one magneto or applying carb heat.

Note: Without the engine running, if you point into wind with the controls in the neutral position, you will move backwards with the wind.

STEP TAXI

As anyone who has tried water skiing will know, you are not supposed to assist the process by making any movements - the idea is to let the skis do the work and get onto a "step" once you hit a certain speed (you are actually hydroplaning on top of the water rather than being in it). So it is with floatplanes.

Note: Because you use full power to get on to the step, and are therefore travelling faster, you need extra caution when taxying. Naturally, the water rudders are retracted! Turns of more than 30° require considerable experience as the centrifugal force involved may tip the machine over.

Note: A phenomenon known as *porpoising*, where the nose starts pitching up and down, should be stopped before the oscillation becomes uncontrollable. Do this by closing the throttle and pulling the control column completely back as the nose rises.

You get on the step by holding the control column fully back and applying full power. The nose will rise as you accelerate. When it stops rising, ease the column forward until the nose is just above the horizon and the aircraft accelerates a little more, at which point you should reduce power or you will become airborne.

Use the rudder to turn, but use aileron as well to keep the outside wing up and counteract centrifugal force.

RUNUPS (NOSE HIGH)

These are usually done before the pre-takeoff checks, but can be performed during the takeoff run. They should not be done downwind because of engine cooling and spray problems. Check the takeoff run area while you are taxying as the nose-high attitude will make it difficult later.

Nose-high taxying is also used for helping with turns into the downwind position, but should not be done for too long as the engine may overheat.

Note: Only experienced pilots should use the nose-up mode when turning downwind in strong winds. Average pilots should sail backwards.

Takeoff

The best conditions for takeoff are with the current and into wind.

With the water rudders up, point into wind and apply full power with the stick or control column fully back. Once the nose has risen as far as it will go, ease the column forward to a roughly neutral position. As the centre of water pressure moves back along the floats, the aircraft will move up onto the step, and it may veer slightly to the left from the propeller torque. A slight check back on the control column should fix that.

At some stage, when flying speed is reached on the step, the aircraft will fly itself off the water. lower the nose slightly to keep yourself in ground effect as long as possible (assuming no obstacles!) This helps you land better if the engine fails. Having said that, if the water is glassy, you need to establish a positive rate of climb as soon as possible. Using an external visual reference such as a lump of rock or a tree can be helpful with this.

Note: The most efficient planing angle of the floats is when their tails almost, but not quite, touch the water, to obtain the least resistance. It is something that needs to be learnt early on.

Remember the takeoff attitude - you will need it for landing!

GLASSY WATER

Glassy water takeoffs require a longer distance because there is no wave action to help the floats break free from the water tension.

ROUGH WATER

Here, you are trying to get off the water as soon as possible, with as little speed as possible. Once on the step, keep the nose high so that the wave impact happens against the step compartment, but without the rear part of the floats in the water.

Apply takeoff power as the bows of the floats are rising on a wave, to stop them digging in and to keep spray away from the propeller.

Note: This procedure could turn into a series of bounces across the waves, and you may get thrown into the air at minimum flight speed. A little extra flap should stop you landing back on to the water.

CROSSWIND

You use the ailerons to keep the upwind side of the aircraft from being lifted out of the water before you reach flying speed. Some pilots may roll a float out of the water completely to keep the aircraft positively on the water and reduce the resistance from the water.

Note: Do not lift the upwind float during takeoff! You might skip sideways and ground loop!

DOWNWIND

One obvious hazard is that you need more distance for takeoff. A less obvious one is that, as soon as you raise the water rudders, the aircraft will try to weathercock into wind, so you will need a bootful of the normal rudder. It can be made more effective by keeping the flaps up until you build up some speed so that they do not blank it out.

Landing

Note: You can land in an area that is considerably smaller than what you will need to take off in!

The best conditions are into the current and the wind.

You use the same attitude to land as you had for takeoff, and you have to maintain it after you touch the water. Normally, with a landplane, you relax on the controls as soon as you land. Only after you come off the step do you do this with a floatplane.

ROUGH WATER

As with the rough water takeoff, the attitude should be set so that the step compartment of the floats (the strongest part) takes the brunt of the landing on top of a wave.

Be ready to apply power after severe bounces. If the aircraft starts porpoising, take off again.

GLASSY WATER

A smooth, mirror-like surface is useless for depth perception (clear water doesn't help, as you will be referring to the surface underneath), so you should try to use an external reference as well as an increased instrument scan (there is a *lot* going on!) For this, land close to the shore, parallel to it (there won't be any wind).

This is always a power-on landing, initiated about 100-150 feet above the surface.

The flaps should be set for the best lift/drag ratio and the usual landing attitude set and rigorously maintained. Use the power for a 50-100 feet per second rate of descent, anticipating a slowdown as you enter ground effect in the last 10-20 feet, just before touchdown.

Drive the machine on to the water - that is, keep the engine running until touchdown and ease the throttle back once contact is made, keeping the control column back. *Do not attempt to round out or feel for the surface.*

Keep the attitude until the aircraft settles into taxi mode.

Note: Glassy water landings use up a considerable amount of space!

EMERGENCY LANDINGS

Surface contact should be made as evenly as possible, with water rudders up and stick/column held fully back.

On glassy water, land as close to the shore as possible.

You and your passengers should be familiar with the problems of underwater egress (you will probably be upside-down and disoriented - many people drown in otherwise survivable accidents).

CROSSWIND

Crab into wind to get rid of drift. Close to the water, straighten with rudder, lower the upwind wing and take up the landing attitude. Land on the upwind float first, but the other one should touch at pretty much the same time anyway. Keep the ailerons into wind, retract the flaps and wait for the aircraft to slow and settle into taxi mode.

DOWNWIND

These should be avoided, as the high groundspeeds involved tend to make the machine pitch forward on touchdown. There will also be a longer ground run, but you knew that already.

After Landing/Docking

Retract the flaps straight after touchdown and lower the water rudders after entering taxi mode.

The engine must be shutdown before you can stop the machine, so you will be docking without power and brakes. As with the preflight, make sure there is nothing that can damage your aircraft while you are drifting, *before* you turn the engine off. Be prepared for weathercocking! Open the doors and brief the passengers early.

Once the engine is off, get out onto the float and catch the aircraft against the dock yourself, unless you are sure that any "helpers" actually know what they are doing.

Tie the machine down as appropriate.

INSTRUMENTS

Flight instruments must be able to be read easily, in terms of position, lighting and clarity. They can have up to four sub-systems, not all of which will be in the same case:

- Detection (e.g. temperature probe)
- Measurement (aneroid capsule)
- Coupling (suitable linkage between measurement and indication)
- Indication (Pointer, or digital display)

Displays can be *circular* (linear or non-linear), *straight* (like a tape) or *digital*.

Instruments can also be classified into four groups, after the variations in properties of certain materials against variations in temperature:

- Expansion
- Vapour-Pressure
- Electrical, based on:
  - Resistance, or
  - Increase in electromotive force

Most will be electrical.

Lighting

White lighting is usually combined with grey cockpit interiors because:

- you have unrestricted use of colour
- warning indicators become more prominent
- black instrument cases against a grey background emphasizes their size and shape

Individual instruments may be lit by:

- Integral lighting, which is built into the instrument
- ring, eyebrow, or post lighting, all of which are fitted to the outside of the instrument case
- floodlighting

PRESSURE

In many systems, the pressure of a liquid or gas must be measured and indicated, either directly, where the source of pressure is connected to the instrument (mostly Bourdon tubes), or remotely, where it can be some distance away, with electrical signals being sent instead. Such systems would have a transmitter at the pressure source and an indicator on a panel. This means you won't have yucky fluids in the cockpit, and you don't have to carry a lot of plumbing. Indicators can be based on synchronous receivers, DC or AC ratiometers or servos.

Pressure is the *force per unit area*, which may be measured by comparing it against a liquid of known density, or having it act in a known way and measuring the force produced. In aviation, atmospheric pressure is usually expressed by the *Hectopascal* (hPa), which is made up from 100 Pascals. The older unit is the millibar (mb) which is one-thousandth of a bar, or 1,000,000 dynes per square centimeter (100,000 Pascals). Thus one millibar equals 100 Pascals or one Hectopascal.

Pressure Sensing

Aneroid gauges use a metallic pressure sensing element that flexes under pressure. *Aneroid* means *without fluid*, or *not wet* (depends on which book you read), to distinguish between aneroid and hydrostatic gauges, which do use fluid, although aneroid gauges can be used to measure liquid pressure.

The pressure sensing element may be a Bourdon tube, a diaphragm, a capsule, or bellows, all of which will change their shape in response to the pressure. The deflection is transmitted by a suitable linkage that will rotate a pointer around a graduated dial, or activate a secondary transducer that might control a digital display, the most common of which measure changes in capacitance that follow the mechanical deflection.

DIAPHRAGMS

Diaphragms are simply circular metal discs that are corrugated to give them strength, to provide larger deflections. They are used to detect low pressures. One side of the disc is exposed to the pressure to be measured, and the other is linked to the indicating mechanism.

CAPSULES

A capsule consists of two diaphragms placed face to face and joined at their edges to form a chamber that may be completely sealed or left open to a source of pressure. They are also used for low(ish) pressures, but are more sensitive than diaphragms.

BELLOWS

In gauges that sense small pressures or differences, or require an absolute pressure to be measured, the gear train and needle may be driven by an enclosed and sealed bellows chamber, called an *aneroid*, as used in aneroid barometers, altimeters, altitude recording barographs, and the altitude telemetry instruments used in weather balloon radiosondes. The sealed chamber is used as a reference pressure and the needles are driven by the external pressure. Bellows are an extension of the diaphragm, but operate like a helical compression spring - indeed, there may even be a spring to increase the *spring rate* and to help the bellows return to its normal length once the source of pressure is removed.

Airspeed indicators and rate of climb indicators (*variometers*) have connections to the internal part of the aneroid chamber and to an external enclosing chamber.

THE BOURDON TUBE

The most common pressure sensor was invented by French watchmaker Eugene Bourdon in 1849, in which a C-shaped elliptical hollow spring tube is sealed at one end, with the other end connected to a source of pressure. The pressure differential from the inside to the outside causes

the tube to change from an elliptical to a more circular shape, and to straighten out, rather like an uncoiling hose. Which way it moves is determined by the curvature of the tubing, as the inside radius is slightly shorter than that on the outside, and the ratio between the major and minor axes depends on what sensitivity you need - the larger the ratio, the greater it is.

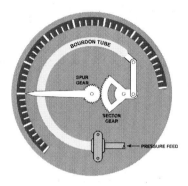

The end result is that a specific pressure can cause movement for a specific distance. When the pressure is removed, the tube returns to its original shape. To do this, the material used requires a form of heat treating (spring tempering) to make it closely retain its original shape while allowing some elasticity under a load. Beryllium copper, phosphor bronze, and various alloys of steel and stainless steel are good for this purpose, but steel has a limited service life due to corrosion, stainless steel alloys add cost if specific corrosion resistance is not required, and beryllium copper is usually reserved for high pressure applications. Most general use gauges use phosphor bronze. The pressure range of a tube is determined by the *tubing wall thickness* and the *radius of the curvature*.

In summary, a Bourdon-based gauge uses a coiled tube which causes the rotation of an indicator arm connected to it as it expands due to pressure increase.

MANOMETER

The term *manometer* is often used to refer specifically to liquid column hydrostatic instruments (see also *Meteorology*). Hydrostatic gauges (like the mercury column manometer) consist of a vertical column of liquid in a tube whose ends are exposed to different pressures, with the difference in fluid height being proportional to the pressure difference.

However, the simplest design is a closed-end U-shape, one side of which is connected to the region of interest. A force equal to the applied pressure multiplied by the area

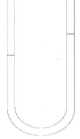

of the bore will force the liquid downwards until, eventually, the two levels will stand the same distance above and below the original level. If you take into account the area of the tube bore and the density of the liquid, you can calculate pressure from the difference in the levels. Any fluid can be used, but mercury is preferred for its high density and low vapour pressure, so the tube can be shorter.

Manometers are used for calibration purposes.

TEMPERATURE

Knowledge of the air temperature is needed for performance calculations, anti-ice control and calculation of true airspeed (TAS), amongst other things.

The quantity of heat contained in a substance is a measure of the kinetic energy of the molecules it contains, depending on the temperature, mass and nature of the material concerned. For example, a bucketful of warm water will melt more ice than a cupful of boiling water because it contains more heat. Thus, two bodies containing the same amounts of thermal energy may not have the same temperature, because temperature is a measure of the *quality* of heat (or the rate at which molecules are moving), which means it cannot strictly be measured, but only compared against some form of scale.

There are two ways of measuring temperature (or rather the average kinetic energy of molecules), called *Fahrenheit* or *Celsius*, and it's a real pain to convert between the two. The quick and easy way is to use the scale on the back of a flight computer:

but here are the calculations for people who want to show off:

F – C $Tc = (5/9)*(Tf-32)$

C – F $Tf = ((9/5)*Tc)+32$

16°C is equal to 61°F, 20°C is 68°F and 30°C is 86°F, for gross error checks and quick conversions - however, given

the standard of performance charts in the average flight manual, doubling the Celsius amount and adding 30 to get Fahrenheit, or subtracting 30 from Fahrenheit and dividing the remainder in half to get Celsius is probably good enough!

The Fahrenheit scale assumes that water freezes at 32°, and boils at 212°. Celsius starts at 0° and finishes at 100°, which is more logical, but the scale is coarser. The *freezing level* (in flight) is where the temperature is 0°C.

Static Air Temperature (SAT)

This is the ambient temperature, often called the *Corrected* or *True Outside Air Temperature* (COAT), once all the errors are sorted out. It is the temperature that would be recorded if you were able to stop the aircraft dead whilst still flying (i.e. with nothing frictionally induced).

In simple terms, SAT = OAT.

Total Air Temperature (TAT)

At higher speeds, compression (of the air) against the aircraft surfaces means that whatever temperature is indicated will be considerably warmer than the OAT (this affects helicopters because of the speed of the rotor blades). At speeds above 0.2 Mach, the boundary layer can be slowed down or stopped (relatively speaking) and be affected by adiabatic compression that will raise the temperature. The difference is called *RAM rise*, and the resulting indicated temperature is RAT, or *RAM Air Temperature*, which is therefore equal to SAT + RAM Rise.

TAT is technically the maximum rise possible, and can be thought of as the *indicated* air temperature, or what the aircraft feels, which is the same as the OAT plus the effects of adiabatic heating. It represents the temperature of air which has been brought virtually to rest (relative to the aircraft), during which process kinetic energy is converted to internal energy, after the full effect of heating from compressibility, or adiabatic heating.

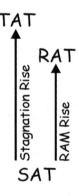

TAT is always warmer than SAT, and the difference varies with Calibrated Air Speed.

RECOVERY FACTOR

To compute TAS, the air data computer converts total air temperature to static air temperature, as a function of Mach number, because SAT cannot be measured directly. If you don't have an air data computer or a Machmeter, you can obtain TAS as a function of calibrated airspeed and local air density (or static air temperature and pressure altitude which determine density) on the E6B.

The difference between TAT and SAT is also known as the *stagnation rise*, and the proportion of stagnation temperature that can actually be sensed by the aircraft instruments is the *recovery factor* or *K value*, which is governed by the thermometer. With a Rosemount probe, the K factor is assumed to be 1.0, hence its other name of *Total Air Temperature Probe*. However, with bimetallic or liquid/vapour filled thermometers, and more basic electrical ones than the Rosemount, mentioned overleaf, K is normally around 0.75-0.85, being the temperature of air which has been brought only *partially* to rest.

With a recovery factor of 1, a thermometer is therefore measuring TAT, which is SAT + 100% of stagnation rise. If a thermometer has a recovery factor of 0.8, it is measuring SAT + 80% of the stagnation rise. If the recovery factor is zero, it is measuring SAT only.

Thermometers

BIMETALLIC STRIP THERMOMETER

Below about 150 kts, a thermometer like the one shown below is good enough for getting the OAT. The probe sticks out directly into the airstream, and the dial is inside the cockpit. The works consist of a helical bimetallic strip in a tube, which twists as the temperature changes, and moves the pointer.

The probe cannot be shrouded from the Sun, and it is necessarily mounted next to the fuselage skin, so its readings can be affected by kinetic heating, even at the low speeds associated with helicopters - at 150 kts, the rise can be in the order of 3°.

Being crude instruments, they are also subject to other errors, so a professional rule of thumb is to assume an error of about 2-3°.

WHEATSTONE BRIDGE

The Wheatstone Bridge was invented by Samuel Hunter Christie in 1833 and improved and popularised by Sir Charles Wheatstone in 1843. It measures an unknown

electrical resistance by balancing two legs of a bridge circuit, one of which includes the unknown component:

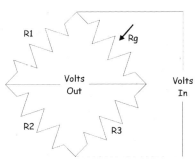

4 resistors arranged in a diamond have a DC voltage applied across the top and bottom. When the output voltage across the middle is zero, the bridge is balanced. As the bridge becomes unbalanced, the varying voltage across the middle can be measured with a voltmeter. In this case, it powers a wiper arm that is positioned by a servo loop, and how far the arm moves is a measure of the temperature change - this movement positions the needle on the gauge. The advantage is that changes in the sensor voltage do not affect accuracy.

THE ROSEMOUNT PROBE

Otherwise known as the *Total Air Temperature Probe*, this has a small (i.e. quick reacting) resistance coil inside concentric cylinders, mounted on a streamlined strut around 50 mm or so from the fuselage skin, which therefore has little influence on it (skin temperature can be increased by kinetic energy). The probe is open at the front with a smaller hole at the back to allow air to continuously flow in. There is also a venturi at the front to encourage water and dust particles to separate as the air speeds up, so the aircraft must be moving for it to work. A heating element prevents icing, and is self-compensating, in that, as temperature rises, so does resistance in the element, which reduces the heater current. Although the heater affects the temperature sensed, the error is small, around 1°C at Mach 0.1 and 0.15°C at Mach 1.0, so helicopters aren't affected.

Aside from skin temperature, direct sunlight will give an artificially high reading and, when flying from cloud to clear air, readings will be low for however long it takes for moisture to evaporate from the bulb or element in the probe. Rosemount probes are used on larger helicopters, such as Pumas.

ERRORS

Instrument error comes from the usual imperfections in manufacturing and can be sorted out by fine calibration.

Environmental error is caused by solar heating or icing. The Rosemount probe has a heater for the latter problem, and probes are usually mounted on the underside to keep them in shadow, but the residual effects of environmental error can only be minimised, and not corrected for. Some heating is caused by compression as air is brought to rest, which is the difference between SAT and TAT, so it is only a problem when you need to find SAT. There is also frictional heating in the boundary layer, but both heating errors can be fully compensated for, either automatically or by calculation.

Flat plate sensors, with their sensing element flush with the aircraft skin, are susceptible to environmental errors because of their relative lack of shielding. They are affected by frictional heating in the boundary layer (not compressibility), and instrument error.

TEMPERATURE COMPENSATION

Various methods can be used to make an instrument over- or under-read according to which way the temperature is going. For example, a thermal junction can get hot by itself, which will vary the emf it produces and give you false readings.

In mechanical terms, a bimetal strip made of invar and brass or steel can be attached to a capsule to make it expand or contract slightly, or you could arrange to vary the resistance of an electrical current.

FLIGHT INSTRUMENTS

Flight instruments are laid out in a *T arrangement*.

The artificial horizon is in the centre, because it is a primary instrument (it tells you which way is up), the heading indicator is below, No 1 altimeter at the top right, with the vertical speed indicator below, and the airspeed indicator is at the top left with the turn coordinator underneath.

The idea is to have the most important instruments as close together as possible to reduce the scanning distance.

A *primary instrument* is one which gives instant and constant readouts (also called *direct*). A *secondary instrument* is one that you have to deduce things from, such as the altimeter increasing, telling you that the pitch must have changed (you might also say that the altimeter gives you an indirect indication of pitch attitude). The ASI and VSI also give indirect indications of pitch, and the HI and TC indicate bank. Note also that a primary instrument will tell you at what rate things are changing, but a secondary one will only indicate that change is taking place.

They are further grouped under the headings of *pitch*, *bank* and *power*.

Pitch

- *Artificial Horizon* (Attitude Indicator). The most important pitch instrument, because it gives direct, instantaneous readings.

- *Altimeter*. Although it indicates pitch indirectly, it is a primary pitch instrument. Its readings will lag more at higher altitudes.

- *Airspeed Indicator*. A secondary pitch instrument, although its value becomes less at higher airspeeds, as changes are more pronounced and the range indicated by the needle is less and more difficult to read. Any given power setting has only one pitch attitude where altitude and airspeed are constant.

- *Vertical Speed Indicator* (VSI). A secondary pitch instrument, which should be used with the altimeter. It will give a brief reverse indication if abrupt control movements are used.

Bank

- *Artificial Horizon* (Attitude Indicator). Also the most important bank instrument, for similar reasons under *Pitch*, above.

- *Heading Indicator*. An indirect instrument, because if you change heading, bank must be involved somewhere.

- *Turn Coordinator*. As it shows a rate of turn (3° per second for rate 1), it is an indirect indication of bank.

Power

Power instruments are not strictly in the traditional T, but you have to check them anyway. The Airspeed Indicator is a secondary power instrument, as it changes in relation to power application.

A turbine engine has to operate within certain limits - it must not be run too fast, or too hot, or have too much strain imposed on it. The relevant gauges (in a helicopter, anyway) are the N_1, or compressor RPM, the TOT, or Turbine Outlet Temperature, sometimes known as T4, and the torquemeter, respectively. *Stop raising the collective when you reach the first of these limits.* **Maximum Continuous Power** is the setting that may be used indefinitely, but any between that and maximum power (usually shown as a yellow arc on the instrument) will only be available for a set time limit. Such ratings are there to conserve engine life as much as possible, to maximise servicing intervals.

An instrument may contain *overspeed detectors* in the form of pointers or warning lights. These may only be reset by engineering, for obvious reasons.

A red triangle, or dot, or diamond on an engine instrument face or glass indicates the maximum limits for high transients, as found when starting

THE TACHOMETER

Engine RPM are a direct indication of power, so the tachometer is a primary engine instrument. Turbines rotate so fast that the numbers are too large to make sense of, so percentages are used instead (that is, 100% means full power). In a helicopter, the engine and rotor RPM (R) needles usually sit on top of each other in the same *dual tachometer*, although they can be separate, as in the R22. In powered flight, the needles are joined; in autorotation, they are split:

On a turbine helicopter, the big needle labelled T above left would represent the turbine RPM (N_2), and there will be a smaller gauge showing "gas producer", or N_1, RPM. The other big needle (R) is for Rotor RPM.

The mechanical tachometer is found only on light piston-engined aircraft. There is a direct drive (up to 2 m long) from the engine to the indicator, inside which a magnet is turned inside an aluminium *drag cup* to set up eddy currents that make the cup turn at the same speed as the magnet. The cup is supported on a shaft to which is attached a pointer and a controlling spring which is there to oppose the turning force so that, for any one speed, the eddy current drag and spring tension are in equilibrium, and the pointer is steady.

On more modern aircraft, tachogenerators driven by the engine can put out DC, or single- or three-phase AC, which can drive a voltmeter calibrated in RPM. The lack of moving parts allows engines to be further away from the cockpit, and you don't need power supplies. With the DC version, output voltage varies with RPM, and drives a moving coil indicator which needs a commutator and carbon brushes, so there is wear and sparking which can cause radio interference (or fires). Also, voltage loss in transmission leads to indication errors. A *single-phase brushless AC generator*, on the other hand, has its output rectified to DC, so the mechanical problems are not there, but indication errors are. One disadvantage of a single phase AC generator tachometer is the possibility of the values transmitted being affected by line resistance. On the other hand, spurious signals from a DC generator commutator are avoided and the information is independent.

A *Three-Phase AC Tachogenerator* has its *AC* frequency varying with RPM, to drive a *squirrel cage motor* at the instrument. Frequency is proportional to transmitter drive speed and the speed indicating element is an asynchronous motor driving a magnetic tachometer. These normally rotate slightly slower than the generator, with the slip depending on the torque required. Motors that rotate at the same frequency as the AC generator are *synchronous* squirrel cage motors. Because frequency is sensed rather than voltage, voltage losses are not a problem, but extra wiring is needed to carry three phases.

INDUCTION TACHOMETER

This does not need a direct engine drive. RPM is sensed by a magnetic probe next to a toothed wheel, called a *phonic wheel.* The probe is used to count the passage of teeth on the wheel by changes induced in the field. Thus, the operating principle of the induction type of tachometer is to *measure the rotation speed of an asynchronous motor energised by an alternator.* The signal from a transmitter with a magnetic sensor connected to an RPM indicator is an AC voltage whose frequency varies with RPM signals that are converted to square pulses which are counted. On older aircraft, the half-wave AC signal (see *Electricity*) is passed through a transformer to create high voltage and low current, then averaged to become a DC output (high voltage, low current signals lose less strength over long cable runs). The half-wave AC signal can be squared off into digital signals, which do not rely on voltage levels to signify information, but the *presence* of a signal, as with any computer. However, this needs an external power supply. Power failure is indicated by a power-off flag or the indicator needle moving off the scale.

MANIFOLD PRESSURE GAUGE

The *Manifold Pressure* gauge shows pressure inside the inlet manifold, in inches. The theory is that the higher the pressure is, the more the amount of fuel/air mixture that is potentially available. When the engine is running, MAP is below atmospheric pressure because of the pressure drop across the butterfly valve (the engine is sucking air in). When the engine is stopped, the MAP will be at atmospheric pressure (you keep MAP constant as you increase altitude by opening the throttle). Power increases because exhaust back pressure falls, which improves scavenging. The equivalent in a turbine helicopter is the *torquemeter*. A break in the line between the MAP gauge and the induction system is indicated by the gauge registering prevailing atmospheric pressure. The gauge uses an aneroid pressure diaphragm.

TORQUE

This is the measure of the power output of a turbine engine. In the accessory gearbox on the Bell 206, for example, two gears slide against each other as power varies. One is fixed, and the other is free to open or close a small hole through which oil moves - the more the power demand, the more the oil flows and the more the torquemeter reads. The principle is that, "when the flow through a variable orifice remains constant, differential pressure across it is inversely proportional to its area".

TEMPERATURE

Operating at a higher than intended temperature will cause loss of power, excessive oil consumption and damage to the engine.

In a piston-engined helicopter, the *Cylinder Head Temperature* (CHT) gauge (which uses a thermocouple) shows the temperature of a selected cylinder, which is not necessarily the hottest one (usually a rearmost in a horizontally opposed engine). Knowledge of the *Exhaust Gas Temperature* (EGT) is needed for leaning the mixture efficiently. The probe is in the exhaust manifold.

On a turbine-engined helicopter, depending on where it is measured, the temperature gauge may be called any of the following names:

- TGT - *Turbine Gas Temperature*
- EGT - *Exhaust Gas Temperature*
- TOT - *Turbine Outlet Temperature*

It's also called the ITT in the Bell 212.

High temperatures in the 700-1000°C range are measured with *thermocouples*, which are based on the idea that dissimilar metals welded together can create an electrical potential at their junction, proportional to the temperature (the very small voltages are detected by a *galvanometer*). In other words, the voltage output is determined by the difference in heat between the two ends, provided the cold end is maintained at a constant temperature (intermediate metals in the circuit will not modify the emf either if their contact points are kept at equal temperatures).

Thermocouples are wired in parallel so the failure of one does not stop the whole system. External power is not needed, so when you shut down, you can check that the TOT is not moving rapidly out of limits.

FUEL GAUGES

Fuel quantity is measured by the level in the tank, but may be shown in volume or weight. It can be measured by *float type* (resistance) or *capacitive* contents gauges.

Note: Although many fuel gauges are accurate, they should never be relied upon as the final guide to what you have in the tanks, especially if they are calibrated with lbs or kg - fuel weight (per gallon) varies with specific gravity and temperature, so instrument readings will vary as well.

Reading the book *Free Fall*, about the Gimli Glider is very instructive about this - a 767 had to make a dead stick landing at Gimli (in Manitoba, Canada) after running out of fuel in the cruise, due to a combination of circumstances, including misleading fuel gauges and confusing lbs for kg (actually, the whole episode is very instructive about CRM).

FLOAT TYPE (RESISTANCE)

This consists of a resistive circuit using floats connected to a Wheatstone Bridge circuit. The float may be made of specially treated cork, or a sealed lightweight metal cylinder. It is attached to an arm that is pivoted to allow angular movement that is transmitted to an electrical element consisting of a wiper arm and a potentiometer (variable resistance), so, as the fuel level changes, the float arm's movement alters the resistance. Ohm's Law determines the current flow, which is fed to an indicator.

Float type indicators provide information on *volume*, whose indication varies with the temperature of the fuel.

One advantage of float-type fuel gauging systems is their easy construction. Neither are they affected by voltage variations (if a galvanometer is used), but they are influenced by *aircraft attitude, acceleration,* and *temperature variations.*

CAPACITANCE TYPE

The capacity of a capacitor depends on the nature of the dielectric in which it is immersed (see *Electricity*). Fuel has twice the capacitance of air so a full tank has twice the capacitive reactance as an empty one. A simple capacitance system will consist of a variable capacitor in the fuel tank, an amplifier, and an indicator. The complete circuit forms an electrical bridge that is constantly being rebalanced around the differences between the tank and reference capacitors. The signal is amplified and used to drive a motor inside the indicator.

A *capacitance probe* that runs the full height of the tank consists of two tubes, one inside the other, with fuel between them. The two tubes are fed with AC so the "capacitor" formed by the tubes (fuel is the dielectric) charges and discharges alternately. The amount of discharge varies according to whether the dielectric is fuel or air, so the electrical signal produced is proportional to the tank's contents.

On their own, the detectors can only measure the height of fuel (volume), so a datum or *reference capacitor* compensates for density to ensure that weight is indicated correctly (if a question does not specify otherwise, assume you have a compensated system, as most aircraft use

them). Compensation works on the basis that variations in fuel capacitance follow permittivity, which describes how an electric field affects and is affected by a dielectric. Thus, permittivity relates to a material's ability to transmit (or "permit") an electric field. For example, in a capacitor, an increased permittivity allows the same charge to be stored with a smaller electric field (and a smaller voltage), leading to increased capacitance.

To ensure that only permittivity is measured, the compensator unit is placed in the bottom of the tank so that it is always covered with fuel, which means that capacitance is not measured by fuel quantity. When temperature increases, permittivity will increase and so will capacitance, and the bridge circuit becomes unbalanced. The voltage so produced drives a motor that drives a potentiometer that decreases the resistance. As this is biased towards a full tank, an increase in fuel quantity is indicated. Indication errors will still be there because density also varies with temperature, but these are minor in comparison, so errors are minimised.

Indication errors will still be there because density will also vary with temperature, but these are minor in comparison with permittivity, so errors are minimised.

There are many sensors connected in parallel, because fuel has a habit of sloshing around - this ensures that a more accurate average reading is taken. There is always a zero signal which is suppressed by the signal from the probes. If it fails, your gauge will suddenly read empty, or whatever the manufacturer chooses. A test routine simulates the empty signal. If a fuel tank with a capacitive contents system has water in it, but no fuel, the gauge will show an inaccurate value. If a temperature rise increases the fuel volume, the fuel weight remains the same.

OTHER INDICATIONS

Fuel low warnings usually give warning from the *supply tanks*, which may be fed from others, as with the Bell 206L, or the 407. *Fuel flow* may be displayed on a cockpit gauge and passed to the autopilot and navigation systems.

PITOT-STATIC SYSTEM

This consists of a series of pipes through which air flows to feed three common instruments on your panel; the altimeter, airspeed indicator and vertical speed indicator. The total and static pressures are sensed, measured and compared to allow speed, altitude and its rate of change to be indicated.

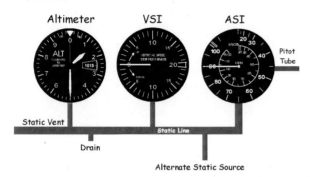

An aircraft is acted on from all directions by *static pressure*, which is fed into the system through static lines that are connected to static ports or static vents on *both sides* of the machine, to ensure that they balance out when it yaws, or does strange manoeuvres. They may or may not be heated (generally not on smaller machines). The static pressure is so called because it remains pretty much the same. It's actually the normal barometric pressure that decreases with height, so any changes in it are slow in comparison. Information from the static ports may also be fed to non-flight systems, such as an autopilot or a flight director.

Aircraft intended for IFR work will have an *alternate static source*, which takes its feed from inside the aircraft in case the main one starts leaking or gets blocked, either through ice, a bird strike, or whatever. When used, some error will be introduced into the instrument readings because the cabin air pressure is lower than that on the outside due to airflow over the cabin, so airspeeds and altitudes will read *higher* than normal. The VSI will show a momentary climb as the alternate static source is selected, then it will stabilise and produce normal readings. If the alternate source gets blocked, or you don't have one, smashing your

way into the VSI (preferably not the ASI or altimeter) will have the same effect.

The *pitot tube* (pronounced pee-toe) is used to detect *total pressure* (as mentioned by Bernoulli), and it is connected to the

airspeed indicator. Total pressure (sometimes called *stagnation pressure*) is the pressure obtained when a moving gas is brought to a stop through an adiabatic process - in this case, it includes the static pressure that affects the aircraft from all sides, and an extra element that comes from forward movement, since the pitot tube is pointed towards the direction of flight. If the fluid (air) is an ideal one (meaning not viscous), total pressure is equal to the sum of potential energy, kinetic energy and pressure energy, but the first is ignored in a pitot tube, and the kinetic energy is converted to pressure energy anyway.

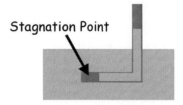

Stagnation Point

This creates an equal volume above the level of the flow, which is *dynamic pressure*, and the difference between it and static pressure is a measure of airspeed.

The formula for *dynamic pressure* is:

$$\text{Dynamic Pressure} = \tfrac{1}{2}\rho V^2$$

Where ρ (the Greek letter "rho") is air density and V the true velocity. As you can see, its strength depends of the speed of the relative airflow, and its density. The $\frac{1}{2}$ in the formula assumes the fluid is an ideal one, so the shape of the body is ignored.

The pitot tube may be heated to stop it icing up, so watch your hands (tell the passengers). If it's not at the front, it will be in another relatively undisturbed place, parallel to the relative airflow for best effect. Sometimes, a static source will be in a pitot head, as a small hole or series of holes around the side of the base.

Errors

Errors in measurement will affect displayed speed, height and vertical speed. Accuracy depends on the shape of the probe and where it is placed. The total *pressure error* comes in two categories, *position* or *configuration error* (inherent from the design), and *manoeuvre error*, from the way you handle the machine, and which mostly affects the VSI. Position error is defined as the *amount by which the local static pressure differs from that in the free stream airflow.* The ASI and altimeter can develop positive or negative position errors.

Configuration errors will have been established during flight testing, and can be displayed on calibration cards or programmed out by electronics, if you have them. Standby instruments, however, will not have the luxury, and will have uncorrected errors given on a calibration card.

The greatest pitot-static system errors are found when manoeuvring.

Air Data Computer

The traditional pitot-static system uses a lot of pipes to get its work done. The ADC was developed in an attempt to reduce the plumbing:

It is a black box in a centralised location that receives inputs from the usual sources and translates them into electrical equivalents for transmission to the relevant indicators, which have no pressure sensing elements, so they can be simpler (and cheaper) to make.

Pressure sensing is done with *transducers*, which use the E and I bar arrangement described in *The Altimeter*, below, as a pick off for the signals.

The data can be fed to the autopilot and Flight Director, Flight Management System, GPWS, area navigation aids, instrument comparison systems, etc. On the very latest systems, the feeds to the pilots' instruments also go to the EFIS signal generators to be converted for electronic display. There are two ADCs in most modern air transport aircraft to provide redundancy.

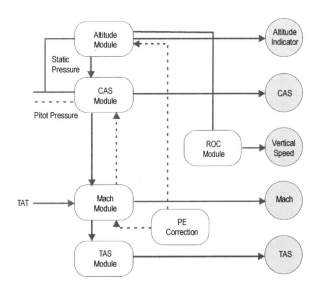

THE ALTIMETER

This is actually a barometer with the scale marked in feet rather than millibars (technically a *manometer*). As you go up, pressure is less, so the altimeter translates air pressure into an *estimate* of altitude, although it will be better sealed than a barometer, so that air pressure in the cockpit doesn't affect it - the only pressure that should be there is static pressure from the pitot-static system. The readings could be inaccurate due to temperature and pressure variations from standard.

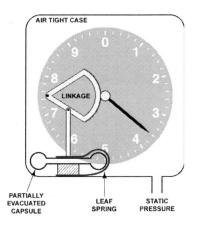

Inside a *sensitive* altimeter are *two* aneroid capsules (vacuums), which are corrugated for strength and kept open with a large leaf spring (a *simple* altimeter is a little more basic, with only one capsule - they are commonly used as cabin altimeters on pressurised aeroplanes since, at high altitudes, the capsule's movements are difficult to detect). The capsules' movements as you go up and down are magnified through the spring by a "suitable linkage" that connects directly to the pointer, using jewelled bearings. If the capsules expand, as they would when you go up, the pointer increases the reading. There is also a temperature compensation system to correct any spring and linkage tensions. Outside, there is a small knob, linked to a subscale which is visible through a small window. Rotating the knob causes the subscale to move and adjust the instrument to an *altimeter setting* (see *Meteorology*).

True altitude is shown from pressure altitude, so only in standard ISA conditions will the true altitude be indicated. For example, when it is extremely cold (below about -16°C), it will be a lot lower than shown, so corrections must be applied (altitudes given with radar vectors from ATC are corrected already). If this is something you need to take note of, you could perhaps mark the corrections directly on to the approach chart, next to the heights they refer to (you must recalculate *every* significant height). Again, see *Meteorology.*

The dials work like a clock. The long, thin pointer indicates hundreds of feet and the short, wide one, thousands. A very thin one, maybe with an inverted triangle at the end, as above, shows feet in ten thousands.

Caution: The three-needle display can be easily misread.

Servo Assistance

The *servo-assisted altimeter* typically uses a digital readout. In this instrument, the aneroid capsules are connected to one end of a pivoting magnet (an I-bar) which influences an E-bar that has windings on each of its arms:

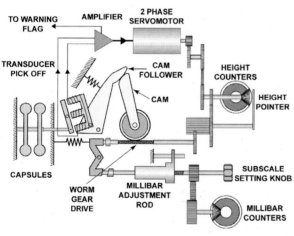

An AC current is fed to the primary winding on the centre arm, and as long as the gaps between the E and the I bars are equidistant, no voltage is induced in the coils on the other arms. The E-bars are wired in opposite directions and are connected in series to an amplifier unit - one example of the use of transformers.

Once the capsules increase or decrease in size, however, the gaps vary in size to create different magnetic fluxes and an output voltage that will be in or out of phase with the voltage in the primary coil, according to the direction of the displacement. Its magnitude will vary with the amount of the deflection.

The signal goes to the amplifier, then to the servomotor control winding so that the pointer and height counters are driven in the relevant directions. At the same time, the servomotor gear train rotates a worm gear that rotates the cam and cam follower to try and balance the magnetic fluxes at the I-bars, reaching the null point when the aircraft is levelled off and no more voltages are produced.

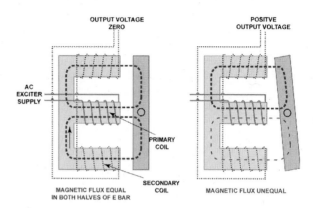

Turning the altimeter setting knob on the front drives the worm gear directly. All this complexity allows increased sensitivity at higher altitudes, as the aneroid capsules only have to drive the I-bar and not the whole instrument. The rest is done by the servo motor, which removes lag and pressure errors, and can drive more robust displays.

Encoding Altimeter

An *encoding altimeter* is used with a transponder in Mode C so that your altitude can be shown on a radar display.

The encoding assembly is mechanically activated by the aneroid capsule. Older versions consist of a light source, various lenses and an encoder disc with a special pattern on it (in eleven concentric circles) that works like a bar code when the light is reflected from it to produce binary inputs that correspond to 100-ft increments in altitude. One turn of the disc covers the complete range of the altimeter. Naturally, there are now digital versions that can also be fitted externally.

Note: The adjustment knob on the altimeter does not affect what ATC see on their radar screens! All encoding systems transmit your altitude corrected to 29.92 inches, or 1013.25 hPa. The ground equipment makes any regional corrections directly. You won't get into trouble for small deviations, say, of 200 feet or so, but you may be treated as an amateur and directed around their airspace, rather than being allowed a more direct routing.

Datums

Height is the vertical distance from a particular datum, usually in the case of aviation from the surface of an airfield. *Altitude* is height above sea level. *Elevation* is the vertical distance of a point on the Earth's surface from mean sea level.

Indicated altitude is what is shown on the dial at the current altimeter setting. *Calibrated altitude* is the indicated altitude corrected for instrument and position error. *True Altitude* is the actual one above mean sea level, taking the above errors into account, plus air temperature and density (absolute altitude is the actual height above the surface, and is produced by a radio altimeter).

You can calculate true altitude with a formula. First, subtract the ground elevation from the indicated altitude, and divide by 1,000 feet to get a single decimal number. Next, multiply that figure by the difference between the ISA temperature and the indicated one. Multiply that figure by 4 ft to get the amount to be subtracted from the indicated altitude. Thus:

$$\frac{\text{Ind Alt-Elevation x OAT-ISA x 4 ft}}{1,000}$$

On the flight computer, put the PA against the OAT in the window and read the true altitude on the outer scale against the indicated one on the inner scale.

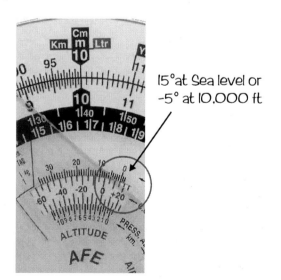

15° at Sea level or
-5° at 10,000 ft

Pressure altitude is the height of a particular pressure setting, usually 29.92" or 1013.2 mb, but could be any other, such as 700 mb, as on high level weather charts. QNE (1013.2) makes your altimeter read Flight Levels. *Density altitude* is the pressure altitude corrected for non-standard

temperature. The *altimeter setting* (QNH) is the pressure at a point (or *station*, to be technical), corrected for temperature and reduced to mean sea level under standard conditions, so if you set it on your scale, you will see altitude (your height above mean sea level), or the airfield elevation if you are on the ground.

Errors

Instrument and position errors are calculated by the various manufacturers, and will be found in the flight manual. Position error arises because there is no perfect place to put the static ports (or the pitot tube, for that matter, for the ASI). It is generally greater at low IAS as the angle of attack is abnormal, but manoeuvring doesn't help. On an aircraft with 2 altimeters, and only one compensated for position error, in straight symmetrical flight, the lower the speed, the greater the error will be between them, but the ADC should compensate (a non-compensated altimeter, however, will indicate a higher altitude). If the static source on the right gets blocked, in a sideslip to the right, the altimeter will over-read.

Altimeters also suffer from:

- *mechanical error,* or *instrument error,* due to misalignment in linkages and gears

- *temperature error,* particularly when cold (see the *Meteorology* section). When temperatures are above ISA, true separation will be greater, and *vice versa.* The error will be around 4 ft per thousand for every degree of deviation, and the same deviation is assumed to apply for all heights. If the temperature is lower, *you* are lower!

- *elastic error* (or *hysteresis* - an irregular response of the capsule to pressure changes, which varies substantially with time passed at a given altitude)

- *reversal error,* a momentary display in the wrong direction after an abrupt attitude change

- *time lag* from the distance a pressure change has to travel in the pipes, at its worst during steep altitude changes. Due to lag, the altimeter will under-read in a climb, and *vice versa*

If the static line becomes blocked, the reading will not change from the point where the blockage occurred.

If you didn't adjust your instruments, and were flying between areas with different air pressures, you would not be at the height you thought you were. As an example, when flying from high to low pressure, your altimeter would over-read (from HIGH to LOW, your instrument is

HIGH), so you would be lower than planned and liable for a nasty surprise. Conversely, if a flight is made from an area of low pressure into an area of high pressure, without the altimeter setting being adjusted, the altimeter will indicate lower than the actual altitude above sea level. The same goes when you move between areas with different temperatures - for an aircraft at a constant indicated altitude over a warm air mass, the altimeter reading will be less than true altitude. Going into a colder air mass, it will over-read.

Altimeter Checks

Altimeters must be checked before flight. Rotating the knob through ±3 inches should produce a corresponding height difference of about ±300 ft in relevant directions. Set the scale to the current setting. The altimeter should indicate the field elevation, plus the height of the altimeter above it, within ± 50 ft. Both altimeters (if you have two) should read within 50 feet of each other.

An Airspeed Indicator is simply a pressure gauge with its dial marked in knots instead of PSI. Its airspeed indication is determined by the dynamic pressure it senses by capturing Total Pressure then subtracting static pressure so that dynamic pressure is isolated inside its capsule. Any change in dynamic pressure expands or contracts the capsule, and it is this movement which determines the position the needle on the dial.

Airspeed Indicators are calibrated so that IAS = TAS at ISA mean sea level. If you climb at constant IAS, you will be climbing at a constant dynamic pressure, but air density decreases, so you need more V^2 to produce the same dynamic pressure.

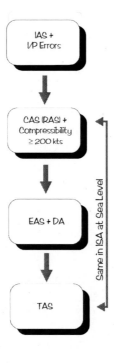

MACHMETER

See the end of this chapter.

AIRSPEED INDICATOR

To find airspeed, you need to compare the general pressure outside (the static pressure) with the dynamic pressure from the aircraft's movement through the air, so this instrument is connected to both the static and dynamic pressure systems. It's similar to the altimeter inside, except that the capsule is fed directly with dynamic pressure, and its size will vary in direct proportion to any increase or decrease. The otherwise gas-tight instrument casing (outside the capsule) is fed with static pressure, so dynamic pressure is isolated. The needle, being connected to the capsule (through a suitable linkage), will therefore read airspeed directly.

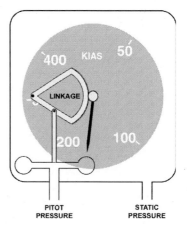

Note: Some aircraft, such as the Bell 407, have a dampened needle, which will indicate the speed you have been, and not the speed you are at.

The combination of static and dynamic pressure is the *stagnation pressure*, because airflow is being brought to rest inside the pitot tube, or stagnating.

The ASI may be calibrated in knots or mph, that is, a rate of change of distance per unit of time, several variations:

- *Indicated airspeed* (IAS) is read directly, without corrections

- *Calibrated airspeed* (CAS) is the IAS corrected for instrument and position errors, which are highest at low speeds (IAS and CAS will be about the same at speeds above the cruise). It's known by older pilots as the *Rectified Air Speed* (RAS), and is a measure of the dynamic pressure at *low speeds*. Instrument and position errors can be corrected out by the Air Data Computer in modern aircraft. *An aircraft always takes off at the same CAS*

- *Equivalent Airspeed* (EAS) is CAS compensated for compressibility, (*not* density!) or factors arising from high speeds above around 300 kts. It does not consider density error, and is effectively IAS/CAS where such errors are small, such as in helicopters. EAS is a measure of dynamic pressure *at high speeds*, which is always lower than or equal to CAS, because, as the air is compressed inside the pitot tube, the dynamic pressure is greater than it should be, and the correction is a negative value, so it could be regarded as a form of error. TAS (below) can be obtained from EAS and Density Altitude. When descending at a constant CAS, EAS increases, and *vice versa*. EAS explains the aerodynamic behaviour of an aircraft - it is what keeps the aerofoils in the air! The bridge between EAS and TAS is Density Altitude

- *True Air Speed* (TAS) is the CAS corrected for altitude and temperature, or density (remember its original calibration is based on the standard atmosphere). *It is the only speed* - the others are pressures! The slide rule part of the flight computer is used to calculate these, discussed below. On average, the TAS increases by 2% over the IAS for every 1,000 feet. Refer to the *Performance* chapter for a discussion on the effects of air density on TAS. TAS is used for navigation.

You can find TAS from the CAS and Air Density, which can be derived from Pressure Altitude and temperature which, in an exam, may involve a conversion from Fahrenheit to Centigrade (and from miles per hour to knots). Thus, in ISA conditions at sea level, CAS = TAS. However, as an example, given an altimeter setting of 30.40", an indicated altitude of 3450', an OAT of 41°F and an IAS of 138 mph, find the TAS in knots

For the moment we will take CAS as 118 kts, having converted 138 mph to 120 kts and looked it up on an imaginary graph (if there isn't one, the question will contain the information required). 41°F also converts to 5°C. The PA is found in the usual way, remembering that 1" is equal to 1,000'. The difference between 29.92" and 30.40" is 0.48, or 480 feet, which gives 2970' when subtracted from 3450' (29.92 is the "higher" figure in terms of distance above ground).

The TAS is 122 kts, and the Density Altitude (out of interest) is 2500'. If the TAS were over 300 kts, you would have to apply a compressibility

correction, which will always bring TAS and CAS closer together.

- If you maintain a constant CAS and level, when flying from a warm air mass to colder air, TAS will *decrease* as air density *increases*, and *vice versa*.

Colour Coding

There are various colour codes for ASIs, which are handy if you don't have the flight manual to hand. The *green arc* covers the range of speeds for normal operations, the yellow arc is the caution range (that is, not to be used for long periods of time, and the red line is the speed not to be exceeded, V_{NE}. The blue line on a helicopter ASI is V_{NE} in autorotation.

The "normal" V_{NE} varies inversely with altitude, decreasing as you go higher. For example, on the Bell 206, when below 3000 lbs MAUW, you have to decrease V_{NE} by 3.5 kts per 1000 feet. On a Bell 212 at 9,000 feet, it could be as low as 80 kts.

Errors

The ASI suffers from position and attitude errors, plus those from the instrument itself, and lag. It is very susceptible to position error, which can be up to 10 kts at low speeds (check the flight manual). However, density error is also important, since changes in air density affect the dynamic pressure, and make the ASI under-read (the ASI only reads TAS when density is standard, so to find it you have to apply a correction to CAS). The effect of temperature extending and contracting the linkages is fixed by a bi-metallic strip that distorts to correct the expansion.

At high speeds (over 300 kts TAS) a further correction is made for Compressibility Error, from air being compressed when it is brought to rest in the pitot tube.

If the pitot tube and its drain get blocked, the airspeed indicator will read high in the climb, low in the descent

About 10% of indicated vertical speed should be used to determine the number of feet to lead by when levelling off from a climb or descent

and not change at all when airspeed varies. This is because only the static pressure is changing, so they are behaving like altimeters (a typical icing situation). Thus, as you get higher, the instruments will over-read, and there is a danger that you will try to bring the speed back until you stall (without knowing why) which is what happened when the crew of one large jet missed the checklist item for the pitot heat. As static pressure *increases*, the ASI reading will *decrease*, and *vice versa*. If the drain hole remains open, however, IAS will read zero, as there is no differential between static and dynamic pressures, due to the drain hole allowing pressure in the lines to drop to atmospheric. A leak in the pitot total pressure line of a non-pressurised aircraft would cause an ASI to under-read.

If the static port gets blocked, the pressure inside the instrument will remain the same, and will become relatively low or high (over-read or under-read) as you descend or climb, respectively. The ASI will still read correctly in the cruise as long as the OAT remains the same but, in the descent, it will over-read as it moves into higher pressure, and you will be closer to the stall than you think. In the climb, the aircraft will appear to be underperforming as the thinner air imparts less of a dynamic force.

V-Speeds

Speed	Explanation
V_{LE}	Max gear extended
V_{LO}	Max gear operating
V_{NE}	Never Exceed speed. A red line on the ASI of a helicopter is the V_{NE} for power on, and a blue line is that for power off. V_{NE} may not be exceeded under any circumstances because it concerns aerodynamic and structural limitations.
V_{NO}	Normal Operations. 10% less than V_{NE}.

VERTICAL SPEED INDICATOR

There is a capsule inside this, too, but it is connected only to the static system. However, there is a *restrictor*, or *calibrated leak* between the inside and outside of the capsule that makes the pressure outside lag behind, so the VSI measures the *rate of change* of *static pressure*. It detects the rate of change of static pressure with height, based on pressure difference between the capsule and case. It is otherwise called a *variometer*.

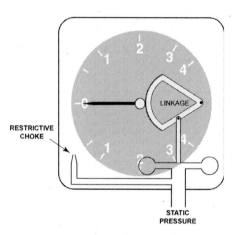

In other words, the difference of pressure between two chambers is measured, with one chamber (the capsule) being inside the other (the case). Static pressure goes to the capsule, then through the metering unit to the case, so the pressure inside the case is lagging behind the capsule.

During level flight there is no pressure differential across the metering unit, but in a descent (for example), static pressure increases and flows into the capsule and case. The capsule will expand as normal, but the restrictor will keep the pressure inside the case relatively low and create a differential that distorts the capsule one way or another and the suitable linkage transfers the movements to the dial to show climb or descent. However, the case pressure must be kept lower than the capsule pressure and made to change at the same rate to obtain a constant differential.

Increased velocity through the restrictor means decreased pressure, after Bernoulli, and the case has a greater volume than the capsule, so the process is slow enough to allow the aircraft to stabilise before anything needs to be done. In fact, the capsule leads the case by about 4 seconds.

A complex choke system self-compensates for temperature, density and air viscosity, using two capillary tubes to give a laminar flow and two sharp-edged orifices for a turbulent flow. Errors that result from the two types are of opposite sign and cancel each other out.

The VSI is a trend *and* a rate instrument, showing the direction of movement (up or down), and how fast you're going, in hundreds of feet per minute on a logarithmic scale, with zero at the 9 o'clock position, so it is horizontal during straight and level flight. Any movement up or down is shown in the relevant direction.

Errors

Aside from the usual position error, the VSI suffers from lag, which may last up to 6-8 seconds before the air inside and outside the capsule stabilizes. This means that, for example, once you level off and the altimeter is stable, the VSI takes a few more seconds to settle to neutral. There is also *reversal error*, which occurs when abrupt changes cause movement briefly in the opposite direction. In the hover, the VSI often shows a slight descent.

If the static source becomes blocked, pressure differentials disappear and the instrument reads zero.

IVSI

An *instantaneous VSI* uses two accelerometers in the static line, or a static input to an acceleration pump, to reduce lag errors, which unfortunately introduces turning errors. The accelerometers consist of two small cylinders with weights inside (they act like pistons), held in balance by springs and their own mass. The weights are centralised when stabilised in the climb or descent, but, when levelling, they act in opposing directions to sharply reduce instrument indications by puffing air into the appropriate places (inertia causes an immediate differential pressure).

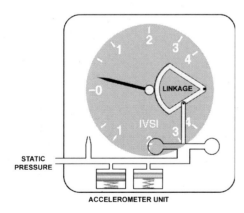

ACCELEROMETER UNIT

When returning to level flight from large angles of bank, the IVSI will initially show a climb. If the turn is maintained it will stabilise to zero, and then indicate a descent on rollout. Thus, IVSIs should not be relied upon while initiating or ending turns at bank angles of more than about 40°.

THE COMPASS

The Earth has its own magnetic field, which resembles a doughnut, in that the lines of force are more or less parallel with the curvature of the Earth but increase their angle towards the Poles until they move vertically downwards in a circle surrounding the true pole.

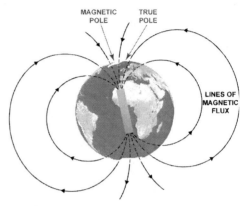

Although the origin of the Earth's magnetic field is not known, *the Earth is regarded as a magnet with its blue pole near the North pole and the direction of the magnetic force pointing straight down to the earth's surface* (exam answer). In fact, the geographic North Pole is magnetically a South Pole, and *vice versa*, which is why the North end of a compass needle points to it. As the compass needle tries to follow the lines of force, it will try to dip near the Poles, to a point where it is almost vertical and actually unreadable due to the vertical component of the Earth's magnetic force, which is called Z. The other bit is H, the directive component, which is zero at the pole, and maximum at the Equator (Z is the other way round). H is approximately the same at magnetic latitudes 50°N and 50°S.

As the compass needle tries to follow the lines of force, it will try to dip near the Poles, to a point where it is almost vertical and actually unreadable due to the vertical component of the Earth's magnetic force, which is called Z. The other bit is H, the directive component, which is zero at the pole, and maximum at the Equator (Z is the other way round). H is approximately the same at magnetic latitudes 50°N and 50°S.

Dip should obviously be minimised as much as possible, and is why true tracks and headings are flown in those areas - the North and South magnetic Poles are the only places on the Earth where a freely suspended magnetic compass will stand vertical. *Magnetic dip is the angle* between the horizontal and vertical forces acting on a compass needle toward the nearer pole. Its existence is why the limits of a magnetic compass lie between 73°N and 60°S (the magnetic compass is most effective about midway between the magnetic Poles). An *aclinic line* is a line representing points of zero magnetic dip. As the magnetic pole and lines of force do not coincide with either the true poles or lines of longitude, there is a system of accounting for magnetic variation, discussed in *Navigation*.

A direct reading compass has a pivoted magnet that is free to align itself with the horizontal part of the Earth's magnetic field.

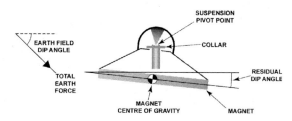

It must have certain properties to do this:

- *Horizontality.* The needle must dip as little as possible. This is done by making its centre of gravity lie below the pivot point, with pendulous magnets, which opposes the vertical component of the Earth's magnetic force (Z). Although there is still a residual dip, if it is less than 3° at mid-latitudes, it is OK. There is also a collar and sleeve assembly that stops it falling apart when inverted

- *Sensitivity.* This can be improved by increasing the length and/or the pole strength of the magnet. However, two short magnets will do just as well, and they can also be employed as the weights under the pivot point mentioned above. Pole strength can be increased by using special alloys. In addition, you could use a jewelled pivot to reduce friction, and a suspension fluid which both lubricates it and reduces the effective weight of the whole assembly. Modern compasses are sensitive, down to .01 gauss, but even that gives excessive hunting (in fact, you need gyro assistance when the magnetic field is below about .06 gauss)

- *Aperiodicity.* The ability to settle quickly after a disturbance, which is helped by the (transparent) suspension liquid. The two magnets above are also useful here, as they keep the mass of the assembly near the pivot, reducing inertia. Light alloys reduce inertia even more. Thus, *the mass of the assembly is kept close to the compass point, and damping wires are used*

Being magnetic, the compass will be affected by all the fields generated by the aircraft itself, causing a phenomenon called *Deviation*, which is discussed in the *Navigation* chapter. To try and eliminate errors, particularly magnetic dip, a remote indicating gyrocompass may be used, which is slaved to a DGI (see below). The master unit is mounted near the rear of the aircraft, so it is removed from as much influence as possible (hence the term *remote*). It contains a gyroscope under the influence of a magnetic element.

E2B

A typical E2B standby compass (left), as used in most aircraft today, consists of a floating inverted bowl suspended on a pedestal in kerosene, for damping.

The bearings are marked on the outside of the bowl, and there are two parallel magnetised needles inside, suspended under the pivot point, as mentioned above. Here is what the insides look like:

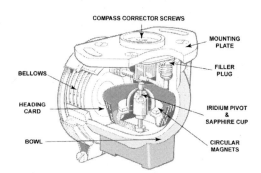

Unfortunately, although the centre of gravity's position below the suspension point assists with minimising the effects of Z, it also creates errors when accelerating or turning.

Acceleration Errors

These are caused by inertia on East-West headings. Because the C of G of the compass is under the pivot point, accelerating makes the bulk of the compass lag behind the machine and displace the C of G aft of the pivot point. If you were just going N-S, all you would get is extra dip, but because you are going East or West, the North bit of the compass is pointing to the side of the aircraft, and the displaced C of G, not being vertically in line with the pivot point, goes towards North and creates a couple that causes the compass to turn clockwise to read less than 90° during the turn. A deceleration would have the opposite effect.

There is also a complementary effect from the vertical component of the Earth's magnetic force (Z) which imposes a turning force on the dipped end of the magnet - since the magnet can only turn by rotating about the pivot, the effect is created in the same way.

In the Northern hemisphere, acceleration causes Easterly deviation on easterly headings and *vice versa*.

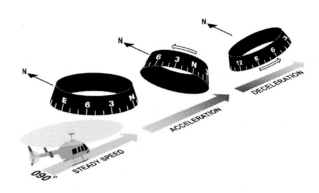

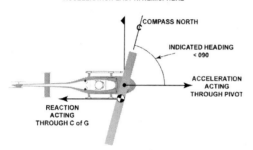

ACCELERATION EAST N. HEMISPHERE

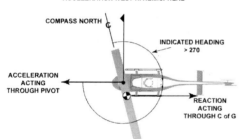

ACCELERATION WEST N. HEMISPHERE

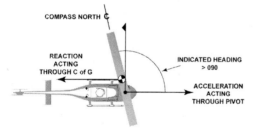

ACCELERATION EAST S. HEMISPHERE

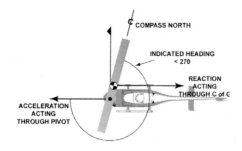

ACCELERATION WEST S. HEMISPHERE

The watchword here is ANDS - *Accelerate North, Decelerate South*, or SAND in the Southern Hemisphere. Accelerations produce apparent turns towards the nearest Pole, and decelerations towards the Equator.

During deceleration after landing on runway 18, for example, a compass in the Northern hemisphere would indicate no apparent turn.

Turning Errors

These happen during turns through North or South - the compass lags on Northerly headings and leads on Southerly ones making it look as if you're turning slower through North and faster through South. Since a turn could be regarded as an acceleration, for the same reasons as mentioned above, as you bank facing North, the pivot point and C of G are displaced in the same way, with the same effect on the North seeking pole, so the needle turns by itself in the same direction as the turn. The C of G (behind the pivot) becomes subject to gravity (Z) and twists the compass card. At Rate 1, it may look like you are not turning - any steeper, you could be going backwards!

On Southerly headings, the machine will be turning against this inclination, so will read the opposite way, so don't straighten up until the compass has gone past the heading you want. The Z field effect is also active here, and is complementary.

To put it another way, during turns through the nearest Pole, the compass will be sluggish, so you need to roll out early. During turns through the furthest Pole, the compass will be lively, so roll out late. A displacement of the magnet in a clockwise direction viewed from above causes the compass to under-read, and vice versa. You therefore get the most *turning* errors through North or South, and the most *acceleration* errors through East or West. In view of this, it follows that, before you start relying on the compass (either to navigate or align your DGI), make sure

Nippy through North

Sluggish through South

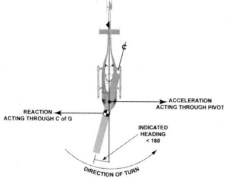

LEFT TURN THROUGH SOUTH, N. HEMISPHERE

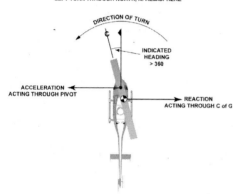

LEFT TURN THROUGH NORTH, N. HEMISPHERE

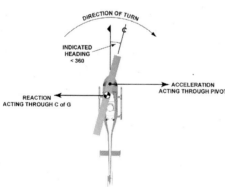

RIGHT TURN THROUGH NORTH, N. HEMISPHERE

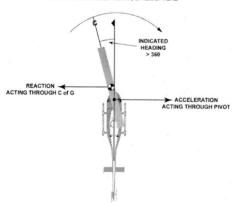

RIGHT TURN THROUGH NORTH, S. HEMISPHERE

you are in steady, level flight. Also, make turns gently, as the swirling fluid keeps the compass moving afterwards.

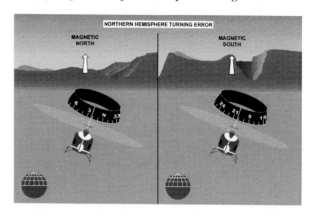

The Compass Swing

Aircraft themselves have built-in magnetism. Its influence on a compass is made up broadly of 3 components:

- *Hard iron*, or metal which can act as a permanent magnet. Permanent magnetism in an aircraft arises chiefly from hammering and the effects of the Earth's magnetic field during manufacture, or sitting for long periods on one heading. There are vertical and horizontal effects, and it is corrected with magnets

- *Soft iron*, or metal which only produces a magnetic influence when affected by the Earth's field. This is because the lines of force flow more readily through metals than they do in air. It has vertical and horizontal elements, the latter being residual and not easily corrected. The effect of this depends on the heading and attitude of the aircraft, and its geographical position

- *Electrical*. Current flowing through a conductor produces a magnetic field

There are also effects from vibration and lightning strikes.

Even though modern designs reduce aircraft effects as much as possible, there are always *residuals* to resolve. They are sorted out by measuring the effects on the aircraft's compass against a Master compass, and introducing fields of equal magnitude but opposite polarity to counteract them. The corrections are applied to horizontal hard magnetism (which changes with heading) and vertical soft (latitude).

For	Steer
000	001
045	043
090	089
135	133
180	184
225	223
270	269
315	316

Airfields and maintenance areas have clear areas in which

© *Phil Croucher, 2007*

this can be done. The figures are written on the deviation card.

A compass swing should be done:

- on installation of the compass in the first place
- as per maintenance schedules
- whenever there is any doubt about accuracy
- after a shock to the airframe or a lightning strike
- if the aircraft has been left standing for some time or has moved to a significantly different latitude
- if any major component or electrical installation has changed

GYROSCOPES

Typically, three cockpit instruments are under gyroscopic influence, the *Attitude Indicator* (artificial horizon), *Directional Gyroscopic Indicator* (DGI) and *Turn Indicator or Coordinator*. The first two are typically suction-powered and the last by electricity. A gyroscope is a heavy rotating mass on a vertical or horizontal axis, suspended in *gimbals* which are in *frames*. Its operation depends on the *resistance to deflection* of the spinning wheel or disc.

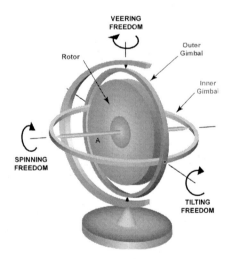

You need a gimbal for each axis you need to measure, so an artificial horizon has 2, as it measures pitch and roll.

Rigidity

The spinning allows the gyro to maintain its own position in space (*rigidity*), regardless of whatever it is attached to is doing. In other words, it resists attempts to displace it from its position. If you attached one to a camera, for example, and used the camera in a helicopter, the helicopter could be bumping around all over the place due to wind or pilot input, and the camera would not move from where the operator put it. The same applies with the instruments mentioned above, as we shall shortly see. Rigidity can be improved with *faster spin speeds*, or by increasing the gyro's *peripheral mass* or its *radius*. The greater the rigidity, the more force will be required to move the spinning gyro.

Precession

Another property gyroscopes have is *precession*, meaning that a force applied to the spinning mass is felt 90° away from where it is applied, in the direction of rotation. More technically, it is the *angular change in the plane of rotation under the influence of an applied force.*

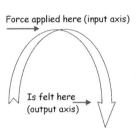

The cyclic control inputs on a helicopter have to allow for this, because the rotor disc is actually a large gyro - even though you make an input for forward flight, the movement applied to the rotor head is done several degrees beforehand. A more mundane example comes from riding a bicycle - when you apply a force to turn one way or another, it is done at the top of the wheels, but the turning movement appears 90° later, hence the turn. The rate of precession varies with rigidity - the greater the rigidity, the slower the precession will be.

In fact, the rate of precession depends on the strength and direction of the applied force, the rotor's moment of inertia and the rotor's angular velocity.

Wander

When a gyro moves from its preset position through precession, it is said to *wander*. When the movement comes from an applied (i.e. actual) force, it is called *real wander*. Unwanted real wander, or *random wander*, may arise from imperfections such as bearing friction or imbalance which will affect the motion. Turbulence alone will not cause precession, but it will enhance random wander.

The gyro is *drifting* when the axis wanders *horizontally*, and *toppling* when it wanders *vertically* (the word *toppling* also indicates a gyro operating outside its limits and unable to give correct indications). Thus, a gyro with only a vertical axis cannot drift (a gyroscope's axis of rotation defines its orientation. A vertical gyro has its axis in *Earth Vertical*, as opposed to aircraft vertical, and a horizontal gyro is in *Earth Horizontal*, but more properly aligned with North).

As this only really concerns a *Directional Gyro Indicator* (DGI), any further discussion will be continued there.

Power

As mentioned, gyroscopic instruments are made to spin through suction or pressure (heading and attitude indicator) or electricity (turn instruments). With the former, air is usually *sucked out* of the casing, and vanes (small bucket-shapes) on the gyro mass catch the movement and force it to go round (vacuum system). The suction gauge on the instrument panel is always part of the checklist before flight to ensure you have enough for the instruments to work properly. If it is reading very high or very low, the filters are blocked or equipment worn, respectively. The rest of the vacuum system has a pump driven by the engine, a relief valve, an air filter, and enough tubing for the connections. Higher rotational speeds can be obtained with electrical gyros, however, especially at altitude, and the casings can be sealed. It is also possible to design gyros with complete movement through 360°.

Tip: During startup checks, pull and hold any erection or caging knobs *before* turning the power on, as the parts inside can clash against each other as they spin up (just one of those little things a pilot can do to save long-term maintenance costs).

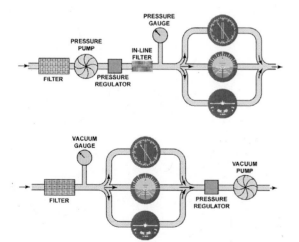

Electrical Gyros

At high altitudes, suction-driven gyros can lose their rigidity because there is a decrease in the amount of vacuum that they can produce. They also require large amounts of plumbing. Some of these problems can be resolved with electrical gyros, whose advantages include:

- Faster spin speed, therefore greater rigidity

- Spin speed is easier to maintain

- The container can be sealed to keep dirt out

- More stable operating temperature

- The ability to work at higher altitudes

- Acceleration errors are minimised because there is no heavy mass underneath the gyro, but if there are, they will be due to the mercury sloshing around in the switches

The power supply is usually 115v 400 Hz 3-phase AC (AC motors tend to be used in artificial horizons, while DC is used in turn and bank indicators). Fast erection involves giving the motors a higher error signal, which can be done in unaccelerated flight.

Refer to the *Artificial Horizon* for more information.

ARTIFICIAL HORIZON

Otherwise known as the *attitude indicator*, this instrument represents the natural horizon and indicates the pitch and bank attitudes, that is, whether the nose is up or down, or the wings are level or not.

The spin axis is *vertically mounted* (in line with Earth Vertical) so the housing (and the aircraft) can rotate around its vertical axis, at right angles to the one in the DGI. The whole assembly is inside an *outer gimbal*, which is Earth Horizontal.

The instrument's C of G is below the suspension point, so it is nearly vertical already when it is switched on, which reduces the erection time. In the suction-driven version, four *pendulous vanes* cover holes through which air tries to pass, but is blocked by the vanes as long as the instrument is vertical. When it is off the vertical, the vanes, which are suspended from a pivot and kept vertical by gravity, open the hole by differing amounts to let more or less air through as required, to provide the correct precessing force. In other words, the pendulous vane stays vertical, but more of the hole is exposed as the instrument moves.

Aircraft Pitched Nose Up

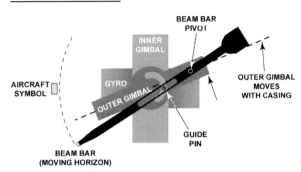

The aircraft symbol is attached to the casing and therefore the aircraft. The *horizon bar* (which stays in line with the Earth) is connected to the rear of the frame and to the housing with a *guide pin*, so when the nose pitches up, the outer gimbal comes off the horizontal. The movement is amplified by the beam bar and the guide pin is driven down - in a descent it goes up. Rolling rotates the instrument case.

With all the rotating parts, there is bound to be friction, which will cause some errors in the readings. Others include *acceleration error*, during forward movement (as in a takeoff) which gives a false climb to the *right* - this is because of the pendulous mounting - the heavy bottom of the (suction) gyro suffers from inertia and creates an imbalance between misplaced centres of gravity (roll error) and closing one of the suction ports (pitch error) - the effect is similar to the compass. The resulting forces precess 90° away for false readings.

Deceleration shows a false descent and roll to port. An

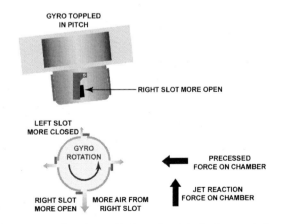

instrument showing a climb to the right indicates pitch and roll errors.

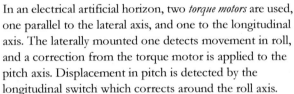

Electrical Version

In an electrical artificial horizon, two *torque motors* are used, one parallel to the lateral axis, and one to the longitudinal axis. The laterally mounted one detects movement in roll, and a correction from the torque motor is applied to the pitch axis. Displacement in pitch is detected by the longitudinal switch which corrects around the roll axis.

Levelling switches are sealed glass tubes containing 3 electrodes (one at each end and one in the middle) and a small blob of mercury. An inert gas is also present to stop any arcing as the mercury comes into contact with the electrodes. The glass tubes are set at right angles to each other on a switch block behind the gyro housing.

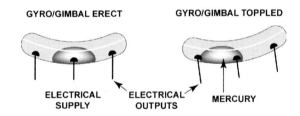

In the normal operating position, the mercury is in contact with the centre electrode, which is connected to the reference winding. If a displacement happens, the mercury makes contact with one of the side electrodes which completes a circuit to the relevant part of the control winding to apply the necessary torque correction. In fact, the voltage to the reference winding is fed via a capacitor and, as we know, this will cause the current to lead the voltage by 90°. As there is no capacitance in the control winding, it lags the reference winding by 90°. the resulting magnetic field rotates the stator in the required direction, at the same time cutting the conductor in the squirrel-cage winding and inducing a further magnetic field that makes the rotor follow the stator field.

This is immediately opposed because the rotor is fixed to the case, so a reactive torque is set up to cause the required amount of precession to correct the instrument.

HEADING INDICATOR (DGI)

This is used to give a stable heading reference free from compass errors. It works in a similar way to the artificial horizon, except that the spin axis is *aircraft horizontal* in the *yawing plane*. The casing turns round a horizontally tied gyro, which has a compass card mounted on it, so the aircraft rotates around the compass card.

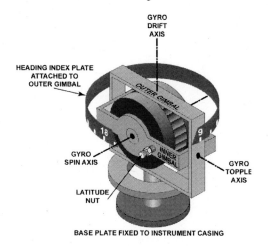

The instrument is air driven. To help with re-erection after toppling (*fine toppling*), the mass of the gyro is spun at 10,000-12,000 RPM, with air jets from twin sources, very close to each other. When the gyro does not lie in the yawing plane, one jet (the drive component) will be pushing the gyro round, but the other (erection component) will strike the rim and cause a precession force at the top which will tend to re-erect it (below). Electrically driven gyros use a *slip ring and commutator*.

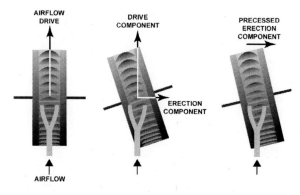

Apparent wander comes from the Earth's movement, or, more technically, when it *appears* to wander to an outside observer. In other words, assuming it stayed in one place, the gyro may still be pointing in the same direction, but at a different part of the Earth after a short time, because the Earth is spinning as well. It is a very similar thing to

convergency - if the gyro starts off being aligned with a meridian, it will be at a different angle with respect to any new one in a given period. In the picture below, it will have drifted clockwise at 15° per hour.

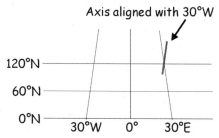

Apparent drift is zero at the equator, as the meridians are parallel to each other, but it can be calculated, although things get more complicated if the gyro is in an aircraft which itself is moving, when *transport wander* is added to the mix This *astronomic precession* (*Earth Rate*) is valid whether the aircraft is on the ground or in the air. All this causes the spin axis to go right (i.e. under-read) in the Northern Hemisphere, and left in the Southern (over-read). Eastward flight increases apparent drift, and Westward flight reduces it, so errors will be more than 15° per hour, and less, respectively. N/S travel will only affect DGI readings as far as the latitude in the formula changes, so mean latitudes are used.

Apparent drift can be found by multiplying 15° by the sine of the latitude to find the error in degrees per hour. The sign will be negative in the Northern Hemisphere because the gyro under-reads as the Earth rotates - that is, if you sat on the ground facing East, the DGI would progressively reduce its readings. In flight, this would be modified by transport wander, so if you held a steady heading of 090°, because the gyro is under-reading, you will be turning away to the *right* of earth track and your *true heading* is *increasing*. With transport wander, flight to the West will cause over-reading, and Eastward flight will cause under-reading (in the Northern Hemisphere).

Because of wander (real or apparent - see above), unless you have a slaved compass (meaning automatic), you should *synchronise* (technical term) this instrument with the magnetic compass every 10-15 minutes or so, remembering, of course, to do it in level, unaccelerated flight. You may get erroneous readings if the aircraft adopts unusual attitudes.

Gyromagnetic Compass

A direct-reading compass's indications get weaker near the poles, are subject to turning and acceleration errors, and can only be read in one position in the aircraft. The Gyromagnetic Compass attempts to resolve these problems by stabilising (gyroscopically) a magnetic compass and providing electrical outputs to the instruments that need to be read by the crew. It is continually sampled for errors and the corrections are made to the gyro. Of course, gyros also suffer from errors, so a compromise is achieved between the two, to reduce the errors of each (that is, providing short-term and long term corrections to cover the compass and gyro, respectively). In practice, the gyroscope is aligned initially to a magnetic meridian and precessional forces are applied to maintain this, based on information from the *fluxvalve detector*. Arrangements are made for signals to be suppressed whenever the system is subject to any of them, and the device will function just as a DGI.

The three main components are:

- The *fluxvalve*, which is the detecting element (compass) that provides long-term azimuth reference for the gyroscope. It will be found as far away from external magnetic influences as possible, say, in a tailboom

- The *Transmission and Display System* is simply the mechanism by which information is sent to the parts and instruments that need it. It includes a feedback system to keep everything synchronised

- The *Gyroscope* provides short-term stability for azimuth reference. It will have two degrees of freedom and the input axis will be vertical (which means that the spin axis is horizontal)

The most significant errors are:

- *Apparent Wander* (Earth rotation and change of position)

- *Gimballing*

- *Mechanical Defects*

The wander rate, in case you're interested, can be used in the Arctic to help keep the aircraft straight when the astro-compass cannot be used. Calculations are made and the heading reset, rather than the DGI, based on entries in the gyro log.

FLUX VALVE

In basic terms, electrical detection of the horizontal component of the Earth's magnetic field is done by placing two identical parallel permalloy strips on top of each other, with a primary winding that is fed with 400 Hz AC wound in series round them in opposite directions. The two poles of the resulting electromagnet thus cancel each other out, and in the absence of any other magnetic source, the total flux in the secondary winding, which is wound round the whole assembly, is zero.

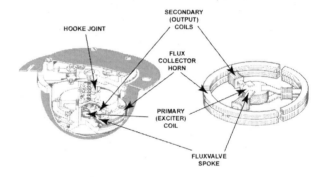

The Earth's magnetic field at that point will induce a current in the secondary that can be detected. That is, any component of the Earth's magnetic force that is parallel to the permalloy strips will have no effect on the strip momentarily saturated in the same direction, but it will be reduced in the opposite direction of the other.

As a result, an emf is induced in the secondary at twice the frequency of the excitation in the primary,

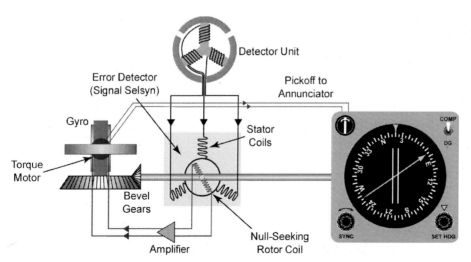

varying with the component of the Earth's magnetic field that is parallel to the strips. Three such devices are arranged at 120° to each other in a circular arrangement:

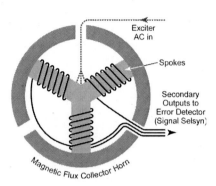

The flux valve assembly is not free to rotate (the detector unit is fixed, so it rotates with the aircraft), but it does dangle from a *Hooke's Joint* (the technical term is *pendulous*) in a remote part of the aircraft, so it will swing within limits of ±25°, although it is oil-damped within its case (or by using *slow-acting torquers*). This is to capture as much of the Earth's H force as possible, rather than the Z force which will produce turning and acceleration errors.

The problem is that, unless there is constant *change* of flux, nothing can be detected, since there is no induced voltage (this would happen if you were on a constant heading). Also, the same induced voltage would represent two headings 180° apart. To sort the second problem out, the detector element has three spokes at 120° to each other, encircled by a rim with three gaps in it to create three individual flux collectors (see above).

For the first problem, an AC current is introduced on top of the horizontal component of the Earth's horizontal magnetic field (H), so that it has a different effect on each spoke. At the centre, and therefore serving all three spokes, is an *exciter coil* which is fed with 400 Hz single-phase AC, as a primary winding. This induces an 800 Hz single phase AC current in the secondary, or pick-off, coil, which is wound around the arm of each spoke. The magnetic polarisations are reversed with each AC reversal, and the peak values are just enough to saturate the soft iron cores at the 90° and 270° phase points.

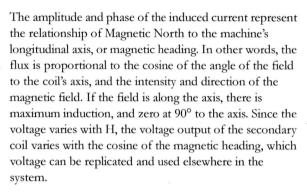

The amplitude and phase of the induced current represent the relationship of Magnetic North to the machine's longitudinal axis, or magnetic heading. In other words, the flux is proportional to the cosine of the angle of the field to the coil's axis, and the intensity and direction of the magnetic field. If the field is along the axis, there is maximum induction, and zero at 90° to the axis. Since the voltage varies with H, the voltage output of the secondary coil varies with the cosine of the magnetic heading, which voltage can be replicated and used elsewhere in the system.

Heading information from the flux valve is sent directly to the *error detector*. Error signals are provided by the rotor coil in the first place, which sends negative feedback to the *amplifier* (then the annunciator and gyro) when HDG is not aligned with Magnetic North. After going to the *selsyn unit* (self-synchroniser), the signals go to the *annunciator*, which is what the pilot sees. The selsyn is like a flux detector in reverse, in that it has the same coil arrangements inside. More details under *Synchronisation*. The torque motor precesses the directional gyro in the horizontal plane. Any gimballing errors are due to banked attitudes, and will disappear after the turn is complete.

The *synchronisation knob* is there for manual correction of gross topple in level flight. In other words, it has the same function as the caging knob.

SLAVING

The current produced by the detector unit flows along suitable cables to the *receiver stator*, which is followed by a *null seeking rotor* contained in a *control transformer*. The rotor's output is taken to *azimuth precession coils* which have permanent magnets in them. If the rotor is not at right angles to the field set up by the stator coils, a current flows through the precession coils to impose a force on the permanent magnet, which torque causes the gyro to precess in azimuth. As the gyro precesses, the rotor is repositioned by mechanical feedback until it reaches a null position, where everything is correctly aligned.

TURN COORDINATOR

This is actually a combination of two instruments, one power driven, and the other not. The idea is to measure the *yaw* rate for low *bank* rates, and since yaw and bank have to be measured, the instrument is made sensitive to both by having its axis (i.e. the gimbal ring) *tilted upwards* by about 30-35°, though it is less sensitive to roll. Displacement remains constant for a given bank, regardless of airspeed. A small aircraft tilts to indicate whether you are banking, so it is a useful backup to the artificial horizon, especially since the gyro is electrically operated and not affected if the suction system fails (although it gives you a rudimentary indication of bank, turns without the other instruments are done with timing). It becomes very useful when you are not able to use the full panel, as the amount that the wings of the aircraft move also indicates the rate of turn.

The instrument is sensitive to yaw and roll, because the gyro's axis (i.e. the gimbal ring) is *tilted upwards* by about 30-35° to make the gyro sensitive to banking as well as turning, though with less sensitivity to roll. Displacement remains constant for a given bank, regardless of airspeed.

When the wings in the little aircraft hit one of the lower marks you are in a Rate 1 turn, which takes two minutes to go through 360°, making 3° per second (you can also add 7 kts to 10% of your airspeed to get a rough guide to the bank angle required). Underneath is a ball in a clear tube containing fluid, for damping purposes, called an *inclinometer*. It is subject to gravity (weight) and centrifugal force, and will be thrown one way or another if the aircraft is not in a coordinated turn. In a *slip* (left, below), the rate of turn is too slow for the bank, so centrifugal force will

be less, and the ball will not be thrown out so much. It will therefore be on the *inside* of the turn (decrease the angle or increase the rate to correct). In a *skid*, the turn is too fast, so more centrifugal force causes the ball to be displaced more, to the outside of the turn (right, below).

Correction is the opposite of the slip. If you are out of balance, the instrument will under-read, so you will go past your turn.

Rate of turn indications are only accurate at the speed for which the instrument has been calibrated, though these are not serious (around 5%). The angle of bank to obtain a given rate of turn increases with TAS, but you shouldn't need to make any calculations - the instrument reads correctly automatically. If the gyro rotates too slowly, the device will have less inertia and be less rigid, so it will tilt less and indicate a slower rate of turn than you are actually doing. Turn radius is directly proportional to TAS, and inversely proportional to the rate of turn.

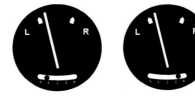

Turn And Bank (Slip) Indicator

This instrument (see bottom pictures) also has an inclinometer underneath, but it has a vertical needle instead of a horizontal small aircraft. As such it will only give you the *rate* of turn, since it is only sensitive to yaw. It has the spin axis athwartships (across the aircraft, so it spins up and away from you), with each end of the spindle held in place with a spring, so it can only move in two axes, none of them vertical.

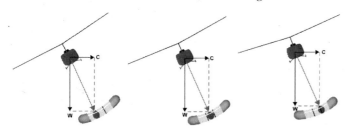

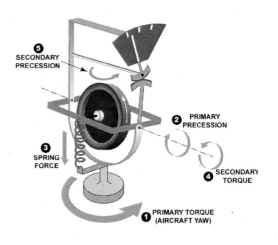

The spin rate is 10,000 RPM, and there are mechanical stops to keep it from going more than 45° either side of the centre.

The gyro is aircraft horizontal with 2 planes of freedom. During normal operation, the spring keeps the spin axis horizontal so the turn pointer is at zero, and the gyro's rigidity will tend to keep it there. The yaw induced when you turn is precessed to the top and bottom of the gyro. As the springs stretch to cope with gyro movement around the longitudinal axis, they apply a force that produces a *secondary precession* equal to and in the same direction as the rate of turn. In other words, a turn makes the gyro move, to create a primary precession that stretches a spring that creates another in the same direction as the original force.

Without the spring, you would still see a turn indication, but would have no idea of its magnitude, so the spring controls the angular deflection of the gimbal ring and introduces its own precessing force. As the precession is equal to the rate of turn multiplied by the angular momentum, the force is a measure of the rate of turn.

All errors cause the instrument to under-read, except when the rate of turn is less than rate 1, when rotor speed is faster than normal, and the springs are slack. The ball is sensitive to gravity and centrifugal force.

FLIGHT MANAGEMENT SYSTEMS

A Flight management System is defined by the exam as a *Global 3D Flight Management System*. A true FMS, if you have one, normally consists of 2 Flight Management Computers and 2 CDUs:

The CDUs (see next column) are the interface between you and the FMCs. The FMS first came to prominence with the Airbus A320, to manage the flight path.

It combines data from various sources, such as navigation systems, the Air Data Computer, route information and operating requirements, to provide a centralised source of information and control for navigation and performance,

if only to help manage fuel costs by calculating optimum levels, etc. (using a *cost index*). The Flight Management Computer, for example, holds a Navigation and a Performance Database into which custom routes can be stored, on top of standard SIDs, STARs and approach plates (in ROM, so they can't be altered). From this information, the FMC can automatically tune navaids to get radio fixes, which are combined with INS or GPS data to find your position. As a result, it can compute any displacement from track to generate guidance signals.

Central control means, for example, that you will select radio and navaid frequencies through the FMS control panel, or MCDU, as shown above - you will not see separate radio or navaid boxes in the cockpit. In other words, the MCDU is the principal pilot interface to the FMS and any other systems that interact with it. You enter data with the *alphanumeric keyboard* and *line select* keys.

The alphanumeric keys are used to make entries to the *scratchpad*, which is actually the bottom line of the display that behaves rather like a one-line wordprocessor, in that the contents of the line can be edited in the normal way. In other words, it is a working area where you can enter and/or verify data before it goes into the system (in fact, information in the scratchpad does not affect the FMS until it is moved to another line on the display). Data is kept in the scratchpad through mode and page changes.

The keys represent the same characters as they would on any keyboard, except that the **SP** button is the space bar.

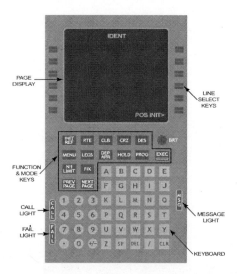

Most aircraft have a single FMC with dual MCDUs, which can each be used to enter data (not simultaneously). If the crew give complete navigation and performance control to the FMS, this is called *managed guidance*. A dual system can be used in several ways. In *Master/Slave* mode, one unit is for input, with that data being shared by the other - they share each other's information, in fact. Each FMC controls its associated AFCS and navaids. When operated *independently*, one unit can display performance pages, for example, while the other displays navigation data - the point is that one does not interfere with the other. *Single mode* exists where only one FMS is operational. *Backup mode* exists when the FMC has failed in certain areas but still retains limited function.

In flight, the FMS will continuously compute position from the IRS, VOR, DME and ILS as required. The priority for the most accurate fix is a DME/DME crosscut, then DME/VOR, then VOR/VOR, and IRS last. It will tune DME frequencies in sequence according to route information in the navigation database. Despite all that, you should still monitor your position carefully.

The FMS will normally be linked to the autopilot and flight director, and if automatic flight is not available, the FMS can at least drive the Flight Director so you can fly manually. Of course, to do its job properly, the system needs information, such as clock time, aircraft weights, fuel loaded, winds, ISA deviations, etc., particularly *databases* of waypoints, navaids, airways, procedures, airports, and other navigation data.

Horizontal Situation Indicator

The HSI (just about) qualifies as a FMS because it displays heading and navigation information in one place to provide a clear air picture. In other words, it is a gyro compass with the VOR and needle included, but there may also be a DME readout.

From the *Radio Navigation* section (just to reinforce the point), here is a comparison of the HSI against the OBI - you are heading 320°, and both instruments have the 120° *inbound* radial selected. Notice how the HSI presents the information clearly, but the OBI says something quite different - if you had no heading information, you might not realise you were going the wrong way!

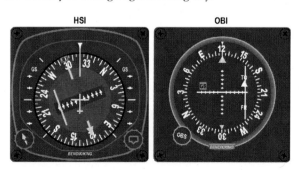

The HSI allows you a vertical perspective of your position in relation to navaids. When slaved to a compass, magnetic turning and acceleration errors are removed, together with gyroscopic drift error.

Flight Director

The Flight Director's job is to reduce your workload by indicating the manoeuvres to execute, achieve or maintain a flight situation. It does this by presenting data as control commands to show you the optimal way to achieve your flight path. In other words, the flight director gives you directions regarding *how to position of the controls* rather than the attitude of the aircraft. This means you get no information about the flight path, for which you need a separate navigation display. You can use the flight director without the autopilot being engaged, meaning that you manipulate the controls, although the autopilot can use the FD to tell you what it's doing.

The FD will be in a display which is a combination of the artificial horizon, localiser & glideslope, altimeter, etc. so not only does it tell you which way up you are, it also tells you where to go, during an approach, at least. Its official purpose is to provide information to allow you to return to a desired path in an optimal way.

The visual guidance can come in the shape of a V-bar:

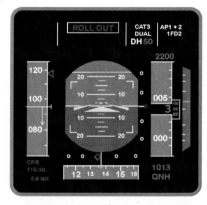

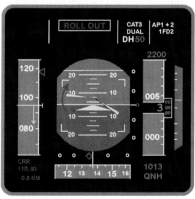

A two-cue system might use command bars: In fact, the original FD was Sperry's Zero Reader, which was a cross-pointed indicator rather like the modern ILS display:

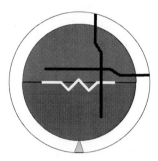

The horizontal bar is associated with the pitch channel, and the vertical bar with roll. You get information about the direction and amplitude of the corrections to be applied to the controls. They will centralise once the inputs required are enough.

Command bars may be displayed when flying manually or when the autopilot is engaged.

EFIS

Conventional instruments can go wrong, and tend to spread themselves out around the cockpit, so you need three pairs of eyes in a big machine to keep track of them all. They also have to be continually monitored.

The *Electronic Flight Instrument System* replaces the traditional ones with CRT or LCD displays, or at least flat computer panels, hence the occasional reference to the *Glass Cockpit*. These have no moving parts, and can be switched to show different instruments, or duplicate information, which is helpful if one fails. In emergencies, you can isolate some instruments for closer scrutiny.

A complete installation consists of one system each for the Captain and the First Officer.

With the glass cockpit, a lot of information can be concentrated into a small space, and the associated computers can take on a lot of the monitoring tasks, so you only need to pay them any attention when something actually goes wrong (see *Alerting*, below). EICAS & ECAM, from Boeing & Airbus, respectively, are well known monitoring systems, but they all have an EFIS at the front end.

These are typical EFIS displays:

Full Mode (VOR & ILS)

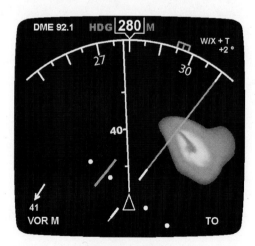

Expanded VOR

© *Phil Croucher, 2007*

Other information that can be displayed includes graphics of the aircraft systems, checklists, maps from the GPS, etc.

The technology involves small computers using solid-state (i.e. no moving parts) 3-axis gyros and accelerometers to derive altitude, magnetometers to find heading, and pressure transducers to find air data (airspeed & altitude), all displayed on flat screens, through suitable software. Because of the potential problems with software, any EFIS system will be backed up by selection of traditional instruments, or another, separate, EFIS system.

The benefits of using EFIS include:

- Increased reliability

- The output of many instruments (typically 6) can be combined into one, leading to greater situational awareness

- You can put other information on, such as checklists and weather

- Colour

EADI/PFD

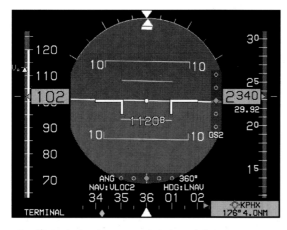

This display by kind courtesy of Chelton Flight Systems. For details of screen operations, see also *Computers, Etc*

The *Electronic Attitude Direction Indicator* (EADI) or *Primary Flight Display* (PFD) can combine the aircraft attitude display with the DGI - if you look carefully, you will see that the traditional T arrangement is preserved in one small space.

The attitude information could come from the IRS, if there is one, or more traditional gyroscopic sources. When the right equipment is switched in, you could also get ILS localiser/glideslope information, groundspeed, flight director commands, radio altitude, etc.

Between 1000-2500 ft AGL, radio altitude is shown digitally in white, with the Decision Height in green. Below 1000 ft, it will change to an analogue presentation, namely a white circular scale which unwinds as you descend and erases above the present height. The DH will be shown as a magenta marker on the circular scale.

With 50 feet to go, the marker changes to flashing amber.

EHSI/ND

The *Electronic Horizontal Situation Indicator* (EHSI) or *Navigational Display* (ND) tells you where you are in one of three modes that have different capabilities (the modes are selected on the EFIS control panel, like this Boeing one:

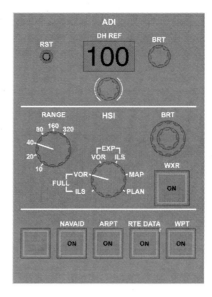

MAP

MAP mode is used for general bread-and-butter enroute navigation. It is oriented to the aircraft heading or track, which can be shown in True or Magnetic (True is automatically selected above 73°N and 65°S.

The aircraft's position is at the apex of the white triangle at the bottom of the screen and the track is represented by a white line extending away from it (see the Expanded version on the previous page. Range markings are selected through the panel above). It normally points to the 12 o'clock position, except in heading mode where it will only do so in nil wind conditions.

A magenta line represents the active route, and the *active waypoint* is the one the system is currently navigating to.

If you want a different heading than that chosen by the FMS, you must use the magenta heading select marker.

Wind speed and relative direction are shown in the bottom left hand corner.

PLAN

This display allows you an overview of the whole or parts of the route, but is not displayed in real time, except for the information at and above the expanded rose. *You cannot normally display wind and weather in this mode.* (depends on the manufacturer). You might use it to see the effects of changes in the route before entering them into the FMC.

VOR/ILS

In full mode, you get an electronic representation of the traditional HSI (see previous page). You will get wind, but not weather, information. In expanded mode, weather information is available.

SYMBOLS AND COLOURS

For the exam, know the JAR 25 symbol colours - such as for armed and engaged modes, heading select and track lines, and off-route airfields, to name but a few. Some questions ask you to identify the mode, or extract information from sample displays, like tracks between waypoints in plan mode. For example, active flight plans and waypoints are *magenta* in MAP mode. Otherwise, general colours are:

- GREEN: Active or selected mode, changing conditions

- WHITE: Present situation and scales

- MAGENTA: Command information, weather radar, turbulence

- CYAN: Non-active and background information

- RED: Warning

- YELLOW: Caution

- BLACK: Off

There are many symbols. Most are self-explanatory or from other systems.

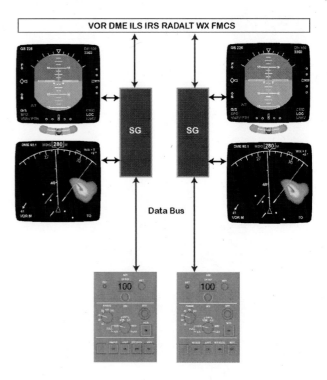

A third (centre) symbol generator may be involved if the left or right unit fails. If two generators are used and one fails, the remaining one can supply both sides, but the information would be the same. Switching is pilot controlled.

AIRSPEED TAPE

The traditional round instruments have now been replaced by tape technology, which I find harder to assimilate information from, but there you are. The V_{NE} could be represented by a red horizontal line.

ALTIMETER TAPE

This appears on the opposite side of the PFD to the speed tape. Most of its information comes from the ADS, and it is fairly self-explanatory.

RADIO ALTIMETER

A radio altimeter is a self-contained on-board aid which indicates the *true height* of the lowest wheels or skids with regard to the ground at any time. Data supplied includes the distance between the ground and the altimeter. Radio altimeters (with audio) are required equipment on helicopters over water. As a result, they are only active below about 2,500 ft. Low altitude radalts are used for precision approaches, with accuracy of ± 2 ft between 0-500 feet or ± 5%, whichever is the greater.

A *continuous wave* FM radio beam in the SHF band is directed towards the ground in a 30° cone, and the signal is reflected back to the aircraft. Continuous wave (as opposed to pulse) eliminates minimum target reception range, since the time delay for a pulsed signal would be too small to measure properly (as well, the antennae cannot switch between transmit and receive that quickly). As the potential time interval is very small, you need separate transmitter and receiver aerials.

The transmitted frequency sweeps up and down through about 200 MHz either side of 4300 MHz, instead of a time delay being measured. The difference between the transmitted and returning frequencies is a measurement of height. Compensation is made for aerial (residual) height and wiring, and to account for signal processing time, so the altimeter reads zero when the wheels touch down (placing the aerials near the gear means the radalt will also read zero when the nosewheel is on the ground).

For most radio altimeters, when a system error occurs during approach, the height indication is removed.

TCAS/ACAS

Airborne Collision and Avoidance Systems (ACAS) provide you with an independent backup to the Mark 1 Eyeball and ATC by alerting you to collision hazards. TCAS (the T stands for *Traffic*) is actually the system developed by the FAA, whilst ACAS is the generic name used by ICAO. *Your aircraft's ACAS capability is not normally known to ATC*, unless you mention it on a flight plan. Basic systems (TCAS I) just provide warnings of traffic without guidance. TCAS III (under development) gives horizontal and vertical guidance.

However, TCAS II, the current equipment, provides advice in the *vertical* plane, as a:

- **Traffic Advisory** (TA), or a warning, telling you where nearby *transponding aircraft* are, or a

- **Resolution Advisory** (RA) which also provides avoiding action by making suggestions about what to do, *in the pitch plane only*.

This is because all systems depend on azimuthal accuracy, which is not terribly good, and why TCAS II makes you climb or descend to avoid traffic (TCAS I leaves it up to the crew to work out any avoiding action and hope the other guy does the same!)

In view of the above, TCAS I can be regarded as a VMC aid, and TCAS II as an IMC aid, although it is possible, of course, to use TCAS I in cloud. There is only one TCAS II installations in the helicopter world, because the original specifications were based on fixed wing practice and have not been modified as yet. Each installation of TCAS I has to be individually certified because it may interfere with TCAS II.

The system uses four antennae, a computer *and a transponder* to continually survey the airspace around you and predict the flight paths of likely intruders, based on Mode C or S transponder signals from other traffic (that is, *it will not see non-transponder equipped aircraft, or obstacles*).

TCAS imagines a small amount of airspace around your aircraft called a *collision area*, in which, predictably, it thinks a collision is possible. Once per second, an area at least 15 nm ahead and 7.5 nm behind is scanned for *intruders*, which are aircraft that might enter the collision area within the next 35-48 seconds. They will be shown on your PFD with a symbol representing the grade of threat, plus numbers representing the intruder's height and + or - sign. An up or down arrow also tells you whether it is climbing or descending if its rate is more than 500 feet per minute. Traffic more than 5 nm away (*surveillance targets*) have hollow white or cyan diamonds. Inside 5 nm, the symbol becomes solid, for a *proximity target*.

A TA (*Traffic Advisory*) is given when the symbol changes to a solid yellow or amber circle as the intruder becomes a potential threat. When the symbol becomes a red square the intruder is an immediate threat and an RA (*Resolution Advisory*) is given which includes avoiding action. You might see a modified VSI:

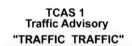

TCAS II can display on its own screen, as shown above, on weather radar, EFIS, a variometer (VSI) with an LCD display, and others.

TRAFFIC ADVISORY

A TA alerts you that an RA (see below), requiring a change in flight path, may follow - it is displayed 35-48 seconds from the time the intruder aircraft is predicted to enter the collision area, displaying range, bearing and altitude, but remember that this system relies on transponder-equipped aircraft receiving information from others. Also, the equipment cannot resolve with complete accuracy the bearing, heading or vertical rates of intruding aircraft, so you should not rely solely on TAs. Look where the conflicting traffic is supposed to be, and get ATC to help. Otherwise, manoeuvre away from the collision risk. Once clear, advise ATC. The Warning Area extends 20-30 seconds from when an intruder would enter the collision area, which is when RAs are issued.

RESOLUTION ADVISORY

An RA is meant to advise you of vertical manoeuvres required for separation from a threat. It will appear on the screen as a red box, or square - red for danger and a box because if you don't follow an RA that's where you will be.

Other traffic not assessed as a threat is indicated by a hollow white or cyan diamond. A *corrective advisory* calls for a change in vertical speed (or something different to what you are currently doing) and a *preventive* advisory restricts it. All RAs are corrective except MONITOR VERTICAL SPEED, which is a *preventative* RA. With a PRA, you should avoid deviation from the current vertical rate, but no changes should be made to that rate.

A response should be initiated immediately (not in the opposite direction), and crew members not involved should check for other traffic. Once adequate separation has been achieved, or there is no longer a conflict, you should return to your intended flight path, and inform ATC, because you have just deviated from a clearance (you are immune from enforcement action in this case). An RA may be disregarded only when you visually identify conflicting traffic and decide that no deviation is necessary. If an RA and ATC conflict, the RA wins. Use TCAS as a keyword when telling ATC what you are up to, as in *TCAS Climb*, or *TCAS Descent*.

Nuisance or false advisories should be treated as genuine unless the intruder has been positively identified and shown visually to be no longer a threat.

Only the USA *requires* the use of ACAS/TCAS, but it may be used elsewhere, with suitable approval.

POINTS TO WATCH

TCAS II can handle multiple intruders, and you could get multiple advisories when your workload is very high, which is why you can turn RAs off. Another time when you might want to do this is when operating OEI, because a climb RA could demand a higher ROC than that available. Descent RAs are inhibited anyway when below 700 ft AGL, to avoid CFIT. TAs and RAs are inhibited below 400 ft AGL.

Emergency Locator Transmitter (ELT)

If an aircraft crashes, the severe G-forces can be utilised to trigger a G-switch that activates a battery-powered transmitter.

In theory, the transmitter's siren-like tone, operating on 121.5 and 243.0 MHz, and latterly 406 MHz, should be heard by aircraft passing overhead, who "guard" these frequencies when the radio isn't needed for something else (when flying between oil rigs, for example, the second radio is routinely tuned to 121.5 MHz). The hearing of an ELT signal should be reported to ATC who should then instigate a search.

An obvious limitation is that another aircraft must be within range and listening to receive the signal., which was one reason why the international COSPAS-SARSAT search-and-rescue satellite (SARSAT) network was developed in 1985 - it is a better system for receiving signals. Another reason was to find the location of each activation, which was overflying aircraft were unable to do. The 121.5 MHz system uses Doppler analyze a received signal and locate the beacon, since it doesn't send coded signals. This is only accurate to within 12 nm., so a circle with that radius would cover 452 square nautical miles.

The older generation 121.5 MHz ELTs have proven to be highly ineffective, because they have a 97% false alarm rate and only activate properly in only 12% of crashes.

406 MHz ELTs dramatically reduce the false alert impact on SAR resources, have a higher accident survivability success rate, and decrease the time required to reach accident victims by an average of 6 hours.

Some countries are phasing out 121.5 MHz satellite alerting. In Canada, this will happen on February 1st, 2009.

An ELT that uses 406.025 MHz can punch through overhead cover such as leaves, aside from allowing better Doppler accuracy to within 2 nautical miles, which is equivalent to an area of about 13 square nautical miles.

Every 50 seconds a 5-watt signal is sent in a .05-second coded location-protocol message which contains the aircraft's registration and manufacturer's serial number, along with the beacon identification code and country of beacon registration. The message format eliminates false alarms from other electronic equipment such as microwave ovens and electronic scoreboards.

There are 5 types of ELT: automatic ejectable, fixed automatic, automatic portable, personnel and water activated.

Alerting

There are standard methods of bringing unusual occurrences to the notice of pilots. They include *visual* (lights, gauges, displays), *aural* (bells and sirens, sometimes voice, as in GPWS) and *tactile* (stick shakers).

The three levels of alerting are:

- **Warnings** (Level A) - Red in colour, could be flashing

- **Cautions** (Level B) - Amber in colour

- **Advisory** (Level C) - White in colour

Off flags are used to signify whether an instrument is working properly or not:

The flags might come on if:

- electrical power is lost

- a gyro is operating at too low a speed

- the signal received by a navigation instrument is either non-existent or too weak

Note: The absence of warning flags no guarantee that the instrument is working correctly! You must monitor all instruments!

INSTRUMENT FLYING
••

The Instrument Rating is more than a check on your ability to fly without looking out of the window. As it is supposed to be a commercial flight, and therefore conducted "expeditiously" (though not without due regard for safety!), the examiner will be evaluating your ability to work under pressure, your liaison with ATC, knowledge of weather and minima, etc. In fact, the assessment will include cockpit checks and altimeter setting procedures (especially checks for icing), and your display of Captaincy. In this respect, *do not use non-standard procedures or R/T!*

Note: The instrument experience you get with your basic licence does *not* qualify you for instrument flying! You must learn to overcome many of your body's limitations to do it properly.

Note: This chapter assumes that you have assimilated the knowledge in *AGK Instruments* and *Radio Navigation*.

Although accurate (and smooth) flying is important, good IFR work is based on correct procedures, and a methodical routine, plus anticipation (a good IFR pilot stops problems happening rather than just reacting to them). Given two marginal candidates flying a test within the accepted limits, the one with better procedural tactics and a systematic way of working will be in a better position for a pass, if the examiner is in a good mood. It does not matter whether you can fly the machine so much as fit into a very complex system without screwing it up for everybody else. You've proved you can fly an aircraft - now you've got to show what you can do with it.

In some countries, such as Canada, the ride will be multi-crew, even if it is in a single-engined helicopter! In others, such as the UK, the examiner is an "intelligent passenger", meaning that, if asked, he is able to set an altimeter or check for icing, but otherwise will let you get on with it, until you do something dangerous, at which point he will take over, or he might want to issue essential instructions.

If you have passengers on board, your flying must be smooth - just imagine they have a cup of coffee in their hand, and try not to spill it! You must be able to hold an attitude, and change it, but this, unfortunately only comes with experience. As you get used to a particular machine, you will remember how much movement of the collective relates to one bars' width of the artificial horizon.

Tip: For your instrument ride, be *very* familiar with the particular machine you are going to use - you'll look less like a dork if you're not hunting around for switches!

Precise pitch control is important - overcontrolling is too easy to do, particularly at high speeds, so your touch should be light but positive, almost letting the aircraft carry on by itself (use the trim). After setting pitch with the artificial horizon, it is usual to check the secondary pitch instruments, as the a/h can give slightly false indications after a turn. The technique is to make small corrections then cross-refer. Each manoeuvre has an associated primary instrument, discussed below, or at least one that needs checking more frequently. In level flight this would be the altimeter; in a climb, the ASI, bearing in mind that deviations may show up more quickly on a supporting instrument, such as the VSI in level flight (you are overcontrolling if your VSI indicates more than a 200 fpm rate of climb or descent). As speed increases, your control movements must get progressively smaller, but you shouldn't need to move the horizon bar more than one width anyway, below about 300 kts, and a half-width above that.

After a while you develop your peripheral vision to read all the instruments at once, which is easier to do than it sounds. Even later than that, if you fly a particular machine regularly, you get so used to the positions of the engine instruments, for example, that you treat the cockpit as one big picture and soon detect any abnormal changes. Digital displays make this more difficult, of course.

Tolerances

You must stay within certain bounds of accuracy:

- Height - ±100 ft
- Headings - ±5°
- Tracking - ±5°
- Speeds - ±5 (kts/mph/whatever)
- ILS - up to ½ scale deflection (Loc/GS)
- Overshoot action - +50 and -0 feet of DH/DA
- Maintaining MDA/MDH - +50 and -0 feet

Tolerances are *outer limits* - you should not be consistently high or low, so be seen to be making corrections!

They can be slightly wider during asymmetric operations.

Using The Instruments

There are only three - *Scanning*, *Interpretation* and *Control*, which should be integrated into a smooth process.

The equation *attitude + power = performance* means setting the anticipated attitude first, then applying power for an expected performance. Put another way, a known attitude plus a known power setting produces a predictable result. This means that you will have to memorise the power settings for each manoeuvre or procedure, plus the corresponding positions of the miniature aircraft against the artificial horizon in the attitude indicator.

The two most important instruments are therefore the attitude indicator and whatever shows you the power being used, which could be a Manifold Pressure Gauge in a piston engined machine or a torquemeter in a turbine. For this reason, they are called *control* instruments. The others in the traditional T are *performance* instruments since they show you the effects of whatever power/attitude combination you have set. They are important because the power instruments cannot tell you if you are keeping to your desired flight path.

Tip: One of the most useful tools is the trim control, if you have one, which should be used after every attitude change - it will reduce a major part of your workload.

As well as the control and performance instruments, you have the navigation instruments, plus miscellaneous ones, like gear indicators, engine oil pressure, etc.

A *primary instrument* is one which gives instant and constant readouts (also called *direct*). A *secondary instrument* is one that you have to deduce things from, such as the altimeter increasing, telling you that the pitch must have changed (you might also say that the altimeter gives you an indirect indication of pitch attitude).

Each manoeuvre has an associated primary instrument, or at least one that needs checking more frequently. In level flight this would be the altimeter; in a climb, the ASI, bearing in mind that deviations may show up more quickly on a supporting instrument, such as the VSI in level flight (you are overcontrolling if your VSI indicates more than a 200 fpm rate of climb or descent). As speed increases, your control movements must get progressively smaller, but you shouldn't need to move the horizon bar more than one width anyway.

Here is a comparison:

Instrument	Direct	Indirect
ASI	Airspeed	Pitch

Instrument	Direct	Indirect
Altimeter	Altitude	Pitch
VSI	ROC/ROD	Pitch
DGI (Heading)	Heading	Bank/Balance
Turn & Bank	Yaw, Coordination	Bank
Turn Coordinator	Yaw, Roll, Coordination	Bank
Compass	Heading	Bank

They are further grouped under the headings of *pitch*, *bank* and *power* (refer to the *Instruments* chapter).

SCANNING

To see the results of the changes you make on the control instruments, you have to keep an eye on more than one. The most efficient way of doing this is to scan them in a regular pattern. Scanning is a *continuous and logical observation of the flight instruments*.

As mentioned above, instruments are grouped for easier assimilation of information. One way of reading them (called the *radial scan*) is to start with the artificial horizon in the centre, and look at the others in turn, always returning after each check:

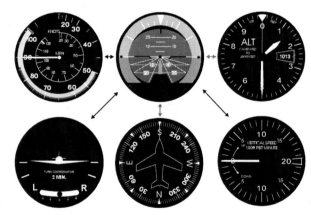

However, there are many other methods, including my own weird version of partial panel, and some people go round in a circular fashion, but the radial scan is the official doctrine, because priority is given to the artificial horizon - that is, you start there, hop out to a performance instrument (as to which one depends on what you are doing), and back again. If you want to go to another performance instrument directly, you must route through the artificial horizon (just to confuse matters, a radial scan that uses particular instruments more frequently to get the relevant information is also called the *selective* radial scan).

© *Phil Croucher, 2007*

To use a radial scan effectively, you need to be asking:

- What information is needed?
- Which instruments give that information?
- How do you check if they are is reliable?

For example, in the picture above, to maintain straight & level flight, the priority is given to the artificial horizon, altimeter and DGI, represented by the blue arrows. The others are scanned less frequently in a cross-check.

Since the artificial horizon is the most important instrument, take time to get familiar with the relative positions of the miniature aircraft, beginning, of course, with straight and level, when the wings should be in line with the false horizon. It will look different on the ground, so find out what it looks like in flight so you can set it before takeoff. The next good one is climbing or descending, which is usually one or two widths of the miniature wings above or below the line.

Cross-checking is important. For example, when trying to maintain a particular speed, ensure that the altimeter is reading correctly as well as the ASI, because you may have inadvertently started climbing or descending. This will affect what power setting you use.

Note: It is possible to fixate on one instrument if you get concerned about the information it provides.

INTERPRETATION

You need to apply your understanding of the operating principles of each instrument to gain the best mental picture of your aircraft's situation and the conditions under which it is operating. This will involve a combination of instruments for each manoeuvre.

CONTROL

Precise pitch control is important - overcontrolling is too easy to do, particularly at high speeds, so your touch should be light but positive, almost letting the aircraft carry on by itself (use the trim). The technique is to make small corrections then cross-refer.

Partial Panel

Sometimes, an instrument will fail, or a system that controls more than one, in which case you have to interpret the remainder in a different way to get the information you need. Typically, you might be left with the turn coordinator as a replacement for the artificial horizon, the compass and the pressure instruments.

It actually isn't that hard to do, even if you are relying mainly on secondary information, but you have to do timed turns (2 minutes for 360°) instead of just using the DGI, so you must include the clock and compass in your scan, although you won't get much sense out of the latter until it has settled down after the turn is complete. The first left or right mark on the turn indicator indicates a rate 1 turn under normal conditions, but 10% of your speed + 7 (kts) is probably more accurate. The instrument that helps most in this situation is the turn coordinator.

Reminder: When going for a Southerly heading, you need to go past the heading you want on the compass by 20° or so. For Northerly headings, you need to anticipate it.

Tip: An alternative is to use the ADF to maintain a consistent heading, as keeping its needle steady is a lot easier than following the compass. Naturally, you will have to cross-check the readings! You could also use the compass presentation on your GPS.

Manoeuvres

STRAIGHT & LEVEL

In theory, you are supposed to alternate between the artificial horizon and VSI in this manoeuvre, since the latter is more sensitive, but that also means it oscillates during turbulence. Some pilots use the altimeter instead, and only use the VSI for keeping an eye on the rate of climb or descent. However, it is useful for *maintaining* straight & level flight, in which case your corrections should be small because of the VDI's sensitivity. If you like, the altimeter is for coarse adjustments (half a bar's width or more) and the VDI for fine tuning. The rate of scan to the VSI should be three or four to one for the altimeter, which ratio can be lessened in turbulence, always remembering to route through the A/H.

Maintain heading with the DGI.

Use plenty of friction on the collective, as an aid to stopping you making any power changes unless you have made a large altitude error, say greater than 100 feet. You can make small changes in level with the cyclic, but not for more than one bar width. Hold the new attitude until the error is corrected.

Note: Although the tolerances for height control are ±100 feet, some companies will expect ±20.

TURNS

Turns should all be done at rate 1, although the only time this is critical is in the hold at 100 kts, which requires 17° of bank - any other angle will ruin the hold.

Calculate the angle of bank for a rate 1 turn by taking 10% of groundspeed and adding 7 kts - at 150 kts, try 22°. Here is the formula:

$$\frac{Speed}{10} + 7$$

For the radius of turn at Rate 1, divide the TAS by 180 for the radius in nm.

Use the A/H, and the rudder once you have started banking. Start timing on roll-in, roll out after 10 seconds - at the angle required, centralize the controls, and start the rollout within about ½ the angle of bank of the desired heading. To prevent overcontrolling, do not use more bank than the turn.

CLIMBS

From the cruise, raise the nose to what you think would be a good attitude (you will get used to what it might be as time goes by). Keep level, watching the ASI reduce to climb speed, then add the required power when it gets there and trim out. Anticipate the levelling off altitude by about 10% of the rate of climb (i.e. 50 feet for 500 feet per minute), pushing the nose forward gently to level off at the cruise altitude, and holding the power until the speed increases. Then reduce the power, and trim again.

Tip: If you can manage to peak the levelling process about the width of the needle above the height required, so you are in a descending attitude when you finally level, it will help performance, and provide a "step" to keep the machine ahead of the game.

DESCENTS

You need 1000 feet per minute unless you are on final approach.

Reduce the power and keep the machine level. As the ASI approaches your descent speed, select the right nose-down pitch, keep the speed and trim. Anticipate your cleared level by about 10% the rate of descent, level, adjust power and trim.

Alternatively, when within 100 feet of the target altitude, level off with the correct power and finish off by adjusting the attitude.

UNUSUAL ATTITUDES

These may be defined as an attitude, or combination of attitudes, involving pitch or bank angles over 30°. They may be caused by anything from turbulence or input from a passenger in the front seat. If the attitude is extreme, some older gyro instruments may topple, so use secondary indications as well, to identify the attitude (are you climbing, descending, or turning?) then apply the proper methods.

Calculations (Rules of Thumb)

Most revolve around losing or gaining a specific number of feet over a given distance, as you would when having to arrive at a fix at a specific altitude, which is why you are given the distance to run when approaching. First of all, find out how far you have to go, then how long it will get there, based on your groundspeed. Dividing the height to be lost by the time to get there reveals how fast you have to come down. Looked at another way, you could find out when to start a descent, knowing you have to come down at a fixed rate. Here, you have to start with the time to descend at the fixed rate, look at your groundspeed and work backwards to see where to start. At 500 feet per minute, which is quite common, the altitude you need to lose (in thousands) multiplied by two is the same as the time needed to descend, in minutes. All you need to do then is apply the groundspeed. For example, to lose 6,000' at 500 fpm needs 12 minutes. At 120 kts, therefore, you need to ask for descent 24 miles out.

These sort of calculations are also useful for glideslopes. Once groundspeed is known, this formula gives you the rate of descent to maintain 3°:

    3° rate = ½ gspd x 10

You could also multiply the groundspeed by 5, or 6 if you want a 3½° glidepath. A 3° glideslope requires 300 feet per nm ROD, so with 2½ nm to go, you should be at 750 feet (2½ x 300). To find the DME point where the glideslope will be intercepted, take your height above ground, divide by 1000 and multiply by 3, so 3000 feet is 3 x 3 = 9 DME. Intercepting a DME arc should be done with a lead based on ½% of the groundspeed, or groundspeed divided by 200, with the answer in nm. So, if the arc is 12 nm and your groundspeed is 100 kts, start turning (at Rate 1) at 12½ nm. The lead for levelling off should be 10% of the climb or descent rate, so at 500 fpm, move the nose at 50'.

Calculate the angle of bank for a rate 1 turn by taking 10% of groundspeed and adding 7 kts. At 150 kts, try 22°. Start timing on roll-in, roll out after 10 seconds. For the radius of turn at Rate 1, divide the TAS by 180 for radius in nm.

To calculate groundspeed in a hurry, figure out the angular difference between your track and the wind direction, take the answer away from 90 and apply the result to the clock face to find a proportional factor. Thus, if the wind angle is 260° and your track is 210°, the difference is 50°. Away from 90, this is 40, or two-thirds (of an hour). If the wind speed is 20 kts, you would take away 14 from your groundspeed.

Your maximum drift (in degrees) is:

$$\frac{Windspeed \times 60}{TAS}$$

Your actual drift can be calculated by applying the clockface method used for groundspeed to the max drift. If you had a max drift of 15°, and the difference between your track and wind direction was 40°, that would be two-thirds, so actual drift would be 10°.

Operating Minima

There are weather conditions under which you're not allowed to land, attempt to land, or take off. A minimum cloud base and visibility is laid down, based on national regulations, ATC, or hard objects (obstacles), in that order. The highest will determine the minimum altitude for that route or sector (that is, each intended track between reporting points), which will ultimately depend on the accuracy of your position, your maps and the characteristics of the area, in terms of weather or terrain. There are different definitions, depending on the airspace, but they all provide you with a lowest safe altitude you can use in an emergency.

You are responsible for ensuring that before takeoff you've got minima for the relevant times at every destination and at least one suitable alternative, which must be noted on the Operational Flight Plan if you intend to use them (this can mean up to 8 airfields if you include takeoff alternates - see below).

While you're not allowed to reduce the limits given, you are actively encouraged to increase them if you think it's necessary. As they're calculated for fog conditions with little or no wind, you should make due allowance for rain and/or crosswinds. Naturally, minima are not valid if anything affecting their calculation has been changed through NOTAMs, or as instructed by ATC.

Minima not in the Airways Manual can be worked out with figures in the Ops Manual, in which case, one copy

must be kept in Ops, and another on board. They will be higher than the precalculated ones, because they come from blanket figures which allow for aircraft in lower performance groups avoiding obstacles visually if an engine fails on takeoff, so Cloud Ceiling figures will vary according to where you can start to construct your Net Flight Path data (see *Performance*). If that happens at 300 feet (that is, your engines are assumed to be working till then), expect a 300 ft Cloud Ceiling.

The same principle goes for RVR figures, which are related to the time required to see and avoid obstacles - if you're going at 90 knots, 1400 ft RVR (a quarter of a mile) will give you thirty seconds between seeing and missing anything. RVR is the distance you can see in the direction of take-off or landing, determined by a certain procedure, usually with the aid of a *transmissometer* or two, and based on runway lights at setting 3. The distance given is taken as the RVR for the time being, that is, only valid for a short time.

For helicopters, you need a ceiling 200 ft above the minimum for the approach and visibility at least 1 sm, but never less than the minimum visibility for the approach to be flown, which can be applied to both precision and non-precision approaches.

It's a good idea, in a commercial environment, to have something up your sleeve, by which I mean what do you do if the ILS goes off halfway down an approach? Many ILSs use an NDB as an outer marker, so why not be prepared to convert to an ADF approach? or a VOR (or whatever)? As a professional, you should not expect to land from an approach, so you don't get fixated and try to get in when you shouldn't. Non-standard minima must be retained with flight documentation.

ALLOWANCE FOR WIND SPEED

Within 20 nm of ground over 2000 ft amsl, increase MOCA/MORA by:

Elev (ft)	0-30 Kts	31-50 Kts	51-70 Kts	+ 70 Kts
2-8000	+ 500'	+1000'	+1500'	+2000'
+ 8000	+1000'	+1500'	+2000'	+2500'

This is because venturi effect over a ridge makes the altimeter misread, as well as causing turbulence and standing waves. A combination of all this, plus temperature errors (see below), can make an altimeter over-read by as much as 3000 feet.

TEMPERATURE CORRECTION

When surface temperature is well below ISA, correct MSAs by:

Surface Temp (ISA)	Correction
-16°C to -30°C	+ 10%
-31°C to -50°C	+ 20%
-51°C or below	+ 25%

There is a more detailed chart in the CAP. ATC should be advised if they are applied to FAF crossing, procedure turns or missed approaches.

Flight Planning

Refer to the *Flight Planning* chapter for the normal stuff. This is just a mention of the things you need to make sure you have or check before you start:

- Enroute Charts
- CFS
- Flight Manual, with checklists
- NOTAMs and Supplements
- Weather for departure, destination and alternates
- Area forecasts, with upper wind and surface analysis & prognosis charts

Departures

In Canada, takeoffs are governed by *visibility*, but to ensure that obstacles are cleared, you may have to follow specific routes. If they cannot be cleared, the use of ceiling and visibility minima ensures that they can at least be seen and avoided. Normally, a straight departure is used, within 15° of the centreline, but a *turning departure* helps when it has to be more than that (this may need speed adjustment to cope with the turn).

IFR departures assume that you will be at 35 feet over the departure end of the runway, get to 400 feet above the airfield elevation before proceeding on course (BPOC), maintaining a climb rate of at least 200 feet per nautical mile throughout (at 120 kts, this is 400 fpm, or 300 fpm at 90 kts). Get those figures into your head. If all engines are assumed to be working until a certain height, do not take off if the cloud ceiling is below it, as you must see and avoid obstacles. The 35 feet at the end of the runway can be 17.5 feet if you include the Clearway as part of your Takeoff Distance Available (see *Performance*). However, you still have to get up to 35 feet before the end of that.

Tip: ATC always change things to help traffic flow, and they often tell you to just revert to the previous clearance when the panic's over, so get into the habit of writing everything down, particularly radio frequencies, as you may need to return to the previous one if you can't make contact on the new one (also, change to the new on one the *other box*, if you have one). Certainly, write down the levels you are cleared to. If you are not sure about clearances, ask ATC to repeat them. They won't mind - they don't want to see you splattered all over the runway any more than you do.

Tip: Make sure you can read any shorthand you use!

DO NOT RUSH. Hustle, yes, but don't rush, or you will forget something.

Note: The obstacle clearance on an instrument departure assumes that all engines are operating. *Using a published procedure does not guarantee obstacle clearance if an engine fails*, so you must limit the weight of your aircraft accordingly. However, there may be procedures that allow obstacles to be avoided laterally which include a turn (or a series of turns) based on specific headings or tracks.

DOCUMENTATION

IFR documentation covers two areas - *en-route*, for larger areas, and *terminal* for the vicinity of major hubs, that is, for more localised areas, such as approach charts, SIDs and STARs. Enroute charts are based on the Lambert projection, and those for more densely populated areas will be of larger scale.

Note: Being a Lambert projection, a straight line is as close as possible a great circle, but because of the (small) inherent errors, you would be wise to add a small buffer if your track takes you past a prohibited area or anywhere else you shouldn't be!

PREFLIGHT STUFF

Check that the RVR/cloudbase are within limits all the way round the route. A cloudbase of 200 feet is assumed, and the aircraft has been out overnight in icing conditions.

Tip: If the weather is bad, the examiner may elect to go anyway, since no real passengers are involved, once you have demonstrated a go-no go decision.

STANDARD INSTRUMENT DEPARTURE

The SID is intended to save time on the radio and a lot of admin. It will be a preselected route outbound, issued on a chart, and all the controller will need to say is something like "Alpha 1 Departure", for you to look it up and know the way to go, in terms of heights and waypoints to be reached at specified times. Noise abatement will have been factored in, as will the performance requirements above. The SID terminates at the first fix, facility or waypoint of the enroute phase after the departure procedure.

TAXI

First of all, organise your cockpit. Have all the charts you need to hand, in the order you want to use them, together with any writing instruments (you can never have enough!). Although a pencil with an eraser on the end is useful, in real flying you have to keep your scribblings for about 6 months, if memory serves me correctly, so you may as well get used to using a pen and just crossing out any mistakes. Remember that crossings out in documents must be readable.

A useful item for keeping charts in is an ordinary menu holder, as used by restaurants (just the right size for Jep charts). Being clear, they can be written on with a marker, in case anything gets changed by NOTAM, or you have to apply altitude corrections when its cold (it's best to mark them directly). Having said that, instructions from ATC, such as those to maintain a level, will be temperature compensated anyway.

Don't forget a stopwatch, which should be easily seen without moving your head.

After starting, while waiting for the engines to warm up, tune and identify the navaids, get the ATIS, then go to the ground frequency to get your airways clearance (at some airports, you need start clearance for the engines). Tell them the ATIS code, so they know you're up to date, your destination and the altitude you intend to fly at (this helps them match your flight plan). If ATC have the clearance to hand they will give it to you straight away, as it clears their desk a little bit, but you will have all the time it takes to get to the holding point to receive it, since you can't take off without it, although it's best to take it when stationary.

Typically, you can expect:

- Ident
- Clearance Limit
- Route
- Altitude
- Departure, and other instructions
- Special instructions
- Traffic information

Having received taxi clearance, as you proceed, check your instruments by turning, ensuring that the turn indicator

shows left (for example), the ball is out the right way, the artificial horizon stays steady and the compass and heading indicator decrease their readings. Do the same for turning right. In a helicopter, you would do this in the hover (slightly higher than normal), nudging the cyclic slightly left and right, forward and back, and pedals left and right.

Somewhere on the SID chart will be a procedure for communications failure, which you should study thoroughly, as reading it while you have an emergency is not what you want to be doing! Take some time to review the departure clearance, or SID, and any last minute modifications from ATC. Think about what you might do if an engine or a radio fails, and go through the drills quickly (if two-crew, you would tell the other pilot).

Then, tell ATC you're ready for departure and line up on the runway when cleared (in Europe, do not use the words "take off" unless actually cleared to do so - always refer to it as *departure* until then. Ever since two 747s collided at Tenerife after a clearance was misheard, they've been really twitchy. Come to think of it, it's a good practice, anyway).

If offered takeoff from an intersection, be sure the remaining runway length is enough, as there's nothing so useless as runway behind you (well, OK, fuel in the tanker is pretty useless, too, as is air above you, and approach plates in the car). You won't fail a test by taking the trouble to taxi to the end of the runway.

TAKEOFF MINIMA

The takeoff minima box is at the bottom left of the aerodrome map in the CAP. In it, the runways available will be listed with either a ½ or a * next to the number:

```
Rwy 15: ½
Rwy 33: *
```

The ½ (mile) means you can take off in any direction and not hit anything if you satisfy the climb performance requirements above, assuming you base the takeoff on a runway. The * means you have to look elsewhere for further information, luckily not far - just to the middle bit of the same airfield map. There you will find conditions that will keep you clear of obstacles for different visibilities - ½ (again) and SPEC VIS.

For example, if you choose ½ mile visibility, you may have to maintain a minimum climb gradient (to find out the corresponding amount of feet per minute, there is a chart in the CAP General pages). If this cannot be done, then you may have to depart visually under SPEC VIS requirements (that is, *specified visibilities* based on your aircraft category. Performance affects the airspace and visibility needed for manoeuvres under IFR. The most significant factor is speed, and five categories of aircraft have been established.

The speed used is the IAS at the threshold, or V_{AT}, which is 1.3 times the stalling speed (V_{SO}) in full landing configuration at max weight. Speed categories are:

Category	Threshold Speed
A	< 91 kts
B	91-121 kts
C	121-141 kts
D	141-166 kts
E	166-211 kts

They are directly linked to airspace and obstacle clearance requirements.

The associated visibilities in miles against categories are:

A	B	C	D
1	1.5	2	2

If you are a Cat C aircraft, for example, you need 2 miles visibility.

When the airfield is NOT ASSESSED, you are on your own with regard to obstacle clearance. If you cannot comply with any requirements (your aircraft may not be powerful enough), any alterations are down to you. If there is no published visibility, you can cook up your own procedure, but visibility may never be less than ½ m. For takeoff, helicopter visibility is half the CAP value, but not less than ¼ m.

Sources of information for visibility include *RVR*, *observed visibility* and the *PIC*, in that order. If any of the first two exist, the PIC is automatically out of the loop. If the RVR is less than the observed visibility, it is deemed to be due to a "localised phenomenon" and takes second place. What this means in practice is that you take the highest of the RVR or visibility, provided it is at least ½ mile for aeroplanes and ¼ mile for helicopters.

The PIC's decision comes into play when the above are not available, such as when the FSS is closed, or there are no facilities anyway (in this case it will help you to remember that runway edge lights are 200 feet apart. Also, that the touchdown zone is the first 3,000 feet or third of the runway, whichever is greater). It might be prudent to take note of the ceiling if you think you might want to come back in straight away or are departing from a NOT

ASSESSED field and are getting out by using the Missed Approach procedure (that is, you have to find the Missed Approach Point first). If you can't get back in, you need a takeoff alternate - the rules for choosing alternates in general are given below.

TAKEOFF

When lining up, check that the heading indicated corresponds with the runway direction (some of these things can slave 180° out). The localiser needle should be centred, or the VOR needle, if it's more or less on the runway, as many are. Check the transponder, note the time and go through the checklist.

CLIMB

After lifting off, ensure that you have a positive rate of climb, and that you seem to be going in the right direction (check the DGI). Leave power on a little longer than you would for VFR flight or, in other words, don't be in such a hurry to reduce it, always bearing in mind the takeoff power limitations. Trim.

If in a TCA, you may be told of a frequency to change to before you take off, or be advised afterwards once you are clear of traffic. It helps the new controller if you state your call sign, departure runway, passing altitude and the one you are cleared to (it will all be written somewhere, but it saves looking it up). If you are not given a frequency, advise the tower of the one you are changing to when the time comes.

Check the OAT and icing every 1,000 feet, or whenever you feel it is appropriate.

En Route

In the enroute phase, you get a bit of time to scratch your head and do a bit of housekeeping, plus a little anticipation. For example, you could update the weather for the destination, prepare the next navaid and ATC frequencies on the other box, make position reports, get any appropriate clearances, brief anybody you have to and do any prelanding checks (and revise with ATC if over 3 minutes' difference. Also tell them if your TAS varies by more than 5%).

Report reaching and leaving all altitudes, and the ones you are passing (up or down) on initial calls, together with the one you are cleared to, just in case the previous controller hasn't transferred the information (it happens). When given a climb or descent, ATC will assume you are doing so at 500 feet per minute for propeller aircraft, or 1,000 fpm for jets.

*It used to be, when the RVR was less than 1200 feet, that you were prohibited from shooting the approach past the Final Approach Fix. One night, an CRJ made an approach in fog to a runway, got off the centreline, and contacted the ground in the go-around. A higher RVR (3/4 of the Advisory Visibility) is now required for Commercial Operators unless you have an Operations Specification (clause in your Operating Certificate) that allows something lower (1/2 the Advisory Visibility). General aviation folks still use the 1200 RVR - see CAR 602.129

Always climb well in advance of an increase in minimum IFR altitude.

Usually, further clearance is given well before you reach clearance limits, but if not, you must hold at the limit, at the assigned altitude, to at least the last time given.

At each checkpoint (navaid, marker), use the 5 Ts:

- *Time*. Punch the clock as soon as you are overhead or get station passage, as even a second will affect the outbound in a hold.

- *Turn*. Get moving in the direction desired.

- *Throttle*. Adjust power as necessary for descent or climb.

- *Tune*. Make sure the navaid is still working (flags, or audio for NDBs).

- *Talk*. Tell ATC what you are doing, if required.

As you get closer to the approach point, start thinking about the Missed Approach and how the wind will affect your hold timing and headings.

Approach - 602.127

Anticipate this by getting the current ATIS, so you at least know what the weather is like. Check the winds against runways, and select the most suitable for an approach, unless otherwise instructed by ATC. Check the visibility (RVR) and see whether an *approach ban* is in effect, in which case you can make plans for your alternate early. At busy terminals, there will be an arrival frequency. At the other extreme, in uncontrolled airspace, make broadcasts and listen on the MF.

Once you know you are on your way in, and which runway you are going to use, you can tune and identify the aids to be used. Make sure you have clearance! And for the missed approach!

To simplify things, some airports may use a *Standard Terminal Arrival Route* (STAR), which works the same way as a SID does, only in reverse. Controllers sometimes forget that fast descent in unpressurised aircraft can hurt the ears, so try asking for it early to allow it to be more gentle. Just shove the nose down a few degrees with the same power setting, and you will gain a few extra knots.

Approaches are either *precision* or *non-precision* - the former has electronic guidance in *azimuth* and *elevation* (that is, left and right, and up and down), and the latter azimuth only (left and right), meaning that the descent path has to be judged by the pilot (you are given a descent gradient which can be converted into a rate of descent based on your

groundspeed). Good examples of a precision approach are an ILS or PAR, or even MLS. A non-precision approach is basically anything else, such as VOR or ADF, or a *Localiser Only* ILS. The difference between the two is easy - *Decision Height* (DH), used on precision approaches, is height-based, in that you go directly down to it, and go-around if you don't see the ground. In other words, the vertical element is started at a precise point, and you likely have the runway in sight at the decision altitude, rather than looking for it in a visual manoeuvre, and reconfiguring the aircraft in a hurry.

Minimum Descent Height (MDH), on the other hand, is time-based, in that you set the stopwatch on leaving the fix and look up to see if you can see the ground at the time you calculated from your groundspeed, having reached the MDH. For this reason, non-precision approaches need to be flown accurately with regard to speed, otherwise your calculations will be out.

Tip: If you get given an emergency that requires you to slow down after the FAF, don't forget to recalculate the timings, or ask for them to be done by the examiner.

Tip: Don't forget to take note of the compass correction card, or you could be a couple of miles off track as well.

On the approach chart there is a guide as to how long it will take to get to the threshold after passing the beacon, based on your aircraft category (see below) and therefore groundspeed. You stay at MDH once you get down to it, and go around after the time if you don't see the runway.

*You can start an instrument approach regardless of the reported RVR or visibility, but you cannot go beyond the outer marker (or equivalent) if either are less than the minima. If it falls below that after that point, you can carry on down to DH/MDH.

If there is no outer marker (or equivalent), this decision must be taken before 1000 feet above the aerodrome on the final approach segment.

You can proceed beyond DH/MDH and complete the landing if the required visual reference is established at the DH/MDH and is maintained.

RVR can only be the same as or greater than met visibility, never less.

Unless otherwise authorized, you must comply with the approach procedures - that is, once accepted, you may not deviate from the clearance. If no specific instructions are given, you must inform ATC of your intentions, as they may be filtering other people in - this also applies to potential missed approaches. If left to your own devices with respect to altitude, you can descend in your own time to the lowest of:

- MEA

- Transition Altitude

- MSA (on the approach)

- 100 nm safe altitude

- at least 1000' above the highest obstacle inside 5 nm (1500 or 2000 within 10 nm depending on mountainous zone).

The altimeter must be set for the aerodrome where the approach is to be conducted before you start.

A non-precision approach is characterised by large "steps", that is, major descents at certain stages, requiring large power changes that can be a pain with an engine out, so it's often a good idea to keep a consistent glide path as much as possible, remembering that the minimum heights at each step are just that - minimum heights. There's nothing to stop you being above them if you are actually descending under control. In other words, MDA (or any altitude, for that matter) is a height *below which you must not descend*, and not (necessarily) a height at which you must fly for the procedure, so you don't have to go to it immediately and make work for yourself in the final stages if you have a problem. In other words, it is a *limit* and not a *target*. My own preference is to descend down to around 100 feet above, and nudge my way down.

You may obviously go down further if you can see where you're going (that is, you have established visual reference), but this should be at *normal touchdown speed*. It is a good idea to get down quickly enough to allow yourself at least a short time in level flight - ideally, at the circling radius or the visibility limits, especially as the MAP is often past the point from where a safe touchdown can be made. Going down to MDA too soon can be a recipe for disaster, because you will be dragging in for many miles in a low altitude, low speed, high power configuration, with a restricted view due to the unusually high nose attitude. In marginal conditions this can lead to a subtle and unobserved entry into a descent. If you can't see anything by your estimated time of reaching the threshold, you must go around (more technically, if you don't have visual reference at the MAP, start the Missed Approach).

Performance affects the airspace and visibility needed for the manoeuvres required. The most significant factor is speed, and five categories of aircraft have been established for approach purposes.

The speed used is the IAS at the threshold, as mentioned under *Categories*, above. They are directly linked to airspace and obstacle clearance requirements.

Tips: On an ILS (especially with an engine out), remain at the procedure turn exit height until you intercept the glideslope, instead of descending straight away, which gives you more time to settle the needles down. If a DME arc (see below) is part of the approach, there will be an *Intermediate Fix* which allows you to leave the arc and get established inbound to the FAF. Do not descend until you are inside the IF.

Once established inbound, say so ("established inbound").

Note: ICAO defines "established on course" as being within half full-scale deflection for an ILS or VOR/TACAN/RNAV/GPS procedure and within $\pm$ 5° of the required bearing for the NDB. This ensures that you stay within protected airspace during an approach. You are not established until you are within these limits.

The next report will be "Outer Marker Inbound" as you pass the FAF at the correct altitude on a non-precision approach, or on the glidepath when using the ILS. This is the start of the Final Approach Segment, which ends at the Missed Approach Point, both described more fully below. Here, you descend to the MDA or DH, depending on the type of approach.

 Follow the cross formed by the two needles - the further down the slope you are, the more you use attitude and not power to keep them in the middle, as long as it doesn't get ridiculous (in a helicopter use the collective).

Once established on the localiser, you need the correct power setting for a descent rate of approximately 387 feet per minute, depending on your aircraft category. Don't forget to reduce power (in a piston) about 1 inch per 1000 feet, because the atmospheric pressure will increase and so will your engine power, which will cause you to go above the glideslope if you do nothing about it. However, you will still need enough over for a slight tendency to ride up on the glideslope near decision height, so you don't head for the ground if you relax the pressure. Get the proper wind correction by making adjustments into wind until the needle stabilises.

Tip: The wind backs and slows down the nearer it gets to the ground, so check your wind corrections!

Watch for 100 feet above the DH and make a call to yourself. If you get visual reference, you can ask for a contact approach, or you may be cleared for a visual approach. When you break out of cloud, keep your drift angle and don't be tempted to point the nose at the runway. RNAV approaches (especially those based on GPS) often have lower minima because the approach can be more aligned with the runway, eliminating the need for circling or visual manoeuvring.

The *decision bar* across the runway lights 1 000 feet back from the threshold is quite useful for estimating your visibility (if there is a moving strobe, or "rabbit", it is at the point where the strobe stops). So, if you can't see the threshold, you can at least try to see the bar, which is a series of white lights across the ones in line with your approach. Use the distance from the markers to gauge how far you can see.

An approach has up to five segments:

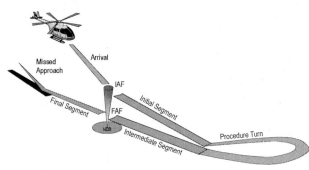

ARRIVAL SEGMENT

Where you transfer from enroute, ending at the *Initial Approach Fix* (IAF - below)

INITIAL SEGMENT

From the IAF to roughly the end of the Procedure Turn (the inbound track), if a FAF is available.

INTERMEDIATE SEGMENT

Preparing for final approach, starting at the end of the initial segment and ending at the *Final Approach Fix* (FAF), which is usually the same beacon as for the IAF (i.e. the Outer Marker). Descent is kept as shallow as possible, as it is where speed and configuration are adjusted, and obstacle clearance reduces in the primary area.

PROCEDURE TURN

This is a reversal mechanism, designed to turn you round 180° in a controlled manner, so you come back in on the same track you went out on. The official definition is *a turn made away from a designated track followed by a turn in the*

opposite direction to intercept and proceed along the reciprocal of the designated track.

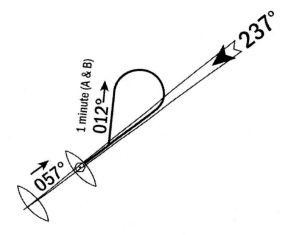

The procedure turn involves timings, based on speeds, that should keep you inside a safe area (from obstacles, that is). The basic one, as above, is to fly outbound for whatever time it says on the chart, turn left 45° (takes 15 seconds at rate 1), fly a straight track for 45 seconds or so (with wind allowance), turn right 180° until you can intercept your original track going the other way. If you got it right, you should be able to intercept it at 30° *without overshooting* (watch out for tailwinds). The turn is designated left or right according to the first turn.

80/260° turns are popular, too, which are more circular:

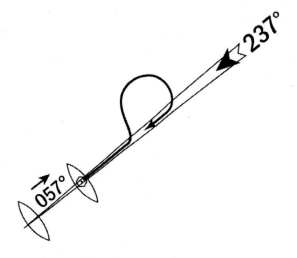

You can normally substitute one kind of turn for the other, unless specifically excluded. However, a specified 80/260 turn is mandatory. Since it occupies less space along the track, you will return to the final approach track around 1 nm closer to the FAF, although this is allowed for if the turn is specified.

BASE TURN

The *base turn* is more or less the same thing, but you turn at the fix:

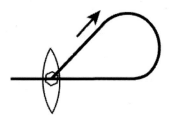

It officially consists of a specified outbound track and timing or DME distance from the facility, followed by a turn to intercept the inbound track where tracks are not reciprocal, or a turn executed during initial approach between the end of the outbound track and the beginning of the intermediate or final approach track.

The turn from the facility is 60° if you go outbound for 1 minute, or 70° if you go outbound for 2 minutes.

A base turn may not be substituted for a procedure turn and *vice versa*.

RACETRACK PROCEDURE

A racetrack procedure is similar to a holding pattern, but used when a reversal procedure is not practical - there may not be enough distance to accommodate the normal loss of altitude, or there may be something in the way that affects the turn. In effect, all you do is establish a hold and extend the outbound leg for 2 or 3 minutes, then turn inbound.

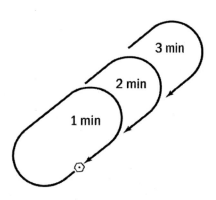

Entry into the racetrack is similar to that of a hold, but on the parallel entry you must intercept the inbound QDM instead of flying direct to the facility having turned inbound, and on the offset entry, the time on the 30° offset track is 1 minute 30 seconds, after which you are expected to a heading parallel to the outbound track for the remainder of the outbound time.

If the outbound time is only 1 minute, the time on the 30° track shall also be 1 minute.

PROFILES

Of course, all this twisting and turning is no good without descending. Here's how an approach might look from the side on a typical approach chart:

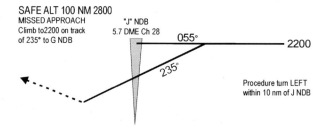

In this case, you have to stay level at 2200 feet outbound (the *platform height*), and remain there until you have completed the procedure turn (that is, within 5° of the inbound track, or intercepted the glideslope, having been cleared for descent). Be aware that sometimes, on an localiser-only approach, ATC will often put you below the platform height, with the resulting confusion, because you have to check your height against distance, and therefore need to start in the right place.

FINAL SEGMENT

This covers alignment and descent for landing, in between the FAF and Missed Approach Point (optimum and maximum distances for the *Final Approach Fix* (FAF) are 5 and 10 nm, respectively). A *Straight-in Approach* (aligned with the runway centreline) are used as much as possible, which means, especially for non-precision approaches, within 30°, otherwise a *Circling Approach* is appropriate.

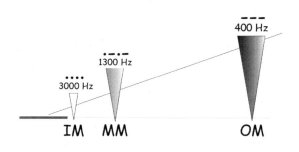

The Marker is a fix or facility (usually a 75 MHz beacon) that allows verification of the glide path/altimeter relationship. In other words, you should be at a certain height when you pass it. The marker performs two functions, as the IAF and FAF.

On reaching the DH or MDH, you must go-around if you do not establish visual reference. If the glidepath goes, it becomes non-precision approach. Remember to apply temperature corrections if it's very cold (see *Air Law*).

DME ARC

Viewed from above, the end result looks more like a polygon than an arc, and the bigger the "arc" is, the easier it is to fly, since it will be flatter. Although obstacle clearance for an arc is 100 feet out to 2.5 nm, it still helps to stay slightly inside the arc, and to use an RMI, but it isn't impossible without one.

The first turn should be made at 90° to the track, making allowance for the wind. That is, you start with an RB of 90° (left or right, as convenient), then allow the RMI needle to stray 5-10° behind. Your DME distance will increase slightly. Then turn enough to bring the needle the same number of degrees ahead of the abeam point, carrying on this way to keep the arc, cross-checking with the DME distance. In theory, with nil wind, you could describe a perfect circle by keeping the RB at 90°, but it almost never happens.

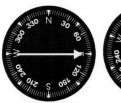  

For example, if you need is a 10d arc, once you have your starting heading, turn by 10° every time the DME ticks up by 0.1d. If it keeps increasing, turn 20° next time, and if it decreases too much, only turn 5°.

When coming off the arc to intercept a radial or bearing, anticipate the movement by about 5° (below about 150 kts, leave yourself ½ nm or so).

If intercepting a localiser, try to have it tuned on the No 1 box, and use the VOR for the lead radials on No 2.

Circling (Visual Manoeuvring)

Circling is visually manoeuvring to a runway or FATO (for helicopters) after an Instrument Approach to another one, or the same one if the approach is not straight in (more than 30° off, in fact). You could also be going to an airfield that is very close to high ground, and to keep the required clearance you arrive at the threshold too high for a proper approach. Minima for this will give the necessary obstacle clearance but, in mountainous areas, account will also be taken of height and effect on turbulence. The circling area is constructed by drawing an arc from *each threshold*, and joining them with tangents. It might be related to aircraft category, speed, wind (25 kts) and bank angle (average 20° or Rate 1, whichever is less). If you have to bank more than 30°, consider setting yourself up again. It also helps to keep a little above the MDA, say 50 feet, but remember you are also below normal circuit height. Since, by definition, the weather is bad (or you wouldn't be using it), set your radios and machine up for the missed approach before you reach MDA, in case you get clag on the downwind leg.

Sectors may be prohibited to avoid significant obstacles.

Circling height will be in the Airway Manual, precalculated to a standard formula; otherwise, just add 300 feet to the highest obstacle within 5 nm of the airfield (provided the result is above 500 feet agl). Descent below MDA/H should not be made until either visual reference can be maintained, you can see the threshold and you can avoid obstacles once in a position to carry out a landing (it is assumed that you keep all these in sight). If you lose visual reference, you must initiate a Missed Approach - make an initial climbing turn toward the landing runway and overhead for the track.

You can get a reasonably accurate circling visibility in metres by multiplying the circuit speed in knots by 20, that is, if speed = 120 knots, visibility must be 2400m. You should not descend below minima until aligned with the runway, except to 500 feet agl on base leg at your discretion if you have the whole of the runway continuously in sight. The minimum MDH and visibility for visual manoeuvring are 250 ft and 800m for helicopters, and as per this table for aeroplanes:

Aircraft Category	A	B	C	D
MDH (ft)	400	500	600	700
Min Met Vis (m)	1500	1600	2400	3600

Approach Charts

Below is a simplified example of a typical approach chart.

At the top is the procedure name - check you're using the right navaid (it sounds silly, but mistakes do happen). Also check the place and the date, which should not only be current, but should also be the same as the one the copilot is using.

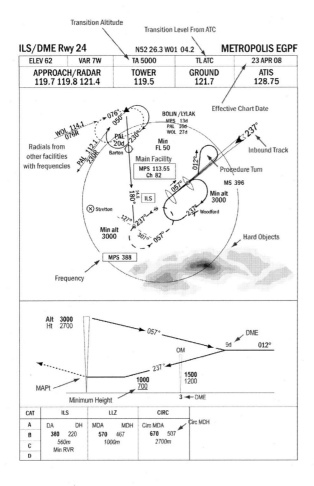

Underneath, in separate boxes, you will find the radio frequencies you will need, starting with ATIS, if there is one, through arrival, tower, ground and departure, loosely in the order they will be used. On the extreme right is the elevation of the field, so you can cross check your altimeter settings. A comparison with the *Touchdown Zone Elevation* will give you an idea of whether you have to cope with an up- or downslope. The next box down, the largest one on the page, is the plan view of the procedure. At its bottom left is the safe altitude for 100 nm around. It is important to note where you are if ATC give you different

routings, particularly if, for example, they give you an extended downwind leg that takes you off the chart.

Underneath the plan view is the side view. Although its size is small, it is arguably the most important one on the chart, since it gives you the heights to be at every stage. Naturally, it should be read in conjunction with the plan. Underneath all that might be a list of the appropriate Decision Heights or Minimum Descent Altitudes, based on the aircraft groups above.

Holding

Holding is a procedure that keeps you more or less in one place if you have to wait for the weather to clear, for example, or for ATC scheduling purposes, or you have something to sort out. Technically, it is *a pre-determined manoeuvre which keeps an aircraft in a specified airspace while awaiting further clearance.*

Note: You are holding because there is a delay in the system, so do not fly around at maximum airspeed burning the precious fuel that you will need in your now extended flight.

Tip: The hold is your friend if you have a problem!

Patterns are usually right-handed racetrack patterns (known as *standard* patterns), but they may occasionally go to the left (*non-standard*) or have a different outbound leg time, which is usually up to 1 or 1½ minutes, depending on your height. In other words, the standard hold should take four minutes (although ICAO don't specify a total time - it's a good exercise for meeting EATs, and it is a matter of professional pride to many pilots to arrive over the holding point precisely on time).

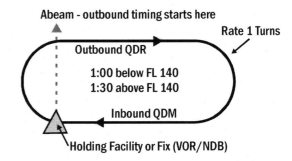

Note: A 1-minute inbound leg is a North American thing.

Tip: During a flight test, the primary goals are to establish and track the QDM, and time the outbound leg properly for one still air minute.

The *Minimum Holding Altitude* (MHA) is the lowest altitude that guarantees signal coverage, communications and obstacle clearance. It is based on a clearance of at least 984 ft above obstacles in the area, and is rounded up to the nearest 50 m or 100 ft. However, over high terrain or in mountainous areas, obstacle clearance up to 600 m (1 969 ft) accommodates the possible effects of turbulence, downdrafts and other phenomena concerning the performance of altimeters.

In a standard holding pattern, the bank angle should be the lesser of 25° or a turn rate of 3° per second (Rate 1), whichever requires the lesser bank (calculate Rate 1 with 10% of your speed +7 kts). This means that your speed should be reduced in the hold, for two reasons. One is that you cannot keep to 25° bank if you are going too fast (over 180 kts), and you need endurance speed anyway to stay there for the maximum economical time. If you cannot conform to a holding pattern, you should inform ATC as soon as possible and request a revised clearance.

Tip: When holding on a VOR, bug the outbound heading, and set the CDI on the inbound QDM. Start turning on station passage (after the flag has moved to FROM), and time the outbound leg when the flag appears after the cone of confusion, or at wings level.

You must fly your headings accurately on the outbound leg, and note the time when passing over the facility at the end, which should be three minutes after the abeam.

This routine should help:

- **Time** - stop the clock - check the timing and restart the time when abeam

- **Turn** - rate 1 to outbound heading

- **Talk** - to ATC

- **Torque** - Descend if appropriate and when cleared

Correcting For Wind

The outbound timing is corrected for wind velocity to keep you inside the primary holding area, especially when there is only an NDB available with which to fix your position. In the UK, at least, it should take you 3 minutes from the abeam position to the overhead.

You adjust the *outbound* leg for wind direction and speed so, if the inbound leg is into wind, you cut the outbound short by whatever amount is appropriate (usually 1 second per knot), plus double the drift correction you would use inbound. If the inbound leg has a tailwind, you add a few seconds to the outbound leg.

The reason for the double drift is that you only have the one leg to make the correction on - if you were simply

flying the track inbound with no correction, you would have to apply three times the drift to take account of the turns, but this takes your outbound heading closer to the wind vector, which will affect your groundspeed, so double drift is normally used (treble drift would also involve drift angles over 45°, which is not recommended).

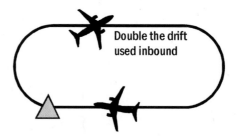

Double the drift used inbound

Even then you will be inside the normal path as you start going outbound, and outside it as you finish, with the wind from the left, so expect the relative bearing to be up to 45° just before you start to turn inbound (it's normally 30°). One suggestion is 3 x drift if the wind is compressing your hold, and 2 x drift if the wind is expanding your hold.

For timing, a good rule of thumb with an inbound headwind is to subtract 1/3 of the time inbound from the outbound leg. Otherwise, add 1/3. Another one is to reduce outbound time by one second for every knot of headwind - 10 kts would give you 50 seconds (by now, the wind has taken you past the abeam point anyway). Yet another is that if it takes 45 seconds from the overhead to the abeam position, take a further 45 seconds for the bit between the abeam position to end of the outbound leg.

Rough Guide: Use either 0°, 5° in light winds, 10-15° in moderate breezes or 20-30° in strong winds. If it gets to howling gale or storm force then just be glad you got back over the aid in time!

As a reminder, the outbound timing below FL 140 is 1 still air minute.

In addition to starting the timing when abeam the fix (or wings level, if the abeam point cannot be determined), it's a good idea to note the timing from wings level inbound as well, so you get a better idea of how to adjust the outbound. Another good clue as to how the outbound leg is doing is to keep an eye on the relative bearing of the beacon - it should be around 30° from behind if you are anywhere near the correct position (known as the Gate).

If you are inside the hold, the tail of the ADF needle will be at the 30° point ahead of time, so correct to that heading (fly the gate) until the end of the outbound leg time, then turn inbound (you might expect to use a lesser rate of turn). For example, if your outbound QDR is 274 your gate in still wind will be 124 (304). If you reach your gate at 50 seconds, fly 304 for 10 seconds.

If the reading is more than 30°, you are too wide or too slow and can expect to increase the rate of turn to recover your timing. If all is going well during the turn inbound, 30° after turning (say at 60° to go), you should be within 10° of the QDM. Also, carry out 90°, 60° and 30° checks on the turn inbound - at 90 to go you should see +5 of the QDM, with 60 to go you should see the QDM, and with 30 to go, -5 of the QDM. If you don't see those figures, you need to roll out early if you are tight or keep rolling if you are wide.

DME Holds

DME holds are actually between two distances - the inbound fix is at the smaller one, and you start turning inbound when you reach the larger (that is, the outbound leg terminates as soon as you get to the limiting DME distance). They are more often than not given to turbine aircraft, with the leg length given with the clearance.

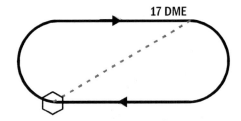

17 DME

Entering The Hold

There are 3 ways of doing this, *direct*, *parallel* and *offset* (or *teardrop*), all according to the *magnetic heading* you are using when you approach the facility. Which you use depends on the direction the fix is approached from, and where the inbound heading of the hold lies. Within 5° of two, you can use either. The almost vertical line in the diagram below is actually offset by 20° from North. Using the correct entry procedure (and speed) keeps you in the safe area. A 6-second delay is assumed between reaching the fix and initiating the entry.

The sectors concerned are created by extending the QDM through the facility and drawing a line at 70° through it (subtract 70° from the QDM for a right hand hold, and add 70° for a left hand hold). A non-standard hold simply has all the entry sectors reversed.

DIRECT

Approaching from **Area 3**, adopt the pattern straight away, delaying the turn onto the outbound heading by 10-15 seconds so as not to be too close to the beacon if you are approaching from across or outside the pattern.

Note: As you can be anything up to 110° off the QDM on arrival at the fix, considerable errors can creep in. You will need to make adjustments to the normal holding procedure if you cross the fix displaced from the QDM by more than 30°.

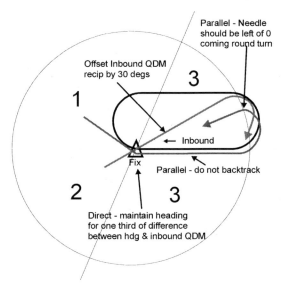

For example, from the non-holding side (lower part of Area 3 above), if you arrive at the fix displaced by more than 30° from the hold QDM, you must maintain the heading for 5 seconds for each 30° of displacement before turning to the outbound heading. If you were approaching at 90° to the QDM, you would wait for 15 seconds. On the holding side (upper part of Area 3), you initially fly outside the pattern, stopping the turn at 90° to the QDM for the same 5 seconds for each 30° of displacement, so if your inbound heading is 210°, you would use 10 seconds.

PARALLEL

From **Area 1**, the parallel entry requires you to go overhead the fix, fly parallel to the inbound QDM a short distance away (that is, going the wrong way, and *not* backtracking) for 1 still air minute, then make a turn into the holding side to fly directly to the fix (if you were a perfectionist, you might turn a little more to the left and intercept the proper inbound QDM, making the subsequent hold more accurate for a better idea of your timing). You may want to start timing at wings level to get a reasonable separation from the beacon before turning back. After that, make all turns to the right.

OFFSET

An approach from **Area 2** requires the *offset* (or *teardrop*) entry. In this case, after the fix, turn to an angle which is 30° less than the QDR on the holding side. Continue across the hold for 1 still air minute until you're in the area of a normal turn in, then turn right to join the inbound QDM.

A quick method of figuring it out is to superimpose the pattern on the compass card and place your thumb under the right side to move it upwards 20° for a standard (right hand) pattern. In the above case (on the right), you are approaching the hold from the North, and the hold's inbound heading (relative to your current heading) is in the parallel entry sector. If the hold's inbound track was 090°, you would enter direct.

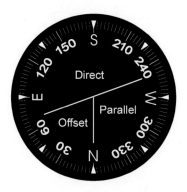

The VOR

The only real difference is what happens at the overhead, which is difficult to assess because of the cone of confusion. At the heights normally used by helicopters, this should last for about 10-15 seconds, so you should assess station passage as being 5-7 seconds after the OFF flag appears.

Leaving The Hold

When given the hold in the first place, you will also be given a time at which you can expect to leave it, in case your radio fails, and the aim is to adjust the patterns to leave the holding fix as near as possible to it. In fact, the holding clearance will include that to the fix itself, the direction to hold from it, the inbound track, DME distances (if holding over one), the altitude or flight level to be maintained and the time to *Expect Further Clearance* or *Expect Approach Clearance*.

If you are proceeding nicely through an approach, but do not receive further clearances when expected, hold on the inbound track at the point you are cleared to until the clearance time, all turns to the right unless published otherwise. If you cannot get in touch with ATC, carry out the appropriate communications failure procedures (squawk 7600, etc.) in the *Communications* chapter.

Some holds are on the charts, and therefore "published". If you are cleared to depart one at a particular time, you can either go there and hold till that time, reduce speed to make the departure time, or use a combination of both.

RUNWAY VISUAL RANGE

Approaches are governed by RVR, which is the maximum horizontal distance that can be seen from pilot's eye level at a typical touchdown on the centreline. It is measured automatically by a *transmissometer*, and there should be one at the start of the runway (A) and one at mid-point (B). The idea behind RVR is to provide consistency in the reporting of visibility where runways are concerned.

RVR can be compared against ground visibility as follows:

Ground Visibility	RVR
1 mile	5000 feet
¾ mile	4000 feet
½ mile	2600 feet
¼ mile	1400 feet

APPROACH BAN

There is an approach ban (meaning that you can't go past the outer marker or final approach fix - see 602.12) when the RVR values are less than:

RVR*	Helicopters
A only	1200
A/B	1200/0
B only	1200

However, the ban does not apply if the RVR changes once you have passed the FAF on final approach, or you are on a training flight and a missed approach will be initiated at or above DH/MDA, or you are on a Cat III approach. In addition, if the RVR is fluctuating rapidly *above* and below the minimum, or is below it due to a localised phenomena with ground visibility above ¼ m.

In short, you can make an approach if:

- the lowest reported RVR is at or above minima

- is fluctuating rapidly *above* and below it and the ground visibility is reported above ¼ m, regardless of RVR

- RVR is unreported or unavailable

- you are on a training flight, planning for a missed approach.

A Cat III approach (602.120) must not be continued beyond the outer marker (or equivalent) unless the RVR is at or above the minima in the CAP.

Landings - 602.128

Maximum descent on final approach after passing the FAF is 6.5%.

When the weather is bad, and the lighting fairly flat, the runway could be subject to certain optical illusions:

Problem	Illusion	Risk
Downslope	Too low	High approach
Upslope	Too high	Low approach
Rain	Closer	Low approach
Narrow	Too high	Low approach
Wide	Too low	High approach & flare
Bright lights	Too low	High approach

In rain, a hilltop half a mile away can look 250 feet lower when viewed through water drops on the windscreen which, if you will remember the discussion on airflow in *Principles of Flight*, will not blow away because of the boundary layer. Using a water repellent is best. It's bad enough coming up to an airfield VFR in such conditions when your eyes are used to the gloom, but there's a short time between breaking out and adjusting your vision for the clues you need. The danger lies in fitting the aircraft attitude to what you expect to see, and end up in an unusual attitude very close to the ground - one reason why airlines use the autopilot for as long as possible. Helicopters, in particular, suffer from this, when the landing site appears in the bottom of the windscreen when the nose is up, and you think you are too high.

Without proper visual reference, approaches may not continue below Decision Height or Minimum Descent Altitude. Any part of the runway or aids associated with it (such as lights) that allow you to judge your position and speed relative to the normal flight path is called the

Required Visual Reference. You should, therefore, be able to see certain items at minimums, to include the runway, its markings, approach or centreline lights, VASIS, etc. If you don't get the required visual reference at the correct point in an approach, you must go around.

Alternate Aerodromes - 602.122

Unless otherwise authorized under an AOC, you must nominate a suitable alternative destination in your IFR flight plan or itinerary, with the ceiling and visibility at or above the minima in the Canada Air Pilot *at the ETA*. This ensures you can land somewhere if your original destination becomes unavailable - as mentioned before, no professional expects to land from any approach. If your departure point is below landing minima, you might also need a departure alternate.

To increase your chances of actually getting in somewhere, alternate minima are higher than for destinations for flight planning purposes, but normal figures apply once you have to use it (the reason why they are higher is that the conditions at your destination would have to be pretty bad to need an alternate for weather reasons, and weather that bad spreads a long way).

However, an airfield can only be nominated as an alternate if it meets certain minima. The standard if there are two precision aids available (straight in to separate runways) is the greater of a 400-foot ceiling and 1 mile visibility (400-1), or 200 - ½ above the lowest usable HAT and visibility, assuming a TAF is available. The HAT is the figure in brackets after the DH/MDA on an approach chart (see below). Where one precision approach is available, it's 600-2 or 300-1 above the HAT and vis, and for a non-precision approach, it's 800-2 or 300-1 above the HAT/HAA and vis (the HAA applies to circling).

600-2 and 800-2 are *standard minima*, but if they are the highest, you can use a *sliding scale*, meaning that 700-1½ or 800-1 are the equivalent of 600-2, and 900-1½ or 1000-1 are the equivalent of 800-2. Although the rules do not specifically say they don't apply to helicopters, their use of a sliding scale is limited anyway because they can use half the CAP visibility values (but not less than one mile).

Check the TAF for the time you will arrive, looking for the keywords, BECMG, PROB and TEMPO:

- *BECMG*. When conditions are getting better, use the end of the time period as a reference. When they are getting worse, use the beginning (in other words, take the better part of the period). In neither case should minima go below requirements for the aerodrome.

- *TEMPO*. Should not be below the (higher) alternate minima.

- *PROB*. Should not be below normal landing minima.

Anything in those times below minima scrubs the aerodrome as an alternate. With no IFR approach, the forecast weather must be at least 500' above a minimum IFR altitude allowing a VFR approach and landing. If a TAF is not available, the forecast weather must be at least 500 feet above the lowest usable HAT/HAA with visibility at least 3 miles when an aerodrome advisory is used. If you're relying on a GFA, the lowest weather goes up to 1000 feet and there must be no cu-nim around (the vis is still 3 miles).

The HAT and HAA are used to calculate the ceiling. As mentioned, look for the figures in brackets after the DH:

```
3500   (321)  1
```

Since ceiling values come in 100-foot increments, you need to round down if the extra is below 20, and up otherwise - in the case above, you would call it (400). To get the forecast ceiling, subtract the airfield elevation from that reported in the GFA, or whatever, in which all heights are ASL.

The last figure is the *advisory visibility* - meaning that, in this case, with a cloudbase of 400 feet, you should have a "reasonable expectation" of getting in from up to a mile away (this also means that it's a good idea to try and get down to MDA before that figure to give you the best chance of landing at normal speed).

So, when calculating the figures, add your 300-1 to get 621, or 700 feet and 2. Thus, this particular airfield would be legal for an alternate with a precision approach, but not with a non-precision approach.

Missed Approach

There are three phases to one of these, as well:

- *Initial* - from the MAP to where climb is established.

- *Intermediate* - from the start of the climb until 50 m obstacle clearance (track may be changed by no more than 50°).

- *Final* - from the 50m point to where a new approach or return to enroute can be initiated.

The Missed Approach is assumed to be initiated above (or not lower than) DH or MDH. Sometimes, it is a fix or specified point, which is useful for timing purposes.

A missed approach must be initiated if you don't see the ground by the time you either reach DH/MDH or the MAP, whichever is earlier, or you might hit something. It is quite an urgent procedure - you have just tried to get as close to the ground as the height of a small apartment block, which is a pretty fine tolerance, given the velocities involved, and you don't want to be there if you can't see where you're going, so the routine is to add full power, then get the gear up, if you have it. Remember the attitude, add the power and the performance will be there.

If no instructions have been received from ATC, follow the published ones. If you still don't get any by the time you reach the Missed Approach Holding Fix, hold there in a standard pattern on the inbound track. If you have to leave the circling procedure, one suggestion is to go to the centre of the airport, and follow the procedure for the approach you just did as closely as possible. The Missed Approach Procedure starts at the *Missed Approach Point*. The initial section (of the Missed Approach) ends when established in the climb.

CVFR

Controlled VFR clearance is obtained by VFR aircraft before entering Class B airspace, after which they behave in all respects the same as IFR ones, except to IFR weather, which they must avoid, if necessary by leaving the airspace by direction or descent.

Routes in Uncontrolled Airspace

IFR and night VFR flights must be done on air routes, unless otherwise allowed under CASS. Except when taking off or landing, or being radar-vectored by ATC, you must always be at or above the MOCA on an airway or air route, and the minimum altitude where an IFR chart is relevant (you may not fly passengers in a multi-engined aircraft under IFR or VFR at night unless its weight allows you to maintain MOCA with one engine out).

Multi Crew

Essentially, the PF (*Pilot Flying*) stays on instruments down to minima, and shouts something like DECIDE when appropriate (depends on Company SOPs). If the PM (*Pilot Monitoring*) says GO AROUND, the PF stays on instruments and does the go around. If not (that is, the response is "Visual, I have control"), the PF hands over to let the PM do the landing (although the PNF can take control at any time on getting the visual reference). The duties should be assigned by the PIC, but many let the P2 do the approach and landing, so they can keep an overview and monitor the process. However, transitioning from instruments to visual at a critical point of the flight is not necessarily a good idea when the weather is really bad - handing over to someone who has had their head out of the cockpit at least a bit of the time is a better choice, particularly as there will be no-one on instruments if you have to go back into the soup. Letting one pilot do it all is best when the break is relatively high.

TAKE-OFF BRIEFING

There must be a clear division of responsibilities between handling and non-handling pilots, with special emphasis on the monitoring role of the latter, bringing to the former's attention any significant deviations. As said elsewhere, every commander has a training role, to help the P2 gain experience; the P2 is trained to handle emergencies, and good CRM allows you to make use of that ability so you can keep command; in other words, don't automatically take over in an emergency, but keep the big picture- use the P2 as an autopilot. In general, the PM should select and identify aids, make radio calls, look out for other aircraft and the visual reference for landing, call deviations and heights on finals, loudly and clearly enough for the PF to hear them, until at least after climb power has been set.

THE MACHMETER
· ·
Aircraft push waves ahead of them, which bunch up as the speed of sound is reached into a *Mach Wave* (named after Ernst Mach). Mach numbers (designated with the letter *M*) have no units, but denote a ratio between two speeds, namely TAS compared to the local speed of sound, as seen with this formula:

$$M = \frac{TAS}{S}$$

where S is the local speed of sound (Mach 1) which, luckily, varies only with temperature (pressure and density cancel themselves out). It is found thus:

$$S = 38.94 \times \sqrt{°Kelvin}$$

The result is in knots, and to get Kelvin, add 273 to the Centigrade. In other words, the speed of sound is proportional to the square root of the absolute temperature, so height doesn't have much to do with it.

For example, at MSL in ISA, it will be 661.32 kts. It is the same at FL100 if the OAT is 15°C.

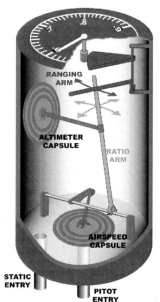

One problem is that the airspeed around the aircraft varies, so you will get different local Mach numbers. We are interested in the *Free-Stream Mach Number*, which is assumed to be at a point in the flow far enough away to be unaffected by the aircraft, and is found with the formula above. M_{CRIT} is discussed under *High Speed Flight*. The *Critical Drag Rise Mach Number* is the speed at which there is a significant rise in drag from the formation of shockwaves, also called the *Drag Divergence Mach Number*. The *Detachment Mach Number* (M_{DET}) is where the bow shockwave attaches to the leading edge, above which there is only a small movement with an increase in speed (and above which all local Mach numbers are supersonic).

Dynamic pressure is measured by an airspeed capsule inside the machmeter, while the static pressure is measured by an aneroid capsule. They are at right angles to each other and a complex linkage detects their movement ratios. In other words, an ASI and an altimeter (in the same casing) feed their movements to a *main shaft*, which is connected to a *ratio arm*, then a *ranging arm*, to the *indicator* (rat ran in). When altitude decreases, the ratio arm slides to the end of the ranging arm, which reduces the ASI's involvement in the whole affair. As you go higher, it slides to the root, giving it more influence. Thus, the Mach number is found by dividing the dynamic pressure by the static pressure - *there are no temperature sensors*.

In the climb, speed of sound decreases because the temperature does, so you must reduce TAS to keep the Mach Number constant. A climb at constant IAS means an increasing TAS and a decreasing speed of sound (from the temperature), so TAS and Mach No will increase.

On the whizzwheel (flight computer), if you set the *Mach Index* opposite the temperature, you can read the speed of sound directly against the inner scale 1.0. In the picture on the right, the Index (a double-headed arrow) is in a window at the bottom. TAS 280 corresponds to a Mach No of 0.424.

If you set the PA against CAS, the Mach number is in the appropriate window.

You can go the other way and find the TAS from the OAT and Mach number. The formula is simply:

```
TAS = S X Mach No
```

You need the temperature to find S first (see above). On the computer, line up the Mach Index with the OAT in the TAS window and look for the TAS on the outer scale opposite the Mach No.

Be aware that the Mach index on CR computers (as shown) is designed to work with *indicated* temperature.

Errors

The machmeter does not suffer from density error because it cancels out on both sides of the equation, but it is prone to instrument and pressure errors (which are actually very small, so indicated Mach number is taken as the true Mach number. If the pitot source becomes blocked, the Machmeter shows the same errors as an ASI. The Mach Number will remain unchanged until static pressure changes in a climb or descent. In a climb, the airspeed capsule will have excess static pressure, so will cause the instrument to overread (and under-read in a descent).

Blocked static sources mean that excess static pressure is trapped in the *case* and cause the instrument to under-read (in a descent it will overread). If the static line fractures inside the pressure hull, static pressure will be too high and it will under-read. Likewise, if the pitot line leaks, the instrument will under read.

Remember the sequence *ERTM* - if the Mach number remains constant with altitude (the last letter), the other speeds reduce, with *Equivalent* (E), *Rectified* (R) and *True* (T) airspeeds reducing most, in that order.

At high speeds, temperature will become artificially increased at speeds above about 300 kts, because of compressibility (this is already accounted for in the CR flight computer, so don't add any figures again from charts or tables).

RADIO NAVIGATION

5

The other relevance of AC as used in aircraft is that it is the basis of radio waves, which we use to convey information. The sound of a rotor blade slap from 1100 feet away will take one second to reach your ears, but air travelling at that speed would be ten times more powerful than a hurricane, so the sound you hear is not *in* the air - rather the sound changes the characteristics of the air instead. The effect is rather like the example of electrons moving down a cable given in the previous section. One pushed in at one end affects the others in line until one falls out at the other end, so it is easier to imagine a wave of compression pushing air particles in front of it before it affects your eardrums. If this is done too slowly, though, the air particles have a chance to get out of the way, so the effect is not noticeable below a certain rate of vibration, or *frequency*. In vibrating, the sound waves also move up and down. This depth of travel from peak to trough over a complete cycle is the *amplitude*, or the volume.

However, a sound wave will still only travel so far by itself, which is why it needs help, in the shape of a *carrier wave*, to move over longer distances. The carrier wave is created at radio frequency (the RF carrier), and a sound wave (the AF signal) is piggy-backed on to it, so that an electronic copy of the original signal is made. The two signals are then decoded at the receiving end - a radio receiver is a device for splitting up the two waves and amplifying the result, since the signal when it hits the aerial is quite weak (if you could actually transmit a sound wave, it would be so long that huge aerials and extremely large coils and capacitors would be needed to do the job).

The information to be sent *modulates* (i.e. varies) the carrier wave through *amplitude* (power) or *frequency*. The former is typically used in aviation:

and the latter by FM music stations (*frequency modulation*), but many customers, such as forestry, also use it for communications.

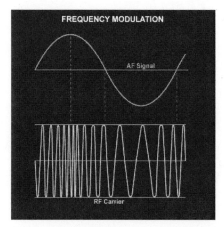

Note: Although Marconi transmitted the first CW signal, a Canadian, Reginald Fessenden, transmitted the first *voice* signal from Massachusetts to ships along the Eastern Seaboard. Mind you, Nikola Tesla was ahead of them both - Marconi did what he did with 17 of Tesla's patents.

Anyhow, a *modulator's* job is to combine the signals from the radio and audio amplifiers:

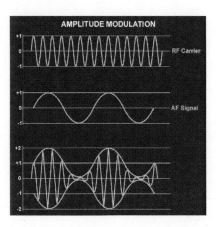

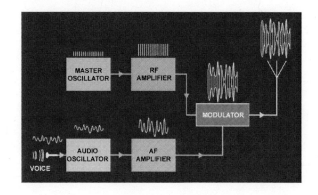

A *demodulator* will reverse the process at the other end - a device that performs both functions is called a *modem*.

There will be an RF amplifier at the end of the receiving aerial that produces a stronger copy of the signal that was sent out from the transmitter. This is fed into a detector that produces a feeble copy of what originally went into the audio amplifier (from the microphone), then into an audio amplifier for a quick boost before an exact copy of the original speech comes out of the loudspeaker.

The simplest method of transmitting information is to turn a signal on and off in a recognisable code, as used by older NDBs which break the signal in a pattern matching the Morse Code ID of the station, called *Wireless Telegraphy*, or *continuous wave* (CW).

Otherwise, to impose information on a signal, you can adjust the amplitude, the frequency, or the phase, if the frequency of both waves is the same.

HOW IT ALL WORKS
. . . .

Way back when, Maxwell discovered that a changing magnetic field produces an electric field, and *vice versa*, but Faraday had to ask him to put his calculations into language a layman could understand! Hertz later produced a circuit in which a pulse from an induction coil charged a capacitor until its insulation broke down and produced a spark. The spark was recreated in a receiving loop of wire that had a gap in it, placed not too far away.

If you put a capacitor and inductor in series with a resistor and an AC supply, the current will oscillate at a *resonant frequency* although, in practice, frequencies near the resonant one will be affected as well, so the circuit will be sensitive to a *range* of frequencies.

Referring back to *Electricity & Magnetism*, a coil and capacitor in parallel behave like a flywheel and a spring. When a capacitor is charged, it is storing electrical energy, as we know. When it discharges through the coil, and the magnetic field collapses, an emf is induced, which tends to keep things flowing in the same direction, to charge the capacitor up the other way. Then it discharges again and the process continues in a repeating cycle until all the energy is transformed into heat and electromagnetic waves, so to maintain the pace you must feed energy into the circuit at appropriate points in the cycle.

This tuned circuit is connected to an aerial and earth, and the capacitor is adjusted until the resonant frequency of the circuit matches the frequency of the signal. As there is

now a maximum impedance to that frequency, a large voltage (at that frequency) is produced across the circuit.

Sidebands

When you combine two AM signals, they naturally occupy more space, or take up a larger bandwidth*. When a carrier is modified by a frequency lower than itself, the boundaries of the total band are effectively two extra frequencies, being the equivalent of the *sum* and *difference* frequencies of the carrier and the modulator, so you get three in total, namely the carrier *plus* the audio and the carrier *minus* the audio. The extras are called *upper* and *lower sidebands*, which are exact mirrors of each other, in terms of power and information carried:

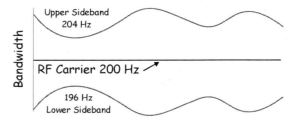

An FM signal has many sidebands and therefore needs more bandwidth.

A neat trick is that you can remove the carrier and eliminate a sideband, or transmit one sideband only, adding what was taken away *at the receiver*, which means you don't need so much power to transmit (for the same distance), and the signal doesn't take up so much space, so you get more channels with which to work. In effect, you can transmit with *narrower bandwidths*. This is *Single Sideband Transmission*, or SSB. Traditionally, the upper sideband is used above 10 KHz, and the lower one below.

BANDWIDTH

*Like a road, whatever you transmit over must be "wide" enough to carry the traffic you intend to send over it. The "width" of any signal is known as its *bandwidth*, but a transmission medium will also have a bandwidth, and here, the term is twisted slightly to mean the width it is *able to provide*, rather than the *width it occupies*. The aim, when matching signals to media, is to ensure that the signal bandwidth does not exceed that of the intended link, or that your car is not too wide for the road. So officially, the bandwidth is the difference between the highest and the lowest range of frequencies that a signal occupies. As an example, 3,000 Hz is a wide enough spread to carry voice information, and if you used it to modify a carrier wave of 3 MHz (3,000,000 Hz), your bandwidth will range from 2,997,000-3,003,000 Hz (the boundaries of the bandwidth being the sum and difference frequencies mentioned above). Unofficially (and more commonly), the term defines the amount of information that can be carried by any media, or signal, (that is, capacity) in a given time. For example, the bandwidth of an FM signal is larger than that of an AM one, which is why FM is only suitable for use at VHF and above where there is stacks of room.

Wavebands

The range of electromagnetic waves is quite large (see right), but radio waves only occupy a small part of it, actually between about 3 KHz to 3,000 GHz. This area is split up by International agreement between the people who wish to use it, and consists of frequency ranges, or bands, that share similar characteristics:

Band	Frequency	Aid	Wavelength
VLF	3-30 KHz		10-100 km
LF	30-300 KHz	NDB, LORAN	1-10 km
MF	300-3,000 KHz	NDB	100-1000 m
HF	3-30 MHz	HF, SSB	10-100 m
VHF	30-300 MHz	VOR, LLZ, VHF	1-10 m
UHF	300-3,000 MHz	DME, SSR, GP, GPS	10-100 cm
SHF	3-30 GHz	AWR, MLS	1-10 cm
EHF	30-300 GHz		1-10 mm

An invisible connection between two points is called a *field* - since radio depends on the interplay of electricity and magnetism, there is an electromagnetic field joining your radio with whatever is transmitting.

A change of one type of field causes a change in another, so if you vary an electric field, it will induce a magnetic field and *vice versa*, which is how an aerial is used to transmit - flip-flop movement of electricity up and down its length creates a magnetic field that forms concentric lines of force around it, at 90° to the electric field (the lines of force, in fact, would look rather like a laminated doughnut if you could see them).

Put another way, the antenna becomes charged with electrons which leak back the other way when the current reduces to zero. This leaking back (or collapsing) creates a magnetic field, so the current and magnetic field will be increasing while the electric field is reducing, reaching their maxima and minima at the same time (see *Antennae*, below). Then the whole process reverses and repeats itself at a frequency of several million times a second.

Around the aerial, the emf and current are never in step, because the electric field appears a quarter of a cycle before the magnetic field, but about a quarter of a mile later they align themselves properly, and grow and collapse together. The trick in the first place is to flip-flop the electricity so fast along the antenna that it effectively falls off the end and keeps on going, which doesn't happen below a certain frequency anyway. Because the current needs to lag behind the emf, you need a coil in the transmitting circuit to stop things starting and stopping too suddenly. The capacitor will now take a fraction of a second before it starts to discharge, creating the disparity.

Although the transmitted power remains constant, some energy is absorbed by the Earth and the ionosphere. Land absorbs 3 times as much as the sea does, and the rate of absorption *increases* with an increase in frequency. With the ionosphere, the absorption rate *decreases* with an increase in frequency.

The remaining energy has to spread itself over a wider area, so the signal gets weaker (attenuates) with distance away from the transmitter (plus coastal refraction and diffraction). The circumference of the wave front increases as the wave spreads, reducing the amount of energy per unit of length. The power of the transmitted signal fades in an *inverse square relationship*, meaning that a signal 2 nm from its source will have a quarter of the strength of one only 1 nm away. Put another way, you need 4 times the power to double the range of transmission

Radio waves generally take the scenic Great Circle route, which means that they travel in a straight line (see *Navigation*) but may have their direction changed through:

- **Refraction**, which is the *bending* of a wave, typically inside the ionosphere (discussed under *Sky Waves*)

- **Reflection**, from a flat surface such as the Earth or the ionosphere, like light off a mirror, but after reflection, a phase shift will occur, which will depend on the angle at which the surface was struck, and the wave polarisation, discussed below

- **Diffraction**, around corners or following the curvature of the Earth, which can extend ranges beyond the horizon (line of sight

Cosmic Rays	
Gamma Rays	
X Rays	
UV	Light Waves
Visible Light	
IR	
Radar	
FM	Radio Waves
TV	
AM	

GROUND (SURFACE) WAVES

Ground waves are associated with LF/MF waves, and may go directly to their destination (close to the ground), or curve to follow the Earth's surface, depending on the frequency, although friction with the ground and the widening circumference of the wave will eventually weaken their power, cause them to curve downwards and eventually be absorbed by the ground.

The rate of attenuation of a surface wave is around 3 times greater over land than it is over the sea. Typical figures for maximum range are 100 and 300 nm respectively, with high power transmitters. Ground waves are sometimes called *Surface Waves*, and their following of the Earth's curvature is caused by *diffraction*. The lower the frequency, the more it has an effect, and the better the bending.

A *ground-reflected wave* is actually a direct wave (below) that hits the ground first.

DIRECT WAVES

These are contained within the troposphere, and are otherwise known as *tropospheric waves*. They are also *line-of-sight*, meaning that anything in the way, like hills or buildings, will have a detrimental effect (direct waves will not bounce like those used with HF, below).

They are associated with VHF and above, and you will get best reception if the transmitter and receiver are in sight of each other, but, in practice, you can expect a little more than that, actually to just beyond the horizon, due to effects like refraction and diffraction (the calculations are in the *VOR* section). The actual figure is greater by a factor of around 4/3. Air-ground transmissions are limited to 25 nm in the UK, up to 4,000 feet for tower frequencies and 10,000 feet for approach.

SKY WAVES

A *space wave* may leave the antenna at an upward angle, or be bounced off the ground. Otherwise it will be a *sky wave* when headed for the ionosphere, where it might be refracted downwards again, if the angle is right, and reach further distances (on HF).

THE IONOSPHERE

This is a region where the Sun's UV rays dislodge electrons from the gas molecules, making them positively ionized (and therefore charged) and creating several conductive layers a couple of miles thick around the Earth, starting about 60 miles up, but lower during the day, and varying with the seasons (they are not spheres, but change their shape constantly).

The ionisation makes the gases (nitrogen and oxygen) conductive, like a fluorescent light. The nitrogen is ionised at the higher levels - lower down it is the oxygen. This happens mostly during daytime and is at its minimum just before sunrise. In other words, air is a good insulator in the lower parts of the atmosphere, but ionisation makes it more conductive as you go up. *Recombination* is the process where electrons and atoms get back together again, starting during late afternoon and early evening, and continuing overnight.

The ionosphere depends directly on the Sun's radiation, so the way the Earth moves around the Sun affects the ionosphere's characteristics (the angle of elevation of the Sun changes frequently, which accounts for variations in its height and thickness). Some of these changes are predictable, and some are not, but all of them affect the propagation of radio waves.

The regular variations can be 27-day, daily and 11-yearly (from sunspots), but the daily ones have most effect on aviation operations. As the atmosphere is bombarded by waves with different frequencies, they produce 4 cloud-like layers of electrically charged gas atoms, between 50-300 km above the Earth, called the D, E (Heaviside), F1 and F2 layers (Appleton).

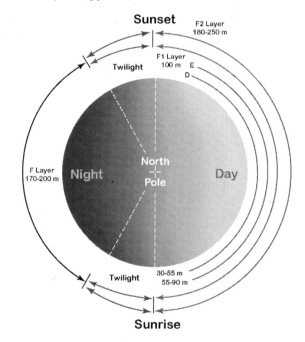

The first was discovered by James Van Allen in 1957, hence its naming as the Van Allen belt. UV rays with higher frequencies can penetrate deeper into the atmosphere so they create the lowest ionised layers.

- The **D layer** sits between 50-100 km high *during the day*. Ionisation is low because fewer UV waves penetrate to this level. The D layer refracts VLF, as long as large antennae and high power transmitters are used, but it absorbs LF and MF waves, so the range during daytime is about 200 miles

- The **E layer** is higher, between 100-150 km, and almost disappears by midnight. It allows medium-range communication on LF and HF bands

- In daylight, the **F layer** splits into the **F1** and **F2 layers**. It is responsible for most HF long-distance communication. During maximum sunspot activity, F layer atoms can stay ionised all night. For horizontal waves, the single-hop capability can be up to 3000 miles, and more with multiple hops

REFRACTION

Anyhow, any wave that hits the ionosphere is bent, as the side of the wave that hits one of the layers of the ionosphere first starts to speed up (because of the reduced dielectric constant from ionisation), which makes it turn. The effect is similar to that of light refraction in water which makes an object appear to be displaced.

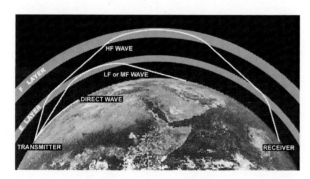

Eventually, if the angle is increased, the bending will be enough to bounce the wave back to Earth (we won't get into Moon bouncing here!) The angle at which this first happens is called the *critical angle.*, which is the smallest angle that will allow a wave to be refracted and still return to Earth. Any rays more vertical than this angle are called *escape rays*. The *critical frequency* depends on the density of the layer concerned. If a wave passes through a layer, it can still be refracted from a higher layer if its frequency is lower than that layer's critical frequency.

The lower the frequency of a wave, the more rapidly it is refracted, and the larger will be its critical angle, but the less the distance it will travel. A 20 MHz wave will be detected further from the transmitter than a 5 MHz one.

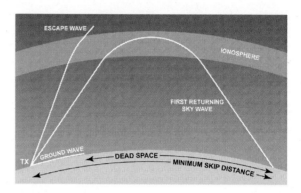

The first wave to reach the ground after being refracted is called the *First Returning Sky Wave*, until the maximum range is reached. When a wave leaves an antenna, the ground wave will be detected until it fades, or attenuates. Between that point, and where the first sky wave comes from the ionosphere, is an area where nothing is heard, a *skip zone*, or *dead space*.

The skip distance is the Earth distance taken by a signal after each refraction, or the distance covered by the first sky wave. 30 MHz signals do not return because they are too high in frequency, being at the bottom of the VHF band (15-25 MHz is more typical for bouncing). You can refract off the ionosphere and back off the ground several times for multiple hops.

Surface and atmospheric attenuation *increase* with frequency, while ionospheric attenuation *decreases*. Ground range increases if critical angle, frequency, dead space and skip distance decrease, and *vice versa*.

Thus, we depend on the ionosphere for all HF contacts beyond the ground-wave zone. It moves all the time, itself being dependent on the intensity of particle and wave emissions from the Sun, so propagation is affected considerably by the ionosphere's movement, which is why the ADF suffers from what is called *night effect* just after sunset and before sunrise when the needle swings erratically (on the other hand, during the night is when you will receive distant stations best). Refraction can occur in many ways, from:

- The **ionosphere** (see above)

- **Coastal effects** (a wave crossing at anything other than a right angle will be bent)

- **Atmospheric conditions** - under certain inversion conditions (mostly in the morning), a phenomenon called *ducting* occurs, which enables VHF/UHF waves to travel unusually large distances because of the ratio of the wavelength to the depth of the inversion

Ducting is exceptional *super-refraction*, which occurs when the trajectory of a radio beam bends towards the earth's surface more than normal, or rather, at such a rate that its elevation change with distance is less than normal. The bending could be strong enough for the beam to bounce off the Earth's surface. When a radar beam is involved, this will increase ground clutter.

VLF signals can travel long distances through a similar process involving the ionospheric layers and a *conduit wave*, which is *reflected* rather than *refracted*.

Generally, HF communication is always possible when the frequency is low enough to be refracted and high enough not to be attenuated. Unfortunately, the only information we have about the above changes are usually derived from statistical sources, such as a monthly mean max usable frequency, and so on.

With HF, frequencies need to be higher during the day or when you are at greater range from the station. At night, you can use lower ones, generally about half (that is, use *Double During Day*), which is something to be aware of when you are operating at a remote base and you use HF to keep in touch with the Operations office. Generally, you might leave the office with a selection of five frequencies you can use depending on the time of day.

The upshot of all this is, if you rely on radio waves for approaches to airfields, you should be aware that they bend at certain times of the day (e.g. dawn/dusk) and over certain terrain, such as mountains, where you could also get *multipath propagation*, as signals are received from many sources and will be out of phase with each other at the antenna. Sometimes, in those circumstances, waves will cancel each other out.

FREQUENCY SELECTION

For successful communication on HF between two points at any given time of the day, there exists a maximum frequency, a lowest frequency and an optimum frequency.

As the level of ionisation is less in the ionosphere by night than it is by day, you have to lower the frequency to obtain the same type of refraction. Luckily, attenuation is reduced at night as well, so this is mitigated slightly. The MUF not only varies with path length and between day and night, but also with the seasons, meteor trails, sunspots, and other cosmic disturbances. This is why HF transmitters have to use a wide range of frequencies between about 2-20 MHz to get through.

OPTIMUM WORKING FREQUENCY

The *optimum* usable frequency, where attenuation is minimum for the range obtained, or where you have the least number of problems, is the best theoretical frequency, being one that brings the skywave back to the receiver. It is the frequency that causes the first returning sky wave to fall just short of the receiving station, so that when it drifts, the station will still pick it up.

This frequency should be high enough to avoid the disadvantages from multipath fading, absorption and noise, but not so high as to be affected by rapid changes in the ionosphere.

It is about 85% of the ....

MAXIMUM USABLE FREQUENCY

This is the point at which refraction is no longer possible.

LOWEST USABLE FREQUENCY

This is the point below which refraction cannot start.

Antennae

An antenna is a conductor (or a group of conductors) that can radiate or collect electromagnetic waves. Looked at another way, it is a device that can convert electrical energy into electromagnetic energy and *vice versa*.

A certain length of straight wire will possess a natural amount of inductance and capacitance, which will correspond to a particular wavelength, since the length of a radiated wave depends on their product. This means that you will be able to receive suitably strong signals on that wavelength without any additional circuitry. However, it is not practical to carry around a range of antennae, so adding a capacitor or coil to the mix will allow you to artificially adjust the natural wavelength of the antenna to suit a variety of circumstances. For example, a normal VHF antenna would be about 15 cm long, but using complex circuitry allows you to electronically shorten it.

There are two basic classifications of antennae, namely *Hertz* (half-wave) and *Marconi* (quarter wave). Hertz types are also known as *dipoles*, and are usually positioned well above ground, radiating horizontally or vertically (see *Polarisation*, below) for frequencies of 2 MHz and above. Marconis are perpendicular to the Earth and have one end grounded to it, used for frequencies below 2 MHz.

It is not essential for a circuit to be in resonance for radiation to take place, but as the radiation is proportional to the flowing current, which is maximum at resonance, the antenna is always practically tuned.

POLARISATION

Electromagnetic radiation is comprised of the E and H fields, which stand for electric and magnetic, respectively. The electric field arises from voltage, and the magnetic one from current. The two act at rightangles to each other.

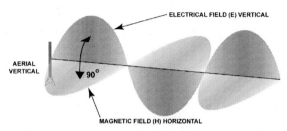

A wave's *polarisation* is noted with reference to the *electrical* field, so a *vertically polarised* wave has a *vertical* electric field, which will come from a vertical aerial (for efficiency, the receiver must have the same orientation). For example, NDBs are vertically polarised, whilst VORs are horizontally polarised. However, a vertical slotted aerial will produce a horizontally polarised wave, and *vice versa*.

In general, polarisation does not change over short distances. However, over long distances, especially at high frequencies, it can be drastically changed.

DIRECTIONALITY (DIRECTIVITY)

A straight antenna will radiate in all directions, but *parasites* (additions to the antenna structure) or shaping (as with radar) can make the wave more directional:

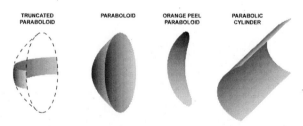

However, some directionality can be achieved with just two dipoles.

One by itself would radiate equally in all directions, but if a second, not fed with power, is placed a quarter of a wavelength away, it behaves like a resonant coupled circuit which has oscillatory currents induced in it. These currents re-radiate, and the quarter-wave spacing causes it to be in such a phasing as to cancel out the original radiation on that side, and to reinforce it on the opposite side, so the second dipole has the same effect as a reflector (see *Radar*), and gives you a marked gain in signal strength in a particular direction. Below is the principle as used with the VOR, described below.

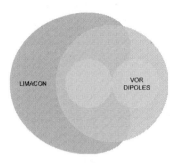

The greater the number of dipoles in an array, the narrower and more intense will be the beam of radiation. For example, N dipoles will take in N times as much RF power as one, if they are not too close to each other.

GAIN

The ratio between the amount of energy propagated in a particular direction and that which would be propagated if the antenna were not directional is called antenna gain.

RECIPROCITY

This is the ability of an antenna to be used for transmitting and receiving.

TRANSMITTING SIGNALS

When an alternating current is applied to one end of a straight antenna, the wave travels to the other end, where it can go no further. This is a point of high impedance, so the wave bounces back towards where it came from. Although there is some loss from resistance, the wave is reinforced at the start point with more energy, which results in continuous oscillations that are sustained with suitably timed impulses. There is also a high voltage at the *start* point, meaning the centre of the wire has minimum voltage. The maximum movement of electrons is also in the centre, so it has a low impedance there. The meeting of these two stresses sets up a standing wave which makes the particles oscillate all the time. Standing waves can be kept going with the minimum expenditure of energy.

The length of the antenna must allow the wave to travel from one end to the other and back within one cycle, and the wavelength is the distance travelled within that cycle.

THE INDUCTOR RADIATOR

We know that oscillating currents can be set up in a simple circuit that contains a coil and a capacitor, and that the oscillations can be kept going with suitable circuitry.

Unfortunately, for every short section of loop in a coil that radiates electromagnetic waves there is another that carries the current in the opposite direction which largely cancels it out, because each turn in the coil goes up one side and down the other. However, the cancellation is not complete, depending on your position relative to the antenna. For example, in this picture of the loop aerial associated with a non-directional beacon, you would receive no net radiation looking at it as you are, directly at the loop.

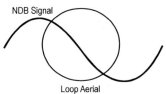

However, if you were to look at the loop from the side, and therefore with one side of the loop closer to you than the other, the difference between the up and down side of the loop is enough to cause waves to radiate in a particular direction if they are alternating fast enough. This works best if the diameter of the coil is half the wavelength because the radiation from both sections pull together, but this method is still not terribly efficient.

THE CAPACITOR RADIATOR

There is a capacitor in an oscillatory circuit, which can be replaced by long wires that can be opened out vertically so that the lines of force can create large loops with current flowing in the same direction in all parts. As there is no return path, those currents cannot be neutralised.

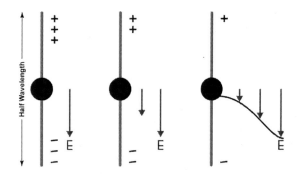

In the picture above, the upper half of the wire has a full positive charge and the lower half an equal negative charge, producing an electric field with a full value. As the charges decrease, the electric field also decreases and the original maximum electrical field is radiated away (the perpendicular magnetic field is not shown for clarity). These are the conditions that alternate continually, causing the wire (antenna) to radiate.

Each half of the wire (antenna) is therefore charged positively and negatively in turn, but the centre is at zero alternating potential - the maxima are reached at the ends, which are always at opposite polarity (except instantaneously twice every cycle when they are at zero).

The relationship between an antenna and the Earth is a capacitative one, with the air between them as a dielectric

Since the simple straight wire possesses inductance and capacitance, and resistance is relatively small, it can be classed as a resonant circuit with its own natural frequency. This arrangement, that is, two wires connected centrally against each other is known as a *dipole*.

RECEIVING SIGNALS

In simple terms, the antenna catches a radio wave and a small electrical current with the same waveform as the incoming signal is induced in it through an electronic tide. In practice a *selection* of frequencies is captured because an antenna is cut for the middle of the frequency band you want (half wavelength is good, but a quarter is often used).

The signal passed on to the radio set after being received is at the *resonant frequency of the antenna*, with a few signals on either side for good measure. This signal is amplified and selectivity improved with a *tuned circuit*, where capacitive reactance cancels out the inductive reactance. Some other signals do get through however, so *filters* eliminate them in later stages. In the end, all radio frequencies will finally be extracted, leaving only a low-level audio signal to be amplified and sent to your headset.

Calculations

Electromagnetic energy travels at a constant speed of 300,000,000 metres per second, abbreviated with the letter C (remember $e = mc^2$?)

In nautical miles, the figure is 161,800.

The distance travelled by a wave at that speed is called the wavelength, or λ for short. Thus:

$$\lambda = \frac{C}{F}$$

F is the frequency. For simplicity, use metres and seconds when playing with the above formula. So, if you wanted to find the wavelength of a wave with a frequency of 300 KHz (the answer is 1000 m):

$$\lambda = \frac{300000000}{300000}$$

VOR

• •

Very High Frequency Omnidirectional Range is a ground-based short range navigational aid that broadcasts on VHF, using the *phase difference* between two signals to signify your direction from the transmitting station as one of 360 radials *from* a station. The frequency range is between 108-112 MHz on even decimals, plus 50 KHz (to prevent confusion with the ILS), and 112-118 on odd and even, plus 50 Khz (in the exam: 108 to 117.95). Receivers with integrated DME normally select the associated Y channel (those with two decimal places) automatically, while stand-alone receivers display X and Y channels separately.

VORs represented on maps have a compass rose round them, aligned with Magnetic North. They are a pain to shut down and realign, which is why a VOR's variation will often be different from its aerodrome.

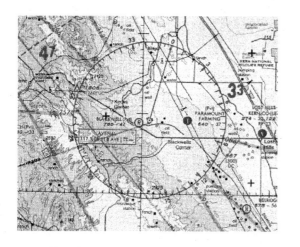

VORs are not sensitive to heading, as is the ADF (below), because they show *track*. A VOR transmits a coded signal that indicates the bearing of the receiver *from* the beacon, which is magnetic, using the variation *at the station*. The bearing is called a *radial*, of which there are 360.

The *Station Identifier* is transmitted in Morse every 15 seconds (4 times a minute), and you must confirm the frequency and ID before using a VOR for navigation. If there is no ID, but behaviour is otherwise normal, the system is on maintenance (you may sometimes hear a Morse test code of ▬ ··· ▬).

The transmitter sends out a 30 Hz FM *reference signal* in all directions, which is received by all stations at the same phase. Rotating around this reference signal is another one whose *amplitude* is varied to produce a polar diagram called a *limacon*, which is similar in shape to the cardioid used by the ADF (below), but without an absolute null point,

rotating electrically at 30 times/second (there is some signal strength at the minimum). This rotating signal will be out of phase with the reference signal by the amount of degrees it has rotated round the circle, so the phase of this signal received in the aircraft depends on its bearing from the station (which is why it's called a *variphase signal*). Both signals are in phase at 0°, or North, 90° out when East, and so on. For each degree moved, the signal changes phase for the same amount, which is how your direction is determined. Because the signal is frequency and amplitude modulated, it is classed as an A9W signal (Doppler VOR has its modulations the other way round).

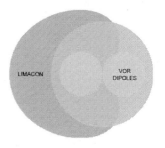

Overhead the beacon, you will be in a *cone of confusion*, the same as you would be with any antenna - this is an area where no signal is received, so the TO/FROM flags disappear and the alarm flag comes up. The ICAO limit for the cone is 100° across, and the width can be worked out by finding the tangent of the angle and multiplying it by your height, to get the answer in feet (FL 360 = 6 nm). During this *station passage*, just ignore the signal or use something else.

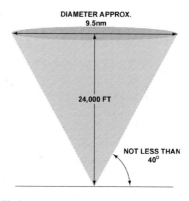

There will also be ambiguities *abeam* the beacon - 90° either side of the selected radial there is a *zone of ambiguity* up to 10° across where the flag will not show at all, and the indications should therefore not be relied upon.

Deep in the bowels of the aircraft will be a large black box, connected to a *remote indicator* in the cockpit, that might also double as an ILS display:

This one has 4 dots plus a circle, so each one is 2°, for an overall width of 10°. For 3 dots plus a circle, each one is 2.5°.

Once you select a radial by turning the *Omni Bearing Selector* (the small knob just under the dial), the *Course Deviation Indicator* (CDI) needle will be in the centre (if you are exactly on the selected radial), or either side of it, up to 10° away, so each dot left or right represents 2°, if there are 5 on your display (2½° with 3). In the picture above, there are 4 small dots on each side and a big one in the middle.

When the needle is in the middle, you will be on the selected radial, which traditionally is *from* the station when on the same side, shown by TO/FROM Flag, which, on later instruments, will be a small white triangle pointing in the relevant direction. If the indicator shows *To*, you are on the *reciprocal*, or on the other side. In the example of the display above, the radial selected is N, or 360°, because the *From* flag is showing (as the needle is two dots left, you are actually on the 004° radial). Thus, when holding *inbound* on the 240 radial, your heading should be 060°. This is a common trap in exam questions (and check rides) - if you are tracking inbound on a radial, set the reciprocal at the top of the display, as radials go *from* a station. All you have to do then is watch the needle - if you are going away from a station on a radial, and the needle is pointing left, then you fly left until it centres.

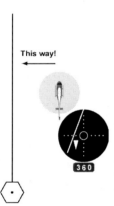

This way!

If you are going to the station, then you fly right. The thing to remember is that the needle always points to *where the radial is*, which has *nothing to do with the heading of the aircraft* (remember this for exams). All you do is follow the needle. In short, the radial is where the needle is, and you do not necessarily turn that way to get to it - sometimes, having the needle on the left means turn right! *Only if your heading is the same direction as the OBS will it be on the correct side.*

As an example, here is a comparison of the HSI against the OBI - you are heading 320°, and both have a setting of 120° *inbound*. Notice how the HSI presents the information clearly, but the OBI says something quite

different - if you had no heading information, you might not realise you were going the wrong way!

For any radial, there are boundaries formed by the CDI and the To/From indicator, creating quadrants around the station (that is, four distinct areas). You will be in one of them. You can therefore take the indications from two VOR stations, draw the lines of position (i.e. bearings) from the compass roses and the intersection point is your position (left). Remember to ensure that the CDI is centred in both cases and the FROM flags are showing. For example, in the picture below, which displays would the pilot see, and in what order, for the helicopter moving from A to B?

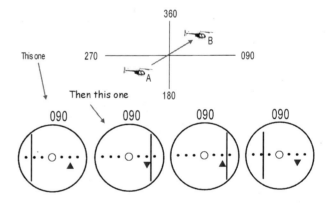

When tracking along an airway, tune and identify the station you are going from, track the selected radial until near the mid-point, then tune and identify the next station. The TO/FROM flag should change over. If you have to use another VOR for a fix as a reporting point along the airway, select the required radial, and when the needle is centred you are over the fix:

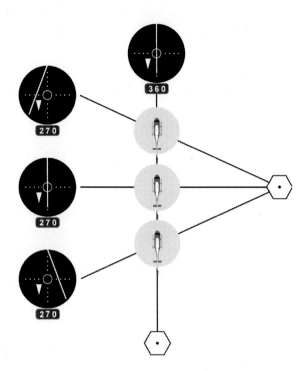

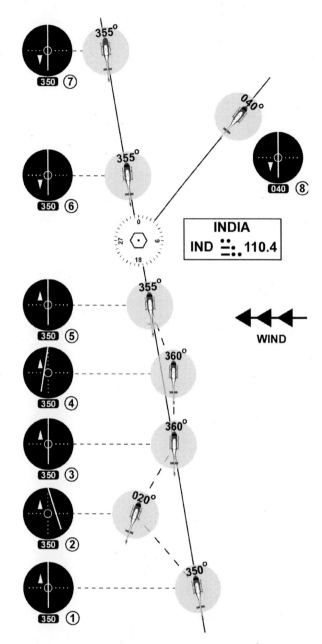

In the exam, you will need to determine whether you have passed a radial or not. In this case, the needle will be to the left if the station is on the left, and *vice versa* if you are not there yet, assuming your heading is the same as the OBS. Otherwise, the needle will point the opposite way if you have already gone past (oops!)

To intercept a radial inbound, tune and identify the VOR station, then select the reciprocal of the desired radial by turning the OBS until you get a TO reading. Fly to whichever side the needle is displaced, turning the shortest way to a heading 90° away from it, until the needle starts to move, at which point reduce the intercept angle to 45° (left). As the needle centres, reduce the intercept angle again and maintain the track with suitable adjustments for drift. Do the same outbound, except look for a FROM reading. A good rule (inbound and outbound) is to subtract the intercept angle if the needle goes left, and add if it goes right to find the heading to steer. For example, 280°-90°=190°. To bracket for drift, turn onto a zero wind heading and see what the drift actually is. Get back on track, make a large correction the opposite way and see what happens. Get back on track and half the original correction. Keep on until the correct heading is found.

Here are the needle movements and the responses of an aircraft as it drifts off to the left and comes back on course:

Range

If using the VOR at high altitudes, you might get station overlap and erroneous readings, so, if VOR bearing information is used beyond the published protection range (see the AIM), errors could arise from interference from other transmitters. You could also be out of range.

The (theoretical) reception range for VHF transmissions can be estimated with this formula:

```
NM = 1.23 X √Height AGL
```

It's simple Pythagoras, since it involves right-angled triangles. Technically, the *Height AGL* above is the height of *both* antennae (i.e. transmitter and receiver), in feet, added together, so the formula could also read:

```
NM = 1.23 X √H1 + 1.23 X √H2
```

In real life, the results from the formula above will vary if the transmitter is weak, there is something in the way, or the receiver is not working properly.

If a radio beacon has an operational range of 10 nm, by what factor should the transmitter power be increased to achieve 20 nm? Four.

Time to Station

You often need to know the time it will take to get to a station (well, you will in the exam, anyway), which is simply found by turning 90° from the inbound radial and noting the seconds taken to go through a number of them. To get the time in minutes, divide the time just noted by the number of radials (degrees) gone through. All you need do then is use the groundspeed (or TAS in an emergency) to find your distance. It is a variation of the 1 in 60 rule.

For time to station, the formula is:

$$\text{Time (mins)} = \frac{\text{Mins x 60}}{\text{Degrees}}$$

On the flight computer, set minutes on the outer scale, and degrees on the inner one. Read the answer on the outer scale opposite the 60 arrow.

In the picture above, the speed triangle (60) is opposite 120 (knots or gallons) on the outer scale, which means it will take 6 minutes to go 12 nautical miles, or 6.5 to use 13 gallons, and so on.

For the distance, try:

$$\text{Distance} = \frac{\text{Mins x GS}}{\text{Degrees}}$$

For example, your relative bearing to a fix is 315°, which 3 minutes later is 270°. What is the distance from the fix if ground speed of 180 knots?

The difference between bearings is 45°, so 540 divided by that is 12 nm.

Airways

If you are 100 nm from a VOR, and if 1 dot = 2°, how many dots deviation from the centre line of the instrument will represent the limits of the airway boundary?

Airways are normally 5 nm wide either side of the centreline, so, applying a variation of the 1 in 60 rule:

$$\frac{5 \text{ x } 60}{100}$$

The answer is 3°, or 1.5 dots deviation.

An airway 10 nm wide is defined by two VORs with a bearing accuracy of ± 5.5°. To ensure accurate track guidance within the airway limits, what is the maximum distance apart for the transmitters? Answer: 105 nm.

The system is limited to about 1° of accuracy. One degree at 200 nm means a width of 3.5 nm.

Testing

Some airfields have low power test equipment (2 watts) transmitting on 114.8 (usually, but you might get 108.0 from a repair station), identified with the ATIS, so have a pen ready to save you writing it down again later (the ID may just be a series of dots). The system is intended for ground use, although it can be used when airborne (there will be certified airborne check points), but you could always get to a position on a known radial and check the readings. As you move the OBS, you can expect the usual indications relating to the bearing selected (which is why two transmitters are used, to save you moving the aircraft to the radials). With the needle centred, the instrument should read 000° FROM or 180° TO at any point within the airport, with an accuracy of ± 4° (± 6° when airborne).

In fact, transmitter error (or FM/AM synchronisation, at least) should be within ±1°. The system should shut down automatically if it gets outside that. Phase comparison error should not be more than ±3°, and station errors should be within ±1°. The nominal accuracy is ±5°.

Problems

Although the VOR is less subject to static and interference than an NDB, and it is much more accurate, the transmissions depend on line of sight, and there are suspect areas at 90° to a radial (zones of ambiguity), and overhead (cone of confusion), as mentioned above. In addition, certain rotor RPM settings can cause fluctuations up to ±6° (change them slightly before saying the instrument is U/S).

Transmissions may be adversely affected by uneven propagation over irregular ground surfaces, and if bearing information is used beyond the published protection range, errors could be caused by interference from other transmitters.

Doppler VOR

Using Doppler allows the frequency of a signal to decrease when the distance between the beacon and aircraft increases, and *vice versa*. It is a system that is useful for removing site errors, and allows you to use a VOR in hilly country. The transmitter has one antenna that transmits a 30 MHz signal omnidirectionally (the reference signal), which is surrounded by about 50 others which are energised in sequence at 30 Hz, anticlockwise. The result is a Doppler shift that makes the transmitter look as if it is advancing and retreating 30 times a second.

To get the reference 30Hz signal, the VHF carrier is AM modulated with a 30 Hz sine wave signal, horizontally polarised against noise. As it is a reference signal, its phase is independent of the aircraft position. The other (FM) signal has a phase that changes 1 degree for each degree change in bearing around the VOR station. It leads the reference signal by a phase angle equal to your bearing from the station.

A sub-carrier at 9960 Hz above and below the carrier frequency is introduced into the mix, in the form of two sidebands, to separate the 30 Hz signals. The sidebands are made to rotate electrically 30 times a second, so their frequency changes after Doppler. Thus, the sub-carrier effectively becomes *frequency modulated* at 30 Hz.

The end result is signals that are the opposite way round to a normal VOR, but the equipment in the aircraft doesn't notice the difference because the signals are in phase in the required places.

ADF/NDB

An *Automatic Direction Finder* (ADF), also known as a *radio compass*, is a device in an aircraft that picks up signals broadcast on the Medium wave band by *Non Directional Beacons* (NDBs), so called because they radiate in all directions, using *surface waves*. The approved ICAO range for aeronautical NDBs is between 200-1750 KHz, but that part of the radio spectrum also includes commercial radio stations, whose use in IFR work is not allowed because of the problems involved with identification, and there are no guarantees of consistency of service, but they are useful to listen to on long journeys (and yes, the needle still points to the station). If there is no ID, but the system otherwise appears to behave normally, the system is undergoing calibration or maintenance.

Transmissions are not dependent on line of sight, but utilise ground waves, so the system is good over long distances, although there are a few problems, mentioned below. It is possible to get 1,000 nm range over sea and 300 nm over land if the power is high enough, but since better systems have come along, NDBs are now only used as enroute navaids on airways, homing beacons for instrument approaches and markers for the *Instrument Landing System* (ILS), with a typical range of about 35 nm.

Power affects NDB range (in nm) by a factor of 5 times the square root of the power in watts:

$$\text{Range (nm)} = 5 \times \sqrt{\text{Power (W)}}$$

The minimum signal to noise ratio is 3:1 for ICAO, but it's 5:1 in the UK. ICAO also requires ±7° accuracy.

The primary function of the ADF receiver is to determine the bearing of an *incoming NDB signal*, which is *vertically polarised*. To do this, it uses a *loop aerial*.

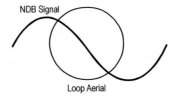

When the loop is square (across the bearing) to the beacon, the signal reaches both sides of the loop at the same time and there is no signal detected. When the loop is sideways-on, however, the signal reaches one part of the loop first. The second part will be out of phase, so a current will be generated, which drives an electric motor to continually seek the null position. It is phase sensitive, so it can always turn the shortest way. Various stages of

*This is useful knowledge if you want to do an NDB approach to a coastal aerodrome in mountains as the sun is setting!

magnification inside the receiver help this along, but they need not concern us here. The point is that the detected signal is not what is actually used to determine the bearing, but the *null signal point*, since the current flow is slow to build up and break down, and is a bit on the woolly side anyway. The null point is much sharper and easier to find.

Because the current flows in the opposite direction depending on the position of the loop, you also need some way of determining which end is what, otherwise you could be 180° out. A single vertical aerial called a *sense antenna* helps here - the signals are combined algebraically and the magnitude and polarity of the sense aerial arranged to be identical to the loop. The result is a polar diagram called a *cardioid*, with only one null point.

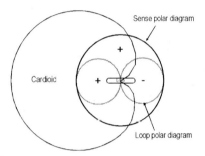

On one side of the loop, the diagrams are positive and combine, but on the other, one is positive and the other negative. Thus, they cancel out, hence the null point on one side. The modern (and more stylish) equivalent is a small housing with two coils at right angles to each other, wound on ferrite cores. They are connected to the stator coils of a *goniometer* which points the needle.

Limitations*

Limitations of the system include:

- *static*, including local thunderstorm activity, which is likely to cause the greatest inaccuracy

- *station overlap*, when NDBs have the same frequency, which is why they are not supposed to be close to each other. Because this is more pronounced at night, it can easily be confused with *night effect*, below (promulgated ranges are not valid at night for this reason). This will have the greatest effect on ADF accuracy, particularly at night

- *night effect*, where the needle swings erratically, at its strongest just after sunset and before sunrise. The loop is designed to receive surface waves - any others resulting from sky waves produced when the ionosphere de-energises and gets higher will be out of phase and confuse the system. If the

ionosphere is not parallel with the Earth's surface, they will also arrive from different directions. Check for an unsteady needle and a fading audio signal. *Promulgated ranges are not valid at night*

- *quadrantal error*, or variations caused by the aircraft itself, in the same way as it might affect a compass. The signal is reradiated by the airframe and the receiver gets an additional (much weaker) signal to contend with. The greatest error lies at 45° to the fore and aft axis, hence the term *quadrantal*. Modern systems have corrector boxes for this

- *mountain effect*, or variations caused by reflections from high ground, where two signals might be received at once from different paths

- *coastal refraction*, from radio waves in transit from land to sea, or parallel to the coast, because they travel slightly faster over water. This makes you aircraft appear closer to the shore. This effect is most noticeable at less than 30° to the coastline (i.e. an acute angle), and at lower frequencies, so expect errors if you are using an NDB inland directly in front of or behind you. The effect is to make the aircraft appear closer to the shore. With two NDBs, one 20 nm, and the other 50 nm inland from the coast, and if the coastal error is the same for both, the error seen by an aircraft over water will be greater from the beacon that is further away

- *Identification*. Since there is no flag indication of failure, as there is with the VOR, you should continuously monitor the station ID when relying on the instrument. Aside from that, the only way of knowing about problems is seeing the needle rotate to the right if the signal is not received

The most common error, though, is failing to recognise *station passage* - if you are directly over the beacon, it will swing around all over the place and be confused with one of the above, or failure of the instrument, where the needle just rotates to the right. This is the same cone of confusion effect that VOR has (above).

Use

The ADF is normally tuned with the function switch in the ANT position (it stands for *antenna*). This removes the needle from the loop and saves wear and tear as it tries to point at every station you tune through - here, the sense antenna is used by itself to obtain the ID. Once there, return the switch to the ADF position (or COMP, on some sets).

As always, check - in this case, ensure that the needle points vaguely where you expect it to.

The TEST button spins the needle 90° from its tuned position, and back, to indicate a good signal. BFO means *Beat Frequency Oscillator*. The BFO switch also uses the sense aerial by itself to detect the modulated Morse identifier. Hearing this by itself helps you tell if there is any fading (night effect) or noise (thunderstorms, interference). The tone you hear when this switch is activated is put there by the ADF receiver, since a carrier wave by itself cannot be heard.

When an incoming RF signal is present, the BFO produces a small AC current which differs from the RF by around 2 KHz. The RF and BFO outputs are fed to the frequency mixer (heterodyne), where they are subtracted from one another to produce a *difference* or *beat* frequency (the same principle is used in modern telephone tones). The beat frequency is amplified and fed to a loudspeaker which produces a steady AF of 2 KHz, within the human hearing range. If the incoming RF stops, no sound is heard from the loudspeaker.

The fixed card display (*goniometer*) has a compass rose with 0° representing the nose of the aircraft at the top of the instrument, and a needle that points to where the signal is coming from, in this case 010° (including thunderstorms if they are stronger than what you are tuned into).

Thus, if a station is ahead, the needle will point to 0°, or 180° if it is behind. However, if you made no allowance for wind, and just pointed the nose of the aircraft at the station (*homing*, as opposed to *tracking*), you would actually follow a curved path towards it.

Allowing for drift lets you keep a straight track, which is needed for airways (see *Tracking*, below). If you are heading to a beacon maintaining a relative bearing of zero, and the magnetic heading decreases, you have some right drift, and *vice versa*.

Unfortunately, working with fixed cards involves some maths. First of all, though, some definitions:

- *Magnetic Heading* - angle between longitudinal axis and magnetic North
- *Relative Bearing* - the angle between the aircraft's longitudinal axis and the NDB, which is what you read directly from a fixed card ADF
- *Magnetic Track* or *Bearing* - the angle between aircraft position and the NDB, either to or from

Take note of this formula (you will need it in the exam):

        MH + RB = BTS (MB)

In other words, the magnetic heading plus the relative bearing gives you the bearing to the station:

MB = MH + RB

My **B**uddy
Must **H**ave
Red **B**lood

See *Navigation* for an explanation of Magnetic Heading

Taking the example on the left, the formula would read:

        324 + 46 = 010

You can get the relative bearing like this:

        BTS - MH = RB

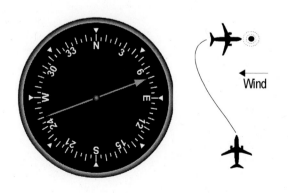

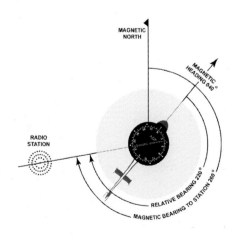

If you split the display into two halves, based on a line between 0° and 180°, and call the right half plus, and the left minus, you can use the needle's position in either to find the track to a station. For example, if the needle is in the right half (the plus segment), add the heading to the relative bearing to get the track. If it is in the left, take it away (work the needle back from zero in this case). Whilst turning right, the aircraft heading will increase while the relative bearing decreases, and *vice versa*. As long as you remain on the same bearing, the amount of heading change will always equal the change of ADF indication.

RMI

The *Radio Magnetic Indicator* is a combination of ADF indicator and slaved compass that replaces the fixed card with one that moves, so the top of the instrument represents the aircraft's compass heading (which includes deviation) and the needle points to the QDM (or QDR, if you look at the other end), which saves you doing the calculations above in your head.

In other words, it always displays the present heading and bearing, and does some of the work required by a fixed display. There may also be a repeater needle from the VORs giving you the same information relative to the stations they are tuned to. In the example on the left, the heading is 139°, and the ADF QDM is 077°. The VOR needle is pointing to a QDM of 210°.

The RMI does not need a TO/FROM flag, as there is no 180-degree ambiguity. With the VOR, the tail of the needle on the RMI indicates the bearing received *at the aircraft*. In other words, the signal left the VOR on whatever bearing it shows. Change it to True using the variation at the VOR.

As a point of interest, the VOR needle on an RMI will always read correctly if any deviation occurs, but headings and ADF readings will be in error by the deviation. This is because the ADF needle will naturally point towards the transmitting station, regardless of what the compass rose does. The VOR QDM, on the other hand, is created *within the instrument* by subtracting the aircraft heading from the

QDM and applying the difference clockwise round the dial from the lubber line. Deviations are automatically applied because the number cruncher ensures that the VOR needle moves in the same direction for the same amount as the compass rose.

For either needle, however, if it is off to the left, you fly left, and *vice versa*.

Position Fix

For a fixed card ADF, find the relative bearing to each station and add them to your heading to get the tracks to the stations. Then find the reciprocals and plot them outwards. Along an airway, to find where you are in relation to an intersection, you will already know the bearing to station (BTS), because it will be on the map. Using the formula:

$$RB = BTS - MH$$

you can find what the needle will indicate when you get there.

Time to Station

As with the VOR, note the seconds taken to go through a number of degrees on the relative bearing, and divide the time just noted by the number of degrees gone through to get the time in minutes. Then use groundspeed (or TAS in emergency) to find your distance.

Tracking

To find an intercept heading, just add or subtract the intercept angle to the track you wish to establish, as with an airway. It's common to use 90° inbound and 45° outbound, but use whatever ATC and circumstances (or exam questions) dictate (30° is nice). Note the track, and add or subtract your heading, as appropriate, to get the expected relative bearing when on track, which you will be when the needle of a fixed card points to it. With an RMI, just watch the needle.

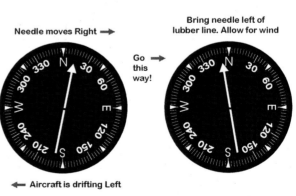

When drifting, the needle will always point to the side of the aircraft the wind is coming from, so corrections inbound should always be made that way, ensuring that the needle goes to the *other* side of the lubber line once a corrected heading is established. For example, if you want to track 090°, and the wind is coming from the right, to be on track you want to end up in a situation where the heading is an equal amount of degrees the other side of the lubber line as the needle is, such as a heading of 110° (*plus* 20 of the lubber line), looking for a 340° relative bearing (*minus* 20 of the lubber line). Or, for a track of 090°, your heading might be 070° while the ADF needle points to 110° (heading - 20°, looking for + 20° from the needle). If you are going the same way as your track, the needle will tell you which way to go. If it is on the left, your track will be on the left, and *vice versa*. Just turn whichever way until the needle reads the desired intercept on the opposite side.

A good ploy is to allow the drift to happen until you get a positive reading, say 10° port, double it the other way (go 20° starboard), and when you are back on track, reduce it by half (10° in this case) to hold it. This is called *bracketing*. When tracking *outbound*, however, you want to end up with the needle on the same side as the wind, so, although you are still looking for the plus 20, minus 20 equation, the needle would be pointing at 160° RB (when you make your initial turn, the needle looks like it's going the wrong way, but you get used to it). In short, if the pointy end moves to the right of a line between 0° and 180°, fly right, as drift is to the left, and *vice versa*. If you want to decrease the bearing to or from a beacon, make the needle's reading decrease - for example, if the track is 270° and you want to approach or depart on 260° (decreased), change your heading so the needle reads less by suitable amount for a cut and then wait until the heading is less by the same amount the needle is more.

To put it even more succinctly - push *to* the needle when flying towards an NDB, and drag *from* it when flying away!

AIRWAYS

The information from navaids becomes less reliable the further away you get from them, so corridors are defined, within which the signals can be counted on.

For VORs, the corridor width starts 5 nm either side, diverging at 4° for 70 nm, until 20 nm wide. The width remains constant between 70-140 nm, where it diverges

again at 4° until a width of 40 nm is reached at 280 nm out, at which point it remains constant.

For NDBs, the corridor starts 5 nm either side, diverging at 7° until a width of 20 nm is reached at 40 nm out, remaining constant between 40-80 nm out, thereafter diverging at 7° until 60 nm wide at 245 nm, then remaining constant.

DME

Distance Measuring Equipment is secondary radar (see *Radar*, below), but in reverse. It measures the time difference between *paired pulses* being sent from an aircraft, and received back on different frequencies, 63 MHz away from each other (there are 126 DME channels). In other words, the aircraft is the first to transmit on UHF, then the DME transmitter returns the signal (with the same pulse spacing), plus 63 MHz, after a 50 microsecond delay which is subtracted during the number-crunching (the delay reduces the chances of uncoordinated activity when the interrogating aircraft is near the station). Two frequencies are used because, otherwise, the first pulse received would be the ground return from below. Similarly, the ground station could self-trigger from other sources, such as those being bounced off a building. *Jittering* is used on the PRF so the DME's own pulse can be identified. That is, only signals with the same jittering pattern are replied to, because they are unique to each aircraft. *Aircraft DME receivers do not lock on to their own transmissions reflected from the ground as they are not on the receiver frequency - the interrogation and reply frequencies differ.*

DME is UHF-based, between 962 and 1213 MHz, so a typical frequency is 1000 MHz. Its purpose is to continuously display your distance from the station to which it is tuned.

DME is normally based with a VOR or TACAN and has a range of about 200 nm, ± 6, with an accuracy better than ½ nm or 3% of the distance, whichever is the greater. Thus, when the DME is co-located with a VOR, the two signals combined will give you a position based on a radial from the VOR and how far away on that radial you are. *Co-located*, with respect to a VOR/DME pair, means within

2,000' on an airway, and 100' on an airfield. *Associated* means that one callsign ends with a Z, and that they are within 6 nm, but not close enough for co-location. The maximum distance between VOR and DME/TACAN ground installations with the same morse ID is 600 m.

DME is rarely set up by itself, so it is not normally tuned directly - you usually select a VOR or ILS frequency and the DME reading will come up automatically, since the frequencies are usually paired. In other words, you select a VHF frequency to receive a UHF signal. The ident, however, is higher pitched than that of a VOR, so you can identify it between VOR idents on the same frequency (it is transmitted only once to the VOR's four). By convention, frequencies requiring only one decimal place are known as *X channels*, and those with two are *Y channels*.

X and Y Channels are used to make more efficient use of the bandwidth available and reduce interference. They are distinguished by pulse spacing. On the X Channel, interrogation and reply pulses are separated by 12 microseconds, and Y Channel interrogation pulses by 36 microseconds, with replies 30 microseconds apart. DME/P uses different figures. The reason for the spacing is that, in mode X, the received frequency is 63 MHz below the aircraft transmission frequency for channels 1-63 and 63 MHz above it for channels 64-126. This is reversed in Mode Y, that is, the ground frequencies for channels 1-63 and 64-126 are 63 MHz above and below the aircraft frequencies, respectively, so the transmissions are in the air-to-ground band.

Instruments in the cockpit will not only show your distance to a station, but will calculate the rate of movement and display the groundspeed (just multiply the distance flown in 6 minutes by 10 if yours doesn't). The reason it's not completely accurate is because the distance measured is the *slant range* from the station, and not from your equivalent position on the ground, although at long distances and lower altitudes, this will be minimised. In practical terms, the difference is insignificant when more than 10 miles from the station, and the *maximum error occurs overhead* - at 12,000 ft, the instrument would read 2 nm, and 4 nm at 24,000 ft, and so on.

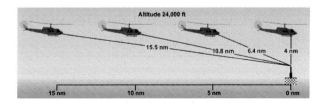

Simple Pythagoras will give you the real distance:

$$D = \sqrt{(S^2 - A^2)}$$

D is the ground distance, *S* is the readout (slant range) and *A* is your altitude in *nautical miles* (above the DME source).

The slant range itself is calculated by:

$$\text{Range} = \frac{\text{Time } (\mu s)}{12.4}$$

Examples: At FL 210, you will not receive any distance indication from a DME station approximately 220 nm away because you are below the line of sight altitude. If the time taken for an interrogation pulse to travel to the ground transponder and back is 2000 micro-seconds, the slant range will be 165 nm. An aircraft at FL 370, 15 nm from a DME station 1000 feet AMSL, will have a DME reading of 16 nm.

The most accurate calculation of your ground speed will come from a DME on the flight route, meaning that you will be tracking directly to or from the DME.

The ground station can only respond to a certain number of interrogations in a given period of time - generally, it can handle only up to 100 interrogations before *beacon saturation* occurs. If too many aircraft are interrogating it, the receiver will automatically be desensitized so it can hear and reply only to the strongest. Busy airspace can result in shorter-than-normal DME reception range, particularly with lower-powered DME units. An aircraft DME in tracking mode that subsequently experiences a reduction in signal strength will switch in the first instance to *memory mode* so it has something to work on until the signal gets better. A DME experiencing difficulty with locking on will stay in search mode, but will reduce the PRF to up to 60 PPS after 15 000 pulse pairs have been transmitted. Display counters rotating aimlessly throughout their range indicate that the airborne receiver is conducting a *range* search.

Errors

ICAO specifies that range errors should not exceed ± 0.25 nm plus 1.25% of the distance measured so, at 100 nm, the maximum should not exceed ± 1.5 nm.

TACAN

This is a pulse-based military navigation system operating in the UHF band (*Tactical Air Navigation*), which can be used by the DME circuitry in your aircraft (*not* the VOR - military aircraft have a display which is not compatible). When a TACAN is co-located with a VOR, the resulting VORTAC will show DME readouts automatically when you tune the VOR, since the frequencies are paired. Of course, a military machine can pick up the complete TACAN signal, which provides range, radial speed and bearing information, in a manner more suited to military operations than traditional methods.

RNAV

Area Navigation is a generic name for systems that allow navigation over wide areas - it was originally coined for a way of electronically moving navaids, VORs in particular, to other places enroute, which implies that you must be within the operating range of the navaids concerned. For example, you could tell the black box the distance and bearing of your house from the nearest VOR and it would present all the signals as if the aid was actually there. On a direct route with no specific navaids to aim for, you could shift all nearby ones to fit on your direct track so you had a series of phantom stations in the shape of instant VORs (*phantom waypoints*) to use. Thus, RNAV describes ways of flying directly across country without doglegging all over the place, or where you don't have to pass over a radio fix, which saves fuel and makes better use of airspace.

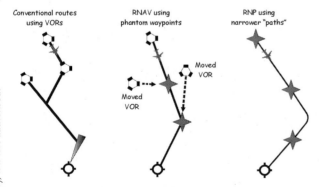

| Conventional routes using VORs | RNAV using phantom waypoints | RNP using narrower "paths" |

The concept is illustrated in the picture above. Although not on the helicopter exam syllabus, RNP (*Reduced Navigation Performance*) has been included as an example of modern techniques which can use curved paths and narrower airways.

ICAO Annex 11 defines Area Navigation (RNAV) as "a method of navigation which permits aircraft operation on any desired flight path within the coverage of station-referenced navigation aids or within the limits of the capability of self-contained aids, or a combination." An RNAV waypoint could be *a geographical position derived from a VOR radial and DME distance* but, in the USA at least, RNAV is no longer VOR-based.

Nowadays, RNAV can be based on VOR/DME, LORAN and Omega, not forgetting GPS. Some systems have their own tuners and can automatically set up DMEs, etc. according to signal strength for best position lines (the most accurate RNAV fixes come from DME/DME). A VOR does not have to be in range when entered, but must be when used, otherwise erratic indications may be experienced when flying towards a Phantom Station at low altitudes close to the limits of reception. In fact, the system will go into DR (*Dead Reckoning*) mode when receiving only one VOR, or if there is no bearing and distance information, using whatever TAS is coming from the ADC, heading from the compass and the last computed wind velocity.

RNAV displays information with reference to the *active waypoint*, and *not* the navaid on which it is based. That is, TO/FROM flags will flip over at the waypoint, regardless of where the VOR being used is. *Filters* limit the rate of change of VOR bearings, where they arise from multi-path reflections (site error). Close to the beacon, DME range sets the maximum rate, as the bearings change fast anyway, and errors might occur. On approach, 1 dot's deviation is equal to ¼ nm, and 1 nm en route, where 5 dots span half the airway. One of the functions of the Course-Line-Computer is to transfer the information given by a VOR/DME station into tracking and distance indications to any chosen Phantom Station or waypoint.

Types of System

In **direct ranging** systems, the signals from two stations, such as VORs, are enough for a position fix where they cross. In **hyperbolic systems**, a bearing is based on a phased or time difference between two ground stations, as with LORAN or Omega (or Decca), where three stations are needed for two bearings (Decca uses three Slaves for each Master). It is an inexpensive method, but relies on ground stations being operational.

B-RNAV is the basic system, with an accuracy of ± 5 nm for at least 95% of the time, as for RNP5. This can be achieved with VORs (up to 100 nm apart)/DME, DME/DME, LOC, GPS and a mix of INS/IRS. Precision

Area Navigation (P-RNAV) has the same accuracy as RNP1, meaning ±1 nm on 95% of occasions, and will be controlled by the FMS (one exam answer requires *a track-keeping accuracy of 0.5 nm standard deviation or better*). P-RNAV must be referenced to WGS 84.

VOR/DME (Rho-Theta)

As mentioned above, the VOR/DME station can be offset electronically to any desired position within its range of promulgation. A VOR does not have to be in range when its details are entered into the system, but must be when used, otherwise erratic indications may be experienced when flying towards a Phantom Station at low altitudes close to the limits of reception. In fact, the system will go into DR (*Dead Reckoning*) mode when receiving only one VOR, or if there is no bearing and distance information, using whatever TAS is coming from the ADC, heading from the compass and the last computed wind velocity.

Filters limit the rate of change of VOR bearings, where they arise from multi-path reflections (site error). Close to the beacon, DME range sets the maximum rate, as the bearings change fast anyway, and errors might occur. On approach, 1 dot's deviation is equal to ¼ nm, and 1 nm en route, where 5 dots span half the airway. One of the functions of the Course-Line-Computer is to transfer the information given by a VOR/DME station into tracking and distance indications to any chosen Phantom Station or waypoint.

Trivia: The Greek letter R (*Rho*) stands for range, and *Theta* is an angle, so a Rho-Theta fix involves a range and an angle, as you would get from VOR/DME.

DME/DME (Rho-Rho)

Here, DME receivers are used in conjunction with a microprocessor to measure the distance from two DME receivers for a position fix. Some systems have their own tuners and can automatically set up DMEs, etc. according to signal strength for best position lines (the most accurate RNAV fixes come from DME/DME).

Global Navigation Satellite System (GNSS)

There are two satellite systems currently available, with another one to follow. The one supplied by the USA is called *GPS*, and the Russian system is *GLONASS*, which cannot be used under all circumstances.

Although the American GPS system is still usable, it is relatively old technology and originally designed for

military use, so for modern purposes, continual workarounds have to be made, which often turn out to be more expensive than starting from scratch. *Galileo* is a European system that should be operational by 2008 (the first satellite was launched on the 28th December 2005). It uses 30 satellites, and the signals will overlap with GPS with *spread spectrum* technology unscrambling the mess.

RNAV is supported, but GNSS can provide better instrument approach paths, including vertical navigation, which can reduce delays and diversions.

For IFR purposes, certain standards must be met:

- *Accuracy* in terms of *position error*, or the difference between the estimated and actual positions

- *Integrity* is the measure of trust that can be placed in the information supplied by the system, including the timely issue of warnings

- *Continuity* is the system's capability (expressed as a probability) to perform. That is, there must be a high probability that the service will be available throughout a full approach procedure

- *Availability* is the time during which the system can deliver the above for a specific phase of flight

Satellite signals are not only used for navigation, but also to provide specialised clock systems for various earthbound systems, such as cell phone networks and TV stations, since the satellites all have atomic clocks on board. ATC use it for this purpose as well.

GPS

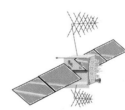

The *Global Positioning System* was originally set up by the US military to help submarines get lost more accurately, based on Doppler Shift, as one of six satellites passed overhead. Now the system is managed by an executive board that ensures that all users' needs, including civilians, are considered. It also now uses 24 satellites (with at least 21 operational at any time, although there have recently been up to 26 or 28 on line - the extras allow orbital manoeuvres and maintenance) to give extreme accuracy at a much reduced cost compared to, say, INS (the original satellites are now used to monitor the atmosphere). The phrase *Full Operational Capability* means that all 24 satellites are working. *All In View* means that a receiver is tracking more than the required 4 satellites, and can instantly replace a lost signal with another already being monitored. *Search The Sky* is a procedure that starts after switching on a receiver to check that no stored satellite data is available.

Satellites are spread between 6 circular planes, with 4 in each one. GLONASS uses 3 planes at 60° to the Equator. To stop them hitting US satellites, they fly lower.

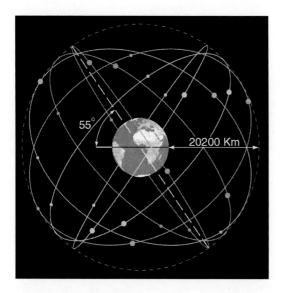

GPS orbits cross the equator at a 55° angle (or, rather, *the inclination of the satellite's orbit to the equatorial plane is 55°*), so you won't see a satellite directly overhead when North of 55° N or South of 55° S, although this does not affect polar service, because, at high latitudes, receivers can see satellites over the other side of the pole, so more satellites can actually be visible at high latitudes than elsewhere (they never go right over the Poles). Where the satellite goes South to North it is in the *ascending node*, and in the *descending node* when it goes the other way.

Although it is guaranteed to be kept running for the foreseeable future, in (US) National Emergencies it may be unavailable, which is why it is still only acceptable as a backup to certificated radio-based navigation aids, at least under JAA. In addition, the satellites are not always in an optimal position (you can get RAIM holes), and interference can affect their signals, including jamming. If the position fix from the GPS differs from that of conventional navigation systems by an unacceptable amount, or the RAIM information is suspect, the flight may be continued, but using conventional navigation systems, so *prescribed IFR equipment must be installed and operational*. The datum for altitude information when under IFR or conducting approaches is *barometric altitude*.

The system consists of three basic elements:

- The **Space Segment**: the satellites, which transmit signals that are useable by the receivers

- The **Control Segment**: ground stations, etc., that track the satellites and monitor their status

- The **User Segment**: receivers that select satellites automatically, track signals and calculate the time taken to reach the receiver

 Contrary to popular belief, satellites are not geostationary, but move around the Earth every 12 hours, 20 200 or so km above the WGS 84 ellipsoid. However, at least 5 should be visible at any point over the Earth at any time, though you could get a problem flying through the odd ravine way up North, especially as their transmitting power is only around 50 watts, or rather less than the average light bulb. The signals themselves have less strength than a Christmas tree light, which is why they are easily jammed.

GPS is a position-finding device, and can calculate distance, track and speed from your changing position, but it does not know what heading you are on unless you tell it. It can also give altitude information, but 3D readouts require 4 satellites, without the benefit of RAIM (see below). GPS readings are referenced to a mathematical model, such as WGS-84, to minimise the influence of the ionosphere, comparing the model against the signals received. *Calculated heights are above the WGS 84 ellipsoid.* They can be converted to others inside most receivers.

The system works by *satellite ranging*, or measuring the distance to several satellites. For example, you must be somewhere on the surface of a sphere centred on Satellite A, and similarly for Satellite B.

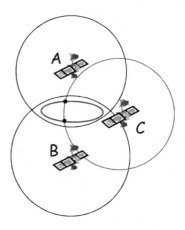

In fact, you must actually be somewhere on the circle formed where they intersect. If you then bring in Satellite C, the three spheres intersect at only two points, and you must be at one of them (there are techniques for deciding which one).

Thus, in the beginning, the only known locations are those of the satellites your receiver can see- the system tracks their positions to within about 1 m, from 12,000 miles up, at 7,000 mph! Then it calculates the distances to them based on the time it takes for their signals to get there, that is to say, *the distance between a satellite and a receiver is determined by the time it takes for the signal to reach the receiver, multiplied by the speed of light*. If you are off by even 1 millisecond, your position would be in error by over 300 km, so, for 1 m accuracy, time measurement must be accurate to within 3 nanoseconds. Satellites therefore use atomic clocks, for high precision, and continuously transmit their positions, plus a code number in a set code, at exactly the same time. In fact, the timing accuracy is down to one billionth of a second, and the pseudorandom code is repeated every millisecond (the General Theory of Relativity predicts that time runs slower with more gravity, and the atomic clocks in satellites indeed run slightly faster than they would on the surface, so corrections have to be made continually). The set code appears to be random, but isn't, which is why it is called *Pseudo-Random Noise Code*. It is the means by which a receiver recognises signals from a particular satellite, or differentiates between them.

Since the transmission time is known, the distance the signal has travelled can be calculated from the time of arrival. The receiver matches each satellite's code with an identical copy in its database. By comparing any shift with its internal clock, it can calculate a *pseudo-range*, which is similar to comparing a broadcast copy of a song against one already playing on a CD player - if they both started at the same time, the received one would be slightly behind from the time delay. If several "songs" are received at the same time from multiple sources, the GPS receiver can correct for errors in its own clock and determine actual travel times. In other words, when your GPS receives the satellite signal, it compares the received code with what it generated internally. If the signal has the same code that was transmitted 2 seconds ago, it knows it has taken 2 seconds for the signal to arrive.

The principle used is that, if three perfect measurements can locate a point in space, four imperfect ones can eliminate clock offsets, or cancel out some timing errors. An error is therefore deliberately introduced, and algebra is used to compute where all possible points could

intersect. The result given is your position. Because it is calculated, the word *pseudo* is used. In other words, the measured distance between a satellite and a receiver is called a *Pseudo-Range* because the calculated range includes receiver clock error. The parameters that can be determined by a GPS receiver tracking signals from 4 different satellites are *latitude*, *longitude*, *altitude* and *time*.

Satellites transmit on two UHF carrier frequencies, L1 and L2, which are US designations. The (higher) L1 frequency is 1575.42 MHz and L2 is 1227.60 MHz. The (digital) information is superimposed on them, as it is with any other radio signal. Being digital, the data consists of long strings of 1s and 0s, which are simpler to transmit, more reliable and error-free, and less prone to jamming because *error redundancy checking* (see *Computers, etc.* in AGK) can be used. The basic elements transmitted are:

- offset of the clock from UTC
- ephemeris data
- ionospheric delays

The signals are line-of-sight, and will not pass through water, buildings or solid objects in general, although they do pass through clouds, glass and plastic (regardless of that, though, the best conditions for reception are in clear areas with open skies). The most accurate fix comes from 3 satellites with a low elevation above the horizon, 120° from each other and a fourth directly overhead. The three types of data superimposed onto the L1 and L2 carriers are the *Navigation Message*, the *C/A (Coarse Acquisition) Positioning Code* and the *P (Precision) Positioning Code*.

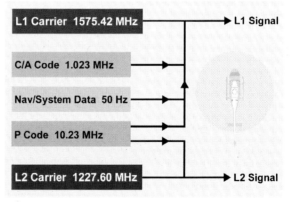

A *Standard Positioning Service* (SPS) is available to all for general use from civilian signals on L1, together with S/A. PPS (or *Precise Positioning Service*) Code is for the military and broadcast in an encrypted fashion on L1 and L2 (the Y channel).

Differential GPS uses at least fifteen minutes' worth of data collected at a stationary location, combined with a precisely located reference point. Satellites are kept in line by an atomic clock at a ground master station within 70 nm, and aircraft use crystal oscillators to increase accuracy to within 1-3 metres with a correction signal from the ground station. The nearer the receiver is to a DGPS ground station, the more accurate is the fix.

Although the orbital paths of GPS satellites could theoretically be predicted under Kepler's laws of planetary motion, the assumption that the Earth is a perfect sphere of uniform density is not correct, and gravity from other heavenly bodies (e.g. the Moon and the Sun) have their own effects on top of Earth gravity. There is also very slight atmospheric drag, because satellites are not travelling in a perfect vacuum, plus the impact of photons of light emitted by the sun both directly and reflected off the Earth and Moon. This *solar radiation pressure* is a function of a satellite's size and orientation, distance from the sun, etc., but the end result is that satellites headed towards the Sun are slowed down, and accelerated when headed away. This *clock drift* is virtually impossible to estimate accurately, and is the largest unmeasurable source of error. Actual satellite locations must therefore be measured periodically. The four unmanned monitoring stations send location information to the Master Station in Colorado where a master list is maintained. As the data is needed by all users, it is periodically uplinked to individual satellites, in two parts called the *almanac* and the *ephemeris*.

Almanac data describes approximate orbital data over extended periods of time. As each satellite contains almanac data for the entire constellation, a GPS receiver only needs to download it from one satellite to figure out the approximate location of them all. Almanac information is transmitted every 12.5 minutes and takes 12.5 minutes to download (30 seconds per data frame), so it will take at least that time before accurate fixes can be determined. This data becomes stale over time or if you move the receiver to another location more than several hundred kilometers away (the initial setup is known as a *cold start*). **Ephemeris information** contains precise location information of individual satellites and the parameters needed to predict their positions for the near future. Unlike almanac data, each satellite transmits only its own ephemeris data, so the receiver must gather it from each one in view. Ephemeris data is transmitted every 30 seconds, and takes 12 seconds to download. It is considered valid for up to 4-6 hours (the data stream contains an indication of validity).

Note: *Receivers calculate the elevation and azimuth data of a satellite relative to the antenna from the Almanac data transmitted by the satellites. Almanac data in the receiver is used for fast identification of signals from visible satellites.*

The *mask angle* is the lowest angle above the horizon from where a satellite can be used. Signals from it contain the time (from four atomic clocks) and its position, plus error correction. From this, the pseudo-range of the satellite can be computed, which is called that because it is not directly measured, but calculated, so it is subject to error, particularly delays as signals pass through the ionosphere.

For each satellite, the pseudo-range is added to the *ephemeris data* (or exact position in space), and triangulation used to figure out the receiver's position. As mentioned above, you need 4 satellites for a 3D position, which includes height above Mean Sea Level, or altitude. Such height readouts should not be used for navigation by themselves, as they are referenced to the WGS-84 spheroid, so the current altimeter setting should be put into the receiver if you want to use them (the techies at Garmin say the term Mean Sea Level is used generically, as the difference is close enough with the accuracy available).

SIGNAL AUGMENTATION

Selective Availability, where there was a deliberate fudging of the signal (by dithering the clock signals) to make it less accurate for non-military receivers, is now inoperative, because various other ways of improving or maintaining accuracy to the proper standards required for aviation have been developed which made it redundant. However, some early systems cannot take advantage of even this potential improvement.

ABAS

The *Aircraft Based Augmentation System* includes *Fault Detection* and *RAIM*.

Receiver Autonomous Integrity Monitoring makes sure satellites are working properly by verifying the signals, so an extra satellite is needed to detect corrupt information. For the bad signal to be isolated, you need one more (in fact, a 5th satellite is for checking errors, while the 6th is a stand-in). Without RAIM, you have no assurance of accuracy, and you need 4 satellites for a 3D fix.

Note: RAIM is the equivalent of an OFF flag.

FDE (*Fault Detection & Exclusion*) can tell which satellite is faulty and exclude it from the calculations. For it to work, you need at least six satellites with good positioning. For avionics that cannot take advantage of SA being discontinued, average RAIM availability is 99.99% when en-route and 99.7% for non-precision approaches, assuming 24 operational satellites and mid latitudes. FDE availability ranges from 99.8% for en-route to 89.5% for non-precision approach. Otherwise, there is virtually 100% RAIM availability when en-route and 99.998% for non-precision approaches. FDE availability ranges from 99.92% (en-route) to 99.1% (non-precision approaches).

Most aircraft systems can accept input from an altitude encoder. This is called *baro-aiding*, which essentially reduces the number of satellites required by one, further increasing the availability of RAIM and providing an additional measure of tolerance to satellite failures.

IRS systems can also be used with GPS inside aircraft.

SBAS

Satellite Based Augmentation Systems use ground-based reference stations to monitor satellite signals and relay data to master stations, which assess signal validity and compute error corrections. The *Wide Area Augmentation System* allows GPS to be used throughout a flight, including a Cat I precision approach. Satellite signals are received by precisely surveyed ground stations, which detect errors and send them to a Master Station (WMS), which in turn adds correction information based on geographical area and uplinks a correction message to a satellite for rebroadcast. This improves the 95% signal accuracy from 100m to 7m, but it can be better than 2 m.

When SBAS integrity messages are used, the additional satellites that would be required for RAIM are not needed, because the messages are available wherever the satellite signal can be received. WAAS currently uses two satellites over the Atlantic and Pacific Oceans.

GBAS

Ground Based Augmentation Systems have corrections sent directly to aircraft receivers from ground stations at airports, typically within about 30 nm. There is a monitoring function in the ground station to assure the integrity of the broadcast.

RECEIVERS

Single channel receivers move from one satellite to the next in sequence. Although this can be very quick, it is still not fast enough for navigation. *Multi-channel* receivers (most suitable for aircraft) continuously monitor position data whilst locking on to the next satellites. *Continuous receivers*, with up to 12 channels, can eliminate GDOP problems by watching more than four satellites.

ERRORS

- Satellite clock drift (see above)

- Ephemeris (position)

- Propagation delay, such as through the ozone layer

- Receiver noise. Antennae should be fitted on the upper fuselage near the Centre of Gravity

- Multi-path reflection

- C/A Selective Availability (see above)

- GDOP/PDOP. When satellites are too close to each other, vertical and horizontal position accuracy is degraded, resulting in *Geometric (Position) Dilution of Precision*. ICAO requires a PDOP/GDOP of less than six for en-route navigation, and three or less for non-precision approaches. The normal accuracy of 100 m for 95% of the time assumes a PDOP of 3 and a range error of 33.3 m (range errors are multiplied by PDOP to obtain stated accuracies)

OPERATION

Although it is tempting to use GPS all the time, remember that it is electrical, and therefore reserves the right to go offline at any moment, without warning. The antenna in a GPS is live as well, and equally liable to stop working. A GPS may also have a database of airspace and frequencies inside - although not so important for VFR use, it is still the mark of a professional to keep it up to date.

DISCHARGE DETECTORS

Otherwise known as *Stormscopes*, after one manufacturer, these detect lightning discharges and display them on a green screen in the cockpit. They work in a similar way to an ADF with its needle pointing towards a storm. Cheaper models have to be cleared every time you change heading. Because lightning varies, a strong signal may be mistaken for a storm, and *vice versa*.

VDF

The purpose of *VHF Direction Finding* is to provide directional assistance in times of difficulty, rather than for general navigation, so a typical frequency it might be used on is 121.5 MHz. One or more ATC stations can get a bearing for you to steer (QDM) to get to their location from your transmissions, so *the minimum equipment is a*

VHF radio. A direction-finding station can only find your position in relation to itself, when working alone - to get an exact position, you need two or even three more, who will all report to a Master Station.

The full range of services available could include:

- Emergency Cloudbreak

- Emergency No-compass Homing

- Homing

- Fix

- Track-out Assistance

- Time & Distance Estimates

However, the ICAO recommended practice recognizes only homing, with no compensation for wind drift, which is actually the only element that most pilots are aware of, receive training on, or use. In Canada, VHF-DF equipment is provided at 27 FSS, two Towers and one RAAS site.

Being based on VHF, VDF is subject to the usual limitations (line of sight, multipath, etc.), so the higher you are, the better the results you will get. You must transmit for a few seconds for a bright line to spread from the centre of a screen to the outside which is marked with compass bearings. The following services are available, assuming no wind:

- **QDM** - magnetic bearing *to* (i.e to be steered, with no wind)

- **QDR** - magnetic bearing *from*

- **QUJ** - true bearing *to* (to be steered, with no wind)

- **QTE** - true bearing *from*

When a position is given in relation to another point, or in lat & long, it is a **QTF**. When positions are given by heading or bearing & distance from a known point that is not the station making the report, the known point shall be from the centre of an aerodrome, a prominent town or geographic feature, in that order.

A series of bearings is a QDL (so QDL QDM means several QDMs). QGE is the distance from the relevant point. A QGH is a letdown where ATC give you headings to steer, based on VDF bearings). Older equipment uses a cathode ray tube on which the line appears (like a radar sweep) pointing to where your transmission is coming from. More modern digital equipment uses a circle of LEDs at 10° intervals, which will show the same information, with a digital readout in the centre. Accuracy

comes in these classes, in relation to bearing or position, and will be included in the transmission:

Class	Bearing	Position
A	±2°	5 nm
B	±5°	20 nm
C	±10°	50 nm
D	<C	<C

RADAR

The use of radar *improves aircraft spacing and safety* - the word stands for *Radio Direction and Ranging*, without which it is arguable whether the Allies would have won World War II. Although the Germans had it, too, it was Dowding's organised use of the information it provided that produced the edge. The Germans thought the war would be over soon and slowed down its development in 1940, and used it mainly for shipping anyway. By the time they realised they had to catch up, it was too late.

The system was called RDF (*Radio Direction Finding*) until 1943, when the name was changed to harmonise with the Americans (in those days it just about got the distance right). It works on the basis that microwave pulses can reflect (or echo) off objects, with a proportion of the energy expended returning to the transmitter to be processed. The "blips" representing the objects are displayed on a Cathode Ray Tube and an air traffic controller can see the relative positions of aircraft reflecting any pulses. The radar beam is rather like that from a flashlight, as the antenna focusses the pulses into a beam with the most energy concentrated in the centre.

You can calculate the distance between the transmitter and the object because the speed of the radio wave is known, and the direction the antenna is pointing at the time supplies the bearing. It takes 12.36 microseconds for a radio wave to travel out and back for each nautical mile of range, or 123.6 microseconds for each 10 nm.

The VHF portion of the electromagnetic spectrum does not allow the bandwidth required for the short pulses that allow good target definition, so the UHF bands were used (today, it is SHF). Thus, radar is limited to line of sight.

In most countries, outside of terminal control areas, radar is used more as a monitoring device, but in others, such as the USA, you are more or less under radar control all the time and very rarely follow a flight planned route.

The word *pulses*, mentioned above, means that short bursts of electromagnetic energy containing 1000 cycles or so are mixed with relatively long periods of silence (*relatively long*, in electronic terms, means somewhat less than a thousandth of a second). This is known as *primary radar*, and it has a few limitations. First of all, radio signals weaken over distance and, since the pulses have to make two journeys (there and back), the range of a target is necessarily limited. Secondly, the blip on the screen is quite large, and aircraft very close together cannot be distinguished, unless the beam is narrow enough to pass between them. Finally, radio waves can be bent by the atmosphere or screened by objects, such as mountains or buildings, and different aircraft return signals differently, in terms of shape or surface. *Continuous Wave radar* is used in radio altimeters and the Doppler system.

The radar antenna is expected to act as a transmitter (horizontally) and a receiver (vertically), for which it should be able to produce a thin beam, and receive a wide one, respectively. Because of this, there will be imperfections in design, which will produce unwanted radiations known as *sidelobes*. A *parabolic dish* can produce a focussed beam, but it will spread with distance.

The generated pulses travel through either coaxial cable or a hollow tube called the *wave guide* (which requires pressurisation to ensure the proper conditions for microwave conduction). The energy passes through an electronic switching device called the *duplexer* that directs outgoing pulses to the antenna and incoming pulses from the antenna to the receiver.

The antenna is a shaped antenna:

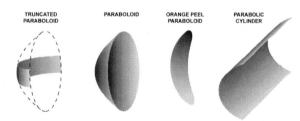

| TRUNCATED PARABOLOID | PARABOLOID | ORANGE PEEL PARABOLOID | PARABOLIC CYLINDER |

After transmission, the reflected energy is directed back to the wave guide where it travels past the duplexer which directs the returns to the receiver. The receiver converts the microwave returns to electrical signals that are amplified and sent to the *Plan Position Indicator* (PPI), which anyone else would call the display.

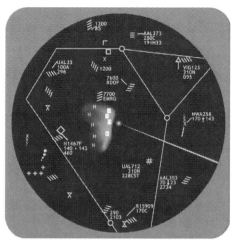

Its timebase (the frequency with which the picture is repainted) is linked to the antenna, in that when it passes through North, so does the beam painted on the display. As a pulse is fired off, a spot of light moves from the centre of the tube to the outside, reaching the circumference before the next pulse goes. The effect is a line of light rotating round the screen, at 60 RPM.

When a return is received*, the electron flow is increased and display intensity increases to a spot which fades away slowly as the line moves on. Range markers are displayed with a saw-tooth wave. By making the grid (brilliance) negative, the fly-back is suppressed, meaning that you won't see the lines where the pulse flies back from the end of one line to the beginning of the new line.

The larger the dish, the narrower the beam width will be - for example, a 30" dish produces one 3° wide, and 12" gives 7°, assuming the same frequencies. A short pulse length with a narrow beam gets the best picture.

The *cosecant squared* antenna is used mainly with airborne weather radar in MAP mode, because a larger area of ground is illuminated by the beam, producing echoes whose signals are practically independent of distance. When looking at the ground for mapping purposes at fairly close range, the beam must be widened vertically as well as having its energy distribution controlled so that returns from longer range (the top of the beam) are of similar strength to those from shorter range (the bottom of the beam). The strength of the signal vertically within the beam depends upon the square of the cosecant of the angle of depression, so more energy is radiated in the upper part of the beam than the lower part.

Any range detected will be a slant range, as per DME, and maximum range will be determined firstly by the *Pulse Repetition Frequency* (PRF), because pulses have to return to the transmitter before the next ones are sent, plus the *Pulse Interval* (PI). They are related as follows:

$$PRF = \frac{1}{PI}$$

Examples: Assuming sufficient transmission power, the maximum range of a ground radar with a PRF of 450 pulses per second is 333 km. At 1200 pulses/sec, around 69 nm. A ground radar transmitting at a PRF of 1200 pulses/second will have a maximum unambiguous range of approximately 67 nm.

In transmit mode, the pulse of energy is sent, then the antenna is converted to a receiver for a set time, to receive the reflected returns. This is done thousands of times a second as the antenna moves over its range. The number of times a pulse is sent per second is the *Pulse Repetition Frequency* (PRF), and is the main reason for a maximum range. Minimum range, on the other hand, is set by *pulse width,* because a long pulse could still be receiving part of an echo from one target while starting to get the information from a second, if they are close together. However, a longer pulse carries more energy and would return a stronger signal, so there is a balancing act to get the best all-round results.

The *Pulse Recurrence Period* (PRP) or *Interval* (PRI) is the time it takes to transmit the pulse then wait for its return. If all this happened inside a second, the PRP would be 1 second. As mentioned, the number of pulses per second is the PRF, so the further the target is away, the longer must be the PRP and, by extension, the PRF.

With continuous wave radar, the minimum range restriction is removed. To double the range, you must increase power 16 times.

Moving Target Indication

MTI makes use of Doppler to eliminate returns from fixed objects such as hills or buildings. The radar will only display returns that show a Doppler shift, i.e. moving targets, but a target maintaining a constant range would not show up.

Secondary Surveillance Radar

This is a development of a system introduced during the Second World War called *Identification Friend or Foe* (IFF), which was supposed to distinguish between friendly and enemy aircraft (friendly aircraft had a small transmitter that gave a distinctive periodic elongation to the blip on the screen, so anything with a primary blip was an enemy). It was codenamed Parrot (or Canary) by the British, which

probably has something to do with the current use of the word *Squawk* to mean *transmit the relevant codes*, which you dial up on the transponder in your aircraft, and which will appear next to your blip with your height readout, depending on the type of transponder you have.

SSR improves on the primary radar mentioned above by using double-pulse secondary equipment to provide more information, hence the name. Participating aircraft carry a *transponder* (for *transmitter/responder*) that receives the interrogation pulse from the transmitter (1030 MHz ±0.2 Mhz), superimposes information on it and sends it right back on another paired frequency (1090 MHz). This means, first of all, that the range of operation can be doubled immediately, and, secondly, that the blip on the screen can be made much smaller, together with information that makes it more easily identifiable to ATC, because the pulses can be coded. As well, there is no storm clutter, as the principle of echo return is not used. Computer trickery can provide predicted tracks and collision warnings, amongst other things.

The following information can be seen on the screen:

- Pressure Altitude
- Flight Level
- Flight Number or Registration
- Groundspeed

A controller for example, will give you a number to *squawk*, which you dial up on the transponder, and which will appear next to your blip with your height readout, depending on the type of transponder you have.

There are standard numbers to squawk, when not otherwise instructed, which are:

- 0000 - malfunction
- 2000 - from non-SSR area

You cannot set the number 8! Watch for this in questions that ask you to choose between valid codes

In emergency, squawk:

- 7500 - Hijack*
- 7600 - Communications failure
- 7700 - Emergency

You will be given details of other traffic according to the clock system, such as "fast mover at 6 o'clock", based on the track seen on the radar. When fitted, *transponders should be used at all times*. When changing squawks as instructed, take care not to dial up the emergency ones by mistake, and *do not switch the transponder to standby* during the change to avoid it, as senior pilots often do, because this will remove your display from ATC's screen and cause all sorts of alarms to happen.

MODE A/B

Mode A is the regular variety, based on the original IFF, which just displays the code you select in the aircraft - you get this just by turning the switch to ON. In other words, it is for basic identification.

The spacing between the leading edges of the 1st and 2nd pulses determines the mode of operation. In answer to an interrogation, a Mode A transponder will transmit up to 14 pulses 8 microseconds apart, the first and last ones being *frame pulses* (F1 and F2), which are always there and enclose the whole signal so it doesn't get confused with others. The 12 that are left can be there or not in up to 4096 (2^{12}) combinations, from 0000 to 7777. The *ident pulse* is transmitted for up to 20 seconds, 4.35 microseconds after the last frame pulse when you press the button.

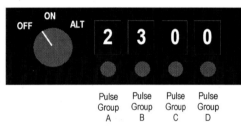

Each number selection knob controls 3 pulses (pulse groups A, B, C & D). 2300 (for example) produces the binary codes of 010, 110, 000 and 000. 0 means Off, or no signal, so selecting 2 means that only pulse 2 of Pulse Group A is transmitted. Selecting 3 requires pulse 1 plus pulse 2 of the B group (refer to *Binary Arithmetic* under *Computers, Etc.* for more information). There would therefore only be 3 pulses between the frame pulses, which saves on transmission bandwidth.

MODE C

This adds altitude to the mix - a Mode C transponder is directly attached to an *encoding altimeter* (or, more precisely, an *altitude digitiser*, which selects a different code to that selected in the window), but only Pressure Altitude information based on 1013.25 (or 29.92) information is sent from the aircraft - the conversion to local pressure, if required, is done inside the ATC computer. *ATC will not be able to see changes when you move the altimeter subscale*. Mode C is selected by switching to ALT, after switching on for Mode A. The pulses are 21 microseconds apart. You should always use Mode C unless directed otherwise.

In Mode C an air traffic controller's presentation gives information regarding your indicated flight level that is accurate to within ±50 ft.

Both Modes A and C suffer from interference, otherwise known as *fruit* and *garble*.

MODE S

S stands for *Select*. It allows each aircraft to have a unique code, and respond only to requests directed to it (A and C transponders respond to all requests). In this way, you can increase the capacity of the system.

Mode S uses a 24-bit address, which reduces mistakes and allows the system more capacity and efficiency. For example, Mode S transponders have 20-foot resolution of altitude data, while Mode C has 100-foot resolution. It can also provide two-way data link communications on 1030 and 1090 MHz, used in the case of TCAS for manoeuvre messages, but also as a backup for VHF voice.

Weather Radar

Although it shares the same name, this is not a good system for detecting other aircraft or ground returns because it is tuned to the average size of raindrops. In fact, the primary purpose of weather radar is to detect the sort of rainfall that would indicate thunderstorms and their associated turbulence. It therefore relies on your interpretation of the contents of the screen display for best results.

Two frequency bands are used, such as *C band* (4000-8000 MHz), and *X band* (8000-12500 MHz). C band illuminates storms beyond nearby precipitation better, but X band has more resolution, although its higher frequencies are subject to absorption, and scattering from smaller raindrops. The wavelength is about 3 cm (at 10 GHz, or maybe 9375 MHz), to detect a 1½ cm raindrop - in fact, ½ the wavelength is the optimum object size for detection. Thus, cumulus clouds are most readily detected by airborne weather radar when using the weather beam, but it cannot detect snow or clear air turbulence. When used for navigation, AWR is only a *secondary* means.

Note: Weather radar is required on helicopters that can carry more than 9 passengers under IFR or at night when current weather reports indicate that thunderstorms or other potentially hazardous weather conditions, regarded as detectable with airborne weather radar, may reasonably be expected along the route to be flown.

The antenna (scanner) is kept inside a *radome* in the nose of the aircraft, and there is an RT box containing the

transmitter/receiver, together with a scope in the cockpit. The antenna inside the radome can be parabolic or flat, sweeping through 45-60° either side of the nose - the flat scanner reduces power demand and sidelobes. In *weather* mode, the beam is narrow (pencil) and cone-shaped. For mapping, it is wide and fan-shaped (effective up to 50-60 nm), but for long range mapping, you should use weather mode anyway, because the narrow beam goes further (more power is concentrated in it).

Weather radar detects rainfall to *avoid* (not penetrate) severe weather, as many large raindrops in a small area are a dead giveaway for thunderstorms or, rather, their activity is - turbulence is proportional to the rate at which rainfall increases or decreases over a given distance. Whether you want to go towards the area concerned depends on the intensity of the echoes received, the spacing between them and the capabilities of the pilot and aircraft.

Note: A clear area on the radar screen (say between significant echoes) doesn't mean there is no cloud or precipitation, as minute droplets, ice, dry snow and dry hail have low reflective levels, if at all - clear areas between echoes does not necessarily mean you can see your way between them.

In fact, a clear area is more likely to indicate large water droplets, as they will totally absorb the energy as they approach the size of the radar wave, and the screen will not be able to display the remaining thunderstorm area behind the point of complete attenuation (absence of returns produces a use for the stray side lobes mentioned above, in that the downwards one produces a ring on the screen at the same range as your height above ground, so you can check if the equipment is working). Thus, the greatest echoes come from rain, and drop size is more important than their number. Normal weather radar cannot detect turbulence, but Doppler radar can.

Note: Because of attenuation, a weak return does not mean a less violent storm - you could just be too far away from it to get decent information.

Operation is quite simple, but full use on the ground should be avoided (not below 500 feet, in fact, because the radiations will affect people or equipment). Naturally, you've got to check the equipment before departure, but most sets have an internal procedure for this. When you

do switch it on, it should be set to *Standby* for at least 3 minutes first, to allow things to warm up (when not in use, the set should always be set to SBY to keep the (roll and pitch) stabilisation gyros running - it stops them crunching together as the aircraft moves). Ground testing requires *tilting up* in weather mode.

You will have several scan ranges to choose from, possibly from 250 miles down to 5, but 80 is adequate, which is about what you would get with a 10 inch antenna, the usual fit in small aircraft. The smaller it is, the wider the beam and the dispersal of energy, which means that a lot of it will pass by whatever storm is around, giving you an indication very much less than the true hazard. You would be safe to assume that whatever you see on the screen is in reality one or two levels more severe.

Once airborne, there is a *tilt* capability which will point the antenna up or down so you can adjust for the aircraft attitude and get more detail about approaching storm cells, but don't expect to see the tops of a storm, because the crystals won't reflect the energy in the first place, and your beam focussing will be too narrow to include it. The tilt control is the most important key to a more informative display in moderate rain, and should be used often to get a better 3D picture. To ascertain whether a cloud return on an AWR is at or above the height of the aircraft, the tilt control should be set to 2½° up, assuming a beam width of 5°.

In the same way, you will also get ground echoes, which are good for detecting the enemy coast ahead, but only because water will absorb the echoes and you will see a big black hole instead. Buildings and the like won't reflect properly at all - you might just see a mass of confusing colours (that's what the MAP selection is for, but that's not wonderful, either). MAP Mode uses a *cosecant radiation pattern*, so you can scan a large area producing echos whose signals are practically independent of distance.

In MAP Mode, a fan shaped beam effective up to 50-60 nm is used, but the pencil-shaped WX beam is preferable beyond that because more power is concentrated in it. Also, MAP Mode uses a *cosecant radiation pattern*, so you can scan a large ground zone producing echos whose signals are practically independent of distance.

If you haven't got the luxury of colour and computer-controlled echo highlighting (and have to rely on steam), there are distinctive storm patterns to look out for:

- *The Hook.* These stick out from a cloud, and will suggest strong wind circulations, like tornadoes, which are found in thunderstorms with a marked windshear in the middle levels

- *The Finger.* This is like a spur out from a cloud, not quite as curled as the hook. The trick here is to look at the edges - sharp contours mean a growing storm, while fuzzy ones mean a dissipating storm

- *The U-shape.* This is like a valley in a mountain, with strong updraughts surrounded on three sides by the sort of heavy precipitation associated with downdraughts

- *Scalloped edges.* When round a cloud outline, particularly at the back end of a storm, they signify severe attenuation due to heavy precipitation

Shapes can change quickly, so they need careful monitoring (hail shows up better when the gain is reduced). The heaviest precipitation, and heaviest turbulence, will show up as black holes, or in red, which will be best detected in *Contour mode* (where high rainfall rates, or maximum cell activity, appears in Red).

Tip: Radar signals weaken, and might show the end of the weather falsely.

Iso-Echo (for mono screens) produces a hole in a strong echo when the returned signal is above a pre-set value. *It is used to detect areas of possible severe turbulence in cloud.* The edges of the hole that actually appears on the screen have the same rainfall rate, and is like a contour line, hence the name. When the line is narrow, there is a strong intensity gradient, so avoid hooked echoes, especially rapidly changing ones. In fact, you should beware of thin lines of whatever colour.

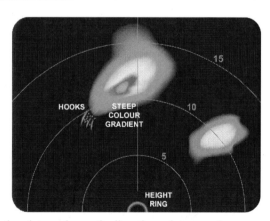

In the picture above, the line along the centre is your intended track, and the curved lines are your range markings, so there's something nasty lurking 10 nm away slightly on your port side, with a little finger (or hook) in front of you which may or may not be producing some

rainfall. The colour zones closest together indicate the greatest turbulence. Note the colour progression from green to yellow to red, and possibly magenta for maximum severity. By changing the scale to 10 nm, the returns on the radar screen should increase in area and move nearer to the top of the screen.

Note: Targets separated by a distance less than the beam diameter will merge and appear on the display as one.

Avoid the brightest returns (i.e. those that are changing rapidly, or contouring, or coloured magenta or red) by at least 20 nm. Above the freezing level, make it 5 nm and 10 nm when below. If you see anything at all between 50-70 nm, keep well away from it. The minimum height above a storm should be 1,000 feet for each 10 kts of wind speed.

After switching on, if a single very bright line appears on the screen, the scanning of the cathode ray tube is faulty. If the display collapses in on itself, suspect the power supply.

Ground Radar

Those used for longer range, such as those covering airways and larger airspace, tend to have lower frequencies and longer wavelengths, lower PRFs and larger pulses to get maximum range with as little attenuation as possible. Where shorter range is good enough, say, for use near an aerodrome, short frequent pulses are used to get better picture definition. In addition, antenna rotation will be higher because shorter range radar will be used when things are changing quickly.

A typical long range coverage will be up to 250 nm, with a preferred frequency of 600 MHz and a 50 cm wavelength. Shorter range coverage is provided by.....

PRECISION APPROACH RADAR (PAR)

PAR is primarily used by the military, which is high-definition in nature, because it uses the 9-10 GHz range and has a 3 cm wavelength, similar to weather radar, so weather clutter can be a problem (meaning you may be denied its use when you need it most!) It uses two radars (and antennae) to give horizontal and vertical guidance to aircraft on final approach up to about 10 nm within 20° of final track and 7° of elevation. It's supposed to be a landing aid, not one for sequencing or spacing aircraft, and it may also be known as *Airport Surveillance Radar* (ASR). Since the range is 10 nm, PAR is limited to the final stages of approach. The display is in two parts - the upper giving altitude and distance information, and the lower azimuth and distance.

The controller will give you the headings to fly, plus position information with regard to the glidepath, but only if you are dangerously low will positive height information be given. In the final stages you will be told not to acknowledge the instructions as things will be happening hard and fast. As your height is monitored, the heights to which you can descend before overshooting will be lower.

PAR's usefulness lies in the fact that navaids are not required and neither is a compass, as the controller tells you to turn left, right, descend, etc. Also, since acknowledgements are not required, you can listen over an ADF or VOR if your radio doesn't work.

ILS

This is a precision approach system using a VHF transmitter for horizontal guidance (the *localiser*), with a 1.4° wide beam, and a UHF one for vertical, which usually produces a 3° *glideslope*. The localiser beam is transmitted from the *far end* of the runway, (i.e. the upwind end) about 300 m out across the extended centreline (if not, it is known as *offset*), and the glideslope is generated somewhere in the first 300 m upwind of the *threshold*, off to one side by about 150 m. Its signals are only valid down to the lowest authorised Decision Height

The *Threshold Crossing Height* (TCH) is where the glideslope antenna should be to ensure that the wheels don't hit the ground if they hang too far below the cockpit.

The impression given is that two narrowly focussed beams intersect to provide the guidance but the "beams" are created electronically *by the equipment in the aircraft* (that is, voltages are produced from the radio signals). This means you can get on-course or on-glidepath indications regardless of your position, as was found by an Air New Zealand 767 in July 2000, which got down to 400', *6 miles short of the runway* (check your distance and altitudes, and do *not* use equipment on test!)

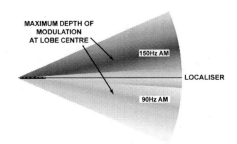

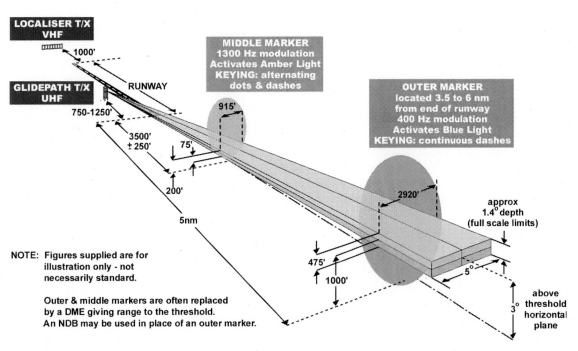

The localiser transmits two overlapping lobes of radio energy on VHF, the one on the left during approach being A2 modulated at 90 Hz, and the other also A2 at 150 Hz. If the depth of modulation of both lobes appears to be the same, the receiver assumes you are on the ILS QDM in the centre, or following the *equisignal*. The greater the difference in modulation depths, the more the indicator needle is displaced. For example, if an aircraft is receiving more 90 Hz than 150 Hz modulations from the localiser, the instrument indication will show *fly right*.

Note: ICAO defines "established on course" as being within half full-scale deflection for an ILS or VOR/TACAN/RNAV/GPS procedure and within ± 5° of the required bearing for the NDB. This ensures that you stay within protected airspace during an approach. You are not established until you are within these limits.

The normal approach is called the *front course*, and is used with the other components of the system. The course line along the extended centreline in the opposite direction is called the *backcourse*. Unless your system has reverse-sensing capability, you have to do the opposite of what the needle says when inbound along the back course (as you would when outbound along the front course). Disregard glideslope indications on a backcourse, unless there is one on the chart.

The glidepath transmissions are done in a similar way, but on UHF (between 329-335 MHz), with the frequencies paired with localiser ones (the upper lobe is the 90 Hz one). However, ground reflections from the lower lobe produce *side-lobes* which can give false indications. Luckily, these should be above the real glidepath, but you should still be aware of them. Watch for high rates of descent, and check altitudes against distances. Glidepath calculations in exams are simply variations on the 1 in 60 rule - you should be at the Middle Marker at about 200 feet (around 3500' from the threshold), and the Outer Marker at 1400 feet (3° is a descent rate of about 5 times groundspeed in knots). One dot means 50 feet at the Outer Marker, and around 8 feet at the Middle Marker. *There is virtually no guidance below 100 feet* - remember this if you decide to bust minima at any time. The glideslope actually flares at around 25-30 feet, so if you follow the needle, you will start to climb at that height (autoland compares sink rate against radalt indications to cover for this).

ILS transmitters are sensitive to vehicles, etc., around them, which is why there are *ILS Critical Areas*, in which such movement is restricted. The reason why pre take-off holding areas are sometimes further from the active runway when ILS Category 2 and 3 landing procedures are in progress than during good weather operations is that aircraft manoeuvring near the runway may disturb the guidance signals.

The signals received in the cockpit are translated onto an instrument like the one on the top left. The vertical needle shows whether you are left or right and the horizontal one tells you whether you are high or low. In the example, you are on the glideslope and left of the localiser, so you "chase the cross" to get back on, that is, fly level to the right. Below, on the left is a picture of it combined with other stuff in a *Horizontal Situation Indicator* (HSI). The glideslope indicators are on either side, and the rest of the instrument behaves like an RMI.

Note: The OBS doesn't work when the VOR instrument is used for the ILS.

The frequency range for the localiser lies between 108-112 MHz, on odd decimals, within which there will be 40 channels, so a typical frequency is 109.15 MHz. The glideslope has the same number, between 329-335 MHz, with the frequencies paired. *Glidepath* means any part of the glideslope intersecting the localiser.

Markers & Beacons

Three beacons (radiating at 75 MHz) are used on the way down the glideslope so you can tell how far you've got to go, as a gross error check against false signals. The Outer Marker is at about 5 miles, which often coincides with, or is replaced by (in Canada), an NDB or DME, and the Middle Marker at about ½ mile from the threshold (where you should be around 200 feet off the ground), plus an inner marker just before the threshold, at DH, though they are not present in some countries (it's mainly for Cat II approaches - see below).

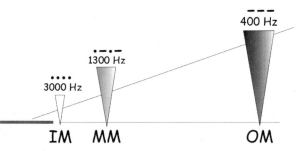

© *Phil Croucher, 2007*

At the middle marker, the box you have to be in to be within the first dots horizontally and vertically is 75 feet wide and 35 feet high (in something large, the wingtips are likely outside). The markers don't have to be tuned, as they have their own identification.

In the cockpit, the outer marker produces a blue flashing light within a couple of degrees of the overhead (for a number of seconds at a particular speed). The middle marker is amber and the inner one white, if used. They all beep as well, using different tones (400, 1300 and 3000 MHz if you really want to know) in Morse. The OM uses three dashes at two per second, the MM dot-dash-dot-dash at two per second, and the inner marker four dots at 6 per second. You may be lucky and have a DME to help.

Tip: When coming down the glideslope, don't forget to adjust your heading as the wind slows down and backs nearer to ground level.

Gradients, Etc

The outer marker of an ILS with a 3° glide slope is 4.6 nm from the threshold. Assuming a glideslope height of 50 ft above the threshold, what is the approximate height of an aircraft passing the outer marker?

$$\frac{\text{Range From Threshold (ft)}}{60} \times \text{GP Angle} = \text{Ht (ft)}$$

Substituting:

$$\frac{27968}{60} \times 3 = 1398.4$$

Add the 50 ft above the threshold to get 1450 ft, in round figures.

A strong headwind causes a *decrease* in groundspeed and rate of descent, and a tailwind does the opposite.

RATE OF DESCENT

You can use the slide rule on the flight computer to solve these as a proportion problem if you remember that, using the 1-in-60 rule, for a 3° glidepath, you need to lose around 300 feet for every 1 nm - at 60 kts, this would be 300 feet per minute. If you put the 60 kt index on the slide rule against 300 on the outer scale, you can read 450 fpm against 90 kts, and so on........

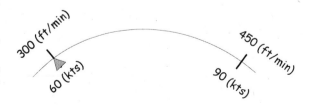

For a 3° glideslope, you can also use groundspeed divided by two, then multiplied by 10. For example, at 400 kts you get 200, times 10, for 2000 ft/m. For a 2.5° glideslope in the above problem, just put the index against 250, or 350 for a 3.5° glideslope, and so on. The rate of descent required to maintain a 3.25° glide slope at a groundspeed of 140 kt is approximately 800 ft/min.

What approximate rate of descent is required to maintain a 3° glidepath at a groundspeed of 90 kt? 450 ft/min.

Range & Coverage

The localiser range and coverage is:

- 10 nm, 180° off the centre line
- 17 nm, 35° off the centre line
- 25 nm, 10° off the centre line

For steep approaches, the figures change to:

- 10 nm, 35° off the centre line
- 18 nm, 10° off the centre line

You should be able to get the glideslope signal up to 10 nm. The approximate angular coverage of reliable navigation information for a 3° ILS glide path out to 10 nm is 1.35° above the horizontal to 5.25° above the horizontal and 8° each side of the localiser centreline. An aircraft tracking to intercept the localiser inbound on the approach side, outside the published ILS coverage angle may receive false course indications.

ILS is 4 times more sensitive than the VOR, so full deflection is 2½ °, as opposed to 10° (½° per dot), with a width of 700 feet at the threshold. One dot means you are 300 feet off course at the Outer Marker or FAF, and 100 feet off at the Middle Marker. If the localiser is more than 30° away from the centreline, it is an *offset localiser*.

Category I

A Category IILS is the basic variety that brings you down to a 200 ft DH.

Category II

This takes you further down, to as low as 100 feet DH and RVR 300m.

Category III

A Cat III ILS glidepath transmitter provides reliable guidance information down to the surface of the runway.

MLS

• •

The *Microwave Landing System* is an ideal replacement for the ILS for complex approaches that require many heading and height changes, such as in mountains.

It uses a time-referenced scanning beam with *differential phase shift keying* (see *Computers, Etc* in AGK 2) to provide guidance for 3D positioning on approaches that can be curved with varying glide paths, especially useful in mountainous areas. It suffers less from interference than ILS (it is insensitive to geographical siting), and has more channels. Information can be displayed in the cockpit through normal or multipurpose displays. The identification is a four-letter code beginning with *M*, transmitted in Morse at least 6 times a minute. The azimuth station is broadly equivalent to the ILS localiser, but does a lot more, transmitting over 200 channels between 5031-5090 MHz on the SHF band (or C Band). The *elevation station* uses the same frequencies, but the signals are *multiplexed*.

The azimuth transmitter at the upwind end of the runway (same as the ILS) provides a fan-shaped horizontal approach zone with approach signal accuracy to ±40° either side of the centreline to at least 20 nm and 20,000 feet (15° above the horizontal in elevation). The transmitted beam sweeps back and forth between the limits of coverage, and a complete scan includes two sweeps. An aircraft on the side where the sweep starts will have a shorter interval between them than an aircraft on the far side, which is how its position is determined. The elevation transmitter is at the downwind end of the runway and works in much the same way.

The back azimuth at the other end of the runway, on the other hand, is ±20° to 7 nm and 5,000 feet, and is used for missed approaches, etc. However, it transmits at a lower data rate as its requirements are less.

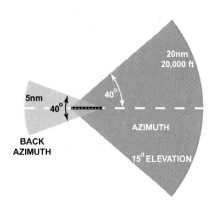

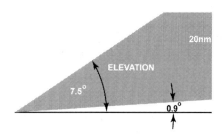

MLS uses a co-located *Precision DME* to provide distance information. The *DME/P* is similar to the normal type, but works between 962-1105 MHz (the L Band) on a paired frequency system, and is more accurate (down to 100 feet). Without precision DME, MLS assumes the same status as an ILS.

RADIO COMMUNICATIONS

Pilots need a radio licence to use the airwaves, which will be a limited version of an amateur radio licence. It is normally a separate piece of paper, which needs you to pass an exam before it is granted, but it does last for life and requires no revalidation. Although your use of the airwaves is limited, you still need to know the rules so that other people don't suffer.

In Aviation, using non-standard phraseology can be fatal. The phrase:

"Advise ready for taxi, use caution, company pushing out of XYZ"

is not a clearance to pushback, even though it might sound like one. Similarly, an instruction to conduct runup checks on the other side of a runway you would have to cross to get there is not a clearance to do so.

As further examples: The words *"request Federal Aid"* in one message were interpreted to mean that a hijack was in process, rather than the intended request for FAA clearance expressed in a joking fashion. The figures 210 by themselves could mean a Flight Level, a heading, or a speed to be maintained.

Communications should be restricted to what is required for the task in hand. Obscene language is prohibited, and using the air-to-air frequency to talk about personal matters is highly unprofessional. This is because anyone with an emergency can't send a MAYDAY until you have stopped talking. The only time you can interfere with another station is when you have to send a higher priority message (see *Categories Of Messages*, below). It is also an offence to use a callsign for a purpose other than that for which it is notified.

Within about 200 nm of an ATC station (depends on your height), VHF is normally used - over a 1 hour flight, it is easily possible to use over 10 frequencies. Unless there are relay stations along your route, or there are special arrangements to patch into the telephone system, as used in Canada, after that distance you will need to use HF. When even HF is no use (it is often drowned out by static), messages are often relayed between aircraft. As a result of the problems, HF communications have to follow the procedures described in this chapter have to be followed more strictly.

One of the main reasons for RTF congestion is having to send extra messages because people don't use the radio properly, which includes using *concise and unambiguous phraseology*. Controllers are also not supposed to transmit during takeoff, or on the last part of final approach or the landing roll, unless safety is a factor (you are working hardest at these times and don't need distractions). Most of them realise that you can't change frequency in the hover.

You are bound to preserve the *secrecy of communications*. That is, you may not say anything about, or even the existence of, any transmissions received, transmitted or intercepted by a radio station, except to whoever is supposed to receive it in the first place, or a properly appointed official, which may be someone who operates a retransmission service (naturally, this does not apply to distress messages, or those relating to safety, such as severe weather, or addressed to *All Stations*). Messages should be as brief as possible, consistent with getting the point across because, as soon as someone presses their transmit button, nobody else can use the system. Thinking about what you are going to say before you speak will help with this - if it is a long message (say filing a flight plan), write it down first, and break frequently, in case anyone is trying to get an emergency message out.

Naturally, a continuous listening watch should be maintained at all times, for airmanship, but especially when transiting controlled airspace during notified hours of watch. You must report your position and height on entering and just before leaving an ATZ.

Due to licence restrictions, aircraft equipment is meant to have as little power (around 250 watts) and as few controls as possible, including displays, so some frequencies may not be completely shown - 122.075, for example, comes up as 122.07 (usually, you will pull one of the knobs to get the extra bit). In fact, everything should be preset. The standard channel spacing is 25 kHz (if the last digit displayed includes 2 or 7, your equipment is capable of 25 kHz operations), so a 760-channel transceiver is necessary. In some areas of Europe, channel spacing has been reduced to 8.33 kHz.

The primary medium for aeronautical communications is VHF (AM) in frequencies between 118 - 136.975 MHz.

The *Squelch* quietens down the output when no signal is being received, so you don't get continuous earfuls of white noise. A signal coming in cancels this and activates the audio (a variable squelch merely determines the signal level when this occurs). The correct procedure with the Squelch, therefore, is to rotate the knob until the hiss just stops, and leave it there, although it is true to say that this will hide a weak signal, so lifting the squelch may help you hear it, if you are far away.

The reason you might say Two Thousand Four Hundred rather than Two Four Zero Zero is that it can be construed as To Four Zero Zero, as in Cleared To Four Zero Zero

There are one or two points about radios that aren't often taught properly during training. The first is to wait a split second to speak after pressing the transmit button, which gives all the relays in the system a chance to switch over so your message can get through in full, that is, not clipping the first bit. Secondly, whenever you get a frequency change *en route*, not only should you write it down on your Nav Log, but change to the new frequency *on the other box*, so you alternate between radios. This way, you have something to go back to if you can't get through on the new one (although it is appreciated that this could create difficulties with two station boxes which must be switched every time).

Primary reference documents for this subject are ICAO Docs 4444 (Air Traffic Management), Doc 9432, and Annex 10, included on the CD.

English must be used for air–ground communications unless an alternative has been arranged with ATC beforehand.

Categories Of Message

Messages must be dealt with in this order:

- Distress
- Urgency
- Direction Finding
- Flight Safety (ATC messages, avoiding weather)
- Meteorological
- Flight Regularity (parts and materials)
- UN Charter
- Government messages
- Service communications
- All others

General Operating Procedures

A message consists of four parts: The *Callup*, The *Reply*, The *Message* and The *Acknowledgement*.

LETTERS

To make transmissions clearer, letters are pronounced in certain ways, as shown in the table below. Speak all words plainly and clearly, with none of them running together and no accentuation. Do not shout, or speak too quickly. Although the phraseology can be a bit longwinded (*day-si-mal* for decimal, for example), and you may feel a bit stupid pronouncing some of the words, remember they

are that way to reduce ambiguity, which would have been handy in Tenerife when two 747s collided with each other because the clearances got confused (see *Human Factors*). The word *decimal*, by the way, is an ICAO word, replaced with *point* in the USA).

Letter	Word	Speech	Morse
A	Alpha	**AL**FAH	▪-
B	Bravo	**BRAH**VOH	-▪▪▪
C	Charlie	**CHAR**LEE	-▪-▪
D	Delta	**DELL**TAH	-▪▪
E	Echo	**ECK**OH	▪
F	Foxtrot	**FOCK**STROT	▪▪-▪
G	Golf	GOLF	--▪
H	Hotel	HO**TELL**	▪▪▪▪
I	India	**IN**DEAH	▪▪
J	Juliet	**JEW**LEEETT	▪---
K	Kilo	**KEY**LOH	-▪-
L	Lima	**LEE**MAH	▪-▪▪
M	Mike	MIKE	--
N	November	NO**VEM**BER	-▪
O	Oscar	**OSS**CAH	---
P	Papa	PAH**PAH**	▪--▪
Q	Quebec	KEH**BECK**	--▪-
R	Romeo	**ROW**MEOH	▪-▪
S	Sierra	SEE**AIR**RAH	▪▪▪
T	Tango	**TANG**GO	-
U	Uniform	**YOU**NEEFORM	▪▪-
V	Victor	**VIK**TAH	▪▪▪-
W	Whiskey	**WISS**KEY	▪--
X	X-ray	**ECKS**RAY	-▪▪-
Y	Yankee	**YANG**KEY	-▪--
Z	Zulu	**ZOO**LOO	--▪▪

NUMBERS

Number	Speech
0	**ZERO**
1	WUN
2	TOO
3	TREE
4	**FOW**ER
5	FIFE
6	SICKS
7	**SEVEN**
8	AIT
9	**NINER**

Numbers (as used for altitude, cloud height, visibility and RVR information) should generally be spoken individually, except for whole thousands (or hundreds) where they occur as round figures. 65 is therefore *six-five*, while 2000 is *two thousand*. Eleven thousand is *One One Thousand*. In other words, combinations of thousands and whole hundreds must be transmitted by pronouncing each digit in the number of thousands, followed by the word *Thousand*, followed by the number of hundreds, followed by the word *Hundred*. For example:

- Altitude 800 (Eight Hundred)
- 1,500 (One Thousand Five Hundred)*
- 6,715 (Six Seven One Five)
- 12,000 (One Two Thousand)
- 200 (Two Hundred)

Use the word *decimal (daysimal)* when you need a decimal point - *one one six decimal two* means 116.2. Altitude above sea level is expressed in thousands of feet, plus hundreds, but flight levels use separate digits, so 2500 is said as two thousand five hundred, but FL 100 is *flight level one zero zero*. Express a heading separately, e.g. *two five zero* for 250°.

MORSE CODE

Although the codes (see above) are printed on maps, etc., it's still a good idea to learn them, even if only to keep your job in an airline (many make it a requirement to have at least 6 words a minute). It also stops you peering at your map in the murk and moving your head around too much. Amateur radio clubs are a good source of inexpensive training materials. Starting off at a high speed is best, with the simplest letters. E, for example, is one dot (*dit*). Listen to a stream, picking out that letter, then add another, such as T, which is a dash (*dah*), then I (2 dots), M (2 dashes) and so on. In a few days you could be up to 20 wpm.

TIME

Time is expressed in terms of the 24-hour clock, based on UTC (*Universal Co-ordinated Time*), or what used to be called Greenwich Mean Time. The letter *Z* (for *Zulu*, meaning GMT - sorry, UTC) is used as shorthand in things like flight plans, etc. The first two figures of a 24-hour time represent the hour past midnight, and the second two the minutes past the hour, so 2345 means 45 minutes past eleven in the evening (take away 12), or a quarter to midnight. If you see a timegroup:

220345Z

It means a quarter to four GMT on the 22nd of the month. Usually, you only transmit the numbers for minutes ("arriving at 45"), but this only relates to the *current* hour, and if there will be no misunderstanding. If there is any possibility of confusion, or you mean another hour, include the other figures. Time is normally given to the nearest minute, except that control towers may state

the time to the nearest half minute when issuing a taxi clearance to a departing aircraft.

You can *Request a Time Check* from ATC at any time.

TRANSMISSION TECHNIQUE

Assuming you are within the performance range of your equipment, and after listening out first, to make sure you don't interfere with another transmission, call ATC, using their name, and normal conversational tones (no need to shout!), followed by their function, as in *London Tower*. Then use the words *This Is*, followed by your own identifier (you should use the full callsign on initial contact with ATC, but you can subsequently use any abbreviations they make. See *Callsigns*, below). Normally, your callsign is the same as your aircraft's markings, unless you have applied to ICAO for permission to use a company name or a flight number. Include the frequency you are on, in case they are listening to several, so they know which button to push, then the word *Over*, as an invitation for them to respond:

> *"London Approach, this is Charlie Papa Alpha Charlie Oscar on one one eight decimal two, over."*

Maintain an even rate of speech, not above 100 words per minute, with a constant volume, avoiding hesitation.

ATC will reply with your full callsign, but may well shorten it afterwards, to the country letter followed by the last two of your registration, as in *Charlie-Charlie Oscar*, if there is no confusion with another aircraft. You can use it from then on. Don't be concerned if there is a short delay - the controller might be writing down your details first, or may even have to put down the coffee (in Canada, you may be on a remote link). If you receive no reply, wait ten seconds before trying again.

If the field has an ATIS (continual weather broadcasts, every half hour), you should obtain the information and include the code letter with your initial call:

> *"with information Delta."*

The format is the same if ATC call you first, but you can omit the word *over* if the reply is obvious and there will be no misunderstanding.

STANDARD WORDS & PHRASES

If you need to make a correction, say the word "Correction" followed by the last correct word or phrase before continuing. If you need to get something repeated, use the words *say again* (if you say *repeat*, you might well get an artillery barrage, because that's what the gunners use!)

You can specify parts of a message by saying *say again all after*, or *all before*....

A message from ATC to all stations listening out on a frequency would be a *general call*, and be preceded with the words *All Stations*. A message to multiple stations can be done in any convenient sequence, but the replies must be in the order given.

Phrase	Meaning
Acknowledge	Confirm that you have received this message
Affirm	Agreement
Approved	Permission granted for proposed action
Break	Separation between parts of a message
Break Break	Separation between parts of a message when busy
Cancel	Annul previously transmitted message
Changing to	Going to another frequency
Check	Examine a system
Cleared	Proceed under the conditions specified
Confirm	Did I get that right?
Contact	Get in touch with....
Correct	That is correct
Correction	Oops - made a mistake
Disregard	Ignore my last
Go Ahead	Proceed with message
How Do You Read?	What is my readability?
I say again	I repeat
Monitor	Listen out on (frequency)
Negative	No, or not correct
Out	This conversation is over - no reply is expected
Over	I have finished speaking and I expect a response
Read Back	Repeat the message back exactly as received
Recleared	Ignore your last clearance and receive a new one
Report	Pass me the following information (as in Report altitude).
Request	I would like......
Roger	The last messages has been received (if not understood!)
Say again	Repeat what you just said
Speak Slower	Reduce your rate of speech
Standby	Wait to be called
Verify	Check and confirm
Wilco	Your instructions will be complied with (Will Comply)
Words Twice	Send (or will send) every word twice

The word *To* is omitted from messages relating to Flight Levels:

Climb Flight Level 100

HELICOPTERS

Helicopters are different! There is some standard phraseology that is unique to their operation. Firstly, the manufacturer's name or model as a prefix in the callsign may be replaced with the term *helicopter*. In addition, these terms have specific meanings:

Phrase	Meaning
Lift	A manoeuvre where the helicopter gets airborne and enters the hover
Hover	A manoeuvre where the helicopter holds position whilst airborne in ground effect, waiting to proceed. Spot turns, etc. are allowed
Air Taxi	Proceeding at a slow speed above the surface, normally below 20 kts in ground effect
Ground Taxi	Movement in contact with the ground, under a helicopter's own power (for wheeled helicopters, to reduce downwash)
Taxi	Ground or Air Taxi, according to preference
Hold	Come to a standstill - either hovering or on the ground (on the ground if ground taxiing)
Touchdown	Come into contact with the surface

CALLSIGNS

You should use your full callsign until it is abbreviated by ATC, then you can use the shortened version.

For example, under ICAO, the abbreviated form of XY-ABC should be X-BC, so *Cherokee XY-ABC* would become *Cherokee BC*. In Canada, however, C-ABCD would be shortened to just BCD.

Once satisfactory communication has been established, and there will be no confusion, you are allowed to abbreviate a ground station's callsign.

Talking to Air Traffic Control

ATS units are identified by the name of the location, then the service available:

- *Centre*: En route area control, including RAS and FIS

- *Approach*: Approach control when a separate function

- *Departures*: Departure control when a separate function

- *Final/Director*: Radar control providing vectors onto final approach

- *Tower*: Aerodrome control or aerodrome and approach control from a control tower

- *Ground*: Surface movement control

The name of the location or the service may be omitted once satisfactory communication has been established. An ACC has a *Control* suffix.

On a typical flight, you might talk to several ATC departments, loosely in the following order (some may be combined at smaller airfields). In general, the procedure for outbound aircraft is:

- Obtain the ATIS or current weather

- Request startup clearance, stating the ATIS version you have, but....*

- Obtain taxi instructions (up to a limiting point - normally the holding point of the runway in use)

- *Obtain departure clearance or instructions while taxying, which is difficult in the hover, so maybe get it beforehand.

- Change to Tower for takeoff clearance, also difficult in the hover, so you will often taxi on the Tower frequency

On the way back in:

- Obtain the ATIS or current weather

- Request joining instructions, stating the ATIS version you have

- Report position in the circuit, such as downwind, finals, etc (the *finals* call is made within 7 km. *Long finals* is at 15 km)

- If ATC require you to *Go Around*, they will say so, at which point you climb away and start the circuit again. You can initiate a Go Around at any time by saying *Going Around*

GROUND CONTROL

The Ground Controller handles all movements on the manoeuvring area, including aircraft and vehicles, and possibly start clearances (departure clearances given by Ground are *not* clearances to takeoff!) Typically, you would be talking to Ground up to the holding point, and afterwards when landing - this helps ATC with planning and keep the tower frequency clear (but a helicopter may taxi on the Tower frequency, as your hands are full in the hover). It also reduces fuel waste from delays. It helps if you say where you are, and include the current ATIS:

"C-PACO on Helipad 1 with Bravo, request start"

Bravo is the latest ATIS. You will get an acknowledgement, with the current QNH.

TOWER

For traffic close to the aerodrome, including the circuit. After takeoff, you may be asked to change to Approach (below), but, more typically, you will stay with the Tower until clear of the area. Taxi instructions will contain a clearance limit, meaning a point beyond which you must not go without further permission. This will normally be the holding point of the runway in use (you are automatically cleared across those on the way, *holding short* when you get there), but may be elsewhere if they are busy. On a large airfield, taxiways to be used will be included:

"Taxi to the hold for 19, via taxiway Alpha, then Bravo."

However, helicopter operations are a lot more informal at smaller airfields.

APPROACH

Sometimes known as *Radar*, these controllers sit in a darkened room in front of radar screens, so have no visual contact with the traffic they are dealing with (don't worry, they are fed frequently). Approach controllers guide the aircraft during its approach or departure to or from the airport. Mostly, arrivals and departures are handled by a single approach unit but, at busier airfields they may be separate, with different controllers, callsigns and frequencies.

If told to *continue*, because of traffic on the runway, that is *not* a clearance to land - you still need permission. If the runway is long enough, in daylight, you may be allowed to *land after* whatever is on it already. The words "go around" mean "initiate a missed approach".

Canadian ATC Services are divided into:

- **VFR Control** at controlled airports and subdivided into:

  - Airport Control Service

  - Radar Service, if a Tower Radar Plan exists

- **IFR Control** at area units and subdivided into:

  - Area Control Service. Area controllers are not necessarily based at an airport, and control aircraft that are passing through their airspace without landing.

  - Terminal Control Service

- **Information Services** which include AMIS, for use by Air Defence Units, Alerting Service and FIS

- **Supplementary Services** which include Altitude Reservation & ADCUS, for Customs alerting

There is some blurring between them and controllers do not always make it clear what service you are getting.

Overseas, you might also find:

- A *Radar Advisory Service* which is only provided under IFR, regardless of the weather. You will be given the bearing, distance and height of known conflicting traffic, plus *advisory* avoiding action, which should nevertheless not be ignored. If you do, you must advise ATC. You remain responsible for terrain avoidance.

- You can get A *Radar Information Service* (RIS) under IFR or VFR. You still get information on conflicting traffic, but without avoiding action. You are responsible for separation from other aircraft and terrain avoidance.

- A *Flight Information Service* is *not* a radar service. It is merely someone to talk to.

RADAR IDENTIFICATION

You can be identified by information from yourself (position reporting, or in relation to a prominent object), by making turns that can be seen on radar, or by identing with SSR (SSR is the only one that does not require a backup).

RADAR VECTORING

The phrase *Under RADAR Control* is only used when a radar control service is being provided, meaning that you must do what you are told. ATC will assume responsibility for separation and terrain avoidance.

You may be given specific vectors for lateral separation purposes, and left to resume your own navigation when it is completed (they may be nice and tell you where you are). *Orbits* (complete turns) may be used for delaying purposes or for increasing separation.

You should be advised if radar identification is lost, or about to be lost, and appropriate instructions should be given. Heading information and instructions are in degrees magnetic.

Clearances and Readbacks

You must comply with any clearances received and acknowledged. If you don't like them, you should say so at the time, since an acknowledgement without further comment is taken as such. Clearances are valid only in controlled airspace, and there will be some form of the word "clear" in the text to identify them. Clearances must always be read back (you don't need to read back the wind velocity). You must also comply with instructions in the same way, unless safety is a factor. An instruction will be identifiable, but the word "instruct" may not be included. Clearances should be given slowly and clearly, and not when pilots might be doing something important, like taxying, or lining up for takeoff, or hovering. All clearances should be read back, to ensure that they have been received and transmitted properly in the first place, to the right aircraft.

If a clearance or an instruction is not suitable, you may request and, if practicable, obtain an amended one. Clearances are passed slowly and clearly, since you will need to write them down, and preferably before startup, since you will not want to be bothered when taxying, etc. They will contain the aircraft identification (as per the flight plan), the clearance limit (usually the destination) and the route, levels, changes and any other instructions, especially about departure manoeuvres.

Control is based on *known traffic only*, so you are still responsible for safe procedures and good judgement - clearances do not constitute authority to violate the rules! Information about flight conditions is meant as assistance or reminders.

Aircraft moving to control areas within 30 minutes of each other must be coordinated before departure clearance is issued.

You should start a transmission with the callsign of the service provider followed by the aircraft callsign. When a readback of an ATC message is required, you should terminate the read back transmission with the aircraft's radio callsign.

These clearances should be read back in full:

- Taxi instructions

- Clearances to enter, land on, take off from, cross, backtrack and hold short of the runway in use

- Heading, speed and level instructions

- Altimeter settings

- Transponder codes

- Airways or route clearances

- VDF information

- Frequency changes

- Type of radar service

Route clearances must be read back completely. Others (including conditional clearances) need only contain key elements and include sufficient detail to clearly indicate that they will be complied with. Use the words *Unable To Comply* if you have a problem with a clearance.

CONDITIONAL CLEARANCES

A conditional clearance depends on the actions of another aircraft, such as when being given clearance to cross a runway after a taxying aircraft has passed. Correct identification of the aircraft involved is essential. Conditional clearances must be given in this order:

- Identification

- The condition (specify)

- The clearance

For example: "C-PACO - Behind the A 340, Line up and wait". Your reply: "Behind the A 340, Line Up and wait, C-PACO".

Note: This implies the need for you to identify the aircraft or vehicle causing the conditional clearance.

Readability Scale

To check a radio, call up another station (if they're not busy) and ask how they read you (don't take more than about ten seconds). They will reply with a readability grading on the following scale:

- 1 - unreadable

- 2 - readable now and then

- 3 - readable with difficulty

- 4 - readable

- 5 - perfectly readable

"Reading you Strength Three", for example.

Weather Information

ATC will happily provide weather information if required, but it helps to keep the airways clear if you use the following automated services.

ATIS

This is routine information for departing and arriving aircraft supplied by a continuous and repetitive broadcast on discrete VHF frequencies and/or VOR, and possibly NDB (but not ILS) at major aerodromes. The *Automatic Terminal Information Service* reduces congestion on VHF frequencies, although it may have its own channel. You should listen to it and take down the details before you contact ATC, inbound or outbound. On first contact with ATC, you should state the version you have received, such as "Information Golf", or whatever. ATIS broadcasts should be updated whenever a significant change occurs, and should not last over 30 seconds.

These are the items transmitted in the correct order:

- ATIS ID

- Time (24 hour clock)

- Wind Velocity (Degrees/Knots)

- Visibility (Metres)

- Low Cloud (oktas/feet)

- Medium Cloud (oktas/feet)

- High Cloud (oktas/feet)

- Temp/Dew Point (Degrees)

- Altimeter (hPA/Inches)

- Runway in use

- Anything else useful, such as runway missing, lights out, etc.

Scattered, with reference to cloud cover, means that half, or less than half, of the sky is covered (3-4 oktas). *Broken* means 5-7 oktas, and *overcast* means 8 oktas (100%).

In Canada, CAVOK (Cloud and Visibility OK) means more than 6 staute miles visibility and no cloud below 5000 feet (abroad it might be reported in km). Visibility less than 1 mile is reported in 1/4s or 1/8s.

VOLMET

This is usually transmitted over HF for long-distance flights (North Atlantic and Arctic for Canada), but can be found elsewhere. It consists of long readouts of TAFs and METARs in a sequence, so if you miss the aerodrome you want, just wait for it to come round again. Many airfields have it available over the telephone.

Transfer Of Communication

When ATC want to hand you off to another ATS unit, they will say something like:

> *Contact Ground (or whatever) on (frequency)*

> *Contact London on 118.75*

Radio Failure

ICAO Annex 10, Vol II refers.

Try another frequency, or talk to other aircraft first. Make sure also that the facility is not closed, and that you are not out of range. If all that fails, essentially, you must comply with the last clearance, which hopefully included permission to land or clear the area. If you don't need to enter controlled airspace, carry on, maintaining VFR as necessary; don't enter it even if you've been previously cleared. If you must do so, divert and telephone for permission first. If you're already in controlled airspace, where clearance has been obtained to the boundary on leaving, or the field on entering, proceed as planned. If in doubt, clear the zone the most direct way as quickly as possible, avoiding airfields, and making blind transmissions, in case the transmitter is working. If you are in a circuit, and your radio fails, repeatedly switch the landing lights on and off.

Squawk 7600 for communications failure. If you can hear ATC they will likely ask you to push the ident button if you cannot transmit.

IFR - 602.137

If you are in or have received a clearance to enter controlled airspace, you must listen out on the appropriate frequency for messages or further clearances, set the

transponder to 7600 and try to establish communications with ATC any way you can. Otherwise, refer to the Canada Air Pilot and the CFS. If in VMC, continue VFR and land as soon as practicable.

If you cannot continue under VFR:

- Use the last cleared routing, or the last vectored fix, or that which would have been given, or the flight planned route, in that order.

- Use the highest of last assigned altitude, minimum IFR altitude (as per airspace) or that which might have been expected (if the failure happens during radar vectoring, climb immediately to minimum IFR altitude) while proceeding to the fix or facility associated with the procedure. ATC know pretty much when you are going to get there, because you have a flight plan in, so they will clear the way. When you get to the facility or fix, go straight into the full procedure, without holding, as they will want you on the ground as soon as possible - that is, do it quickly, but be safe.

- Start the descent procedure at the original or amended ETA, that last notified or the last expected approach time.

EAT, or *Expected Approach Time*, is when ATC estimates an arriving aircraft, following a delay, can leave the hold to complete an approach. Changes over 5 minutes should be communicated as soon as possible. If you have received and acknowledged holding instructions, you should leave the hold at the cleared time, EFC or EAT. If an approach does not begin at the holding fix, leave at EAC. If you have no EAC time, when you arrive at the clearance limit, go to a fix where the approach begins. Finish the descent or approach as close as possible to ETA (within 30 minutes). If you have received and acknowledged holding instructions, you should leave the hold at the cleared time, EFC or EAT. If an approach does not begin at the holding fix, leave at EAC. If you have no EAC time, when you arrive at the clearance limit, go to a fix where the approach begins. Finish the descent or approach as close as possible to ETA.

On a transborder flight to the USA, the requirements are essentially the same, but you are responsible for obeying US requirements.

VFR

In Class B, C or D airspace, you must either land at the aerodrome controlling the zone (see NORDO), or leave by the shortest route. Set the transponder to 7600 and inform ATC as soon as possible. Outside the airspace, continue under VFR to the nearest suitable aerodrome, set 7600, use NORDO. If all else fails, enter the airspace squawking 7600, use NORDO and confess to ATC.

NORDO

The procedure for arriving at an aerodrome without using a radio is to approach the circuit from upwind, join crosswind at circuit height and join the downwind leg. Keep watching for traffic and light signals.

Look for traffic before turning finals, and make another circuit if no permission for landing is given. After landing, taxi to the ramp.

SPEECHLESS CODE

Under ICAO procedures, one short press of the transmit button means *Yes*, and two means *No*. Three means *Say Again*, and four (*H* in Morse) is a request for homing. One long press mans *manoeuvre complete*, and one long, two short and one long (*X* in Morse) means *Bugger, I've got another emergency* - (joke!)

However, in Canada, the ATC MANOPS (Manual of Operations) only covers asking a pilot to change squawk, squawk ident, go to standby & back or change heading in the event of loss of aircraft transmit.

RECEIVER FAILURE

Make reports at scheduled times or positions, preceded by the phrase "Transmitting Blind due to receiver failure".

Distress & Urgency Procedures

An emergency exists the moment you become doubtful about position, fuel, weather, or anything else that could affect the safety of your flight. The first transmission should be on the frequency in use at the time, then the international one of 121.5 MHz, followed by others.

The first station receiving a Distress or Urgency call (see below) should *acknowledge it* and take immediate action to ensure that the necessary information is made available to ATC and the operating agency, and take control of communications if necessary, including issuing imposing radio silence by saying *Stop Transmitting - MAYDAY*, after which everyone should shut the heck up. If and when the threat is over, the Distress call must be cancelled by notification on ALL frequencies on which the original message was sent.

INTERCEPTING DISTRESS TRANSMISSIONS

Distress transmissions are normally given out on the frequency in use at the time, but when over the high seas, say when flying offshore, you will typically be guarding one of the distress frequencies, either *121.5 MHz, 243 MHz* or *2182 KHz* for merchant shipping. ELTs operate on 406 MHz.

If you hear a distress transmission, you must:

- Record the position of the craft in distress (take a bearing)
- Inform the appropriate ATS unit or RCC
- At your discretion, whilst awaiting further instructions, proceed to the position given

Once there, if a rescue is in progress, do not interfere without checking with whoever is in charge.

If you need to direct another craft to the scene, circle it at least once, fly low just in front and rock the fuselage, then fly off in the direction you want them to go.

You can use the same signals when they are finished with, but fly behind instead. In theory, they should hoist the *Code Pennant*, which is a flag with vertical red and white stripes, close up, or flash a series of *Ts* in Morse Code with a lamp. On the other hand, they could just turn in the direction requested. A blue and white chequered flag means *Much Regret, Unable* (i.e. *NO*), as does a series of *Ns* in Morse.

DISTRESS

The Distress call (MAYDAY) is used when threatened by *grave and imminent danger* and in *most urgent need* of *immediate assistance*. You can use the letters SOS in Morse Code (··· --- ···), or the spoken words MAYDAY, repeated 3 times, followed by relevant details, like your position, and what is happening:

> MAYDAY MAYDAY MAYDAY
> *Callsign (e.g. C-JLBI)*
> *Type (e.g. Helicopter)*
> *Nature of emergency (e.g. Total Engine Failure)*
> *Intentions of PIC*
> *Position (e.g. 20 Miles E of London VOR)*

Repeat as necessary. You can also fire rockets or red lights at short intervals, and parachute flares. Control of distress traffic is the responsibility of the aircraft in distress.

To cancel a MAYDAY:

- State MAYDAY once

- Say ALL STATIONS three times

- Aircraft ID

- Station called

- Time

- Name of station in distress

- DISTRESS TRAFFIC ENDED

- Station called

- OUT

Distress frequencies are:

- 121.5 MHz - VHF Aeronautical Emergency Frequency

- 243 MHz - UHF Military Emergency Frequency

- 500 KHz - MF International Distress Frequency

- 2182 KHz - MF International Distress Frequency (this is officially in the MF band, but most HF radios can deal with it)

The squawk code for an emergency is 7700.

Tip: If you don't have time to change the squawk, keep pressing the Ident.

URGENCY

The Urgency call (or "PAN") spoken three times, indicates a very urgent message concerning the safety of a ship, aircraft or other vehicle, or of some person on board or in sight, but immediate assistance is not required. It has priority over all other messages except Distress (above). If you just wish to mention you are compelled to land, but don't need help right away, switch the landing lights and/or navigation lights on and off in an irregular pattern.

Include as much information as you can, but especially:

- Name of station addressed

- Aircraft identification

- Nature of urgency condition

- Intentions

The phrase *PAN PAN MEDICAL* means that the following message concerns a protected medical transport using aircraft assigned exclusively to medical transportation.

AIR LAW

6

The government often has to make laws about subjects it knows nothing about, or cannot keep up with, or which are strictly for a local area (i.e. bye-laws), so it may grant a suitable person or authority (e.g. an Aviation Authority, such as Transport Canada, or the Minister) the power to make laws on its behalf, which saves much time.

This is known as *subordinate legislation* (or more commonly, and wrongly, as *delegated legislation*). The Canadians call it *Administrative Law*, which is a better name.

Legislation about Aeronautics in Canada comes from Parliament, like any other law in Canada does, but some of it originates from International requirements, because Canada belongs to the *International Civil Aviation Organisation*, or ICAO. The following bit is a brief description of how it all fits in, although it is not required for the exams, so you could skip a few pages straight to *Canadian Aviation Regulations* if you wish. However, reading it may put a few things in perspective - some of the subjects in the exam syllabus are there not because Transport Canada requires them, but because ICAO does. The most obvious example is Human Factors, but the radio stuff counts as well, as does Accident Investigation.

One direct benefit for pilots is that countries that subscribe to ICAO recognise to greater or lesser degrees the licences of other countries, so a Canadian pilot going to work in the UAE would, in theory, only have to take an Air Law exam to get a UAE licence (note, however, that this does not work to the same extent in JAA countries (Europe), although certain exemptions are granted).

INTERNATIONAL AIR LAW

One idea behind this concept is to reduce a phenomenon known as *conflict of laws*, and the resulting confusion that could arise where, say, a claim for damages is brought in a French court in respect of injury to a Canadian whilst travelling on a ticket bought in Holland for a journey from Germany on an Italian plane. Another intention is to *foster international trade*.

International Air Law has mainly evolved through various International *Conventions* or *Treaties* which form the basis of Public International Law, which can be incorporated into the law of individual states, as with the *Chicago Convention of 1944*, which established *International Standards* and *Recommended Practices* (with which, over the high seas, you must comply, and inform ICAO if you don't).

A *Convention* is an agreement that many nations are at liberty to enter into (*multilateral*) and the word *Treaty* indicates agreements between two (or more) States that bind only themselves (*bilateral*). As you will see below, conventions can cover many subjects, including standards for navigation equipment, but they can also establish governing bodies, such as the *International Civil Aviation Organisation*, established by.........

The Chicago Convention 1944

This is arguably the most important legislation that affects aviation, because most of the countries in the world subscribe to it and adopt it as all or part of their own aviation legislation. Otherwise known as the *Convention on International Civil Aviation*, the parties to the Chicago Convention recognised that, after World War II (which actually ended in 1945), the future development of international civil aviation would be a major help in creating and preserving friendship and understanding among the nations and peoples of the world, whilst recognising that its abuse can become a threat to general security. Not only that, the air transport industry was considered to be at risk. The idea was to avoid friction and promote cooperation between nations and peoples to foster peace, by agreeing to develop international civil aviation in a safe and orderly manner, establishing international air transport services based on equality of opportunity, operated soundly and economically.

One of the most important results of the Convention, as it is called, was the formation of ICAO in 1947, under Article 43, whose standards and practices are used all over the world, with the odd difference here and there (they will be described in the AIM of whatever country).

The *International Air Transport Association* (IATA) is a private organisation formed by the airlines, which has strong links with ICAO and governments, and is often used as an agent for inter-airline cooperation. IATA has many committees, but the most significant is *Traffic*, which negotiates many arrangements between states and airlines. However, most helicopter pilots will only become aware of IATA when dealing with Dangerous Goods, because IATA issue their own Regulations.

ICAO Documents

Part of ICAO's job is to issue *Standards and Recommended Practices* (SARPs), so ICAO shoves out a lot of paperwork in the course of its working life.

ANNEXES (SARPS)

The Chicago Convention lists 18 Annexes in Article 90, which contain *Standards and Recommended Practices* which the various member countries of ICAO adopt as the source documents for their own legislation (the word *shall* indicates that you are reading a *Standard*, and the word *should* indicates a *Recommended Practice*):

- *Annex 1* - Personnel Licensing
- *Annex 2* - Rules of the Air
- *Annex 3* - Meteorological Services for International Air Navigation
- *Annex 4* - Aeronautical Charts
- *Annex 5* - Measurement Units
- *Annex 6* - Aircraft Operation
- *Annex 7* - Nationality and Registration Marks
- *Annex 8* - Airworthiness
- *Annex 9* - Facilitation (entry and departure for passengers and baggage)
- *Annex 10* - Aeronautical Communications
- *Annex 11* - Air Traffic Services
- *Annex 12* - Search and Rescue
- *Annex 13* - Investigation of Accidents
- *Annex 14* - Aerodromes
- *Annex 15* - Aeronautical Information Services
- *Annex 16* - Environmental Protection 1 - Noise
- *Annex 17* - Security, for a program at each international airport, by each contracting state
- *Annex 18* - Dangerous Goods

SARPs are finalised by the *Air Navigation Commission*. The standards in the Annexes are to be considered binding for member states that have not notified ICAO about any national differences (they are listed in the AIM). Deviations must be reported to ICAO for publication in a supplement to the Annex concerned.

PROCEDURES FOR AIR NAVIGATION SERVICES (PANS)

PANS are procedures that have been adopted by the ICAO Council for worldwide use. They can contain new procedures or those which are complex, or which are not quite suitable for SARPs. In other words, they are *detailed guidance documents issued by ICAO, containing operational practices that are beyond the scope of SARPs, but which are nevertheless subject to a measure of uniformity*. They come in three sections:

- **PANS-ABC** - ICAO abbreviations and codes
- **PANS-OPS** - Aircraft Operations
  - Volume 1 - Flight Procedures
  - Volume 2 - Construction of Visual & Instrument Procedures
- **PANS-RAC** - Rules of the Air & Air Traffic Services

PANS do not carry the same legal force as Annexes, but they are nevertheless observed as strictly as law. For example, the ICAO document about Aircraft Operations is DOC 8168-OPS, affectionately known as PANS-OPS, in which Vol I describes flight procedures (i.e. approaches, etc), and Vol II is for people who develop them, so the working pilot will only be remotely bothered about Vol I. PANS-RAC covers Rules of the Air and Air Traffic Services. If you end up flying long haul across the North Atlantic, you will become very familiar with it.

REGIONAL SUPPLEMENTARY PROCEDURES

SUPPs contain stuff that is too detailed, or changes too much, for Annexes. They augment PANS and modify the SOPs contained in them for the various regions.

International Air Transit and Air Transport Agreements

As scheduled services were excluded from the Chicago Convention, their rights and privileges were dealt with in the *International Air Services Transport Agreement* and the *International Air Transit Agreement*, both also initiated at Chicago in 1944.

The former allows the carriage of traffic between the State of Registration of an aircraft and any other State, and the latter allows aircraft of states party to it to overfly or make tech stops in the territory of other contracting states. However, the main outcome was certain freedoms, commonly known as the *five freedoms*, although there are actually up to eight or nine.

THE FIVE FREEDOMS

These are granted between States after negotiation. The first two arise from the Air Transit agreement and, being *technical rights*, have no commercial implications, but the others, from the Air Transport agreement, being *commercial rights*, do - number Five allows another State's airline to pick up from yours and transport to another.

- *One* - to fly across territory without landing

- *Two* - to land for non-traffic purposes (such as technical stops)

- *Three* - put down passengers, mail and cargo taken on in the owning State

- *Four* - take on passengers, mail and cargo destined for the owning State

- *Five* - take on passengers, mail and cargo destined for any other Contracting State, and put them down (nothing to do with *cabotage*, below)

OTHER FREEDOMS

These are not so widely accepted, because they evolved as workarounds for some minor problems arising from the fifth freedom:

- *Six* - start in another State, and go through the State of Registry (base nation) to a third (combination of 3 and 4)

- *Seven* - revenue traffic between two States, neither being the State of Registry (i.e. by the carrier of another State)

- *Eight* - operate an internal service within another State (*cabotage*). In other words, carriage of revenue traffic between two points in one State by the carrier of another State

- *Nine* - Code sharing. Carriage of passengers by airlines other than the one booked. 2 or 3 airlines are often shown as operating one flight

The Tokyo Convention 1963

This relates to offences committed on board, but not by, aircraft (it is penal law). It was an attempt to unite against threats to security, like hijacking or terrorism. It covers *damage caused in the territory of a contracting state, or in a ship or aircraft registered therein, by an aircraft registered in another contracting state.*

- Article 3 says that the State of *Registry* has jurisdiction over offences and acts committed on board, and should take necessary measures to prove it

- Article 4 says that other States may not interfere with aircraft in flight to exercise criminal jurisdiction over an offence committed on board, except when it has an effect on its territory, has been committed by or against one of its residents, is against its security, is a breach of any of its aviation rules, or such exercise is necessary under an international agreement

The Tokyo Convention also describes the authority and responsibilities of the PIC, who has final authority as to the disposition of the aircraft while in command.

If a person commits, or is about to commit, an unlawful act on an aircraft, the commander may impose reasonable measures, including restraint, to:

- protect the safety of the aircraft, persons and property on board

- maintain good order and discipline

- enable handover to the authorities by removal or refusal to allow the people on board

Other crewmembers and passengers may be dragged in to assist as necessary.

In a hijacking situation, the obligation of a State is the *provision of navaids, ATS* and *landing clearance.* A contracting State must take measures for the safety of passengers subject to unlawful interference until their journey *can safely be continued.*

Isolated parking positions must be established for aircraft subject to unlawful interference. The minimum distance from other aircraft, buildings, etc. is 100 m.

When an aircraft subject to an act of unlawful interference must depart from its assigned track or level, the PIC must attempt to broadcast warnings on the VHF emergency frequency.

The Warsaw Convention 1929

Relates to liability and its limitation for death or personal injury, or loss or damage to baggage or cargo (if it didn't exist, airlines would soon go bankrupt). It applies to international carriage of passengers, luggage or goods by aircraft for reward, but includes free carriage by aircraft in an air transport undertaking.

The carrier is liable for damage sustained on board, including embarkation and disembarkation (except if the passenger's health was the cause of death or injury). For baggage or cargo, the liability exists when the stuff is in the carrier's charge. Having said all that, in 1995, the *Airline Liability Conference*, under IATA modernised the Warsaw Convention. Essentially, it laid down that compensation for international passengers would no longer be limited by it.

TICKETS (ARTICLE 3)

The carrier must issue a document indicating departure and destination points, including stopping places (the same applies to luggage, covered in Article 4).

The absence, irregularity or loss of a ticket does not affect the contract of carriage under the Convention, but if a passenger is accepted without a ticket, the carrier cannot rely on limited liability.

AIR WAYBILLS (ARTICLE 5)

The equivalent of a ticket for cargo is the *air waybill*, which must be in three parts. The first must be marked "for the carrier" and be signed by the consignor, as must the second part, which must be marked "for the consignee". The third must be signed by the carrier and handed to the consignor after goods have been accepted. The carrier must sign before the cargo is loaded, and may ask for more than one waybill if there is more than one package.

If the paperwork isn't done properly (or, more correctly, the consignor isn't warned about liability), the carrier cannot rely upon it.

The Hague Convention 1970

This concerns the suppression of unlawful seizure of aircraft, and the rules for establishing jurisdiction.

The Montreal Conventions

The 1971 version dealt with unlawful acts against the safety of civil aviation (air rage, etc.), particularly sabotage, but mainly acts other than hijacking. The 1998 version concerned unlawful acts of violence at international airports, and the 1991 one was about international marking of plastic explosives for easier detection.

The Rome Convention 1933

To cover liability towards people and goods on the ground or damage caused by foreign aircraft to third parties on the ground.

People who suffer damage only need to prove that it was caused by an aircraft in flight, or anything falling from it, to get full compensation, but not if the damage did not arise as a direct result, or if it results from mere passage through airspace under existing regulations. The liability for compensation lies with the *operator*, but only up to a sum in line with the weight of the aircraft. Although compensation is limited, it may not be if the damage was caused by intent or theft of the aircraft.

CANADIAN AVIATION REGULATIONS

These come in several parts:

- The *Aeronautics Act*, which is the enabling legislation

- *CARs*, which tell you *what* is to be done, or what *can* be done

- *CARs Standards*, which tell you *how* it's to be done

They are collectively known as CARs, and do not apply to the military doing their normal thing, models, rockets, hovercraft or wing-in-ground-effect machines.

Regulations (and Standards) are divided into nine parts:

I	General Provisions
II	Aircraft Identification
III	Aerodromes and Airports
IV	Personnel Licensing and Training
V	Airworthiness (ignored here)
VI	General Operating & Flight Rules
VII	Commercial Air Services
VIII	Air Navigation Services
IX	Repeals & Coming Into Force

Note: In this book, the regulations follow the order of ICAO Annexes.

Luckily, the working pilot only needs to bother with Parts I, VI and VII, that is, *General Provisions, General Operating and Flight Rules* (subparts 1, 2 and 5) and *Commercial Air Services*. Where a Standard relates to a Regulation, the numbering will be similar; *icing*, for example, would be covered by *Regulation* 602.1 and *Standard* 622.1. Each regulation comes in three parts, such as:

600.01.101.01

which represent the *Part* (600), *Subpart* (01) and *Regulation* (101.01), respectively. Anything in Part 6, for example, would therefore start with 600 (although each subpart is split into Divisions, the only way to find out about them is to look in the index at the beginning of the Part itself). Amendments may not be made to CARs unless people have been consulted under *CARAC Management Charter and Procedures*, and more than 30 days has elapsed, unless urgently required for safety reasons.

Enforcement

Exemptions may be made if they are in the public interest and don't affect safety. Otherwise, relevant parts of the Act apply to everyone and everything related to aviation in Canada, and all Canadian aircraft (including passengers and crew) and people holding Canadian aviation documents outside Canada. Everyone exercising the privileges of a Canadian aviation document (and every Canadian aircraft), in a foreign state, must comply with the relevant laws of that state.

Everyone doing anything outside Canada that would be illegal inside Canada may be proceeded against and punished where they are found in Canada, as if the act had been committed there. The registered owner, operator or PIC of an aircraft may be proceeded against on behalf of another person unless it was in the possession of yet another person without consent. The operator of an aerodrome or other aviation facility may be proceeded against on behalf of another person unless offences were committed without consent. You have not committed an offence if you try as hard as possible to prevent it.

Documents & Admin

If you hold a Canadian aviation document, are the owner, operator or PIC of an aircraft to which one relates, or have one in your possession, you must produce it to a peace or immigration officer or the Minister (i.e. Transport Canada) when requested.

Unless you're a military pilot, or a foreign one from a contracting state, undergoing training (with no passengers carried), you must hold, and be able to produce *during your duties*, an appropriate permit, licence, rating and medical certificate (a pilot's licence consists of three parts, namely the licence itself, a radio operator's licence and a medical).

You cannot lend a Canadian aviation document to anyone not entitled to it, or allow them to use it, mutilate it, alter it or render it illegible.

RETURN OF DOCUMENTS

Canadian aviation documents must be returned immediately after the date of suspension or cancellation.

SUSPENSION, CANCELLATION, RENEWAL

Notices of suspension or cancellation after a contravention must state what the alleged contravention was, and the duration of any suspension. The notice must be sent by personal service, or registered or certified mail, to your last address, and doesn't take effect until thirty days after it has been served or sent. A request for review by a tribunal does not automatically stay proceedings, but you can apply for one in writing.

A notice of suspension issued because of an immediate threat to aviation safety must include the effective date of the suspension and the conditions under which it may be terminated. The threat concerned must also be specified, and, as above, and it takes effect immediately after receipt. Similarly, a notice of cancellation or suspension on medical grounds must include the effective date and details of the suspension, or conditions under which it is terminated. These suspensions may also be appealed by applying to a tribunal within 30 days of being served, but the tribunal cannot stay their suspension or cancellation pending appeal.

A Canadian aviation document may also be suspended, cancelled or not renewed if you voluntarily surrender it, it is mutilated, altered, or rendered illegible, the aircraft to which it relates has been destroyed or withdrawn, or the service it relates to has been discontinued.

RECORD KEEPING

Recording systems, including computer or microfiche, that are not based on paper entries, must be protected against loss, destruction or tampering, and paper copies must be produced on reasonable notice.

Alterations should be done so the original entry can still be seen, with a note as to why the alteration was made, when and by whom.

LICENSING (ICAO ANNEX 1)

Examinations

Unless authorized by an invigilator, you may not copy or remove any portion of the text, give it to or accept it from anyone, give or receive help to or from anyone, or use any aid or written material, or you will be barred for up to a year from a retake.

All memory must be cleared from calculators or hand-held computers before and afterwards in the presence of the invigilator. The latter must also have been designed for flight operations and approved.

You must be competent in one of the official languages.

PREREQUISITES - 401.13/421.13

You must meet standards regarding medical fitness and identification (that is, a permit, licence or other official document with your signature and photograph), with a recommendation from the instructor responsible for your training, plus the proper experience. Military pilots, however, just need proof of wings. If you have a foreign licence, a letter is not required if you are applying for the equivalent Canadian one, but the paperwork must have been done in the previous 24 months. Recommendation letters may only be used once. Proof of medical fitness can be an appropriate Medical Certificate, Medical Assessment Letter (Form 26-0417), Civil Aviation Medical Declaration (Form 26-0297), temporary Medical Certificate or Medical Exam Report assessed by the RAMO (see under relevant licence, below).

Before taking exams, for a Pilot Permit-Gyroplane, -Recreational - Aeroplane, or a PPL, you must have 10 hours in the same category, or hold a valid Pilot Permit for ultralights. For a Class 4 Instructor Rating, you need to complete 50% of the flight training, and all the ground school. For a higher class, you must have 50% of the experience required. An IR requires at least 20 hours of instrument flight or ground time. Otherwise, you need at least 50% whatever is required.

When it comes to flight tests, for a Pilot Permit - Gyroplane or a PPL you need at least 35 hours in the same category or aircraft, and for a Pilot Permit - Recreational - Aeroplane, at least 25 hours. Otherwise, it's at least 75% of whatever is required for the licence. Commercial candidates who are not in an approved integrated course must complete the written exam before the flight test. Instrument and instructor candidates must complete all requirements before the flight test.

PROOF OF CITIZENSHIP AND AGE

You can use:

- Citizenship certificate
- Certificate of Registration of Birth Abroad
- Birth or baptismal certificate (or certified copy) issued in Canada or a state whose citizens do not need a passport to travel there
- Passport. With no expiry date, get attestation from your State
- Aviation licence showing relevant citizenship
- Canadian Immigration Record and Visa, or Form IMM1000, as issued to landed immigrants (or the new landed immigrant card)

Medicals - 404

Canadian medical requirements stem from ICAO. If you have a higher licence, and wish to use privileges for a lower one, the validity is automatically extended. Validities on certificates supersede CARs. Before you have one, you, as a holder of a Canadian aviation document imposing certain standards, should advise the physician or optometrist. They, in turn, must advise the authorities of any defect affecting your licence, if they suspect you are in aviation.

Medicals are only valid *if you meet the initial issuing requirements.* A Board of Inquiry or insurance company may interpret the words "medically fit" a little differently than you think if you fly with a cold or under the influence of alcohol. In any case, you should talk to a medical examiner as soon as possible in the case of:

- admission to a hospital or clinic for over 12 hours
- surgery or other invasive procedures
- regular use of medication
- regular use of correcting lenses

Currently, your medical certificate, once issued, lasts for four renewals, stamped by the doctor at each one.

CATEGORY 1

Required for an ATPL or CPL, valid for 12 months under 40 and 6 months if over, plus the remainder of the month of issue. Your first one requires an ECG and Audio test, the former being repeated every two years between 30-40 years of age and every year over 40, and the latter at the first medical after 55. Otherwise, your vision must be at least 20/30 for each eye and you only need a chest x-ray at the initial exam if a respiratory problem is suspected.

CATEGORY 2

For Air Traffic and Flight Engineer Licences.

CATEGORY 3

For PPLs and Student Pilot Permits. You need an ECG for the first one after the age of 40. You should hear the examiner whispering softly 6 feet away, otherwise you will need an audiogram. Each eye must be 20/30, and you only need a chest x-ray at the initial exam if a respiratory problem is suspected. It is valid for 60 months under 40 and 24 months if over, and counts for gyroplane and balloon pilots as well. Medicals for Student pilots last for 60 months regardless of age. Overseas, validity periods last only for 24 months.

CATEGORY 4

For Recreational Pilot Permits (see below). You just need to sign a declaration (Form 26-0297) which is countersigned by any physician.

Commercial Pilot Licence - 401.30/420.30

PRIVILEGES

You may exercise the privileges of a PPL, a VFR OTT rating (aeroplanes) or act as PIC or co-pilot in a commercial air service if a single-crew aeroplane is endorsed on your licence. You may also act as copilot if the aircraft has a minimum flight crew requirement of more than one pilot, but that type must be added to your licence (see *Type Ratings*).

You may not fly at night with a licence issued for day flying.

AGE

You must be at least eighteen.

MEDICAL FITNESS AND VALIDITY

You must have a Cat 1 Medical, which is valid for 12 months under 40 and 6 months over that, but you may exercise PPL privileges until the end of the PPL period. The licence is maintained by a Category 1 Medical Certificate.

KNOWLEDGE

You must complete at least 80 hours *commercial* ground school, covering the usual stuff, and get at least 60% in the mandatory areas of the CPL exam. If you don't already hold a PPL(H), you must do another 40 hours commercial ground school for the CPL, for a total of 80 hours.

EXPERIENCE

You need at least 200 hours (in aeroplanes), of which at least 100 is PIC, including 20 cross-country. After your PPL, you must do 65 hours' commercial training in aeroplanes, at least 35 hours dual, including 5 at night (at least 2 cross-country), 5 hours cross-country (by day), which may include that done at night and 20 hours instruments on top, of which up to 10 may be done in a simulator.

You also need 30 hours solo, 25 of which must emphasize your general flying skills, to include a cross-country inside at least a 300 nm radius from the departure point and at least 3 landings at points other than that of departure, with 5 hours solo by night, to include at least 10 takeoffs, circuits and landings.

SKILL

You must have done a flight test in the last 12 months, but you have to write the exam first.

RESTRICTED LICENCE - DAYLIGHT FLYING

If you don't manage the night hours, you can still get a licence, but restricted to day only, if you have the total dual and solo. The restriction will be removed once you gain the hours.

If you hold a licence for the other class with a night rating, the night experience may be reduced to 5 hours, including 2 dual night, 1 solo night and 1 dual instrument.

CREDITS

If you hold a CPL(H), your ground school is reduced and you may write a shorter, alternate category exam that has a pass mark of 60%.

Your DND wings are the equivalent of the ground school, written exam, course and PPL requirements, if you have the experience, which must include at least 10 hours in aeroplanes in the last 12 months. You must get at least 60% in the ARPCO exam.

CREDITS FOR FOREIGN APPLICANTS

If you hold an ICAO licence, your CPL (or higher) exempts you from ground school. If you hold an FAA aeroplane certificate, the requirements are even further reduced.

ATPL - 401.34/421.34

PRIVILEGES

You may:

- exercise privileges of private and commercial licences for the appropriate class

- with a Group 1 IR, act as PIC or co-pilot of a two-crew aeroplane in a commercial air service if the type is endorsed on your licence

AGE

You must be at least twenty-one.

MEDICAL FITNESS AND VALIDITY

You must hold a Category 1 Medical, which is valid for 12 months if you are under 40 and 6 months if you are over, but you may exercise PPL privileges until the end of the usual PPL period. The licence is maintained by a valid Category 1 Medical Certificate.

KNOWLEDGE

You need at least 70%.

EXPERIENCE

The training for an unrestricted CPL, at least 1500 hours (900 in aeroplanes), to include at least 250 hours PIC, which may include up to 100 under supervision. Both must include at least 100 hours cross-country, at least 25 hours by night.

Also, 100 hours night (P1 or P2), at least 30 in aeroplanes. 200 hours cross-country as co-pilot in an aeroplane that needs one, or 100 additional hours cross-country as PIC, which may have been part of the 250 hours mentioned above, and 75 hours instruments, of which up to 25 hours can be done in approved ground trainers, and up to 35 hours in helicopters. Instrument ground time does not count toward the total 1500 hours.

SKILL

In the last 12 months, you must have demonstrated in a multi-engined aeroplane with no central thrust configuration, and fitted for IFR in controlled airspace, competence in appropriate normal and emergency flight procedures and a Group 1 instrument rating (you can only have a group 1 for the initial issue).

CREDITS - EXPERIENCE

A DND applicant with a Group 1 IR (unrestricted), or on a helicopter needing a copilot, covers skill requirements.

Holders of a valid FAA ATPL have met the skill requirement, and their examination requirements are reduced.

TRAINING (PIC U/S) - 421.11

Operators with large machines may supervise co-pilots so they can build PIC time, if Transport Canada agrees they are capable. Supervisory pilots must be briefed by Transport Canada. The time may be acquired in the co-pilot's seat if the PIC functions concerned can be performed from it, otherwise, you must have at least ten hours in the pilot's seat. The time must include at least the flight functions of a PIC, including flight planning, takeoff, landing, en route flying and approach (not taxying) and at least one takeoff and landing for each 10 hours flight time.

For an ATPL - Aeroplane, you can claim up to 100 hours PIC U/S, if you hold a CPL - Aeroplane with multi-engined and suitable type ratings, a Group I IR and at least 150 hours PIC in aeroplanes. For an ATPL - Helicopter, you can claim up to 150 hours PIC U/S with a CPL(H) and a suitable type rating, plus over 100 hours PIC helicopters.

You must get the time in the 12 months before applying. You must submit a personal log (or other reliable record) with a summary of P1/US time and total takeoffs and landings, and indicate the portions claimed on the application form.

Foreign Licences - 421.07

For non-residents. A Foreign Licence Validation Certificate is normally valid for a year. You must provide the licence, a letter of request, and the reasons why it is needed, such as flight testing, private flying, ferrying, etc. If the medical lasts longer than the ICAO standard, the validation is limited to Canadian airspace, and the validation period to no longer than the Canadian medical.

Type Ratings - 401.40/421.40

You can find out the minimum crew for any aircraft in the *Minimum Crew Document*, which could be a type approval certificate, flight permit, flight manual or POH. Some machines need two pilots for IFR and can get by with one under VFR.

Required for every high performance or multi-crew aeroplane on your licence.

AEROPLANE - TWO CREW

KNOWLEDGE

You need ground and flight training on type and, for a PPL or CPL, at least 70% in either the Type Rating-Aeroplane (IATRA) or ATPL written exams (SAMRA and SARON), in the last 24 months, but you must also have 50% of the hours for the ATPL to do the latter. If you have an ATPL, you are exempt the writtens.

EXPERIENCE

Complete flight training on type and have over 250 hours on aeroplanes.

SKILL

You must have passed a PPC on type in the last 12 months.

AEROPLANE - TWO CREW-CRUISE RELIEF

You must hold a CPL or ATPL, and Group 1 IR.

KNOWLEDGE

You must complete ground and flight training on type, and, if you only hold a CPL-Aeroplane, within the previous 24 months, get at least 70% in either the Type Rating-Aeroplane (IATRA) or ATPL (SAMRA & SARON) exams. If you hold an ATPL already, you don't need to take exams.

EXPERIENCE

Complete flight training on type and have at least 250 hours on aeroplanes.

SKILL

You must pass a PPC, excluding takeoffs and landings, on type within the previous 12 months.

HIGH PERFORMANCE AEROPLANE

KNOWLEDGE

Complete type ground training.

EXPERIENCE

Do the flight training and have over 200 hours on aeroplanes.

SKILL

Within the previous 12 months, pass a qualifying flight under a Transport Canada Inspector or a qualified person.

SECOND OFFICER

EXPERIENCE

In the last 12 months, you must have done type-related training by an approved institution.

SKILL

You must pass a Second Officer proficiency check on type.

CREDITS FOR DND APPLICANTS

Active and retired members of Canadian Armed Forces with their wings meet the qualifying flight requirement above, if they have at least 10 hours PIC on type or qualified as PIC during the previous 24 months. The PPC requirement is met if they have acquired at least 50 hours on the appropriate type or have qualified as PIC during the previous 24 months.

CREDITS FOR FOREIGN APPLICANTS

The qualifying flight mentioned above is not needed if you acquire least 10 hours PIC on the appropriate type in the last 12 months. The flight itself may be done under a qualified person licensed by a Contracting State, if you submit a letter from the State's Licensing Authority (or other acceptable source), confirming the personal log entry, and the qualification of the person who supervised the flight.

If you have a two-crew type rating, the PPC requirement is met with at least 50 hours on type in the last 12 months. It may be performed by a qualified person licensed by a Contracting State if you submit a letter from the State's Licensing Authority, or other acceptable source, confirming the personal log entry and the qualification of the person who supervised the PPC.

AIRCRAFT TYPE

The type must be in the Canadian Civil Aircraft Register, except for aircraft purchased abroad with a provisional Canadian C of R, or those manufactured in Canada where no type approval has yet been issued, but a certification flight test program is being conducted (only to flight test pilots and flight engineers employed by the manufacturer, or Transport Canada), or aircraft not in the Canadian Civil Aircraft Register where a Canadian type approval, or a Canadian approved type certificate has been issued.

Night Rating - 401.42/421.42

For the PPL, as you need a minimum amount for the CPL and ATPL anyway.

EXPERIENCE

You must have at least 20 hours, including at least 10 at night, to include at least 5 hours dual (with 2 cross-country), and 5 solo, including 10 takeoffs, circuits and landings, and 10 hours dual instruments. Up to 5 of the 10 hours dual instruments may be instrument ground time, as long as it is on top of the night time.

SKILL

In the last 12 months, you must have successfully completed a qualifying flight under a Transport Canada Inspector or other suitably qualified person by demonstrating the skills in the Flight Instructor Guide-Aeroplane (TP 975).

CREDITS

If you have a night rating in another category, the total of 20 hours is reduced to at least 5 in the relevant class, which must include at least 2 hours dual night, 1 hour solo night, and 1 hour dual instruments, which must be in addition.

Instrument Rating - 401.46/421.46

Group 1 covers multi-engined aeroplanes, Group 2 multi-engine centre line thrust and single engined aeroplanes, Group 3 single engined aeroplanes.

PRIVILEGES

You may use your licence under IFR, and privileges of VFR OTT.

REQUIREMENTS

KNOWLEDGE

At least 70% in INRAT, after gaining over 50% of the total time and 20 on instruments (flight or ground). If you fail, you must wait at least 14 days for a resit.

EXPERIENCE

At least 50 hours cross-country as PIC (10 in the appropriate category) and 40 on instruments, of which up to 20 may be done on the ground. The 40 hours must include at least 5 hours dual from an instructor, in aeroplanes (for Group 1, 2 or 3), or in helicopters (Group 4). You also need 15 hours dual under an IFR instructor, with one dual cross-country flight under simulated or actual IMC of at least 100 nm, under an IFR flight plan to include at, two different locations, an instrument approach to minima.

SKILL

You must pass a flight test under the Flight Test Standards-Instrument Rating (TP 9939E), or an IFR PPC under Part VI or VII, as applicable.

CREDITS FOR DND APPLICANTS

You can use a military instructor to get the experience above. You are exempt the flight test if you have your

wings or hold an appropriate unrestricted Canadian Forces IR, and you have the experience above.

FOREIGN APPLICANTS

You can use a foreign military instructor to get experience if they have equivalent qualifications.

VALIDITY - 421.48

24 months, calculated to the first day of the twenty-fifth month following the month the test was conducted, although you can get one for less than that. Put another way, it's 24 months, plus the remainder of the month of issue. If you renew in the 90 days before it was due to expire, you can claim the original validity date, that is, you get 27 months.

RECENCY

You must have done the test in the appropriate group (aircraft or sim) within the past 12 months. In the previous 6 months, you must have done 6 hours on instruments and 6 approaches to appropriate minima (aircraft or sim, simulated or actual) - this may be done while instructing. Alternatively, do a PPC including the instrument stuff in CASS.

RENEWAL - 421.49

You must pass the flight test. If your IR expired more than 24 months ago, you must also get at least 70% in INRAT, although you are exempt if you also hold a CPL or ATPL from a Contracting State and pass their IR test working commercially outside Canada in the previous 12 months, and give Transport Canada a copy of the paperwork.

You are also exempt INRAT if you hold a Second Officer Rating or a Flight Engineer Licence and you work for hire or reward for a Canadian air carrier operating aircraft requiring a Second Officer or a Flight Engineer, and you previously held an IR and CPL.

If you hold a Canadian Forces unrestricted IR and your civil IR expired more than 24 months ago, you don't need to take INRAT if your pilot licence is valid and your Forces renewal was done in the appropriate type.

An IR can be extended for up to 90 days if the application is made while it is valid and you can prove you haven't been able to take the test.

Recency - 401.05/421.05

Unless you're a flight engineer, you must have acted as PIC or P2 in the last 5 years, or 12 months if you do a check ride (flight review) with an instructor who certifies your log book, and you pass any exams required here, like

PSTAR. The review must include all items in the flight test for normal issue.

The certification in the log book is:

"This is to certify that the skill requirement for _____ has been met"

and must have date, name, signature and licence number of the instructor.

You must also have passed a recurrent training program within the previous 24 months and, if you carry passengers (that is, other than an examiner), within the previous 6 months, in the same category and class or equivalent simulator (unless it's a glider or balloon), have performed 5 night or day take-offs and landings (for a day flight), or 5 night take-offs and landings, if wholly or partly by night.

The following count as a recurrent training program:

- a flight review done by an instructor in the same category, covering items in the initial flight test.

- attendance at a safety seminar from Transport Canada

- participation in an approved recurrent training program to update knowledge of human factors, meteorology, flight planning and navigation, and aviation regulations, rules and procedures

- completion of the most current annual self-paced study program in the Transport Canada Aviation Safety Newsletter, which covers the subjects referred to above. Keep it as proof.

- completion of a training program or PPC under Parts IV, VI or VII (i.e. commercial)

- the issue or renewal of a pilot permit, licence or rating, including night, VFR OTT, instrument, multi-engine, instructor, landplane or seaplane. Completing the written exams counts as well.

A second officer must have acted as such on an aircraft in the previous 5 years and, if a passenger or trainee is on board, the previous 6 months, have acted as second officer in an aircraft or equivalent simulator of the same type.

Personal Logs - 421.08

These must be maintained by applicants for, and holders of, flight crew permits, licences or ratings to record experience concerning their issuance, and recency. Only holders or persons authorised by them can make entries.

Aside from your name, personal logs should have the date of the flight, type of aircraft and registration, crew position, flight conditions (day, night, VFR, IFR), places of departure and arrival, intermediate take-offs and landings (aeroplanes), flight time, methods of launch and inflation, as applicable.

Flight time is the total time from when an aircraft first moves under its own power with the intention of taking off until it comes to rest after the flight, so it includes taxi time, or time with skids on the ground (helicopters). This is what goes in your log book. *Air time*, on the other hand, is between wheels or skids off and when they touch the Earth again. This is what goes in the Journey Log (some Journey Logs have columns for both). Flight time may be written down as *PIC* (sole manipulator of the controls), *P2* (co-pilot) or *Dual*. An instructor would log PIC, while a student would log dual. Where two licensed pilots are practising instrument flying, the one not designated as PIC should log dual. Where dual controls are fitted, whoever is the PIC must be decided before takeoff.

If you lose it, an Affidavit or Statutory Declaration sworn before a Commissioner of Oaths will do instead, with evidence, such as journey log entries. If you can't provide it, the experience is only good for a CPL. You must also complete all exams and tests required. The Affidavit must contain a breakdown of appropriate flying experience, including:

- day and night, P1, P2 and dual

- cross-country by day and night, P1, P2 and dual

- instrument trainer time

- aircraft types and registrations

- names of employers and dates of employment

It must also contain an explanation of how you lost the log and a statement declaring that all attempts to reproduce its entries have been unsuccessful.

A foreign licence holder may be credited with minimum experience in ICAO Annex 1 for the licence held.

VFR OTT Rating - 401.44/421.44

These may be issued for aeroplanes or helicopters, and one counts for the other. They are not automatically included on the PPL (A) or (H), and the CPL (H) and ATPL (H) - they must be endorsed with the rating before you can use it.

KNOWLEDGE

You must acquire a standard of knowledge under the Flight Instructor Standard - VFR OTT.

EXPERIENCE

At least 15 hours dual instruments, of which up to 5 may be done on the ground. Training must be as per the Flight Instructor Standard - VFR OTT.

SKILL

You must reach the skill level in the Flight Instructor Standard - VFR OTT.

CREDITS

If you hold, or have held, an IR, you can have a VFR OTT rating upon request.

CREDITS FOR DND APPLICANTS

If you hold, or have held, a Canadian Forces IR, you meet the Knowledge, Experience and Skill requirements above.

CREDITS FOR FOREIGN APPLICANTS

If you hold, or have held, a foreign Instrument Rating, you meet the Knowledge, Experience and Skill requirements above.

Flight Instructor - 401.61

Only flight instructors may train unlicensed pilots.

You must pass the appropriate flight test, a refresher course (the rating will be renewed from its last day), and have at least 300 hours training in the last 24 months, having recommended at least 80% of candidates for passes on the first attempt (the renewal is based on at least 5 flight tests). If you renew twice by another means, you must take a flight test the third time. If the rating is, or has been, valid in the previous 12 months, you must pass the appropriate test. If it has been invalid for between 12-24 months, you need a recommendation from a Class 1 Instructor and must pass the flight test. For over 24 months, you must also pass the exam under *Knowledge* (below) for the rating.

Ratings can be extended for up to 90 days if the application is made while the rating is valid, and you can show you haven't had a chance to get it renewed in the 90 days before it was due to expire.

CLASS 4 - 421.69/77

SUPERVISION REQUIREMENT - 421.62

You must be employed as an instructor by an FTU and be under one of its supervising instructors (i.e. a suitable Class 1 or 2 Instructor), except for ultra-lights. Supervisors must review each student's training program and records (for each first solo and test recommendation), and carry out flight progress checks at any time, but at least once before first solo and before the final test.

PRIVILEGES

You may:

- conduct dual instruction for a pilot permit or licence, or endorsement of a night or VFR OTT rating on the latter
- authorize trainees for solo flight
- recommend trainees for tests
- recommend a trainee for a night or VFR OTT rating
- instruct on ultra lights without being supervised

PREREQUISITES

Before starting flight training, for aeroplanes, you must have a CPL or ATPL (Aeroplane) and at least 20 hours instrument time, of which at least 10 must be in flight. Before ground training, you only need to have passed the CPL written exam and flight test.

KNOWLEDGE

You must have at least 25 hours ground school, to include practical application of the basic principles of learning and instruction, preparation and use of lesson plans, procedures for planning and presenting preparatory ground instruction, pre-flight briefings, in-flight instruction, and post-flight debriefings, theory of flight for air exercises, aircraft flight manuals and operating limits, presentation of pilot decision-making concepts, and the use of the *Transport Canada Flight Instructor Guide*, *Flight Training Manual*, CARs, Part IV and the *Flight Test Standards*.

EXPERIENCE

You must have at least 30 hours dual instruction on overall pilot proficiency and the presentation of all exercises in the *Flight Instructor Guide*, with at least 5 hours training in the teaching of instrument flight skills. Up to 5 of the 30 hours may be done in an approved simulator or flight training device.

SKILL

You must pass the flight test in the *Flight Test Standards*.

CREDITS

If you hold, or have held an instructor rating for aeroplanes (when applying for an helicopter rating, and *vice versa*), gyroplanes, gliders, balloons or aerobatics, you are exempt 10 of the 25 hours ground school. The same goes for an ATPL, or a teaching certificate issued by provincial or territorial authorities (you can't claim both). An aeroplane instructor rating exempts you from the helicopter written exam, and vice versa.

If you hold, or have held, a Helicopter Instructor Rating, you are exempt 10 of the 30 hours' dual, and the 5 hours' training in the teaching of instrument flight skills. An ATPL-Aeroplane exempts you from 10 of the 30 hours' dual. The reverse is true for helicopters.

A Canadian Forces QFI/QHI Category for single-engine aeroplanes or helicopters, as appropriate, gets you up to 15 hours equivalent experience towards the 30 hours of dual instruction for the opposite category.

If you hold, or have held, in the last 24 months, an Instructor Rating from a Contracting State, you are exempt 10 of the 25 hours ground school, or 15 if the rating is in the appropriate category.

If you hold, or have held, in the previous 24 months, a rating from a Contracting State, you are exempt 10 of the 25 hours ground school, and can claim up to 15.of equivalent experience towards the 30 hours dual instruction.

VALIDITY

To the first day of the thirteenth month following the month the test was conducted.

CLASS 3 - 421.70/78

PRIVILEGES

You may exercise the privileges of a Class 4 instructor and act as CFI of a flight training unit (aeroplanes only) if you are the only one.

PREREQUISITES

You need to be a Class 4 Instructor, but not if you are a Canadian Forces QFI or an instructor from a Contracting State, if the state has a reciprocal agreement, and the rating was not based on one from a State without agreement.

KNOWLEDGE

A Forces or foreign instructor with at least 750 hours ab-initio instruction experience must complete ground instruction (i.e. no specified minimum) to cover the Knowledge requirement for a Class 4 Rating, obtain a letter of recommendation from a Class 1 Instructor before

attempting the written exams, and get at least 70% in each. With between 300-750 hours, you must also do at least 10 hours ground instruction.

EXPERIENCE

You must have conducted at least 100 hours dual instruction for the issue of a pilot licence - Forces, or foreign instructors as above are exempt.

SKILL

You must complete an "Instructor's Training Record While Under Direct Supervision" form, proving you have authorized at least 3 students for their first solos, recommended at least 3 for flight tests, and conducted at least 50% of their last 10 hours dual instruction. If these requirements are met, you don't need a flight test, unless the application coincides with the expiry of a Class 4 Rating. If you are subject to follow-up action about your Flight Test Record under Section 421.67, you cannot upgrade from a Class 4 to a Class 3.

If you are a Forces or foreign instructor, as above, you need some dual instruction under a Class 1 Instructor, who must give you a letter of recommendation for the flight test, as described in the *Flight Test Standard Flight Instructor Rating-Aeroplanes, Helicopters, Aerobatic (TP5537)*.

PERIOD OF VALIDITY

Initially, to the first day of the 25th month following the month the most recent Class 4 test was conducted, or from the date of the Class 3 test.

CLASS 2 - 421.71/79

PRIVILEGES

You may exercise the privileges of a Class 3 instructor, supervise a Class 4 instructor and act as CFI of a flight training unit.

PREREQUISITES

You must have held a Class 3 Rating in the previous 12 months and meet the following knowledge, experience and skill requirements.

KNOWLEDGE

In the last 24 months, you must have got over 70% in the exams.

EXPERIENCE

You must have at least 500 hours instructor time, including at least 400 hours dual instruction for the issue of a civil pilot licence or military wings, and have recommended at least 10 applicants for the recreational, private and/or commercial flight test (up to 3 may be for the recreational test - aeroplanes).

SKILL

You must complete the flight test in the *Flight Test Standard-Flight Instructor Rating-Aeroplanes, Helicopters, Aerobatic* (TP5537). If you are subject to follow-up action about your Flight Test Record under Section 421.67, you cannot upgrade from a Class 3 to a 2.

PERIOD OF VALIDITY

To the first day of the 37th month after the month the test was conducted.

CLASS 1 -421.72/421.80
PRIVILEGES

You may exercise the privileges of a Class 2 instructor and conduct ground school and flight training for instructors.

PREREQUISITES

For an initial Class 1 Rating, you must have held a Class 2 in the last 12 months and meet the following knowledge, experience and skill requirements.

KNOWLEDGE

For aeroplanes, you must, within the previous 24 months, have obtained at least 80% in the Flight Instructor Rating-Instructional Techniques (AIRAT) exam.

EXPERIENCE

You must have, in aeroplanes, at least 750 hours of flight instruction, including at least 600 hours dual for the issue of a civil pilot licence or military wings, and have recommended at least 10 applicants for the recreational, private and/or commercial flight test (up to 3 may be for the recreational test - aeroplanes).

SKILL

You must complete the flight test in the *Flight Test Standard - Flight Instructor Rating - Aeroplanes, Helicopters, Aerobatic* (TP5537). However, if you are subject to follow-up action about your Flight Test Record under Section 421.67, you cannot upgrade from a Class 2 to a 1.

PERIOD OF VALIDITY

To the first day of the 49th month after the month the test was conducted.

Crew Member Qualifications - 722.65, 724.108

PPC - 723.88, 724.108

Must be done by a Transport Canada inspector or approved company check pilot under Schedule II for helicopters, in the aircraft or approved simulator, covering the aircraft, its systems and components, proper control of airspeed, direction, altitude, attitude and configuration under the operating manual, Flight Manual, Ops Manual, SOPs, check list, etc. Also, departure, enroute and arrival instrument procedures, adherence to approved procedures and qualities of airmanship when selecting a course of action. Procedures not approved in the flight sim must be done in the aircraft. PIC and 2IC checks must be done in the applicable seats.

If you pass the PPC, your IR is renewed as well, so IR manoeuvres must be included if relevant. If you renew a PPC or competency check within 90 days of its expiry, the validity period is extended by 24 or 12 months, respectively, so you can get an extra three months. PPCs must also be done on a combination of a Level 4 or higher training device and a full flight sim, or a combination of a Level 6 or higher and the aeroplane, if a sim is available in North America.

The level of checking on a sim must be part of the training program approval for each type. Procedures not approved for the device must be completed in the aeroplane. The configuration of the training device must closely resemble that of the aeroplane used.

Proficiency checks must use normal seats and consist of a demonstration of PF and PNF duties, constructed with minimum disruption in a logical continuous flow reflecting a normal flight profile and must not be conducted as an isolated group of emergency procedures and drills. However, the person conducting the check may require any manoeuvre or procedure from the appropriate Schedule as necessary. PPCs are transferable between operators operating the same equipment.

VALIDITY PERIOD - 722.67/723.91

12 months, but 24 if additional training (such as a Competency Check) has been given. If training has expired for 24 months or more, initial type training must be passed. The same applies to the PPC or competency check, after doing initial ground and flight training.

COMMERCIAL AIR SERVICES

Although CARs splits this into five types, that is, *Foreign, Aerial Work, Air Taxi, Commuter* and *Airline* (Private Operators are covered in Part VI, but that only applies to large aeroplanes), the general principles and paperwork involved in running them are the same, just more complex as you go up the scale.

The Rules In General

If you charge to carry people or freight, you require an *Air Operator Certificate* (AOC), which is granted by Transport Canada. The only exemptions are military or model aircraft, rockets, hovercraft or wing-in-ground-effect machines, which are exempt from CARs anyway, so government departments have to follow the rules, too. Otherwise, section 700.02(1) says:

> *"No person shall operate an air transport service unless the person holds and complies with the provisions of an air operator certificate that authorizes the person to operate that service."*

- *air transport service* means a commercial air service for transporting persons, belongings, baggage, goods or cargo in aircraft between two points

- *commercial air service* means *any* use of an aircraft for hire or reward

- *hire or reward* means any payment, consideration, gratuity, benefit, directly or indirectly charged, demanded, received or collected by any person for the use of an aircraft

- *person*, according to the Interpretation Act (sect 35), includes artificial persons, such as government departments and limited companies

Paragraph (2) of section 700.02 extends the above to aerial work, and paragraphs (3) & (4) exempt farmers and sightseeing operations by FTUs from them.

Except for ultralights or sightseeing, *aerial work* involves carrying people other than crew members (that is, not passengers in the normal sense), helicopter Class B, C or D external loads, towing (except glider towing by a flight training unit) or the dispersal of products. *Air Taxi* rules apply if you run an air transport service or do sightseeing, with single-engined or piston multi-engined aircraft weighing 8168 kg (19,000 pounds) or less, carrying under nine passengers. *Commuter operations* do the same, only with bigger machines, that is, multi-engined weighing under 8 618 kg (19,000 pounds), but carrying between 10-19 passengers, or turbojets with a Maximum Zero Fuel Weight below 22 680 kg (50,000 pounds) carrying less than 19. Anything bigger comes under airlines, including helicopters that can carry over 20 passengers.

Transport Canada, of course, can vary the above any time.

Before you do anything, though, you need an *Operator Certificate* (see below), unless you are a farmer using your own machine for spraying within 25 miles of the centre of your farm, or you have a flight training unit operator certificate and are using a single-engined aircraft in Day

VFR for sightseeing with less than 9 passengers, and you are an instructor. Neither do you need a foreign AOC (see 701.01/721.01) for an overflight of or a technical landing in Canada (unless you want to do something weird, like takeoff or land below limits), or you are in a foreign state aircraft, that is, a civil aircraft owned by and exclusively used in the service of a government. You do, however, need a flight authorisation, which must include certain minimum information. If you want a **foreign AOC**, you must also hold one in your own state, and perform the same services in both places.

Private Pilots

As a PPL holder, you may only take money (or the equivalent) as the pilot of aeroplanes or helicopters if:

- you own or operate the aircraft and the flight is for purposes other than hire or reward, that is, passengers are only carried incidentally. Only the passengers may share costs for fuel, oil and fees against the aircraft.

- you are employed full-time for another (i.e. not flying) purpose, or you are a volunteer for a charitable, not-for-profit or public security organization and the flying is incidental. If you own the aircraft, you must be paid on distance travelled or hours flown, up to your DOCs and fees charged against the aircraft. If you rent it, you can include the rental costs.

Air Operator's Certificate

Any Canadian, a citizen, permanent resident or corporation of a foreign state that already holds one in that state and meets the requirements may hold an AOC. A citizen, permanent resident or corporation of the USA or Mexico may hold one for aerial work in the shape of a *specialty air service*, for which authorisation is required.

You must operate safely, that is, with a decent organizational structure, operational control system, training and maintenance programs. Ground handling services and equipment must also be adequate, as must the aircraft, for which you must have legal custody and control of at least one in the relevant category, for which you may also need a MEL.

The management must be employed full-time and consist of at least an Ops Manager, Chief Pilot, and, if you don't have an AMO certificate, maintenance manager, and a flight attendant manager if you want to run an airline. In between those, you can expect to employ the usual fleet managers, safety officers, etc., if required. You can

If this page is a photocopy, it is not authorised!

contract management out, but the other operator must have a similar AOC and comply with *Commercial Air Service Standards*.

You also need an Ops Manual (see *Documents and Records*, below).

Private Operator Passenger Transportation - 604/624

This only concerns large or turbine-powered pressurized Canadian *aeroplanes* used for non-commercial transport of passengers (i.e. company aircraft carrying company personnel only), where they are not already covered under an FTU or Commercial Requirements (Part VII). It does *not* apply to helicopters. The idea is to bring some control to a largely unregulated environment, and the rules are essentially the same as for Commercial Air Services, including Flight & Duty Time.

The process is administered by the *Canadian Business Aircraft Association*, from where you get the operating certificate.

Flight & Duty Hours - 700.14

There is a 14-hour basic working day, inside which you can fly as many hours as you can cram in, allowing for refuelling, rest breaks, etc., except when you do a 15-hour day, or on single-pilot IFR, when you may be restricted to 8 (below), though it is possible to extend the duty day for unforeseen circumstances, like weather. The initial description of this is in CARs, Part VII, Subpart 0, so start looking at paragraph 700.14. It's further amplified in CASS (*Commercial Air Service Standards*), in paragraph 720, etc. These are the only two places you will find it. Further differences are in your Ops Manual, as the Company can get exemptions.

YOUR RESPONSIBILITIES

Firstly, you must inform the Company when you become aware that either flight or duty times will be exceeded. This means *all* flights done by you, including instruction, private and military. You should also make the best use of any opportunities and facilities for rest provided, and plan and use your rest periods properly. In short, you should not act as a crewmember (and should not be expected to) if you believe you are (or likely to be) suffering from fatigue which may endanger the safety of an aircraft or its occupants.

MAXIMUM FLIGHT TIMES - 700.15/720.15

In general, unless your Ops Manual says otherwise, your total flight time (not duty hours) must not exceed:

- 1200 hours a year
- 300 hours every 90 days
- 120 hours every 30 days, or 100 on call
- for commuters and airlines, 40 hours in 7 consecutive days
- for aerial work or air taxi, 60 hours in 7 consecutive days
- single-pilot IFR, 8 hours a day

However, for aerial work, air taxi, or non-scheduled stuff, for any 6 separate periods of 30 days in a year (that is, 180 days non-stop if you wish), the above can be *increased*, but *may not exceed*:

- 1200 hours a year
- 900 hours every 180 days
- 450 hours every 90 days (reset to zero with 5 off)
- 210 hours every 42 days (reset to zero with 5 off)
- 150 hours every 30 days (reset to zero with 5 off)
- 60 hours in 7 consecutive days
- single-pilot IFR, 8 hours a day

In other words, you can reset your hours to zero in the above-mentioned areas 6 times a year. You must get 5 days off *before* and *after* assignments over 27 days, with the maximum being 42 days (there are often extensions for emergencies, like fires).

If you reach any limits, you may not continue or be scheduled for duty until you've had the rest period, unless "unforeseen operational circumstances" apply, but the original times must have been planned realistically.

MAXIMUM DUTY AND REST PERIODS

After your duty day (to include 15 minutes for after-flight duties in commuter or airline operations with aeroplanes), you must have a *minimum rest period*, defined in only one place in CARs, right at the front, under *Interpretation*, where it says you should be free from all duties, not be interrupted and be able to get at least *8 hours' sleep* in suitable accommodation, travel there (and back) and take care of personal hygiene. Realistically, therefore, the rest period should be about nine hours long. It's an hour extra anyway for spraying, with 5 hours of sleep taking place between 2000 and 0600 hours. Time spent on essential duties required by the Company after duty are not part of a rest period.

If you get time off during the day, that is, your duty time includes a rest period (a *split duty*), you can go beyond the basic day by half the rest period up to 3 hours, if you have been given advance notice and you get 4 hours uninterrupted in suitable accommodation. This covers situations where you deliver people to a place and wait for them to come back. In other words, you can claim some of the period spent hanging around in the middle as "rest" and tack it on to the end of the basic working day. You can plan to do this from the start, extending the duty time by half of the "rest" taken. This means that the maximum time you can possibly be on duty is normally 17 hours, if you have 6 hours off during the day (18 if you do the 15-hour day allowed for 6 months of the year). Your next rest period must be increased by at least the extended time.

For spraying, the system is similar, except that you don't count the hours from the start of the first duty, but can consolidate the two periods as one. In other words, you cannot extend the total of 14 hours, but you can spread it over different parts of the day. You also need rest periods that allow at least 9 hours sleep in suitable accommodation, one of which must be between 2000-0600, and you must receive at least 5 days free from duty every 30 days.

Generally speaking, though, most people in aerial work or air taxi, or with a helicopter (not on scheduled passenger services or heli-logging) extend to 15 hours, if the following rest period is extended by the same amount (1 hour) *or* you do less than 8 hours' flying a day (you can do this for 6 months, if you look at 720.15). Transport Canada can issue a special permission for 15 hours, so check your Ops Manual. In this case, it appears that your next rest period must be an hour longer than the standard minimum, or you can't do more than 8 hours flying the next day. Spray pilots are restricted to 14 hours anyway.

UNFORESEEN CIRCUMSTANCES

You can extend by up to 3 hours if the subsequent rest period is increased by at least the extension. You must notify the operator (see the Ops Manual) of the length of and reason for the extension, with the paperwork being kept until the next audit. Transport Canada must be notified as soon as practicable.

Flights must be planned within the maximum flight and duty times, taking into account pre- and post-flight duties, the flight(s), forecast weather, turn-around times and the nature of the operation.

DELAYED REPORTING TIME

If you are notified of a delay of over 3 hours in reporting time before leaving your place of rest, duty time starts 3 hours after the original reporting time.

TIME FREE FROM DUTY

A *day off* means you were assigned no duties, and not expected to be available inside an hour, or be at a specified location. For commuter and airline operations using aeroplanes, or when on call, you must have at least 36 hours a week or 3 days in every 17 days (all in one go) - on *deployed operations* (that is, you are working at another base for at least 10 days), the 3 days in 17 may be replaced by 4 within 19.

For aerial work, air taxi and helicopters, 13 days every 90 or 3 every 30, although you can be assigned duty for up to 42 days after 5 days off instead of the latter requirement. You must, in any case, have 5 days off after every assignment over 27 days. In other words, before and after any assignment of duty over 27 days, you must have 5 days off, and the maximum assignment is 42 days.

POSITIONING

You must have an additional rest period of at least half the time spent travelling over your maximum duty time.

CREW MEMBERS ON RESERVE

You can either be *On Standby, On Call, On Reserve* or *Free of Duty*. For the first, you must be in a specified location and available inside an hour - for the second, the location requirement is removed (it's really for commuter/airline work). When on reserve, the notice period is over an hour, with each day having an uninterrupted rest period scheduled in advance, giving you at least 8 hours' sleep. There are 3 ways of dealing with this:

- You get 24 hours' notice of when your rest period will start, and how long it will be. It cannot start more than 3 hours earlier or later than the preceding rest period, or more than 8 hours in a week (1.1 hours a day). So, if your first rest period starts at 8 in the evening, the next one must start between 5 and 11 (pm), and those for the rest of the week around 7-9.

- You get at least 10 hours notice, free of all duty.

- You get no duties and are not interrupted between 2200 and 0600 hours.

Most companies use the third. If the above cannot be complied with, that is, you get no notice at all, your maximum duty time is 10 hours, and the next rest period must be increased by 5 hours (actually half the duty time).

You must be able to obtain at least 8 consecutive hours' sleep a day while on reserve. You must be given either 24 hours notice of the start and duration of the rest period, which cannot shift more than 3 hours earlier or later than the preceding one, nor more than 8 hours in a week, 10 hours notice of the assignment, with no duty in them, or no duty time and no interruptions between 2200-0600 local time.

If the above conditions cannot be complied with, the maximum duty time is 10 hours, and the subsequent minimum rest period must be increased by at least one-half the length of the preceding duty time.

CONTROLLED REST ON THE FLIGHT DECK - 700.23/720.23

Where one pilot is allowed to grab a few Zs while the other remains alert.

TRAINING

You must receive training in the program as well as in the general principles of fatigue and fatigue countermeasures.

PRE-FLIGHT ACTIVITIES

The PIC must decide if operational considerations allow rest on the flight deck, based on guidelines developed by the operator. Rest periods will be planned at a pre-flight briefing to anticipate and maximize sleep opportunities and manage alertness. The briefing can occur in flight, and must include the choice of rest sequence, planned and unplanned wake-up criteria, transfer of control procedures and co-ordination with flight attendants.

PRE-REST PERIOD

Activities should take about 5 minutes and include the transfer of duties, an operational briefing, completion of physiological needs, co-ordination with flight attendants and time to become comfortable in the flight deck seat.

REST PERIOD

Only one crew member at a time can rest while others remain alert, although an alertness monitor may be used as a backup. The resting crew member's duties must be completed by the non-resting crew members. All crew members must remain on the flight deck throughout the rest period, which can only be up to 45 minutes to avoid sleep inertia when awakened. Rest periods can only occur during cruise and must be completed at least 30 minutes before planned TOD, workload permitting. More than one sleep opportunity may be taken by crew members.

POST-REST PERIOD

Unless required for abnormal or emergency situations, you must get at least 15 minutes without duties before resuming normal duties, and an operational briefing.

LONG-RANGE FLIGHTS - 700.22

Except within Northern Domestic Airspace, a flight, or a series terminating more than 4 one-hour time zones from the departure point must be limited to 3 sectors and be followed by a rest period at least equal to the preceding duty time. The maximum number of sectors that may be completed after a transoceanic sector is one, excluding one unscheduled technical stop.

CUMULATIVE TIMES

There are no cumulative limits for duty hours, only flight times.

RULES OF THE AIR (ANNEX 2)
•••

Aircraft bearing the nationality and registration marks of a Contracting (ICAO) State must obey these Rules of The Air (Annex 2), wherever they may be, but local state rules take precedence. However, over the high seas, the Rules apply without exception, except where a State has supplied "an appropriate ATS authority", in which case the ICAO rules become subordinate to it.

Compliance & Authority

In flight or on aerodromes, you must comply with:

- The *General Rules*

plus, when in flight:

- The *Visual Flight Rules*, or
- The *Instrument Flight Rules*

according to the flight conditions. It is the responsibility of the PIC to comply with them, whether at the controls or not, but the Rules may be departed from *when absolutely necessary* in the interests of safety. Before starting a flight, the PIC must become familiar with *all appropriate information*. This should include (when not near an aerodrome, and when IFR), current weather reports and forecasts, allowing for fuel requirements and alternative courses of action.

The PIC has final authority as to the disposition of an aircraft *while in command* - for aeroplanes, this is between when the doors are first closed and opened again at the

If this page is a photocopy, it is not authorised!

end of a flight. There seems to be no equivalent definition for helicopters.

Intoxicating Liquor, Narcotics or Drugs

You may not act as pilot or flight crew while under the influence of intoxicating liquor, or any narcotic or drug, by which your capacity to act as such is impaired.

PSYCHOSOMATIC SUBSTANCES

People whose functions are critical to safety (e.g. safety-sensitive personnel) must not act as such while under the influence of psychosomatic substances that impair human performance.

Protection Of Persons & Property

NEGLIGENT OR RECKLESS OPERATION

Aircraft shall not be operated in a reckless or negligent manner that may endanger life or the property of others.

MINIMUM HEIGHTS

You may not fly over any congested area of a city, town or settlement, or over open-air assemblies of people, below a height that allows you safely make an emergency landing (that is, without undue hazard to persons or property on the surface), except when taking off or landing, or with permission. IFR and VFR restrictions have their own headings, below.

Aircraft Restrictions

DROPPING OR SPRAYING

This must be done under conditions prescribed by the appropriate authorities and clearances supplied by the relevant ATC.

TOWING

This must be done under conditions prescribed by the appropriate authorities and clearances supplied by the relevant ATC.

PARACHUTE DESCENTS

Aside from emergency descents, these must be done under conditions prescribed by the appropriate authorities and clearances supplied by the relevant ATC.

ACROBATIC FLIGHT

This must be done under conditions prescribed by the appropriate authorities and clearances from ATC.

Formation Flight

This must be done by *pre-arrangement with the PICs concerned.* In controlled airspace, it must also be done under conditions from the relevant ATC, which shall include:

- operating as a single aircraft for navigation and position reporting
- separation between aircraft is the responsibility of the flight leader and the PICs, including when they are joining up and breaking away
- aircraft must be at least 1 km horizontally and 30 m vertically from the flight leader

Unmanned Free Balloons

Their operation must minimise hazards to persons, property or other aircraft, under Annex 4.

Prohibited, Restricted and Danger Areas

Identification includes the nationality letters (such as EG for UK) of the State which has established the airspace, plus the letters *P, R* or *D* for *Prohibited, Restricted* or *Danger,* area, respectively, followed by a number. Numbers must not be re-used for at least a year after the area concerned is cancelled. Aircraft must not fly in any such areas that have had their particulars published, except under conditions applied by or with permission of the relevant State (over whose territory the areas are established).

Avoiding Collisions - 602.19

There are rules about how aircraft should be flown around other traffic, e.g. *not in such proximity to other aircraft as to create a collision hazard.* Even when you have right of way, you must take any necessary action to avoid collision (in other words, even with clearance, commanders are responsible for not hitting other machines). Another aircraft with an emergency gains priority over you. If you must give way, you must not pass over or under, or cross ahead of, the other aircraft unless you are far enough away not to create a risk of collision, taking due note of wake turbulence. Aircraft with right of way should maintain course and speed.

A glider and whatever is towing it are *one aircraft* under the towing PIC.

APPROACHING HEAD-ON

If there is a danger of collision, each must alter course to the right.

OVERTAKING

You are overtaking when you are approaching another aircraft from behind *at less than 70° from the longitudinal axis*, which means that, at night, you should not be able to see its port or starboard navigation lights. Aircraft being overtaken have right of way, and the overtaking aircraft, whether climbing, descending or in horizontal flight, must keep out of the way by altering course to the right (*well clear* on the ground) until well past and clear, even if their relative positions change.

CONVERGENCE

If a steady relative bearing is kept between two aircraft at the same altitude, they will eventually collide. When two aircraft are converging in this way, the one coming from the right has the right-of-way, except that:

- power-driven, heavier-than-air aircraft (flying machines) give way to airships, gliders and balloons

- airships give way to gliders and balloons

- gliders give way to balloons

- power-driven aircraft give way to aircraft that are towing or carrying loads

When two balloons converge at different altitudes, the higher one must give way.

LANDING

Except where ATC dictate otherwise, or in emergency, aircraft landing or on finals have right of way over others in flight or on the ground or water. Where several are involved in landing, *the lowest has right of way*, as long as it does not cut in front of another on finals, or overtake it. However, power driven heavier-than-air aircraft must give way to gliders. *An aircraft whose pilot is aware that another is compelled to land shall give way to it.*

TAKING OFF

Aircraft taxying on the manoeuvring area must give way to those taking off or about to take off.

SURFACE MOVEMENT

If there is a danger of collision between two aircraft taxying on a manoeuvring area:

- when approaching head on, or approximately so, each shall stop or, where practicable, alter course to the right to keep well clear

- when converging, the one with the other on its right shall give way

- aircraft being overtaken shall have right of way, and overtaking aircraft shall keep well clear

Aircraft taxying on manoeuvring areas must stop and hold at all runway holding positions unless authorised by the Tower. They must also stop and hold at all lighted stop bars, and may proceed further when the lights are switched off.

Emergency vehicles must be given priority over aircraft landing and taking off.

Details of position markings and signs are set out below (Annex 14).

Lights & Signals

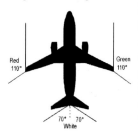

If more than one light is needed to comply with the Rules of the Air, only one should be visible at a time. Where a light must show through specified angles horizontally, the light should be visible from 90° above and below. Lights showing in all directions must be visible from any point horizontally and vertically. You may switch off or reduce the intensity of flashing lights if they *adversely affect the performance of your duties*, or subject outside observers to harmful dazzle.

Anti-collision lights are intended to attract attention to your aircraft, and navigation lights are intended to show your relative path to an observer. Navigation lights are set up so that only one can be seen by another aircraft at any time. Anticollision lights are seen from all directions. Other lights may be displayed if they cannot be mistaken for them. Between sunset and sunrise, you must show anti-collision and navigation lights. On the manoeuvring area, in addition, aircraft must display lights that show extremities of the structure (unless the aircraft is stationary and otherwise lit up adequately), and engine running lights (a red one must be displayed when the engine is running in any case).

By day, anti-collision lights must be used in flight.

Simulated Instrument Flight

Fully functioning dual controls must be installed and a fully qualified pilot must occupy the other seat (presumably trained to fly from there) with suitable vision forwards and sideways. If not, an additional observer in full communication with the safety pilot must be carried to fill in the gaps.

Operations Near Aerodromes

Aircraft on or near an aerodrome must, whether or not in an ATZ, observe other traffic to avoid collisions, conform with or avoid the traffic pattern, make all turns to the left on approach or takeoff, unless otherwise instructed, and land and take off into wind, unless the runway configuration or ATC dictate otherwise.

Aircraft Manoeuvring on Water - 602.20

Aircraft or vessels coming *from the right* have the right-of-way. If you are approaching another aircraft or vessel head-on, you must alter heading to the right to keep well clear. Aircraft or vessels being overtaken have the right of way, and overtakers must alter heading enough to keep well clear.

Aircraft landing on or taking off from the water shall, as far as practicable, keep well clear of all obstacles and avoid impeding their navigation.

At night, lights conforming to the *International Regulations For Preventing Collisions At Sea* (Revised 1972) must be shown, unless it is impractical, in which case lights conforming as closely as possible must be shown.

ATS Flight Plan

There are many reasons for filing flight plans - first of all, they help get you slotted into the system, even if it isn't quite the route you asked for. Next, they help with radio failures, as, once you're in the pipe, so to speak, everyone knows where you're supposed to be (more or less) and can act accordingly. Then there are forced landings, where an educated guess may be made as to your position, followed by statistics, and, finally, because the law says you must, under certain circumstances (International flights, for example, *always* require a flight plan, as does IFR flight in controlled airspace).

Tip: Filing a flight plan also ensures that your destination is notified of your timings.

Officially, you need to file a flight plan before any flight:

- within controlled airspace under IFR

- in advisory airspace when you need advisory service. Advisory routes must be crossed at 90° at the appropriate IFR level

- in designated areas or along routes where ATC provide flight information, alerting and SAR services, and where they liaise with military units and ATC from other States to avoid interception for identification

- across international borders

- under Special VFR if you wish the destination aerodrome to be notified

- over 40 km when MTOM exceeds 5700 kg

They are also *recommended* for flights over water more than 10 nm from the coast and/or flight over sparsely populated or remote terrain.

In Canada, a flight plan must be filed for all commercial flights, except those under VFR taking off and landing at the same aerodrome. This includes positioning, private and line training. You can file one at any time at your discretion, but don't forget to close it properly, or you will be overrun by C130s. An *itinerary* is enough for other flights, such as local area training flights, or air tests. There must be a responsible person on the ground to monitor flight progress, and alert the emergency services if you do not arrive at the SAR notification time or within 1 hour of ETA (24 hours for an itinerary).

You should always file a plan as far in advance as possible, but at least 30 minutes for a flight in Canada - try 60 minutes to the USA. The same form is used for itineraries and flight plans, and they are usually filled in the same way. The differences are in the AIM/AIM, with some examples.

You must stick to the flight plan unless a request has been made for a variation and a *clearance obtained*. In an emergency, you can do what you need and sort it out afterwards. For inadvertant changes:

- Deviation from track - regain track as soon as practicable

- TAS variations - you must inform ATC if the average variation of your TAS is expected to be more than ±5% from that given in the flight plan

- ETA changes - if the ETA for the next applicable reporting point, FIR boundary or destination aerodrome (in that order) is going to change by more than three minutes, you should inform ATC

In controlled airspace, you must report to ATC the time, your position and level at whatever reporting points or intervals of time as may be established, or as directed. The *standard position report* contains the aircraft identification, position, time, flight level/altitude, next position and time over, ensuing significant point, in that order.

VFR

You must file a VFR Flight Plan or Itinerary wherever you go, unless you are within 25nm of the aerodrome. The latter can be left with a Responsible Person, who undertakes to notify the authorities if something happens. Otherwise, you may file a plan or itinerary with ATC, a FSS or a CASS. The itinerary can just be something like a notice board or map on the wall (you don't need a written copy in any case for flights beginning and ending on the same day at the same aerodrome).

You must inform the relevant people of any changes to the route, the duration of the flight or destination, so that SAR is not alerted unnecessarily.

INTERNATIONAL

International flights always require a flight plan, but flights from Canada to the USA are not foreign for this purpose. If you are near the USA border, you need to file at least an hour ahead (remember also that Customs are not advised until a departure time is received).

IFR

IFR flights require a flight plan, too, but an IFR Itinerary is acceptable if the flight is wholly or partly in uncontrolled airspace, or you are unable to transmit the required information for a flight plan.

You should notify ATC as soon as practicable of changes to cruising altitudes, routes, destination and changes in TAS of more than 5%. In controlled airspace, you must get clearance before making them.

COMPOSITE VFR/IFR

You can mix portions of the flight and obey the relevant rules for each part. If you go VFR first, you must contact ATC (or an FSS) before entering controlled airspace - clearance is not automatic, and you must remain VFR until you acknowledge it.

OVERDUE AIRCRAFT

You are overdue on a flight plan immediately after any SAR notification time, or within 1 hour after the last reported ETA (24 hours for an itinerary).

INTERMEDIATE STOPS

You can include several short stops, maybe for refuelling or picking up passengers, but not on a single IFR flight plan (it only works for VFR flight plans or VFR/IFR itineraries. All you need to do in the Route section of the ICAO form is repeat the name of the place you are stopping at and include the length of the stop, as in

CYHX (0+20) CYHX. The total elapsed time (EET) to destination should include all stops, but this will only activate SAR after the normal period - if you want it for each leg, you must file a plan for each one…..

CONSECUTIVE PLANS

Only one plan in a series will be allowed for an initial departure from the USA, otherwise they must all be in Canada. The series must fall within 24 hours, and you must supply at least the departure points, altitudes, routes, destinations, ETDs and EETs, alternates, fuel, TAS, souls on board and where arrival reports will be filed.

CROSS COUNTRY IFR TRAINING FLIGHTS

Officially, these are flights with no intermediate stops, making IFR approaches at points along the route. The places where you want to do the approaches should be in the information box of a single flight plan, with the times you think they will take (do not include them in the EET). You will be cleared to final destination but, if this is not practical, you will get later variations with your initial clearance. You will get clearances for missed approaches with the initial approach clearance at each enroute point, or holding instructions if things are busy.

ARRIVAL REPORTS

An arrival report (for IFR) is normally automatically filed for you by the Tower or FSS (you can, in fact, file an arrival report before landing, due to an exemption in an AIC). If you become VFR, you can cancel IFR, but you end up with no separation, and must still file an arrival report on landing, as your plan is still active.

On a plan to a remote aerodrome under controlled airspace, you will likely be cleared in the descent through an approved procedure. If you cannot reach ATC to give an arrival report, you can use various means, including the telephone, relay through other aircraft or close it while you can still talk to them. If there is not an approved procedure, you will be cleared to the MEA and told of the appropriate minimum IFR altitude. If you then get to the MEA, and have no visual reference, you could request descent to the MOCA for 30 minutes (the MEA is protected).

VFR RELEASE

You can request a departure maintaining VFR until an IFR clearance can be received. You will be given a time, altitude and location for contact with ATC. Such a departure may not be approved by an IFR unit.

© *Phil Croucher, 2007*

FORMAT

The ICAO plan is used for everything. Here are the details:

AIRCRAFT ID

The call sign. Without a company callsign, use the aircraft registration.

FLIGHT PLAN

PRIORITY	ADDRESSEE(S)
<< ≡ FF →	

	<< ≡

FILING TIME	ORIGINATOR
	<< ≡

SPECIFIC IDENTIFICATION OF ADDRESSEE(S) AND/OR ORIGINATOR

3 MESSAGE TYPE   << ≡ (FPL   Blank if only one

7 AIRCRAFT IDENTIFICATION   ▪ C P A C O   No Hyphens

8 FLIGHT RULES   ▪ V

TYPE OF FLIGHT   G   << ≡

9 NUMBER   ▪ [▲]   TYPE OF AIRCRAFT   B H 0 6

WAKE TURBULENCE CAT   / L

10 EQUIPMENT   ▪ S D I C   << ≡

13 DEPARTURE AERODROME   ▪ C Y L L   A for Altitude   F for Flight Level

TIME   0 6 0 0   << ≡

15 CRUISING SPEED   ▪ N 0 1 0 0   LEVEL ▲ A 0 1 5 →   ROUTE   B C N   D C T

N for Knots

	<< ≡

16 DESTINATION AERODROME   ▪ Z Z Z Z   See 18

TOTAL EET HR. MIN   0 1 1 5

ALTN AERODROME   → E G G W

2ND ALTN AERODROME   →

18 OTHER INFORMATION   D O F / 0 7 1 1 1 2   D E S T / 5 2 0 1 N 0 0 0 2 W

Date Of Flight (5 days ahead)

) << ≡

SUPPLEMENTARY INFORMATION (NOT TO BE TRANSMITTED IN FPL MESSAGES)

19 ENDURANCE   Dry Tanks

→ E /   HR MIN ▲   0 2 3 0   → P /   PERSONS ON BOARD   0 0 3

Cross out what you **don't** have → R /

EMERGENCY RADIO
UHF ☒   VHF ☒   ELT ☒

SURVIVAL EQUIPMENT   → ☒ /   POLAR ☒   DESERT ☒   MARITIME ☒   JUNGLE ☒   → JACKETS ☒   / LIGHT ☒   FLUORES ☒   UHF ☒   VHF ☒

DINGHIES
→ ☒ /   NUMBER [ ]   → CAPACITY [ ]   → COVER ☒   → COLOUR [ ]   << ≡

AIRCRAFT COLOUR AND MARKINGS
A /   White with red/blue stripes

REMARKS
→ ☒ /   [ ]   << ≡

PILOT IN COMMAND
C /   SMITH   ) << ≡

FILED BY   SPACE RESERVED FOR ADDITIONAL REQUIREMENTS
Please provide a telephone number so our operators can contact you if needed

FLIGHT RULES & TYPE OF FLIGHT

The former goes in Box 8. V=VFR, I=IFR, Y=IFR/VFR, Z=VFR/IFR (put the changeover point in the route section). Where the change is composite, (VFR/IFR/VFR) the first takes precedence (Y in this case).

Next is the type of flight. The first character is C=Controlled VFR, D=Defence VFR, E=Defence Itinerary, F=Flight Itinerary. The second is G=General Aviation, S=Scheduled, N=Non-scheduled, M=Military, X=Other. An Aztec on an itinerary could use FG.

NO & TYPE OF AIRCRAFT, TURBULENCE CATEGORY

Box 9 is also in 2 parts. The first is the number of aircraft. The next is the type (e.g. BH06 for a Bell 206). H=Heavy (above 300,000 lbs), M = Medium (15500-300000 lbs) and L = Light.

EQUIPMENT

Box 10, for comms, nav and transponder, in that order (COM, NAV, SSR). N=None or unserviceable. S=Standard, that is, VHF, ADF, VOR and ILS. C=LORAN, D=DME, F=ADF, G=GPS, H=HF RTF, I=INS, J=Data Link, K=MLS, L=ILS, M=OMEGA, O=VOR, R=RNP certified, T=TACAN, U=UHF, V=VHF, W=RVSM certified, X=MNPS certified, Y=CMNPS certified, Z=other. For SSR, N=Nil, A=Mode A, C=Mode C, X=Mode S without ident and PA, P=Mode S with PA & no ident, I=Mode S with ident & no PA, S=Mode S with ident & PA. SD/C is commonly used for standard equipment with DME and Mode C transponder.

DEPARTURE AERODROME

In Box 13, use the ICAO code from CFS (CYHX=Halifax).

DEPARTURE TIME

Anticipated time in hours and minutes UTC, preferably over 30 minutes ahead, or an hour near the USA border, up to 24.

CRUISE SPEED, ALTITUDE, ROUTE

Box 15 is for the flight planned TAS. N=Knots, M=Mach Number. For cruising level, A=Altitude in hundreds of feet ASL (e.g. A050). F is for Flight Level. Under *route*, include speed and altitude changes, airway numbers and waypoints on the route. DCT (Direct) is assumed unless they are included. IFR routes should be used when available, as per IFR charts.

DESTINATION, EET, SAR, ALTERNATE

In Box 16, use the ICAO code as per the CFS. The EET can include the number of days. Use your own SAR time, up to 24 hours after ETA. You don't need an alternate on a VFR plan or itinerary, but if you need one that doesn't have an ICAO ID, use ZZZZ and place the details in Box 18 with /ALTN after.

OTHER INFORMATION

Use 0 if you have nothing else to add. For a transborder flight to the USA, use ADCUS and the number of US citizens to prepare customs, but they are not advised until a departure time has been received.

SUPPLEMENTAL INFORMATION

Fuel endurance (to dry tanks) in hours and minutes goes in Box 19. Place an X through the U and V if you do not have the VHF and UHF emergency frequencies (243 & 121.5 MHz). Cross out the E under ELBA if you don't have an ELT. If you do, they types are: A or AD=Automatic Ejectable or Deployable, F or AF=Fixed or Automatic Fixed, AP=Automatic Portable, W or S=Water activated or survival, P=Personnel (non-fixed). Cross out survival equipment you don't have, and add with whom arrival reports are filed. Finally, your name and licence number, and who to notify if SAR is initiated.

Signals

INTERCEPTION

Under Article 9 of the Chicago Convention, contracting states reserve the right to stop aircraft from other states flying over of its territory. As a result, aircraft may need to be led away from an area or be required to land at a particular aerodrome. A copy of the interception procedures must be carried on international flights.

If an aircraft assumes a position slightly above and ahead of you (normally on the left), rocks its wings, then turns slowly to the left in a level turn, you have officially been intercepted. Your response should be to rock your own wings and follow (the intercepter will normally be faster than you, so expect it to fly a racetrack pattern and rock its wings each time it passes). After interception, try to inform ATC and make contact with the intercepting aircraft on 121.5 or 243 MHz. You should also squawk 7700 with Mode C, unless otherwise instructed.

If the aircraft performs an abrupt breakaway manoeuvre, such as a climbing turn of 90° or more without interfering with your line of flight, you have been released. If it lowers its gear and descends to a runway, you are expected to land there (the accepted phrase, if you can communicate, is *Descend*). However, you can make an approach to check the area, then proceed to land. Lowering your gear or showing a steady landing light means you acknowledge the instruction. Flashing the landing light means the area is unsuitable, as does overflight with the gear up somewhere between 1000-2000 feet. At night, the substitute for rocking wings is irregular flashing of navigation lights.

Here are some pertinent phrases:

Phrase	Meaning
Callsign	My callsign is....
Cannot	Sorry, can't do that.....
Am Lost	Where the hell am I?
Wilco	Your instructions will be complied with
Mayday	Help!
Hijack	Have been hijacked
Land	I would like to land at....
Descend	I require descent
Repeat	Say that again
Callsign	What is your callsign?
Recleared	Ignore last clearance and receive a new one
Descend	Descend for landing
You land	Land here
Proceed	You may proceed

Lights & Pyrotechnic Signals

Sent from the Tower to NORDO aircraft, or those with radio difficulties. Acknowledge by rocking the wings or flashing the landing lights once.

Signal	To air	To ground
Steady red	Give way to other aircraft - keep circling	Stop
Red pyro/flare	Do not land for time being	
Red flashes	Airport unsafe do not land	Move clear of landing area
Green flashes	Return for landing	Cleared to taxi
Steady Green	You may land	Clear to take off (not a vehicle)
White flashes	Land after continuous green. After green flashes go to apron	Return to starting point
Bursting red/green stars	You are in or near a danger area; push off	
Blinking rwy lts		Ground personnel clear areas

Visual Flight Rules (VFR) - 602.114

Although the airspace you fly in comes in seven varieties (Class A, B, C, etc.), it is, essentially, controlled or uncontrolled. As the names imply, in the first you do as you're told (by ATC), and, in the second, you, as pilot, are responsible for the safe conduct of the flight, which means avoiding obstacles and other aircraft, which you can only do if you can see them. The official definition of a flight under VFR is "one conducted under Visual Flight Rules", conveniently leaving out what the Rules are.

The Visual Flight Rules govern flight in *Visual Meteorological Conditions* (VMC). A flight may only be conducted under VFR if the conditions exist all the way along the route. When the weather gets so bad that you can't see where you are going, *Instrument Meteorological Conditions* (IMC) apply, and you must fly under *Instrument Flight Rules* (IFR), below, although you can fly IFR at any time, even in VMC (you just have to obey tighter rules for obstacle clearance, etc., since you're not supposed to be looking out of the window). The definition of IMC is actually a negative one, being "weather precluding flight in compliance with Visual Flight Rules", and where this happens could depend on the type of airspace you are in, as well as the weather. Class A airspace is always IFR, for example, as are some control zones.

CONTROLLED AIRSPACE - 602.114

You must have visual reference with the surface with at least three miles visibility, and be at least 500 feet vertically and 1 mile horizontally from cloud. In addition, inside a control zone, ground visibility must not be less than three miles, and you should not be below 500 feet AGL, except when taking off or landing.

UNCONTROLLED AIRSPACE - 602.115

You may not start a VFR flight unless the weather reports indicate that the conditions will allow it.

AT OR ABOVE 1,000 FEET AGL

You must have at least 1 mile visibility by day, 3 miles at night, and be 500 feet vertically and 2,000 feet horizontally from cloud.

BELOW 1,000 FEET AGL

At least one mile visibility by day (unless authorised by an AOC or flight training certificate), three miles at night, and clear of cloud.

Airspace	Grd vis	Horiz cld	Vert cloud	Ht
Control Zone	3m	1m	500'	500'
Controlled	3m	1m	500'	n/a
Uncontrolled > 1000'	1m	2000'	500'	n/a
Uncontrolled < 1000'	1m	Clear cloud	Clear cloud	n/a

MINIMUM VISIBILITY - 702.17/722.17

For ½ mile visibility in uncontrolled airspace, helicopters must fly at a speed that allows obstacles to be seen and avoided. Advisory speeds are.

Visibility (m)	Speed (Kts)
800	50
1500	100
2000	120

The pilot must also have at least 500 hours (commercial) PIC time.

VFR OVER-THE-TOP - 602.116

This is flying over the top of a solid bank of cloud, where you can't see the ground, but you can see where you're going. It must be authorised in an AOC.

You can only do this in the cruise by day at least 1,000' vertically from cloud, or if you have a vertical distance between layers of at least 5,000', with over 5 miles visibility and destination weather is forecast for scattered cloud or clear and visibility of at least 5 miles with no precipitation, fog, thunderstorms or blowing snow from 1 hr before to 2 hrs after ETA, based on a TAF. Otherwise, the after ETA time increases to 3 hrs.

One particular point to note with OTT (and night) flight is that you must carry *all relevant charts and publications* for the proposed route and probable diversions, which essentially means you can't go without a map. Your choices are VNC, WAC or VTA. Normal VFR flight doesn't require charts, but you must be familiar with appropriate available information for the trip.

CPL or ATPL holders may fly VFR OTT, but the rating needs to be specially endorsed on helicopter licences and aeroplane PPLs. RPP holders may not.

SPECIAL VFR FLIGHT - 602.117

This is used when you can't comply with IFR in a control zone - at night, it is only used for landing at the destination. It's a legal technicality, used to allow VFR aircraft to fly in an area where the law says only IFR aircraft may fly. Visibility must be at least ½ mile for helicopters, and 1 mile for everything else. You must also be clear of cloud and able to maintain visual reference with the surface, and obtain clearance from ATC before doing so, which means you need radios. Helicopters must also fly slowly enough to avoid collisions with other traffic or obstacles.

On your request (it is never volunteered), permission will be granted if traffic permits. SVFR may be authorised by a non-radar equipped control tower and an FSS, but remember that *Special VFR only applies in a control zone* - although you might be able to get to the edge of a zone under it, you might not be able to go further because the ½ mile limit (for helicopters, anyway) may increase to 1 mile outside the zone if you cannot comply with low visibility requirements.

MINIMUM ALTITUDES

Unless taking off, approaching or landing as described in 602.12, or as allowed under 602.15, you may not overfly a built-up area or open-air assemblies of people, unless you are high enough to land without creating a hazard to people or property on the surface and, in any case, at least 1,000 feet above the highest obstacle within 2,000 feet from an aeroplane, 500 ft above the highest obstacle within 500 ft of a balloon, or 1,000 ft above the highest obstacle within 500 ft of anything else.

Otherwise, you may not fly closer than 500 ft to any person, vessel, vehicle or structure (for sections 602.13, 14 and 15, you are "overhead" within 500 feet horizontally from a helicopter or balloon, or 2,000 feet otherwise).

Balloons must have enough fuel to fly clear of the built-up area, allowing for variations in take-off Weight, temperature and actual and forecast winds. If the area is inside Class C airspace, you must get clearance before taking off. You may take-off from such a place in a balloon with permission from the owner of the launch site, there is no special aviation event being held, the local authorities don't object, the diameter of the site is at least 100 feet or the greatest dimension of the balloon plus 25%, whichever is the larger, and the take-off point is upwind of the highest obstacle in the take-off path by its height, and you can maintain a positive rate of climb to at least 500' above the highest obstacle within 500', or, where the flight path is directly over residential or commercial buildings, or an open-air assembly of people, using the maximum safe rate of climb.

You can land in a balloon to avoid endangering people on board, but you must tell ATC, before or as soon as possible afterwards, with the time, registration, location and reasons. See also 602.16 and 18.

You may not fly over an aerodrome below 2,000 feet.

In Class B airspace, you must be on a CVFR flight plan, meaning that you are under IFR, but in VMC.

In Class C TCAs, check out the CFS and/or VTA chart. To establish initial contact, give your type and identification, your position relative to a published callup point, altitude, destination and route, transponder and ATIS codes.

Watch out for Fur Farms, which have chrome yellow and black stripes painted on roofs or pylons, although that's a little difficult on pipeline or powerline survey and they just appear out of the blue, so to speak. Also, overfly herds of caribou and other wild animals at over 2,000 feet.

The term for holding when it comes to VFR aircraft is *orbiting*, which will be over a known location. You are responsible for obstacle clearance.

HELICOPTERS

To operate over built-up areas at altitudes and distances less than those in 602.14, or to conduct a landing or take-off within the built-up area of a city or town (see also 702.22/722.22), an Aerial Work Zone plan must be submitted to Transport Canada at least 5 working days ahead, to include:

- certification that the municipality has been informed
- purpose of the flights
- dates, alternate dates and proposed times
- location
- type of aircraft
- altitudes and routes, on a map
- hazard procedures & precautions
- contact name

For a helicopter carrying a jettisonable external load, also include a description and number of the loads, and security arrangements. If you will be operating to a roof top, add safety precautions for forced landings onto or load penetration through it.

Instrument Flight Rules (IFR)- 602.121

Generally, all flights in IMC must be conducted under IFR, although you can actually fly IFR at any time, even if the weather is clear - for example, you must obey IFR rules at night. The essential difference between IFR and VFR is that tighter margins are applied for avoiding obstacles and choosing your altitude according to your direction (the *Quadrantal Rule*). To start a flight under IFR, the weather must be *equal to or better than* specified minima at the destination or its alternate. In Class A, B, C, D, E or F Special Use Advisory airspace, you must also have ATC clearance, and observe any conditions included.

IFR clearances can be received in plain language, or as a *Standard Instrument Departure*. They must be read back, except where a SID is in force and you got the clearance on the ground before departure, or by electronic means. However, ATC may request a read back at any time. You may deviate from clearances and instructions as far as necessary to avoid a collision, if you are responding to an advisory from ACAS or TCAS, or GPWS. As soon as possible afterwards, however, you must carry on with the last clearance or instruction, and inform ATC. The rest of this, including operating minima, etc. is covered in the *Instruments* chapter.

MINIMUM ALTITUDES

The MOCA (below) must be at least 2000 feet above the highest obstacle within 10 miles of the centre line of the route, and at night under VFR, at least 1,000 feet above the highest obstacle within 3 miles.

Otherwise, you must be at or above 1,000 feet above the highest obstacle within 5 nm from your estimated position, or 2,000 feet in mountainous regions 1 or 5 (as per the *Designated Airspace Handbook*), or 1,500 feet in areas 2, 3 or 4.

During the day, under VFR, an aeroplane may not fly less than 300 feet AGL, or nearer than 300 feet to any obstacle.

A higher minimum altitude requirement may be specified by NOTAM.

For each route segment, the MEA must be at least equal to the MOCA for navigational signal coverage, rounded up to the nearest 100 feet. Each route must include the FROM/TO route segment, track, MOCA, MEA, distance between fixes or waypoints and navaids.

Records of company routes must be kept in a form and format similar to the catalogue of approved routes.

If the above procedures are followed, a pilot may use routes not yet contained in the record of company routes.

VFR at night or IFR flights must either have working navaids or an approved long range nav system, so for navaids other than those publicly available, you must get the permission of the owner/operator so you know their condition. If you can't get it, you must have instructions on how, and whom to contact, to confirm that the navigation aid is in service.

Flight visibility must be at least 3 miles under VFR at night.

Unless otherwise authorised, foreign operators may only, in uncontrolled airspace, conduct IFR or night VFR flights on air routes.

Minimum Obstacle Clearance Altitude (MOCA)

The lowest altitude for an airway or route segment in which an IFR flight may be conducted. It gives you 1,000 ft of clearance above all obstacles inside the lateral limits defined by navaids (see below), in non-mountainous regions, but does not account for reception range, as does the MEA, which will be higher.

Minimum Enroute Altitude (MEA)

Similar to MOCA, but guarantees navaid reception.

Minimum Sector Altitude (MSA)

Found on approach plates, based on a 25nm circle round a navaid, giving 300m above the highest obstacle.

Decision Height (DH)

Officially, "a specified height at which a missed approach must be initiated during a precision approach if the required visual reference to continue the approach to land has not been established." In other words, it's the height at which you must go around if you can't see anything vaguely resembling a runway or the approach lights. It's where a decision must be made whether to carry on towards the runway or get the heck out. A precision approach is an ILS, MLS or PAR, typically where you have to maintain a constant glidepath.

Minimum Descent Altitude (MDA)

MDA is "a specified altitude referenced to sea level for a non-precision approach below which descent must not be made until the required visual reference to continue the approach to land has been established."

There's no real decision here - you are just not allowed below that height on a non-precision approach. If you do gain visual reference, the approach is essentially terminated to carry on visually. It is time-based, in that

you set heading for the runway on a track from the beacon for a time based on your aircraft category (which is in turn based on speed).

Refer to the *Instruments* chapter for more about this.

Minimum Holding Altitude (MHA)

The lowest altitude that guarantees signal coverage, communications and obstacle clearance, so it's the same sort of thing as the MEA.

NO ALTERNATE - 703.31/723.31, 724.27

The flight must be operated under a Type C Control System. Otherwise, as for:

Foreign

The Ops Manual or equivalent must contain procedures, flight followers must be aware of the situation and have current weather readily accessible. PICs must be familiar with diversions, and the destination must be within three hours planned time from the departure. For at least two hours either side of the ETA, there must be no risk of fog or similar restriction to visibility below three miles, no risk of thunderstorms or freezing precipitation, a ceiling of at least 1,000 feet and a visibility of at least three miles. You must also be authorised by your State.

Quadrantal Rules

What height you fly at depends on the direction you are flying, for which, unless told otherwise, you use magnetic track in the SDA and true track in the NDA.

VFR BELOW 18,000 FEET

2,000 feet separation, as follows (but not below 3,000 feet):

000-179°	180-369°
Odd levels + 500 feet (3500, 5500 etc)	Even levels + 500 feet (4500, 6500 etc)

IFR/CVFR BELOW 18,000 FEET

2,000 feet separation, as follows (but not below 3,000 feet):

000-179°	180-369°
Odd levels (3000 5000 etc)	Even levels (4000 6000 etc)

Exceptions in CFS do not apply to VFR flights. High level airspace may be structured for one-way traffic at times, and non-appropriate levels will be used.

REGISTRATION MARKS (ANX 7)

Note: Annex 7 contains only standards, not recommendations (i.e. you *shall*).

Registration marks are assigned by the state of registry or a *common mark registering authority*. The common mark is selected from the series of symbols in the radio call signs allocated to ICAO by the ITCU.

The *nationality mark* is the one that tells you what country the aircraft belongs to, as assigned by ICAO (e.g. *G* for UK, *N* for USA), and registration marks are *combinations of letters or numbers* assigned by the State of Registry, which should not be confusable with the five-letter combinations used in the *International Code of Signals*, or other common groupings used in aviation, so any containing the word PAN or the letters XXX or TTT should not be used. The nationality and registration marks are separated by a hyphen. Otherwise, marks must be in Roman characters and be displayed to their best advantage, according to features of the aircraft, and be clean and visible. They must also be on a fireproof metal plate in a prominent position on the fuselage, wing (microlight), or basket or envelope (balloon).

The Certificate of Registration should be kept on the aircraft (Chicago Convention Article 29).

Unless in an exhibition, air show, movie or television production, marks must be visible and displayed to Aircraft Marking and Registration Standards. Foreign aircraft must comply with their own State laws.

Unless registered before January 1, 1974, or it is a vintage aircraft, the nationality mark for a Canadian aircraft is the letter "C", with a combination of four letters as the registration mark. Otherwise, the letters "CF" and three letters are used, which can, however, be changed to "C" plus "F" and another three, which you must do anyway if you repaint it. All changes must be notified to Transport Canada in writing. Special registrations must be used within 12 months of being issued.

Aside from maintenance or by official request, marks may not be removed or changed unless the aircraft is permanently withdrawn or exported. Alternative sizes, locations or colours may be specified for former military aircraft and replicas.

Specifications for Marks - 202.01/222.01

Unless for production test, customer acceptance, manufacturing or export flights (where marks may be removeable, but must not come off or become erased during operation), marks must be displayed and fixed to a Canadian aircraft as follows:

GENERAL

Painted on, or done with a similar degree of permanence, distinct and not obscured or confused by other symbols or letters, in Roman capitals without ornamentation, formed by solid lines that contrast with the colour of the aircraft, with at least 5 cm (1.970 inches) between the edge of each letter and each edge of the surface on which they are displayed. The nationality and registration marks must be separated by a hyphen.

HELICOPTERS OR GYROPLANES

You can choose between once parallel to the longitudinal axis each side of the fuselage or cabin, below the window line as near to the cockpit as possible, or one on each side surface of the tail, or once on each side of the upper engine or transmission cowling of the main rotor assembly, where the cowlings are over the main cabin. If you don't have marks on the bottom of the fuselage or cabin, the side marks above must be 30 cm (11.8") high, or as high as possible, allowing for a border of 5 cm (1.970"). However, they must always be at least 15 cm (5.9"), except for gliders, amateur-built aircraft and ultralight aeroplanes, which must be at least 7.5 cm (3").

SPECIFICATIONS FOR LETTERS

Must be next to each other in a series, of equal height, at least 15 cm (5.9 inches) on a heavier-than-air aircraft, and 50 cm (19.68 inches) on the bottom surface of a wing. Those on the bottom of the fuselage or cabin of a rotorcraft must be the lesser of 50 cm (19.68 inches) or four-fifths of the width of the fuselage or cabin. Letters on a lighter-than-air aircraft must be at least 50 cm (19.68 inches) high.

The width, except for "I", "M" and "W", must be two thirds of the height. The letter "I" must be one sixth of the height, while "M" or "W" must not exceed it.

A hyphen must be two-thirds the height of any letter. The thickness of letters or hyphens must 1/6th of the height. Spaces between letters and hyphens, must be at least one quarter of the width of the letter "C".

MARKS DISPLAYED AT AN ANGLE

They must all be the same angle, not more than 35° either side of the perpendicular (height is measured at right angles to the base line). Width and spacing (including the hyphen) are measured parallel to the base line, between the outside edges of each letter and the hyphen.

Application for Registration Marks - 222.02

Must include manufacturer's name, model and serial number, its location, and whether the aircraft is new, used or being manufactured. You also need the applicant's name and address, telephone number, evidence of qualification to be the registered owner (except Her Majesty in the right of Canada or a province), an estimated date when registration will be applied for and evidence that the aircraft is not registered in another country. To reserve a mark, you need the applicant's name and address, telephone number, evidence of qualification (except Her Majesty in the right of Canada or a province), and the fee.

Former Military Aircraft & Replicas

Apply in writing, including evidence that the aircraft retains its colours and original markings, and suggested clearly identifiable alternatives.

Alternative Sizes or Locations - 222.06

Apply in writing with evidence that the structure prevents marks being displayed properly, with suggested clearly identifiable alternatives.

Aircraft Registration - 202.13

All aircraft operating in Canada, except hang gliders or parachutes, must be registered, either in Canada, or a contracting or foreign state by agreement. For production test, customer acceptance, completion of manufacturing or export flights, registration is not required with written authorisation. Any Canadian over 16 can be a registered owner, as can an entity formed under the laws of Canada, or a province, if it provides a certified copy of its incorporation certificate, or equivalent, and meets certain requirements about the keeping and preservation of records, reporting (unless exempt) and, while the aircraft is registered in Canada, more than 60% of the flight time every six months is in Canadian airspace. The C of R is cancelled automatically if the above qualifications lapse.

The term *Canadian* is defined under the *Canada Transportation Act* as "a citizen, permanent resident, **corporation** or other entity incorporated or formed in Canada that is **controlled in fact by Canadians** with at least 75% voting interest owned or controlled by Canadians". This is to stop corporations using Canada as a flag of convenience.

Corporations that are not Canadian-controlled can be registered owners if the aircraft is used on Canadian business, that is, flying primarily in (including into or out of) Canada (see 222.15). Records showing that the flights were primarily in Canada must be kept for three years (see also *Journey Logs*).

TYPES OF REGISTRATION

An aircraft can be registered as:

- a *state aircraft*, which is a civil aircraft owned by and exclusively used in the service of a government in Canada.

- a *commercial aircraft*, for Aerial Work, Air Taxi, Commuter or Airline operations, or in a flight training unit.

- a *private aircraft*.

A provisional registration can be issued for importation, or a temporary one if the paperwork is not yet available. If it is, a continuing registration may be issued, and an interim registration is automatic, once only, if the new owner is qualified and any part of custody and control is transferred, or any information, like a change of address, is changed.

Identity for Registration - 202.18

Usually established by the fuselage or hull, so when scrapped, an aircraft officially ceases to exist. A balloon takes its identity from its envelope.

Certificates of Registration - 202.25

These can be provisional, temporary, interim or continuing. A temporary one is for when paperwork is not there for a continuing one, and it expires or is cancelled on the earliest of:

- the date in the temporary certificate

- the last day of the three months (90 days) after the issue date

- the day there is a change in legal custody and control

- the day a continuing C of R is issued.

The C of R has 5 parts and must always be carried, unless registered in a non-contracting foreign state or one with an agreement that allows it to do so, in which case an authorisation must be issued. Part 1 (white) is the certificate itself, Part 2 (white) is the application, Part 3 (pink) is the change of ownership form, Part 4 (white) is an interim certificate and Part 5 is the change of address card.

As well as the above, the C of R of a Canadian aircraft is cancelled where:

- an owner dies, is dissolved or amalgamated with another, or ceases to be qualified.

- the lease is extended and Transport Canada is not told within 7 days

- unless it is undergoing restoration or is an ultralight, the aircraft has not been flown in the last 5 years

- an aircraft registered as an ultralight is no longer one

- custody and control documentation ceases to be in effect, unless the registered owner retains custody and control afterwards and submits notification (including the day it ceased), and a true copy of the new document, within 60 days

- an aircraft is destroyed, permanently withdrawn, is missing (with the search terminated) or has been missing over 60 days. Transport Canada must be notified within 7 days of your becoming aware.

- there is misrepresentation or fraudulent documentation in the original application.

INTERIM REGISTRATION - 202.36/222.36

The new owner (or registered owner, if just changing information) must complete the back of the C of R, send the Continuing one to Transport Canada, and retain the Interim on board.

C OF R LOST OR DESTROYED - 202.27

It may be replaced on written application from the registered owner, assuming registration requirements continue to be met.

AMENDMENT OR REPLACEMENT - 202.28

Transport Canada may request the return of a C of R for amendment or replacement, within 7 days of receipt.

Transfer of Legal Custody and Control - 202.35

You have legal custody and control of a Canadian aircraft when you, as owner, have complete responsibility for its operation and maintenance. When you transfer any part of it, the C of R is cancelled, and any transfer notified in writing within 7 days. If the new owner meets the requirements, an interim registration is granted, but only on one occasion. It expires on the earliest of the last day

of the three months following the date of the transfer, the day of any further transfer of any part of custody and control or the day a continuing C of R is issued.

For changes to name, address, etc., an interim registration is also granted, expiring as above. An interim C of R is not transferable.

Importing an Aircraft

You must state the name of the manufacturer, the model and serial number, whether it is new or used, proposed dates for importation, destination, and the name, address and telephone number of the owner. First, however, you need a provisional C of R, which may contain conditions, such as dates and destinations. It expires, or is cancelled, when the aircraft arrives, after a test flight is completed, is operated on a date not specified, or in a different manner.

Exporting an Aircraft - 202.38

Where a Canadian aircraft is sold or leased to an unqualified person, and is not in Canada at the time, or it is expected to be exported, the Canadian marks and Mode S transponder address must be removed from all avionics, and Transport Canada notified in writing within seven days. Copies of all agreements must be provided and the C of R returned.

Reporting Requirements - Registered Owners Canadian Aircraft - 222.15

You must keep the entries in the journey log for three years after the year in which the flight time is accumulated and make it available to Transport Canada for inspection upon request.

Reports must be made inside the seven days after the last day of the sixth month following the month it was registered, and the last day of every six month period thereafter, indicating the total time in each period, and in Canada, which includes non-stop flights between two points, where one is in Canada. Ignore emergency, maintenance or refuelling stops.

Registration Requirements - 222.16

Except for provisional registrations, the application must be signed in ink, by each owner, an authorized officer for an entity or Her Majesty. Authorised officers (or agents) must provide proof of their authority. It must be accompanied by the bill of sale, lease, will or other legal document establishing the applicant as the owner, and evidence that the aircraft is not registered in a foreign state. One owner must be nominated for receiving requests, notices and other documents sent by Transport Canada (a request, notice or document is given to each owner if it is given to a nominee, at the last address in the Canadian Civil Aircraft Register). A registration mark must have been issued.

Except for an ultralight, the aircraft must be eligible for a flight authorization under Part V.

A photograph of the plate that identifies the make, model and serial number must be provided to Transport Canada, on request.

Removal of Marks - 202.61

If the C of R of a Canadian aircraft expires or is cancelled, Canadian marks must be removed within 7 days of receipt of a request to do so. You may not make a fraudulent notification.

Canadian Civil Register - 202.69

An entry will be made for each Canadian aircraft with a continuing or temporary C of R, with the name and address of each owner, the registration mark and other particulars, all of which will be removed if the certificate expires or is cancelled, or any part of custody and control is transferred to somebody not qualified.

Registered Owners

You must, within seven days, notify Transport Canada in writing of any change of name, address, or loss of qualification.

Aircraft Information - 202.46

You must inform Transport Canada, in writing, of your aircraft's location and whether it is serviceable, within 7 days of receipt of a request to do so, including where and when it might return to service. If it is permanently withdrawn, whether or not it has been, or will be, disposed of, and the manner of disposal, must also be specified.

Foreign Aircraft - 202.42 (222.42)

Except for ultralights at Canadian special aviation events, foreign-registered aircraft can only operate in Canada up to 90 days a year, unless the state is a contracting state, and the operator is either the foreign state itself or a citizen or incorporated entity of it - if the latter, the operation must be under an AOC. Parts of a day count as one, and the aircraft is in Canada once inside Canadian airspace.

An ultralight must only be operated inside Canada by its owner at the special aviation event concerned, within a 5-mile radius, under the procedures in Subpart 3 of CARs

Part VI and the authorisation. Transport Canada needs to know the location and duration of the event, which must not last more than 14 days, and the owner's state does not require it to be registered within it.

Aircraft Registered in a Foreign State - 202.43

An aircraft registered in a non-contracting state, or one without an agreement that allows it to be operated in Canada, must carry its authorisation on board.

Operation of a Leased Aircraft by a Non-registered Owner - 203

The term *Canadian Air Operator* includes FTUs and private operators - an *operator certificate* includes an AOC, an FTU operator certificate and a private operator certificate. The term *lease* means an agreement in respect of the operation of an aircraft that specifies a start and end date, gives the lessee legal custody and control and the right to exclusive possession and use of the aircraft during its term, and may include provisions about operating the aircraft for hire or reward. A leasing operation means the operation of an aircraft under this Subpart.

APPLICATION - 203.02 (1)

This Subpart applies to the following persons:

- a Canadian air operator leasing a Canadian aircraft from another Canadian operator

- a foreign air operator leasing a Canadian aircraft from a Canadian operator under Part IV, VI or VII

- a Canadian air operator operating under Part IV, VI or VII leasing an aircraft registered in a foreign state

- a foreign air operator that leases a Canadian aircraft from a Canadian aircraft manufacturer.

This Subpart does not apply in respect of the operation of a private aircraft.

LEASING OPERATIONS - GENERAL - 203.03 (1)

If you want to operate aircraft as part of a leasing operation and you are not the registered owner, you need an authorization as below, unless:

- each party holds a Canadian operator certificate for the type

- the lessee is qualified to be the registered owner of a Canadian aircraft

- the maintenance control system referred to in section 406.35 or 706.02 and the approved maintenance schedule (see subsection 605.86(2)) are, during the term of the lease, equivalent for the lessor and the lessee

- the crew members are employed by the lessee

- the registered owner informs Transport Canada in writing, no later than seven days after the start of the lease, of:

  - the registration mark, model designation and serial number of the aircraft

  - the names, addresses and telephone & fax numbers, and facsimile numbers of the registered owner and the lessee

  - the Canadian operator certificate number and the approved maintenance organization certificate numbers of the lessor and the lessee

  - the start and end dates of the lease

  - the name of the person responsible for the maintenance of the aircraft during the term of the lease

  - the address of the main maintenance base for the aircraft

If all the conditions have been met, an authorisation will be issued specifying conditions that must be met. It expires on the earliest of:

- the date on which the lease is terminated

- the date specified in the authorization

- the date on which the certificate of registration of the aircraft is cancelled

- the date on which the operator certificate is suspended or cancelled

- the date on which there is a change in any of the information that was submitted in support of the original application

The authorization must be carried on board, as must a leasing advisory, if provided.

INTERNATIONAL OPERATIONS - 203.04 (1)

If either the lessor or the lessee is not a Canadian, permission is required from each State. If a third State is involved, the laws of that State must be observed.

REGISTRATION OF LEASED AIRCRAFT - 203.05

The certificate of registration of a leased Canadian aircraft operated under 203.03 remains valid regardless of any changes in the legal custody and control of the aircraft at the start or end of the lease or where the Minister has issued an authorization at any other time.

FORWARDING OF AIRWORTHINESS DIRECTIVES - 203.06 (1)

For a Canadian aircraft, the registered owner shall, immediately on receipt of the authorization, forward to the lessee all applicable airworthiness directives.

For a foreign aircraft, the Canadian lessee shall ensure that the aircraft conforms with all applicable airworthiness directives.

MAXIMUM NUMBER OF LEASED AIRCRAFT - 203.07 (1)

The number of leased aircraft registered in a foreign state must not exceed 25% of the total number of aircraft registered to the Canadian air operator, rounded to the next highest whole number. Neither shall a Canadian air operator lease to foreign air operators more than 25% of the total number of Canadian aircraft registered to that Canadian operator, rounded up to the next whole number.

LIMITS ON PERIOD OF OPERATION - 203.08

A Canadian air operator may only have one authorisation to lease a foreign aircraft for more than 24 months in any period of 30 consecutive months, or an aircraft may only be subject to one lease for more than 24 months in any period of 30 consecutive months.

SUBMISSION OF SIGNED LEASE - 203.09

A signed copy of the lease must be provided to Transport Canada within 7 days.

AIRWORTHINESS (ANNEX 8)

Annex 8 prescribes the minimum standards for aircraft that overfly or land in State territory (the *international* carriage of passengers and cargo). Related to this is Annex 6, Part 1, Chapter 5 (*Performance*), and JAR/FAR 145. Standards apply to the complete aircraft, including power units, systems and equipment. Airworthiness operation limitations must include all limiting mass, C of G position, mass distribution and floor loading information.

The State of *Registry* determines continued airworthiness. When an aircraft is no longer airworthy, permission can be obtained from it to fly it without fare-paying passengers on board to where it can be restored to an airworthy condition.

The certificate of airworthiness is required by Article 31 of the Chicago Convention, issued (or rendered valid) by the State of Registry, whose responsibility it is to develop and adopt requirements to ensure continued airworthiness. An aircraft is "airworthy" when it complies with the flight manual, any placards, and the ICAO Airworthiness Technical Manual. The captain is responsible for ensuring airworthiness before flight (engineers sign for their *work*, not the aircraft).

Maintenance can be *Scheduled* or *Unscheduled*, which basically speak for themselves. Both are supposed to ensure that an aircraft is kept at an acceptable standard of airworthiness. Depending on the performance category and its maximum authorised weight, there will be different schemes covering this, but the nature of General Aviation means that aircraft are very often not seen by an engineer from one check to the next (but the owner/pilot can do some elementary tasks, as described below).

Types of check include 50-hour and 100-hour, which can be extended by 5 or 10%, respectively, for scheduling, but this should not be used as part of normal operations (lack of planning on your part doesn't justify an emergency on an engineer's part). In between, there will be times when components need to be changed, either on a planned or emergency basis.

The *Maintenance Schedule* contains the name and address of the owner or operator, and the type of aircraft and equipment fitted. It lays down when every part of the machine will be inspected, with the type and degree of inspection, including periods of cleaning, lubricating and adjustment. They are written specially for each aircraft, and are subject to Transport Canada approval before moving to a new one.

After work is done, an *Aircraft Maintenance Engineer* (AME) signs a *Maintenance Release*, which means that the work done meets any applicable standards and the aircraft is released back into service. However, you are still responsible for ensuring that the aircraft is airworthy. Not being an engineer, the only way you can find this out (aside from a thorough preflight) is to check the Journey Log before flight, in which you should find an *alert card* which shows when the next servicing is due. Simply subtract the current aircraft hours from that figure to find out how many hours' you can do before the next check.

After an abnormal occurrence (like a lightning strike or heavy landing), the aircraft must be inspected (and not flow until it has been done). If nothing has to be taken apart, the inspection can be done by the PIC, but I would suggest you need technical qualifications to know that you don't need to take anything apart in the first place.

People To Sign a Maintenance Release

AMEs, or anyone authorized to sign under the laws of a state that is party to an agreement or a technical arrangement with Canada, or qualifications deemed sufficient. Also, the owner of an amateur-built aircraft, or someone authorized to sign by an AMO.

Maintenance under Part IV must be done under a maintenance policy manual (MPM) established by the holder of an AMO certificate issued under Section 573.02 with a rating of a category appropriate to the work performed; or a foreign document equivalent to an MPM, established by a maintenance organization approved under the laws of a state that is party to an agreement with Canada and the agreement provides for such certification.

Maintenance under Part IV or VII

Except for balloons, maintenance must be carried out by an approved maintenance organization (AMO) with a maintenance policy manual (MPM), or the foreign equivalent.

Duplicate Inspections

A duplicate inspection is first made and certified by one qualified person and subsequently made and certified by another. One is required when stuff like engine or primary flight controls have been modified, repaired, replaced or disassembled. Away from base, this may be carried out by a pilot qualified on type.

Elementary Work

This is technically maintenance but, for CARs purposes, it means specific tasks not subject to a maintenance release, so you don't need an AME to do them.

A licensed pilot, who is also the owner or operator of an aircraft, may perform elementary work on it. Under normal circumstances, it is limited to piston-engined, private unpressurised aircraft below 5700 kg. Details of the work (that is, tyre and safety belt replacement, checking cylinder compression, changing fuel, oil or filters, replacing fuses, bulbs or reflectors, cleaning replacement of fluids or lubrication not involving disassembly and cleaning and replacing spark plugs) must be entered in the

Log. As said above, elementary work does not need a maintenance release. In a commercial environment, this work may still be done, but must be authorised by whoever is in charge of maintenance for the company. People so authorised must be trained and do the job at least once under an AME or organization holding an Approved Training Organization Certificate under Subpart 566 (the supervising AME need not hold any special rating).

Defects

MINIMUM EQUIPMENT LIST

The company will hold permission for you to operate with some equipment unserviceable for a limited time, subject to the *Minimum Equipment List* (MEL), which is based on the Master MEL produced by the aircraft manufacturer (there are none approved for aircraft less than a certain weight). A Master MEL will not necessarily apply to everyone, as circumstances differ, so operators must prepare their own, which may not be less restrictive than the Master. It will be found in the Ops Manual, Part B, *Type Technical Information.*

MELs are lists of systems and equipment installed on an aircraft, showing how many of them can be defective and for how long. In other words, they are changes to the type design that do not require recertification. In some cases, additional restrictions are applied - for example, you may have to troubleshoot, inspect or secure items as conditions to be met before takeoff. As the MEL is a detailed list, it follows that *any item not on it must be working* at the time of dispatch. However, MELs are usually black-and-white and only address operation (or not) and not degraded performance, such as unusually slow landing gear or excessive fuel consumption, which means that not every possible combination is allowed for, or the additional workload from multiple defects. You still therefore need to exercise some professional judgement, but there are circumstances where operation is definitely not permitted and, although you are given the authority to operate with specified equipment unserviceable, you don't have to if you don't think it's safe (which is a point you may have to argue sometimes with your employer). When in doubt, consult an engineer, but remember that their signature in the log book only guarantees their work, so the responsibility is still yours. Once an MEL is approved, compliance is mandatory. They are not transferable between operators.

If you have a problem before taxying out, you would refer to the MEL. Once you start taxying, you would consult the Ops Manual.

CONFIGURATION DEVIATION LISTS

CDLs are the structural equivalent of MELs, allowing operation with minor bits missing, like fairings, access panels, vortex generators and static discharge wicks. They take no account of dents, distortion, etc.

DEFERRED DEFECTS

These are defects which will not prejudice the safety of a flight, but should be rectified as soon as practicable after it. For example, the minimum navigational equipment for IFR operations in most areas is 2 VOR + 1 ADF or 1 VOR + 2 ADF, ILS, DME, Transponder, Marker and 2 720 channel VHF Comms. However, you can fly when one of the above is unserviceable if it is not reasonably practical to effect repairs or replacements before taking off, especially as outside maintenance should not be used without approval.

If you, as commander, are satisfied that the forecast weather conditions, latest route information, regulations, etc. allow your flight to be safely made, you are allowed to complete one flight to a place where repairs may be effected.

Note: The idea is to get you to a place where a defect can be fixed, or to fly while awaiting spares - it's not for skimping on maintenance.

As a general rule, a defect will only be allowed for a *return* to base; only under exceptional circumstances should you *depart* with one (see *MEL*, above). Defective equipment should be isolated from the remainder of the relevant system by removing fuses, blanking pipelines, locking selectors, or anything else that will promote safety, including labelling the equipment as defective (on gauges, the label needs to be placed so that no readings can be taken). Because you must be aware of the condition of an aircraft to exercise proper judgement, all defects should be entered in the relevant part of the Technical Log. The aircraft should not then fly until they are either cleared or deferred, which means that it can be scheduled for a more convenient time, such as the next service, when the machine is in the shop anyway. Details of deferred defects should also be recorded on the *Deferred Defects Sheet*, which is carried with the Log. A new Log page must then be started, but if, for any reason, the same page must be used (you might have run out), the defect(s) must be clearly identified by numbering. When a deferred defect is finally cleared, the entries are made on the current Log page and DD Sheet (not the originals), cross-referencing the original number, rectification action & clearance certification.

FACILITATION (ANNEX 9)

This concerns the ease with which passengers and cargo can come and go between countries with the minimum of paperwork (Article 37 of the Convention refers, as amplified by Articles 22 and 23). It therefore deals with such subjects as customs & immigration, and anything else dealing with the *safety*, *regularity* and *efficiency* of air navigation:

> *States agree to adopt all practicable measures, through special regulations or otherwise, to facilitate and expedite navigation by aircraft between the territories of contracting States, and to prevent unnecessary delays, especially in administration of the laws relating to immigration, quarantine, customs and clearance.*

Aircraft not engaged on scheduled international air services flying to or through any designated international airport under Article 24 are admitted temporarily free of duty, and may remain there without security or customs duty being required.

Aircraft of other contracting States not on scheduled international air services (i.e. general aviation aircraft) may, subject to the Convention, make flights into or non-stop in transit, and to stop for non-traffic purposes (refuel, emergency) without prior permission from the State concerned. However, they may have to follow prescribed routes for safety or security reasons. Assuming they are engaged in such services, they may also take on or discharge passengers, cargo or mail, subject to State regulations (see Article 7, *Cabotage*). No more advance notice than that required for ATC purposes and the authorities concerned is required. The minimum notification required for a non-scheduled flight from one State to another is the information in a flight plan at least two hours ahead of its arrival at a previously designated international airport.

Documentation

You need the same documentation when arriving by air as if you had come by ship.

GENERAL DECLARATION

This is a customs form, when inbound or outbound from a country. It consists mainly of information about the route and date of flight, the aircraft and the state of health of the crew on board. If the same information is available in other ways, it should not be required. It is signed by the PIC (who is responsible for its completion), or an agent. You need two copies outbound, and three inbound.

INBOUND AND OUTBOUND AIRCRAFT

Document	Outbound	Inbound
General Declaration	2 copies	3 copies
Cargo Manifest	2 copies	3 copies
Simple Stores List	2 copies	2 copies

Embarkation/Disembarkation cards may be required by some States. These must be available free of charge and completed by passengers in legible handwriting unless block lettering is specified.

Inadmissible passengers will be transported away from the State of arrival *by the operator*, who may recover costs from them.

Inspection of crew members and their baggage must be done as expeditiously as possible. States must accept oral declarations of baggage from passengers and crew.

CREW MEMBER CERTIFICATE (CMC)

The CMC is an ID card for crews (flight and cabin), which is valid for the term of employment. It is an alternative to a licence, which doesn't have a photo, and therefore isn't enough for identification purposes. They may be used for temporary admission to a State, and don't require a passport or visa, if you stay within the bounds of the relevant city and depart on your next scheduled flight.

BAGGAGE/CARGO

Unaccompanied baggage must be cleared by a simplified procedure distinct from that normally applicable to cargo.

TELECOMMUNICATIONS (ANNEX 10)

You can only use English. Refer to *VFR Communications* for more details.

AIR TRAFFIC SERVICES (ANX 11)

Whether you need ATC or not depends on the *type of traffic* and its *density*, with due allowance being made for the weather and "other factors". Once that has been sorted out, the airspace is carved up and designated according to the services provided (see *Airspace Structure*).

ATC's mission in life is to *prevent collisions* and *expedite traffic* (exam question). They also provide flight information, but this takes second place, although they make every effort. IFR flights can get information about severe weather, forecasts, navaids and aerodromes, and anything else that is relevant.

The information is disseminated through various offices, including *area control centres, terminal control units, control towers* and *Flight Service Stations* (FSS).

ATC units use UTC, in 24-hour clock format. Clocks must be accurate within ±30 seconds, or 1 second for data links.

Services Provided

FLIGHT SERVICE STATIONS

You can expect the following services from an FSS:

- *En Route Flight Information Service.* Allows pilots to get and pass flight information, or report emergencies. Relays position reports and clearances where radio reception is poor (maybe contact your company).

- *Airport Advisory Service,* such as wind, preferred runways, time on departure, altimeter settings, air and ground traffic, etc. etc., that allow pilots to execute safe and expeditious departures and arrivals at controlled airports.

- *Remote Aerodrome Advisory Service* (RAAS). Weather, runways, NOTAMs, PIREPs, traffic, etc. As the office where the information is coming from is remote, you are responsible for mandatory procedures. A Remote Communications Outlet (RCO) may be involved (below).

- *Vehicle Control Service* (VCS). Controls vehicles on manoeuvring area when the tower is closed, or during FSS hours when there isn't one. Not available with RAAS.

- *Flight Plan Service.* Includes weather and NOTAMs, and itineraries. Helps you collect the information for a safe flight.

- *Surface Weather Observing Service.* Collects, disseminates surface weather data.

- *Aviation Weather Information Service* (AWIS). Tailored for preflight and enroute stages, to help decisions.

- *Aviation Weather Briefing Service* (AWBS). An interpretive preflight and enroute briefing service from certain FSSs within a region. The service is toll-free, and you can expect to see satellite and radar images. People are trained to cover all weather problems. Long range cover is available, too. In the CFS, this is signified as W1.

- *VFR Alerting Service.* Notifies SAR with communications searches if VFR flight plans or itineraries are not closed on time, or overdue reports are not received.

- *Aeronautical Broadcast Service.* ATIS, weather broadcasts, etc.

- *Navigation Assistance Service.* VDF service in emergency, potential or otherwise, or on request. Others depend on facilities.

- *Navigation Aids Monitoring Service.* Checks out VORs, ADFs, etc.

- *NOTAM & PIREP service.*

- *Fixed Telecommunications Service.* The FSS will be connected to a larger system so information can be spread easily between ground stations and aircraft.

- *Paid Communications Service.* Private companies can use their facilities, too.

Most FSSs are open 24/7. Wind direction and speed is given to the nearest 10° and 5 knots.

REMOTE COMMUNICATIONS OUTLETS

RCOs are VHF transmitters established miles away from the operating agency. They are used for aerodromes without much traffic, and therefore do not justify the cost of a full time FSS specialist. When communicating with one, you will actually be talking to a specialist in a larger airfield somewhere else. Where the distance is long, the comms link might be a telephone line, as found in a *Dial-Up Remote Communications Outlet* (DRCO).

To activate it, press the transmit button 4 times, with not more than 1 second between presses. You should hear the normal sounds of a telephone call being established. Then a plastic voice will say "link established", after which you treat it as a normal radio conversation, with some delays between responses. The plastic voice will say "call terminated" when you disconnect.

You can get *Flight Information Service Enroute* (FISE) on the enroute frequency and RAAS on the MF.

AIR TRAFFIC CONTROL SERVICE

- *Aerodrome Control Service*, from towers to aircraft and vehicles. The callsign is *Tower* or *Ground*, as appropriate. In a control zone, the Tower provides separation between Special VFR and IFR flights (exam question). In low visibility, ground movements are kept to the minimum, with protection for ILS/MLS sensitive areas. Emergency vehicles get priority

- *Area Control Service*, from *Area Control Centres* (ACCs) for IFR & CVFR flights in control areas. Their callsign is *Control*, and they are supposed to achieve separation between controlled flights

- *Approach Control Service*, for arriving and departing flights. Their callsign is *Approach*. It might also be *Radar*, or *Talkdown* for PAR

ALERTING SERVICE

This must be provided for aircraft using ATC, on a flight plan or otherwise, or which are the subject of unlawful interference (officially, the service notifies appropriate organisations about aircraft needing SAR, and to assist as required - usually done by a *Rescue Coordination Centre*, or RCC). Alerting is done by the ATS unit responsible for the aircraft at the time (exam question), and the decision to initiate it is the responsibility of the flight information or control organisations. Alerting Service and FIS are often provided by the same unit (yet another). The states of emergencies are divided into three phases, which are:

- *Uncertainty* (INCERFA), which exists after 30 minutes with no communication, or appearance after ETA, whichever is later

- *Alert* (ALERFA) exists with apprehension as to the safety of an aircraft or its occupants after failed attempts to get in touch, it fails to land within 5 minutes of ETA or a clearance, it is believed to be under unlawful interference, or other information implies trouble short of a forced landing

- The *Distress phase* (DETRESFA) exists where there is reasonable certainty that an aircraft and its occupants are threatened by grave and imminent danger or require immediate assistance - e.g. fuel exhaustion or forced landings

FLIGHT INFORMATION SERVICE

To supply pilots in *C-G airspace* with information about such things as *navaid unserviceability* or *hazardous conditions*, such as volcanic ash, etc., especially that which might not have been available on takeoff or might have developed since then. Their callsign is *Information*.

BROADCASTS

ATIS (*Automatic Terminal Information Service*) is broadcast on available VHF frequencies, VOR and NDB (not ILS) at major aerodromes (you can use it as an ID on instrument rides), to reduce congestion on VHF frequencies, although it may have its own channel. You should listen to it and take down the details before you contact ATC, inbound or outbound. ATIS broadcasts should be updated whenever a significant change occurs, and should not last over 30 seconds. The information given need not be repeated, except for the altimeter setting.

AIRSPACE RESERVATION SERVICE

From the *Airspace Reservation Unit* (ARU) and ACCs to provide reserved areas in controlled airspace, and to give out information concerning them (includes military areas).

AIRCRAFT MOVEMENT INFORMATION SERVICE

From ACCs to inform air defence units about flights in the ADIZ.

CUSTOMS NOTIFICATION SERVICE (ADCUS)

From ATC units (on request) to advise customs in advance of transborder flights at specified points of entry.

RADAR SERVICES

Radar allows the best use of airspace by reducing separation between aircraft, and the provision of information, such as traffic and weather. If SSR is available without primary radar, it will not be possible to detect all aircraft.

ATC know which aircraft they are talking to by position reports, identifying turns or transponders. You will be told of any change in the identification status. However, radar identification doesn't stop you being responsible for the disposition of your aircraft, including collision avoidance and obstacle clearance, although ATC accept responsibility for the latter when vectoring IFR and CVFR flights enroute and IFR ones on approach until within the final approach area.

TERMINAL CONTROL SERVICE

From IFR units (ACCs) or *Terminal Control Units* (TCUs) for IFR and CVFR flights in specified control areas.

TERMINAL RADAR SERVICE

An extra from IFR units to VFR aircraft in Class C airspace.

RADAR ADVISORY SERVICE

This can be requested at any time, but is usually used in IMC, so you should not accept vectors if they take you there and you are not qualified. This can be time wasting, especially if it's a clear day and you're continually given vectors downwind that take ages to catch up on; although you are not obliged to accept the advice, you must inform the controllers, as you must if you change heading or altitude. Once advice is refused, you become responsible for traffic separation, although you are always responsible for obstacle avoidance and obtaining clearances.

RADAR INFORMATION SERVICE

For informing pilots of the bearing, distance and level of conflicting traffic. Controllers do not offer avoiding action, and updates are only done at pilot request if there is a definite hazard. The responsibility for separation is that of the pilot. RIS is normally only available within 30 nm of an Approach radar head.

RADAR VECTORING

This is achieved by giving you *specific headings* to maintain desired tracks. It may be used when separation is necessary, for noise abatement, when requested or if an operational advantage would be gained. You should be vectored along routes or tracks that you can easily monitor (just in case the radar fails), but you will be told where you are being vectored to, and when it stops (this can be assumed if you are bound for a final approach or traffic circuit and are given clearance). Otherwise, it continues until you leave the coverage area, go into controlled airspace or are transferred to a unit without radar. You should not be vectored into uncontrolled airspace, unless it's an emergency or you are dodging nasty weather.

The *minimum radar vectoring altitude* is the lowest one that still clears obstacles and does not trigger GPWS, and is used to make the transition to an approach easier, but it may be lower than the minimum altitudes on your chart. If you are cleared to a lower altitude, ATC are responsible for obstacle clearance until you can start an approach (i.e. terrain clearance is with the controller). If the radio fails, be prepared to get back up to at least flight planned altitude or MSA in a hurry.

When IFR in controlled airspace, and advised that radar service is terminated, you should *resume normal position reporting*.

As mentioned, the primary duty of a unit providing radar control is to *separate traffic*. To this end, one function of radar control in approach areas is to provide *surveillance radar approaches*.

An SRA terminates 2 nm from touchdown., except when, as determined by ATC, the accuracy of the equipment allows a lesser distance. In that case, distance and level information must be given every ½ nm. When SRAs continue to the threshold, transmissions should not be interrupted for intervals of more than 5 seconds while the aircraft is within 4 nm from touchdown. A missed approach must be ordered by the controller if you are not visible for the last 2 nm.

IFR Separation

VERTICAL

Standard separation between aircraft is 1,000 feet vertically at or below FL 290, and 2000 feet above that.

However, when your altimeter is set below 29.92", there will be less than 1,000 feet between your aircraft and one at 18,000 feet using 29.92", so the lowest available is actually FL 190 between 28.92-29.91" and 200 for 27.92-28.91". Naturally, if the altimeter setting is 29.92" or higher, the lowest FL is 180.

HORIZONTAL

ATC separate aircraft laterally by treating each procedure or navaid as being inside a little pocket of "protected airspace", taking into account the navigation skills and equipment of an average pilot. As long as the areas allocated for aircraft do not overlap, separation is regarded as being provided. In low level airspace the full width of the airway is protected.

To help with this, your equipment must be calibrated regularly, and you must keep to the centreline of the tracks you wish to fly (although you should regain track immediately, remember your customers may have coffee in their hands, and a screaming turn to the right will not be appreciated! Just make the turns nice and smooth or, better yet, don't stray off in the first place). If you find yourself in the wrong place, tell ATC straight away.

On approach, the basic horizontal dimensions of intermediate, final and missed approach areas are protected, and should not overlap with aircraft holding or en route, or on an adjacent approach. It is your responsibility to remain within the areas when cleared, and tell ATC when you can't, so they can allow more space for aircraft following.

Transition Altitude & Level

The Transition Altitude is the altitude at, or below which, any reference your vertical position is based on altitude (which itself is based on QNH). Any higher, you have to use *Flight Levels*. A transition altitude is normally specified for an aerodrome by the State in which the it is located. For ICAO, the height of the transition altitude is as low as possible but normally at least 900m (3000'), rounded up to the nearest 1000. In Canada, it is 18,000 feet.

The Transition Level is the lowest available flight level when the altimeter is set to 29.92/1013.2, including when the altimeter setting is more than standard. However, if it is is less than standard, the transition level will be higher than that. The difference between transition altitude and transition level is the *transition layer*. The Transition Level is always higher than the Transition Altitude. When two are combined, the higher is used.

Flight level zero is at the atmospheric pressure level of 1013.25 hPa.

ATC Procedures

In IMC, ATC only provide traffic separation. When being vectored for an approach, ATC is responsible for collision avoidance and obstacle clearance. When radar identified, the PIC is responsible. Clearances or instructions are only valid in controlled airspace.

SPEED ADJUSTMENT

Aircraft under radar control may occasionally be asked to increase or decrease speed to help traffic flow. Very often, you can be slipped in before an approaching aircraft if you open up the throttle a bit. On the other hand, you may be catching up with one that is a little slow. Speed changes will be requested in 10 kt units, and you should keep within ± 10 kts of that requested. You don't have to accept any changes if they are unsafe, of course, and once a clearance is issued, the adjustment is normally cancelled.

You should reduce speed to the maximum extent possible within 3,000 agl and 10 nm of an uncontrolled aerodrome.

Airspeed Limitations - 602.32

However, the maximum speed below 10,000 feet (ASL) within controlled airspace is 250 kts, and below 3,000 feet (AGL) within 10 nm of a controlled airport, 200 kts (250 uncontrolled), unless on departure, climbing above 10,000 feet, the safety speed is higher, or under a special flight operations certificate (an airshow).

The minimum speeds used by ATC when issuing adjustments are 250 kts above 10,000 feet ASL over 20

nm from the destination, and 210 kts below that. Inside 20 nm, turbojets must be above 160 kts, and propeller aircraft 120 kts.

PARALLEL OFFSET

This means flying a parallel course to an assigned route, offset by a certain distance, used, for example, when you need to change altitude while following another aircraft. Navigation is the pilot's responsibility. When regaining the original track, alter heading by 30-45° and report when complete. The instruction will include the miles right or left of the original track and the time it will end.

STRUCTURED AIRSPACE

High level airspace may be structured for one-way traffic at certain times, and non-appropriate levels will be used. However, aircraft against the flow will be assigned proper levels where possible.

HOLDING PATTERNS

These keep aircraft over a particular point until they can be fitted into the traffic flow further onwards. Refer to the *Instruments* chapter for information on how to use them.

CONTACT & VISUAL APPROACHES

If you are clear of cloud with 1 nm visibility, with a *reasonable expectation* of getting to the destination on a published instrument approach, you may be authorised to depart from the procedure to proceed visually. Such a *contact approach* must be requested by you, and traffic conditions must allow it. In addition, you are responsible for obstacle clearance, noise abatement and obeying airspace restrictions, being at least 1,000 feet above the highest obstacle within 5 miles from your estimated position until you have enough visual reference to land. It follows that familiarity with the area is a good idea if you want to find the destination in poor visibility. Throughout all this, ATC will ensure separation from other IFR aircraft and will issue missed approach instructions if they don't think you will get in. You will still be responsible for obstacle clearance.

A *visual approach* may be undertaken by IFR aircraft in VFR conditions, with authorisation from ATC. If you are under radar control, you may request vectoring to where you can start a visual approach if the ceiling is at least 500 feet above the minimum vectoring altitude and the visibility is at least 3 sm. You must also be able to see the airport (or the aircraft in front of you if it is controlled).

If you accept such a clearance, you are responsible for keeping away from traffic you are told to follow (controlled aerodromes) or which may be unknown (uncontrolled), adequate wake turbulence separation, navigation to final approach, keeping to noise abatement procedures and keeping away from Class F airspace.

Missed approach instructions will not be given, as you are under VFR, and you must remain so, even if a landing cannot be undertaken.

IFR IN VMC

You may cancel an IFR flight plan in VFR conditions outside Class A or B airspace, if the weather is not expected to revert to IFR, and you continue with IFR procedures. However, you need to file a VFR flight plan, if required, as you cannot simply convert IFR flight plans.

ATC may give IFR clearance for departure, climb or descent under VFR to a time, altitude or location, outside Class A or B airspace below FL 600, if weather permits.

Clearances, Instructions - 602.31

A *controlled flight* is any flight subject to ATC clearance, which is *authority to proceed only as far as known traffic is concerned.*

You must comply with any clearance received and acknowledged. If you don't like it, you should say so at the time, since an acknowledgement without further comment is taken as such. Clearances are valid only in controlled airspace, and there will be some form of the word "clear" in the text to identify them. Clearances must always be read back. They are passed slowly and clearly, since you will need to write them down, and preferably before startup, since you will not want to be bothered when taxying, etc. They will contain the aircraft identification (as per the flight plan), the clearance limit (usually the destination) and the route, levels, changes and any other instructions, especially about departure manoeuvres. Control is based on *known traffic only*, so you are still responsible for safe procedures and good judgement - clearances do not constitute authority to violate the rules!

If a clearance or an instruction is not suitable, you may request and, if practicable, obtain an amended one. Having accepted clearance for an approach, you may not deviate without further clearance. If a specific approach is not mentioned, tell ATC which one you are doing.

Clearance to land, or any alternative clearance, received from a non-radar controller should normally be passed to the aircraft before it reaches 2 nm from touchdown.

You must also comply with *instructions* in the same way, unless safety is a factor. An instruction will be identifiable,

but the word "instruct" may not be included. Information about flight conditions is for assistance or are reminders.

Aircraft moving to control areas within 30 minutes of each other must be coordinated before departure clearance is issued.

APPROACH CLEARANCES

When direct controller-pilot communications (DCCP) are active, ATC will normally advise pilots of the ceiling, visibility, wind, runway, altimeter setting, approach aids and conditions, etc. immediately before or after descent clearance is given. If you tell them you have the current ATIS, they will only give you the altimeter setting.

If you are going to an airport underneath controlled low level airspace with a published approach procedure, you will be cleared out of the controlled airspace vertically via the procedure. Without a published procedure, you will be cleared to MEA and asked about your intentions (strictly honourable, of course). If you cannot cancel IFR at that point, ATC will provide protection down to MOCA for 30 minutes. You can cancel IFR, leave the airspace horizontally or ask to go to another airport.

When you get clearance for an approach, its name will indicate its type if you are required to stick to a particular procedure. If you get visual reference with the ground before completing it, you should carry on unless cleared otherwise. If you will be given another runway than that in the approach, the runway number will be given in the clearance as well (in this case, if you have to go around, use the missed approach procedure for the original runway, not the landing one).

Having accepted clearance for an approach, you may not deviate from it without further clearance. If a specific approach is not mentioned, tell ATC which one you are doing. This includes the tower and FSS.

If no other instructions are given, you may descend to the lowest of the MEA, transition altitude, approach MSA, the 100 nm safe altitude, or at least 1,000 feet above the highest obstacle within 5 miles (1500' in mountainous areas 2, 3 and 4, and 2000' in 1 and 5).

Where pressure variations are high, or temperatures are very cold, you should operate at least 1,000 feet above MEA within designated mountainous regions.

Airspace Structure - 601.01

Airspace can be restricted, according to the density of the traffic in it, the nature of the operations, the level of safety required and the National interest. The airspace over Canada is split up, according to the use made of it.

CANADIAN DOMESTIC AIRSPACE (CDA)

This includes all airspace over the Canadian land mass, the Arctic, the Archipelago (assorted islands) and any high seas underneath the bound. It is split into the Southern Domestic Airspace (SDA) and Northern Domestic Airspace (NDA). The difference is that magnetic tracks are used in the SDA, and true tracks in the NDA. The above boundaries are also used for:

ALTIMETER SETTING REGIONS - 602.35

The NDA boundaries (above) coincide with the *Standard Pressure Region*, where 29.92" is usually set on the altimeter for altitude reference. On departure within the region, however, use the *current altimeter setting* (from observations in the last 90 minutes) right up to the cruise level, where you set 29.92" just before reaching it. On arrival, just before starting descent, use the setting of the intended destination. In the hold, keep the standard setting until the lowest flight level in the hold.

The *Altimeter Setting Region* is the same size as the SDA, and is where you must use the current setting of the nearest station so, when landing, set the altimeter to whatever is in use at your destination.

When going from the ASR to the SPR, set 29.92" immediately *after* crossing the boundary, unless told otherwise. When going the other way, set the current altimeter setting of the nearest station immediately before crossing the boundary.

Airspace below 18,000 feet is *Low Level Airspace*. Predictably, that from 18,000 feet upwards is called the *High Level Airspace*.

LOW LEVEL CONTROLLED AIRSPACE

Consists of control area extensions, control zones, high level airways and airspace, low level airways, Arctic, Northern and Southern Control Areas, TCAs, transition areas, restricted airspace, advisory airspace, military operations areas and danger areas, from 2200 feet to 17,999 feet.

A control zone is an area round an aerodrome (usually 7 nm radius, but can be 3 or 5, and Class C, D or E) where IFR and VFR aircraft are controlled by ATC. The normal height is 3,000 feet AGL (actually above aerodrome elevation). If the weather is below VFR in a control zone, you must ask for Special VFR clearance before flying in it.

A *Control Area Extension* is extra airspace for controlling IFR aircraft at busy airfields, usually starting at 2200 feet AGL and stretching to 18,000 ASL, although outer portions may be higher.

A *Terminal Control Area* (TCA) is for IFR aircraft within a 45 nm radius of the primary aerodrome, up to 9500 feet for the last 10 nm. Between 12-35 nm, the height will be 2200 feet. The military version (MTCA) speaks for itself.

A transition area starts at 700 AGL and ends at the first boundary of controlled airspace. It is also meant for IFR aircraft and will be at least the size required for instrument approaches, although it normally has a 15 nm radius.

ICAO AIRSPACE CLASSIFICATIONS

Controlled airspace is classified into Class A, B, C, D, E, F Special Use Restricted or F Special Use Advisory.

Note: In Canada, visibility is in statute miles and distance from clouds in thousands of feet.

CLASS A

This means most airways, and main control zones and control areas. Separation is provided for IFR aircraft only (VFR is not allowed), from 18,000 ft to FL 600. Since clearance to enter is required, you need continuous two-way radio communication.

CLASS B

Separation is provided between all aircraft, IFR or VFR, from 12,500 feet (or MEA, whichever is higher) to 17,999 feet. It may contain a control zone and TCA. Clearance is required from VFR aircraft before entering, and position reporting is required, so you need a minimum level of radio/nav equipment for continuous two-way radio communication. Unless you can get Special VFR, you must leave when conditions demand IFR. In UK, Class B airspace only exists above FL 245 (Upper Airspace).

Visibility must be 8 km above 10,000 feet and 5 km below that, *clear of cloud.*

CLASS C

Separation is between IFR aircraft, with VFR separated from IFR. VFR aircraft have to look out for themselves and require clearance to enter, so they also need a 2-way radio. They may get traffic information and conflict resolution. If there is no ATC, Class C airspace reverts to Class E. There are no speed restrictions when IFR, but the VFR limit is 250 KIAS, below 10,000 feet. Does not yet exist in UK.

Visibility must be 8 km above 10,000 feet and 5 km below that, 1500 m horizontally and 300 m vertically from cloud.

CLASS D

Control zones and areas of lesser importance, so IFR and VFR traffic is allowed, but separation is provided only between IFR aircraft. However, they are informed about VFR flights (VFR traffic details are also given to VFR flights). The maximum speed is 250 kts IAS for IFR and VFR up to 10,000 feet. For VFR flights, visibility must be 8 km above 10,000 feet and 5 km below that, 1500 m horizontally and 300 m vertically from cloud.

Two-way radio communication is required, as is clearance to enter, so the *minimum radio equipment*, when asked, is *VHF comms.* For the Canadian version of Class D, you only need to establish contact with ATC before entering, so if they reply and ask you to stand by, you can carry on. If ATC is not available, Class D reverts to Class E.

CLASS E

Anything that is still controlled airspace, but not meeting the requirements above, like low level airways, control area extensions, transition areas or control zones without a control tower. IFR and VFR flights are permitted, but separation is only between IFR aircraft. All flights receive traffic information as far as is practical.

The maximum speed is 250 kts IAS for IFR and VFR up to 10,000 feet.

For VFR flights, visibility must be 8 km above 10,000 feet and 5 km below that, 1500 m horizontally and 300 m vertically from cloud.

Two-way radio communication is required for IFR flights, as is clearance to enter.

CLASS F

Advisory Routes, where some limitations are imposed. Separation is between IFR aircraft as far as practicable (with advisory service) and all flights get flight

information on request. Clearance is not needed to enter., but IFR flights need two-way radio equipment. ATC advisory service is provided to all *participating* IFR traffic, and Flight Information Service to other flights.

For VFR, visibility must be 8 km above 10,000 feet and 5 km below that, 1500 m horizontally and 300 m vertically from cloud. At and below 900 m, or 300 m above terrain, whichever is higher, 5 km vis, clear of cloud, in sight of land or water.

Maximum VFR speed is 250 kts IAS for IFR and VFR up to 10, 000 feet.

In Canada, Class F Advisory is used for air shows and the like, and VFR aircraft should avoid it unless taking part. A=acrobatics, T=training, F=aircraft testing, P=parachuting, S=soaring, M=military, H=hang gliding. Class F Restricted needs advance permission, as it may be a danger area, a rocket range, or similar (check the NOTAMs).

R=Restricted, D=Danger, 100=BC, 200=Alberta, 300=Saskatchewan, 400=Manitoba, 500=Ontario, 600=Quebec, 700=Atlantic, 800=Yukon, 900=NWT.

CLASS G

Anything not designated as A, B, C, D, E or F, where ATC has no authority, so it's free airspace. There's no separation service, but Flight Information Service is provided if required.

For VFR, visibility must be 8 km above 10,000 feet and 5 km below that, 1500 m horizontally and 300 m vertically from cloud. At and below 900 m, or 300 m above terrain, whichever is higher, 5 km vis, clear of cloud, in sight of land or water.

UNCONTROLLED AIRSPACE

Consists of high and low level air routes, restricted airspace, advisory airspace, military operations areas and danger areas, plus the bits underneath the Northern and Arctic Control areas. Uncontrolled airspace is G, F Special Use Restricted, F Special Use Advisory.

The dimensions of the above are in the Designated Airspace Handbook, as are air defence identification zones, altimeter setting regions, standard pressure regions, mountainous regions, holding points, reporting points, intersections, control towers, military TCAs, flight information regions, etc., etc.

AIR ROUTES

Low level *Airways* exist between 2200 (AGL) and 17,999 feet (ASL), and are Class E airspace. Low level *Air Routes* are the same size, but are Class G, uncontrolled, and start at the surface.

The dimensions depend on the reliability of signal coverage. VHF airways (that is, defined by VORs) are 4 nm wide either side of the centreline, increasing outwards to where the 4½° lines cross the width. For LF/MF airways (using NDBs), substitute 4.34 and 5°. Air Routes are known by two letters and a number, like RR3, or RB4.

When the width of an airway increases due to splay, the diverging lines from the facilities cross the basic airway width at *50.8* nm for VHF and *49.66* nm for NDB.

Airways have one letter and a number (G1). The letter usually represents a colour, either Green or Red (East-West) or Blue and Amber (North-South). Remember that the airspace within the dimensions is *protected*, meaning that, if you are trying to get into an aerodrome with no approach procedure, you have some breathing space in which to manoeuvre.

FLIGHT INFORMATION REGION

Airspace of defined dimensions extending upwards from the surface, where flight information and alerting services are provided. There are 7, namely Vancouver, Edmonton, Winnipeg, Toronto, Montreal, Moncton and Gander.

TRANSPONDER AIRSPACE - 601.03

Consists of all Class A, B and C airspace, and any Class D or E in the Designated Airspace Handbook. Refer to Secondary Surveillance Radar under *Electricity & Radio* for procedures and methods of use.

IFR OR VFR IN CLASS F SPECIAL USE AIRSPACE - 601.04

You must be authorised (see the *Designated Airspace Handbook*), if activities are not hazardous and access does not jeopardize security.

IFR IN CLASS A, B, C, D, E OR F AIRSPACE - 601.04

You must be authorised by ATC, or Transport Canada. The operation must be in the public interest and not likely to affect aviation safety.

VFR IN CLASS A AIRSPACE - 601.06

You must be authorised by Transport Canada, and the operation must be in the public interest and not likely to affect aviation safety.

VFR IN CLASS B AIRSPACE - 601.07

You must be authorised by ATC, or Transport Canada. The operation must be in the public interest and not likely to affect aviation safety. If you cannot maintain VMC as cleared, you must request Special VFR (in a control zone), or an amended clearance to maintain VMC, or go IFR. Once outside a control zone, you cannot continue with Special VFR minima, but must revert to 1 sm visibility and remain clear of cloud, in the case of a helicopter, for example (Special VFR limits are half a mile visibility and clear of cloud).

VFR, CLASS C & D AIRSPACE - 601.08

You must have clearance before entering Class C airspace, but you merely need to establish two-way communication for Class D. If you can't maintain it, you may still enter, in daylight in VMC, if you get clearance first. Class C and D airspace become Class E when ATC is not in operation.

SEARCH & RESCUE (ANNEX 12)

SAR must be provided on a 24-hour basis, with no overlap on coverage areas. Each SAR region must have a *Rescue Coordination Centre* (RCC). SAR assistance is given regardless of nationality.

Procedures

AT THE SCENE OF AN ACCIDENT

The PIC should:

- keep any craft in distress in sight until no longer required

- determine his own position

- be able to report as many details as possible to the RCC, including:

    - type of craft in distress, ID and condition

    - position, time in hours and minutes UTC

    - number of people observed, and if they have abandoned the craft

    - number of persons observed afloat

    - apparent physical condition of survivors

- act as instructed by the RCC

The first aircraft on the scene should take control, until the first SAR one arrives. If it cannot communicate with the RCC, it should hand over to an aircraft that can.

INTERCEPTING DISTRESS TRANSMISSIONS

Distress transmissions are normally given out on the frequency in use at the time, but when over the high seas, say when flying offshore, you will typically be guarding one of the distress frequencies, either *121.5 MHz, 243 MHz* or *2182 KHz* for merchant shipping. ELTs operate on 121.5 MHz and 406 MHz.

If you hear a distress transmission, you must:

- Record the position of the craft in distress

- Inform the appropriate ATS unit or RCC

- At your discretion, whilst awaiting further instructions, proceed to the position given

If you need to direct another craft to the scene, circle it at least once, fly low just in front and rock the fuselage, then fly off in the direction you want them to go.

You can use the same signals when they are finished with, but fly behind instead. In theory, they should hoist the *Code Pennant*, which is a flag with vertical red and white stripes, close up, or flash a series of *T*s in Morse Code with a lamp. On the other hand, they could just turn in the direction requested. A blue and white chequered flag means *NO*, as does a series of *N*s in Morse.

GROUND-AIR VISUAL SIGNALS

Survivors can communicate with SAR aircraft visually by making signals on the ground. They should be at least 8 feet high (or as large as possible) with as large a contrast as possible between the materials used and the background.

Need Assistance	V
Need Medical Help	X
No	N
Yes	Y
Going This Way	←

Rescue units can use these (mostly double symbols):

Operation Complete	LLL
Found all personnel	LL
Found some personnel	++
Cannot continue - going home	XX
Split into different groups in directions indicated	← →
Aircraft in this direction	→ →
Nothing found but continuing	NN

AIR-GROUND VISUAL SIGNALS

Indicate your understanding of the ground signals above by rocking your wings in daylight or flashing your landing lights twice at night (or nav lights if you haven't any landing lights).

DROPPABLE CONTAINERS & PACKAGES

Those containing survival equipment should be coloured (with streamers):

Red	Medical Supplies/First Aid
Blue	Food and Water
Yellow	Blankets/Protective Clothing
Black	Miscellaneous (stoves, shovels, etc.)

Use a combination if the goods are of a mixed nature.

ACCIDENTS & INCIDENTS (ANNEX 13)

An Aviation Occurrence is any accident or incident associated with the operation of aircraft, or a situation that could lead to one. After any occurrence, the TSB must be told as soon as possible (see the AIM for how). You can make reports in confidence under the *Confidential Aviation Safety Reporting Program* (CASRP).

Aircraft Accident

A reportable one occurs when:

- anyone is killed or injured from contact with the aircraft (or any bits falling off), including jet blast or rotor downwash

- the aircraft sustains damage or structural failure

- The aircraft is missing or inaccessible

between the time any person boards it with the intention of flight, and all persons have disembarked (ICAO definition). This does not include injuries from natural causes, which are self-inflicted or inflicted by other people, or to stowaways hiding in places not normally accessible to passengers and crew. *Significant* or *Substantial Damage* in this context essentially means anything that may involve an insurance claim, but officially is damage or failure affecting structure or performance, normally meaning major repairs.

Under ICAO, a *fatal injury* involves death within 30 days. A *serious injury* involves:

- more than 48 hours in hospital within 7 days

- more than simple fractures of fingers, toes and nose

- lacerations causing nerve or muscle damage or severe haemorrhage

- injury to any internal organ

- 2nd or 3rd degree burns or any over 5% of the body

- exposure to infectious substances or radiation

The *Transportation Safety Board* of Canada (TSB) investigates aircraft accidents, and has teams of investigators on 24-hour standby to go worldwide. Its function is not to apportion blame, but to *ensure that accidents don't happen again*.

POST ACCIDENT PROCEDURES

The pilot or senior survivor, Company or aerodrome authority (in that order, if practical) should take as much as possible of the following action after evacuating passengers to either a sheltered location upwind of the aircraft, or into the liferaft:

- Prevent tampering with the wreckage by ANYBODY except to save life, avoid danger to other persons or prevent damage by fire, for which turn the fuel and battery OFF - disconnect it if there is no risk of a spark, but the TSB won't like you to touch too much, so remove only emergency equipment, like first aid kits or survival packs, noting where you got them from. Account for all people on board. Attend injured and cover bodies.

- Activate the distress beacon and maybe use aircraft radio equipment. Prepare pyrotechnics, select, and prepare a helicopter landing site or lay out search and rescue signals.

- If people or communications are close, send for assistance.

- If rescue is likely to be delayed because of distance or failing daylight, prepare suitable shelters, distribute necessary rations of food and water. If necessary, find fresh water.

- Inform the Company (Ops Manager, Chief Pilot) by the quickest and most private means of:

  - Aircraft and Reg No

  - Time, position of accident

  - Details of survivors

  - Nature of occurrence or other details

- Notify Police, Fire, Ambulance, ATC, Gas/Electricity

- Note weather details.

- Make sketches, take photographs. Preserve and protect documents.

AIRCRAFT ACCIDENT REPORTING

All phone calls and actions taken should be recorded by the person receiving the initial notification - continuous watch should be kept for at least 48 hours or the duration of the process, whichever is longer. Callers should be identified, to ensure it is not a false alarm and to ensure it is indeed a company aircraft. No information should be released without Company authority, mainly for liability reasons.

The Company Accident Report form should be completed, in addition to complying with the laws and regulations of the country of registration and the country in which the accident or incident occurred. If there is any doubt, the occurrence should be reported as an Accident; it can be reclassified later.

The Company should form an Accident Board, consisting of people with varying qualifications as deemed necessary. This won't be done on the spot, there should be a permanent list somewhere. Only allow 1 photographer and reporter on the scene (let them fight it out amongst themselves).

The accident investigation kit should include a cellphone/satphone, camera, tape recorder, GPS, large-scale map, magnifying glass, compass, tape measure/ruler, plenty of pens and paper (for witness statements and diagrams) first aid kit (to include tweezers), ruler, a packet each of latex and leather gloves, dust masks, tie tags, surveyor flags and tape, labels, torches, fluid sample bottles, and anything else for the circumstances (duct tape, restricted access signs, etc).

If you get there before the TSB, take notes, keep detached and don't disturb anything, unless it's going to blow up or catch fire, which would destroy any evidence, including documentation, needing to be preserved. When taking photographs, you will need overall scenes, and pictures of gauges, etc. Include anything (such as the ruler in the accident kit) that will indicate scale. As for statements, don't put words in witnesses' mouths; just take down what they say.

All documentation relating to the aircraft or pilot should be impounded.

FLYING AFTER AN ACCIDENT

Crew members should remain on site, unless medical treatment or examination is required, and may not be scheduled for flying duties until authorised by the Chief Pilot in consultation with the Medical Examiner. No comments should be made until either they feel fit to do so, or a night's rest has passed since the accident, whichever is sooner.

Incident

Any happening other than an accident which hazards or, if not corrected, would hazard any aircraft, its occupants or anyone else, not resulting in substantial damage to the aircraft or third parties, crew or passengers. In Canada, this refers to aeroplanes over 5700 kg MAUW and helicopters over 2250 Kg.

You may have to submit a written report within 48 hours.

EXAMPLES

Precautionary or forced landings, due to engine or tail rotor control failure, an external part of the aircraft becoming detached in flight, contaminated fuel, forced, unscheduled, changes of flight plans from by the failure of aircraft instruments, navigation aids or other technical failure, obstructions on rig landing platforms or other landing sites, loss of an external load, with no third party claim, bird strikes, Airprox, in-flight icing, crew incapacitation. The ICAO bird strike information system is *IBIS* (exam question).

SERIOUS INCIDENTS

These are nearly accidents, or have serious potential technical or operational implications, or may result in disciplinary action against aircrew or engineers. The 'Serious' classification is normally made by the senior person on the operation as soon as possible after the event and before the crew or aircraft fly again, mainly to preserve their recollection of the incident or to ensure their fitness for duty rather than for disciplinary reasons. Away from base, you should load a replacement CVR or CVDR and return the others to base. Both should be disabled after shutdown to prevent data being overwritten when power is re-applied. A near-collision needing an avoidance manoeuvre is a serious incident, as is fire or smoke in the passenger compartment.

AERODROMES & AIRPORTS (ANNEX 14)

An aerodrome is generally any place for landing aircraft that fits the official definition, which is, broadly, being set apart for the purpose, including any necessary buildings. *Aerodrome Traffic* is all traffic on the manoeuvring area of an aerodrome, and flying in its vicinity.

An airport is an aerodrome with an aviation document in force, so it has to meet a higher level of safety. It would typically be used for passenger-carrying commercial flights, for example. It is also required for those in built-up areas. Offshore oil rigs are also covered by Annex 14.

Full details of handy places to land, including heliports (see below) are in the *Canada Flight Supplement*, or CFS, which you need a good knowledge of for your commercial ride. An aerodrome or airport listed in it that does not need previous permission for use is for public use. Where permission is required, you either need to get it first, or just provide prior notice, so they can get the sheep off the runway (actually, it's so they can get the latest information, but you know what I mean).

You may not:

- walk, stand, drive, park anything, or cause an obstruction, without permission from the operators or ATC

- tow aircraft on active areas at night, without wingtip, tail and anti-collision lights, or light from the towing vehicle

- park, or leave an aircraft, on an active area at night without wingtip, tail and anti-collision lights, or lanterns hanging from the wingtips, tail and nose

- operate a vessel on, or cause obstruction on the surface of, a water area that must be kept clear, when ordered to leave, or not approach it

- remove, deface, extinguish or interfere with markers, markings, lights or signals for air navigation, without permission from the operator and ATC

- display a marker, marking, sign, light or signal likely to be hazardous by causing glare or confusion with, or preventing clear sight of, another one

- allow a bird or animal in your custody to be unrestrained inside an aerodrome or airport, except to control others

- discharge a firearm within or into an aerodrome or airport without permission

- display a marker, marking, light or signal that may cause a person to believe a place is an aerodrome when it is not

Fire Prevention - 301.09, 302.11

Except for flarepots, smoking, sparks and open flames are not allowed on an apron, an aircraft loading bridge, a gallery or balcony near an apron, or where a fire hazard could be created, unless during maintenance or servicing with permission from the aerodrome operator. Smoking, may be allowed in an enclosed building or shelter on an apron if a fire hazard is not likely.

Registration - 301.03

Aerodromes are *registered* when their information is in the CFS or *Water Aerodrome Supplement*. Changes must be notified immediately.

Wind Direction Indicator - 301.06

Must be a conspicuously-coloured truncated cone, visible from 300m (1,000 feet) above and illuminated at night, unless the wind can be determined by radio or other means, like smoke or wind lines on water. They must be removed if an aerodrome is closed permanently.

A dry TC windsock (as used at airports) is horizontal at 15 kts, 5° below the horizontal at 10, and 30° below at 6 kts.

Lighting - 301.07

A runway used at night must have a line of fixed white lights on each side, visible for over 2 nm in all directions, unless it is impractical (there may be no electricity), in which case you can use a fixed white light in a safe place at each end for alignment, and white reflective markers on the sides, if they are effective from over 2 nm when aligned with the centre line. The lines of at least 8 equidistant lights or markers must be the same length (at least 420m) and parallel, and the same distance apart as the runway width during the day. The distance between each in the line must be at least 60 m (200 feet), with each light or marker opposite to another.

A taxiway used at night needs a line of fixed blue lights or retro-reflective markers parallel to each other on each side at least 60 m apart.

When a manoeuvring area or a heliport is closed, the lights shall not be operated or markers kept, except as required for maintenance.

At night, unserviceable portions of the movement area must use fixed red lights, red retro-reflective markers or floodlighting. An aircraft parking area must use blue lights or retro-reflective markers, at least 60m (200 feet) apart, or floodlighting.

ARCAL stands for *Aircraft Control of Aerodrome Lighting*. It works by clicking a sequence on the transmit button, within 15 nm of the aerodrome concerned. Use the sequence when starting the approach, even if the lights are on already, as this will restart the timing mechanism. A Type J ARCAL requires 5 keys within 5 seconds. A Type K needs 7 to start with, but you can adjust the intensity to low, medium or high with 3, 5, or 7.

A flashing white beacon used to identify the aerodrome at night will flash a Morse Code letter about 3-4 times a minute (see CFS).

Operations at or Near Aerodromes

There must be no likelihood of collision with other aircraft or vehicles, and the aerodrome must be suitable for the intended operation. This means observing other traffic and conforming to or avoiding the traffic pattern, together with making all turns to the left inside the traffic circuit, except when otherwise specified in the CFS or by ATC. You must also land and take off into the wind, where practicable, unless otherwise authorized by ATC. You must maintain a continuous listening watch on the appropriate frequency, or keep a watch for visual instructions from ATC.

Controlled Aerodromes

You must get clearance from ATC to taxi, take off or land. Unless authorized by them, you may not fly below 2,000 feet over an aerodrome except when landing or taking off, or you are in the service of a police authority, are saving human life, on fire-fighting or air ambulance operations, administration of the *Fisheries or Coastal Fisheries Protection Act*, administration of national or provincial parks, flight inspection, aerial application or inspection, highway or city traffic patrol, aerial photography conducted under an AOC, helicopter external loads, or flight training.

Uncontrolled Aerodromes

These have no control tower, or have one that is closed. They use a common frequency so that all aircraft using it can keep track of what's going on and broadcast their intentions to other traffic. Direct your call to a station or broadcast to local traffic if nobody answers, and keep listening. Maintain noise abatement procedures.

Broadcast your departure intentions before moving on to the runway. Afterwards, monitor the frequency until well clear, normally 5-10 nm, looking out for aircraft entering downwind. You can depart on course straight ahead, turning when well clear of the circuit, or from the crosswind or downwind leg.

On arrival, report position and altitude, intentions and ETA well beforehand. Report joining the circuit, and do so from the upwind side, turning crosswind across the runway then downwind at 1,000 feet AGL. Alternatively, join straight in downwind at circuit height. If you need to check the wind and runway condition from the overhead, do so well above circuit height and complete the letdown on the upwind side. Don't forget to report on finals and when clear.

MANDATORY FREQUENCY (MF)

One is assigned to some uncontrolled airports, and must be used for all transmissions with its area of coverage. It's usually found at airports with an FSS.

AERODROME TRAFFIC FREQUENCY (ATF)

Used for airfields that don't meet the specs for an MF. If no Unicom exists, the ATF will be 123.2. The difference between an ATF and an MF is that, with the former, the appropriate procedures should be followed and, in the latter, they must be followed.

VFR AND IFR WITHIN MF AREA - 602.97

Normally, you must have suitable radio equipment, and maintain a listening watch on the specified frequency, but if a ground station is in operation, you can give prior notice, if you ensure there is no likelihood of collision, and you enter the circuit from where you can complete two sides of a rectangular circuit before turning onto finals.

GENERAL MF REQUIREMENTS - 602.98

Reports must be made on the MF to the ground station with it, or broadcast, if a ground station is not in operation.

BEFORE MANOEUVRING AREA

Report your intentions beforehand.

ON DEPARTURE - 602.100

Before moving onto the take-off surface, report your departure intentions, ensure there is no likelihood of collision with another aircraft or a vehicle during take-off, and report departing the circuit.

ON ARRIVAL - 602.101

When VFR, you must report at least 5 minutes before entering the MF area, giving position, altitude, estimated time of landing and arrival intentions. You must also report downwind, on finals and clear of landing surface.

CONTINUOUS CIRCUITS - 602.102

You must report joining downwind, on finals (stating intentions) and when clear of the landing surface.

FLYING THROUGH AN MF AREA

Report at least 5 minutes before entering, giving your position, altitude, estimated landing time, intentions, and when clear.

IFR APPROACHES OR LANDINGS - 602.104

You must report your intentions 5 minutes before you estimate commencing approach (with your estimated time of landing), when commencing a circling manoeuvre, and as soon as practicable after initiating missed approach.

You must also report passing the fix outbound (for a procedure turn) or when you first intercept the final approach course, passing the final approach fix (or three minutes before the estimated time of landing), and on finals.

Controlled Airports

2-way radio communications are normally required. Where ATIS is available, you should take the details before transmitting, and inform ATC what version you have, so they know whether you're up to date.

ATIS (*Automatic Terminal Information Service*) is typically broadcast on a VOR frequency at major aerodromes (you can use it as an ID on instrument rides), although it may have its own channel. This relieves ATC of a lot of work, and saves the airways getting clogged up, but they will still give you the current altimeter setting. So, the pre-departure routine is to listen to the ATIS, contact the ground frequency (if there is one) for taxi clearance, then tower for takeoff, remaining there until you clear the zone.

Where runways cross each other, watch out for a *Hold Short* clearance, which is intended to stop you entering the wrong runway. It must be read back.

When arriving, you still need the ATIS before contacting ATC, which should naturally be done before entering the control zone. They will need to know your identification, aircraft type, position, altitude, ATIS version, transponder code and intentions. You should then be cleared to the circuit or a position for further clearance.

DO NOT TRY TO TURN BACK TO THE FIELD IF THE ENGINE FAILS ON TAKEOFF - LAND STRAIGHT AHEAD.

READ THAT AGAIN.

AND AGAIN

Land and Hold Short

These operations involve landing on one runway and making sure you don't encroach on another crossing at an intersection, or even another taxiway or some other reason for stopping (if there's another runway across your path, you could be arguing with a 737). Although it is used for convenience and in the interests of keeping traffic moving, you have the final authority to refuse a LAHSO clearance, as the final responsibility lies with you. Although such a clearance must be carried out, you can still reject a landing.

Standard Traffic Circuit

The circuit (round a runway) is *part* of an aerodrome traffic pattern, and *not* the *traffic pattern* (which actually starts when you enter a control zone and ends in the downwind leg). The ICAO definition of a circuit is *the specified paths to be flown by aircraft operating in the vicinity of an aerodrome*. It is not just a way of making sure that everyone follows the same one-way route around an airfield, but also a good exercise in precision flying. The existence of the circuit is the reason why airfields have to be avoided by a minimum distance.

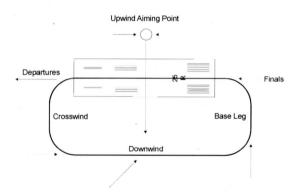

Such paths include the *crosswind leg*, which is at right angles to the runway, and is turned onto after takeoff (the circuit is usually left handed). The *downwind leg* is parallel to the runway, and goes the opposite way to the runway in use - you make the "downwind" call just after turning on to it. The *base leg* is also at right angles, but in the opposite way and at the opposite end to the crosswind leg, from which you turn onto *final approach* (more than 4 nm away, it is a *long final*). Again, make "base" and "final" calls just after the turn (on an instrument approach, you might call *Beacon* rather than Final).

The takeoff phase lasts until 500 feet, where you make a 90° turn crosswind to level off at circuit height (usually 1000 feet, but check, in case they surprise you). Another 90° turn takes you downwind, and you report being on the downwind leg when more or less abeam the tower. You also do your pre-landing checks, but leaving the landing gear for the base leg, which is another 90° turn at the end of downwind.

While in the circuit, keep a good lookout and be very aware of your position relative to other aircraft, adjusting your spacing as necessary. Use the downwind leg to plan your final approach, according to conditions.

In Canada, there are different ways of joining the circuit, depending on whether you need a radio or not for a *Mandatory Frequency* (MF) or *Aerodrome Traffic Frequency* (ATF). Control zones, with control towers, are obviously MF areas, but some lesser ones have only an aerodrome advisory from a Flight Service Station or a remote FSS, and they too are MF areas. In an MF area, everyone must have a radio and be communicating on the MF. Other aerodromes have nothing, or perhaps a UNICOM which has no authority or responsibility. They are not MF areas even though they have some assigned Aerodrome Traffic Frequency for use if you have a radio.

Join the circuit either straight into the downwind, or from the upwind (dead) side into mid-downwind (merging level into the downwind leg from the inactive side, having made a descending left-hand turn from at least 500 feet above circuit height). When crossing the aerodrome to check for landing information (to see the windsock, etc.), you must do so well above circuit height (at least 500' above). With an aerodrome advisory service available inside an MF area, join at 45° into the downwind, on base leg, or directly into final on a slow day.

You leave the circuit straight ahead (terrain permitting). In an MF area you must announce that you are departing the circuit (CAR 602.100). Don't make any turns until clear, after reaching circuit altitude.

All the above, of course, can be varied by ATC at any time.

LIGHTING

A heliport used at night must be illuminated with floodlights. If the take-off and landing area is rectangular, its boundary must have at least 8 fixed yellow lights or retro-reflective markers (one at each corner), no more than 13m (42.5 feet) apart. If circular, at least 5 lights or markers must be placed up to 13m (42.5 feet) apart.

Floodlighting must illuminate the perimeter, which may also have lights or reflective tape in the same pattern as the takeoff and landing area. If possible, the aiming point should have a triangle made out of 6 red lights.

If markers are used, a light source must show the location of the heliport, or, if there is only one path for approach and departure, two lights to show the approach orientation. Preferred approach and departure routes must be shown by 5 yellow or white omnidirectional or sequenced flashing lights.

Radio-controlled lighting must comply with Schedule II. Flare pots may be used as temporary lighting.

Runways & Taxiways

Runways are built for the so-called *critical aircraft*, that is, the one that uses it most of all and requires the most length. Naturally, larger ones can be accepted, but special performance procedures will probably need to be complied with. The width will be proportionate to length, but not above 200 feet.

TODA

Runway (TORA)	Clearway
25 R	Stopway

Emergency Distance

Details are declared by the Airport Authority and published in the AIM, although they can be found in many other publications. This declared distance is either the *Take-off Run Available* (TORA) or *Landing Distance Available* (LDA), as appropriate. Any areas at the ends unsuitable to run on, but still clear of obstacles, are called *Clearways* - the *Take Off Distance Available* (TODA) is TORA + Clearway. Part of the Clearway that can support an aircraft while stopping, although not on takeoff, is declared as *Stopway* which may be added to the TORA to form the *Emergency Distance Available* (EDA), and marked with yellow chevrons. This is the ground run distance available for an aircraft to abort a take-off and come to rest safely - the essential point is that Stopway is ground-based and clearways are not, so they can be included in performance calculations (see *Flight Planning* for more about this).

The end of the runway is called the *threshold*. Any obstacles interfering with the glideslope may need it to be *displaced* a certain distance, but the area behind it can still be used for taxying and takeoff runs, even if it not for landing. The *Touchdown Zone* is the first third of the runway or the first 3,000 feet, whichever is greater (edge lights are 200 feet apart).

Runways are named after the direction they are facing in, without the last number. For example, one facing West, or 270°, would be called Runway 27. In fact, the naming is to the nearest tenth degree, so one facing 067° is actually Runway 07. A T after the number (as in 07T) would be a True direction, as used in the NDA. Parallel runways will also be known as *Left* or *Right*, but if there were 3, they would be designated *Left*, *Centre* or *Right*, for example 22L, 22C, 22R.

Where no runways are available, the takeoff and landing areas will be marked with pyramidal or conical markers (orange & white for airports, orange for aerodromes).

A *radio altimeter operating area* provides a smooth area from which to obtain information for the autoflare. It should extend at least 300 m into the pre-threshold area, and 60 m either side of the extended centreline. Obstacles interfering with the glideslope may need the threshold to

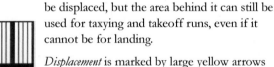

be displaced, but the area behind it can still be used for taxying and takeoff runs, even if it cannot be for landing.

Displacement is marked by large yellow arrows pointing towards the new threshold - a white painted transverse stripe drawn across a runway indicates a temporarily or permanently displaced one (see left). The threshold will be relocated if part of the runway is closed, and crosses will be used instead of arrows. A displaced threshold affects only the LDA for approaches to it - reciprocal directions are not affected.

CONTAMINATION

Whenever there is water on the runway, surface conditions are described (with its depth) as:

- *Damp* - there is a change of colour due to moisture

- *Wet* - the surface is soaked, but no standing water

- *Water patches* - significant patches of standing water*

- *Flooded* - there is extensive standing water visible*

*You might get aquaplaning.

The three states of frozen water to be reported are:

- *Dry Snow.* That which can be blown if loose or, if compacted by hand, will fall apart on release. The SG will be up to, but no including, 0.35

- *Wet Snow.* That which, if compacted by hand, will stick together and form a snowball. SG is from 0.35 up to, but not including, 0.5

- *Slush.* Snow that has been compressed into a solid mass that sticks together and resists further compression. SG is 0.5 and over

BRAKING ACTION

Code	Estimated Action	Measured Coefficient
1	Poor	< 0.25
2	Medium-Poor	0.26-0.29
3	Medium	0.30-0.35
4	Medium-Good	0.36-0.39
5	Good	0.40 and above

Markings & Signals

To a certain extent, you can tell from the air how suitable a runway is for your aircraft by the markings painted on it (which should be white). For example, a *non-instrument* runway over 5,000 feet long looks like the top one:

The first big markings are 1,000 feet from the end, and the smaller ones occur every 500 feet afterwards. An *instrument runway* (above, right) has a 500-foot marker first, where the wheels are supposed to hit (the reason that touchdown is made well into the runway is that, if you sink, at least you are likely to hit concrete). In addition, if there is a windsock at each end of the runway (on the left side), it is over 4,000 feet long. Otherwise, it will be at the mid-point. If it's a Transport Canada windsock (fly close to see the small print), the runways are likely to be on an airport.

At least 6 unidirectional lights at the runway end should show red in the runway direction. Threshold lights (and wing bar lights) should show green in the approach direction.

Two or more white crosses (with arms at 45° to the centre line) along a section or at both ends of a runway or taxiway mean the section between them is unfit for aircraft movement.

A mandatory instruction sign has white text on a red background.

MARKERS AND MARKINGS - 301.04

When closed permanently, all markers and markings must be removed, except for manoeuvring areas, which must have relevant markings painted on afterwards. If the surface is snow-covered, is unsuitable for painting, or the closure is temporary, you can use a conspicuously coloured dye or material. Unless on a water aerodrome, red flags or cones must be placed along the boundary of an unserviceable movement area. For periods over 24 hours, where a runway (or part of it) is closed, closed markings under Schedule I must be placed as follows:

- if longer than 1220m (4,000 feet), one at each end and additional ones at least every 300m (1,000 feet).

- if between 450m (1,500') and 1220m (4,000'), one of at least half the dimensions in Schedule I at each end and additional ones the same size midway between them.

- if shorter than 450m (1,500 feet), one of at least half the dimensions in Schedule I at each end.

When part of a taxiway is closed, there must be a closed marking at each end.

For a helicopter take-off and landing area, a closed marking must be over the H, or the centre of the area.

TAXIWAYS

When the cockpit remains over the centre markings, the clearance between the outer main wheel and the edge of the taxiway should be at least a distance based on the wingspan - 7.5 m for aeroplanes under 15 m span, up to 23 m for those under 65 m. The distance should be maintained when the taxiway curves.

HOLDING POINTS

A non-instrument runway will have a yellow single solid and a single dashed line across the taxiway (the dashed line is on the runway side). An instrument runway has a double set of each (an *A Pattern*) going to the runway (on the way back, they tell you when you are clear, when *all parts* of the aircraft have crossed the line).

A *B Pattern* looks like a ladder (left), and is used to protect ILS/MLS signals, so it is not so much a holding point, but a boundary line. An *intermediate* holding position marking is a single broken line.

There may also be a red marker board either side of the taxiway:

Lighting

Approach lights (and their supports) must be frangible for the last 300 m before the threshold. Any beyond that over 12 m high must be frangible for the top 12 m. Supporting structures surrounded by non-frangible objects only need the bit above them to be frangible.

Aeronautical ground lights must be operated:

- continuously during darkness after the end of evening civil twilight until the beginning of morning civil twilight

- when required for the control of air traffic

- at any time when their use, based on weather, is considered desirable for the safety of air traffic

Lights on and near aerodromes that are not intended for en-route navigation may be turned off if no likelihood of regular or emergency operation exists, as long as they can be turned on again at least *one hour before an expected arrival*. A *Barrette* is 3 or more aeronautical ground lights closely spaced.

One trick for remembering what lights do is to remember that *omnidirectional lights* are intended for use when circling (runway end lights should therefore be unidirectional, for example, as they must be seen down the runway).

RUNWAYS

Runway *end* lights should show *unidirectional red* (at least 6) in the direction of the runway. Runway *threshold* lights should show *unidirectional green* in the approach direction. Centre line lights for the last 300 m should be red.

Runway edge lights are fixed and (variable) white, except for those between the end and a displaced threshold, which are red (because you can't use the area for landing). However, the remote end (the least of the final 600 m or one-third) of an instrument runway may show yellow, and be omnidirectional for circling. Approach lights may be used for centreline guidance when the whole of a runway is used for takeoff when it has a displaced threshold (however, they shouldn't dazzle pilots). Centreline lights on rapid exit taxiways are alternating green/yellow.

TAXIWAYS

Taxiway edge lights are fixed omnidirectional blue, although some may be shielded to prevent confusion.

Paved taxiways should have green centre line markings, for continuous guidance between runways and aircraft stands, but alternating yellow/green ones indicate an ILS sensitive or critical area (the nearest to the perimeter is always yellow).

A stopbar across a taxiway shows red lights 3 m apart. Stopbars are used when RVR is less than 350 m, and must be controllable by ATC. If the RVR is less than 550 m, and there are no stop bars, runway guard lights should be used.

Signs

 A *mandatory instruction* sign has white text on a red background, found at holding positions, etc. *Information* signs have black text on a yellow background (the other way round for a location sign, and a yellow border if it is stand-alone).

A *runway vacated* sign would be at the end of the ILS/MLS sensitive area.

Signs must be lit at night or in bad visibility (with RVR below 800 m).

Airport Fire Fighting

The idea is to *save lives* during emergencies on airports or aerodromes, so the main task is to get passengers and crew out of dangerous situations which, of course, doesn't mean they can't deal with others at the same place. How many firefighters and how much equipment you need is based on the longest aeroplanes using the airfield and their width, that produce an *aerodrome category*, determined from a table in Annex 14. The most important factors are training, effectiveness of equipment and speed of response. Normal response time should be 2 minutes (not more than 3) to each end of the runway in optimum visibility and surface conditions.

Visual Aids For Navigation

An aerodrome must have at least one wind direction indicator (*windsock*), which must be visible from aircraft in flight or on the movement area, and free from the effects of air disturbances from nearby objects.

A *landing direction indicator* (which should be in the form of a letter T) must be in a conspicuous position, typically in the signals area (see below). It should be white or orange, depending on which provides the best contrast, and be lit at night. A white T with a disc above (for airborne machines) and a single black ball suspended from a mast (for those on the ground), mean that the directions for takeoff and landing are not necessarily the same.

There must be a *signalling lamp* in the control tower, capable of producing red, green and white signals which can be aimed at the target. It should be able to transmit Morse signals at up to four words per minute.

SIGNALS AREA

This provides basic information about an aerodrome to aircraft in flight without the need to use a radio. It is a small square surrounded in white that contains relevant symbols, situated next to the control tower.

The principal requirement of a signals area is that it must be visible from the air (obvious, really - it should actually be visible from above 10° above the horizontal from 300 feet). It should be on an even horizontal surface and be at least 9m square. Its colour should contrast with those of the panels used, and it should be surrounded by a white border at least .3 m wide.

Visual Approach Systems

Approach lighting works backwards from the threshold for up to 3,000 feet for precision approach runways. It has a purpose other than to show you the way in at night - it's also meant to help you transition to the visual after coming out of the clag.

When approaching visually to a runway, it's also useful to have something to help get the glideslope right (lateral guidance is provided by the runway lights). Those described here use different coloured light patterns to show whether you are on a glideslope, too high or too low. They will be situated to the left of the runway threshold and visible up to about 5 nm by day and 20 nm or more by night. Their sphere of influence is ±10° of the extended centreline, up to 4 nm. There are various designs, and *what you use depends on what you are flying*. You may need more eye-wheel height! In the CFS, they may be designated as V1, V2 or V3, or P1, P2 or P3.

You should remain on the indicated glideslope until you need to go lower for a safe landing.

VASIS

The *Visual Approach Slope Indicator System* is a group of four lights (2-bar), which provide an aiming point about 1,000 feet into the runway, based on a glideslope of 3° (usually).

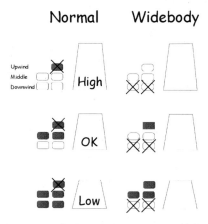

The light bars are called *upwind* and *downwind*. There's a middle one for the 3-bar version - normal aircraft use the middle and downwind ones, and widebodies (i.e. high-cockpit) use the middle and upwind (far) ones. This gives an aiming point further in, so the gear clears the threshold. *Normal* means an eye-to-wheel height of up to 25 feet (e.g. DC-8). Widebodies have up to 45 feet.

A *Tri-Color VASI* uses red, green and amber to indicate low, on the glideslope and high, respectively. Their range is around ½ to 1 mile during the day and 5 miles at night (depends on visibility).

A *Pulsating VASI* (PVASI) uses a single light source to project a two-colour approach indication. When very low or very high, the light pulsates more in relation to your distance away, red or white, respectively. Otherwise it is steady white for on the glideslope when using one system, and alternating red and white on another.

A *T-VASIS* uses 10 lights, with 4 horizontal ones in the middle and the other 6 as 3 vertical groups above and below, which only appear when you are low or high. If you do things properly, you will arrive at the threshold at 45 feet. All lights are white, except where a gross undershoot is involved, when they turn red. Lights above the horizontal 4 are the fly down lights, whereas those appearing below are the fly up ones.

Note: An AVASIS is an Abbreviated VASIS for aircraft with an eye-wheel height of 10 feet.

PAPI

The *Precision Approach Path Indicator* does the same thing as VASIS, but with 4 lights in a row. When on the correct slope, the two lights nearest the runway are red and the two furthest ones show white. Three whites and a red mean slightly high, and three reds and a white means slightly low. Four of each is way too much. When on the glideslope, you should see red lights over white ones ("red on white, you're all right"). If you are too low, you will see red over red ("red on red, you're dead"). When the approach is correct, you will be clear of obstructions within 6-9° either side of the centreline up to 4 nm out, with safe wheel clearance over the threshold.

Note: An APAPI is an Abbreviated PAPI with only two lights for aircraft with an eye-wheel height of 10 feet.

Frost on the front lenses may cause colour mixing and cause a false fly down signal.

AERONAUTICAL INFO (ANX 15)

The process of Aviation needs a huge flow of information in order to run smoothly - technically for its *safety*, *regularity* and *efficiency*, since wrong information can be dangerous. Many accidents have happened because crews have input wrong information, intentionally or otherwise. As with all computers, if you put garbage in, you get garbage out. The role of such support services became more important with the advent of *RNAV* (Area Navigation), *RNP* (Required Navigation Performance), *Computer-based navigation systems* (INS/IRS)

All the above systems require accurate information for their operation, which is obtained from the publications issued by Aeronautical Information Services, such as NOTAMS, etc. To ensure uniformity and consistency, States are urged to *avoid Standards and Procedures other than those established for international use.*

States are required to either provide such services themselves, or in conjunction with another, or through non-government agencies which meet the standards. The responsibility, however, still lies with the State, and information published on its behalf must show where the authority comes from, as well as being accurate, timely and of the quality expected by ICAO. States must share information, in English, with place names spelt as per local usage, and any translations in the Latin alphabet. Published coordinates must conform to WGS-84.

If a 24-hour service is not provided, services must be available from two hours before and after a flight in the area of responsibility, or at other times by request.

Aeronautical Information Publication

The AIM is a summary of the rules and regulations that affect aviation (similar documents are issued by all countries) or, in other words, a publication containing aeronautical information of a *lasting character essential to air navigation*. As such, it is not the final authority for the rules you have to obey, but the law that backs it up is. A clue as to what is or isn't supported by law is given by the word "shall". The AIM should be easy to use in flight, and it is split into these parts in Canada:

- GEN (General)
- AGA (Aerodromes)
- COM (Communications)
- MET (Meteorology)
- RAC (Rules Of The Air & Air Traffic Services)
- FAL (Facilitation)
- SAR (Search & Rescue)
- MAP (Aeronautical Charts & Publications)
- LRA (Licensing, Registration & Airworthiness)
- AIR (Airmanship)

Permanent changes are issued as *AIM Amendments*. Temporary changes of long duration (3 months) and those of short duration containing extensive text or graphics are issued as *AIM Supplements*. Supplement pages are coloured, so they stand out, preferably in yellow.

Note: In Canada, the AIM is being replaced by the Airman Information Manual. It is mentioned here in case you fly abroad later.

AIRAC Canada

A notice issued weekly to give advance notice of changes within Domestic Airspace.

Aviation Notice

This will contain information specific to a region, or short term stuff that only requires reading once.

NOTAM

A *NOTice to AirMen* is a warning or notice about anything that might affect a flight that is either temporary or happened too late to be in charts, etc., such as changes to frequencies or serviceability of navaids, or hazards. They are in the list of items to be checked before flight and can be obtained by telephone, from an ATC office or over the Internet.

NOTAMs do not amend the AIM, but they may affect the information it contains - for example, a permanent danger area will have its hours of operation published in the AIM, and variations published by NOTAM. A temporary danger area, on the other hand, may be *activated* by NOTAM (where a permanent danger area has two upper limits, the higher one is raised by Notam). In fact, a NOTAM is generated and issued whenever its information is:

- *Temporary* and of *short duration*, or of *long duration* made at *short notice*, except when it contains *extensive text and/or graphics* (information of short duration with extensive text and/or graphics is published as an *AIM Supplement*)

- Permanent, but operationally significant

Operationally significant means the establishment, closure or significant changes in the operation of aerodromes or runways, or the operation of aeronautical services, electronics, aids to navigation (frequencies, ID, etc), visual aids, fuel, SAR facilities, firefighting, hazards to air navigation (obstacles), and the like.

These items are *not* covered by NOTAM:

- routine maintenance work on aprons and taxiways which does not affect the safe movement of aircraft

- runway marking, when operations can safely be conducted on other available runways, or the equipment can be removed when necessary

- temporary obstructions near aerodromes that do not affect the safe operation of aircraft

- partial failure of lighting where it does not directly affect aircraft operations

- partial temporary failure of air-ground communications when suitable alternative frequencies are known to be available and are working

- the lack of apron marshalling services and road traffic control

- the unserviceability of location, destination or other instruction signs on the aerodrome movement area

- parachuting in uncontrolled airspace under VFR, when controlled, at promulgated sites or within danger or prohibited areas

- other information of a similar temporary nature

DISTRIBUTION

NOTAMs are issued in three categories to addressees for whom the information has direct operational significance, if they would not otherwise have 7 days prior notification (exam question). The categories are:

- *NOTAMN* - one with new information

- *NOTAMR* - one replacing a previous NOTAM

- *NOTAMC* - one cancelling a previous NOTAM

Temporary NOTAMS must include an expiry date, which may be estimated (with an EST suffix).

A checklist of valid NOTAMs is distributed over the AFTN at regular intervals of up to a month, to the same distribution list as the NOTAMs themselves.

SNOTAM (SNOWTAM)

Tam

A small white Scottish terrier (see left). Seriously, a NOTAM about *snow, ice and standing water on aerodrome pavements,* valid for up to 24 hours, but reissued if there is a significant change in conditions, including the coefficient of friction or the type or depth of deposit, available width of runway or conspicuity of lighting.

The relevant form has *17 sections.* If the cleared length of runway is less than the published length, it would be displayed in Box D, with the cleared length in metres.

ASHTAM

A NOTAM about operationally significant changes in volcanic activity. Codes are:

- *RED.* Volcanic eruption in progress or likely. Ash plume/cloud reported/expected above FL250

- *ORANGE.* Volcanic eruption in progress or likely. Ash plume/cloud not reported/expected above FL 250

- *YELLOW.* Volcano known to be active or activity increased or decreased from Red or Orange. Not currently dangerous but exercise caution

- *GREEN.* Volcanic activity has ceased or returned to normal state

Aeronautical Information Circulars

AICs contain information that does not qualify as AIM information or NOTAMs. They contain amendments to the AIM, but not officially.

SECURITY (ANNEX 17)

The aim of aviation security is to safeguard international civil aviation against acts of unlawful interference.

ATC must be informed if unlawful interference occurs on a flight. If this cannot be done by the PIC, the hijackers must do it (joke).

ICAO

Annex 17 requires States to establish national civil aviation security programs:

- Stopping unauthorised weapons and explosives being carried on board (the PIC must be notified of those used by air marshals)

- Not to mix transit pax or baggage with people not subject to screening - passengers who have been screened for security must not mix with unscreened passengers before boarding, otherwise they must be rescreened

- Carriage of people subject to proceedings (prisoners, etc.)

- Not transporting baggage for passengers not on board without extra security

- Adequate measures against hijacking

State assistance to aircraft subjected to acts of unlawful seizure include provision of navaids, air traffic services and landing permission, as may be required under the circumstances.

Measures must be taken, as far as practicable, to detain such aircraft on the ground, unless there is an overriding duty to protect human life, with due consultation between the State of the incident and the Sate of the operator. The State must take adequate measures for the safety of the passengers and crew until their journey can be continued.

The States of Registry and of the operator must be informed, together with all States whose citizens have been harmed or detained as hostages, and who remain on board, not forgetting ICAO.

If 7500 is selected on the transponder, absence of a reply to a request for confirmation is taken as confirmation. Naturally, you must make a full report afterwards. Following unlawful interference, try to keep the track and level until at least able to tell ATC what's going on. Otherwise, try to broadcast warnings on 121.5 MHz or use 7500.

The minimum isolation distance on the ground from a hijacked aircraft is 100 m, away from normal activities.

ADIZ

The *Air Defence Identification Zone* is looked after by the military, who like to know who is going in and out. The plan should be filed before entering the ADIZ (or taking off within it) and a position report made as soon as practicable after takeoff. A VFR plan should indicate the estimated times and points of entry. Changes should be reported within ±5 minutes and 20 nm.

ESCAT

These rules establish priority for aircraft in times of war or national emergency, Testing occasionally takes place over communications facilities, which you should acknowledge and carry on with whatever you were doing.

DANGEROUS GOODS (ANX 18)

This is covered in Section 7, *Operational Procedures.*

PANS-OPS

Much of this concerns IFR flight (approaches, holding patterns, etc.), but there are some items of interest to the VFR helicopter pilot.

Altimeter Setting Procedures

Cruising levels are expressed in terms of *flight levels*, when above the Transition Altitude, and *altitudes*, when *at or below* Transition Altitude. The change in reference is made, when climbing, at the Transition Altitude, and, when descending, at the Transition Level.

The *Transition Altitude* is the altitude at, or below which, any reference your vertical position is based on altitude (which is based on QNH). Any higher, you have to use *Flight Levels*. A transition altitude is normally specified for an aerodrome *by the State in which it is located*. It is as low as possible, but normally at least 3000 feet, rounded up to the nearest 1000.

The *Transition Level* is the lowest available flight level available above the Transition Altitude when the altimeter is set to 1013.2 mb, so it would normally be FL 30 in UK, including when the QNH is more than standard. However, if the QNH is less than standard, the transition level will be higher than that. The Transition Level is determined *by the ATS unit concerned*, since it varies with pressure from day to day, and it is always *higher* than the Transition Altitude. The difference between transition altitude and transition level is the *Transition Layer*, which will be *more than zero and less than 500 feet*.

When passing through the transition layer, report flight levels when going up and altitudes when going down - the Transition Level is the latest point at which you change from standard setting to QNH. In other words, when descending to go below Transition Level, if you are cleared to a Flight Level, you must keep 1013.2 set on your altimeter. If you are cleared to an altitude, and no more FL reports are needed, set the QNH as soon as you start descending and report altitudes. Flight level zero is at the atmospheric pressure level of 1013.25 hPa. Consecutive Flight Levels are separated by intervals of at least 500 feet.

Crews should communicate with boom or throat microphones when below Transition Altitude or Level.

ALTIMETER SETTING REGION - 602.35
The same dimensions as the SDA. Just before taking off, all altimeters must use the setting or elevation of the nearest station. In the cruise, you must use the nearest station along the route or nearby, if over 150 nm apart. Use destination settings just before commencing descent.

STANDARD PRESSURE REGION - 602.36
The same dimensions as the NDA. Just before taking off, all altimeters must be on the setting or elevation of the aerodrome. Before reaching the appropriate flight level, use 29.92" or 1013.2 mb. In the hold, before landing, set the aerodrome setting just before the lowest flight level of the procedure. Otherwise, the destination setting must be set just before commencing descent.

BETWEEN REGIONS - 602.37
Except where authorized by ATC, when going from the ASR to the SPR, set all altimeters to 29.92" or 1013.2 mb immediately after entry into the SPR. The other way, use the setting of the nearest station along the route or nearby, if they are more than 150 nm apart, immediately before entry into the ASR.

Within 20 nm of ground over 2000 ft amsl, increase MOCA/MORA by these amounts, against windspeed:

Elev (ft)	0-30 Kts	31-50 Kts	51-70 Kts	+ 70 Kts
2-8000	+ 500'	+1000'	+1500'	+2000'
+ 8000	+1000'	+1500'	+2000'	+2500'

This is because the venturi effect over a ridge makes the altimeter misread, on top of causing turbulence and standing waves. All this, plus temperature errors (see below), can make one overread *by as much as 3000'*.

When the surface temperature is well below ISA (below -15°C), correct MSAs by:

Surface Temp (ISA)	Correction
-16°C to -30°C	+ 10%
-31°C to -50°C	+ 20%
-51°C or below	+ 25%

PRE-FLIGHT CHECKS
Rotating the knob must produce a corresponding height difference in relevant directions. At a known elevation on the aerodrome, vibrate the instrument by tapping, unless mechanical means is available:

- Set the scale to the current altimeter setting. The altimeter should indicate the elevation, plus the height of the altimeter above it, within ± 50 ft.

- With both on the altimeter setting, indications should be within ±50 feet of aerodrome elevation, and 60 feet of each other.

TESTING
All VFR aircraft in Class B airspace, and all IFR aircraft, must have had an altimeter and static pressure system check in the last 24 months.

Transponder Operation
When a serviceable transponder is carried, it must be operated at all times during flight, regardless of whether a transponder is required for that airspace (SSR is required above FL100, and when IFR below that).

Normally, unless you have an emergency, a communications failure, or are subject to unlawful interference, you must operate the transponder in Mode A as directed by ATC or as prescribed by regional air navigation agreements. In the absence of both, squawk 2000.

Other standard numbers to squawk, when not otherwise instructed, are:

- 0000 - malfunction
- 2000 - from non-SSR area

In emergency, squawk:

- 7500 - Hijack*
- 7600 - Communications failure
- 7700 - Emergency

*Absence of a reply is confirmation that the selection is not accidental.

Note: *You cannot set the number 8* - watch for this in questions that ask you to choose between valid codes.

Transponder codes must always be read back.

When unlawful interference is suspected, and where *automatic distinct display* of 7500 and 7700 is not provided, the controller can verify his suspicions by setting the SSR decoder to 7500 then 7700.

Mode C must be operated continuously, unless otherwise directed by ATC. The tolerance level for Mode C level information is within ±200 feet of the assigned level (you must report within ±100 feet, when Mode C is operated).

When asked to *squawk ident*, your return becomes temporarily brighter, so you can be positively identified. Do this only when requested. If the ident doesn't work, a controller can ask you to switch to standby to avoid a turn for identification. The term *recycle* means reselect the assigned code. Modes and codes must be read back.

If a transponder fails during flight in a mandatory area (i.e. *after departure*), you may go to the next planned destination, then complete an itinerary or go to a repair base, as permitted by ATC. It is possible to enter controlled airspace without the required equipment, but ATC must be asked first. Permission is always subject to traffic. If your transponder is unserviceable before departure and you can't fix it, you can take off for a place where repairs can be done. Again, ATC must be informed, preferably before the flight plan is submitted (put an N in Section 10 of the flight plan form, or whatever character represents partial serviceability).

For more about transponders and how they work, refer to Section 6b, *Radio Navigation*.

ACAS

If your flight path has to be altered because of ACAS advisories, the deviation must be limited to the minimum extent necessary. You must promptly revert to the terms and conditions of any clearances previously issued once the conflict is resolved, and notify ATC as soon as practicable of the scope of the deviation, including its direction and when it ended.

MISCELLANEOUS

Aircraft Operating Over Water

Except when taking off or landing, a land aircraft may not fly beyond where it could reach shore if an engine fails, unless authorised in an AOC. If doing so, however, helicopters must have an approved emergency flotation kit and fly high enough to allow time for them to inflate before touching the water. Life preservers must be carried within reach of each person with their seat belts fastened, and you may need a liferaft. The Ops Manual must include passenger ditching procedures and a requirement to file a flight plan or itinerary, and flights conducted over water more than 15 minutes at normal cruising speed from shore or from a suitable aerodrome must be capable of direct flight following with radio.

Carriage of People on Aerial Work - 702.16/722.16

Must be a crew member or maintenance technician trainee, someone undergoing training for essential duties during flight, a fire fighter or fire control officer being carried in a forest fire area, be being carried to an aerial work site, perform an essential function to do with the aerial work and is necessary to accomplish it. May also be a parachutist if you are authorised in your AOC. During helicopter external load operations, people not essential during flight are carried only with a Class D load complying with subsection 702.21(1), except for crew undergoing training, or fire fighters carried only with Class B equipment necessary for fires within a forest fire area. Aircraft equipment must comply with 605 and people must be briefed under Section 722.23 of the Aerial Work Standard. Parachutists and jumpmasters are essential during flight and do not require an Operations Specification.

Passengers in Single-Engined Aircraft - 703.22/24

You may not carry over 9 passengers in single-engined aeroplanes, but you can in Transport Category helicopters, if the pilot has passed a single-engine PPC on one of the single-engine types operated, and the AOC contains authorisation.

Passengers may not be carried in single-engine helicopters at night or under IFR.

Towing VFR at Night (Aerial Work)

Must follow Section 602.14 (low flying) over built-up areas unless otherwise authorized, taking account of hazards if an inadvertent release happens. The tow must be jettisonable and lighted, having been tested in Day VFR. Departure and approach paths must not go over built-up areas. Only crew members and people with essential in-flight duties must be carried. The PIC must have at least 10 hours towing in the last 6 months.

The object being towed must not be a glider, taking into account proximity to a lighted glider recovery aerodrome. Flights must be coordinated with ATC. Operational restrictions and procedures must be in the Ops Manual.

TOWING VFR OTT (AERIAL WORK)

Flights must follow Section 602.15 (i.e. less than normal low flying minima) only on pre-planned routes or areas with no hazards. You must be able to descend in VMC. The tow must be jettisonable and have been tested in Day VFR. Flights must be coordinated with ATC. Operational restrictions and procedures must be in the Ops Manual.

TOWING UNDER IFR

No chance.

DISPERSAL OF PRODUCTS VFR AT NIGHT

Only under VFR, with a discernible natural horizon. The dispersing area must have been surveyed by day and obstructions marked for night. The pilot must be familiar with the flight path and obstructions beforehand. The aircraft must have a lighting system for obstacles, and operational restrictions and procedures must be in the Ops Manual.

DISPERSAL OF PRODUCTS VFR OTT/IFR - WEATHER ALTERING

Must be coordinated with ATC, with no hazards to people or property on the surface, with restrictions and procedures in the Ops Manual.

SINGLE-ENGINE AIRCRAFT VFR AT NIGHT/IFR - PAX TPT

Only in factory built, turbine-powered aeroplanes with an engine MTBF of 0.01/1,000 or less established over 100,000 hours in service. You may not fly over Designated Mountainous Regions 1 and 5 and you must be properly trained. If a foreign aircraft, you must be authorised by your State.

AEROPLANE EQUIPMENT

Two attitude indicators, powered separately and independently, two independent power generating sources, each capable of sustaining essential flight instruments and electrical equipment, an auto-ignition system, or a specification in the Ops Manual that continuous ignition must be ON for take-off, landing and flight in heavy precipitation, a chip detector system for excessive ferrous material in the engine lubrication system, a radar altimeter and a manual throttle which bypasses the FCU if it fails.

VFR AT NIGHT

Nobody, other than crew members, people essential during flight and parachutists (when authorized), can be carried over Designated Mountainous Regions 1 and 5, and equipment, pilot qualifications and restrictions must be included in the Ops Manual. You must also carry maps. Parachuting must be within 10 nm of the departure point.

IFR

Flights must not be over Designated Mountainous Regions as defined in the Designated Airspace Handbook (TP 1820), and aircraft equipment, pilot qualifications and restrictions must be in the Ops Manual.

VFR NIGHT, NON-CREW ON BOARD, NO IR

Only with crew and people essential during flight. The area must have lights on the surface for visual reference and a discernible horizon. Flights must be on pre-planned plotted routes with the PIC familiar with navigation procedures, and aircraft equipment requirements, pilot qualifications and restrictions must be in the Ops Manual.

1,000' OTT IFR

Not allowed in Class A or B airspace, but in Class C or D, you must be at least 1,000 feet above cloud, haze or other phenomena that has a well-defined top, with at least 3 sm visibility and maintain the appropriate cruising altitude, as well being authorised by ATC.

Fuel Dumping - 602.30

This may not be done unless necessary for aviation safety, and all measures are taken to minimize danger to human life and damage to the environment.

Aircraft Operating Over Water - 702.20/722.20, 703.23

Helicopters only, with approved flotation kit, except for fire suppression or fish stocking if the essential people on board have life preservers and have been instructed in ditching and evacuation (the details must be in the Ops Manual). Over the water, you must be high enough to inflate the floats. Life preservers for each person on board must be within reach when seat belts are fastened. When over 15 minutes at normal cruising speed from shore or a suitable aerodrome with passengers, you must have direct air-ground flight following and the Ops Manual must include equipment, procedures and restrictions.

Pilot's Compartment

Inspectors producing ID must have free and uninterrupted access to the pilot's compartment. The Inspector may choose the most suitable seat.

Noise Criteria - 602.105

You must follow noise control requirements in the CFS.

Flight Control Locks - 605.29

These must be incapable of becoming engaged when the aircraft is operated, with an unmistakable warning whenever they are.

Operating Restrictions and Hazards - 601/621

FOREST FIRES

Not below 3000 feet within 5 nm, or in any airspace in a relevant NOTAM, unless under an appropriate fire control authority, or are Transport Canada performing their normal duties.

MARKING AND LIGHTING OF HAZARDS

A building, structure or object, including one of natural growth, that is hazardous to aviation safety because of height and location must be marked and lit under the Standards Obstruction Markings Manual.

PROJECTION OF DIRECTED BRIGHT LIGHT SOURCE - 601.20

You may not project a bright light into navigable airspace if it creates a hazard to aviation safety or cause damage to an aircraft or injury to persons on board, unless authorised. Neither may you fly an aircraft into such a light, unless authorized.

Aircraft Icing - 602.11

You may not attempt to take off in an aircraft with frost, ice or snow on any of its critical surfaces (see *Icing*), except that frost under the wings caused by cold-soaked fuel may be present, if the maker's instructions have been obeyed.

If frost, ice or snow may reasonably be expected to stick to the aircraft, you may not attempt to take-off unless it has been inspected immediately beforehand, or under an authorised inspection program (the latter is required for airlines). The inspection must be performed by either the PIC, a designated crew member or someone who has passed an aircraft surface contamination training program.

Crews must immediately report frost, ice or snow on wings to the PIC, who must ensure they are inspected before takeoff. Before an aircraft is de-iced or anti-iced, the PIC must ensure that crew members and passengers are informed.

Radiocommunications - 602.122

See *Communications*.

PRE-FLIGHT AND FUEL REQUIREMENTS

Carry-on Baggage, Equipment and Cargo

Must be stowed as in the type certificate, or restrained so they don't shift during movement. Anything in a passenger compartment must be packaged or covered to avoid injury to people. Safety equipment, normal and emergency exits accessible to passengers, and aisles between flight deck and passenger compartments must not be blocked.

If the aircraft can carry more than 10 passengers, and passengers are carried, no passenger's view of any sign must be obscured, unless an alternative exists. Passenger service carts and trolleys must be securely restrained during taxi, takeoff, landing and turbulence as directed. Video monitors suspended from the ceiling and extending into an aisle must be stowed and securely restrained during take-off and landing. Crew members must be able to reach all parts of the compartment with a hand-held fire extinguisher.

Crew Member Instructions - 602.87

Crew members must be instructed about their duties and the location and use of normal and emergency equipment.

Fuel Requirements - 602.88

This Section does not apply to gliders, balloons or ultra-lights.

When VFR in an aeroplane, you must *start with* enough fuel to get to the destination and fly for 30 minutes at normal cruising speed (45 minutes at night, and 20 minutes for helicopters).

When IFR in a propeller-driven aeroplane, you must have enough fuel to approach at the destination, carry out a missed approach, land at an alternate and still have 45 minutes' worth left. If you don't have an alternate, you can carry out the missed approach at the destination. In a jet-engined aeroplane or helicopter, the remainder reduces to 30 minutes in both cases.

You must also carry fuel for taxiing and foreseeable delays before takeoff, weather, foreseeable air traffic routings and traffic delays, landing at a suitable aerodrome in case of cabin depressurization or failure of any engine at the most critical point, and any other foreseeable conditions that could delay your landing.

PASSENGER BRIEFINGS - 602.89

Passenger handling itself is a specialised task. As I've said before, in General Aviation you're very much involved with your passengers, who will usually get quite excited and engage you in conversation about all manner of things. Of course, a frequent business traveller may not get this familiar, but you might still be asked to join them for lunch; not only out of courtesy, but also as cheap entertainment-if you're not a good conversationalist when you start your career, you'll very soon learn! Other little things are good for customer relations, too, such as helping them with their belts, checking they're OK and settled down just before take-off and during the flight, and generally looking after their well-being. All this is pure salesmanship. A lot of repeat business comes from a company's pilots' relationships with passengers, and if you're not naturally gregarious (a good mixer), think twice about charter work as a long-term way of earning a living.

How to handle passengers in general is very much a matter of Company policy. Some like to be spoken to, some don't, but there are some small attentions you can give without being obtrusive. Just going round checking seat belts and doors helps (never trust a passenger to shut doors properly), as is a look over your shoulder before take-off and occasionally during the flight. People new to flying are fairly obvious, and they may not appreciate such commonplace occurrences (to you, anyway) as noise, turbulence, pressure changes, strange noises from the front (stall warnings, gear coming up and down, etc.), or lack of toilets.

However, CARs imposes on you the responsibility for the safety and well-being of your passengers. You will find you are supposed to brief them before every flight, or at least take all reasonable steps to do so.

A lot depends on what your passengers doing at the destination - if you're shutting down, tell them to stay seated until everything stops. If it involves a running disembarkation, one passenger should be briefed to operate the baggage door and do the unloading.

Transistor radios, tape recorders and the like should not be operated in flight as they may interfere with navigation equipment (or even the fly-by-wire systems). If you don't believe me, tune to an AM station, as used by ADF, on a cheap radio and switch on an even cheaper calculator nearby - you will find the radio is blanked out by white noise. In fact, the radiations from TVs and radios come within the VOR and ILS regions as well. Although cell phones are cleared for use near heart monitors (in hospitals), they do so at low power when inside range of a cell. Once in an aircraft, and a long way away from a transmitter, they put the power up and then become dangerous - a couple of hundred phones in an aircraft can therefore create havoc.

Anyway, as I said, you, as commander, are responsible for ensuring that all passengers are briefed, or have equipment demonstrated, as outlined below. One member of the flight or cabin crew should be responsible for cabin safety from the time the aircraft is accepted for flight, until all the passengers have been offloaded at the end of it.

Pre-flight

Whoever it is should confirm that the passenger compartment contains emergency equipment in appropriate stowage(s), seatbacks are in the upright position and lap straps and/or harnesses are ready (neatly arranged seatbelts always give a good impression, or, rather, untidy ones don't). Tables should be folded and stowed, and catering secured. Unless weight and balance allows random seating, passengers should be shown, or conducted to their seats.

Once they are seated and you have their attention, give them a briefing in a calm and authoritative manner, and be as interesting and informative as possible, with a bit of humour if you can; some passengers may be experienced air travellers, others may not. The idea is to ensure they will retain enough to react sensibly in an emergency which, it should be emphasised, is unlikely to occur.

Before take-off and landing (and whenever you deem it necessary, e.g. during turbulence), they also need to be told (don't just show them the card) about the aspects involved in various aspects of aircraft operation, in particular the following:

- Your authority as aircraft Commander.

- Methods of approaching the aircraft, in particular avoiding exhausts and tail rotors - if nearby aircraft have engines running, it could mask the sound of a closer one. Pitot tubes are especially sensitive (and hot!) Children should be kept under strict control. Wait for signal from pilot. Used crouched position in pilot's view. Take off loose objects, hats, etc.

- Dangerous Goods and hazardous items that must not be carried. Bear scares (pepper sprays) must not be in the cabin. No objects above shoulder height - carry equipment horizontally. Long items should be dragged by one end. Do not throw cargo.

- Methods of opening and closing cabin doors (inside and outside) and their use as emergency exits. Not leaving seat belts outside. Where not to step and what to hold on to. Sharp objects must be handled carefully when working with floats installed.

- When they can smoke (not when oxygen is in use!)

- Avoidance of flying when ill or drunk - not only is this dangerous to themselves, but if they are incapable next to an emergency exit, others could suffer too.

- How to use the seat belts and when they must be fastened.

- What not to touch in flight.

- Loose articles, their stowage (tables, etc.) and the dangers of throwing anything out of the windows or towards rotor blades or propellers.

- Use and location of safety equipment, including a practical demonstration (if you intend to reach a point more than thirty minutes away from the nearest land at overwater speed, you need to do this with the lifejacket, maybe in the terminal). When oxygen needs to be used in a hurry, adults should fit their masks before their children.

- The reading of the passenger briefing card, which should be of at least Letter size, so it doesn't get lost in a pocket. It should also be as brightly coloured as possible, so it catches the eye. Particular things to place on this card that always seem to be forgotten include instructions not to inflate lifejackets in the cabin and full door opening instructions (don't forget any little bolts that may be about).

- The brace position (including rear-facing seats). If you ever have to give the order to adopt it, by the way, don't do it too early, otherwise the passengers will get fed up waiting for something to happen and sit up just at the point of impact.

- How long the flight will be, and how high you will be, what the weather will be like.

You might want to adapt the following sample brief:

"Welcome aboard this flight. I am the commander and I must ask you to take notice of any instructions you may be given by myself or my crew, and this includes any given by signs.

If I have to land quickly or in an emergency, I will tell you in enough time for you to prepare properly. You will know it's an emergency, because you will hear me say something like "Oh sh*t"(Only joking).

Emergency exits include the window there and the door by which you came in. Full instructions for each are on the briefing card, which I would like you to read thoroughly, as it gives further instructions for the lifejacket, should it be required, under your seat. Other emergency equipment includes fire extinguishers which are there and there, and the First Aid kit there. The Emergency Locator Transmitter is here, with the On switch clearly marked.

For take-off and landing, please ensure that seat backs are upright and all loose articles are stowed away. You may not smoke during taxi, take off and landing, please do not throw anything out of the windows.

Finally, the flight should take about 1 hour, and I hope you enjoy it."

In-flight and pre-landing briefings may be given by a crew member, or with illuminated cabin warning signs. In an emergency during flight, passengers must be briefed on relevant emergency action.

The following items must be demonstrated:

- the use, fastening and unfastening of safety belts/harnesses.

- use of oxygen masks when appropriate.

- location and use of life-jackets, if takeoff or approach will be over water, or when the flight will be more than 50 nm from shore. The demo can be done before boarding.

Before Take-off:

- When, where, why and how carry-on baggage must be stowed.

- The fastening, unfastening, adjusting and general use of safety belts or harnesses

- The requirement to obey crew instructions regarding seat belts or Fasten Seat Belts and No Smoking signs, and their location.

- When seat backs must be upright and tables stowed.

- Where emergency exits are and, for passengers near exits, how they work.

- Location and advisability of reading safety cards.

- Location and use of emergency equipment, e.g. ELT, fire extinguisher, survival gear (including access if locked away), first aid kit and life raft.

- Using passenger operated portable electronic devices.

- The location and operation of the fixed passenger oxygen system, including masks and the actions to obtain and use them and activate the flow of oxygen. This must include a demonstration.

- Location and use of life preservers, including removal from stowage/packaging and a demo, when to inflate.

- After take-off, if not already done, that smoking is prohibited, and advisability of using safety-belts or harnesses during flight.

- In-flight for turbulence, when seat belts are required and stowing of carry-on baggage.

- Before getting off, the safest route away and relevant dangers, such as pitot tubes, propellers, or engine intakes.

- If no more passengers have boarded for subsequent take-offs on the same day, the pre-take-off and after take-off briefings may be omitted if a crew member has verified that all carry-on baggage is properly stowed, safety belts or harnesses are properly fastened, with seat backs and chair tables secured.

- For helicopters, add instructions for immersion suits and, for wide-bodied machines, how to get out in a roll-over by using the under-seat frame of cabin seats as a ladder, and special instructions with external fixtures. (e.g. ski racks).

Individual Safety Briefing

This must include any information from the standard safety briefing and safety features card that the passenger would not be able to receive during the normal briefing, and additional information for their needs, such as special brace positions, exits, etc.

Such passengers need not be re-briefed after a crew change if the crew member that gave the individual briefing advises the new crew of its contents, including any special information.

A passenger may decline an individual safety briefing.

Preparation for Emergency Landing

Where time and circumstances permit, this must consist of instructions about safety belts or harnesses, seat backs and tables, carry-on baggage, safety features cards, brace position (when to assume, how long to remain), and life preservers.

Safety Features Card

Something to read for passengers - it may look something like the picture on the left. It must contain applicable information, including that smoking is prohibited, each type of safety belt or harness (when to use, how to fasten, tighten and release), when and where carry-on baggage must be stowed and any other related requirements and restrictions, and correct positioning of seat backs and tables for takeoff and landing. In addition, emergency procedures and equipment, including the oxygen system, showing mask location and presentation, the actions to obtain the mask, activate the flow of oxygen and correctly don and secure the mask and priority for people assisting others, location of first aid kits, fire extinguishers, ELTs, survival equipment and, if the stowage compartment is locked, how to open it.

Also, the appropriate brace position for impact, the location, operation and method of using each exit, the safest and most hazard-free escape route following evacuation, the attitude of the aeroplane while floating, location of life preservers and correct procedures for their removal from stowage or packaging, donning and use for adult, child and infant users (including when to inflate), location and use of life rafts and location, removal and use of flotation devices. The card must bear the name of the operator and the type, and contain only accurate safety information for the type and configuration, with clear separation between each instructional procedure. All actions for multi-action procedures must be in the right sequence, clearly identified and depicted.

EMERGENCY EQPT - 723.82

If the water temperature is below 10°C, everyone in a helicopter must wear a survival suit (technically, the suits must be provided, and the PIC must direct them to be worn, but the effect is the same - see 602.63). On top of lifejackets and survival equipment as below, power driven aircraft also require:

- normal and emergency checklists or placards as per the flight manual

- for VFR OTT and Night VFR and IFR, relevant charts and publications

- hand held extinguisher in the cockpit, available.

- first aid kit

Survival Equipment

Over land, unless:

- you're in a balloon, glider, hang glider, gyroplane or ultra-light

- within 25 nm of departure point in contact with a ground station

- you are in a multi-engined aircraft South of 66.5 N in IFR in controlled airspace or along designated air routes

you must carry suitable survival equipment (for season, area, etc.) to start a fire, provide shelter and water and make signals. You can use different equipment as per the ops manual, and you don't need it in an area and season where survival of people on board is not jeopardized.

Life Preservers & Flotation Devices

Over water (including taking off or landing) beyond a point where you could reach shore if an engine fails, each person on board must have a life preserver or other individual flotation device, easily accessible when seated.

A land aeroplane, gyroplane, helicopter or airship over 50 nm from shore must have a life preserver for each person.

Life Rafts and Survival Equipment - Flights over Water - 602.63

You must carry life rafts for everyone on board over 25 nm or 15 minutes at cruising speed, whichever is less, from a suitable emergency landing site. Distances and times are doubled if you can carry on with a failed engine.

Life rafts must be easily accessible, installed in conspicuously marked locations near an exit and equipped with an attached survival kit, suitable for season, area, etc., containing at least a pyrotechnic signalling device, a radar reflector, a life raft repair kit, a bailing bucket and sponge, a signalling mirror, a whistle, a raft knife, an inflation pump, dye marker, a waterproof flashlight, a two day supply of water (based on one pint per day per person) or a means of desalting or distilling salt water for the same amount, a fishing kit, a book on sea survival and a first aid kit containing antiseptic swabs, burn dressing compresses, bandages and anti-motion sickness pills.

A list of survival equipment must be on board with information on how to use it, together with a survival manual appropriate for the season and climate.

First Aid Kit Contents

Must contain the supplies and equipment for a Type A kit as per Schedule II of Part V of the Aviation Occupational Safety and Health Regulations, and 1 pair of latex gloves.

Emergency Medical Kit

Must be carried on aeroplanes with more than 100 passenger seats.

PASSENGER & CABIN SAFETY
••

Safe Movement of Passengers

Aircraft should be parked to avoid exposure to hazardous conditions, to which passengers must be alerted. There must be guidance and escorts along safe routes, smoking restrictions must be enforced and entertainment system headsets that decrease awareness of other traffic or limit reception of audible direction or warning signals are not worn. Passengers must be briefed on how to safely get on and off when engines are running, and passengers on float planes must be alerted to their unique hazards.

Fuelling with Passengers on Board

The pilot must supervise, and be near the main exit (there must be at least two on larger aeroplanes) to immediately communicate with and assist the evacuation of passengers in an emergency. One must be the entry doors through which the passengers embarked.

Two-way communication must be maintained between ground crew supervising fuelling and qualified personnel on board. All exits must be clear of obstructions and available for evacuation.

On-board APUs discharging into the zone should not be started after filler caps are removed or fuelling connections are made. If an APU is stopped during fuelling it must not be restarted until the flow of fuel has ceased and there is no risk of igniting fuel vapours, unless the flight manual dictates otherwise.

Electrical power supplies must not be connected or disconnected, and equipment likely to produce sparks or arcs must not be used, including combustion heaters in or near the aircraft and photographic equipment within 10 feet (3 m) of the fuelling equipment or the fill or vent points of the fuel systems. Smoking is not permitted either. Fuelling must be suspended when lightning is within 8 km.

Known high energy equipment such as HF radios and weather radar must not be operated, unless the flight manual allows otherwise.

"No Smoking" signs must be illuminated, and passengers must not smoke, operate portable electronic devices or otherwise produce sources of ignition.

Portable Electronic Devices

Transistor radios, tape recorders and the like should not be operated in flight as they may interfere with navigation equipment (or even the fly-by-wire systems). If you don't believe me, tune to an AM station, as used by ADF, on a cheap radio and switch on an even cheaper calculator nearby - you will find the radio is blanked out by white noise. In fact, the radiations from TVs and radios come within the VOR and ILS regions as well. Although cell phones are cleared for use near heart monitors (in hospitals), they do so at low power when inside the range of a cell. Once in an aircraft, and a long way away from a transmitter, they put the power up and then become dangerous - a couple of hundred phones searching for a cell in an aircraft can therefore create havoc.

Here are some other examples:

- On an MD 87, failures in flight mode annunciator No 2 occurred while two video cameras were being used in the cabin. On another one, an uncommanded change of modes in the flight management system occurred when a CD player was used.

- On a DC 10 (as it was then), there were ADF bearing discrepancies when two Gameboys were being used.

- On a 727, coming down the ILS, between 2000-3500 feet, the flight director vertical bar and localiser needle both moved to the left when some clown used a cellular phone.

- On an MD 80, the wrong flight level was captured when another idiot used an FM digital receiver.

- A 747-400 started oscillating left and right of track as two passengers were using laptop computers.

PROHIBITED DEVICES

Any transmitting device intentionally radiating RF signals.

PERMITTED DEVICES WITHOUT RESTRICTIONS

Hearing aids, pacemakers, electronic watches and properly installed equipment.

PERMITTED DEVICES WITH RESTRICTIONS

Personal life support systems may be operated during all phases of flight, if it does not interfere with aircraft systems or equipment. Portable two-way radio devices may be used only when the aircraft engines are not running, except the APU. They may not, however, be used during the passenger briefing. Other portable electronic devices may not be used during take-off, climb, approach and landing.

When interference with the aircraft's systems or equipment is suspected, crew members must confirm passenger use, instruct them to terminate, prohibit suspected device(s), and recheck the aircraft's systems and equipment.

Note: Lithium Ion batteries, as found in most modern laptops and Portable Electronic Devices, can overheat and burst into flame. In 2004, they were banned in the US as cargo on passenger planes, but, due to the combination of the manufacturing process, where even a nano-sized particle of dust can cause a problem, and the falling quality control due to the economic climate, the incidents have been increasing, so be wary about putting such devices in a remote baggage compartment, as found on the Bell 212.

DOCUMENTS & RECORDS

The stuff listed below should be carried on all flights:

- Certificate of **A**irworthiness*
- Certificate of **R**egistration*
- **R**adio Station Licence*
- **O**perator Manual (i.e. flight manual)
- **W**eight and Balance report
- **J**ourney Log* (but see below)
- **I**ntercept Orders (see below)
- **L**icences of flight crew*, to include radio and medical certificates

*Required by the Chicago Convention, Article 29

Remember the above with the acronym ARROWJIL, made up from the bold letters. Commercial flights also need an Ops Manual. ICAO also require a passenger list* or cargo manifest*.

Flight Authority - 507

All Canadian aircraft and those operated in Canadian airspace, other than ultra-lights and hang gliders, must have a document that says they are fit for flight.

Unless surrendered, suspended or cancelled, it remains in force for the time or number of flights specified, or indefinitely, if the aircraft continues to meet the conditions under which it was issued.

CERTIFICATE OF AIRWORTHINESS

Issued at the beginning of an aircraft's service, and remains valid by proper loading, obeying the flight manual, completing all scheduled maintenance,

completing the AAIR (see below), complying with all ADs, performing proper daily checks as per the flight manual and having all no-go defects rectified before flight.

Items to be checked regarding the certificate before flight include making sure the nationality and registration match, as does the type designation and serial number, the date of issue (if more than a year ago, check the AAIR is present), the signature and seal. Otherwise, refer to Section 507.06.

A Special C of A is for amateur-built aircraft.

FLIGHT PERMIT

These are required for situations where the aircraft is still safe, but there is no C of A, or it has become invalid, such as when a maintenance check runs out away from base and you have to get the machine home (if you are already on your way back, but are delayed through weather or ATC, you may complete the flight if the check runs out during it, but you should have planned things properly in the first place. Stopping for fuel does not count).

A specific-purpose flight permit need not be carried in Canadian airspace, if an entry is in the journey log with the details. Neither does a flight permit need to be carried on a balloon if you can lay your hands on it before and after the flight.

Refer to Section 507.06, or Chapter 507 of the Airworthiness Manual.

ANNUAL AIRWORTHINESS INFORMATION REPORT

An AAIR keeps the C of A valid (see above) and must be submitted annually by the owner of a Canadian aircraft (except ultra-lights), under Chapter 501 of the Airworthiness Manual, unless it is out of service, no later than the anniversary of when the flight authority was issued, unless agreed otherwise. The pink copy stays with the flight authority.

Its purpose is to collect data and satisfy the reporting requirement of the annual inspection procedure.

Radio Station Licence

This is automatically renewed each year, as long as the fee is paid.

Certificate of Registration

All aircraft operating in Canada, except hang gliders or parachutes, must be registered, either in Canada, or a contracting or foreign state. For production test, customer acceptance, completion of manufacturing or export flights, registration is not required with written authorisation.

Any Canadian over 16 can be a registered owner, as can an entity formed under the laws of Canada or a province. The term *Canadian* is defined under the *Canada Transportation Act* as "a citizen, permanent resident, corporation or other entity incorporated or formed in Canada that is controlled in fact by Canadians with at least 75% of the voting interest owned or controlled by Canadians". This is to stop corporations using Canada as a flag of convenience.

Corporations that are not Canadian-controlled can be registered owners if the aircraft is used on Canadian business, that is, flying primarily in (including into or out of) Canada (see 222.15). Records showing that the flights were primarily in Canada must be kept for three years (see also *Journey Logs*).

An aircraft can be registered as:

- a *state aircraft*, i.e. a civil one owned and exclusively used by a government in Canada

- a *commercial aircraft*, for Aerial Work, Air Taxi, Commuter or Airline operations, or in a flight training unit

- a *private aircraft*

A provisional registration can be issued for importation, or a temporary one if paperwork is not yet available. If it is, a continuing registration may be issued, and an interim registration is automatic, once only, if the new owner is qualified and a part of custody and control is transferred, or any information, like a change of address, is changed.

IDENTITY FOR REGISTRATION PURPOSES

Usually from the fuselage or hull, so when they are scrapped, the aircraft officially ceases to exist. A balloon takes its identity from its envelope.

CERTIFICATES OF REGISTRATION - 202.25

These can be provisional, temporary, interim or continuing. A temporary one is for when there is no paperwork for a continuing one, and it expires or is cancelled on the earliest of:

- the date in the temporary certificate

- the last day of the three months (90 days) after the issue date

- the day there is a change in legal custody and control

- when a continuing C of R is issued.

The C of R has five parts, and must always be carried, unless the machine is registered in a non-contracting foreign state or one with an agreement that allows it to do so, in which case an authorisation must be issued. Part 1 (white) is the certificate itself, Part 2 (white) is the application, Part 3 (pink) is the change of ownership, Part 4 (white) is an interim certificate and Part 5 is the change of address card. As well as the above, a Canadian C of R is cancelled where:

- a registered owner dies, is dissolved or amalgamated with another, or is not qualified.

- the lease is extended and Transport Canada is not told within 7 days

- the address is changed and Transport Canada is not told within 7 days

- unless it is undergoing restoration or is an ultra-light, the aircraft has not been flown in the last 5 years

- an aircraft registered as an ultra-light is no longer one

- custody & control documents cease to be in effect, unless the registered owner retains custody and control afterwards and submits notification (including the day it ceased), and a true copy of the new document, within 60 days.

- an aircraft is destroyed, permanently withdrawn, missing (with search terminated) or has been missing for over 60 days. Transport Canada must be notified within 7 days of your becoming aware.

- there is misrepresentation or fraudulent documentation in the original application.

INTERIM REGISTRATION - 202.36/222.36

The new owner (or registered owner, if just changing information) must complete the back of the C of R, send the Continuing one to Transport, and retain the Interim on board.

C OF R LOST OR DESTROYED - 202.27

It may be replaced on written application from the registered owner, if the requirements continue to be met.

AMENDMENT OR REPLACEMENT

Transport Canada may request the return of a C of R for amendment or replacement, within 7 days of receipt.

Route Guides & IFR Charts

You need a route guide so you can get around the airways without messing things up for anybody else. Any used must be the current ones, as amended. Although the symbols and keys are generally printed on them, it is still a good idea to know at least the basic ones for use in a hurry, and to impress examiners. Because they are included, they have not been reproduced in this book.

The *Low Altitude* charts (LO) are for use up to 17,999 feet in Canadian Domestic Airspace, and anywhere else Canada has responsibility. There are 10, on 5 sheets, back to back. *Terminal Area* charts come on both sides of one sheet, also valid up to 17,999 feet. They are available for Edmonton, Vancouver/Victoria, Calgary, Saskatoon, Regina, Winnipeg, Windsor, Toronto, Ottawa, Montreal, Quebec, Moncton, Halifax and Gander.

LO and Terminal charts are revised every 56 days, and updated by NOTAM. Full details about how to get them are in the MAP section of the AIM, where you will also find version information on the first page, to see if your map is up to date.

The CFS is a supporting document for charts and approach plates, and lists aerodromes that are an advantage to the aviation community, that is, open to the public, used by more than one aircraft and have telephone access - fuel would be useful as well. It is a joint civil and military publication issued every 56 days. Any part of it that is incorporated by reference into CARs becomes part of CARs and therefore part of the law of the land, so watch it.

ATS Flight Plan

See under *Rules Of The Air (Annex 2)*.

Operational Flight Plan - 723.18, 724.17

VFR at night flights within an aerial work zone and day VFR flights do not need an operational flight plan. For local flights (within 25 nm), or those ending at the departure point, this need not be a formal document unless specified in the Ops Manual. The same goes for routes with cruise segments of less than 30 minutes. For Day VFR, the flight plan or itinerary will do instead. Otherwise, minimum contents for IFR and night VFR are:

- operator's name
- date
- registration & tail number
- type and model
- flight number
- type of flight (unless all the same)
- PIC
- Departure aerodrome
- Destination aerodrome
- Alternate
- Routing(s)
- Specification of way points for special operations requirements
- planned cruise altitudes
- planned cruise TAS
- planned cruise IAS
- winds
- temperature
- ground speed or wind in cruise
- estimated time enroute
- time from destination to alternate
- distance to destination and alternate
- fuel burns
- fuel required
- weights - total FOB, zero fuel weight and planned MTOW
- signature of PIC or alternative
- POB

The plan may be computer generated or produced manually from charts and tables by the crew, in which case an approved form displaying the above information with enough space to make entries as the flight progresses must be used. The Ops Manual must specify how formal acceptance of the operational flight plan by the PIC shall be recorded.

Journey Log

A system for recording defects and maintenance between scheduled servicing, as well as information relevant to flight safety and maintenance. In other words, the formal communication between flight crews and engineering.

The aircraft may never be more than 25 nm away from it, so it normally must be on board, except if you do not plan to land and shut down anywhere other than the point of departure, or you are flying a balloon and the log is immediately available before and after the flight.

Single entries for a series of flights may not be made unless they are done by the same pilot, or a daily flight record is used as per Section 406.56. Dual signatures are required when engine or primary flight controls have been modified, repaired, replaced or disassembled.

Entries must be retained for at least one year, or three years if the aircraft is registered under Section 202.15(3) to a corporation that is not Canadian-controlled and the journey log is used a record of their flight time in Canada. It must also be kept for three years after the date of removal of service. The requirement to transfer two entries from the old journey log when starting a new one is no longer in force - instead, there must be an "unbroken chronological record" (605.94(4)).

Unless recorded in the operational flight plan or flight data sheet, the PIC of an aircraft in a commercial air service and operating in international flight must record in the journey log the following:

- names of the crew and duties

- places and times of departure and arrival

- the flight time

- the nature of the flight, i.e. private, aerial work, etc

- any incidents or observations relating to the flight.

Company Operations Manual

The Ops Manual is like the Standing Orders or SOPs (*Standard Operating Procedures*) issued by any military unit, hospital or other type of large organisation. It's a book of instructions that are constant, so that Company policy can be determined by reference to it, containing information and instructions that enable all Operating Staff (i.e. you) to perform their duties. It's partly to save you constantly pestering Those On High, but mainly for situations where you can't speak to them anyway and need information with which to make decisions. As part of the Operating Staff of a Company, you are subject to the rules and requirements in it, and it's your responsibility to be fully conversant with the contents at all times. You will be expected to read it at regular intervals, if only because it gets amended. Amendments, when issued, consist of dated and printed replacement pages on which the text affected is marked, ideally by a vertical line in the margin. On receipt of an amendment list, those responsible for copies of the manual incorporate the amendment in theirs

and record it on the form in the front. You should find a proposal form for changes somewhere as well.

The prime objective for the Ops Manual in the first place is to promote safety in Company flying operations. As the authorities are involved, it's therefore compiled in accordance with the law (in fact, as far as you are concerned it is the law) and all flights should be conducted to the standards set out in it. Usually in several parts, it can be a single volume with a small operator, or several in the average airline.

Although the manual is supplemented by statutory instructions and orders, not all of them will be mentioned. It doesn't mean that you should ignore those that aren't, but being acquainted with all regulations, orders and instructions issued by whoever is all part of your job. Naturally, references to publications mean the current editions, as amended. When mentioned in the Ops Manual, they acquire the same legal force.

There will be several copies of the Manual around, the numbers issued differing with the size of the Company, but the typical distribution list below should be regarded as a minimum; each aircraft will have its own copy.:

Copy	Who has it
1	Master Copy-Operations Manager
2	Authorities (Transport Canada)
3	Chief Pilot
4	Training Captain
5	Maintenance Organisation
6+	One per aircraft or pilot

A large airline will likely have its own print shop just to produce Ops Manuals and amendments. For more about these, see *Operational Flying*.

CONTENTS - 702.82, 723.105, 724.121
IFR AND VFR AT NIGHT

Preamble about use and authority of manual, table of contents, amendment procedures, amendment record sheet, distribution list and effective pages, copy of AOC and Operations Specifications, management organization chart, duties and responsibilities of management and ops personnel, description of operational control system (i.e. flight authorization and planning, fuelling, weight and balance, weather minima, passenger briefing, emergency stuff, etc.). See CARs for full list.

DAY VFR

Similar to the above. Refer to CARs for differences.

Abbreviated for Owner/Pilot, one Aircraft, Day VFR

Table of contents, amendments, effective pages, copy of AOC and Operations Specifications, weight and balance system, emergency and survival equipment carried, overdue procedures, reduced VFR limits in uncontrolled air space and accident/incident reporting.

Abbreviated for Parachute Jumping, under 7 aircraft

Preamble, TOC, amendments, effective pages, copy of AOC and Operations Specifications, weight and balance, emergency & survival equipment, overdue procedures, accident/incident reporting and procedures for day/night VFR.

Aircraft SOPs - 723.107, 724.124

With significant differences in equipment and procedures between types, SOPs, which may be in the Ops Manual, must show registrations of applicable aircraft, but if the information is in another publication on board, it need not be repeated. SOPs must include:

- *General* - TOC, effective pages, amendments, preamble, communications, crew co-ordination, use of check lists, standard briefings and calls.

- *Normal Procedures* - Weight and balance, ramp procedures, battery/APU starts, taxi, take-off and climb, cruise, descent, approaches (IFR, visual, VFR and circling as applicable), landing, missed approach and balked landings, stall recovery, refuelling with people on board, on-board navigation and alerting aids and check lists.

- *Abnormal and Emergency Procedures* - Emergency landing/ditching - with and without time to prepare, incapacitation two communication rule, bomb threat and hijacking, engine & propeller problems, fire, smoke removal, rapid decompression, flapless approach and landing, in-flight icing.

Aeroplane Operating Manual - 724.123

Must have a table of contents, list of effective pages, amending procedures, preamble, identification of the aeroplane by type and registration, and operating procedures and limitations that are not less restrictive than those in the flight manual and CARs.

EQUIPMENT REQUIRED

Power-driven Aircraft - Day VFR - 605.14

Daylight exists half an hour before sunrise and after sunset, or whenever the Sun's disc is less than 6° below the horizon (in case you're in the North, where the Sun doesn't really set). This equipment is a minimum:

- sensitive altimeter adjustable for barometric pressure in controlled airspace

- an airspeed indicator

- magnetic compass or direction indicator independent of electrical systems

- tachometer for each engine and or rotor with limiting speeds established by the manufacturer

- oil pressure indicator for each engine, if applicable

- a coolant temperature indicator for each liquid-cooled engine

- an oil temp indicator for each air-cooled engine with a separate oil system

- manifold pressure gauges for each reciprocating engine with a variable-pitch propeller or in a helicopter, supercharged or turbocharged engines

- fuel quantity indicators for each main fuel tank, a landing gear indicator, visible from crew seats

- radio equipment for two-way communication in Class B, C or D airspace, an MF area (unless under subsection 602.97(3)), or the ADIZ

- radio equipment suitable for Subpart 4, or Subpart 3, 4 or 5 of Part VII

- in Class B airspace, navigation equipment for flight plans

- radio nav equipment for Subpart 4 of Part VI or Subpart 5 of Part VII

Power-driven Aircraft - VFR OTT - 605.15

You need equipment as for Day VFR (above), plus:

- anti-icing equipment for each airspeed system

- a gyroscopic direction indicator or stabilized magnetic DI

- an attitude indicator

- a turn and slip indicator or turn coordinator, unless you have a standby AI usable through attitudes of ± 80° of pitch and ± 120° of roll for a helicopter, in which case you may use a slip-skid indicator

- in the NDA, a non-magnetic means of establishing direction.

- radios for 2-way communication on appropriate frequencies

- radio navigation equipment suitable for safe navigation

Power-driven Aircraft - Night VFR - 605.16/625.16

Night is from half an hour after sunset to half an hour before sunrise, or whenever the centre of the Sun's disc is more than 6° below the horizon (for when the Sun doesn't really set). Equipment is as for Day VFR, plus:

- a turn and slip indicator or turn coordinator, unless you have a standby AI usable through flight attitudes of 360° of pitch and roll for an aeroplane, or ± 80° of pitch and ± 120° of roll for a helicopter, so you may use a slip-skid indicator

- an adequate source of electrical energy for all of the electrical and radio equipment

- spare fuses for at least 50% of the total number of that rating

- if an aerodrome is not visible from the aircraft, a stabilized magnetic or gyroscopic DI

- in the NSA, a non-magnetic way of establishing direction

- for an airship in controlled airspace, radar reflectors capable of a 360° reflection

- illumination for instruments

- when carrying passengers, a landing light

- suitable position and anti-collision lights

Lights must not be mistaken for, or downgrade the conspicuity of, a light in the navigation light system, unless you are doing aerial advertising.

For night VFR flight under Subpart 4 of this Part or Subparts 2 to 5 of Part VII, you also need:

- an attitude indicator

- a vertical speed indicator

- anti-icing equipment for each airspeed system

- an OAT gauge

POSITION AND ANTI-COLLISION LIGHTS 605.17

Aircraft must show a steady green light of at least five candela to starboard through 110° from ahead horizontally, with a steady red on the other side, and a steady white of at least three candela through 70° each side of dead astern horizontally. If more than 2 metres from the wing tip, another may be put at the tip. Note that the boundaries are parallel, so only one light can be seen.

Position and anti-collision lights must be on between sunset and sunrise, unless it affects safety.

Power-driven Aircraft - IFR - 605.18

For day flying, as for Night VFR, except illuminations (last 3), plus:

- an adequate source of electrical energy for all of the electrical and radio equipment

- spare fuses equal to at least 50% of the total number of fuses of that rating

- if an aerodrome is not visible, a stabilized magnetic or gyroscopic direction indicator

- in the NDA, a way of establishing direction not reliant on magnetic sources

- for airships in controlled airspace, radar reflectors capable of a 360° reflection

By night you need this as well:

- illumination for instruments

- when carrying passengers, a landing light

- suitable position and anti-collision lights

- an attitude indicator

- a vertical speed indicator

- anti-icing for each airspeed indicating system

- an OAT gauge

- a power failure warning device or vacuum indicator showing the power available to gyroscopic instruments from each power source

- an alternative static source for the altimeter, airspeed indicator and vertical speed indicator

- enough radios for two-way communications

- enough radio nav equipment to allow you, if a failure occurs, to proceed to the destination or another suitable aerodrome, and, in IMC, to complete an instrument approach and conduct a missed approach.

If this page is a photocopy, it is not authorised!

Oxygen Equipment and Supply

Air pressure forces oxygen into the blood, so the higher you go, the less effective this will be. The net result is that you must use oxygen when the cabin pressure is lower than 10,000 feet (see also *Human Factors*). In a *steady flow system*, oxygen is fed to a mask with a face piece and a plastic bag that can expand. The bag is a *rebreather*, because it allows air to be reused to a certain extent. Flow must be adjusted for different altitudes. If it is not enough, the flow indicator will show a red line. *Demand* oxygen systems only provide it when the person inhales.

UNPRESSURIZED AIRCRAFT

All crew and 10% of passengers; at least 1 passenger	Entire flight over 30 mins between 10000-13000 feet ASL
All persons on board	Entire flight above 13000 feet ASL or at least 1 hour for air transport.

Use of Oxygen - 605.32

For over 30 minutes between 10-13,000 feet ASL, each crew member must use supplemental oxygen. All persons on board must use it for all flight above 13,000 feet ASL. The handling pilot must use an oxygen mask if the aircraft is not equipped with quick-donning oxygen masks at or above FL 250, or it does have them, but above FL 410.

Flight Data Recorders

These aircraft must have a suitable Flight Data Recorder:

- after July 31, 1997 or, for aircraft operated under Part VII, after February 28, 1997, multi-engined turbine-powered aircraft capable of carrying more than 10 passengers, made after October 11, 1991.

FDRs must record at least the time, PA, IAS, vertical acceleration and magnetic heading. When carrying passengers, you must add force on the control column, rudder pedals or control wheels, or their positions, the position of horizontal stabilizer, out-of-trim condition, whether the auto-pilot is on or off, engine power (torque, RPM, fuel flow), ambient air temperature and pitch attitude.

There are also requirements as to how data is recorded, according to how many seats the aircraft has. When required, FDRs must be on continuously from the start of take-off until the completion of landing.

An FDR may be missing under an MEL. If there isn't one, you can fly without one for 90 days if the CVR is working and the failure date is in the technical records.

Cockpit Voice Recorders - 605.34

Must continuously record voice signals transmitted from, or received in, the aircraft about its operation, the aural environment of the flight deck, including each microphone used by a crew member, the intercom and PA system, and identification of navaids. If the aircraft is made after October 11, 1991 and brought onto the register after the effective date of this standard, you also need a time scale, and must record the uninterrupted audio signals received by a boom or mask microphone (which must be used below 10,000 feet AMSL). Information must be recorded for the duration of the flight or the last thirty minutes, whichever is less.

These aircraft must have a suitable Cockpit Voice Recorder:

- after July 31, 1997 or, for aircraft under Part VII, after February 28, 1997, multi-engined turbine-powered aircraft capable of carrying more than 6 passengers, for which 2 pilots are required.

When required, CVRs must be operated continuously from when power is first applied before flight to when it is removed afterwards. You cannot erase relevant communications from a CVR.

A CVR may be missing under an MEL. If there isn't one, you can fly without one for 90 days if the FDR is working and the date of failure is in the technical records.

Transponder and Automatic PA Reporting Equipment - 605.35

Except balloons or gliders, aircraft flying where a transponder is required must have one with pressure-altitude reporting, unless under an MEL. Otherwise, you may go to the next landing point and thereafter, under ATC instructions, to complete a planned schedule or proceed to a maintenance facility if safety will not be affected and the request was received before the airspace was entered.

ELT - 605.38

These must only be switched on in emergency, but may be tested in the first 5 minutes of any hour, for 5 seconds (exam question). Just turn the thing on and listen out - you will hear a siren-like sound.

Accidental activations should be reported to the nearest ATC unit, especially if the unit malfunctions, in which you need to report the model number and any details. The device should then be switched off.

If you hear an ELT signal in flight, notify ATC of your position and altitude, with the time you first heard the signal and the signal strength. If you lose the signal, report this as well. Do not attempt SAR yourself. If the signal is constant, it may be your own aircraft. ELTs must be fitted as follows, (and armed):

Aircraft	Operation Area	Min Equipment
All aircraft except *	Over land	One ELT of AD AF AP A or F2.
Large passenger transport multi-engined turbo-jets	Over water where life rafts are required	Two ELTs of Type W or S or one of each
All other aircraft requiring an ELT	Over water where rafts required	One ELT Type W or S

* gliders, balloons, airships, ultra-lights or gyroplanes, multi-engined turbo-jets over 5 700 kg (12,500 lbs) in IFR in controlled airspace over land, and south of 66 30' N, or those registered in contracting states, with a serviceable radio transmitter for SAR purposes having a distinctive audio signal, and capable of communication on 406 MHz. Also training aircraft within 25 nm of the aerodrome of departure, those on flight tests, new aircraft in operations incidental to manufacture, preparation or delivery, or under 605.39.

USE OF ELTS

ELTs must meet ICAO specifications and be capable of broadcasting simultaneously on 121.5 and 406 MHz. They must also be registered.

If you require an ELT, you may operate without a serviceable one if there is an alternative that:

- is identified in the information section of a flight plan or flight intinerary

- can provide immediate notification of a distress situation (without activation by a crewmember) to either a Joint Rescue Coordination Centre (JRCC) or a third party that can transmit the information to a JRCC

- allows aircraft location within 2.7 nm

- is registered in the Transport Canada database

There may also be other terms and conditions in an MEL.

Standby Attitude Indicator

Needed by all transport category aircraft. Must be powered independently of the electrical generating system, work without selection after total failure, continue reliably for at least 30 minutes afterwards, operate independently of any attitude indicator system, with the indicating instrument plainly visible to any pilot and illuminated during all operations.

Safety Belts - 605.22

Aircraft, other than balloons, must have seats and safety belts for each person on board, except infants, unless a type-certification exists for a safety belt for two people. Safety belts must have a metal-to-metal latching device. However, for people on stretchers or in incubators (or similar), parachutists or those working near an opening in the aircraft structure, you can use a system secured to the primary structure.

SHOULDER HARNESSES - 605.24

Required for:

- Flight attendant seats on transport category aeroplanes

- Front seats or those on the flight deck, except small planes made before 18/07/78

- Forward- or aft-facing seats on small aeroplanes made after December 12, 1986 with an initial type certificate for under nine passenger seats.

- All seats on normal or transport category helicopters made after 16/09/92.

- Aerobatics

- Class B, C or D external loads on helicopters

- Aerial application, or aerial inspection other than flight inspection for the purpose of calibrating electronic navaids below 500 feet AGL.

CARs does not specifically state in so many words that shoulder harnesses must be worn in helicopters (or anything else, for that matter) but 605.25 (1) requires the PIC to direct all persons to fasten safety belts during movement on the surface, take-off and landing and at any other time deemed necessary. 702.44 (and 703.69) require that the pilot seat and any beside it are equipped with a safety belt that includes a shoulder harness. 605.24 (4) requires normal or transport category helicopters manufactured after September 16, 1992 to have each seat with a safety belt that includes a shoulder harness. Since the definition of a seat belt mentions a shoulder harness, a reasonable person would conclude that if a belt comes with one, it should be used, except for rear seats in machines manufactured before Sep 16, 1992. However, such instructions may well be in an Ops Manual.

Note: If you don't wear shoulder straps, you will jackknife over the lapstrap and your head will hit whatever is in front of it at 12 times the speed it is coming the other way. Also, tolerance to forward deceleration reduces to below 25G, from a normal total of over 40. Passengers in the oil patch might like to know that.

GENERAL USE OF SAFETY BELTS AND RESTRAINT SYSTEMS

All people must fasten safety belts during movement on the surface, take-off and landing and at any time you consider it necessary. This also applies to child restraint systems, those used by parachutists and people working near an opening in the aircraft structure.

If you expect more than light turbulence, flight attendants must discontinue their service, secure the cabin and occupy a seat, fastening the safety belt. In turbulence, if considered necessary, the in-charge flight attendant must direct all passengers to fasten their safety belts and all the other flight attendants to discontinue their duties relating to service, secure the cabin and occupy a seat, fastening the safety belt. The PIC must be informed.

Once directed to do so, every passenger who is not an infant must ensure their safety belt or restraint system is fastened. Infants with no restraints must be held securely in the passenger's arms. Otherwise, restraints must be properly secured. No passenger must be responsible for more than one infant.

CREW MEMBER SAFETY BELTS - 605.27

Crew members must be seated at their stations with safety belts fastened during take-off and landing, and at any time the PIC directs. Flight attendants must also do so whenever directed by the attendant in-charge. However, if the safety belt sign has been used, this does not apply if you are performing duties relating to safety, if you are a flight attendant performing duties relating to passengers in light turbulence, or you are occupying a crew rest facility in the cruise and the restraint system is properly adjusted and securely fastened. At least one pilot must be at the controls with safety belt fastened during flight.

CHILD RESTRAINT SYSTEM - 605.28

The person using it must be accompanied by a parent or guardian who will attend to their safety, their weight and height are within the specified range, there is a legible label indicating the applicable design standards and date of manufacture, it is properly secured by the safety belt of a forward-facing seat that is not in an emergency exit row

and does not block access to an aisle, and the tether strap is used under the manufacturer's instructions.

A seat designed to reduce occupant loads, such as crushing or separating components, must not be a hazard.

Every passenger responsible for a people using child restraints must be in an adjacent seat, familiar with installation and how to use them.

De-Icing or Anti-icing Equipment

If icing conditions are reported or forecast, your aircraft must be adequately equipped, unless current weather or pilot reports indicate that icing conditions no longer exist.

Anti-icing systems prevent ice forming, and de-icing systems remove it afterwards. The most common form of the former system in small helicopters is for the engine air inlet, mostly operated with bleed air from the compressor above 4°C, though some specify 5° (TwinStar), whenever moisture is visible.

Very few small helicopters have de-icing, but larger ones do, like the Super Puma's heating elements along the leading edges of its rotor blades. See also *Icing*.

FLIGHT TRAINING UNITS - 406 (426)

To operate a flight training service in Canada using an aeroplane or helicopter, you need a flight training unit operator certificate. However, you can operate a flight training service without one if you hold a private operator certificate or an AOC, the aircraft is specified in them, and the training is other than toward obtaining a recreational pilot permit, a PPL, a CPL or a flight instructor rating, or the trainee is the owner (or a member of the family) of the aircraft, or a director of a corporation that owns it.

Alternatively, the aircraft must have been obtained from a person who is at arm's length from the instructor, and the training is other than toward a recreational pilot permit or a PPL (there are certain conditions attached to this - such as notifying Transport Canada in advance).

Eligibility to Hold FTU Operator Certificate - 406.04

You can hold a certificate if you are a Canadian, or a citizen, permanent resident or corporation of the USA or Mexico.

Notification Requirement - 406.05

If you use a glider, balloon, gyroplane or ultralight in Canada, you must notify Transport Canada in writing of the legal name, trade name and address of the operator of the FTU, the base of operations, category of aircraft, type of training and the name of the instructor responsible for operational control.

The above information must be provided before training, within 10 working days of any change and on the service being discontinued.

Issuance/Amendment of FTU Operator Certificate - 406.11

You must have a suitable management organization, qualified ground and flight instructors to cover all authorized training and a full-time CFI who meets the requirements of Section 406.22. You also need legal custody and control of at least one Canadian registered aircraft, and all must be properly equipped for the area and type of training.

As part of your application for a certificate, you must provide information about the main base, and include written permission from the Local Airport Authority (LAA). If not available, and you haven't actually been denied operations, access can be demonstrated by other means. You also need the name of the CFI, supported by a resume, as in Section 406.21, the name of the person responsible for maintenance, under Section 406.36, the aircraft to be operated, including category, class, type and registration, the type of training and proposed route for the solo cross-country training flight as per Section 406.55.

On top of all that, you must have a copy of the flight training program outline, as in Section 405.13, a copy of the statement signed by the CFI, under Section 406.22, the proposed maintenance control system, including the maintenance control manual, under Section 406.38, written confirmation of insurance coverage against injury or death to passengers, and public liability, as required by Sect 606.02-Liability Insurance, form 26-0380-Statement of Intent completed and signed, and form 26-0344-Application for Flight Training Unit Operator Certificate completed and signed.

For temporary operations at satellite bases, you must provide information about the base, the person responsible for training operations there, arrangements for maintenance, the aircraft to be operated, including category, class, type and registration, the type of training, the proposed route for the solo cross-country training

flight as outlined in Section 406.55, if applicable, the period of operation, a copy of the flight training program outline, under Section 405.13, and a statement signed by the CFI accepting the responsibility for supervision of training operations.

Appointment of CFI - 406.21 (426.21)

A CFI must be an instructor who meets Section 406.22. Changes must be notified to Transport Canada within 10 working days. You can operate up to 60 days without one, if there are extenuating circumstances and proper supervision is available, not affecting safety. Transport Canada must approve and you must comply with the relevant standards. Under the same circumstances, you can operate for up to 6 months with a CFI subject to a prohibition regarding the exercise of the privileges of a permit, licence or rating under Section 404.06.

The CFI's medical may be invalid for up to six months if that person remains a full-time employee, and responsible for all non-flight duties required, and other staff can carry out airborne duties.

QUALIFICATIONS

You can be a CFI where an instructor rating is required, with a Class 1 or 2 Instructor Rating for the category, or a Class 3 Rating for aeroplanes if no other instructor is employed at the FTU. If an instructor rating is not required, you must be qualified under 405.21.

If you are operating a glider, balloon, gyroplane or an ultralight, you must hold a pilot permit or licence for the category of aircraft, and a flight instructor rating.

RESPONSIBILITIES

Operational control, the overall pilot training program, supervision of other instructors, including supervising Class 4 instructors by Class 1 or 2 instructors, approving ground instructors, the quality and content of ground school and flight training, the content and accuracy of Pilot Training Records, course reports, student pilot permits issued, licence applications and other relevant documents, ensuring that instruction is based on the contents of the appropriate Flight Instructor Guide and Flight Training Manual, ensuring that the daily flight record is used for operational control, ensuring that the regulatory and licence standards publications including CARs, AIM Canada, CFS, Water Aerodrome Supplement, Flight Instructor Guide and Flight Training Manual, and the training manual on human factors are readily available to trainees and amended, maintaining current copies of training publications, charts, maps and any other material, ensuring that all solo flights are properly authorized by a flight instructor and acknowledged by the trainee, decisions with respect to flight safety during flying periods, and confirming the continuing validity of staff licences and ratings.

Instructor Records - 406.25 (426.25)

Those for ground instructors must have the name and date of appointment. For flight instructors, name, permit or licence number (with ratings and dates), next medical.

Maintenance Control System - 406.35

That is, policies and procedures regarding maintenance of aircraft operated, as described in the Maintenance Control Manual (MCM).

PERSON RESPONSIBLE - 406.36/426.36

Needed by all FTUs, and must be authorised to remove aircraft from operation, where justified because of non-compliance with these Regulations or of a risk to its safety, people or property. If the FTU holds an AMO certificate as per Section 573.02, the person appointed above is the person responsible for the maintenance control system of the AMO, appointed under paragraph 573.03(1)(a).

Such a person must demonstrate (to Transport Canada) knowledge of the planning, implementation and direction of the maintenance control system and pass an exam on CARs, unless already holding a pilot or an AME licence, and have not been convicted more than once in the past 5 years of contravening with full knowledge "mens rea" the Aeronautics Act or CARs. Management functions may be assigned for specific activities, including removal of aircraft from operation as above, if the assignment and functions are in the MCM.

MAINTENANCE PERSONNEL AND FACILITIES - 406.37/426.37

Must be provided by the flight training unit. There must be enough staff for the initial development of the maintenance schedule, scheduling and performance of maintenance within it, the accomplishment of ADs, operation of the evaluation program, the proper dispatch of aircraft with regard to spare parts and defects, authorising personnel as necessary and the initial development and updating of the maintenance control manual (see below).

Facilities, technical and regulatory data, supplies and spare parts must include a place of business (with fixed address), a means of communication (telephone, fax, etc.), devices used to establish when maintenance is required (planning boards, card files, or a computer system), necessary equipment and tools for elementary work or servicing, supplies and spare parts for timely rectification of defects and a secure, dry storage area for technical records.

MAINTENANCE CONTROL MANUAL

Copies, or relevant parts, must be available to each person performing or certifying a function in it. Amendments must be submitted to Transport Canada for approval when instructed and inserted within 30 days of approval.

The manual must contain a Table of Contents, an amendment control page, a List of Effective Pages (with each page numbered and dated), the legal name, trade name and address of the flight training unit, the location of bases, the category, class, type and number of aircraft operated, a statement confirming that the manual and incorporated documents reflect the FTU's means of compliance with Section 406.35, details of any assignment of functions, the amendment and distribution procedure, methods used to record maintenance, details of maintenance schedules, procedures ensuring that only parts and materials meeting the requirements of CAR 571-Aircraft Maintenance Requirements are used, a description of the procedure for recording empty Weight and Balance information, technical dispatch procedures, defect recording, rectification and control procedures, service difficulty reporting and the evaluation program.

MAINTENANCE ARRANGEMENTS - 406.39/426.39

Maintenance can be done outside Canada by a person or organization without an AMO certificate with a Maintenance Specification, including details of the relevant portions of the MCM provided to them, the maintenance to be performed and records to be kept by the person performing the maintenance. The person or organization must be approved under the state that has an agreement with Canada that provides for recognition of the work performed, or approved by Transport.

Persons or organizations performing maintenance on the FTU's aircraft must have adequate facilities, equipment, spare parts and personnel where the maintenance is to be performed and a suitable AMO certificate. Transport Canada must issue a maintenance specification. The maintenance required must be clearly defined and made under the maintenance control manual, or approved by Transport Canada.

EVALUATION PROGRAM - 426.47

This ensures the maintenance control system (including schedules) continue to comply with the regulations, by periodic verifications of all aspects of the systems and practices used, to ensure compliance with regulations and approved procedures - just like a Quality Control system (ISO 9000 or similar). It must be responsive to changes, and address the need for amendments to the MCM or Maintenance Schedules, which must be reviewed periodically for compliance with current requirements, including the use of detailed checklists. The elements it must contain are listed in CARs.

TECHNICAL DISPATCH PROCEDURES - 406.40

An aircraft must be airworthy, appropriately equipped, configured and maintained for its intended use, and maintained under the FTU's maintenance control manual.

DEFECT RECTIFICATION & CONTROL PROCEDURES - 406.41

Policies and procedures must exist for recording defects and their rectification, including those detected during operation or elementary work or servicing, and recurring defects (where a failure is repeated 3 times, on a particular aircraft, within 15 flight segments of a previous repair).

MAINTENANCE PERSONNEL RECORDS - 406.46/426.46

Must be retained for at least 2 years after an entry is made and contain all appointments and personnel qualifications, authorisations to perform elementary work under CAR 406.43, and all training conducted under CAR 406.45.

TRAINING PROGRAM - 426.45

Must include initial and update training so people remain competent and are made aware of changes to regulations, and any additional training. It may be part of an AMO system if in the MCM and requirements here are in the AMO manual.

FACILITIES AT BASE - 426.52

There must be communication with the nearest FSS, continuous use of facilities with adequate classrooms, training aids, continuous use of dispatch facilities with spaces for flight planning, pre- and post-flight briefing, which may be within reasonable distance of a satellite.

DAILY FLIGHT RECORD - 426.56

Must be retained for at least 2 years after an entry is made and include date, registration, PIC, trainee, exercise or lesson, instructor's authorization, trainee's acknowledgement, time up & down, air time, flight time.

Aircraft Registration Requirements

Must be registered in Canada under Part II or in another contracting state, in which case Transport Canada must authorize its operation, and, except for ultralights, the type must be approved for Canada.

Aircraft Flight Authority

A C of A must be in force for an aeroplane or helicopter, or a flight authority for a glider, balloon or gyroplane.

Safety Belt and Shoulder Harness Requirements

Each front seat must have a safety belt that includes a shoulder harness.

Checklists

Must be readily available to each crew member.

Aircraft Operations - 406.51

For PPL, CPL or instructor training, you must have access to at least one Pt V aeroplane certified for spinning. For a helicopter pilot permit-recreational, PPL, CPL or instructor rating, you must have access to at least one helicopter capable of full-on autorotations.

Dispatch of Aircraft - 406.53

Aircraft must be maintained under a maintenance control system.

Aircraft Operating over Water - 406.54

Except when taking off or landing, you may not go beyond a point where a land aircraft could reach shore if an engine fails.

Solo Cross-country Routes - 406.55

Transport Canada must be notified in writing of the planned route of the solo cross-country flight originating from any base.

Journey Log Entries - 406.57

A person must be designated.

Flight Training at a Satellite Base - 406.58

An instructor (not a Class 4), must be responsible for training operations and ensure that a qualified instructor is on duty when solo flying is going on. A Class 4 instructor may not conduct training at a satellite base unless a Class 1 or 2 instructor is on duty.

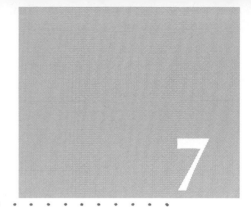

FLIGHT OPERATIONS

7

T his chapter covers things you can do with aircraft of an operational nature. However, it only deals with items required for the exams - for more on each subject, refer to either *Operational Flying* or *The Helicopter Pilot's Handbook*, by the same author.

FUELLING

Jet and piston fuels mix differently with contaminants (particularly water), which is due to variations in their specific gravities and temperatures. The specific gravity of water, for example, is so close to Avtur that it can take up to 4 hours for it to settle out, whereas the same process may take as little as half an hour with Avgas. As a result, there is always water suspended in jet fuel, which must be kept within strict limits, hence two filtration stages, for solids and water. The latter doesn't burn, of course, and can freeze, but it's the fungi that gather round the interface between it and the fuel that is the real problem - it turns into a dark-coloured slime which clings to tank walls and supporting structures, which not only alters the fuel chemically, but blocks filters as well. Not much is required for this - trace elements are enough, although, in reduced temperatures, dissolved water will escape as free water, and look like fog. Aviation fuel is "clean" if a one-quart sample is clear of sediment when viewed through a clean, dry, clear glass container, and looks clear and bright.

Note: It has been found that when visible water is present in jet fuel containing anti-icing additive, the additive will separate from the fuel and be attracted to the water. After a certain amount, thought to be about 15%, the density of the new liquid changes so much that it is not identified as water, and will therefore pass through water filters, and will not be detected by water finding paste. Where the ratio becomes 50%, as much as 10% of whatever is going through the filter could actually be water, which is very likely to get to the engine, since the filters on the airframe itself are not as restrictive.

Turbine aircraft at high altitudes use fuel heaters (actually heat exchangers based on bleed air or engine oil) to melt the ice crystals that form in the fuel up there.

Aircraft parked overnight should ideally have tanks completely filled to stop condensation, but this is impractical if you expect a full load the next morning and don't have room for full fuel as well, in which case be prepared to do extensive sampling from the tanks. Half filled drums left overnight should not be used for the same reasons, but, in remote places (like the Arctic), fuel is a precious commodity and you think more than twice before discarding any (as it happens, drums are scarce too, and they may get used for all sorts of things, particularly diesel for drills, so beware - always smell the contents first). Full drums are usually delivered to a remote cache by Twin Otter or something, and they should be sealed straight from the refuellers-as you tend to use any remainder in a very short time, this can be minimised somewhat. Look for a fill date, as fuel over two years old should be looked at sceptically. Also look for a large X, which is the accepted symbol for contamination, although not everyone has a black marker with them.

An unofficial, but excellent substitute for water paste or detectors with jet fuel is food colouring, which you can at least get in the local grocery store, even if you're in Baffin Island. All you need is one drop - if there is no water, it will disperse evenly over the surface. If there is water, the food colouring will go directly to the water droplets, which will be more visible anyway from the colour.

Drums should not be stored vertically for long periods, because the bungs are not airtight, even though they might stop fuel from leaking out (although it is good idea to stand them vertically for about half an hour before you use the fuel). When the contents contract as the air cools overnight, water inside the rim and collecting around the bung can be sucked in as well, so either store the drums on their sides, with openings at 3 or 9 o'clock, or stick something underneath at 12 o'clock that causes the drum to slant enough to stop rainwater collecting and covering the bungs. Other openings or connections should be protected with blanks or covers, or at least have their openings left facing downwards. Drain plugs, valves, filter bowls, sumps and filter meshes should be checked daily for sediment, slime or corrosion. Always have spare filters.

The reason why long-term storage is not good for fuel (up to two years for drums is the accepted maximum) is partly because of daily temperature changes. When it is warm, the fuel expands and some of the vapour-air mixture is driven out. When it gets colder, the fuel contracts and fresh air is sucked in, to mix with more vapour. As the cycle repeats itself, the fuel inside gradually loses its effectiveness. Humidity will mean that water vapour will get in, too, and condense into liquid. The presence of oxygen will also cause a gum to form, which is more apparent when fuel evaporates (the fuel filter is designed to remove it).

Containers should be filled to 95%, and sealed tightly, where the temperature is mostly below 80°F, out of direct sunlight - the 5% airspace allows room for expansion.

Each day before flying, and when the fuel is settled, carry out a water check in aircraft and containers (but see below, for drums). Collect samples in a transparent container and check for sediment, free water or cloudiness-if there is only one liquid, ensure it is not all water. The instructions for using water detectors are displayed on the containers. In the Arctic, unless there is a thaw in Summer, separated water will be frozen in the bottom of the drum, and you will only have to worry about that in suspension. Water-finding paste, however, will not detect suspended water, and is as an additional test, not a replacement for a proper inspection. Oxidised fuel is darker than normal with a rancid smell (rotten eggs indicates fungal activity).

Naturally, only competent and authorised personnel should operate fuelling equipment, who must also be fully briefed by their Company. In practice, of course, refuellers know very well what they're doing, but you should still be in full communication with them. In general, the following precautions should be taken:

- Documentation must reflect the fuel's origins and its correct handling.

- Vehicles must be roadworthy and regularly inspected.

- Fire extinguishing equipment must be available and crews familiar with its use.

- Barrels, when used, should be undamaged and in date (give-aways for this include faded labels). Over long periods, a fungus can grow, which will clog fuel lines. When checking a drum, have it standing for as long as possible, but at least half an hour (although the benefits of this are negated when drums are stored on their side at the fuel cache and you need the fuel in a hurry). Place a block of wood at some point between the bungs, so that dirty fuel is kept more away from the openings and any garbage at the bottom is away from the bottom of the standpipe. Then draw a sample from as far down as you can through a water detector. If you put the standpipe in, block the top with the palm of your hand, and pull it out, you can empty the standpipe into a container to make this easier. Smell the contents - don't trust labels or colours if the seal's broken. Also, get used to the weight - water weighs more and avgas weighs less than turbine fuel. An **X** on the drum means contamination. Secure it afterwards so it doesn't roll around the landing.

- Run fuel for a few seconds to clear the pipes of bugs and condensation, etc., that may be downstream of the filters.

- Maintain a clear exit path for removal of equipment in emergency.

- The aircraft, fuelling vehicle, hose nozzle, filters or anything else through which fuel passes should be electrically bonded before the fuel cap is removed. The accepted procedure is drum to ground, drum to pump, pump to aircraft, nozzle to aircraft then open the cap. The reverse when finished. Be particularly careful when it's cold, as the air might be dry, and airborne snow particles add their own friction and static. However, according to NFPA 407, App A A-3-4, if the machine and drum are bonded, they don't need to be grounded. This is because "it does not prevent sparking at the fuel surface" (NFPA 77, Recommended Practice on Static Electricity). The National Fire Protection Association is the authority on this subject). It's not only the movement of fuel through pipes and filters (especially filters) that generates static, but also a fault in some part of the system may apply a voltage to the nozzle. Plastics don't help, and using chamois as a filter is dangerous. If you do feel the need to ground anything, salt water is better than permafrost.

- Don't refuel within 100 feet of radar equipment that is operating. Only essential switches should be operated, with radio silence observed.

- Avoid fuelling during electrical storms, and don't use bulbs or flash equipment in the fuelling zone. Non-essential engines should not be run, but if any already doing so are stopped, they should not be restarted until fuel has ceased flowing, with no risk of igniting vapours.

- Brakes or chocks should be applied, but some places require brakes off when near fixed installations.

- Take out rescue and survival equipment so if it blows up you still have it.

Most important is daily checking, before flying.

Note: *Fuel can burn you.* High vapour concentrations will irritate the eyes, nose, throat and lungs and may cause anaesthesia, headaches, dizziness and other central nervous system problems. Ingestion (like when siphoning) may cause bronchopneumonia or similar nasties, including leukemia and death. If you get it on your clothes, ground yourself before removing any and rinse them in clean water. Fuel spills must be covered with dirt as quickly as possible. Otherwise, everyone not involved should keep clear - at least 50m away, but for exceptions see later.

Fuel density changes with temperature - on a hot day, you won't get as much in, and will get less endurance. So, the colder the temperature, the heavier the fuel. In general, you can take avgas as 6 lbs per US gal, Jet A at 6.8 lbs and Jet B at 6.5.

Passengers on Board

Not normally, especially with engines running, but in certain circumstances (i.e. casevac, bad weather, no transport, or on an oil rig) it may be permitted, if:

- Passengers are warned that they must not produce ignition of any substance by any means (including electrical switches). They must also remain seated, with belts/harnesses unfastened.

- "Fasten Seat Belt" signs are off, and NO SMOKING signs on, with sufficient interior lighting to identify emergency exits.

- A responsible person is at each main door which should be open and unobstructed.

- Fuellers are notified if vapour is detected in the cabin.

- Ground activities do not create hazards: the bowser or installation should not stop people leaving in a hurry.

- ATC and the Fire Authority are informed.

- Fire extinguishers are nearby.

BIRD & WILDLIFE HAZARDS - CAR 302/RAC 1.15

In Canada, the concern is not only for aircraft, but also the birds, as they can pollinate flowers and remove insect pests from commercial food crops and forest species. One pair of Warblers, for example, can remove caterpillars from over 1 million leaves within the 2-3 week period that they are feeding their nestlings.

Prevention is better than cure, and you may like to avoid birds as much as possible rather than hit any. Notifications of permanent or seasonal concentrations are found in NOTAMs, and other information is found on the ATIS or from other crew reports, but birds are mostly attracted by open refuse tips and least attracted by long grass. Otherwise, you can expect them at bird sanctuaries or along shorelines or rivers in Autumn or Spring - migratory birds use line features for navigation as well, but they don't necessarily keep 300m to the right (joke). Migration routes typically follow mountain ranges or coastlines, and may utilise updrafts and other wind patterns or avoid barriers like large stretches of open water. In fact, routes out and back are often different. There are bird migration maps in the AIM, RAC 1.15.

If you see a potentially hazardous flock of birds you should *climb at a safe speed* and inform ATC if possible. If you get a birdstrike, stop and inspect the damage. If you can't, make sure you have controllability before trying to land again - fly the aircraft first. After landing, report the incident on the appropriate form.

Noticeably fewer birdstrikes occur at height, so try to fly as high as possible, certainly above 1500 or even 3000 ft (40% of strikes occur on the ground, or during takeoff and landing. 15% occur up to about 100' agl. One of the highest so far hit a DC-8 at FL 390).

Speed is also a factor (*Niering* 1990) because half the speed means a quarter of the impact energy. Since the highest risk occurs under 500 m, the lower you go, the slower you should be.

A short delay on the approach could mean the clearance of a group of birds, as they do move in waves. Groups of birds will usually break away downwards from anything hazardous, so try to fly upwards if possible. You could also use landing lights to make yourself more visible, especially where two are flashing alternately. Avoid freshly ploughed or harvested fields, and beware of updraughts in mountains areas, where birds will be trying to get some free lift. Birds are most active at dawn and dusk.

Windshields

The force from a bird impact increases with the square of the speed - at 110 kts, the impact from a 1 lb bird can exceed 1200 lbs sq/inch (the force is actually determined by the square of your speed multiplied by the mass of the bird). The problem is that, below a certain weight, the windshield will only be designed to keep out rain and insects. However, a hot windshield is more pliable and less likely to shatter if it gets hit - some aircraft need these on for take-off and landing, but if there is nothing in the flight manual, use 15 minutes.

Overheating is as bad as underheating, so be wary if your aircraft has been left in the sun a long time.

Migratory Birds

Although most birdstrikes happen between July-October (during daylight hours), the chances are 5 times higher during the migratory season (*Jerome* 1976).

A migratory bird is one that has a seasonal and somewhat predictable pattern of movement (birds migrate to increase their chances of breeding). More than 90% of Canadian birds are migratory. Neotropical migratory birds breed in Canada and the United States during Summer and spend Winter in Mexico, Central America, South America or the Caribbean islands. A more strict definition says that they are "Western Hemisphere species in which the majority of individuals breed North of the Tropic of Cancer and Winters south of that latitude".

There are about 200 species, with the majority being songbirds like warblers, thrushes, etc., but there are also many shorebirds such as sandpipers, plovers, and terns, raptors (hawks, kites and vultures), and a few waterfowl (such as teal). Although not technically a Neotropical bird, the champion is the Arctic Tern, that can cover 22,000 miles (35,400 km) annually between the Poles.

Most long-distance migratory songbirds and shorebirds, and some waterfowl, migrate at night in cooler temperatures and calmer air, where predators are few. Others, such as hawks and vultures, may utilise daylight because they soar and glide on rising currents of air, or because they feed on flying insects that are active then.

Large birds may use a V-formation (echelon) to conserve energy due to drag reduction - individual savings can be between 12–20%.

Birds choose flight altitudes according to where the best winds are found. Because winds at higher altitudes are stronger than those below, they fly higher with tailwinds and lower with headwinds. They also fly higher at night and when crossing large bodies of water.

Around 90% of strikes occur below 2,000 m (*Satheesan* 1990). 75% of songbirds fly between 500 and 2,000 feet (150- 600 m), but most do so within the following ranges:

	Feet	Meters
Songbirds	500-6,000	150-2,000
Shorebirds	1,000-13,000	300-4,000
Waterfowl	200-4,000	60-1,200
Raptors	700-4,000	200-1,200

Bar-headed Geese are known to cross the Himalayas at 29,500 feet (9,000 m). The world record holder is a Ruppell's Griffon Vulture seen at 37,000 feet (11,300 m.)

The migratory bird regulations prohibit the killing of such birds through the use of an aeroplane, but I suspect you should include helicopters. Low flying aircraft in particular can severely damage their harvesting areas, particularly those for geese. Assistance may be sought from Game officers whose contact details are listed in RAC 1.14.2.

Note: Wildlife hazards include the following list, which is not exhaustive, in descending order of risk to either side:

- deer
- geese
- gulls
- hawks
- ducks
- coyotes
- owls
- rock doves and pigeons
- bald and golden eagles
- sandhill cranes
- sparrows and snow buntings
- shorebirds

- blackbirds and starlings

- crows and ravens

- swallows

- mourning doves

- herons

- turkey vultures

- American kestrels

- wild turkeys

- cormorants

WINTER OPERATIONS

Although colder air means there's less danger of exceeding temperature limits, there are hazards, too, including freezing precipitation, low ceilings and cold temperatures. Rapid changes in these are typical, and it's possible to get weathered in for days at a time, so don't forget your chocolate bars.

The Weather

In the Frozen North, the best conditions are in late winter or early spring, with a major problem being darkness. Once the snow is down, the air is quite dry and it can stay clear and cold for long periods, so you can ignore fog and the rest until it gets a bit warmer.

Above the 60th parallel, don't expect the weather to behave rationally at all. For example, further South, the East wind is responsible for bad flying conditions, but up there the West wind is the one to look out for, as well as large swings between low and high pressure which will often bear no relation to what the weather is doing (so don't rely on cloud shadows over the ground as an indicator of surface wind speed). Aside from barometric changes, look out for wind shifts, which will bring changes in wind speed and amounts of blowing snow and less visibility - even a difference of 100 feet in elevation can mean the difference between snow or not. Temperature changes often mean bad weather is approaching from the North - if it drops, expect ice crystal fog, which is the low level equivalent of contrails made at high altitude, and created by air disturbance, which could actually be from the aircraft itself. Rising temperatures will produce melting and poor visibility. The chill factor from rotors can reduce the ambient temperature by several degrees.

When it gets to below -20 or so, contact gloves will prevent your skin freezing when it comes in contact with cold metal, which is a more efficient conductor of heat than air is. You may also need sunglasses. Always dress properly-in a forced landing it could be that the clothes you wear will be the only protection you have. Also, being cold when you are actually flying is a Flight Safety hazard - metal foot pedals will conduct heat away from your boots very quickly. Extra time for planning should always be allowed and the pre-flight inspection should include you-being improperly dressed and making a series of short exposures will fatigue you more quickly, especially when the clothes you are wearing are bulky and awkward to move in. Maintain blood sugar levels as more calories are consumed in the cold (you need 3000 calories a day in the Arctic in Winter). If the air is very dry, you will lose fluids more quickly through the usual ways, but especially breathing. Losing 10% causes cause delirium, and a 20% loss is fatal. You could try and eat snow, but the conversion to water takes more energy, so melt it first.

Preserve your machine's heat as much as possible on the ground, by covering vital areas as soon as possible after landing, not opening and closing doors too much, etc. It's very important that it does not get so cold that it won't start again, so you might consider starting up every couple of hours or so, which will both use fuel and battery capacity - certainly, in the average car, it takes about half an hour's driving to replace the energy taken by one start, and I'm sure it's worse with an aircraft - a depleted battery will sooner or later mean an expensive hot start. At the very least, remove the battery and keep it warm. If you see fan heaters around the helipad, they are for putting under the covers to keep the engine and gearbox warm (all night). Light bulbs are good, too, around the FCU.

Special attention should also be paid to the following:

- That correct oil and grease is used and special equipment (like winter cooling restrictors) is fitted to keep engines warm. For Bell 206s, at least, below -40C, your oil must meet MIL L7808 specifications, and you will need fuel additives in all fuels other than JP4 below -18C. **Note**: It has been found that when visible water is present in jet fuel containing anti-icing additive, the additive will separate from the fuel and be attracted to the water. After a certain amount, thought to be about 15%,the density of the new liquid changes so much that it is not identified as water, and will therefore pass through water filters, and will also not be detected by water finding paste, which is not, in any case, intended to detect water in suspension. Where the ratio becomes 50%, as much as 10% of whatever is going through the filter could be water, which is very likely to get to the engine, since the filters on the airframe itself are not as restrictive.

• Use deicing fluid if possible - scrapers do not leave pretty results. Fluid, if it's thick enough, helps prevent further ice forming (see the tables in Chapter 6). Don't forget to fit engine blanks, etc. before using them. Deicing fluids are also good degreasers.

• That windscreens are defrosted (keep moving a mechanical heater around, or it might melt the perspex). Don't forget to have a cloth handy for wiping the windscreen from the inside when it mists up.

• You have proper tie-downs and pitot/engine covers, static vent plugs, etc.

• That heating systems are working properly and don't allow exhaust into the cabin (if you get regular headaches, check for carbon monoxide poisoning).

• De-icing and anti-icing equipment is working properly and that all breather pipes, etc. are clear of anything that could freeze.

• That the aircraft has not been cold soaked below minimum operating temperatures. If so, there are particular (and tedious) ways of starting the machine again, which essentially involve preserving the heat from repeated attempted starts so the engine compartment can warm up, with a ten-minute gap between each, removing and replacing engine blankets every time. In case you were wondering, cold soaking occurs when the aircraft and fuel become colder than the ambient temperature, which can happen over a cold night or at high altitudes, and it becomes a problem because heat is conducted more quickly away from precipitation, making ice formation easier. A 737 took off from Toronto, which was cold, and arrived in Nassau, which was warm, with heavy frost on the upper wings (it was melted by refuelling with warmer fuel).

• That frost, ice and snow has been removed, particularly on lift-producing surfaces. If you leave hoar frost on the fuselage (only if it can be seen through), beware of flying into cloud where more

will stick. It must be removed from where its dislodgement could cause ingestion, e.g. engine cowlings.

• Check particle separators as water seepage may have frozen inside the engine, resulting in abnormally high N_1 and JPT.

• That the skids are not frozen to the ground. On a solid surface, you might be able to rock the machine using the tail. Otherwise, use the pedals with a little collective just before takeoff.

• That you unstick windscreen wipers and moving parts (including rotors) by hand, or you will strain the motors.

• That control linkages and movement are checked.

• That pitot heat is checked by hand - don't accept a flicker on the ammeter.

• Water drains are not frozen.

• That carb heat is checked.

Static becomes problem when it's cold, as snow and air can be very dry and therefore good electrical insulators - a helicopter can retain its normal static charge efficiently when landing on snow (before refuelling, remove your survival kit, so if it blows up you've got something to wear after you've warmed your hands in the fire).

When possible, the first start of the day should be an external one. With a turbine in cold weather you can expect a lower achieved N_1 before light up with abnormally high JPT peaks, eventually settling down lower than normal. Oil pressure will be slow to rise, but high after starting - do not go above ground idle until pressures are in the green and will stay there as you increase the throttle. Temperature, on the other hand, will be very slow to rise at all, and you want the transmission to be at least indicating something, which will mean the engine oil is OK as well, as it gets hot quicker. Allow the electrics to warm up as well - even the knobs can get brittle.

Don't wind up too quickly in case you spin or yaw on the pad, especially if there's an engineer on a ladder doing a leak check. If the machine has been frozen to the ground, one skid may come free first and cause a rollover. Taxi slowly with caution if the taxiways are clear of snow. If not, taxi higher and slightly faster then normal to keep out of the snow cloud. If you have wheels, act as if you have no brakes.

Marshallers should be well clear and move slowly themselves. If the heater is required to be off in the hover, ensure the blower is on, to help clear the windscreen.

Whiteout

See under *Visibility* in the *Meteorology* chapter.

The Cruise

Mountain wave clouds can be loaded with heavy ice at remarkably low temperatures (remember that low pressures and low temperatures will cause your altimeter to read high). When using anti-icing, take into account the inaccuracy of the temperature gauges, so if you must turn it on at 4°, and the temperature gauge is only accurate to within 2, start thinking about it at 6°.

Wet and sticky snow has more chance of icing, and is associated with low visibility, which would indicate that you shouldn't be flying anyway. Luckily, light powdery snow tends not to accumulate, but will still give you the leans. Whatever type you fly in, use snow baffles.

Visibility, by the way, includes the inside! When it's very cold, water vapour (from clothes, breath, etc.) will freeze on the windscreen, so warming up the machine before passengers get in will help a lot.

Navigation

Sun Tables are used for resetting your DI in the Arctic, with true sun bearings taken every 20 minutes or so (assuming you can see it), based on the fact that we know where the Sun will be with reference to True North for a given time, date, latitude and longitude. Having obtained the local time, look in the tables for the Sun's bearing, point the nose towards it and set the DI to True North. The two types of navigation are True North and Grid North (to find Grid North, add your longitude to True North, and vice versa).

In True North navigation, headings have to be measured from your point of departure, using the longitude of your departure point as a base line. Every time you cross a longitude, you add a degree going East, and subtract going West, so if you cross 10 longitudes enroute on a heading of 090T, your return heading will be 280T, not 270.

Many pilots drop dye balloons en route so they can find their way back. Others fly low enough to create a disturbance in the snow surface with their downwash, with the obvious dangers.

Landing

Landing Sites should be selected with a view to pulling out of a resulting snow cloud if necessary. That is, you may need to escape somewhere.

The colour of ice can be a good clue as to its suitability. White or blue is the thickest, and therefore safest, whereas black ice may have running water underneath and will be quite thin (for this reason, avoid inflows or outflows of streams or rivers). Granular, dirty looking ice is melting. Large puddles or sheets of water are also a dead giveaway. However, ice is never really safe - it doesn't matter how many heavy water trucks the customer may have parked there that week, helicopters vibrate a lot more than trucks do or, more particularly, in a different way, and the hole punched through for the hosepipe has already weakened the structure. Also, however thick they tell you the ice is, you have no way of knowing whether it is actually supported by water underneath (the level may have dropped), or whether any running water has eroded the under surface. Neither do you know whether any snow on top has shielded the ice from the cold, or whether the Sun's rays have reacted with bare ice to act as a lens and create temperatures dangerously close to a thaw, during which ice several feet thick can often become composed of long vertical needles, known as candle ice (read those old Hudson Bay survival manuals). Try and land somewhere else first.

Shut down carefully on an icy surface, anticipating ground spin. After shutdown, fill any fuel tanks to prevent condensation, always being aware of the next payload. Remove batteries if temperatures are forecast to be below -10°C. Try to park the machine facing the sunrise, so the Sun's warmth can help with de-icing the windscreen.

Also see that the battery is fully charged before departing from base, and consider taking a spare, together with an external start cable- if the ship's battery runs down completely, the plates will become sulphated and won't actually hold a charge so, even if you start from an external source, you won't be able to start again without one if you shut down. A good ploy is to use the external battery for operating electric fuel pumps, etc. Check that heaters, blowers, etc. work and that snow deflectors are fitted. Also, note whether tie downs and covers are serviceable. De-icing fluid cans should always be carried, as should a small amount of food. If all this becomes too much, consider a support vehicle.

REMOTE OPERATIONS

Because of the difficulties of communication in remote areas, Ops, or someone responsible, must know where you are. If you have to make a forced landing, you must ensure that the Company is notified together with the appropriate ATC, so that overdue action is not started unnecessarily. In the Sparsely Settled Area of Canada you must be able to communicate with a ground station from any point along your route, which means using SSB HF (5680 KHz), unless within 25 nm of your base or an airport.

When leaving passengers in an isolated position, make sure of a couple of things. Firstly, everyone understands the time (and date) of pickup, the location and the method of backup transportation. Also, keep a record of the names, all relevant grid references, etc. Learn how to use the "man overboard" facility on your GPS, so you can go back immediately to your last position.

Keep in mind the recovery problems should the engines fail to start after a shutdown; always position as close as possible to a track or road to save trouble later (engineers like being near a pub as well, if you can manage it). The track or road will also help as a line feature to make your way back with if you wander off and get lost.

Don't let your fuel get too low - it's usually delivered to accurate GPS co-ordinates, which may be on top of a frozen lake so the drums will sink in Spring and not be there when you want them. Either that or Ops may have written them down wrongly. My point is that the added stress of looking for fuel that isn't there when you're short is not what you need.

Assuming passengers don't carry too much baggage, you should be able to carry a few home comforts, such as a tent, a stove that runs on aircraft fuel, high-calorie food and a sleeping bag rated for the temperatures you expect to meet. Keep it out of the aircraft when refuelling, so you don't get left with nothing if it catches fire.

If you're forced down, the first task (if necessary) is to assist survivors and apply First Aid, after turning on the ELT, and the second to provide shelter (once the ELT is on, leave it on, as that will make best use of the batteries). The absence of food and water should not become a problem for some time if everyone's had their breakfast - even in the Arctic, in Summer, there's plenty of water around, but you would still be wise to boil it first, for at least 5 minutes, as cold does not kill germs. Try not to eat or drink at all for the first few.

MOUNTAIN FLYING

Note: This covers the basics for exams only.

Refer also to the *Meteorology* chapter for wind behaviour.

Look out for a book called *Designated Mountain Areas*, which tells you which parts of the country are mountains or not.

In the mountains, general principles common to other areas will be vastly different. You must be prepared to adapt your flying techniques as the need arises, for the peculiarities of the region and the type of aircraft. In other words, have not only Plan A, but Plan B, C, etc. up your sleeve, because, very often, once you've looked at a site and gone round for finals, you will find a cloud has got there before you! You cannot afford to assume that a particular situation is the same as, or similar to, any other you might have encountered previously. You can also expect fog, especially in the early morning, which will often stick to the sides of valleys for quite some time. Sometimes, you can create your own clouds, by pulling down warm air from an inversion above.

However, air behaves the same way round pointy bits of ground whatever its height above sea level, and this includes flying around buildings (we will look at laminar flow shortly). The big difference here is that you have less power to play with, hence the mention of density altitude.

Performance changes drastically when both temperature and height increase-just the opposite to flying in cold weather, but you knew that anyway. As far as altitude is concerned, low-level operations (below about 5000 feet) probably won't need you to get too concerned, apart from taking notice of airspeed placards and power limitations, because some of the power lost with altitude is regained with cooler temperatures. You will find that at least 75% power is available to a fair height, but be careful (some pilots report no real difference up to 8500 feet).

Power available is reduced with height (and temperature), and rotors turn at the same speed, so, as you increase altitude, higher pitch and power settings will be required (in some helicopters, like the 500C, the rotor blades will stall before you reach engine limits). The dynamic pressure applied to the ASI is also reduced, so IAS will read less in relation to TAS, so, if you maintain a particular airspeed, your groundspeed will increase accordingly, and you will be going faster than you think. The ASI will also be slower to react.

Density Altitude is your real altitude resulting from height, temperature and humidity. The more the density of the air decreases for any of those reasons, the higher your machine thinks it is. The effects are found at sea level, as well as in mountains, when temperatures are high - for example, 90° (F) at sea level is really 1900 feet as far as your aircraft is concerned. In extreme situations, you may have to restrict your operations to early morning or late afternoon in some areas.

Larger control movements will be needed, with more lag, so controls must be moved smoothly and gradually, or the effects may well cancel each other out - you may be on the ground well before that large handful of collective pitch even takes effect! Rotor RPM will rise very quickly with the least excuse.

Your maximum weight for a given altitude (and vice versa), as well as cruising speed in relation to them both should be known, at least approximately, in advance. You also need to know the Hover ceiling In and Out of Ground Effect (HIGE/HOGE) for any weight, so you know you can come to a low hover properly, however briefly, and recover from an unsuitable landing site (hovering should actually be minimised, partly because you can't rely on ground effect being present, and you have less power anyway, but also because you need to keep a little up your sleeve if the wind shifts, or you begin to lose tail rotor authority. Having said that, no-hover landings are not recommended, because of the chances of snagging the skids on something). Check the performance charts in the back of the Flight Manual, and start practising hovers about 1-2 feet off the ground, bearing in mind, of course, that the said charts were established by test pilots, in controlled situations.

If you allow for these effects during flight planning, fine, but it's easy to get used to a particular place and air density and a corresponding take-off run, base leg, etc., and you may get caught out one day when things change.

Illusions

There is a psychological aspect to mountain flying. In the initial stages, it requires a good deal of self-control, as you overcome a certain amount of fear and tension, which is not good when you need to be relaxed on the controls. You will also have to cope with some optical illusions.

Almost the first thing you will notice is the lack of a natural horizon, and will maybe want to use the mountain tops or sides as a substitute. This, however, may cause a climb, or other exaggerated attitudes, and make it difficult to estimate the height of distant ground, either from a cockpit or on the ground itself, so you will find it best to superimpose a horizon of your own below the peaks. This

is where using your instruments will help, both to keep attitude and give you a good idea of your height and speed (but you're not supposed to be instrument flying!)

Close to the ground, you will get an impression of increased speed, especially near to a ridge. For example, climbing along a long shallow slope is often coupled with an unconscious attempt to maintain height without increasing power so, unless you keep an eye on the ASI, you will be in danger of gradually reducing speed-if your airspeed is reducing, then either the nose has been lifted or you're in a downdraught (downdraughts will be associated with a loss of height or airspeed for the same power). You can also tell if you're in a downdraught by watching the position of the nose-if it yaws into the slope, the air is flowing downwards and vice versa. A lack of cloud above, i.e. descending air, is also a possible indication.

Downdraughts can frequently exceed your climbing capabilities. Strong updraughts can suspend you in mid-air with zero power - if the air subsides suddenly, you will be going down faster than you can apply it. Do not fight it, but guide the aircraft towards a lifting slope, or try for a cleaner column of air.

Approaches to pinnacles (or roof-top helipads) should be steeper than normal as the wind strength increases, because the *demarcation line* between smooth and turbulent air becomes more vertical:

The rate of descent should be controlled with collective, and the rate of closure with the cyclic.

NIGHT FLYING

Night flying can be pleasant - there's less traffic, you tend not to go in bad weather and the air is denser, so the engine and flying controls are more responsive (if they're heavy, the instructor has his hands on as well). There is no VFR at night, so you have to go under IFR (which is not the same as going IMC). You certainly need the same equipment as for IFR and daytime flying, as per Annex 2.

Searching for an overdue aircraft in low light conditions causes lots of problems, and route planning should take account of this. Otherwise, it's much the same as for day, though there are some aspects that demand some thought. Plot your route on the chart in the normal way, but navigate with electronic aids, or features that are prominent at night, such as town lighting, lighted masts, large stretches of water (big black holes), aerodromes, motorways, etc. It's often convenient to go from lighted area to lighted area, but this depends on what you're flying over. However, the easiest way to get around is to know the area you are flying in. Get used to it by day as much as possible, and establish some good safety altitudes.

Refer to *Human Factors* for night flying illusions.

Taxi higher and slower than by day, making no sideways or backwards movements. In autorotations at night, use a constant attitude, at whatever speed is comfortable, to keep the beam from the landing light in the same position on the ground, because otherwise it will shine up into the air when you flare, from which position it's no good to you at all.

WAKE TURBULENCE
· ·

A by-product of lift behind every aircraft, (including helicopters) in forward flight, arising from induced drag, particularly severe from heavy machines, and worst at slow speeds, as on takeoff or landing. Wake vortices are horizontally concentrated whirlwinds streaming from the wingtips, from the separation point between high pressure below and low pressure above the wing. Air flowing over the top of the wing tends to flow inward due to the reduced pressure sucking it in, while that under the wing tends to flow outwards because it is of higher pressure and pushes outwards. Where the lower air curls over the wingtip, it combines with the upper air to form a clockwise flow (on the left wing - on the right it is counter clockwise).

Wake generation begins when the nosewheel lifts off (i.e. as lift is generated) on take-off and continues until it touches down again after landing:

Rotation Point   Safest Area   Touchdown Point

Vortices (one from each wing) drift downwind, at about 400-500 fpm for larger aircraft, levelling out at about 900 feet below the altitude at which they were generated. Eventually they expand to occupy an oval area about 1 wingspan high and 2 wide, one on each side of the aircraft. The distance between them will be about ¾ of the wingspan or rotor disc:

The heavier and slower the aircraft, the more severe the vortices will be, and flaps, etc. will only have a small effect in breaking them up, so even clean aircraft are dangerous.

The effects become undetectable after a time, varying from a few seconds to a few minutes after the departure or arrival, although they have been detected at 20 minutes. Vortices are most hazardous to other aircraft during take-off, initial climb, final approach and landing, but you should be careful any time you are within 1,000 feet below and behind a heavy aircraft.

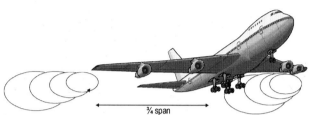

¾ span

Those from large aircraft tend to move away from one another so, on a calm day, the runway itself will remain free, depending on how near the runway edge the offending wings were. They will also drift with wind, so your landings and takeoffs should occur upwind of moving heavy aircraft, before the point of takeoff and after that of landing. Inside a vortex core, you could get roll rates as much as 80° per second and downdraughts of over 1500 feet per minute, so avoid them.

A crosswind will increase the movement of the downwind vortex and decrease that of the upwind one. A light wind of 3-7 knots could mean the upwind one actually stays in the touchdown zone and the downwind one moves to another runway. Since a tailwind can also move the vortices of previous aircraft into the touchdown zone, a light quartering tailwind is the most dangerous position to be in.

Although there is a danger of shockloading, the biggest problem is loss of control near the ground. You are safest if you keep above the approach and take-off path of the other aircraft, or land beyond its touchdown point (or lift off before its takeoff point) but, for general purposes, allow **at least 3 minutes** behind any greater than the Light category (especially widebodies) for the effects to disappear (but see the table below).

Aircraft are grouped into these categories:

Category	ICAO & Flt Plan (lbs)
Heavy (H)*	300,000 or more
Medium (M)	12,5000-300,000
Light (L)	12,500 or less

*The word "Heavy" must be used after the callsign in any initial contact with ATC

Although ATC will normally suggest an interval, this table can be used as a guide, although there are no guarantees, whatever separations are given:

Lead Aircraft	Following Aircraft	Min Dist
Heavy	Heavy	4 nm
Light	Heavy	6 nm
Medium	Heavy	5 nm
Light	Medium	4 nm

Helicopters

Rotor downwash is wake turbulence from helicopters, which is easy to forget when hovering near a runway threshold or parked aircraft with little wind (although it's quite useful when crop spraying). Otherwise, the effects are similar to fixed wing, in that you get vortices from each side of the rotor disc, but the lower operating speed means they are more concentrated.

Downwash also creates dust storms and can lift even heavy objects into the air, instantly presenting *Foreign Object Damage* (FOD) hazards to engines, main and tail rotor blades (so don't bolt your FOD, it gives you ingestion! - old RAF joke, on which I hope there's no copyright). Plastic bags or packaging sheets are FOD, too. Generally speaking, the larger the helicopter, the greater the potential danger (obvious, really). Bell 212, Sikorsky S76 and smaller machines are *Light*, in terms of the above table, but size is not significant when creating vortices; use the table for comparison purposes when avoiding other types. The rotor wake changes within three distinct speed ranges:

- *Up to 20 mph*, the air moves primarily downwards, most of it descending from the outer edges of the blades, so you get a relatively calm area around the fuselage (in other words, you are in the middle of a ring, like a doughnut - you can see this by hovering over water)

- *At 18-22 mph* (on a Bell), the annular ring shortens in the direction of movement to become an ellipse, coinciding with translation. Above 20 mph, the annular ring disappears, and a large

amount of separate, small airflows coalesce to provide an area of ill-defined downward airflow

- *Above 35 mph*, two distinct rotating vortices are formed from directly behind the machine to a long way behind, assuming no outside influence (they are fully developed about 1 rotor diameter behind the mast, and can be sustained for up to 2500 feet). Each vortex starts from where the annular ring would be in the hover, and is relatively calm in the center (in fact, the centre-to-centre distance between them is just under the rotor diameter, and slightly displaced from the centre towards the retreating blade). Regard them as large funnels extending rearward and downward, getting bigger as they go. There is still a downward flow.

DANGEROUS GOODS (ANX 18)

The carriage of dangerous goods by air may only be done with the approval of the relevant National Aviation Authority (FAA, CAA, Transport Canada, etc.), as per ICAO Annex 18, which is otherwise known as the *ICAO Technical Instructions for the Safe Transport of Dangerous Goods by Air*, and what is incorporated into national laws to give them effect (permanent approval is given in your company's AOC, so check your Ops Manual for further information). Airlines use another document called the *IATA Dangerous Goods Regulations* (referred to as the *Regulations*, described below), which is compiled from Annex 18, but much easier to use, and sometimes more restrictive, due to industry practice and other operational considerations. Because of this, although it has no official force, the Book is accepted as a *working*, or *field document* for non-airlines, even though it says clearly in the front that it does not apply to them (1.2.1). In the event of a legal dispute, the ICAO Technical Instructions prevail.

The Technical Instructions are supposed to provide the basis under which Dangerous Goods can be transported safely by air, at a level that ensures no additional risk to the aircraft or its occupants (in other words, an *incident* is not supposed to lead to an *accident*). The classifications inside it are determined by a UN sub-committee of experts.

For our purposes, the term *Dangerous Goods* includes anything that poses a significant risk to health, safety or property *when transported by air*, including aerosols, solvents, paints, chainsaws, matches, stoves, car batteries, gas tanks and even magnets or perfume under the right circumstances - in other words, mostly stuff that anyone may have at home, but subjected to the adverse forces involved in transportation, such as expansion and compression, or simply being handled differently (fuel evaporates more quickly at altitude). Even a 9-volt battery can generate enough heat to start a fire when its terminals are shorted out. Dangerous Goods could be toxic, flammable, corrosive, infectious, radioactive or explosive, or a combination, and the rules apply regardless of the reason for their movement, commercial or private. Many items already carried in an aircraft are hazardous, including fuel, ethylene glycol, methyl alcohol, halon, hydraulic fluid, carbon monoxide, etc., but they will be exempt from the regulations to a certain extent, because they are needed for airworthiness purposes, or for sale to passengers (perfumes, or alcohol).

Everyone in the transport chain (including passengers) needs to be aware of the dangers, and their responsibilities, and your company has a legal liability to ensure that employees are trained properly. As a working pilot, flight attendant, or a member of the ground staff, you really only need an awareness of the subject, since you have no authority to change any paperwork or play around with packaging, but if you are a *shipper*, your knowledge needs to be much more extensive (it's very easy for you to change roles, because, out in remote places, your passengers may well turn up with dangerous goods and expect you to handle all the details).

Dangerous Goods actually come in nine classes, described below, which should have a diamond-shaped label on their packaging to identify them, like the one on the left (the number at the bottom identifies the hazard class). Sometimes, there will be two labels, where a substance or material comes with more than one risk, in which case, one will be a *primary* and the other a *secondary* label (secondaries do not have classifications). *Handling labels* (e.g. "This Way Up") are

rectangular. On the left is a typical situation in which the label will be used, on the side of a fuel bowser, and the first thing that a firefighter will look at when called to an incident.

Packing Groups indicate degrees of danger within classes, which leads nicely to one key to the safe transport of Dangerous Goods, which is packaging - *single packaging* means things like oil drums or propane cylinders, by

themselves. *Combination packaging* covers batteries or bottles, etc. inside boxes that keep them safe (in other words, there is some element of doubling up, like with a crate of beer - the beer is in the bottle first, which then is in a crate). If you need it, approved packaging can be obtained from various manufacturers (see the IATA regulations), but it will be relatively expensive, since they have a hold on the market. However, if you ship the goods in *Limited Quantities*, specialised packaging may not be needed, though it should still be of good quality. *Salvage Packaging*, which is not usually seen, is not for shipping, but recovering Dangerous Goods after an incident.

After packaging, the other key to safe transport is *training*, the idea being to make sure you know how the stuff is packaged in the first place and what to do if it leaks or is otherwise damaged, because it may affect the flight characteristics of your machine, and the way an emergency is handled by people on the ground. Recurrent training must take place at least every two years. Another reason for training is to ensure that the security paper trail is preserved - since, in theory, it is the *shipper's* responsibility to ensure that Dangerous Goods are packaged properly, the only way everyone else knows what is in the box is by reading the paperwork. Thus, as with the rest of the aviation industry, much of what you do is based on trust, and you shouldn't really be carrying anything without pieces of paper stating that all regulations have been complied with. In fact, there can be severe penalties involved if things aren't done right (in the USA, especially, including custodial sentences, as the engineers who put the oxygen generators on the flight that ended up in the Florida Everglades found out), so it is to your benefit that you learn what you can. What knowledge is required at each level in the chain is in the Regulations, but, generally speaking, the average person would need to know what Dangerous Goods are, the general philosophy behind them, limitations, passenger and crew allowances, recognition of undeclared Dangerous Goods, labelling & marking, storage and loading, the *Notification To Captain* (NOTOC) and what to do in an Emergency. Thus, you should be able to:

- Define and identify Dangerous Goods by their 9 classes, including those that are forbidden, permitted or exempt

- Use the IATA Regulations Book (actually, the *List of Dangerous Goods*) and apply its information

- Check that packing instructions have been followed

- Verify that marking and labelling is correct, or be able to do it yourself

- Verify information on a Shipper's Declaration, or complete one yourself

- Verify the information on an Air Waybill, or complete one yourself

- Store, handle or load Dangerous Goods

- Know how to notify the PIC of Dangerous Goods loaded

- Know the difference between *Operator's* and *Shipper's* responsibilities

- Know what to do in an emergency

The safest way, of course, is not to transport Dangerous Goods at all, but you still need to recognise them in order to exclude them, and there is often a commercial demand to move such cargoes to remote places, where air transport provides the only way in, aside from walking, and passengers, bless them, will hardly ever tell you what's in their baggage anyway. In other words, we need to get the job done with an element of risk management. If risk cannot be eliminated, then those goods are likely prohibited anyway, or at least subject to severe restrictions (the IATA Regulations list around three thousand items by name and quantity allowed).

Applicability

As mentioned above, the IATA Dangerous Goods Regulations apply to:

- all IATA airlines

- any that are party to Cargo Traffic Agreements

- any shippers and agents offering shipments to them

At first sight, therefore, it would appear that anyone who is not an airline is exempt, but ICAO Annex 18 still applies, as amended by your national legislation.

The problem is that it was all written for major air carriers, and can be very restrictive for small operations, particularly when spraying or on fire suppression, so some exemptions are allowed in certain areas. Most are based on common sense, in that your aircraft may be too small to separate goods that require to be kept apart, or you may not even have a cargo hold, but certain things are *not allowed* in *any* aircraft under *any* circumstances, particularly non-refillable gas lighters and those that leak in reduced pressure, or "strike anywhere" matches (they are listed in the Regulations).

Exemptions

Approval is not required if the goods are required for the job in hand, airworthiness of the aircraft, or are extras for the health of passengers and crew, such as fire extinguishers, first-aid kits, insecticides, air fresheners, life saving appliances, pyrotechnics in survival kits and portable oxygen, or anything to do with catering or cabin service (like dry ice, or items for sale on board). Generally, however, spares and replacements for the exempt articles above should be treated as Dangerous Goods.

Neither do you need approval for veterinary aids or humane killers for animals (if used in flight), aviation fuel and oil in aircraft tanks, materials in hoppers or tanks for aerial application. However, exemptions for dangerous goods used for aerial work differ from state to state - refer to the State of operation for details. In the USA, for example, this would be 14 CFR Chapter 1, and in Canada, the TDGR (*Transport of Dangerous Goods Act*) *Section* 12.12. Others include TDGR 12.4: Explosives Class 1.4S, 12.5: Forbidden Explosives*, 12.9: Limited Access, 12.16: Emergency Response.

*Must be listed as a category of operations in the operations manual.

Common sense applies with exempt goods, in that the containers must be properly constructed, staff must be trained, and the items stowed properly. If spraying, the aircraft must be properly ventilated, and you can even carry medical goods on flights before and after patients have been offloaded, if it's impractical to offload them as well. Pesticides could be exempt in safe containers of less than 220 litres, the aircraft is cargo only, there is adequate ventilation, no smoking and local authorities are informed.

Some dangerous goods that are not permitted may be carried (see Table 2.3.A in the IATA Regulations for the full list), and they come in three groups:

GROUP 1

These need approval from operators (check your procedures), with the PIC notified as well:

- Wheelchairs or other battery-powered mobility aids with spillable batteries, *as checked baggage*, and *upright*, with batteries securely attached and disconnected, with terminals insulated against short circuits. If not upright, batteries must be removed and carried upright in strong, rigid, leak-proof packaging (labelled *Battery wet, with wheelchair* or *Battery wet, with mobility aid*, with a *Corrosives* label and marked for orientation). Spill-resistant vent caps should be fitted

- Mercurial barometers or thermometers carried by representatives of government weather bureaux or similar official agencies, as *carry-on baggage only*. The items must be in strong outer packaging, with a sealed inner liner or bag of strong leak-proof and puncture-resistant material impervious to mercury, to stop it escaping from the package, irrespective of its position

- Insulated packaging containing refrigerated liquid nitrogen, otherwise known as *Dry Shippers*, to transport non-dangerous goods at low temperature (in other words, the packaging itself is the dangerous goods!) The packaging must not allow build-up of pressure within the container or the release of any nitrogen, whichever way up it is

GROUP 2

These only require operator approval:

- Dry ice, for perishable items, as checked baggage, not above 2 kg, and the package must allow release of the gas.

- Small gaseous oxygen or air cylinders, required for medical use.

- Not more than 5 kg of securely boxed ammunition (cartridges) for sporting weapons, in **Division 1.4S**, for that person's own use, securely boxed and *in checked baggage only*. Cartridges with explosive or incendiary projectiles are *not* permitted (Division 1.4S is for cartridges packed or designed so that dangerous effects are confined within the package, unless degraded by fire, and which do not hinder fire fighting). Allowances may not be combined.

- Wheelchairs or other battery-powered mobility aids with non-spillable batteries, *as checked baggage*. Batteries must be securely attached and disconnected, with terminals insulated against short circuits.

- Up to 2 small non-flammable gas cylinders in self-inflating lifejackets, and 2 spares.

- Heat producing articles, such as underwater torches and soldering irons, which must be disabled.

- As checked baggage only, one small chemical oxygen generator for respiratory aid (available on the retail market), per person, if (without

packaging) it can withstand a 1.8 m drop onto a rigid, non-resilient flat horizontal surface, in the position most likely to produce damage, without loss of contents and without actuating. There must be at least 2 positive means of preventing unintentional actuation and, at 20°C, no external surface may exceed 100°C. It must be in the manufacturer's original packaged, which must include a sealed outer wrapping against being tampered with, and be marked to indicate compliance with the above.

GROUP 3

These do not need prior approval at all:

- Alcoholic beverages in receptacles under 5 litres, containing 24-70% by volume, up to 5 litres per person

- Non-radioactive medicinal or toilet articles (including aerosols, hair sprays, perfumes, medicines containing alcohol), and, in checked baggage only, aerosols which are non-flammable, non-toxic and without subsidiary risk, for sporting or home use. Not more than ½ ltr or ½ kg per item, total 2 litres or 2 kg

- Small CO_2 cylinders for mechanical limbs, etc., and spares for long journeys

- Safety matches or lighters, for use *on one's person*. 'Strike anywhere' matches, lighters with unabsorbed liquid fuel (other than liquefied gas), lighter fuel and refills are *not permitted* (safety matches will only self-ignite with certain materials, where strike-anywhere matches can ignite with friction against most solids)

- Radio-isotopic pacemakers or other medical implants (including Lithium-powered) for medical purposes

- Hydrocarbon gas powered hair curlers, if the safety cover is securely over the heating element. No gas refills, one per passenger or crew member

- Small personal clinical thermometers containing mercury, cased.

FORBIDDEN

Aside from strike-anywhere matches, disabling devices, such as mace, pepper spray, etc., are prohibited on the person, in checked and carry-on baggage, although, in Canada, pepper spray may be carried externally in a ski basket or similar (they use it against bears). Security-type attache cases, cash bags, etc. that use Lithium batteries are also forbidden.

What To Look For

Sometimes, Dangerous Goods are not obvious. *Hidden* Dangerous Goods could be in the item itself or the packaging. Otherwise, here are just a few items the average pilot might come across and their characteristics:

- *Aerosols* - changing cabin pressure and temperature may result in leaks if the can is not properly sealed. They could also explode if they get overheated from being left in the sun. In addition, the CFC propellant, which is now politically incorrect, has been replaced with butane, which is flammable

- *Aircraft Spares* - explosives (flares, etc.), chemical oxygen generators, compressed air, paint, fuel in equipment, etc.

- *Auto Parts* - these may contain wet batteries, hydraulic fluid (in shocks, etc.), nitrogen, air bag inflators, paint, etc.

- *Camping Equipment* - metal bottles could contain flammable compressed gas or liquid (cooking gas, etc.).

- *Chemicals* - most are dangerous. Always be suspicious! Swimming pool chemicals contain chlorine, which is an organic peroxide

- *Cryogenic Liquids* - this includes low temperature gases, such as liquid nitrogen, CO_2, etc. These are dangerous because your skin will stick to the container if it's cold, and the gas will cause suffocation in confined spaces

- *Dental Apparatus* - flammable resins or solvents, compressed or liquefied gas, mercury and radioactive materials

- *Diagnostic Specimens* - these may contain infectious substances - in fact, *anything* medical should be regarded with suspicion

- *Diving Equipment* - may contain air cylinders with compressed air or other gases, although emptied ones should be OK. Diving lamps have lead-acid batteries

- *Drilling or Mining Equipment* - may contain explosives

- *Dry Cell Batteries* - although not on the list, make sure they don't short out

- *Electrical Equipment* - may contain magnetised material or mercury

- *Electrically Powered Apparatus* - wet batteries (wheelchairs, golf carts)

- *Frozen Food* - may be packed in dry ice (don't confuse fumes with smoke!)

- *Fireworks* - these are explosives

- *Gas Cigarette Lighters* - the cheap non-refillable ones are a pain in the *** - they are dangerous because they leak under the slightest pressure

- *Gas Cylinders* - if filled, only as cargo

- *Household Cleaners* - these can contain chlorides, ammonias, oxidisers, etc. (and even have their own "dangerous" symbols). Ammonia reacts with oxidisers to produce toxic fumes

- *Household Goods* - may include flammable materials, cleaners (see above), aerosols, paint, etc.

- *Instruments and Machine Parts* - may contain mercury, chemicals, solvents, grease. Be especially careful of racing car stuff, and items used for rock shows and movies

- *Lab Test Equipment* - may contain chemicals, solvents, etc. Dental Apparatus may contain resins or solvents

- *Magnets*

- *Matches* - these may not be in checked baggage, but are allowed on a passenger's person. Book matches can easily come apart and strike against another book if packed too tightly against each other. *"Strike anywhere" matches are not allowed*

- *Mercury* - toxic fumes at high temperatures and low pressures. Liquid mercury penetrates aluminium to turn it brittle and weak, so will cause severe structural damage to an aircraft

- *Paint* - should be accepted as cargo only, since most paints are flammable, even if they are water-washable. This includes enamels, lacquers, woodstain, thinners, etc. Reduced pressure can also cause the container to pop open

- *Passenger Service Units* - may contain oxygen generators, which are definitely Dangerous Goods

- *Photographic Equipment* - corrosive chemicals that attack most types of metal used in aircraft construction. They can also cause severe burns

If a package is damaged during loading, you must arrange for its removal

- *Power Tools* - petrol engines, with fuel tanks, power riveters (explosive)
- *Safety Equipment* - Liferafts will contain firemaking equipment, and may even inflate themselves
- *Vaccines* - aside from their own danger, they may be packed in Dry Ice

Units of Measurement

Primarily, the metre (m), kilogram (kg), litre (l) and kilopascal (kPa), or decimals of them all, if clearly specified. Conversion tables are in App B of The Regulations.

Metric units must be used in the Shipper's Declaration.

Responsibilities

Responsibility for compliance lies with the *sender* of Dangerous Goods

There are many people in the chain, and each one needs as much information as possible. The operator (carrier) has the final word as to whether any item should be accepted for transport, and has the right to impose special conditions.

EMPLOYERS

Responsible for making sure that their employees obey the regulations and that they are properly trained, including the issue of appropriate certificates. There is also a requirement to display posters in appropriate areas. Information must be provided to employees as to how they should carry out their duties.

CARRIERS (OPERATORS)

Responsible for goods while in their care. For example, if a label comes off once the package is consigned, the carrier must replace it. Carriers (or their acceptance staff) must not accept any package or overpack unless it is properly packaged, marked and labelled, with *two copies* of a Shipper's Declaration. Neither may they accept leaking or damaged packages, or any marked *Cargo Aircraft Only* for transport on passenger-carrying aircraft. They must use an *acceptance checklist* when accepting Dangerous Goods.

PASSENGERS

Passengers, of course, are not especially trained, but they should still be made aware of the dangers. Information given to them must, at least, consist of prominently displayed notices and information on tickets, or even asking questions at check-in.

SHIPPERS

Responsible for classifying and preparing goods for shipment, including documentation, such as the *Shipper's Declaration*, of which there must be 2. This means determining the classification (including hidden hazards), packing it and labelling it properly.

Training

People working with Dangerous Goods who are not trained must work under the direct supervision of someone who is - such training must be directly relevant to the duties. You are officially trained when your employer considers you so and gives you a certificate.

TRAINING CERTIFICATE

The Training Certificate must show the place of business of the employer, employee's name, the date the training certificate expires, preceded by the words "Expires on", and the aspects of handling, offering for transport or transporting of dangerous goods for which the person was trained for. The certificate must be signed by the employee and by the employer or another employee acting on behalf of the employer or, in the case of a self-employed person, by that person. The Training Certificate is valid for 24 months if issued to a person who is identified in Part 1, Chapter 4 of the ICAO Technical Instructions. A copy must be kept for two years from the date of expiration. Training Certificates are not transferable, but a document issued to a foreign member of the flight crew of an aircraft registered in an ICAO state indicating that the crew member is trained, can be a valid Training Certificate, under ICAO Article 33, when that document is valid in the Member State (check your national regulations - this is so in Canada).

On the request of an inspector, trained people must produce Training Certificates issued to them by their employers.

Undeclared Dangerous Goods

Occasions where undeclared or misreported Dangerous Goods are discovered in cargo or baggage must be reported to the authorities, in an attempt to ensure it doesn't happen again.

Carriage of Employees

When carrying dangerous goods which can only be carried on a cargo aircraft, company employees can also be carried in an official capacity, that is, having duties concerned with the preparation or undertaking of a flight or on the ground once the aircraft has landed.

Classes & Labelling

Packages containing dangerous goods must have diamond-shaped labels that indicate their characteristics by class or division (numbering is for convenience, and does not mean that Class 1 is more dangerous than 9).

- 1 - **Explosives** (Black on Orange) - normally forbidden

  - 1.1 - Mass explosion hazard - REX

  - 1.2 - Projection hazard - REX

  - 1.3 - Minor blast or projection hazard - REX/RCX/RGX

  - 1.4 - No significant hazard - REX

  - 1.5 - Very insensitive - mass explosion - REX

  - 1.6 - Extremely insensitive - no mass explosion - REX

- 2 - **Gases**

  - 2.1 - Flammable (White on Red) - RFG

  - 2.2 - Non-flammable non-toxic (White on Green) - RNG/RCL

  - 2.3 - Toxic Gas (Black on White) - RPG

- 3 - **Flammable Liquids** (White on Red) - RFL

- 4 - **Flammable Solids**

  - 4.1 - Solids (Black on Red/White stripes) - RFS

  - 4.2 - Spontaneous (Black on White, Red lower) - RSC

  - 4.3 - Water reactive (White on Blue) - RFW

- 5 - **Oxidising Substances**, Organic Peroxide

  - 5.1- Oxidising substances (Black on Yellow) - ROX

  - 5.2 - Organic peroxides (Black on Yellow) - ROP

- 6 - **Toxic & Infectious Substances**

  - 6.1 - Toxic substances (Black on White) - RPB

  - 6.2 - Infectious substances (Black on White) - RIS

- 7 - **Radioactive**

  - Category I - (Black on White) - RRW

  - Category II or III (Yellow with White lower half) - RRY

- 8 - **Corrosives** (Black on White) - RCM

- 9 - **Miscellaneous** (Black on White) RMD

You may see other labels, belonging to different hazardous alert systems, such as WHMIS, or even household, or consumer labels, as found on domestic products.

CARGO-IMP CODES

These are the alphanumeric equivalent of the labels, being sets of three letters to be used on flight documents. They are mostly listed above, except, these which will also have their own square label:

- MAG - Magnetised Material

- CAO - Cargo Aircraft Only

- RCL - Cryogenic Liquid

As well, handling labels will have special instructions, like "This Way Up" (2 off, on opposite sides - see above, right), or "Cargo Aircraft Only" (a square one, next to the hazard label). Packages must be marked with the shipping name and UN or ID number. Items packed under *Y instructions* (Section 5) must show the words *Limited Quantity* or *Ltd Qty* (they must also be in Authorisation, in the Shipper's Declaration).

There will also be red-hatched labels to identify Dangerous Goods that have been leaking or are subject to some sort of incident reporting, or for Excepted Packages.

Irrelevant labels should be removed or obliterated.

The UN symbol means that a package has been designed, tested and manufactured to UN specifications.

Multiple Hazards

As mentioned above, there can be two hazards, one of which will take precedence. Table 3.10.A lists some, except classes that always come first:

- 1, 2 and 7

- 5.2 and 6.2

- self-reactive items, and solid desensitised explosives from 4.1

- pyrophoric substances in 4.2

- Anything in 6.1 with Packing Group 1 vapour inhalation toxicity

Otherwise, classes or divisions at intersections of lines in Table 3.10.A are the primary risk. Outer packages may contain more than one item of Dangerous Goods, as long as they don't react dangerously with each other and cause combustion, evolution of gases, corrosion or formation of stable substances. They should also not require segregation.

TWO OR MORE DANGEROUS SUBSTANCES

The technical names of at least two predominant constituents must be shown. For a subsidiary risk label, the component requiring the use of that label must be included, along with qualifying words, such as mixture, or solution. For example, "engine cleaner" will not have its own listing - it is actually a mixture of gasoline and CTC, with a flash point lower than 23°C, coming under 6.1, so it should be called *Flammable Liquid, toxic*.

ONE DANGEROUS SUBSTANCE

If you have a mixture of one listed item, and one not, you should use the listed name, with a qualifying word, such as mixture or solution.

Packaging

Single packaging contains a substance directly, such as a bottle of beer. *Combination packaging* means an outer casing containing inner packaging, which can be treated separately, such as a crate of beer bottles. *Composite*

packaging is similar to combination, but the inner and outer items are treated as one unit. You can mix dangerous goods in an outer package as long as they don't react with each other or otherwise require segregation (see Table 9.3.A), but see also Section 5.5. The same applies to an *overpack*, which is used to combine packagings for convenience, like shrinkwrap (Sect 5.0.1.5 and Appendix A).

Not all Dangerous Goods have the same degree of hazard. Depending on the danger, goods can also be classified into *Packing Groups*:

Group	Danger
I	Great
II	Medium
III	Minor

There is an alphabetical list of Dangerous Goods (the IATA book, section 4.2), where goods have their Class and Packing Group determined for you, with maximum quantities, type of label, etc. Packing instructions are in Sect 5. Be aware that you might need specific containers for certain items. Where more than one hazard is involved, a label must be used for each one.

Packaging must be of good quality and constructed and closed to prevent leakage under normal conditions. Materials used must not react with the goods they are supposed to protect. Enough space must be left in liquid containers to allow for expansion, and there should be absorbent materials to take up leaks.

Packages or overpacks must not be loaded onto an aircraft or a ULD unless they have been inspected immediately beforehand. On unloading, they must be inspected for damage or leakage. If either exists, the position the package occupied must also be inspected. Leaking packages must be removed, and safe disposal arranged. Carriers must replace missing labels in transit. Explosives and detonators must be in their original packaging, and separate from each other. Damaged goods must *not* be carried at all.

Packages must also be secured on board to prevent any movement that would change their orientation.

Documentation

This is part of the (extremely important) communication process, so that everyone knows where the Dangerous Goods are, what's supposed to be in them, what to do if they leak or get damaged, or in any other emergency where outside agencies need to know as well. In addition, the paperwork allows for planning, in case any of the Goods needs to be separate.

ACCEPTANCE CHECKLIST

Required by all operators, and must be used when accepting Dangerous Goods. It basically should ensure that an operator's responsibilities are covered (see above).

SHIPPER'S DECLARATION

Copies should be kept for 2 years, and 2 copies must be given to the carrier, one to be sent with the consignment. The retained copy should be readily available until the items get to their destination.

Metric units must be used.

AIR WAYBILLS

These must show Dangerous and non-Dangerous Goods separately, in that order, except for dry ice used as a refrigerant. They must include one or more of the following statements in the Handling Information box:

- *Dangerous Goods as per attached Shippers Declaration*
- *Dangerous Goods - shippers declaration not required*
- *Cargo Aircraft Only*

NOTIFICATION TO CAPTAIN (NOTOC)

The PIC must be notified in writing of any Dangerous Goods on board the aircraft, and where they are. The document concerned must include at least this information:

- Air Waybill number
- Shipping name & UN number (when assigned, such as Acetone UN1090).
- Class or division, subsidiary risks and, for explosives, Compatibility Group
- Packing group (when assigned)
- Number of packages, net quantity or gross mass per package
- Loading location
- Confirmation of no evidence of damaged or leaking packages.

Typewritten signatures are not acceptable.

Acceptance, Handling and Storage

It is the *shipper's* responsibility to ensure that all is correct (the carrier is responsible for *care in transit*). Before Dangerous Goods are accepted, though, an *acceptance check* ensures that packages, overpacks and containers are not damaged or leaking, are correctly marked and labelled, and documents are correct, according to the Technical Instructions (there should be an example form in the Ops Manual). Unless you loaded it yourself, you must be informed of any Dangerous Goods on your flight with a Notification To Captain (NOTOC).

The loading routine is generally to:

- Fill out a Shipper's Declaration
- Notify the PIC
- Inspect for leakage and condition before loading (see *Acceptance Checklist*)
- Keep a copy of the paperwork.
- Supervise loading and segregation* as required.

*Dangerous Goods, especially toxics, must not be loaded, stowed or secured near foodstuffs, people or live animals (including crews). Those that react with each other should be separated as per the Technical Instructions (see table):

Class or Div	Class or Division							
	1	*2*	*3*	*4.2*	*4.3*	*5.1*	*5.2*	*8*
1	Note 1	Note 2	Note 2	Note 2	Note 2	Note 2	-	Note 2
2	Note 2	-	-	-	-	-	-	-
3	Note 2	-	-	-	-	x	-	-
4.2	Note 2	-	-	-	-	x	-	-
4.3	Note 2	-	-	-	-	-	-	x
5.1	Note 2	-	x	x	-	-	-	-
5.2	Note 2	-	-	-	-	-	-	-
8	Note 2	-	-	-	x	-	-	-

An "x" at the intersection of a row and column means that packages containing these classes of dangerous goods may not be stowed next to or in contact with each other, or where they would interact if a leak occurred. Thus, a package containing Class 3 dangerous goods may not be stowed next to or in contact with a package containing Division 5.1 dangerous goods.

- **Note 1** - See 7:2.2.2.2 - 7:2.2.2.4 of the ICAO Technical Instructions

- **Note 2** - This Class or Division must not be stowed together with explosives other than those in Division 1.4, Compatibility S.

- **Note 3** - Packages containing dangerous goods with multiple hazards in the class or divisions which require segregation in accordance with Table 7-1 need not be segregated from other packages with the same UN number

How to use the IATA Book

The IATA Dangerous Goods Regulations are more restrictive than ICAO Annex 18, and you will see where when you see a pointy hand symbol, like the one on the right. The book itself is divided into ten sections, and subsections are indicated with decimal points, so Section 4.2 is subsection 2 of Section 4. Paragraphs are also numbered, as with *4.2.3* (all are in the Table of Contents). There is also an index and an Index of Tables at the back, together with appendices, but it isn't wonderful.

Here is a sample line out of 4.2 followed by a brief description of the sections:

- *Section 1 - Applicability.* Who and what the regulations apply to, with exemptions, such as medical, animals, etc., plus responsibilities of shippers and training, which may be superseded by National Regulations

- *Section 2 - Limitations.* Goods which are totally forbidden under any circumstances, and those which may be carried with approval, hidden hazards, stuff that can be carried by crews, the property of the carrier and those which are exempt anyway, special provisions for States and operators

- *Section 3 - Classification.* What is in each class, what packing groups indicate

- *Section 4 - Identification.* Official shipping names (in the blue pages). 4.2 is the alphabetical list, and 4.3 is the numerical cross reference, with UN numbers in numerical order to help find the names. 4.4 contains special provisions

- *Section 5 - Packing.* Yellow pages, with details of containers, etc. and packing instructions. No substitutes!

- *Section 6 - Packaging Specifications and Performance Tests.* Mainly for packing manufacturers to make sure their materials do the job

- *Section 7 - Marking and Labelling.* Hazard and handling Labels

- *Section 8 - Documentation.* Waybills, Shipper's Declarations, etc., with examples

- *Section 9 - Handling*

- *Section 10 - Radioactive Material*

- *Appendix A - Glossary*

- *Appendix B - Nomenclature.* Units of Measurement, etc.
- *Appendix C - Organic Peroxides*
- *Appendix D - IATA Member List*
- *Appendix E - Competent Authorities.* By country
- *Appendix F - Packaging Manufacturers, etc.*

First, you need to know what you are dealing with. Section 4 has some blue pages that contain shipping names of just about everything you can think of, together with an ID

number, its classification, what label is required, whether it can go in passenger or cargo aircraft, etc. Take particular note of any symbols nearby, and check for their meanings in Appendix B. In particular, † means look also in Appendix A. There is a numerical cross-reference in Sect 4.3. A * symbol requires a technical name in brackets after a generic name.

Here is a sample line out of 4.2 followed by a brief description of the columns:

UN/ ID no.	Proper Shipping Name Description	Class or Div.	Sub Risk	Hazard Label(s)	PG	Passenger and Cargo Aircraft				Cargo Aircraft Only		S.P. see 4.4	ERG Code
						Ltd Qty							
						Pkg Inst	Max Net Qty/Pkg	Pkg Inst	Max Net Qty/Pkg	Pkg Inst	Max Net Qty/Pkg		
A	B	C	D	E	F	G	H	I	J	K	L	M	N
1863	Fuel, aviation, turbine engine	3		Flamm. liquid	I	-	-	302	1 L	303	30 L	A3	3L
					II	Y305	1 L	305	5 L	307	60 L		3L
					III	Y309	10 L	309	60 L	310	220 L		3L

- *Column A* - The UN or IATA ID number
- *Column B* - Name and description of item, with the proper shipping name in bold type. Descriptive text is in small print
- *Column C* - Class or Division
- *Column D* - Class or Division of subsidiary risks
- *Column E* - Labels required
- *Column F* - Packing Group
- *Column G* - Limited Quantity instruction number for shipments allowed on passenger and cargo aircraft (see Sect 5 - they have a *Y* before the number)
- *Column H* - Max net quantity per package for limited quantities. If there is nothing, limited quantities do not apply
- *Column I* - Packing instruction number for shipments allowed on passenger or cargo aircraft. The word *forbidden* in I & J means the item cannot go on passenger aircraft
- *Column J* - Max net quantity
- *Column K* - Packing instruction number for cargo-only aircraft
- *Column L* - Max net quantity for cargo-only shipments

- *Column M* - Special provisions (contained in Section 4.4)
- *Column N* - ERG Code (Emergency Response Drill Code)

The words *Not Restricted* in columns I & J and K & L mean the item is not considered dangerous. If the material you are dealing with does not appear in the blue pages, check in Section 3 to see if its properties match the classes described there, assuming it isn't forbidden under Sect 2.1 in the first place. Use Table 3.10A to determine the primary hazard if necessary. If it isn't in Section 3 either, it is not subject to the regulations. Radioactive material is covered separately in Section 7.

Next, determine whether it is to be sent on passenger or cargo aircraft. Columns G-L of the blue pages will tell you whether it's forbidden or not, and what quantities can be taken in what packaging. If it is allowed, find the Packing Instruction number (columns G and I), any quantity limitations in one package (H and J), and any variations imposed by States or operators in Section 2.9.2 or Section 2.9.4, respectively. For example, Fedex will not accept Nitric Acid over 40% concentration. You can ship goods in Limited Quantities with ordinary packaging provided it is of good quality. The letter G refers to Gross Weight.

Then check the packaging requirements under Section 5. At the top of each yellow page in there, you will find variations by State and Operator. Select the packaging from the choices available, stick the labels on, prepare the waybill and sign the Declaration. A *Y* designation means Limited Quantity packaging that requires special marking. Non-essential labels must be removed. For example, ID 1863, *Fuel, aviation, turbine engine*, needs a flammable liquid label and may only be carried in limited quantity packaging, 10 litres at a time in Grp III packaging on passenger aircraft (instructions are in Sect 5, Y309). Otherwise, if the aircraft is cargo only, the packages can contain up to 220L.

Emergency Procedures

A Dangerous Goods accident is one which results in fatal or serious injury to a person, or major property damage (that is, one that might involve an insurance claim - a serious injury requires hospitalisation for more than 48 hours within 7 days from the date of the injury). An incident results in injury to a person or property. Both must be reported within 72 hours.

The general procedures include:

- Advise your immediate Supervisor (check the Ops Manual)

- Isolate the package, avoiding contact with the contents (if unable to do that, wash everything, don't eat or smoke, keep your hands away from sensitive areas and get medical assistance)

- Stay on site until names are noted

You must inform the appropriate Air Traffic Services Unit of any dangerous goods on board, especially the proper shipping name, class/division and identified subsidiary risks, the compatibility group for explosives, the quantity and the location on board.

Ultimately, the State in which the incident occurred must be informed (actually, CAA, FAA, Transport Canada, etc.).

More information is in the *ICAO Emergency Response Guide*, document 9481.

METEOROLOGY

8

We have weather because the Earth is heated unevenly as it rotates, and the air surrounding it contains varying amounts of moisture. In balancing out the uneven heating, large quantities of air transport vast amounts of moisture (including the heat it contains), and dump it in varying places around the Earth. In brief:

- Differences in air temperature create the winds - a partial vacuum that heat creates at the surface causes air to rush in and fill the space left behind

- The Earth's spin twists the wind direction

- Pressure decreases with height, and subsequently the temperature under Charles' law

- Cooler air cannot hold so much water vapour, hence clouds

Essentially, the more heat and moisture there is in the air, the more energy it contains, with the more potential for rough weather, such as thunderstorms.

Tip: The temperature and dewpoint figures in weather reports give you the best clues.

There is a net poleward transport of heat from the Equator that helps keep the average temperature of the Earth at around 14°C. Water vapour also contains (latent) heat, which is how it moves heat around so well - when it condenses out, the heat is released (this is a substantial energy release the case of thunderstorms and hurricanes).

The energy for all this originally comes from the Sun. The proportion of the Sun's energy that actually reaches the surface of the Earth can vary from place to place according to how much is reflected back into the atmosphere and the kind of surface it reflects from, but all this is discussed later.

THE ATMOSPHERE

Around the Earth is an ocean of gases, called the *atmosphere*. 21% of the bottom part of it, luckily for us, is oxygen, but 78% is nitrogen, with 1% of odds and ends, like argon (0.9%) and CO_2 (0.03%), and others, that need not concern us here, plus bits of dust and pollutants (the nitrogen, as an inert gas, keeps the proportion of oxygen

down, since it is actually quite corrosive). What does concern us, however, is the 2% of the Earth's total water supply that can also be found as a gas (water vapour), a liquid (clouds or rain) or a solid (ice). Because it weighs five-eighths of an equivalent amount of dry air, the water vapour will also reduce your engine's punch, but that's the subject of the *Performance* chapter. The water vapour content on average is around 1%, but can get as high as 4%. *The troposphere contains more than 90% of all water vapour.*

Thus, the atmosphere provides oxygen, and filters out harmful cosmic rays, aside from helping to regulate the Earth's temperature. It is split into four concentric gaseous areas, according to the mean variation of temperature with height. Starting from the bottom, these are the *troposphere, stratosphere, mesosphere* and *thermosphere*, although the last two are not of much concern to the average pilot. The first two are, however, and the boundary (or demarcation line) between them is the *tropopause*, where any clouds are made of ice crystals.

It normally represents the maximum limit for winds and clouds, because that's where the temperature abruptly stops decreasing with height, resulting in a stable layer above, and its height varies around the Earth, although clouds and moisture can still sometimes be found in the stratosphere. For exam purposes, the troposphere ranges (on average) from the surface to 11 km (7 miles), the stratosphere between 11-50 km, and the mesosphere between 50-80 km (the stratosphere is isothermal between 11-20 km). Just to

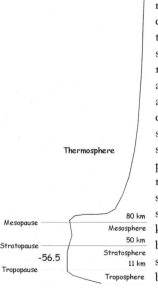

put things in perspective, if the Earth were a ball 1 metre across, the troposphere would be about 2 mm thick. Half the mass of the atmosphere is in the first 5 km.

Over the Equator, the tropopause can be found at around 16-18 km, far higher than it is at the Poles (8 km), because the air is warmer there and has expanded, taking the tropopause with it. For example, North of 60°N in Winter, it will be found at about 29 000 ft. At 50°N, at around 36 090 feet (average 11 km). The height of the tropopause can be locally affected by the movement of various airmasses, so you can get sudden variations in the relatively smooth line shown below.

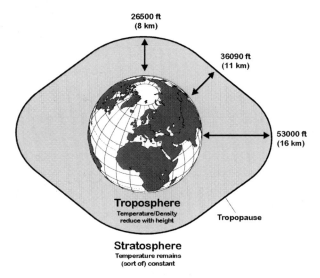

In other words, *the average temperature of the troposphere determines the height of the tropopause*, although the temperature of the tropopause itself is determined by its height. The *lowest* tropopause temperature is around -75°C at its *highest* point at 16 km around the Equator, otherwise it will be more like -56.5°C and -45°C at the Poles (the heights will vary by a couple of thousand feet between January-July).

At 40°N and 60°, the tropopause changes height quite abruptly, and can fold over, which is an instrumental factor in the formation of *jetstreams*. Luckily, this is not relevant for helicopters, except that jetstreams can affect the weather at lower levels, and *vice versa*.

So, underneath the tropopause is the troposphere, and above it is the stratosphere, where the temperature remains relatively constant with height, although you can detect a gradual increase above 20 km because it is heated by ozone that absorbs UV radiation from the Sun. When you're up that high, the ozone levels are above toxic limits, so the air needs to be filtered before it comes into the

cabin. Cosmic radiation also needs to be noted, but that's only relevant for Concorde, which doesn't fly any more.

Temperature *decreases* with height in the troposphere, officially until the rate is less than 2°C per 1000 feet. This is because *Boyle's law* dictates that, as pressure decreases, so does the temperature, resulting in *adiabatic cooling*.

Adiabatic means that the air gets hot, or cold, all by itself, according to whether it is being compressed or expanded - no energy is added or taken away, or exchanged with the outside world. As air expands, the molecules have more room to move around in, so they slow down, which has the effect of reducing the temperature. Similarly in reverse.

The troposphere is where almost all the weather happens, because it contains more than 75% of the mass of the atmosphere. About half of that is below 16 500 feet.

Climate

The *climate* of an area (dealt with later) is its average weather over long periods, and weather is what happens when the atmosphere is affected by heat, pressure, wind and moisture, but heat has arguably the most effect, since changes in weather tend to occur when the temperature changes, along with pressure, of course. A *micro-climate* is a small-scale weather pattern that concerns a local area, like valleys affected by Fohn winds.

The Gas Laws

There are three variables when it comes to gases - *pressure*, *density* and *temperature*, which are all intimately related. For example, if a gas were restrained in a rigid container, increasing the temperature would increase the pressure inside it, and *vice versa*. If the container were not rigid, the density could vary instead. The density of the air will also affect aircraft performance.

The *kinetic theory of gases* (from Maxwell, from Bernoulli's ideas) states that gases are comprised of molecules that are in constant motion, and their properties depend on this motion. In other words, the volume of a gas is the space through which molecules are free to move. From *Avogadro's Law*, which states that equal volumes of all gases at the same temperature and pressure contain the same number of molecules, you can deduce that the same number of molecules (of all gases at the same temperature and pressure) should have the same volume.

The average kinetic energy increases with temperature, and *vice versa* (this also applies to liquids and solids). Contributions to the kinetic theory of gases include:

- **Charles'** Law, from a frenchman, Jacques Charles, which states that, if the *pressure* remains constant, there is a proportionate change in temperature with volume, meaning that, the hotter a gas gets, the more space it takes up, or the more you compress it into a smaller space, the hotter it gets, and *vice versa*. If you double the temperature of a gas, you double its volume. Put another way, equal volumes of different gases expand equally for the same temperature if the pressure is kept constant. Also, equal increases in temperature result in equal increases in pressure if the volume is kept constant. This law helped Charles make the first meteorological flight in a balloon, taking a barometer with which to work out his height. Ultimately, this law states that density of a gas is inversely proportional to absolute temperature

- **Boyle**, an Irish physicist, discovered that, for a perfect gas, if *temperature* remains constant, the volume of a gas varies inversely with its pressure, so if you double the pressure of a gas, you halve its volume. Thus, density is directly proportional to pressure, so if density doubles, so does pressure

- **Dalton** says that the total pressure of a mixture of gases is the same as the sum of the *partial pressures* exerted by each of the gases in the mixture, assuming they don't react chemically with each other, which is relevant when it comes to dealing with oxygen. In other words, each gas's pressure contributes a part of the total according to its constituent proportion, or exerts the same pressure that it would do on its own, and the total pressure of the mixture is equal to their sum. This allows meteorologists to figure out how much water vapour there is in a given parcel of air

DENSITY

Density is the mass per unit volume, assigned a value of 1225 grams per cubic metre at sea level. It is *directly* proportional to *pressure* (Boyle) and *inversely proportional* to *temperature* (Charles), or proportional to pressure divided by temperature:

$$\rho = \frac{P}{T}$$

If you increase the pressure on the air in the rigid container above, its volume will decrease, but its density will increase. If the air is heated, the opposite happens.

The combination of the above is used to formulate the *General Gas Law,* expressed in the following equation for dry air, which is a simplified version of something much more complicated:

$$\rho = \frac{P}{RT}$$

ρ (the greek letter *rho*) represents density, R is a constant value that varies according to the gas, P means Pressure and T means temperature. The formula is used when developing density altitude charts. It states that, if temperature remains constant, density will increase as pressure does (do the math) or, if pressure remains constant, the density increases as temperature decreases.

Thus, pressure falls as you climb, and so does density, but the temperature falls as well, which creates a slight increase in density that offsets the effect slightly. As pressure reduces more than temperature does with height, the general trend is for density to decrease with height as well, but the change is not linear. However, 3% per 1000 feet is a good rule of thumb.

At the surface, density increases with latitude, stays constant at 26 000 feet and decreases with latitude above that, so if you want better performance above the tropopause, don't fly near the Poles! (At upper levels, density is lower over the Poles due to the high concentration of air in the lower levels). At sea level, a gas has a third of the volume it would have at 27 500 feet.

PRESSURE

(See also *Instruments*).

Pressure is the force per unit area exerted on any surface that might be in contact with the gas, commonly expressed in lbs per square inch (psi) or dynes per square centimetre. 1000 d/cm^2 equals 1 millibar.

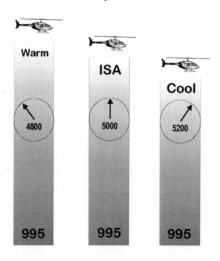

The atmospheric pressure at any point is the weight of the column of air above it, up to the tropopause. Pressure decreases as you go higher, simply because the column of air above you gets shorter.

All three columns in the picture above contain the same weight of air, and the barometric pressure will read the same on the ground, but if you move the cold helicopter to the warm column at the same level, there will still be some air pressure above it, and the altimeter would have a lower reading. The pressure in warm air is therefore higher than it is at the same level in cold air, so the *rate of change of pressure* with height is lower in warm air than it is in cold air. The rate is also faster at lower altitudes, other things being equal. Thus, in warm air, your altimeter will under-read, and *vice versa*.

The Sun

The Sun's diameter is 865,000 miles, or 109 times that of the Earth. Although its surface temperature may be high (5800 Kelvin), some scientists (like Herschel) have proposed that its *centre* is actually cold, like the middle part of a candle flame which won't burn anything. We feel its effects as heat and light, but it also throws out magnetic, or cosmic, rays, which vary in an 11.5-year cycle, signified by *sunspots*, that affect radio propagation, and radio hams pay close attention to them. Nobody really knows what sunspots are, but they could be gaps in the Sun's own atmosphere which allow us to see its dark centre. They were originally discovered by the ancient Chinese, and rediscovered in 1952. In 1982 it was also found that the Earth's magnetic field vibrated in sympathy with the bombardment of electrons and protons from the Sun. There is more about the Sun in *Navigation*.

66° 30' N or S defines the extremities of perpetual darkness or daylight (i.e. the Arctic and Antarctic circles, derived from 90° minus 23½°), so to see a rising and setting Sun, you must be below 66°.

Tip: One finger width equals approximately 60 arcminutes of the Sun's movement, or one degree, over 4 minutes, which is kind of useful when figuring out how much time is left before sunset.

The Earth receives about 2 billionths of the Sun's total radiation, equal to about 23 billion horsepower - more energy per minute than is used on the Earth all year. The electromagnetic energy from the Sun is received in three ways:

- *Ultraviolet waves*, which have the highest frequency and which are absorbed by oxygen and ozone

- Waves from the *visible spectrum* which, when mixed in equal proportions, produce white light

- *Infrared waves*, which have the lowest frequency and which are absorbed by CO_2 and water vapour. They can be seen by some animals

The *Solar Constant* is an average value of 1370 watts per square metre.

The Sun's rays have already been depleted on their way through the atmosphere, of course, in the formation of ozone (O_3) at between 15-50 km up (which acts as a screen to keep out ultraviolet rays), and being absorbed by CO_2 and water vapour, (the concentration of ozone is greatest in the lower part of its layer, while the increase in temperature is greatest in the upper part). Another small amount is reflected back from clouds, leaving about 50% to be actually absorbed by the Earth's surface. This is the credit side of the Earth's *solar budget*, which is the difference between solar energy received and reflected back (the two are only equal at 38° latitude).

For a given amount of sunshine, the rate at which the surface heats up depends on:

- The **angle of incidence** of the rays (see below)

- **Dampness of the ground**, or moisture content of soil (absorbs heat)

- **Nature of the surface** - sandy surfaces warm up quicker, but granite surfaces keep heat longer. Snow surfaces don't change much. Water is slow to

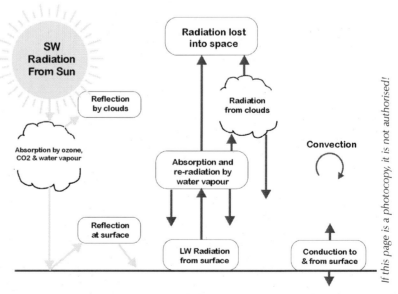

heat, because the rays travel far in, and are widely spread

- **Colour of the surface** - the darker the area that is hit, the more absorption that takes place, and the more heat that is generated

- **Foliage cover** - trees will absorb rays before they hit the ground during the process of evaporation from the leaves

- **Reflection** from the ground

HEAT EXCHANGE

The wavelength of radiated energy is inversely proportional to the temperature of whatever is emitting it. As the Sun is very hot, its radiations are of shorter wavelength than those from the Earth, which has a much lower temperature (in fact around 99% of the Sun's energy is emitted in the shorter wavelengths). This is a similar (but not identical) effect to that produced by the glass in a greenhouse, that lets short wave radiation (light) in, and is less transparent to the longer infrared radiation going out. Essentially, energy radiated from the surface of the Earth is absorbed by CO_2 (plus other gases, including water vapour) which act as a thermal blanket around the Earth, and is reradiated back towards it.

THE GREENHOUSE EFFECT

The Earth is about 33° warmer than it would be without its atmosphere. The difference is called the *Greenhouse Effect*, and the gases that help the process along are called the *Greenhouse Gases*. The heat-trapping gases include CO_2, water vapour, methane (mainly from cows - 300 litres from one every day!), sodium dioxide, plus a few others. The difference between the solar energy received and that reflected back is also called the *Solar Budget*. The quantity of radiation going in and out is only equal at 38° latitude.

In short, whatever radiation gets through from the Sun heats the Earth's surface, which conducts heat to the layer of air closest to it. Air particles heated this way expand and rise, to carry the acquired heat upward until the temperature equalises with the surrounding air. *Turbulence* has a similar effect, and there is also *latent heat transfer*, which occurs when heat absorbed during evaporation at the surface is released when condensation occurs. Finally, some direct transfer of heat is done when short wave radiation is absorbed by the ozone layer.

The Seasons

We get seasons (and varying day lengths) because the Earth is not vertical in space - it is inclined at an angle of 23½°, so that different areas are pointed towards the Sun in their turn, and receive sunlight for longer periods each day, hence Summer.

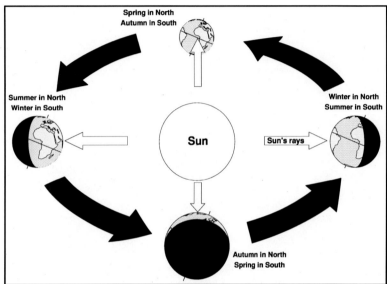

The paradox is that, in the Northern Hemisphere's Winter (on the right, below, where it is tilted *away* from the Sun), the Earth is at its closest point to the Sun (according to Kepler's Laws), proving that the Earth's heat is self-created.

The resulting coolness occurs because the rays strike at an angle of incidence that spreads them over a wide area, reducing their concentration (they have also travelled further):

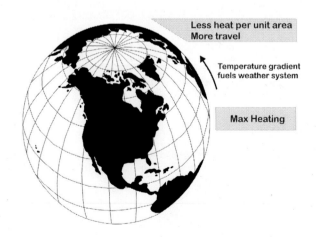

© *Phil Croucher, 2007*

There is more movement in the Northern Hemisphere than the Southern Hemisphere because there are more land masses for the air masses to interact with.

PRESSURE PATTERNS

A column of air above any point has weight, which is commonly measured in terms of *millibars* (or *hectopascals*) or *inches of mercury*, and called the *atmospheric pressure*. Variations in atmospheric pressure can be traced directly to variations in air density, which in turn are often caused by temperature differences.

To make sure that everyone works on the same page, a couple of typical scientists went to a typical place on the South coast of England many years ago and measured the temperature and pressure, which turned out to be 1013.25 millibars (29.92" of mercury) and 15.5° Centigrade. This was adopted as the *International Standard Atmosphere*, and now everyone who makes altimeters, or whatever, calibrates them with it so everybody is on the same page. The pressure actually works out to be around 15 lbs per square inch, which equates to 20 tons on the average person. In short, *ISA is a standard that provides universal values of temperature, pressure, density and lapse rate, by which others can be compared.*

In the standard atmosphere, ½ sea level pressure is obtained at 18 000', one third at 27 500' and ¼ at 33 700'. Thus, pressure decreases with height, but not linearly (a layer 1 millibar deep is about equal to 27 feet at sea level - at 3 000 feet, it's 30 feet, or around 90 feet at the heights jets fly at, i.e. 35 000 feet. **Note:** this is only in meteorology). The sea level pressure on which the standard atmosphere is based relates 1" of mercury to 1,000 feet of altitude, so you would expect to see an altimeter read 1 000 feet less if you set it to 28.92 instead of 29.92 inches. Some countries use *hectopascals*, or *hPas*, instead of *millibars*, which contain 1000 Pascals. Many people also use them interchangeably.

Another quality of a column of air is that it gets cooler with height, as well as less dense, so the standard atmosphere is also taken as decreasing at 1.98°C per 1,000 feet (6.5°C per 1 000 m) up to 36,090 feet (11 km), remaining at -56.5°C up to 65,600 feet. This is called the *standard lapse rate*, which is really an average, and used for convenience, since the lapse rate actually changes from day to day. The *Jet Standard Atmosphere* is another standard which decreases at 2°C per 1,000 feet, to finish at -65°C at 65 600 feet.

Finally, the air gets thinner with height - at approximately 18 562 feet, it is 50% of its density at sea level, so the millibar - sorry, hectopascal, is worth 50 feet. This also means less oxygen, and difficulty in breathing, but this is covered elsewhere. Thus, the actual pressure at a given place depends on its *height*, and the *temperature* and *density* at that point (see *Density Altitude*, below).

Station Pressure

Station pressure is the actual atmospheric pressure at a particular place, without any corrections or adjustments. Several readings are taken through the day, converted to sea level pressure (using ISA) and marked on a map, with the ones that are equal connected up. The lines that join the dots are called *isobars* (*iso* is Greek for *same*), and will be 4 hectopascals apart, counting up and down from 1000. The closer they are together, the more the millibars drop per mile and the more severe the pressure gradient will be, so you get stronger winds (air moves from high to low pressure, and wind arises from horizontal pressure difference).

Isobars are like contours, and make common patterns, two of which are the *low* or *high*, other names for *cyclone* and *anti-cyclone*, respectively (nothing to do with the cyclones that seem to damage trailer parks). Another name for a low is a *depression*. The exact position of a system will be marked by an X.

The red arrows *across* the isobars are wind directions after the *Coriolis Effect* has come into force in the Northern Hermisphere. The movement is in the opposite sense (inward becomes outward) in the Southern hemisphere.

The patterns are round, being circles of isobars, and difference between them is simple; a high pressure area has most pressure in the middle, whilst a low has the least. In other words, the air in a high is descending (and diverging), and that in a low is ascending (and converging), so the weather is settled in the former and tends to instability in the latter, since upwards movement implies clouds forming. So, if you were flying from East to West, you would be best going South of a High and North of a Low, in the Northern Hemisphere.

In temperate latitudes, you will find calm winds and haze in the centre of a Summer High. An Icelandic Low will be deeper in Winter because temperature contrasts between Arctic and Equatorial regions are greater.

In the diagram overleaf, the air is going into the High at the bottom, twisting to the right, moving from the bottom left to the top right, where it comes out of the page again. As mentioned previously, air moves up in the first place from solar heating, and any rushing in along the surface to replace it leaves a gap elsewhere, which is itself replaced with descending air. A dry, sunny region, for example, will get very warm from intense surface heating, and create a

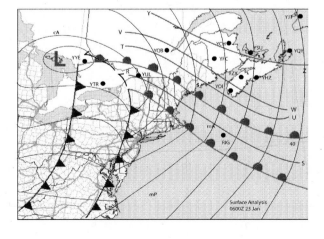

Fronts SFC 0050-0149Z Thu 01 Feb 07
Sea Level Pressure SFC 2150-2249Z Wed 17 Jan-07
Station Plots SFC 2150-2249Z Wed 17 Jan 07

thermal low. Such a non-frontal thermal depression will form over land in Summer. An *orographic* or *Lee* low exists in the leeside of a range of hills after the air has gone over and round the range, where it gets compressed after being forced round. As the air behind the barrier has not been compressed, it is at a relatively lower pressure. A difference of 2 or 3 mb can mean a difference of nearly 100 feet.

A *complex low* is one with several fronts and air masses overlapping each other. When asked questions, try to create a 3D image that will show you which fronts and air masses are on top or below to get the sort of weather on the ground.

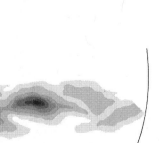

You might often see a *secondary low*, which can be a smaller one inside a larger system that forms at the tip of the warm sector (see *Frontology*), in which the weather is more intense as it feeds on its bigger brother, although the winds will be lighter between them. A secondary low can also form in the cold air advection in the wake of a cyclone. In any case, it will tend to move around the primary Low in a cyclonic sense (i.e. clockwise).

Lows are generally found meandering around the Equator and in temperate latitudes, where they tend to dominate the weather scene with clouds and rain.

Other patterns are the *trough*, which is a longish area of low pressure, like a valley, with U-shaped isobars, and V-shaped ones along fronts. Its opposite number is the *ridge*, found off a High, also U-shaped. A *col* is a neutral area between highs and/or lows.

However, just because cloud is mostly absent in a high, don't expect clear skies, as the descending air might trap haze or smoke, leading to a phenomenon called *anticyclonic gloom* near industrial areas. As an example, this is what the Persian Gulf looks like on a hot VFR day:

Sometimes, areas of layer cloud may also get caught if they are below an inversion (discussed below). The only way it can be cleared is with low level heating (usually insolation or advection) or by strong cooling of the air above the inversion, due to advection. As an example of the influence a high pressure area can have, a strong one commonly sits over Eastern Canada in late Spring because most of the Hudson Bay is still frozen. It is very good at stopping the movement of other systems and weather. There are permanent ones over the poles, as well, not to mention the Siberian high with an elongated section that stretches back into NW Europe in April. When this happens, the clockwise flow brings in warm moist Mediterranean air over Italy, up the Alps and into the upper atmosphere. This air takes longer to slow and cool down, so over NW Europe there is a high tropopause

height in April with a cold temperature. With such *blocking highs*, the normal Easterly movement of depressions and fronts becomes more South-North, or *meriodional* (in line with meridians), a good illustration of which is the *Bermuda High* which is a semipermanent feature in that general area*. It can be responsible for thunderstorms, high density altitudes and low visibility in haze - the clockwise circulation sends warm, damp ocean air up the Eastern half of the United States, which destabilises in the warmth of afternoon heating, to cause thunderstorms. One blocking anticyclone in the Northern Hemisphere is a quasi-stationary warm anticyclone between 50°-70°N.

*Note: "The Azores High" really means a succession of highs that happen to be stagnating in that position.

From this, you will gather that high pressure systems are relatively sluggish, both horizontally and vertically.. Subsiding air is compressed and warmed (which makes them generally cloudless), with saturated air doing so at a slower rate, so you can expect an inversion if a high starts in a region already containing cloud (the air over the cloud is warmed more than that in the cloud). If the air above the cloud is cooled overnight, the layer of stratocumulus that forms will persist, leading to the anticyclonic gloom mentioned above as pollution is trapped underneath at the lower levels. However, if warming can occur in the layer below the inversion, it will be weakened.

Movement of any system can be judged best from the change of pressure as shown in *Station Circles*, described at the end of this chapter. This *pressure tendency* is a small amount per hour in whatever direction.

Geostrophic (Coriolis) Force (Effect)
A major pressure system does not necessarily take the air it contains with it when it moves (like the waves in the sea, which don't actually move, but bob up and down to give the illusion. It's the *swell* that is responsible for the movement of large bodies of water). For true air movement, you need a pressure gradient. Under normal circumstances, air would simply move from high to low pressure, *across* the isobars (due to the *Pressure Gradient Force*, or PGF, shown below).

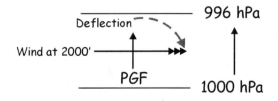

However, this is only true around the Equator. In the Northern Hemisphere, air actually moves clockwise round a high pressure area and anticlockwise round a low, because the Earth is spinning, and deflects normal air movement, until eventually the wind blows *along* the isobars (instead of across) at around 2,000 feet (the middle arrow pointing right above). Thus, an imaginary force *appears* to act at right angles to the rotating Earth, causing a moving body to follow a curved path opposite to the direction of the Earth's rotation.

Not only that, the Earth moves faster at the equator than it does at the Poles, so, if you throw something from the North Pole to the Equator (B to A, on the left), progressively more of the Earth's surface would pass under its track, giving the illusion of the object curving to the right (or West of A) as it lags behind - the Earth is moving slower towards the North. If you threw whatever it was the other way, it would "move" to the East of B, because you are adding the Earth's movement at both latitudes. That is, B will be moving slower relative to A. In other words, a bullet might fly in a straight line, but its target will move to the right

This apparent movement (East or West) is like extra centrifugal force, which is called in some places the *Coriolis Effect*, but actually is *Geostrophic Force* when it refers to air movement, although no "force" is involved, hence the use of the word "effect". That is, the wind at 2,000 feet is assigned a geostrophic property, which is only true when the isobars are straight and parallel. They are mostly curved, so the geostrophic wind becomes the *gradient wind*. The extra energy to keep the air curving comes from the *cyclostrophic force*, which is similar to centripetal force, as it operates inward. Around a low, it is the difference between PGF and GF - around a high, between GF and PGF. The geostrophic wind is the imaginary wind that would result if the Coriolis and Pressure Gradient forces are balanced. When the air starts to move faster, the geostrophic force is increased and deflection starts again. Coriolis force is directly proportional to wind speed, in that it is zero when the wind is still and at its maximum when the wind is at maximum speed. It is also zero at the Equator and large at the Poles (meaning that the above relationships break down near the Equator, and isobars cannot be used to represent weather patterns. Streamlines are used instead).

In any case, wind in a *low* would be *lower* than the equivalent geostrophic wind, and *higher* round a *high*. In the case of a low in the Northern Hemisphere, the centrifugal force goes in the same direction as the Coriolis force. Since the forces must remain in balance, the Coriolis force weakens to compensate and reduce the overall wind speed (the PGF doesn't change), so the wind will back, tend to go inwards and contribute towards the lifting effect, since it is forced up, to cause adiabatic cooling, and precipitation. Inside a high, air movement (winds), will tend to increase with the help of centrifugal force, other things being equal, contributing towards the subsidence and adiabatic warming from compression. However, this is offset by the pressure gradient in a low being much steeper, creating stronger winds anyway. This is known as the *isallobaric effect*, since lines joining places with an equal *rate of change* of pressure are *isallobars*. Centrifugal force helps a low by preventing it being filled, and causes a high to decay by removing mass from it.

Over the sea, the geostrophic effect will be less, giving about 10° difference in direction, as opposed to the 30° you can expect over land (the speed reduces to about 70% over water, and 50% over land). If the winds are high, you could get into a stall on landing as you encounter *windshear*, of which more later.

According to Professor *Buys Ballot's Law* (a Dutch meteorologist), if you stand with your back to the wind in the Northern hemisphere, the low pressure will be on your left (on the right in the Southern hemisphere). The implication of this is that, if you fly towards lower pressure, you will drift to starboard as the wind is coming from the left (a common exam question). It's the opposite way round in an anticyclone. Buys Ballot's Law, by the way, had already been deduced by US meteorologists William Ferrel and James Coffin, but they didn't get to be famous. Note that it does not always apply to winds that are deflected by local terrain, or local winds such as sea breezes or those that flow down mountains.

B

A

Earth Movement

WIND

The Earth is heated unevenly. Air at the Equator becomes warmer than it does at the Poles, so it expands upwards around the middle of the Earth and contracts down to the surface higher up the latitude scale. This general trend gives rise to regular patterns of air movement, in the shape of winds that were well known to navigators on the high seas, such as the *trade winds*, caused by the Coriolis effect, which makes air accumulate (for example) in an Easterly direction at around 30° of latitude in a general area of high pressure right round the Earth (the air flowing poleward is bent eastward by the Coriolis force, resulting in mass of air accumulating aloft, hence the high pressure in this belt). Out of that high pressure, some air flows to the South West, and some to the North East. As well, air from the Poles, settling down and flowing South, creates weather fronts (see *Frontology*) when it meets the warmer air.

Wind moves from high to low pressure, just like the air that emerges from a pricked balloon. It is expressed as a velocity, so it needs direction and speed to fit the definition. The wind always comes *from* somewhere, expressed as a *true bearing* in weather reports (*magnetic* from the Tower), so a *Southerly* wind is *from* 180°. The speed is mostly in knots, or nautical miles per hour, as if you didn't know already. Wind direction is measured with a *wind vane*, while speed is measured with an *anemometer*, which should be placed on a mast 6-10 m above the runway and calibrated after *Saint Venant* (to allow for compressibility) for best results. 10 m is used to make sure that the wind is not affected by small local obstacles. A *pressure tube anemometer* works in the same way as a pitot tube. A more common type has three cups on stalks that are driven round by the wind, and the speed of rotation gives the wind speed.

Obstacles interfere with the wind in different ways. A forest is like large brush, slowing it down and mixing it up. It will tend to build up before an obstacle and create turbulent eddies behind it. This is one effect that will result in *gusts* and *lulls* as the speed varies (the effect of turbulent mixing and friction, or breaking the flow into eddies is a far more important factor). *Gusts* are rapid changes of speed and direction that don't last long, whilst *squalls* do. A gale has a minimum wind speed of 34 kts, or is gusting at 43 kts or more.

Prevailing Winds

Prevailing winds blow more from one direction than any other, and will be a characteristic of a particular region, so they are influential in the placement of runways. In desert and polar regions, they produce sand dunes and snowdrifts.

The arctic and subtropical areas of the Northern hemisphere have a generally East to West movement of weather systems - Polar easterlies carry storms, as do the North-Easterly trade winds. The prevailing Westerlies, which are typically found at 50°N, but can affect the Polar regions, drive mid-latitude storms from West to East.

There are three major components of global air circulation:

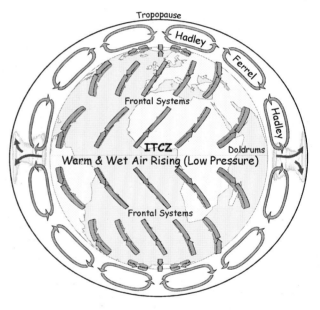

TRADE WINDS

Trade winds blow from SE in the Southern hemisphere and NE in the Northern Hemisphere. They are powered by the difference in temperature between the Poles and the Equator and occur only in the lower part of the troposphere. They are more pronounced over the oceans.

Sir Edmund Halley deduced the causes of tropical trade winds and monsoons through observations made over two years off the West Coast of Africa. In 1735, George Hadley, a London lawyer (go figure) also deduced that the western movement of the winds arose from the W-E rotation of the Earth. Instead of going straight to the North Pole, the warm air from the Equator is affected by the Coriolis force that makes it accumulate in the subtropical latitudes and sink to the surface at around 30°

latitude, creating a *subtropical high*. The sinking air goes back to the Equator from NE to SW, courtesy of Coriolis.

The resulting circulation, that is, up at the Equator and down again at 30° N & S was called a *Hadley cell*, as shown below, with Tropical and Polar versions. This circulation effectively transfers concentrated heat energy from the Equator to higher latitudes and, combined with the Earth's spin, produces prevailing global wind patterns, such as the trades, or *tropical easterlies* (warm sea water is also moved by wind-driven currents).

Between the Hadley cells are *Ferrel cells* in the mid-latitudes, where the outflowing winds clash to form frontal waves. They are named after the William Ferrel mentioned above, who was a mathematician. He found that the sinking air from the Hadley cell at the surface made its way Poleward, then deflected right at about 60°, to produce prevailing Westerlies that flow SW-NE.

The area where the trade winds from the Northern and Southern hemispheres meet is called the *Intertropical Convergence Zone* (ITCZ), which is an area of low pressure that goes right round the Equator, known to sailors as the *Doldrums*, or areas of complete calm either side of the equator, where the only movement of air is up (although it slides horizontally North and South once it hits the tropopause). The only wind is caused by air getting sucked in from areas just outside. The ITCZ particularly affects West Africa between 10° and 20° N, and the Northern coasts of the Arabian Sea in July, when it reaches its maximum Northerly position of 15° to 20° N. It can produce extremely bad weather over a wide area.

As the trades converge, warm, moist air is forced upward, to condense any water vapour as it rises and cools, resulting in a band of heavy precipitation (i.e. frequent and widespread thunderstorms) around the Equator which moves seasonally towards the most intense solar heating, or warmest surface temperatures. Thus, the doldrums move with the Sun according to season - a weak trough called the *Equatorial Trough* circles the Earth close to the Equator and migrates North and South, following the Sun. The winds at Equatorial latitudes flow more across isobars than along them, but they tend to be weak anyway, as they are created more by diurnal heating and cooling. This is towards the Southern Hemisphere between September to February, reversing direction in time for Summer in the Northern Hemisphere. However, in oceanic longitudes it is stationary just North of the Equator, which means more rain as it gets hotter. In January, between Dakar and Rio de Janeiro, it can be found between 0°-7°N.

WESTERLIES

The winds that branch North and South in the upper regions above the Equator are called the *anti-trade winds*, and they divide again at about 25° latitude. One branch continues towards the Poles to form upper Westerlies. The other descends to pile up in the lower levels at 30° latitude to create a zone of calm air with fair weather called the *Horse Latitudes*. This descending air divides yet again to flow towards the Poles and the Equator, the latter creating the trade winds.

The air currents moving towards the Poles from the Horse latitudes are deflected Eastwards to merge with the prevailing Westerlies between 30° and 60° latitude. The *Roaring Forties* are winds found between 40° and 50° S that are able to blow at gale force across vast stretches of open sea because there is nothing in the way.

POLAR EASTERLIES

As cold air that accumulates at the Poles spreads out to move towards the Equator, it is deflected by the Coriolis effect to become the Polar Easterlies.

Mountain Winds

Understanding how air moves around terrain is one of the keys to good mountain flying. Winds can increase your operational ceiling, payload, rate of climb, range and cruise speed. They can also do the opposite, and be very difficult to predict, with formidable up- and downdraughts associated with them. When cruising downwind, along a lee slope or not, sudden wind reversals could make you exceed V_{NE} or even take away your airspeed.

The area of lift from high ground is greatest where the air is made to move sharply in a different direction, and, in line with Bernoulli, the greatest windspeed is found at the top of the crest, where it has to move a greater distance in the same time:

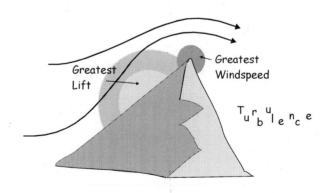

There are several types of wind, which can be loosely grouped into *prevailing* or *local*, with the latter subdivided into other types, such as valley, anabatic, katabatic, mountain waves, chinooks, etc., and which are infinitely variable (glacier winds descend 24 hours a day). The *prevailing wind* is steady and fairly reliable, and starts to affect you from about 6,000 feet AGL upwards. Indeed, upper winds can come from many directions at different levels, and are usually the opposite of lower winds. With mountains, they also acquire a vertical element.

Local Winds, on the other hand, have effects in a more limited area. Valley winds can be felt up to 2500 feet above the valley floor, and reach their peak strength around mid-afternoon. Inside mountains, the same venturi effect that causes a wing to fly or pulls fuel vapour into the throat of a carburettor will cause the wind to speed up as it passes through narrower channels or along valleys (the *Mistral* is a good example).

A katabatic wind is one that flows down an incline that is influential in causing the wind in the first place, which would include the Chinook or the Santa Ana

Cool air on a slope that is generated overnight with radiation cooling will flow down, because it is more dense, and therefore more subject to gravity, causing a *katabatic* wind. It's the same effect as in a closed room on a cold day, where there is a draught near a window even when nothing is open - the air next to the window is cooled, and flows downwards. The katabatic effect usually happens around sunset and overnight (when the heating effect of the Sun is lost), and its significance is not just that you might get some wind from somewhere you don't expect (and downdraughts from severe slopes), but also that it slips underneath the air not in contact with the slope - if there is a river at the bottom of the valley, the extra moisture could also cause fog, so be careful when flying to valley airfields in the evening. Katabatic winds tend to stay within 500 feet of the surface, and can arise quite suddenly, even up to gale force. Glaciers have permanent katabatic winds.

An *anabatic* wind flows *up* a hill, due to ground heating and air expansion during the day. It is not a regular thermal movement, that is, the whole layer does not move vertically away from the slope, but is rather a *slide* of the layer up the hill, so, to get any lift benefit, you have to fly close to the surface. Anabatic winds are quick to decline with cloud cover.

THE DEMARCATION LINE

The demarcation line is the point at which smooth air is separated from turbulent air around a peak, rather similar to that over an aerofoil. In the picture on the left, the snow follows the demarcation line. Above or to the windward side (on the left), air is relatively smooth and upflowing - below, or to the right, in the lee, it is downflowing and turbulent. The demarcation line steepens as wind velocity increases (and the severity of the slope), as does the area of downflow, and moves toward the top of the hill.

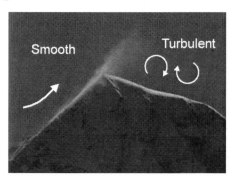

So, in general, air moving up is smooth (left of the line above), and that moving down is turbulent (to the right). You can visualise the difference if you think of a waterfall, and the state of the water before and after dropping over the edge. As a guide to wind speed, the snow in the picture is light and powdery, so it might be around 10-15 kts.

MOUNTAIN WAVES

When a mountain range has an airflow at the 10,000 foot level, greater than about 20 knots (depends on the size of the range), blowing broadside on (within about 30°) and over it in stable conditions*, *standing waves* can exist downwind, noticeable by turbulence and strong persistent up and downdraughts. At that speed and angle they seem to hit a resonant spot.

Note: The wind speed and direction should be more or less constant up to about 18,000 feet, although it doesn't have to be particularly fast over the peaks.

Downdraughts can be particularly dangerous when flying towards a range into a headwind, as the airflow follows the general shape of the surface, so you will experience a strong downdraught just before the ridge:

Note: This does not just apply to light aircraft! 747s have lost complete engines in mountain wave downdraughts, but the most common problems are severe reductions in rates of climb and excessive rates of sink.

*The "stable conditions" are actually a layer of stable air sandwiched between less stable layers above and below

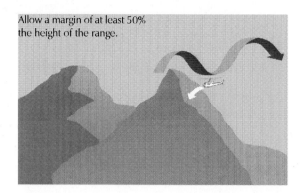

Allow a margin of at least 50% the height of the range.

The wind needs to be fairly straight in direction, so warm sector winds and jetstreams can be very conducive to the formation of waves. The waves will be more dangerous in Winter simply because the wind speeds are stronger, and there will be a longer wavelength. There can be several miles between their peaks and troughs, which can extend between 10,000-20,000 feet above the range and up to 200 or 300 miles downwind:

Rotors are always in circular motion, constantly forming and dissipating as water vapour is added and taken away. They are dangerous, and the most turbulence will be found in them, or between them and the ground. Rotor clouds are formed in the same way as lenticular clouds, that is, from air forced upwards and condensing, then dissipating as they proceed downwards in the wave.

If the rotor forms within an inversion, warm air from above is rotated downward and heated further as it is compressed. On the other way up, cold air is expanding to cool further. Thus, very cold air ends up lying over warm air and conditions are extremely unstable.

As a clue to the existence of waves, you will see a *cap cloud* over the top of the range, creeping down the *lee side* (downwind), as a result of the downdraught.

It disappears as air descends and warms adiabatically.

At the crest of each wave, there will be a *lenticular cloud*, with a *rotor cloud* downwind from each one (the lowest in the system). This is a lenticular cloud viewed from above:

Lenticular clouds are a form of altocumulus that remain stationary with reference to the ground, and will produce airframe icing.

Watch out for long-term variations in speed and pitch attitude in level cruise (the variations may be large). Near the ground in a mountain wave area, severe turbulence and windshear (below) may be encountered, especially at the bottom of a rotor where you may get a performance decreasing shear if you are going in the same direction as the wind. The quickest way out of severe turbulence is up, with the next best directly away from the range. Flying parallel to the range in an updraught, avoiding peaks, gives most comfort.

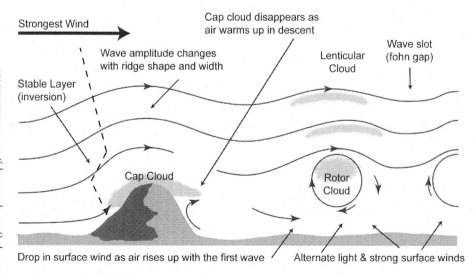

Strongest Wind

Cap cloud disappears as air warms up in descent

Wave amplitude changes with ridge shape and width

Wave slot (fohn gap)

Lenticular Cloud

Stable Layer (inversion)

Cap Cloud

Rotor Cloud

Drop in surface wind as air rises up with the first wave

Alternate light & strong surface winds

© *Phil Croucher, 2007*

An aircraft affected by mountain waves can expect severe turbulence below any rotors, downdraughts that may be stronger than the rate of climb and greater than normal icing in associated clouds

Windshear

This is the name for sudden airspeed changes over about 10 kts resulting from sudden horizontal or vertical changes in wind velocity - more severe examples will change not only airspeed, but vertical speed and aircraft attitude as well. Officially, it becomes dangerous when variations cause enough displacement from your flight path for substantial corrective action to be taken; *severe* windshear causes airspeed changes greater than 15 kts, or vertical speed changes over 500 feet per minute. Expect it to occur mostly inside 1,000 feet AGL, where it is most critical, because you can't quickly build up airspeed (remember that altitude is money in the bank, but speed is money in the pocket).

Although mostly associated with thunderstorms (see below), where you have the unpredictability of microbursts to contend with, it's also present with wake vortices, temperature inversions, mountain waves and the passage of fronts, not forgetting obstructions near the runway, and can occur over any size of area. You can even get it where rain is falling from a cumulus cloud, as the air is getting dense from the cooling, and will therefore fall quicker. Helicopters, especially, can suffer from windshear above and below tree top level in forest clearings, when a backlash effect can convert any headwind to tailwind.

All fronts are zones of windshear - the greater the temperature difference across them (over 10°C), the greater the changes will be. The surface wind speeds associated with a front, particularly over rough ground, can influence windshear production (friction + windspeed + instability = mechanical turbulence). Warm fronts tend to have less shear than cold ones, but as they're slower moving, you catch it for longer. In general, the faster the front moves (say, over 30 kts), the more vigorous the weather associated with it; if it goes slower, the visibility will be worse, but you can still get windshear even then and for up to an hour after its passage.

Warm air moving horizontally above cold air can produce turbulence at the point where they join, as would be typical with an inversion, at around 2,000-4,000 feet with a windspeed of 25 kts or more. In a valley, in particular, when the moving warm air hits a mountainside, it will be forced downwards, but unable to penetrate the cold air, so it is forced to move over the top of that in the valley bottom, so watch out on those cold, clear mornings.

The most significant effect of windshear is, of course, loss of airspeed at a critical moment, similar to an effect in mountain flying, where a wind reversal could result in none at all! You would typically get this with a downburst from a convective type cloud, where, initially, you get an increase in airspeed from the extra headwind, but if you don't anticipate the reverse to happen as you get to the other side, you will not be in a position to cope with the resulting loss. This has led to the windshear classifications of *performance increasing* or *performance decreasing* (see *Microbursts* below).

Windshear is *occasional* if it exists for about a third of the time, *intermittent* between then and two thirds, and *continuous* over that. The alert is given when the mean surface wind is over 20 kts, and the difference between it and the gradient wind is over 40 kts. There also needs to be a temperature difference of 10° between the surface and 1,000 feet and Cbs or heavy showers within 5 nm.

MICROBURSTS

These are small, intense downdraughts that spread out in all directions when they reach the surface, commonly associated with thunderstorms in the mature stage. You are most likely to encounter them within 1,000' of the ground, that is, right on the approach. They are most dangerous where the vertical push converts to the horizontal, between the base of the microburst and the ground - you could get a vertical speed of over 6000 feet per minute and a horizontal one over 45 kts, with a 90-knot shear across the microburst. The diameter of any damage will be up to 4 km, and the duration from 1-5 minutes from first striking the ground, or more, though the maximum intensity is in the first 2-4 minutes. The vertical windshear is expressed in kts/100 feet.

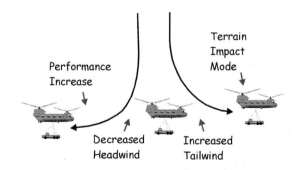

A transit through a microburst involves a performance-increasing shear to start with, followed by a performance-decreasing one, because the downflow divides at the surface (although the burst might be "only" 45 kts, the complete shear will be double that). With the former, you get more airspeed and lift from either increased headwind or decreased tailwind, taking you above the glidepath - recovery involves reducing power and lowering the nose, and using a higher power setting than before when re-established, or the aircraft will sink. The latter is the opposite, of course - you lose airspeed, the nose pitches down and altitude decreases. Recover by increasing power and setting it to less than the original when established (you will need more power and a higher pitch attitude to stay on the glideslope).

The helicopter on the left in the picture above gets an increased headwind, so power is reduced to compensate. This takes effect just as the downburst is encountered, and the headwind becomes a tailwind, so IAS decreases.

Being so close to the ground, you are likely to be taking off or landing, and therefore more vulnerable. The angle of attack reduces inside a downburst, because induced flow increases, so collective should be increased on entry, and reduced (quickly) on exit. Where the air is dry, the microburst will become more vigorous, because the dry air absorbs any moisture, cooling the air and making it more dense, so it falls faster. For more on Wake Turbulence, refer to the *Operations* chapter.

SQUALLS

A squall is a sudden increase of at least 16 kts in average wind speed to a sustained speed of 22 kts or more for at least one minute.

Upper Winds

The height of a particular air pressure depends on the sea level pressure (the starting point) and the air temperature, which becomes very significant at higher levels. For example, an indicated height of 30 000 feet in the tropics would be a true height of around 32 000 feet. Over the Poles, where it is colder, it would be more like 28 000 feet. This height difference is due to the slope of the millibar surface (in this case 300 mb) being followed.

As mentioned previously, a chart depicting upper winds using contours represents these slopes and would look like a landscape when viewed in 3D.

JETS

A jet is a narrow band of strong winds. It is formed from temperature gradients, which will tend to follow the ground position of any fronts, since it is thought that frontal systems percolate downwards from jets rather than grow upward from the surface. The winds in a jet change direction and speed constantly, at which points high and low pressures form, and either go with the flow or develop into something stronger - such positive and negative acceleration points are used by forecasters to predict frontal movement. A surface low is usually equatorward of the jetstream, moving nearer the centre as it deepens, and it will cross at the point of any occlusion.

POLAR FRONT JET (JETSTREAM)

This is the most commonly known jet, otherwise known as the *jetstream*. In both hemispheres, it is typically found between around 30,000 - 40 000 feet, where there is a marked contrast in temperature, just under the tropopause, where it has been lowered after the *Polar Front* has moved towards warmer air at the Equator.

The Japanese used jetstreams to bomb the USA and Canada from balloons, called Fugos, although only 6 people were ever killed, out of 9000 launched. Around a thousand reached America, from Alaska to Mexico

The Polar Front is where cold polar air meets warmer sub-tropical or temperate air in mid-latitudes, which means a rapid change in temperature over a short distance, known in the trade as a *marked temperature gradient*. Thus, a jetstream will be found moving along an area of greatest temperature *contrast*, particularly between Polar and Tropical air, with the cold air on the left in the Northern Hemisphere and on the right in the Southern Hemisphere, looking downstream. The contrasts produce different thicknesses in the atmosphere above them, which serves to intensify any pressure gradients aloft, flowing from South to North, being deflected to the East by Coriolis force as they accelerate to form a river of air.

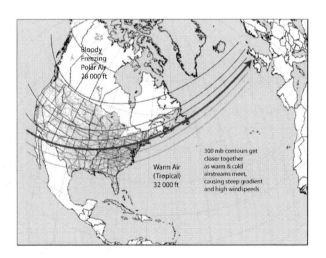

Contrasts are greater in Winter, so winds will be stronger then. A Polar Front jetstream blows all the year round.

The wind gradient will be greatest between the surface and the tropopause, because the air above the tropopause is more or less isothermal. Because the cold air undercuts the warmer air, the interface is sloping, which makes the core look, to a ground observer, as if it were in polar air,

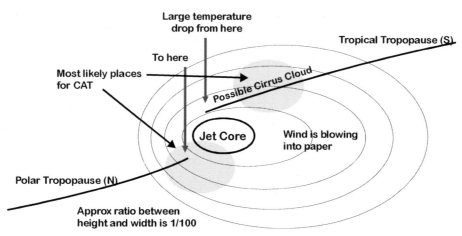

Large temperature drop from here

To here

Tropical Tropopause (S)

Most likely places for CAT

Possible Cirrus Cloud

Jet Core

Wind is blowing into paper

Polar Tropopause (N)

Approx ratio between height and width is 1/100

SUBTROPICAL JET
This is caused by slight temperature contrasts along the boundaries of the Hadley and Ferrel cells in subtropical latitudes. The STJ can usually be found between 25 & 35°, at the 200 mb level.

Between Stockholm and Rio at FL 350 in July, you might encounter a Polar Front Jet, then 1 or 2 Sub Tropical Jets.

LOW LEVEL NOCTURNAL JET
A band of unusually strong southerly winds between 700 and 2000 feet AGL, developing overnight on the Great Plains in the USA, or the Prairies in Canada, or over Southern Queensland or the Northern Territories during Winter in Australia. As a nocturnal inversion develops, the wind near the top can increase to speeds much higher than would be indicated by isobar spacing (say 30-40 kts). It starts at sunset, gets to a maximum a couple of hours after midnight and decreases as the inversion is destroyed.

These jets advect large volumes of warm, moist air Northward from the Gulf of Mexico into the central USA. This is a major factor in the development of thunderstorms in the afternoon and evening.

Low level jets can also be found just ahead of fronts and along a physical barrier such as hills or escarpments (funnelling also creates them).

Hurricanes

A *severe tropical cyclone,* or *revolving storm,* to give a hurricane its proper names, is a non-frontal low that starts over a tropical ocean, that is, in low latitudes where the Coriolis Force is very small, around a core of extremely low pressure, although they do not form near the Equator.

They are classified according to their average one-minute wind speeds - a *tropical depression* or *cyclone* has sustained wind speeds up to 34 kts and a *tropical storm,* between 35-64 knots. Proper hurricanes, or *typhoons* in Asia, are over 65 knots, but in the centre, or the *eye,* the wind speed will be light - 10-20 kt winds are common (the eye can be well observed from a satellite).

Hurricanes arise because vast amounts of water evaporate and are carried upwards on spiralling air currents (the spiralling comes from the Coriolis effect), then the water vapour condenses on to hygroscopic nuclei, releasing

although it is actually in the subtropical warm air mass, between the two tropopause levels. The core is a Westerly tubular ribbon of high-speed air with a circular rotation, when looked from behind or in front, with the rising air being tropical, so you might see cirrus on the equatorial side, although clouds are not usually associated with jetstreams, which makes them more difficult to detect.

From Summer to Winter, the Polar front jetstream over the North Atlantic moves towards the South and speed increases. When crossing a jetstream at right angles in Western Europe, 3 000 feet below the core, with decreasing OAT, the prevailing wind would be coming from the left. If you proceed poleward through a Polar jetstream, the temperature will decrease, and *vice versa.*

Jetstreams are at least 60 kts in strength (more typically 100, or even 150 kts, but 200 kts is rare), and may only be a few hundred miles wide, but they can be thousands of miles long, containing extreme turbulence, which can extend to around 15,000 feet below the tropopause, usually on the polar side - also, head wind components will naturally increase your fuel consumption for the trip. The approximate ratio between height and width is 1:100. The length, width and height of a typical mid-latitude jet stream are respectively 1000 nm, 150 nm and 18 000 ft.

The area of a Polar front jet with the highest possibility of turbulence is, looking downstream, to the left. The most effective way to combat this is to change your flight level. A frequent location of CAT is where the jetstream curves poleward from a rapidly deepening surface low. Jetstreams over 110 kts may have significant turbulence in the sloping tropopause above the core, in the front below the core and on the low pressure side. Maximum winds in a jetstream occur near a break in the tropopause, on the Polar side.

massive amounts of heat that makes the air rise quicker and create vast updraughts that will pull up air from the surface, so the main source of energy is latent heat from the condensation of water vapour. In the end, the whole process keeps repeating itself.

The intense low pressure around a hurricane will lift the sea surface up slightly, and the bulge will push water ahead of the hurricane into very large waves, enough to create a wall of water if it hits land. Hurricane movement is erratic and difficult to predict, but they tend to move to the Northwest (in the Northern hemisphere) in the lower latitudes, and more to the Northeast once they get far enough North to hit the prevailing Westerlies. However, a likely track in the Caribbean is West, turning North East.

Hurricanes only develop where a large area of the sea gets up to 27°C - the water's high specific heat allows the warm waters to persist long after Summer, so you can expect them to occur mostly in the NW Pacific, affecting Japan, Taiwan, Korea and the Chinese coastline, that is, in the Western parts of tropical oceans, because there is more humidity from the long sea passage of the trade winds (they are known as *typhoons* there). There are usually no hurricanes in the SE Pacific and S Atlantic because of the low water temperatures, although there was one in the South Atlantic in 2004 or 2005.

The hurricane season is mainly between July-November (Summer & Autumn), and they occur mostly along the SE coast of the USA. In the Southern hemisphere, the season is from November to March.

Tornadoes

These are rotating funnel-shaped clouds coming downwards out of convective clouds, usually thunderstorms. They can touch the ground, with a typical diameter of less than 50 m, and can lift very heavy items and transport them for several miles. Their exact cause is still not known, but the pressure inside a tornado can be as low as 150 mb. Such a vacuum can be effective - in St Louis, Missouri, in 1896, a pine plank was forced by the high winds that were created from the sharp pressure differentials through a solid iron girder that was supporting the Eads bridge.

Each Spring (for example), cool dry air from the Rockies in Canada collides with hot, humid air from the Caribbean to create two great weather fronts that meet in Oklahoma, Kansas and Texas (Tornado Alley) which start rotating as the hot air rises and the cool air sinks. The peak season for Tornadoes in this area is between March-June. Otherwise, they are most likely in the North Atlantic during Spring and Summer.

A *waterspout* is a gentler cousin of the tornado, coming from a weaker type of cloud, which doesn't mean they're not as destructive.

Other (Local) Winds

Local winds are those that do not arise from patterns of isobars or contours, but are controlled mainly by differences in surface heating. In fact, coastlines, mountains and valleys have more effect on local winds - so much so that the airflow is often across any isobars (they blow for too short a time for coriolis to have much influence). Many local winds are due to diurnal, orographic or seasonal effects, and are so regular that they have their own names:

- The *Pamperos* comes from a marked advance of cold air in S America
- The *Chinook* is a warm, dry, katabatic fohn-like wind that comes off the Rockies near Calgary, Alberta, and other places to the North

DIURNAL EFFECTS

There are naturally occurring daily changes of pressure around the globe, with two maxima and minima at the same local times, namely 10:00/22:00 and 16:00/04:00. In low latitudes (i.e. nearer the Equator), interruptions to this schedule may signify an impending tropical storm.

Because of this, the surface wind increases speed and veers during the day in the Northern Hemisphere, and *vice versa* by night. In the Southern Hemisphere, it increases and backs by day, decreasing and veering by night. Because of this effect, many local winds can be predicted with clock-like regularity. Veering is a clockwise change in wind direction with height or time - backing is the reverse.

The *diurnal variation* actually refers to temperature differences, which is what is ultimately responsible for winds in the first place, although there are diurnal pressure variations, too. The variations are greatest in calm conditions, with no cloud, over land. In desert regions, the difference between day and night temperatures can be as much as 25°C, while over the sea, usually less than 1°C.

LAND & SEA BREEZES

These arise out of a temperature difference between land and sea areas. Air over land warms up and cools down faster than that over the sea, because land has a lower specific heat than water does and needs less heat to warm it up. Thus, temperature changes over land will occur a lot more frequently than they do over the sea. When the land is warmer than the sea, the air over it becomes less dense and the space left by the rising air is filled with an extra component coming from over the water to produce a *sea breeze* which is added to any existing wind (in fact, a relatively high pressure is created at about 1000 feet over land, to produce a pressure gradient aloft).

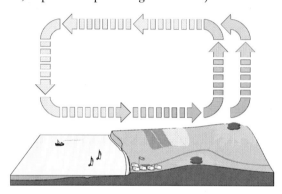

With lower pressure at the same height over the water, there will be air movement towards the sea, at the upper levels (because the column of warm air is taller, and the relative pressure is higher), which will subside to come back towards the land. At night, the process is reversed to get a land breeze. However, land areas are poor conductors of heat and will only be affected through a shallow layer. As a result, land breezes are weaker because the temperature differences are smaller and so is the local pressure gradient.

A prevailing wind can oppose a sea-breeze and delay its development, or go with it and increase its speed, although, at latitudes greater than about 20°, Coriolis can change the direction of a sea breeze.

If a convergence is created, sea breezes can be strong enough to create their own cold fronts, well inland*, and even trigger thunderstorms, as the colder sea air undercuts the land air.

*In Australia, for example, sea breezes have been encountered 400 km away from the sea.

THE BAROMETER

This is an instrument that measures atmospheric pressure, using mercury or an evacuated capsule, hence the *aneroid* (no fluid) barometer (*baros* is Greek for *weight*). The

mercury barometer is quite simple - a long test tube with a vacuum inside is inverted and its end placed into a quantity of mercury. Air pressure makes the level rise or fall, and the height of its column in the tube is measured. You could actually use any liquid, but mercury is very dense, which means you can have a shorter tube.

Aneroid barometers are smaller and used in confined spaces, particularly instrument panels, but they are calibrated against mercury barometers. A device that measures pressure changes over time (with a moving pen over a moving paper drum) is called a *barograph*.

THE ALTIMETER

This is simply an aneroid barometer calibrated in feet rather than millibars or inches of mercury (its inner workings are described fully in *AGK Instruments*). It measures the pressure difference between a selected pressure surface and that at the level of the aircraft.

You would be very lucky to hit the standard atmosphere more than, say, 25% of the time, so you need a means of adjusting any instruments based on it to cope with the differences. An altimeter has a *setting window* in which you can adjust the figures of a *subscale* for the correct pressure on the ground by turning a knob on the front. This is actually part of a very important preflight check, where you make sure that if you turn the knob to the right, the height readings increase, and *vice versa*.

Also, in a pre-flight operational test, the tolerance is ±50'. If you've got two altimeters, they should be within ± 50

feet of each other (in other words, they can misread by nearly 100 feet and still be useable).

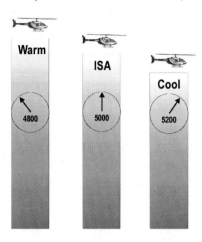

If you didn't adjust your instruments, and were flying between areas with different air pressure, you would not be at the height you thought you were, so your relative height to hard objects, that is, obstacles, such as mountains, television masts, etc. will not be maintained. As an example, when flying from high to low pressure, your altimeter would over-read (from HIGH to LOW, your instrument is HIGH), so you would be lower than planned and liable for a nasty surprise. It's therefore much safer to be going the other way (that is, from LOW to HIGH, where your instrument is LOW). You can check what the difference is with simple maths, using the figures given above of 1" being roughly equal to 1,000 feet. Remember that an increase in pressure equals a decrease in altitude, so if you start with 29.92, then go to where it's 30.92, the altimeter reading would be 1,000 feet *less*, even though the figures themselves increase.

To convert from inches to millibars, in case you have an old altimeter, start at 29.92 and find the difference between it and the current pressure. Divide the difference by 0.03" inches and apply the result to 1013. In other words, 1 Mb (hPa) is equal to 0.03". For example, if the current pressure is 30.02, that is, 0.1" above 29.92" (or 3 x 0.03), add 3 Mb and set 1016. A more formal way is to use this formula:

$$\frac{millibars}{1013.25} = \frac{ins}{29.92}$$

Better yet, here is a table:

hPa (Mb)	Inches (of Mercury)									
	0	1	2	3	4	5	6	7	8	9
970	28.64	28.67	28.70	28.73	28.76	28.79	28.82	28.85	28.88	28.91
980	28.94	28.97	29.00	29.03	29.05	29.08	29.11	29.14	29.17	29.20
990	29.23	29.26	29.29	29.32	29.35	29.38	29.41	29.44	29.47	29.50
1000	29.53	29.56	29.59	29.62	29.65	29.68	29.71	29.74	29.77	29.80
1010	29.83	29.86	29.89	29.92	29.95	29.97	30.00	30.03	30.06	30.09
1020	30.12	30.15	30.18	30.21	30.24	30.27	30.30	30.33	30.36	30.39
1030	30.42	30.45	30.47	30.50	30.53	30.56	30.59	30.62	30.65	30.68
1040	30.71	30.74	30.77	30.80	30.83	30.86	30.89	30.92	30.95	30.98

The standard atmosphere has a temperature element that also affects the altimeter. Remembering that, as we said above, air density decreases as it gets warmer, a point in your imaginary column of air above a station would be higher on a warm day than otherwise (see left). If, therefore, as is typical near the Rockies in Winter, the air is *very much* colder than standard (actually below about -16°C), you will be lower than you should be (actually, the phrase above is still valid, in that going from HIGH *temperature* to LOW, your instruments will be HIGH). A *cold low* will lower True Altitude to a point where it is dangerous to fly in mountains.

This is serious stuff because, in low temperatures, combined with other effects caused by movement of wind over ridges, you could be *as much as 3000 feet below your projected altitud*e, which could really spoil your day (although when coming down the ILS, you are relying more on a radio signal than the altimeter). More practically, you could have a 150-foot difference on a published minimum of 500 feet and be too close to the ground. Another factor that arises from the above diagram is the creation of a wind purely from the temperature difference.

The cooler column has a lower pressure at a given altitude, and the warmer one has a higher pressure, causing air to move, from left to right, in this case, so, applying Buys Ballot's law, low temperature is on the left in the Northern Hemisphere if you stand with your back to the wind. The vertical distance between two pressure levels is less in cold air, as pressure decreases at a greater rate. Pressure in the upper levels depends on the mean temperature of the column of air beneath the point concerned.

In simple terms, when the surface temperature is well *below* ISA (starting at -16°C), correct your altitudes by:

Surface Temp (ISA)	Correction
-16°C to -30°C	+ 10%
-31°C to -50°C	+ 20%
-51°C or below	+ 25%

But here is an abridged table covering the lower levels:

°C	ISA Dev	Height above touchdown or above aerodrome in feet								
		200	**300**	**400**	**500**	**600**	**700**	**800**	**900**	**1000**
-0	-15	20	20	30	30	40	40	50	50	60
-10	-25	20	30	40	50	60	70	80	90	100
-20	-35	30	50	60	70	90	100	120	130	140
-30	-45	40	60	80	100	120	130	150	170	190
-40	-55	50	80	100	120	150	170	190	220	240
-50	-65	60	90	120	150	180	210	240	270	300

The table is rounded up to the nearest 10 feet. For example, at -20°C at 500 feet, your altimeter should be reading 570 ft to ensure a height above ground of 500 ft.

Just remember that, when temperatures are *less* than ISA, you will be lower than the altimeter reading, so *add* any values in tables to published altitudes or heights, and you *must* advise ATC that you are doing so. You can refuse IFR assigned altitudes if temperature error reduces obstacle clearance limits to an unacceptable level, but once the assigned altitude has been accepted, you cannot adjust it for altimeter temperature error.

When the aerodrome temperature is -30°C or colder, add 1000 feet to the MSA to ensure obstacle clearance.

Altimeter Settings

The *altimeter setting* (QNH) is the *station pressure* reduced to mean sea level under ISA temperatures and standard lapse rates, that is, taking the elevation of the aerodrome into account, expressed in inches of mercury (Hg) in North America, or hectopascals in Europe. It is what your altimeter must be set to when flying near aerodromes or other places that may issue it, because otherwise it will only tell you your height above the point you started from. Its other importance is its use on weather maps to create isobars, as mentioned before. To adjust station pressure for sea level, take the elevation and get its equivalent in inches. 500 feet would therefore be 0.5", which is *added* to

whatever the reading is, because the sea is *lower* and would give lower figures anyway. MSL pressure is station pressure corrected to sea level using the average temperature over the last 12 hours.

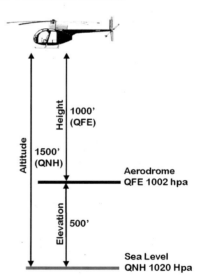

Note: The word *height* refers to distance above a ground-based datum. The word *altitude* is used for distance above *sea level*, so the helicopter on the left has a height of 1000 feet (above the aerodrome, or QFE) and an altitude of 1500 feet (above the sea, or QNH). When using the *standard setting* of 1013 hPa or 29.92 inches (QNE), above the *transition level*, your vertical displacement is expressed in

Flight Levels, which are the altimeter readings with a digit knocked off the end - FL 30 is an altimeter reading of 3000 feet when set to standard.

The barometric pressure is constantly changing and varies from one place to another. What would happen if you departed the spot in the diagram above and returned several hours later to find the pressure of 30.12 inches had reduced to 29.38? The altimeter would be over-reading by 530 feet and you would only be 470 feet off the ground (30.12 - 29.59 = 530, 1500 - 530 = 970 AMSL = 470 AGL). Thus, the altimeter needs constant updating.

These settings are used throughout a flight:

- The altimeter setting is used for general transit, below the transition altitude. It is the aerodrome pressure to one that would theoretically exist at sea level at that point - this is done because reporting stations are not all at the same level. You add the pressure change for elevation above sea level on a standard day. It is forecast for one or two hours ahead over large areas

- The "standard" setting is 29.92" (1013.2 mb), used for Flight Levels above the transition altitude

Note: The altimeter setting is the *Lowest Forecast Pressure* for a complete region, valid for a considerable time, so don't expect accurate height indications!

Pressure Altitude

Pressure altitude is the height within the standard atmosphere that you may find a given pressure, usually 29.92" or 1013 Mb, but actually whatever you set on the altimeter - if you set 1013 on the subscale and the needles read 6,000 feet, the PA *for that setting* is 6,000 feet. PA is a favourite starting point for any calculations for performance, TAS, etc. If the sea level pressure is different from 1013, obstacle clearance heights and airfield elevations, etc. must be converted before using them. To do this, get the local altimeter setting, find the difference between it and 29.92 (or 1013), convert it to feet (1"=1,000 or 1 mb=27 feet at sea level), then apply it the *opposite* side of 29.92. You could also get PA from the altimeter itself, by placing 29.92 or 1013 in the setting window, and reading the figures directly.

The significance of this concerns performance - if the pressure on the surface is less than standard, you are effectively at a higher altitude, and your machine will not fly so well. You often need to be able to calculate the likely pressure altitude of a location beforehand so you know what your performance will be.

For example, for a helipad on the side of a mountain at 400 feet above sea level, with an altimeter setting of 29.72, your PA at that location would actually be 600 feet, since the difference between 29.92 and 29.72 is 0.2, or 200 feet *added*, and where you would enter your performance charts, since they are calibrated for standard atmosphere (the altimeter setting is *below* the standard pressure, so your answer should be *above*). Again, you are *adding* because the sea is *lower*, and the figures ought to be higher. In the exam, write down 29.92 first, then subtract the altimeter setting and multiply by 1,000. If the answer is negative, take it away from the elevation. If it's positive, then add. The same principles apply if you are using millibars and 1013, where 1 Mb = 27 feet in the lower levels.

Pressure levels with altitude are:

Height	Pressure Level
Surface	1013
10 000	700
18 000	500
24 000	400
30 000	300
34 000	250
38 000	200
58 000	100

Density Altitude

This is the *altitude in the Standard Atmosphere at which the prevailing density occurs*, meaning your real altitude from the effects of height, temperature and humidity, and is used to establish performance, as it is a figure that expresses where your machine thinks it is, as opposed to where it actually is - see also the *Performance* chapter. For now, it is *pressure altitude corrected for non-standard temperature, or* the true air temperature at a given level. Thus, pressure altitude has the same value as density altitude at standard temperature.

To find DA on the flight computer, set the aerodrome elevation or Pressure Altitude against the temperature in the *airspeed* window. The DA is against the datum arrow in the PA window. If you want a formula:

$$PA \pm 118.8 \times ISA\ Dev$$

(Multiplying ISA Deviation by 120 is good enough).

Corrected Altitude

This is *indicated altitude* corrected for temperature. True Altitude is indicated altitude corrected for the fact that non-standard temperatures lead to non-standard pressure lapse rates.

TEMPERATURE

· ·

The words *air temperature* refer to the amount of heat contained in the air, represented by the kinetic energy of its molecules rubbing against each other. The faster they move, the hotter it is, and *vice versa*. Heat is the sum total of energy possessed by the moving molecules of a body - temperature is the rate at which those molecules oscillate. As you heat an item, its molecules need more room in which to oscillate, so it expands. As the distance between the molecules grows, the molecular force that keeps them together gets weaker.

As mentioned above, most, if not all, of the Earth's heat comes from the Earth itself, that is, from below. The Sun's rays do not produce heat (or light) until they hit something (which is why it's cold and dark in space), so the air will get warmed by *conduction* from the ground which has been heated up by them, known as *insolation*. In other words, *terrestrial radiation* and *conduction* are primarily responsible for heating the lower atmosphere.

Glider pilots and anyone who has done basic physics will know that lighter areas radiate heat better than dark areas do, so different parts of the earth will produce different amounts of heat, and *thermals*, which is what keeps gliders up in the air (for exam purposes, thermals are called *convection currents*, and they are just rising parcels of warm air). The ocean is always slower to warm up than the land, as are any marshy areas and forests, because the Sun's rays penetrate further and are weakened as a result. By comparison, rocks, roadways and pavements are very quick, so, as a general rule, the drier the surface, the better for producing thermals (any moisture will require energy to warm it up first, which retards any output of heat). Along with surface characteristics, the latitude of a place will have an effect on local temperature, because the amount of insolation will vary. In the same way, if you apply an equal amount of heat to various substances, some will warm up quicker than others - the standard for comparison is that applied to water, which has a specific heat value of 1. Smaller quantities increase temperature more rapidly.

Since the Earth does not get hotter and hotter as the Sun shines on it, it follows that heat must be radiated away somewhere. This explains the difference in temperatures between day and night, known as *diurnal variation*. The temperature begins to rise shortly after sunrise (after an initial dip) because the Sun's radiation exceeds that of the Earth, and starts to fall mid-afternoon, when it falls below, carrying on through the night until the process starts

again. This is less marked over water, which reacts more slowly. In fact, changes over the sea will not be much more than 1°C. The *maximum variation* (exam question) would happen inland with clear skies over a dry area, such as the desert. Clouds will also absorb and reflect some energy from the Sun during the day, and act as a blanket overnight to stop heat being radiated away, further reducing diurnal differences. Clouds can reduce the normal 50% insolation the Earth might receive on a sunny day right down to 15% (the remainder is reflected back by clouds and the atmosphere). Windspeed and relative humidity will also have an effect.

There are two ways of measuring temperature (or rather the average kinetic energy of molecules), called *Fahrenheit* or *Centigrade* (*Celsius*), and it's a real pain to convert between the two. The quick and easy way is to use a flight computer, but here are the calculations for people who want to show off:

F - C $Tc = (5/9)*(Tf-32)$

C - F $Tf = ((9/5)*Tc)+32$

16°C is equal to 61°F, 20°C is 68°F and 30°C is 86°F, for gross error checks and quick conversions - however, given the standard of performance charts in the average flight manual, doubling the Celsius amount and adding 30 to get Fahrenheit, or subtracting 30 from Fahrenheit and dividing the remainder in half to get Celsius is probably good enough! The Fahrenheit scale assumes that water freezes at 32°, and boils at 212°. Celsius starts at 0° and finishes at 100°, which is more logical, but the scale is coarser. The *freezing level* (in flight) is where the temperature is 0°C.

For each °C of cooling, a gas will reduce its volume by 1/273. -273°C is equal to 0 K (*Kelvin*), or *Absolute*, which is the point at which all molecular motion is supposed to have stopped, and therefore has the least kinetic energy. Alternatively, you could say that 0°C is equal to 273 K (or A), from which you can deduce that the 1° steps in both scales are the same (*Rankin* is an absolute scale with the same divisions as Fahrenheit - add 459.69 to Fahrenheit totals. Kelvins are base units rather than a scale, so they don't carry a degree sign).

Thermometers are covered in the *Instruments* chapter.

Inversions

We have already seen that the standard reduction of temperature with height is 1.98°C per thousand feet. Where it remains constant, there is an *isothermal layer*. Where it *increases* (typical in anticyclonic conditions), you have an *inversion*, but the lapse process stops at the tropopause anyway, so the stratosphere would be a good place to find an inversion. Thus, a temperature inversion exists where the air temperature *increases* with altitude instead of decreasing. In other words, cold air will be underneath warmer air, which can happen during the passage of a cold front, or a cooler onshore breeze might be flowing over warm sea water. Cool air that is rising will lose its buoyancy and be stopped from rising further upon reaching its equilibrium level. In a thunderstorm, this happens just above the tropopause, where the cloud material settles into a layer that causes the anvil shape.

Overnight radiation cooling of air at the surface can cause an inversion too, as can katabatic winds in the mountains that settle in valleys. It is also a possible consequence of subsidence - the stable layer at some height in the low troposphere of an older high in the mid-latitudes is a *subsidence inversion,* which can be responsible for trapping thick haze and smoke in the lower levels. More permanent inversions are associated with large high-pressure systems, where descending currents of air near the centre cause the air to warm up by compression, so the air at middle altitudes becomes warmer than that at the surface.

Performance is affected by variations in temperature, and inversions will do so adversely. Large ones encountered shortly after takeoff can seriously degrade climb performance, particularly when you're heavy. Even a small one in the upper levels can prevent you reaching a preferred cruising altitude. At lower levels, expect deteriorating visibility, as an inversion can prevent fog clearance for prolonged periods until blown away by horizontal movement of air (to improve your chances of seeing the surface, fly higher above a mist layer). Below a low level inversion, visibility is often moderate or poor because there is no vertical exchange to carry pollutants and haze into the free atmosphere (industrial pollutants, especially incinerated pesticides during the stubble burning season, collect at the base of an inversion - they can be trapped within it, but surface-based pollutants cannot ascend into the inversion layer.

Winds tend to be stronger above an inversion, so above and below, the wind is likely to change significantly in speed and direction. A strong low level inversion promotes vertical windshear.

When flight planning, you can find the top of an inversion (assuming the air below it is well mixed, as it would be in the presence of insolation) by allowing 400 feet for every degree of difference (in Celsius) between the temperature and dewpoint.

ISA Conversions

Many exam questions involve comparing the ambient temperature against what it should be under ISA conditions. Although the reduction is technically 1.98°C per 1000', 2° is often used for convenience, as is done with the *jet standard atmosphere*, which doesn't have a tropopause - a point to watch with questions that take you above 36,000 feet. -60°C at 40,000' is ISA -4.2.

You might be asked what the temperature deviation is at FL 290, when the OAT is -47°C? First of all, find out what the temperature difference from sea level *should* be, so, using 2°C per thousand feet, we find it should be 58° lower (29 x 2). Given that the temperature at sea level is always 15°C in ISA, subtract one from the other to get -43°C (-58+15). As the OAT is -47°C, the temperature deviation is ISA - 4°C (that is, 4° colder than it should be). In short, find ISA by multiplying the altitude in thousands of feet by -2 and adding 15, then apply deviation. Height changes by 4% for every 10° deviation.

The other way round, you could have to find temperature, given a deviation at a flight level. If it's ISA -7°C at FL 250, +15 (ISA) - 50 (25 x 2) gets us -35°C, normal ISA temperature. Applying the deviation, which is colder, we get -42°C.

Tip: To find out what the standard temperature should be at any level, line up the two tens on the inner and outer wheels of your flight computer and take a look in the altitude window against the height you require.

15° at Sea level or -5° at 10,000 ft

MOISTURE

A given parcel of air can hold a certain amount of moisture at a certain temperature. This ability is increased as the air gets warmer, and decreased as it gets colder. The source of such water vapour is mainly evaporation from oceans, lakes, vegetation, etc. As particles of exposed water break off into the air, the *average* rate of motion of those left behind decreases, which is detected as cooling, thus, heat energy is seen as being used up as molecules break away, and is regarded as being hidden within the vapour as *latent heat*.

Latent Heat

In the solid and liquid states, water molecules are bound strongly together, but in the gaseous state, the bond is weak. Rather a lot of energy is required in the form of heat to make it weak - 600 times more, in fact, than is required to raise the temperature of water by 1°C. The heat energy that is used to break the bonds is absorbed by the water vapour, from which position it is used to keep the molecules apart, which is required for the water vapour to remain as a gas. Because this energy is stored with the water molecules, it is known as latent heat, and it accounts for how water vapour is able to transport large amounts of heat, albeit hidden, around the globe. The heat is released again when the water vapour condenses, warming the surrounding air. As it is now less dense, the warmed air will rise.

Dewpoint

This is the temperature at which cooling results in 100% saturation, or the point at which water vapour begins the process of condensation (at constant pressure) into visible water droplets, so, if the temperature and dewpoint at an airfield are the same, it will take very little incentive for clouds to form - the further apart they are, the less likely you are to get cloud, and therefore icing if the temperature is low enough (however, the warmer the wet air is, the more likely you are to meet bad weather). Without hygroscopic nuclei for the water particles to bind on to, condensation may not actually occur, even when air cools below its dewpoint (*supersaturation*).

Constant pressure is mentioned above because pressure changes when air is lifted, so the dewpoint can change with altitude.

Humidity

The *absolute humidity* is the actual mass of water vapour in a given volume of moist air, expressed in grams per cubic metre (i.e. as a volume). Over the sea, it is usually at its minimum at dawn, and at its maximum shortly after noon, because of the temperature (opposite to relative humidity).

The *Humidity Mixing Ratio* is also the actual mass of water vapour in a given mass of air, but expressed in grams/kg, or as weight rather than volume. *HMR for saturation* is the maximum mass that *could* be contained.

RELATIVE HUMIDITY

For a particular temperature, relative humidity can tell you how close the air is to being saturated. It is a measure of how much moisture an air parcel is holding against what it *could* hold at that temperature (and pressure) or, in other words, the *percentage saturation*, which will *decrease* if the air gets warmer, as when subsiding in a high pressure area, because temperature is raised by compression, and it can absorb more moisture. Thus, the amount of water vapour that air can hold is determined by the temperature:

Temp	*Vapour*
30°C	27 gms/kg
15°C	11 gms/kg
0°C	4 gms/kg

Relative Humidity is officially defined as the vapour pressure (or mixing ratio) divided by the saturation vapour pressure (or saturation mixing ratio), multiplied by 100. It is *not* the dewpoint divided by the temperature!

Humidity is also known as *vapour pressure*, because water vapour exerts its own partial pressure. At saturation point, this will be maximum. As air rises, it expands, and reduces its pressure, and hence the partial pressure, which ultimately reduces the dewpoint.

Relative humidity could change as a result of the air absorbing more moisture, say when moving over the sea, but it is more likely to change quickly through temperature changes (including diurnally with the Earth's atmosphere), at least for our purposes. On a typical day, relative humidity is high in the morning (as it is cooler) and lower in the late afternoon (when it gets warmer).

Relative humidity can also indicate the drying power of the air, since evaporation is most intense at high temperatures and low humidities, and *vice versa*.

Water added to air makes it moister, and less dense, and more likely to rise.

MEASUREMENT

The *hygrometer* is an instrument that measures how wet the air is. A piece of human (or horse) hair, which gets longer as it gets moister, is laid out against a calibrated scale of known humidities (its length increases by about 2.5% between 0-100% relative humidity). A "suitable linkage" transmits its movements to show relative humidity.

Another method is to use two thermometers inside a *Stevenson's screen* about four feet off the ground. One measures the temperature of the ambient air, and the other has its bulb surrounded with wet muslin, using distilled water. If the air is dry, the water in the muslin will evaporate and make the remaining water cooler (due to the *latent heat of evaporation*) and the wet-bulb thermometer will indicate a lower temperature. Thus, the drier the air is, the greater will be the difference between the readings (the closer they are together, the less likely is the risk of frost). Relative humidity is then deduced with the use of tables, or a *tephigram*. A Stevenson's screen has louvred sides to stop the Sun's rays affecting the thermometers, while still allowing a free flow of ambient air across them.

The *dewpoint depression* is the difference between the temperature and the dewpoint, while the *wetbulb depression* is the difference between the wet and dry bulb temperatures. The dry bulb temperature is the actual temperature, while the wet bulb temperature is the temperature air will cool to when water evaporates into unsaturated air. *When the air is saturated, the dewpoint is equal to the wet bulb temperature and the actual temperature.*

In unsaturated air, the dewpoint is always lower than the wet bulb temperature because, as air is saturated, the temperature decreases, while the dewpoint increases.

Mostly, air is made to reach its saturation point by force, such as being moved up the sides of mountains or over large areas of slower moving air (*large scale ascent*) and, if the conditions are right, cloud will form. In fact, the ways of cooling air are many. Where horizontal movement over a cooler surface is involved, it is called *advective*, as found in the Atlantic provinces of Canada, when moist air passes over the cold Labrador Current.

The convection currents we have already met cause adiabatic cooling by lifting air so that it expands and cools, and expansion cooling is really the same thing caused by upslope movement or mechanical turbulence, another name for low level air being mixed and moved upward (*adiabatic* means that no heat is removed or added - temperature changes happen in other ways, i.e. from expansion or compression. That is, work is done at the expense of internal energy). A good example of "upslope

fog" occurs over the Canadian prairies when air is moving from East to West (Winnipeg is about 800 feet ASL, Regina to the West is about 1900 feet ASL, and Calgary, in the foothills of the Rockies, is about 3500 feet ASL).

Radiation cooling tends to happen overnight with clear skies, when the Earth's heat radiates out into space and the air next to the ground gets cold enough to condense out any moisture it contains. If the winds are light, just enough to stir things up (3-5 kts), fog will form, predictably called *radiation fog*, with typical vertical extent of up to 500 feet. A good rule of thumb is that when the T/Td spread is below 5°F, with radiational cooling occurring, fog is possible.

If there is no wind, you will just get dew on the ground, and if the wind is too strong you will get low level stratus cloud. The most common way for it to dissipate is through the Sun's heat raising the temperature above the dewpoint (usually by 10 in the morning, and the visibility will get worse before it gets better), but winds help, as does a drier airstream to absorb the moisture. Below is a picture of the process happening in the Rockies.

Night-time cooling is less over water than land, as water traps heat. Clouds have an effect because they absorb radiation themselves. The *topographical effect* results from cold air getting trapped in valleys and lower areas, and the stronger cooling is more conducive to fog formation.

Note: *Deposition* occurs when water vapour goes directly to the solid state (i.e. ice) without a liquid stage. *Sublimation* is when it goes the other way, that is, ice is converted directly to water vapour (actually, the word is used for both directions as well).

Lapse Rates

The lapse rate is the *rate of change of temperature with height* (usually a decrease).

ENVIRONMENTAL LAPSE RATE

This is the actual measured change, which is about 6.5°C per 1000 m (1.98°C per 1000 feet). However, it does vary, depending on local air conditions.

ADIABATIC LAPSE RATE

This is a theoretical rate which can be calculated, and there are two variations:

DRY ADIABATIC LAPSE RATE

The DALR is the (constant, fixed) *decrease in temperature of unsaturated air with height* at a rate of 3°C per 1,000 feet* or 9.8°C (10°C) per 1,000 m (*Dry* in these circumstances just means a relative humidity of less than 100%). *Adiabatic* means that no heat is exchanged with the surroundings - the air warms up and cools down due to pressure (height) change, with no external heat or moisture added or removed. Such a parcel of air rising through the atmosphere will find the surrounding pressure to be less, so it will expand. The molecular energy is spread out into a larger volume, which is detected as cooling the air. If it were to descend again, it would end up at the same temperature it started with. After the dew point, however, you need to consider......

*In practice, there is an excess of around 1° near the ground, so the first 1 000 feet should really decrease at the rate of 4°C per 1,000 feet. This is called *super-adiabatic*, and it is not a factor for the exams, I'm just being picky.

SATURATED ADIABATIC LAPSE RATE

The SALR allows for *latent heat*, or the energy that is released when water condenses. Latent means *undeveloped*, implying that an amount of heat is lurking in the background waiting to do something, so when the water vapour condenses out, the air parcel will get warmer as energy is released into it. Converting water from one state to the other requires energy, which originally comes from the Sun's rays during evaporation, and is stored with the vapour, as the water molecules must be kept apart with that energy. Condensed water molecules are strongly attracted to each other, and are balanced by equally strong repulsive forces. The energy that goes with the vapour is the *latent heat of vapourisation*. When vapour condenses back into a liquid the latent heat is released into the surrounding air as *sensible heat* and affects the SALR.

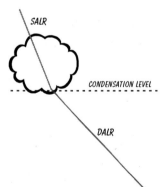

The presence of latent heat means that the air will cool more slowly. In fact, there can be so much heat released that flight in normally stable layer cloud can be quite bumpy, from internal eddying. Latent heat leads to the *Chinook*, which is a dry, warm*, downslope wind in the lee of the Rockies, commonly found from Calgary southward all the way through to Colorado, that can raise the air temperature to over 20°C in Winter. This is probably why the native Indians called it the Snow Eater, which is what the name *Chinook* means.

*With the Chinook, the air on the windward side is so cold (and therefore stable) that it does not rise up the slope (it is said to be blocked). The wind at higher levels is diverted down the lee slopes instead. As the air in this wind has very little moisture to start with, its descent produces more warming, hence the warm and dry characteristics.

Saturated air made to rise by the mountains cools at SALR, and when it descends on the other side, having dropped its moisture, it warms at twice that, i.e. DALR, so you get a dry, warm wind with clear skies.

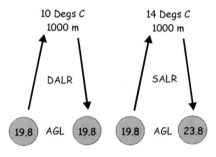

In California, it causes fires. In the Alps, it is known as the *Föhn Effect*, which is the correct term for the exam. Being downslope, it is a katabatic wind.

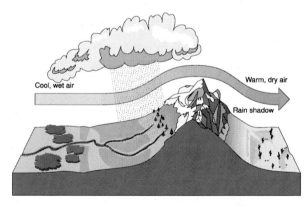

The SALR can range from 4°C to as high as 9°C per 1000 m, but the average for exam purposes (for lower levels anyway) is 6°C per 1000 m, or 1.8°C per 1000 feet, for

Europe. The reason for the variation is simply that warm air can hold more moisture - and there is more latent heat with which to warm the air as condensation takes place. This also explains why high clouds are thinner - there is less moisture to condense out because the air is cooler.

THE BRADBURY RULE

The rate of closure of the HMR against the DALR is around 2.5°C per 1000 feet, or 1°C per 400*, so, when finding out a freezing level, find the cloud base, then switch to the SALR (the dew-point lapse rate is 0.6°C per 1000 feet). To find the cloudbase, just multiply the difference between the surface temperature and dewpoint (Tdry-Tdew) by 400 to get an approximate height.

*This rule of thumb is named after the glider pilot/meteorologist Tom Bradbury. It is a better method for predicting the base of cumulus cloud TAFs, which usually give the lowest base during the forecast period.

Note: This only works if cumulus actually forms.

For example, if the ground temperature is 10°C, and the dewpoint 7°C, the cloudbase should be at 1,200 feet (3 x 400). Then divide whatever the dewpoint temperature is by 1.8 and add the converted number in thousands of feet to the cloudbase to get the freezing level. Divide 7 by 1.8 to get 3.8889, which becomes 3889 feet, so the freezing level is at 5089 feet.

Stability

Remembering the previous mention of convection currents, you can see that air has vertical movement as

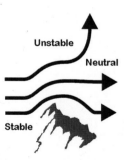

well as horizontal. The less movement there is, the more stable the air is, and the less bumpy, because it tends to resist vertical motion - a parcel of air in stable conditions will tend to return to its original level after rising or sinking. On the other hand, a parcel in unstable air will rise or sink more quickly - that is, it will continue accelerating.

A cold air mass moving over a warmer surface will be unstable because the lower layers will pick up moisture and temperature, which will be warmer than the surrounding air. This heating from below causes the lapse rate to steepen, and the moisture makes the air less dense. This will carry on into the night over the sea, as the water will keep its heat better than land will. On the other hand, a warm air mass over a cold one will have its lower layers

reduced in temperature, possibly as far as an inversion, which is about as stable as you can get.

Instability arises when air is upset by small disturbances, such as when air warmer than that surrounding it begins to rise, as it is bound to do, because it is less dense. It may have been lifted in the first place by *convection, convergence, mechanical turbulence, orographic* (over a geographic barrier, like a mountain range) or *frontal* means. The warmer it is when it starts, the more energy the bubble has to keep going, but it's really the lapse rate that determines when it stops (well, OK, humidity counts as well). As it rises, air expands, and cools, matching the air around it, until it eventually cools off quicker than the surrounding air, and stops. Once it becomes saturated, though (and cloud forms), cooling slows down and allows the ascent to continue further, because the condensation releases heat and gives the (now less dense) parcel of air a boost (so if the air is already hot and moist before it hits relatively cooler air, say from the Caribbean, thunderstorms are highly likely). In addition, the air containing water vapour is less dense.

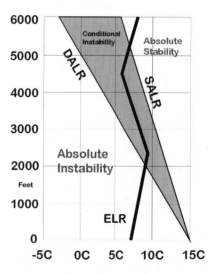

If the environmental lapse rate lies to the left of the DALR (being steeper), air is *absolutely unstable*, which is quite a rare condition. If the lapse rate is between the DALR and SALR (that is, between 1.8 and 3°C per 1000 feet), it is *conditionally unstable*, meaning stable when dry, but unstable if saturated. To the right of the SALR, limited convection is possible, and to the right of the isothermal (i.e. vertical), you get total stability from an inversion. Thus, in flight, you can estimate the stability by the *rate of change* of temperature with height - the more rapid the change, the more instability there is. You can infer stability from a low rate of change or even an inversion. If the lapse rate above the condensation level is greater than the SALR, the rising air actually gets warmer than that around it, which will give intense ascents and be instrumental in forming thunderstorms. Then all you need is a *trigger action* to cause condensation.

In summary, stability affects the type of clouds and precipitation, visibility, wind strength and turbulence. Stable air can produce poor visibility at low levels, constant drizzle, light or calm winds with layer cloud, and no turbulence. Unstable air, on the other hand, tends to be associated with good visibility, heavy precipitation, heap clouds, strong winds, turbulence and storms.

CLOUDS

Clouds are symptoms of the weather - in theory, if you know what clouds belong to what weather systems, you can deduce what weather is coming, and when, based on the known movement characteristics of those systems. For example, if you see wisps of cirrus cloud approaching from the West, you know that in around 15 hours it will be raining continuously from low, grey cloud, and you might encounter freezing rain, because that's what happens with a warm front, and they move at around 15-20 knots, assuming they are not blocked by something like a high pressure system. If you notice that the wind has picked up and the altimeter setting has dropped a bit, you would know it is quite close. Similarly, if you see Cu or Cb clouds, you know the air is unstable.

The amount of cloud in the sky is reported in *Oktas*, or eighths of the sky area. *Opacity* is a function of cloud depth and droplet distribution. The *cloud base* is the height of the first available cloud above the official aerodrome elevation, although this may differ between countries (in the USA, for example, it is the height of the base of a cloud layer, of which there can be many). It can be measured by releasing a balloon which ascends at a known rate and timing its disappearance into cloud. At night, beams of a searchlight can be reflected, and the angles calculated with an *alidade*. In a *cloud base recorder*, a narrow beam of light continually swings from near the horizontal to the vertical. Inside, a photo-electric cell only receives light from the vertical, and for any cloud base, there will be only one angle that provides this. However, these are now largely obsolete, and the *laser beam ceilometer* is now in widespread use.

Cloud names were coined by an amateur meteorologist, Luke Howard, in 1803, who based them on the Latin words for *hair*, *heap*, *layer* and *rain-bearing* (*cirrus*, *cumulus*, *stratus* and *nimbus*) not to mention *middle* and *broken* (*alto* and *fracto*). Others, as modifications, were added by Kaemtz and Renou, whose work was followed by scientists at Upsala University.

Clouds form in the first place because air contains water vapour, and because the air is cooled, causing the vapour to condense out at the saturation point (it binds on to *hygroscopic nuclei*, the official name for dirt, which can include pollen and pollutant particles). Air holds more vapour when it is warm, and a given amount can become saturated in two ways - you can either add more water vapour to it, or reduce its temperature. The excess vapour changes from gas to liquid, with the droplets *coalescing* into clouds as they collide. When they get heavy, they fall under gravity. The *Bergeron-Findeisen* theory says that some water droplets turn to ice and grow after sublimation of water vapour and collision with supercooled water droplets (see *Icing*). However, I have seen snow materialise out of the sky in Northern Canada (e.g. formating on nothing at all), and favour the coalescence theory, since Bergeron-Findeisen doesn't explain clouds in Summer that have no freezing level. However, coalescence does tend to occur in warmer and deeper clouds.

Cooling occurs when air expands as it is forced upwards in various ways:

- Uplift over a land or air mass (orographic lifting). The exact type depends on the stability (or otherwise) of the air

- Convection currents, such as thermals rising from a heated surface

- Frontal lifting

- Eddying (at the surface, or at the boundaries of two layers of air)

- Waves in the lee of mountains

- Uplift from a depression

Clouds affect surface heating by shielding the Earth and absorbing the Sun's Rays, or acting like a blanket to keep the heat in at night. Those above the freezing level are largely ice crystals. Otherwise, there are two main types, *layer*, or *heap*, associated with stable and unstable conditions (below), which might also be called *stratiform* or *cumuliform*, meaning horizontally or vertically developed, respectively. There are a further three classifications based on the height of the cloud base, namely:

The limits of each classification vary with latitude (and the troposphere). Low clouds do not have a prefix added to their name, medium cloud has *alto* in front and high clouds have *cirro*. *Nimbo* means rain-bearing

Low (Strato)

From SL to about 6500 feet, consisting mainly of water:

- **Stratus** (St), thin, uniform, low, boring, associated with relatively stable air. Not much precipitation. At ground level, is called fog or mist. Caused by large areas cooling, rather than individual pockets of air, as with cumulus

- **Stratocumulus** (Sc). Like stratus, but cumulus-like, with small globules popping up here and there, and well-defined bases. Often formed in eddy currents which cause stratus to clump up, because the stratus tops will be cool from reflecting the Sun's rays and the bases warm from absorbing the Earth's infrared radiation. Can also form from cumulus joining up under an inversion. Sc can produce light rain or snow - heavy showers will come from embedded cumulus

- **Nimbostratus** (Ns). Thick, dark, low rain cloud, typical in warm fronts, which may be found through all layers, but at least starts in the *alto* range. Moderate to heavy continual rain or snow

Middle (Alto)

Between 6 500-23 000 feet, made of water, ice, or supercooled water droplets, depending on temperature:

- **Altocumulus** Similar to Sc (above), but higher. Size is between 1 & 3 finger-widths, with shading (not dark and gloomy, like stratus)

- **Altostratus** (As), similar to stratus, but higher, medium sheet greyish or bluish cloud, any thickness up to 10-12,000'. No ground shadow

High (Cirro)

Between 16 500-45 000 feet, made of ice crystals, so they have some transparency:

- **Cirrocumulus** (Cc) is high sheet cloud, made of small cloudlets (for want of a better word) which do not cast shadows, looking like a mackerel sky

- **Cirrostratus** (Cs) translucent high cloud, very delicate, made up of ice crystals. When in front of the Sun, you may see a halo round it

- **Cirrus** (Ci) is a high and fibrous filament indicating that a warm front is around 200 nm away. Otherwise known as *Horse tails*, or *Mares' tails*, they are precipitating clouds but the precipitate evaporates well before reaching ground level - the falling ice streaks form the distinctive filaments

Other

- **Heap clouds** (i.e. vertically developed):

  - *Cumulus* (Cu), are small amounts of heap cloud at low and medium levels, looking a bit like small balls of cotton wool (see left) with flat bases. It's actually *convection cloud*, which gives you a clue as to how it is made, and glider pilots seek out the thermals underneath them for the lift they provide (when a cumulus cloud is removed from its thermal, it can still grow from the latent heat that is released inside it making it warmer than its surroundings to cause it to float upwards). In strong winds, you might see them in long lines (called *cloud streets*, or *radiatus*), and you will get showers from larger ones. So-called "fair weather cumulus", typically seen on a nice Summer's day, normally forms directly as such, but (less commonly) can develop from stratus or strato-cu that has broken up with morning heating (they can also spread out into strato-cu or alto-cu in the presence of an inversion). Characteristics of cumuliform cloud include large water droplets, instability, turbulence, showers, and mainly clear ice. *Cumulus Congestus* is cumulus with a large vertical extent. *Mediocris* are as tall as they are wide, and *Humilis* are the smallest, being wider than they are tall. "Fair weather" means they do not produce any precipitation.

  - **Cumulonimbus** is towering stormcloud, which may appear spontaneously over flat lands or be part of an advancing front associated with a depression (left). "Towering" means up to as much as 60,000 feet, and the anvil shape at the top is due to it meeting the tropopause, where temperature starts to remain constant, stopping the cloud's ascent. Cbs are mostly found around late afternoon, and can project into the stratosphere. They are cumulus congestus until the upper regions turn into ice crystals. See also *Thunderstorms*

- *Lenticular*, found at the crest of standing waves formed in the lee of mountain waves

Precipitation

This comes from anything with *nimbo* in its name. It will be continuous from stratiform clouds, and intermittent from cumuliform clouds, from which *Virga* comes - it evaporates before reaching the ground, and looks like streamers just below the cloud base, but avoid it, because it is turbulent.

Precipitation is the end result of a chain of events that starts with the cooling through ascent of a parcel of dirty moist air ("dirty" meaning that it contains microscopic particles that water can bind on to). Once the saturation point is reached, condensation occurs and droplets coalesce to fall out as rain, snow, or whatever, according to temperature. Precipitation in mid-latitudes is likely to be drizzle. Nitrogen oxides from lightning discharges can attract water droplets that can be a contributory factor in forming.........

HAIL & SLEET

Hail forms from large water droplets forced above the freezing level, although there is also an accretion and growth process as well. Early studies said that hailstones were recycled through the cloud depth, but others indicate that they can grow while suspended in a strong updraught before falling out. Snowflakes are combined ice crystals which come from the freezing of water vapour without going through a liquid stage. Sleet is half-melted snow, that begins to unfreeze during descent below freezing level when it is quite high above the surface.

Ice usually forms on aircraft during flight in cloud, but it can happen in the clear.

TURBULENCE

This is found in cloud and clear air (that is, *Clear Air Turbulence*, or CAT), and usually comes from friction when air currents mix, from various sources, such as *convective*, *orographic*, *windshear* and *mechanical*, and is reported as:

- *Light*, with small changes in height or attitude, near stratocumulus

- *Moderate*, more severe, but you are still in control. The ICAO definition is: *There may be moderate changes in aircraft attitude and/or altitude but the aircraft remains in positive control at all times. Usually, small variations in air speed. Changes in accelerometer readings of 0.5 to 1.0 g at the aircraft's center of gravity. Occupants feel strain against seat belts. Loose objects move about. Food service and walking are difficult.* Good indicators are Cumulus-type clouds, which may also warn you about....

- *Severe*, with abrupt changes, and being temporarily out of control, indicated by Cumulonimbus and lenticular clouds, if there are many stacked on top of each other. Expect the latter when winds across mountain ranges are more than 40 kts

- *Extreme*, impossible to control

If turbulence is likely, use the turbulence speed in the flight manual, which will be rather less than normal. Advise the passengers to ensure their seat belts/harnesses are securely fastened. Catering and other loose equipment should be stowed and secured until the risk has passed.

THUNDERSTORMS

The Earth has a surplus of electrons, and the ionosphere doesn't - if you take the air between them as a dielectric, you have a very large capacitor (see *Electricity* in *AGK*) with a potential difference between its "plates" in the order of 360,000 volts, reducing with height at about 100 volts per metre (the body's resistance is high, so you don't notice the 200 volts between your feet and your head). However, capacitors leak, and they break down when one plate gets overcharged and the dielectric becomes a conductor (it gets ionised). The thunderstorm replenishes the Earth's negative charge through this mechanism, and it is estimated that, at any time over the planet, there are over 40,000 active thunderstorms. The power contained in a thunderstorm is more than 4 nuclear bombs put together (some say 10), which is a very good reason to avoid flying through them. Lightning itself is a discharge of around a million volts with an associated current of between 10,000-40,000 amps, heating the air up to 30,000°C. This can fuse sand or start a fire.

The airflow is greatly disturbed anywhere near a thunderstorm, usually noticeable by strong up- and downdraughts, together with heavy rain and lightning, or even tornadoes, mentioned below. Because of the inflow of warm air and the outflow of cold, the gust front can extend up to 15-20 miles ahead of a moving storm. Avoid them even at the cost of diversion or an intermediate landing, but should this be impossible, there are certain things you can do, mentioned later.

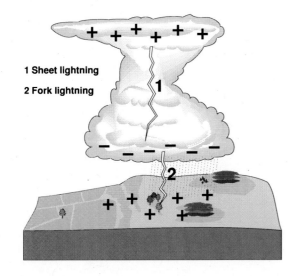

1 Sheet lightning

2 Fork lightning

In the picture above, there is a positive charge in the anvil. There is a negative charge in the freezing layers, and a

positive charge below. Once the charge becomes high enough, the natural resistance of the air is breached and you get a lightning discharge (there are negative cloud base to positive ground strikes, and highly positive anvil cloud to positive ground strikes). Once a contact is made, say with a flagpole, air molecules will heat up enough to reduce the air's resistance even further, to allow more charge to flow.

It can be at least as dangerous up high as way down low - you can expect anything from lightning and turbulence to icing and hail, each with hazards of their own - lightning, for instance, could explode a fuel tank, and strikes can occur up to 20 nm from a storm cell. Not only that, even over baby ones near to larger storms, you will need at least 5000 feet clearance - *sprites* have been known to go up 75 miles into space (for the exam, clear the top of a severe thunderstorm by 1,000 feet for each 10 kts of wind). Similarly, try not to fly underneath, either, or make steep turns. The currents inside a thunderstorm will easily be enough to suck in the average helicopter, or spit it out. Closer to the ground, the eddies will slow down vertically, but they will also go sideways and mix together, getting just as bumpy in the clear air.

Pressure usually falls rapidly as a thunderstorm approaches, then rises rapidly with the first gust. It returns to normal after it passes. The wind, too, will change as outflow changes to inflow. Atmospheric changes are at their lowest value when the thunderstorm is approaching.

An *embedded thunderstorm* will have penetrated overlying bands of stratiform cloud on its way up, and been completely obscured by other types of clouds.

To start a thunderstorm, you need *moisture* (high relative humidity), a *steep* (unstable) *lapse rate* and a *lifting*, or *trigger*, *agent*, which could be orographic, convective, frontal or nocturnal, as occurs in the midwest plains after night-time radiation from the cloud tops, which would increase lapse rates (of course, you could get two trigger actions, as when a front hits the Rockies). On the left is a picture of a thunderstorm in the early stages of development. The instability and moisture content determine the severity of any storm, and a high temperature and dewpoint close together are a good early warning as the air is hot, and contains lots of vapour. Convective activity over land in mid-latitudes is greatest in the Summer, in the afternoons, so you can expect local isolated thunderstorms arising from thermal triggering mostly in the mid-afternoon, from warm updraughts.

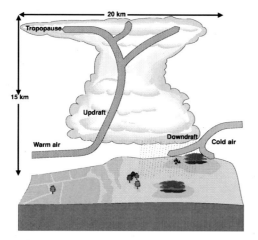

During the *development, or cumulus* stage, several cumulus clouds will begin to merge, where the system consists *mainly of updrafts*, and will grow to around 4 miles wide at the base and 20,000 feet in height. That is, warm, moist unstable air is forced to rise because of the trigger agents mentioned above. Water droplets are merging as well, to form larger raindrops, which get to be a hazard once they get above the freezing level and become supercooled (see *Icing*, below). When they are big enough, they will fall, and pull cold air down with them (and drier air in from above), which is where the downdrafts come from. The drier air causes some evaporation, which absorbs latent heat and makes the air even colder, to fall faster. So, rain at the surface is a good indication of the transition to ….

The *mature* stage is distinguished by rainfall, but mostly by downdraughts and updraughts. As well, rotor winds characterised by roll clouds are most likely to occur here.

When wet-bulb cooling occurs in the middle and upper levels of a thunderstorm, the cooling of the air causes it to become negatively buoyant (i.e it sinks), and accelerate toward the earth's surface causing a derecho, a macroburst or a microburst. In other words, cold air from high altitudes is forced down to balance the powerful updraughts caused by the warm air rising inside the cells. The cold air spreads out when it hits the ground to form a

cushion, or *cold dome*, ahead of which are more, called *downbursts*, which may themselves contain *microbursts*, which, technically, are concentrated inside a 4 km radius. Expect lightning as well at this stage, which comes from the friction between up- and downdraughts and between water and air molecules.

Thus, a well-developed line of thunderstorms pushes a mass of cold air in front of it, which forces warm air up, to form more storm cells. The leading edge of cold air becomes the windshift line, only sometimes marked by roll cloud.

As the top of the cloud reaches the tropopause, inversion conditions stop the ascent and strong upper winds produce the distinctive anvil shape.

The main characteristic of *dissipation*, which is the third stage and starts once the updraughts cease, is a *downdraught* and *disappearing cloud*.

Although the clouds associated with a thunderstorm may extend for some distance, a thunderstorm is actually a collection of several cloud cells in varying stages of development, with varying diameters, typically a few hundred feet across. The different cells may be developing, maturing or dissipating at rates of their own, which could form their own trigger actions and make the storm self-perpetuating. Otherwise, development normally takes 20-30 minutes, the mature stage between 40-60 minutes and dissipation starts after 2 hours.

Air Mass thunderstorms mostly arise from surface heating - in the mature stage, rain falls through or immediately beside the updraught, inducing frictional drag to retard it and turn it into a downdraught. This will reduce the cell's lifecycle to somewhere between 20 minutes and 2½ hours. In a *Steady State* thunderstorm, this will be several hours because the precipitation falls outside the downdraught. Tornadoes often form with steady-state thunderstorms associated with cold fronts or squall lines.

A *severe thunderstorm* has surface winds over 50 kts and hail more than ¾" across. *Cumulonimbus Mamma* clouds often occur with violent thunderstorms and tornadoes. The temperature band for lightning is between +10° to -10°C.

Squall Lines

A *squall line* is an unbroken line of thunderstorms, which can be hundreds of miles long and which Murphy's Law dictates will be right across your flight path (they will be too wide for a detour and too severe to penetrate).

Squall lines occur under the same conditions as thunderstorms and can appear anywhere that air is moist and unstable, but often ahead of cold fronts in late afternoon or early evening, or before a "dew point front", which separates air masses that only have different moisture levels. They are the product of severe cold frontal conditions, where a cold front nudges under the warm sector (watch for an acute bend in isobars at the front, or low roll cloud across the advance). They can move so fast that they can get embedded into the warm frontal cloud. However, the normal propagation method comes from a line of updraughts along an outflow boundary from a thunderstorm, spreading out as they hit the ground and nudging air upwards to its dewpoint. Precipitation falls behind the system, and a classic squall line has the updraught along the front and the downdraught on the back.

The following clues will help you detect squall lines before flight:

- A well defined warm sector, with high dewpoints, especially ahead of and parallel to the cold front (hot moist air has a lot of energy)

- Cold air aloft, where any warm air rising into it gets a buoyancy boost (watch for a trough aloft). Jetstreams can give air a similar boost as it gets sucked up from lower levels

- Strong Southerly winds just ahead of the cold front

Air Traffic Control Considerations
Obtain clearance from, or notify, ATC so they can separate you from others. If you can't, keep manoeuvres to a minimum, and inform them ASAP.

Takeoff and Landing
Not if thunderstorms are overhead or within 5 nm. The same goes for refuelling!

ICING

Ice adversely affects performance, not only by adding weight, but also by altering the shape of lift producing surfaces, which changes your stalling speed - autorotation in a helicopter could therefore be a lot more interesting than normal (the US Army found that ½" on the leading edge of a rotor blade reduces your lifting capacity by up to 50%, and increases drag by the same amount) - if your engine stops, you could really fall out of the sky! On top of that, fuel could freeze in wing tanks, as could control surfaces, and slush picked up on take-off could stop the gear from operating, as well as instruments. For exam purposes, the effects of icing include:

- reduced lift
- increased drag
- increased weight
- increased stalling speed
- increased fuel consumption
- inefficiency of engine operation

Also jammed controls and interference with radios

Zero degrees is actually when water becomes *capable* of freezing, from which you can infer that it doesn't necessarily do so. A *Supercooled Water Droplet* is one below freezing, but not frozen. It gets away with this from the absence of hygroscopic nuclei to bind on to.

When such a droplet strikes an airframe, however, just below 0°, some of it will freeze on impact, releasing latent heat and warming the remainder, which then flows back, turning into *clear ice* when the freezing is slow, which can gather without noticeable vibration. In other words, the airframe will act as one giant ice nucleus, and the freezing is *behind* the point of impact, and therefore behind the influence of deicing equipment, where it can pile up and distort the lift-producing surfaces. 1/80th part of a SWD will freeze on impact for each degree below zero, assuming a large droplet - small ones will form *rime ice* - see below. The worst place to penetrate cumuliform cloud is between 0 to -10°C, where most SWDs are - you are most likely to find large ones in the lower levels of cloud that has formed in unstable air (cumulus), in temperatures only a few degrees below freezing, and you can expect clear icing from them.

Rime ice comes from smaller SWDs well below 0° (actually from -10° to -20°C), when freezing is fast. It is opaque and granular and moves forward as it builds up on sharp surfaces like antennae. On a helicopter rotor blade, it is more likely to occur on the top rather than the leading edge. Below -40°C, you will likely only encounter ice crystals, which will not stick to the aircraft, or *very small* SWDs. However, ice accumulation is too unpredictable to assume anything - you can get severe icing in towering cumulus down to -25°C. It is worst at the top of CBs.

In summary:

- *Clear icing* happens most often in cumuliform cloud between 0 and -10°C

- *Rime icing* favours stratiform clouds and is found between -10 and -20°C

- The most dangerous temperature range is between +5 and -5°C, because SWDs are larger, as warmer air holds more moisture. The fluid that runs back can freeze well away from deicing equipment

Icing equipment is not certified if you are carrying deposits from ground operations or storage, so ensure that *all* frost, ice and snow is removed *before* you get airborne, if only because the aircraft systems don't get really under way till then. The trend now is towards a "clean aircraft concept" which, essentially, means that nothing should be on the outside of an aircraft that should not be there, except, perhaps, for deicing fluid, but even that is suspect.

Note: Very few helicopters have decent deicing systems - and even then they are large ones with electrically heated blades, etc. that are not certified for anything more than light icing conditions, and then only for short periods. Smaller helicopters only have engine *anti-icing*, which must be used *before* ice forms. In the USA, *forecast* icing conditions are construed as *known* icing conditions, so read the flight manual!

Ice should be removed from at least all critical areas in the 5 minutes before takeoff, including hoar frost on the fuselage, because even a bad paint job will increase drag, which is relevant if you're heavy, and it will have a similar effect (*hoar frost* is a light frosty deposit that typically appears on a parked aircraft after a clear cold night, and both temperature and dewpoint of the collecting surface are below freezing. It can usually be seen through). These areas include control surfaces, rotors, stabilisers, control linkages, etc. Hoar frost comes about through *deposition*, where water vapour changes directly into ice crystals. A heavy coat of frost will increase stall speed by 5-10%. If it comes to that, ice, snow or frost about as rough as medium sandpaper on the leading edge or top of a wing reduces lift by 30% and increases drag by 40%. Fine particles the size of a grain of salt even sparsely distributed

(say, 1 per square centimetre) can destroy lift enough to prevent takeoff.

 Normally, the Captain must check that no ice accretion is present on the airframe before takeoff, except as mentioned in the Flight Manual. The best way to detect it is with the *Mk 1 eyeball* (on the left).

The ability of an object to accumulate ice is known as its *catch* or *collection efficiency*, which is inversely proportional to the shape of the surface. In other words, a sharp-edged object is better at catching ice than a blunt-edged one is, because it deflects air less (but speed is also a factor). Due to the speed and geometry of a helicopter's main rotor blades, for example, their catch efficiency is greater than that of the fuselage, so ice on the outside of the cabin doesn't relate to what you might have on the blades, although they rotate so fast that they are always a degree or so warmer. Canadian Armed Forces tests show that you can pick up a lethal load of ice on a Kiowa (206) rotor blade inside 1-6 minutes, although it's true to say that 206 blades, being fairly crude, don't catch as much as more sophisticated ones, such as those on the 407. If the rate of catch is low and the droplets are small, you can expect to see rime ice rather than clear ice. In cumulus cloud, you are most likely to see clear ice with a high catch rate. It's the *rate of accretion* that's important, not the type of icing, although clear ice is definitely worse than rime ice, since the latter contains air bubbles and is much lighter and slower to build. It also goes forward from the leading edge as opposed to spreading backwards. Variations on clear ice are *freezing rain* and *freezing drizzle*, both of which have larger droplets and are caused by rain falling through colder air, becoming supercooled and turning into ice pellets as they come across freezing temperatures (if you get wet snow, it's colder upstairs or, rather, it's above freezing where you are). In layer cloud, the amount of liquid water will increase with height and become at its maximum near the cloud tops when temperatures are not far below freezing.

Although aircraft are different, expect icing to occur (in the engine intake area, anyway) whenever the OAT is below 4°C, but check the Flight Manual. Clear ice is found most often in cumulus clouds and unstable conditions between 0 and -10°C, and rime ice in stratiform clouds between -10 and -20°C (exam questions). The most serious risk is on the front surfaces of the aircraft (another exam question). Remember that icing equipment, if you have it, is there to get you through light-moderate icing in a relatively short time - not to operate there continuously.

Ice is reported as:

- *Trace*, meaning slight, non-hazardous, perceptible

- *Light*, with occasional use of deicing equipment. Flights over 1 hour might be inadvisable

- *Moderate*, where use of above equipment is necessary. Time to consider diversion

- *Severe*, where the equipment is useless and you must divert

Note that the above levels relate to *rates* of ice accretion, not *amounts*. The most danger lies in supercooled precipitation.

Pitot head, static vent and fuel vent heaters should be on whenever you encounter icing, together with anything else you feel is appropriate. Otherwise, you need warmer air to get rid of ice effectively - just flying around in clear air can take hours to shift it, but you could at least say you won't get any more. Aerodynamic heating comes from air friction, which may get rid of ice, but only at high speeds, so will not likely benefit helicopters, except for rotor blades, which may be warmer by 1° or so, from their speed. Climbing out is often not possible, due to lack of performance or ATC considerations, and descending has problems, too - if you're getting clear ice, it's a fair bet the air is warmer above you, since it may be freezing rain, from an inversion, probably within 1,000 feet or so, as you might get before a warm front, or after a cold one. The most dangerous position to be in is in rain - it is quite common to fly above a freezing level (always being aware that there may be two!) if there is no moisture around.

In this position, landing on your first attempt becomes more important as you are unlikely to survive a go-around without picking up more. You basically have three choices, go up, down or back the way you came. Going up is a good first choice if you know the tops are nearby, if only because you won't have a chance to do so later, but you present more of the airframe to icing risk, which is why there is often a minimum speed for climbing in icing conditions, slightly more than normal (a zoom climb will help). To keep out of trouble, before going, check that the freezing level is well above any minimum altitudes, which will help get rid of ice in the descent. Try to make sure the cloud tops are within reach as well, or that you have plenty of holes.

DE-ICING FLUIDS

De-icing fluids are only required until you get airborne, after which the ship's systems should be able to take over.

The aircraft's rotation speed determines which fluid is appropriate, as it should shear off during the takeoff run.

Note: Fluids used must be safely stored, labelled, handled and applied. Unqualified liquids, such as Isopropyl alcohol, may be classed as flammable dangerous goods, meaning that only limited quantities may be carried, and that you need training

The main types are what used to be known as AEA (*Association of European Airlines*) Type I (unthickened) with a high glycol content (at least 80%) and low viscosity, and Type II (thickened) with a minimum glycol content of at least 50% which, with a thickening agent (one or two teaspoons of cornflour), remains on surfaces for longer. The idea is to decrease the freezing point of water but, as the ice melts, the fluid mixes with the water, both diluting it and making it more runny (what's left after repeated applications to combat this is of an unknown concentration, and may refreeze quickly). Type I is primarily intended to be a heated *deicing* medium for smaller aircraft rotating over 60 kts. Type II was developed for *anti-icing*, for aircraft with rotational speeds over 100 kts. Type III is similar to Type II, but is an *anti-icing* fluid for aircraft rotating over 60 kts. Type IV is also similar to Type II, but with significantly longer *holdover times* for aircraft rotating over 100 kts. It is otherwise known as Union Carbide Ultra fluid and is green, and needs care to provide uniform cover, especially over any Type I fluid that is already there.

Note: Do not use Type II or IV fluids on aircraft for which they are not approved, as they have been known to pool in aerodynamically quiet areas and refreeze.

Holdover time is the estimated time that fluid will prevent frost or ice forming, and the accumulation of snow on protected surfaces. It begins at the final application and expires when the fluid loses its effectiveness. The oldest coat will break first. It can be affected by high winds or jet blasts damaging the fluid film, and temperature, humidity, etc. The one-step deicing method uses heated fluid but, although quick and simple, uses more fluid when chunks of ice, etc. have to be flushed off. The two-step method has a deicing and an anti-icing portion, which uses less fluid. A heated, diluted fluid (Type I) is used for the first, with hot water or a mix of FPD and water. A more concentrated, cold one (Type II), plus water, is used for the second application (Type II fluid applied cold increases its thickness and holdover time. Although heating a fluid increases its *deicing* properties, unheated fluids are more effective for *anti-icing*).

A Polar Front depression starts to form in the West Atlantic and moves at around 20 kts towards the European continent, so its life cycle lasts for about a week

Freezing Point Depressant fluids (FPD) are supposed to help the deicing process and provide a protective film to delay the formation of frost, ice or snow. They are highly soluble in water, but ice is slow to absorb it, or melt (heating helps). Once the FPD becomes diluted, it may start to run off. The remaining mixture of water and FPD could freeze with only a slight decrease in temperature. Any residue on engine or fan compressor blades will also reduce performance or cause a stall or surge, aside from getting vapours in the cabin as soon as things start to heat up (makes you wonder why they use it). Because of possible dilution, it is standard practice to ensure that the remaining film has a freezing point at least 20°F below the ambient temperature.

GENERAL PRECAUTIONS

Deposits must be swept from hinges and system intakes, and the sprays should not be directed to them, as the fluid may be further diluted by the melting ice it is designed to remove, and may refreeze. It may also cause smearing on cockpit windows and loss of vision during takeoff.

Afterwards, confirm that flying and control surfaces are clear and move over their full range, and intake and drain holes are free of obstructions. Jet engine compressors should be rotated by hand to ensure they are not frozen. Don't forget the undercarriage.

AIR MASSES

A large body of air will have the characteristics of its origin (the *source region*), particularly with regard to moisture and temperature. To acquire the characteristics required to meet the classification, a mass of air has to stay in one place for several days in a more or less uniform place, so one definition of an air mass could be *a huge body of air with uniform properties of temperature and moisture*. For the necessary stagnation for air to acquire such characteristics, light winds are needed, so a source region is likely to be subject to high pressure.

Air masses are basically *Arctic* or *Polar*, *Tropical* or *Equatorial*, *Maritime* (sea-based) or *Continental* (land-based). There is no Equatorial Continental because there is no land mass in the region large enough to produce the required effects. Arctic and Polar air only really differ at upper levels, otherwise they are much the same, especially at the surface.

Thus, air masses vary as to moisture content and temperature. It's what happens when one moves away from its source region that is important, as well as what happens when it mixes with others - refer to *Tornadoes* to see the effects that occur when N Westerly airflow meets S Easterly airflow over the USA. Air masses of the same type mix well, but others don't, and will produce problems at the transition point (the process in an air mass that leads to widespread NS and AS cloud is *lifting*). Air from the Azores would be warmer and more humid than North Russian air. Europe in Summer is affected by Tropical Continental air from the South Balkans and the Near East, but the main air masses that affect Canada are:

- *Continental Arctic* (cA), which is stable, dry and very cold from polar land regions, with little energy. In winter, if cA moves South over the Great Lakes, expect heap clouds and snow showers over Southern portions. It is centred on the North pole.

- *Maritime Arctic* (mA), moist and cold, from polar oceans.

- *Maritime Polar* (mP) comes from temperate oceans, so it will be moist and slightly less cold.

- *Maritime Tropical* (mT), moist and warm, from tropical oceans. In early Summer, you can expect fog as it moves over the Great Lakes.

All can be modified if they move over different areas. Maritime Tropical, for example, will become Maritime Polar if it moves North for long enough.

Advection means horizontal air movement, as opposed to convection, which means vertical movement. Advection fog arises from the same process as cloud formation, except for its direction.

Most of the time the weather in the Arctic is clear and cold and the only reduction to visibility is from high winds and blowing snow. However, systems from the Aleutian Low often move into AK, BC and AB westward, mostly associated with mP air masses.

The *stability* of an air mass is affected by its *origin* and *how it got to where it is*.

FRONTOLOGY

A front is a line of discontinuity, or a narrow transition zone between air masses where they are forced to mix, even though they don't want to. Otherwise, the boundary between two air masses might occupy several kilometres.

The process starts in mid-high latitudes when low pressure systems form along the boundary between cold polar air and warmer air from temperate zones. Some parts of the boundary being faster than others causes them to catch up and the end result is that warmer air is forced upwards. The weather associated with fronts depends on the air masses concerned and the way in which they interact - if the warm air that is forced upwards is dry and stable, for example, you won't necessarily see any clouds.

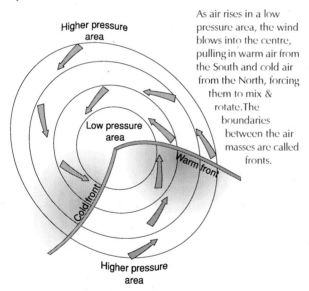

Higher pressure area

Low pressure area

Warm front

Cold front

Higher pressure area

As air rises in a low pressure area, the wind blows into the centre, pulling in warm air from the South and cold air from the North, forcing them to mix & rotate. The boundaries between the air masses are called fronts.

The narrow part (depicted by the red or blue line) is actually the ground position, as the effects of a front with height are felt for some distance either side. The difference is usually in temperature (which can actually be very small), but may be purely due to moisture content. Fronts are always associated with depressions, which are

sometimes referred to as *frontal waves*. A series of fronts or depressions, one after the other, is referred to as a *Westerly Wave* (an *Easterly Wave* is a wave in a trade wind belt from E-W with severe convective activity in the rear of its trough). Depressions usually form on cold or stationary fronts, and will rotate *anticlockwise* around a low.

Warm tropical air could be forced over colder arctic air, for example, because it is less dense and, if moist, will form a typical cloud structure that we can use to tell when a front is coming. The name of a front, that is, *warm*, or *cold*, comes from whichever air mass is overtaking the other, whereas the type of weather you get is determined by the stability and moisture content of the *warm air mass*. The actual temperature is less important than its relationship to that of the surface it is passing over.

The *Polar Front* is where South- and North-Westerly airstreams meet to form long series of depressions, starting off the Atlantic Coast of North America. It is the boundary between polar and tropical air (Polar Front depressions move along it toward the East, being most Southerly during Winter). In Summer, you can generally expect to see the Polar Front range from *Newfoundland* to the *North of Scotland*, and, in Winter, further South from *Florida* to *South-West England*. It lies in a trough of low pressure with highs on each side - interaction between them cause a bend, or wave, in the Polar front, and so the whole process starts. A *dew point front*, or *dry line*, forms when two similar air masses with only a moisture difference between them meet. Other than that, there is little contrast across it.

Frontogenesis is the term for the forming of a front, and *frontolysis* the one for its dissipation. The cold air mass does not move at a *stationary front* (where surface winds tend to flow parallel to the frontal zone), and you get an *upper front* with any temperature gradient aloft. To try and find where a front might be on the surface (looking at a weather map in the exam), look at the temperature, pressure, dew point and wind velocity as depicted in station circles. On the ground, watch for the wind picking up, and the altimeter dropping slightly. In fact, knowing the signs given out by an approaching front can be very useful when operating in remoter places. You need to watch these items:

• *Wind speed and direction*. Winds veer as a front approaches and back as it passes. For a cold front, they will start from the South and end up Westerly or North Westerly - with a warm front, look for winds to start from the East (ish) and end up in the South (ish). Any farmer will tell you that the wind will reverse direction as a thunderstorm approaches. With a stationary front, surface winds will tend to flow parallel to the frontal zone

- *Temperature.* It gets colder as a cold front passes, and warmer as a warm front goes by. The greater the temperature difference, the more violent the passage will be

- *Humidity.* Humidity will be high, and the temperature and dew points will be close together with a cold front passage. If the temperatures are both high, there will more of a likelihood of thunderstorms, due to the energy in the air. The temperature and dewpoint spread will widen once the front has gone through, and humidity will decrease. These effects will not be so noticeable with a warm front passage, since the slope is shallower

- *Clouds.* Cold fronts and warm fronts bring cumuliform and stratiform clouds, respectively

- *Pressure trends.* Pressure always falls as a front approaches, because massive amounts of air are being lifted. The faster the rate of change, the more severe the weather is likely to be, and it may include thunderstorms and heavy rain. Pressure will rise again after the front passes by

It's best to fly toward fronts, to get the best weather to find your way home in if things deteriorate rapidly, as they tend to do. Also, make frequent updates to your altimeter settings, or use the *Regional QNH*, which is a *prediction* of the lowest sea level pressure over the next hour.

The Warm Front

This exists where warm air overtakes a colder air mass and is forced upwards, meaning clouds. Its symbol on a weather map, resembling beads of sweat, is shown on the

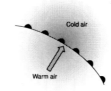

left. The frontal slope has a gradient of somewhere between 1:150 and 1:200, although the clouds themselves will be about 5 miles high, starting with Nimbostratus at more or less ground level, through alto-stratus to cirrostratus. When flying towards it, you would see the clouds the other way round, of course, so once you start seeing cirrus clouds, you know that a warm front is somewhere ahead, anywhere between 300-600 miles away, or nearly 24 hours at a typical speed of about 25 kts, so have an overnight kit if you have to wait it out (rain will typically be 200 miles ahead). You can use the typical slope figure to work out the cloud base in front of the system. At 100 miles, it will be 2,640 feet, which comes from 1/200*100, making half a mile, multiplied by 5280 (feet).

Clouds will therefore appear in this order as you fly towards a warm front - cirrus, cirrostratus, altostratus, stratus and nimbostratus. The extensive cloud layers are caused by unstable warm air overrunning retreating cold air, with a high moisture content. As such, the precipitation will change from steady rain to heavy showers.

The shallow slope ensures that whatever is coming will last some time, and you can expect the pressure to fall, the cloud to get lower, the wind to back and increase in speed, rising humidity, bad visibility, drizzle and rain, though not necessarily in that order. The freezing level will be lower in front than behind, and the slope means that freezing rain will be falling on anything underneath (see diagram above), so if you are flying towards a warm front, or towards the rear of a cold front, in between their freezing levels and that in the warm sector, watch out! Supercooled

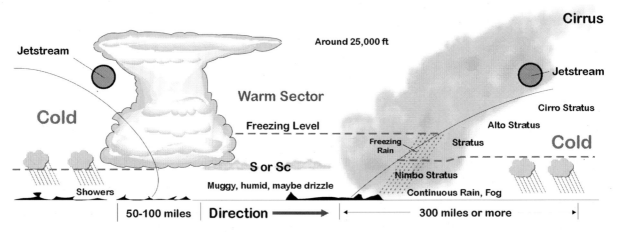

Jetstream — Cold — Warm Sector — Around 25,000 ft — Cirrus — Jetstream — Cirro Stratus — Alto Stratus — Freezing Level — Freezing Rain — Stratus — Cold — S or Sc — Muggy, humid, maybe drizzle — Nimbo Stratus — Continuous Rain, Fog — Showers — 50-100 miles — **Direction** — 300 miles or more

water droplets from above will freeze onto your cold airframe. Once you see ice pellets, expect freezing rain next (exam question). If you are thinking of trying to descend out of it, remember that the cloud base lowers in precipitation.

As the front passes, you will experience *frontal fog* in front (from the added water), followed by advection fog afterwards. The rain will stop, then become drizzle under an overcast sky, and the wind will veer. As humidity rises to saturation point, visibility could be poor. You will then be in the warm sector, where conditions will be more settled for a few hours (the pressure will rise abruptly), with broken or overcast stratus, just a few hundred feet thick. The further you are away from the low centre, the more the cloud is likely to break up, but don't be fooled - high ground upwind could be holding the cloud back, giving a false impression that the system has passed on. The warm sector is called that because it has the warmest air of the whole system, stuck as it is between the warm and cold fronts.

For the exam, when asked to predict the future position of a warm front (and the type of weather), use the direction of the isobars in the warm sector, since the front moves parallel to them. As warm air finds it hard to displace cold air, a warm front will move at about half the speed of a cold front in the same conditions.

After the warm sector comes......

The Cold Front

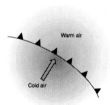

This has a much steeper slope (1:50) and brisker activity, with more of a likelihood of thunderstorms, because the wind field convergence is typically stronger along cold fronts, providing a greater forcing mechanism. The rain becomes more showery and the wind veers more, to the West or Northwest. Pressure gets higher, and temperature and humidity decrease. In temperate climates, large amounts of Cu-nim are unusual at this point, but they are not over continental land areas. The rain belt is relatively small compared to the warm front, and visibility will improve markedly.

A cold front moves at about the speed of the wind perpendicular to it just above the friction level (i.e. about 2,000 feet, for 15-25 kts), but they are faster in Winter because the air is colder and exerts greater pressure. However, friction with the ground will slow the lower

levels, so there is a bulge effect along the leading edge. The friction, often coupled with strong heating from below as the cold air crosses warmer ground, often creates gusty wind conditions. The weather is generally colder after its passage, and with less cloud, because pressure is greater to the West and less to the East, limiting the inflow of air.

Expect questions on weather at a cold front, and after its passage (pressure rising, fair weather cumulus and good visibility, because the turbulence has removed the pollution from the lower layers). The associated weather is actually determined by the stability and moisture content of the warm air mass, the speed of the front, and steepness of the frontal surface. Wind shifts will be usually more pronounced (in fact, it will veer about 30° and increase in speed).

The Occlusion

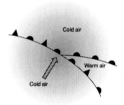

Cold fronts move faster than warm fronts. When one catches up with the other, the warm sector (the bit between a warm and a cold front) is lifted from the ground, leaving only one front on the surface (the rate depends on the temperature difference between the air masses). Of course, the end result is that you get two fronts, one on top of the other.

Surface wind can be the first clue that this is happening.

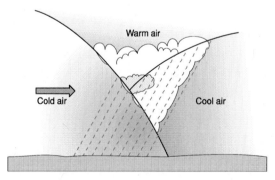

If the air behind the cold front is the coldest, you get a *cold front occlusion*. If the air is the warmer of the two, you will get a *warm front occlusion*, even though the two air masses are cold, relative to the warm front. However, the essential point is that warm air is forced aloft to condense and form clouds.

You get more rain with a warm occlusion, plus a quicker transition from warm to cold front weather.

A cold occlusion is more or less the same as.......

Trowal

A *Trough of Warm Air Aloft*, again from a cold front catching up with a warm one. Trowals (occlusions) are parts of systems in their decaying state. They are found on constant pressure charts above 700 mb (around 10,000 ft), and can affect surface weather quite severely. Jetstreams are found poleward. See also .....

Cold Pool (Cutoff Low)

A cold pool is a cold air block (a *warm dome* is a warm air block), and is otherwise known as a *trough aloft*, or a *cutoff low*, meaning there is no connection with the prevailing westerlies. They are isolated upper level lows found South of the Polar front jet, usually most evident in the circulation of the temperature of the middle troposphere and may show little or no sign on a surface chart (look for a low pressure aloft on a 500 hPa chart).

Once cold air from the source region above is caught up in mid-latitude depressions, its characteristics are altered. Warming from below (over relatively warmer sea surfaces, for example) leads to instability, and, with moisture (after the sea passage), cloudy convection (showers, thunderstorms) is triggered. The cold pool will move with the general flow, and will eventually warm out (disappear) after sensible and latent heat exchanges. A pool of cold air can also become detached at lower latitudes, that is, away from the mid-latitude westerly zone, and drift slowly over relatively warmer seas, (like the Mediterranean), and lead to intense convective development, often taking on marked cyclonic characteristics through the troposphere, and giving rise to locally severe conditions due to heavy rainfall, severe thunderstorms and squally winds.

VISIBILITY
••

Defined as the greatest horizontal distance a dark object (of known dimensions) can be seen and recognised against a light background, usually prominent objects from the tower, or a measure of the opacity of the atmosphere in a particular direction. The *prevailing visibility* is the greatest met or exceeded through at least half the visible horizon. This, of course poses a problem at night, so *night visibility* really refers to how far you would be able to see in daylight. Visibility may be reduced by fog, mist, cloud,

precipitation, sea spray, smoke, sand, dust and industrial haze, etc. Here is a reminder of how bad it can be:

The best visibility in haze is obtained when down-sun and up-moon.

Fog

This is essentially cloud at ground level, which officially exists when you can't see more than 1,000 metres due to water droplets in the air, so it's not cloud really, because you can't see anything at all in clouds, but the process of formation is the same, with the other difference being that fog forms downwards and clouds form upwards - therefore you can't fly under fog. In homogeneous fog, visibility is generally less than RVR.

- *Radiation fog* forms over land, preferably low-lying, when temperatures approach the dewpoint with very slight winds (2-8 kts), and where moisture is present. It doesn't form over the sea, because the diurnal temperature variation is less. It is often found in the early morning after a clear night, since it likes high relative humidity, light winds and clear skies. Its vertical extent is typically 500 feet, and it usually clears quickly, once the Sun's heat gets to work, often getting worse before it gets better. If the windspeed is too low, water cannot be held in suspension, so it falls out as dew. If it is too high, you will get low stratus. It disperses with wind, heat, or a drier air mass. You can expect the densest type of radiation fog the night after an afternoon of heavy rains (say after a slow moving front, where skies clear late in the day), in low lying areas, which, naturally, is where you will find most airfields.

- *Upslope fog* forms from adiabatic cooling of moist, stable air as it moves up slopes.

- *Advection fog* arises from warm air flowing over a cold surface, and it can be encountered immediately after the passage of a cold front. Advection simply means the movement of air in bulk - warm advection means warm air replacing colder air, and *vice versa*, as you would find with fronts. It is not the same as radiation fog because air movement is involved, and the coolness does not arise from diurnal variations, but longer periods, as with the sea, where this type of fog is commonly found (*Steam Fog, or Arctic Smoke,* comes from cold air moving over warm water). Over land, it could arise from a warm, moist air mass flowing over cold ground. Winds over 15 kts will lift advection fog into a layer of low stratus or stratocumulus.

- *Hill fog* is low cloud covering high ground, which may or may not have contributed to its formation.

- *Frontal fog* may simply be low cloud touching high ground, or come from rain falling through unsaturated air beneath.

- In *shallow fog*, you may be able to see the whole of the approach and/or runway lights from a considerable distance, even though reports indicate fog. On descending into the fog layer, your visual reference is likely to drop rapidly, in extreme cases from the full length of the runway and approach lights to a very small segment. This may give the impression that you're pitching nose up, making you more likely to hit the ground after corrective movements. You should be prepared for a missed approach whenever you have the slightest doubt about forward visibility.

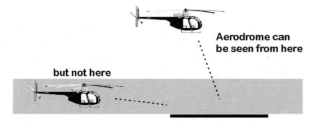

Aerodrome can be seen from here

but not here

Mist

Essentially, thin fog, and the same definition applies, except that the visibility is over 1,000m, being reported at 5000m.

Whiteout

This is defined by the American Meteorological Society as:

"An atmospheric optical phenomenon of the polar regions in which the observer appears to be engulfed in a uniformly white glow".

That is, you can only see dark nearby objects - no shadows, horizon or clouds, and you lose depth perception. In other words, you are unable to distinguish between the ground and the sky - the snow-covered surface cannot be detected by the naked eye because of the lack of normal colour contrast. Whiteout typically occurs over unbroken snow cover beneath a uniformly overcast sky, when the light from both is about the same. Blowing snow doesn't help, and it's particularly a problem if the ground is rising. In fact, there are several versions of whiteout:

- *Overcast Whiteout*, which comes from complete cloud cover with light being reflected between a snow surface and the cloud base. Perspective is limited to within a few feet, but the horizontal visibility of dark objects is not materially reduced

- *Water Fog.* Thin clouds of supercooled water droplets contacting a cold snow surface. Horizontal and vertical visibility is affected by the size and distribution of the water droplets [1]

- *Blowing Snow.* Winds over 20 kts picking up fine snow from the surface, diffusing sunlight and reducing visibility

- *Precipitation.* Small wind-driven snow crystals coming from low clouds with the Sun above them. Light is refracted and objects obscured caused by multiple reflection of light between the snow covered surface and the cloud base. Spectral reflection from the snow flakes and obscuration of landmarks by the falling snow are further complications.

Once you suspect whiteout, *immediately* climb or level off towards an area where you can see things properly. *Do not be tempted to go on instruments.* Better yet, put the machine on the ground before you get anywhere near whiteout conditions.

Flat light is a similar phenomenon, but comes from different causes, where light is diffused through water droplets suspended in the air, particularly when clouds are low. *Brownout* comes from blowing sand or dust.

MET SERVICES & INFORMATION

The meteorological service operates a vast intelligence system that gathers information every half an hour and transmits it to a central point for analysis. Even ships at sea contribute information. The reports are combined with the findings of a low-orbit satellite that flies round the world every 107 minutes. It measures wave-heights, amongst other things, whilst others might look at conditions in the troposphere and stratosphere. A Cray computer crunches the results and the information is used to try to forecast the weather.

ATIS (*Automatic Terminal Information Service*) is broadcast on available VHF frequencies, VOR and NDB (not ILS) at major aerodromes (you can use it as an ID on instrument rides), to reduce congestion on VHF frequencies, although it may have its own channel. You should listen to it and take down the details before you contact ATC, inbound or outbound. ATIS broadcasts should be updated whenever a significant change occurs, and should not last over 30 seconds. The contents of an ATIS broadcast are mentioned in the *Air Law* section.

VOLMET is usually transmitted over HF for long-distance flights (North Atlantic and Arctic for Canada), but can be found elsewhere. It consists of long readouts of TAFs and METARs in a sequence, so if you miss the aerodrome you want, just wait for it to come round again. Many airfields have it available over the telephone.

Otherwise, there are all sorts of facilities available over the Internet, by telephone, fax or radio. Mostly, though, you will be dealing with your local *Flight Service Station* (FSS), which will provide the *Aviation Weather Information Service*, or AWIS (W2 in the CFS). The *Aviation Weather Briefing Service* (AWBS), however, is more advanced because it is used for long range flights as well. It is not always found at an FSS - you mostly see it at AES offices (W1 in CFS).

The PATWAS is the *Pilot's Automatic Telephone Weather Answering Service*, which pretty much speaks for itself - you use a touch tone telephone to get a continuous recording of meteorological information. Check the CFS for where you can get it.

The *Transcribed Weather Broadcast* provides continuous aeronautical and meteorological information on L/MF and VOR facilities.

Some FBOs have access to a private system based on DUATS computer terminals. DUATS stands for *Direct User Access Terminal System*. The FBOs will have computer terminals that connect directly to the system, but you can also dial into it from home once you register. Again, check the CFS for availability.

TAFs

Terminal Aerodrome Forecasts describe forecast conditions at an aerodrome for between 9 and 24 hours. The maximum validity will be 30 hours as of Fall 2008. They are not available for offshore operations, and are only issued after 2 consecutive METARS (which will look suspiciously similar - in fact, many groups in METARs are found in TAFs, but differences are noted below). A TAF may be sub-divided into 2 or more self-contained parts by the abbreviation 'FM' (from) followed by the time UTC to the nearest hour, expressed as 2 figures.

Note: The term CAVOK (*Ceiling and Visibility OK*) is not used in TAFs in Canada.

MESSAGE TYPE

TAF or TAF AMD, for amended. The amended forecast will have AMD inserted between TAF and the aerodrome identifier, and will cover the remainder of the validity period of the original forecast.

STATION IDENTIFIER

4-letter ICAO indicator for aerodrome.

DATE AND TIME OF ISSUE

A 6-digit code, with the date as the first two, then the time in UTC.

VALIDITY PERIOD

A METAR reports conditions at a specific time, but the TAF has the date and time of origin, followed by the start and finish times of its validity period in whole hours UTC, e.g. TAF EGLL 130600Z (date and time of issue) 0716 (period of validity 0700 to 1600 hours UTC).

WINDS

To the nearest 10°, in knots, magnetic. 000000KT is calm, VRB means variable, less than 3 kts. Gusts are in 2 digits. WS means windshear, when significant, with speed and direction at a height.

HORIZONTAL VISIBILITY

Only minimum visibility is forecast; RVR is not included.

WEATHER

If no significant weather is expected, this is omitted. After a change group, however, if the weather ceases to be significant, 'NSW' (no significant weather) will be inserted.

A minus (-) means light, no sign is moderate, and + means heavy. It is described in 7 ways, such as SH for showers, DR for drifting, FZ for freezing, MI for shallow, BL for blowing and BC for batches.

FC=Funnel Cloud (Tornado), TS=Thunderstorm, DZ=Drizzle, FG=Fog (< 1 km), BR=Mist (> 1 km), GS=Small Hail, FU=Smoke, SS=Sandstorm, VA=Volcanic Ash, PO=Dust/Sand, RA=Rain, SG=Snow Grains, PL=Ice Pellets, IC=Ice Crystals, SA=Sand, SN=Snow, HZ=Haze, GR=Hail, DU=Dust, SQ=Squall, DS=Duststorm.

CLOUD

Up to 4 cloud groups, in ascending order of bases, and cumulative, based on the amount of the sky covered, in eighths, or oktas. The cloud ceiling is the height of the first layer that is broken or overcast. The first group is the lowest individual layer; the second the next of more than 2 oktas and the third the next higher of more than 4 oktas. A group has 3 letters for the amount (FEW = 1 to 2 oktas, SCT, or scattered = 3 to 4 oktas; BKN, or broken, = 5 to 7 oktas, and OVC, or overcast = 8 oktas) and 3 for the height of the cloud base in hundreds of feet above ground level. For clear sky, expect SKC. VV means vertical visibility in hundreds of feet which, if you get it at all, means an obscured ceiling. CB means thunderstorms and is added as necessary. Clouds may cover the sky, but not conceal it if transparent, hence the term opacity.

SIGNIFICANT CHANGES

As well sa 'FM' and the time (above) significant changes may be indicated by 'BECMG' (becoming) or 'TEMPO' (temporarily). 'BECMG' is followed by a four-figure group indicating the beginning and ending of the period when the change is expected. The change is expected to be permanent, and to occur at an unspecified time within it. 'TEMPO' will similarly be followed by a 4-figure time group, indicating temporary fluctuations. 'TEMPO' conditions are expected to last less than 1 hour each time, and collectively, less than half the period indicated.

PROBABILITY

Probability of a significant change, either 30 or 40%. The abbreviation 'PROB' will precede the percentage, followed by a time group, or a change and time group, e.g.:

    PROB 30 0507 0800FG BKN004

or

    PROB40 TEMPO 1416 TSRA BKN010CB

EXAMPLE

    CFYK 0615 VRB06KT 9999 SCT 030

was issued at Yellowknife for 0600-1500, with variable wind at 6 kts, visibility more than 10 km and 3-4 oktas of cloud at 3000 above the airfield elevation.

METARs

Meteorological Aerodrome Reports are compiled half-hourly or hourly while the office is open, about 15 minutes after observations are made. The elements of a report are separated with space, except temperature and dewpoint which use a /. Missing information has the preceding space and that element omitted.

METARS are reports, not forecasts, but you may see an outlook tagged on the end after the word TREND. They represent a 2-hour period from the time of the observation. NOSIG means no significant changes expected in the next 2 hours.

Countries may modify the code - for example, the USA reports temperature and dewpoint in °C and uses current units for the remainder of the report.

MESSAGE TYPE

METAR means a routine actual weather report. SPECI means a significant change off the hour.

STATION IDENTIFIER

4-letter ICAO indicator for aerodrome, plus time of observation in UTC.

WINDS

The first three numbers are the direction to the nearest 10° and the next two the speed in knots. G means Gusts. 000000KT is calm, VRB means variable, less than 3 kts.

HORIZONTAL VISIBILITY

The minimum is in metres, followed by one of the eight points of the compass if there is a difference in visibility by direction, as with 4000 NE. If the minimum visibility is between 1500-5000 m in another direction, minimum and maximum values, and directions will be given, e.g. 1400SW 6000N. 9999 means 10 km or more, while 0000 means less than 50 m.

    CFYK 231020Z 02006KT 4000 0900NE
    R27/0600U R32/0150D PRFG OVC007
    12/11 Q1028

In the example above, 4000 is the prevailing visibility, which is the best figure that can be applied to at least 50%

of the horizon (contiguously or otherwise), so if the visibility varies from 8 km down to 4000 m for at least half of the visible horizon, the prevailing visibility is 4000 m.

If the visibility in a particular direction is less than 1500 m or is less than half of the prevailing figure, the lowest visibility observed (900 m above) is reported, with the direction (NE - NDV means *No Directional Variation* of visibility sensors). If the lowest value applies in several directions, the most operationally significant one is given. If the visibility is fluctuating wildly (such as with a rapid shower transition), only the lowest visibility is reported.

With an automated system, NCD is inserted in place of the cloud code when no cloud has been detected and the absence of CB or TCU cannot be detected. On the other hand, NSC means that the system is capable of detecting their absence

RUNWAY VISUAL RANGE (RVR)

RVR figures are assessed when the visibility gets below 1500m. If the touchdown visibility is less than 400m, all three parts of the runway are reported. Between 400-800m, the mid- and end-points are only given if they are less than the touchdown zone. Above 800m you only get them if they are lower than 800m.

An RVR group has the prefix R followed by the runway designator, then an oblique stroke followed by the touch-down RVR in metres. If RVR is assessed simultaneously on two or more runways, it will be repeated; parallel runways are distinguished by L, C or R, for Left, Central or Right parallel respectively, e.g. R24L/1100 R24R/1150. When the RVR is more than 1500m or the maximum that can be assessed, the group will be preceded by P, followed by the lesser value, e.g. R24/P1500. When less than the minimum, the RVR will be reported as M followed by the minimum value, e.g. R24/M0050.

PRESENT WEATHER

Any precipitation. A minus (-) means light, no sign is moderate, and + means heavy. It is described in 7 ways, such as SH for showers, DR for drifting, FZ for freezing, MI for shallow, BL for blowing and BC for batches. See under TAFs for other codes.

The abbreviation UP indicates when it has not been possible to identify precipitation using automatic observation. REUP should be used to indicate that the automatic system has been unable to identify a recent precipitation.

CLOUD

Up to 4 cloud groups may be included, in ascending order of bases. A group has 3 letters for the amount (FEW = 1 to 2 oktas, SCT, or scattered = 3 to 4 oktas; BKN, or broken, = 5 to 7 oktas, and OVC, or overcast = 8 oktas) and 3 for the height of the cloud base in hundreds of feet above ground level.

Apart from significant convective clouds (CB) cloud types are ignored. Cloud layers or masses are reported so the first group represents the lowest individual layer; the second is the next individual layer of more than 2 oktas; the third is the next higher layer of more than 4 oktas, and the additional group, if any, represents significant convective cloud, if not already reported, e.g.:

    SCT010 SCT015 SCT018CB BKN025

The symbol /// denotes that the automated station cannot detect the type of cloud group at this level. ////// is used in front of CB (or TCU) where the automatic system has detected a CB (or TCU) and where the coverage (or height) of these clouds has not been measured

CAVOK AND SKC

CAVOK will replace visibility, RVR, weather and cloud groups when visibility is 10 km or more, there is no cloud below 5000' or the highest MSA, whichever is greater, and no cumulo-nimbus; and there is no precipitation, thunderstorm, shallow fog or low, drifting snow. Otherwise, the cloud group is replaced by 'SKC' (sky clear) if there is no cloud report.

AIR TEMPERATURE AND DEWPOINT

Shown in °C, separated by /. A negative value is indicated by an 'M' in front of the appropriate digits, e.g. 10/M03 or '01/MO1'

PRESSURE SETTING

QNH is rounded down to the next whole millibar and reported as a 4-figure group preceded by 'Q'. If less than 1000 Mb, the first digit will be '0', e.g. 'Q0993'.

QNH is the QFE reduced to MSL under ISA. Although the met office would correct for temperature and pressure, for our purposes, only pressure is used, at 27 feet per mb (hPa) at sea level through to 50 feet at 18,500 feet (if you want to include temperature, use the average below the aircraft). QFF is similar, but using the long term monthly mean temperature and humidity, and is closer to reality.

If this page is a photocopy, it is not authorised!

RECENT WEATHER

Significant weather seen since the previous observation, but not currently relevant, will be reported with the standard present weather code preceded by the indicator 'RE', e.g. 'RETS'.

WINDSHEAR

Included if windshear is reported in the lowest 1600 feet, beginning with 'WS': 'WS TKOF RWY20', 'WS LDG RWY20'.

RUNWAY STATE

For snow or other contamination, an 8-figure group may be added at the end.

TREND

For when significant changes are forecast during the next 2 hours. The codes 'BECMG' (becoming) or 'TEMPO' (temporarily) may be followed by a time group (in hours and minutes UTC) preceded by one of 'FM' (from), 'TL' (until) or 'AT' (at). These are followed by the expected change using the standard codes, e.g. 'BECMG FM 1100 250/35G50KT' or 'TEMPO FM 0630 TL0830 3000 SHRA'. Where no such significant changes are expected, the trend group will be replaced by the word 'NOSIG'.

DENEB

Fog dispersal is in progress.

Area Forecast

This covers several hundred square miles. Cloud bases are reported above sea level.

SIGMETs

Warning of serious weather, covering 60 minutes flying time ahead of the aircraft.

AIREPs

Reports by pilots, commencing with *UA*. *UUA* is *urgent*. AIREPs are similar to position reports in content, except that they also have met information at the end, like temperature, wind, turbulence, icing and other relevant information.

AIRMET

A telephone service for people without access to charts, etc. with information in plain language for certain areas (see AIM MET section for contact numbers).

They are valid for 8 hours, and are issued 4 times a day, with an outlook of 6 hours:

0500-1300 UTC	to 1900
1100-1900 UTC	to 0100
1700-0100 UTC	to 0700
2300-0700 UTC	to 1300

Radar & Satellite

Radar or satellite images give a good overview of a situation:

Note: Remember that weather radar is supposed to detect *raindrops* and *hail*, not cloud droplets, so you will generally only see the thicker parts of clouds.

The Meteosat series of geostationary satellites fly about 36,000 kilometres above the Equator. Their orbit time is exactly 24 hours, which is how they stay in the same place over the Earth's surface. They can take pictures every 15 or 30 minutes, but resolution is limited due to distance.

Moreover, the image is distorted due to the angle from which it is taken

Polar Orbiters, on the other hand, fly 800 km above the surface, to provide high resolution images. They make 14 orbits per day (around 102 mins for each orbit) passing close to the poles. Between one orbit and the next, the Earth rotates 25°. Thus, they can take only four useful images per day of any particular place.

CHARTS

....

Weather information is issued in many ways, including the charts mentioned below. Those showing *expected* patterns are *prognosis* charts, but you can bet they won't be anything like what you see when you get there.

Graphical Area Forecast

The GFA was introduced in April 2000. It's not one, but a series of six charts (actually, three sets of two) showing the most probable weather below 24,000 feet amsl at a particular time for a particular region, which could be Arctic, Yukon-Northwest Territories, Nunavut, Pacific, Prairie, Ontario-Quebec and Atlantic. There is one for the ocean West of the Arctic, but you only get that if you ask for it. They are issued 4 times a day, about half an hour before the periods they relate to, which are 0000, 0600, 1200 and 1800 UTC, so expect to see 24 pieces of paper across your desk in the course of a day. One GFA will therefore consist of 6 pieces of paper, which is what you will get in the exam.

The period covered is 12 hours for each issue, with an IFR outlook for another 12 under the comment box, although it's possible that new charts will have been issued. If amended, they will have the letters CCA for the first revision, CCB for the second, and so on, in the first line of the title box. As mentioned, you will get three sets of two, for the start, middle and end of the period. Of each group, one will show clouds and weather, whilst the other shows what you might expect in terms of icing, turbulence and freezing level.

Naturally, over a fax line from a flight service station, all you will get is black and white, and probably not very readable at that, but colour ones are available from NAV Canada, at **www.navcanada.ca/flight/**.

THE CHARTS

On the top, overleaf, is a clouds and weather chart. The one underneath it is for icing and turbulence. When asked to check the weather at a certain time (it will usually be near the end of the period), don't do the computations from the first GFA chart, but the one just before the time required. Get used to making deductions, as a typical question might ask for the conditions in a descent just when the edge of a cloud area is over the destination, so brush up your interpolations. Also, know your symbols.

The chart is split into several areas:

- The information box (the big one on the left) has the pictures.

- In the title box at the top right is the chart name, from the GFA domain, with the type of chart, underneath which are the issue and valid times.

- A limited supply of symbols is in the legend box, with a scale in nm.

- The comments box contains any the forecaster cares to make.

The IFR Outlook is a summary for the next 12 hours.

Points to note (for exams):

- Heights are above sea level, unless noted otherwise, and in hundreds of feet. Only base and tops of clouds are given. Scalloped areas indicate organised clouds.

- Visibility is given only when below 6 sm. Over that, it is shown as P6SM.

- Wind is given only above 20 kts, or gusts 30 kts +.

- All fronts are included, as are highs and lows. As with normal weather maps, isobars are 4 mb apart. There will be an arrow with a number next to it, showing the direction and speed of movement (in the exam, don't deduce it from the first chart - look at all the charts before answering a question about this). The letters QS mean *Quasi-Stationary* where movement is less than 5 kts.

- Use the abbreviations in TAFs and METARs to describe ground-based layers like fog (but see below). Only mentioned when vis is expected to be less than 6 sm.

- Only moderate or severe icing is shown, although bases, tops and type will be covered. Icing areas are surrounded with blue dots.

- Only moderate or severe turbulence is shown, together with its type, such as CAT, etc. Bases and tops are shown the same way as clouds are.

The freezing level is a red dashed line used like a contour, beginning at the surface and continuing at 2,500' intervals.

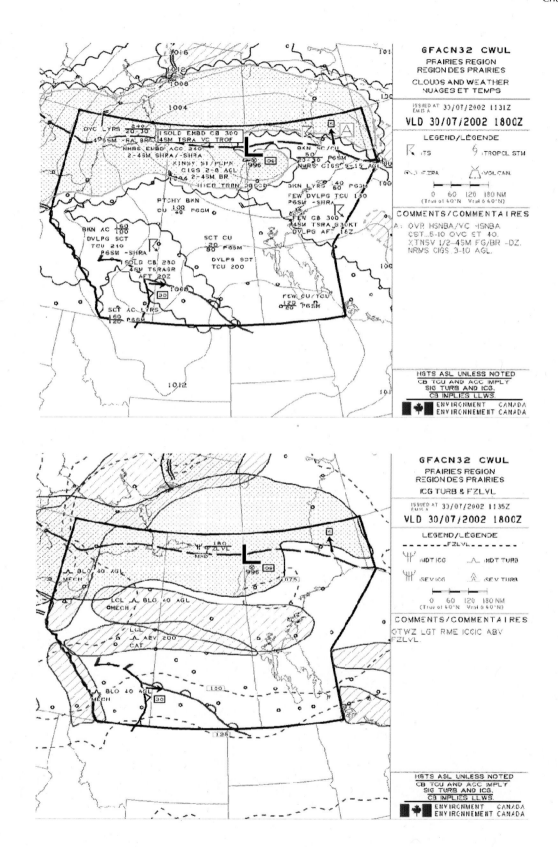

CLOUDS

Tops and bottoms of forecast clouds will be shown, up to 24,000 feet ASL, but the tops of convective clouds will be shown above that (cirrus clouds are not shown at all).

Convective clouds will also be named - other types will be only when significant. The borders will be enclosed in scallops containing a description and the heights in hundreds of feet (see left). In the case on the left, the bottoms of broken cumulus will be 2,000 feet, and the tops at 8,000.

Where the visibility is expected to be over 6 miles, and organised clouds not forecast, there will be no border, but a statement of SKC, FEW or SCT. Multiple cloud layers are indicated separately inside, based on the amount at that level, not the total. Surface-based layers are shown as OBSCD (obscured).

VISIBILITY

Given in statute miles, up to 6. Above that, it is indicated as P6SM. Thus, obstructions to vision are only mentioned under 6 miles. A dashed line as a border indicates intermittent or showery precip. A solid line means continuous.

WINDS

Sustained windspeeds over 20 kts are shown with wind barbs. A G means *gusts*, with the peak value in knots.

 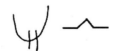

ICING & TURBULENCE

Icing is shown for moderate and severe levels, with bases and tops, in the same way cloud is shown, but with a different symbol (far left). The symbol for turbulence is to its right.

FDAs

Forecasts for Upper Level Winds and Temperatures, prepared twice daily for various altitudes, as tabulated figures:

	3000	6000	9000
YVR	9900	2415-07	2430-10
YYF	2523	2432-04	2338-08

You have to interpolate for the height you will be at which, in the exam, will be nowhere near any of the lines in the table - for example, at 7,500 feet, the figures would be something like 2422-8. A minus sign means temperatures below 0°C. Wind velocity is in degrees true and knots, 9900 means *light and variable* and high winds are above 18,000 feet.

The Station Circle

Weathermen use a station circle (or model) to describe the weather where their observations are made. Below is a decode of the symbols:

N	Total cloud	Nh	Sky covered low/mid cloud
dd	Wind dir (T)	h	Cloudbase
ff	Wind spd in kts	CM	Middle cloud
VV	Visibility in miles	CH	High cloud
ww	Present weather	TdTd	Dewpoint
W	Past weather	a	Barograph trend
PPP	Pressure in mb	pp	Pressure change in last 3 hrs
TT	Air temperature	RR	Precipitation
CL	Low cloud	Rt	Time precip began or ended

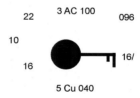

In the example on the left, the dark circle means the sky is covered with cloud (it would have white and black quadrants otherwise), the temperature is 22°C, and the dewpoint 16°C. The wind is from the East at 15 kts - if the wind is calm, there will be a second circle around the first. The visibility is 10 sm in rain. The middle cloud is 3/10 Alto-Cu at 10,000 feet. Low cloud is 5/10 Cumulus at 4,000. The sea level pressure is 1009.6 and the trend over the last 3 hours is a steady increase of 1.6 mb.

The wind barbs are on the clockwise side in the Northern Hemisphere, and the anticlockwise side in the Southern Hemisphere. A triangle (instead of a circle) indicates an automatic reporting station.

○	Clear	⌐	Smoke
◑	1/8	•	Rain
◕	SCT	’	Drizzle
◑	3/8	▽	Shower
◑	4/8	✳	Snow
◑	5/8	∾	Frz Rn
◕	BKN	=	Fog
●	7/8	∞	Haze
●	OVC	$	Dust
⊗	OBSC	⊹	Blow Sn

FRONTAL PASSAGE

You can tell the position of fronts between stations just by looking at the station circles. These items will change as a front goes by:

- Wind veers (marked clockwise change in arrow direction)

- Pressure drops as fronts approach, steadying after warm fronts, rising after cold ones

- Temperature changes according to the type of front

- Weather will start with moderate continuous rain ahead of the warm front to drizzle in the warm sector, followed by heavier intermittent or continuous precipitation at the cold front, then nil (or showers) afterwards

- Clouds follow the pattern in the diagram above

- Visibility improves significantly behind the cold front

Upper Level Charts

These are also prognosis or analysis charts, but based on a particular pressure level, so the real altitude represented will vary a great deal (they will be lower as you go North, because it gets colder there). They are based on the relationship between winds and temperature, in that a height of a pressure surface will increase as it gets warmer and *vice versa* (the same principle as with altimeter errors). Here are the approximate heights the charts represent:

Pressure (mb)	Height ASL (ft)
850	5 000
700	10 000
500*	18 000
400	24 000
300	30 000

*18,000 feet is about halfway up the atmosphere in terms of pressure, meaning that near the midpoint of the troposphere, so 500 mb charts give a good average view of what's going on. In fact, it shows both the broad scale of event at the higher levels, but some of the lower storm systems can also be visible.

Upper level features tend to lag behind those on the surface - that is, an upper trough associated with a surface front would lie further to the West. Winds will also tend to increase with height.

Because pressure in the upper levels is dependent on the mean temperature of a given column of air; a low mean temperature through a column of air in the troposphere produces low pressure aloft, and a high mean temperature produces a high, resulting in a pressure gradient high up in the atmosphere, where air will flow.

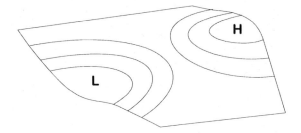

In other words, once a pressure level is high because of the air temperature, there will be a gradient between it and colder air, which will be lower - air will flow from high to low pressure, but the root cause will be temperature. Eventually, geostrophic force will make the wind veer to the right, to blow parallel to the imaginary isobars.

The values used are direction relative to True N and speed in knots.

Buys Ballot's Law is still good - in the Northern Hemisphere with your back to the wind, the cold air will be to the left* and the thermal wind will blow parallel to the isotherms, with low temperatures to the left. Speed will be inversely proportional to the distance between the isotherms, meaning that the strength of the wind will depend on how steep the slope is.

For example, two points with the same surface pressure of 998 hPa are 200 nm apart in the Northern Hemisphere. The mean temperature between the surface and 20,000 feet at Point A is -2°C and -10°C at Point B, to the South. What is the wind velocity at 2,0000 feet halfway between A and B?

As the mean temperature changes by 8°C, the temperature gradient is 4°C/100 nm. The height of the layer is 20,000 feet, so the wind speed at that level is 80 kts (4 x 20). Since the points are N-S with respect to each other, Buys Ballot's law gives you a Westerly wind, or 270/80.

As both points have the same surface pressure, there is no geostrophic wind at the surface, otherwise you would have to add it to the thermal wind to get the upper wind (just draw a diagram).

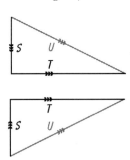

Isotherms of mean temperature are roughly parallel to lines of latitude, and the average thermal wind is westerly outside the tropics. From this information, you can deduce the direction of the surface or upper wind, depending on which one you know already. For example, if the surface wind is Northerly, and the thermal wind is westerly, the upper wind will be backed in relation to the surface wind (left, top). Similarly, a Southerly surface wind will veer towards the thermal (bottom).

Westerly winds will increase their speed but keep their direction, while Easterly winds will decrease in speed, then veer or back to become light Westerly. In the tropics (between 0-20°), winds up to 40,000 feet will be Easterly.

*Although the contours look the same as isobars, and the wind will behave the same way, remember the surface chart is based on sea level pressure, and the ones here show the *altitude* of the pressure level, so a Low really is lower than a High, instead of indicating an area of rising air, as it would on a sea level chart. Also, there will be lines joining points of equal temperature (isotherms) and windspeed (isotachs), which are both dotted and easy to confuse with each other. *High level winds are the sum of the vectors of the low-level winds and thermal components.* Buys Ballot's law applies with temperature as well, except that you stand with your back to the thermal component, and closely space isobars still mean a high gradient and hence stronger winds. Look for jetstreams around closely spaced isotherms and isotachs. You can detect CAT by comparing charts for vertical windshear gradient over 6 kts per 1,000 feet, and horizontal shear over 40 kts per 150 miles.

While an isobar connects points of equal barometric pressure normalized to sea level, an *isohypse* connects points of equal geopotential height (they are also called *height contours*). As well, isobars are plotted only on surface charts while isohypses are found on upper air charts. An isohypse, or *height contour*, represents the distance from zero geopotential meters (at about sea level) to the pressure level of interest. Its value depends on the average temperature and moisture content of the air underneath.

Low isohypses values indicate colder air (troughs) while high isohypse values (ridges) indicate warmer air. Moisture has a minor effect on height as compared to temperature - moist air will have a little higher isohypse value than dry air at the same temperature because moist air is less dense. If an *isohypse* of the 500 hPa pressure surface is labelled as 552, it means that for all connected points, topography is 552 decameters above MSL.

The relevance of upper level charts is that they give you a better idea of the real movement of air masses and hence the sort of weather coming your way. Although the winds follow the contours, remember that the 500 and 850 mb charts can often oppose each other. Upper winds are also stronger because the density is less. Half the density, say at 20,000 feet, is double the speed. Wind direction is given relative to True North, in knots. The best approximation of wind speed at FL 250 is obtained from interpolation between the 500 and 300 charts, taking into consideration the significant weather chart. Laying a temperature and humidity chart over them is helpful - if low level winds are warm and moist, expect instability and thunderstorms, particularly if upper winds are cool. If things are the other way round, expect an inversion and poor visibility (from industrial haze), albeit no clouds. If it's very dry at higher levels, moisture will be sucked out from lower ones - with no saturation there will be no clouds, but good visibility. The idea is to get a 3D picture of what's going on upstairs - for example, the slope will always be downward, toward the colder air mass.

The Captain is responsible for checking, before flight, that the aircraft's weight is such that the flight can be safely made, and that any cargo is properly distributed and secured

FLIGHT PLANNING

Weight and balance must follow the Flight Manual, to ensure that an aircraft is safely loaded. As the Flight Manual forms part of the Certificate of Airworthiness (or Permit to Fly), if its conditions are not met, the flight becomes illegal, and any insurance is invalidated.

The Mass & Balance limitations for any aircraft are found in the Flight Manual and may (or may not) be repeated in Part B of the Ops Manual. The details for a particular aircraft, after being weighed, will be found in the *Weight & Balance Schedule*, tucked away in the Technical Log, the Flight Manual, or the aircraft document folder. In the exam, you will get to use a specimen loading manual.

UNITS & CONVERSIONS

There are many ways of expressing mass and volume, and considerable care must be used to ensure that the correct ones are used - and not just for the exams. Fuel gauges, especially, come in all sorts of varieties.

Units of volume in general use are Imperial Gallons, US Gallons and Litres. Units of mass (weight) are pounds (lbs) and kilograms (kg). To convert from one to the other, you need to know the *specific gravity* of the liquid concerned, based on that of water, which is taken as 1, since 1 Imperial Gallon of it weighs 10 lbs. For example, as fuel is less dense than water, a typical SG value (found in most flight manuals) for jet fuel is .79. Here are some other examples:

Fuel	lbs per Imp Gal
80/87	7.2 (.72)
100/130	7.3 (.73)
115/145	7.4 (.74)
JP-1	8 (.8)
JP-4	7.8 (.78)

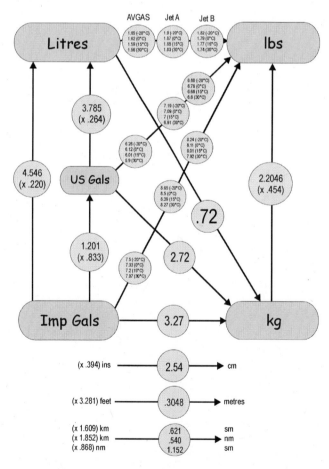

Conversion Chart
Multiply in the direction of the arrow - divide the other way (figures in brackets are the multiplication factor if you don't want to divide).

WEIGHT

It's well known that every aircraft has a Maximum Takeoff Mass, which is the heaviest with which you may get airborne (although you may not always be able to use it - see below). It's also well known that aircraft will fly overweight to a certain extent, if only because there's a tolerance range in the performance figures - ferry flights frequently do so (with approval), with the extra weight being fuel, but having the ability doesn't mean that you should. You will at some stage be under some pressure to take an extra bit of baggage or top up with that bit of fuel that will save you making a stop en route, but consider the implications. Firstly, any C of A (and insurance cover) will be invalid if you don't fly within the limits of the flight manual, and, secondly, you will be leaving yourself nothing in hand for turbulence and the like, which will increase your weight artificially. The designer will have allowed for 60° turns all the way up to MAUW, but not heavier than that. The effects of overloading include:

- *reduced acceleration capabilities* (leading to longer takeoff and landing distances). Takeoff and safety speeds will be affected as well.

- *decreased climb capability* (watch for those obstacles)

- *reduced range, ceiling, manoeuvrability, braking* and *power margins*. Control ranges will certainly be affected

- *Possible structural damage*

The Aircraft

New aircraft are normally weighed at the factory and may be used without reweighing if the records have been adjusted for alterations or modifications.

Although sometimes a weighbridge can be used if the aircraft is small enough, the empty weight is usually determined by measuring the downward force at each wheel, skid or jacking point. Since the station numbers are known, you just need to combine the figures to get a weight & balance.

For example, after weighing a helicopter, the following values are noted:

- Forward point: 350 kg

- Aft right point: 995 kg

- Aft left point: 1 205 kg

What is the longitudinal C of G position in relation to the datum 4 m in front of the rotor axis, knowing that the

forward point is at 2.5 m forward of the rotor axis and the aft points are 1 m aft of the rotor axis?

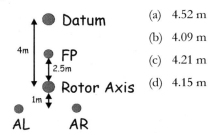

(a) 4.52 m

(b) 4.09 m

(c) 4.21 m

(d) 4.15 m

The answer is 4.52 m. The total weight is 2550 kg (350 + 1205 + 995). The forward point is 1.5 m behind the datum (4 m - 2.5), so the forward point's moment is 350 x 1.5 = 525. The rear points' moment is 2200 kg (from 1205 + 995) x 5 (from 4 + 1), which equals 11000. Now, divide the total moment by the total weight (11525/2550) to get approximately 4.519607843, the nearest answer.

Each part weighed is called the *reaction mass* - so the sum of them all is the total mass. The *reaction moments* for each *reaction point* are added together and divided by the total mass to get the ship's C of G.

The Load

Generally, actual weights must be used, meaning that you must physically weigh your passengers and cargo, but, under some circumstances, you can use *Standard Masses* for convenience, described below.

Here are the relevant definitions: (exam questions may expect you to know whether to include crew or not):

- The *Manufacturer's Empty Weight* (MEW) is that in the Weight and Centre of Gravity Schedule, which is established by weighing before the machine is used for commercial air transport. It is the weight of the empty aircraft, plus integral equipment and fluids in closed systems

- The *Aircraft Prepared for Service Weight* (APS Weight) includes all operational equipment (cabin seats, life rafts, life jackets, portable ELTs, inlet screens, hook, hoist, etc). It excludes the flight crew, fuel and payload

- The *Operational Empty Weight* is the MEW (above) plus operator's items, such as crew, their baggage, unusable fuel and oil, emergency and catering stuff, paperwork, etc (otherwise known as the Variable Load)

- The *Dry Operating Weight* is the OEW, plus items for specific types of flight

- The *Disposable Load* includes freight, passengers and usable fuel and oil (*payload* and *fuel*)

- The *Useful Load* is the payload, or disposable load without fuel, oil and consumables

- The *Maximum All-Up Weight* (MAUW) is the maximum certified aircraft gross weight

- The *Restricted Takeoff/Landing Weight* (RTOW/RLW) is the maximum aircraft gross weight for performance (e.g. weight restriction for Category "A" requirements)

- The *Maximum Taxi (Ramp) Weight* is the maximum weight at which the aircraft may be moved, under its own power or otherwise. It is the sum of the Maximum Takeoff Weight plus fuel for taxi and runup. It can therefore be higher than MTOW, and you should be able to burn off the difference before takeoff to reach the Takeoff Mass

- The *Zero Fuel Mass* is the weight of an aircraft, above which, any increase in weight must consist entirely of (usable) fuel. It is normally relevant for aeroplanes to prevent the wings being stressed from there being too much weight in the cabin, since the fuel tanks are in the wings, but in helicopters assumes an importance for C of G and controllability issues

- The *Maximum Landing Weight* is there to help prevent the impact with the runway being transmitted through the undercarriage to the rest of the aircraft, which can only happen if the weight is kept within certain limits (it also assists in reducing downward velocity). This weight may very well be restricted performance-wise in a similar way to Take-off Weight, and could equally be a factor in further reducing your payload at the start of a flight. It's actually the Zero Fuel Weight, plus reserve and alternate fuel

Note that the Empty Weight and the payload will not change during flight, but the fuel load will, and may change the C of G, of which more later. The mass of the fuel must be determined with the actual density or, if not, the density calculated under a method in the Ops Manual.

Maximum Takeoff and Landing Weights are there because of structural and performance limits, plus aerodynamic reasons and weather. They are affected by such things as:

- Pressure Altitude

- Temperature

- Space available. If you have to do a vertical climb or descent, you will need more power and maybe have to reduce weight

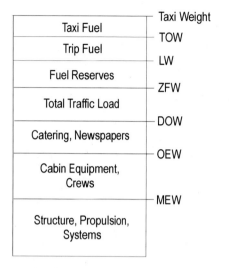

PROCEDURE

First, you need to determine the Maximum Takeoff Weight, which may need to be adjusted for the conditions under which the aircraft has to operate. Write this down on a piece of paper for now.

Then you need to find the APS Weight, which is derived from the aircraft's Basic Empty Weight, plus that of the crew. The Basic Weight will be found in the Weight & Gravity Schedule, in the aircraft's technical documentation. It will have been written out by the maintenance department, and may include different weights and moment arms for different configurations, such as dual flight controls, etc. Subtract the APS Weight from the MTOW to find the Disposable Load, e.g.:

```
3150  (MTOM)
2060  (BEM of 1875 + Crew)
1090  (Disposable Load)
```

You must fit the fuel and passengers in the remainder, so subtract the fuel required for the trip from the Disposable Load, to find the Traffic Load, or what the customer is paying for. If the Traffic Load available is not enough, you must either reduce it, or the fuel, which means you must stop en route to pick up some more.

STANDARD WEIGHTS

Passengers and checked baggage must normally be weighed, unless you have an arrangement with your Inspector for a *load plan*. Standard weights can be used when things are happening quickly and you cannot weigh things (except when passengers weigh more than shown):

Summer		Winter
200 lbs (90.7 kg)	Males (>12)	206 lbs (93.4 kg)
165 lbs (74.8 kg)	Females (>12)	171 lbs (77.5 kg)
75 lbs (34 kg)	Children (2-11)	75 lbs (34 kg)
30 lbs (13.6 kg)	Infants (0-<2)	30 lbs (13.6 kg)

The figures include carry-on baggage so, if there is none, reduce them by 13 lbs. Add 13 lbs for clothing in Summer and 14 lbs in Winter to actual weights.

Fuel and oil have standard weights, too, although technically the weight of fuel in the machine changes with temperature (check the flight manual). For exam purposes, jet fuel is 6.5 lbs/US gal and oil as 7.5 lbs/US gal.

DISTRIBUTION & LOADING

There are two aspects to loading an aircraft, the weights themselves and their distribution, and you sometimes get some nasty surprises - unusually shaped fuel tanks mean that you won't get a straight line variation; every fuel load will have a different moment arm, principally because the fuel tanks have a C of G system all of their own, running separately from the aircraft (even in small ones, like the Bell 206 or 407). In this case, it's not enough just to subtract the closing fuel moment from the starting one - for example, say 1,000 lbs has a moment of 1843 and 300 lbs has 558. The result for 700 lbs of fuel may not be 1843-558 (1285), but the actual figure of 1294, which is enough of a difference to cause an insurance company to have qualms about paying up after an accident.

The Centre of Gravity of any object is a point inside it where its weight (or gravitational attraction) passes through, or where its mass is concentrated. It could be described as the average location of its weight force, or better described as its point of balance. The location of the C of G depends on the object's shape, density and the external gravitational field. If a vertical line through the C of G lies outside the base on which the object relies for support, it will overturn, unless you do something to counterbalance the force:

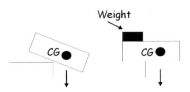

It is interesting to note that a lighter weight than the one shown above, but further away from the CG (if there were room) will have the same restraining effect. In the bottom diagram below, the beam is balanced even though different weights are suspended from it - the difference is compensated for by each one's distance from the fulcrum:

Loads in aircraft work the same way.

The Centre of Gravity, therefore, of an aircraft, is the imaginary point around which its weight forces are said to act. It is normally referenced to the longitudinal axis, and the details for any aircraft will be found in its Flight Manual. The range in which the C of G works, or, rather, its limits, are determined by aircraft stability and manoeuvrability - when outside the design range, control movement is affected.

Incorrect loading naturally affects aircraft performance, and will possibly prevent the thing from even getting airborne. Limitations to be considered include:

- *Limiting mass* (the heaviest weight you can fly with, which may be restricted for performance reasons)

- *C of G position* (too far forward or aft will affect the range of operation of the flying controls)

- *Mass distribution* (too far over to one side may affect your lateral C of G, or stop people getting out in emergency)

- *Floor loading* (the structure will be stressed for a certain weight per area)

The *reference datum* is an imaginary point from which all calculations start and where some C of G ranges are expressed (for example, *106 inches aft of datum*). Mostly, it is somewhere around the nose, to keep the values positive.

The *moment arm*, or *balance arm*, is the distance from the reference datum to the C of G of a mass. It may be measured in Imperial or Metric units, and you must use the same ones throughout (the expression *station* may also be used). To get the C of G of an aircraft, you multiply the weight of each item in it by the arm of the location it occupies to get the *moment*, or the amount of leverage that item contributes (for example, a 200 lb load 6 feet behind the datum would have the same downwards force as a 100 lb load 12 feet from it - the moment is the mass of an item multiplied by its distance from the datum). Then add the moments and divide that total by the total weight. Because you might end up using very long numbers, sometimes you use a *moment index*, the result of dividing the moment by 1,000 to make the figures more manageable.

The aircraft itself will have an arm and a moment from when it was last weighed, which is where you start. You can find it in the *weight and balance schedule*, and it may be varied if you add or take off various items of equipment.

Here is a simplified typical calculation (the principles are exactly the same for larger machines, just with more seats):

Item	Wt	Arm	Moment
Aircraft	1881	116.5	219137
Front pax	185	65	13000
Rear Pax	185	104	19240
Baggage	50	147.50	7375
Zero Fuel CG	2301	112.45	258756
Fuel	310	110.7	34273
Total	**2611**	**112.22**	**293025**

The total C of G for takeoff is 112.22, obtained by dividing the total moment figure (293025) by the total weight, or mass (2611).

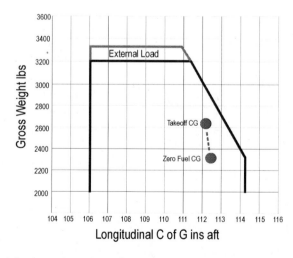

The procedure, then, is to multiply the weights by the arms to get the moments, and divide the total moments by the total weights to get the C of G. Next, refer to the flight

manual to see if the figure fits into the authorised range on the graph - simply take the all-up weight you end up with, and the final C of G, and line them up horizontally and vertically. If they are inside the envelope, you are OK, but don't forget you have to land again! Your C of G may be fine for takeoff, but check again after fuel has been used!

Changes

One day you might have to shift the load. Here's how to figure out what to move and where:

$$X = \frac{W \times D}{d}$$

where:

X	Weight to be moved
W	Total weight of aircraft
D	Distance the C of G is out
d	Distance between old and new locations of load moved

So, if your gross weight is 3000 lbs, your load is 1½ inches outside the envelope (aft), to be moved from the baggage compartment to the rear seats, all of 34 inches, you need to move 133 lbs to get back in limits:

$$133 = \frac{3000 \times 1.5}{34}$$

Rearranging the formula a bit, you can work the above out on the flight computer.

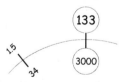

Note that the total weight has not changed. Remember also that the C of G will follow the weight, that is, if the movement is forward, the C of G will go that way, as well. To find a change in C of G:

$$D = \frac{X \times d}{W}$$

LEMAC

Because a wing's aerodynamic characteristics are related to *chord length*, it's helpful on large aircraft to refer to the C of G's position relative to the chord, which is actually difficult to measure due to the shape of the wing, so the *Mean Aerodynamic Chord* (MAC) is used instead, with the allowable C of G range expressed in percentages of it (%MAC). It is the average distance from the leading to the trailing edges of the wing, or the chord of an imaginary rectangular one with the same centre of pressure. As with the "normal" C of G, it can be used to predict the handling characteristics of the aircraft, which are normally acceptable at the 25% average chord point.

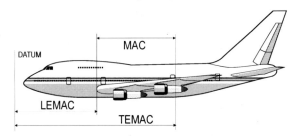

LEMAC is the distance from the datum to the leading edge of the MAC, at the front, and TEMAC is the distance to the trailing edge, at the back. LEMAC is therefore 0% MAC and may also expressed as a distance aft of the datum. So, the C of G will lie somewhere between LEMAC and TEMAC, depending on the weight and configuration. This formula calculates the %MAC (use the same units):

$$\text{\%MAC} = \frac{\text{CG-LEMAC}}{\text{MAC}} \times 100$$

Find the conventional C of G first, then divide its distance aft of LEMAC into the MAC (TEMAC minus LEMAC). The reason you need to know the %MAC settings is because some jets have their horizontal stabiliser trim settings marked in this value (the figures are a product of the C of G and flap setting). Others, such as the 737 have them marked in units of nose up trim, and you will need to look in the trim tables to get the settings for a given C of G. To convert %MAC figures back to an arm (for C of G change - see below), first convert the C of G as %MAC to C of G in ins aft of LEMAC:

$$\text{CG (aft LEMAC)} = \text{CG\%MAC}/100 \times \text{MAC}$$

Then just add the figure obtained above to the distance from Datum to LEMAC.

Floor Loading

Passenger seats occupy the whole floor space evenly; this load-spreading principle needs to be borne in mind with freight (cargo is best distributed like passengers would be), which makes it easier to provide decent restraint on each pack, because access areas to exits above and around the cargo are needed for *when the load has moved* after an emergency stop. Loads should be restrained with nets or straps (or a combination) and must distribute the load over available fixtures, such as seat attachments. In emergency, you can use seat belts (see *Tiedowns*, below).

Some aircraft have a proper cargo fit, but problems arise where one that normally carries passengers is used without modification, which is why you may need to be certificated on your training forms as being cleared to change the aircraft layout. Naturally, in small aircraft where the emergency exits are obvious, this really only involves removing the seats, because the aim is just to substitute loads that use the same fixtures and locations, but where you get involved in removing galleys and otherwise converting the cabin in larger ones, the exercise becomes a little more difficult (just because a Flight Manual contains details of freight loading limitations, don't assume that any modifications you make are permitted - those figures may only have been used for basic certification).

The floor of the machine, including baggage compartments, will not be able to take more than a certain amount of weight per square foot, usually expressed in pounds. For example, one might like 100 lbs/sq foot. The more floor area a load takes up, the less weight per square foot it will exert (*load spreading*).

To find the floor area taken up, find what it is in square inches, then divide by 144, so a pallet 37" x 39" will take up 10.02 sq ft (refer to the *Limitations* section in the Flight Manual). To find what the floor can hold in that area, multiply it by the floor load limit, then subtract the weight of the pallet and fixings to find what you can put on it.

In the real world, however, you more often have to find an area that will take a particular pallet, since it will be inconvenient to break it down. As above, you first find the area from the dimensions, then divide it into the total weight of the item - the limit must be above this weight.

TIEDOWNS

When loading cargo, it is important to use the tiedown points provided, since they have been designed to provide restraint in the usual attitudes of flight. However, very often, cargo is loaded onto passenger seats, but it should

Proper Planning Prevents Poor
Performance

Well begun, half done

still be restrained, using at least the passenger seat belts.
This is because it may move in flight, and in doing so, it
will affect the C of G.

As to when a shift of cargo becomes important has not
officially been defined, but a common-sense interpretation
would be "when it changes the C of G of the helicopter"
to quote one inspector.

FLIGHT PLANNING

This may appear tedious in the early stages, but planning is
actually around ¾ of a trip - you're not just getting paid
for the flying! The more planning you do, the more
answers you will have to hand when things go wrong and
the better the trip will be, as any plan you have spent time
over is better than one cooked up on the spur of the
moment. If you get into a little routine, the process will
become speedier as time goes by. One good example of
the need for thorough preparation is a flight in
deteriorating weather. If you should suddenly find yourself
in cloud, do you know what the MSA is and what heading
will keep you away from high ground? And who to call? I
thought not! This is stuff you should know before you go!
In general, you need to know:

- The use of charts and other aids to find out
  bearings and distances

- How to calculate the fuel required, and how to use
  it efficiently

- How much payload your machine can carry as a
  result, and how it might affect your takeoff and
  landing weights, and techniques, although this is
  more to do with performance

GENERAL PLANNING

However, for the general planning required for a trip,
points to remember (in more or less this order) are:

- Airspace you will fly through (controlled or
  uncontrolled). There might be several factors that
  affect your choice of route:

  - Routes inbound and outbound (ATC
    sometimes have preferences)

  - Restricted areas

- Radio frequencies required

- Maps and preparation

- NOTAMs

- Weather (destination and alternates, including
  takeoff), including enroute forecasts, weather and
  winds, etc. If no met information is available for
  the destination, you must have 2 alternates

- Minima (when IFR)

- Minimum safe altitudes, and performance

- Best level for performance and comfort
  (Quadrantal Rule)

- Best level for winds aloft

- Fuel required

- Weight & Balance

- Documents required to be carried

- Flight plans

- Aircraft serviceability

After all that, select the route from the map, writing down
the tracks and distances on the PLOG (below), then apply
the wind to find out the resultant headings and
groundspeeds.

Always ensure you are using the same units, that is, don't
mix magnetic and true headings and wind directions.
Either apply the magnetic stuff to everything before you
start, or work it all out in true and apply the magnetic
variation at the end.

ATC flight plans are covered in Section 1 (*Air Law*).

THE PLOG (FLIGHT LOG)

The letters are short for *Progress Log*, or a sheet of paper which tabulates the details of a particular flight, used for flight planning and checking progress on the actual trip. In commercial companies, it must be kept as a record of the flight (I'm told that a navigation log used to be just that - the progress of a ship was carved on a lump of wood). Once you've drawn your proposed track on the map, you put its details in the appropriate boxes on the plog, work out the wind, obtain your intended heading and groundspeed, apply the magnetic variation, calculate the fuel required, fill 'er up and you're ready to go.

Below is a sample form, partly filled in with details of a proposed trip from Yellowknife (CFYK) to Fort Smith (CBDI) - it's taken from the D-13 WAC chart. Notice that the Flight Level (or altitude, in this case) is higher than the Safety Altitude, which I've taken from the biggest blue figure in the lat/long boxes en route, plus a bit for mother. The figure would look something like this on a chart:

$$6^8$$

Meaning 6,800 feet is the minimum height you want to be for safety.

The figures for an alternate have been left out for clarity, but you should always choose one and work out the figures for it in the same way, before you go - by definition, an alternate is for when you *really* need one, and there's never enough time to do things on the run. When planning a trip with a lot of legs, my own preference, if there's room, is to leave a line between each one, in case you do have to change things, or you note any differences, such as wind velocity, and work out a new groundspeed.

When planning a trip with a lot of legs, my own preference, if there's room, is to leave a line between each one, in case you do have to change things, or you note any differences, such as wind velocity, and work out a new groundspeed.

Different organisations will have their own version of the above form, but this is more or less like what you will see in the exam. The only things that are missing are boxes for fuel flow and weights at relevant points.

The tactics are to fill the form up to the groundspeed column first, meaning you are just using the triangle of velocities at this stage, with information in the question itself. Find the climb and descent groundspeeds (check the question), deduce the distance travelled, and subtract the figures from the first and last legs. Once you know your groundspeeds and distances, you can figure out how long each leg will take, which is the starting point for fuel calculations. In an exam, don't forget to apply magnetic variations to the w/v, unless the tracks are given as True.

Time	From	To	FL/ Alt	Safety Alt	TAS	W/V	Track T	Drift	Hdg T	Var	Hdg M	G/S	Dist	Time	ETA
1200	CFYK	CBDI	3500	2500	90	180/15	150			-26			175		
Alternate												Totals →			

Otherwise, there's not much else you can usefully put in at this stage, so get your whizzwheel and see if you can fill in the rest, given that the wind velocity is 180/15. If you want to cheat, the picture below will show you what it should look like.

TOC/TOD

To calculate these, find the mean height and temperature for the mean TAS, then the mean W/V for mean heading and groundspeed. Figure out the times based on the height change and rates of climb or descent, then use mean groundspeed. Then work inwards from the start and end points of the journey for distance and time.

Time	From	To	FL/ Alt	Safety Alt	TAS	W/V	Track T	Drift	Hdg T	Var	Hdg M	G/S	Dist	Time	ETA
1200	CFYK	CBDI	3500	2500	90	180/15	150	+5	155	-26	129	78	175	135	1415
Alternate												Totals →			

FUEL

Around half the takeoff weight of modern jets consists of fuel, as lots of it is burned en route. Because fuel efficiency depends a lot on the altitude flown, careful planning is essential, especially when fuel takes up space that can be used by fare-paying passengers. An MD-11 burns 16,000 lbs an hour at FL 350, but *26,000* at 11,000 feet (it will also go a lot slower). Around 3-4% of fuel is burnt just to carry the rest of the fuel, so it makes sense to carry as little as possible, especially when you have to climb to higher altitudes, but often the fuel at home base is cheaper that that you get elsewhere, so a little sacrifice is often necessary to save money in the long run (carrying extra fuel for economic or planning reasons is called *tankering*). Contrast this with the GA habit of filling up as often as possible.

Very few aircraft will actually take a full load of passengers and fuel, so you need to know how long it will take between two points, find out how much fuel it will take, *then* fit the passengers in. *Do not put the passengers in first and fit the fuel in afterwards!* Not unless you plan to stop en route, at least. Of all the things there is absolutely no excuse for in Aviation, running out of fuel is one of them! If you have to take less fuel, then you will have to stop and pick up some more on the way, or leave someone behind. If you take the same fuel anyway, you will be overweight, with not enough power in the engines to get you out of trouble, and *invalid insurance*.

You will need more to counteract the effects of ice. Fuel flow should be adjusted if you plan to use specialised equipment in flight, such as heaters, or not use anything essential, such as an engine. Don't forget, on the exam, that you have to calculate fuel for the alternate as well.

Fuel and oil consumption rates and weights should be in the Flight Manual. It's usual to keep a check on the fuel contents to see if things are going according to plan, keeping track of fuel consumption. When it comes to flying bigger machines, however, it all becomes much more critical. When heavy at the wrong level, you could be burning uneconomical amounts relative to what you would burn when lighter at a more sensible level - jet engines are that sensitive. The weights of fuel carried can account for significant differences in airspeed and/or performance as it is burned off, but this is covered more under *The Cruise* (see *Performance*). The main thing to bear in mind is that your weight at the end of a leg will be a lot different than that at the start of it, and so will the fuel flow, which changes in sympathy. You therefore have to

get used to making educated guesses as to the mid-leg weight to get a mean fuel flow.

For example, if the aircraft weighs 126,000 kg at the start of a leg, the associated fuel flow is 7500 kg/hr, and the leg time is 35 minutes, you can immediately round the time up to 36 minutes for a mid-point time of 18 minutes. You could probably assume 7000 kg/hr, which means just under 120 kg per minute. 18 minutes at that rate means you will burn off 2160 kg, meaning that your approximate mid-leg weight is 124,000, which is what you use to enter the charts (use the right line).

The plan should be to arrive over the destination in a position to make an approach, overshoot (missed approach) and fly to an alternate, and still have enough to hold for 45 minutes (30 for a turbo jet) at the alternate. Even then, you must still be able to carry out an approach and landing, so you should carry enough for the estimated time to destination, plus 5% for contingencies, time to alternate, and holding fuel.

Fuel Management

Jet engines are more efficient at higher altitudes because less fuel is needed for a given thrust, due to the reduction in lift and drag, and lower temperatures through the inlet cause a significant reduction in *Specific Fuel Consumption* (SFC), up to the tropopause. However, after a certain flight level, fuel flow increases, because of an increased drag penalty from the excessive angle of attack needed to create enough lift (if it goes high enough the machine will stall). This flight level is the *optimum altitude*, and is a function of fuel flow and TAS, which reduces as you climb at a fixed Mach number into colder air.

Jets also work best at the top end of the RPM range, at around 90%.In other words, they produce a lot of power, but use a lot of fuel doing it, especially at low level - at 35,000 feet, thrust is only 39% of that at sea level, compared to 80% at the tropopause (having said that, the bypass ratio is reduced high up, so the optimum altitude for a fanjet may be slightly lower).

Jets also work best at the top end of the RPM range, at around 90%. In other words, they produce a lot of power, but use a lot of fuel doing it, especially at low level - at 35,000 feet, thrust is only 39% of that at sea level, compared to 80% at the tropopause (having said that, the bypass ratio is reduced high up, so the optimum altitude for a fanjet may be slightly lower). Because piston engines keep their RPM and internal temperatures more or less constant, the Specific Fuel Consumption won't change much, but turbine engines change RPM constantly, so the best SFC, and range, is found at higher power settings. Turbines burn much more fuel per horsepower when run at low speeds - in fact, a larger one can burn up to 40% more fuel than a smaller engine at maximum power, which means that your payload will be smaller because you must carry more fuel. The reason a turbine is less efficient at low power is firstly because there is less heat inside, so the *Delta Temperature* between the inside and the cold air outside is less, reducing the incentive for the hot air to rush out. Another reason is that the blades inside are optimised for a the best angle of attack, and if the airflow is wrong, engine efficiency is reduced because more work has to be done to compress the air. This will use more fuel.

A jet's efficiency comes from range, not endurance, so you must plan to get as far as possible in any flight (see *Specific Ground Range*, below). It follows that long range flights need huge fuel reserves, another good reason for planning, because the Commercial Guys would rather you carried passengers than fuel, unless it is more expensive at the destination (you are always walking a fine line with complex aircraft). *Tankering* is the term used for carrying more fuel than you need for commercial reasons. The Flight Manual (or Ops Manual) should have graphs for determining cost benefits. If you do fly for endurance, though, you must go for the lowest fuel flow at the highest levels, and at speeds which give the minimum drag (although these will be increased slightly at lower levels and decreased at higher ones to improve handling).

For *minimum time*, max thrust is used for the highest Mach number. The idea for a minimum time route is to choose an altitude that gives the greatest groundspeed for TAS under forecast winds, which is found by plotting the track for an hour or so over several headings, then repeated over the whole route. This is how the NAT track system works.

For *maximum range*, the cruise climb, in an ideal world, means climbing steadily as fuel is used up, that is, you climb initially to the most efficient level, and keep going steadily up until you reach the TOD as weight reduces, but this is not convenient for ATC, especially on NAT routes (in fact the only aircraft to use it was Concorde because it was by itself), so, in practice, a *stepped climb* is used, where you go up four thousand feet at a time, having started 1000 feet above the ideal starting altitude, and flown until you are 3000 feet under the next one, for the Quadrantal Rule. Your range is about 95% of the maximum available.

However, stepping should only be considered if it is going to use less fuel than you are currently - doing it before the machine is ready costs fuel which cannot be recovered

later (the climb itself takes fuel, as it is done at climb thrust rather than cruise thrust, as in a drift climb, which needs about 30 minutes at the higher level to justify).

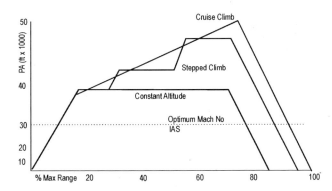

Another method is to set constant power and accept increasing airspeed, particularly when using constant alpha, as with the Falcon 20F, but this makes ETAs harder to calculate, so you can set a target airspeed and reduce power as fuel is used instead. With TAS constant, drag reduces as weight decreases and your range is 80-90% of the maximum available.

Maximum range in any aircraft is achieved when the ratio between distance covered and fuel flow is maximum, meaning that maximum range requires minimum fuel flow, for a given distance. Fuel flow in a propeller aircraft is proportional to power, so maximum range will be achieved when the power required for a given distance covered is at a minimum. Power required in straight and level flight is drag x TAS, and increasing TAS equates to increasing the rate of distance covered, so, for maximum range, you must fly at the speed at which the ratio of TAS to drag is at a maximum, where the TAS is higher, at altitude. The best range height for most jets is around 40,000 ft, although the BAe 146 likes about 30,000 ft.

Each unit of fuel allows the engine to deliver a certain amount of power for a certain amount of time. This product is a fixed quantity, in that if you vary power or time, the other quantity has to change - double the power, you halve the time, and so on. Thus:

```
Work Available = Drag x TAS x Time
```

or:

```
Power x Time = Drag x TAS x Time
```

Cancelling out Time on both sides, we get:

```
Power = Drag x TAS
```

Now, *TAS x Time* is the same as the distance travelled, so you can rewrite the above to read:

```
Work Available = Drag x Distance
```

or:

$$\text{Distance} = \frac{\text{Work Available}}{\text{Drag}}$$

Note that the *weight* of the fuel determines your range - each pound of it has a specific value of heat that creates horsepower or thrust, so the denser your fuel is, the further you can fly (check the specific gravity. This is why pounds or kilograms are used for calibrating fuel quantity gauges. Unfortunately, fuel is delivered to you in gallons or litres, so correct conversion is important. As a rule of thumb, for Jet A, take the weight in lbs, add half, then divide by 10 to get US gallons. 2000 lbs is therefore approximately 300 US gallons, at the usual fuel weight of 6.76 lbs/gal.

Since *Work Available* is a fixed quantity, drag must be minimised to maximise the distance flown. Maximum Range speed is therefore the same as that for Minimum Drag, or V_{MD}, which is not affected by height (it's an aerodynamic property, and is expressed in terms of IAS). TAS increases, of course, but so does power required, so the two effects tend to cancel each other out, and range obtainable is not much affected by height either.

The manuals will normally quote two cruising speeds, *High Speed* (.85 Mach) and *Long Range* (.82 Mach), with the latter being chosen for economy - you choose a reasonable speed which reduces as fuel burns off and weight decreases - there are charts for this, which will give you cruising air miles per lb of fuel. In fact, a compromise technique is used, using a constant Mach number until mass decreases enough for a climb to where you can regain the speed, roughly every two hours.

Because fuel flow varies due to weight at the start and end of each leg, when using fuel flow charts, etc., you should estimate the mid-weight for the leg in question, because it would be artificially high at the start. It need not be exact, as you only need an average fuel flow. Thus, you need to learn to interpolate between columns and rows. Check if the tables are for each engine.

EPR gauges also become inaccurate in turbulent air, so you might have to use N_1 settings instead, from a *Turbulent Air Penetration* table. In severe turbulence, since the AI does not read correctly, you should set power for the recommended rough air speed (check the tables) and maintain a level attitude, regardless of altitude and air speed variations.

For most trips, fuel management revolves around getting the maximum range for a given amount of fuel or, looked at another way, how little you can get away with on a fixed distance. However, occasionally you are asked to hold, or patrol, and the question of how long you can stay airborne arises, namely endurance. The amount of fuel burnt per unit of thrust is called the *Specific Fuel Consumption*, or SFC. For jets, it reduces with altitude up to the tropopause, where it remains constant. It's different for turboprops, because they can run without producing thrust (which actually comes from the prop). With them, SFC improves with altitude, but propeller tip speeds limit their altitude anyway. After full throttle height with pistons, fuel consumption *increases* with altitude.

The optimum cruise level for a turbojet is where you can obtain the best angle of attack at max continuous power, which will increase as fuel is burned off. A constant Mach cruise is held near the optimum level, and power is reduced to maintain it, since the speed to maintain optimum level also decreases, and constantly changing speed and altitude is inconvenient. Maximum Range Speed comes out of the Lift/Drag curve. For prop-driven planes, this coincides with L/D_{MAX} but, as with best ROC, turbojets achieve this at higher speeds, where there is a maximum difference between the square roots of the lift and drag coefficients (where a straight line from the origin hits the bottom of the curve).

For a headwind, speed up to minimise the time affected - 10% increase in airspeed gives more than a 10% increase in groundspeed (for example, at 100 kts, with a 40-kt headwind, adding 10 kts gives you a groundspeed of 70 kts, which is 16%). With a tailwind, slow down and let the wind do the work. As weight decreases with fuel usage, you could either increase altitude to improve SFC or decrease speed to keep the best L/D ratio (the optimum angle of attack will not change). However, although fuel usage decreases with height, so does the TAS, which offsets most of the advantage gained, so altitude is not always the answer, especially if the winds change. Thus, fuel calculations are done by counting units of fuel per unit of distance over the ground.

The initial climb is at a constant IAS, which means an increase in TAS up to the changeover level. The climb thereafter is at a constant Mach No, which means a decrease in TAS. Initial descent is done at a fixed Mach number, so the IAS and TAS will be *increasing*. After the descent changeover level, a fixed IAS value is used, so the Mach number and TAS *decrease*.

Early descent from cruise altitude can result in a fuel penalty of around 30 kgs per minute for some jets, not helped by incorrect selection of descent speed, which could add 10-20 kgs on top.

RECIPROCATING ENGINES

In the cruise, you should reduce power and lean the mixture, which will reduce the fuel consumption and reduce wear on the engine. In the CAA book, data is in tables for various power settings. Generally, the higher the RPM, the greater the speed, but at the expense of fuel economy, range and endurance. The lower the RPM, of course, the fewer number of times the engine goes round, and the less fuel is used. Calculating the Specific Air Range (the fuel used per Nautical Air Mile) can help you compare the various options. That is, find out how far you can go for each pound of fuel. Note that twin-engined aeroplanes have higher power and fuel consumption, so there will be a significant difference in fuel required for descent.

SPECIFIC GROUND RANGE

Knowing the SGR is useful when IFR and planning on particular fuel consumption, but actually burning something entirely different. It also gives you an idea of the most efficient cruising altitude, allowing for winds. Thus, the best altitude for *range* (see below for endurance) will be what gives you the most SGR, and you will need to find the groundspeed first.

Divide fuel flow by groundspeed to get lbs per nm, or the other way to get nm per lb of fuel, if those units are used, e.g. 600lb/hr at 120 kts is 5lb/nm or 0.2 nm/1lb fuel. Thus, if an aircraft at FL 320 has a TAS of 494 kts, a headwind component of 50 kts and a fuel flow of 7900 kg per hour, its fuel burn would be 17.8 kg/nm. At FL 350, with TAS 486 kts, head wind 55 kts and fuel flow of 7500 kg/hr, it might be 17.4 kg/nm. Other things being equal, the best FL for range would therefore be FL 350. If you had 21,500 kg in hand, you would get 1236 nm out of the old bus. To get the same at FL 320, the headwind would need to reduce to 40 kts. The reciprocal of the 17.4 kg/nm above is .056 nm/kg. Here is a handy formula:

$$NGM = \frac{NAM \times G/S}{TAS}$$

NGM = *Nautical Ground Miles*, and NAM = *Nautical Air Miles*.

SPECIFIC AIR RANGE

This is similar to the above, except that TAS is divided by fuel flow to get nautical *air miles* per lb (fuel flow is therefore TAS divided by SAR, which improves with altitude). It is affected by fuel flow, TAS, IAS, time, EPR, temperature, altitude, Mach number.

$$NAM = \frac{TAS}{Flow \ (ph)}$$

In an exam, you may well have to calculate TAS from the Mach number.

The *Optimum Altitude* is where maximum specific air range is attained.

ENDURANCE

Sometimes you just have to keep up in the sky for short periods, possibly to wait for some radiation fog to burn off, or when holding (see below). Whereas flying for range is more concerned with *specific* fuel consumption (per nautical mile, for example), endurance flying is more to do with *gross* fuel flow, or how much is burned off per hour, in terms of weight. Fuel flow is least when thrust is least, so you are getting maximum (level flight) endurance at the IAS for minimum drag (V_{MD}), because, in level flight, thrust is equal to drag.

You need to run the engines at max continuous RPM to get the required thrust most economically, which also means doing it at the right altitude, since jet engines are less efficient when lower (RPM must be severely reduced to get the lower thrust). The greater the power/weight ratio, the greater will be the optimum altitude.

HOLDING

There will be Holding Tables in the performance charts to calculate the equivalent of fuel burned in a particular time. Questions might ask what EPR, IAS and fuel flow you get for a certain height and weight. Remember that the figures given are *per engine*, so multiply as necessary.

FLIGHT MANAGEMENT SYSTEM

This will control most flight profiles. The one in the 737 allows for four different speeds: ECON (controlled by a cost index in the database), LRC, Manual or RTA, which means that speed will be adjusted to meet a Required Time of Arrival. The autothrottle normally takes care of the speed.

The FMS optimum altitude will be where 90% thrust produces 1.32 V_{MD}, as modified for the cruise wind and cost index. Of course, ATC don't have the same computer, so you will find that most Ops Manuals require flight within 200 feet of the optimum altitude. You might want to select a higher level at first so the optimum level climbs up as weight reduces.

The maximum altitude is limited by:

- absolute ceiling

- pressurisation ceiling

- C of A maximum altitude*

- Buffet boundary

*This is usually taken from the pressurisation ceiling anyway.

The cruise buffet boundary is normally the lowest and most limiting, with the absolute limit last, except when very light.

IFR

Journeys are split into specific phases, such as *start*, *checks*, and *taxi* (that is, before take off), *take-off* and *climb* (another phase), *cruise* and *descent* (yet another), *approach* and *landing*, plus 10%, plus *missed approach* and *diversion* to the alternate. Then there's holding at the alternate, unusable and contingency fuel, which covers errors in forecast winds, navigation, ATC restrictions and individual variations from standard fuel consumption. By arrangement, block figures can be used which ignore the take-off and climb. In fact, headings required are:

- *Start*, taxi and run-up (plus icing systems and APUs)

- *Departure* and enroute climb

- *Route* fuel, to include climbs

- Approach

- Missed Approach

- *Alternate Fuel*. Enough for a missed approach from MDA at the destination, climbing from missed approach altitude to cruise altitude, cruise to TOD, to execute an approach and landing at the alternate

- Reserve

- Contingency Fuel

FUEL MONITORING

Fuel checks should be done at regular intervals (usually over each waypoint), so you can compare actual consumption to planned consumption. This allows you to detect excessive fuel consumption early, in which case, you could reduce power, change altitude or divert (don't forget

to tell the engineers the engines might be suspect), or make sure you have enough to finish the flight. The checks would either be noted on the PLOG or plotted on a graph.

Point of No Return

Also known as the *Point of Safe Return*, this is the furthest point you can fly to and return to a landing point behind you (usually your point of departure), based on a given amount of fuel, which usually, for obvious reasons, takes account of a certain amount of reserves (so-called "dry tanks" PNR is *not* a good idea). After the Point of No Return, you do not have enough fuel to return home on a navigation leg, hence the name. It is purely a fuel (actually, an endurance) problem, having nothing to do with distance, so if your PNR is beyond the destination, so much the better.

The principles are good for other scenarios, too - your destination might get socked in underneath a warm front, so you would need to know the last position enroute that would allow you to go to an alternate behind you, away from the front where the weather is better. Once you know that PNR, you would check the weather at the original destination and make the decision whether to abort or not when you start to approach it. In this case, another definition of PNR is the greatest distance you can go past an airfield, and return to it with the required reserves intact.

For planning purposes, assuming still air, the PNR is the maximum point (or furthest from departure) possible, as any tailwind outbound becomes a headwind homebound, and the detrimental effect is experienced for longer than the beneficial effect. That is, you will spend longer beating headwinds than the benefit gained from tailwinds. If you estimate the same fuel for each leg of an out-and-back trip, and assume that the head- and tailwinds will cancel each other out, you will run out of fuel not too far from home. *As soon as a wind gets involved, you need more fuel than you would in still air.*

Example: Every day, you fly from Rainbow Lake (where there is no rainbow and no lake!) in N Alberta to Shekhili compressor station, at which there is no fuel. The distance is 50 nm each way and cruise speed 100 kts. Fuel consumption is 29 US gals per hour. On a nil-wind day, therefore, it should be half an hour each way but, with 20-knot tailwinds outbound, you get there in only 25 minutes. The journey back, on the other hand, takes 37.5 minutes, which is 62.5 minutes total. This may not sound much, but with 60-knot winds, you would be flying for 35 minutes longer than expected, and the figures get worse with longer stage lengths, etc. The PNR will always tend towards the departure point, meaning that distance to PNR is greatest with zero wind, and reduces in windy conditions, regardless of direction.

The formula below can give you a patrol time in a *radius of action* problem, which is the same thing, (the edge of the radius is your limit to use the same fuel to get back to base, useful in the Arctic, over water, or in similar hostile territory).

The simple calculation takes no account of changes in TAS or fuel flow - both will change if an engine fails. If you have to calculate this after an engine failure (in real life, not the exam), refer to *Specific Ground Range*, above, and add the fuel used per mile out and back together. Then divide the result into the endurance. In other words, calculate the fuel used per nautical mile out and back to get the fuel used for each nm radius of action (fuel flow divided by groundspeed). Divide it into the PNR fuel available (endurance) to get the distance to the PNR.

Otherwise, to get the simple (normal) PNR time in minutes:

$$\frac{E \times H}{O + H}$$

where E = endurance (in minutes) to where you only have reserves left, O = gspd on (kts) and H = gspd home (kts). All it does is find the ratio of the groundspeeds and divide them into the endurance, assuming normal TAS. For example, with 3 hours' endurance, and a 90 kt groundspeed outbound, with 150 kts home:

$$\frac{180 \times 150}{90 + 150}$$

$$\frac{27000}{240}$$

The answer is 112.5 minutes, based on a ratio of 9:15. Just apply the groundspeed to get the distance if you want to mark it on the map, or work it out with this:

$$\frac{E \times O \times H}{O + H}$$

To shuffle the first formula around a bit:

$$PNR \ (Time) = \frac{E \times H}{O + H}$$

$$PNR \ (Time) = \frac{H}{E} \qquad \frac{}{O + H}$$

Take a journey 390 nm long, with a groundspeed out of 240 kts, and back of 210 kts, place the combined groundspeeds (bottom part of the formula) on the inner scale against the groundspeed home on the outer, and read the time to PNR (182 mins) against the endurance (390 mins) on the inner scale:

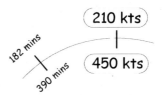

Find the distance in the usual way. As a gross error check, add the totals for the two legs together and check the sum against the endurance.

The PNR moves *into wind* from the mid point, which will be half the endurance in nil wind conditions (this is a useful check for gross error). The exam does not necessarily take account of the TAS changing as weight decreases, multiple tracks or climb and descent figures, but they are something you might want to consider in real life.

Use full TAS to find out when you would get to the PNR, so you know what to do if an engine fails. For radius of action, you would mix airspeeds (full TAS on, reduced back), so you know how long you can fly on a tank and still get back, even if an engine fails.

For multiple legs, work the flight forwards, dividing the flight into sectors (takeoff, climb, etc.) and back from landing until you find the critical sector, where the fuel out and back equals the amount you can lift. Do the PNR on the critical sector.

Critical Point

Otherwise known as the *Point of Equal Time* (PET), or the *Equi-time Point* (ETP), this is the point at which it's just as quick to go on to a destination or go back to an airfield behind you - useful if you have an emergency and want to land as soon as possible. This can also mean the point at which it will take equal time to either of two airfields, not necessarily in front or behind you. It has nothing to do with fuel, so the fact that you have the CP doesn't mean that you necessarily have the range.

The simple formula to find the distance is:

$$\frac{D \times H}{O + H}$$

where D = total distance. Use T instead to find the *time* to the CP:

$$\frac{T \times H}{O + H}$$

The other letters are as used with the PNR formula, but the speeds could be reduced ones after the CP if an engine fails. If you have multiple legs (say, on an airway route), just add them all up and treat them as one distance. The CP also moves into wind from the mid-point.

You can do this (and PNR) on the slide rule by placing the groundspeed home on the inner scale against groundspeed out on the outer scale. Then look for two numbers which, when added together, comprise the distance or *Time To Turn*, as appropriate (187.5 and 112.5 for the above example). A better way would be to shuffle the above formulae around:

$$\text{CP(Distance)} = \frac{D \times H}{O + H}$$

$$\frac{\text{CP(Distance)}}{D} = \frac{H}{O + H}$$

Then say you had a distance of 920 nm to go, with a groundspeed out of 240 kts and one home of 210 kts and a flight planned time enroute of 230 minutes. Find the time and distance to the Critical Point.

First, line up the sum of the groundspeed home and out (450 kts) on the inner scale against the groundspeed home on the outer scale:

The corresponding times and distances will appear opposite each other. The time to the CP (107.5 mins) is against the flight planned time of 230 minutes, and the distance (430 nm) is against the total distance. Always add the totals up (there and back) to see if they are the same.

To calculate the CP for a trip along an airway, or a series of waypoints, add all the distances together and treat them as one in the formula.

The CP can differ depending on the type of emergency. If it's a medical one, for instance, or a disruptive passenger, your aircraft will have no change in performance and you won't lose any airspeed. However, if you lose an engine, it will all change drastically. As most aircraft keep similar fuel

flows with less airspeed with one engine out, this means effective range will decrease by whatever percentage. This is where proper reserves become important, because that slower speed will eat into whatever you planned to have left over.

So, to summarise, use relevant reduced airspeeds after engine failure, but *full airspeed* to calculate ETA at the CP. That is, you calculate the position with reduced speeds first, then find out when you will get there at full speed.

The CP will move into wind from the halfway point, where it will be in nil wind conditions. To find out exactly where (in terms of mile into wind), use this formula:

$$\frac{\text{Half Distance} \times \text{Wind}}{\text{TAS}}$$

Note: Neither PNR or CP take account of drift down, etc., so if you get a question involving anything that will affect your O and H speeds, do those calculations first.

MAPS

When planning a flight, the first thing to do is to draw a line on the map to represent the track you wish to fly. You can find the length of the track simply by comparing it against the lines of longitude nearby.

Find the mid-point of the track you have drawn and mark it with a cross. Then maybe mark the line at 10 nm intervals (or split the two halves into quarters), depending on how long the line is (this one's a bit short). You might want to draw dotted lines branching out at 10° from the origin, but these may be left out once you know what you're doing. When learning they are very useful when calculating drift once you find the wind is different from that forecast and you need to recalculate on the run. The less you have to do in the air, the better, as your first priority is to fly the aircraft, and you don't want to start getting rulers out and spreading your map around. In fact, you will find that a lot of your job lies in the planning - your time in the air is a relatively small part of the process. If it isn't, there's something wrong.

A good alternative to using ten-minute marks is to find prominent features and mark an ETA against them, as mentioned above.

NOTES

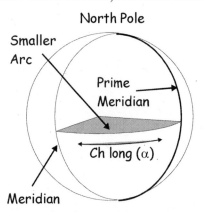

NAVIGATION

Navigation involves taking an aircraft from place to place without reference to the ground, except, perhaps, for checking that you've got the right destination! To do this without radio navigation aids, a system called *Dead Reckoning* is used, which is actually short for *Deduced Reckoning*, based on solving a *triangle of velocities* with a flight computer, discussed below.

The biggest mistake people make when starting to fly is to confuse *navigation* with *map reading*, which is used when you need to know your position precisely, as when doing survey, or as required by a customer. As far as navigation goes, however, you only really need your location in terms of something like "10 miles SE of a radio beacon", or similar. This allows you to sit back and enjoy the ride a bit more, or devote your attention to something slightly more useful. First, though, we need to get acquainted with the Earth, which is the third planet away from the Sun and the fifth largest in the Solar System.

It is not round, but flatter at the Poles than it is at the Equator (the bulge in the middle is due to the vast centrifugal forces and helps to stabilise the spin).

Note: As the Earth, like all planets, is not a perfect sphere, its "radius" can mean various things. The radius of the Earth at a point on the surface is the distance from the centre to the *mean sea level* at that point, which varies from about 6 356.750-6 378.135 km. The IUGG value for the equatorial radius of the Earth (the *semi major axis*) is 6378.137 km (3963.19 statute miles), for an equatorial circumference of 40, 075 km (24, 901.5 miles).

Between the Poles (the *semi-minor axis*), the circumference is 40 008 km (24 859 miles), so the Earth is larger round the Equator than it is through the Poles by just under 22 nm, or 41 km. The difference is called the *compression ratio*, and the value for the flattening is 1/298.

For this reason, the Earth should be called an *oblate spheroid*, or an *ellipsoid* but, for our purposes, it is a sphere.

On the surface it is around 12 miles from the top of the tallest mountain to the bottom of the deepest ocean.

If this page is a photocopy, it is not authorised!

POSITIONAL REFERENCE

A Positional Reference System identifies any position on the surface of a sphere. Since the Earth is a sphere (well, nearly, anyway) we have to use *polar co-ordinates*, using the angles θ and φ, otherwise known as *latitude* and *longitude*, respectively.

The word *position* means a place that can be positively identified, and which may be qualified by such terms as *estimated*, *nil wind*, etc.

To help find yours, a series of lines running North-South is drawn from Pole to Pole through the Equator, called lines of *longitude* (the North Pole is the one at the top). They may also be called *meridians*, when split in half, and by convention are drawn for every degree you go round the Equator, of which there are 360. Also, by convention, they start at Greenwich, in London (with the *Prime Meridian* at 0°), and are calculated to 180° East or West, which is the maximum figure. The opposite of a meridian (on the other side of the Earth) is an *anti-meridian*.

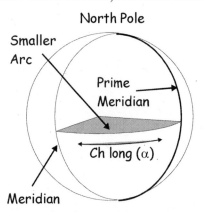

Longitude is the distance East or West from the Prime Meridian. Technically, it is the *smaller arc of the Equator between the PM and the one through the point concerned.*

Since the Earth takes nearly 24 hours to spin on its N-S axis, 15 lines of longitude represent 1 hour, and it is noon when the Sun is overhead (*transiting*) any particular meridian. The spinning is anticlockwise at 15.04° per hour when viewed from the top of the Earth (West to East), so the Sun and other heavenly bodies will appear to move the other way, that is, to rise from the East and set in the West.

Having only one vertical line, however, is not enough to find a position with, since you could be anywhere on it, so more imaginary lines are drawn, horizontal this time, and parallel to each other, North and South of the Equator, up to 90° each way, called lines of *latitude*. They go across lines of longitude, and indicate your position North or South of the Equator, from 0° (at the Equator) to 90° at whichever Pole. The latitude of any point is the *arc of the meridian*

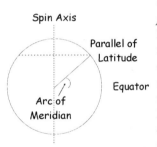

between the Equator and the parallel through the point (see left), or that represented by the angle between the plane of the equator and the line from the point of interest to the centre of the sphere. More simply, it is the distance North or South of the Equator.

Remember: True North is the direction of the observer's meridian to the North Pole.

Important latitudes include the *Tropic of Cancer* (23° 27' N), the *Tropic of Capricorn* (23° 27' S), the *Arctic Circle* (66° 33' N), and the *Antarctic Circle* (66° 33' S). There are many variations, but *geodetic latitude* and *geocentric latitude* are two discussed below, under *Geodetic/Geocentric Systems*.

Note: Lines of Latitude (*parallels*) are always parallel to each other, whereas longitude lines (*meridians*) converge towards the Poles.

The imaginary parallels are also fixable by natural means - the Sun, Moon and planets pass over the Equator, for example, and the tropics of Cancer and Capricorn represent the limits of the Sun's travel North and South as it rises and sets every day. Thus, only between the two Tropics is it possible for the sun to be at its zenith, and only North or South of the Arctic and Antarctic Circles, respectively, is the midnight sun possible (remember this with questions concerning the Air Almanac). Until the 1770s, however, when John Harrison invented a marine chronometer which only lost 5 seconds in two months, you could not fix longitude with any degree of precision, because time was measured by the cabin boy turning a glass with sand in it over and over.

When giving position, latitude is always given first, as in 45°N, 163°W. Note the way the meridians slant towards the top of the map below. All is explained shortly!

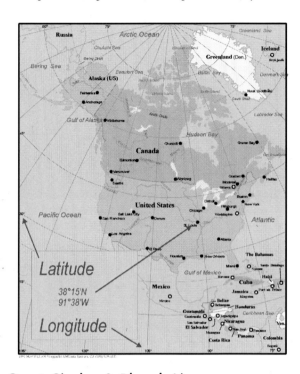

Great Circles & Rhumb Lines

Great Circles have planes that go through the centre of the Earth, or, in other words, are circles whose radius is that of the Earth, so they will always bisect it. The definition includes lines of longitude and the Equator. Since meridians are half lines of longitude, they are semi-great circles, so a meridian and its antimeridian together make a Great Circle.

The Equator is a great circle midway between the Poles, and parallels of latitude are small circles constructed with reference to the Equator. The angular distance between them along a meridian is latitude.

Although Great Circles are the shortest distance between two points on the Earth's surface, the angle created when they cross a meridian changes every time, except N-S or E-W, of course (see *Convergency*), so your course is continually under review. Rhumb Lines, on the other hand, cut each meridian at the same angle, and, in so doing, maintain a constant direction with respect to True North. They are not straight (being concave toward the nearer Pole), because the meridians converge, so they are longer in distance than Great Circles (see the red line, below). However, the difference between them is not worth worrying about below about 1,000 miles, for the convenience of steering one track.

Trivia: The word *rhumb* comes from the angle measurement representing the "point" on old-fashioned compass cards. With 32 rhumbs in 360°, a rhumb is 11¼°. Rhumb lines are also called *loxodromes*, which comes from the Greek for *slanting path*.

A rhumb line always spirals toward a Pole, unless it is actually going East, West, North, or South, in which case it closes on itself to form a parallel of latitude (small circle) or a pair of meridians. All lines of latitude are rhumb lines, as are meridians, but the Equator and meridians are great circles as well.

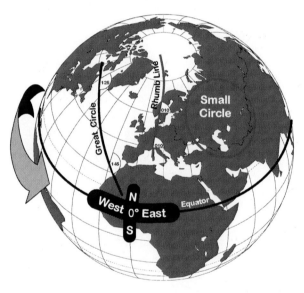

Speed & Distance

Distance is the length of a line separating two points, although this becomes more complicated on a sphere, where the line becomes curved.

Distance along a parallel of latitude is also known as *departure*, or *change of longitude*. Here is the formula again:

```
α (nm) = ch long (mins)x cos lat
```

Otherwise, horizontal distance is measured in metres, kilometres or nautical miles, and speed is a *rate of change of position expressed in those units*, per hour, minute, or whatever (a **knot** is 1 **nautical mile** per hour. It was originally measured by allowing a long rope to stretch out behind a ship with knots tied in it at regular intervals, hence the name). For aircraft, we must deal with *airspeed*, *groundspeed* and *relative speed*, discussed elsewhere in this section.

For navigation, a typical length can be expressed as:

*   A **kilometre**, which is 1000 metres, and was originally 1/10,000,000 of the distance between the Equator and either Pole on a meridian passing through Paris. 8 km equals 5 statute miles. As a rate, it is expressed in km/hour

*   1 **nautical mile** (nm) is taken as 6080 feet, or 1852 m (ICAO), which is slightly more than:

*   A **statute mile**, which is 5280 feet and is an Imperial measurement. In aviation, it is used only in visibility reports in some countries. 1 nautical mile is equal to 1.15 statute miles

The distance between parallels of latitude is 60 nautical miles, because 1 nm is the distance subtended by 1 minute of latitude, although it varies between the Poles and the Equator because the Earth bulges in the middle. The length of a nautical mile at these points is 6108 and 6046 feet, respectively, but 6080 is used for calibration and navigation in general, and is actually only correct at 48° latitude. One minute of longitude, however (i.e. along a parallel), will only be 1 nm *at the Equator*, due to convergency, where the distance between meridians gets smaller toward the Poles. You can find the true length of a degree at any latitude by multiplying the change of longitude (in minutes) by the cosine of the latitude, so at 60° N, the distance between meridians is 30 nm (this is the *departure formula*, which is only accurate along one parallel).

On the flight computer, discussed later, you can find out departure quite easily. Say from York (roughly 54°N), you need to find a ship just East of the Isle Of Man, which is more or less on the same latitude, but 3° to the West, or 180 minutes, which *at the equator* would be 180 nm. The cosine of 54° is the same as the sine of 90°- 54°, which is 36°, so:

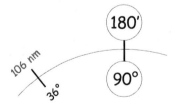

You have 106 nm to travel, so it will take around an hour at 100 kts.

Convergency

Convergency is the angle of inclination between two meridians. It is zero at the Equator, and 1° at the Poles, but otherwise varies at the *sine of the latitude*. It can be calculated between any two points at different latitudes, unlike departure - simply take the change of longitude and multiply it by the sine of the *mean latitude*.

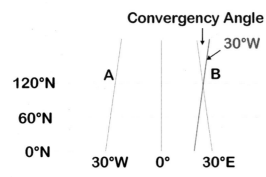

Convergency Angle

On the right hand side of the diagram, the 30°W meridian has been transferred across from its original position. The difference between points A and B is the *earth convergency*.

The *convergence factor* is the rate at which a straight line on the chart is changing its direction with respect to True North. In most cases, and near the parallel of origin of a Lambert chart, this will be very close to the rate at which a Great Circle track changes.

Conversion Angle

The *conversion angle* is the difference between a rhumb line and a great circle at each end of a line joining two points - it is half the *convergency*, described above. At the halfway point, the two lines are parallel, which is why you should measure your track at the mid-point if you use a chart where straight lines are great circles. (i.e. most flight planning charts).

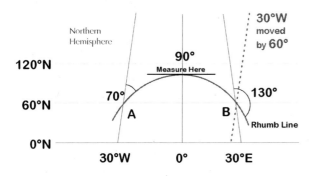

The relevance of this lies with plotting radio bearings on Mercator charts, on which great circles are curved and

which must therefore be converted to Rhumb Lines, which are straight, for plotting and fixing purposes.

Rhumb lines are always curved, except on Mercator charts.

EXAMPLE

What is the direction of the Great Circle track at each end of a line joining the points 30°S 130°E and 30°S 160°E? These are both on the same latitude, to make it easy, so the rhumb line track is 090° or 270°, depending on which way you go. The picture below is based on Mercator (with parallel meridians), since this is where the difference between Great Circles and Rhumb Lines is most relevant.

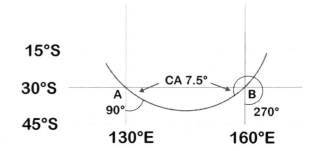

The formula for convergency is:

```
ch long x sin mean lat
```

or:

```
30 x sin 30
```

Conversion angle is half that value, so:

```
½ x 30 x .5 = 7.5°
```

The Great Circle Tracks are 097½° and 262½°.

DIRECTION

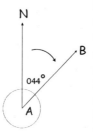

Direction is the position of one point relative to another, regardless of the distance between them, measured in an angular fashion. It is expressed with reference to either True or Magnetic North, depending on whether magnetic effects from the Earth itself are taken into account. All meridians run North to South - the direction North is along any meridian going towards the North Pole (i.e. up, towards the top of the Earth).

A *bearing* is the clockwise angle between North and any line between two points. In the case on the left, B is on a

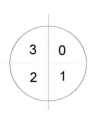

bearing of 044° from A, in relation to North. The opposite is the *reciprocal*, quickly found by adding or subtracting 180°, that is, 224°.

The complete circle of direction (or *compass rose*) is split into 360 *degrees*, which in turn are split into 60 *minutes* and 60 *seconds*, so the complete expression of an angle is in degrees, minutes and seconds - 30° 45' 53". North is 0°, so, going round the clock, East is 90°, South is 180° and West is 270°.

Tip: Adding or subtracting 90° is easier if you remember that each quadrant of the compass rose (that is, every 90° segment) starts with a different number, 0, 1, 2 or 3, so if you are in the second quadrant and want to turn left, you start with a heading beginning with 1 and will end up on one beginning with 0. Similarly, in quadrant 3, you might start on, say, 210 and end up on 300 if you turn right. The first two digits of the final bearing will add up to the same number as those of the one you started with, so, starting at 140°, turning right, you know you will finish up on 2-- something. As the first 2 digits of the original heading are 1 and 4, the next digit on your final heading will be 3, as 2 and 3 make 5. Thus, final heading is 230°.

As with any rule, there are exceptions, but these are few, so they are easy to remember. 100° and 110° have reciprocals of 280° and 290°, respectively, which means that the first number is 2 when it should be 3, but the addition side still works. The last exception is 010°, for which the reciprocal is 190°, but the first two digits on each side still add up.

Magnetic Bearings

One problem is that a compass does not point towards True North, but Magnetic North, since the Earth generates its own magnetism (see also *The Compass* in *Instruments*) - and the two Norths (or Souths) do not coincide at their respective Poles.

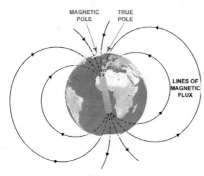

The geographic North Pole is magnetically a South Pole, which is why the North end of a compass points to it. By convention, the North Pole is blue and the South Pole is red. The North Magnetic Pole was discovered by Soviet explorers to be the rim of a magnetic circle 1000 miles in circumference, around 600 miles from the true Pole.

The next problem is that magnetic force is not constant over the globe - it may be varied by local deposits of metals under the ground, for example, and bend the magnetic flux lines. The way to Magnetic North will therefore vary across the ground from place to place, and a freely suspended compass will turn to the direction of the *local* magnetic field (because the *Horizontal Component* is toward Magnetic North). As well, the lines of force will be vertical near the poles.

VARIATION

Magnetic variation is the angle between True North and Magnetic North.

On a map, or chart, which would be drawn initially for True North, there is a dotted line called an *isogonal* that represents the local magnetic variation to be applied to any direction you wish to plan a flight on.

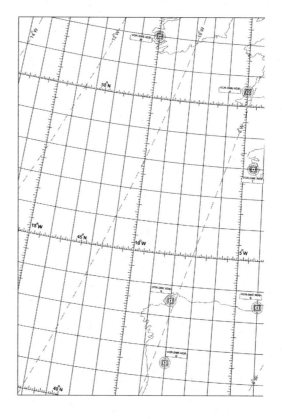

Variation is westerly where it is to the left of the meridian, and Easterly when to the right. It also changes every year, since the magnetic pole moves East, about one degree every six years (completely round the North Pole in 960 years). *The charted values of magnetic variation normally change annually due to magnetic pole movement causing values at all locations to increase or decrease.* When plotted, isogonals are accurate worldwide to ±2°.

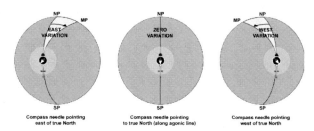

Compass needle pointing east of true North | Compass needle pointing to true North (along agonic line) | Compass needle pointing west of true North

An *agonic line* exists where magnetic variation is zero, or where True and Magnetic North are both the same. There's one near Frankfurt, running North/South. The maximum variation you can get is 180°.

The phrase to remember is *Variation East, Magnetic Least, Variation West, Magnetic Best*, that is, if the variation on your map is, say, 21° West, the final result should be 21° *more* than the true track found when you drew your line. If you travel over many variations, use an average about every 200 miles. Variation on a VOR bearing is applied *at the station*, and on an ADF *at the aircraft*.

DEVIATION

We saw above that the magnetism from the Earth will vary the direction displayed by a compass. The aircraft's own magnetism, created from large amounts of metal mixed with electrical currents, plus any residual magnetism from hammering, etc. during manufacture, will do something similar, called *deviation*, which is applied to the magnetic heading to get *Compass Heading*.

The net result of an aircraft's magnetic forces is represented by a dot somewhere behind the wings or rotor head. On Northerly headings, the dot lies behind the South part of the needle and merely concentrates the magnetic force. On Easterly headings, however, the dot is West of the South part of the needle and causes an Easterly deviation. Similarly, when heading West, a Westerly deviation is caused.

The phrase here is *Deviation West, Compass Best, Deviation East, Compass Least*, similar to Variation. So, if deviation is to the *left* of magnetic North, the difference is *added* to the course for the correct magnetic heading.

Deviations will be displayed on a small correction card next to the compass, and they are obtained after a *compass swing*, a complex procedure normally done by an engineer. There will be an area on every aerodrome well away from buildings, etc. set aside for it. Allowing for deviation is called *compensation*.

For	Steer
000	001
045	043
090	089
135	133
180	184
225	223
270	269
315	316

$$HDG(T) \pm VAR = HDG (M)$$

$$HDG(T) \pm VAR \pm DEV = HDG (C)$$

Deviation will be labelled + or - in the exams.

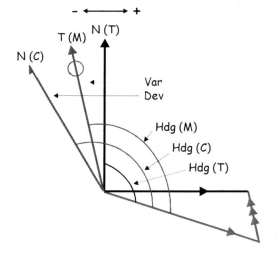

TIME & TIME ZONES

We know that the Earth, with 8 other planets (making 9), revolves round the Sun, although, to be picky, Pluto is not considered to be a real planet, because its orbit intersects with Neptune's - it is referred to by astronomers as a dwarf planet. There are also about 2000 minor planets and asteroids. 1 year is the time it takes a planet to go once round the Sun, in the Earth's case being 365¼ days (the odd quarters are consolidated every four years into one day in a leap year, and 3 leap years are suppressed every 4 centuries). While it is going round the Sun, the Earth spins on its axis once nearly every 24 hours, and the Solar System itself is creeping towards the star Vega, but that need not concern us right now. The speed of the Earth's orbit around the Sun is 66,600 mph, or 18.5 miles per second, much faster than a bullet. Because the Earth rotates from West to East, the heavenly bodies appear to revolve about the Earth from East to West.

Kepler's Laws Of Planetary Motion

Copernicus first proposed that the planets revolved around the Sun, but Johannes Kepler determined that:

- each one moves in an ellipse, with the Sun at one focus (it's an ellipse rather than a circle because there are influences from outside the solar system)

- the radius vector (the straight line joining the Sun and any planet) sweeps equal areas in equal time, so they speed up and slow down to compensate

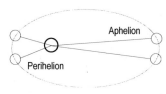

The *perihelion* (1-10 Jan) is where the Earth is closest to the Sun, and the *aphelion* (1-10 Jul) is where it is furthest away. The Earth moves faster round the Sun at the perihelion, although it looks as if the Sun is moving faster.

At perihelion, Earth is about 91 million miles from the Sun; it moves outward to around 95 million miles at aphelion, so the difference in distance is only about 3%.

The problem with the elliptical orbit and the different speeds is that the length of the *apparent solar day* varies, so the *mean solar day* is used as an average, at 24 hours (the apparent solar day is the time between successive transits of the real Sun). Thus, a (non-existent) Mean Sun actually transits any meridian at noon, hence the expression *Local Mean Time* (LMT), which is the time at a particular meridian. The time of transit of the real Sun over a meridian is *Local Apparent Noon*. Your watch would have to change its speed continually if it tried to track the real, or apparent (visible) Sun.

The difference between a solar and a mean day is never more than a minute, but the results are cumulative - the real Sun is about 16 minutes ahead of the mean Sun in November and 14 minutes behind it in February. The Air Almanac uses mean Solar time.

The word *transit* means the passage of a heavenly body over the meridian of a place on the Earth (or through the field of a telescope) - the time difference between two transits is called a *day*, and we have to cope with transits of the Sun and the fixed stars, so we have two types of day. *Sidereal time* (star time) is kept with regard to the fixed stars, which appear fixed only because of their distance from us (it's actually time measured by the apparent diurnal motion of the vernal equinox, which is very close to, but not identical with, the motion of stars. They differ by the precession of the vernal equinox relative to the stars, but you knew that already ☺).

To all intents and purposes, therefore, the Earth rotates 360° in one *sidereal day*, which is regarded as a constant figure against the stars, even though, technically, it isn't. A sidereal day lasts 23 hours and 56 minutes (of solar time), which is about 4 minutes less than a solar day, because the Earth's direction of rotation and its orbit round the Sun are the same. Thus, to make up the time, the Earth must rotate an extra 0.986° between solar transits, so in 24 hours of solar time, the Earth will actually rotate 360.986°. In other words, during the course of one (solar) day, the Earth has moved a short distance along its orbit around the sun, and must rotate a little bit more before the Sun reaches its highest point at any given place. The difference between clock time and Apparent Solar Time is called the *Equation Of Time*, which comes from two causes: the Earth's orbit being an ellipse and the earth's tilt.

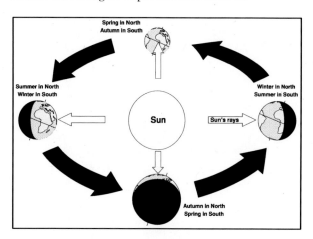

The Earth does not spin vertically, like a top, but is inclined at 23½° from the vertical over a 41,000-year cycle. The *obliquity of the ecliptic* actually ranges over 22.1-24.5°, so the Earth, in this respect, behaves rather like a ship caught in the swell of the sea as it nods back and forth. When the inclination points towards the Sun (left below), the Northern Hemisphere days are long and the nights are short. The day when this is at its maximum value is the *Summer Solstice* on June 21 (Solstice is Latin for *Sun Stand Still*). The *Winter Solstice*, when the inclination is at its maximum *away* from the Sun is December 21. In other words, the Sun sets further South each day, until, on December 21st, it starts moving North again. On June 21st, it stops going North to go South.

Time

In navigation, time can mean either a specific hour of the day, or a time interval. After Einstein, the state of motion and location of the clock used to measure it became an important part of its measurement, particularly with satellite operation. Days and nights are of equal length on the Spring and Autumn *Equinoxes*, March 21 and September 23 (Equinox means *Equal Night*), because the spin axis is vertical to the Earth's orbit. The Equinoxes are the times year when the relationship between the length of day and night, as well as the rate of change of declination of the sun, are changing at the greatest rate.

Trivia: The Moon rises and sets at the same points as the Sun, but at opposite solstices. For example, it rises at midwinter at the same place the Sun does at midsummer. The Earth and Moon also rotate round each other, round some pivotal point, as they proceed on their way around the Sun. Even more strange is that the Moon fits exactly over the Sun when superimposed on it.

The beginning of the day at any location is when the Mean Sun is in transit with its anti-meridian, or when the Sun is on the opposite side of the Earth to the point in question. This would be midnight, or 0000 hours Local Mean Time (LMT). Similarly, when the Sun is in transit with the meridian concerned, it will be Noon, or 12:00 hours. The angle between a meridian over which a heavenly body is located and where you are is the *Local Hour Angle*, or LHA.

The *Prime Meridian* is the standard to which all local mean times are referred. Local Mean Time there used to be called *Greenwich Mean Time* (GMT), but is now referred to as *Universal Coordinated Time*, or UTC, which is more accurately calculated, but can be regarded as the same for our purposes (GMT itself only came about because of the railways - previously, every part of Britain ran its own time scheme). The Greenwich day starts when the mean Sun transits the anti-meridian (180° away), and transits the Easterly ones before it reaches Greenwich. The local mean time in those places will therefore be *ahead* of UTC, and that of those West will be *behind*. When doing calculations, revert everything to UTC first, and don't forget the date!

THE INTERNATIONAL DATE LINE

This is where a change of date is officially made, mainly the 180° meridian which bends to accommodate certain islands in the South Sea and parts of Siberia. As you cross it, you can gain or lose a day, depending on which way you are going. When solving time problems, however, calculating in UTC usually sorts things out automatically.

Since we take (more or less) 24 hours to go round the Sun, in one hour we move through 15°, or we take 4 minutes to go through 1°. Similarly, in 1 minute we transit 15 minutes, or take 4 seconds to go through 1 minute (just to remind you, a degree is split up into minutes, which in turn are split into seconds).

STANDARD TIMES

To save you adjusting your watch constantly as you move round the Earth, some countries adopt standard times, that is to say, legal authorities allocate a standard amount East or West of Greenwich. For example, Canadian time zones are:

Zone	Convert (UTC-)
Newfoundland	3.5
Atlantic	4
Eastern	5
Central	6
Mountain	7
Pacific	8

They don't necessarily coincide with the correct longitude lines, but are aligned with province boundaries, for convenience (some towns in Northern BC keep Alberta time). In theory, standard time is based on the LMT 7.5° either side of a regular meridian, divisible by 15°.

DAYLIGHT SAVING (DST)

This was originally set up in UK during the First World War in an attempt to keep people out of pubs during working hours, and to make them get up earlier so they could use the daylight. Essentially, clocks go forward one hour for the summer - in *Spring* they go *forward*, in *Fall*, they *fall back* (Windows will tell you automatically!)

INTERNATIONAL ATOMIC TIME

Since 1 January 1972, UTC has been linked to IAT, which is based on an atomic clock, and which has shown that the length of the average day is increasing by about 2 milliseconds per century, due to tides, winds and other types of friction. To compensate for this, a leap second is inserted or omitted on a day decided by the International Time Bureau. It last happened in 1989.

The Air Almanac

This is a document published by some Government department in the darkest places of Ottawa that lists the activities of the Sun and other planets. From it, you can find out what time the Sun will rise and set, etc.

Standard times around the world are in three lists on pages A20-A23, *Fast on GMT*, *Slow on GMT*, and *Keeping GMT*.

List I - PLACES FAST ON G.M.T. (mainly those EAST OF GREENWICH)

The times given below should be } *added* to G.M.T. to give Standard Time. *subtracted* from Standard Time to give G.M.T.

			h	m					h	m
Admiralty Islands	...		10		Estonia	...	...		03	
Afghanistan	...	...	04	30	Ethiopia	...	...		03	
Albania*	...	...	01		Finland	...	...		02	
Algeria*	...	...	01		France*	...	...		01	
Bangladesh	...	...	06		Iran‡	...	...		04	

*Summer time may be kept in these countries
‡ The legal time may differ from that given here

Check the footnotes!

List III - PLACES SLOW ON G.M.T. (WEST OF GREENWICH)

The times given below should be } *subtracted* from G.M.T. to give Standard Time. *added* to Standard Time to give G.M.T.

			h	m					h	m
Argentina	...		03		Chile‡	...	...		03	
Azores	...	...	01		Colombia	...	...		05	
Bermuda*	...	...	04		Cuba*	...	...		05	
Canada	...	...			Ecuador	...	...		05	
Alberta*	...	...	07		Grenada	...	...		04	

At 105° 45' E, at noon LMT, what is the GMT?

105 x 4 = 420 mins, or 7 hours. 45 divided by 15' = 3 mins. Greenwich is least because the location is East, so 12 (noon) - 7 hrs 3 mins is 04:57 GMT

At 147° 28' W, at 1327 LMT, what is the GMT?

147 x 4 = 588 mins, or 9:48 hours. 28 divided by 15' = 2 mins. Greenwich is best because the location is West, so 1327 + 9:50 23:17 GMT

SUNRISE, SUNSET

There are also tables in LMT that tell you when the Sun rises and sets, varying with date and latitude (between 60°S to 72°N). At the Equator, Sunrise is always 0600 and Sunset at 1800. Except in high latitudes, the times of Sunrise and Sunset vary only a little each day, so they may be taken as the same for all latitudes.

Notice that the Sun rises later and sets earlier as latitude increases in Winter, but it rises earlier and sets later in Summer. However, outside the latitudes above, the Sun will not set in Summer, or rise in Winter. An open square box at the top of a column means the Sun is visible, and a filled in box means it isn't. 4 hash marks (////) means continuous civil twilight:

Lat	July							
	1	4	7	10	13	16	19	22
°	h m	h m	h m	h m	h m	h m	h m	h m
N 72	■	■	■	■	■	■	■	■
70	□	□	□	□	□	□	□	□
68	□	□	□	□	□	□	////	////
66	////	////	////	////	////	////	////	////
64	////	////	////	////	////	////	////	////
62	////	////	////	////	00 19	00 51	01 11	01 27
N 60	01 01	01 09	01 17	01 26	01 36	01 45	01 55	02 05
58	01 47	01 52	01 57	02 03	02 09	02 16	02 24	02 31
56	02 16	02 19	02 24	02 28	02 33	02 39	02 45	02 51
54	02 38	02 41	02 44	02 48	02 52	02 57	03 02	03 08
52	02 55	02 58	03 01	03 04	03 08	03 12	03 17	03 22
N 50	03 10	03 12	03 15	03 18	03 22	03 25	03 29	03 34
45	03 39	03 41	03 43	03 46	03 49	03 52	03 55	03 58
40	04 02	04 03	04 05	04 07	04 09	04 12	04 14	04 17
35	04 20	04 21	04 23	04 24	04 26	04 28	04 31	04 33
30	04 35	04 36	04 37	04 39	04 40	04 42	04 44	04 46

To find the time of sunset at 55°N on July 12th in the table, first interpolate for the latitude, so you end up with 02 38 on the 10th, and 02 42 and a bit on the 13th. With 4 minutes between them, the answer is 02 40

Sunrise or Sunset occurs when the Sun's upper edge is on the viewer's horizon, which will be affected by atmospheric refraction - when you see the Sun for the first time, it is still half a degree below the horizon, but this will not affect the figures as they are based on visible phenomena.

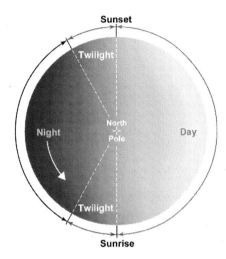

The Almanac also has tables for Sunrise and Twilight, but the process is the same. It deals with the real Sun, but the times are in LMT.

In fact, it is refraction that accounts for twilight. *Civil twilight* exists when the sun is within 6° of the horizon, and *nautical twilight* when between 6-12°. Between 12-18° below, you get *astronomical twilight*, and *legal twilight* happens 30 minutes before sunrise and 30 minutes after sunset. Remember that the figures are tabulated according to *local mean time*, which is based on the mean Sun, which doesn't exist. You will also have to interpolate, since not every day is shown, or every latitude. You can guarantee that any questions will land right in the middle! You may be asked when before or after sunrise you will arrive at a place, or duration of twilight.

The Sun is also used, with other tables, to get a True Bearing, with which to set your DGI, which is very handy when up North.

Tip: The shadow of a pen or pencil on a sheet of paper helps find the position of the sun on overcast days.

You could also use the heading of a known feature, such as a runway, or, in emergency, the compass, and subtract the variation, but that won't be so accurate.

Tip: Another way to determine true heading is to ask your GPS (if it is capable) for the true bearing to an NDB. Then subtract your relative bearing for the true heading.

MAPS & CHARTS

The words *map* and *chart* are used interchangeably, but there is no accepted definition of the difference. Officially, a chart will show parallels and meridians with minimum topographical features, and be used for plotting (see the example under *Variation*, above), while a map will show greater detail of the Earth's surface, so maps are for looking at, and charts are for working on!

The point about them both is that they are small scale representations of the Earth's surface that are only accurate within a relatively small area, since you are trying to show a 3 dimensional object on a 2 dimensional surface. The further from the *centre of projection* you go, the  more the distortion you get but, to all intents and purposes, it can mostly be ignored in its general area. You can see the problem if you try to flatten a globe, and the Equator and poles pose special problems because their meridians are parallel and converging, respectively. There are many ways of adjusting for this, and each suits a different purpose, so lines drawn on maps based on different projections will not cross through the same places (watch those danger areas!) When producing maps and charts, a reduced model of the Earth is used, so the compression factor is so small that it can be ignored.

Projections

The term *projection* means that an imaginary light is placed inside a model of the Earth and the shapes of the land masses are projected onto a piece of paper, which could be *conical* (Lambert), *cylindrical* (Mercator) or *flat*. All projections require sophisticated mathematical techniques to be effective.

The quality of *orthomorphism*, or *conformality*, which is the more modern term, that all charts should strive for, means the scale is correct in all directions, or at least within a very small area if the scale varies, and bearings are correctly represented. That is, the scale at any point is independent of azimuth, meaning that, for a short distance in any direction, it will be equal, so the outlines of the areas to be portrayed must conform. In addition, parallels must always cross meridians at right angles. Otherwise, no chart is perfect, as you will find when you try to fold them!

Lambert's Conformal - VNC/WAC Charts

Imagine the Earth with a light shining at its centre, then place a cone on top. If it could shine through the crust, an image of the Earth will be projected onto the cone. Where the cone meets the earth, the shadows of the land formations will be accurate, but will be out of shape the further North and South you go. This is the *conic projection*, the basis of the Lambert Conformal, and what most of today's aeronautical charts are based on, as the meridians will be straight, even if they converge towards the North. On a Lambert, Great circles are assumed to be straight lines (actually they are very shallow curves), and rhumb lines will be curves concave to the nearer pole. The word *conformal* means that a straight line approximates a Great Circle. Great Circles that are not meridians are curves concave to the Parallel of Origin.

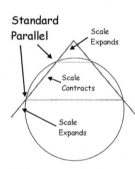

Johannes Lambert overcame the problem of scale expansion in the 18th century by pushing the imaginary cone further into the Earth's surface, to cut it in two places instead of one. This gives it two *Standard Parallels*, or points where scale is correctly shown (and where the *nominal scale* is). To be sure, there is a slight contraction between them, but this is insignificant (1% or less) if two-thirds of the chart are between the Parallels. The *Parallel of Origin* is midway between them, where the scale will be smallest. Outside the standard parallels, the scale expands, and will be greatest at the top and bottom of the chart. Thus, the Lambert is not technically a constant scale chart, but is regarded as such because, with careful positioning of standard parallels, the errors can be reduced to less than 1%. *On a Lambert conformal conic chart, the distance between parallels of latitude spaced the same number of degrees apart reduces between, and expands outside, the standard parallels.* Scale is constant along a *parallel of latitude*.

However, although chart convergency is constant (the meridians being straight lines), it varies on Earth with the sine of the latitude, both being equal to each other at the Parallel of Origin, therefore chart convergency is equal to *d long* x *sin PO* (the sine of the Parallel of Origin is sometimes called the *constant of the cone*). Towards the Equator, chart convergency is *greater* than that on the Earth, and *vice versa*.

As a reminder, if you draw a straight line joining two points of different longitude, the angular difference between the initial and final true tracks is equal to chart convergency.

Here is a good example of a Lambert Projection. Note the converging meridians, and the curved parallels of latitude, which are *arcs of concentric circles*.

As with the Mercator (see below), variation for NDB bearings should be applied *at the aircraft*, and for VOR/VDF *at the station*. However, for NDB bearings, you also have to apply convergency between the aircraft and NDB to make it correct.

Mercator

The Mercator projection does things differently. Instead of a cone, the Earth is surrounded with a vertical cylinder, touching at the Equator. Archimedes did it first, using an imaginary light at the centre of the Earth, but Mercator varied the vertical scale inversely to the cosine of the latitude so that the longitude scale is constant (in degrees) and that North always points North. This is because the light projection (actually the *cylindrical gnomonic*) becomes very distorted in polar areas.

One degree of latitude at 60° is twice as large as it is at the Equator because the cosine of 60 = ½. The unavoidable E-W stretching away from the equator is accompanied by a corresponding N-S stretching, so, within relatively small areas of the map, dimensions have the same scale in N-S and E-W directions, ensuring that directional vectors have the same bearings on the map as they do on the Earth.

Meridians now do not converge, but are parallel, equally spaced, vertical straight lines, so rhumb lines are accurate, but the distance between latitudes increases away from the centre. Since the Earth distance between parallels of latitude remain the same and the *chart distance increases*, the *scale* of a Mercator chart *becomes larger* with increase in latitude, expanding as the *secant* of the latitude, or the reciprocal of the cosine. This is not significant below about 300 nm, but you should always use the scale near the distance to be measured. *Parallels of latitude on a Direct Mercator chart are parallel straight lines unequally spaced.* Meridians are *parallel, equally spaced, vertical straight lines*, so it is *not* possible to represent the North or South Poles.

The Mercator is conformal, which means that angles and small shapes are represented correctly, but the scale varies greatly away from central parts of the map, so it does not show equal areas. Greenland on a Mercator looks as big as South America, even though it is only one eighth as big, but small portions of the coast (or any small region) will keep their shapes.

Shapes, therefore, will be accurate where the cylinder touches the surface, but distortion will be much greater further away. Since rhumb lines on this projection are straight lines, it follows that great circles must be curved, in this case, concave to the Equator (except meridians and the Equator itself). That is, the rhumb line is always nearer the Equator. As bearings are correctly represented, the chart is also orthomorphic. The Mercator projection is the one mostly used for plotting charts between 70°N and 70°S, as constant headings (as rhumb lines) are easier to use than great circles and a straight line on the mercator represents your actual path over the Earth. Also, around the Equator, there is very little distortion.

The rhumb line looks shorter than the great circle because of scale expansion. The relevance of this lies with plotting radio bearings, because radio waves take the shortest way (great circles, which will be curves), so long distances need the conversion angle applied to plot them as straight rhumb lines - in fact, an *ABAC scale* on the chart will do this for you. Complications also arise from whether the plot is done at the aircraft (ADF) or the station (VOR/VDF), and where you apply variation and conversion angles. Thus, *radio bearings on Mercator charts must be converted to rhumb lines.*

For NDB bearings, calculate the True Great Circle bearing of the NDB *from the aircraft*. Derive the rhumb line bearing from the aircraft to the station by applying the conversion angle *towards the Equator*. Add or subtract 180° from the rhumb line bearing to find the True rhumb line bearing of the aircraft from the station.

For the VDF/VOR, calculate the True Great Circle bearing *from the station*. Derive the rhumb line bearing from the station to the aircraft by applying the conversion angle *towards the Equator*. This is the True rhumb line bearing of the aircraft from the station.

TRANSVERSE MERCATOR - VTA CHARTS

Within 10° or so of the Equator, scale error on a direct Mercator is only 1% or so, but there's no reason the cylinder has to touch at the Equator.

The Transverse Mercator is a *horizontal* cylinder projection, on which a rhumb line is no longer straight, a straight line represents a great circle, and, with the exception of the Equator, parallels of latitude appear as *ellipses*. The *Central Meridian* (CM), or Meridian Of Tangency, which can be any meridian, where the cylinder touches the sphere, coincides with the relevant longitude, so True North and Grid North are the same along it, and the scale is exactly correct. However, because rectangular grid lines are based on the CM, moving East or West means applying some sort of *grivation* (see *Grid Navigation*, below). A scale factor also has to be applied as you move around to convert ground distances to measured distances. To reduce this, the projection uses two North-South lines with a scale factor of 1, so in the centre the correction is less than 1 (0.9996 for the UTM), while outer parts have it greater than 1. Parallels, except for the Equator, are ellipses. The Transverse Mercator's advantages include accuracy, over small areas, at least, and it is used for long, narrow areas, such as countries with a great N-S extent, or which are not very wide. Wide countries are split into zones, for which see......

UNIVERSAL TRANSVERSE MERCATOR

Because the Transverse Mercator is very accurate in narrow zones, it has become the basis for a global system, in which the globe is subdivided into narrow longitudinal zones, which are projected onto a Transverse Mercator projection. A grid is then superimposed on the projection, which is actually what is used to define your position (grids are easier to use than latitude and longitude).

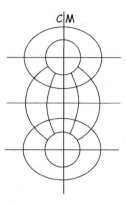

Knowledge of the UTM is not required for the exam, but is included because you will come across it in your career.

It all started when the US military imposed standards on a system that was already in use by the British, Portuguese, French and Belgians for mapping Africa, since they were the colonial powers.

The system uses sixty 6° longitude *zones* and twenty 8° latitude *bands* between 80° S to 84° N, giving 1200 areas overall (you have to go up to 84°N to get to a point north of Greenland).

Longitude zones are numbered 1-60 starting at 180°W, and can be thought of as individual strips of the Earth's surface that have been cut at the poles and peeled back, so they can be "laid flat" as the basis for smaller maps.

See also *Grid Navigation*, below.

OBLIQUE MERCATOR

This projection is used specifically to produce charts of a great circle route between two points, i.e. strip charts. The *Meridian Of Tangency* is any great circle other than a meridian. The cylinder round the Earth is neither vertical nor horizontal, but is skewed, hence the name *oblique*.

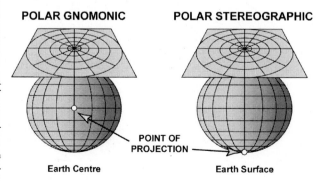

Polar Stereographic

These charts are used in polar regions, because the others cannot cope with convergence that well (in fact, they are a good complement to UTM). To get the details correct, the paper is held flat over the top of the Pole and the imaginary light projected straight up from inside the Earth to it. This is the result:

PROPERTIES

Parallels of latitude are concentric circles, and the spacing between them *increases* away from the Pole, so the scale expands away from the Pole, like with Mercator (to find latitude difference, subtract the radii). On a Polar Stereographic chart whose tangency is at the pole, Great Circles, with the exception of meridians, more closely approximate a straight line the the higher the latitude. Rhumb lines, except meridians, are curves concave to the Pole. The value of the convergence factor is 1.

POLAR NAVIGATION

Up there, it's darker for longer and there are fewer navaids (those that do exist are oriented to True North). The compass begins to get unreliable (the rate of magnetic variation changes quicker nearer the Poles), and there is increased deviation from the aircraft's own magnetic field, so realigning the DGI is also a problem, especially as it wanders in the long term. Not only that, communications are difficult, as well, but that's the subject of another chapter.

Areas above 65°N are officially known as *high latitudes*. A *polar track* exists where part of it crosses an area where the horizontal component of the earth's magnetic field is less than 6 micro-teslas.

Inertial Reference Systems are used to overcome these problems.

Grid Navigation

In higher latitudes, where the meridians converge greatly, your course will cut them at wildly different angles, so your heading needs to be changed continuously if you use standard navigation techniques. In fact, every time you cross a meridian, the change is 1°, and the nearer you get to the Poles, the quicker the change is - essentially, you must keep changing the magnetic heading to steer a straight course. If you look at the picture overleaf, you can see the angular differences in starting and ending points relative to the Poles. So how can you get your True Heading when the compass doesn't work?

Grid navigation uses an arbitrary grid overlaid on a projection (Polar Stereoographic or Transverse Mercator near the Poles, usually) for direction reference, which compensates for massive changes in variation and convergency where the meridians disappear up their own orifice. As it also means you don't need to worry about magnetic variation (because magnetic variation changes rapidly, too), the gyro heading can remain the same, regardless of what your magnetic compass says (when you get above a certain latitude, you reset your (unslaved) DGI to align with the grid system *before* the compass becomes ineffective, so you can find your way back if something goes wrong). Although the original purpose of grid navigation was to assist with navigation at the Poles, it can actually be used at any latitude.

Note: Grid Nav requires a stable gyro (i.e. one that has very little random wander), so that your alignment with reference to Grid North can be maintained as long as possible - for every degree of compass error, you will drift around 5 miles off per hour. You must also set your latitude nut correctly to allow for Apparent Wander.

The Polar Stereographic (or Lambert in sub-polar areas) is used because, on them, a straight line approximates a Great Circle.

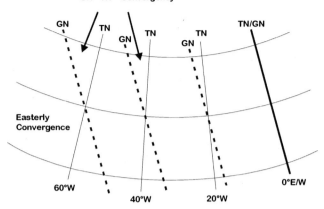

A *reference meridian*, or *grid datum*, (usually Greenwich in the Northern regions) is selected and Grid North is assumed to be at an infinite distance along it (that is, the Datum Meridian is laid along 0-180°). *Grid Meridians* are then drawn parallel to the *Datum Meridian*, so they point North as well, and the direction of any tracks measured from them will be *Grid Direction*. The difference between the grid and True tracks is simply *convergence* (and on a Polar Stereographic, convergence is the change of longitude). The only place where there is no difference between True North and grid North is along the Greenwich Meridian. Thus, your longitude and the convergence factor of the chart govern the angle between Grid and True North.

Grid North is West of True North if you are West of the Greenwich meridian, and *vice versa*. In the diagram overleaf, the Grid North line to the East of point A is pointing to the *left* of the True North meridian at 40°W, although this point is illustrated better with a Lambert

You can see that the transposed 0° line (which is also the grid) creates a greater angle to True North as you go West.

Grid convergence is labelled East or West according to the direction of Grid North relative to True North. That is, it is Easterly when True North is East of Grid North and Westerly when True North is West of Grid North.

Convergence East, True Track Least

Convergence West, True Track Best.

Thus, in the Northern Hemisphere, the chart convergency is equal to the longitude **with the sign reversed** (in the Southern Hemisphere, use it straight). In the diagram overleaf, for example, the track is 090°G. A is at 40°W, so the sign changes to 40°E, True track is least and the calculation becomes:

$$090 - 40 = 050T$$

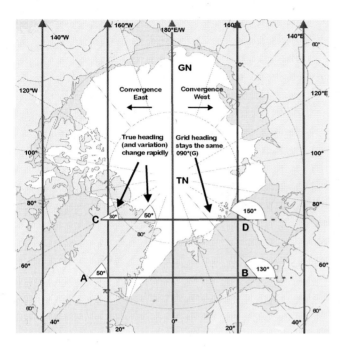

At B, on the other hand, which is at 40°E, you get:

```
090 + 40 = 130T
```

Since grid convergence is always equal to the chart convergency between the datum meridian and the one at your position, if you know the value of one track, you can always find the other.

POLAR ANGLE

Polar angle is used to relate true direction to grid. It is measured clockwise from Grid North to True North. You can convert from one to the other with this formula:

```
GD = True Dir + polar angle
```

To find out the polar angle from the convergence angle, in the Northwest and Southeast quadrants, polar angle is equal to convergence angle. In the Northeast and Southwest quadrants, it is equal to 360° - CA.

GRIVATION

This is the difference between the directions of *magnetic* lines of force and grid North (the grid magnetic angle). You can either convert Grid heading to True, then apply variation, or combine convergency and variation in one step.

The sum of Grid convergence and variation is called *Grivation - isogrivs* join points with the same value. Thus:

```
Grid ±Griv = MH

True ±Varn = MH
```

So, if your Grid Heading is 90° and the Grivation is 30°E, the magnetic heading is 60°.

Grivation East, Magnetic Least

Grivation West, Magnetic Best.

Scale

Because a map is a representation of the Earth's surface, you need to know to what proportion it has been drawn to gauge distances accurately.

Assuming a constant scale, the ratio between distances on a map and the Earth's surface is expressed as a scale based on the map's size. For a scale of 1:500,000 (commonly referred to as a half-mil), one inch on the map is equal to 500,000 inches on the Earth:

There are 63,360 inches to the mile, so an inch on a half-mil map is 7.89 statute miles.

You can tell which chart has a larger scale by looking at the *representative fractions*, obtained by dividing chart distance by Earth distance. Thus, a chart distance of one inch divided by its Earth equivalent of 13.7 nm would be a 1:1000000 map, and of a smaller scale than a 1:500000 (the bigger the number after the colon, or under the dividing line, the smaller the scale is). The representative fraction is always written with the map distance (as the numerator, on top) as 1, regardless of the measurement units.

You find the ground distance between any two points by multiplying the map distance by the denominator so, taking the 1:500,000 scale above, 5 units on the map would be 2,500,000 units of ground distance.

Not everything on a map is done to its scale; if it were, you would hardly see roads and railways, so they are artificially expanded to be visible. The centre of any object is its actual position.

The faster your aircraft flies, the less time you have to check the map, so those made for high and fast flight, or for instrument flying where you can't see the ground anyway, will not have many ground features marked on them, and will be called *charts*, like this one:

If you need to find out what Earth distance is represented by a chart distance, multiply the chart distance by the scale. For example, if asked what distance is represented by 25 cm on a 1/1,000,000 chart, multiply 25 x 1,000,000 to get 25 million centimetres. Divide that by 100 to get metres (250,000), then by another 100 to get 250 km.

Relief

Information about high ground is given in various ways. *Contours* are lines on a map joining points of equal height (or elevation) above sea level, so they are similar to isobars (the closer they are together, the steeper the slope they represent).

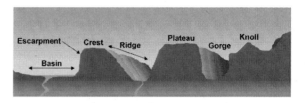

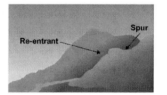

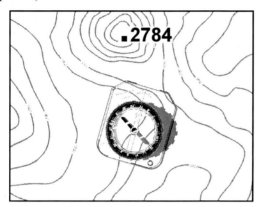

Spot Heights (commonly used on approach plates) show the elevation of prominent peaks with small dots, with the actual height shown next to them. The highest one will be distinguished in some way, possibly surrounded by a square, or printed in bold.

Some maps may give different colours or shading to various layers to make things more obvious, known as *Layer Tinting.*

Otherwise, on a map, expect water to be blue, woods to be green, and railways and power lines to be black.

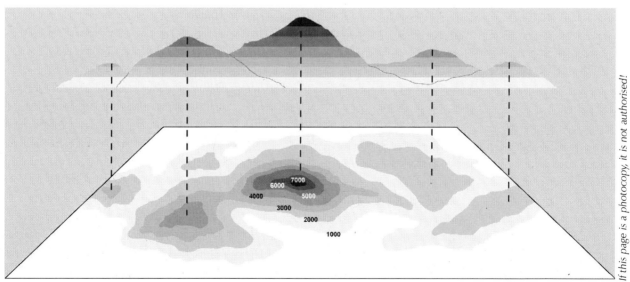

THE TRIANGLE OF VELOCITIES

An aircraft in flight is affected by the wind both along its axis and from the side, or from a head/tail or beam component.

In flying between point A and point B, you will only get there by just pointing the nose in the right direction if there is no wind, or if it is exactly on the nose or tail. This is very rarely the case, so your aircraft would *drift* off course, according to the wind's direction, if you did nothing to correct it. In other words, you would end up a certain distance left or right of the original target if the wind were blowing across your track from the relevant direction (in the early days of the North Sea, when navaids weren't around, pilots would build in a slight error to their calculations, so that they would know which side of the rig they were just in case it all went wrong).

The smart thing to do would be to make a heading correction towards the wind's direction to maintain a straight track. This, unfortunately, inclines the body of the aircraft more sideways to the track over the ground, which reduces groundspeed, because some of the energy from the engine is used to keep it there.

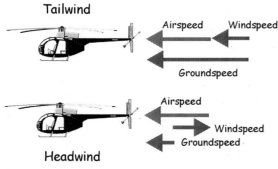

Thus, the speed of the aircraft through the air will not necessarily be the same as its speed over ground - if you are flying into wind, you will go slower relative to the surface, and faster if the wind is behind you.

You work out what the wind's effect on your trip will be by getting the forecast winds from the flight planning office, and working out a combination of three sides of a triangle, called the *triangle of velocities*, because a velocity expresses a combination of speed and direction, and we are concerned with those of your aircraft, the wind and the difference between them.

First of all, though, a few definitions:

- *Track*. The path the aircraft intends to follow over the ground, represented by the line on a map from one point to another (*Track Made Good* is the actual path - the difference between them is *Track Error*)

- *Heading*. The direction the aircraft is pointed in, according to its compass

- *Wind Velocity*. The speed and direction of the wind. The faster your aircraft, the less its effect. Forecast winds are given as True

- *True Air Speed* (TAS). The speed relative to the atmosphere, not necessarily the same as that indicated on your ASI, and not necessarily the same as.....

- *Ground Speed*, or the speed of the aircraft over the ground, because of wind

- *Drift*. The difference between heading and track due to wind, measured *from* heading *to* track

- *Air Position*. The position the aircraft would have reached without wind

- *DR Position*. The calculated position of the aircraft

- *ETA*. Estimated Time of Arrival

- *Fix*. Definite confirmation of position by ground observation, radio aids or astro nav

The velocity of an aircraft in flight (i.e. through the air) will therefore consist of its heading and airspeed. In the top diagram overleaf, the heading is 270°(T) - the single arrow is the symbol for the heading vector, pointing the right way, of course. When plotting, a scale is used, so if the heading vector were 3 inches long, at 50 kts to an inch it would equal an airspeed of 150 kts, or the air position after one hour of flight. If we added the wind speed and direction, the resultant between them would represent track and groundspeed, also to scale (right, middle).

In this case, the wind vector is half an inch long, for 25 kts, from the North. Joining the ends would therefore show your ground position after one hour, and your track and groundspeed, after measurement (you will have deduced already that two arrows are used for the track and three for the wind - the track arrows always go in the opposite direction to the other two). The *drift angle* is the difference between track and heading, measured *from* the heading *to* the track, in this case about 10°, so the track is 260°.

The centre diagram shows what would happen if you simply pointed the aircraft nose towards the West - you would drift to Port for the amount indicated. If you wanted to arrive over the intended destination, you would actually have to point the nose to the right (i.e. Starboard) enough to counteract the drift to the left.

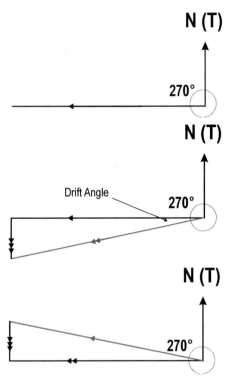

All you need to do now is draw the same wind vector on the *opposite* side of the line, and measure the length and angle of the new line to find out what heading to steer (280°). Don't forget to work out the variation and deviation so that the compass heading is correct.

Dead Reckoning

The only information you have after some time in flight is your air position, based on the TAS and heading(s) you used since you started. In theory, if you then add the known wind velocity for the period, you should get your ground position, which is known as a Dead Reckoning (DR) position, because it has been deduced rather than being positively identified:

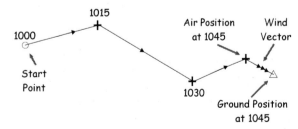

An air plot should be maintained constantly - every time the heading is changed, it should be recorded.

If you happen to fly over an object that can easily be identified from a map, you have a *position fix*, which can be used to find what the real wind is, and your actual groundspeed. On the map, simply connect a line from your air position to the fix, and measure the resulting line between them (the wind vector). The line between your start point and the fix would be the *Track Made Good*, which could be used to solve the above problem on the computer. The length of the wind vector is proportional to the length of time the plot has been running. Otherwise, the unit of measurement is the local nautical mile, conveniently obtained from the side of the chart in use (for most purposes, use the mean latitude. Similarly, where meridians are converging, use the mid-longitude).

When obtaining a fix, VORs are more accurate than NDBs (remember to check line-of-sight in the exam), and a 90° cut is best, always being aware of coastal effect. Unfortunately, multiple position lines meet exactly, and your position is assumed to be in the middle of the resulting *cocked hat*.

Nowadays, since fixes are readily available, the track plot is the favoured method, that is, the wind direction is found from the known parts of the other two sides of the triangle, using the Dalton Computer, as discussed above.

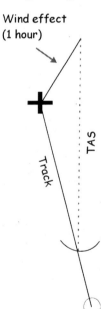

Wind effect (1 hour)

The traditional way for a navigator to do the job without a computer would be to draw the required track on the map, and an hour's worth of wind velocity from the start of that line, to scale. Then, with a pair of compasses opened out to the TAS, an arc would be described on the proposed track (the other point would be placed on the end of the W/V line). Joining the two points would produce the heading to steer to make good the track, and its length would tell you the groundspeed. The angle between heading and groundspeed is the *drift*, which could be assumed to be constant for long enough to draw a predictive series of lines for 6 minutes ahead.

DR involves the calculation of your best known position without navaids or visual fixes. In essence, it involves drawing the equivalent triangles of velocity you would create on your Dalton computer (see below) on a map, as discussed already, although it is important to grasp that the triangle's purpose is more to do with finding directions and speeds rather than finding a position. With no wind, your air position after a period of time would be the same as your ground position. Dead Reckoning attempts to reconcile the two, having taken into account whatever the wind has gotten up to.

As mentioned above, the lines you draw will be to scale, so one 3" long at 50 miles to the inch would represent 150 kts. When climbing and descending, take the mean TAS for the leg, and mean wind velocity.

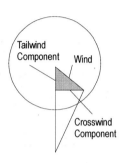

Remember that these velocities go together: *Heading & Airspeed, Track & Groundspeed, Wind Direction & Speed*. Also remember that you have to find mixed pairs, such as heading and groundspeed, rather than the combinations mentioned above, because you start with a mix in the first place (you usually know the airspeed and track already). Given any four, you can figure out the others by measurement, but you can do this mechanically with the *flight computer*. On the left is the triangle of velocities on the Dalton Flight Computer.

LOST PROCEDURE

Assuming you have flown as accurately as possible, and the wind velocity was accurately forecast, and you made no mistakes in your flight planning, you should find yourself pretty much on track throughout the flight. However, life is not always like that, and once in a while you may find yourself unsure of your position, the technical term for being lost. The *circle of uncertainty* is a way of trying to remedy this by allowing a percentage of error and drawing a circle of appropriate size centred on your destination. In theory, you should be somewhere inside it. The diameter will very rarely be more than 10% of distance flown.

You could also find the average heading, wind velocity and TAS to estimate your ground position. Averages are based on two observed fixes.

A useful method of a pilot resolving, during a visual flight, any uncertainty in the aircraft's position is to maintain visual contact with the ground and set heading towards a line feature such as a coastline, motorway, river or railway.

THE FLIGHT COMPUTER

The E-6B was developed in the United States by Naval Lt. Philip Dalton in the late 1930s. The name comes from its original part number for the US Army Air Corps in World War II. It is a device with a sliding scale, marked with drift angles and TAS arcs, with a frosted circular screen on which you can draw the business end of the triangle of velocities:

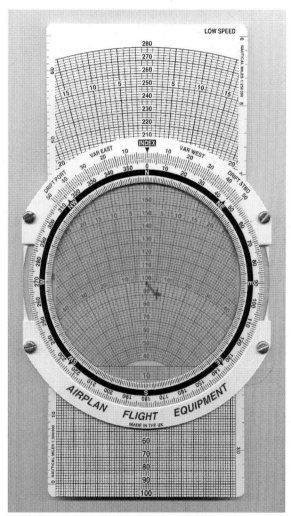

There is a dot in the centre of the screen, around which is a compass rose that can be rotated to bring your heading or track under the lubber line at the top, labelled *Index* in the picture below. All you need to do is draw in the wind vector to see how they all relate to each other.

Note: There will be an instruction book with your computer, so the details here will necessarily be brief.

First, move the sliding scale to make your TAS appear underneath the dot in the centre of the frosted screen (say 100 kts). Then rotate the screen so the wind direction (315°) lines up under the lubber line at the top.

Draw in a line vertically *downwards* from the centre dot equal to its speed in knots (15). This is called the *wind down* method*. Rotate the screen again until the track is under the lubber line (N). The end of the wind line will point to a drift (6° Starboard) and headwind (10 kts), which you just apply to track and airspeed to get the missing bits, namely the true heading to fly (006°) and the resulting groundspeed (90 kts) which you use for flight planning. Then apply magnetic variation and compass deviation to get the heading to fly.

Alternatively, put the wind on as above, align your track with the index and draw a vertical line through the wind dot. Then put the TAS under the grommet (centre dot) and turn the line you just drew until it parallels a drift line. Your heading is at the top, with the groundspeed under the wind dot.

*Wind up is initially slightly simpler if you only want to find the heading you need to fly to maintain a proposed track, but the heading marker will indicate your track and the wind point will be on the TAS, with the groundspeed under the centre dot. When you need to find track from heading and want to find the wind, it is not so easy. For example, in the picture above, you can see immediately that your groundspeed is lower than your airspeed, and that the track is on the right by however many degrees. If you had marked the wind upwards, you would have had to make an extra calculation or at least put the TAS line under the wind dot. You could always use wind up for heading questions and wind down for track questions:

- To find **hdg and g/s**: Mark the wind upwards, set the track at the index, set the TAS on wind mark, read the g/s in the centre, then read the Wind Correction Angle

- To find **track and g/s**: Mark the wind downwards, set the heading at the index, set the TAS in the centre, read the g/s at the wind mark and read the drift angle

CR Series

These were invented by Ray Lahr and marketed by Jeppesen. They are circular, with no sliding scale, and are based on trigonometry (they are easier to work with one hand, but be aware that, as the angle of drift increases, there's a small angular correction to be applied on top).

The cross between the 10 and 20 under the centre of the instrument on the right is the wind velocity (180/15). Its position to the right of the main line going towards TC (True Course) means the wind is coming from the right, and the crosswind component is 2 kts. Looking across from the 20 on the outside scale (bottom right), you will see that 1.3° is the correction to be applied to obtain the heading (the white arrow above the letters TAS must be opposite the aircraft's TAS for this to be correct). The headwind component is 12 kts, which should be subtracted to obtain a groundspeed of 78 kts.

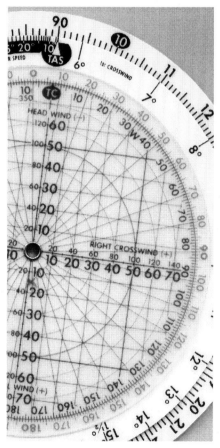

The very small versions of the CR have some functions left out, which are unimportant to most aircraft anyway, to pack everything else in, but don't get one too small, because your eyes won't see the print so well at night.

Slide Rule

On the other side of both types, there is a circular slide rule, with the 60 point on the inner scale conveniently marked to make speed and time calculations easier:

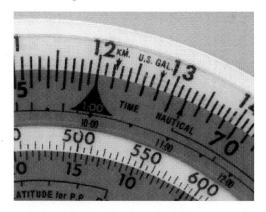

It can be positioned against fuel quantity or distance on the outer scale to read time on the inner scale. As with any slide rule, you need the approximate answer first, as a gross error check and to give you an idea where to put the decimal point (if you were wondering how it works, you are adding *indices*, which is also where logarithms come from, but that is outside the scope of these notes).

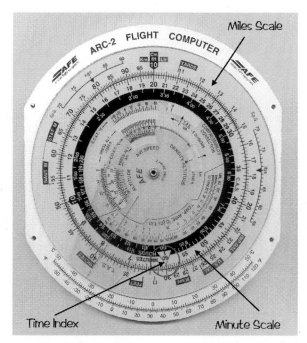

The outer, stationary, scale is called the *miles scale*, and the inner one, which rotates, is the *minute scale*, so distance and time are always opposite each other. There are auxiliary scales in the centre for calculations concerning pressure and density altitudes.

The 60 point in the inner scale is variously called the *time index*, or the *mph* or *gph index*. It is used for any calculations involving time, and will always appear opposite the groundspeed or fuel consumption. In the picture, it is next to 30, which could mean 3, 30 or 300 kts/mph/kilometres per hour, depending on the problem, so you could travel 4, 40 or 400 miles in 80 minutes, respectively. Alternatively, it could mean you travelled 3 miles in one minute, which is 180 mph.

Tip: To find out what the standard temperature should be at any level, line up the two tens on the inner and outer scales and take a look in the altitude window against the height you require.

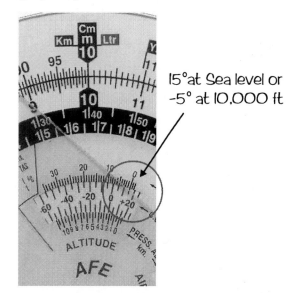

15° at Sea level or –5° at 10,000 ft

Tip: To find Density Altitude, set the aerodrome elevation or Pressure Altitude against the temperature in the *airspeed* window. The DA is against the datum arrow in the DA window. **Note:** Cross check with the formula in *Meteorology*.

The most common problems concern time, fuel consumption and distance, which always oppose each other. Just move the inner scale until the 60 point is opposite the TAS or fuel consumption. Read the time on the inner scale against distance on the outer scale, or fuel if you are checking how much is being used. In the picture on the previous page, the speed triangle (60) is opposite 120 (knots or gallons) on the outer scale, which means it will take 6 minutes to go 12 nautical miles, or 6.5 to use 13 gallons, and so on. It will also take 7 minutes to travel 140 miles, so the slide can be used to solve proportion problems as well. Reduce hours (and proportions) to minutes for simplicity. To multiply normally, place 10 on the inner scale against one number on the outer scale, and read the answer on the outer scale against the other, on the inner scale.

Square roots can be found easily as well (useful for VHF ranges). Find the number you want the square root of on the outer scale, then rotate the inner one until the number opposite 10 is the same as the one against your original number, e.g. 400 will have 2 opposite, as well as against 10.

To find TAS, line up the temperature against the pressure altitude in a window in the rotating slide rule (it may be labelled True Air Speed), then read the TAS on the outer scale against the RAS. Don't forget to allow for compressibility at speeds over 300 kts. In the picture on the left, the temperature is -21°C at 10 100 feet (follow the red line). The indicated airspeed is 177 kts, and the TAS is 200. Notice also that the Density Altitude is 7 200 feet, or 2 550 km.

True altitude is done the same way, using the Altitude window - lining up the same figures for PA and temperature gives you a true altitude of 18 800 ft against an indicated altitude of 20 000.

Conversions are done by lining up arrows on both scales representing the commodities concerned. For fuel weights, you will need the specific gravity, which is 1 for water, and used as a common denominator. It will vary from place to place, but that in the Flight Manual is the one to use. For example, if the s.g. of fuel is taken as 0.8, how much does 1 gallon weigh? The answer is 8 lbs (water would weigh 10). Alternatively, how many litres do you need from the fuel guy if you can carry 2600 kg and the s.g. is 8.2? Try 3170.

In the picture in the next column, the arrow labelled *km* on the outer scale is opposite the one marked *statute* (miles) on the inner scale. All you do is read off the direct equivalent on each scale - 112.5 km equals 70 statute miles.

EXAMPLES

How long will you take to fly 60 nm at 90 kts? Less than hour, so place the 60 index under 90 on the outer scale, move around to 60 and read 40 mins on the inner scale.

How far will you fly in 90 minutes at 105 kts? A quick estimate suggests it will be around 150 nm - place the index against 105 on the outer scale and read off 157.5 on the outer scale against the 9 on the inner scale.

If you travel 47 nm in 24 minutes, what is your groundspeed? Place 24 on the inner scale against 47 on the outer scale and read 117.5 kts against the index.

If you used 40 US gallons over 3 hrs 20 minutes of flight, what is your fuel consumption? 12 US gals/hr.

MISCELLANEOUS
••

The 1 in 60 Rule

This is a common method used in solving tracking problems, based on tangents, which, if you remember from Pythagoras, can be found by dividing the length of the opposite side of the angle to be found by the adjacent side. Or, in terms of aviation, dividing the distance off track by that of the desired track. We needn't go into the proof here, but you can end up with a formula:

$$Error = \frac{Distance\ Off\ x\ 60}{Distance\ Gone}$$

So if, after 40 nm, you are 8 nm off track, your track error angle would be:

$$Error = \frac{8\ x\ 60}{40}$$

or 12°, as indicated against the time index on the flight computer when you line up 40 nm under 8:

This would be doubled the opposite way to get you back on track, then applied as a single figure to keep you there (applying the correction only once would make you parallel the original track).

To track directly to the original destination, you would need an extra bit, called a *closing angle*, which you can find by altering the formula:

$$CA = \frac{Distance\ Off\ x\ 60}{Distance\ To\ Go}$$

Add the combination of closing angle and track error to the heading the appropriate way.

If you were intending to track along a VOR radial, and found you were actually on a different one, you can use the 1 in 60 rule to see whether you were still inside an airway. If the centreline was 045°, and you were on the 040° radial, you would be off track by 5°. If the DME says you are 45 nm away, it's a simple calculation:

$$Dist\ Off = \frac{TE\ x\ Dist\ Gone}{60}$$

The answer is 3.75 nm, so you are OK. It works for glideslopes, too:

$$Height = \frac{GP\ Angle\ x\ Range}{60}$$

SUMMARY

The 1 in 60 rule means that every 1 degree off track represents 1 nm for every 60 travelled. If you just want to parallel the track, alter course by the track error in the appropriate direction. To go to the destination, add the closing angle. To get back on track, alter course by double the track error. Once there, the original track plus or minus the track error will keep you there. Be aware, though, that the time to regain track may be more than that used to create the error in the first place, and that these rules are approximate, because altering heading changes the relationship of the wind to your machine.

Departing On Course

For the most accuracy when learning to fly, it is best to get to a safe height, then set course, making sure you pass the start point in the cruise. Although this means you won't have to make separate calculations for the climb, with more experience, you will be able to climb on course directly from the circuit, making proper allowances.

En Route

Check your DI against the compass every 15 minutes or so. Also, check your fuel state against progress, noting large reductions in particular, as they may indicate that you have left the fuel cap undone (gauges may read higher), or you have a leak. Pre-plan known events for your first leg, such as a noticeable town, a railway and road crossing, disused airfield, etc. Work out when they should turn up with your pre-planned groundspeed, and you can see if you are running early or late.

ESTIMATED TIME OF ARRIVAL (ETA)

Constant revision of groundspeed is important - not only do you need a check on the wind, but ATC also need to know your arrival time (within three minutes) so they can slot you in. Noting your timing between pre-marked points on your map is one method, but a useful mental check is to multiply the distance flown in 6 minutes by 10, so, if you fly 20 miles in 12 minutes, you are doing 100 kts. Alternatively, if you fly a quarter of the total distance in 15 minutes, it will take one hour for the whole leg.

The definition of ETA refers to arrival at the *destination*.

PERFORMANCE

The regulations require your aircraft to have adequate performance for any proposed flight, meaning the ability to get off the ground in the first place and maintain certain rates of climb against distance, so you can avoid hard objects (obstacles), particularly when you can't see them. As a result, performance charts will emphasise rates and angles of climb very strongly (climb requirements are established with one engine working hard for a specified time).

Many accidents are performance-related, particularly when taking off and landing, and especially when the aircraft is heavy, and operating in hot and thin air. Since you are trying to get a large, heavy object into or out of a relatively small place at some speed, the whole point of performance calculations is to ensure that the space *required* for taking off and landing is not more than the space *available*, taking due account of an engine failure right when you don't want it, and that you have enough engine power to cope with the situation. The idea is to keep the aircraft mass within limits during all phases of a flight, because the less the weight of the machine, the better it can fly when less power is available. How much an aeroplane can lift is basically down to speed - the faster you go, the more you can take, but various factors work against this, such as runway length, wind, flap position, braking action, temperature, pressure altitude, etc., which are all described below and included as part of a performance chart in some way.

Unfortunately, the charts in flight manuals tend to be optimistic, and they are based on new machines and skilled pilots in the first place, so, although the graphs will give you a maximum weight for the conditions, you would be wise to give yourself a margin, as the maximum weight is a *limit* and not a *target*.

It is your responsibility to decide whether or not a safe takeoff (and landing) can be made under the prevailing conditions. Performance requirements will be worked out before a C of A is issued, over a wide range of conditions, and they are subsequently incorporated in the Flight Manual, which forms part of the C of A.

The takeoff and landing phases are the most critical, demanding the highest skills from crews and placing the most strain on the aircraft. Because of this, strict regulations govern the information used for calculating take-off or landing performance.

Of course, in the old days (say during the war, or when the trains ran on time), having enough engines to lift the load was all that mattered and no priority was given to reserves of power and the like. Now it's different, and you must be able to keep your machine a specified distance away from obstacles and be able to either fly away or land without damage to people or property (and the machine) if an engine fails.

Aircraft are certified in one of several groups, the one in which it operates depending on its Certification, Max All-Up Weight and the number of passengers it carries. Within these limits you can choose which group to operate in, and come under the appropriate WAT (*Weight, Altitude and Temperature*) limitations; it may be more acceptable commercially, for example, to operate in a lesser group if it enables you to take more payload, and make more money - all you might need is longer runways.

Individual machine performance will vary due to such variables as the age of the airframe and engines, the standard of maintenance, or crew skill and experience, without the engines being adjusted for several seconds after the initial failure. What you can do on one day under a given set of circumstances may well be impossible another time. Performance is therefore a set of average values-particular machines may be better or worse.

The original testing, of course, is done with new aircraft and experienced pilots, and the statistically-derived *gross performance* graphs thus obtained are known as *unfactored*, although they do allow for one or two engines failing (subsequent machines off the production line are assumed to be the same as the first). Gross performance figures equate to an estimated fleet average, and fudge factors are applied to produce *net performance*, so there is a margin if you have a tired engine, or a new pilot, or any other operational contingency that cannot reasonably be foreseen. The Net Takeoff Flight Path is the aircraft's actual or Gross Takeoff Flight path decreased by a margin which, for two-engined aircraft, is 0.8%.

In other words, gross performance (based on demonstrated performance) is the average you might expect if there is a 50% chance you might get better or worse performance, and which should be achieved *if possible*. Net performance is gross performance scaled down to account for various conditions of flight, and the chance of not achieving it is remote, which is why it is used to establish obstacle clearance. Scheduled performance is based on Net performance.

Net performance is the minimum standard for Commercial Air Transport and is based on an incident probability rate of 1:1000000. Performance calculations must legally be done to net standards.

Occasionally, performance data in a flight manual will already be factored, but you will have to check the small print on the chart, in case they surprise you. Figures and graphs are based on Standard conditions which allow for fixed reductions in pressure and temperature with height. As we all know, the real world isn't like that, so these assumptions may not always be true and due allowance must therefore be made for them (if your aircraft is performing sluggishly, you may find it's not the machine, but the conditions it has to work under that are at fault).

You must, (with one engine out) clear all obstacles under the departure track within a defined area by a specified margin, without relying on seeing and avoiding them. The obstacle clearance plane has a slope of 152 ft/nm, which you must remain above, maintaining a climb gradient of at least 200 ft/nm that keeps you above it. If an obstacle pokes its nose into the obstruction clearance plane, it follows that you need a higher climb gradient, which will be specified on the plate.

Note: The obstacle clearance on an instrument departure procedures is based on all-engine aircraft performance. *Using a published procedure does not guarantee obstacle clearance if an engine fails*, so you must limit the weight of your aircraft so that you clear all obstacles during takeoff, after a failure of the most critical engine. However, there may be procedures that allow obstacles to be avoided laterally which include a turn (or a series of turns) based on specific headings or tracks.

Here it is in CARs, Subsection 705.57(1): "No person shall conduct a takeoff in an aeroplane if the weight of the aeroplane is greater than the weight specified in the aircraft flight manual as allowing a net take-off flight path that clears all obstacles by at least 35 ft vertically or at least 200 ft horizontally within the aerodrome boundaries, and by at least 300 ft horizontally outside those boundaries."

All the relevant data will be in the graphs, but some groups have no information at all in some areas. For instance, an aircraft may be assumed to have all engines working until above 200 feet, under which height there is no data for landing or take-off (which is why the take-off minima should not be below this, because you must be visual to avoid any obstacles should an engine fail). Sometimes, there can be no specific provision for engine failure at all. High Performance aircraft are a special case, because they tend to be operated much closer to their limits, which means more planning.

The data needed to check your performance is in the Flight Manual, which will have a supplement if your aircraft is foreign made, or you are using non-standard equipment - these override information in the standard manuals. Accuracy with charts is essential - very often you have to interpolate between figures or lines, and it's a good idea to get used to paralleling lines between the several graphs that may be on one chart. Study the examples carefully and always read the conditions on which the chart is based - helicopter ones, for example, often need the generator switched off.

For performance reasons, flights are split into four phases:

- *Takeoff*, which runs from the start of the takeoff run to include an initial climb to a *screen height* of 35 feet (sometimes 50)

- *Takeoff Net Flight Path*, which starts at 35 feet (or 50, as the case may be) to 1500 feet above the aerodrome

- *Enroute, or Cruise*, which extends from 1500 feet above the departure point to 1500 feet above the destination. You need to be able to cope with an engine failure here, too, but very often the MEA over mountainous areas is higher than the maximum height you can get in that condition. *Drift down* charts allow you to calculate a way out of the area so you can drift down to the OEI service ceiling, for which you must meet minimum altitude conditions so your gradient of descent matches the distance you must travel to clear the area

- *Landing*, from 1500 feet until coming to a complete stop. Sometimes the landing weight determines the takeoff weight. If you add the landing weight and the fuel burn together, then subtract the aircraft and payload weights, you will find out how much fuel you can carry

With performance matters, there are some principles that remain constant:

- Turbojets can only *plan* to use 60% of runway length (70% for turboprops) for takeoff (on the day, use all of it)

- You can only *plan* to use 70% (or 60% for alternates) of the Landing Distance Available (on the day, use all of it)

- You can only *plan* to use 50% of any reported headwind component, and *must* use 150% of any tailwind. This is for several reasons but, mainly, the ROD has to increase to maintain the glideslope, and reducing power in a jet to do this is not good because the engines take some time to spool up, especially from flight idle, which is where the revs will be in a high tailwind. You might also exceed flap speeds, and have less time to set up properly but, more importantly, you will float to bleed off excess speed and lose valuable runway space. Floating will be amplified by the slight increase in airspeed (and lift) obtained from lessening of the tailwind near the ground. Finally, a tailwind makes encountering your own vortices more likely

- You will lose some runway length from lining up

- You must account for weight, altitude and temperature (WAT), and brake energy, for the destination as well. All may restrict your takeoff weight

- You must account for runway surface condition, type and slope

- Distances *required* must not be more than distances *available*

- Mass must not be more than that in the flight manual for the conditions

For **light twin**s, you will invariably need more than whatever is stated in the Flight Manuals. On takeoff, you will need more runway to stop in or take off on if an engine fails, and landing distances are based on normal braking or nil wind:

- Do not assume the OEI Climb chart is a substitute for an accelerate-go chart (assuming you have one - most light twins don't). Engine-out climbs are only done under certain conditions, certainly not with the gear and flaps down, etc. Also, V_{YSE} is assumed

- Check your accelerate-stop distance - your runway length for takeoff should be the *greater* of accelerate-stop or accelerate-go

Since you can't find out V_1 until you know the maximum weight, for large fixed wing aircraft, the general procedure for using charts is:

- Find the lesser of the all-engines and one-engine-out distances (using a zero clearway, zero slope and zero wind length that allows the same weight as the runway you are trying to use, otherwise known as *Distance D*).

- Find the maximum takeoff weights for the balanced field length*, WAT limits, tyre speed limits, or anything else peculiar to your aircraft, such as brakes. In some cases, if the runway length is way over that required, but you are otherwise stopped by WAT limits, you can increase V_2 to increase 2nd segment performance at the expense of extra runway. Make sure none are above the maximum structural takeoff weight.

- If there are no obstacles, take the lesser weight, determine V_1, V_R & V_2, and reduce weight as applicable to suit the V_{MBE} (max brake energy) to get your max takeoff weight. Obviously, if your actual weight is below all these, you have adequate performance. If it isn't, you will either have to kick a couple of passengers off or change one of the parameters (choose a longer runway, for example).

- If there are obstacles, reduce the gross weight until the gradient available matches that required, then add it to the selection of weights to choose from above.

*Balanced Field Length V_1 means that the distance to abort and stop is the same as it is to carry on, assuming engine failure occurs exactly at V_1. In other words, accelerate-stop is the same as accelerate-go. Since it is often safer to carry on, many people use a lower V_1 instead. The term V_1 Cut refers to simulating an engine failure at V_1.

Essentially, you have to allow for differences in pressure, temperature and moisture. If you were taking your helicopter to a higher landing site, and you knew the current altimeter setting, you can calculate the pressure altitude at your proposed landing site with the formulae in the *Meteorology* chapter.

FACTORS AFFECTING PERFORMANCE
•••

Pressure Altitude

If the sea level pressure is less than standard, the air is less compressed, and your engine (and propellers) think they are at a higher altitude and will not perform so well. Thus, when the sea level pressure is *less* than it should be, you are at a *higher* pressure altitude, or the equivalent of being at a greater height. A high pressure altitude means a higher *altitude* rather than higher *pressure*.

So, to use performance charts effectively, you must find the Pressure Altitude you are really at (for how, see *Pressure Altitude* in *Meteorology*), then modify it for temperature by finding.............

Density Altitude

This is the altitude where the air in question matches the ISA density, or where the actual density equals what it would be in the standard atmosphere. In other words, it is your real altitude resulting from the effects of non-standard temperature, but also including height, pressure and humidity, all of which can make the air thinner and which are mentioned below. In standard conditions, the Density Altitude is the same as the Pressure Altitude - as temperature increases above the standard, so will Density Altitude, which can be defined as *Pressure Altitude corrected for temperature*, so once you have found your PA above, you then have to modify it. The details will be in the Flight Manual, although humidity is usually ignored in the average performance chart, because high air density and humidity do not often go hand in hand. However, if there is moisture around, say after a good shower, you would be wise to be careful.

Note: Pressure Altitude has more to do with engine power, and Density Altitude affects aerodynamic efficiency.

Anyhow, the idea is that the more the density of the air decreases for any reason, the higher your aircraft thinks it is. If you look at the lift formula, you will see that the lift from a wing or thrust from a propeller is directly dependent on air density, as is drag, of course. The effects are as valid at sea level as they are in mountains when temperatures are high - for example, 90° (F) at sea level is really 1900' as far as your machine is concerned. In extreme circumstances, you may have to restrict operations to early morning or late afternoon.

Here is a handy chart:

°F/C	60/15.6	70/21.1	80/26.7
1000	1300	2000	2700
2000'	2350	3100	3800
3000'	3600	4300	5000
4000'	4650	5600	6300
5000'	6350	6900	7600
6000'	7400	8100	8800
7000'	8600	9300	1000
8000'	9700	10400	11100
9000'	11000	11600	12400
10000'	12250	13000	13600
11000'	13600	14300	15000
12000'	14750	15400	16000

It shows that, at 6,000 feet and 21°C, for example, you should think in terms of 8,100 feet. If you want to work it out for yourself, try this formula:

$$DA = 145,366[1 - (X^{0.235})]$$

where X is the station pressure in inches divided by the temperature in *Rankin degrees*, which are found by adding 459.69 to Fahrenheit totals.

However, it's much simpler to add 120' to the Pressure Altitude for every degree above ISA at a particular altitude. For every degree below ISA, subtract 120'. Thus:

$$DA = PA \pm (120 \times ISA\ Dev)$$

ALTITUDE

Air density drops off by .002 lbs per cubic foot (i.e. 2½%) for every 1000 feet in the lower layers of the atmosphere.

HUMIDITY

Adding water vapour to air makes it less dense because the molecular weight is lower (dry air is 29 - water vapour is 18). On cold days, humidity is less of a problem because cold air holds less vapour. A relative humidity of 90% at 70°F means twice as much than at 50°F.

TEMPERATURE

As heat expands air, it becomes thinner. Thinner air is less dense (*Boyles Law*). On the surface, an increase in temperature will decrease density and increase volume, with pressure remaining constant. At altitude, however, pressure reduces more than temperature does, and produces an apparent contradiction, where temperature will decrease from the expansion.

PRESSURE

Air density reduces with atmospheric pressure (*Charles Law*). When you compress air, its density increases.

Runway Length

Getting the wheels off the runway is only part of the story. You must also clear an imaginary screen (35 feet) at the end of the *Takeoff Distance Available* (TODA), which is actually the *Takeoff Run Available* (TORA) + the *Clearway*, which is an area at the end of the runway that is unsuitable to run on, but still clear of obstacles, so you can fly over it. The distance to clear the screen is the *Take-off Distance Required*, which should obviously not be more than the TODA, which should not be more than 1½ x TORA.

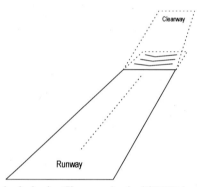

You can include the Clearway in the TODR because it is actually above the ground, over the *Stopway*, which is part of the Clearway that can support an aircraft while stopping, but not under take-off conditions. Clearways are defined rectangular areas that are supposed to protect the initial climbout after takeoff, and should have a slope below 1.25% and be at least 500 feet wide.

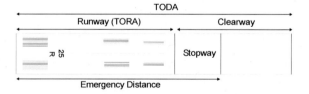

Stopway may be added to the TORA to form the *Emergency Distance Available* (EDA), or the ground run distance available to abort a take-off and come to rest safely. It is marked with yellow chevrons. EDA is sometimes also referred to as the *Emergency Distance* or *Accelerate-Stop Distance Available* (ASDA). The greater the EDA, the higher the speed you can accelerate to before

the point at which you must decide to stop or go when an engine fails (e.g. V_1 - see *V-speeds*, below). Other things being equal, ASD is mainly a function of the speed at which takeoff is rejected (V_1). Increasing flap will increase drag and help with the stopping distance, but the increased lift will decrease the efficiency of the brakes by decreasing the weight on the wheels, and they just about cancel each other out, particularly with the Airbus.

Where the ASDA is equal to the TODA, you have a *balanced field*. The *Balanced Field Length* is where the abort distance is the same as the continue distance, but because of the dangers of stopping in a hurry, V_1 is reduced by many operators for safety, so there is more reject distance to play with.

In short, these distances must be calculated: TORA, TODA, ASDA, LDA. With no clearway or stopway, and the threshold right at the end, they will normally be equal to the runway length (runway available is actually the overall length less distance lost when lining up).

Landing Distance Available must similarly not be less than *Landing Distance Required*. Unless the Flight Manual states otherwise, for propeller driven large aircraft, LDR must be factored by 1.43 to make it 70% of distance available, with no allowance for wet runways. For turbojets, the maximum you can plan to use is 60% (LDR must be increased by 15% if the runway is wet, not to exceed 60% of the LDA - multiply the dry graph result by 1.15).

These limits only apply up to the start of the takeoff roll, that is, they are for flight planning, so you have something up your sleeve. Once airborne, use 100% of anything available.

Tip: In the absence of accurate calculations, aim for 2/3 of the rotate speed by the time you get 1/3 along the runway. Otherwise, abort the takeoff.

Loss of Length Due to Alignment

This depends on the aeroplane geometry and access to the runway. Accountability is usually required for a 90° taxiway entry and 180° turnaround. There are two distances to be considered:

- The minimum distance of the mainwheels from the start of the runway for determining TODA and TORA (L below)

- The minimum distance of the most forward wheel(s) from the start of the runway for determining ASDA (N below)

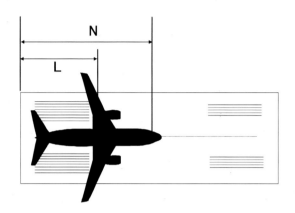

Altitude and Temperature

The higher you are, the less dense the air and the less the ability of the wings (rotating or otherwise) and engines to "bite" into it, thus requiring more power and longer take-off runs to get airborne. Humidity has a similar effect, but is usually allowed for in the graphs.

TODR will increase by 10% for each 1,000-foot increase in aerodrome altitude and 10% per 10°C increase in temperature (factor by 1.1). LDR increases by 5% for each 1,000-foot increase in PA and 10°C increase in temperature (factor by 1.05).

Aircraft Weight

Greater mass means slower acceleration or deceleration and longer distances. TODR will increase by 20% for each 10% increase in weight and LDR 10% per 10% increase in weight (factor by 1.2 and 1.1). Some manuals give take-off and landing weights that should not be exceeded at specific combinations of altitude and temperature, so that climb performance is not compromised. These are known as *WAT limits* (*Weight, Altitude and Temperature*), and are mandatory for Commercial Air Transport flights.

Sometimes rates of climb are given instead, so you need to be aware that a Commercial Air Transport aeroplane must be able to maintain a certain rate of climb depending on whether it has retractable landing gear or otherwise. In a multi, if you can't visually avoid obstacles during climb or descent, you must be able to climb at whatever rate with one engine out at the relevant altitudes and temperatures. This means all obstacles - you can't exclude frangible ones, so you may have to restrict take-off weight.

Runway Slope (Gradient)

Going uphill when taking off will delay acceleration and increase the distance required before V_{LOF} is reached. The converse is true of downhill slopes and a rule of

thumb is that TODR will increase 10% for each 2% of uphill slope, and vice versa (factor both by 1.1).

When landing, an uphill slope aids stopping, thereby reducing LDR. Any gains from landing upslope or taking off downslope should not be made use of but accepted as a bonus (that is, don't use them as part of your planning).

Runway slopes are expressed like climb gradients, being either positive (uphill) or negative (downhill). In the graphs, slopes are factored for as maximum of ± 2%. Another way to look at them is the difference in elevations at either end of the runway, divided by the length, multiplied by 100%.

If the slope is unknown it can be calculated by taking the altimeter setting at each end of the runway and finding the height difference.

Tip: Compare the Touch Down Zone Elevation with the airfield elevation from the approach plate.

When landing on a runway that is useable in either direction, regard it as a 0° slope.

A couple of things to watch for with slopes:

- If the slope is concentrated on one part of the runway (say the first 400 m), the takeoff roll will be even longer

- Upslope ahead causes a visual illusion, leading to a higher than normal nose attitude on rotation, which increases angle of attack and drag, and reduces acceleration

Surface Winds

Headwinds will reduce the distances required and improve the flight path after take-off. Tailwinds have reverse effects and crosswinds may even exceed the ability of the tyres to grip the runway. Aside from handling, crosswinds may also increase the TODR if you need to use the brakes to keep you straight. Forecast winds should be factored by 50% for a headwind and 150% for a tailwind, although this may be allowed for in the charts. TODR and LDR will increase by 20% for each tailwind component of 10% of the lift-off and landing speed (factor by 1.2).

The flight manual will state maximum crosswinds (try *Limitations*). A useful guide (for American machines, anyway) is that the maximum crosswind will be about 20% of V_{SO}. When finding the angle between the wind and the runway, remember that runway headings are magnetic and winds in forecasts are true.

You can also use the crosswind chart to find a limiting wind, or the maximum you can accept from any given angle. Just draw a line upwards from the maximum speed you can accept, and stop when you reach the line representing the wind direction. The curved line at that point (or its interpolation) is the maximum windspeed you can take.

Surface

Performance information is based on a dry, hard surface. A "contaminated" runway has over 25% of its surface area covered with standing water or slush (or loose snow) more than 3mm thick, or compressed snow and ice anywhere along the takeoff run or accelerate-stop surface. However, your flight manual may have different ideas. The 3 states of frozen water from ATC are *snow, ice* and *slush*. Just 13 mm of slush can produce enough drag to equal 35% of a 747's total thrust. At 25 mm, it is equal to 65%. Your takeoff distance can therefore increase from anywhere between 30-100%.

Note: In 1968, tests found that an average runway (that is, not porous or grooved), when wet, has a 2:1 wet:dry stopping ration - in other words, the landing roll *doubled*. This could increase to 6:1 if there were significant rubber deposits, or the runway was otherwise worn. The important factors are loss of friction when decelerating, and displacement of (and impingement drag when accelerating through) whatever is on the surface, so it may be difficult to steer, and take-off and accelerate-stop distances may increase due to slower acceleration, as will landing distance because of poor braking action and aquaplaning (see *Hydroplaning*, below), which is a condition where the built-up pressure of liquid under the tyres at a certain speed will equal the weight of the aircraft. In fact, slush drag increases until you get to around 70% of hydroplaning speed, after which it diminishes to zero when total hydroplaning is achieved. Slush's influence depends on fluid depth and density, and the square of forward velocity - half an inch will increase takeoff distance by 15%. At one inch, it's 50%. 2 inches' worth will stop acceleration completely.

When operations from contaminated runways are unavoidable, *do not* attempt to take off in depths of wet snow or slush over 15 mm, or try to grease it on when landing, or land too far in. *Do* lower the nosewheel as soon as possible, and use reverse thrust, or at least aerodynamic braking. Also, ensure the speed is safe before turning off the runway - the greatest tyre cornering effort occurs with no braking.

The responsibility for assessing runway surface conditions lies with the operator of the airfield, and not ATC, who merely pass it on.

WET (CONTAMINATED) RUNWAY

A runway is wet (or contaminated) when over 25% of its surface is covered with water (or equivalent in terms of loose snow or slush) more than 3mm deep, or when there is enough moisture on its surface to make it appear reflective, without significant areas of standing water (Falcon's definition is less than an eighth of an inch). *Any* compacted snow or ice counts as well. Without a shiny appearance, it is only damp. A wet runway, regardless of braking action, always affects minimum TODR/LDR. If the runway is wet, but the graphs are for dry runways, multiply the graph result by 1.15 (15% - exam question). This will likely mean reducing weight.

DAMP RUNWAY

A runway is damp when the surface is not dry, but the moisture on it does not give it a shiny appearance. You can call a damp runway a dry one, if braking action is good.

DRY RUNWAY

A dry runway is one neither wet nor contaminated, including paved runways specially prepared with grooves or porous pavement and can retain effectively dry braking action with moisture present.

WHEN TAXYING

On the ground, you may need slower taxying speeds and higher power settings to allow for reduction in brake performance and the increase in drag from snow, slush or standing water, so watch your jet blast or propeller slipstream doesn't blow anything into nearby aircraft.

Try not to collect snow and slush on the airframe, don't taxi directly behind other aircraft, and take account of banks of cleared snow and their proximity to wing- and propeller-tips or engine pods. Delay flap selection to minimise the danger of damage, or getting slush on their retraction mechanisms.

COEFFICIENT OF FRICTION

This is the difference between braking action on wet and dry runways, for the same aeroplane at the same speed and mass. As groundspeed increases, so does the difference, so action can only get better if you start higher than .4 and decelerate.

BRAKING ACTION

This table really concerns the action of tears against the runway, but it is worth noting that certification testing may be done with new brakes and tyres - worn ones, as found on most aircraft, probably won't be capable of a high-energy RTO.

Coefficient	Action	Code
> .4	Good	5
.39-.36	Medium-Good	4
.35-.30	Medium	3
.29-.26	Medium-Poor	2
< .25	Poor	1

HYDROPLANING

This occurs when liquid on the runway creeps under the tyres and lifts them completely, leaving them in contact with fluid alone, with the consequent loss of traction, so there may be a period during which, if one of your engines stops on take-off, you will be unable to either continue or stop within the remaining runway length, and go water-skiing merrily off the end (actually, you're more likely to go off the side, so choosing a longer runway won't necessarily help). The duration of this risk period is variable, but will vary according to weight, water depth, tyre pressure and speed. It only needs a tenth of an inch to do this.

Dynamic hydroplaning is the basic sort, arising from standing water (*lift off speed* is the important consideration here). It comes with as two subtypes, *partial* and *full*, both more likely when water depth is over 6 mm. *Viscous hydroplaning* involves a thin layer of liquid on a slippery surface, such as the traces of rubber left on the landing area of a runway which fill in the small holes (one reason why it's dangerous to drive after a rain shower in Summer). In other words, it is caused by a *smooth* and *dirty* runway surface, at a lower speed than dynamic hydroplaning, and you should particularly watch out for the white markings - it can almost be like landing on ice. *Reverted Rubber Hydroplaning* happens when a locked tyre generates enough heat from friction to boil the water on the surface and cause the resulting steam to stop the tyre touching the runway. The heat causes the rubber to revert to its basic chemical properties, i.e. black and runny.

Although there are many contributory factors, the most important is tyre pressure. A rough speed at which aquaplaning can occur is about 9 times the square root of your tyre pressures (see the formula below), 100 pounds per square inch therefore giving you about 90 kts (7.7 times if the tyre isn't rotating) - if this is higher than your

expected take-off speed you're naturally safer than otherwise. The point to note is that if you start aquaplaning above the critical speed, you can expect the process to continue below it, that is, you will slide around to well below the speed you would have expected it to start if you were taking off.

Most factors that will assist you under these circumstances are directly under your control, and it's even more important to arrive for a "positive" landing at the required 50 feet above the threshold at the recommended speed on the recommended glideslope than for normal situations (the positive landing helps the wheels break through the water). Under-inflating tyres doesn't help - each 2 or 3 lbs below proper pressure will lower the aquaplaning speed by 1 knot, so be careful if you've descended rapidly from a colder altitude. Naturally, you should try not to use the brakes, but as much aerodynamic braking as you can, after lowering the nose as quickly as possible to reduce the angle of attack and place weight on the wheels.

The (rotating wheel) formula is:

$$Vp = 34.5 \sqrt{(p)}$$

Vp is the ground speed in knots and *p* is the tyre pressure when using bars (for PSI, use 9 instead of 34.5. The stationary wheel formula uses 7.7, so you might get partial hydroplaning while the wheels spin up).

GRASS

For dry short grass (under 5"), the TODR will increase by 20%, a factor of 1.2. When it's wet, 25% - a factor of 1.25. For dry, long grass (5-10"), TODR will increase by 25%, and 30% when wet (it's not recommended that you operate when the grass is over 10" high).

For dry short grass (under 5 inches), the LDR will increase by 20%, a factor of 1.2. When it's wet, 30% - a factor of 1.3. For dry, long grass (5-10 inches), LDR will increase by 30%, and 40% when wet. For other soft ground or snow, the increase will be in the order of 25% or more for take-off and landing.

The Takeoff

In the range of speeds used for takeoff, thrust will decrease initially because of intake momentum drag (in a high bypass jet), then steady, then decrease a little more, even though ram air effect is building up. For a low bypass, the ram effect will increase mass flow (and thrust) above about 250 kts.

Drag arises from the usual aerodynamic drag, plus wheel drag. The former will increase sharply at the rotation point, while the latter depends on the weight on the wheels and the resistance of the runway surface. The weight on the wheels will reduce as lift takes over, but with thrust reducing slightly during the takeoff roll, the result is that the net acceleration force reduces during takeoff, especially at the rotation point, and so does the rate of acceleration. The rotation speed should therefore be as low as possible, because a small increase in it requires a disproportionate amount of runway to be made available. However, V_R must be greater than stalling speed, for obvious reasons, and V_{MC} so you can keep the thing under control once airborne with an engine out. BUT - the 5° of bank allowed for V_{MCA} cannot be applied at V_{LOF} (lift off speed), which is *higher* than V_R, and occurs *after* it.

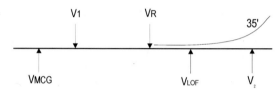

Since V_{LOF} is not normally calculated, V_R is taken as being at least $1.05\ V_{MC}$ to allow for the difference (see also *V-Speeds*, below).

Aircraft tyres are usually rated to 210 or 225 mph. This affects V_R indirectly, since the MTOM becomes the limiting factor, which will affect V_R in turn. However, you have to make some calculations because the tyres are running at a true groundspeed (they are literally on the ground) and V_R is an airspeed, and therefore affected by pressure altitude and temperature.

Obstacles (The Climb)

Takeoff requirements also need to consider obstacles along the takeoff path which cannot be avoided visually. An obstacle is in your path if the distance from it to the nearest point on the ground below your intended flight path is inside the lesser of:

- 60 m, plus half the wingspan, plus an eighth of the distance from there to the end of the TODA

- 900 m

The *Net Flight Path* is made up of segments covering various stages of flight (such as when undercarriage or flaps are raised) and is so called because NET (i.e. factored) performance data is used to assess it. The NFP starts from 35 feet above the end of the TODR (Reference Zero), this being the imaginary screen the aircraft must clear, and must clear all obstacles vertically

by at least 35 ft, or at least 90 m plus $0.125 \times D$ horizontally (where D is the horizontal distance travelled from the end of the TODA, or the end of the takeoff distance if a turn is scheduled before the end of TODA. For aeroplanes with a wingspan of less than 60 m, a horizontal clearance of half the wingspan plus 60 m, plus $0.125 \times D$ may be used).

The top of the screen at 35 feet above the runway is known as *Reference Zero*, which is where the takeoff officially ends and the climb begins, at V_2, in fact.

The various stages of a climb are:

- The first segment starts at Reference Zero and ends when the gear comes up. Transport category aircraft must be able to climb positively during it.

- The second segment lasts until levelling off for the cleanup (usually 400 feet AGL, having gone through V_2, V_3 and V_4 with flaps and power at takeoff settings and the propeller of the failed engine feathered).

- The third segment ends when ready for the enroute climb. It is usually a level burst at 400 feet, during which acceleration is made to V_{YSE}, flaps are retracted and power is reduced to Max Continuous (there is usually a time limit for engines above this).

- The fourth (and final) segment is a climb to 1500', or higher if there are obstacles. The aircraft is clean with Max Continuous power on one engine, the other feathered.

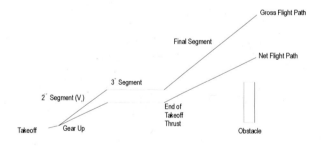

Maximum climb performance in most jets is achieved at a constant IAS until a specified Mach number, which is held constant until levelling off in the cruise.

If an obstacle (including a frangible one) intrudes on the Net Flight Path, then take-off weight must be reduced until it's cleared by the relevant margin, so this may be a determining one in calculating *Restricted Takeoff Weight*. You can make gentle turns to avoid obstacles, and not have to fiddle with take-off weights, and there will be graphs in the Flight Manual allowing you to calculate radii and procedures for it. However, you will need to be visual as well, so a minimum cloudbase is necessary.

If an engine fails in the climb out, normal practice would be to carry on at V_2 to flap retraction height, then return to the point of departure, having jettisoned fuel to get the weight down, but if you can't (maybe the weather) the NFP and MSA must be examined at the flight planning stage. It may even be necessary to climb overhead the airfield to get the height before going for your return alternate.

You must use the one-engine inoperative net flight path data from the point at which full instrument flying commences, or is expected to.

The best Rate of Climb speed is obtained when there is the greatest difference between the power required for level flight and that available from the engines. In turboprops, this will coincide with the speed for the best lift/drag ratio, since power output is relatively constant. Turbojets, however, produce more engine power with speed, which is enough to overcome the extra drag, so the maximum differential between power required and available happens at a higher speed, and best ROC occurs above L/D_{MAX}. There will be performance tables to find time and fuel required for climbs. Remember that headwind and tailwinds will change the distance figures. To cope with this, work out the groundspeed with no wind and apply the corrections then. You can use the whizzwheel to find out the distance and time.

CLIMB GRADIENT

This can be either positive (climbing) or negative (descending) and is usually expressed as a percentage. To get it, divide the height difference by the ground distance travelled, taking the wind into account. Without wind, you get the *Still Air Gradient*. If an aircraft has a rate of climb of 500 fpm and 100 kts TAS, first convert the speed to feet per minute:

$$100 \times 6080 = \frac{10,133 \text{ fpm}}{60}$$

Thus, in one minute you will have flown 10,133 feet through the air and gained 500 feet in height so the gradient will be 500/10,133, or .0493, which, multiplied by 100% gives a Still Air Gradient of Climb of 4.9344, or 5% in round figures.

With 20 kts of headwind, the groundspeed above would be 80 kts.

$$80 \times 6080 = \frac{8106 \text{ fpm}}{60}$$

For a 6% gradient, or thereabouts.

The above method uses TAN (*Opposite over Adjacent*) to calculate the angle, and is what examiners typically expect you to use. However, a more accurate formula:

$$\frac{ROC \times 6000}{TAS \times 6080}$$

uses the SIN (many questions give very little spread between answers, so you may need it).

ROC is in feet/min and the TAS is in kts, while the 6000 is 60 seconds for a minute multiplied by 100%. The 6080 converts kts into feet/min.

The Cruise

This extends from the top of the climb (TOC) to the top of the descent (TOD), when the Captain wakes up. The idea is to use the least fuel, if only because some airlines increase your pay packet, but sometimes, you must get somewhere as quickly as possible, with maximum TAS.

This has already been covered in *Fuel Management* in Chapter 9.

RECIPROCATING ENGINES

In the cruise, you should reduce power and lean the mixture, which will reduce the fuel consumption and reduce wear on the engine. Generally, the higher the RPM, the greater the speed, but at the expense of fuel economy, range and endurance. The lower the RPM, of course, the fewer number of times the engine goes round, and the less fuel is used. Calculating the Specific Air Range (the fuel used per Nautical Air Mile) can help you compare the various options. That is, find out how far you can go for each pound of fuel. Note that twin-engined aeroplanes have higher power and fuel consumption, so there will be a significant difference in fuel required for descent.

In a non-turbocharged aircraft, the TAS increase between 5,000-12,000 is hardly discernible, so you would only go that high if you were getting a good tailwind or the MSA (or weather) forces you - the fuel consumption will be more or less the same at either altitude and the climb will take up more fuel than you save. Turbocharging will increase TAS, so you can decrease power to reduce fuel consumption and engine wear, and increasing range, too.

Landing

Approach is normally done at 1.3 V_{SO} for the weight. As this is an indicated airspeed, the groundspeed might be different - high altitudes and temperatures will increase it, as will a tailwind, of course. Brakes are the most used way of stopping once on the ground (aerodynamic braking is not very good at stopping large aircraft, and reverse thrust is best at high speeds).

SPEED

Peculiar to landing is speed - a higher one naturally requires a longer distance, not only for slowing down, but the FAA have also determined that being 5 knots too fast over the threshold is the same as being 50 feet too high. Aircraft are classified according to IAS at the threshold (V_{AT}), equal to Stalling speed (V_{SO}) x 1.3:

Category	Threshold Speed
A	< 91 kts
B	91-121 kts
C	121-141 kts
D	141-166 kts
E	166-211 kts

At the planning stage for a Class B aircraft, the minimum climb gradient is 300 ft/min climb speed with all engines operating.

Balked Approach Flight Path

A balked approach is a go-around in the landing configuration (gear and flaps down, etc.). It is similar to Net Flight Path, and commences at DH above the upwind end of the LDR. However, you may not be able to complete a balked landing or go around once you have entered a low-energy landing configuration without touching the ground, because your flaps and gear would be set for landing, you would be below about 50 feet, in descent, with the throttle in the idle range and with decreasing airspeed. Balked landings or go-arounds should be initiated before this point is reached - if you put your aircraft in this state, the subsequent board of inquiry would only assume you thought it was safe to do so. As there will be no performance figures in the charts to cover it, this is a high risk experiment - in fact, you might stall if you try to climb before your engines have spooled up.

Diversions

You must be capable of continuing the flight from any point of engine failure at or above MSA to a height above a suitable airfield (within WAT and runway limits), where you must be able to maintain a positive rate of climb. Consideration must therefore be given to height loss, and the likely drift down rate with engine(s) out is established from the Flight Manual. The charts will indicate how quickly you can expect to descend, based on aircraft weight, temperature, altitude, etc.

If the MOCA is quite high (say over the Rockies at 14,000 feet), you're obviously going to be pushed to get there in some aircraft with two engines, let alone one. If you have to go that way and suspect you may have performance problems, you could always work out your Drift Down with the help of an emergency turn, information about which will also be found in the Flight Manual. What you do is establish a point one side of which performance is OK and the other side of which, if you have an engine failure, you make an emergency turn to get yourself away from the area and (hopefully) out of trouble, drifting down to the MEA. Again, the charts will indicate the rate of descent in a turn and all you need do then is ensure that your MSA reduces at a greater rate than your altitude! If you can't comply with any of this, you may have to reduce your weight until you can.

Power Settings

Noise abatement (or looking after your engines) sometimes means reduced thrust on take-off, which obviously tightens performance limits, which will increase all your distances. EPR (*Engine Pressure Ratio*) is how you measure power output on a turbojet or turbofan (turboprops use *torque*). It is the difference between the exhaust and inlet pressures - if it is three times the size out of the back, EPR is 3. However, EPR gauges should not be used by themselves, but cross-referenced with other instruments, especially when the probes might ice up. The relevance of this becomes apparent with an engine failure after V_1, where some aircraft (like those with automatic controls) allow full throttle without exceeding performance limits. Others need the levers to be set more accurately, and a likely idea of what the limits will be before take-off.

EPR settings vary with altitude and temperature. When using the tables, enter with the temperature and pressure altitude, remembering to make adjustments if you use bleed air (check the notes on the chart, which will be set up for a default). As there are so many variables, you might find it easier to create a table:

	Eng 1	Eng 2
Table	2.17	2.18
A/C off	+ .6	
Other		-.5
T/O EPR	**2.23**	**2.13**

If you have an EPR each for temperature and PA (as with the 737), use the lower.

Miscellaneous

Low tyre pressures increase distances required.

Engines Out

The performance loss suffered by a light twin when an engine fails can be over 80%. This is because climb performance is a function of thrust horsepower, which is more than that required for level flight.

If an engine fails in the cruise above the single-engine ceiling, you should slow down to within 5 kts of the best single-engine rate of climb speed (V_{YSE}) and apply maximum continuous power on the other engine(s). If you cannot then climb, at least you might be able to maintain height, or descend more slowly so you reach the scene of the crash slower. Do not go below V_{MCA} (V_{MC} in the US).

You will not be surprised to hear there are tables for fuel dumping. Usually, you find the intersection between the starting and ending fuel weights to find the time required, but don't expect a question in an exam to be so simple - expect to use Zero Fuel Weight.

The time limit for jettisoning fuel is 15 minutes. You must be free from hazards, the discharge must be clear of the aircraft, and controllability must not be affected.

You can also find out the maximum altitude you can maintain with an engine out. On a 737, for example, the engine bleed configuration gives you a choice of three tables concerning the use of anti-ice. You then match the aircraft weight against the ISA temperature.

V-SPEEDS

These are significant aircraft speeds, on large aircraft, calculated for every takeoff, and varying with weight (or mass), that is, they increase as you get heavier (to help with checking how they can vary, look at the trends in pages 64 & 65 of CAP 698). Some, like V_1, are found in tables in the Performance section of the Flight Manual. Typically, you enter a table at the appropriate PA, then go across until you reach the relevant temperature range (making sure you use Centigrade or Fahrenheit). Then go down to the row that has the gross weight and flap settings you want and read the speeds off. Watch for notes at the bottom of the table! Sometimes, as with the DC-9, you have to find the basic speeds first, then apply the above parameters.

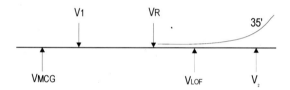

Here are some:

Speed	Explanation
M_{MO}	V_{MO} for higher altitudes, in Mach numbers (the red line on the airspeed/Mach indicator). The changeover altitude is in the POH.
V_A	Manoeuvring speed. The max speed you can make abrupt, full scale deflections of the controls without damage (about twice V_S). Not always the best speed for entering turbulence (see below). Valid only at gross weight. A 20% decrease in weight needs a 10% reduction in manoeuvring speed. Flying just above this speed may cause permanent deformation of the aircraft structure if the elevator is fully deflected upwards.
V_B	Maximum gust or turbulence penetration speed for turbines, at least 10 kts below V_A compensating for the power used delaying the stall and for windshear. Lighter aircraft should be flown slower, as stall speed decreases in line with weight.
V_{BE}	Best Endurance, or the greatest airborne time per unit of fuel, around 75% of V_{BR}.
V_{BG}	Best power-off glide (for greatest distance per unit of height). Distance is affected by a windmilling prop.
V_{BR}	Best Range, or best L/D, and greatest air distance per unit of fuel, decreasing with weight.
V_C	Cruise speed, for the most velocity pr unit of fuel. Around 1.3 x V_{BR}
V_{CEF}	The airspeed at which the critical engine is assumed to fail. It must not be less than 1.05 V_{MC}. See V_1.
V_D	Dive speed, normally at least 25% higher than cruise speed (1.4 x V_{NO}).

Speed	Explanation
V_{DF}	Demonstrated diving speed.
V_F	Flap Speed.
V_{FE}	Max speed Flaps Extended - the top of the white arc.
V_{FO}	Max Flap Operating speed.
V_H	Max level speed at max continuous power.
V_{LE}	Max speed, gear extended.
V_{LO}	Max gear operating speed.
V_{LOF}	Lift Off speed. About 10% above V_{MU}. The speed where the aircraft first becomes airborne, or where lift overcomes the weight.
V_{MBE}	Maximum Brake Energy speed, or the maximum speed on the ground from which a stop can be accomplished within the energy capabilities of the brakes. As brakes turn kinetic energy into heat, it is affected by mass, pressure altitude, temperature and slope, so it is most limiting at high masses, temperatures, pressure altitudes and downhill slopes.
V_{MC}	See below.
V_{MCA}	Minimum Control Speed, for control in the air - the minimum speed at which the aeroplane is controllable with a maximum of 5° bank when the critical engine becomes inoperative with the remaining engines at take-off thrust (i.e. your rudder does not have enough push). It is not connected with stalling speed, and on bigger twins your approach speed can be less - thus, if an engine goes after the point where you can gain speed and reconfigure, you are committed for landing. V_{MCA} decreases with increase in PA, and increase with aft C of G. There is no guarantee that you can maintain altitude, let alone climb - you can only expect to maintain heading. V_{MC} is marked with a red line on the ASI.
V_{MCG}	Ground Minimum Control Speed - the minimum calibrated airspeed on the ground (using only rudder to correct yaw) where takeoff can be safely continued, when the critical engine becomes inoperative and with the remaining ones at takeoff thrust (it is assumed the aircraft has just been rotated, the nose wheel is no longer in contact with the runway, but the main wheels are still on the ground). The distance between where the engine is assumed to fail and the aircraft becomes parallel with the centreline may not be more than 30 ft from the centreline. It decreases as elevation and temperature increase, as there is less yaw from the critical engine (it is producing less thrust from the less-dense air). It is the same as the minimum V_1. Although no account is officially taken of nosewheel steering, in practice, it should be available as well. Factors that reduce V_{MCG} include density altitude, reduced thrust on takeoff, large tail fin or rudder area, forward C of G and engines closer to the fuselage.

Speed	Explanation
V_{MCL}	Approach and Landing Minimum Control Speed - The minimum speed with a wing engine inoperative where it is possible to decrease thrust to idle or increase thrust to maximum take-off without encountering dangerous flight characteristics.
V_{MD}	Minimum Drag - induced drag equals profile drag. It increases with weight and lift. Also means Minimum Descent, or the lowest rate of sink in a power-off glide, which occurs at minimum drag x velocity. The time in flight is affected by a windmilling prop.
V_{MO}	Max operating speed (at lower altitudes), to prevent excess damage from dynamic pressure, relevant to high speed aircraft (same as V_{NE}). Varies with altitude.
V_{MP}	Minimum power, lower than V_{MD}. It is close to V_S.
V_{MU}	Max Unstick speed, or the minimum speed you can fly off the runway without hitting it with the tail (actually, that point is the limiting speed for geometrically limited aircraft - the actual limit is the angle of attack at which you reach the maximum coefficient of lift). As it is established as the basis for V_1 and V_R during manufacturer testing, you don't normally have to deal with it, but it is useful where you just want to get the wheels off a dodgy surface and stay in ground effect until V_{TOSS}.
V_{NE}	Never Exceed speed, around 90% of Dive Speed (V_D). On a turbine, the equivalent is V_{MO} or M_{MO}.
V_{NO}	Normal Operations.
V_R	Rotation Speed, or the IAS at which the aircraft is rotated to the takeoff attitude, whether the engine has failed or not. It is at or just above V_1 (On the 727, they are the same), but must not be less than that, or 1.05 x V_{MCA}. V_R must also be high enough to get to V_2 before screen height. It is a speed that, if maximum rate of rotation was applied, V_{LOF} of at least 1.1 x V_{MU} with all engines operating could be attained, or at least 1.05 x V_{MU} with one engine out.
V_{RA}	Maximum speed in rough air.
V_{REF}	Chosen speed on the approach (ref speed), derived from 1.3 x V_{SO} (stall speed in landing configuration), so it increases with weight.
V_S	Stall speed, or minimum steady controllable speed in flight.
V_{SL}	As above, for specific configuration.
V_{SO}	Stall speed in landing configuration - the bottom of the white arc, decreasing with weight.
V_{SR}	Reference Stall speed.
V_{S1}	Stall speed, clean, power off - the bottom of the green arc on the ASI. It decreases with weight (and unloading manoeuvres). In other words, the conventional stall, with a load factor of less than one.
V_{S1G}	Stall speed, corresponding with the maximum lift coefficient (just before lift starts decreasing). Same as V_{SR}.

Speed	Explanation
V_T	Threshold Speed - V_{REF}. Where you should aim to cross the threshold to ensure the scheduled landing field lengths are consistently achieved. The speeds at the threshold are V_{T0} - all engines operating, V_{T1} - a critical engine out and V_{T2} - two critical engines out. Maximum threshold speed is described below, but the minimum speed is determined by V_{MCL}.
V_{TMAX}	Maximum Threshold Speed - speed at the threshold above which the risk of exceeding scheduled landing field length is unacceptably high. Go-around action should normally be taken if this will be exceeded. It is normally 15 knots more than all-engines operating target threshold speed.
V_{TOS}	Min speed positive climb in takeoff condition, one or more engines out.
V_{TOSS}	Takeoff Safety Speed in a Cat A helicopter (equivalent to V_2). It was developed because it is below Vy, and repeatable, aside from giving a better angle of climb than rate of climb, because you're more interested in clearing ground in a short distance than how fast you're going up.
V_X	Best angle of climb, or the most height in the shortest distance. It decreases with weight, but the angle of attack remains the same. As V_{S1} increases in a turn, the safety gap between it and this speed will be eroded if you attempt a climbing turn. It does not change with altitude, but increases with mass for a jet, and decreases with flap. This does not apply to helicopters because, although, in a vertical climb, it would be zero, at all other times it would be so variable as to be impossible to calculate and below a reliably indicated airspeed anyway. See V_{TOSS}.
V_{XSE}	Best s/e angle of climb.
V_Y	Best rate of climb, or the most height in the shortest time. It occurs with the greatest difference between power available and power required. For a jet, it is quite high, and because the graphs concerned are relatively flat against each other (see left), it can vary widely from the optimum and not affect things much. For a prop aircraft it is quite low, however, and very low climb rates are achieved below it.
V_{YSE}	Best s/e rate of climb, represented by a blue line on the ASI.
V_{ZRC}	Zero ROC - you cannot accelerate, climb or turn, so must reduce drag.

Speed	Explanation
V_1	So-called Takeoff Decision Speed, above which the takeoff is supposed to be continued, and below which abandoned, if an engine fails. It used to be called the critical engine failure speed, also called V_{CEF}, but it is actually the maximum speed at which you take the first actions to abort, or the minimum speed to continue after an engine failure. According to Boeing, if you reach this speed accelerating, you have already made the decision to continue. Thus, it is a performance speed, as the decision to abort must be made beforehand. In other words, it is the speed at which an engine failure is recognised, not the speed at which it occurs. It is entered into the MCDU before flight, and is represented by a 1 on the speed scale of the PFD. Engine failure having been recognised, V_1 is the speed at which the continued TODR will not exceed the TODA, the continued Take-off Run Required will not exceed TORA and the Accelerate-Stop Distance will not exceed the EDEA. V_1 is supposed to give you a safe full stop or a successful engine-out takeoff if something happens, that is, if an engine fails below it, you slam on the anchors, and afterwards, you get airborne and try to fix things in the air. However, high speed rejects are among the top three causes of accidents. Unless you feel things will be uncontrollable, your chances may better in the air anyway (in practice, the only time you would land a large aircraft back on would be if a failure prevented you from actually flying). In any case, you cannot determine V_1 accurately until you know your takeoff weight, which is sometimes not found until you are taxying out and the information transmitted to you over a datalink, so for planning, you work with an approximation, with standard weights. It is a fixed speed concerning engines only, based on weight, flaps, altitude and temperature (nothing to do with runway length), and raising any one of them will raise V_1, and vice versa. You may see the odd table with a correction for very strong winds, but wind otherwise has no direct effect. Treat slope in the same way (a headwind or an upslope will mean an increase V_1). When asked whether a condition increases or decreases V_1, think about committing to flight at a higher or lower speed - for example, if stopping distance has to be increased, or antiskid doesn't work, or you have a tailwind, decrease it, and vice versa. V_1 must not be less than V_{MCG}, and not greater than V_R and V_{MBE}.

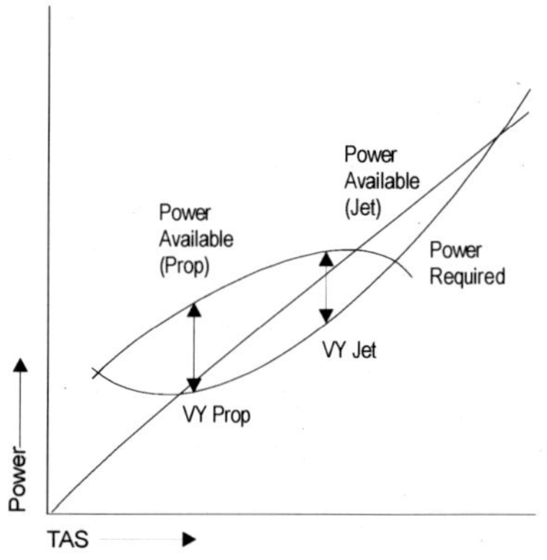

Speed	Explanation
V_2	Takeoff Safety Speed, or minimum safe flying speed if you lose an engine after takeoff, to be achieved before screen height (35') and provides a safe margin above stalling speed for manoeuvring to flap retraction speed (V_3). It must be at least 20% more than stall speed and 10% above V_{MCA}. Weight is the main factor. Calculate for each landing for go-arounds. Because V_X is low for prop-driven aircraft, V_2 will be close to the speed for best angle of climb, and well below for a jet (for which it is an initial target speed - V_4 gives a better climb angle and manageability). On the PFD is it represented by a purple triangle on the speed scale. The lower limits for V_2 are 1.2 x V_S and 1.1 x V_{MCA}. For all engines, a jet is usually accelerated to V_2 +10kt (V_4) after rotation because it gives a better angle of climb, a more manageable pitch attitude and, if an engine fails later, the climb gradient will be better.
V3	Flap retraction speed. The target speed for the screen height with all engines operating, and used to the point where acceleration to flap retraction speed is initiated.
V4	The all engines operating take-off climb speed, to where acceleration to flap retraction speed is initiated. V_4 should be attained by 400 feet.

CHARTS

These may look complex, but once you've figured out the way to enter one performance chart, you can use them all. For exam purposes, the best tip is to read the small print around the graph itself, as this is where you will find the conditions on which the chart is based, such as "generator off", or "anti-icing on".

Below is a typical performance chart (this one is for takeoff distance). Essentially, it's a combination of several graphs in one, each feeding off the other. Usually, you start with something like your weight against Pressure Altitude, go from their intersection to temperature deviation, then runway slope, then the wind component to find your answer. On the right is a simplified one so you can see the procedure clearer.

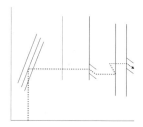

Very often, you have to work backwards, or at least go through the process several times to get what you need.

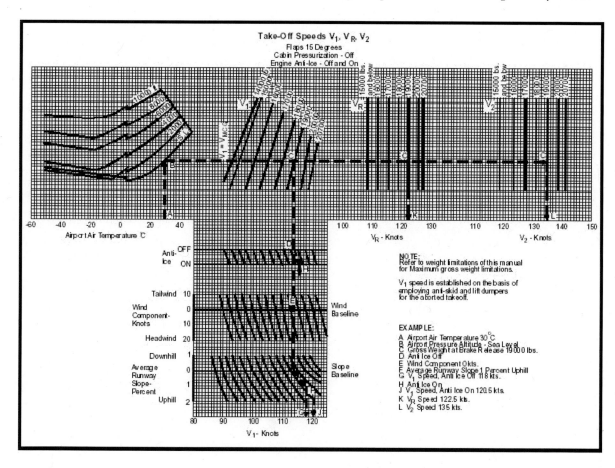

NOTES

GOING FOR A JOB

Inexperienced pilots have a similar problem to people in many other walks of life - they cannot get a job because they don't have the experience, and they cannot get the experience without a job (try being a junior lawyer!). When looking for work with hardly any hours and a licence which is barely dry, you are in a similar position to asking your father for the keys to his new Mercedes so you can go to a party. You have to ask yourself what characteristics you might have that would make your father do such a stupid thing. Or that might make passengers get into a machine with you at the controls, for that matter.

What would your father want to know? That he will get his car back, of course, undamaged, and with no after effects, like traffic tickets. Similarly, a Chief Pilot will need reassurance that you are capable of flying one of the company machines without crashing it, upsetting the customers and being the cause of a subsequent visit from your local friendly Operations Inspector. In this respect your flying ability counts for only a small part of the qualities required - it's the remainder that need to be emphasised when doing the rounds at such a disadvantage (even failing your exams proves persistence if you finally pass them!)

OK, so now you're a Chief Pilot - what would you like to see in someone who walks into the office with a resume in one hand and no doughnuts in the other?

I would suggest a selection from the following would be appropriate:

- A smile on your face

- A firm handshake

- Confidence

- Presentable appearance, including clothing and hairstyle - no shaven heads or curly locks, and especially no earrings.

- Clean vehicle

It's a fact that jobs have been offered just on appearance. I know, because it happened to me, and no-one even asked to look at my logbook or licences (actually, the reason was because my resume was printed, in the days when it was a major achievement to get one typed, but more about those shortly). However, in the normal course of events, for low-timers, visiting as many companies as possible is about the only way to get yourself known.

Just sending a resume is not good enough when they haven't seen you before.

Believe it or not, someone with relatively low experience and who gets on with customers is actually in a better position than somebody the other way round, other things being equal, as experience and flying techniques can be taught - personality can't. Also, get to know lots of people at the bottom levels, because Chief Pilots very often ask the guys on the shop floor if they know anyone when there's a vacancy and, if you are recommended, there's less chance of personality conflicts later (Chief Pilots don't like hassle, but they do like people who are not going to drop them in it, as they carry a lot of responsibility). At least one company I know of gets its pilots in the crew room whenever someone is about to be offered a job, and they take a vote.

Employers like people who have clearly made an effort to know their (potential) jobs, and who clearly absorb information and knowledge about their aircraft and other crew members. In other words, the sort of people who give every impression of being commanders in their own right and can be relied upon in flight and otherwise. Although much of this comes from experience, the potential is often very obvious at an early stage.

Remember also that loyalty goes both ways. Some companies deserve all they get when their pilots disappear in a shortage - with no staff, they can't trade, and they go out of business. It's happened before and will happen again (they forget that companies need good people, but good people don't need companies). On that basis, if you're doing the traditional two years as a hangar rat before you get your hands on a machine, be prepared to move on if it seems like the company are more interested in your cheap labour than training you. In my opinion, in with your normal windscreen-washing, you should be doing the air tests and non-revenue flying, which will not only give you an incentive, but make your subsequent training cheaper by keeping you current. It is entirely possible to get well upwards of 400 free hours a year in a busy company, if you're prepared to end up in strange places for days at a time.

You will have to do a bit of research about every company you target - you will certainly need the name of whoever does the hiring, and the head of the department you want, if they are different (in most cases, it will be the Chief Pilot or Base Manager, or, in other words, someone with local knowledge). Only go to the personnel department as a last resort, and even then just to ask for the right name(s). You need to know the sort of work they do, the type of customers they have, where they operate, and tailor your initial conversation around it, emphasising the benefits you can bring which cause them the least amount of work. For example, in Canada, one of the first questions you will be asked is if your PPC (*Proficiency Check*) is current, because it can be transferable between companies if they operate the same machinery, and they won't have to spend money sorting you out. It's almost guaranteed that the next question will concern either a mountain course or long-lining experience, so be prepared. The point is that their requirement for a pilot is to solve a problem, and you need to be the one with the solution, so get their attention, then create the desire to employ you and, more importantly, do something about it. In fact, the sort of telephone conversation a busy Chief Pilot up to the ears in paperwork would like to hear is something like:

"Hi, I'm a King Air pilot with 1500 hours, available now."

Music to the ears. Just adjust it for your own situation, but only get detailed after you start fishing for what they want. If you get asked any question at all, you've got what is known as a "buying signal", but the question will likely come after a short period of silence, which you shouldn't break. Answering apparent brushoffs with further questions should keep the conversation going. If you can introduce the name of somebody already known to them, so much the better.

THE ADVERT

If there is one, it's usually the last resort for companies who need staff - apart from being outdated anyway, the best jobs are almost always filled by word of mouth, and the ad is placed to satisfy legal requirements, or to wind up the opposition. In fact, the way an advert is worded can tell you much about the company you may be working for.

Read what it actually says. If it states definitely something like "must have 500 hours slinging", it means your application will go straight into File 13 (the waste bin) if you don't. On the other hand, another might say that such experience "is desirable" or "is an advantage"; if you score 6 out of 8 on the requirements, then go ahead. In this case, circumstances will determine what happens to your application, for instance whether there is a pilot shortage or not, or whether the Chief Pilot or the Personnel Department actually wrote the advert (Personnel won't haven't a clue as to what's really required and may have just copied it from somewhere else). Just bear in mind that words like "preferable" also become criteria for *weeding out* applicants if there are a lot of them.

However, your face may fit better than higher-qualified people, and it's a favourite hobby of some pilots to keep applying for jobs anyway, so to help you get on where you may be at some sort of disadvantage (whether you're one of many applicants or you haven't quite got the qualifications required), you may need to employ a few tactics, including your resume.

Tip: One tactic that works more often than not is to apply relatively late, say a week after the ad appears, ensuring that the bulk of applications are out of the way and whoever has become cross-eyed looking at them will get yours when he's back to normal, possibly all by itself so you're noticed more. You also (theoretically) go to the top of the pile. However, *do not miss the deadline* as, even if the Chief Pilot wants you, Personnel will bounce you out anyway. Another is to always make a follow-up call, including after an interview - in some companies, the process is very long and you can easily get forgotten.

Tip: If the ad runs again in a very short time, it means they haven't found anybody - if you didn't have the qualifications the first time round, you may do now!

YOUR RESUME

Applying for a job involves selling yourself, by which I mean that you are the product to be marketed, and the process starts even with the envelope in which you send your details (a full-sized stiff-backed one ensures they don't get creased). It's surprising how many people fail to use the resume and covering letter (they are, after all, a first introduction) as properly as they should be. I have seen very badly handwritten resumes with no idea of spacing on ragged paper that would disgrace a fish and chip shop. This type of introduction says little for your self-image and is likely to go straight into the bin - if it doesn't, it will be a reminder of what you were like long after the interview. *Your resume is your sales brochure.*

Having said all that, in a lot of aviation companies the atmosphere is relatively informal, and, although you need a resume, hardly anyone ever reads it, at least not till you make them do so by turning up on their doorstep, so take the following remarks with as large a pinch of salt as you feel able. You may only be required to fill in an application form (see below), which will also involve a breakdown of hours - usually First Pilot and Grand Totals. The initial contact could well be a faxed one-page letter, with everything relevant on it, and full details when asked.

Tip: Keep a running breakdown of your hours, separate from your logbook and updated monthly, say, in a spreadsheet, which will help you extract these figures when required (it will also be a back-up should the original get lost, but a logbook must fulfil certain legal requirements). Keep columns for specialised stuff.

However, a large company with a personnel department (which therefore deals with several other professions) will expect to get the full treatment. Like flying, the more preparation that goes into your resume, the better the results you will get. Remember, you're trying to beat the opposition, in an environment where the best person for the job frequently gets eliminated early on, and the person who plays the application/interview game best wins. Unfair? Yes, but life's like that, so here's a couple of points to note before we go any further - the resume is not meant to get you a job, but an interview. Secondly, it actually consists of two parts - the resume itself, which contains the usual stuff, and a covering letter, which, being a business document, should be neatly typed or wordprocessed on white letter-sized paper, unless you are specifically told to do otherwise (you might be asked to fill in a form) - it looks more professional anyway.

The letter is actually a focussing device, that should include information that might not belong in the resume, or to highlight anything that might be particularly relevant (from the ad, maybe) and to get it in front of the right person. Ring up to make sure you spell their name right, as "Dear Sir" or "Dear Madam" will often mean consignment to the waste bin immediately. You may also include reasons for wanting to join the company, or, more to the point (salesmanship again), how useful you will be to them, because that's what they're bothered about. You could, for example, cover points mentioned in the advert, or you know that they're concerned about. This is your sales pitch.

Use the word "I" as little as possible, include any reference numbers in the advert, and get the person's job title right. Don't "wish" or "hope" for an interview (salesmen are taught to ask for a sale, so - ask for an interview!). Remember that most resumes look the same, especially if you use a Microsoft Word template!

If you are not replying to an ad, remember that Personnel often do not know about vacancies until actually asked to do something about one, so you need to get hold of the person in charge of the department or base you are interested in. One tactic might be to write to the Big Boss, whereupon it might filter down to the relevant person from above, giving them more of an incentive to do something about it. Don't be shy about this - speculative letters show initiative, which is one quality required when operating in remote places. It also saves them money, if they are actually looking, as recruitment costs money (when talking about yourself, and therefore saying nice things, when you begin to feel slightly embarrassed is the time to stop).

Although it is often said that a resume should fit on one page (and this is good advice), life is never so convenient, and you should always be aware from the start that you might need 2 or even 3, if you include a breakdown of your flying hours. On the one hand, trying to cut everything down when it won't get any smaller is stressful, and on the other, many resume readers (myself included) find it frustrating that more information isn't forthcoming when I want to read it. The trick is to put the information you think might be needed on the first page, and expand it on the following pages, even if you repeat yourself (you could also put it in the covering letter). As a guide, my own procedure is to go through any list of resumes with the requirements of the job in mind, and either highlight any that are already mentioned, or write down any that are not, on the front page as an aid to later sorting. What is relevant depends on the job, but it's a fair bet that licences, types flown, total hours on each and availablility would be a good start - you could probably think of more, but especially include contact details.

Don't bother with referees, as these are usually taken up after the interview anyway.

Having said all that, you should still try to get the information in as short a space as you can without leaving anything out - if you're only going for a flying job, the tendency to include irrelevant information should be avoided, and everyone knows what a pilot does, so your resume will be on the technical side, that is, short, competent and to the point. Management qualifications (if you have them) are not important to somebody who just wants a line pilot (all the advice here should be read in this light - you don't have to include everything). As with all salesmanship, you're trying to make it as easy as possible for the customer, in this case your potential employer, or at least the poor clerk in the personnel office who has to go through all the paperwork before the interviews (it's worth mentioning at this point that the clerk's job is to screen you out, or to discover who *not* to interview). If you feel the need to be more specific, use the covering letter to get your details in front of the right person. The screening out can take place in as little as 8 seconds - the irony is that they use the resume for the process. What do they see in that time? Well, the type of paper, its condition and layout, to mention but a few items (your subconscious can pick up a lot without you knowing). In short, whether you've spent time on it.

You need to use quality paper, A4-sized and white, and therefore inoffensive, but this requirement is really for scanning. Use one side of the paper only with the script centralised, with no underlining or strange typefaces. Leave at least a one-inch border at the top and bottom of the page with a good sized margin on either side. It will cost a minimal amount to get a two-page resume wordprocessed properly and not much more to get a reasonable number photocopied, preferably on to the same paper. Use a spellchecker. Twice.

It should include your career history, commencing with your present position and working back about 5 years in detail, the remainder in brief. The name and town is enough to identify employers with a brief description of their activities, if needed, as aviation is a small world. You may include reasons for leaving your current position but, as said above, when people read a resume they almost always do it with a highlighter in one hand to mark relevant passages for later, and you can almost guarantee that this will be a prime target, so prepare it very carefully.

In summary, the layout must be neat, as short as possible, well spaced and easy to read, with a positive attitude conveyed throughout. Section headings could include:

- *Personal Details*, centred at the top - just name, address and contact number
- *Post applied for* (optional)
- *Profile*
- *Key Skills*
- *Work Experience* (a better heading than career, if you haven't really got one!)

If you don't have much experience, include outside interests that have transferable skills. All other personal stuff (date of birth, etc.) should be at the end, as it bores most readers.

Application Forms

Practice on a photocopy first, and always use the same pen throughout (that is, make sure you're not likely to run out of ink halfway through and have to change colours).

Don't leave blank boxes - use N/A (*Not Applicable*) if one doesn't apply, and never refer someone to an attached resume (that is, attach one if you like, but don't ask them to look somewhere else for information they want *now*).

The "other information" box is the same as a covering letter, so don't miss it out.

THE INTERVIEW

Let us first of all establish what the interview is not. It has nothing to do with your competence as a professional, except for the simulator ride (if one is required). The mere fact that you've been put on any list at all, let alone shortlisted, indicates that your flying abilities are recognised.

On their side, the interview is really to see if your face will fit. They are about to let your personality loose on their customers and they want to see if you will help solve the problem or become part of it. In other words, they are looking for people who know the rules, have common sense, and the personality and tact to apply them. In other words, they are interviewing future *Captains*.

You, as an employee, must create value beyond the cost of employing you. As far as you are concerned, it's a chance to see if you will like the Company, in which case you may find it useful to write down what you want from them.

Note: With reference to value, mentioned above, the cost of employing you is not just your wages - you may have training or health insurance thrown in, plus other benefits, not to mention the staff employed to look after you, or any office you might have. In the first year, you may well cost much more than your salary. Even the interview process can cost thousands!

Interviewing techniques can be very sophisticated. You may be lucky and get away with a quick half-hour with someone who is just as nervous as you are, but the full-blown two day affair with Personality and Psychometric testing is becoming increasingly common. Certainly, it is used by one Electricity Board in the UK, and almost every airline worldwide. The full nine yards might include written maths, intelligence and psychological tests (with over 600 questions), a simulator ride, an interview and a medical (nine yards, by the way, or 27 inches, was the length of an ammunition belt in a B-17, so I'm told). Most questions are relatively simple, but the average time for each is about one minute. Examples are figuring out the next number or symbol in a logical series, identifying how a shape or object would look if rotated, finding words amongst a group of mixed letters, etc. The psychological part is not timed and presents situations and statements to be ranked from 1 to 4 according to which is the most or least like you. Do not try to read into questions or guess what they are trying to achieve, just answer them (don't add your own selections!). There may also be a team exercise, perhaps an evacuation plan for a village about to be flooded, in which you are given priorities and resources. There won't be a right answer - they will be looking for group interactions, such as who takes charge, who sits back and contributes quality input at the right moment, etc.

Anyhow, whatever shape it takes, you must regard the interview as having started whenever you walk through the main door of the building or meet any Company person. You are definitely under observation at lunch (why do you think so many people join you?), and the receptionist has been on the team more than once.

Tip: The problem with lunch (for you, anyway) is that it's an opportunity for many questions that cannot be asked elsewhere, so be even more on your guard.

The interview is therefore even more part of your sales technique. Naturally, you will be smartly dressed and presentable, and you must convince them that they are not so much buying a pilot as peace of mind. Unfortunately, most interviewers make their decisions about you in a very short time, based on what they see, feel and hear, well before the dreaded interview questions even start!

Although unlikely in a pure Aviation company, there may be questions or situations designed to put you on the spot by trying to destroy your composure. To combat this, there are ways of behaving that will give you the most confidence. Don't talk too much, don't be pushy or negative and don't break silences. Awkward questions are mostly to establish the pecking order should you actually join the company later; the answers, to them, are not that important. They may even be there to see how you handle stress and whether you can be intimidated (by passengers, maybe), and the only weapon you have is to practice

beforehand, though it's best to pre-handle certain *types* of question rather than specific ones. You might, for example, be asked how your life will change if you are successful, or even whether you would be happier elsewhere. The majority of questions don't have a right answer - the interviewers are looking at your ability to reason, and justify your answers. Here are some possibilities, based on my own experience and that of others:

- Technical questions on the aircraft flown or from the pilot's exams, such as What is Dutch Roll?, or What are swept wings for?

- What if you smelt alcohol on your Captain's breath?

  Here, they are looking to see if you recognise a dangerous situation, know your responsibilities and have the tact to face up to a Captain. In the real world, in large organisations at least, much of your life will involve covering your backside against other peoples' mistakes or problems. As a first officer, it's your job to challenge the Captain if there is something wrong, but you don't want to give the impression that you're going to cause your own problems later. Reporting someone is almost always the wrong answer, at least for a first response, if only because it's bad CRM! Start with determining whether the aircraft is likely to be damaged (people don't usually deliberately screw up) and from that whether to terminate the sortie or not. In this situation, I would discuss it directly with the person concerned (making sure my facts were right) and leave it up to them to remove themselves from the flight (known as "passing the buck"). I would probably only take it higher if the Captain didn't take the opportunity to fall on his own sword or started intimidating me (escalating the problem is not only for your sake, but the people coming after you who might not have so much courage). In any case, I would ensure the discussion was in the cockpit (where the CVR would be running) or at least in front of credible witnesses.

- What would you do if you realised you had left your licence at home?

  You shouldn't take off without it - an insurance company could use it as an excuse not to pay up if an accident happened. Not only that, the company's operating certificate would be at risk. However, in the US, you could get an official copy faxed to you, which would be legal for 60 days.

- Why do you want to be a pilot?

  The view's good!

- What are your strong or weak points?

- How would you handle a grumpy captain?

  Gently!

- Why do you want to work for us?

- What is the biggest economic threat to this company?

- What does this company fly and to where?

- What is the Boss's name?

- What is the share price?

- Who did you train with?

- Tell us something that taught you about flying.

- Where do you want to be in 5 or 10 years' time?

- Have you ever scared yourself?

- Tell us about you.

- What can you bring to this company?

- Who have been your role models, or have had had the most influence?

- What are your goals? Which have you not achieved?

- What is your greatest accomplishment?

- How would you fly this SID?

- From this photograph of a site in the Antarctic, what's the time of day?

- Having flown various types, how will you feel about coming to work here and just flying one? Will you get bored?

- We start at 0530 every morning. How do you feel about that?

- The Captain continues an approach beyond minimums, telling you he has done it a thousand times and everything's fine. What do you do?

- You smell smoke - what initial action should you take? Then?

- The Captain tells you the smoke is normal and it will clear, but 15 minutes later it's getting worse. If the Captain gives you the same response, what would you do?

- The aircraft is loaded way beyond gross weight, the Captain tells you he does this all the time, and the aircraft will fly. What do you do?

- Once the gear is up, what conversation will you have with the Captain?

None that does not directly concern the operation of the aircraft.

- Put these in order of preference: Small boys, Guns or Flowers

  Flowers (cargo makes more money), small boys do not weigh as much as adults, and guns require too much paperwork

- How would you deal with a personality clash with an arrogant Captain?

- You have the Board in the back, and they insist on getting to a meeting on time. 30 miles out, the destination is under a LVL 6 cell with very little movement. What would you do?

- Besides good pay (*yeah, right - author*) why do you want to be a pilot?

- Say something funny

- What are the goals of the Company?

  Safety, Cost, Efficiency, Customer Care (in whatever order is relevant)

- How are they measured?

  Number of accidents,% spend, Utilisation, Complaints (for example)

- What do you do about sexual harassment?

- *Ask them not to complain (joke)*

- You're in the hotel restaurant on a stop over and in walks the Captain with a skirt on....what do you say?

  It depends on whether its colour clashed with his/her accessories (joke)

- Your career, though progressing nicely, is slow. How do you feel about it?

  Trick question - same as the one that asks if you would actually be happier in another company. You need to show confidence in yourself here.

- How would you rate yourself in relation to communication skills, dependability, and integrity on a scale of 1-10?

- If you attain all your goals as a pilot what do you intend to give back to aviation?

- What is important when managing pressure?

  Prioritisation, Ability to say No, Delegation, Asking for help

Don't forget you are new to the game, so you want standard answers with some common sense thrown in - if your responses don't seem to be what they want, back them up with good reasons why they should be - your training doesn't give you all the answers, but it does qualify you to think for yourself. Although an interview isn't meant to be funny, a couple of good, humorous remarks won't do any harm, but lay off the sarcasm - it doesn't go down well when you're supposed to be dealing with other people. The thing to remember is that all the above questions are based on fear (that you might screw up and make them look foolish, at the very least), so they are at a disadvantage, too. In large organisations, those who make mistakes don't get promoted - it follows, therefore, that people who don't make mistakes increase their chances markedly (you could also take the cynical view that those who do the least work make the least mistakes to its logical conclusion, but we'll ignore that for now).

Talking of which, if you were going for a management job, you might also want to consider:

- The work program is behind, the budget is overspent, and you are given some more work - how would you deal with it?

- How would you deal with someone who continually takes a sick day after returning from holiday or books dental appointments for late morning so they don't come back to work for the day?

- How would you deal with people who won't help colleagues who are returning from a hard day, saying "It's not my job", or "It's not my turn)?

It's certainly not on to slate other companies or be too eager to leave your present one without a very good reason - if you can do either, you can do it to the one you're going for. Do not sit until invited, and if you are not, at least wait until the interviewer sits down. Do not smoke without permission, don't swear, interrupt or "interview" the interviewer, even if he is inept. Nor is it a good idea to argue, be familiar or apologise for yourself. The best tactic is to avoid extremes and place you and your opinions firmly in the middle - be the ideal "Company Person", in fact. By the way, the interviewers to watch out for are the surly or the quiet ones.

Don't even think of mentioning personality clashes or "philosophical differences" as they are more politely known (unless you want to be a trial lawyer!), and DO NOT TELL LIES.

Finally, when asked to do an evaluation ride, don't push off afterwards without helping to put the machine away, or at least offering to help.

OTHER BOOKS BY PHIL CROUCHER
••

The Bell 206 Book

A training aid for people coming to the Bell 206 for the first time, or pilots who have been flying it for years who have been trained up on myth and legend and would like to know how it really works!

ISBN 0-9732253-9-4 $24.95

CARs in Plain English

Canadian Aviation Regulations translated!

ISBN 0-9681928-4-X $44.95

Canadian Professional Pilot Studies

The Canadian version of this book.

ISBN 0-9681928-9-0 $79.95

The Helicopter Pilot's Handbook

What nobody ever tells you! An attempt to gather together as much information as possible for helicopter pilots, old and new, professional and otherwise, in an attempt to explain the why, so the how becomes easier.

"a much needed summary of all the "basics" we live by. It sure is great for an old timer to see how all the things we had to find out the hard way in the 60's and 70's can now be found in a book. A great reference tool." Robert Eschauzier

"In short... great book! Thankfully your book illuminates many of the practical aspects of flying rotorcraft that are missing from the intro texts used during training. I'd equate much of the valuable practical information in your book to the to the same valuable information found in "Stick and Rudder." Ian Campbell

"The chapters covering your experiences and showing 'the real world' of helicopter ops is a worthwhile addition to any pilots library and knowledge bank." Paul

".....an excellent book for pilots interested in a career as a helicopter pilot. It answers all the really hard questions like "how does a young pilot get the required experience without having to join the army for 10 years". Great book for anyone interested in fling-wings!" Reilly Burke, Technical Adviser, Aero Training Products

"Having only completed 20 hours of my CPL(H) in Australia, a lot of the content was very new to me. Your writing style is very clear and flowing, and the content was easy to understand. It's made me more eager than ever to finish my training and get into it. It's also opened my eyes as to how much there is to learn. The section on

landing a job was excellent, especially for this industry that seems so hard to break into." Philip Shelper

"Picked up The Helicopter Pilot's Handbook on Friday and have already read it twice. How you crammed that much very informative info into 178 pages is totally beyond me. WELL DONE. What a wealth of information, even though I only have a CPL-F. OUTSTANDING. I'm starting it again for the third time because I've picked up so much more the second time, that I'll read certainly a dozen more times. I cant wait to apply a lot the ideas and comments that you have supplied. My wife is totally blown away that I've read it cover to cover twice and going around for a third time. She said it must be an outstanding book as I need real mental stimulus to keep me going." Will

"I have only skimmed through the first version. Its already answered and confirmed a few things for me. Just the type of info I am after." Andrew Harrison

"Your book is very good and has been read by a few of the guys here with good 'raps'. particularly the Info on slinging etc. is stuff that is never covered in endorsement training. Certainly a worthwhile addition to any pilot library." Gibbo

ISBN 0-9681928-3-1 $34.95

Single Pilot CRM

Based on the author's successful CRM courses.

"I have nothing but praise. It really is a timely piece of work. I've been through the United Airlines CRM program, and a couple of corporate programs. None of them are geared towards the single pilot environment, and I've always been suspicious that the single pilot environment is a lot bigger than the multi-pilot environment. I really like the phrase 'Company Resource Management' that you suggest. It's a whole lot more appropriate for what we do in the helicopter world. I've read the first 22 pages 3 times so far and I'll probably read them a couple more times before I feel like I've got a handle on them." Mike Fergione

ISBN 0-9732253-7-8 $24.95

INDEX